Digital Rendering for Fashion and Costume

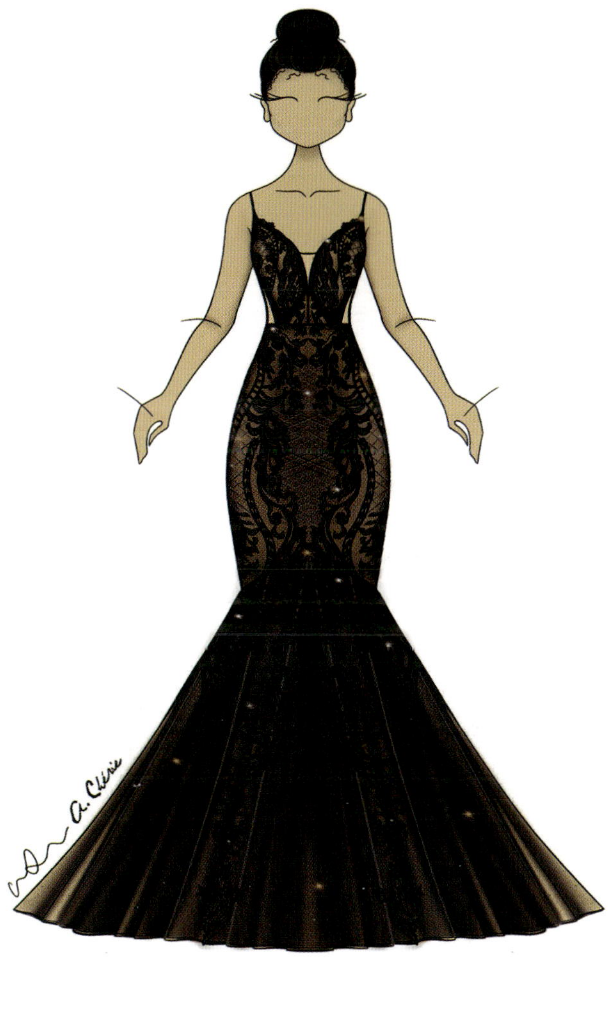

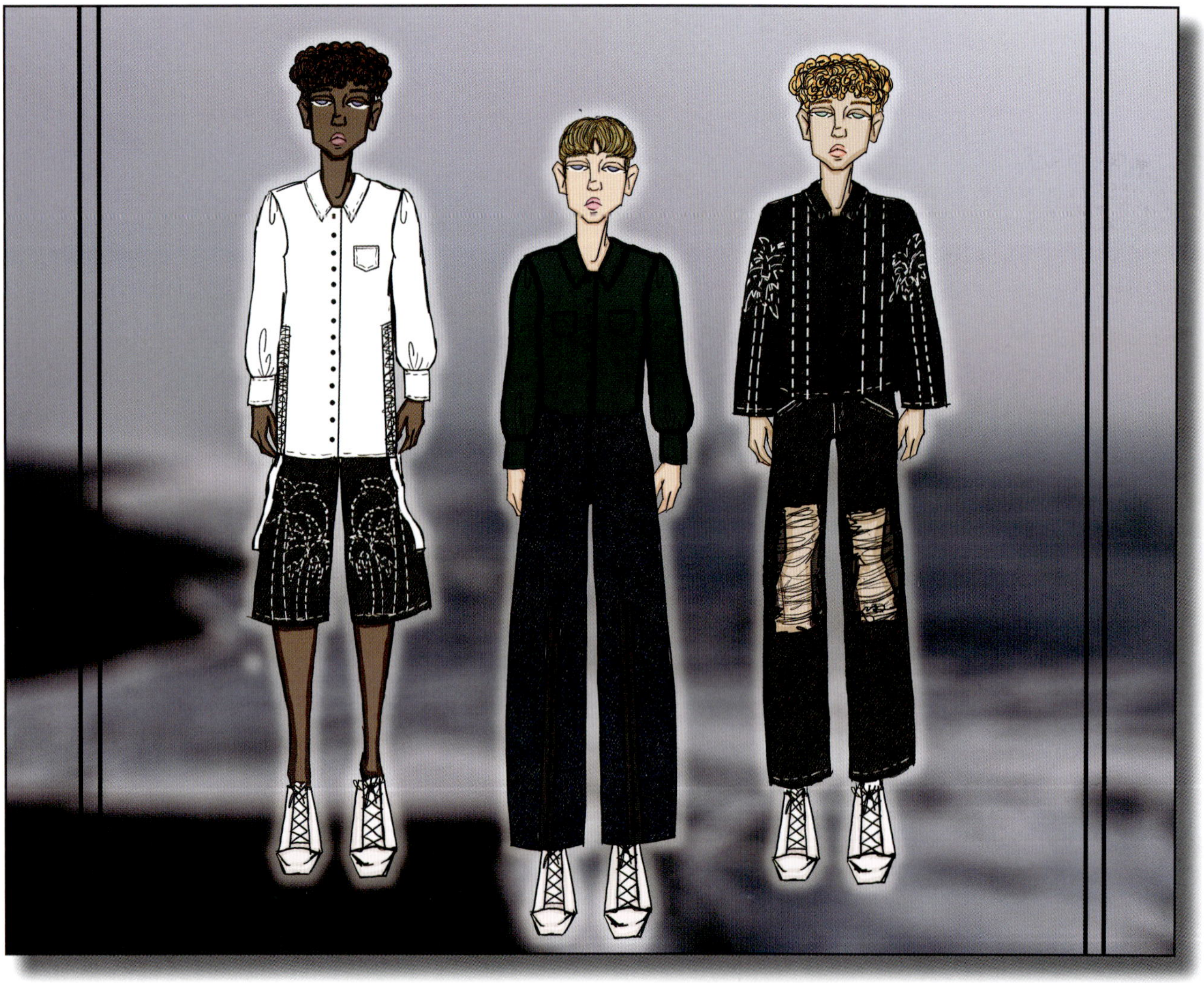

Digital Rendering for Fashion and Costume

Lalon Alexander
Theresa Alexander
University of the Incarnate Word

FAIRCHILD BOOKS
NEW YORK • LONDON • OXFORD • NEW DELHI • SYDNEY

FAIRCHILD BOOKS
Bloomsbury Publishing Inc, 1359 Broadway, New York, NY 10018, USA
Bloomsbury Publishing Plc, 50 Bedford Square, London, WC1B 3DP, UK
Bloomsbury Publishing Ireland, 29 Earlsfort Terrace, Dublin 2, D02 AY28, Ireland

BLOOMSBURY, FAIRCHILD BOOKS and the Fairchild Books logo are
trademarks of Bloomsbury Publishing Plc

First Edition published 2026

Cover design: Louise Dugdale
Cover images: Phamai Techaphan/Moment/Getty Images; Digital illustrations: Lalon Alexander
and Theresa Alexander

A catalog record for this book is available from the Library of Congress.

ISBN: PB: 979-8-7651-0368-5
ePDF: 979-8-7651-0369-2
eBook: 979-8-7651-0370-8

Typeset by Integra Software Services Pvt. Ltd.
Printed and bound in India

For product safety related questions contact productsafety@bloomsbury.com.

To find out more about our authors and books visit www.fairchildbooks.com
and sign up for our newsletter.

To our parents, who are still wondering why neither of us became engineers. Sorry.

*To our many students who have impressed, entertained, challenged,
and downright confounded us over the many years of teaching.*

*And while we're at it, to all our teachers who were impressed, entertained,
challenged, and downright confounded by us over the years.*

Contents

Extended Table of Contents

Chapter 5
Shading, Highlighting, and Giving Life to the Illustration 189

Chapter 6
Adding Texture for Fabrics 219

Chapter 10
Backgrounds and Textures for Layouts 393

Chapter 11
Putting it All Together 411

Chapter 12
Portfolios 451

About the Authors

Dr. Theresa Alexander and Dr. Mary Lalon Alexander are both associate professors in the Juren-Sullivan Fashion Management department at the University of the Incarnate Word in San Antonio, Texas, where they teach hand and digital illustration. Lalon is the Chair of the Fashion Management Department. Theresa also taught hand illustration and computer illustration at Texas Tech University, and hand illustration at the Paris Fashion Institute.

Dr. Theresa Alexander has a BS in Clothing, Textiles, and Merchandising, with a specialization in Fashion Design from Texas Tech University, an MA in Fashion and Textiles with a specialization in Clothing Technology from Nottingham Trent University, and a PhD in Higher Education from the University of the Incarnate Word.

Dr. Lalon Alexander has a BS in Clothing, Textiles, and Merchandising, with a specialization in Fashion Design from Texas Tech University, an MFA in Costume Design from Carnegie Mellon University, an MS in Creativity and Change Leadership from Buffalo State College (SUNY), and a PhD in Higher Education from the University of the Incarnate Word.

Theresa and Lalon Alexander are two sisters, four years apart but more alike than they care to admit. Both sisters have loved illustration since childhood. They always had pencils in hand growing up and *absolutely* had to have the box of sixty-four crayons for school, even though the school only required a box of twelve.

For Lalon, drawing was an iterative process as she started getting good, got compliments, felt good about it and wanted to improve, which resulted in more compliments. Her bookshelf had a Weekly Reader book of *Drawing Fashions* beside a copy of Andrew Loomis's *Figure Drawing for All It's Worth*. She was consumed with gaining more knowledge about how to improve her drawing skills and spent summers taking extra art classes at local museums.

Lalon's first digital illustration was of a lone sheep, using DOS commands to color large individual pixels. She recalls that she did not initially see this mode of illustration as a "game changer" at the time. But, as we know, computer illustration dramatically improved over the next few decades. She was introduced to Adobe Illustrator and Photoshop sometime in the 1990s. Over the years, she has amassed hours upon hours of digital illustration learning. She tirelessly worked her way from terrible through to mediocrity and all the way to "hey, not bad!"

Theresa's journey through illustration was a combination of a love for drawing and a stubborn need for perfectionism. She would spend hours drawing the same thing over and over in order to improve. Once technology became part of her toolkit, innate curiosity also began to drive her progress. Theresa needs to know how things work; therefore, she dives deep into the software to discover the mechanics and possibilities.

The sisters first started with digital illustration programs in the early 1980s using KoalaPainter. Theresa gained further experience using software from Microdynamics. She then started using CorelDraw and Corel Photo-Paint with regularity in the early 1990s when the computer mouse became a regular addition to the PC. Lalon started to become more interested in digital illustration in the mid-1990s. They also used/taught Micrografx among other software before embracing the Adobe products.

As the cliché goes, "the best way to learn something is to have to teach it." Theresa started teaching Computer Illustration over twenty years ago and Lalon started about fifteen years ago. After teaching computer illustration to fashion students for many years, they have had access to more mistakes than most people can imagine. This ranges from the incident of the floppy disk stuck in the drive because a rhinestone was accidentally glued to it, to the incident of the Procreate drawing that was "enhanced" by a fuzzy coworker (read as, "the cat laid on my iPad when I wasn't looking"). Through the years of amassed mistakes and questions, they have stuck to the philosophy that mistakes make for great learning opportunities. So do not ever feel ashamed of voicing the question that your neighbor was thinking! Everyone has questions when learning. That's just how learning works.

Lalon Alexander, MFA, PhD
Chair of the Fashion Management Department
Associate Professor of Fashion Management
Juren Sullivan Center for Fashion Management
University of the Incarnate Word
San Antonio, Texas

Theresa Alexander, PhD
Associate Professor of Fashion Management
Juren Sullivan Center for Fashion Management
University of the Incarnate Word
San Antonio, Texas

Foreword

Paul Tazewell

Early in my career, I was privileged to teach a figure drawing class to a group of eager costume, scenery, and lighting design students during my brief tenure as a faculty member at Carnegie Mellon University. It was in this class that I met a brilliant and talented student, Lalon Alexander. One building block I would emphasize was the importance of understanding the human form, knowing this would be the foundation of every character. Every class began with a live model switching poses every 30 seconds and having students sketch each pose. This foundational base would allow the clothing to speak directly to period and the characters.

Digital Rendering for Fashion and Costume by Lalon Alexander and Theresa Alexander is the first all-encompassing text on digital illustration for fashion and costume. Intended for not only design students but also working professionals who want to transition to digital illustration in a class or on their own.

My process has always been to start the design journey by going to my library of books compiled over the years. Then I work to enhance what I find with images sourced from the internet and various archives. Specific character details evolve from collaborating with each actor and my team and build to become part of the final design.

After the initial phase, I pull out my 3H pencils, sharpener, gum eraser, and sheets of watercolor paper and start to sketch each character. This is how I begin the process of combining research references with the director's and actor's insights. As I sketch, I always keep in my mind the actor that is destined to bring the role to life. My tubes of Windsor Newton watercolors close by, my paint brush in hand, I develop the closest representation of the character to my best ability. Each element, the silhouette, the cut and fit, the specific year, and the fabric choice speaks of how I want the costume to be an extension of the actor's form and what I want that costume to say about that character. I strive for specificity and life that I can conjure in a watercolor sketch; very old school. The watercolor medium speaks to when I entered the profession of costume design and my education leading up to my design career. Watercolors speak to the tactile magic that allows ideas from the brain to combine with information gathered through my eyes to manifest the character onto a page. Sketching allows me to fully understand who that character is I am designing and to perfect how I want to see that character as a three-dimensional (3D) being.

As my career has expanded into designing multiple theater productions at the same time as designing films with thousands of costumes, I have recognized the need to change my relationship to my creative process and the traditional way of rendering characters. I have come to rely on digital rendering whether I am doing it myself or guiding and responding to digital artwork from concept artists that I collaborate with. Expertly written, Lalon and Theresa Alexander's knowledge, expertise, and professional background in teaching fashion, illustration, patternmaking, costume design, textiles, digital design, sewing, costume, paired with their robust comprehension of digital applications makes this text digestible. The authors explore shapes, digital colorizing, skin tone, facial features, hair, shading, highlighting, adding texture to fabrics, styling from conception to finished portfolio-ready illustration. The text is superbly written so that instructors, students, and professionals have a seamless transition to knowledge for primary digital applications. The Alexander's effortlessly guide readers step by step to bring their original renderings to vibrant digital illustration life.

Digital rendering has also become the norm when working with film studios to deliver accurate versions of the actor's face wearing the costumes I have designed. The clarity of this text makes the costume approval process more visually immediate and allows the director and the producers to see the actor that they have cast wearing the design that they are needing to approve. Acknowledging the film studio adage "time is money" a digital costume rendering is the closest that you can get to what the actor will look like when they finally step on set. As always, it is reliant on the costume designer to understand what has been rendered and manifest that design with appropriate fabrication, fit and engineering, and to supervise the makers to create the costume that they desire.

As a successful costume designer, I now rely on the ability to see multiple options for a costume idea using digital costume renderings. I can change the color, the fabric choice, the intricate details. I can add a jacket or remove a jacket, all to perfect what the idea of the costume is and to allow the director to weigh in on some of those options as well. The technology and description provided in *Digital Rendering for Fashion and Costume* teaches students a direct way to explore the best route to take for a character's costume. I am glad to see that the industry exploding for concept artists and character development for film, animation, and gaming. *Digital Rendering for Fashion and Costume* provides readers with the tools to inspire and create in this all-inclusive guide to exacting digital rendering. To learn to digitally render is a beautiful way to see creatives finding a home for their passion and for realizing characters as an integral part of the storytelling process.

Paul Tazewell, Costume Designer
Academy Award for Best Costume Design,
Wicked (2025)
Tony Award for Best Costume Design,
Death Becomes Her (2025)

Preface

What makes a great illustrator? Talent often boils down to a strong affinity for a particular activity. If you enjoy drawing, then you practice it frequently and aim to get better with each illustration. Hence, you become "talented" at illustration. This is good news for everyone. Even if you don't like drawing or think you are bad at it, you can improve with practice and time, so long as you make it a goal and persevere with practice.

Good illustrations do not equate to good designs, but many people do not recognize that. Therefore, it pays to improve your illustration skills for others to perceive you as a better designer. It is completely unfair, we agree. But those are the facts. There are certainly exceptions to this rule, but most people who are not trained in design (and even some who are) fail to understand the difference between good illustration and good design. These may be the people hiring you for the job. So, even if you do not like illustration, you probably want to put in some time to get better at it. This is especially true if you are just starting out and have not yet built up your professional network.

Digital Rendering for Fashion and Costume came about because it is difficult to find a solid all-in-one resource by experts because the technology rapidly changes and designers tend to use different applications to suit their personal preferences.

Digital Rendering for Fashion and Costume is written from more of an illustrator-who-happens-to-use-digital-tools viewpoint rather than a here's-how-to-use-this-one-digital-app-for-this-one-project viewpoint. The idea is to learn about tools you can find and use in most applications to create a good illustration for fashion or costume.

What Courses and Students Can Use this Text?

This text is intended for fashion and costume design students or working professionals who want to transition to digital illustration. The lessons work well for both a traditional classroom and self-learners. The nice advantage to a classroom is the community of learners at hand, ready to provide individual feedback and support. If you are a self-learner, try starting a small group community online or in person to take the learning journey together.

By the title alone, you probably figured out that the lessons in this book show a specialized application to apparel items. Although the content is aimed at fashion and costume students, the information provided is in no way exclusive. If you are a concept designer, game character illustrator, cosplay aficionado, or anyone else interested in rendering clothing on a body, then this text is as much for you as anyone else.

This is not a beginner's book, however. The content is presented for those with some familiarity of the software as well as general illustration and design knowledge. If you are unsure if you are ready to tackle this subject, review the section on "What you should know before going through this book." Multiple texts and online videos are easily accessible about how to get started with the software you choose to utilize. In general, you should have basic working knowledge of Adobe Illustrator and Photoshop or your particular software of choice. Fewer garment illustrators are familiar with InDesign, so basic functionality of the software is covered in the layouts section.

So why fashion AND costume? Why not focus on just one? The authors have training and backgrounds in both industries, plus rendering clothing is one area that the two professions roughly do in the same manner. There are a multitude of differences between the two areas. But communicating a garment design is still communicating a garment design. There are certainly some differences in style, layout, and portfolios, so we will touch on those differences throughout the chapters.

In this text, you will find both specific explanations about how to use these digital tools and holistic explanations to approach your style and design needs.

The authors challenge the reader by not only giving step-by-step instructions to follow and learn, but also discussion topics about the choices made in design communication. With the expertise guidance, this text will help students to produce a better portfolio.

Please note that this book focuses on two-dimensional illustration. Additionally, this book does not cover illustration basics such as figure proportion, line quality, etc. Nor is basic design included. As there are more text-book options for drawing hand and digital technical flats, we do not include that subject matter here.

Check the Extend Your Learning section of the appendices if you need to brush up on any or all the aforementioned subjects. You may need to spend a little time getting to know the basics and can easily return to these lessons when you are ready.

How to Use this Book

The book is designed in sections of building up an illustration from the figure to texture to styles to layout. The learning path works straight through from the first page to the last. However, it can work just as well to pick and choose the subjects in the order you need most to strengthen your skills. Do not be afraid to build your own learning experience based on your needs. For example, you may already be skilled at digitally rendering the figure and color but want to learn more about adding textures or creating your own style. Adjust your learning path as needed to get the most from the lessons.

Many other texts focus on the software platform for the learning path. For this book, we approach your learning from the perspective of an illustrator rather than a software expert. Therefore, for each chapter, you will see instructions for creating the same or similar effects through different software or methods within a software package. The emphasis is on creating the illustration technique instead of the technical software application. So rather than having five chapters on how to use Photoshop to create a rendering followed by five chapters on how to use Illustrator to create the same rendering, we mix the software application instruction in each chapter according to the illustrative end goal, such as creating texture. The purpose of this approach is to make the lessons more relatable to designers and to encourage flexibility in a world of constantly changing software.

Organization of the Text

Chapter 1, Introduction to Digital Rendering for Fashion and Costume, reviews design communication, technical application needs, and what you need to know before starting to use this book.

Chapter 2, Rendering the Figure, explains how to digitally render figures in both Photoshop and Illustrator and how to clean up a scanned analog figure.

Chapter 3, Colorizing, talks about color modes, adding and working with color, and saving color swatches.

Chapter 4, Using and Making Repeating Prints, is about scanning, making, and using repeating prints in both Photoshop and Illustrator.

Chapter 5, Shading, Highlighting, and Giving Life to the Illustration, helps readers give their illustrations life through a variety of shading and highlighting techniques. These methods include painting, using dodge and burn, and using shapes, among others.

Chapter 6, Adding Texture for Fabrics, helps readers learn how to make renderings look more accurate by adding texture. Readers will learn to make textures through painting techniques, filters, layer effects, pattern fills, and a few other methods.

Chapter 7, Faces and Hair, explains some tricks of the trade for creating faces and hair and helps to make an often daunting part of illustration less frightening.

Chapter 8, Style, discusses how to use different tools and settings to make illustrations look more artistic and emulate analog renderings.

Chapter 9, Basics of Layouts for Fashion and Costume, helps the reader take their renderings from a figure to a presentation. This chapter covers mood and inspiration composites, fabric boards, photoshoots, and layouts.

Chapter 10, Backgrounds and Textures for Layouts, covers backgrounds for different purposes and different types of backgrounds, including scenes, textures, and graphic backgrounds.

Chapter 11, Putting it All Together, is a special chapter that covers using software for layouts. This includes how to create boards in Photoshop and Illustrator and an extended section on how to use InDesign.

Chapter 12, Portfolios, is a final chapter that helps the reader assemble their work into a final product. Both physical and digital portfolios are covered, as is the design of resumés and cover letters.

Text Features

Learning Objectives: Each chapter begins with a list of learning objectives to guide them through the chapter and help them understand the major points.

Step by Step Projects: Chapters are built around multiple step-by-step projects to help students learn concepts through doing.

Images: Chapters are image rich. These are a combination of images that guide students through the step-by-step projects, images to explain concepts, and images of artwork for inspiration. Throughout the text we have included student work as well as that of established professionals.

Style Secrets: Style Secret callout boxes provide advice for enhancing and exploring your personal illustration and design style options.

Pro Tips: Pro Tip callout boxes supply more advanced features or technical tips to take your software further.

End of Chapter Summaries: Chapter summaries help students review the key concepts from the chapter.

Key Terms: A list of key terms is included at the end of each chapter for students to use to review their knowledge of chapter concepts and to prepare for quizzes and tests.

Review Questions: A selection of review questions at the end of the chapter help students determine if they understand the chapter content and techniques.

Discussion Questions: Each chapter includes a list of discussion questions intended to help students think about challenging or controversial situations. These questions can be used by instructors in class, on discussion boards, etc.

Commands Introduced: A list of Adobe commands introduced in the chapter is included at the end of each chapter for students to review and practice.

Keyboard Shortcuts: A list of the keyboard shortcuts discussed is included at the end of each chapter to help students remember and practice the shortcuts. Additionally, there is an appendix listing all the applicable shortcuts for Illustrator, Photoshop, and InDesign so readers can look up shortcuts in one location.

Practice Exercises: A selection of practice exercises has been included at the end of each chapter. Readers can use these exercises to practice their knowledge and skills or instructors can assign them.

List of Resources: A list of resources has been included at the end of the book. Here, readers can find links to software and hardware providers, plugin developers, and font and stock image providers.

Extend Your Learning: This appendix provides a list of specialized training providers and useful books.

Glossary: The glossary provides definitions for all of the key terms from the chapters. This will help students clarify confusing terms and study for quizzes and tests.

INSTRUCTOR AND STUDENT RESOURCES

Digital Rendering for Fashion and Costume STUDIO

We are pleased to offer an online resource to accompany the textbook *Digital Rendering for Fashion and Costume*. The online STUDIO is specially developed to complement this book with rich media ancillaries that students can adapt to their visual learning styles to better master concepts and improve grades. Within the STUDIO, students will be able to:

- Study smarter with self-quizzes featuring scored results and personalized study tips
- View instructional videos that accompany each chapter
- Access practice files to download and use for book and video exercises
- Review concepts with flashcards of essential vocabulary
- View a digital gallery of colored renderings from the textbook for students to use as inspiration for their work

The *Digital Rendering for Fashion and Costume* STUDIO can be accessed as follows:

SIGN IN

1. Go to https://www.bloomsburyonlineresources.com/fairchildbookstudios
2. Follow the instructions to enter your unique access code which is printed on the inside back cover of this book. The code is valid for one registration only.
3. Credentials to access the STUDIOs will be emailed once the code has been redeemed.

Having trouble registering or logging in? Be sure you have entered your access code, not your password when prompted.

STUDIO™ will be live within six to eight weeks of the book's publication date.

Instructor Resources

- *Instructor's Guide* provides suggestions for planning the course and using the text in the classroom, supplemental assignments, and lecture notes.
- PowerPoint® presentations include images from the book, providing a framework for lecture and discussion.

Instructor's Resources may be accessed through https://www.bloomsburyonlineresources.com/fairchildbookstudios

Acknowledgments

First and foremost, thanks to the artists who contributed illustrations and artwork for this text. You recognize the value of helping future generations and are a credit to the industry! Thanks to Adrianna Martinez, Alejandra Sanchez, Alexandra McMayon, Ana Stoyanova, Angelica Alarcon, Arlette Benavides, Arti Sandhu, Bryan Ramirez, Carla Bellisio, Cayce Atwood, David Arevalo, Donny Guerra, Emily O'Brien, Fabio Toblini, Frankie Rivera, Grace Kang, Hannah Delmore, Holly Poe Durbin, Jackie Mallon, Jacob Climer, Jasmine Lea Hernandez, Jessica Ozoude, Julianne D'Errico, Julia Robles, Latisha Francis, Liana Hinojosa, Maya Kanawati, Mona Jahani, Nanette Acosta, Natasha Andrews, Olivera Gajic, Papa Oppong, Rachel Anderson, Reagan McGuire, Rebecca Salinas, Ricardo Gutierrez, Ruby Sosa, Ryan Park, Salma Ali, Sam Connor, Shelby Gomez, Stephanie Maiti Marquez, and Veronica Carreon.

We would like to express our gratitude to our many art, fashion, costume, and technology teachers who put up with our pestering questions and self-assured demeanors. In particular, Susan Tsu, Paul Tazewell, Catherine Black, Myra Timmons, Sheri L. Dragoo, and James Glavan.

We also want to thank our twenty-five years' of students that provided much of the troubleshooting experience, pedagogy, and content matter for this textbook. If it could go wrong, you showed us how!

A big thank you to Bloomsbury for allowing us the opportunity to become first-time authors. We would especially like to thank Emily Samulski for encouraging our quirky personalities throughout the writing process. Thanks to Julie Vitale and Edie Weinberg for keeping us on track and preventing us from being "too" quirky.

We greatly appreciate the feedback (good and developmental) from our many reviewers. It was a LOT to read, and we cannot thank you enough for taking the time to comb through it and provide your thoughts:

Carol D'Angelo, University of Hawaii
Amy Dorie, San Francisco State University
Nicolas ChampRoux, Houston Community College
Sherita M. Cuffee, Montclair State University
Julie DeMaggio, Butte College
Mary Elliott, Louisiana State University
Barry Fuhrman, Dallas College
Saul Kapilivsky, Miami International University of Art and Design
Julie Lamarra, Utah State University
Edward Murr, Fashion Institute of Technology
Holly Poe Durbin, University of California, Irvine
Teresa Reynolds
Lori Wahl, University of Idaho
Cheryl Whitaker, Houston Community College

A big shout out to our colleagues at the University of the Incarnate Word. Thanks to our many supporters in the School of Media and Design who encouraged this project and provided advice along the way. We would like to especially thank Melinda Adams, our program chair, for putting up with the many delayed departmental tasks due to, "we're trying to get XYZ of the book done this weekend!" Also, thanks to our (now retired) dean, Sharon Welkey, for encouraging us over the past nineteen years to push ourselves professionally while staying sane.

Finally, thank you to our family. Our parents supported both of us throughout the many years of abundant sequins, fabric shopping, glitter, superfluous art supplies, unnecessary education, and writing, despite the fact that neither of us became engineers. As proper spinsters, we also thank our cats, who simultaneously kept us sane and drove us crazy. (Don't ask about how Fiona deleted half of my layers one day.)

The Publisher wishes to gratefully acknowledge and thank the editorial team involved in the publication of this book:

Publisher: Emily Samulski
Art Development Editor: Edie Weinberg
Senior Development Editor: Julie M. Vitale
Assistant Editor: María Francisca Núñez
In-House Designer: Louise Dugdale
Production Manager: Ken Bruce
Project Manager: Rebecca Willford

Digital Rendering for Fashion and Costume

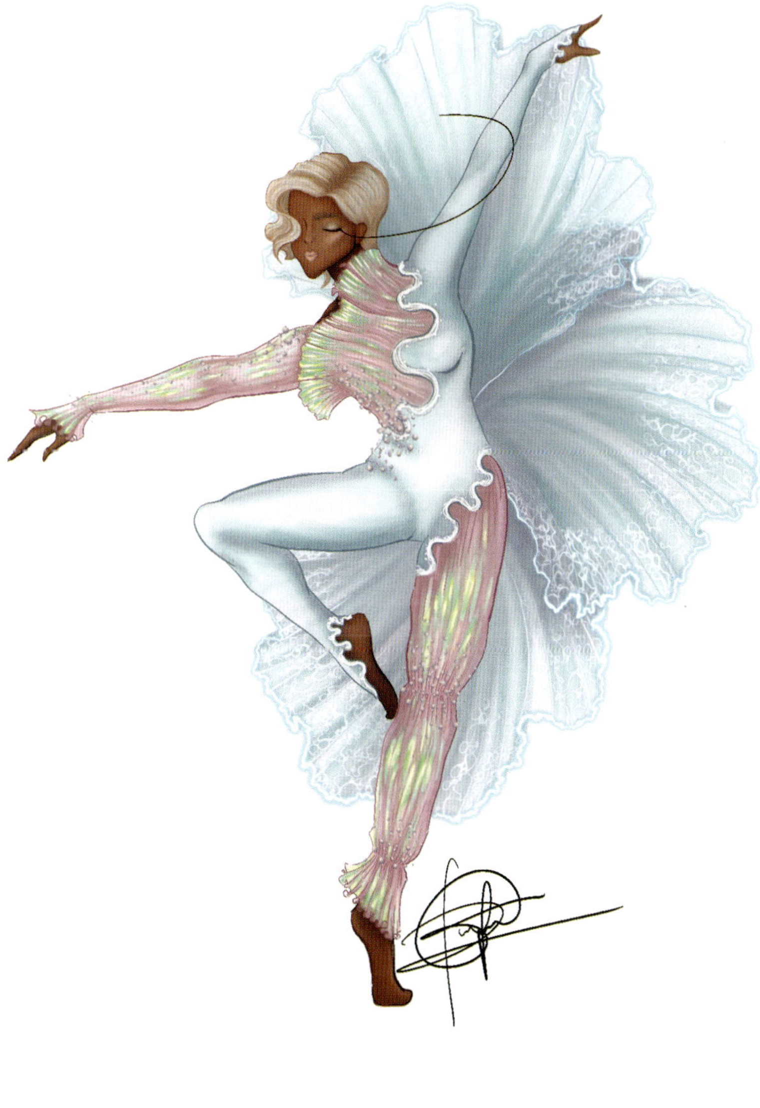

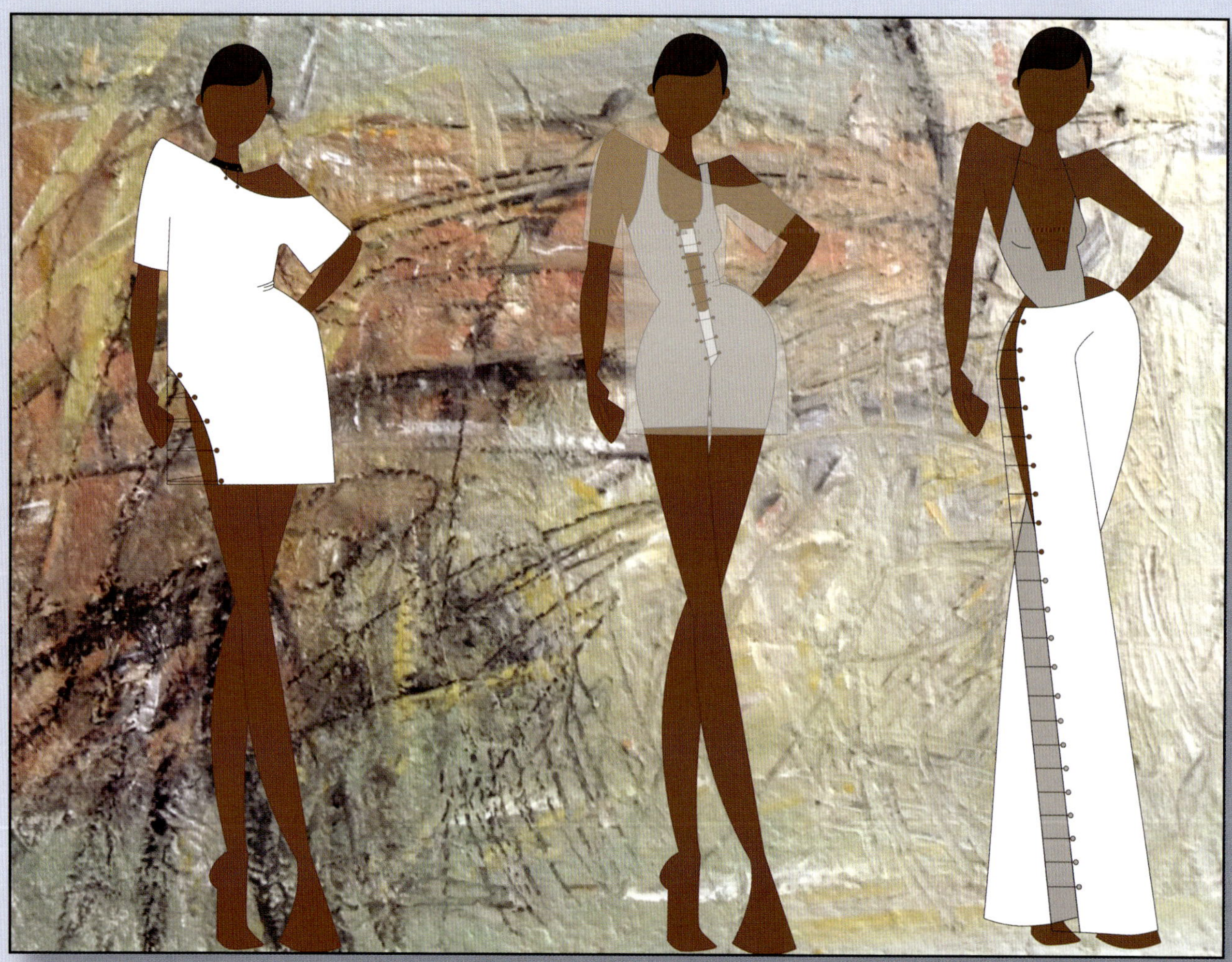

Figure 1.1 Digital rendering can save time and make your workflow more efficient. Are you ready to learn a new skill? Artwork and designs courtesy of Natasha Andrews Instagram: @art.tashatrinae.

CHAPTER 1

Introduction to Digital Rendering for Fashion and Costume

Learning Objectives

After completing this chapter, you should be able to

- Recognize the purpose of this text and how to use this book
- Understand digital and analog design communication
- Assess your digital toolbox
- Describe key digital rendering concepts

Fashion and costume illustrations are as widely varied as the fashion and costume industries. Hand illustrators use a mix of mediums, canvases, and styles to convey their ideas. The last few decades presented a new platform for communicating design needs. You may have picked up this book because it is assigned as part of a class, because you want to venture into the world of digital rendering on your own, or because you are a digital illustration guru who wishes to expand their skills. Whatever your reason, we are glad you joined us.

This book addresses the "how" of digital garment rendering (Figure 1.1). However, the "what" and the "why" are content-specific to the field in which you work or study. There are different communication needs for each industry. To generalize, the fashion industry needs detailed accounts of each garment to communicate how it should be made when the orders are sent to different manufacturers or factories. The costume industry relies on renderings to convey the story through character of a given moment. Often costume designers rely on the help of artisans and technicians to interpret the rendering into reality. As mentioned, these are simple generalizations, and there are always exceptions. There also may be times when a fashion brand requires a stylized sketch and times when a costume shop needs a detailed flat for construction. The content will always be dictated by the context.

If the world of digital illustration is somewhat foreign to you, we encourage you to lean into the discomfort. The graphic designer and illustrator Von Glitschka states that, "Fear is part of learning."[1] This is sometimes difficult, particularly for adult learners, to remember. No one should be proficient or perfect when learning a new skill. Even if you are a skilled hand illustrator, there will many moments of struggle to transition to digital illustration. So, remember to take a deep breath, give yourself a break when things do not go according to plan, and push up your sleeves to start working!

Renderings and Portfolios

Are renderings and portfolios still relevant today? This is an excellent question. The fashion industry has changed dramatically over the past 100 years. There are many jobs in the industry for which a portfolio is entirely superfluous. Seasoned designers often get new jobs through networking and word of mouth. Keeping up with your portfolio is a personal call that may not be necessary according to your circumstances. However, for most entry-level jobs and internships in the design and technical design fields, it can help you get the job. The ability to demonstrate digital illustration skills may open other doors, as well (Figure 1.2). Even if you do not feel the need to keep a portfolio you may want to invest in learning digital rendering to expand your skill base.

In terms of the costume industry for stage or screen, you are often expected to showcase your work. Again, a seasoned designer probably has stacks of old costume plates in a box under the bed and already has an established reputation for their design work. But for those just entering the industry, you will need to demonstrate your design ability through illustrations, visual research, and still shots from productions. A portfolio can help organize and showcase your work to those who have not previously worked with you. Once you become proficient with the software, you may find ways to quickly generate and change ideas for the design team to review and discuss.

A portfolio is an expression of your design ability, illustrative ability, and aesthetics (Figure 1.3). Physical portfolios, meaning a case you carry around with printed designs, may be dwindling in demand depending on your situation. For that reason alone, you may stand out from competitors by keeping it "old school" by bringing your physical portfolio to the interview. Online

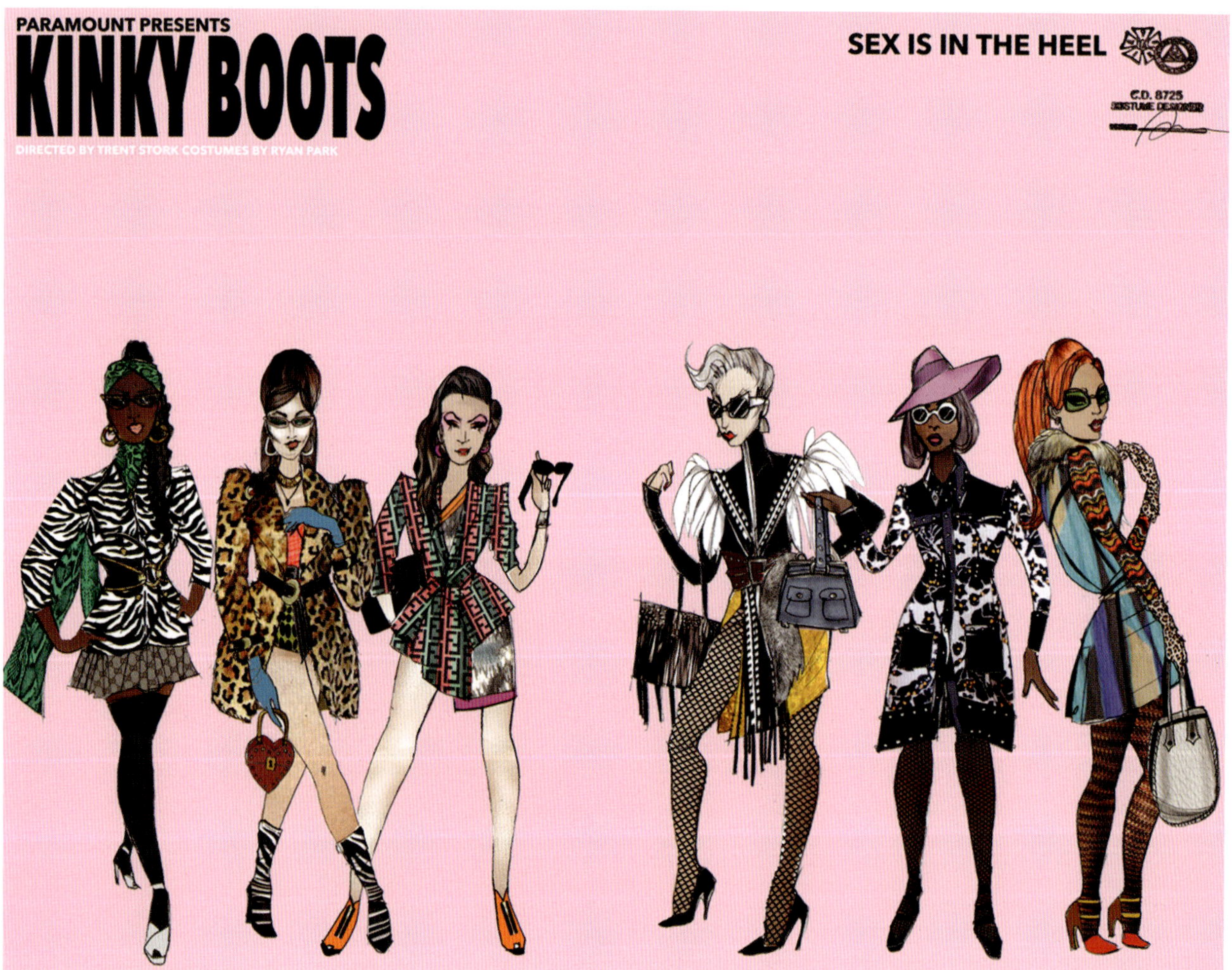

Figure 1.2 Fashion and costume illustrations have some key differences, but far more commonalities. Artwork and designs courtesy of Ryan Park. Ryanparkdesign.com

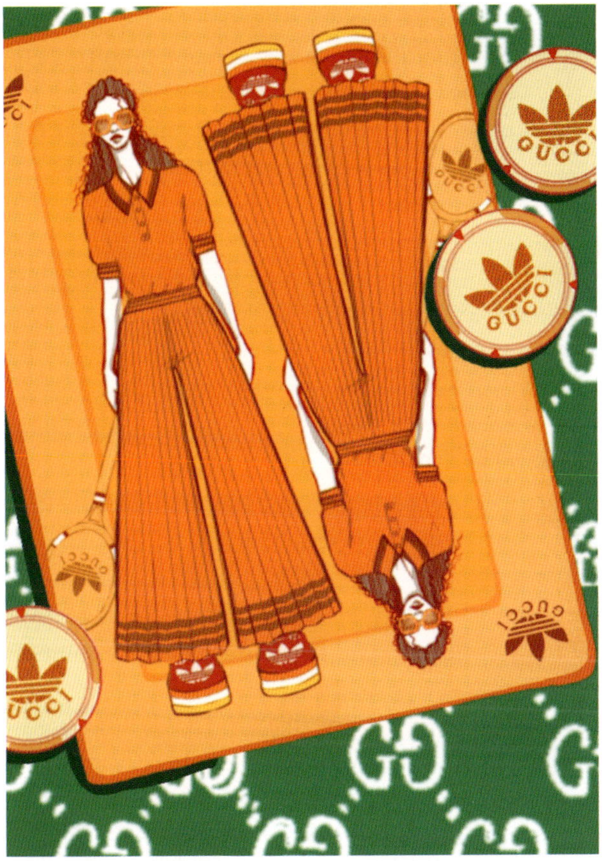

Figure 1.3 It takes time and deliberate practice with any digital illustration software to experience its full range of artistic potential. Courtesy of Hannah Delmore @hannahdelmoreillustration. Hannahdelmore.com.

portfolios are easily accessible and a great way to quickly capture the attention of a potential employer. Whether you choose to utilize a physical portfolio, a digital one, or both, this book will help you on that path.

Who Is this Book for?

This text is intended for fashion and costume design students or working professionals who want to transition to digital illustration. The lessons work well for both a traditional classroom and self-learners. The nice advantage to a classroom is the community of learners at hand, ready to provide individual feedback and support. If you are a self-learner, try starting a small group community online or in person to take the learning journey together.

By the title alone, you probably figured out that the lessons in this book show a specialized application to apparel items. Although the content is aimed at fashion and costume students, the information provided is in no way exclusive. If you are a concept designer, game character illustrator, cosplay aficionado, or anyone else interested in rendering clothing on a body, then this text is as much for you as anyone else.

The Purpose of this Text

This is not a beginner's book, however. The content is presented for those with some familiarity of the software as well as general illustration and design knowledge. If you are unsure if you are ready to tackle this subject, review the section on "What you should know before going through this book." Multiple texts and online videos are easily accessible about how to get started with the software you choose to utilize. In general, you should have basic working knowledge of Adobe Illustrator and Photoshop or your particular software of choice (see Figure 1.4). Fewer garment illustrators are familiar

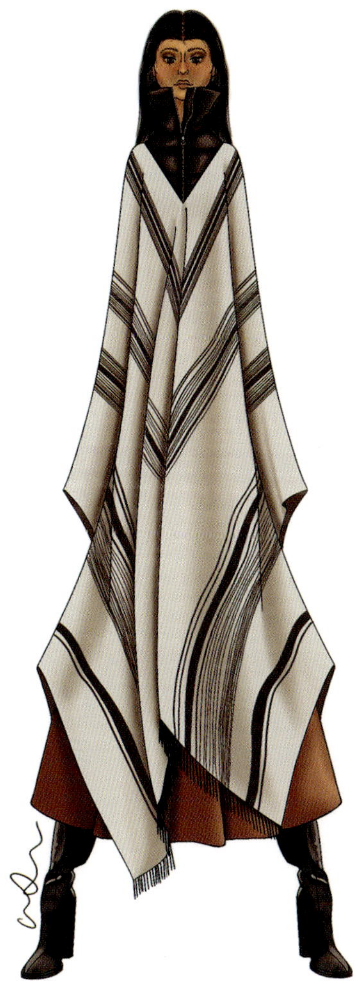

Figure 1.4 As you prepare to learn, remember that it takes time and practice to master the software. What are your learning goals? Courtesy of Alejandra Sanchez.

with InDesign, so basic functionality of the software is covered in the layouts section.

Please note that this book focuses on two-dimensional illustration. Additionally, this book does not cover illustration basics such as figure proportion, line quality, etc. Nor is basic design included. As there are more textbook options for drawing hand and digital **technical flats**, a form of clear technical drawings used frequently in the fashion industry, we do not include that subject matter here (see Figure 1.13). If we could cover all the related areas of instruction this would be a very large book, indeed. Alas, the publisher feels it is important for students to be able to carry your book without a forklift.

Be sure to check the Extend Your Learning section of the appendices if you need to brush up on any or all the aforementioned subjects. You may need to spend a little time getting to know the basics and can easily return to these lessons when you are ready.

How to Use this Book

The book is designed in sections of building up an illustration from the figure to texture to styles to layout. The learning path works straight through from the first page to the last. However, it can work just as well to pick and choose the subjects in the order you need most to strengthen your skills. Do not be afraid to build your own learning experience based on your needs. For example, you may already be skilled at digitally rendering the figure and color but want to learn more about adding textures or creating your own style. Adjust your learning path as needed to get the most from the lessons.

Many other texts focus on the software platform for the learning path. For this book, we approach your learning from the perspective of an illustrator rather than a software expert. Therefore, for each chapter, you will see instructions for creating the same or similar effects through different software or methods within a software package. The emphasis is on creating the illustration technique instead of the technical software application. So, rather than having five chapters on how to use Photoshop to create a rendering followed by five chapters on how to use Illustrator to create the same rendering, we mix the software application instruction in each chapter according to the illustrative end-goal, such as creating texture. The purpose of this approach is to make the lessons more relatable to designers and to encourage flexibility in a world of constantly changing software.

We start with the figure (Figure 1.5). This is the base for your designs, even if the garment extends well beyond human anatomy, such as a large animal costume. The wearer or performer is still at the base of the garment. We then move through adding color and patterns, different texture applications including fabric textures, light and shadow, faces and hair, and finally creating specific styles in the digital format. The content then shifts from individual renderings to layouts. Learn what makes a good project layout, background selections, followed by portfolio layouts and choices.

Each chapter starts with key learning objectives and ends with a summary of the main points. The keywords help the learner to absorb new terminology. Discussion questions are used to prod deeper into the choices we make as designers and illustrators. Review questions help to test what you learned in each chapter along with the tools and shortcuts used. Follow along with the in-chapter lessons by utilizing the exercises files

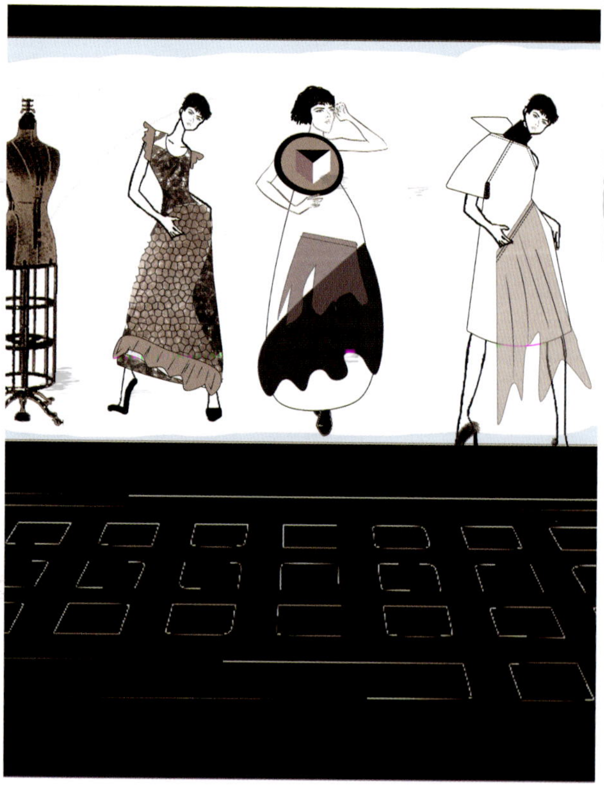

Figure 1.5 How will artificial intelligence affect the design communication world? What opportunities and threats will you face as an illustrator in the future? Artwork and designs courtesy of Julia Robles.

provided through the online resources. Then try your hand with practice exercises and your own illustrations. Along the way you will find Pro Tip callout boxes to provide technical tips and tricks. The Style Secret callout boxes help to develop your style and portfolio while creating a competitive edge (Figure 1.6). Throughout the text we included student work as well as that of established professionals for inspiration.

Through the online website, you can access the files necessary to follow along with the in-chapter lessons as well as other resources to help you. Use these as part of the lesson or for just-in-time help as you learn. Finally, you will find low-stakes review quizzes for each chapter to cement the key learnings as you progress.

If all the above is not quite enough for you, take a look in the appendix. We have included resources for you to explore the options for assets, inspiration, and plugins. Do you crave more learning or need to brush up on your basics before venturing through these lessons? Check out the Extend Your Learning section. The glossary helps to keep up with the terminology when you need it. Finally, we included a common shortcuts list for the main software covered in the text. Ultimately, how you use this book is up to you! You should have plenty of material to start with, though. So let's dive in!

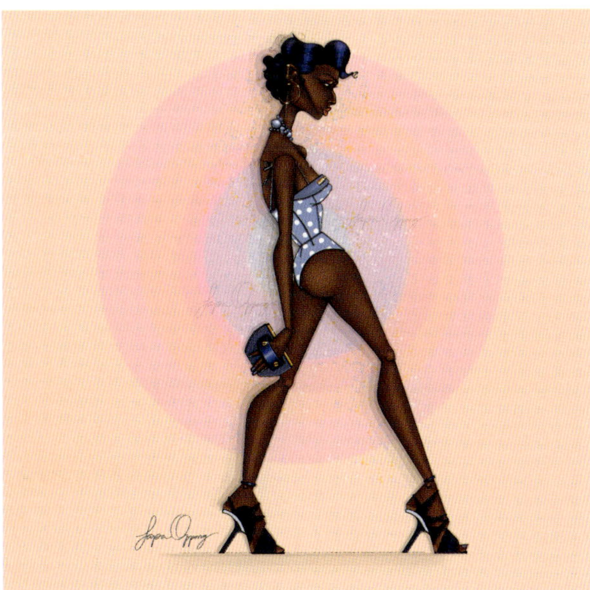

Figure 1.6 Consider what is the best workflow for your skill and needs: partially digital, fully digital, or some other style? "Oscars Awards Look Idea 2" by Papa Oppong. 2023. Made with Procreate for iPad. Copyright Papa Oppong. All rights reserved.

Design Communication: Digital or Analog?

What Is Design Communication?

We use the term **design communication** to mean illustrations of clothing. This is a generic term for either fashion or costume, but indicates the drawing of individual garments, parts of garments, or whole looks. The purpose of design communication is to convey the appearance of the finished product to those who will produce and interact with it.

- Can be used for design decisions and approval of designs
- Can be used to help makers/manufacturers create the design communicated
- Can be used to help sell the designs to retail buyers or to introduce characters to actors/directors (Figure 1.7)
- Can be used to communicate your designs to interviewers/potential employers

You may have other uses for design communication, as well. Whatever your reason, this text will help you to clearly convey your designs to the necessary recipient.

How Do Analog and Digital Illustration Compare?

One style is not necessarily better than the other, but there are advantages and drawbacks to each. **Analog** illustrations, meaning non-digital or by hand, can be practiced practically anytime, anywhere. The supplies can be very basic and easily accessible. Many people grow up drawing and have an intuitive understanding of how to manipulate a pencil with their hands (or other drawing appendage). This probably means you are more prone to pick up an analog tool such as a pencil to quickly work out an idea from your mind.

However, **digital** illustration, meaning that the illustration uses computer technology (Figure 1.8), has become so commonplace that you may risk criticism for not embracing change should you keep to a hand-drawn style. It is also more difficult to alter the hand illustration to meet production changes as they occur. In the

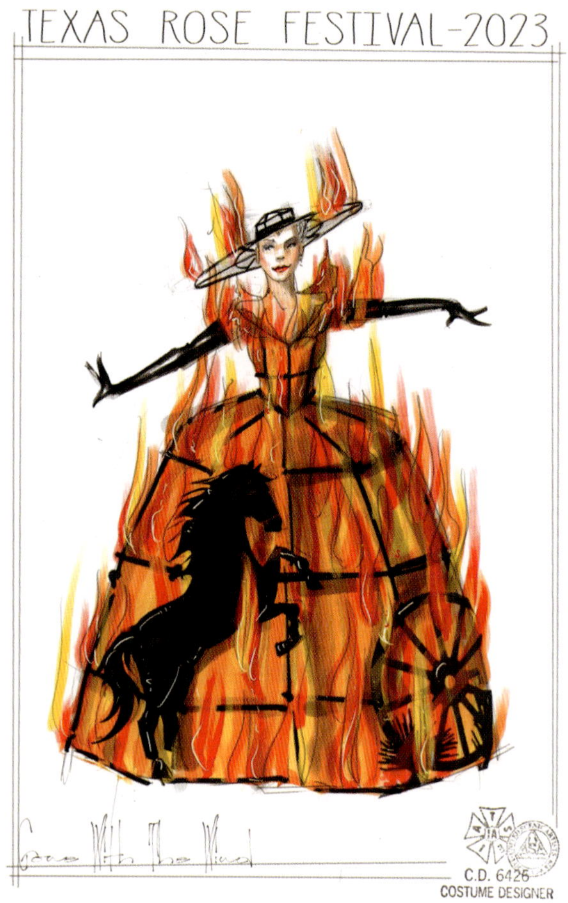

Figure 1.7 Design communication may be very technical or more abstract depending on the industry, the stage of garment production, and the unique context of the situation. Courtesy of Jacob A. Climer.

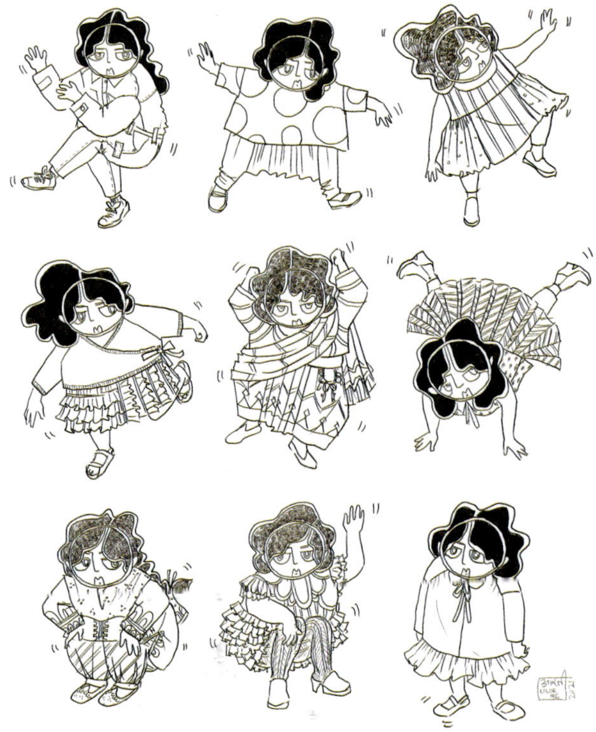

Figure 1.8 Some learners may prefer to create their designs using analog sketches, digital sketches, or a combination of both. Feel free to use what works best for you. Courtesy of Arti Sandhu.

industry, however, you need to practice and become comfortable with computer illustration if that is what your job calls for.

Unsurprisingly, most adults are more comfortable with analog sketches because that is what they grew up with. This may change as children are equally comfortable with having a tablet and stylus in hand as they are with crayons and construction paper. Already this shows in our current undergraduate classes. About half the students prefer to draw on a tablet and never seem to carry paper or pencils!

Now that there is access in most places with global internet reach, digital illustration is not as exclusive as it once was. Additionally, smaller devices make digital rendering apps almost as easy to access as pencil and paper. Many jobs now require the use of computer applications in design communication, which means that it is advantageous to demonstrate. It is easy to change colors or fabric choices if the documents are correctly set up. Plus, you do not need much physical room to work or keep artistic supplies such as paints or markers. However, the devices and applications (and keeping the technology up to date) are costly for most people. A digital divide still prevails in many areas of the world between those with and those without access to resources.

A final consideration is that the Adobe Suite has a steep learning curve that takes deliberate practice. Be prepared to occasionally hit a learning wall that takes time to work through. You may feel frustrated if you have not had to do this for a while.

How Does Hand Illustration Inform Digital Illustration?

Although it is not completely necessary to be a skilled hand illustrator prior to starting digital illustration, there are distinct advantages. Should you already possess rendering skills, you will have a style developed that can translate to a digital medium (Figure 1.9). Additionally, previously honed motor skills will transfer to digital illustration through a stylus and tablet. Styluses have come a long way since first introduced in the market. They have the sensitivity to translate your intuitive stroke style and

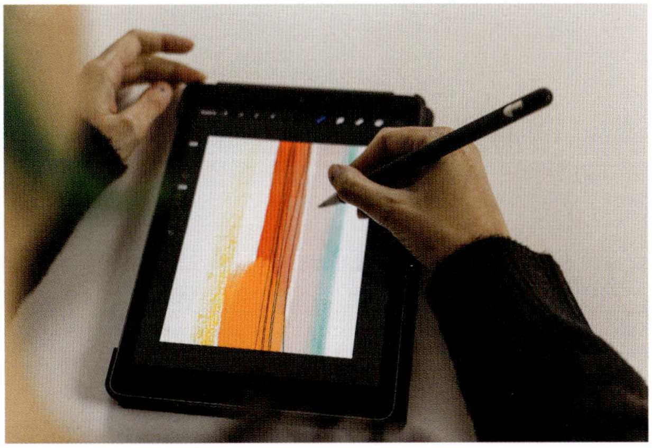

Figure 1.9 Photo of tablet and stylus. The stylus makes the transition from analog drawing to digital drawing more intuitive. Westend61/Getty Images

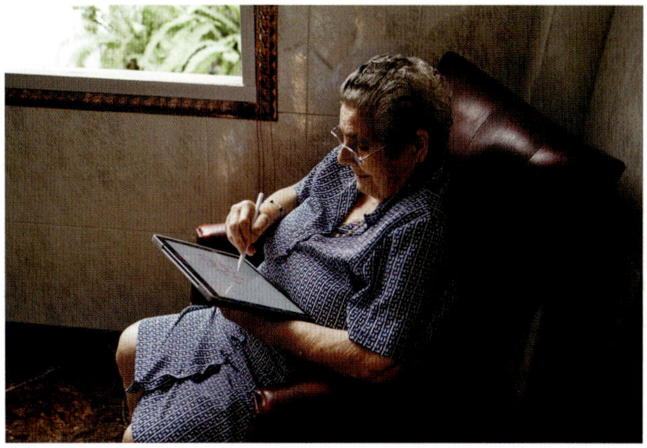

Figure 1.10 Photo of student working on a tablet. Some students are simply faster at the transition to digital artwork like this astute learner. Don't be discouraged if this is not you. You will get it over time. Yoss Sabalet/Moment/Getty Images

pressure to a screen. This skill is a bit harder to transfer via a mouse, but it is still possible.

Hand illustration practice can also help produce confidence in your work. Although this may seem to be a trivial quality, it can be a significant boon when trying to learn digital illustration. To explain, we find that often students who are not confident in their drawing ability struggle more to learn to draw digitally. It appears those who are sure of themselves as hand illustrators are more willing to take risks and learn from failures than those who lack confidence in both hand and digital illustration.

Unfortunately, advanced motor skills and confidence do not decrease the time it takes to progress to a digital medium. All learning requires understanding of the technology before you can transfer hand illustration to digital skills. Some learners may adapt better and faster to a digital medium simply due to an intuitive synchronism with digital logic (Figure 1.10).

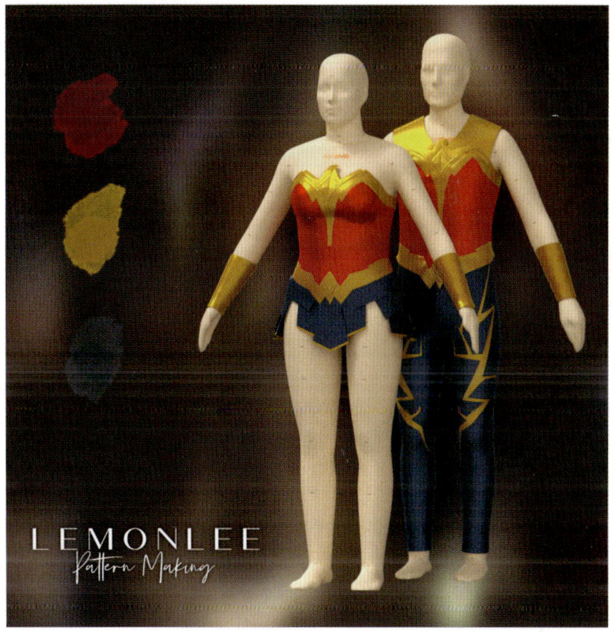

Figure 1.11 3D illustration has many uses, but is generally not the best choice for initial design communication. Photo of 3D work produced by Liana Hinojosa of LemonLee Pattern Making.

How Does 3D Illustration Compare with 2D Illustration?

We mentioned previously that this book sticks with two-dimensional (2D) illustration. Although 3D digital illustration has improved by leaps and bounds, there are some practical reasons to not include such instruction in this text. Generally, 3D illustration has specific end-use applications that for the most part do not align with the purpose of this book. 3D illustration is most commonly used for game character conceptualization or garment sample production (Figure 1.11). You can create similar realistic effects through 2D digital painting, without having to render a 360-degree view that takes more time. For fashion and costume designers trying to communicate initial design ideas, 3D rendering may be an act of time-consuming overkill. At least, it is for the time being.

Additionally, 3D rendering requires specialized skills in certain subject areas, and software that are fundamentally different from the illustration software we are referencing for this book. For example, to use Clo3-D (a 3D rendering software for the garment industry) and similar 3D rendering packages for apparel, you need to be comfortable with patternmaking or draping.

Yes, Photoshop and some of the other artistic software mentioned have 3D tools. However, it helps to first learn 2D illustration before venturing into another realm. As mentioned previously, we can only cover so much with one book. Should someone write an instructional book on this subject matter? Absolutely. Is this that book? Nope.

What about AI?

Artificial intelligence is quickly gaining ground in the artistic world. At the time of writing this book, AI-generated art is readily available and hotly debated. There are still many issues with the quality of the results, but the technology is improving at a rapid rate. Will this change garment illustration and design? Will artists and designers need to look for new jobs? Will it make illustration and design easier or just less "human"? How does AI affect intellectual property copyrights? New technology is always equally exciting and terrifying. One thing is certain, however. We will need to keep an eye on the development of AI art.

AI is already at work with certain digital painting programs. *Content-Aware Fill* and the *Object Selection* tools use a form of artificial intelligence that analyzes the data from the pixels and performs a task based on your input. These tools have been around for a few years and seem less threatening to artists as they are non-generative. However, newer **generative AI** tools such as **text to image** continue to become mainstream. Generative AI creates new content such as images. Text to image is one type of generative AI that has become very popular in the last few years. Programs such as Adobe Firefly, Midjourney, and Image Creator from Microsoft Bing can create new images by analyzing keywords typed in against the vast data set of images available on the internet. Vizcom can take your rough sketches and provide texture, 3D elements, or help you workshop the design. Adobe Illustrator has recently introduced *Generative Shape Fill* and *Generative Vectors*, among other AI tools. Photoshop has introduced *Generative Fill* tools. Generative AI tools are currently being developed faster than the authors can write this text.

If you have never tried working with generative AI before, you should. The fear of generative AI art is certainly understandable. However, this is another tool for art that we all need to at least deal with, if not embrace. We recommend that you take the time to learn to use it while playing around before incorporating it into your artwork. After all, the primary complaint about AI is the copyright issue. Generally, if you agree to the terms of use for the tool, you also agree to allow the parent program access to your artwork. With some programs, they offer a paywall that allows you to keep the rights to your work. As with any new technology, you should investigate thoroughly and use your best judgment. We will explore a few possible uses in the Styles and Background chapters. Hopefully, this will spark some ideas to use these tools in new and unexpected ways.

Technical Applications

Why Adobe?

Adobe applications are currently the most widely used for fashion and costume communication. That fact may change as cheaper and more accessible applications become available and adopted. Procreate, Affinity Design, Clip Studio Paint, and a slew of other artistic software are creating stiff competition for Adobe. Already, about half of our students prefer Procreate because of its intuitive interface and affordability. They often start in Procreate, then move the illustration over to Photoshop when they need the more advanced features.

Adobe Illustrator, Photoshop, and InDesign have many positive qualities to make them the primary contender for digital illustration. First, the artist has total control over all aspects of the work. Very little is automated until you tell it to be so (such as actions or templates). Even the few automated processes, such as photo merging, can be performed manually if preferred. These applications have over three decades of experience in the field as one of the pioneers of digital illustration. They have a strong backbone of developers and dedicated users to help support your journey into digital illustration. Adobe can be relied upon for very powerful tools and professional results. Furthermore, they are very flexible in that there are multiple ways to accomplish the same task. For example, if you want to change the color of one part of the illustration, you have a wide variety of ways to accomplish that task. For the most part, there are at least ten different ways to complete any single action in these applications (Figure 1.12).

Interestingly, the same qualities that make Adobe products a good choice often prove to be obstacles. Illustrator, Photoshop, and InDesign are all very powerful

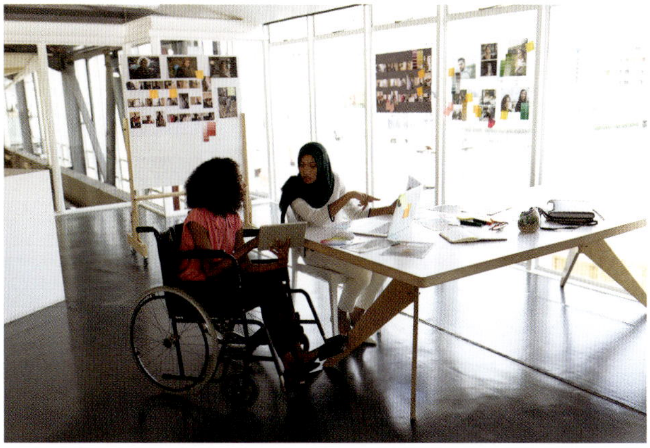

Figure 1.12 Photo of students working on computer. Remember that someone else may show you a different way to achieve results. This is okay! One of the hard parts about this software is that you can get to the same effects via many, many different routes. Wavebreakmedia/iStock.com

tools that put the control in your hands. This means that the programs will do what you tell them to do—*exactly* what you tell them to do, even if you do not know that you told it to do so. These are not intuitive or easy programs to pick up on the fly. You need to deliberately work with the applications on a consistent basis to understand how to fully utilize them. Think of it as trading ease of use for power. The camera app on your phone is simple to use, but you are limited with how much you can edit the photo. Photoshop, by comparison, takes time to learn how to use but allows you to do a nearly infinite number of alterations to a photo.

Additionally, due to the robust nature of these applications, you need a decent computer to run them. Sadly, the "lightweight" computers often suggested for students rarely support the necessary requirements for full Adobe applications. These computers are mostly used for word processing and spreadsheet programs. See the section on software and equipment hardware for more information about the requirements.

Can the Information Be Used in Other Programs?

The short answer to this question is yes … mostly. The longer answer is that it depends upon the functionality of the program that you are trying to use. Each program is built a little differently, although there are some universal concepts about how we build digital artwork. Many of the concepts such as layers, brushes, filters, and blend modes can be found in the majority of illustration-based applications. How you access that function will vary according to the particular software.

Some software programs have a more limited range of their functionality. So, you may not be able to utilize a certain set of instructions if your application does not have that filter or function. This is where your own familiarity with the software of your choice and your personal creativity come into play. You may not have that one particular filter to achieve the specified effect, but you may find one similar or a different way to create the effect altogether. As an example: Procreate does not have a cloud rendering filter used to create camouflage. Instead, perhaps you can make your own brush to achieve a similar look.

How Do the Programs Compare?

There are many digital art programs out there, and more show up on the market every day. It is impossible to create a text to cover every software. However, some of the programs listed below are roughly interchangeable. Meaning, with some minor deduction, you can use the artistic method for one program and utilize it in another. Table 1.1 lays out some key components to consider when comparing the software available. In the table you will see the specified program, primary function, general cost, learning curve, flexibility of the features and tools, general mobility, and hardware requirements. We do not list all software on the market. The estimation of the components for each software is the authors' opinions. For instance, others may feel that Adobe products are very intuitive and easy to learn. We are simply calling it like we see it based upon our own experiences.

In the chart, the cost is depicted as $ to indicate below 25 USD, $$ for 25 to100 USD, or $$$ to indicate above 100 USD per year or per program. The learning curve indicates how easy and quickly a new user can become proficient in the program. Program flexibility is used to communicate how many features and tools are available to use. Mobility means how easy it is to use the program in unconventional spaces. This depends on the availability of the program for mobile devices and how well it operates without an internet connection. Finally, hardware needs indicate the type of device and necessary requirements to run the program.

Table 1.1 Comparison chart showing some of the more commonly used software applications in digital illustration.

SOFTWARE	PRIMARY FUNCTION	COST	LEARNING CURVE	PROGRAM FLEXIBILITY	MOBILITY	HARDWARE NEEDS
Adobe Photoshop	Photo editing and digital rendering (mostly pixel-based)	$–$$$; Adobe offers many plans and options. If you are a student or teacher, Adobe has a discounted subscription. Be aware that it goes up after the first year, though. Fully read the terms of the agreement	Steep	High	Laptop or desktop needed for full features; less functional version available for mobile devices	Robust disk space, RAM, and graphics card for laptop or computer
Adobe Illustrator	Vector-based artwork	Same as above	Steep	High	Same as above	Same as above
Adobe InDesign	Desktop publishing and layout	Same as above	Steep	High	Same as above	Same as above
Adobe Fresco	Digital painting	Free for starter plan, upgrade for premium features or part of the Creative Cloud	Mid	Mid	Fresco works well on a mobile device	Decent—but does not require as much as other Adobe programs
Corel Painter	Digital painting	$$$; student discount available	Steep	High	Low	Similar requirements to Adobe
Procreate	Digital painting	$	Low	Mid	High	iPad
Clip Studio Paint	Digital painting	$$	Mid	Mid	High	Decent—but does not require as much RAM or disk space as Adobe

The first program listed is Adobe Photoshop. This program has become so synonymous with photo editing that it has become a verb. Photoshop, or Ps as we commonly shortcut the name in this book, is primarily a **raster** or pixel-based photo-editing tool. However, it is now used as a digital painting tool just as frequently. Pixel-based systems work with a pixel grid that carries color and value information. When you zoom into a small area on a raster image, you will see the pixel grid. This application is best for more artistic illustrations, any photo editing, and compositing.

Photoshop is a great choice if you like to initially work analog before importing the artwork to a digital format. It is also a good choice for editing any photoshoots of your work. It is available for tablets such as the iPad. The program is not as flexible or robust in tablet form, though. There are distinctive limitations compared to the full desktop version of the program. It is highly flexible and often fun to use but tends to be used less in the fashion industry because technical flats are the main standard (Figure 1.13). Photoshop is generally not the

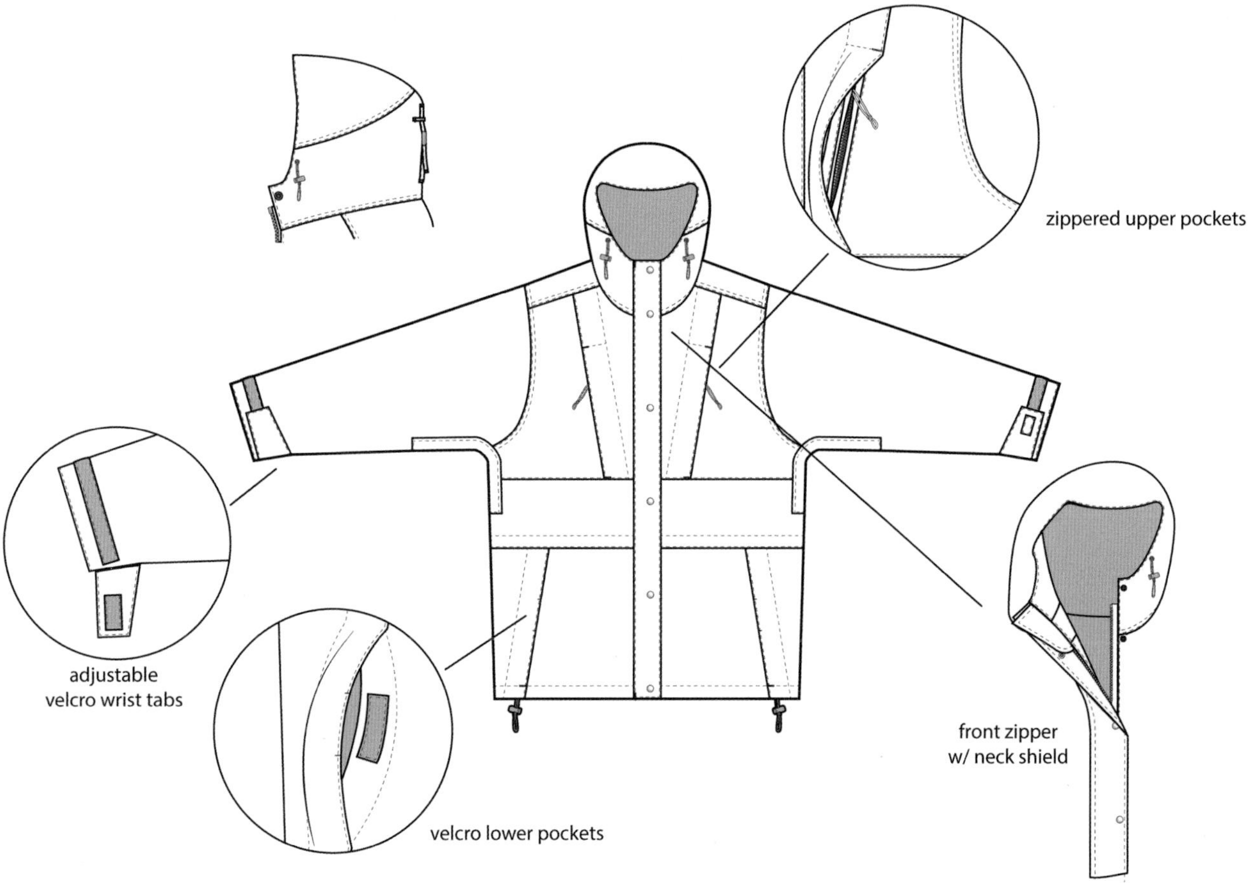

Figure 1.13 Example of technical flat showing all the details of a garment. Artwork by the authors.

best choice for more graphic work such as technical flats or for portfolio layouts.

Adobe Illustrator, in contrast, is primarily a **vector**-based program. This means the artwork is based upon a series of mathematical coordinates rather than a pixel grid. So, no matter how much you zoom in or out, the image will stay crisp. It produces a cleaner graphic style that is better suited to technical flats of garments and logos. This is the most common tool and style used in the fashion industry. Like Photoshop, Illustrator has a mobile device version that is less robust than the full desktop version. It is not a good choice for photo editing or more artistic styles of digital painting. It should be noted that Illustrator has some effects that are pixel-based, whereas Photoshop has some vector-based tools.

Adobe InDesign can easily work with both vector and pixel images. This application is best for portfolio layouts, resumés, and multi-page documents. It excels at pulling multiple elements together for a portfolio or any document with a lot of pages and text. InDesign does a great job of reducing file size through linked files (Figure 1.14). The program is not well suited to creating individual elements such as technical flats, rendered illustrations, or edited photos. It also currently does not have a mobile device version.

We mention Adobe Fresco here because it is built as a digital painting application. It is less functional than Photoshop but works well as a mobile application for sketching and rough painting. Fresco is probably most comparable to Procreate. If you have invested in the Adobe Creative Cloud, this is a great starting place in lieu of purchasing another program such as Procreate. The starter version of Fresco is also available for free and then you can upgrade for the premium features without subscribing to Adobe Creative Cloud.

Corel Painter is less well known and does not currently have a mobile counterpart. However, Painter remains a favorite of some illustrators and concept artists for digital painting. It has very similar functions to Photoshop. However, many feel that Painter has a better brush engine that creates more realistic painterly effects. Painter is currently less likely to be picked up

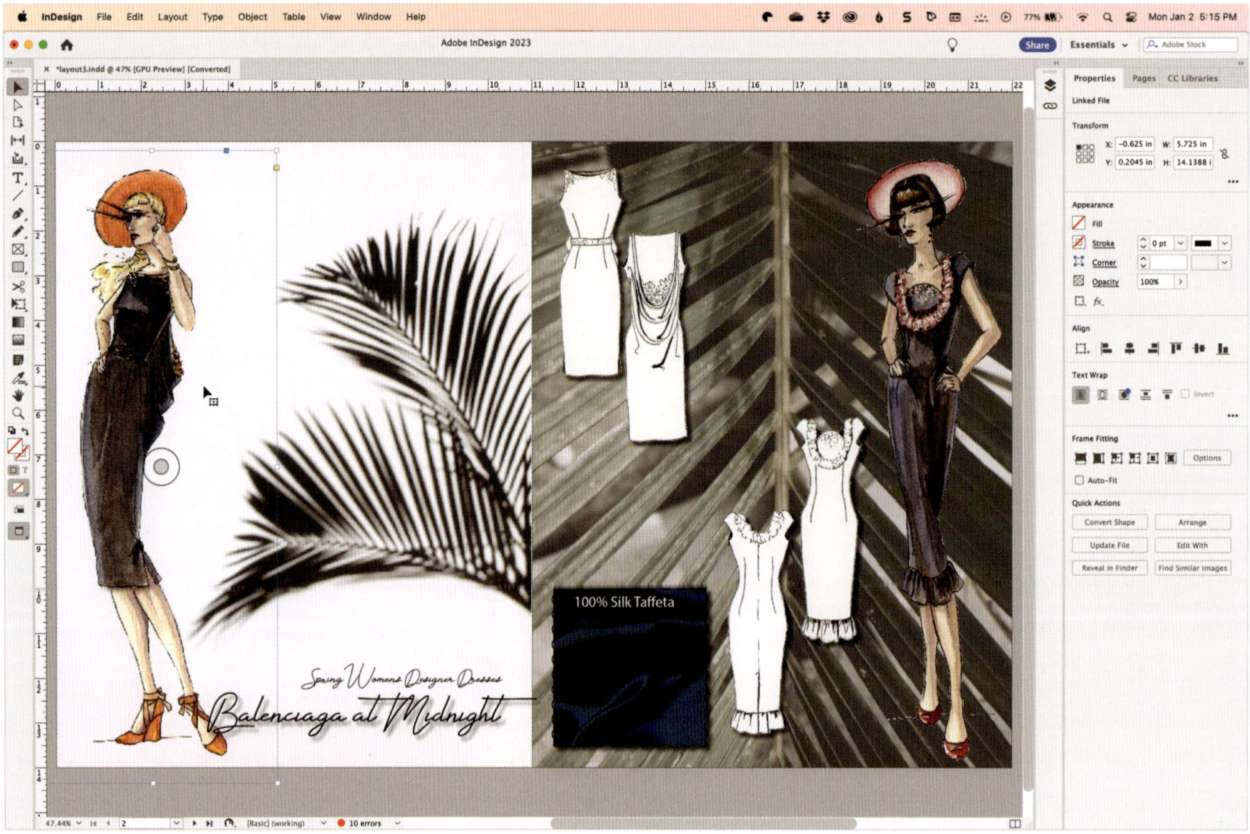

Figure 1.14 Example of portfolio layout in InDesign. InDesign is best for laying out your boards and is not good for creating illustrations or flats. Artwork by the authors.

by new users in the digital illustration world. However, many experienced illustrators use the program regularly for all or part of their illustration process.

Procreate is quickly gaining popularity against the Adobe products. It is easy to learn and is significantly less expensive, which makes it very appealing to new digital artists. It is highly mobile and uses a more intuitive interface. Procreate does face some limitations, however. This program is only available for the iOS platform. That means it is limited to iPads and iPhones. It also does not offer all the robust features available on a program such as Photoshop. This may or may not be an issue for you, depending upon your personal needs. Finally, because of the smaller computing power of a tablet versus a full computer, the file size is limited in Procreate. There are workarounds,[2] but this means you can only produce so many layers per image.

Clip Studio Paint is the final program compared above. You may not be familiar with this application, but it is quickly gaining popularity in the character creation field for gaming and manga. This means that fashion and costume designers will soon start to follow. This software is available for desktop and mobile devices. It costs more than Procreate but less than the Adobe Creative Cloud. The program flexibility also falls somewhere in between the two software, as well. If you are familiar with Adobe Photoshop, the Clip Studio Paint interface will look very familiar. Unlike Photoshop and its mobile counterpart, however, the Clip Studio Paint interface looks the same between the desktop and mobile versions. One interesting feature to note about Clip Studio Paint, however, is the 3D pose feature that allows you to set a pose for reference while sketching.

There are a slew of other programs available out there, and more come onto the market every day. While we do not cover them in-depth here, they may work better for your needs. For example, Krita is an open-source software. This means that the program is available for free so long as you follow their terms of use. Sketchbook Pro, Paint Tool SAI, Affinity Designer, or even Adobe Photoshop Express may be the better option for you (Figure 1.15). Do your research to choose the software that fits your artistic needs, budget, and skill level. There is no right or wrong answer. There is only what is right for you.

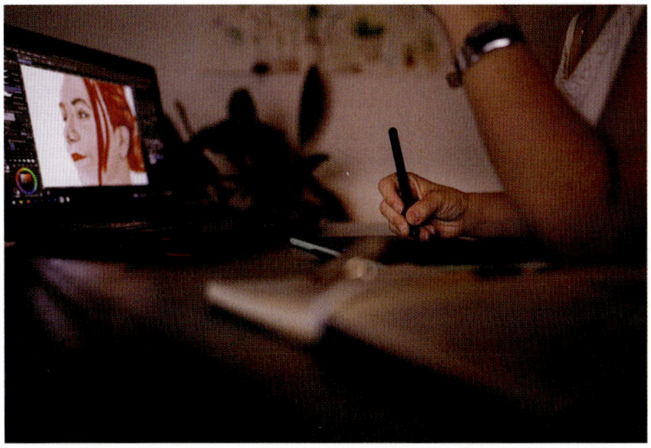

Figure 1.15 Photo of student working on computer. If you already have a device and some graphic application, use that. Don't spend money on other hardware or software until you know exactly what you want. Dusan Stankovic/iStock.com

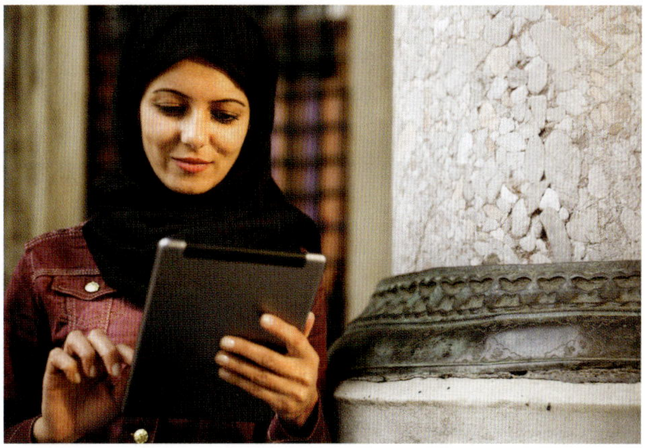

Figure 1.16 Photo of student working on tablet in a museum. The great thing about tablets is their mobility. You may not have access to as many features as a tradeoff, though. Rossella De Berti/iStock.com

What Equipment and Software Do I Need?

If you are deciding to purchase new software, use the information in the previous section to help you choose the best option for your needs. What you currently have is always the best place to start, though. Don't spend more money if you are just starting to learn. If you already have digital artistic software, even if it is not listed above, use that for now. Remember these are just tools. More robust software does not make you a better illustrator any more than buying a top-dollar, high-quality pencil. Once your skills progress, those tools may help you out. But when you are starting to learn, go with what you can afford.

As a side note, some applications offer subscriptions whereas others have you purchase the software outright. You will need to do a little research to see what works best for your budget. Adobe and some of the other packages may offer discounts for students. If you are a formal student at an institution, be aware that some schools offer student access to certain software. Check with your school to see if you already have access to any of the software previously mentioned.

In terms of hardware, you will first need to determine if you want to work on a full computer, a mobile device, or some combination of the two modes. A computer, regardless of desktop or laptop, Windows or Mac, will be a more flexible and robust tool, overall. Because of the increased computing power, the applications will offer more features and tools. Plus, you can generally have larger files with more layers and non-destructive editing. However, these devices generally cost significantly more than mobile options. They are also more difficult (particularly if you have a desktop) to tote around with you.

Mobile devices such as tablets have the advantage of mobility (hence, the title "mobile" devices! Figure 1.16). However, they are more limited in computing power. At least, that is, for the time being, as technology develops quickly. Less computing power means that there will be more limitations in the software flexibility and file size.

Whatever you decide is best for you, be sure to check the recommended requirements for the software you want to use. Usually, they will list "minimum" requirements and "recommended" requirements. Always go with the recommendations, if possible. Only meeting the minimum requirements will result in more crashes, slower actions, more glitches, and occasional lost work. If you do not "speak" hardware and have no idea what the requirements mean when reviewing your hardware, ask for help! You can have your equipment checked by a specialist, look online for tutorials about the subject, or try the chat help feature offered by many of the hardware and software websites.

Along with this, you will want to check that you have some sort of internet connection. Most of the software requires a connection to download and set up. Also, all hardware and software have frequent updates to keep refreshed. If you want to save hardware file storage space, you will need a decent connection to upload and download from your online file storage cloud.

Aside from the primary device you use, you need some way to make your sketches digital. If you like to hand sketch, you will need either a scanner or a camera to import the drawing. A phone or tablet camera is often the most convenient, but it also takes some skill and practice to get a high-resolution, evenly lit, flat photo. Scanners come in a wide variety of price and options, as well (Figure 1.17). If shopping for a scanner, we recommend a flatbed option with a high resolution (300 dpi is commonly recommended).

If using a tablet, consider a drawing stylus such as the Apple Pencil to assist you while working. If using a laptop or desktop, you may want to consider a drawing tablet such as the Wacom Intuos. These will help make the working process feel more intuitive than trying to work solely with a mouse or track pad.

Finally, you may want to look at printer options. Consider the cost and quality of the ink and paper. If you just do not want to invest in one more expensive piece of equipment, do not fret. There are generally plenty of printing sources such as FedEx around most cities.

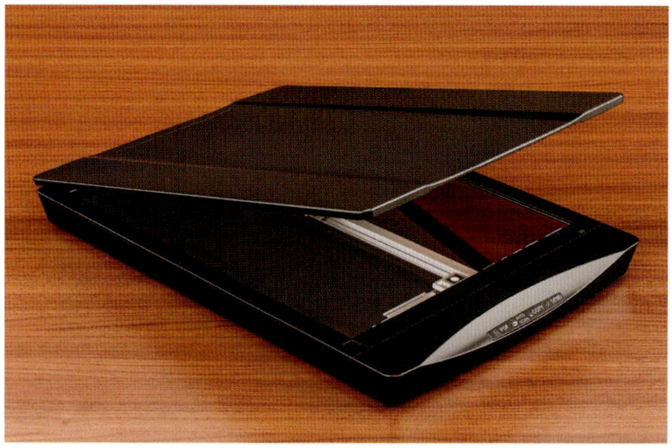

Figure 1.17 Photo of scanner. Remember to check if you have free access to these sorts of tools through your school, public library, or other resource. AlexLMX/iStock.com

Mac or PC?

Should you use a Mac or PC option for digital illustration? The answer is completely dependent upon your personal preferences and comfort. Either platform will work just fine. We cannot tell you which is better for you. We alternate between PC and Mac screenshots to try to balance the platform familiarity for students. Whichever you use, be sure to check your current system aspects and if they meet the recommended requirements for the software and any peripheral equipment you may use.

What Should I Know Before Going through this Book?

This is an intermediate- to advance-level book. Therefore, we make some assumptions about your skill level. To get the most out of this text, you should be able to operate your own device, have basic working knowledge of Adobe Photoshop and Illustrator (or your software of similar choice), and basic proficiency at hand illustration. You should also have a desire and commitment to learn and translate your designs to a digital platform. You should have the time to invest in this learning path. There are no magic wands to instantly understand this medium. We also assume that you have the patience to learn and have a growth mindset. You must accept that there will be failures along the way. That is simply a part of learning. Finally, you should also have basic design knowledge and understand how garments and fabrics behave on the human body. Attention to detail and some sense of color theory help along the way. You do not need to be an expert in any one of these areas. However, you should have a functional knowledge about them as we cannot cover all these aspects within one text!

So, what do we mean by basic working knowledge of Photoshop and Illustrator? You should know how to open, create new, and save documents. For Photoshop, you should be familiar with the *Paintbrush* tool, the *Layers* panel, make basic *selections*, use the *move* tool, and make transformations. To test yourself, can you add the bow to the shirt below (Figures 1.18a and 1.18b)? You will find these files in the STUDIO Access file downloads for

STYLE SECRETS 1.1

Sourcing Your Visual Research

When creating new designs from existing inspiration, be mindful of how you source your visual research. It is tempting to just "grab" images from Google, Pinterest, or whatever image search you prefer. However, you need to be aware of intellectual property. Afterall, you don't want others to use your work willy-nilly, do you?

Chapter 1. Your finished result should look something like Figure 1.18c.

For Illustrator, you should be able to use the *pen* and *arrow* tools. Do you understand how to create new shapes, and how to manipulate the *fill* and *stroke* of objects? To test yourself, can you draw this flat below (Figure 1.19)? Again, the files are available in the STUDIO Access download portal.

If you are not using Adobe products, just be sure that you have a similar basic working knowledge of the program of your choice. We describe some of the primary aspects that are common to most digital illustration software in the Common Tools section. Be honest about your own comfort and skill level. You may need to brush up on your basic skills within the program you are using before trying the exercises in this book. Do yourself a big favor and make sure you have this functional knowledge before you become overwhelmed with the more advanced instructions in this text. Remember, the book will still be here when you are ready!

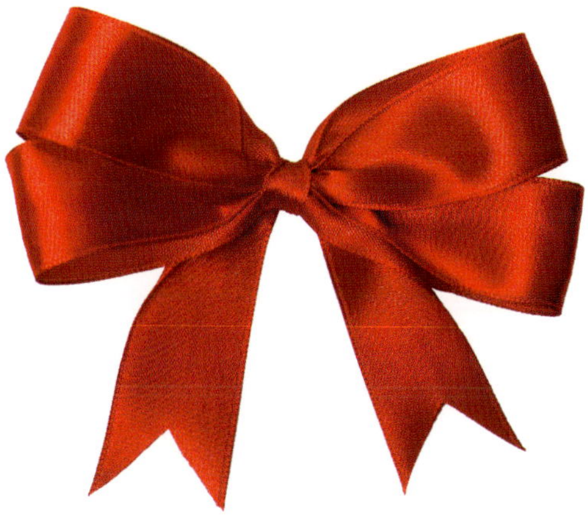

Figure 1.18a The bow image can be found in your exercise files. See if you can select one of the bows from the background and apply it to the shirt image. iMelamory/iStock.com

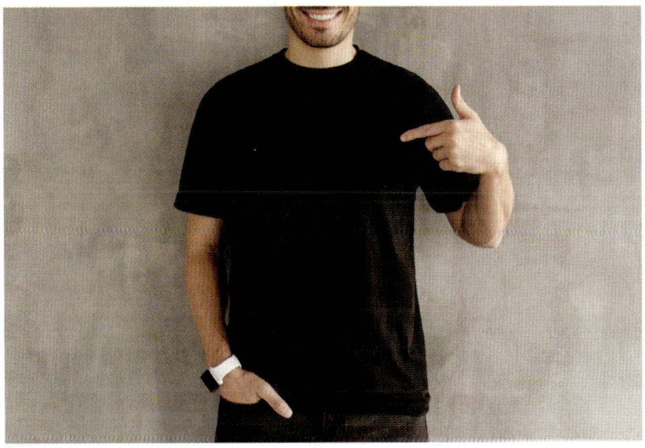

Figure 1.18b Photo of model in a shirt. This photo is also in your exercise files. Damir Khabirov/iStock.com

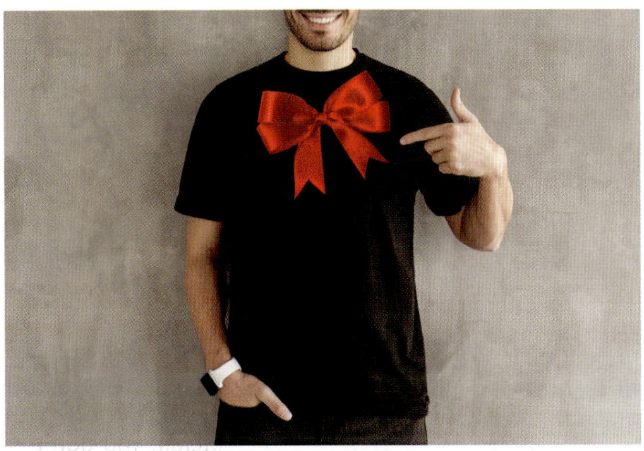

Figure 1.18c Finished image. How does your result compare with this sample?

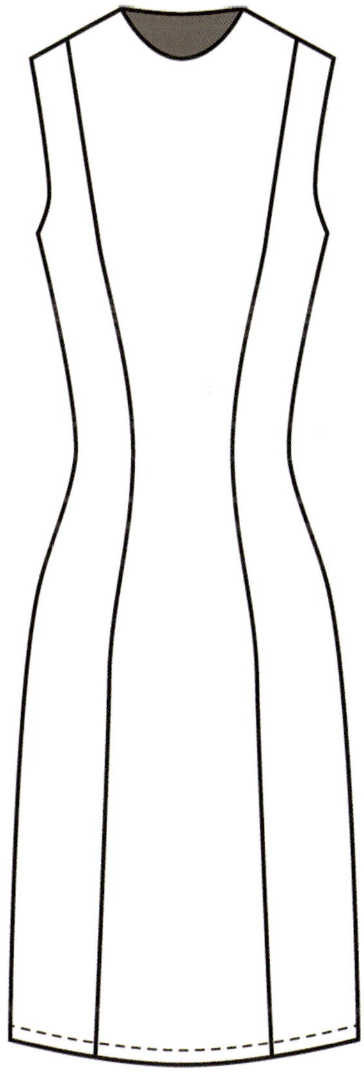

Figure 1.19 Can you reproduce this princess dress flat in Illustrator?

A Note about Troubleshooting Adobe

Adobe is hard. As Zoë Hong says about all fashion, "it's hard because it's hard, not because there is something wrong with you."[3] This is something that takes time and deliberate practice to have a firm handle on it. Here's the deal: you can either have control or you can have ease of use. Think about texting on your phone: it autocorrects your spelling, suggests emojis, and you are stuck with the font used by the application. It's easy to use, but you don't have much control or many choices. It's often frustrating for that reason. How often did you notice an autocorrect mishap after sending? The algorithm in the program tries to out-guess what you intended to write based on a series of if–then situations that may or may not apply to your message intent (Figure 1.20).

Adobe applications give a lot of control and provide a plethora of tools. It does NOT try to out-guess what you intended to do, however. This means that the program does exactly what you tell it to do, whether you know it or not. So, until you are familiar and comfortable with the program, you may accidentally turn on some command or property that results in less than satisfactory outcomes.

All of this means that you must deliberately practice with each program on a regular basis to understand how to fully utilize it. It takes patience. Without an expert over your shoulder to help you troubleshoot, you need to fully explore your mistakes. When something doesn't seem to be working right, don't keep repeating the same command. Try a different command. Look at the properties panel. Play with the options to see if it helps. Search the web for other folks that are experiencing the same issue. Trust us, someone else out there has run across this same issue and posted about it.

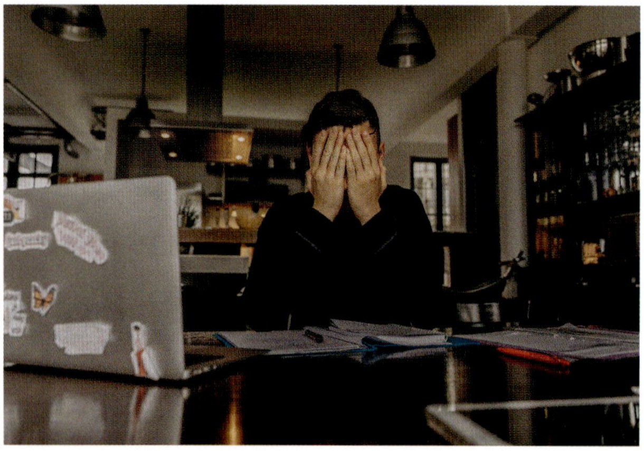

Figure 1.20 Photo of frustrated learner. There will be times when you just want to quit. Remember that it's a journey rather than a destination. Well, unless you have an assignment due tomorrow, that is ... Dusan Stankovic/Getty Images

Now there are times that Adobe experiences hiccups. It takes a lot of space to run these programs, and sometimes glitches occur. If you are getting some weird actions when the command previously worked, try closing and restarting the program. You may need to close and restart the whole device. Check for updates with both Adobe and your main system. If all else fails, contact the Adobe support team for help.

Lisa Carney always says, "first you get good, then you get fast" about Adobe.[4] This is excellent advice. Don't expect to master this stuff in a week, a month, or even a year. Go through the practice exercises before trying the technique on your own work. Sit in on general Adobe classes to understand the program better. Practice regularly, have patience with yourself, and remember, Adobe isn't out to get you. Mwuhaha!

Updates

All software updates frequently, and the programs shown in this text are no exception. Adobe releases a few versions annually and has multiple bug or security updates on a regular basis. The annual versions will include new or altered tools, features, and sometimes interface looks. For the most part, these updates will not dramatically alter the processes shown in this book. The marketing team likes to make the new features look flashy to sell more subscriptions. However, the overall function of the tools and workflow we use only face dramatic changes about every four to eight years. Even when we do start to utilize new tools to make the workflow smoother or faster, it does not mean that the "old way" stops functioning. So do not fret if you see photos of an older version in this text. The instructions still apply!

Common Tools within the Applications

Regardless of the software you use, there are a lot of similarities in the tools. The interface, tool symbol, and feature may have different names and looks, but they essentially work the same way. Following are descriptions of tools and features with which you should be familiar.

PRO TIP 1.1

Use Warm-Ups

Whether you use a mouse or some form of a stylus and tablet, it helps to warm up a little before jumping into your work. We have included some warm-ups for you in the exercise files for this chapter. Utilize them however best suits you. You can aim to become proficient with each task individually before moving to the next, or work through the entire set to improve your dexterity. You can download these files through your STUDIO Access. Figures PT 1.1a and 1.1b show examples of warm-up exercises for the mouse and the tablet.

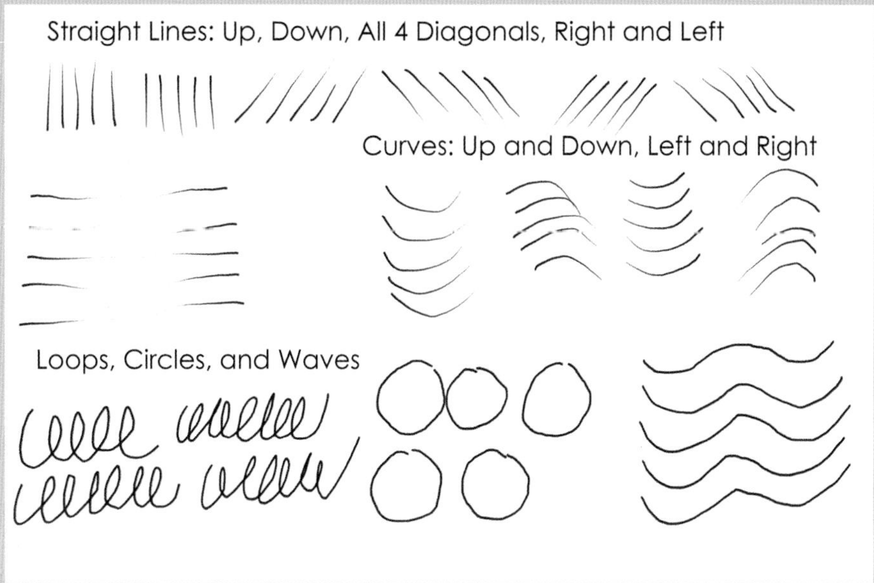

Figure PT 1.1a Mouse warm-up exercises.

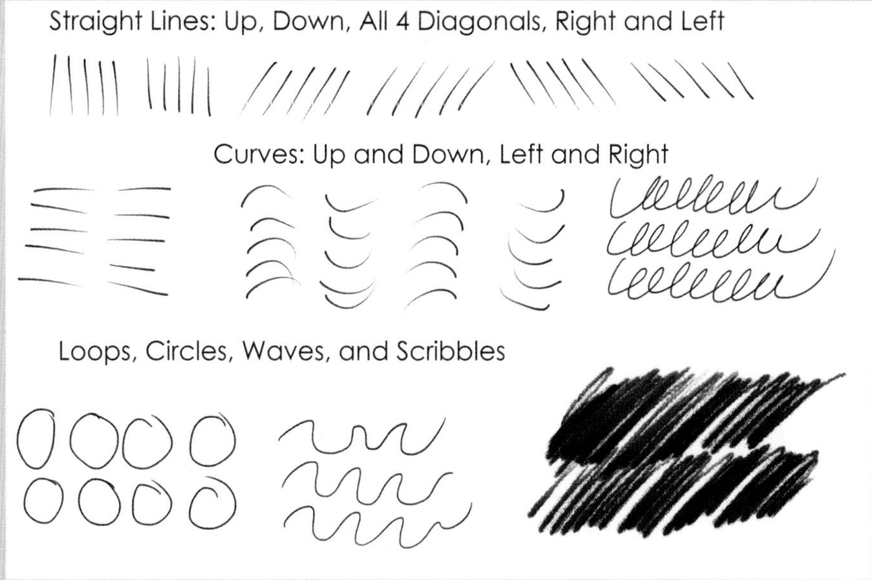

Figure PT 1.1b Tablet warm-up exercise. It helps to warm up your hand with some basic exercises before you start to illustrate.

Layers

Layers are a major feature found in most artistic software applications. Think of layers like sheets of transparency paper, stacked one on top of another. Each sheet contains part of the artwork that adds up to the entire picture. You can move the order of the stack, remove a layer, change the layer, or temporarily turn it off without affecting the other layers. You gain a large amount of flexibility with your artwork with this feature. The primary drawback is, as usual, increased file size as you continue to add layers. This drawback is more of a problem on smaller computing devices such as tablets or phones.

Layers are controlled through a separate panel that will look a little different for each software out there. Take the time to familiarize yourself with how to turn layers *On* and *Off*, *Lock* the layer, move layers, change *Opacity*, and change the *Blend Mode* for a layer. In Adobe, you can bring up the *Layer* panel through the *Window* menu.

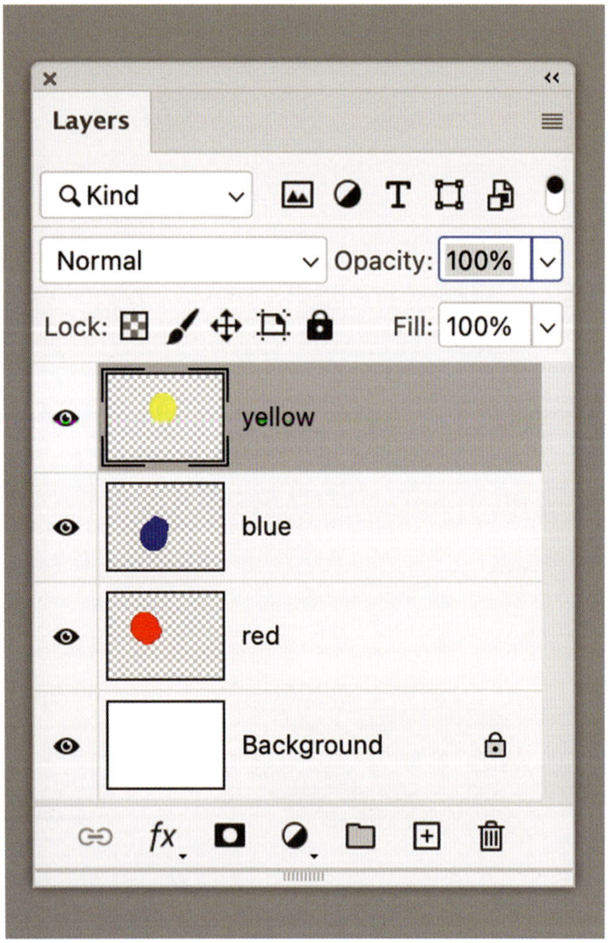

Figure 1.21 Screenshot of the *Layers* menu in Photoshop. Notice that the menu includes its own set of tools and features.

Blend Modes

Blend modes are common for many artistic applications. Blend modes change how the artwork on a layer interacts with the artwork stacked below it. They can be applied to an entire layer or to a particular tool like the *Brush* tool. Most of the software use the same or at least similar language such as *Multiply*, *Soft Light*, and *Overlay*. They are a common part of the Photoshop workflow and other similar digital painting applications.

The best way to understand how *blend modes* work is to play with them. Use a file like the one in Figure 1.22a to see how the different modes react with the layers below them. Figure 1.22b shows the file with the Hard Light blend mode applied.

Selection Tools

Selection tools vary according to whether you are working with raster- or vector-based artwork, and, of course, the specific software.

When working with vector art on the computer, you generally have a *Selection* tool (the black arrow tool in Illustrator) or the *Direct Selection* tool (the white arrow). The difference is that the *Selection* tool chooses an entire object whereas the *Direct Selection* allows you to pick a specific part of an object, such as an anchor or path. Figures 1.23a and 1.23b show the two tools and how they work differently using the exercise file.

However, if you are working with pixel-based art, you will have to use one of several options to select part or all of the artwork. You can choose selections through a drawn perimeter such as a *Lasso* tool, or through some sort of criteria such as a color range. Learning to make pixel selections with the many tool options is something that takes time. Images with "fuzzy" edges such as feathers, hair, or smoke can be frustrating challenges when first learning the software. However, with training, practice, and patience, you will soon get the hang of it. This technology is also rapidly improving, making even the most difficult selections easier than before. Figure 1.24 displays a *Lasso* tool selection using the exercise file.

Transform Tools

Transform tools are common in most art software programs to *Scale*, *Rotate*, *Flip*, *Warp*, and *Distort* part of

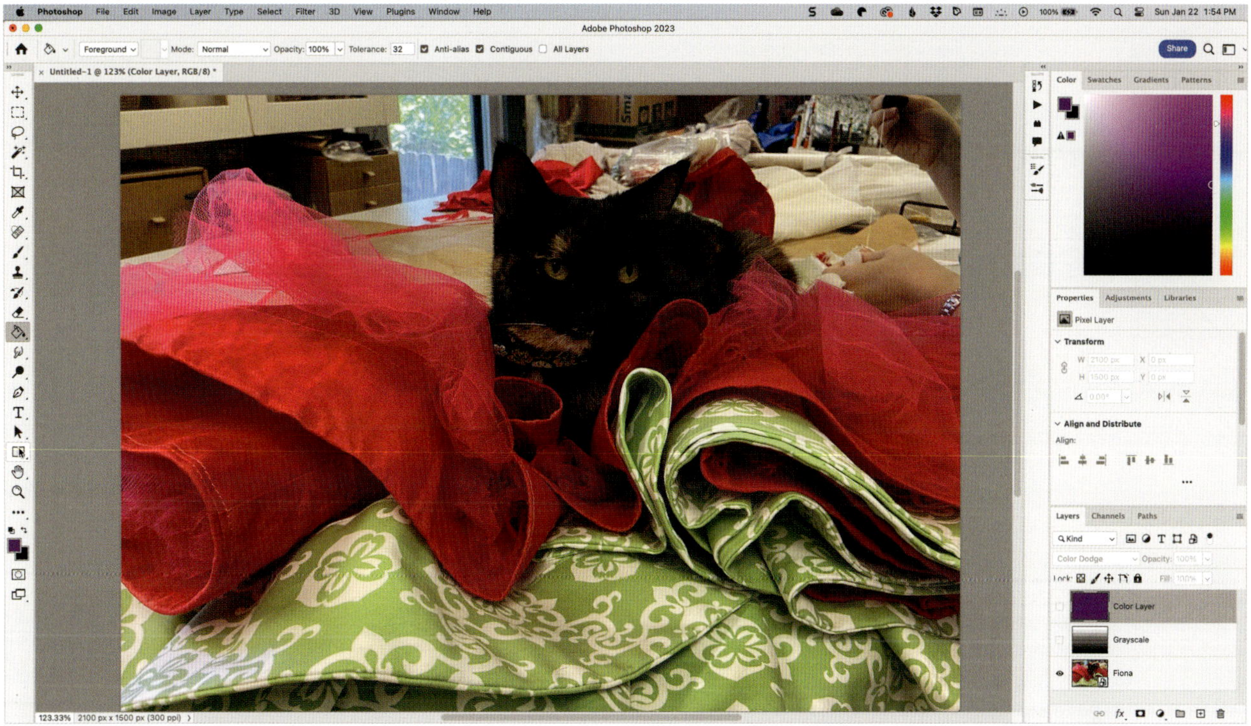

Figure 1.22a Blend mode file. Turn on the *Visibility* of one of the layers above the photo and play with the *Blend Modes* to see the different effects on Fiona the cat.

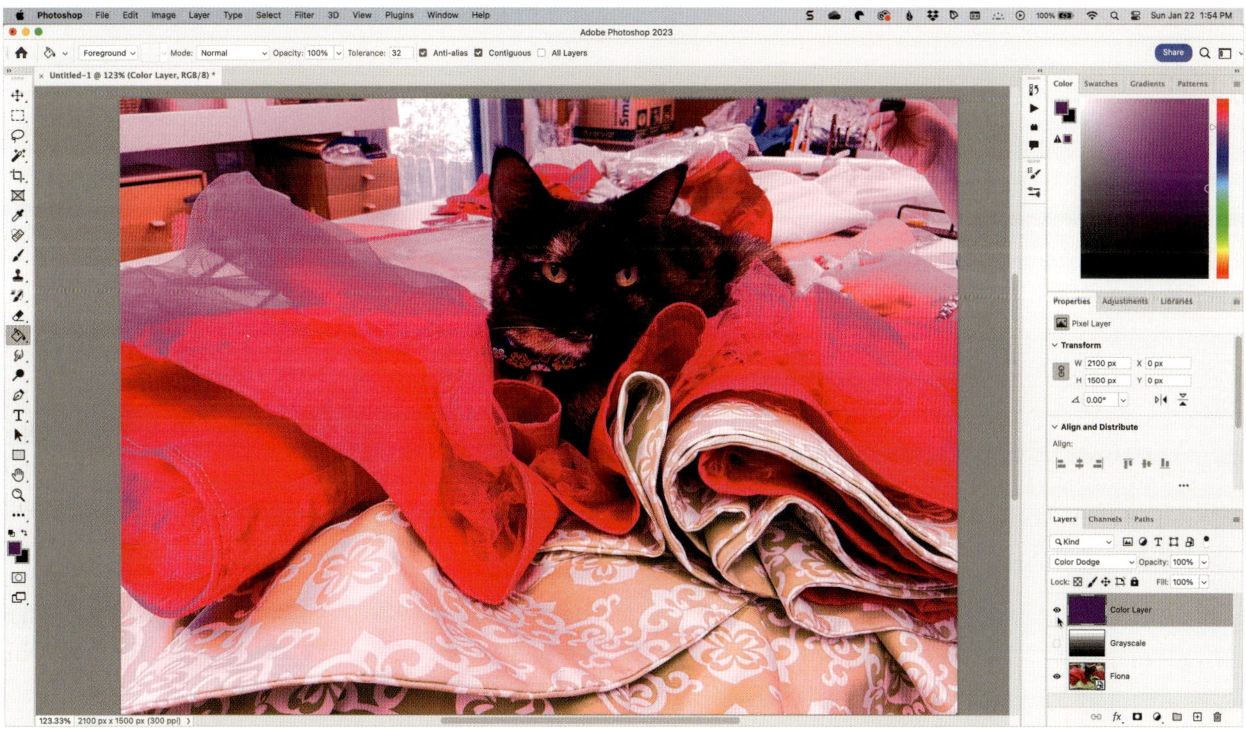

Figure 1.22b Blend mode file with *Color Dodge* mode applied. Isn't Fiona pretty?

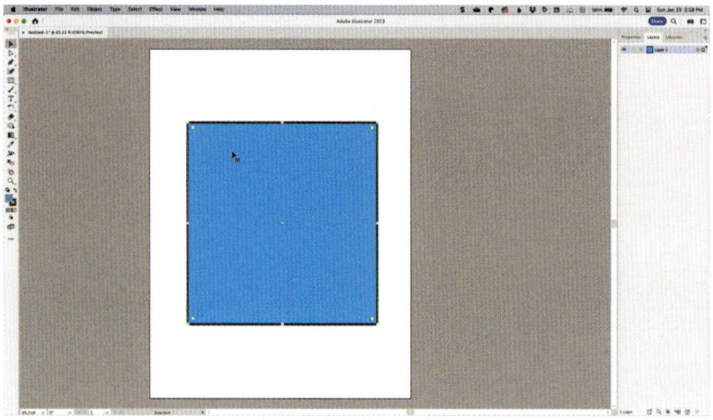

Figure 1.23a Selecting with the *Selection* tool or black arrow in Illustrator. Notice that it selects the entire square. See how all anchor points and paths show as selected? This will allow you to move the entire shape.

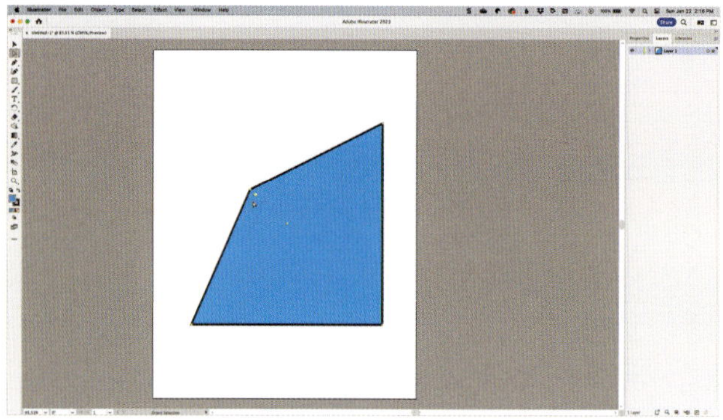

Figure 1.23b Selecting with the *Direct Selection* tool or white arrow in Illustrator. When you choose a particular anchor point, it only selects that point and the paths to either side of it. This allows you to move just the single point selected.

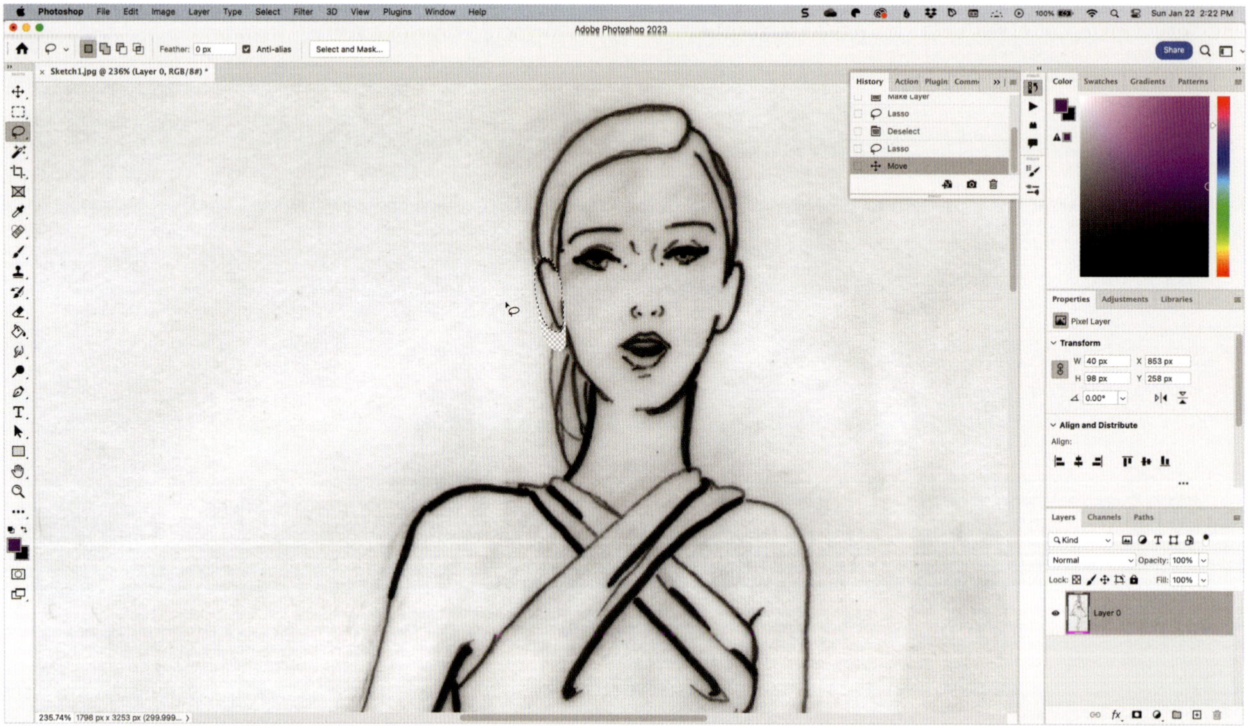

Figure 1.24 Selecting in Photoshop with the *Lasso* tool. The ear was selected with the *Lasso* tool and then moved up to a better position using the *Move* tool.

the artwork. Look for these tools or commands within your software of choice. You will first need to make a *Selection* to use the *Transform* tools. For programs such as Illustrator, you can often find these features as individual tools in the *Tool* menu. In Photoshop, the commands can be found under the *Edit* menu. The *Transform* tools tend to move more than many other features from one program to another. Spend the time to learn where they are and how they work for your software of choice. Figure 1.25 shows part of the exercise file being distorted through the *Scale* command.

Brushes

Brushes are a major feature of all digital art software. Luckily, *Brushes* also tend to be one of the most intuitive features within any graphic program. In Photoshop, Procreate, and most digital painting or photo-editing applications, you select the *Brush* tool, determine the size and style, and start to paint! For Illustrator or other vector-based line work, you need to draw the points and paths, then you can apply a brush style to the line. Figure 1.26 shows a path in Illustrator with a *Brush* style applied.

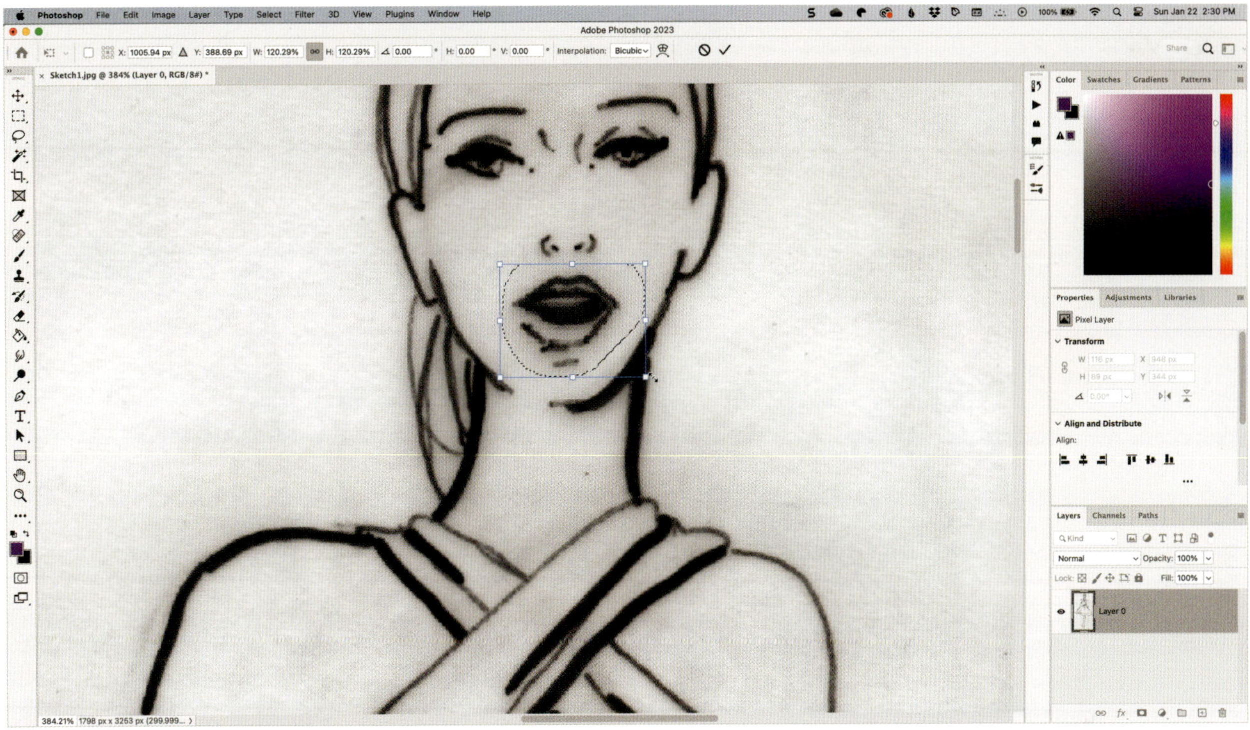

Figure 1.25 Scaling the lips in Photoshop. The lips were selected with the *Lasso* tool, then scaled up with the *Transform* tool found under the *Edit* menu.

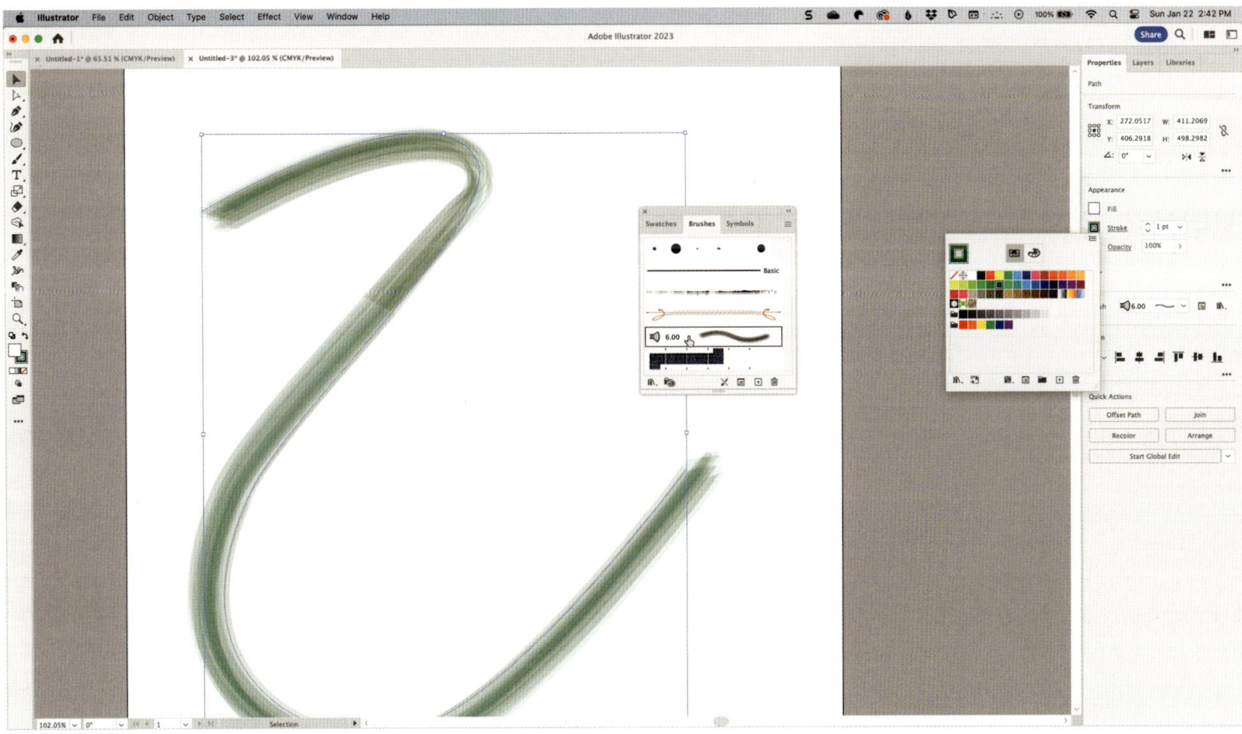

Figure 1.26 Illustrator path with a *Brush* style applied.

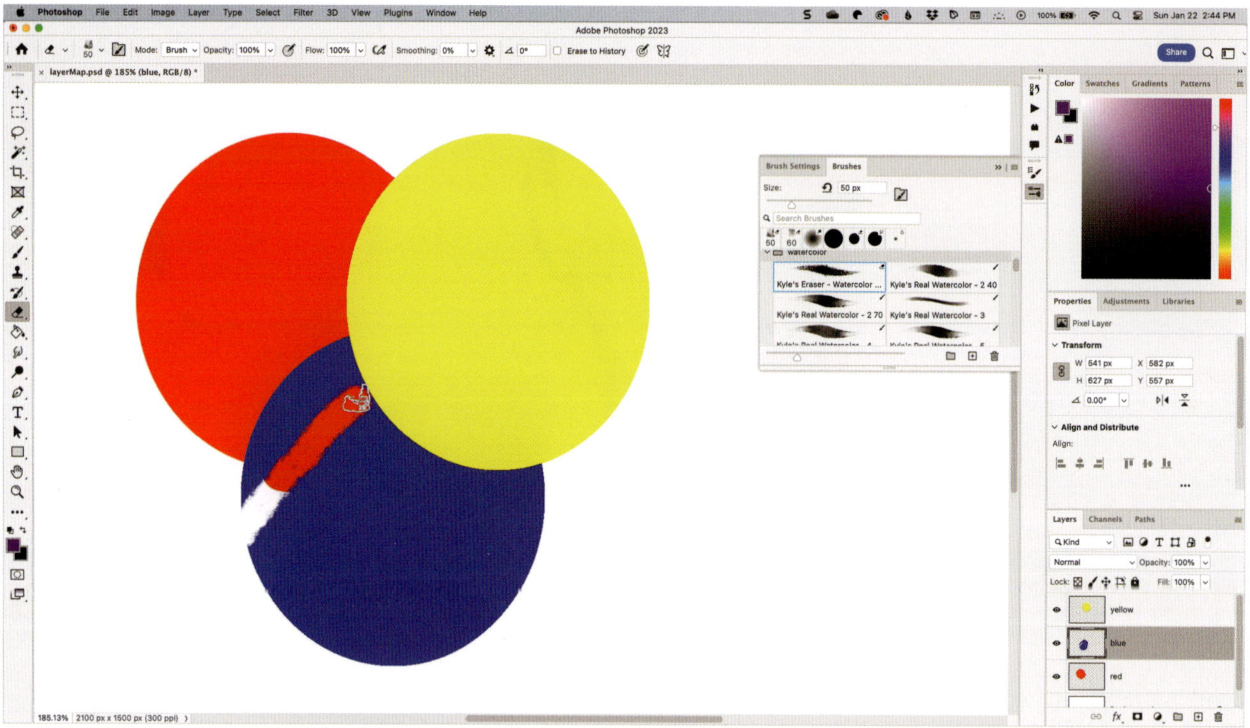

Figure 1.27 *Eraser* tool in Photoshop used with watercolor brush setting.

The great part about brush settings is that you can apply the style to other tools such as the *Eraser*, *Dodge*, and *Burn* tools, or the *Clone* stamp. This makes it easier to use these other tools while keeping the look very natural. You can see the *Eraser* using a watercolor brush setting in Figure 1.27.

Adjustment Layers

Adjustment layers are a feature found in Photoshop and other photo-editing or digital painting programs. You won't find this feature in Illustrator, though, due to the nature of that program. *Adjustment Layers* are exactly what they sound like: layers that allow you to adjust the colors and values of artwork below them. You can also apply adjustment effects without a separate layer if you go through the *Layer* menu in Photoshop. However, the action cannot be undone once you save and close that artwork. Separate *Adjustment Layers* can continue to be tweaked, though. We will use the adjustment features in the color and texture chapters.

Masks

Masks are common for all photo-editing, digital painting, and graphic illustration programs. There are multiple different types of masks, though. **Vector masks** follow a vector **path** on the artwork. **Layer masks** apply the mask to the entire layer to which it is applied (Figure 1.28). **Selection masks** use a pixel selection within your artwork. Whatever the mask, you will see that it is communicated through a black, white, and sometimes gray display. Black indicates the selected area that will be blocked and white shows the areas that will be affected. "Black conceals and white reveals" is a common phrase in the digital illustration world. Areas of gray are just low-opacity black that indicate a transition of the mask. Part will show and part will be blocked according to the opacity of the black.

Two other forms of masking include a **clipping mask** and **Lock transparency**. A clipping mask will clip one layer to another. Meaning, whatever artwork is on one layer can be visually trimmed to fit within the artwork on another layer. Clipping masks work a bit differently between Photoshop and Illustrator. Most notably (and frustratingly) you *Clip* one layer to the one below it in Photoshop, whereas it clips to the layer above it in Illustrator. It's just a convention of how each program is built, but can be easy to forget when you frequently switch between the two applications.

Lock transparency is not really a mask but allows you to paint or apply artwork to a layer that automatically clips to the artwork already laid down on that layer

PRO TIP 1.2

Secrets of Saving and File Size

Stop whatever you are doing right now and save your work! We cannot tell you how many times students and professionals alike spend hours of work on a file only to lose it all to an unexpected power failure, computer crash, or other random mishap. As more and more applications start auto-saving, we become accustomed to not worrying about the save button. Adobe does keep hidden backups as you work but they are, well, hidden. You have to dig through your program files to find them. So, stop and hit the save button now. Make sure you know where you are saving it, too. Look at the storage file path before you hit the "*OK*" button. If you are not sure, click on "*Save As*" to locate the path.

Now that you saved something, let's talk about better ways of saving your work. First, assess what you want to do with the file. Some file types are better for working, some for printing, and others for sending to people. The chances are that you need to do all these things, which is why you will probably need to save different formats of your work. See Table PT1.1 for a comparison chart of the more commonly used file formats for fashion and costume illustration.

Some of the more computer-savvy readers may say, "What about Tiffs or Gifs or other formats?" Tiffs are great for photographs, but we don't use them as often for renderings in the fashion and costume industry. Gifs are mostly used for animated graphics. There are many other great file formats with their own strengths and weaknesses. However, we don't use them much in this text.

So, to summarize, always keep a working copy in the native file format of whatever program with which you work. If you need to send a high-resolution file to a printer, then use a PDF. When you want a smaller image to use for websites or to email someone, then use a JPG. As a side note, be wary of sending your work to others. We talk more about this subject in Chapter 12 on Portfolios.

Finally, we recommend that you set up a system for saving files that makes sense to you. Keep a system of named folders and files. You don't want to have to constantly open "untitled347.psd" to see what image it contains.

Table PT1.1 A comparison chart of the most commonly used file formats in fashion and costume illustration.

FILE TYPE	PROS	CONS	BEST USED FOR
Native file format (.PSD,.AI,.INDD, etc.)	Holds all the information, layers, adjustments, etc. of your work	Tend to be larger file sizes that take more storage	Working files
.PDF	You can choose to flatten the file to save space or keep the layers and editing ability. PDFs will open on almost any device. They are reliable and consistent. They also hold multiple pages	Can still be large files unless you compress the file and/or flatten the image	Sending to a printer or sharing high-quality (printable) images or books
.JPG	Small file size and high compatibility with other devices	PEGs degrade each time you save them, so they are not good as working files. They will not hold layers and only hold a single image	Emails, websites, or lower-quality uploads
.PNG	Holds transparency	Digital use only, will not support CMYK	Not often used for our purposes unless you need to use a "cutout" image (meaning it does not have a background). When working with Adobe products, though, it is unnecessary as the native file formats will serve the purposes for which we might use a PNG

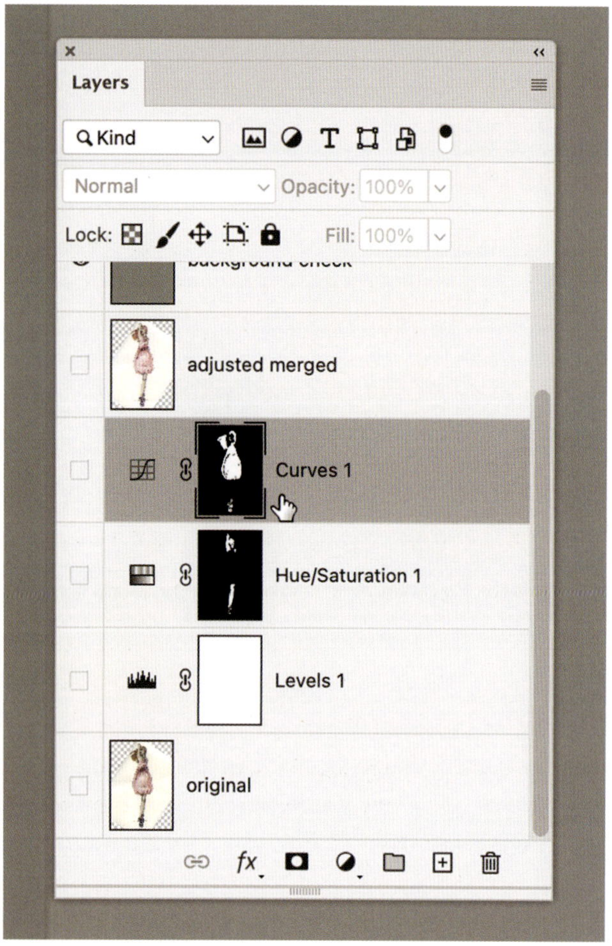

Figure 1.28 Screenshot of *Layer Mask* on a *Curves* layer. The black indicates blocked areas, whereas the white indicates areas that allow the adjustment to show.

(Figure 1.29). So, if you want to paint over a shape, it will only paint within the shape and will not go outside of those boundaries. This is very useful when applying shading to a particular part of the object.

Vector Paths

Vector paths are mostly utilized in graphic programs such as Illustrator. However, they can be also utilized on vector layers in Photoshop. A vector path is made up of **anchor points** containing mathematical coordinates and the paths or lines that connect one anchor point to another. Although vector paths are less intuitive to the analog painter, they are incredibly useful to understand in both the fashion and costume industry. You can make very clear design imagery to communicate necessary details. Illustrator is the primary application used in the fashion industry for tech packs. It is to your benefit to understand how vector paths work.

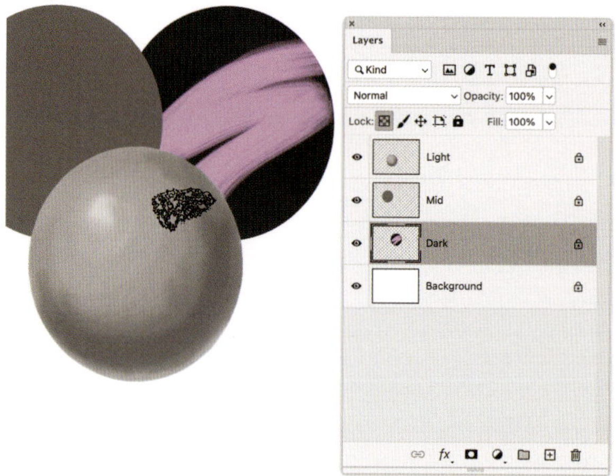

Figure 1.29 Screenshot of a layer with *Lock transparency* engaged. The paintbrush will not be able to go beyond the boundary of the pixels on that layer.

Although it is expected that you have a basic understanding of Illustrator and/or other vector-based graphic applications, it is important to review the difference between a path and a shape (Figures 1.30a–c). Nine times out of ten, if your illustration is not properly filling with color, it is because you have an open path where you should have a closed one. Here is a brief review:

An **open path** is a series of connected vector points that do not close into a complete shape. Open paths that have a fill color will connect the fill from one open end to the other. Sometimes this is not apparent depending on where the open end points are in relation to the

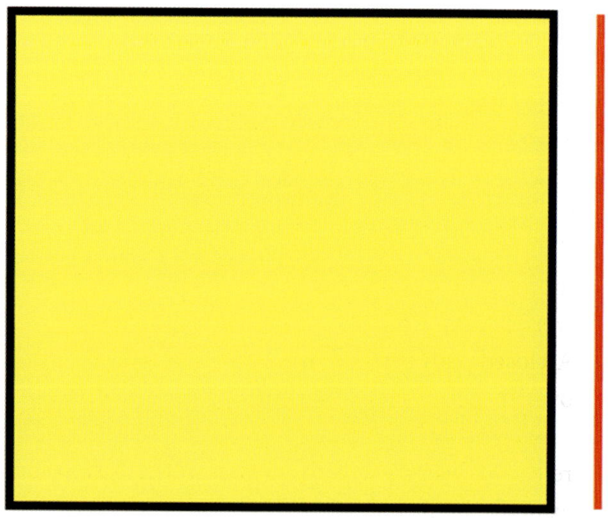

Figure 1.30a The left shows a closed shape with a yellow fill and the right shows an open path with a red stroke.

Figure 1.30b You can see that when the shape is selected, it indicates a path all the way around the rectangle.

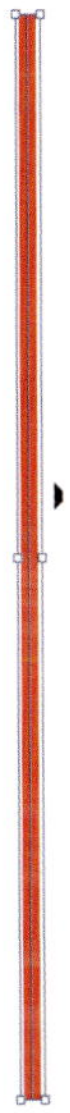

Figure 1.30c The selected path shows a line through the middle to indicate that it is a path with two anchor points.

shape. See Figures 1.31a and 1.31b. This can be deceptive and cause issues later, even if it looks okay for the moment. Therefore, it is imperative to make sure you work in **closed paths** for areas you want to fill with color. A closed path is when the start and end point of a path overlap as one, creating a shape with no open points.

How do you decide when to close a shape? The answer relies on where you want to change the base color. For example, in the t-shirt below, the entire shirt is one color, including the sleeves (Figures 1.32a–b). This means that it can be drawn with one t-shirt shaped outline with open paths for the seams and stitches.

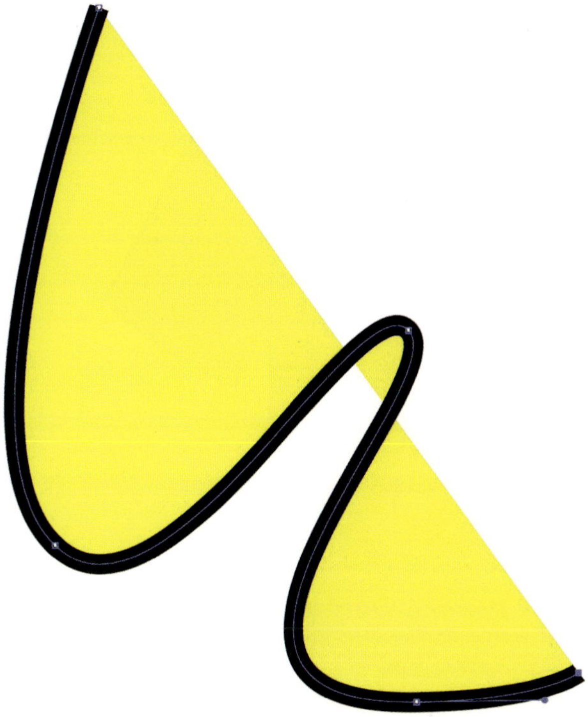

Figure 1.31a The selected path has a black stroke and yellow fill. Notice that the fill connects from one open end point to the other, even slicing through the protruding curve.

Figure 1.31b This can be deceptive if the connecting open points appear to close the shape. Notice that the black stroke does not continue across the top because this is an open path.

However, if you need to make the sleeves another color, then you must produce closed paths that overlap at the armhole seam (Figures 1.33a–d). See how the color does not fill the entire sleeve when it is not a closed path? Even though there is an armhole seam that is part of

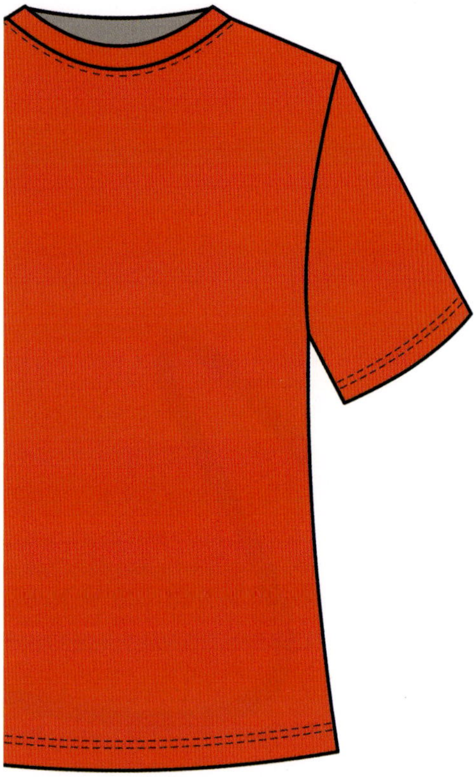

Figure 1.32a If the t-shirt is one color, then you can make a complete shape around the outline of the shirt and add open paths to make the arm seam and stitch lines.

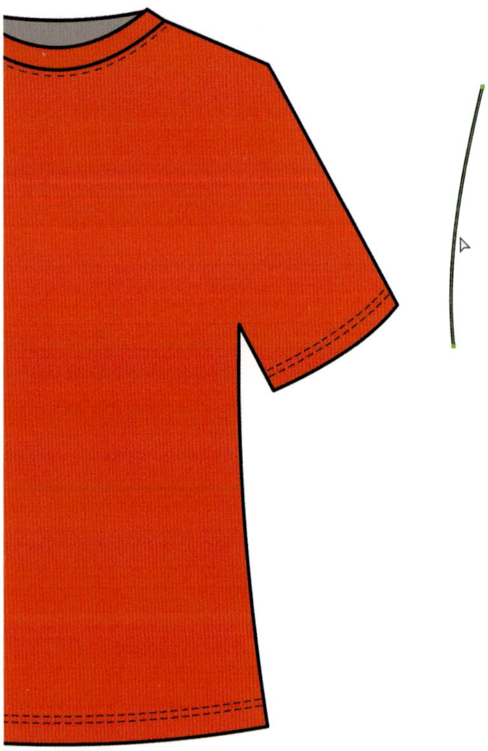

Figure 1.32b This image shows the same shirt with the arm seam moved to the side so you can see the full shape of the solid t-shirt.

the body, and it initially looks complete, it causes issues when you fill the color.

This is a rudimentary concept within vector-based graphic software, but it is imperative that you understand this concept to correctly color your illustration later.

Workflows

How you approach your illustration and coloring process is what we refer to as a **workflow**. There really is no "best" version. Whatever workflow is the easiest and makes the most sense to you will be your best option. First, determine if you are more comfortable with a mix of hand and digital work, or if you want to keep it fully digital. Then you can determine which style of rendering is the right choice for you.

Partially Digital

There is the option to create your illustrations fully by hand, of course. However, we assume that you wouldn't pick up this book if that is what you truly want to stick with. The first step into the realm of digital illustration is to adapt a hybrid approach in which you create your initial illustration by hand and then digitally import it to manipulate through one of the many programs. This may include a rough sketch that you then digitally refine and complete, digitally coloring a pencil illustration, or a finished rendering that only needs some color enhancement through *Adjustment Layer*. Most folks that have a history and comfort with analog illustration tend to start here. Many illustrators stay with this type of workflow and never fully convert to digital. That is perfectly fine!

Fully Digital

If you are comfortable with starting your artwork in the digital realm, then feel free to keep your work fully digital. You can free sketch with a tablet or trace over your analog work or photos to create the initial pose. There's not much to it; just jump in and start drawing!

Other Workflows

In this book, we mostly also follow a workflow in which we create the elements, meaning the individual rendered

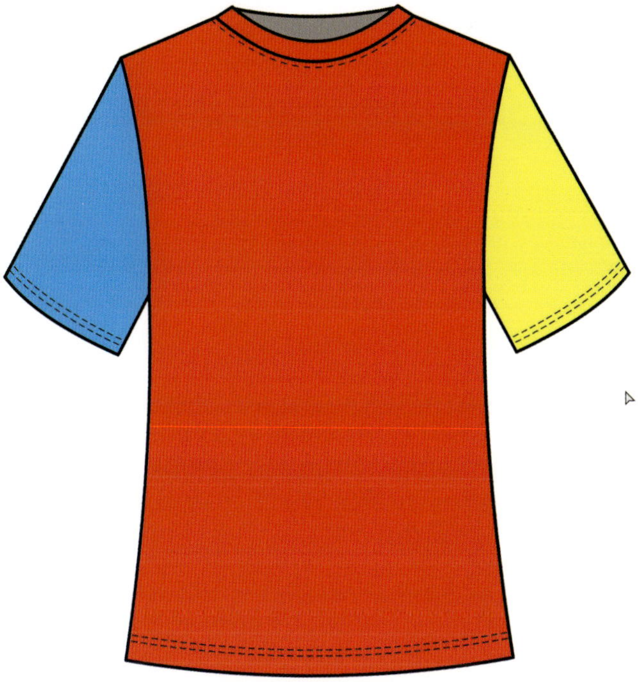

Figure 1.33a In this image, the sleeves are different colors.

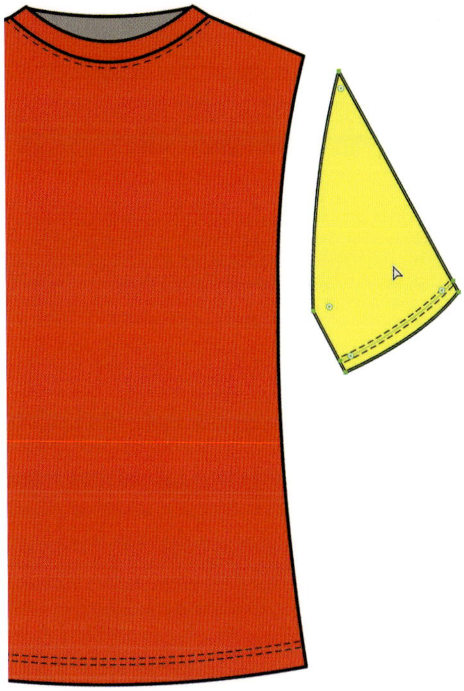

Figure 1.33b Here, the sleeve is moved to the side to see the two complete closed paths: one for the body of the shirt and one for the sleeve. The armhole lines overlap when it is correctly positioned.

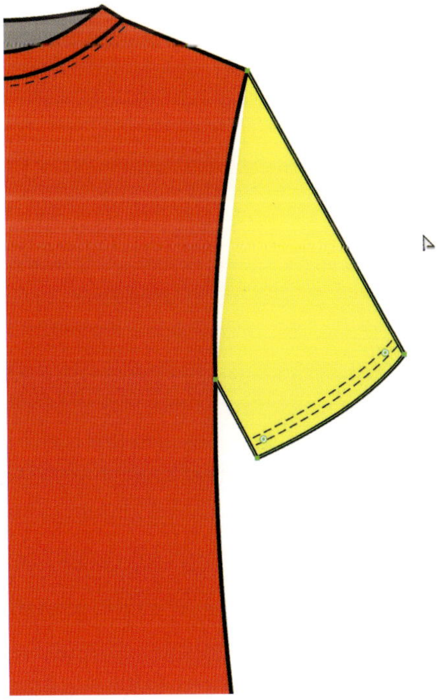

Figure 1.33c Here, the sleeve is an open path rather than a closed path. This causes a gap in the fill between one open end to the other.

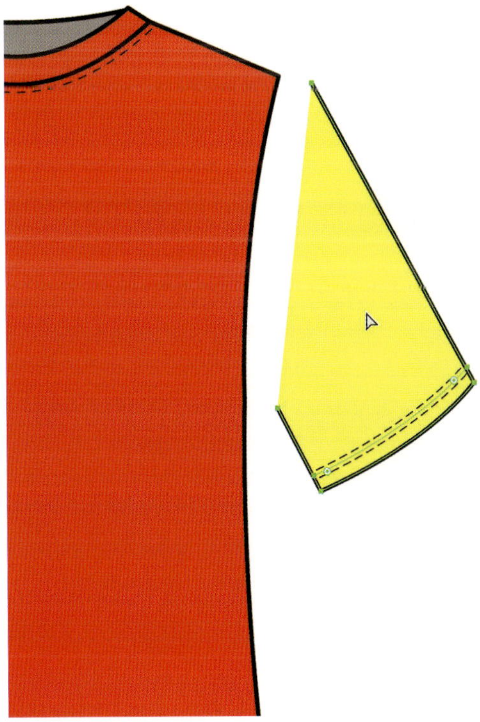

Figure 1.33d When the sleeve is moved to the side, you can see the fill color connecting from one open end to the other. The application does not "know" that you want it to fill over to the armhole line of the shirt body. You must tell it to do that by closing the path with the same curve as used on the body armhole.

figures, before compiling them into a layout. In contrast, some people work completely in one file, creating more of a painting. We recommend the individual elements workflow simply because it is easier to make changes when needed. The fashion and costume design industries often require last-minute changes.

We will talk more about other workflows as we go through the lessons. For example, there are different workflows for color and portfolio layouts. You may want to play around with several options as you learn just to try them out. Most people settle into the style that works best for them. However, you may also find that changing your workflow can sometimes boost your creativity if you are in a rut! Don't be afraid to try something new when your schedule and life permit.

Summary

This is an intermediate text for those wanting to transition their rendered fashion and costume work to a 2D digital format. Determine if you are ready to make the jump to this style of design communication by assessing your personal skills and comfort, software, and equipment. Although Adobe software are the primary platforms used in this text, the lessons are transferrable to other applications. Look through the common tools and features to see if you have a basic understanding of how to start using the lessons in this book to help progress your skills. Now it is time to push up your sleeves and get going!

STUDIO Companion Videos for Chapter 1

Please refer to STUDIO for accompanying chapter video(s).

Keywords

Adjustment layer
Analog
Anchor point
Blend mode
Brushes
Clipping mask
Closed path
Design communication
Digital
Generative AI
Layer mask
Layers
Lock transparency
Open path
Path
Raster
Selection mask
Selection tools
Technical flats
Text to image
Transform tools
Vector
Vector mask
Workflow

Review

1. In your own words, summarize the purpose of this book.
2. If you want to learn more about the basics of drawing the figure, where would you reference in this text?
3. What is design communication and why is it important to your chosen career?
4. Explain the main differences between a raster-based and a vector-based program.
5. How does the brush function work differently for a raster image versus a vector image?
6. Why is it important to use closed paths in vector-based programs?
7. Explain the pros and cons of a partially digital workflow. Do the same for a fully digital workflow.

Commands Introduced

- Adjustment layers
- Blend modes
- Brush tool

- Direct Selection tool
- Lasso tool
- Layers panel
- Lock transparency
- Masks
- Selection tool
- Transform tool

Discussion Questions

1. What are the most important aspects of garment design that you need to communicate for this industry (pick the industry according to your class)?
2. Is it better to have more function or more mobility with your applications and devices?
3. Discuss/dissect methods used by illustrators you admire.
4. Discuss the pros and cons of 3D rendering for garment design.
5. Discuss artificial intelligence-generated art/design in the fashion and/or costume industry. Do you think this is a good or bad development? Defend your opinion.

Practice Exercises

1. Find a professional illustrator whose style you admire. Contact them for an interview to see what software and equipment they prefer. See if they have any advice for a student. This is not as scary as you might think. Many professionals are flattered when someone shows interest in their work and will happily speak with you!
2. Assess your own strengths and weaknesses in this subject area. Make your own learning plan using the text/lessons. Set up a plan with your own objectives, benchmarks, and deadlines.
3. Look up the minimum and recommended requirements of the software of your choice. Check the configurations of your device and compare it to the requirements.
4. If you are using an application other than Adobe, go through and find all of the basic functions. Take the time to learn how to access layers, blend modes, adjustment layers, brushes, etc.

Endnotes

1. Quote permission from Von Glitschka via personal communication, email correspondence January 7, 2023.
2. To "cheat" your way around the limitations of file size and number of layers in tablet programs like Procreate, you can save multiple stages of a file as you build it. Meaning, you can save the first stage of the file with a certain number of layers, then compress it to one layer and reopen the flattened file to continue to add more layers from that point. Save the file once you get it to another stage, flatten it, and start again. This workaround makes it difficult to backtrack to changes in the beginning layers, though. So, while it does function, it does not function very well depending on your needs.
3. Quote permission from Zoë Hong personal correspondence via email correspondence January 10, 2023.
4. Quote permission from Lisa Carney personal correspondence via email correspondence January 3, 2023.

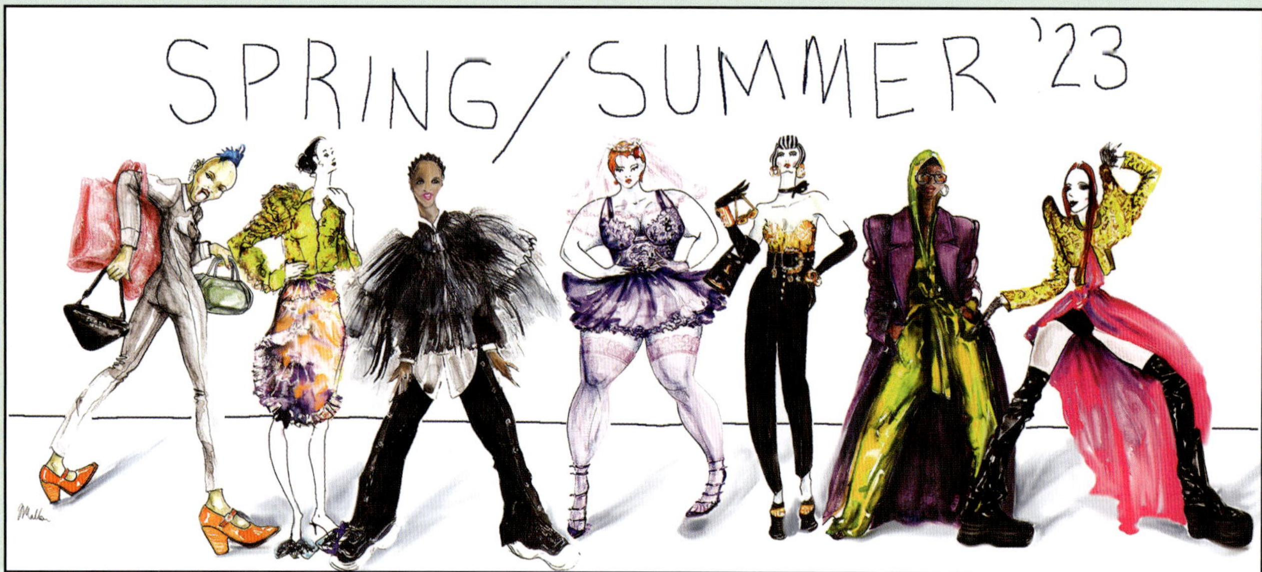

Figure 2.1 Figures are the base for your garments and design communication. Artwork by Jackie Mallon. Instagram: @jackie_mallon1. Jackiemallon.com.

CHAPTER 2
Rendering the Figure

Learning Objectives

After completing this chapter, you should be able to

- Recognize different approaches to digital illustration and rendering
- Develop templates in both Photoshop and Illustrator to assist your illustration process
- Explore how to scan in and utilize a figure in Photoshop
- Develop a digital sketch of a figure in Photoshop
- Utilize a scanned sketch to create a figure in Illustrator
- Demonstrate how to digitally sketch a figure in Illustrator
- Analyze the importance of line quality and how to produce it in both Illustrator and Photoshop

The figure is the base for your rendering and design communication. There are many approaches to starting the sketch, just as those reading this book will have a wide variety of practice and comfort level with illustration of the body and garments (Figure 2.1). Even if you consider yourself a novice at any sort of design communication, remember that the important thing is to jump in and start doing it.

What's Your Style? Recognizing Different Approaches to Digital Illustration and Rendering

Which style is the best? We get this question all the time. There is no "best" version; it depends both on your own personal style and what your client or boss is asking of you. Developing your own illustration style is something that you will create with time, patience, and experience. You may have a dramatic illustration flourish that people admire and gains attention. You may have a more straightforward look that is very detail-oriented. Or you may be in a range somewhere between the two while trying to find your personal style. Spend time looking at other styles for inspiration but do not copy those styles directly. Try to come up with your own look. Spend time deliberately practicing multiple styles until you find what works best for you and your needs.

Whether you sketch analog or digitally to start a project is a personal preference. We suggest that you start with what you are most comfortable, then expand through practice. If you are used to hand illustration and are faster at that method, then start there. Scan your artwork in and start to work with that as a base. If you are comfortable with drawing digitally, then start with that. Experiment with both ways, especially if you have not tried the other version. You never know; you might discover a new way of working that you love.

It is worth mentioning here that developing your own design style and illustration style are separate but related actions. Many people (including trained designers) can't distinguish between a good illustration and a good design. We have seen beautiful illustrations of mundane (and sometimes outright terrible) designs and many "chicken scratch" illustrations of amazing designs. Unfortunately, all too often the good illustration is seen as a better design over the rough illustration without regard to the quality of the design itself. So, what does this mean for you? Well, it indicates that you should put some significant effort into creating a well-polished portfolio when starting out in the industry.

Back to the style question, though. In terms of the platforms, they will produce different looks. Illustrator produces a much more graphic, sometimes cartoonish look. That may be precisely what you need. Photoshop can produce a wider range of looks if you need something more versatile. It is easier to recreate hand media looks such as marker, watercolor, gouache, and colored pencil in Photoshop. It is also easier to use a collage style of rendering. However, this does not need to be an "either/or" situation. Once you start to become comfortable with both formats, you can transfer any project back and forth between the two as needed to create a unique look. You can also incorporate other programs or plugins for certain effects if you like. Artistic styles are covered more in Chapter 8.

PRO TIP 2.1

Using a Reference When Sketching

Many artists who digitally sketch like to have a photo reference or collection of references open while sketching. Most applications will allow for this workflow style. To do so in Illustrator or Photoshop, all you need to do is have your reference image and your blank artboard open simultaneously. Then go to the *Window* menu bar, click on *Arrange*, and chose a tile option that suits you to see both images while working! You can also pull the individual image to a floating window. If using other software, look in the *Help* menu for reference image. There will most likely be a command to allow for this because it is such a common way to work in any illustration field.

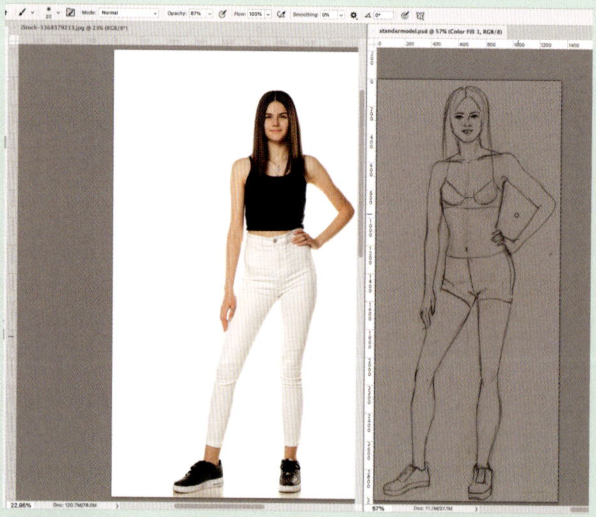

Figure PT2.1 Resource photo and sketch tiled side by side to make it easier to reference. VladimirFLoyd/iStock.com

Using Templates

For those who are less comfortable with illustrating the body, or those who prefer to hand-sketch the body and garment first, you may want to use a template. **Templates** are useful tools in both Illustrator and Photoshop (or any other illustration application for that matter). These are tools to help you improve your skills and gain confidence during the learning process. As you become familiar with the digital tools and illustration in general, you can start to wean yourself from dependence on templates.

With most templates, you want to create your file first. This helps control the size of your work to your parameters. Photos, especially, can be deceptive in size if you are not familiar with understanding file sizes, and you may end up tracing either a very tiny or extremely large image.

If you want to practice making templates, you can use the resource file ModelPhoto1.jpg.

STYLE SECRETS 2.1

Isn't It Cheating?

Some people look down upon tracing from a photo as a form of copying or cheating. Do not be disheartened if you are still learning to draw accurate figures. Remember that most masters learned by copying other paintings or drawings until they learned correct proportions and techniques. This is a learning process to help train your eye and hand. We do not necessarily recommend that you keep to this method for your professional career, but it is a good way to learn correct human proportions and train your eye.

Templates in Photoshop (Ps)

Photoshop is not necessarily set up for template use automatically. However, it is easy enough to make a particular layer into a template that you can turn off or discard later.

Step 1: *Open* your new document in Photoshop to the size you prefer to work with such as 8.5"× 11"or A4.

Step 2: *Place* your photo or scanned sketch. You have the option to place an **embedded image** or a **linked image**. The linked image is appropriate at this stage because you probably won't need the image past the initial stage of using it to help you sketch. The linked image saves space in your file so long as you don't rename or move the file location. If you do, you may need to relink the file if you need to reference it again. Embedded images store with the document file. They do not need to be relinked if you move a file but do make the file size larger.

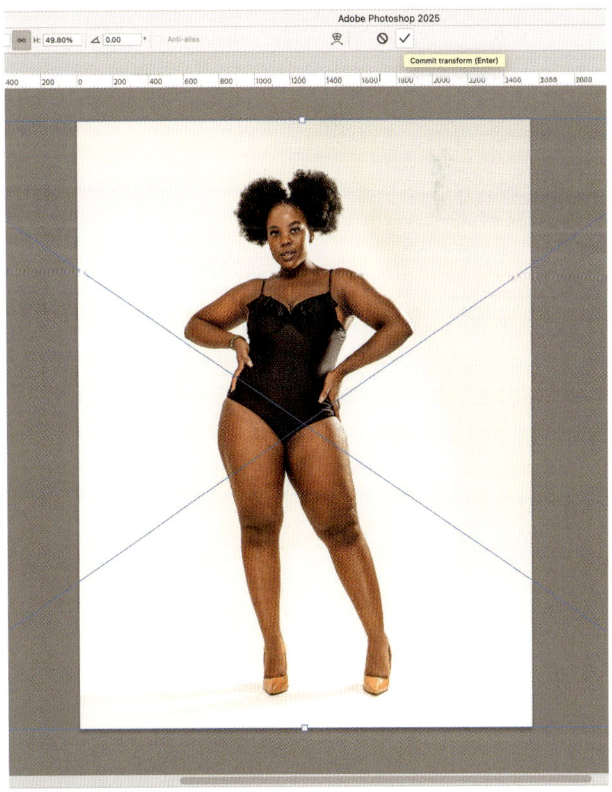

Figure 2.2 Photo *Placed* on document in Ps. Photograph courtesy of Ricardo Gutierrez, R Models Agency.

Step 3: Open the *Layers* panel. Lower the *Opacity* of the layer to your desired level so that you will be able to trace or use the image as a guide, but not be distracted by the colors or unnecessary details. Somewhere around 50% is often preferred.

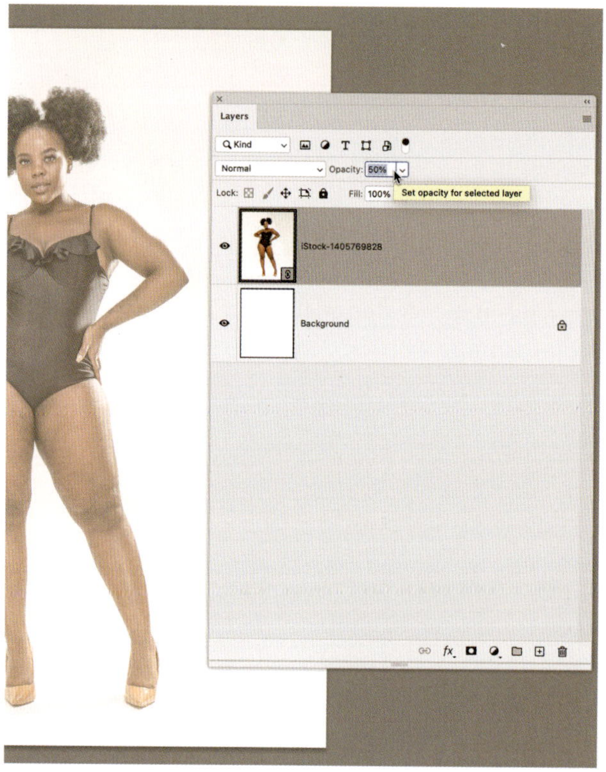

Figure 2.3 The *Layers* panel. Notice that the *Opacity* of the selected layer has been reduced.

Step 4: *Lock* the layer the photo is on by clicking the *Lock* button while on the selected layer.

Step 5: Create a *New Layer* on top of this one by going to the *Layer* menu and clicking on the *New Layer* button. You are set to use the template to start sketching!

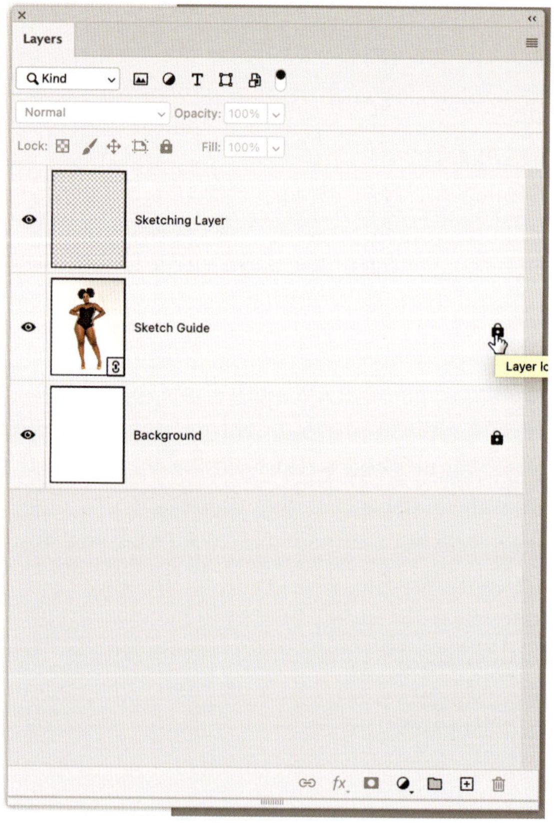

Figure 2.4 The *Layers* panel. Notice that the layer with the photo has been *Locked*. The empty layer above is ready for you to start sketching using your template.

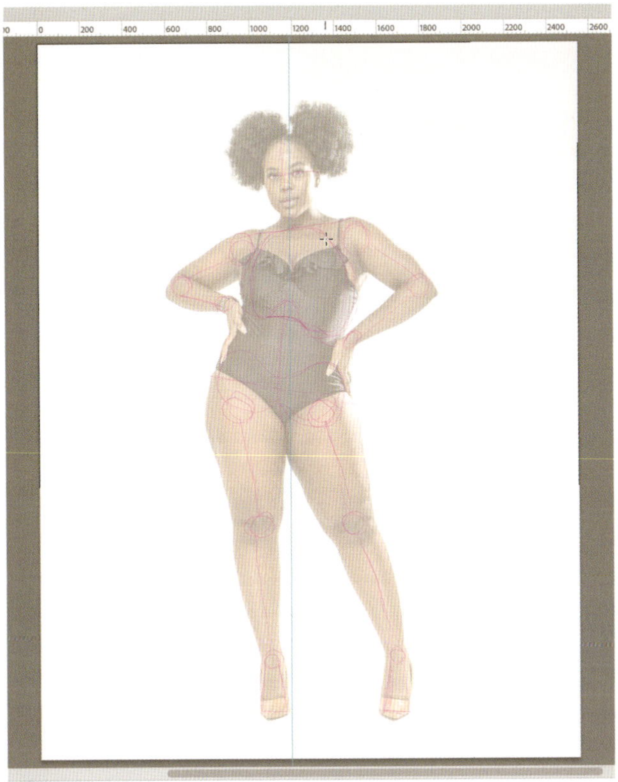

Figure 2.5 This is what your image should look like once it is ready for you to start sketching on the layer above.

Templates in Illustrator

Fortunately, Illustrator is already set up for using templates! It essentially does the same functions as we manually created in Photoshop, but with fewer clicks of the mouse. It bears mentioning that Illustrator will not dim .ai files in template mode for some reason. You will need to manually dim it if you are using another .ai file type for your template base layer.

There are three methods to set up your templates in Illustrator:

Method 1: When you start to open your image, use the command *New from Template*. Navigate to your reference image and click *Open*. This will automatically set up your reference image as a template layer.

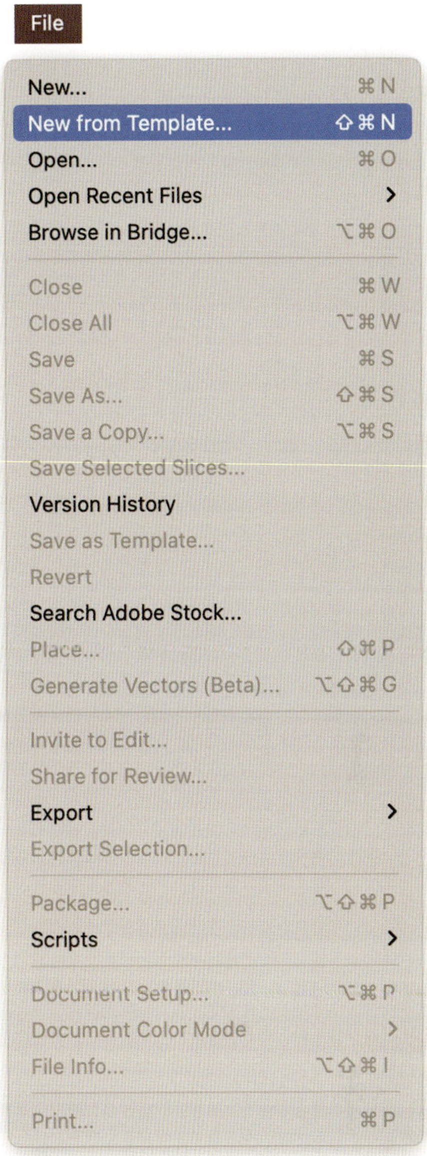

Figure 2.6 In the *File* menu, select *New from Template* to set up a reference image as a template.

Method 2: You can create your *New Document*, then *Place* the image. In the *Place* dialog box, navigate to your image. Before clicking *Place*, tick the checkbox for *Template*. This will place the file as a template in your new document.

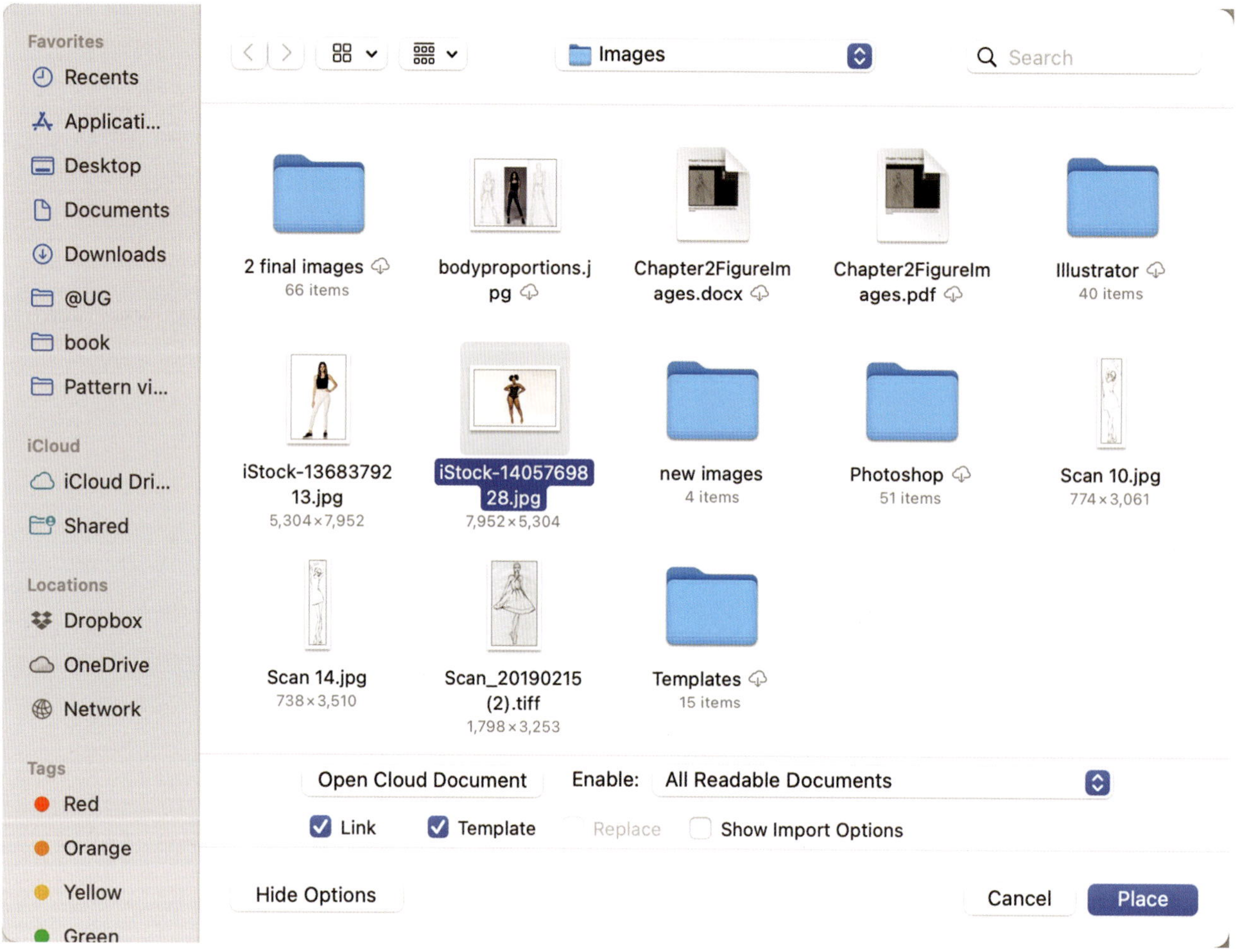

Figure 2.7 *Placing* a file as a template by ticking the checkbox for *Template* in the *Place* dialog pop-up box.

Method 3: You can also do this manually if you prefer!

Step 1: Create a *New Document* in Illustrator set to your personal preferences. We recommend at least 8.5″ × 11″ or A4.

Step 2: *Place* your photo or scanned sketch. Illustrator automatically places a linked file. If you want an embedded file, you will need to go to the *Properties* panel and click the *Embed* checkbox with the image selected.

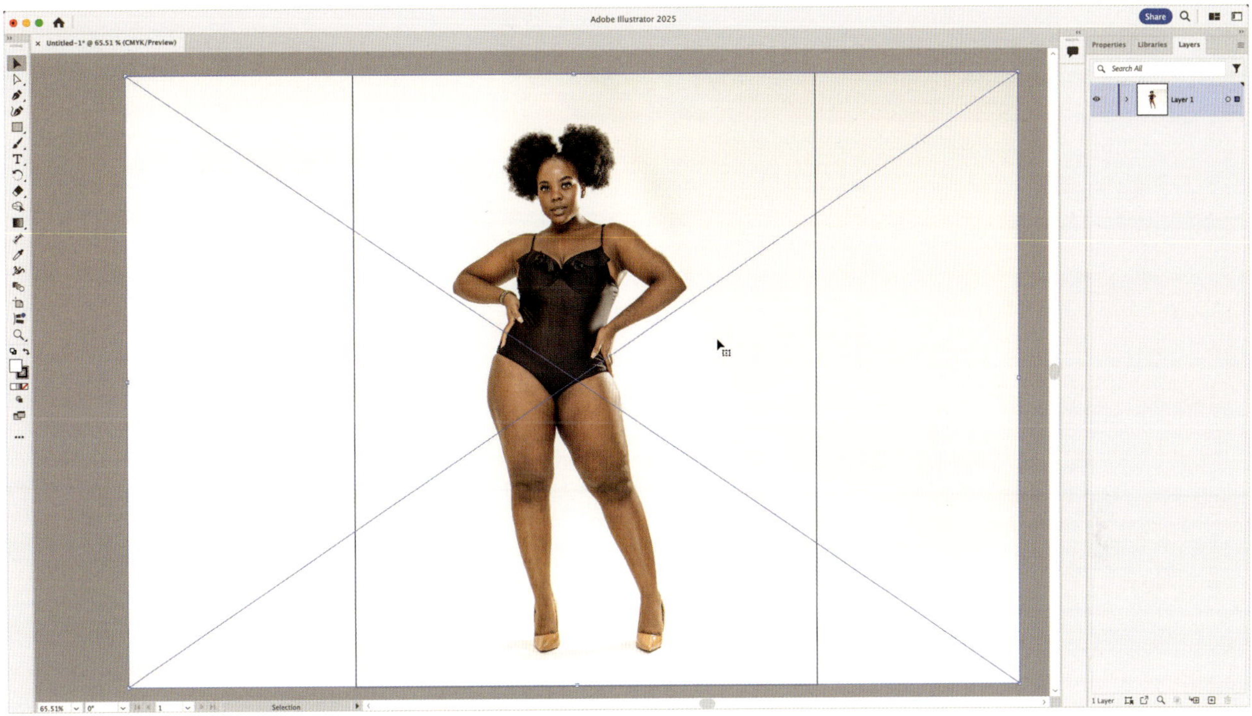

Figure 2.8 Photo *Placed* on document in Ai.

Step 3: Open the *Layers* panel. *Double-click* in the space beside the layer name. This will open a dialog box. Click the *Template* option and adjust the dimming percentage if you like. This automatically locks the layer once you click *OK*.

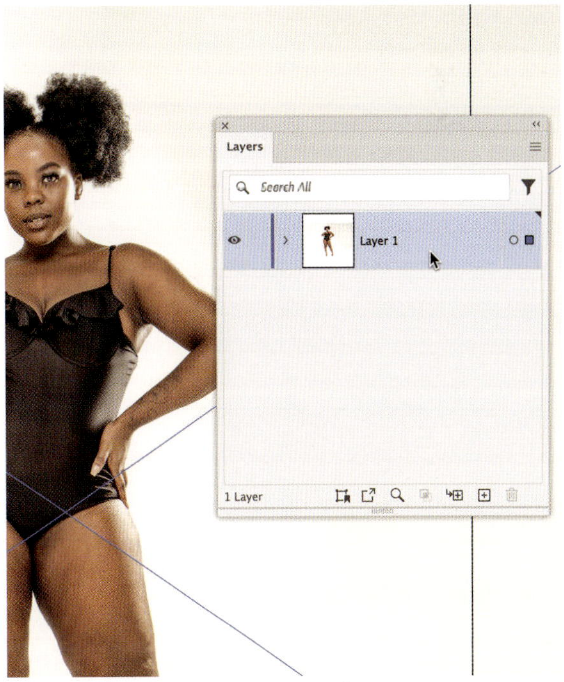

Figure 2.9 The *Layers* panel in Ai. *Double-click* in the space beside the layer name to open the *Layer Options* dialog pop-up box.

Step 4: Create a *New Layer* on top and you are set to sketch!

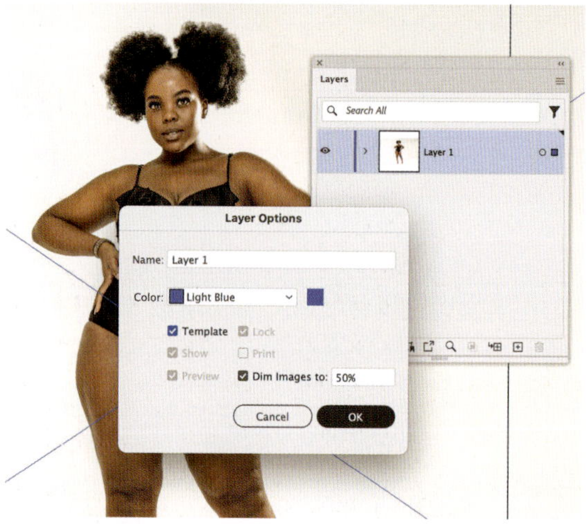

Figure 2.10 The *Layer Options* dialog box. Click the *Template* option and check that the dimness meets your needs. You can readjust it later by reopening the dialog box and changing it if you need.

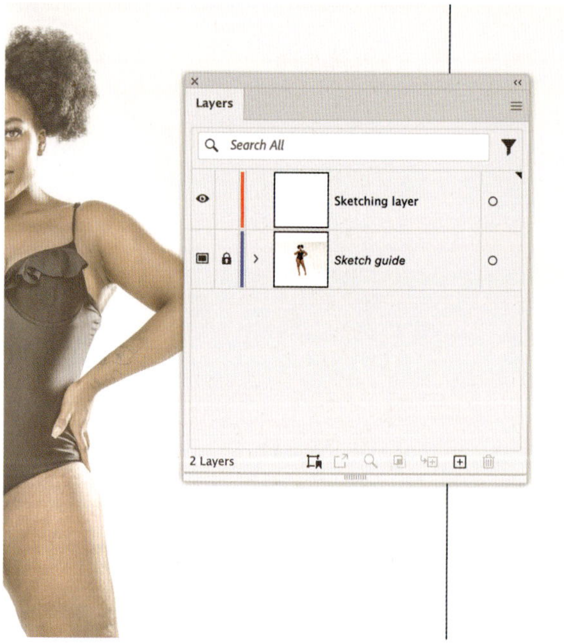

Figure 2.11 The *Layers* menu in Ai. Notice that now the template layer is locked.

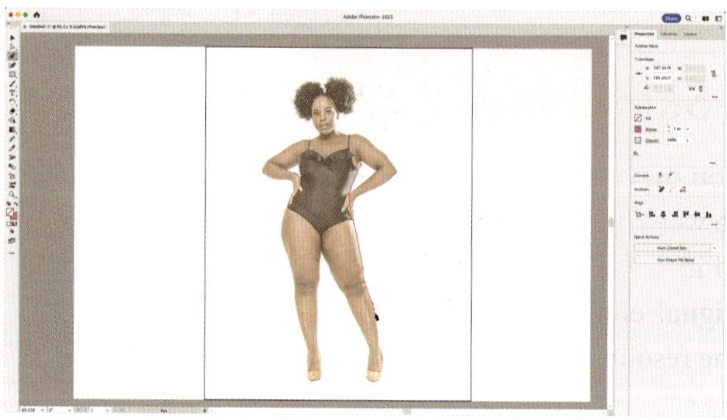

Figure 2.12 This is what your image should look like once it is ready for you to start sketching on the layer above.

PRO TIP 2.2

Grid Help

Many artists prefer to use a grid to help draw from a reference image. Programs such as Procreate have a grid feature that you can turn on in the canvas menu. Photoshop and Illustrator have a grid you can turn on under the view menu. However, if your reference image and your artboard are different sizes, this may cause a bit of trouble making the grids proportional between the two documents. To get around this, you can create a brush in the shape of a grid to click over your image and your drawing canvas. Just use a thin round brush to initially set it up on a blank canvas, then select the lines and create a brush with it. Now you can stamp the brush to create guidelines for drawing from a reference. Do this on a separate layer and transform the stamped grid to a matching ratio between the reference image and your artboard. Turn off or discard the layer once you no longer need it.

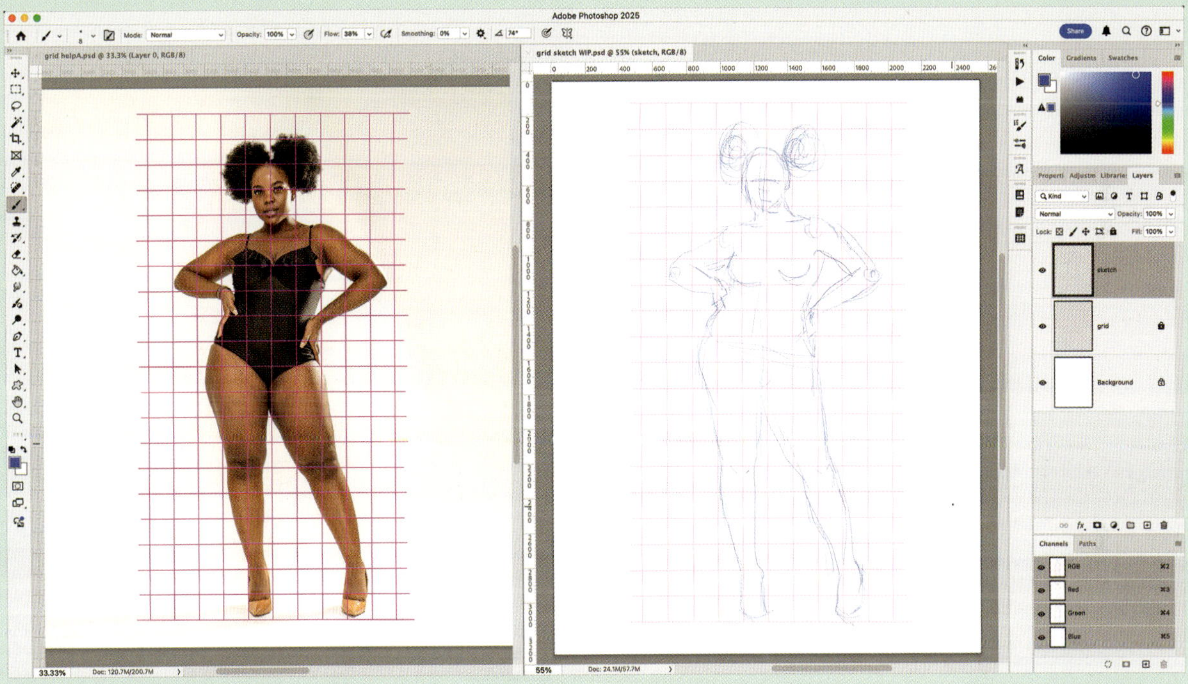

Figure PT2.2 Use a grid-shaped *Brush* in Photoshop to aid the drawing process from a reference image.

Scanning, Tracing, and Sketching in Photoshop (Ps)

You may want to scan in a sketch or finished rendering to work within Photoshop. Both require a little clean-up to improve the image quality and make it ready for any digital enhancements. For these projects, you can use the resource files: Sketch1.jpg and ModelPhoto1.jpg.

If you wish to sketch digitally, you may freehand your sketch, use a template, or use a reference image. For now, refrain from coloring your sketch. We will do this in Chapter 3.

Other raster-based programs such as Procreate, Affinity Designer (using the raster workspace), and Corel Painter will have similar tools and features to Photoshop.

Project 2.1: Scan, Clean, and Prep a Hand Sketch

Step 1: Scan in a clean image. Clean up the drawing as much as possible before scanning with your analog tools (i.e., a physical eraser). This will save time. Often, it takes significantly more time to clean up a sketch on the computer than it does to use an eraser to remove the stray marks and smudges on the hand sketch. You may also want to ink over your pencil lines to make them cleaner and more distinct.

Flatbed scanners tend to work best for importing images. However, you can also take a digital photo to import it. There are also apps available for mobile devices, such as Adobe Scan. These are still not as accurate as a flatbed scanner, but often improve the results of a photo from a camera phone. Be sure to light the sketch well and take the photo from a straight angle. Each scanner and camera will have different settings, so refer to your user manual for instructions to import the image. We recommend a resolution of 300 dpi for most projects.

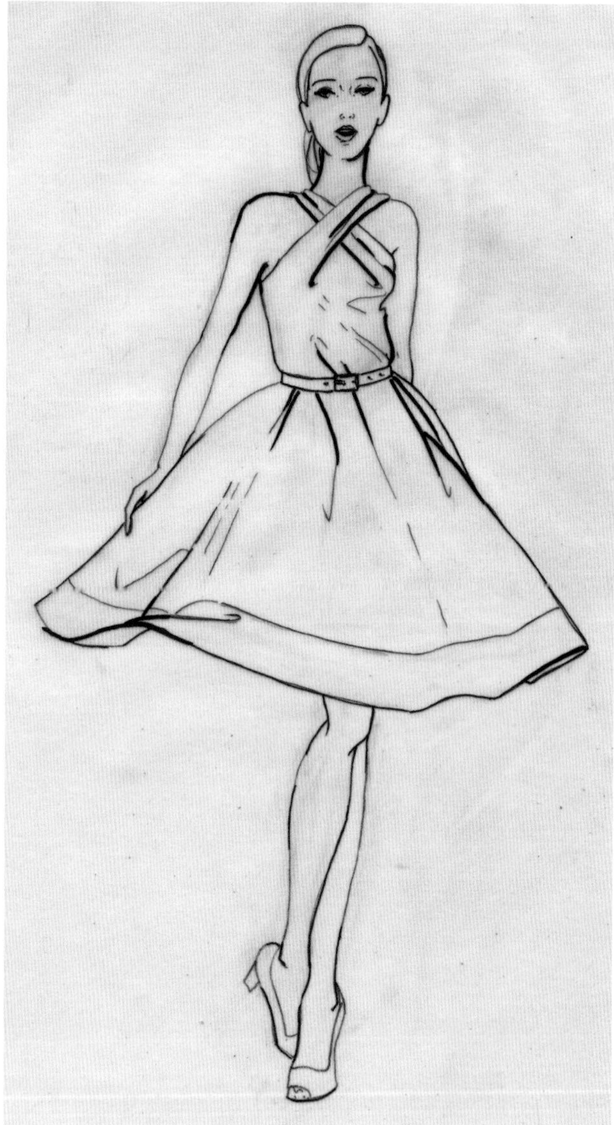

Figure 2.13 Inked and cleaned scanned sketch file: Sketch1.jpg. Artwork by the authors.

Either create a *New Document* to the preferred size and settings and *Place* the image, or *Open* it directly and *Resize* the canvas if needed. To *Place* an image, create a *New Document* in Ps to your desired dimensions. We started with a simple 8.5″ × 11″, 300 dpi document in RGB. You are welcome to adjust this to your personal preferences. We will discuss color more in the next chapter but keep to an RGB color mode for now.

Use the *File* menu to navigate to the *Place Embedded* command. Navigate to the resource file, Sketch1.jpg. Use the bounding box to resize the file when the image appears if needed. Once you are satisfied with the scale, then click the check icon above the image, or press the *Enter/Return* key. We recommend that you place an embedded file rather than a linked file because it will be the basis of the entire rendering. It is also not a particularly large file so it will not impact your working file size much.

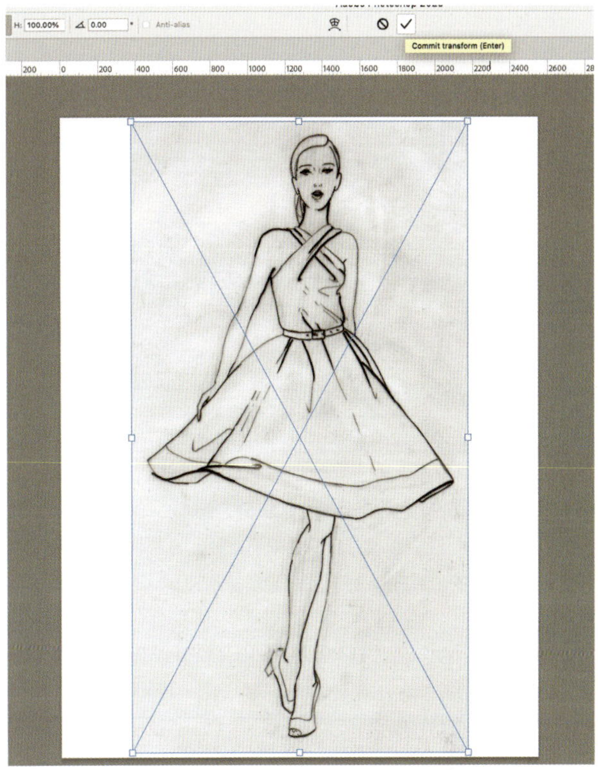

Figure 2.14 Placing the figure on the document in Ps. Once you are satisfied with the scale, *click* the check icon above the image.

Step 2: Clean up the image. There are many adjustment commands that can help clean up a scanned sketch. With time, you will develop your own method that works best for you. For now, use this basic method to achieve good results.

Start with a **Levels Adjustment Layer**. This will help you to get the whites whiter and the darks darker. The goal is to polarize the image to black and white if possible. This makes it easier to render with color later. In the *Layers* panel, click on the *New Fill Layer* button at the bottom of the panel (it looks like a black and white cookie). Choose *Levels* from the list. This will open a new *Levels Adjustment Layer*. If the *Properties* panel is not already open, then open it now from the *Windows* menu. This will allow you to make adjustments.

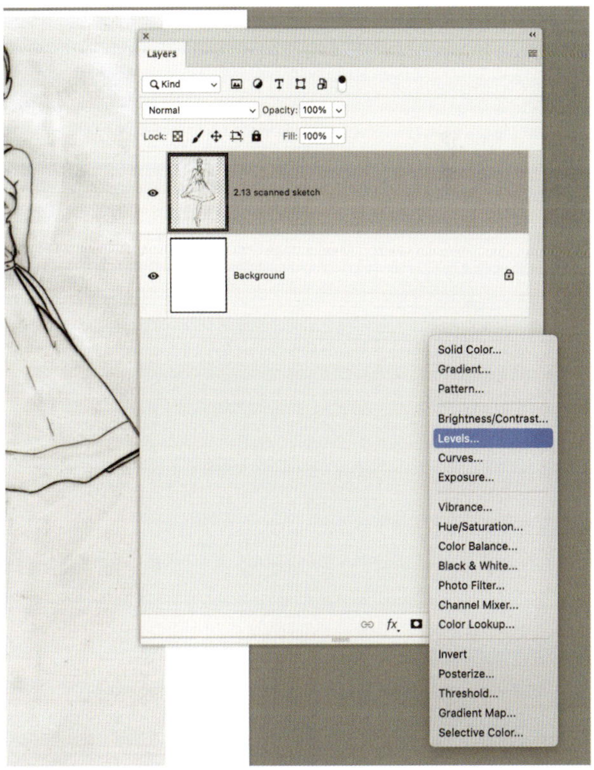

Figure 2.15 In the *Layers* panel, click on the icon for a *New Fill Layer* and scroll to the *Levels* command.

Once you open a *Levels Adjustment Layer*, play with the location of the three arrows below the graph (called a **histogram**) that appears in the *Properties* panel. The best way to understand the results of any command is to hit the buttons to see what they do! Move each of the three arrows—dark, midtone, and light—to see the effect. Notice that the numerical value below each arrow changes as you play with it. Do not worry about the value bar below that area. You do not need it right now.

You can pull the dark arrow right to where the information starts to register on the histogram. Then pull the light arrow left until you start to see the paper background disappear without damaging too much of the sketch line quality. Once you are satisfied with the results, try moving the midtone arrow left or right to make the lines darker or lighter. Much of this is personal preference. However, you are welcome to use the numerical positions in the screenshot until you are comfortable with making your own adjustments. Remember that those numbers will vary with each sketch. It all depends on the darkness of the sketch and the noise around it.

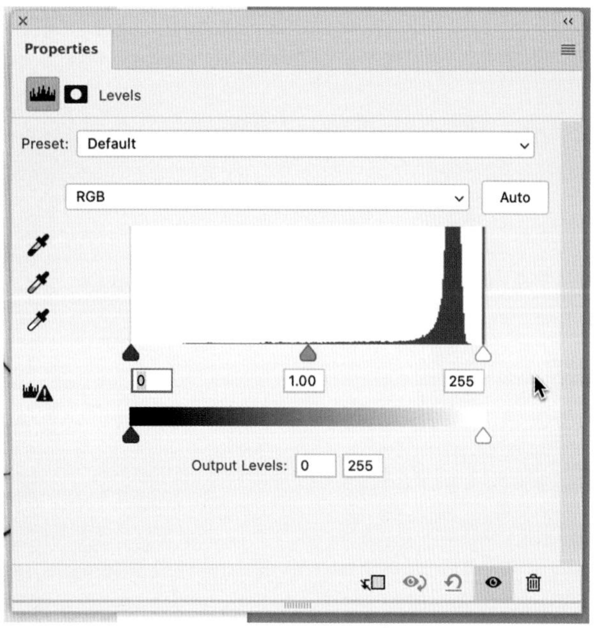

Figure 2.16 The *Levels Properties* panel. Notice the position of the dark, light, and midtone arrows along the histogram.

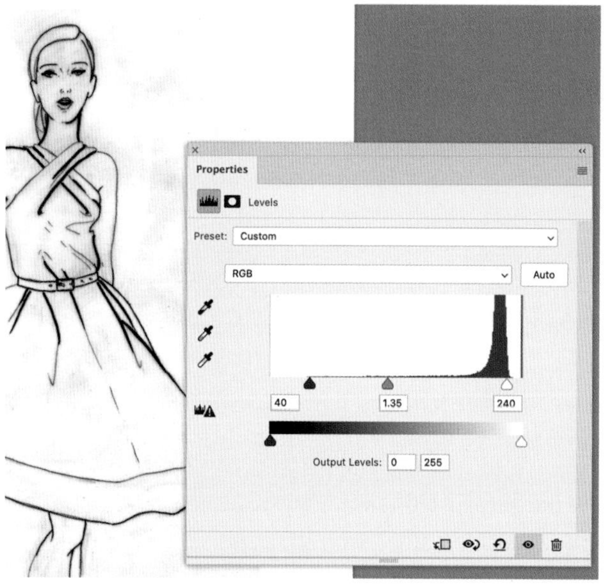

Figure 2.17 The *Levels Properties* panel after making adjustments. This is variable according to your sketch and personal preferences. Your arrow positions may look different from this example.

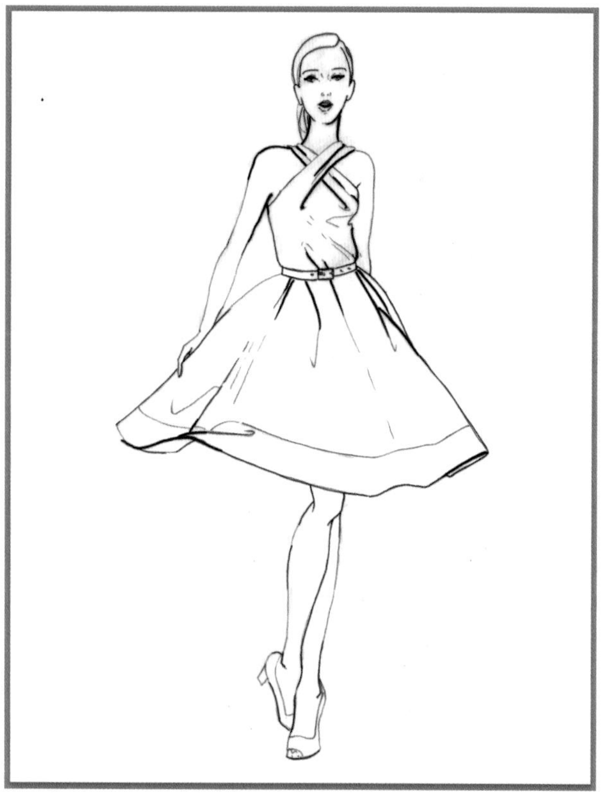

Figure 2.18 The image results after making the levels adjustment. Notice that the background has turned white and disappeared into the artboard.

Step 3: Manually clean up any extraneous smudges. At this point, you want to clean up any extra smudges and correct the sketch line if needed. DO NOT USE THE ERASE TOOL! We know the temptation is strong. However, you will instantly see why the moment you click with the erase tool. It takes away the background, too!

You can clean up those extra marks in a couple of different ways. The most straightforward way is to paint over the marks with the background color. Use the *Eye Dropper* tool from the tool menu to pick up the background color (it may not be exactly white). Then select the *Brush* tool. Use a slightly soft brush (approximately 80% hardness). This allows you to easily cover a smudge without accidentally creating a harsh edge if the color is slightly off.

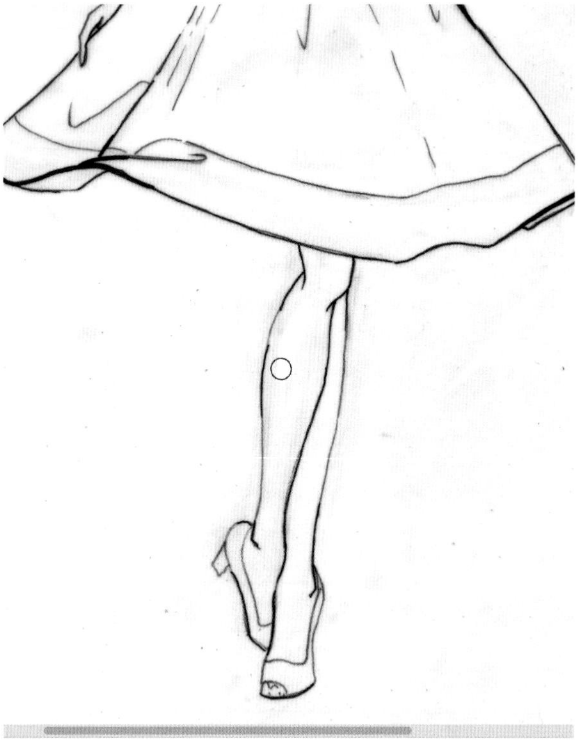

Figure 2.19 Using the *Brush* tool with the background color to correct smudges on the sketch. The brush circle shows a pencil smudge that is partially eliminated using one stroke of the *Brush*.

In some cases, it may be easier to select an area with one of the many *Selection* tools and fill it with the *Paint Bucket* tool in the background color.

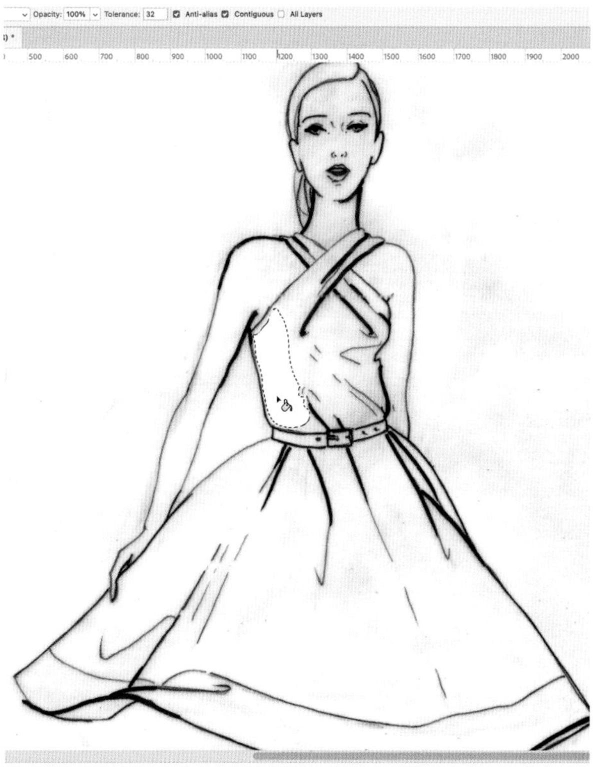

Figure 2.20 Area on side of the bodice selected using the *Lasso* tool and filled with the *Paint Bucket* tool with the background color.

Once you finish cleaning up the smudges and smears, then you may want to carefully adjust your linework using the *Brush* or *Pencil* tool. The *Pencil* tool is simply a brush with specific settings that imitate a pencil quality line. So, once you get used to using the *Brush* settings, you may want to continue with that tool and adjust as needed.

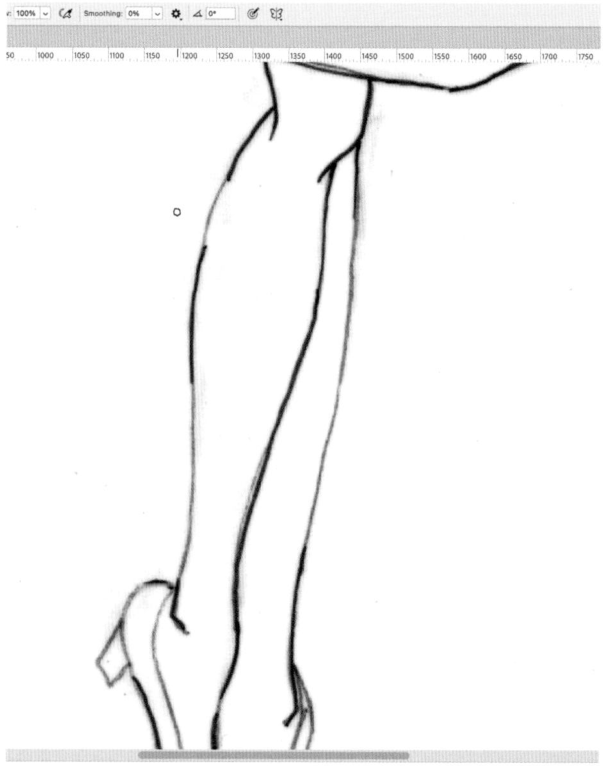

Figure 2.21 The line quality on the leg is a little clunky from the original inking.

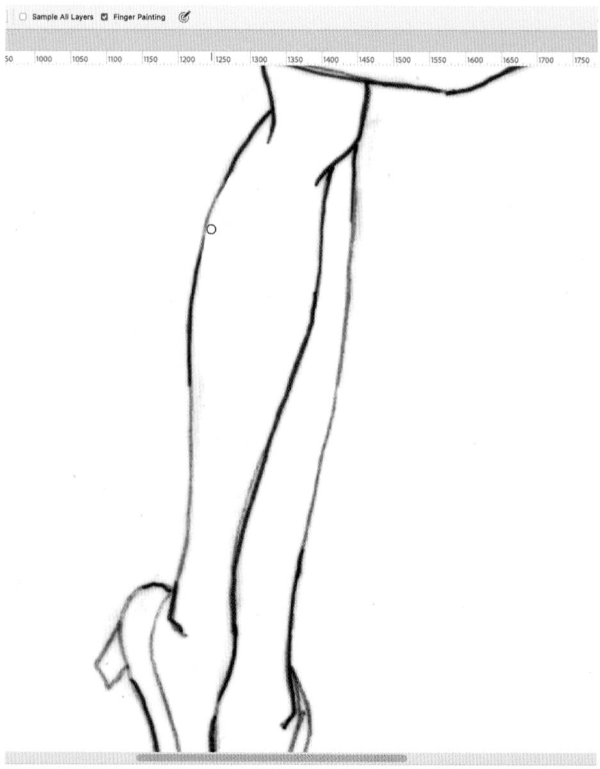

Figure 2.22 Using the *Brush* tool, the line quality is smoothed out to look more natural.

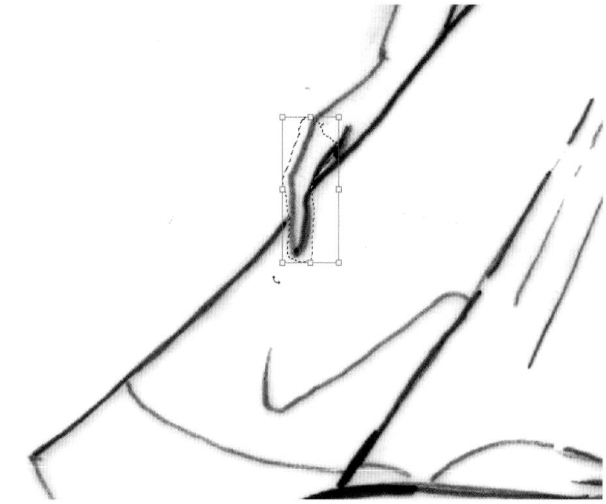

Figure 2.23 If you did not like the original angle of the finger, you can make a selection around that small area.

You can also select specific areas and use the *Transform* tool for corrections. If you do not like the angle or scale of a small area, you can make a selection and then transform it. You will need to fill in the sketch and paper for the transparent areas created afterward.

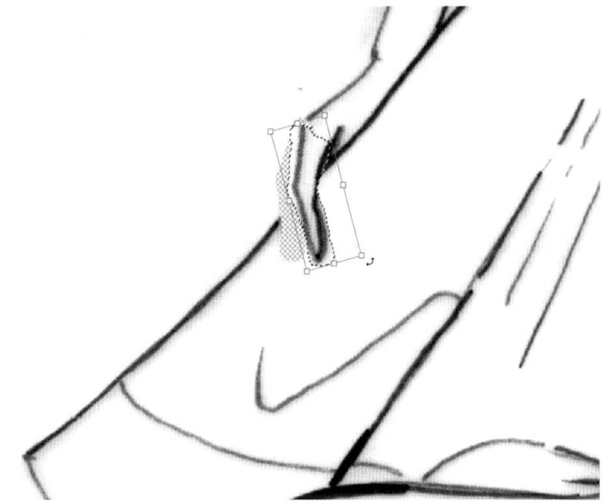

Figure 2.24 Once you have the selection, you can use the *Transform* tools (*Edit* menu → *Free Transform* or with keyboard shortcuts *control+t* for a PC and *command+t* for a Mac). Adjust as necessary.

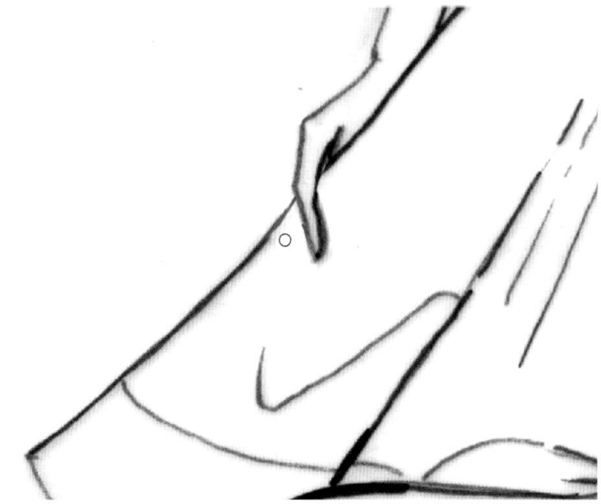

Figure 2.25 Once you are satisfied with the transformation, fill in the transparent areas and missing information of the sketch created from the transformation.

PRO TIP 2.3

Destructive versus Non-Destructive Editing

There is a great amount of debate, mostly due to personal preferences, about working destructively versus non-destructively in Photoshop. Although the name sounds precarious, **destructive workflows** mean that you save file space in exchange for future flexibility. In a destructive workflow, you tend to eliminate layers and options that would allow you to tweak past adjustments. This keeps your file size (often significantly) smaller. However, if you like the ability to make those tweaks in the future, then you can keep a **non-destructive workflow**. You will have larger files that may slow each process down a little (it depends on how large your file gets!).

It works well to use destructive workflows for part of the work, and non-destructive for other parts. In the case of cleaning up a black and white sketch, you are probably safe to work destructively. It is much more likely that any adjustments you make in the future will be to the color layers.

If you are happy with the results of your work so far, you may want to merge all the layers. *Right-click* on any layer in the *Layer* panel to pull up the alternate commands. You can choose *Merge Visible* or *Flatten Image* to reduce the layers to one. This often merges the layers into a Background layer which is locked. If this

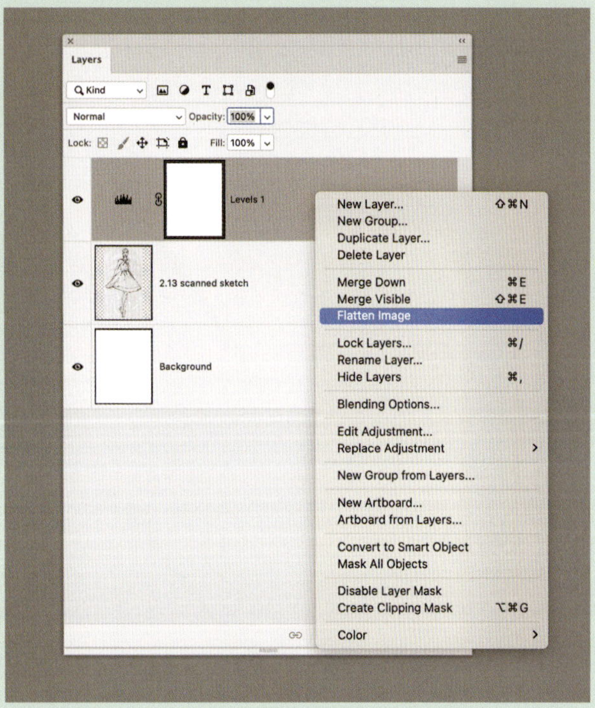

Figure PT2.3a *Right-click* on a layer in the *Layer* panel to *Flatten* the image and reduce the file size.

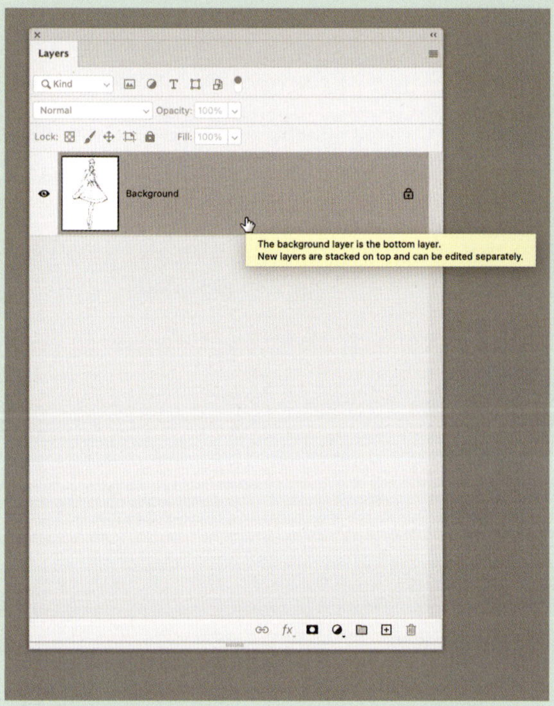

Figure PT2.3b The merged layers created a background layer that needs to be *Unlocked* before proceeding.

is the case (in the *Layers* panel, the layer will say *Background* and show a lock icon beside it), then click on the icon to unlock the layer.

Alternatively, you can use the *Image* menu and select *Levels* from *Adjustments* to make a permanent adjustment without the addition of a new layer.

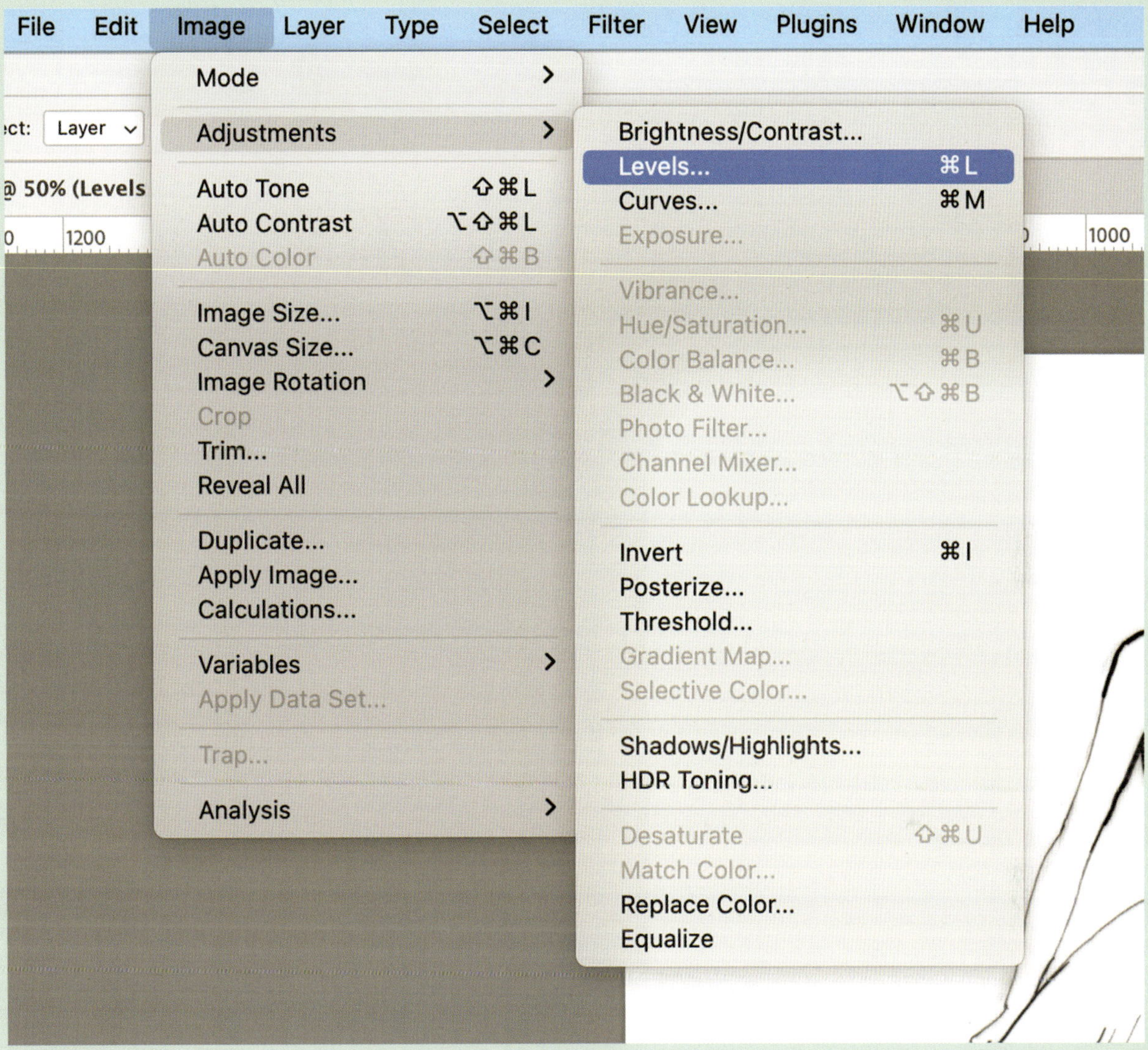

Figure PT2.3c To save file space, you can use destructive editing by selecting the *Levels* command from the *Image* menu at the top of the application.

Another helpful feature to touch up your proportions is the **Liquify** filter. This filter allows you to move the pixels around. It is best used in small doses, as this can distort your pixels if used to excess. There are many useful tools in this filter, but for now we will just focus on one.

It often works better to select a small area with one of the many *Selection* tools. This helps to keep you from distorting the areas around your changes too much. Once you make a selection, go to the *Filter* menu and select the *Liquify* command.

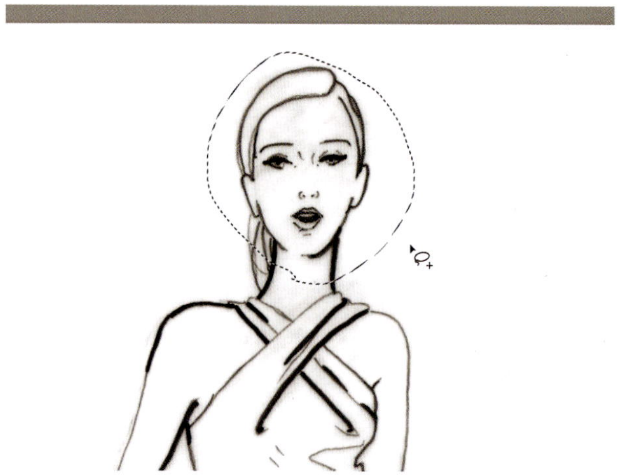

Figure 2.26 Making a rough selection around the head with the *Lasso* tool. We will adjust the ears that were initially drawn too low for the angle of the face.

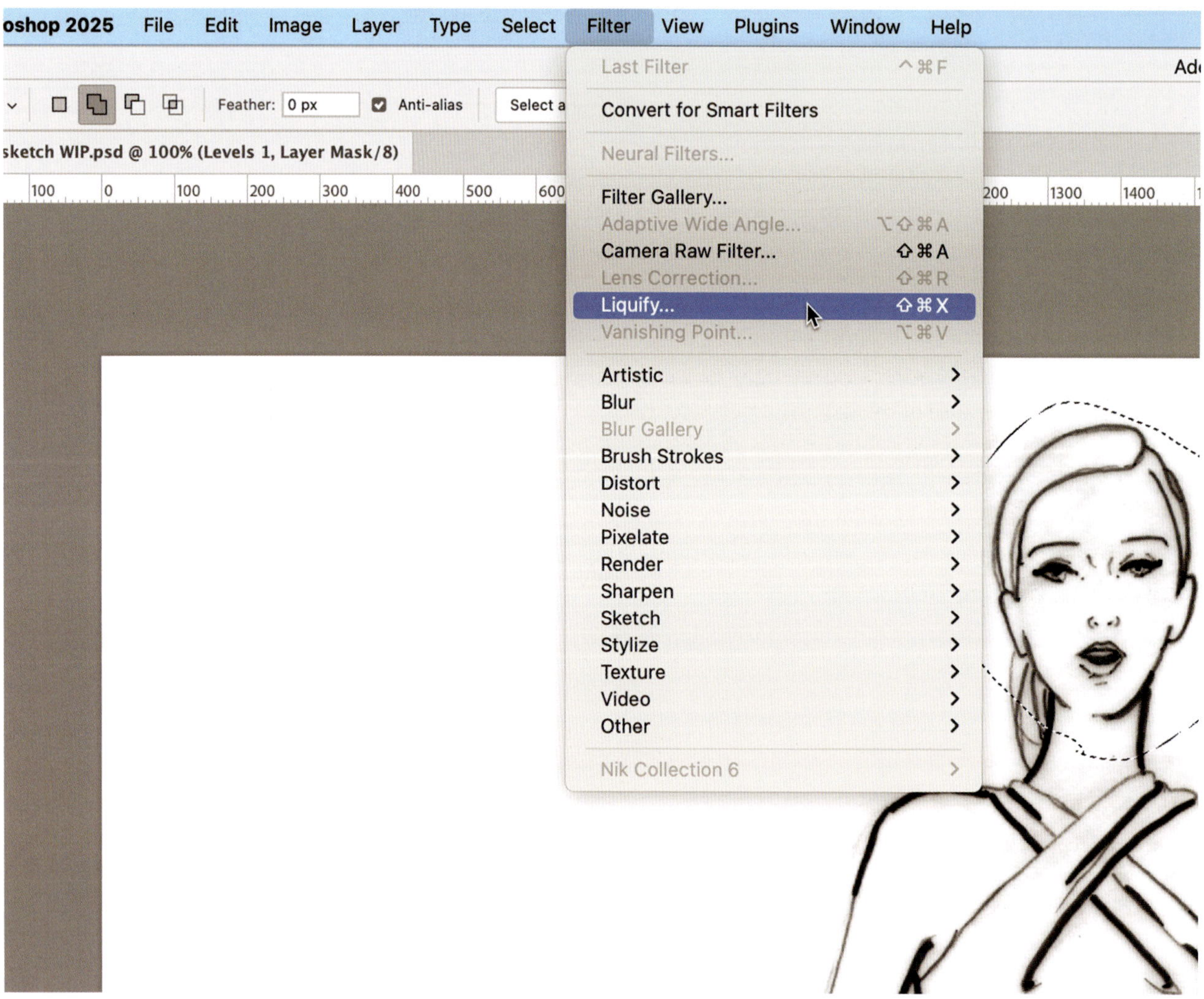

Figure 2.27 Select the *Liquify* command from the *Filter* menu.

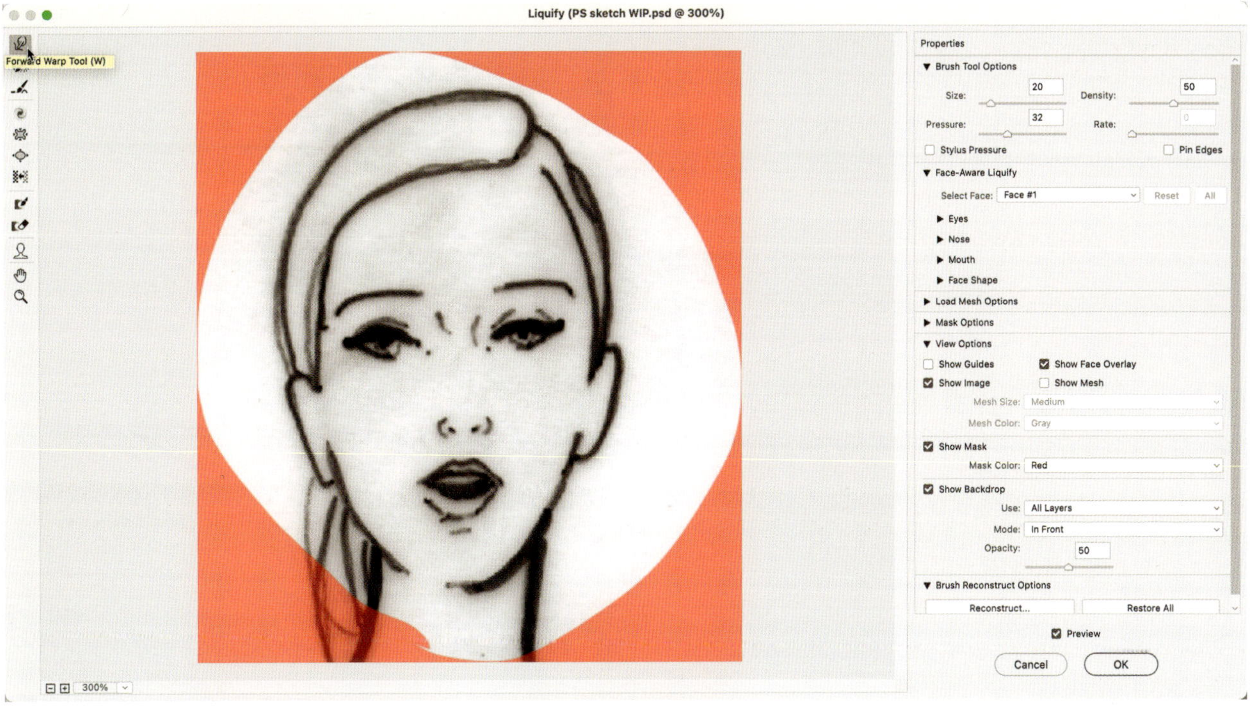

Figure 2.28 The *Liquify* dialog pop-up box. Use the *Forward Warp* tool to make adjustments through small strokes. The red area indicates unselected parts of the drawing.

This will open a pop-up dialog box. The *Forward Warp* tool is found in the upper left corner of the dialog box. With this tool, you can push pixels around. Use very small movements. If you make a big change, it tends to create an odd look because of the distorted pixels. Using small strokes, pull the ear up closer to the sketch's eye level. Once you finish with both ears and any other adjustments you would like to make, click the *OK* button on the lower right side of the dialog box. You can now *Deselect* the area (*control+d* or *command+d*).

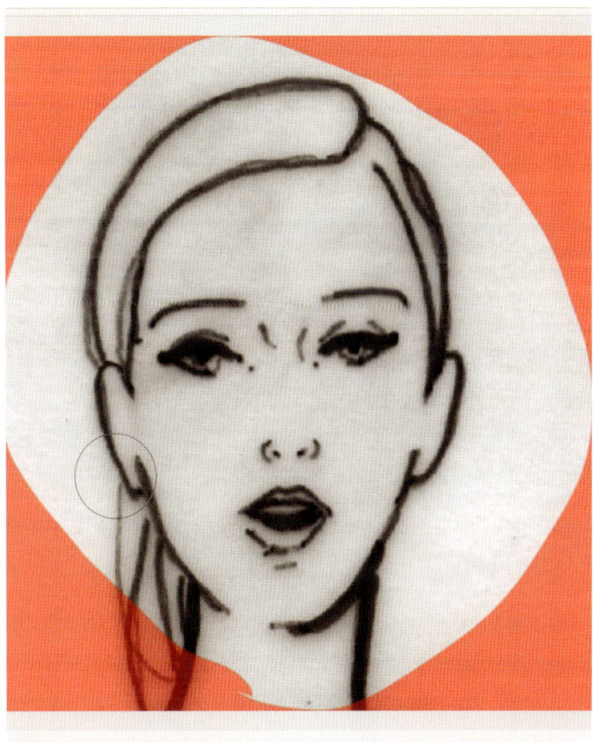

Figure 2.29 Using the *Forward Warp* tool to move the ears up.

Step 4: *Save* your work for coloring! You can use your image again for the other chapters.

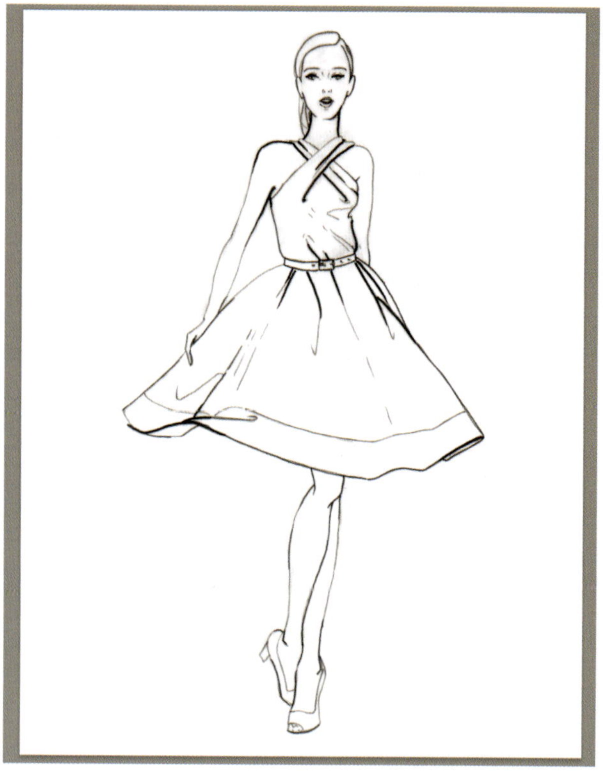

Figure 2.30 The cleaned and corrected sketch ready for coloring.

Scanning and Preparing an Oversized Rendering

Sometimes your original sketch does not fully fit on a scanner bed. You may try taking a digital photo, but sometimes this distorts the proportions if not taken at a straight 90-degree angle to the image. Therefore, it may be easier to scan the image in parts. There is a wonderful feature in Photoshop that will automatically put together images of the same object, so long as there is enough overlap between the images.[1] Be warned, this feature is not available in all apps.

You do not need to have any files open to start. You simply look under the *File* menu for the *Automate* option. Under this option will be the command to **Photomerge**.

Once you click on this command, a pop-up dialog box will appear. It should have *Auto Layout* selected and the *Blend Images Together* box ticked by default. If not, you can make these selections manually. Click on *Browse* to navigate to your scans and select all relevant files.

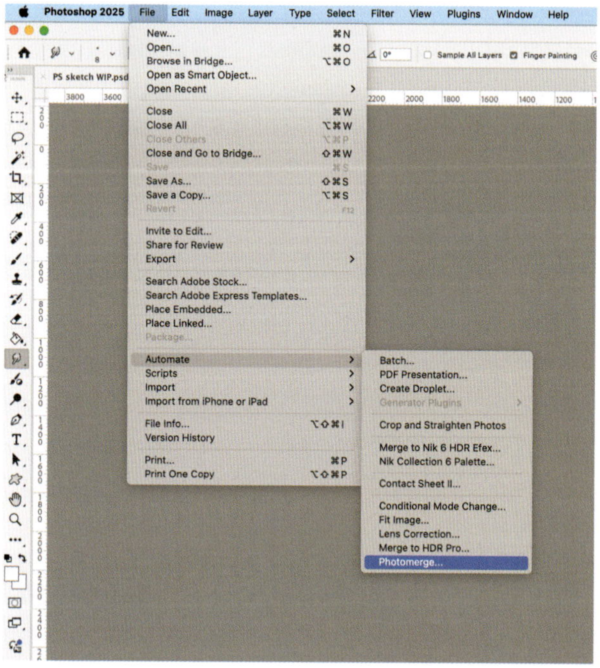

Figure 2.31 The command for *Photomerge* can be found under *Automate* in the *File* menu.

For this example, you can select OversizeSketch1.jpg, OvesizeSketch2.jpg, OversizeSketch3.jpg, and OversizeSketch4.jpg. Use the *Control* or *Command* key to select multiple files. Once all four files are shown in the Source Files field, then click *OK*.

Allow a minute or two for the program to do its work. You may not see any activity for the first few seconds while it is processing, but eventually you will see the program automatically placing the files into separate layers. Once it is done, *Save* your new file. It is now ready to start cleaning up. You may need to *Rotate* the image (found under the *Image* menu) if it compiled the images upside down. This seems to happen about half of the time because the program cannot tell which way up your drawing should be. We also recommend that you make a flattened copy to work with for cleanup. Otherwise, you will have to make adjustments to all the layers, individually. Select all the layers using the *Control* or *Command* key and *right-click* to bring up a menu. Select *Merge Layers*. The merged layer will also save space by eliminating the individually masked files.

Project 2.2: Digital Sketching with or without a Template

Digital sketching is much like sketching on paper. You pick a drawing utensil (choose your *Brush* settings) and start drawing! It takes a while to get used to working on a digital surface, so keep practicing. This is an area of the process in which you may want to explore tablet options.

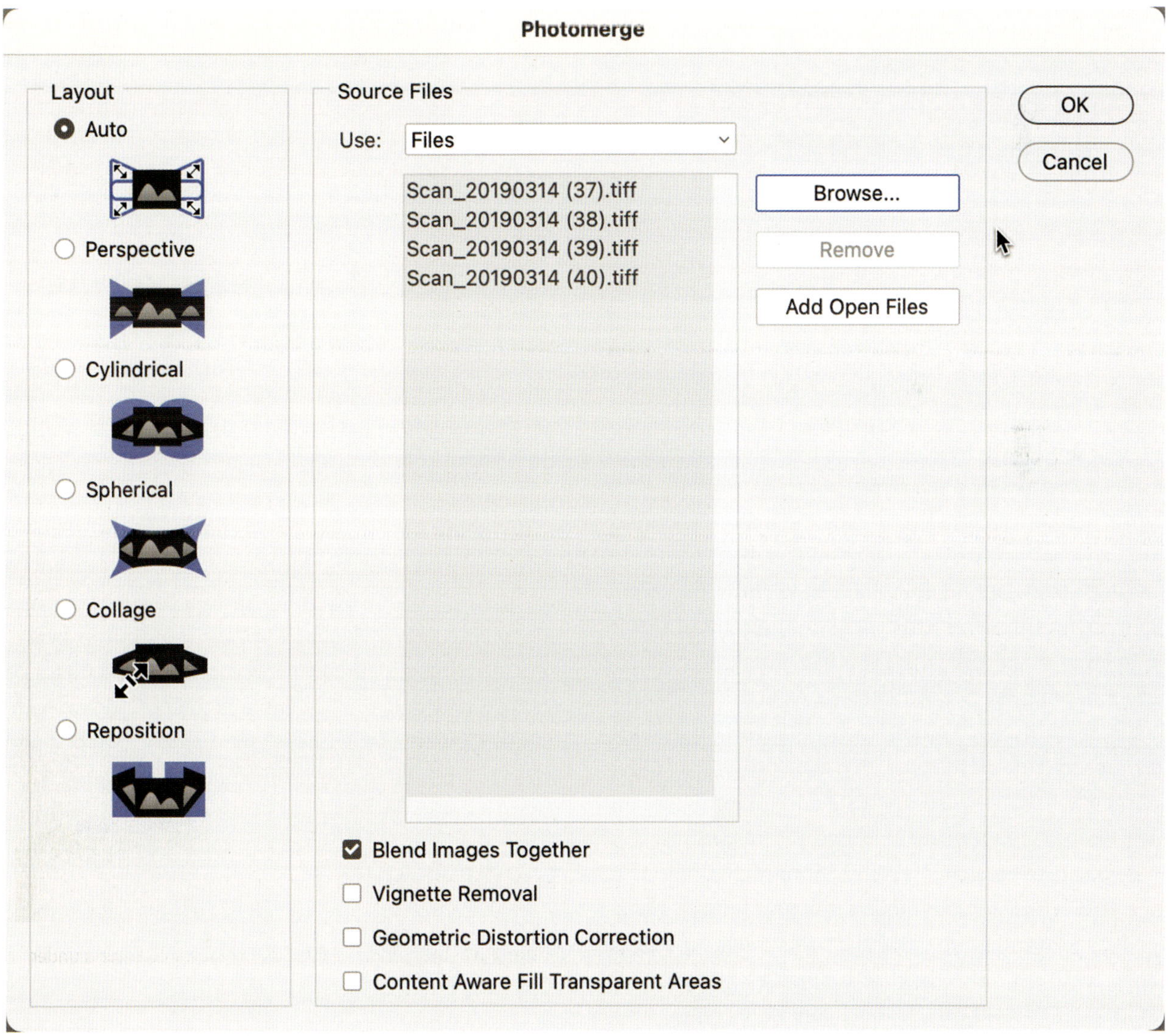

Figure 2.32 The *Photomerge* dialog pop-up box. Check your settings, then browse to the source files. Click *OK* when you are ready to proceed.

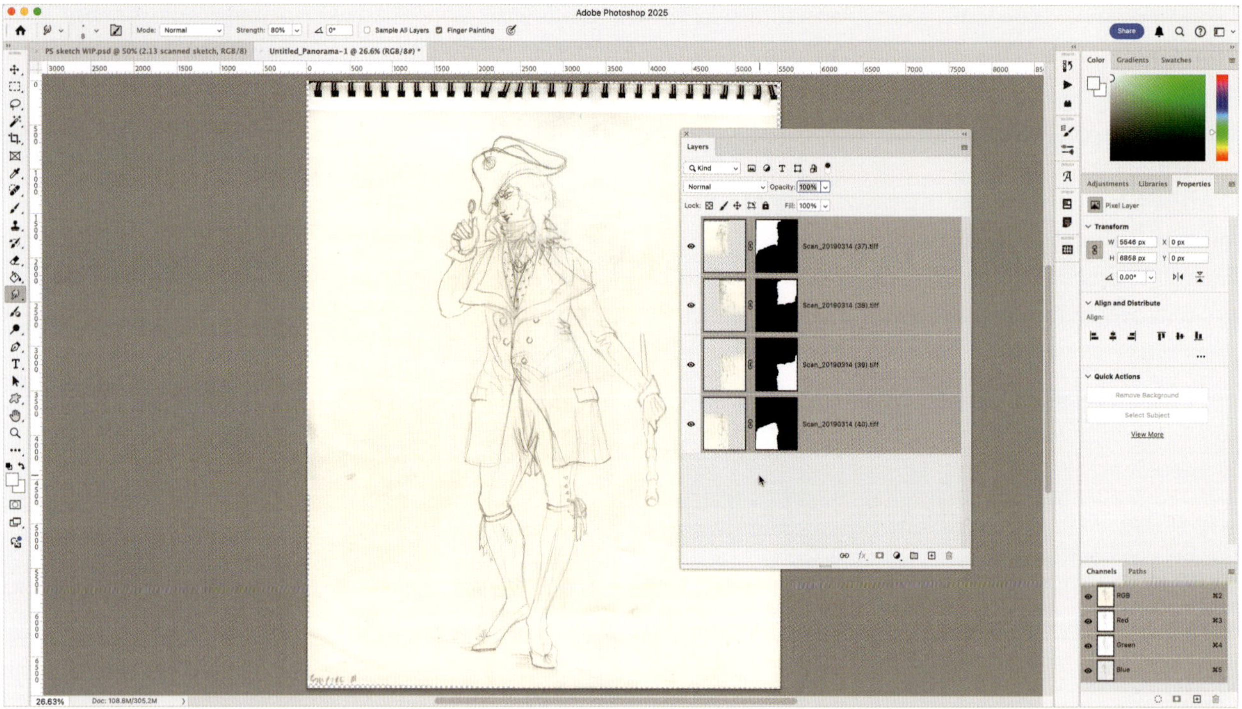

Figure 2.33 The completed photomerged sketch. Notice that each image is on a separate layer with a layer mask to compile the full image. Make a merged copy to proceed with cleaning the sketch.

If working on a laptop or desktop, there are wireless and wired connection drawing tablets of various options and prices. The least expensive ones plug into your computer with a USB, lightning, or other cable and have limited options. Sometimes limited options are better, though! You must watch the screen while your hand is on the tablet making the stylus move, so you will need to practice coordinating your eyes and hands. The more expensive options have a screen on the tablet.

Additionally, standalone tablets, such as the Apple iPad, are useful. Some artists will do their initial sketch on such a tablet with a stylus (like the Apple Pencil) before moving the file to their main computer. You can adhere to the same program, such as Photoshop, on both devices, or you can switch between programs. Many artists like to start with Procreate and then migrate the file to Photoshop for the full range of tool options.

If you are interested in a collage or photobashing style, then you can clean up a model or actor photo (remember to get permission!) and start sketching on a layer above. This can be a very effective and fast technique to get ideas out quickly. Refer to Chapter 8 for more information and inspiration about this style. Essentially, the technique is the same, though. Just start drawing!

Project 2.3: Creating Line Quality in Ps

Line quality can be an important part of your style. Although you can keep a uniform opacity and width of line around your drawing (which is in itself a style), you may want to vary the quality of the line work.

If you use a stylus, you can set the brush to utilize the stylus pressure and tilt for variable line width and/or opacity. This allows you to directly incorporate variable line quality as you sketch. You can also paint in heavier lines after the initial sketch is complete or add them to a scanned sketch. If you need to lighten lines, you can carefully *Erase* part of the line if you digitally sketched on a separate layer. For a scan, you will need to use the *Brush* tool to paint in the background color to lighten a line.

Troubleshooting

There are a few common issues that arise in Photoshop during this process. See if any of these suggestions help with your problem:

"I'm painting with the paintbrush, but nothing is happening."

1. Check that you are on the correct layer in the *Layers* panel. Sometimes you are on an *Adjustment Layer*, or you may have the mask of that layer selected. Stop and check where you are. If you are done with the adjustments at this point, you may want to merge your layers down. There is no major advantage to keep those initial adjustments reversable.
2. Check the size of your brush. It may be too small, or so large that you can't see it on the screen.
3. Check your foreground color. Make sure it doesn't match the background you are painting. You may be making strokes, but they just do not show up against the background.

"I'm trying to paint with the brush but I keep getting the 'no' symbol (a circle with a diagonal slash through it)."

1. Check to see if the layer you are painting on is *Locked*, or if you accidentally selected the *Template* layer to paint (which is locked precisely to prevent you from painting on it!).
2. Do you get an error message when you start to use the *Brush* tool? If so, you are probably working on a *Smart Object* layer. The program will place an embedded image as a *Smart Object*. We will talk more about them later, but the short explanation is that this is another non-destructive workflow feature. You do not really need it at this point. You can either *Rasterize* the layer (Ps will ask if you want to do this when you start to paint on the layer) or you can simply *Merge* your layers into one layer. Either way will work.

"When I try to clean up my scan, I keep getting this gray and white checkerboard instead of the paper."

You are probably trying to use the erase tool instead of painting in the background color. Because the image includes the paper on one layer, it is erasing that layer (the "paper") to what is underneath. As there is nothing underneath, you get the transparency grid.

"I tried to use [pick a command] but I keep getting really odd results that no one can explain."

1. *Save* your work, close the program, restart the computer, and start again. Sometimes the program just picks up a glitch that will not go away until you restart.
2. If that doesn't work, make sure that your device and the software are up to date.
3. Finally, try an internet search to see if others have experienced the same issue and recommend solutions. There are many forums out there in which others found a work-around. If you do not find a solution, then it may be unique to your device. Write into the help/support team of your software first. If they do not have a solution, you may need to take your device to a professional repair center to diagnose the issue.

Scanning, Tracing, and Sketching in Illustrator (Ai)

When creating figures in Illustrator, you have a few options. There is an **Image Trace** tool in Illustrator, but you may find that it is not the best option. You may also want to digitally sketch using the *Pen* tool, *Pencil* tool, or a combination of the two. Creating a sketch in Illustrator may not feel as natural as Photoshop at first. However, like Photoshop, you can use a template or reference image to help as you learn the tools and become more comfortable with the application. Many designers find that they prefer the clean look and graphic tools in Illustrator with time.

Remember that other vector-based platforms such as Affinity Designer (in the vector workspace) will have similar tools to those found in Illustrator.

For these projects, you can use the resource files: Sketch1.jpg and ModelPhoto1.jpg.

Project 2.4: *Image Trace* and Prep

There is a deceptive little tool in Illustrator called *Image Trace*. It sounds fabulous, doesn't it? I scan in my sketch, use *Image Trace*, and then I'm ready to start coloring, right? Not so much—at least not at the moment. Adobe has many talented programmers who make amazing improvements to the functions with every update.[2] So, this is not to say that this will never be the scenario. At the time of this printing, however, the *Image Trace* function should be taken with a grain of salt. Let us use the scanned sketch to see how it works.

Note: Some of the other programs have a similar automatic tracing feature, and some do not. Check the help feature of the program you are using to see if there is any sort of automatic trace feature.

Step 1: When you know you are importing a hand drawing into a vector-based program, aim to connect all the lines, even if with very fine lines. This will help you to keep closed paths where you need them. Otherwise, you may need to manually close the paths with the *Pen* or *Pencil* tool once it is imported. *Open* your image in Illustrator.

Use the *Selection* tool (keyboard shortcut: *v* key) to select the whole image. Look at the *Properties* panel and find a button for *Image Trace*. You can also find the command under the *Object* menu. Select *Image Trace* and a new pop-up dialog box will appear.

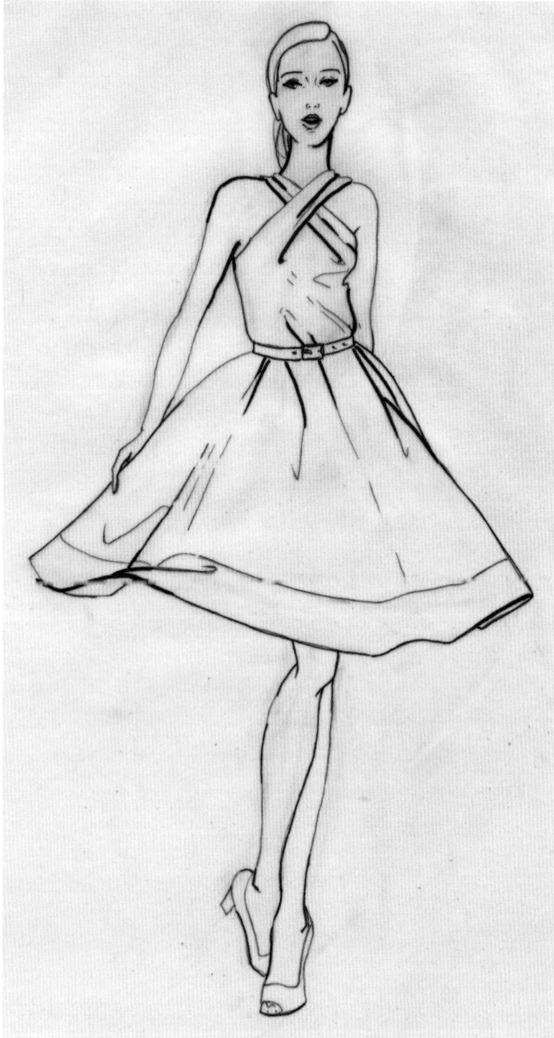

Figure 2.34 Original image, inked and cleaned before scanning.

PRO TIP 2.4

Eye Fatigue

Eye fatigue is common while working digitally for long periods of time. Many artists prefer to add a gray layer below their work to reduce the brightness and eye strain. Turn your sketch *Layer Blend Mode* to *Multiply* to allow the gray layer to show through the white paper of your scanned sketch. If you are sketching directly in the app, you can leave the *Blend Mode* at *Normal* because you are drawing on a transparent layer. Just turn the gray layer on and off as needed to work!

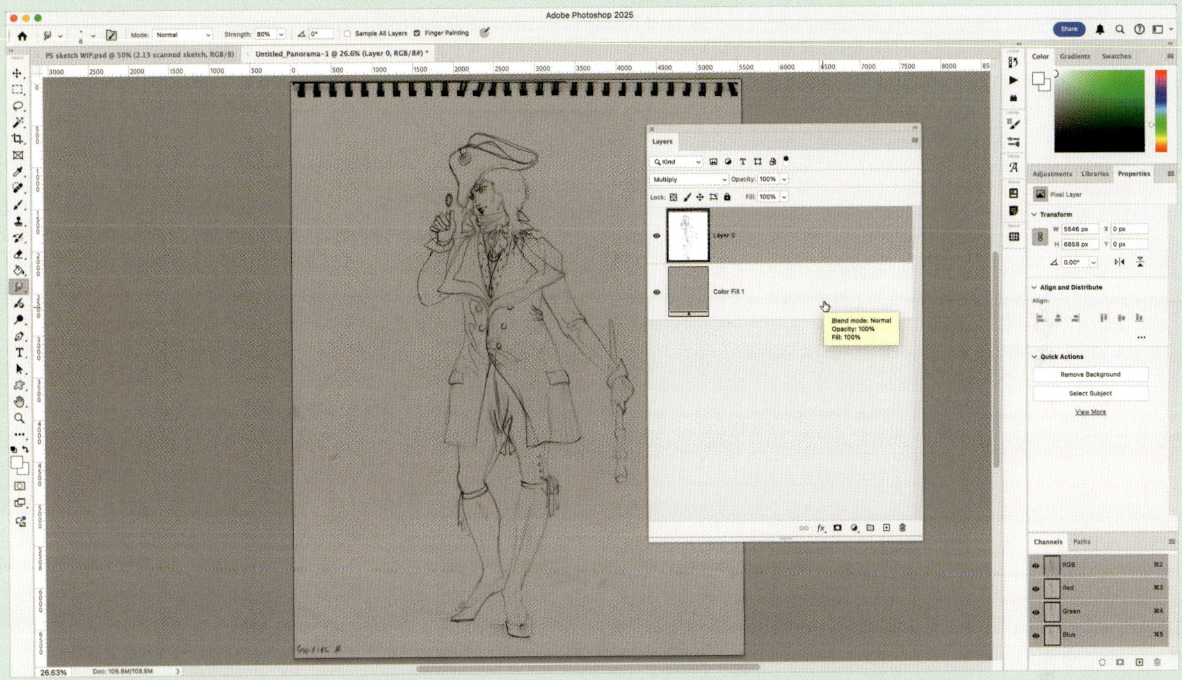

Figure PT2.4 Add a gray layer below your sketch to reduce eye strain when working for longer periods of time. Turn the *Blend Mode* of your sketch mode to *Multiply* to make the white paper color disappear.

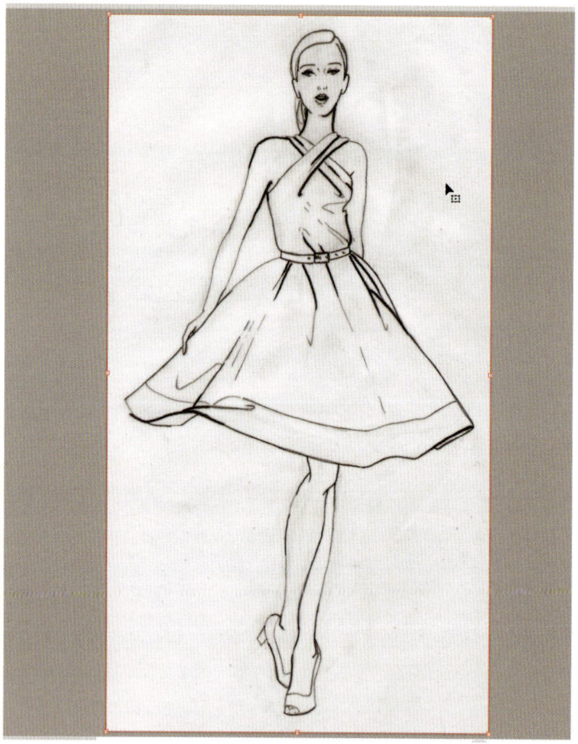

Figure 2.35 The whole image is first selected with the *Selection* tool or black arrow. The *Image Trace* option will not show in the *Properties* panel if the image is not selected. The slight red outline seen here shows that the image is selected. Note that your interface may use a different color to indicate the selected item.

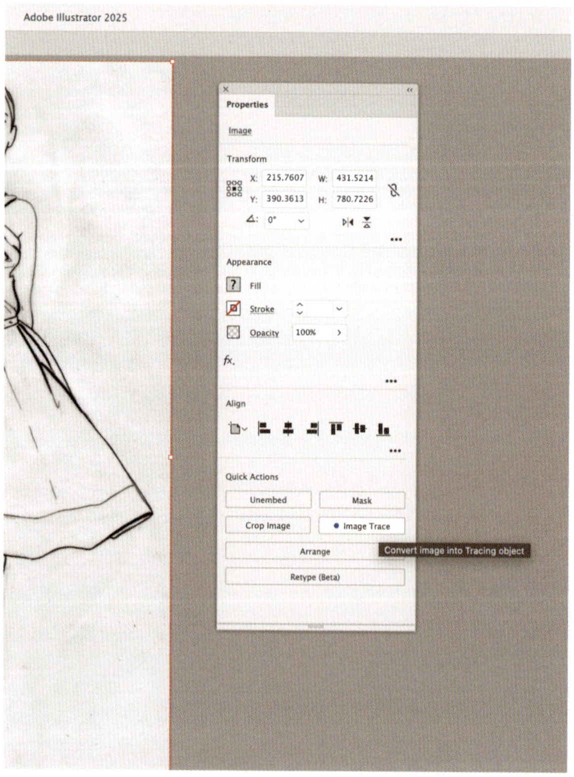

Figure 2.36 The *Properties* panel when the image is selected. Click the *Image Trace* option.

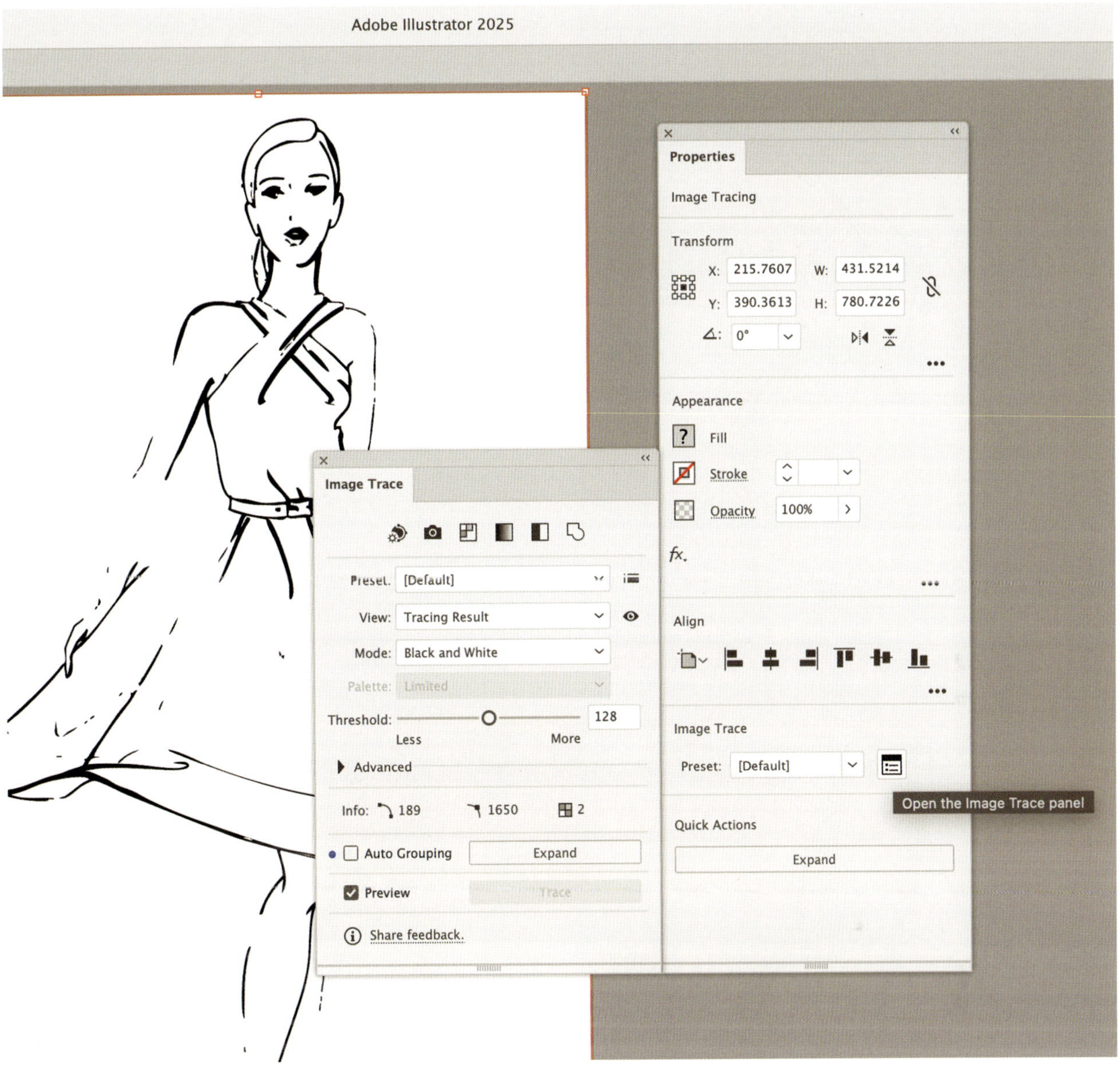

Figure 2.37 Clicking the *Image Trace* option will open the *Image Trace* panel. You can try different presets. Make sure that *Preview* is selected in order to see the results each time, but be warned that complicated images (like photographs) may take a while to process for each change you make. You may also wish to open the *Advanced* options to play with the individual settings.

Make sure that the *Preview* box is checked to see your results. Now try different presets to see the results you get for each. Some produce less than great results (depending on the image you are tracing), whereas others initially look perfect. However, looks can be deceiving! Let us quickly analyze some of the results.

The first two options may produce acceptable results for your needs. However, they often are not sufficient at capturing the quality of the line work. Additionally, while these do not produce an abundance of points and paths (which can greatly increase the file size and complicate the coloring process) they will need additional work with the *Pen* tool to create closed shapes for filling with color. Let us look at some of the other options that initially look promising.

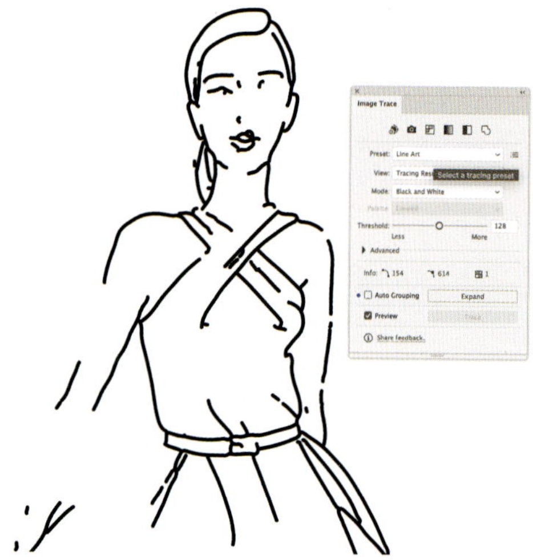

Figure 2.38 This image shows a close-up of the results for selecting the *Line Art* preset. Notice that it eliminates the more delicate line work and flattens the line weight to a consistent width.

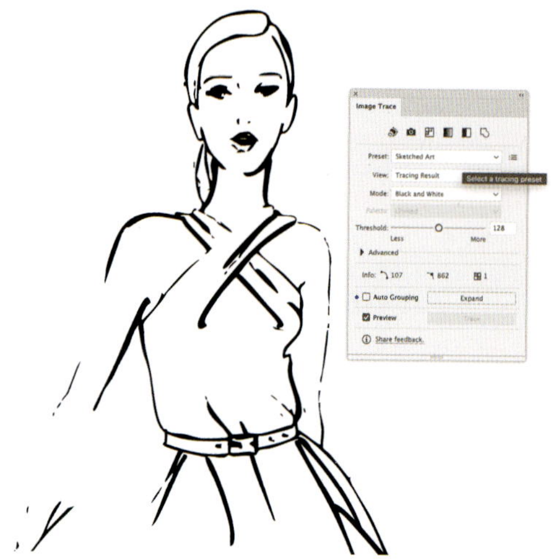

Figure 2.39 This image shows the *Sketched Art* preset. The line weight is improved with more variation. However, the results still eliminate much of the more delicate work.

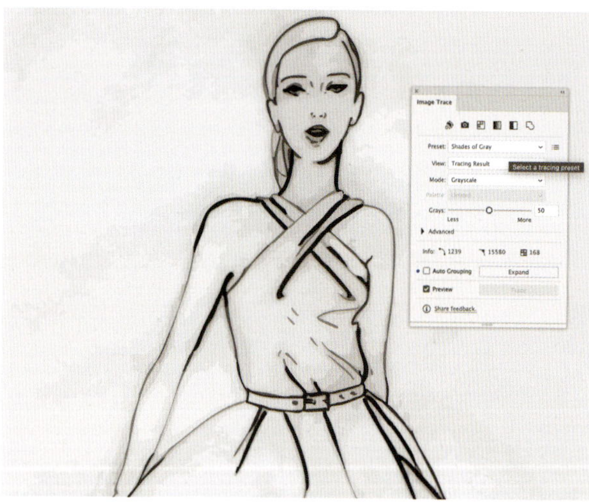

Figure 2.40 This is the *Shades of Gray* preset. At first glance, it seems to do a nice job.

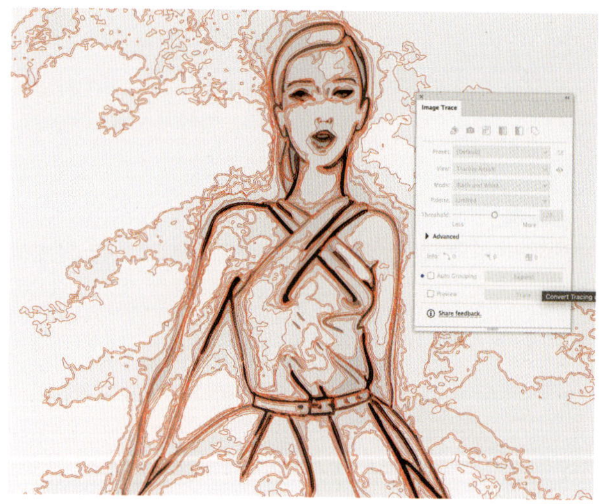

Figure 2.41 Once the result is *Expanded* to show the points and paths, you can see that it creates far more paths than are necessary for our rendering needs.

PRO TIP 2.5

Strike a Pose!

If you want a particular pose or body shape for your illustration but cannot find a photo to reference, try a modeling application or take your own pictures! There are several 3D modeling apps on the market for artists. In these, you can pose a 3D mannequin and dictate the lighting. Some even offer multiple body-type options. You can also find artists' mannequins at a local art store to pose manually, set up your lighting, and take a photo reference. Alternatively, you can also ask a friend to pose while you take your own photos for reference. If you are in costumes, the actors are often willing to pose for you. You can even capture some references of different facial expressions to help you!

The *Shades of Gray* preset captures the line quality very well. Let's **Expand** the result to get a better look. *Expanding* an *Image Trace* will convert the artwork to editable points and paths. While still in the *Image Trace* you will see a command to *Expand* in either the *Properties* panel or the top menu bar. Now you can see that this preset creates a large number of paths, anchors, and unnecessary shading areas for the rendering. Not only does this increase the file size unnecessarily, it also makes it very difficult to color, shade, and apply patterns.

At first, the *Image Trace* function seems very appealing and may look like it generates nice results with certain settings. It is a fast, convenient one-click solution. However, the results are not very useful in the authors' opinion, and it slows down the process overall.

As we need to complete shapes for filling, some of the settings leave too many open paths, while others create too many hidden, closed ones. There are options under the *Advanced* tab that allow you to ignore white areas and reduce points. However, smudges still tend to be picked up and the algorithm for reducing points is not quite as refined as the human eye. As mentioned previously, this function may dramatically improve with future software updates. At the moment, though, it tends to be less helpful for the type of rendering work we do in fashion and costume.

The point of this exercise is less to learn how to do it and more to learn why we do not use it that often. Inevitably, if we do not take a few minutes to show the results of this function, someone will ask why we are not using it. Now you know!

Everyone works differently, however. You may find that this feature functions perfectly for your rendering style and needs. Use what works for you.

Project 2.5: Pen Trace and Prep

Using the *Pen* or *Pencil* tool in Illustrator is the more traditional and reliable way to trace your artwork into a vector image. You can start with your own sketch or use a model photo if you are less confident with sketching bodies. Some use the model photo as a template and essentially trace the outline. You may also want to create and use a grid to proportionally line up your sketch when using a reference photo.

Whether you use a reference photo or not, you will be using the *Pen* tool in Illustrator and other vector-based software. This uses a collection of paths between anchor points. If you are a practiced hand illustrator, this may seem very non-intuitive at first compared with Photoshop or other raster-based software. However, if you only have a mouse and no tablet, this may be an easier option for you.

Step 1: Start by creating *a New Document* in Illustrator. If you would like to use a template, *Open* the file as a template or *Place* it as a template. See the section on templates earlier in this chapter if you need help. Create a *New Layer* above it to start drawing.

Step 2: Use the *Pen* tool (shortcut: *p* key). Open the *Properties* panel and make sure that you have a dark-colored *Stroke* with no *Fill* for now. Some like to work with a black stroke and others prefer a vibrant color that stands out from the background. This is a personal preference.

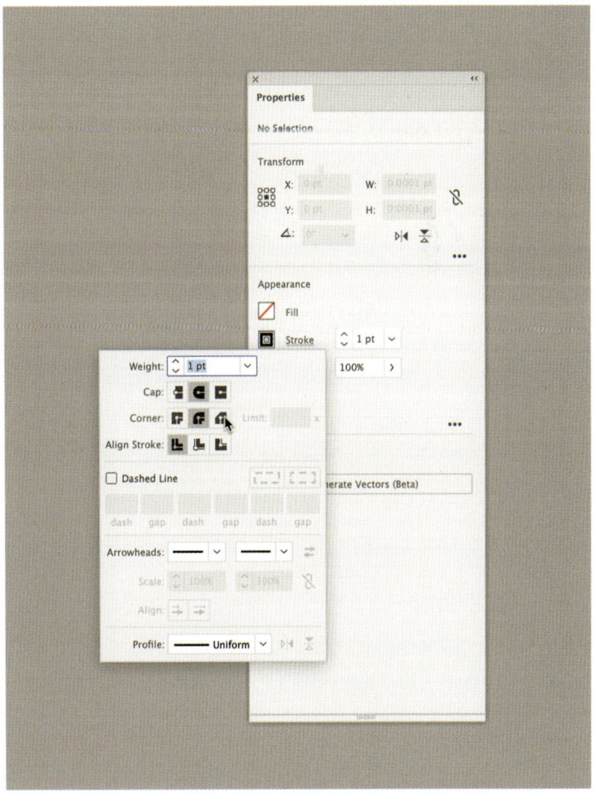

Figure 2.42 Before you start to use the *Pen* tool, check the settings in the *Properties* panel. Turn off the *Fill* for now. Set the color of your *Stroke* to your preference. Keep the weight at 1 point but change the *Caps* and *Corners* to *Round*.

We can fill the shapes later with color, but this allows you to build the figure and still see the template below it if you are using one.

We recommend that you use a 1-point *Stroke* to start. Change the property attributes of the stroke to *Round Corners* and *Round Caps*. This works better for figure and garment rendering. To do this, open the *Properties* panel and click on the word *Stroke* to open the *Stroke* panel. The default stroke is set to *Butt Caps* and *Miter Corners*. Click on the second icon of each to change it to *Round Cap* and *Round Corners*.

Step 3: Remember to think in complete shapes (like a closed fence) when using a vector-based platform. For now, ignore the interior sketch lines. The legs in this sketch are right against each other with no space between them, visually. Therefore, you can trace each leg individually or trace them together as one shape (as seen on the right). Start the first anchor in an area that will eventually be covered up by another layer. In the example on the right, the shape was started just above the skirt line. The skirt layer covers the leg layer, and that top line will not be seen once filled with color.

If you are not very comfortable with using the *Pen* tool yet, you may want to click at each change in line direction, then come back to change the points into curves with the *Anchor Point* tool (usually found below the *Pen* tool in the toolbar). If you are an old hand with the *Pen* tool, feel free to drag out your curves as you draw.

As you go around the shape, be sure that you *click* back on the original starting anchor point to complete the shape. A small circle, like a degree symbol, will appear beside the pen cursor shape. This indicates you are about to close the shape.

If you misplace an anchor, you can select it with the *Direct Selection* tool (keyboard shortcut: *a* key) to move it. Should you need to delete the point altogether, make sure the path is selected, then click on the redundant anchor again with the *Pen* tool. This will eliminate it.

Do not be discouraged if you are frustrated with this method at first. Practice tracing 3–5 figures to really get the hang of it. Remember that you are learning at this stage, and it takes time to build up the knowledge, skill, and speed.

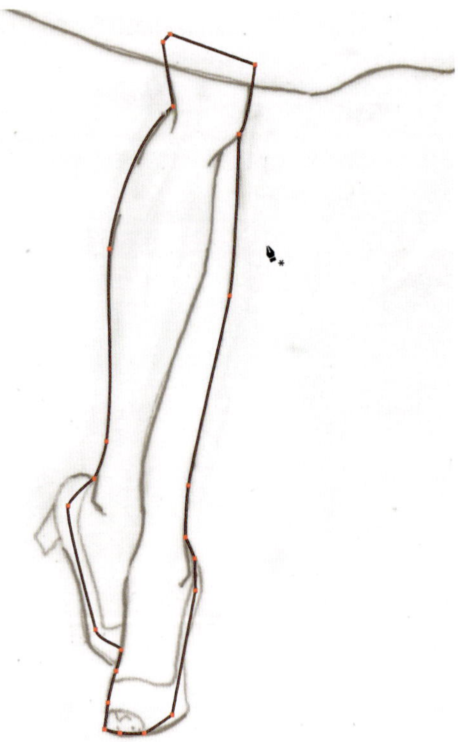

Figure 2.43 Tracing the legs. As the legs are illustrated tightly together, you can trace the outer edge as one complete shape and then fill in the separation between the legs with open paths.

Step 4: Add the interior lines as needed. These will be open paths with no fill. Make sure the completed leg shape is unselected, so you don't accidentally alter what you already completed. Then use the *Pen* tool to click the shape of the line between the legs, at the knee, and at the ankles.

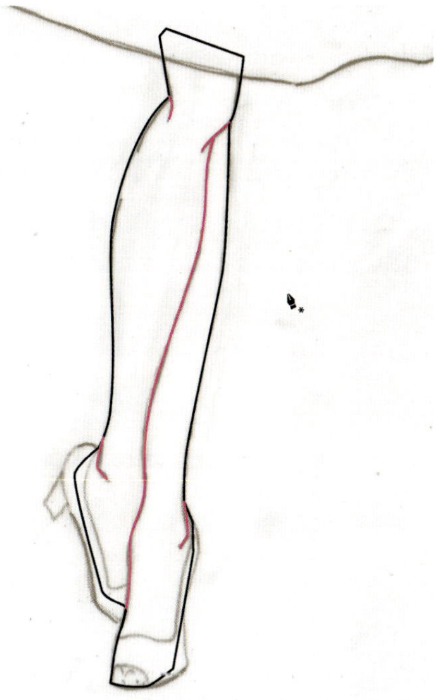

Figure 2.44 Adding the interior open paths for the legs. In this image, the interior lines are colored with a pink stroke to make it easier to see the separation between the open paths and the exterior open path of the legs.

Step 5: Keep going! Go around the whole figure, tracing or drawing shapes and filling in the details with open paths. Keep each major shape on a different layer to keep the file organized for future changes.

Feel free to make tweaks and corrections from the original sketch as you go. We noticed that the ears were too low in the original, so we traced them higher. Also, do not get caught up in making a perfect trace if it will be hidden by another layer later. For the upper body that will be covered by the dress top, we can jump across the body from one arm to the other. Later, the dress layer on top will cover up that part once we fill it with color. This saves the time of trying to trace around the dress twice (once for the dress and once for the body).

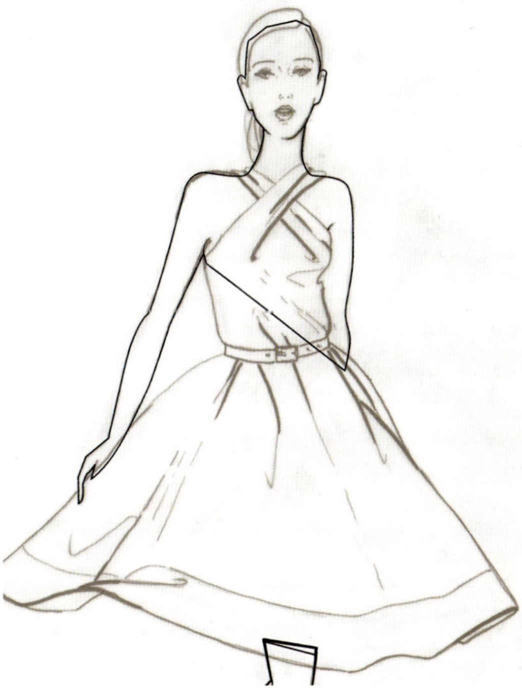

Figure 2.45 In this image, the body that will be the same color is traced with a *Pen* tool. Because the upper dress will cover part of the skin, we can jump from the lower arm to the underarm to simplify the tracing process and save time. Remember that each "area" should be a complete shape to color correctly. Also notice that the ears were traced higher to correct the original sketch.

PRO TIP 2.6

Change Your View!

Remember to zoom in and out while drawing to keep everything in proportion. Do not spend hours working on a closeup of the hand only to zoom out and discover that the proportions are wrong! You may also want to occasionally flip your sketch horizontally to get a different view. Artists commonly look at their work in a mirror during the process to keep the work accurate. Otherwise, our brains tend to compensate and visually correct lines that are, in fact, *not* accurate. It is so easy to flip your image back and forth while working digitally in any program—you should take advantage of this feature frequently. No mirror required!

If you are like most people, your hand is very uncomfortable and less accurate when trying to sketch lines in certain angles. Most pixel-based programs allow you to *Rotate* the view of the canvas to change the angle of your sketch while not affecting the final image. Think of it like turning the paper to get a better angle. In Photoshop, this tool can be found below the *Hand* tool in the main tool menu. You can also use the shortcut *R* to change the view angle.

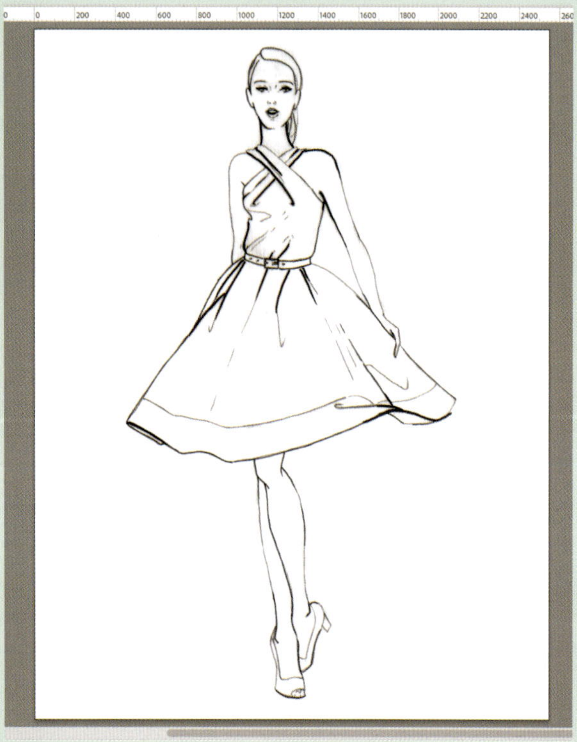

Figure PT2.5a Flip the image occasionally to check your proportions and let your eyes see the results from a new view. Most of the drawing programs easily allow for this command.

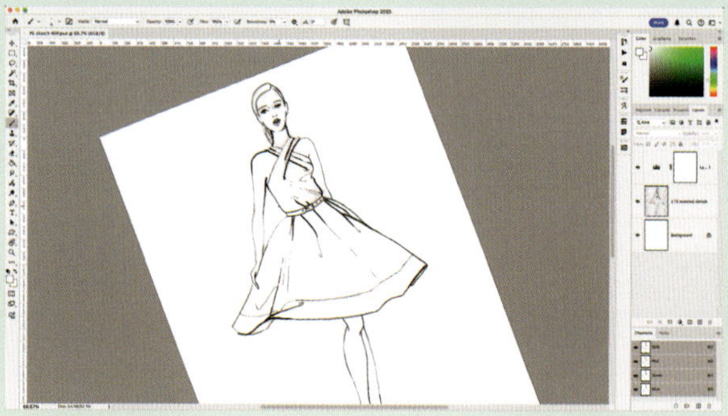

Figure PT2.5b Try *Rotating* your canvas to make it easier on your hand for certain line directions while sketching.

Remember that layer order affects how it is seen. So once an object is filled, it will cover what is underneath it. This means that you can block off shapes below other objects, as seen with the skin that will not show below the dress in this photo.

Although we are not filling the artwork with color yet, these images show how the dress layer in the foreground covers up the top body in the background. The layer order becomes important according to how you made your shapes. Be sure to label your layers to keep them organized. The images are often hard to decipher without labels to help you easily find a particular shape layer. For now, skip the facial features. We will cover this in more detail in a later chapter.

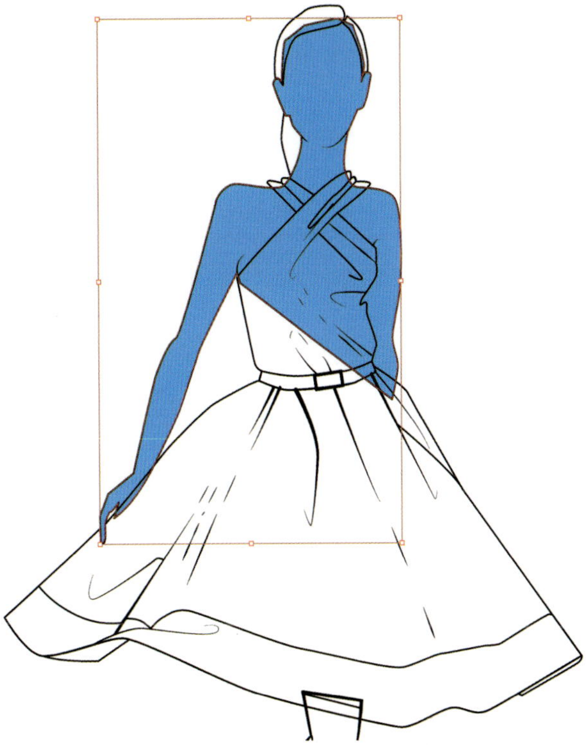

Figure 2.47 This image shows the skin filled in with color. You can see the connection between the lower arm and underarm that will eventually be covered with another layer.

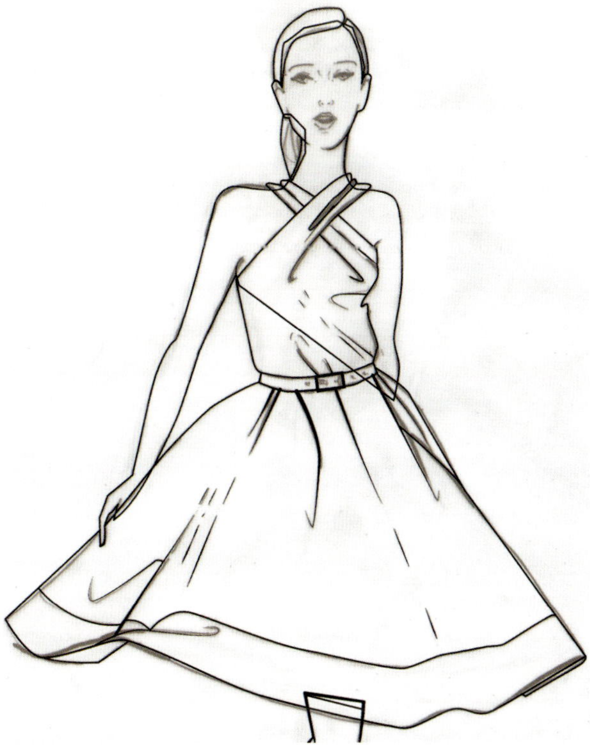

Figure 2.46 Here is the completed, traced image with the sketch still seen through the linework. We are ignoring the face for now and will work on that in a later chapter.

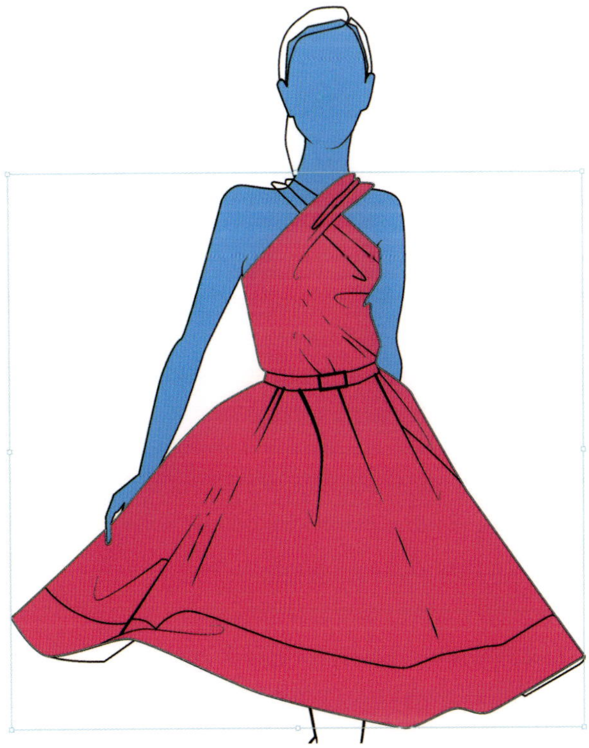

Figure 2.48 Here, part of the dress is filled with color. See how it blocks the skin color below it? The second strap is still not filled, so you can see the line of the neck curve through it.

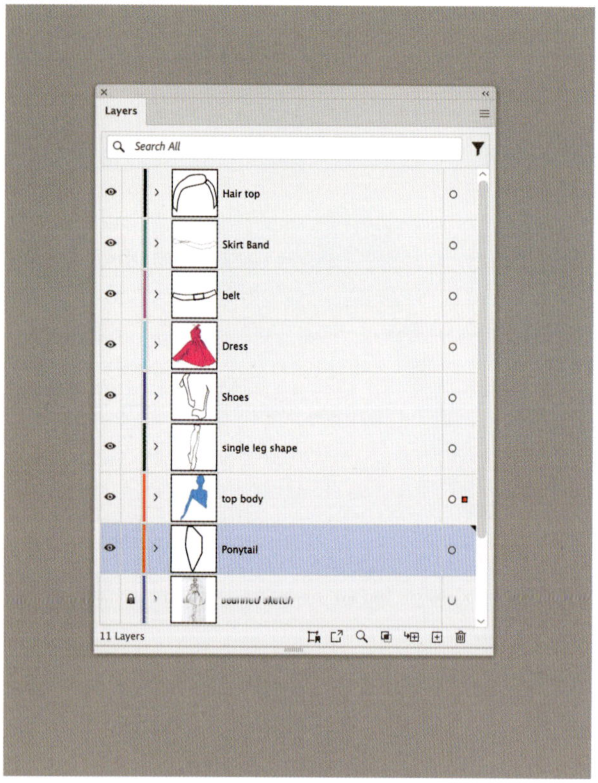

Figure 2.49 The *Layers* panel. Notice the order to have one shape cover another when we get to filling in the shapes with color. For example, the ponytail in the back is on a layer below the top body, which is below the layer for the top of the hair in order for one to block out the other.

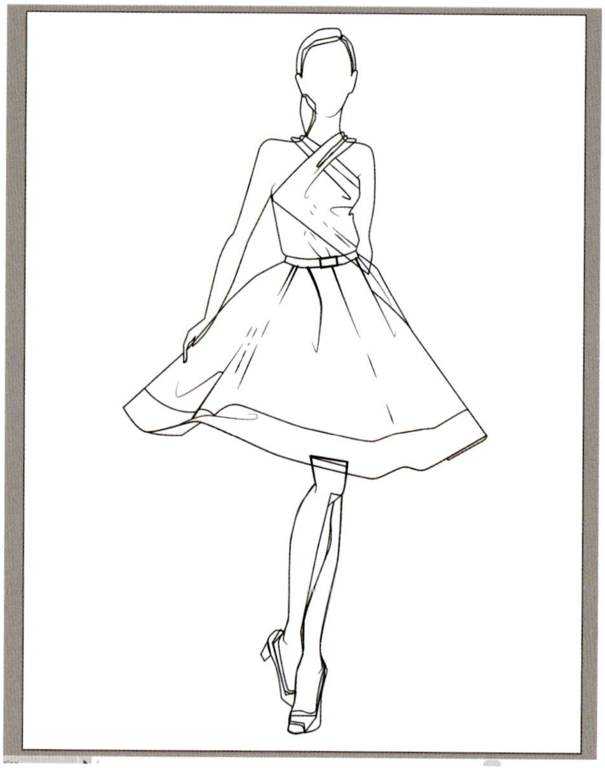

Figure 2.50 The completed illustration using the *Pen* tool to trace a sketch template. None of the shapes are filled with any color, so the extra lines used to complete individual shapes show in this image.

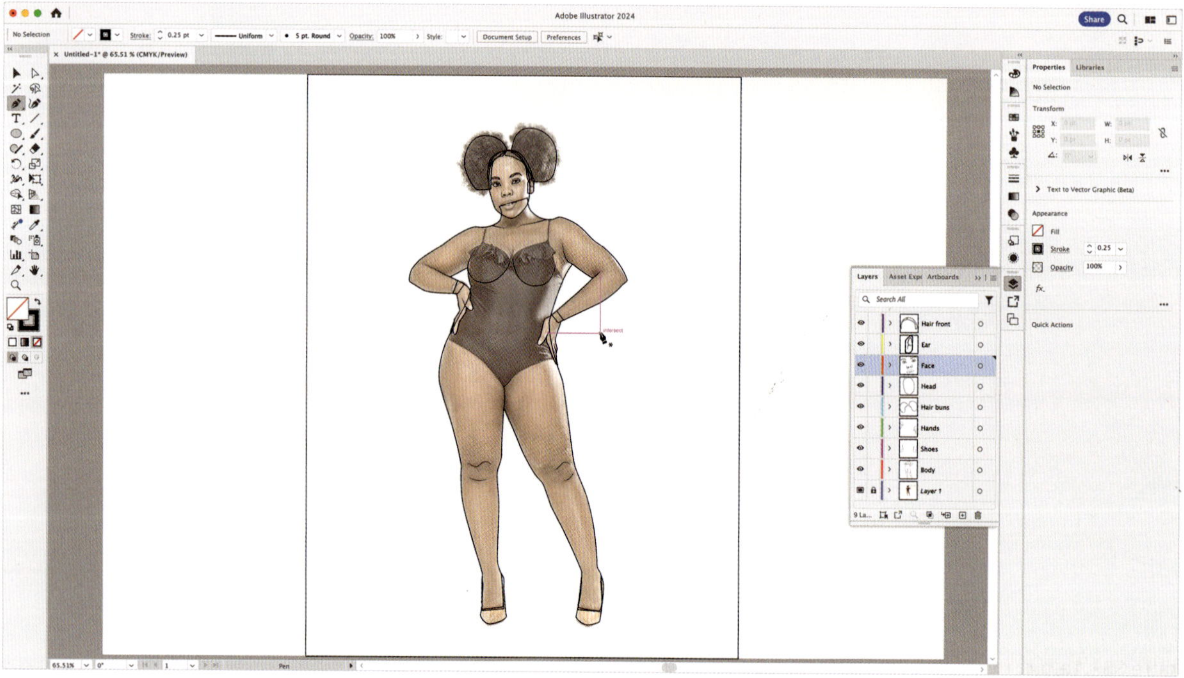

Figure 2.51 Using a photo template to trace with a *Pen* or *Pencil* tool in Illustrator. The photo helps you to get the correct proportions while you are learning. NeonShot/iStock.com

STYLE SECRETS 2.2

A Note about Body Image and the Responsibility of the Fashion Industry

Fashion illustrators have exaggerated the body proportions, especially those of women, since the dawn of commercial fashion illustration. The idea was to make the product appear more alluring and appeal to the vanity of the paying customer. However, there is something to be said for the disappointing effects of the translation to reality. Moreover, few consumers see the illustrations anymore. So why are we still exaggerating and drawing the nine-, ten-, or eleven-head figure? Habit? Some sense of tradition? We need to consider that drawing more representative figures helps to normalize realistic proportions within our culture. If you don't have the expectation to suddenly transform your body through a garment, your ego will take less of a hit when looking in the mirror. The more often we are exposed to images of realistic body types, the less we idealize unrealistic and unhealthy proportions. I appreciate that each illustrator has their personal style but consider if your personal style is perpetuating negative body imagery. The fashion industry is already rife with ethical issues. When you have the power to make a positive change, do it.

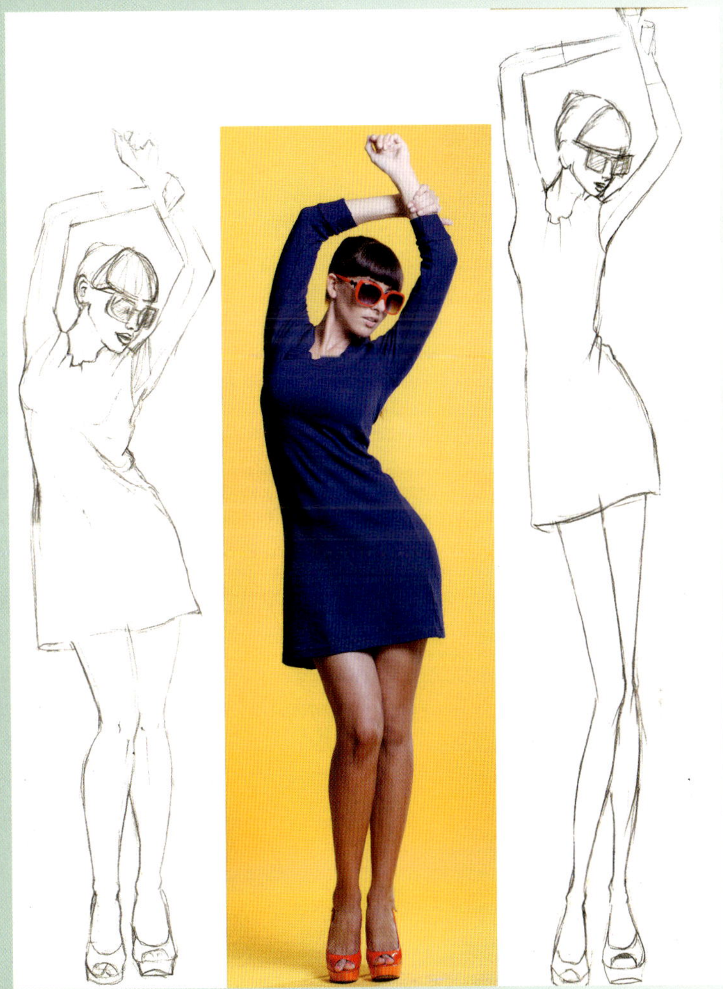

Figure SS2.1a,b,c This side-by-side comparison shows a photo of a model (center) with a proportionally accurate sketch on the left. The sketch on the right is elongated to a nine-head proportion. Which do you prefer? Why? alvarez/uStock.com

Project 2.6: Pencil Tool Sketch

You can sketch directly in Illustrator if you are comfortable with that method. If you have a tablet, this method may work better for you. We have used the *Pencil* tool with the Apple iPad Illustrator app and Apple Pencil quite well. The *Pencil* tool still creates anchors and paths but in a smoother sketching motion rather than a clicking motion. If you have a very steady and controlled hand with the mouse, you may also prefer the *Pencil* tool.

You still want to mentally divide the areas by stacking order and color containment. Make complete shapes, like the legs, together on one layer. Add the open paths for more definition. However, you can use a smooth sketching motion and the program will create anchors, paths, and curves automatically as you draw. If you repeatedly sketch over a particular area, it will keep redrawing the line according to your last hand movement. So, when adding the open path lines like the separation between the legs, you may want to temporarily *Lock* the outline shape path to keep it from accidentally redrawing that shape.

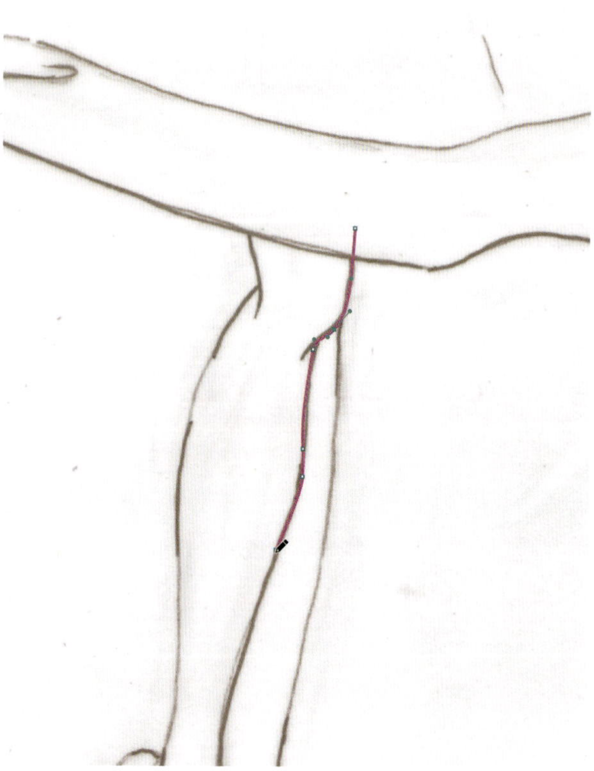

Figure 2.52 Using the *Pencil* tool to draw around the figure. The command will create anchors and curves according to how your cursor or stylus moves around the page rather than relying on you to click where you want an anchor point.

You can still use the *Direct Selection* tool to maneuver individual anchors after you initially sketch it in if you like. You can also mix the tools and use the *Pen* tool for some areas and the *Pencil* tool for other areas.

Project 2.7: Creating Line Quality in Adobe Illustrator

Creating variable line width and opacity in Illustrator is a bit more mechanical than it is in Photoshop. Many like the graphic look and precise control that can be achieved with Illustrator, however.

Method 1: Use the *Strokes* panel for a selected path. This works well with the open paths. Once you have a path selected, open the *Properties* panel and select the *Stroke* menu. Here you can change the *Stroke Width*. You can make it wider or thinner according to the numerical value in the width field. If you need to be more precise than the numbers in the drop-down menu, then click in the field and type a value. For example, you may want to make it thinner than 0.25. You can simply type in a smaller number, such as 0.15.

If you want the line to taper or change in width, then try clicking on one of the *Width Profiles* in the *Stroke* menu. These often have great results for open paths. For closed paths, you may want to try the *Width* tool, as described momentarily, to have a little more control and variance as the stroke moves around a shape.

Method 2: Use the *Width* tool on a selected path. This tool can be found on the toolbar. With a specific path

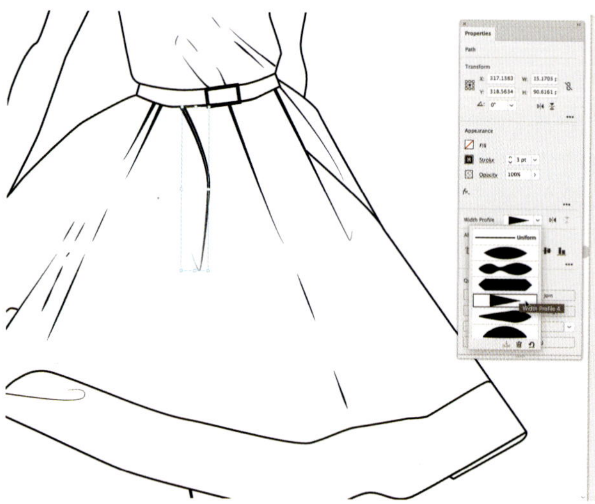

Figure 2.53 The *Width Profile* of a stroke can have very pleasing results for line quality. See how it tapers off to look more sketch-like.

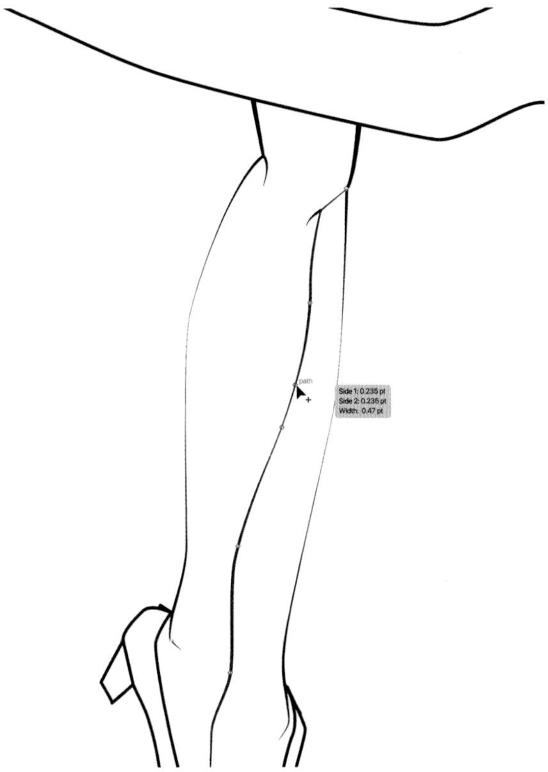

Figure 2.54 The *Width* tool found in the toolbar will allow you to make manual adjustments to the width of a stroke. This works well for closed paths with line quality that the standard *Width Profiles* do not easily address.

selected, pull the width in or out. It will change at that point and will transition back to the original width at the next anchor point. Tweak the path however you like to add variance.

Troubleshooting

The most common issue with Illustrator is that less-experienced (and sometimes very experienced) Illustrator users tend to start laying down anchors and paths without looking at which layer they are on. This results in lost paths that you think should be on one layer but end up on another. Try to keep up with the layer you are on as you draw. If you accidently place a path on a wrong layer, then select that whole path and drag/drop it into the correct layer through the *Layers* panel.

"The pen tool does not show the lines after I make them."

1. Have you checked that you are not on a locked layer?
2. If it seems to be making the line, but then disappears after you click somewhere else, then you probably have no stroke or fill. The anchors and paths are there, but invisible when not selected. Check the *Properties* panel to make sure your stroke has a color and a weight. To look for stray invisible points and paths, navigate to the *View* menu and choose *Outline* view (*control+y* or *command+y*). You can then clean up any unnecessary points. Once you are done, revert to *GPU Preview* (using the same command or keyboard shortcut).
3. Check that you have the *Pen* tool selected. Sometimes we forget and have another tool such as the selection arrow.

"My stroke has a really peculiar shape as I make the path."

The most likely explanation is that you have a fill color turned on. It may be the same color as your stroke and looks like one oddly shaped line. Or you may have the fill and stroke reversed for the same result.

"When I try to turn off the visibility of my reference image, all of my work goes away."

You probably didn't *Lock* the template and drew all of your lines on the same layer as the reference image. You will need to select those paths and drag them to the correct layer. Alternatively, it may be faster to create a *New Layer* below and drag the reference image down to that layer.

"The [pick a command] is acting really weird. What do I do?"

1. *Save* your work, exit the program, and try restarting the computer.
2. Check that the device and software are up to date.
3. Do an internet search to see if others are experiencing the same issue and if they have any solutions.

Mixing the Programs

There is not much reason or advantage at this stage for mixing programs. Some prefer to initially sketch on a tablet in a program such as Procreate or Adobe Fresco, and then import the file to Photoshop to clean up a little more. Everyone has their own preferred workflow. Do not be afraid to experiment to find what works best for you.

You will find as you progress through the lessons that there are things that one program does better than another. Try to limit how much you jump back and forth because you will often have to flatten the image each time. We recommend doing as much as you can in one program before switching to another. When you do need to switch, check that the next program can import the file format you currently have saved. You may want to *Save* a copy so that you can go back to this version if things go wrong in the next program.

When maneuvering from Illustrator (or another vector-based program) to Photoshop (or another raster-based program), you will need to check the resolution settings of the file in Illustrator. The resolution can be found under the *Effects* menu, in the *Document Raster Effects* command. We recommend a high setting to preserve the print quality of the image. You may also want to go ahead and flatten the file to *Save As* a JPEG or other pixel-based file type.

If you want to move the file in reverse (from a raster-based program to a vector-based program) then you probably will want to *Flatten* it and *Save As* a secondary file. The layers can be flattened through the *Layers* panel options. The resolution of that file would have been set from the start when you created the document. Sometimes you need to mix the use of programs to get the best results, so don't be afraid to switch when you need it.

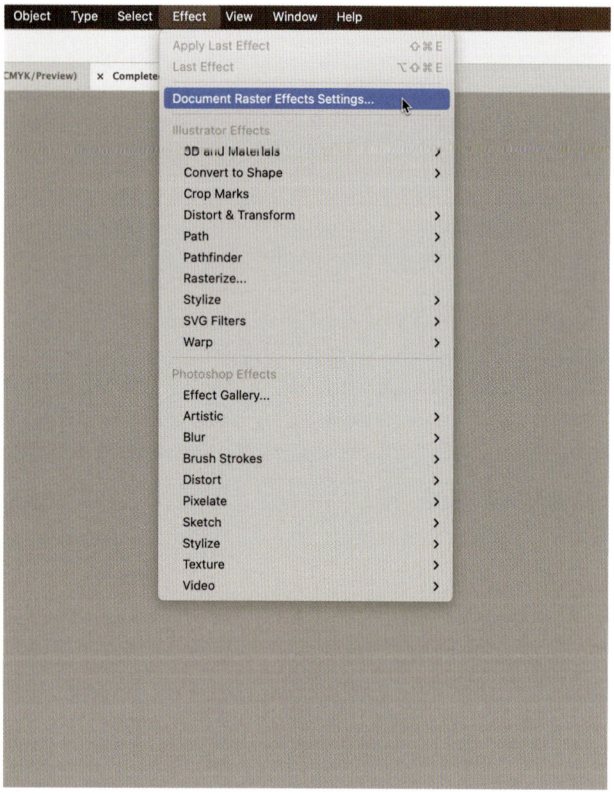

Figure 2.55 To move a file from Illustrator to Photoshop, set the *Document Raster Effects* quality from the *Edit* menu.

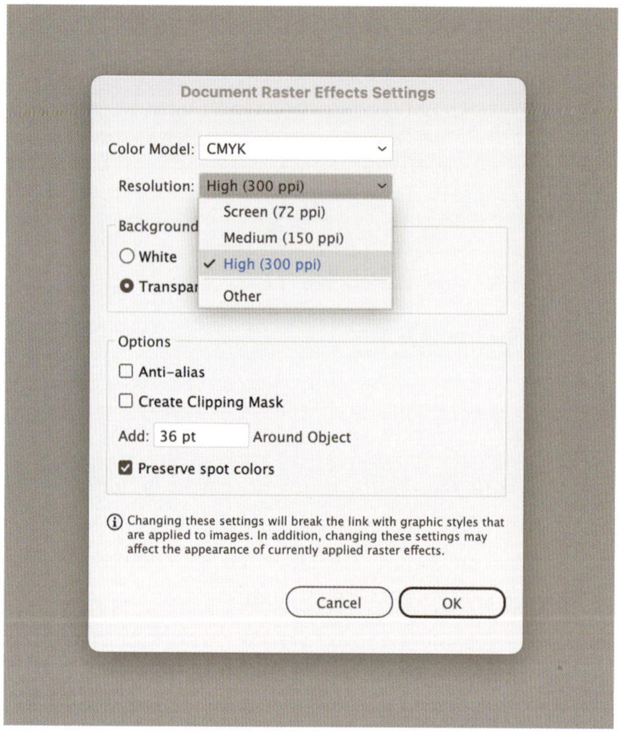

Figure 2.56 This dialog pop-up box will appear. You can keep the default settings for now but adjust the *Resolution* to 300 ppi or higher.

Summary

It is a matter of your personal preferences and design needs as to whether you start with a hand-illustrated sketch or directly sketch the figure into the digital format. If you choose to use a hand illustration, be sure to clean it up before importing. It also helps to ink over your lines to make them darker.

You can use your sketch or a photograph as a template. Essentially, lower the *Opacity* and *Lock* the layer before sketching on a *New Layer*. You may also want to use a grid to help you draw from a reference photo. These techniques help you to learn to draw correct proportions when you are starting to illustrate the figure.

For Photoshop and other raster-based software, you can start with a scanned or photographed sketch to clean up. *Place* the sketch and use the *Transform* tools to manipulate the image to the correct orientation and proportions. Once you complete that, use a *Levels Adjustment Layer* to make the whites whiter and the darks darker. Then you can use a *Brush* with the color of the background to clean up the superfluous marks. Be sure to *Save* your work.

To digitally sketch directly in the software, you will probably want access to a tablet of some sort. *Open* your document and start sketching with a *Brush*. You can use a template of a previous sketch or a photo to help you.

In Illustrator or other vector-based software you can use *Image Trace* to digitally import a scanned sketch, but you may not be happy with the results. The more common way is to trace or draw with the *Pen* or *Pencil* tools. Remember to work in complete shapes to make coloring the illustration easier. You can then use *Width Profiles* or the *Width* tool to change the line quality of the rendering.

If you need to mix the programs, you may do so. They do not seamlessly switch back and forth, so we recommend that you do as much as you want in the first program before switching to the other. *Save* backup copies in case you are unhappy with the results. You are now on your way to coloring the rendering!

STUDIO Companion Videos for Chapter 2

Please refer to STUDIO for accompanying chapter video(s).

Keywords

Destructive workflow
Embedded image
Expand
Histogram
Image Trace
Levels Adjustment Layer
Linked image
Liquify
Non-destructive workflow
Pencil tool
Photomerge
Template

Review

1. Which method of drawing the figure do you think is best if you only have a mouse (no tablet)?
2. List three practices to help draw the figure digitally if you are not comfortable with illustration.
3. What is the difference between the Pen and Pencil tool in Illustrator?
4. Why do you not want to use the Erase tool in Photoshop if you scanned in an illustration to clean up?
5. Why is the Autotrace feature not always the best choice for digitally rendering a scanned sketch?
6. List one way in Photoshop and one in Illustrator to vary the line quality of your illustration.

Commands Introduced

- Brush tool
- Deselect
- Direct Selection tool
- Document Raster Effects
- Embed File
- Expand
- Eye Dropper tool
- Image Trace
- Lasso tool
- Layers panel
- Levels Adjustment
- Liquify filter
- Lock Layer
- New Document
- New from Template
- New Layer
- Opacity
- Open
- Paint Bucket tool
- Pen tool
- Pencil tool
- Photomerge
- Place
- Polygonal Lasso

- Rasterize
- Resize Canvas
- Save
- Save As
- Selection tool
- Stroke panel
- Transform
- Width tool

Keyboard Shortcuts

- Ps: *control+t/command+t* (Free Transform)
- Ps: *control+d/command+d* (Deselect)
- Ai: *v* (Selection tool)
- Ai: *p* (Pen tool)
- Ai: *a* (Direct selection tool)
- Ai: *control+y/command+y* (Outline view)

Discussion Questions

1. How important is illustration style to your future job? Do you think it is more important to draw with a dramatic flair or clean and technically accurate? Why?
2. Do you think it is important to draw figures in accurate proportions or should you conform to the standard fashion illustration proportions (the nine-, ten-, or eleven-head figure) of the past? Explain your opinion.
3. Where do you "draw the line" when borrowing inspiration from others? How do you distinguish between creative license and plagiarism of style? Explain your answer.
4. Do you think it is "cheating" to use a photo of a model or actor as a template for illustration? Explain your opinion.

Practice Exercises

1. Collect ten images of model or actor poses. These should be clear photos that show the figure from head to toe. Look for poses that will show a garment and figure well. You will want mostly forward-facing poses but may want a few that show the back. Stick to one body type for now: men's, toddler's, missy, missy plus, etc. Use these poses for future projects and consider adding to your library as you progress.
2. Create two figures ready for color: one produced in Illustrator, and one produced in Photoshop. Use any of the described methods for each application. Turn in the files in their native file format (.ai and.psd).

Endnotes

1. When scanning a large document in sections, be sure to have plenty of overlapping areas so the algorithm can identify matching areas and overlap them properly. Give it a good 20% overlap to be sure of sucessful results.
2. Image Trace was recently updated in the Beta version of Illustrator. If you are a tech nerd who likes to try out the newest features, look at the Beta option in your Creative Cloud application. You can download the most current version of each program that is not yet officially released.

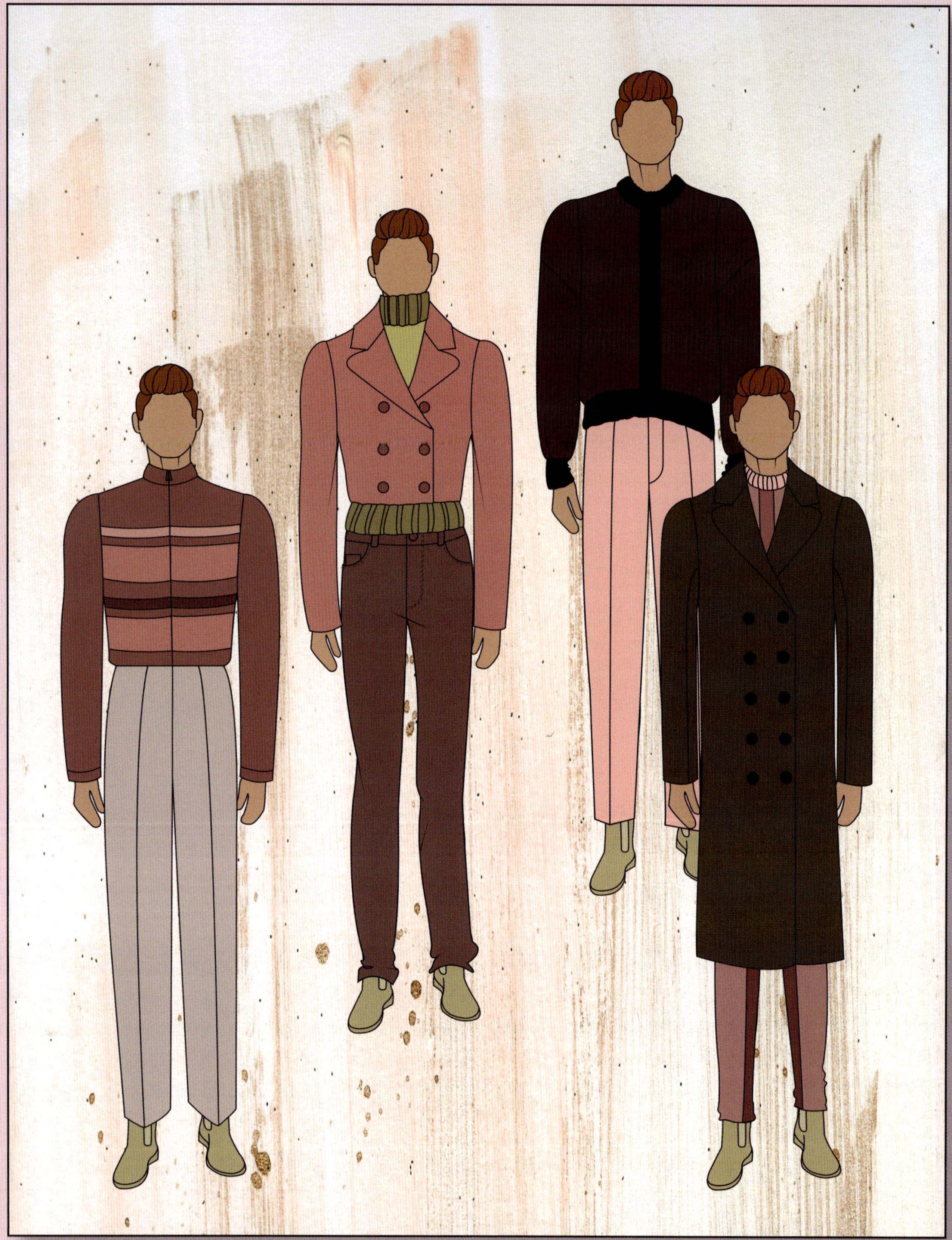

Figure 3.1 Color is an imperitive part of design communication. Artwork by Emily O'Brien. Instagram: @obrieemily.

CHAPTER 3
Colorizing

Learning Objectives

After completing this chapter, you should be able to

- Explore color workflows and differences in color modes
- Start a color library for your renderings
- Digitally adjust a hand-colored rendering in Photoshop
- Add color digitally to a sketch in Photoshop
- Digitally color a sketch in Illustrator

Now comes the fun part! As designers and illustrators, we are naturally drawn to color. You have your figure sorted out, so let's start adding in the color. In this chapter, we will briefly talk about the color modes and how they affect your color work, how to digitally prepare your analog-colored artwork, and how to add color through Photoshop and Illustrator (Figure 3.1).

Color Modes

Most artistic software allows you to choose your *Color Mode* or color system. One mode is not "better" than the other. However, some do produce better results according to your end product. You will have an initial choice to produce the artwork in either *RGB* or *CMYK*. Photoshop provides more choices such as *Grayscale*, *Bitmap*, or *LAB*. Let's briefly explore each option.

RGB is an acronym for red, green, and blue. This is an additive system used for describing how colors interact through light. When you add red, green, and blue together, they produce white. Hence, it is called additive color. Your computer screen, mobile devices, and television all utilize an *RGB* color system. This mode is a good choice when first learning to produce digital illustrations. It is best when you expect to show your work thought a website or social media because the audience views the art through a screen. This is not to say that you can't use *RGB* mode when you want to print an artwork. Items in this mode can be printed as well, although you will experience a slight difference in color from what you see on the screen and how it prints on paper. If you only want to print your work, it is better to use the *CMYK* mode.

Color using pigment utilizes subtractive color and is called **CMYK** for cyan, magenta, yellow, and key color or black. This is the better choice if you only ever plan to print your work. In this system, white is the absence of color, which is why it is called subtractive. You may find that colors tend to be more muted in this system compared to *RGB*. This is simply because light will always show colors more clearly than pigment.

RGB and *CMYK* are the two primary modes found in almost all digital art programs. Some programs such as Photoshop offer other modes such as *Grayscale*, *Bitmap*, and *LAB*. **LAB** stands for lightness-axis, a-axis, and b-axis. This system is a bit harder for beginners to understand how to manipulate properly, but does result in more consistent colors across devices and companies. It is commonly used in the textile industry, so there is an advantage to learning the LAB system.

Grayscale is clearly for items produced solely in a scale between black and white with no other hues. *Bitmap* is a true black and white image with no gray. It is unlikely that you will need either *Grayscale* or *Bitmap* while working in the fashion or costume industries, though.

Of course, if you already created your document for the project in the last chapter, the new document screen is not very helpful. No worries! Look under the *Image* menu in Photoshop. Hover your cursor over the *Mode* feature and notice that you can change your mode here. In Illustrator, you can change the document color mode in the *File* menu.

So, which mode is better for fashion and costume illustration? What if you plan to show your work both digitally and printed? You will find 100 experts that tell you 100 different answers to this question. Our personal preference is to keep it in *RGB* so the colors will show more clearly for digital work and will convert when printing. There may be a slight color difference, so you will always need to print a test copy before creating the final print. Ultimately, the choice is yours, though. There is no right answer. One system is not better than the other. They are simply different.

One final note about color modes. You may have an option to choose the bits for your color mode. For most of what you do in fashion and costume, *8 bit* will be enough. Essentially, the more bits, the more color options you have and the smoother color gradations.

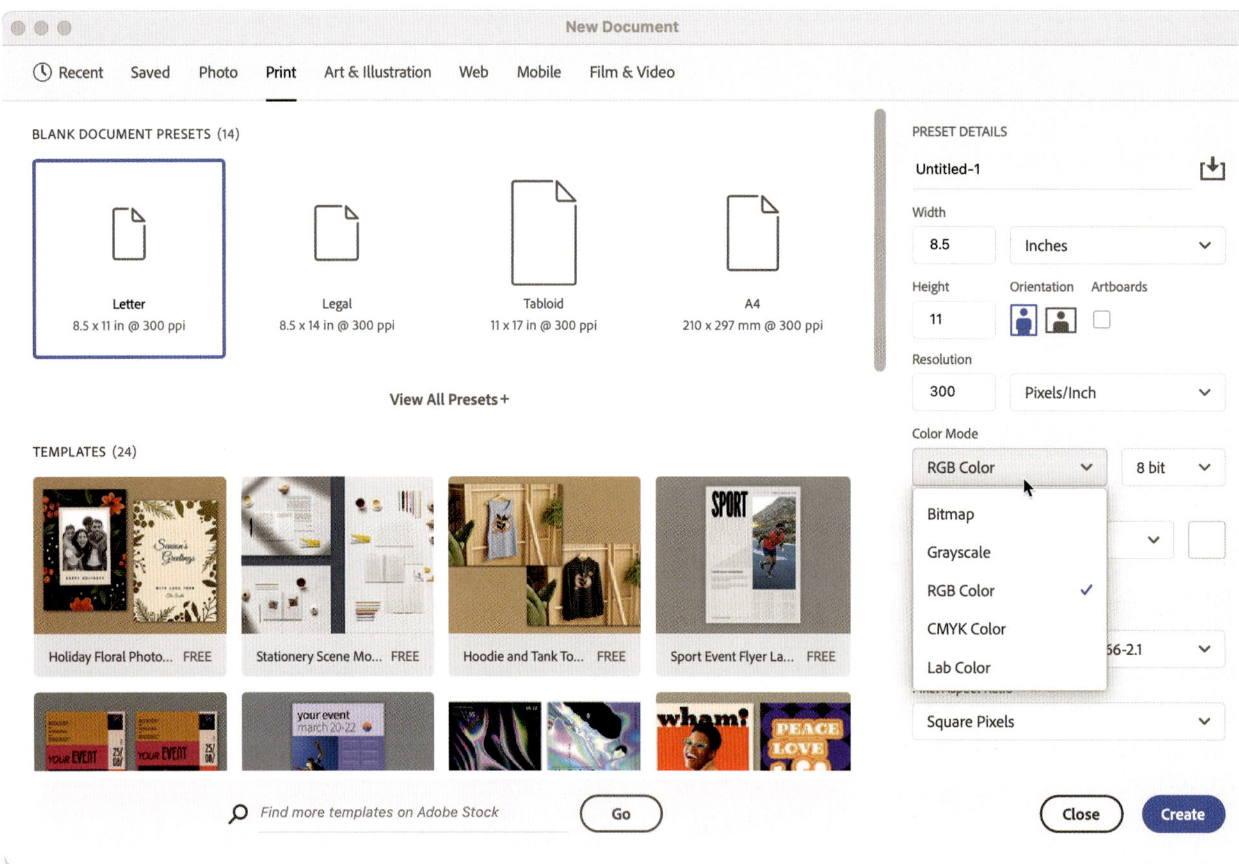

Figure 3.2a When opening a document, check the *Color Mode* options. You will see *RGB* and *CMYK* along with other options, depending on the software.

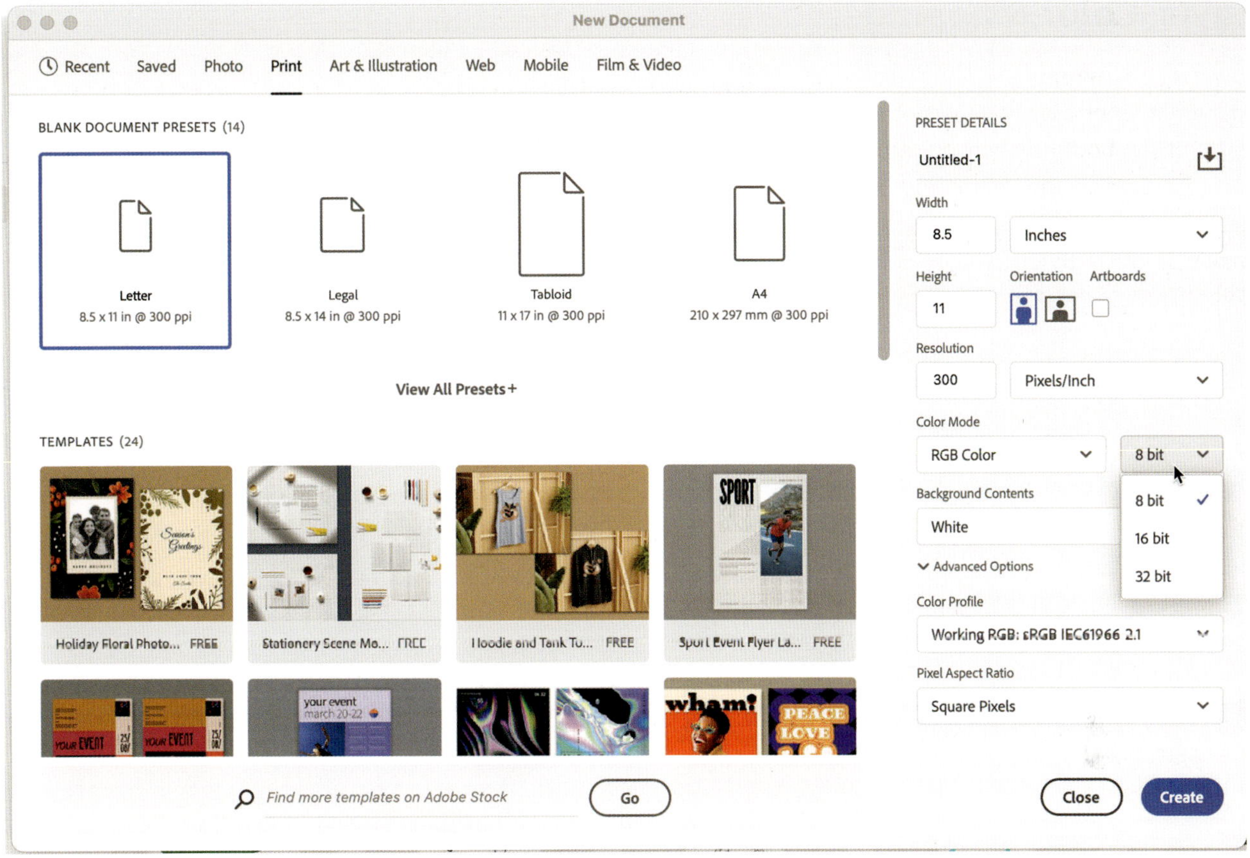

Figure 3.2b In most cases, especially while learning the software, *8 bit* is a good choice. Going up in bits will give smoother transitions and gradation but will also increase your file size.

It also takes significantly more room as you go up in bits, which will slow your computer down as you work. As a learner, there is really no reason to choose more than *8 bit*. As you gain more experience and knowledge, you may find times that it is advantageous to use *16* or even *32 bit*.

Color Workflows

Should you color your renderings by hand or digitally? This is, once again, a personal choice. We highly recommend that you color digitally, though. It is far easier and faster to make changes to fabric colors and textures when you color digitally. That is not to say that it is impossible to do so with hand-colored renderings. You can certainly make color changes through adjustment layers, blending modes and masks in Photoshop. But when you color digitally, you can build the file in such a way as to make on-the-fly changes much more, well, on-the-fly.

Additionally, we make the case for digital coloring because it will help build your skills. Essentially, the more you work in these software applications, the faster you will become at doing so. If you force yourself to always color digitally, then you will gain more experience. Hand rendering may be faster and more comfortable currently, but ultimately you should become faster and more comfortable with digital rendering.

To argue the other side, however, your choice may depend on how often you need to make any changes. How often will you need to change colors or fabrics? Who makes the final decision about colors and fabrics? Are you/they a finicky person? Do you/they like to see options before deciding? If you do not foresee the need to make frequent changes, then feel free to stick with hand rendering. Do what works best for you.

Should you choose to color digitally, there are certain workflow options as to how you may want to approach colorizing. Let's briefly explore each before jumping into the work.

Layer-Color Mapping

Layer-color mapping is the process of keeping items of similar color (usually items of illustrated clothing or parts of the body) on separate layers. By keeping your colors separated and organized, you will more easily be able to make future changes when necessary. It also makes it easier to make layer adjustments to just that color/fabric without affecting others. It is extremely utilitarian. This is the primary workflow demonstrated in this chapter.

For example, you put down a base color that covers the entire object, such as a coat. Then you can shade, highlight, add texture, and add details as necessary to only affect that layer. The layers are stacked from background up to foreground to block any stray coloring below it. This may sound a bit vague and archaic at the moment, but it should make more sense when you practice the coloring assignments! See Figures 3.3a–c to show a simplified version of layer mapping.

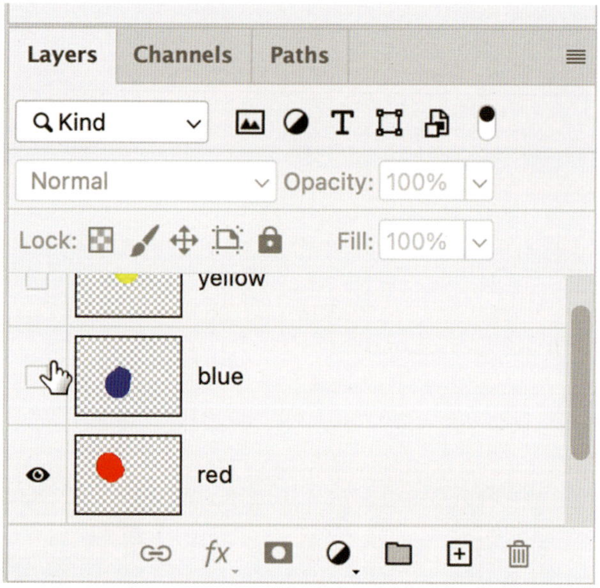

Figure 3.3b Currently, the red layer is showing, but the blue and yellow layer visibility is turned off.

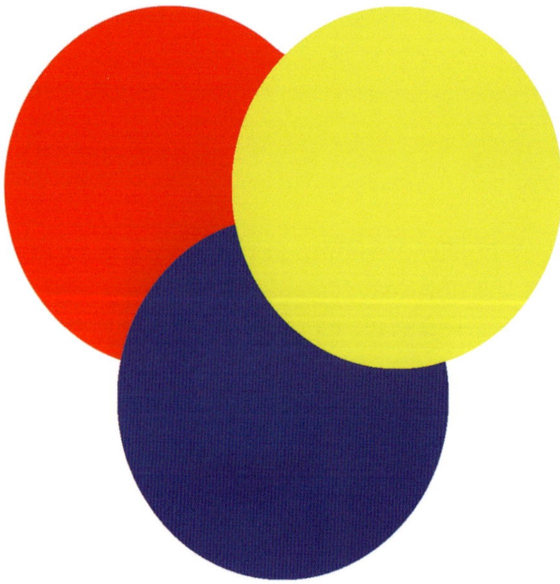

Figure 3.3c When the blue and yellow layers are turned on again, they cover the less-than-perfect red painting. This coloring workflow provides a lot of flexibility for rendering garment designs.

Figure 3.3a Layer-color mapping. The red circle is the lowest layer. Because the blue and yellow circle will cover this one, you don't have to be as precise where another layer will cover it.

PRO TIP 3.1

The Importance of Cleaning Up Your Layers

When first getting used to digital illustration, there is a lot to keep up with! It's easy to push some housekeeping items to the back of your mind and think of them as unimportant. Naming your layers is one habit you need to stay on top of for several reasons.

It may not seem too difficult to mentally keep up with organization right now. However, you will frequently return to a project on another day, month, or even year. Don't be surprised that it takes significant time to reorient yourself to the organization of your own work. This is too much information for your brain to pull out of the weeds, and it shouldn't have to do this when it is easy enough to clean up your layers before closing a project. Allow your mind the freedom to work on the more difficult and creative problems related to the project. Additionally, it is both easier and faster to make necessary changes or updates when you keep an organized workspace. Finally, it helps you to reduce file size by eliminating unused layers you did not originally notice!

Everyone eventually develops their own system of organization. We recommend these tips as you start to think about yours. First, keep to the practice of grouping like objects or adjustments (such as all the highlights for the skin tone) on separate layers. If you put the skin base tone, highlights, and shadows all on the same layer, it will be difficult to tweak only one when necessary.

While you are putting items on their own layers, name them something obvious to you. This second step allows you to come back to the project and know exactly which layer to work on without "digging around." Third, group sections into folders. Put the skin base tone, highlights, shadows, texture, etc. all into a skin folder. It reduces the visual clutter in your *Layers* panel while allowing you the opportunity to apply adjustments to the entire group, such as *Adjustment Layers, Opacity, or blend*, opacity, or blend modes.

Regardless of the system you choose to utilize, practice it regularly. There will come a day when you have hundreds of projects each with hundreds of layers. Save your sanity now by taking a few minutes to organize your layers before saving and closing you work.

Value-Mapping

Without getting too far ahead of the highlighting and shadow lessons, it is worth bringing up **value-mapping** as a color workflow option. Value-mapping, sometimes called tonal mapping, is the process of laying down your grayscale values before applying the hue, or **glazing**. It is based on an analog painting technique. This way of colorizing is more frequently utilized by concept artists or other artists creating more of a "scene" rather than a singular element such as a rendered figure. However, once you understand highlights and shadows (see Chapter 6), you may find that you like this way of working. It temporarily takes away the pressure of choosing colors while determining the highlights and shadows. This workflow is used less frequently for fashion and costume illustration, but that shouldn't stop you from giving it a try! You never know if this will be the right workflow for you. We will cover this workflow more in Chapter 5.

Make a Library

The more you work digitally, the more important it is to keep up with your colors through **Libraries**. Adobe allows you to keep a library, or collection of assets, that is connected to your Adobe ID. Turning your color choices into swatches and saving those swatches with each file is essential (and covered in the lessons below). However, you can also create color **Swatch Libraries** that you can access in other Adobe applications or whenever you have other files open and want to utilize consistent colors. We discuss more about *Libraries* in future chapters.

Working with Color in Photoshop

Let us first look at color in Photoshop. If you have a fully colored rendering, this is the best place to start. When you scan in an image, it becomes a raster image. Therefore, Illustrator is not a good choice to deal with fully colored renderings.

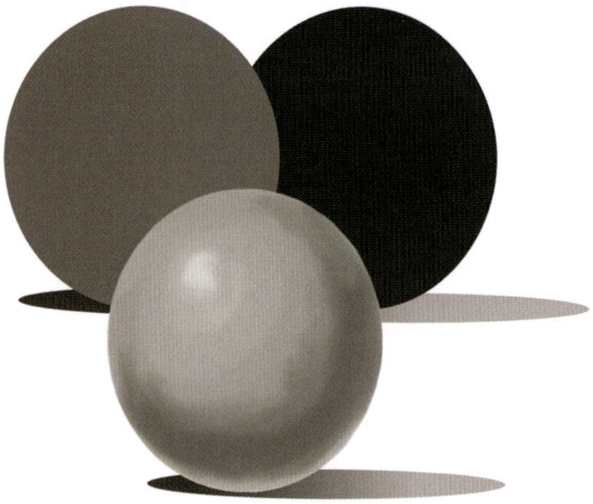

Figure 3.4a Value-mapping. The front sphere is colored in a grayscale value first to determine highlight and shadow, establishing the depth of the scene or figure.

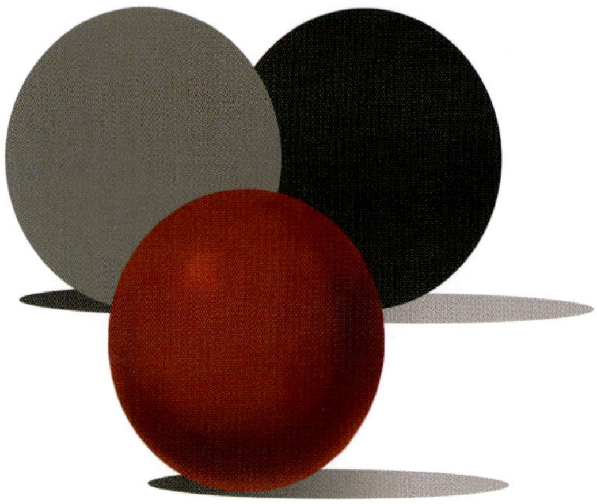

Figure 3.4b Glazing. Once the basic value map is created, then you can go back and add hue information to the value through several means.

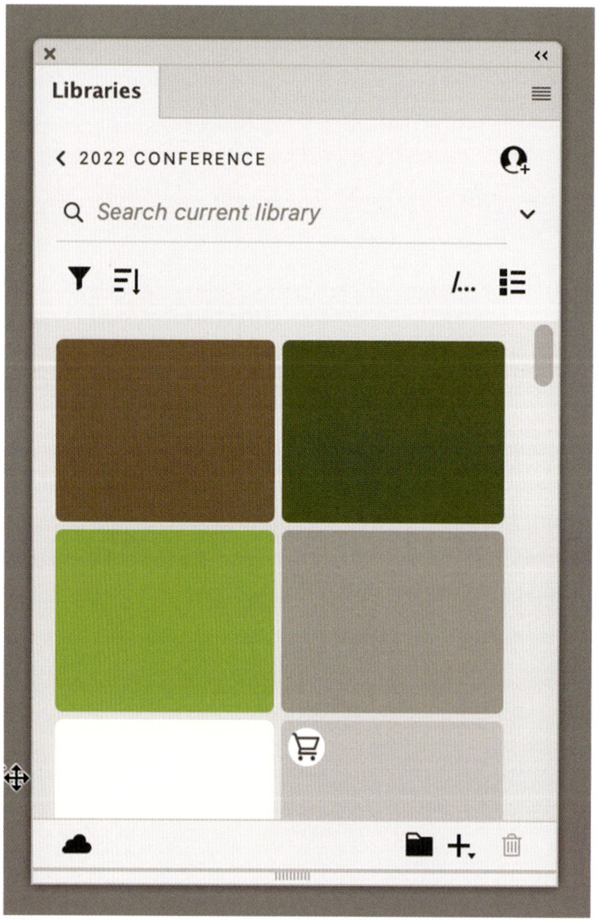

Figure 3.5 Once you make a color *Library*, you can utilize it with any Adobe visual software.

Project 3.1: Scan and Clean Colored Sketch

The colored rendering provided in your exercise files was created with watercolors and scanned at an angle to fit the full figure on the scanner bed. There is quite a bit of work to get this cleaned up and ready for a portfolio layout.

Step 1: *Open* the image and *Unlock* the background layer.

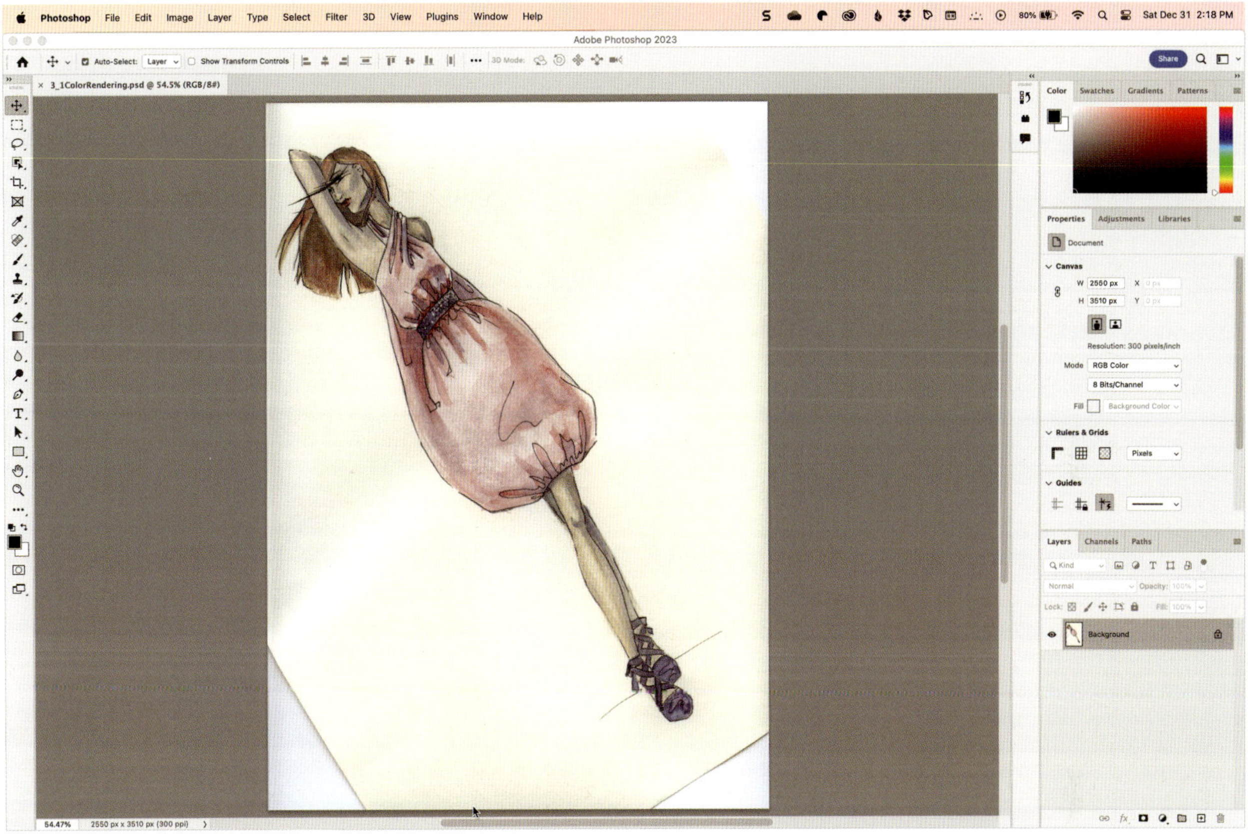

Figure 3.6 *Open* your image in Ps. As you can see, there is a lot of work to get this rendering ready. Start by *Unlocking* the background layer by clicking the lock icon in the *Layers* panel.

Step 2: Make any image transform adjustments. You may need to *Rotate*, *Crop*, *Resize*, or otherwise adjust the image to get it in the correct position and size for your needs. This image was scanned diagonally to get it to fit on the scanner. Therefore, we will need to *Rotate* it.

Under the *Edit* menu is the *Free Transform* command. This will allow you to rotate and resize with your mouse. You can also use the shortcut *control+t* on a PC or *command+t* on a Mac to reach the *Transform* command. If you imported a photo of the rendering, you may need to *right-click* and either *Distort* or *Warp* the image to straighten it out.

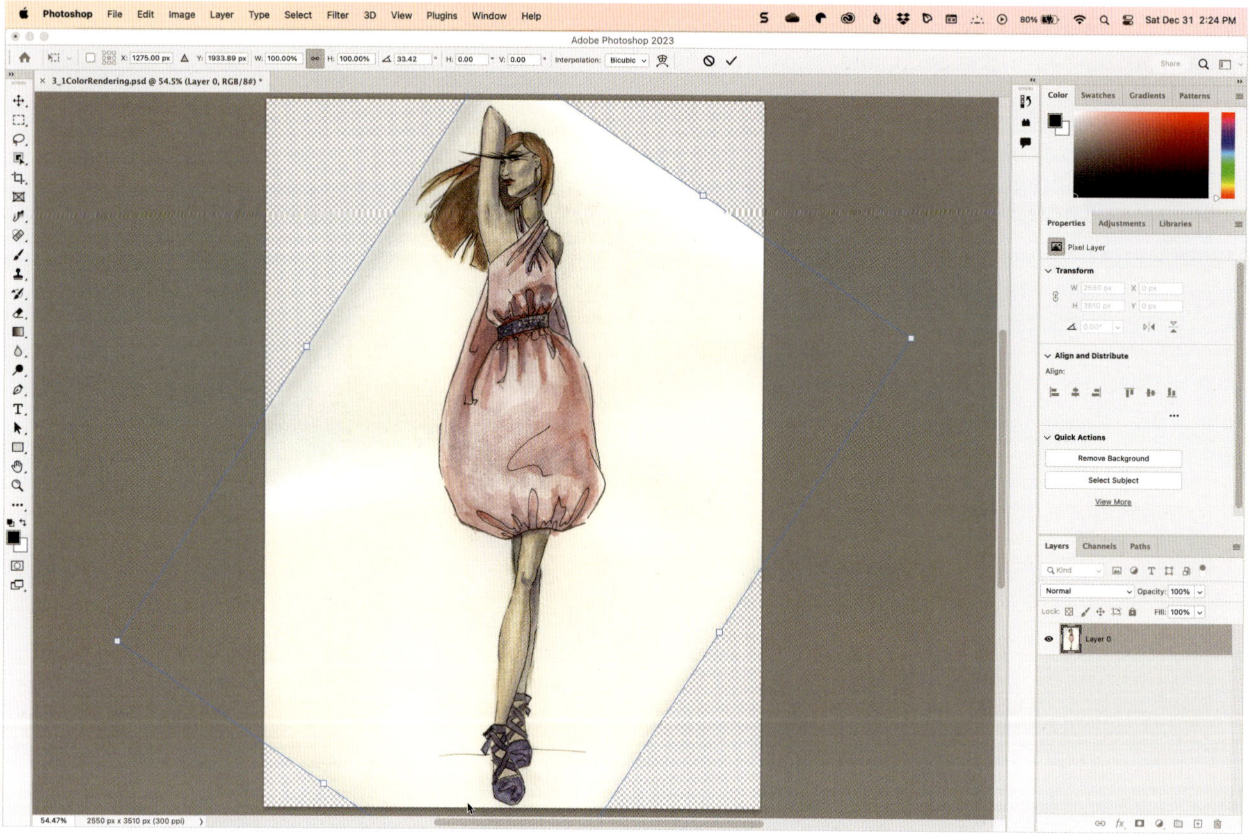

Figure 3.7 A screenshot of the image while *Rotating* and moving. Once you are happy with the position, *click* the check icon in the top *Options* menu or hit *Enter/Return* on the keyboard to accept the changes.

This image just barely fits on the canvas now that it is rotated. If you find that part of the image falls off the canvas, you can resize it to fit the full figure. Let's resize the canvas for a little practice. Under the *Image* menu, you will find the *Canvas Size* command. The *Canvas Size* differs from the *Image Size* command in that *Image Size* will scale the image up and down. *Canvas Size* allows you to change the size of the artboard without affecting the scale of the image.

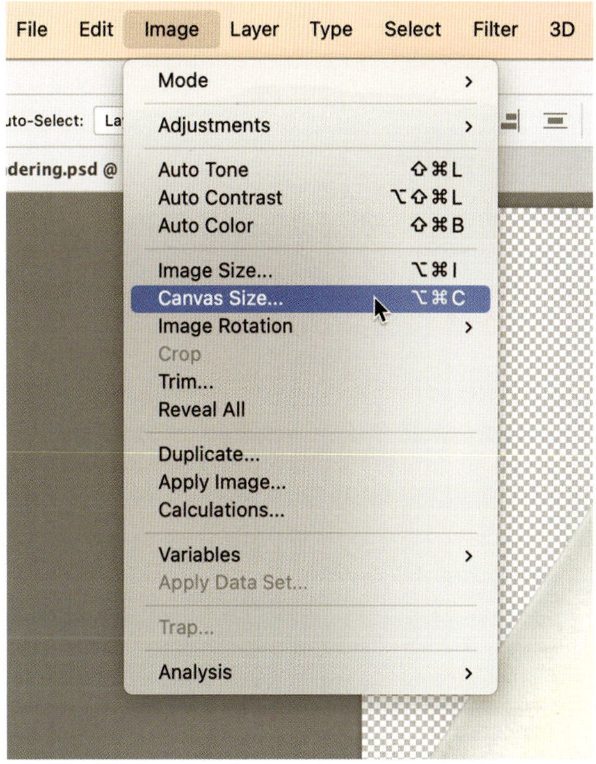

Figure 3.8a You can find the *Canvas Size* command under the *Image* menu. Notice there is a keyboard shortcut (*alt+control+c/option+command+c*) if you prefer to use that instead.

This will produce a dialog pop-up with the *Width* and *Height*. Adobe will do the math for you if you do not want to add up the numbers. Let's add another 50 pixels to give it a little more room. If you are unfamiliar with the size increment, the drop-down menu to the right will allow you to switch it to inches, centimeters, or millimeters. Notice the anchor box below the size fields. This shows how you want to orient the size change. If you only want to add 50 pixels of height to the top and not the bottom of the canvas, then you can click on any of the bottom squares to orient it from the bottom edge. For now, we will leave it in the center square so that it adds to the top (25 pixels) and the bottom (25 pixels).

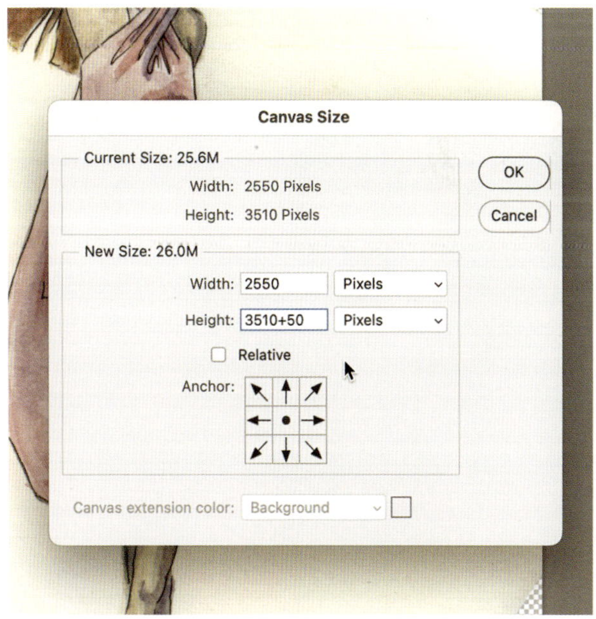

Figure 3.8b A screenshot of the *Canvas Size* dialog pop-up box with adjustment indicated. You can mentally add the 50 pixels to the *Height*, or let Ps do it for you by typing +50 to the number in the field. Keep the anchor in the middle to add to both the top and bottom of the canvas.

Step 3: make initial adjustments. Let's start to clean this image up. As before with the black and white sketch, it is usually best to start with a *Levels Adjustment*. For this image, we brought up the darks to where the graph started to show information but left the lights alone. The midtone arrow will make a big difference in contrast on this image, though.

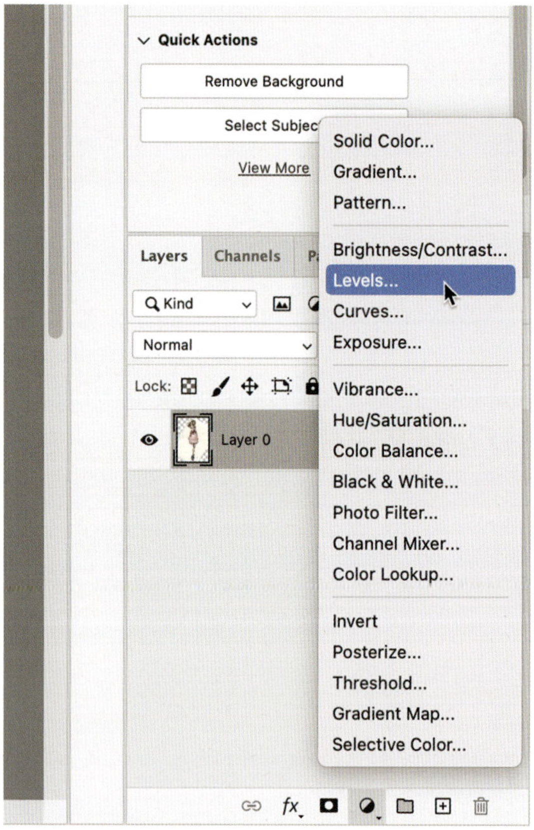

Figure 3.9a A screenshot of the *Layers* panel. Click on the icon for a *New Adjustment Layer* and choose *Levels*. This will create a new layer and open the levels control in the *Properties* panel.

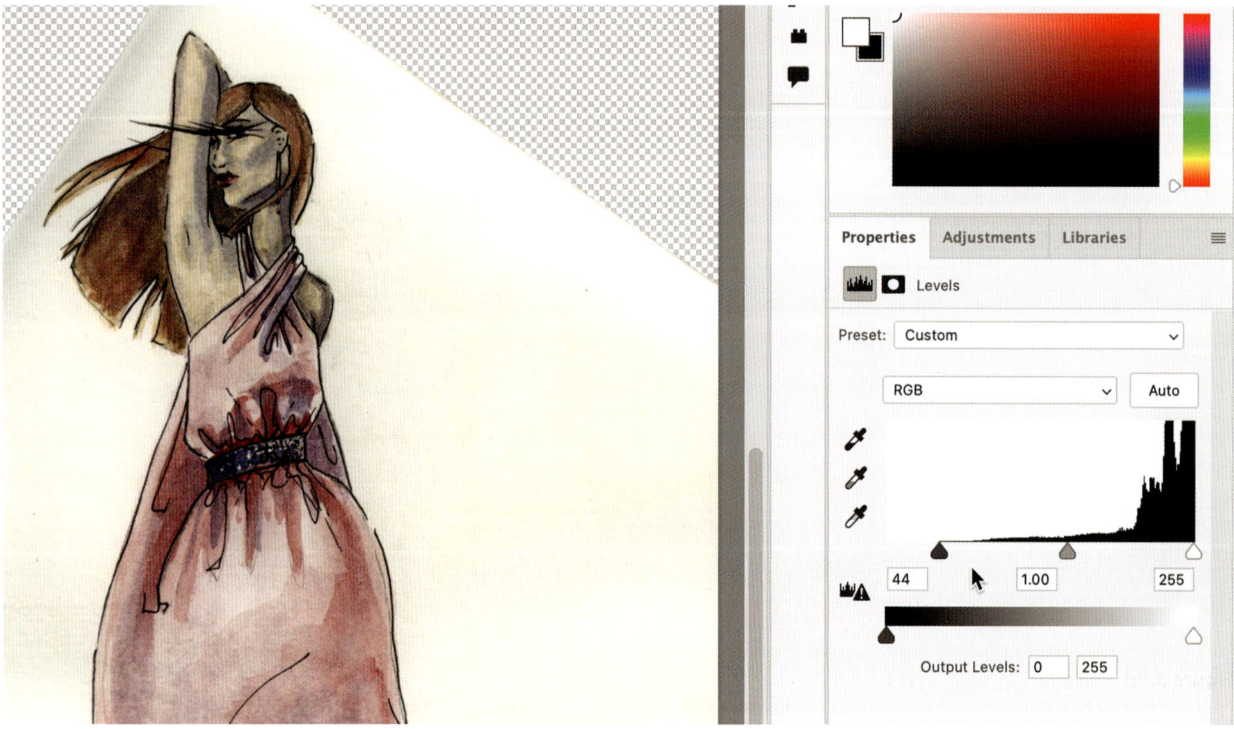

Figure 3.9b A screenshot of the *Levels Adjustment*. Move the darkest arrow up to the point where information starts to show in the histogram. See how this image compares to the next two.

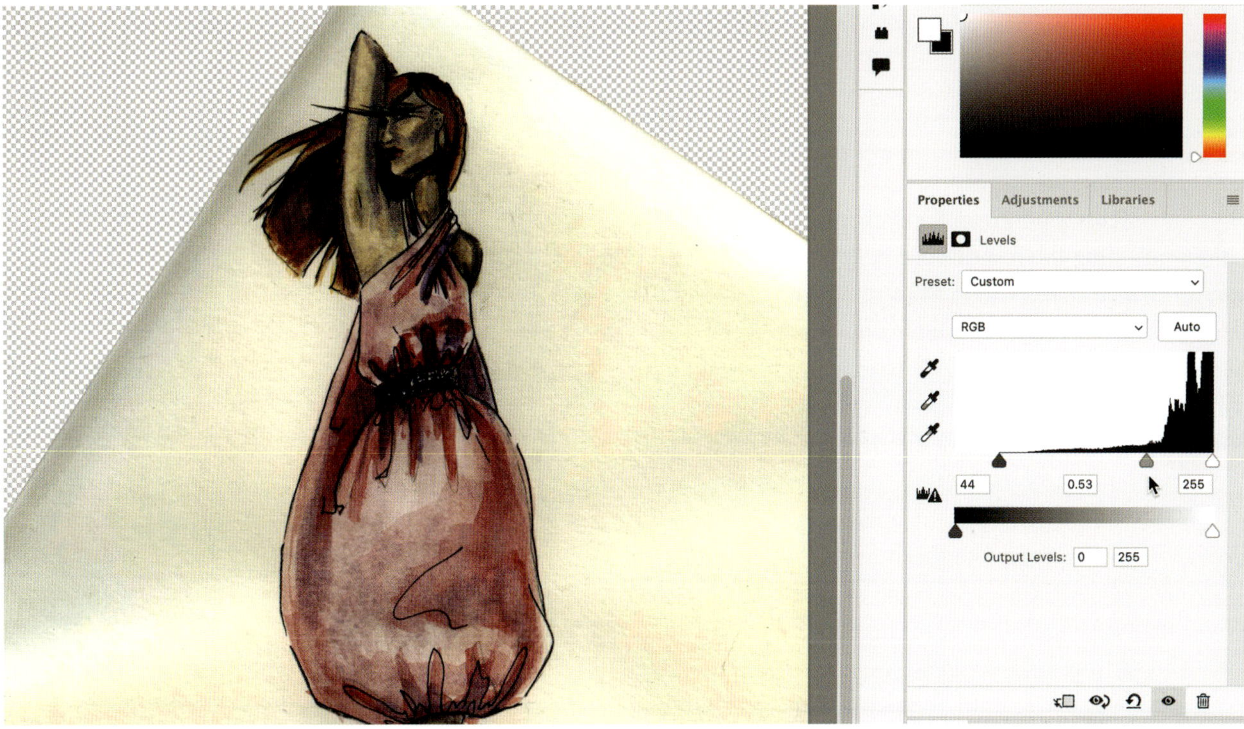

Figure 3.9c Here, the midtones were moved closer to the light end, which allows for more information in the darks and ends up creating more dramatic contrast in the image.

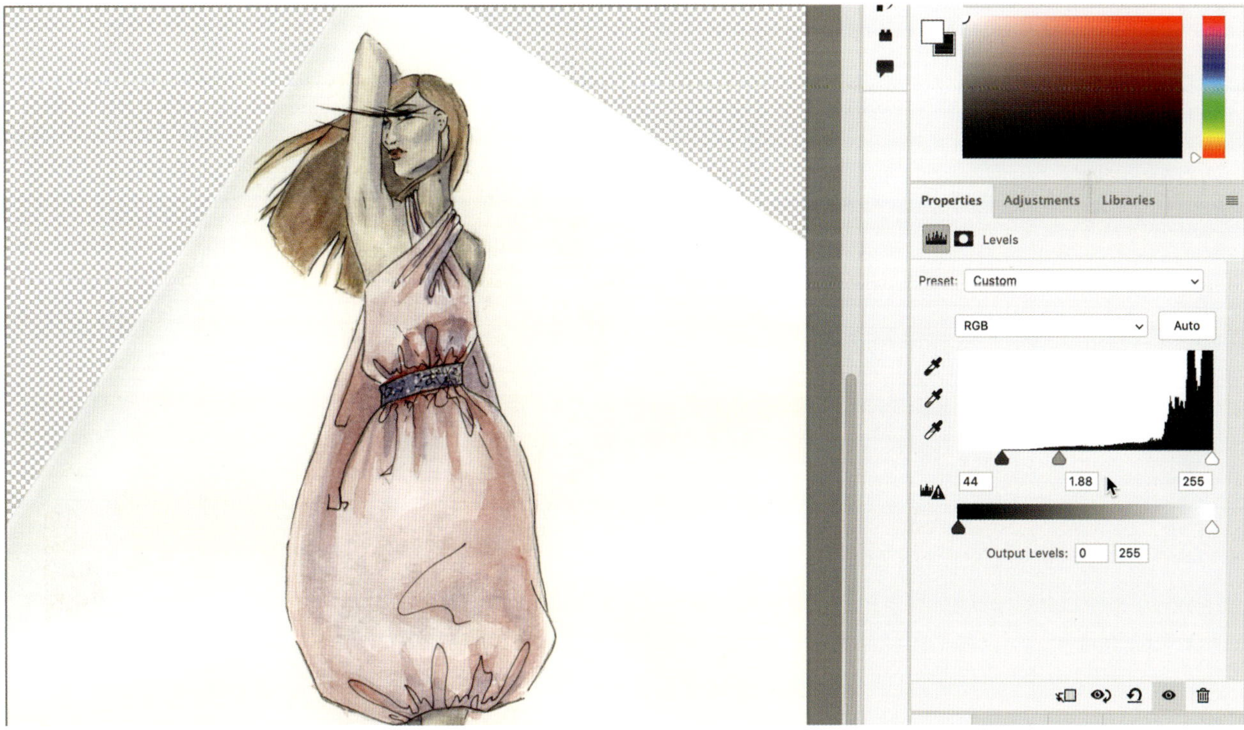

Figure 3.9d Here, the midtones were moved closer to the dark end, which allows for more information in the lights. It seems counterintuitive but does make sense once you understand what is going on. This makes the colors seem more watercolor-like.

This image was originally created with watercolor, and we want to keep that look. Therefore, we pushed the midtones value a bit towards the dark end to decrease the contrast.

Step 4: The colors are still a bit off, particularly for the skin color. She seems a bit green. Let's change the skin tones without affecting the rest of the colors. There are several ways to change colors within Photoshop. The most intuitive is through a **Hue/Saturation Adjustment Layer**. This creates a *New Adjustment Layer* based on the properties of hue, saturation, and brightness, which tends to be an easier way to understand color adjustments.

You can use the *New Adjustment Layer* icon at the bottom of the *Layers* panel to open a *Hue/Saturation Layer*. While the properties are showing, play with each slider first. See how each affects the colors on the image. Notice that the hue slider doesn't necessarily act the way you think it might. You probably won't quite understand what it is doing until you get into understanding the algorithms of the program.[1] For now, just move the slider around until you start to see results that you like.

Let's focus on the skin tone first. Don't worry about how the hair, background, dress, or accessories are affected by the changes at the moment. We will fix that later. Right now, just make your adjustments to give more life to the skin tone.

For this image, we brought the color down to a warmer tone (even though it looks like the slider is in the green range). We also increased the saturation slightly to bring more of that warm tone in. We did not change the lightness. Remember, we are only looking at how this affects the skin tone right now.

Okay, we made our adjustments, but how do we change the other colors back? Notice that when you click back on the *Layers* panel, there is a white page icon

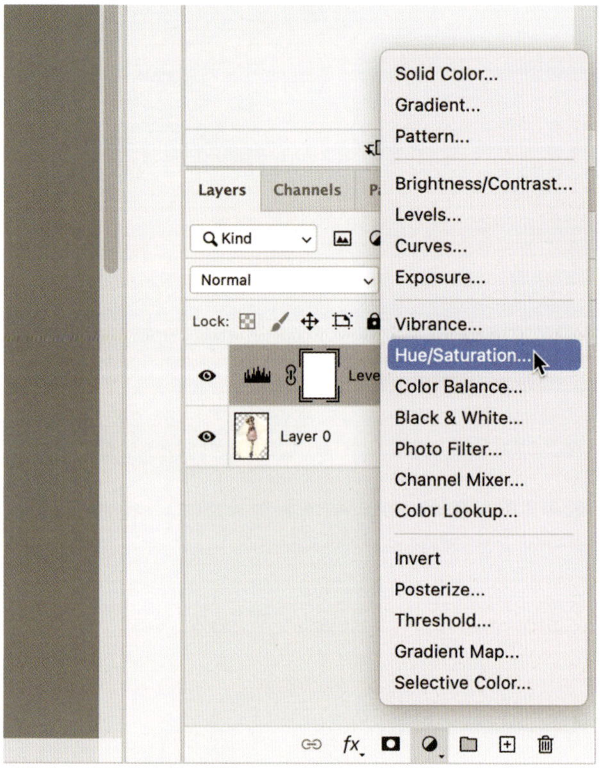

Figure 3.10a Make a *New Adjustment Layer* by clicking the icon at the bottom of the *Layers* panel and choose *Hue/Saturation*.

PRO TIP 3.2

How Math Can Make You a Better Artist

Come back here! I saw you try to skip this section just because you saw the word "math" in the title. Don't be a hater. Give math a chance!

Do you find it frustrating not knowing how numbers relate to hue, saturation, and brightness? Why do your colors become more yellow when you bring down the blue in that curves channel? How on earth are you supposed to "read" a histogram? Why are the hue and color blend modes different?

All these features, and others, are based on mathematical algorithms. You don't need to calculate the math yourself, but it greatly helps to understand what the program is doing. We recommend taking the time to learn more about the more "mysterious" features such as curves, blend modes, channels, hue, value, and even selections. Gaining comprehension of how they work will give you better control when using them. You will save time by knowing exactly how to achieve the desired look rather than just "playing around" with features to see the resulting effects. Additionally, expect more confidence! As you seek to be a better artist, look for videos, text, or courses that explain the math behind the features you use.

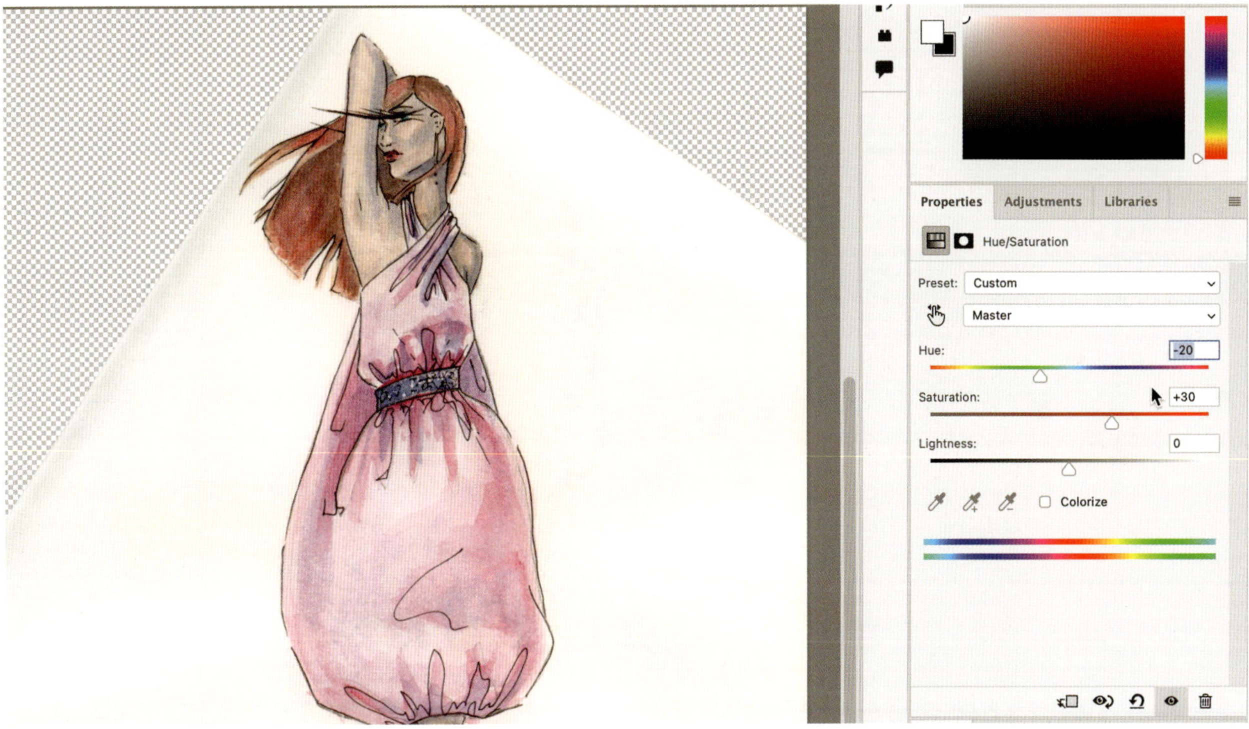

Figure 3.10b A screenshot of the *Hue/Saturation Adjustments* to liven up the skin tone. Nudge the hue down and the saturation up.

next to the adjustment icon. This is a **Layer Mask** that the program adds by default. A *Layer Mask* allows you to direct how much of the change shows on the layer. It works in grayscale. White allows all changes to show (like a clear window). Black blocks out the changes (like when you paint black acrylic onto a windowpane). Anything in between black and white will partially show.

To block out part of the change, we will need to paint on the mask. Make sure the white page icon has the little corner brackets around it on the selected layer. This means we are working on the mask rather than the adjustment. Select solid black for the **Foreground color**. There are two swatches of color shown in the toolbar. The one on top is the *Foreground* color, which is generally the active color you are using when painting. The one below it is called the **Background color**. This is sometimes called the paper color and is what your *Eraser* will fill in where you erase.[2] It is also used with specific filters and effects like the *Render Clouds* filter. For now, just make sure your *Foreground* color is set to black.

Use your *Paint Bucket* tool to click on the image. If you see black showing on your image, then you are on the wrong layer! *Undo* the action (*control+z/command+z*) and check that you have the mask for the Hue/Saturation layer selected. Now the whole layer

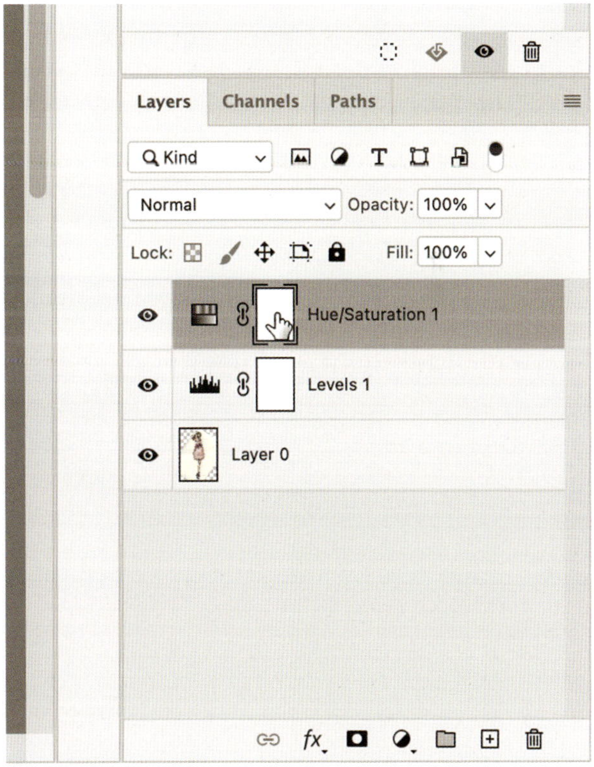

Figure 3.11a The white page next to the adjustment icon is a *Layer Mask*. When it is solid white, the adjustment will be completely visible on the layer below. Click on the white box to make it active. There should be brackets around the corners of the white box icon.

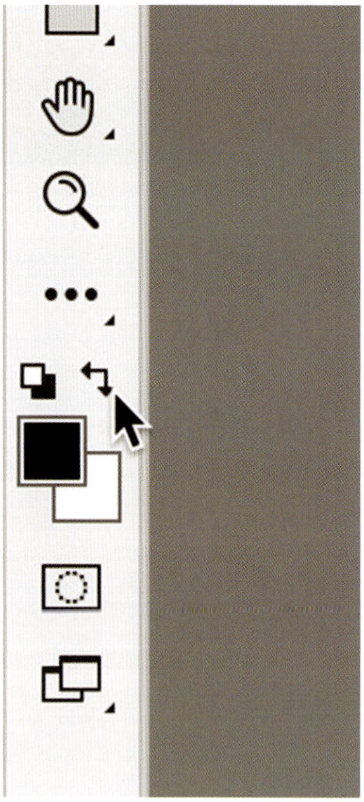

Figure 3.11b A screenshot of the *Tools* panel. Make sure you have black in the *Foreground* (front left box) and white in the *Background* (lower right) color boxes.

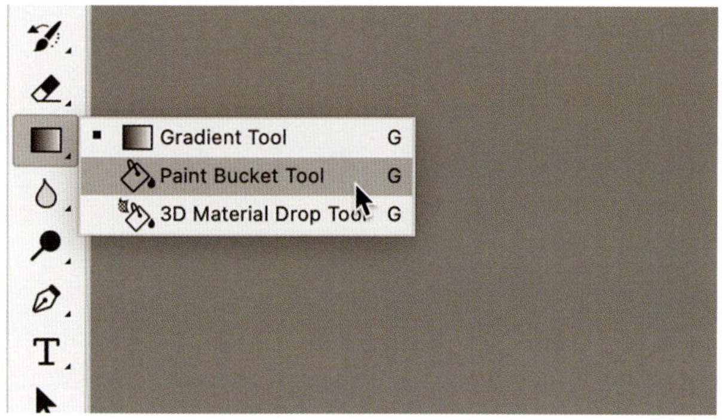

Figure 3.11c Look for the *Paint Bucket* tool in the toolbar. If you don't see it in the icon list, click and hold the *Gradient* tool or *3D Material Drop* tool (whichever is showing). The list of other tools should show. Select the *Paint Bucket* tool.

is blocked. The layer below should look like it did before we applied the *Adjustment Layer*. Paint in the areas you want to show, as so little of the space is using that specific adjustment. Sometimes it is better to start with a blocked mask, and other times it is more efficient to start with an open mask.

With the *Brush* tool, choose a plain, hard, round brush at full *Opacity* for this. Switch your *Foreground* color to pure white. Start to paint over the skin areas. You should see the color shift start to show up on the skin areas as you paint. You will also start to see white blotches show up on the black page icon in the *Layers* panel.

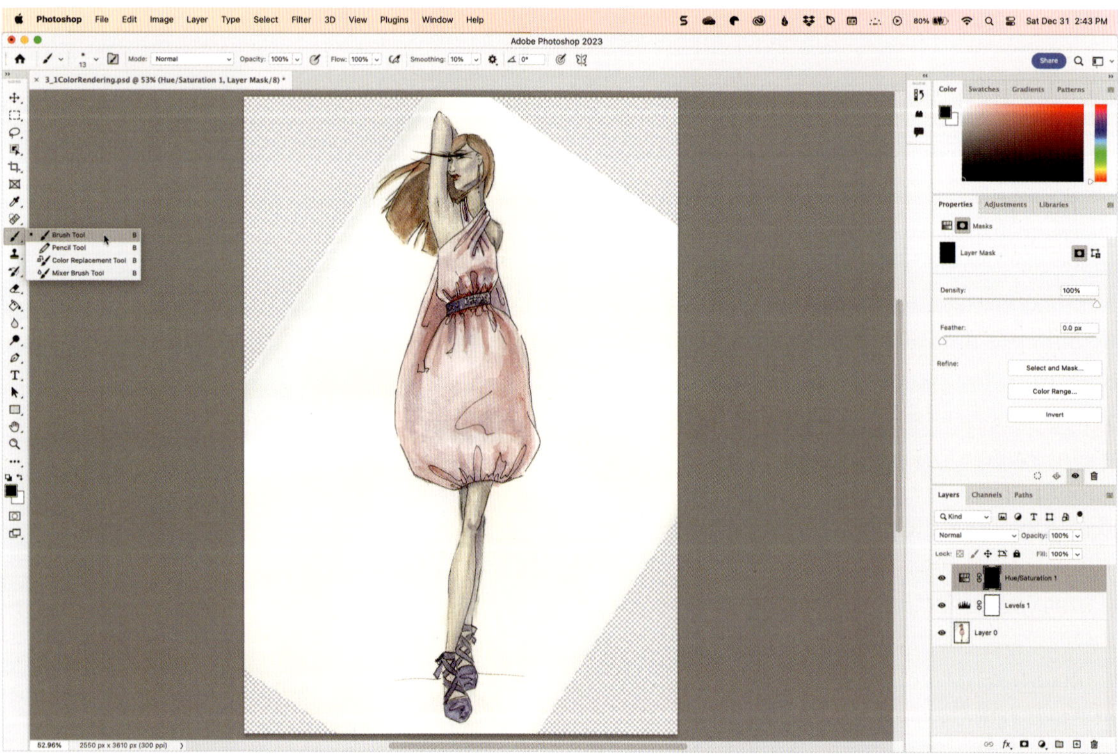

Figure 3.11d A screenshot of the blocked mask. Click anywhere on the image to apply the black fill. Make sure your mask is selected before you apply it to the image. Then select the *Brush* tool for the next part.

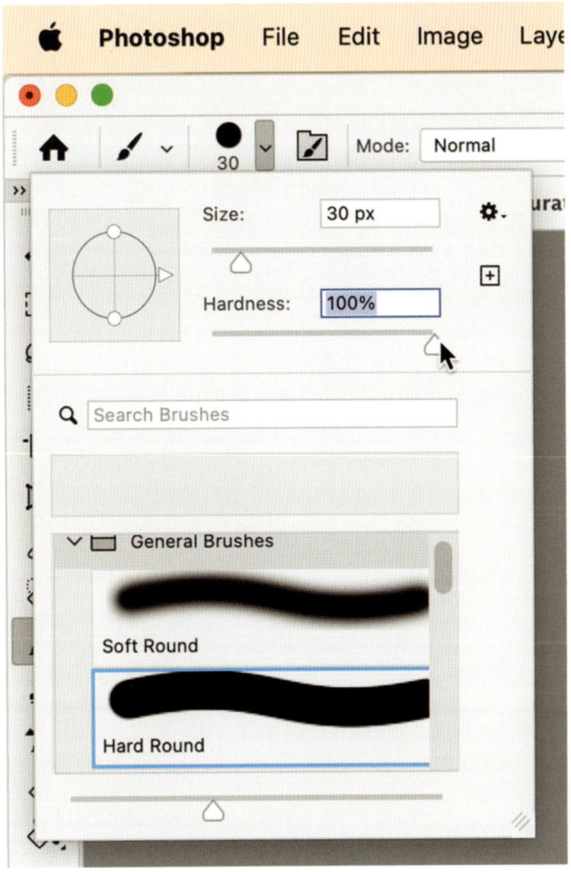

Figure 3.11e A screenshot of the *Brush* menu. This can be accessed through the *Options* menu at the top as shown here, through the *Properties* panel, or if you Open the *Brush* panel.

PRO TIP 3.3

Opacity, Flow, and Fill: What's the Diff?

Some of the cross-application terms used by Adobe are somewhat confusing. Particularly, opacity, flow, and fill may seem similar, but have different effects. Let's start with the easier application for understanding these terms. In Illustrator, you will mostly work with fills. In this program, fills are straightforward. You have a shape and you can add a color or pattern fill to it. **Opacity** in Illustrator affects the transparency of a fill or stroke, depending on what you apply it to, to allow items below to show through.

In Photoshop, you can apply *Opacity* to a brush, a layer, or an effect. Again, it changes the transparency of whatever it is applied to. When painting, you have the option to change the opacity or the flow of your brush strokes. Changing each may seem to result in the same effect at first. **Flow** refers to how much "paint" is loaded onto your digital brush. When the *Flow* is lowered, very little paint will appear as you move the brush. Lowering the opacity will look like it does the same thing, however. The key difference is that flow acts more like a real paintbrush. If you paint in one area for a prolonged amount of time, you will see the paint build up. With lowered *Opacity*, painting in a prolonged area will not result in any build up until you pick up the brush and put it back down for another pass.

Some artists will only use *Opacity* while painting, some only use flow, and others use a mix of the two for different effects. If you are unsure which works best for your needs, try working on a project by only adjusting *Opacity*. Then try working on another project only adjusting *Flow*. Which seems more intuitive to you?

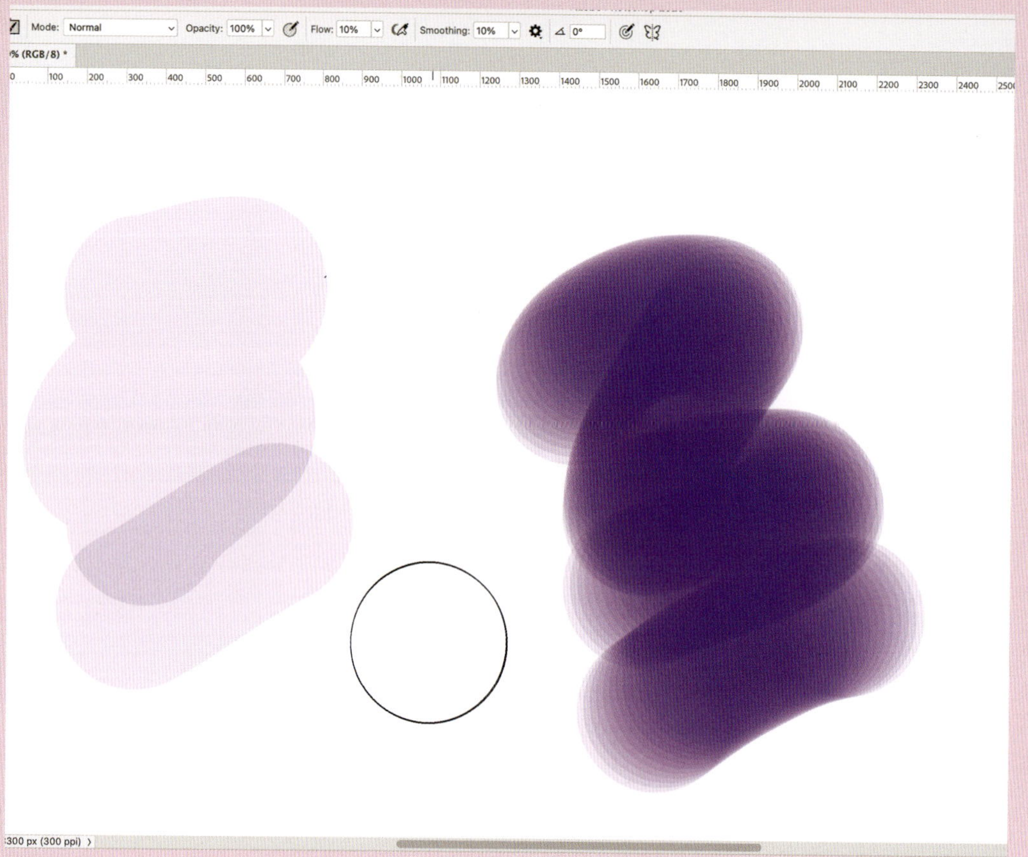

Figure PT3.1 The paint stroke on the left was applied with 10% *Opacity* and 100% *Flow*. The lowest stroke was applied after lifting the brush and setting down again. Notice that the overlapping areas in a single brush stroke lay down an even color whereas lifting and reapplying the brush shows built-up color. The stroke on the right was applied with 100% *Opacity* and 10% *Flow*. On this stroke you can see that the paint will overlap and build up regardless of one stroke or multiple.

You will also notice in the *Layers* panel of Photoshop that you have the option to adjust the opacity and fill. Again, these may seem to do the same thing when first learning the program. *Layer Opacity* changes the transparency for everything on that layer. Fill, in contrast, only affects the transparency of fill effects applied to the layer. This is more clearly seen in certain *Blend Modes* such as *Linear Dodge*. As usual, the best way to learn how they work differently is to play with them while using the program. You can also find additional text that explains the difference more in-depth. Look in the Extend Your Learning appendix for more resources.

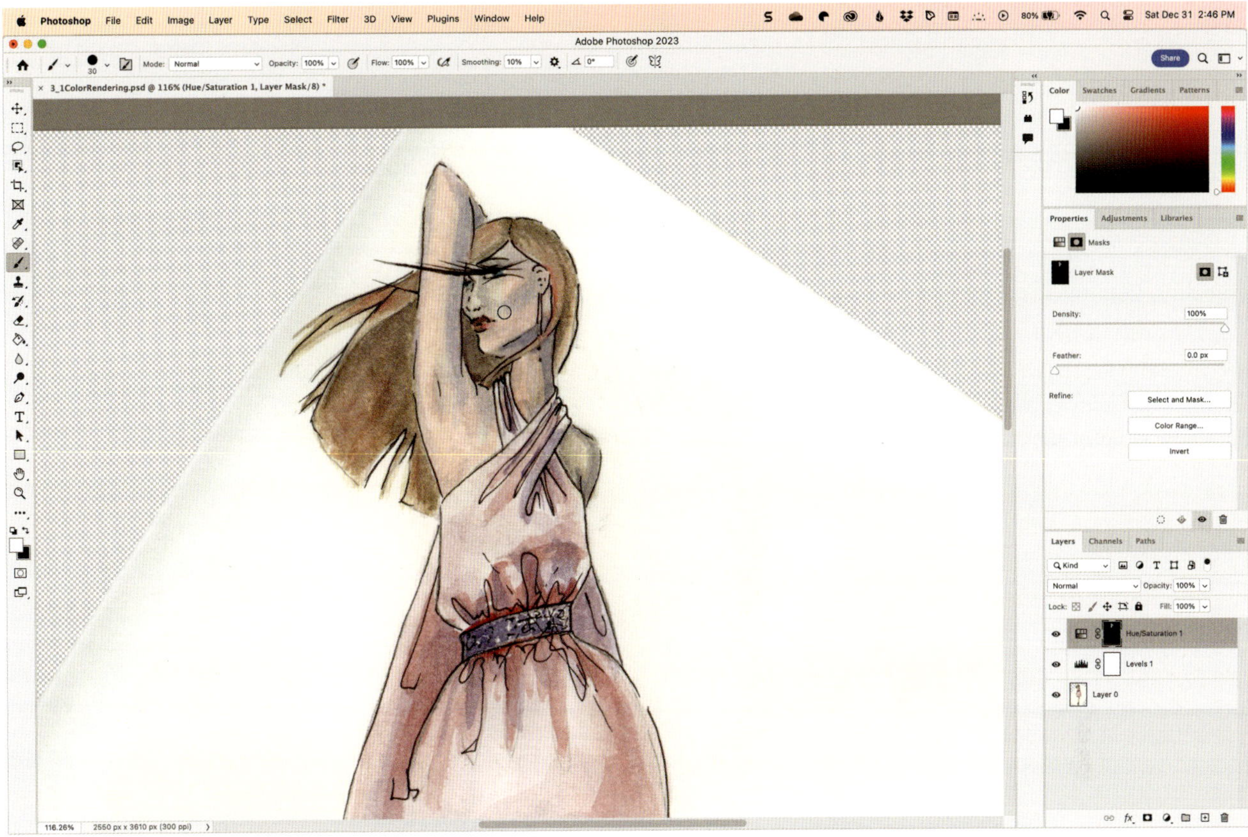

Figure 3.12 A screenshot of masking in the *Adjustment Layer*. Notice that there is a color difference in the face. You can also start to see white start to show on the *Layer Mask* in the *Layers* panel on the right.

Once you mask in the changes, you may need to readjust them. If you like the effect but it is simply too strong, try lowering the *Opacity* of the layer. The *Layer Opacity* can be found in the *Layer* menu and decreases how much of the layer shows, overall. While the *Hue/Saturation* layer is selected, change the opacity percentage in the field located near the top of the *Layers* menu. If you need to tweak the color slightly, then *double-click* on the hue/saturation icon to reopen the panel and make adjustments.

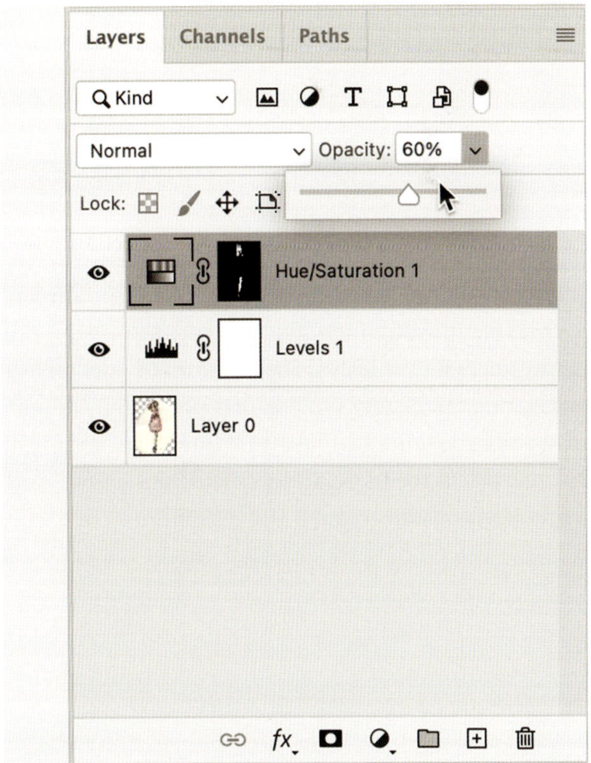

Figure 3.13 A screenshot of the *Layers* panel. The color was a bit too pink, so we lowered the *Layer Opacity* to 60%

Step 5: The skin is fixed, but the dress and hair are still a bit dull. Let's fix that with a different technique called a *Curves Adjustment Layer*. One adjustment method is not necessarily better than another. In fact, there are probably fifty other ways to selectively adjust colors in Ps. We're showing you two of the more common ways. There are a lot of personal preferences within Ps, so don't be surprised if someone else shows you a completely different way to do this. With time and practice, you will develop the workflow and tools that work best for your needs.

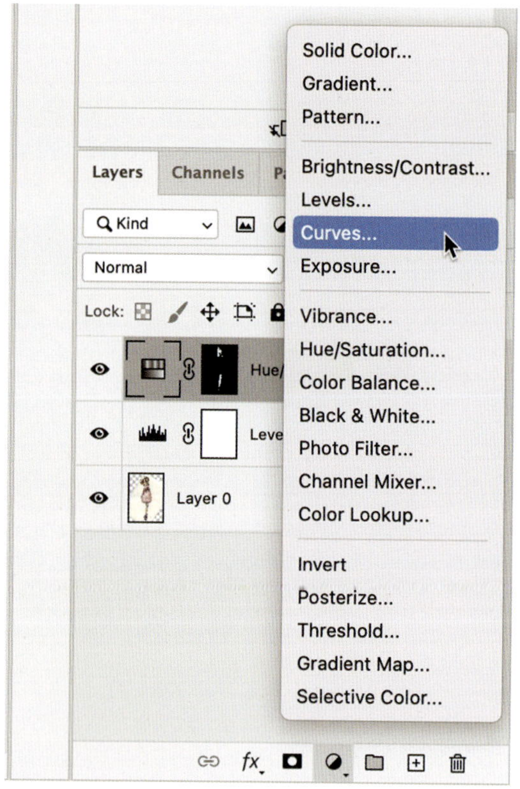

Figure 3.14a Once again, click the *New Adjustment Layer* icon to create a new adjustment layer. This time, choose *Curves*.

Open a *Curves* layer through the *New Adjustment Layer* icon at the bottom of the *Layers* panel. Again, just play around with the histogram at first. Notice that when you click on the histogram, it adds a point. You can pull those points up and down to create interesting effects. If you click on one of those newly created points and drag it completely off the graph, it will disappear.

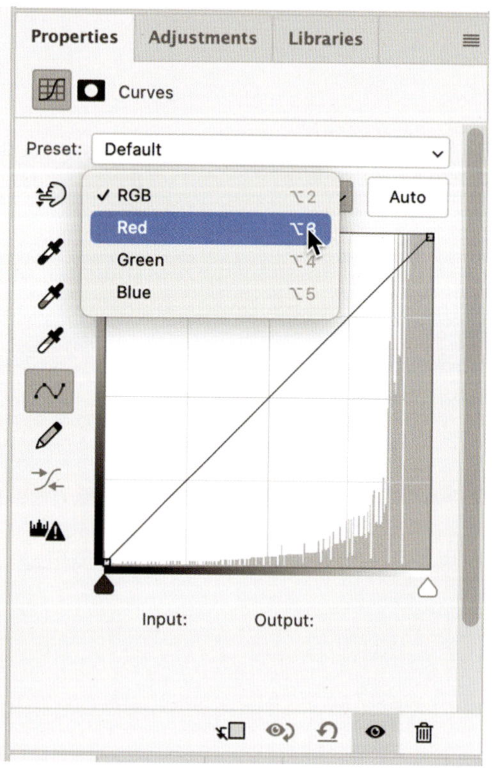

Figure 3.14b A screenshot of the *Curves* in the *Properties* panel. Chose the *Red* channel.

Return this graph back to how you found it and click on the *RGB* field below the *Preset* field. Notice you can choose *Red*, *Green*, and *Blue* individually. Choose *Red* first. The graph will change to a red tint. Click in the middle of the string and pull it up just a little to increase the brightness of the reds within the image. This time we are ignoring the effects on the skin and looking only at the dress and hair.

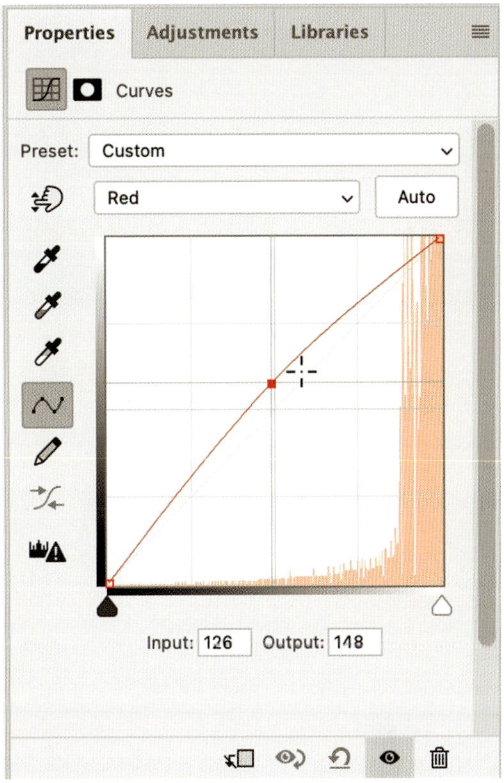

Figure 3.14c On the *Red* channel, pull the middle of the string up slightly to increase the brightness of the reds in the image. See how it changes the colors.

Now switch to the *Green* channel. Pull the middle of the string down slightly to add a little coolness to the reds and make them more magenta. You can try the *Blue* channel as well, but we left that one alone for the color that we liked best.

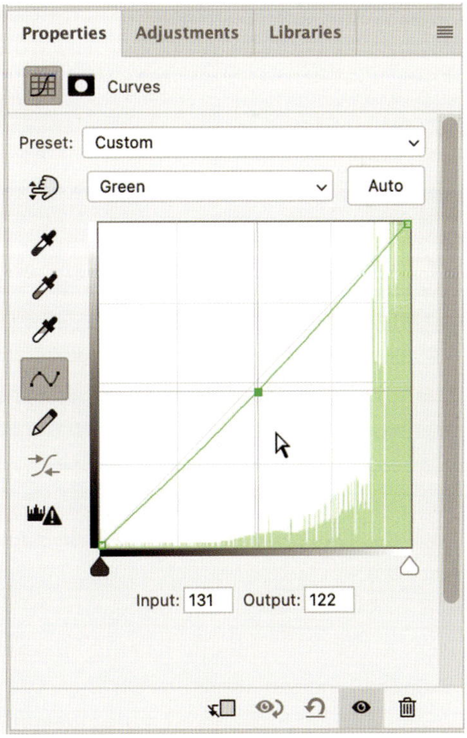

Figure 3.14d On the *Green* channel, pull the middle of the string down slightly to make it more magenta. You can also try the *Blue* channel if you think your image needs it. We left ours alone.

Once you are happy with the results, add black to your mask like before, and start to paint white on the mask on the dress and hair areas. This will allow the adjustments to show through on those designated areas.

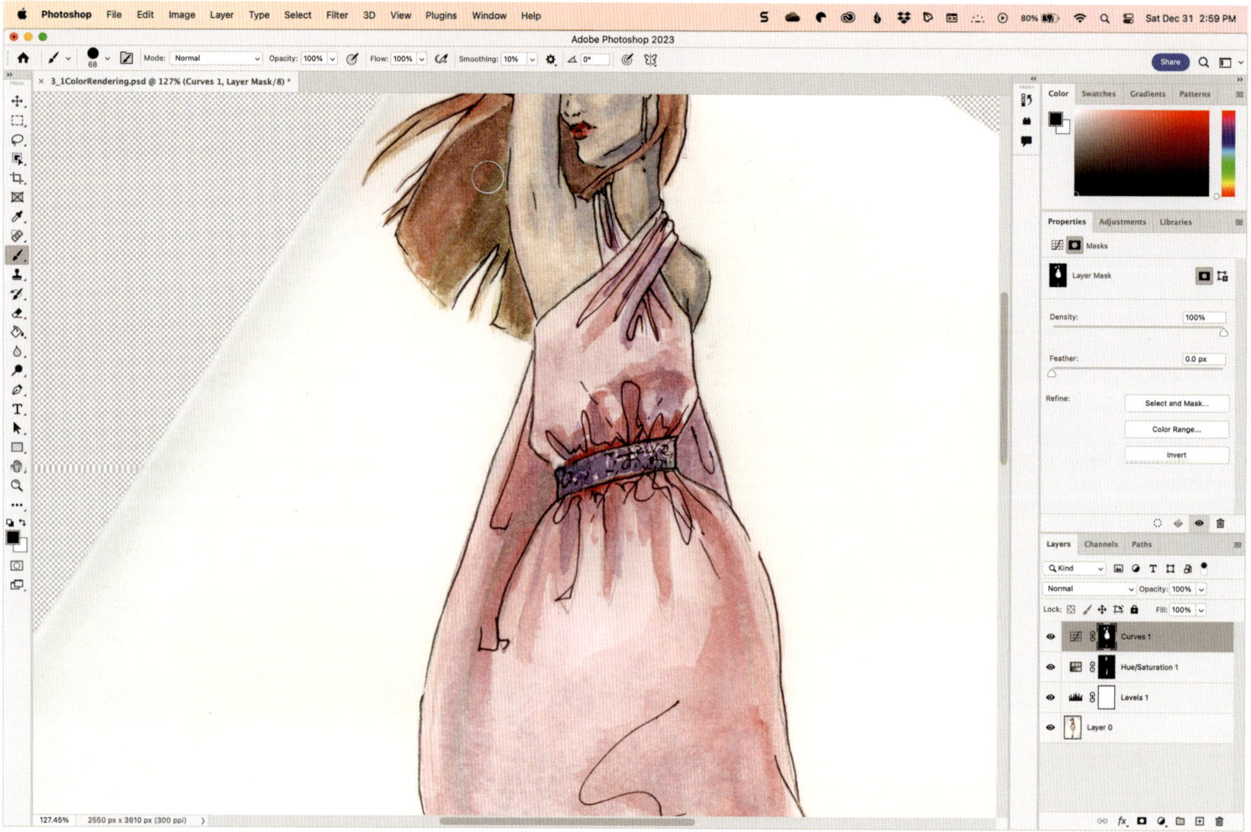

Figure 3.14e A black *Layer Mask* was applied, and the dress and hair areas were painted white on the mask to reveal the curves affect while blocking it from the rest of the image. Remember you can adjust the opacity if you think it is too much.

Make as many adjustments as you like or need to color correct the image. Once you are ready, you can move to selecting the image out from the background.

Step 6: Select out the image from the background. Remember to *Save* your work if you have not already done so! You don't want to lose all of this work. Under the *File* menu, click on *Save* or *Save As*. Or you can use the keyboard shortcut of *control+s/command+s*.

There is a wonderful keyboard shortcut in Ps that is unachievable by any other method. If you press *control+alt+shift+e* (*command+option+shift+e* on the Mac) then it will merge all the visible layers into an extra layer at the top without deleting the original layers! Of course, you can always just *right-click* to either *Merge Visible* or *Flatten Image*, but that would delete your adjustment layers. With the color tweaking, we recommend that you keep those layers intact for later adjustments. If you plan to print this later, you want to leave those layers for future adjustments. The project

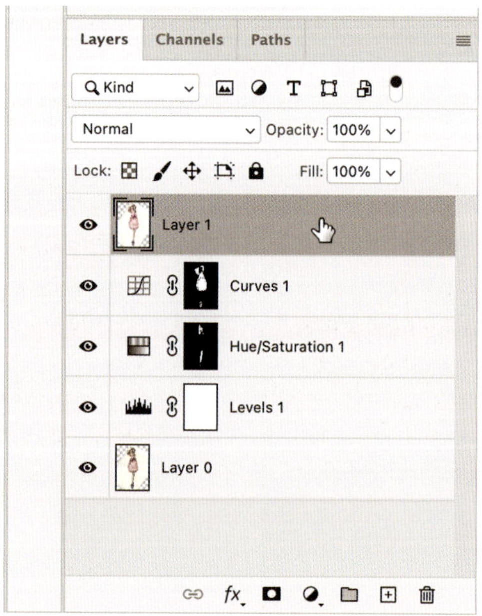

Figure 3.15 A screenshot of adding a merged layer. The new layer will appear at the top of your layer stack once you type the command.

almost never prints the same way you see it on your screen. So, you will need to make some test prints and color adjust as necessary. This keyboard shortcut allows you to put a merged copy at the top while leaving the other layers to change later!

Turn off the *Visibility* of the other layers to see the next effect. Click the eyeball next to all but the top layer. We will use the *Selection* tools for this next bit. Let's look at two different ways to do this.

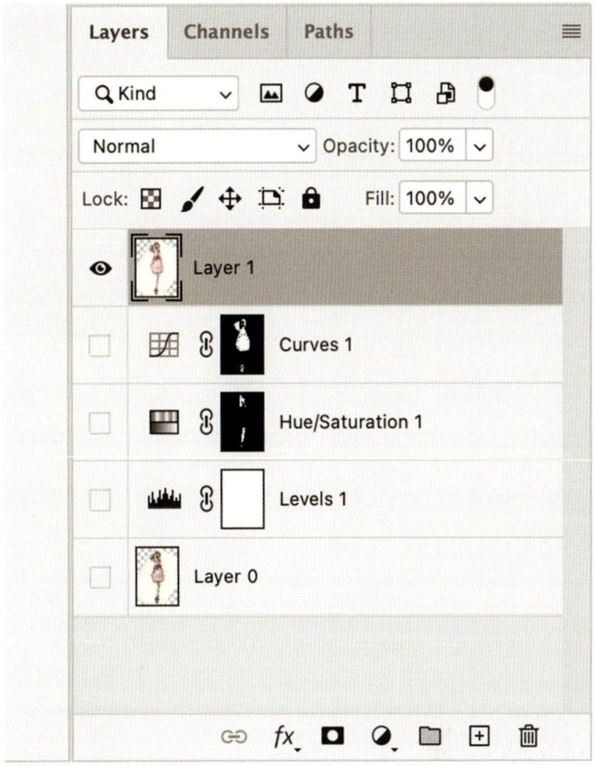

Figure 3.16 With the merged copy at the top, turn off the *Visibility* of all other layers.

Method 1: Selecting with the *Magic Wand* tool. This tool is often cast aside by haters, but it has its uses. For an image such as this, with a relatively clean white background, it is particularly helpful. Look for the *Magic Wand* tool in the toolbar. It may be under the *Object Selection* tool or the *Quick Selection* tool. Make sure you are on the top merged layer. Once you have the tool, click on the white paper. You'll see the "marching ants" that indicate part of your image is selected. Now hit the *Backspace/Delete* key. Voila! The background is gone. This makes it easier to place your figure onto a nice background for the portfolio project.

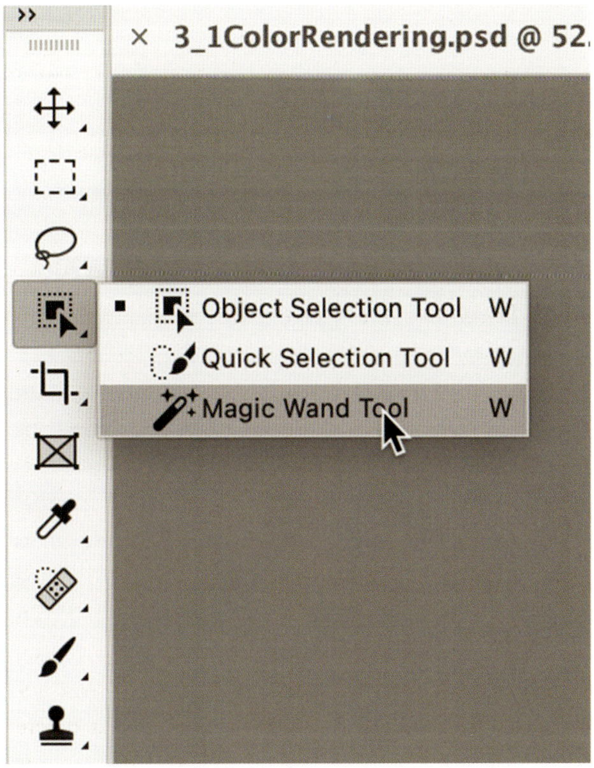

Figure 3.17a A screenshot of the *Tools* bar. Look for the *Magic Wand* tool. If you don't see it at first, look "under" the *Object Selection* tool or *Quick Selection* tool.

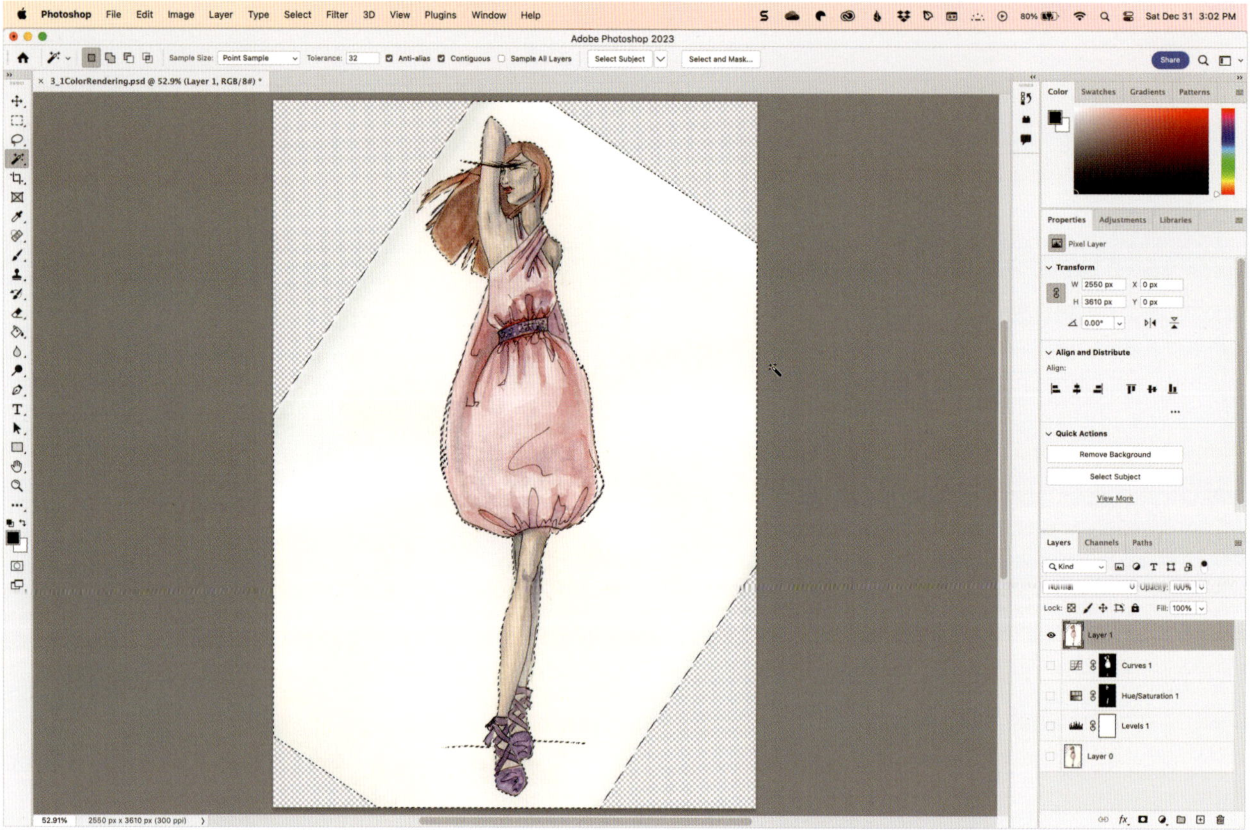

Figure 3.17b The white background is selected with the *Magic Wand* tool. Notice the "marching ants" that indicate a selection.

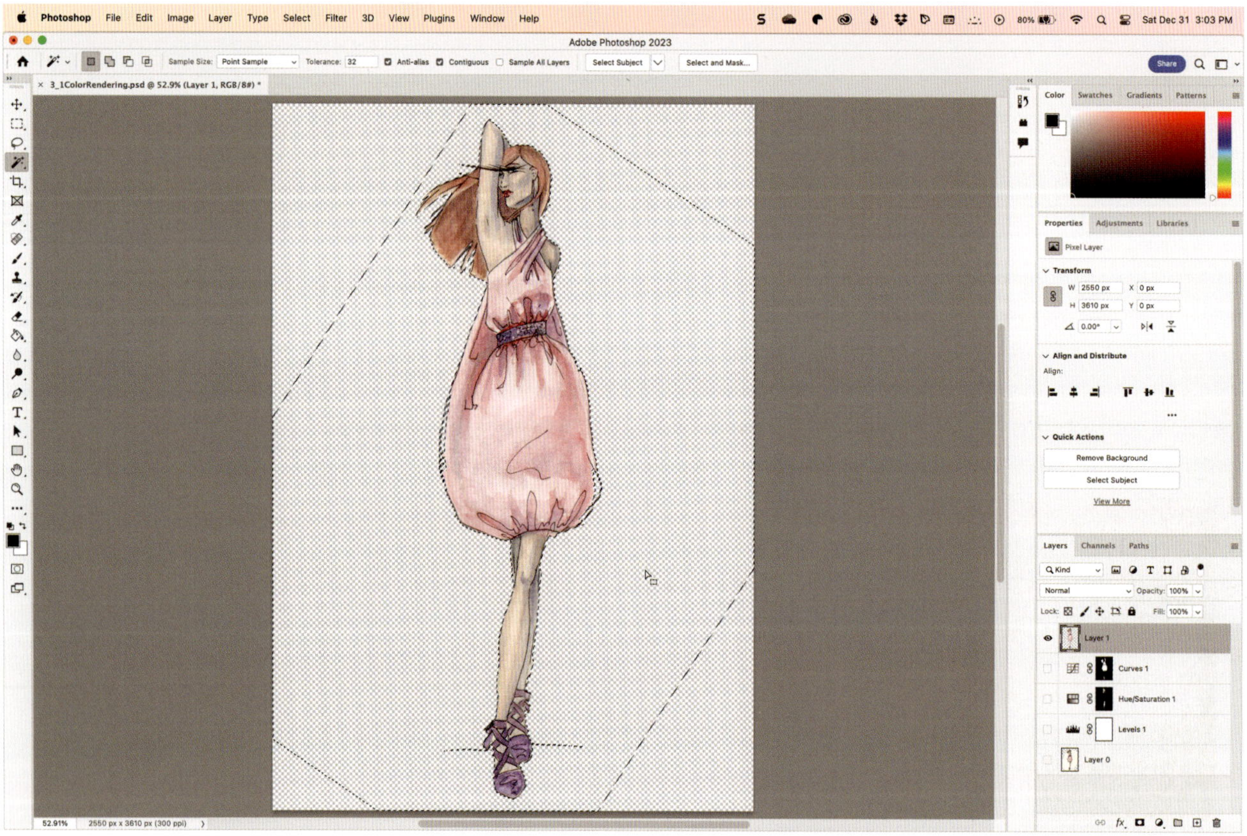

Figure 3.17c The paper background is eliminated, leaving the figure to use in a portfolio layout. If you are happy with the results, you can *Save* the file and it is ready to add to a portfolio project. But wait! You may want to try the second technique before you decide.

You may need to clean up some stray marks that were not included in the selection. On the same layer, use the *Eraser* tool (yes, it's okay to use once you have deleted the paper background) to fully eliminate any erroneous smudges or marks. You can also use it to clean up the edges where the watercolor escaped past the pen lines if you like.

Although the *Magic Wand* worked great for this project, you may have other backgrounds that make it harder to select the foreground figure. Textured/tinted papers or multiple images on one paper may mean that you need a slightly more involved way to pull your single figure out.

Method 2: Using the select and mask method. Use the *History* panel (*Windows menu →History*) or your *Undo* command (*control+z/command+z*) to step backwards and reinstate your background paper with the image. If you still have the area selected, *Deselect* it through the *Select* menu or use the keyboard shortcut *control+d/command+d*. Find the *Object Selection* tool in the same toolbar as the *Magic Wand. Click and drag* a marquee around the rendered figure or simply *click* once in the middle of the figure. This will analyze the color information and create a selection around the figure. This feature does a pretty good job on its own. However, it may need a little refinement.

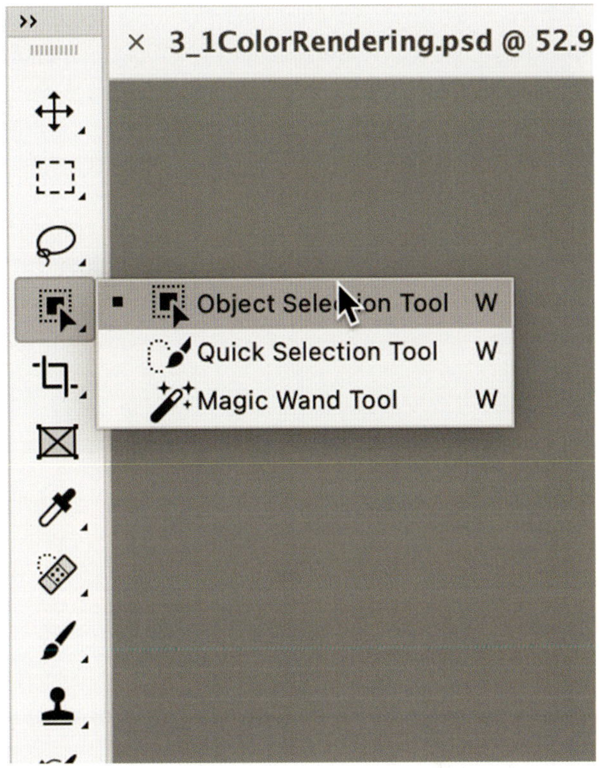

Figure 3.18a A screenshot of the toolbar. Choose the *Object Selection* tool.

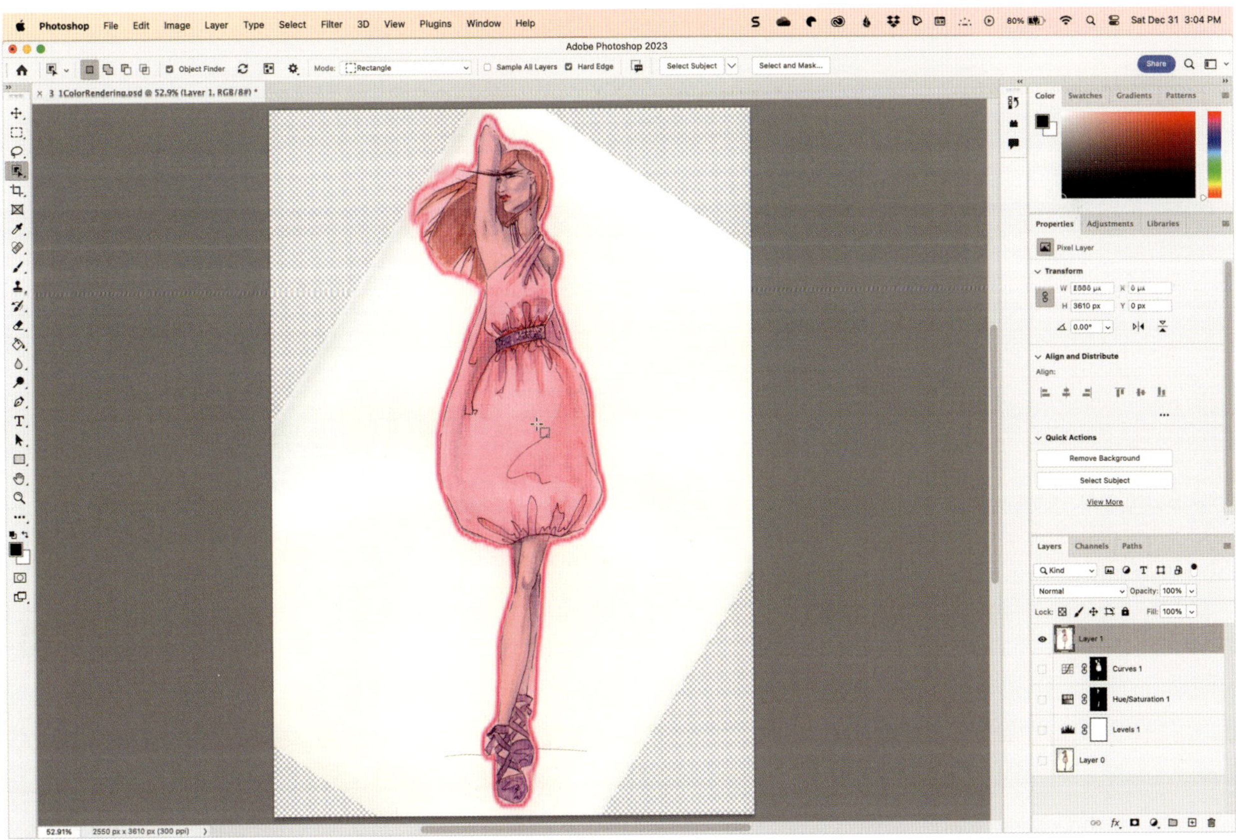

Figure 3.18b The pink overlay indicates your selection. Once made, notice there is the option to *Remove Background* in the *Properties* panel. You will get better results if you choose the *Select and Mask* option in the top *Options* menu, though.

We want to bring your attention to a couple of options while the image has a selection. In the *Properties* panel, you will see a *Quick Action* called *Remove Background*. This will, unsurprisingly, remove the background while you have the figure selected. If you like the results, huzzah! For some, this may not provide the most satisfactory effect, though. Sometimes you simply need to refine the mask with more detail. To achieve this, you will find a button at the top of the *Options* bar called *Select and Mask*.

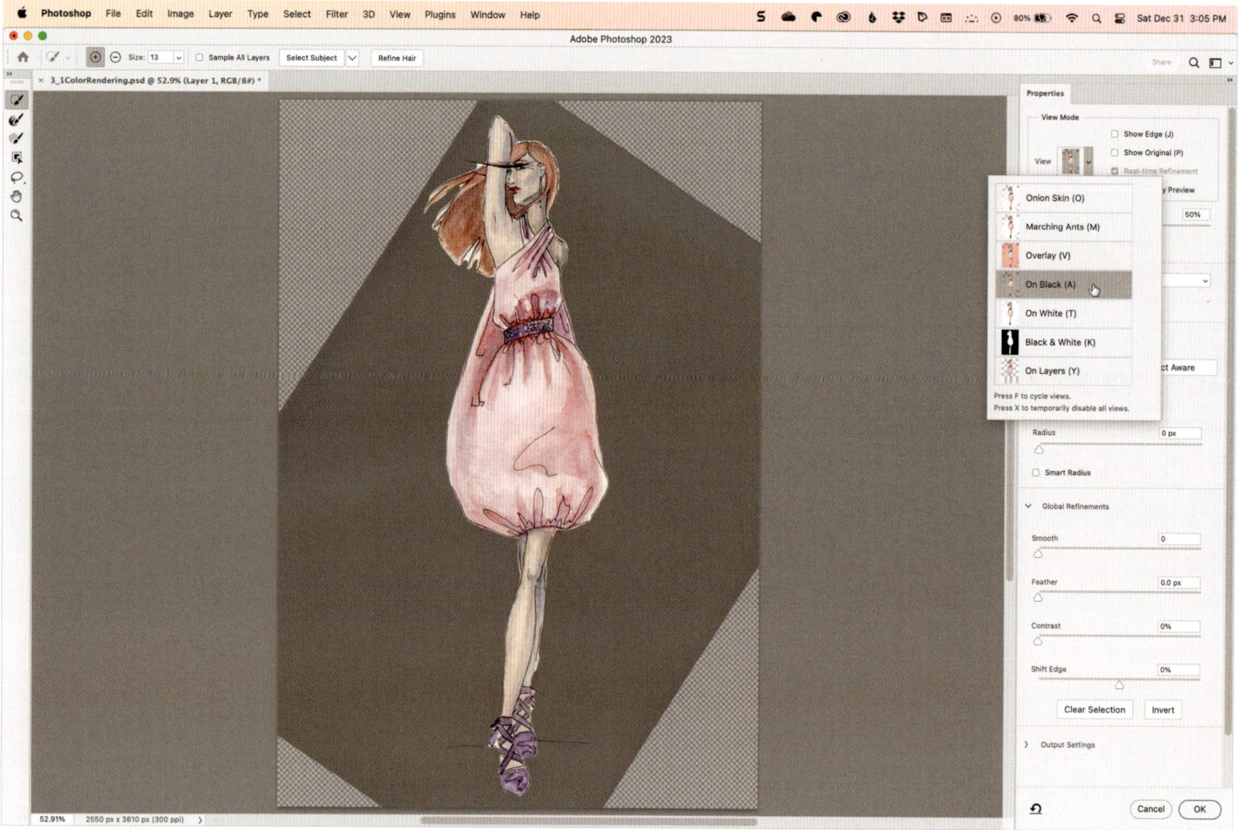

Figure 3.19a A screenshot of the *Select and Mask* interface. On the right-hand side, you can choose a new *View* from the drop-down menu under the small image. Choose the option that makes it easiest to see where your mask is applied. We chose *On Black* for this example.

This button will take you to a pop-up interface. Take a look around. You have tools on the left and a *Properties* panel on the right. You may not see any difference with the image in the middle. The first thing to do is to change the view to make it easier to see what is and is not masked. If this is the case, look at the top of the *Properties* panel in the *View* section. You will see a tiny version of the artwork with a drop-down arrow. *Click* the arrow to choose a more productive view. *Overlay* or *On Black* probably works best for this image. Now you can see what is selected!

For now, leave all the settings in the *Properties* panel alone. Feel free to explore what they do to the mask on your own. Right now, we will use the tool panel on the left. First, *Zoom* in on part of the image to work. Then choose the *Brush* tool. Notice at the top in the options menu that you see *plus* (+) and *minus* (–) symbols. These will affect whether the painted area adds to the mask or subtracts from it. Try the *minus* button and paint around the hair ends. If you go too far into the painting, switch back to the *plus* button. Continue to work your way around the whole image until you are happy with the results.

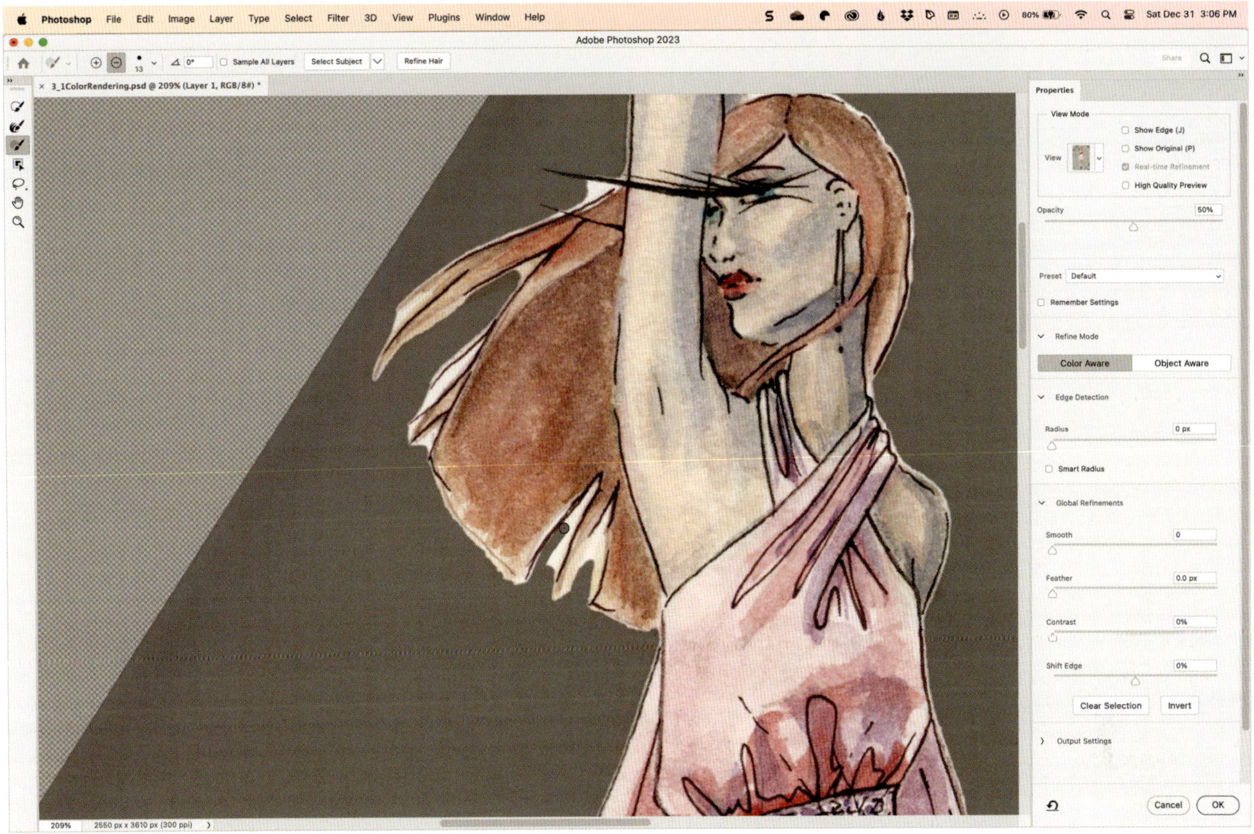

Figure 3.19b Use the *Brush* to add or remove parts of the mask to make it more refined.

Once you are satisfied, look in the *Properties* panel on the right. There is an option to **Feather** your mask. Look at the difference in the selection when you move the slider back and forth. Because this is hand drawn, there is a little softness to the line quality. It will look better if our mask has a small amount of *Feather* applied to soften the transition between the selected and unselected area.

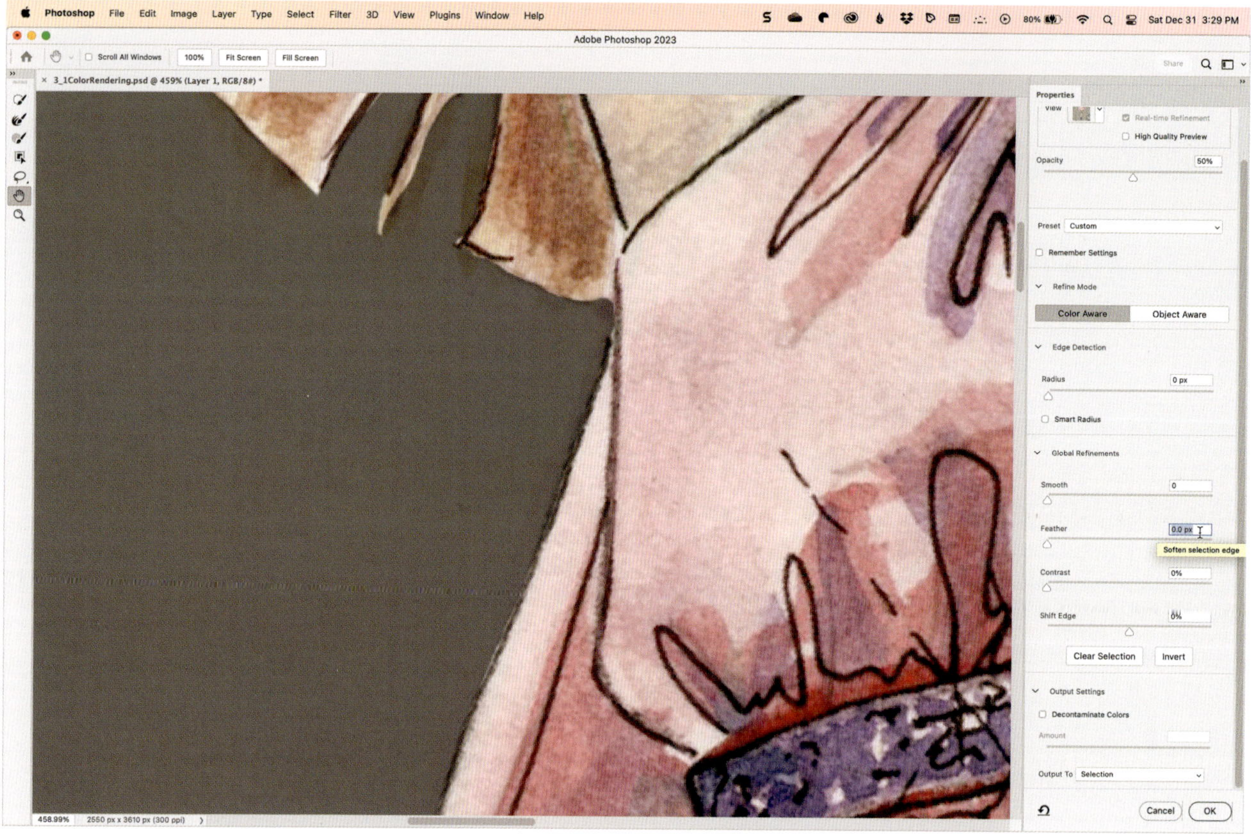

Figure 3.19c A screenshot of the mask with no feathering. Notice the edge sharpness.

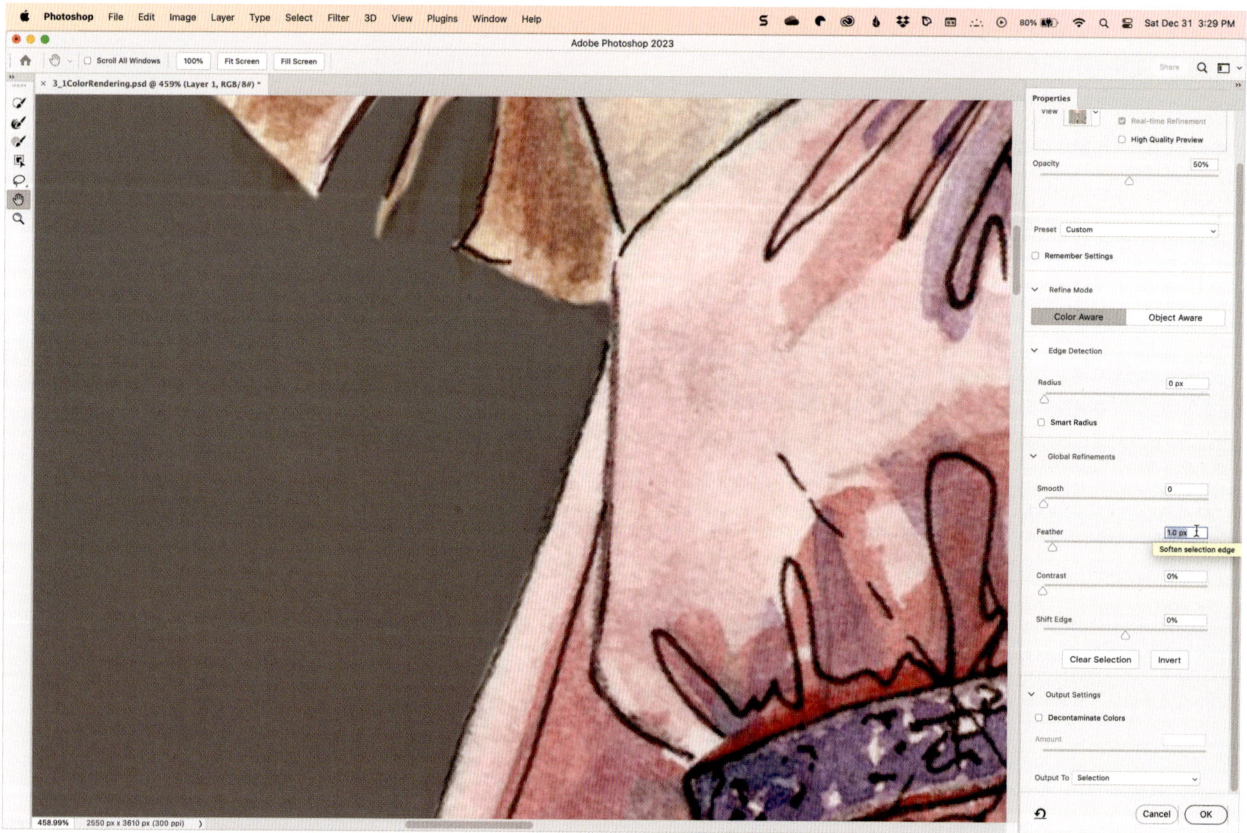

Figure 3.19d A screenshot of the mask with a 1-pixel *Feather* applied. See how it softens the edge slightly?

Then, check the very bottom of the *Properties* panel in the *Output Selection* menu. Notice that you can choose to *Output To* multiple options, including a *New Layer*. If you choose this option and hit *OK* (don't do it yet, though) it will put your selected figure onto a layer by itself, without the background. That's handy, isn't it? However, we want to show you a trick that will prove useful down the line. Leave the *Output To* choice to *Selection* and click the *OK* button.

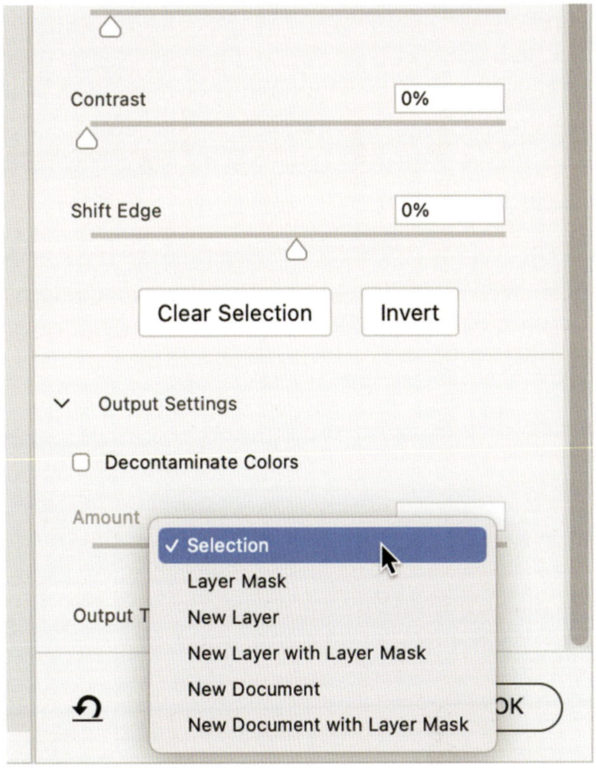

Figure 3.19e At the bottom in the *Output To* settings section, notice that you can change the output. For now, leave it at *Selection*.

This will take you back to the main interface and you will see the marching ants around your figure. While you have the figure selected, use the keyboard shortcut of *control+j/command+j*. This will *Jump a Copy* of your selection to a new layer, all on its own. Why did we make you do this extra step when the *Output To New Layer* would have achieved the same thing? Well, we wanted you to learn that shortcut. It frequently helps when you have a selection that you need to separate to a new layer. Now you know!

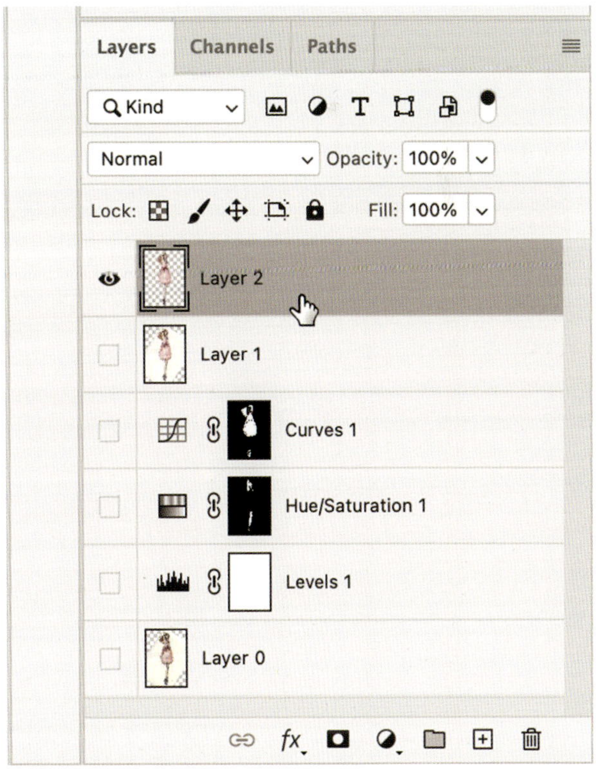

Figure 3.20 *Jump a Copy* of your selection to a new layer using the keyboard shortcut *control+j* or *command+j*. This will pop the selection up to its own layer.

This top layer is all you need to use for a portfolio layer, but you may want to save those other layers in a working file in case you need to tweak your colors later. You can save a flattened file to use for the layout to save space, though. Feel free to keep it in the native file format as well.

Step 7: Continue to make any necessary corrections to select areas of the image if needed. Use what you just learned about adjustment layers and masks to target your adjustments. Remember that the file may print differently from how it looks on the screen, so save a PSD copy in case you need to tweak the colors later.

Before you close your file, you can do a quick check for any stray marks. Add a *New Layer* just below your figure. Fill it with a color. Try a light version, midtone, and dark just to make sure you didn't miss anything. When you are done, either turn off the *Visibility* or *Delete* the layer altogether to save space.

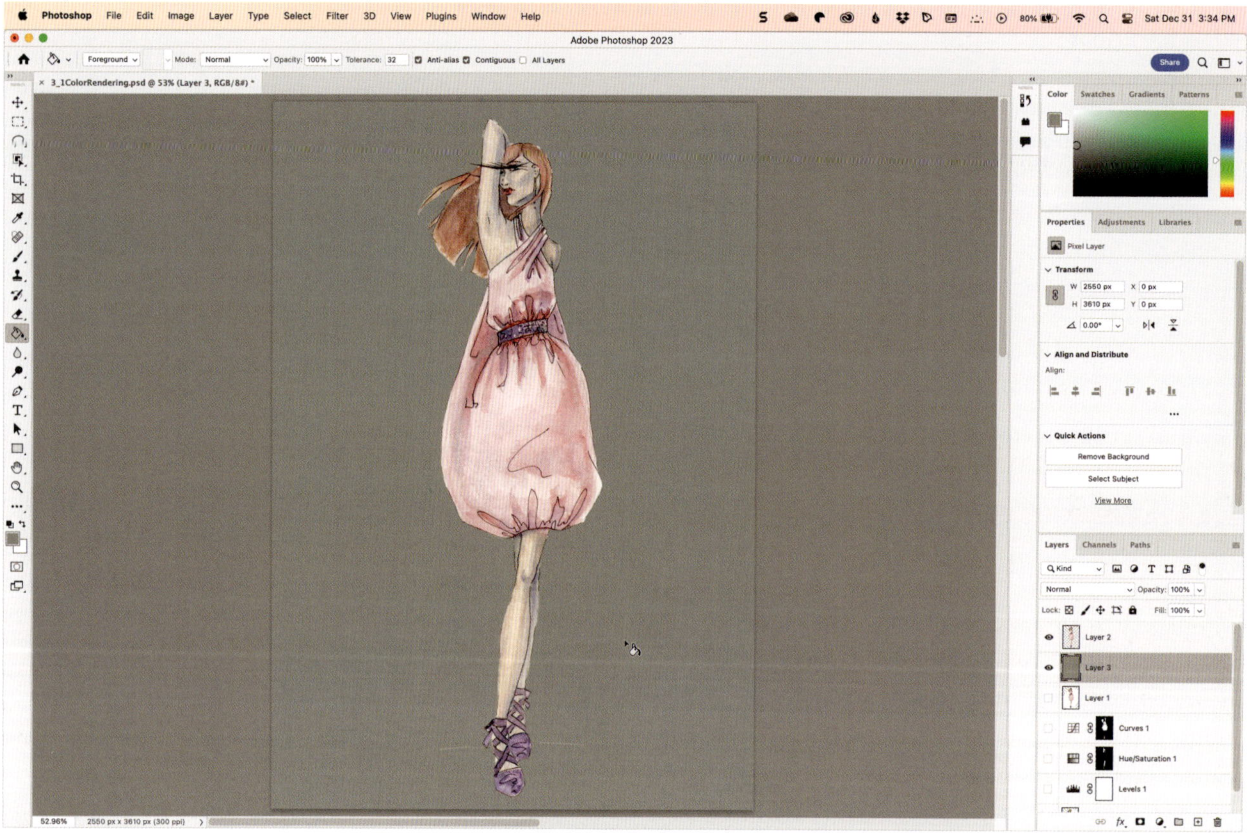

Figure 3.21 You can add a *New Color Layer* below your top figure layer to check for any extra marks that you may have missed. Try changing the color to dark, mid, and light tones to make sure you didn't miss anything.

After all of that, we realized that we did not keep our layers named in the file. Go back and label those layers for later! Finally, you can *Save* and *Close* your file.

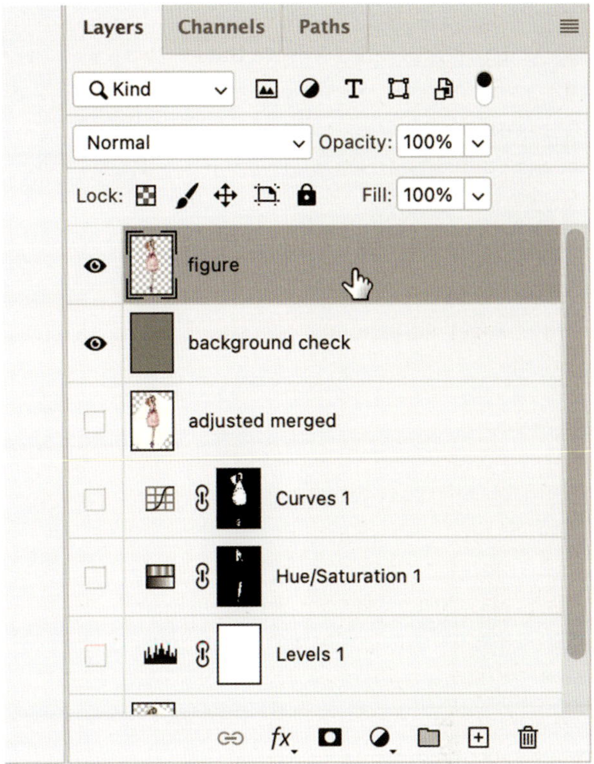

Figure 3.22 Remember to clean up and label your layers for later!

Project 3.2: Base Painting by Layers

If you prefer to digitally color your illustrations (which we recommend) then this project is for you! We will use the aforementioned layer-mapping workflow for this project. We are only adding the base colors at this point, which is preparation for all the other fun stuff you can accomplish digitally with your illustrations! The colors don't matter at this point, so you will see that we use some crazy color choices during this stage. Honestly, it just makes it easier when you don't have to make color decisions at first. You can focus on the technique without the nagging questions of, "Is this the right tone? How will it print?" You might as well have fun with it. Choose a color that just makes you happy for now!

Step 1: In Photoshop, *Open* your prepped figure sketch from Chapter 1 or clean up a new sketch to work with. Remember that the sketch should be on the top layer and set it to the *Multiply Blend Mode*. All color work should be below this layer.

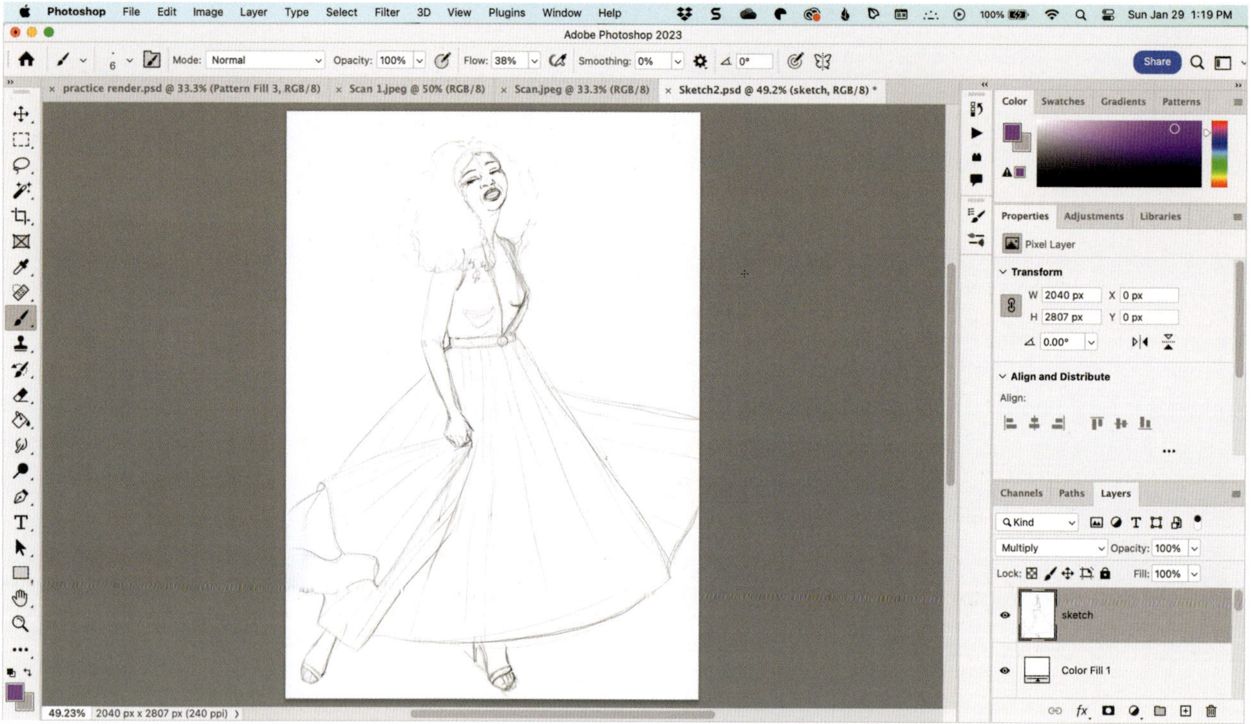

Figure 3.23a Here we have the prepped sketch open in Photoshop with a white color fill layer below it.

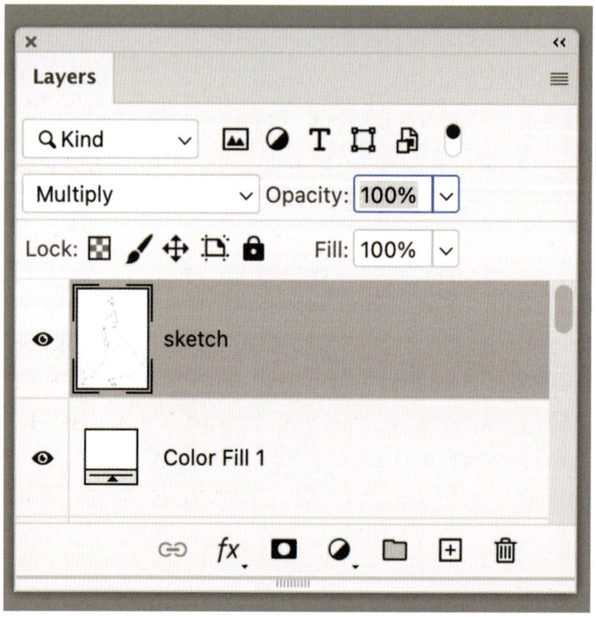

Figure 3.23b Notice that the sketch layer stays at the top of the layer stack. It should be set to *Multiply* for the colors below to show through.

Consider how you want to color your artwork. Think about the stacking order, in particular. If this was a person standing in front of you, what garments would be on top of others? For example, if your figure is wearing a traditional tailored suit, you would have the skin layer towards the bottom of the stack, followed by the shirt, slacks, waistcoat, tie, and finally the jacket towards the top. Take a moment to analyze your sketch. Which layers do you want to separate out, and how do you want to stack them? Go ahead and create a blank layer for each now. Label them so you know which is which. It's easy enough to rearrange the layers through drag and drop if you decide to switch the order later.

Just to remind you, we are only adding flat color at this point. We will cover highlights and shadows in a future chapter. So, the end result of this project may not be as "finished" as the last project. Don't worry: you'll be able to make it fancier as you progress through the next few chapters!

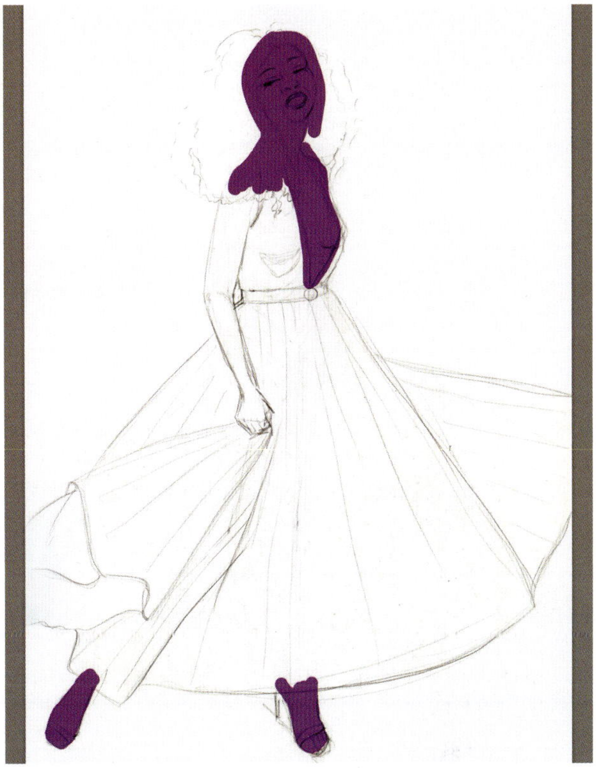

Figure 3.24 We started by painting in the color for the skin layer on this example. It needs to be neat and precise around the areas that don't get covered (for example, the feet) but can be less controlled around areas that will be covered by other layers on top (for example, around the hemline of the dress).

Step 2: On this example, we started with the skin as it is one of the lowest layers (clothes sit on top of your skin, right?). It should be above the background layer, but below the dress in this case. Remember that with layers, whatever is on top will cover up what is below it. So, parts of your coloring work will need to be precise, but others can be a little messier if it is covered. When you look at Figure 3.24, notice that we kept it precise around the feet but less controlled in the areas that will be covered by the dress. The chest and face don't need any precise areas because all edges are eventually covered by the dress and hair!

Notice here that the front arm gets its own layer because it sits in front of the dress. When we adjust colors for the skin tone later, we will need to remember to make the same adjustments to the front arm. Of course, you can also keep the front arm on the same layer as the rest of the skin, but you will need to carefully paint the dress around the arm silhouette. One way is not better, easier, or faster than the other. Choose whichever organizational method makes the most sense to you.

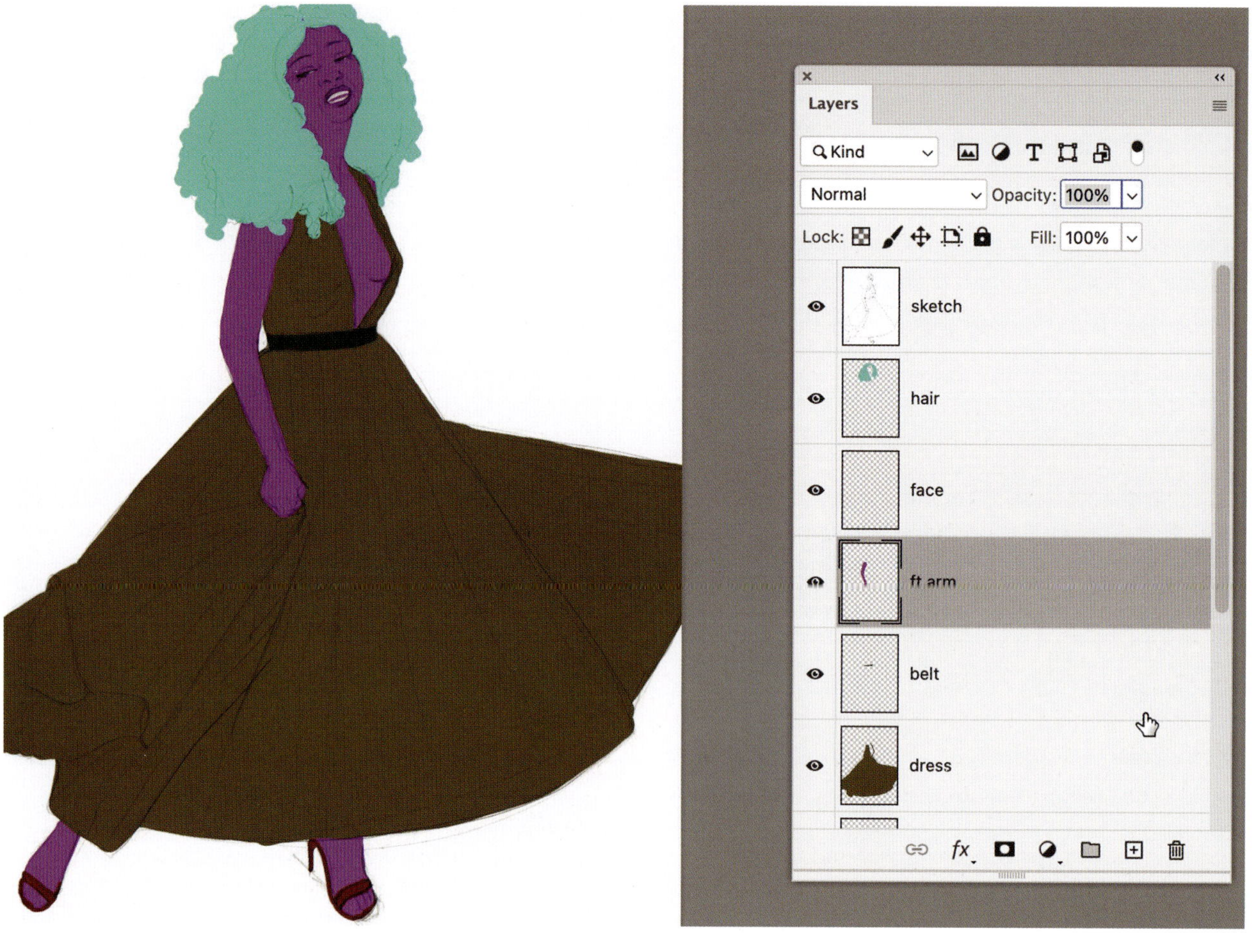

Figure 3.25 We've added a base color to each layer. Notice the stacking order in the *Layers* panel. The dress covers the skin layer, but the front arm is on a separate layer on top of the dress. The hair covers all of it, so it is near the top just below the sketch layer.

Use a plain, round, hard *Brush* and start to color the perimeter. The color does not matter at this point, so don't spend time fretting about choosing the right color. You also don't need a fancy paint brush because we want a flat color. Make sure your brush is set to 100% *Opacity* and 100% *Flow*. You may experience "streaks" if either is less than 100%. Your brush should be small enough to paint the details with precision but large enough to give a good border. You may need to change *Brush* sizes a few times as you work your way around the border.

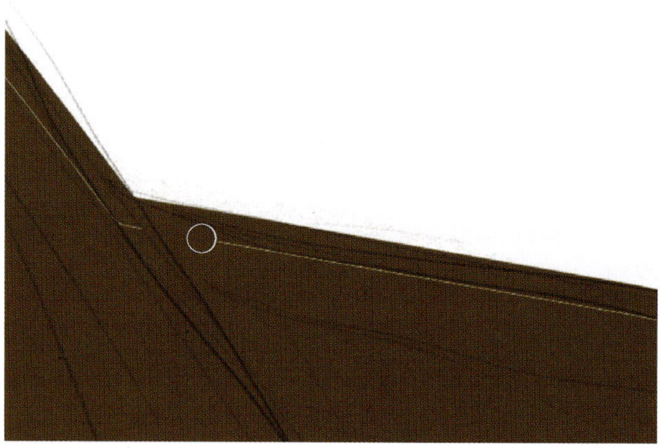

Figure 3.26 When painting in a large area, you can carefully paint around the border, then use the *Paint Bucket* tool to fill in the middle. This leaves a slight gap between the fill and the painted border, however. *Zoom* in and paint over the gap.

Step 3: Once you have colored the border, then either use the *Paint Bucket* tool or *Brush* to fill in the remaining areas. If you use the *Paint Bucket*, note that it creates a little break between the painted perimeter and the fill. You'll need to paint that in to delete the gap.

Step 4: Congratulations! You just set up your first layer. Guess what you need to do now? That's right—fill in all the other areas. Save your work if you have not already done so. We can use this file for the chapters on patterns, highlight and shadow, and textures.

Project 3.3: Change and Save Colors in Ps

If (and when) you find yourself needing to go back to precise colors, you may find it best to make a swatch for reference. Right now, with all flat colors, it's easy enough to just use the *Eyedropper* tool (shortcut *i* or use the *alt/option* key while in the *Brush* tool to pick up a color on the fly). However, once you start adding highlights/shadows and textures, it gets harder to go back to the original base color. Therefore, you probably want to make a swatch for each of your main color choices.

Step 1: Open the *Swatch* panel. If you don't see it, look under the *Window* menu and select the *Swatch* panel. In this panel, click on the folder icon or use the drop-down menu in the upper right-hand side to select *New Swatch Group*. A pop-up dialog box will allow you to name the group. Chose whatever name works for your needs. Click on this folder to select it when it appears in the group list.

Once you have your color selected for the foreground color, click the *plus* icon (+) found at the bottom of the *Swatch* panel. A pop-up dialog box will appear. You can rename the swatch if you like. Notice the small checkbox that allows you to simultaneously *Add to your current library* as you create the swatch. We will come back to this choice in a moment. For now, leave it checked and click *OK*. Your new color swatch will appear in the folder you created!

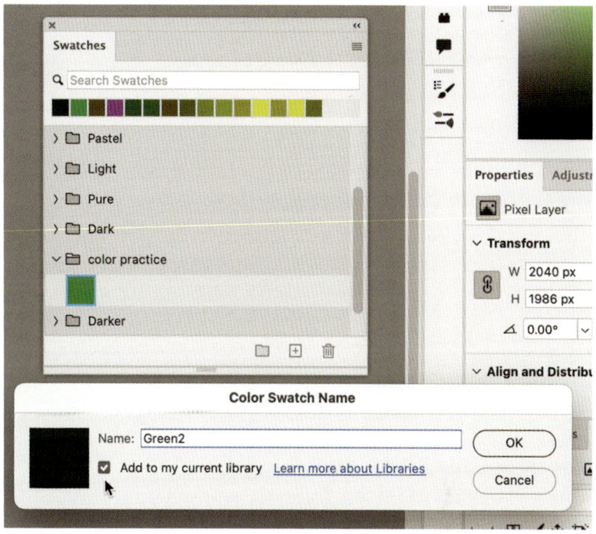

Figure 3.27 When adding a color to the *Swatches* panel, tick the box for *Add to my current library*. This will make your color swatch available across all your Adobe applications.

Step 2: Add as many colors as you need here. You don't have to do anything special to save it. Photoshop keeps it available in that version of the software. If you want to have it available on other versions of the software (for example, if you switch between a desktop and tablet version of Ps) then you will need to export the *Swatch Library* under the drop-down menu. Select the folder you want to export, then choose the command to *Export Selected Swatches*. *Save* the file somewhere you can get to it easily such as a cloud drive. Then you can *Import* the *Swatch Library* into your other device.

The easier way to do this, however, is to put your colors into your **Adobe library**. We brought up

Libraries at the beginning of this chapter. *Libraries* are linked through your Adobe ID. Therefore, any device you sign into will have access to your library. You can save a multitude of assets through this clever feature: colors, graphic elements, actions, styles, etc.

To save a color, you can either have the checkbox clicked when you make a swatch or you can select a color, click on the *plus* symbol (+) in the *Libraries* panel, and select *Foreground color* from the list. If you want to rename it, simply *double-click* on the lower edge of the color that displays the name. To select the color, *click* on it. You can organize your library assets into folder groups. These will be available to you without having to constantly export and import.

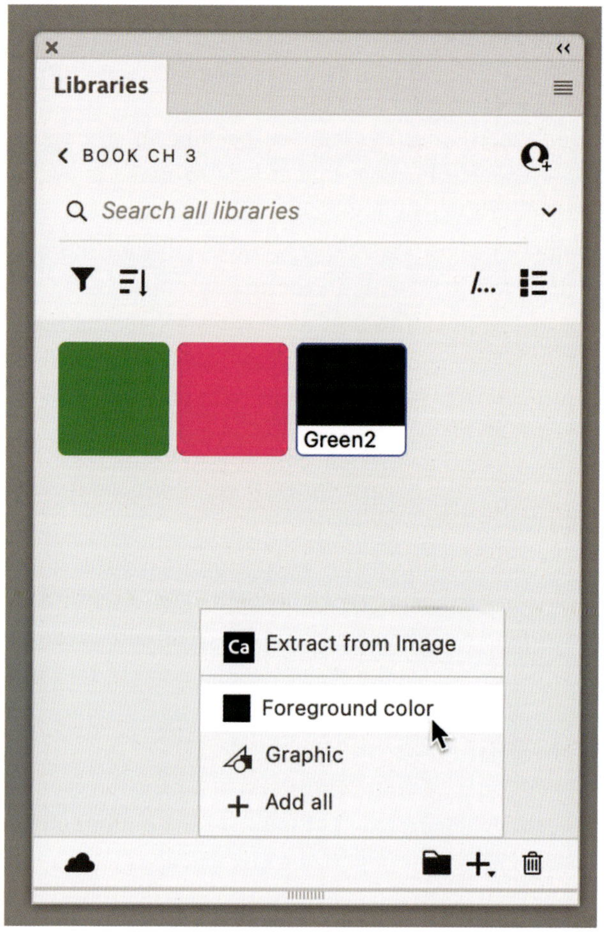

Figure 3.28 To add a color through the *Libraries* panel, click on the *plus* symbol at the bottom of the panel. Then choose *Foreground color* as your option.

Step 3: Now let's adjust some colors. Let's face it, we chose some horrific color combinations! The fastest way is to simply change the color with the *Paint Bucket* tool. Select the layer of the item you want to change such as the dress layer. Select your new *Foreground color*. Use the *Paint Bucket* tool to click anywhere on the dress. Boom! There is your new color. How exciting is that?

That's great, but what if you aren't sure which color to use? Or if the director of your show would like to see a few different options? Maybe you want to show different colorway options for that piece. Well, there are several ways to achieve this.

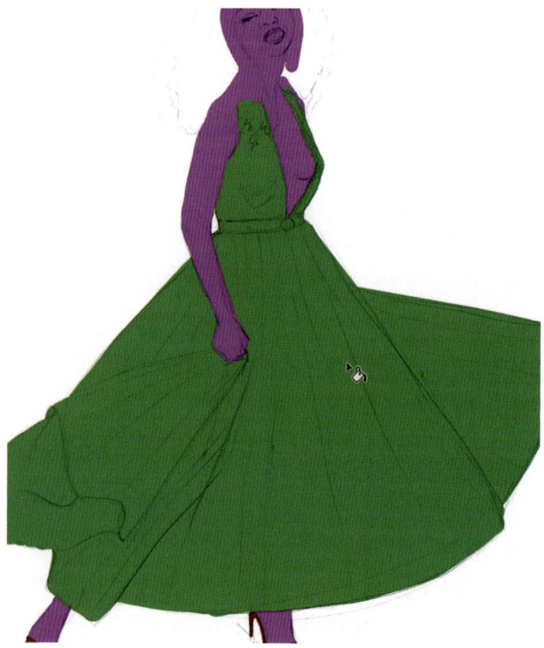

Figure 3.29 After selecting the dress layer and your new *Foreground color*, simply click anywhere on the dress with the *Paint Bucket* tool. There is your new color!

PRO TIP 3.4

Learning Color Theory

Color theory is a massive topic of its own accord. We will not pretend to cover it here, so we recommend picking up some books or classes to better understand the subject. The more you understand about color science and color theory, the easier it will be to control your color needs in a digital workspace. One of the best ways to understand colors is to play with them! Use some sort of analog medium: whatever you have on hand. Paints such as acrylic or watercolor work best, but crayons and colored pencils can be equally instructive! Play and observe what happens when you allow colors to interact with each other. If your base color is red, what happens when you overlap it with yellow? How is that different from overlapping it with green or even black? How does the color change when you use only the barest amount versus adding as much of the color as you can? Have fun while learning. Then pick up a book to learn more about the properties of hue, saturation, brightness, additive versus subtractive color, and color harmonies. This will make you a better artist, regardless of your medium!

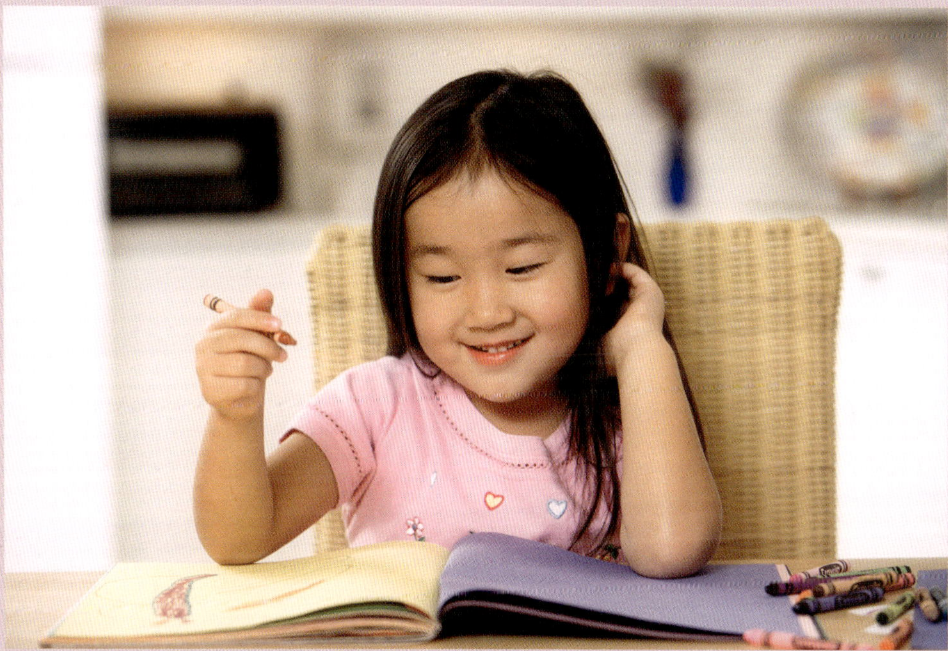

Figure PT3.2 Let out your inner child and play with crayons, colored pencils, or paint to learn how color interacts. Roy Morsch/The Image Bank/Getty Images

Step 4: Try adding a *New Color Fill* layer above your garment. Select the layer you want to change. Use the *New Adjustment Layer* button at the bottom of the *Layers* panel to add a color fill layer. Then clip the layer down to the garment below it. You can do this by *right-clicking* on the color fill layer, or by holding the *alt/option* button while hovering your cursor between the two layers and *clicking*. We refer to this as a Clipping mask. Essentially, the layer below it acts as the mask.

The same clipping action is useful for other types of adjustment layers. For example, you can apply a *Curves Adjustment* layer as seen in Figure 3.31. A *Hue/Saturation*, *Color Mixer*, or *Color Balance Adjustment* layer can be clipped as well. It simply depends on your personal preferences.

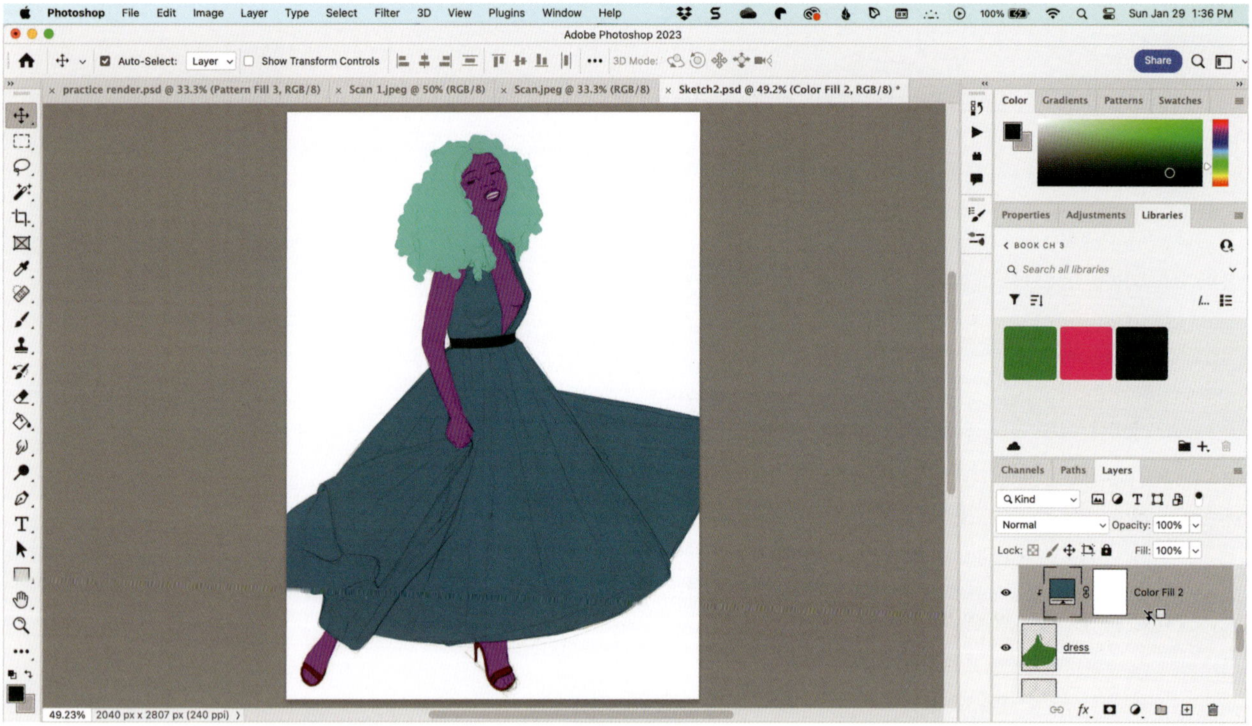

Figure 3.30 With a *New Color Fill* layer added on top of the dress layer, hold *alt/option* down on your keyboard and *click* between the two layers. Notice before you click that the cursor changes to a little arrow pointing down. Once the layer is clipped, the new color will "stick" to the paint layer below it and the layer shows an indent with an arrow pointing down.

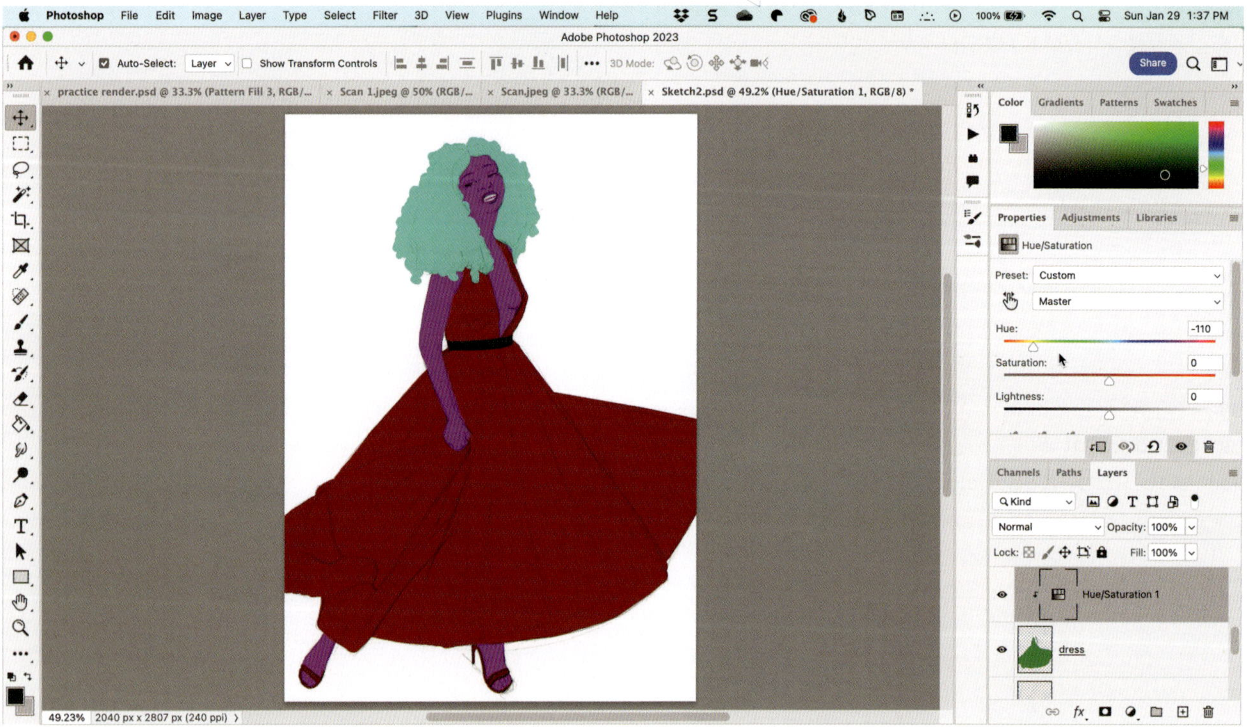

Figure 3.31 We've adjusted the color through a *Curves* layer, then clipped it down to the dress layer. Clipped layers are highly useful!

That wasn't so hard, but what if we have to make the same adjustment to more than one layer? In this example, we have the skin on a lower level but the arm on an upper level. If you used a clipped layer, you could simply duplicate that layer and clip it to any additional necessary layers. Figure 3.32 shows the *Curves* layer copied from the skin layer to the arm layer.

Now, normally, using adjustment layers to change the base layer of skin color is overkill. It's unlikely that you need to show multiple options of skin colors on one figure. However, copying adjustments is very useful when you get to highlights, shadows, and textures.

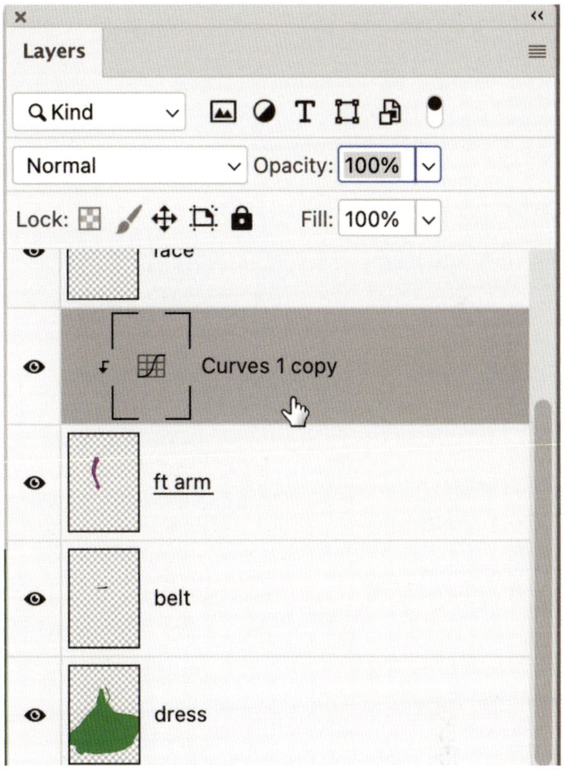

Figure 3.32 We have copied the *Curves Adjustment* layer from the skin layer in the *Layers* panel and applied it to the front arm layer.

Step 5: By the way, to save the illustration with a transparent background we will need to use the *Magic Wand* tool on the upper-most sketch layer. Once you click the *Magic Wand* tool, uncheck **Contiguous** and check *Sample All Layers*. When the *Contiguous* box is ticked, it will only select areas that are touching the color you selected with your wand. If you uncheck it, it will also pick up the background area trapped between the figure's right arm and body. The *Sample All Layers* box means that the program will see all the painted layers as one solid figure. Click anywhere in the background space to select the full background. Now hit the *Backspace/Delete* button. Then, simply turn off the *Visibility* on your lowest color fill layer. Voila! No more background.

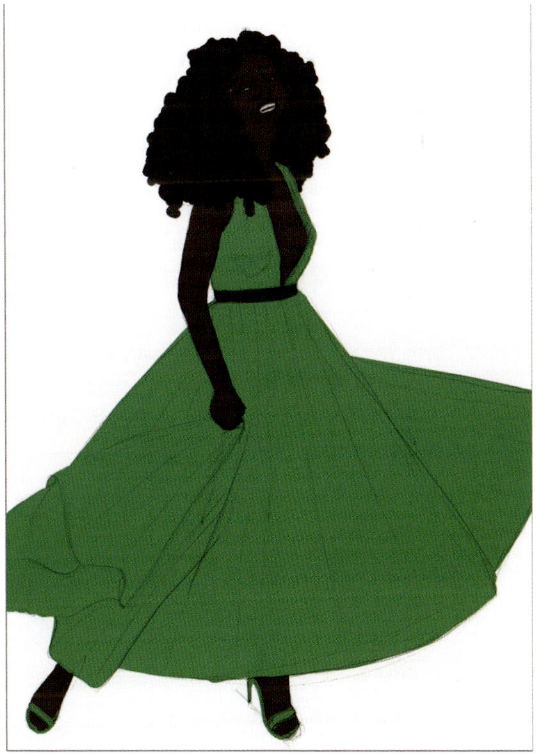

Figure 3.33 All the base colors are laid down on separate layers and our figure is ready for the next chapter.

Step 6: We've had a lot of fun with our grape-colored model! We will go ahead and adjust our model to a more traditional skin tone, though. Figure 3.33 shows our figure, ready for patterns, textures, and depth in the coming chapters!

Troubleshooting

Let's look at some of the more common issues you may encounter when colorizing in Photoshop.

"When trying to paint or otherwise affect a layer, I get a 'no' symbol of a circle with a slash."

This means that you currently cannot change that layer. Check the *Layers* panel. Are you on the correct layer? Is the visibility turned off? Are you trying to paint an adjustment layer? Is the layer locked? These are the main culprits.

"My paintbrush or fill tool seems to have no effect."

Look at the *Layer* panel. Are you painting on a layer or the *Layer Mask*? Is the *Opacity* of the layer turned up? Is it set to the *Normal Blend Mode* or something else?

If you don't see anything out of sorts in the *Layers* panel, look at the *Options* ribbon in the top bar while in the *Brush* tool. Make sure your paintbrush *Opacity* and *Flow* are turned up enough to see the results. Check the *Blend Mode* of the *Brush*. Sometimes the *Brush* you choose changes these settings, or you may accidentally change them without realizing.

"When I am painting, part of the layer below shows through."

1. Check the *Layer Opacity* or *Blend Mode*.
2. If those settings are correct, then look at the *Brush Opacity*, *Flow*, or *Blend Mode* in the top *Options* ribbon. Inevitably, this will cause the colors of the lower layer to show through if your *Opacity* and *Flow* are not all the way to 100% and your *Blend Mode* set to *Normal*.

"When I print my work I see a noticeable variance in the colors between the screen and the print."

1. There are a few things you can check. This often happens if you work in an *RGB* color mode and then proceed to print. The printer, no matter the brand or type, must convert the color information to *CMYK*. Different color modes have different ranges of the color gamut. A **color gamut** is the range of colors available within that mode. Particularly vibrant colors you see on the screen may not be achievable when printed. It's simply due to the difference of colors you can see through projected light versus those available through pigment on paper. You can check this by looking in the *View* menu and selecting *Gamut Warning*, as seen in Figure 3.37a.

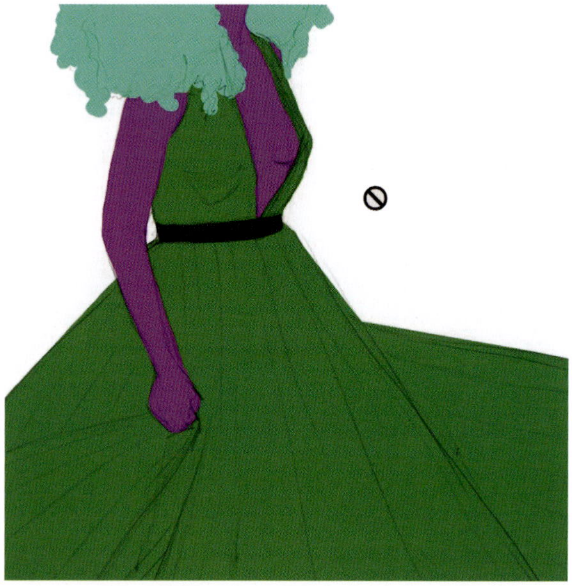

Figure 3.34 Sometimes you may get this "no" symbol when trying to paint. Look at your *Layers* panel first to see which layer is selected.

Any color that falls outside the gamut will show as gray when this option is turned on. You can see in Figure 3.37b that the majority of the colors we chose will not print the way we see them on the screen. Only the belt, shoes, and a few edges darkened by the top sketch layer will print the same color we see on the screen.

You have a few options when dealing with this issue. You can *Save* a printable version and change the *Color Mode* to *CMYK*. There is usually a noticeable "dulling" of the colors, but they will print closer to what you see on the screen. Adjust and tweak your colors to an acceptable version while in this mode.

Likewise, you can simply adjust your colors while in *RGB* and recheck with the *Gamut Warning* feature until you achieve the desired look.

Should you still have issues after dealing with the gamut warning, it may be a matter of color calibration. If the printer is in your personal possession, then you can invest the time and cost to calibrate between your devices. However, if you use a third-party printer, it may not be in your control. You will have to decide if complete control of the final look is worth the time and financial investment for your needs.

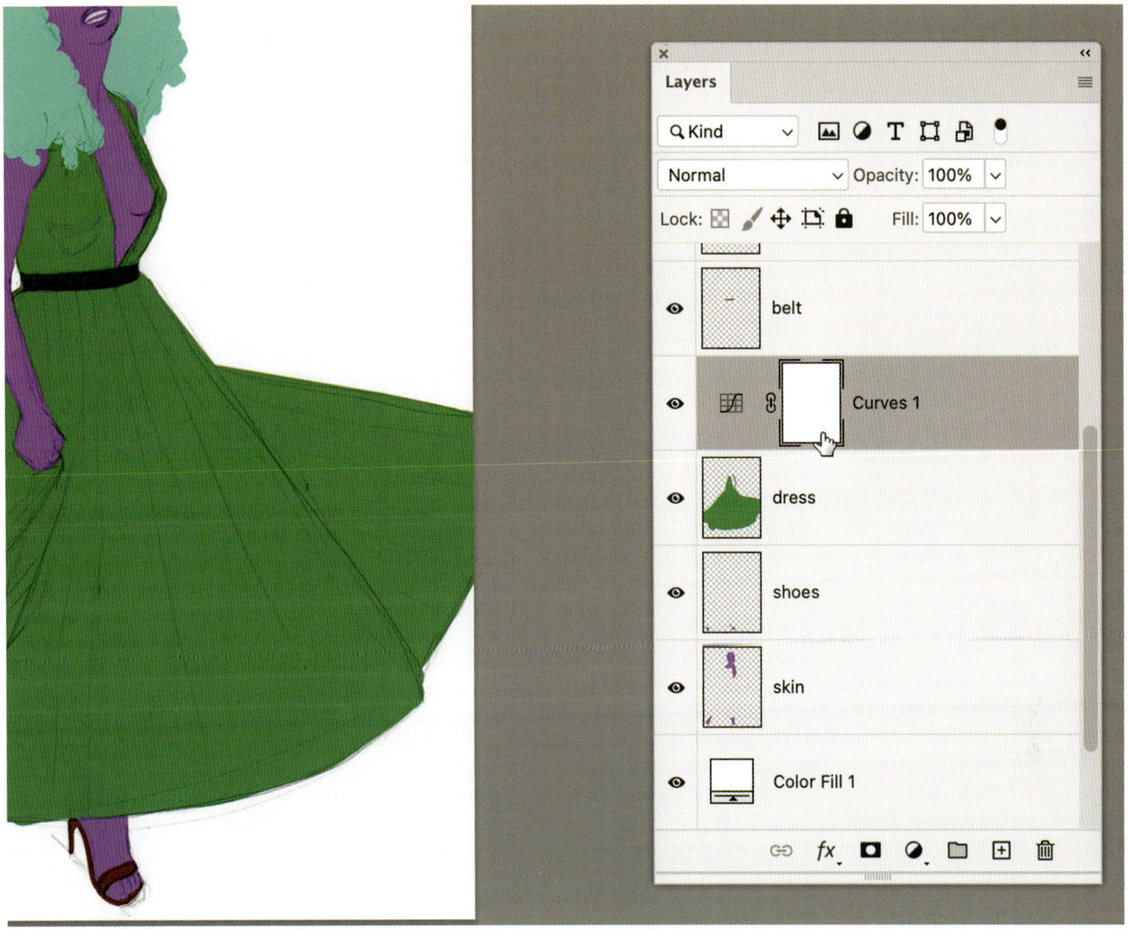

Figure 3.35 If it looks like nothing is happening when painting, make sure you are not on a *Layer Mask* or an *Adjustment Layer*. Click the correct layer you want to paint upon or create a new layer.

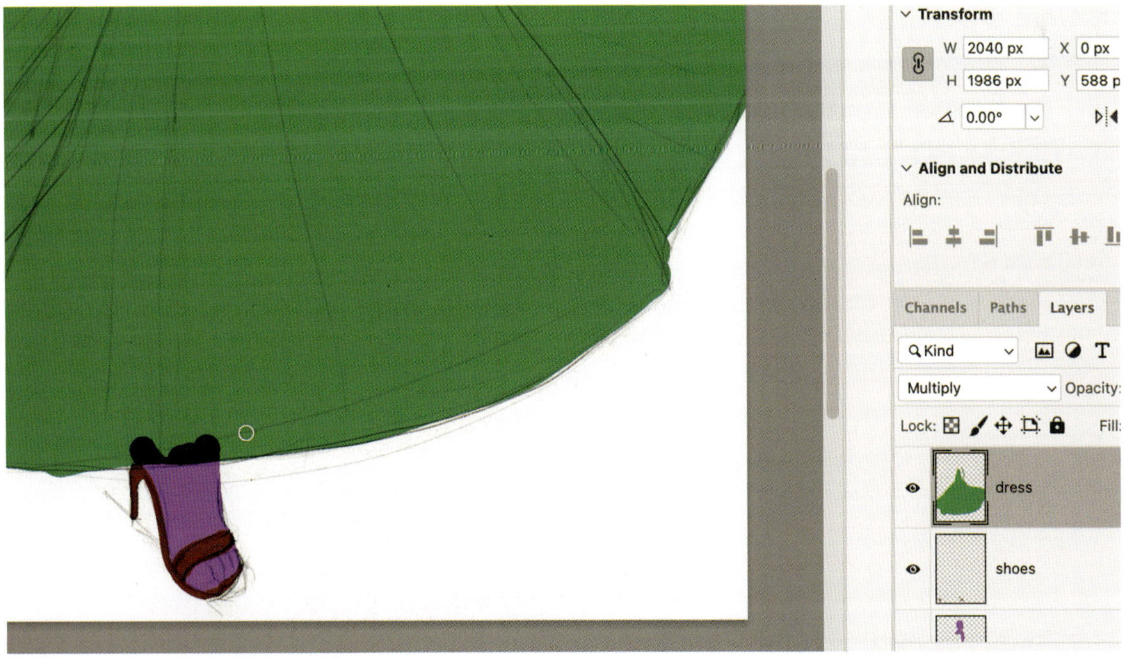

Figure 3.36 Check both your settings and the *Brush* settings if a lower layer shows through to an upper layer. Make sure everything is set to Normal mode and 100% Opacity. Here the dress layer was accidentally set to Multiply and the paint strokes of the foot layer shows through.

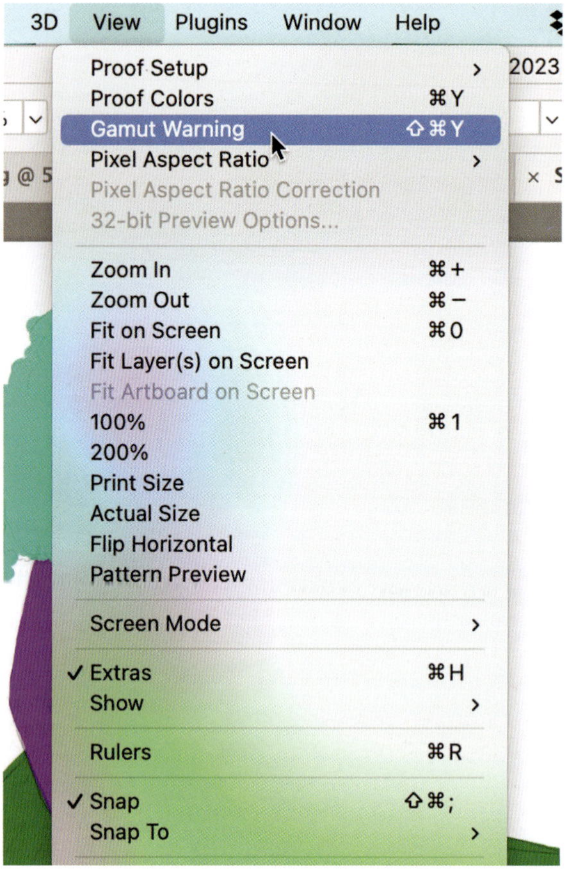

Figure 3.37a In the *View* menu, select *Gamut Warning* to see what falls outside of the CMYK gamut.

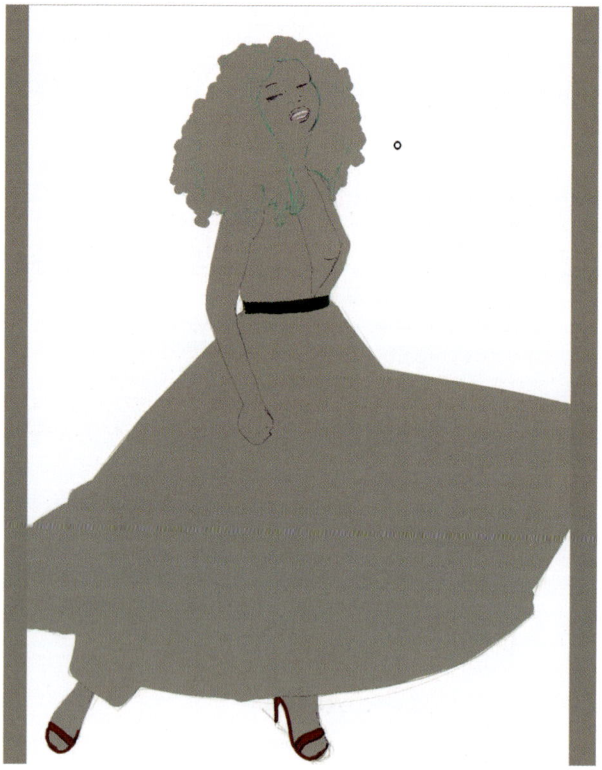

Figure 3.37b When viewing your work with the *Gamut Warning* turned on, the gray areas indicate colors that fall outside of the CMYK gamut.

PRO TIP 3.5

What Is Color Calibration and Why it Is (or Isn't) Important to You

Color calibration is the process of aligning the color consistency across your devices. In essence, it helps to ensure that the sky blue on your monitor matches what comes out of your printer. For some, it is imperative to match colors exactly across all devices within a team or company. For many of us, it's not that big of a deal.

If you want to tighten up your color variance, there are options available for laptops, desktops, and some display tablets. Many operating systems will have some sort of built-in color calibration through the settings. You can easily look up how-to videos or instructions online, depending on the specific device and platform. These solutions depend upon your personal estimations and can be a little tedious. If you want an easier solution, there are online websites, software, and even equipment that you can purchase to help make a more precise calibration.

Keep in mind that although you have control over your personal monitors and printers, you cannot control someone else's output device. Meaning that your project might be the exact color you want on your monitor; however, it may display differently on your friend's monitor. It may also not print the way you want if you send your work to an outsourced print company. If there is a moral to this story, it is that you can control a lot, but you can't control everything!

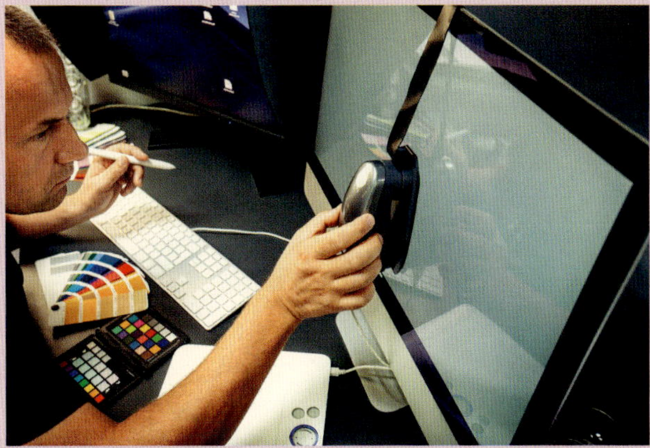

Figure PT3.3 You can purchase equipment to read and help you calibrate the color on your monitor. Avalon_Studio/iStock.com

Working with Color in Illustrator

Illustrator is often dismissed when considering digital artistic rendering due to its graphic nature compared with Photoshop's ability to duplicate traditional painting effects. Although Illustrator is not the best choice for recreating the look of watercolor or oil paints, the graphic quality can be equally rewarding. Try creating a few alternatives of some of your work in both programs to see if one, the other, or both programs in tandem work best for your artistic style.

Project 3.4: Using Fills and Strokes

Step 1: *Open* your Illustrator figure from Chapter 2. Just to keep the visuals interesting, we are using a different model. You will still be able to find this one in the exercise files, though.

Once you have your figure open, use the *Selection* tool (black arrow) to choose one area such as the shirt or skin shapes. With that shape selected, you change the Fill from none to, well, whatever color you like! If you want to change multiple shapes to the same *Fill* color, you can hold *shift* while *clicking* on additional shapes.

Step 2: You can choose *New Swatch Color* from the *Properties* panel or *Swatches* panel, or you may use the *Color Picker* by double-clicking the *Fill* color in the toolbar. If you choose a unique color through the *Color Picker*, you probably want to *Save* it as a swatch so you can easily access the same color again. Now go ahead and start to color all the layers!

You'll notice that we tend to set up the color layers using wacky colors. There is no particular reason for this. It's simply how we started doing it years ago to keep it fun.[3] Then we go back and change them to the correct colors.

Step 3: Once you have selected your colors, you may want to consider changing the *Stroke* colors. In Figure 3.41a, the image is colored with black strokes. This lends itself to a more graphic look. However, you can select a shape and its interior paths, then change the *Stroke* color to a darker version of the same color. This gives a softer look. Compare the two end results. Which style do you like better?

That's it! If you want to make more details, add new shapes or paths to represent those details. If you want to change your colors, go for it. Remember to *Save* your work, though.

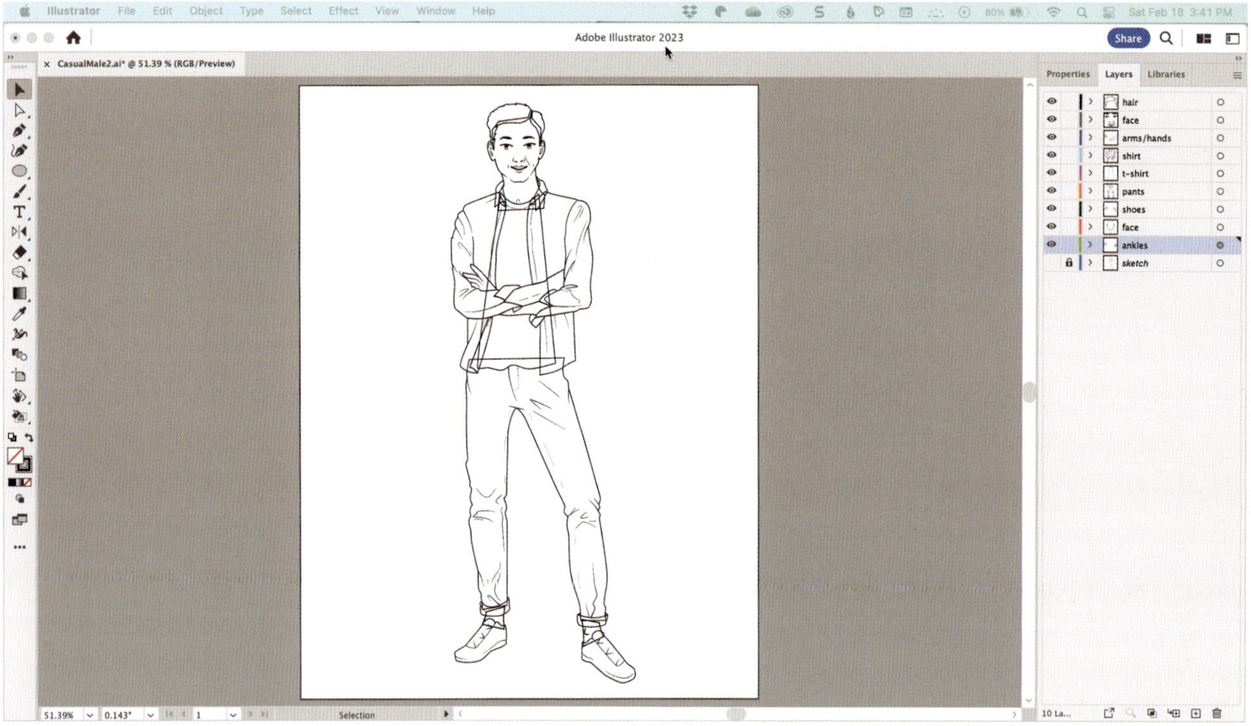

Figure 3.38 This figure is traced with the *Pen* tool in Illustrator, ready for color. There are no *Fills* applied yet, so you can see all the construction lines used to create the shapes.

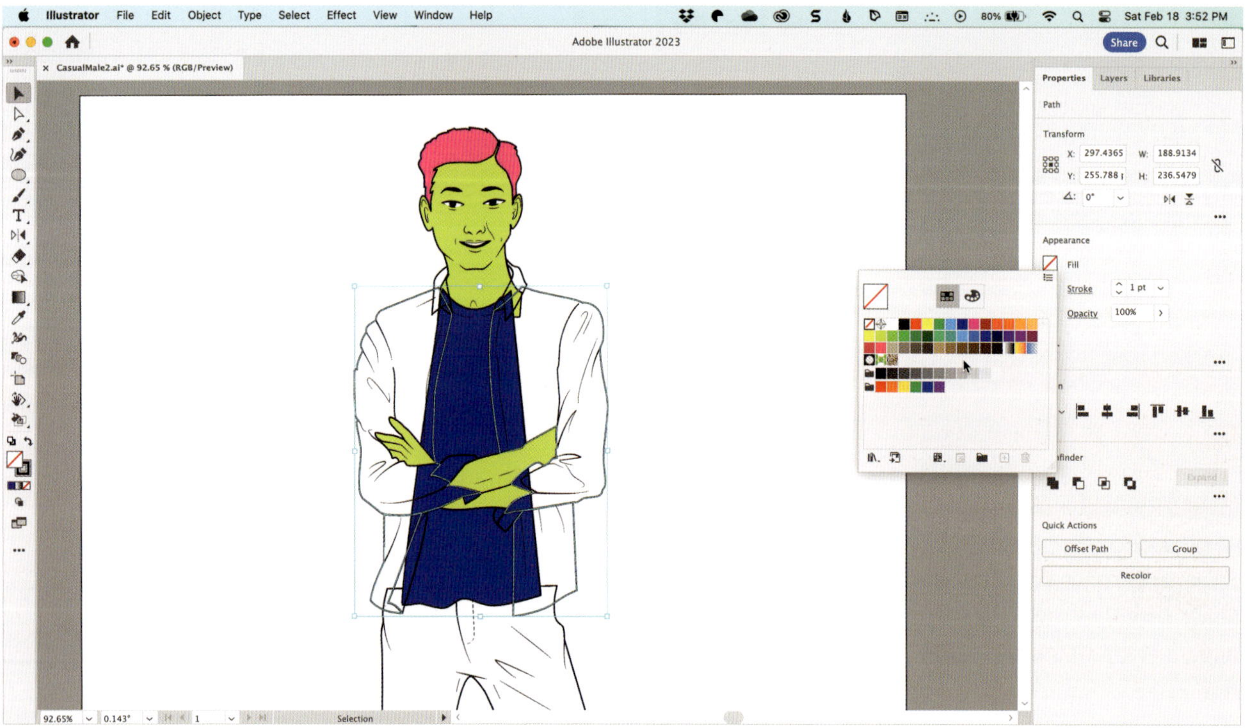

Figure 3.39a The shirt is selected with the *Selection* tool. Because the shirt is several smaller shapes, we hold *shift* while selecting those shapes. In this screenshot, we have already colored the skin, hair, and t-shirt layers.

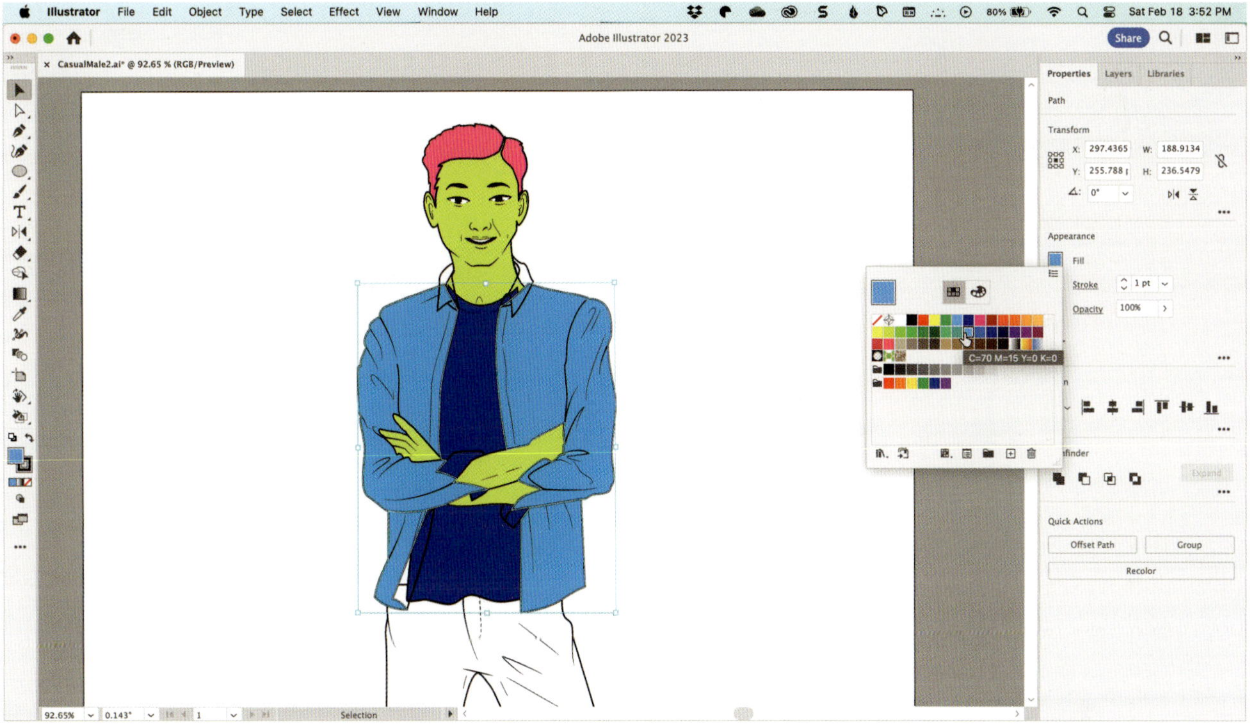

Figure 3.39b With the shirt areas selected, we changed the *Fill* from none to a blue color. If you missed any areas like the collar or cuffs, just select them and individually change the color.

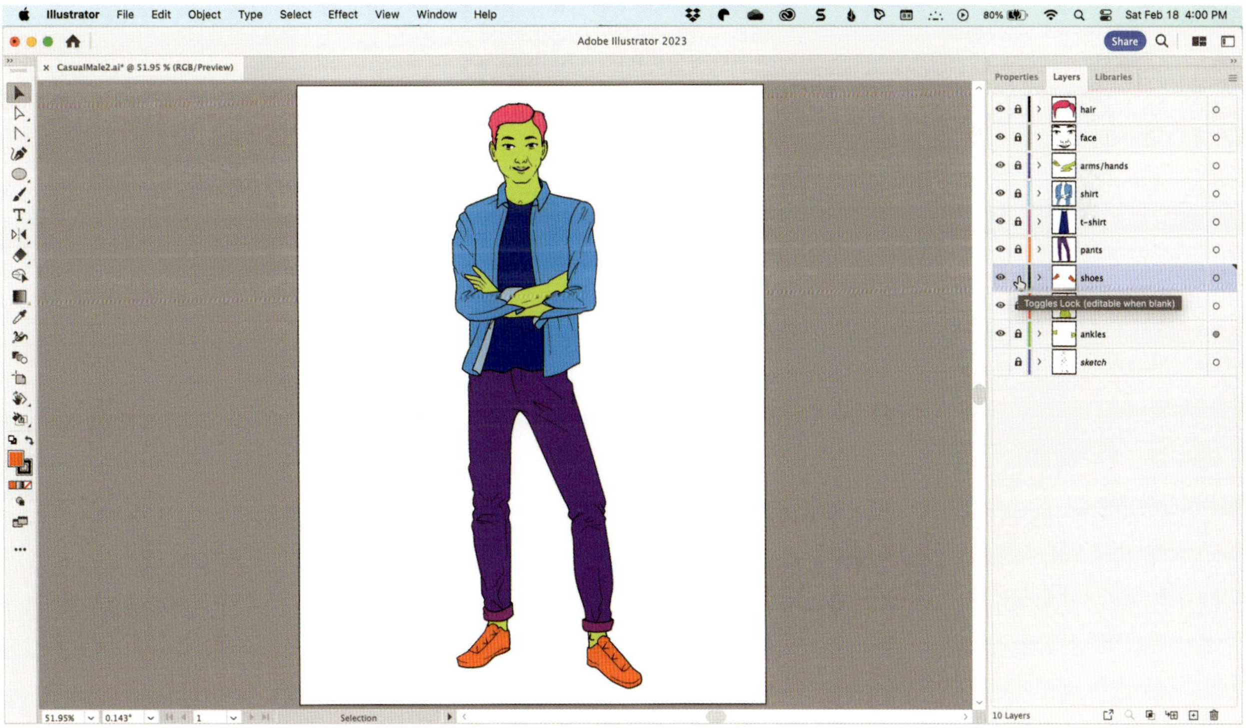

Figure 3.40 Here the image is completely colored. We keep the other layers *Locked* while working on one layer at a time to make selections easier.

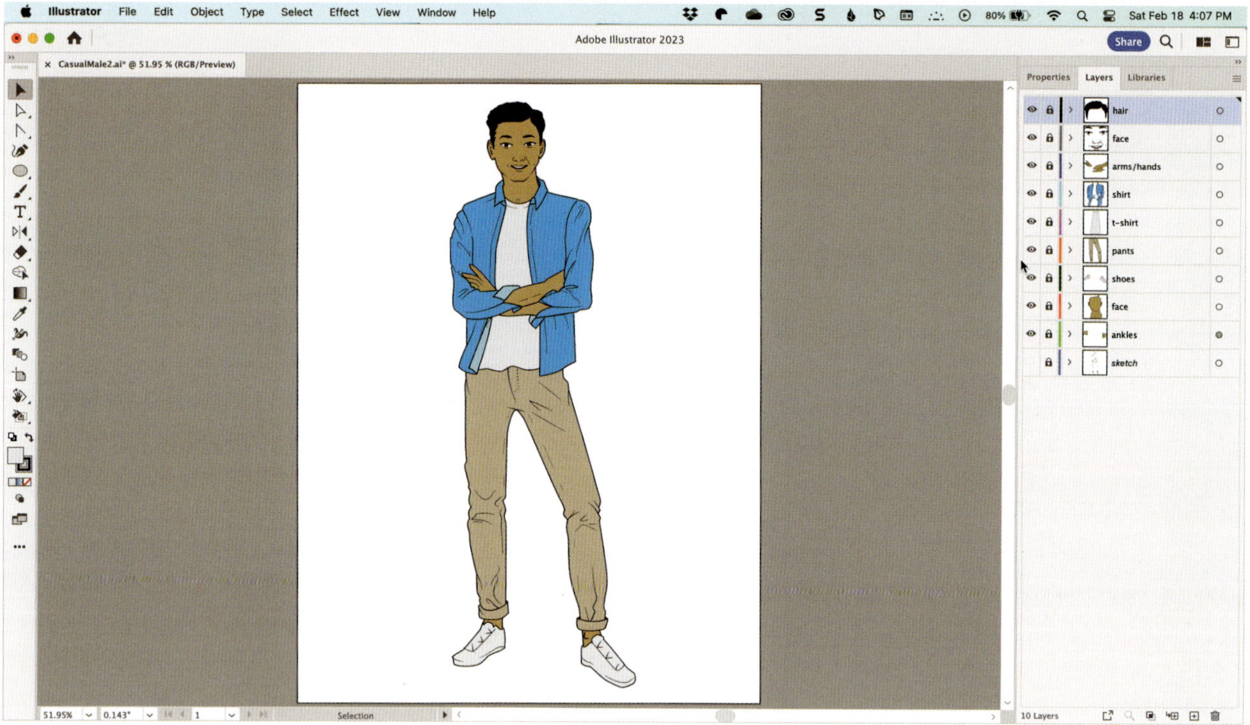

Figure 3.41a Colors changed to a more realistic version. You must admit, it's just not as exciting as the earlier version!

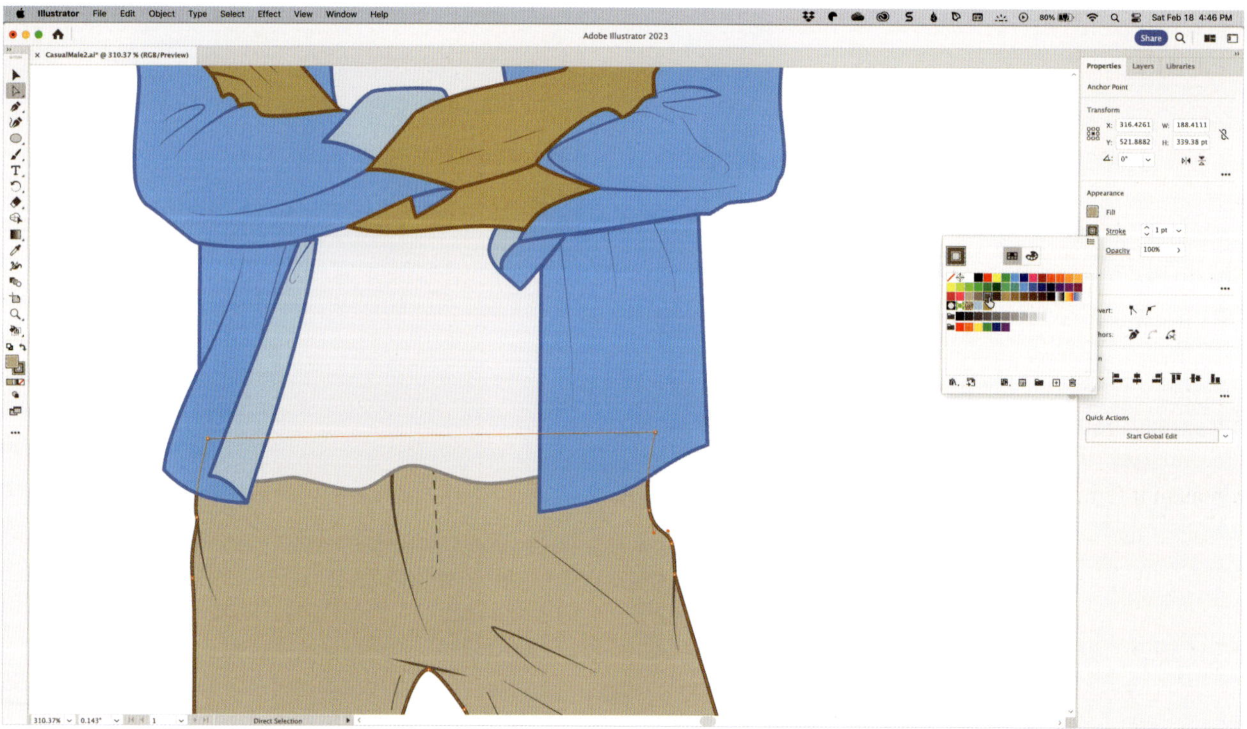

Figure 3.41b *Select* the shape and any interior paths. Change the *Stroke* color through the *Properties* panel to a darker version of the same color.

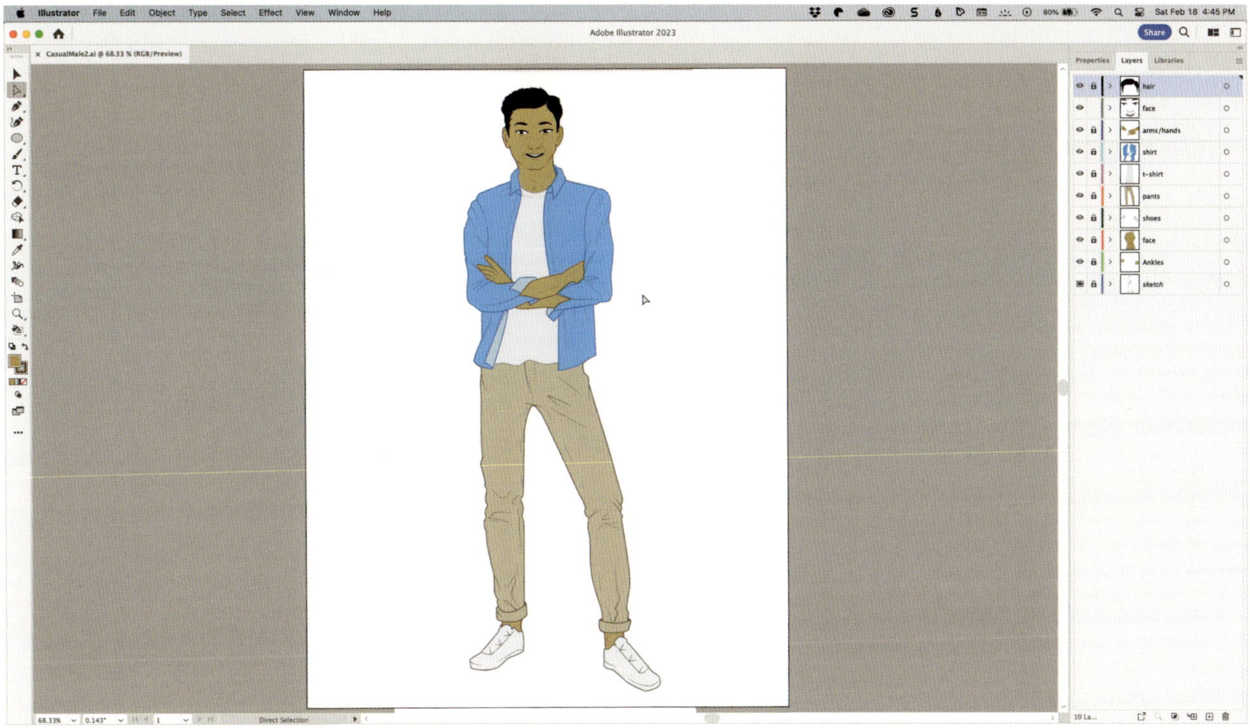

Figure 3.41c Compare this image with stroke colors changed from the original. Which do you prefer?

Project 3.5: Using the Live Paint Feature

The **Live Paint** feature, like *Image Trace*, tends to evoke strong emotions from folks. Some people absolutely love it, whereas others (like the authors) rarely find it useful. We will run through how to use it, regardless. The *Live Paint* feature allows you to add color to an image without creating closed paths with a *Pen* tool. However, there is a reason it tends to be avoided in the fashion industry.

You must have vector artwork to start. However, you don't necessarily need complete shapes for each color variation. You can either use *Image Trace* or use the *Pen* tool to trace the artworks without worrying about closed paths. Exercise file livepaint.ai was produced using *Image Trace*. There are gaps that would cause issues if we tried to fill the shapes normally.

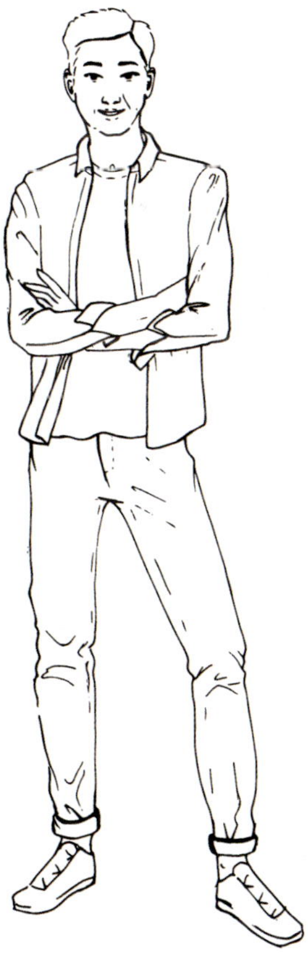

Figure 3.42 This sketch was previously *Image-Traced*. It has a freer line quality that you would not get with a simple *Pen* trace. However, due to the way it is produced, the program does not see the pants, shirt, etc. as closed shapes.

Step 1: To start, select the image. When you use *Image Trace*, the result produces a single object. Therefore, using the *Selection* tool anywhere on the image will select the entire figure. Before you move to the next step, **Expand** the *Image Trace* results. If it is selected, you may find a *Quick Actions* button to *Expand* in the *Properties* panel. *Expanding* a selection will transform it into editable shapes with anchors, paths, and fills. If you don't see it there, look under the *Objects* menu in the top ribbon. There will be a command to *Expand*. Select this to make the image editable. You will be able to click on individual paths and anchors now.

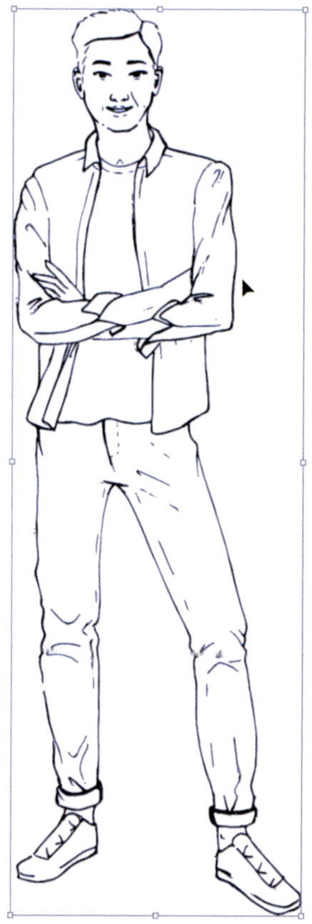

Figure 3.43 Here the figure is selected with the *Selection* tool. Be sure to *Expand* the result. The *Expand* function automatically *Groups* all the paths so one click will capture the entire figure.

Step 2: Look for the *Live Paint Bucket* tool in the toolbar. If you do not see it, don't fret. The *Essentials* workspace does not load all the tools into the toolbar. They have pulled some of the less-frequently used tools and placed them into a separate location. Look at your toolbar. At the base, below the *Fill* and *Stroke* colors and *View* modes, there are three dots (an ellipsis). Click there to open a menu of hidden tools. Look under the paint section to find the *Live Paint Bucket* and *Live Paint Selection* tools. Or you can switch your workspace to *Essentials Classic*, if you prefer. This will also load the full toolbar.

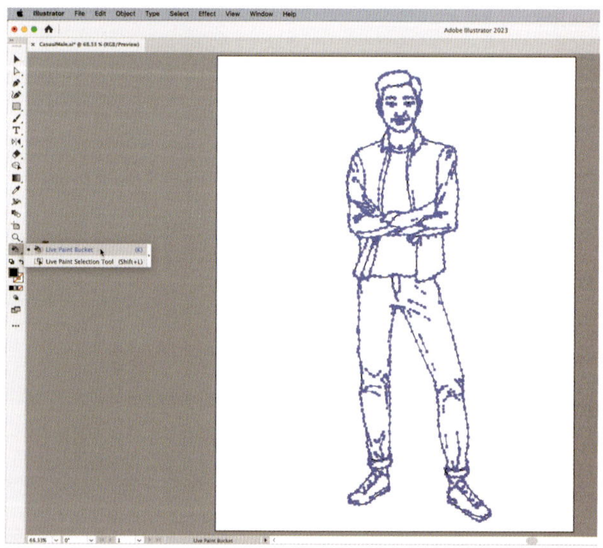

Figure 3.44a Look for the *Live Paint Bucket*. If you don't see it in your toolbar, click on the ellipsis at the bottom of the toolbar to bring it from the hidden menu.

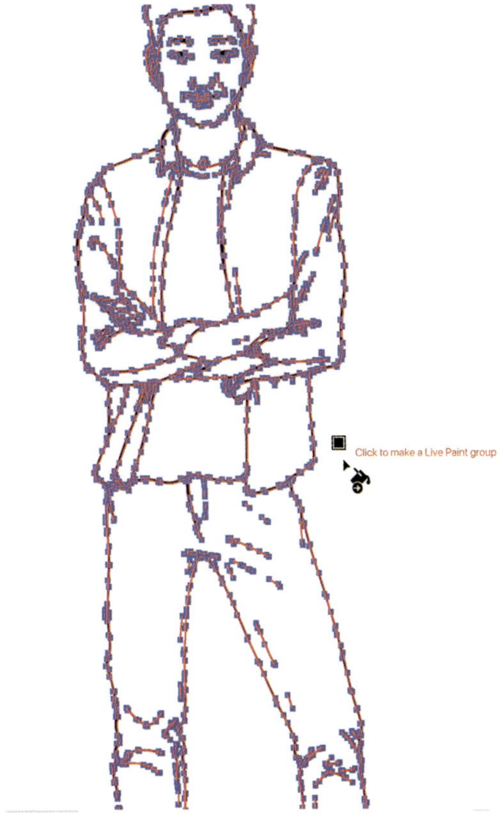

With the *Live Paint Bucket* tool active, click anywhere in the selected image. This will automatically make it a live paint group and start to fill according to where you click. It will start to fill with black color.

Figure 3.44b Once you chose the *Live Paint Bucket* tool, you can click the selected object to make it into a live paint group.

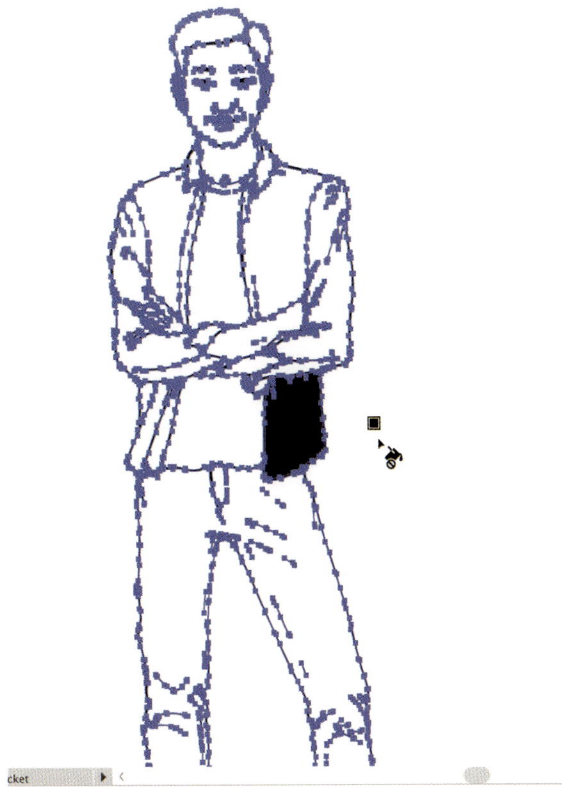

Figure 3.44c Click in an area of the illustration to color it with the *Live Paint Bucket* tool.

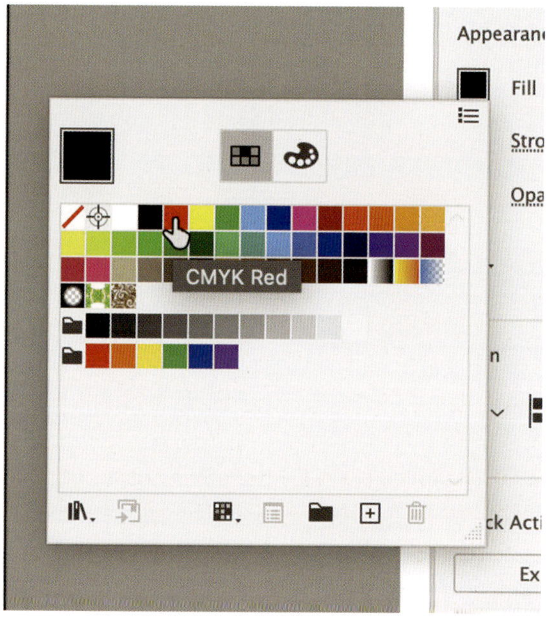

Figure 3.45a Open the *Swatches* panel to choose a new color and activate the color group.

Step 3: To change the color of the fill, open your *Swatches* panel and choose a new swatch. You can also add other color swatches from the *Swatch Library* or create your own color. You will notice that the *Live Paint Bucket* tool looks a little different. Now it shows three tiny swatch colors above the tool. If your cursor does not change, see the explanation in the *Troubleshooting* section.

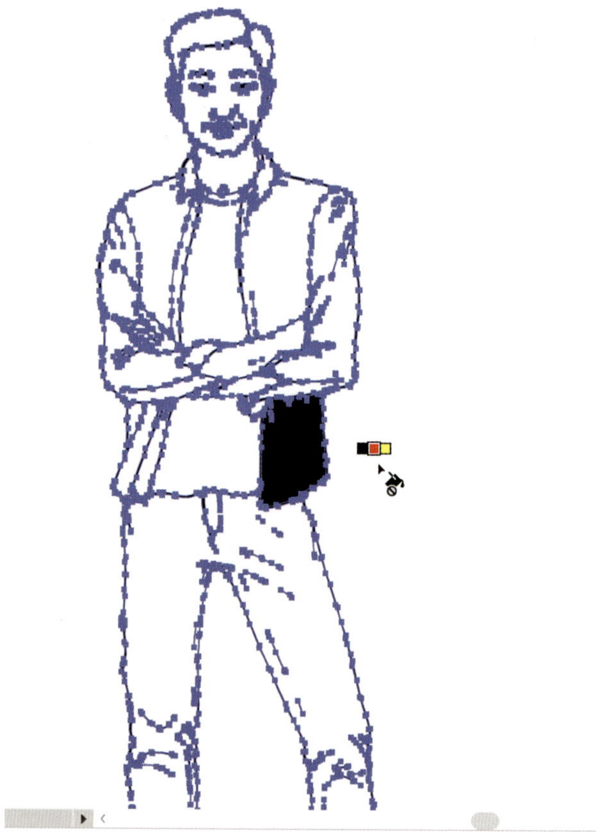

Figure 3.45b After you choose a new color from the *Swatches* panel, notice that the *Live Paint Bucket* shows three colored squares above it. The larger middle swatch is the active color. *Re-click* in the shirt to change it to red.

You can use the *left* and *right arrow* keys on your keyboard to cycle through the colors in your *Swatches* panel. If you want a color that does not show, make sure it is in your *Swatches* panel. The middle, highlighted swatch is the active color. When you click to fill an area, you will see that color appear.

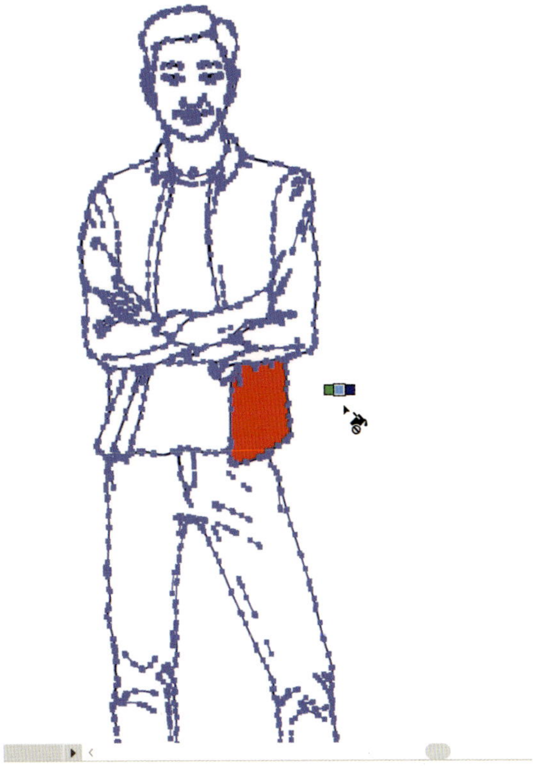

Figure 3.45c You can use the *left* and *right arrow* keys on the keyboard to cycle through the swatches currently in the *Swatches* panel. Remember the middle swatch is the active one and the *Live Paint Bucket* will fill with that color in the next area you click.

Step 4: Go ahead and fill one part of the illustration for practice. Once you are done, use one of the *Selection* tools to click off to the side to *Deselect* the figure. It will help you to see the results. Make sure you did not miss any areas! *Select* the figure again with the *Selection* tool and then pick up your *Live Paint Bucket* to continue filling where necessary.

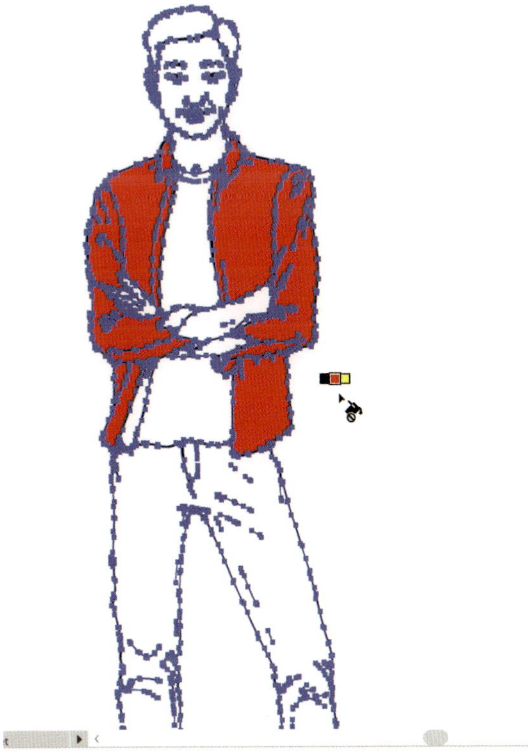

Figure 3.46a Here we have completely colored the overshirt red.

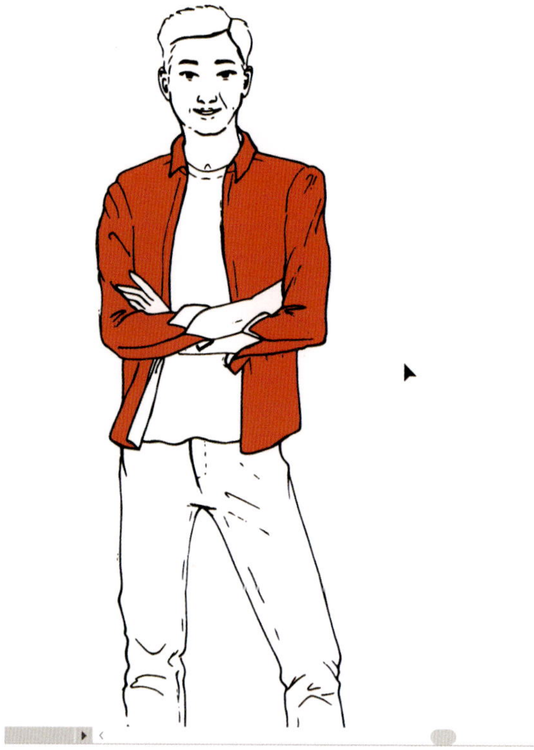

Figure 3.46b Use one of the *Selection* tools and click to the side to *Deselect* the figure. You can see more clearly how the image will appear and if you missed any areas of the shirt.

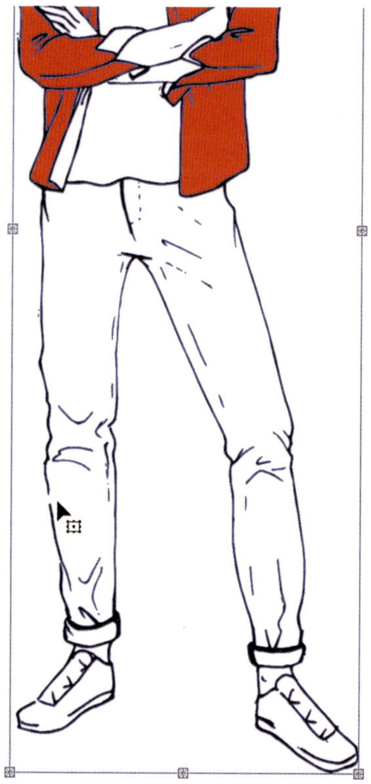

Figure 3.47a Try selecting the pants and filling them with the *Live Paint Bucket* tool. You will notice that it will not fill. This is because there is a large gap in the sketched outline of the pants near the knee.

Step 5: Let's try the pants now to see an issue you may face while using live paint. Notice that the illustration has a rather large gap at the knee of the pants. When we try to fill in the pants with the *Live Paint Bucket*, nothing happens. Earlier we mentioned that you do not need complete shapes for it to fill. So what happened? That gap at the knee is pretty big. Depending on the size of the gap, you have some options.

You may simply use the *Direct Selection* tool to choose one anchor point and drag it up to match the other side of the gap. This solution works well when you can easily see where the gap is located, as in our example. Sometimes you may not be able to see it, though. If that is the case, you can turn on *Gap Detection* through the *Gap Options* menu.

While the illustration is still selected, look in the *Object* menu at the top. Scroll down the menu items until you see *Live Paint* listed. When you hover over those words, you will see another menu open to the side. Look for *Gap Options* and click on it.

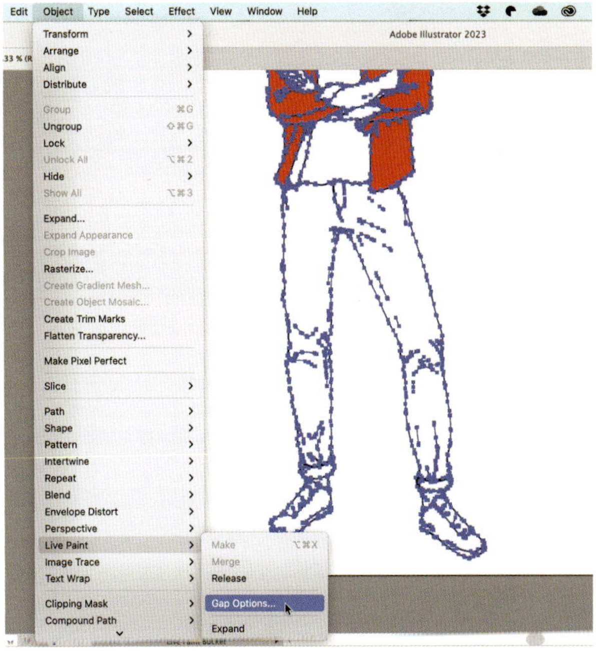

Figure 3.47b One way to deal with the gap in the sketch is to select the *Gap Options* available under the *Live Paint* section of the *Object* menu.

A new dialog box will open. At the top, be sure that *Gap Detection* is ticked on. Immediately below that area will be a drop-down menu for *Paint stops at*. For this illustration, we need to select *Large Gaps*. Before you click *OK*, look at the rest of this menu. It shows the number of *Gaps Found* and offers an option to *Close gaps with paths*. Feel free to try this option. We have had hit-or-miss luck with that option. However, it may improve over time to become more reliable.

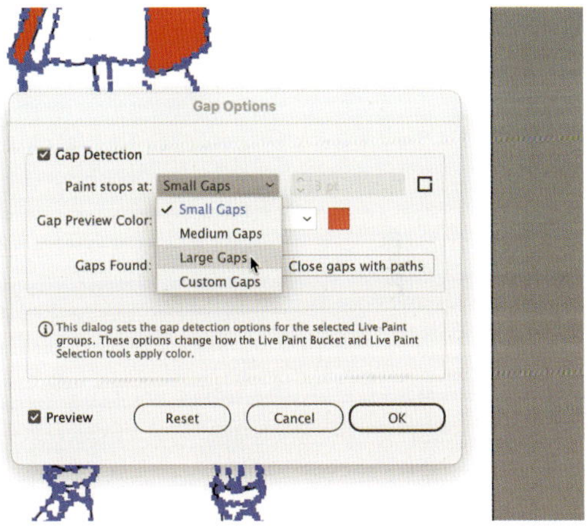

Figure 3.47c A dialog box will appear once you select the *Gap Options*. Make sure that *Gap Detection* is selected and choose *Large Gaps* from the *Paint stops at* menu. Approve the change.

Step 6: Once you select *Large Gaps* for your *Gap Detection*, approve it by clicking *OK*. Then proceed to fill in the pants with the *Live Paint Bucket* tool. You'll notice that it fills in sections. The program cannot distinguish between the perimeter lines and interior lines, so it may close gaps between the illustrated fold lines and the perimeter. Keep *clicking* with the tool until you fill all of the pants. You may need to *Deselect* to check that you caught all the small areas.

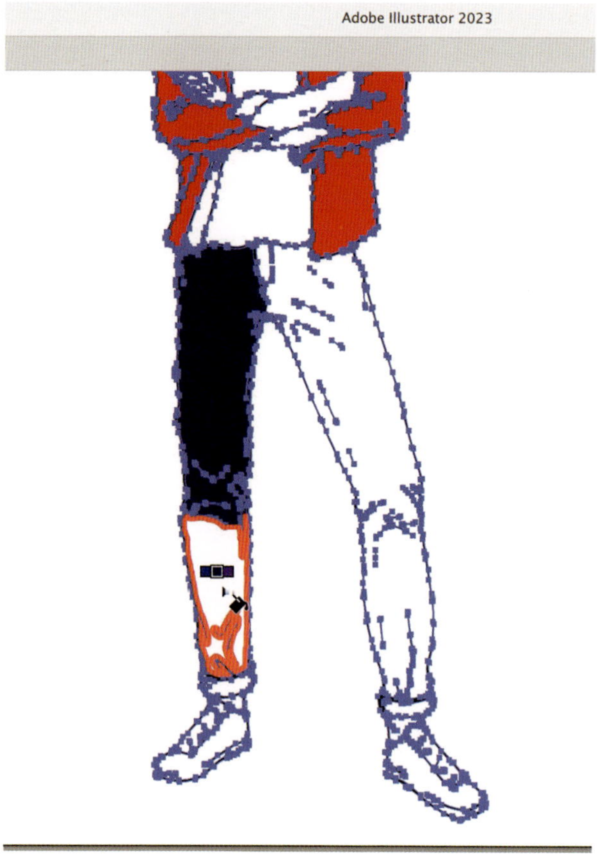

Figure 3.47d Now you can fill in the pants with the *Live Paint Bucket*. Be sure to get all of the sections.

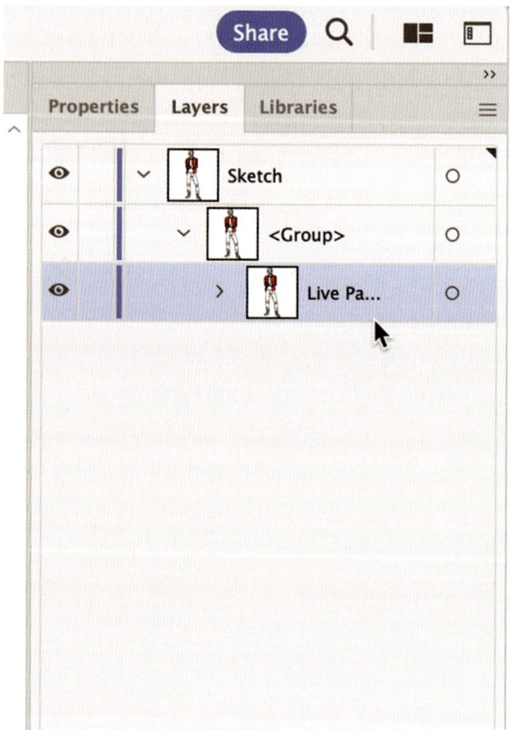

Figure 3.48 One major drawback of using *Live Paint* is that the program *Groups* everything onto one layer. Evaluate if this may or may not be an issue for you.

Step 7: You can continue to fill in the rest of the illustration until you have it all colored. Take a look in the *Layers* panel at some point of the process. You will notice that everything occurs on one layer. In that layer, you will see the image-traced group, followed by the live paint group. It is harder to distinguish which item is which when using the *Live Paint* feature. If this is not an issue for you, then great! Go to town with this function. We find it problematic for keeping the work organized and for adding details such as colored paths. You must drill down into the layer to find what you want to change which often takes time and proves frustrating.

With that said, every illustrator works differently and has different end goals. Do what works best for you.

Project 3.6: Change and Save Colors in Ai

Step 1: Changing colors in Illustrator is very easy. Simply select the object and choose a new *Fill* and *Stroke* color. With the *Live Paint* feature, use the *Live Paint Bucket* to fill with a new color. Note that with a live paint group, selecting the object and choosing a new *Fill* through the *Properties* panel rarely works properly. Often, your line work is viewed as fills, so you end up blanking out the whole illustration. Stick with the *Live Paint Bucket* to recolor if you have a live paint group.

Step 2: If you do not see a swatch that meets your color needs, try loading another library. In the *Swatches* panel, look for the small icon of books. *Click* this and choose a category that piques your interest. Here you can open a pop-up dialog box with other swatches. *Drag* them over to your main *Swatch* panel to access the same color repeatedly.

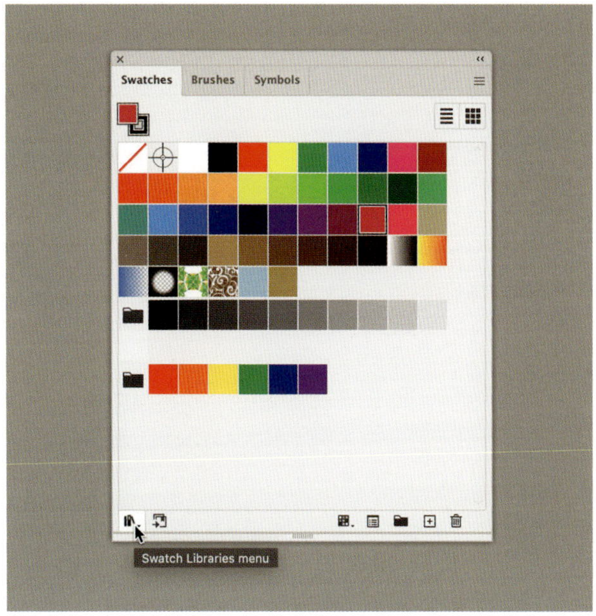

Figure 3.49 In the *Swatches* panel, you can choose new swatch *Fills* or *Strokes*. If you need more options, try opening the *Swatch Libraries* menu.

PRO TIP 3.6

Adobe Color and Other Resources

If you have reached the point of this book when your eyes are glazing over and your forehead has an imprint of a keyboard, take a break and visit color.adobe.com! Even if you don't use other Adobe products, this is a fun website to play with color harmonies. Play around with your anchor color, then choose different options to see what you get with analogous, complementary, or other harmonies. You can also analyze images to extract a theme or gradient or use the accessibility checker. This last feature is extremely helpful for the next time you need to make a visual presentation. Add your background and text colors to see if you pass the contrast and color blindness check! If you have an Adobe ID, you can create and save themes to help with your next project.

Some other fun color resources include plugins such as Coolorus, Mixoos, or Palettator. Do a general internet search for color plugins for the software you prefer. Artist-developers are at work and coming up with fun new additions on a regular basis. You never know what you will find! Remember to do a little research and check out the customer reviews to see if it's the right tool for you, though.

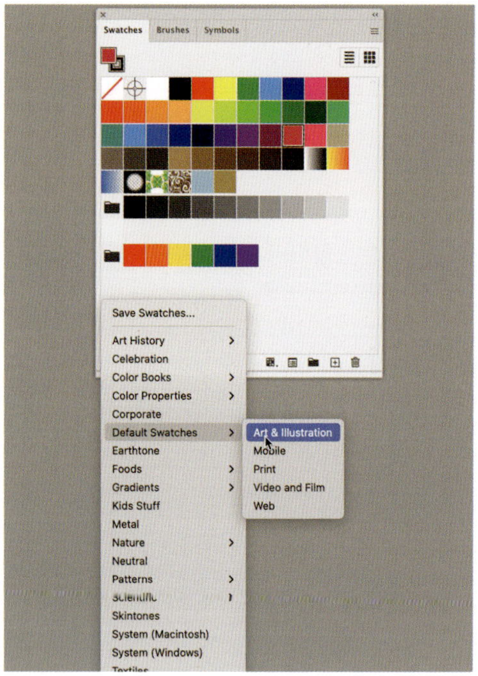

Figure 3.50a To add more swatch colors, chose the book icon in the lower left corner to open the *Swatch Libraries*. Choose a library you would like to explore.

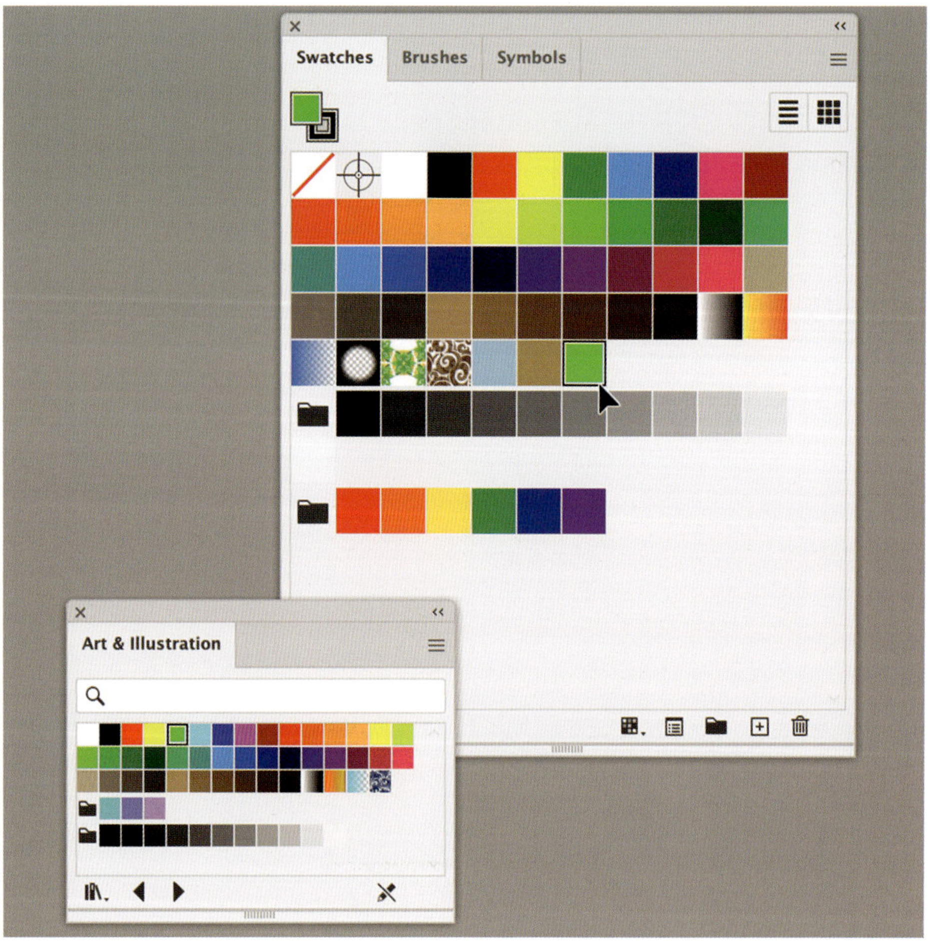

Figure 3.50b When the fresh library option appears, simply *drag* any colors you like to the main *Swatch* panel. You can then *Close* the extra library.

Step 3: Likewise, you can *double-click* on the color to open the *Color Picker* dialog box. Tweak your color as much as needed and close the box. Before you do anything else, *drag* the swatch into the *Swatch* panel or click the *plus* (+) icon to save it with the current file.

When working with color swatches in Illustrator, there are a few options you should be aware of. *Double-click* one of the swatches (any one is fine). A pop-up dialog box appears. Notice that you can rename the swatch and change the color here. You can also put in specific colors according to the color mode. So, if your boss gave you a hex code, just put that code into the # field toward the bottom of the box. Or perhaps they shared a specific CMYK number. Change the *Color Mode* to *CMYK* and adjust the numbers as needed.

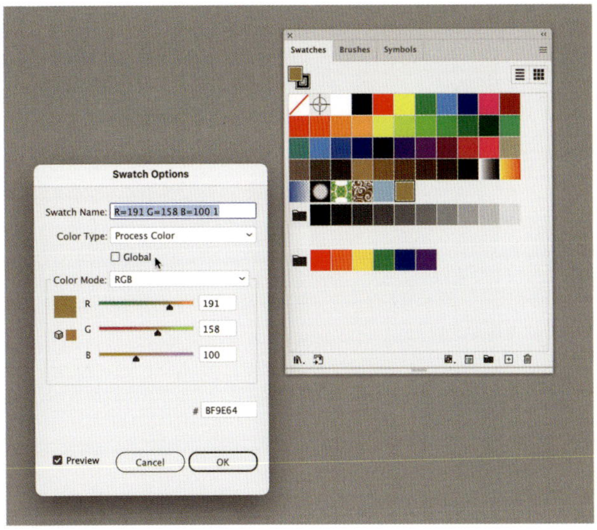

Figure 3.51 *Double-click* a swatch to open the *Swatch Options* dialog box. Here, you can rename a color, tweak the color, or change it to a global color.

You will also notice a check box for **Global Color**. This is a useful option for any color swatch. When part of your artwork is colored with a *Global Color* swatch, you can open the swatch to change it and it will automatically adjust all items colored with that global color swatch. When you color something with a swatch not designated as a global color, you will need to individually change the fill of those items. A *Global Color* swatch is indicated by a white triangle in the lower right corner of the swatch in the menu.

Step 4: If you have a set of colors that need to be accessible for multiple documents, you will need to *Save* your colors in a *Swatch Library*. We recommend clearing any unnecessary colors by *deleting* them from your *Swatch* menu. These are usually the default swatches. There is no reason to save them as they are already in the default color library. Then *click* the first swatch you want to save, hold the *Shift* key and *click* the last swatch to have them all selected. In the *Options* menu at the upper right corner of your *Swatches* panel, you can choose to *Save Swatch Library as AI*.

Alternatively, you can choose the same option through the *Swatch Library* menu at the lower left corner of the panel. Navigate to an easily accessible location and name it something recognizable. You can add it to the default location or put it into a cloud location that is more universally accessible. The default location makes it easy to find if you only work on one device. However, if you find yourself frequently accessing your work from other devices, you may want to put it into a cloud location you can access wherever you have internet access. When you need to load those colors for another project file, simply navigate to the *Swatch Libra* location through your *Load Swatches* option of the *Swatch* panel.

It is also good practice to save your colors to your Adobe library. We have mentioned libraries before and how useful they can be. If you are logged in with your Adobe ID and have access to the internet, you will be able to access any colors, styles, or other assets through your *Libraries* panel. You can also share assets with team members when you have collaborative projects. Simply share the *Library* folder with their Adobe ID.

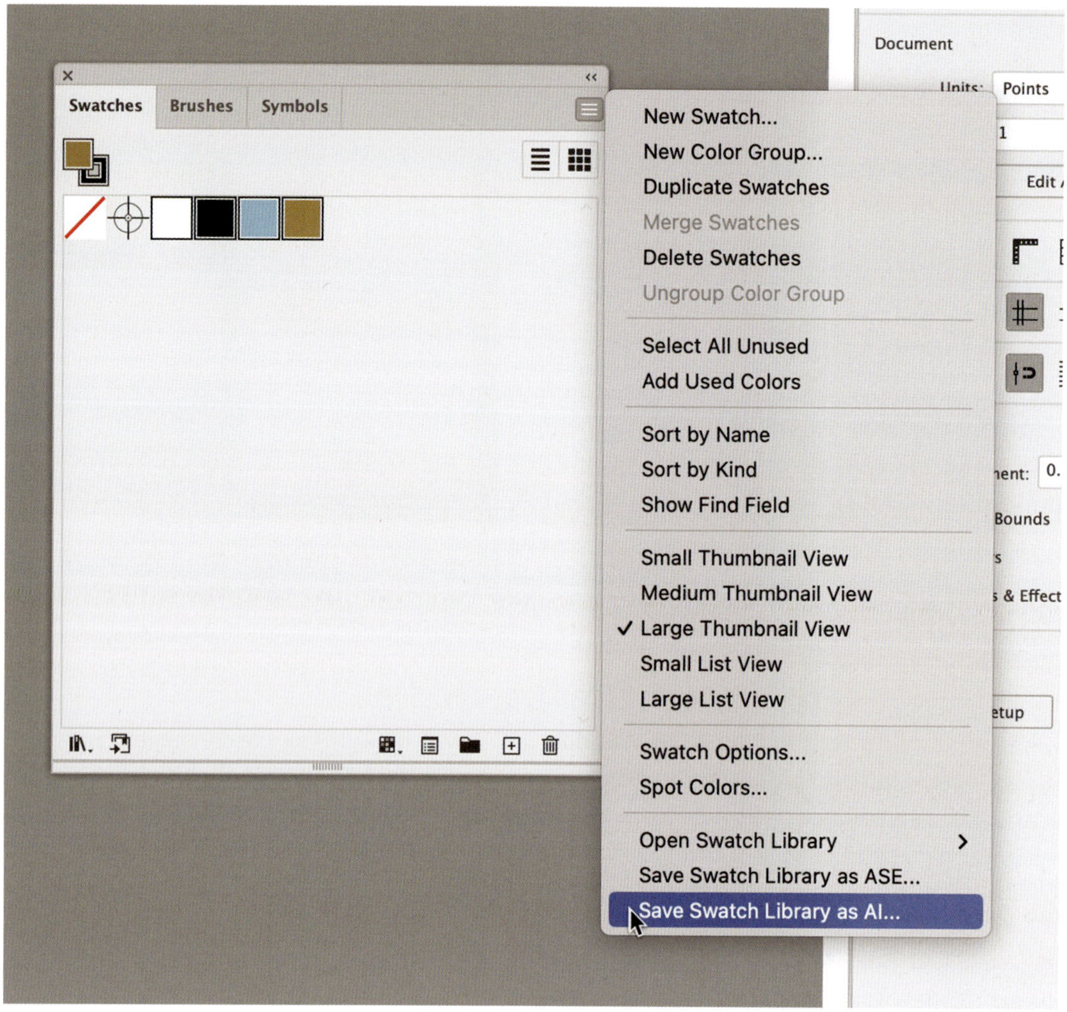

Figure 3.52 To save colors for use with other projects, first reduce the clutter and *delete* any unused swatches. Then *select* the swatches you would like to save and access the swatch *Options* through the upper right-hand corner menu or the *Libraries* menu in the lower left.

Troubleshooting

"I can't get the color to change."

While changing colors may seem fool-proof, you may run into the issue of the color just won't change for you. First, check that the object is fully selected. It should have a highlight color of the layer running through the paths and anchors. It will also have a selection box of the same color around it.

If you have the object selected and still are not able to change the color, look at the *Fill* and *Stroke* boxes. Which is in front? You may be inadvertently changing the color of the *Stroke* instead of the *Fill*.

"I just opened a project and there are no swatches to pick from in the *Swatches* panel."

Should you open a new project and go to the *Swatches* panel only to see black, white, and no fill available, do not

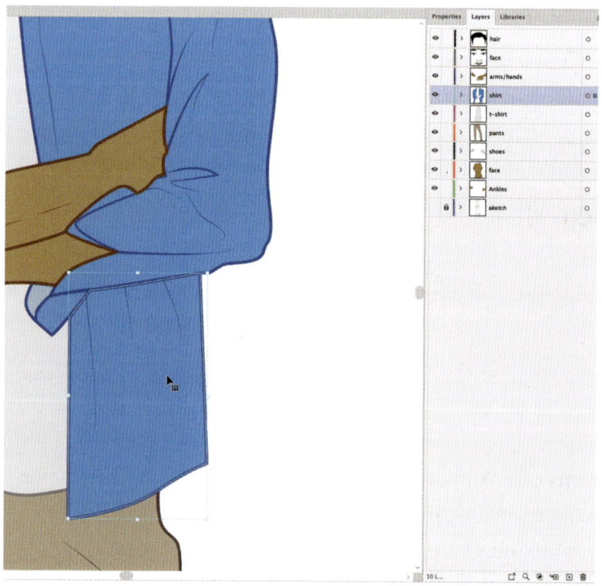

Figure 3.53 Make sure the object is selected when changing colors. You will see it highlighted with the layer color.

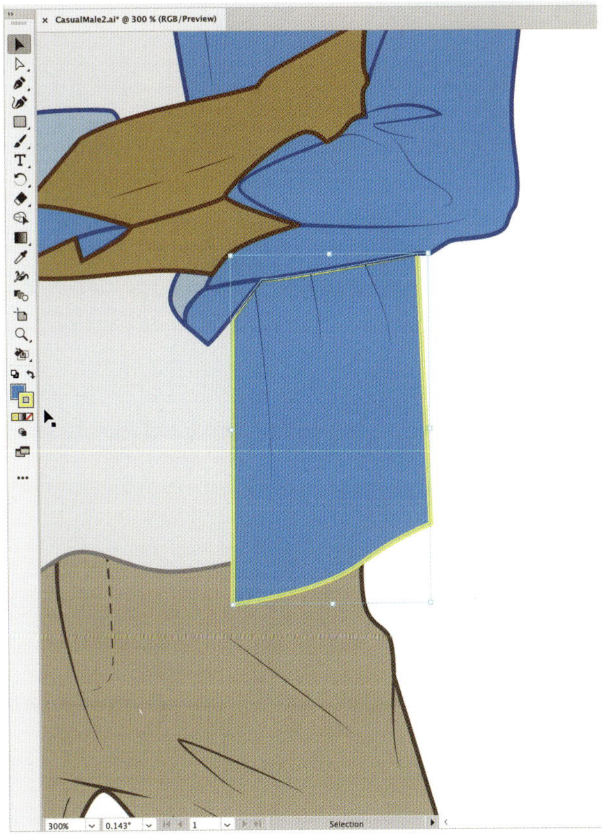

Figure 3.54 Look to make sure you have the *Fill* selected rather than the *Stroke* when changing the color.

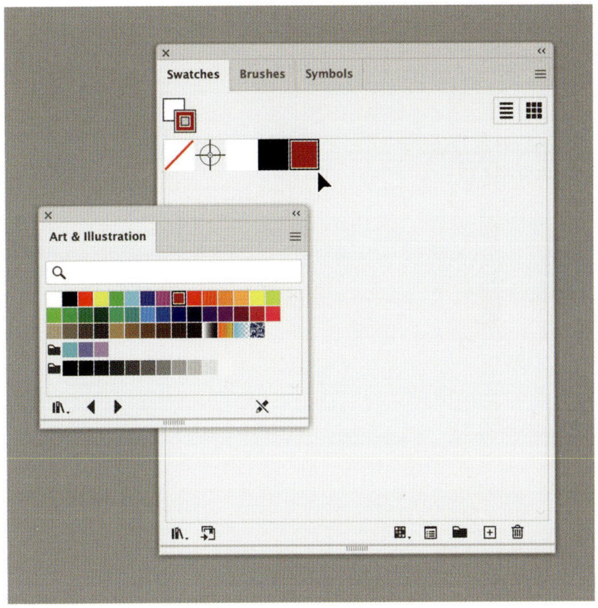

Figure 3.55 If you have minimal swatch colors available for a project, simply open up a *Swatch Library* and *drag* some colors into the main panel.

worry. This sometimes occurs if the file you are opening registers as a black and white image. Simply open one of the *Swatch Libraries* and *drag* some colors into the main *Swatch* panel.

"I can't get *Live Paint* to work."

We described the most common problems of this tool in the Live Paint section. Remember to have the object selected before trying to fill with the *Live Paint Bucket*. If you find that it still will not fill with color, check for gaps in the artwork.

"My *Live Paint* cursor doesn't show three squares."

We mentioned that the *Live Paint* cursor changes from a bucket with a single swatch to a bucket with three swatches when you choose a swatch color. While it isn't the end of the world if your cursor doesn't change, it can be confusing and frustrating. The secret is that you have to choose a color from the official *Swatches panel* to trigger the change. If you choose a color from the toolbar swatch or from a library swatch panel (one that you opened manually), the cursor will not change.

Summary

In the world of digital illustration, you have many options to colorize your work. Consider first if you plan to work mostly in an application like Photoshop or Illustrator. Is your artwork already colored before you scanned it in? Then stick with a program like Photoshop to adjust your contrast and color corrections. *Adjustment Layers* are your best friend in this case. You can also scan in your sketch work and color the layers below the illustration. The top drawing layer should be set to the *Blend Mode* of *Multiply*. Separate your layers according to what makes sense to you and your project.

Paint each item a flat color to prepare your work for future chapters. Remember that the layer beneath will be covered by whatever is above it and paint accordingly.

For artwork in Illustrator, all you need to do is to select each shape and change the fill color. It's that easy! If you prefer *Image Trace* for your linework, you may be better served by the *Live Paint* option, though. Consider what works best for your workflow and end product. Onward to patterns!

STUDIO Companion Videos for Chapter 3

Please refer to STUDIO for accompanying chapter video(s).

Keywords

Adobe libraries
Background color
Clipping mask
CMYK
Color calibration
Color gamut
Contiguous
Expand
Feather
Flow
Foreground color
Glazing
Global color
Hue/saturation adjustment layer
LAB
Layer mask
Layer-color mapping
Libraries
Live Paint
Opacity
RGB
Value-mapping

Review Questions

1. What is the value of keeping your color groups on separate layers? Provide and explain at least three reasons.
2. What are the pros and cons of an *RGB* color space?
3. What are the pros and cons of a *CMYK* color space?
4. What is the difference between *Foreground* and *Background* color in Photoshop?
5. What is an important step to remember after you paint the perimeter of a shape and use the *Paint Bucket* to fill it in?
6. What is the difference between *Filling* a closed path and using the *Live Paint* tool?
7. What are the advantages to keeping your colors stored in a Library?

Commands Introduced

- Brush tool
- Canvas Size
- Clipping mask
- Color Mode
- Curves Adjustment Layer
- Expand
- Gap Options
- Hue/Saturation adjustment layer
- Layer mask
- Layer Opacity
- Layer Visibility
- Live Paint Bucket
- Object Selection tool
- Paint Bucket tool
- Select and Mask
- Swatch Libraries
- Swatches panel
- Transform

Keyboard Shortcuts

- Ps: *i* (Eyedropper tool)
- Ps: While in coloring tool, hold *Alt* or *Option* to temporarily switch to the Eyedropper tool

Discussion Questions

1. Is it better to color your artwork through analog or digital means? Explain your opinion.
2. Do you find that you like Illustrator or Photoshop more at this point? Why?
3. When in Illustrator, do you prefer to trace with the *Pen* tool to make shapes and use the fill to color it, or to use the *Image Trace* with *Live Paint*? Explain your preference.
4. Even if you prefer to color by hand, how can it be advantageous to translate your work to a digital medium? Think about some possible scenarios.

Practice Exercises

1. Use your own artwork to color. Complete at least three figures with three different colorization methods.
2. In Photoshop, open the digital rendering of an artist you admire. Color sample around the image using the Eyedropper tool. Take note of the color combinations used and save any you like as swatches.
3. Start a library of your most commonly used colors for garment renderings.

Endnotes

1. See the Extend Your Learning appendix for more. The hue spectrum is based on a circle (360°). The formula places whichever color you currently have at 0° against the spectrum, which is the position for red hues. For example, if you start with a green hue, it will position it against the red. To turn your green hue to a red color, you will need to move the slider to the left at –120°, around the orange hues on the scale. It is very counterintuitive to beginners. However, with time and training, it will make sense and you can control the outcome with more precision.
2. Paper color is the "old school" name for *Background* color because it was introduced as a system of paper versus drawing tool. Many times the *Background* color does not have any bearing on your actions within the program. However, if you *Erase* to the background, as opposed to erasing to transparency, the selected *Background* color will show. It is also used for certain filters that require two chosen colors or brushes that *Jitter* the color.
3. Actually, this method is helpful to keep students from getting hung up on the "perfect" color and wasting time. That and it is highly entertaining!

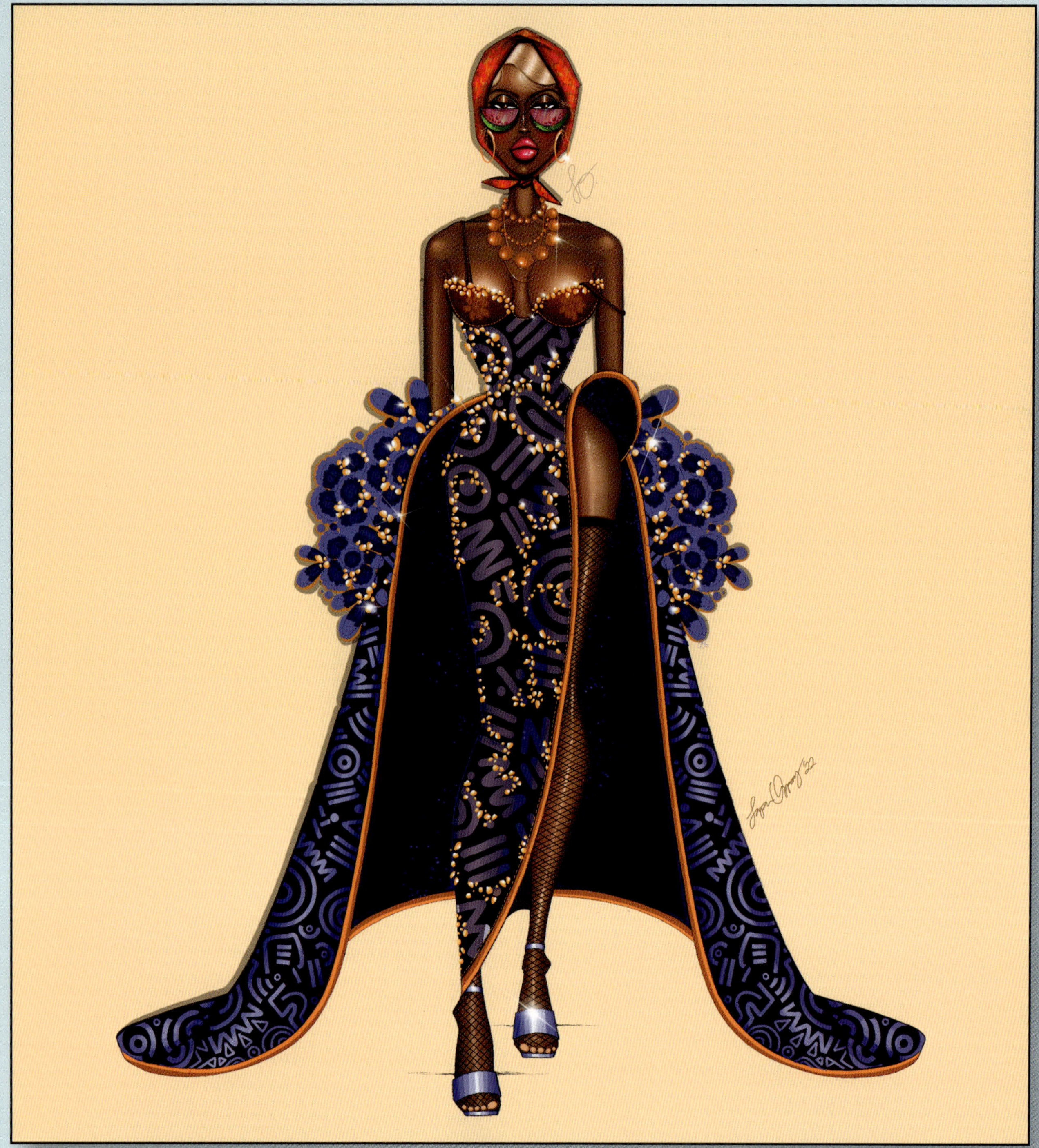

Figure 4.1 Including patterns can amplify any illustration. "Showgirl: Look 3" artwork by Papa Oppong. 2022. Made with Procreate for iPad.

CHAPTER 4
Using and Making Repeating Prints

Learning Objectives

After completing this chapter, you should be able to

- Recognize a repeat
- Create and use your own print in Photoshop
- Manipulate your prints in Photoshop
- Create and use your own print in Illustrator
- Manipulate your prints in Illustrator
- Alter a scanned or photographed print to use as a repeating pattern

Once you add color, you will want to show the surface pattern of your fabrics. Creating a digital repeating pattern is easy enough once you have practiced a few times. Illustrator and Photoshop have similar features when creating prints, but through slightly different routes. And while creating your own repeating pattern is fun, you will probably need to use existing fabric prints for some designs. We will cover it all in this chapter.

The Importance of Showing Your Prints

Color communicates a world of important information. However, it is equally important to properly display any intended prints or visual surface design on your fabrics. A fabric pattern can completely change the look of a design. Prints can help a design stand out from the crowd or camouflage into the background. Regardless of fashion or costume industries, repetitive patterns are essential to design, and consequently, essential to design communication.

Recognizing a Repeat

Before working with repeating patterns, you need to be able to recognize and determine the repeat. A **repeat tile** means that you have the same motif, in the same color and the same orientation, in all four corners of a rectangle. If any detail is different in one of the corners, it is not a true repeat tile. Figure 4.2a shows the repeat tile in the correct position to make a consistent repeat. The repeat tile in Figure 4.2b is incorrectly positioned for a consistent repeat.

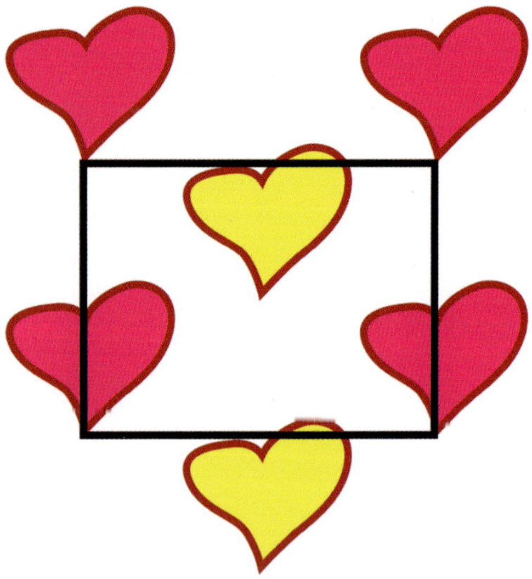

Figure 4.2a Basic repeat. The black rectangle indicates the repeat for this pattern. It goes from dark heart tip to dark heart tip for all four corners. The dark heart will re-form when the patterns are tiled horizontally. The light hearts are split across the top and bottom of the tile and will re-form when the pattern is tiled vertically.

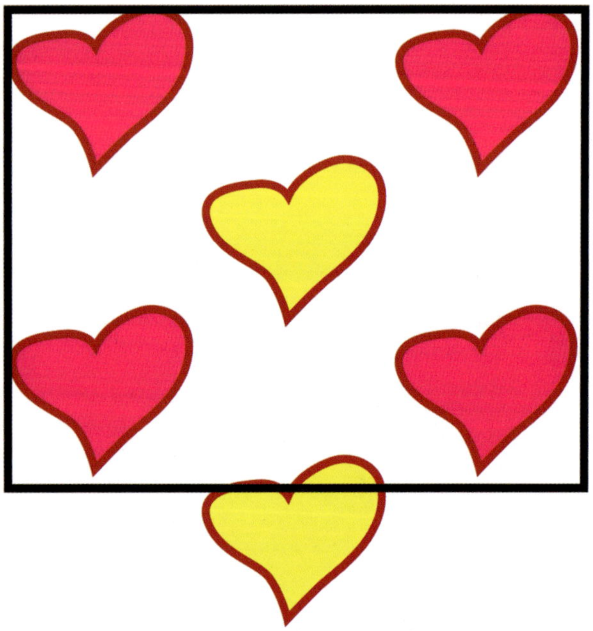

Figure 4.2b Incorrect pattern repeat. In this example, the black rectangle indicates a repeat that is not correct. If tiled, the dark hearts would be too close to each other and the light heart at the bottom of the tile would never have the rest of its shape.

Using Patterns in Ps

Let's start by creating some of your own simple print designs in Photoshop. You can begin with a simple shape and turn it into a repeat. Then we will try something more deliberate like stripes and plaids.

Project 4.1: Creating Patterns in Ps

Print 1: *Open* the exercise file CatTile.jpg. This has already been cropped to a single repeat, so it is ready to turn into a pattern. Go to the *Edit* menu and click on *Define Pattern* as can be seen in Figure 4.3. This will bring a pop-up window in which you get to name your pattern. After you name the pattern and click *OK*, the pattern is saved in the Ps pattern library. This means that you can access the pattern from any function that allows the use of patterns, but only on your specific device.

Print 2: Let's try for a simple stripe next. *Open* a new document in a comfortable size, such as 8.5" × 11" or A4. Turn on the **grid** using the *View menu → Show → Grid*. This is a non-printing tool to assist you with alignment.[1] You may need to adjust your grid before you make your stripe, though. Open the *Preferences* dialog box. In Windows, this can be found under the *Edit menu → Preferences → General*. On a Mac, look in the *Photoshop menu → Settings → General*. You can also use the shortcut keys *control+k/command+k*. On the left side of the dialog box, choose *Guides, Grid & Slices*. The dialog box should look like Figure 4.4. You will see that you can manually adjust your grid. Ours is set to a guideline every 1 inch with 16 subdivisions as seen in Figure 4.5. For stripes, we like to have smaller subdivisions to make smaller stripes. You may choose to work in metric or pixels with a slightly different division. It is entirely up to you.

The nifty part of a stripe is that you only need a narrow strip to create the repeat. Open a new layer above your background (just to keep it tidy) and make sure you are working on that new layer. To create a vertical stripe, draw out a *Selection Marquee* that is about 4 grids high by 16 grids wide anywhere on the page (or whatever comes out to about ¼" × 1"). Fill it with any flat color you like for the main color using the *Paint Bucket* tool. Now draw a new *Marquee* (on the same layer) that is the same height but not as wide to create a stripe. Fill this with another color using the *Paint Bucket* tool. You can stop there or make a few more stripes depending upon your design. Our design can be seen in Figure 4.6.

You are ready to make the pattern. *Marquee* select around the pattern. Your marquee should snap to your fills so long as you have the *Snap* feature turned on through the *View* menu. With the entire thing selected, go to *Edit → Define Pattern*. A new dialog box will appear, and you can name your print however you like!

Print 3: You can use a similar technique to create a plaid next. On a new layer, draw out a square selection (1" × 1" in my case). Fill this with your main color. Create stripes in the vertical direction such as seen in Figure 4.7a. Once you are happy, copy the entire layer by dragging the current layer to the plus icon at the bottom of the *Layers* panel. Use *control+t/command+t* to bring up the *Free Transform* tool. *Right-click* and choose *Rotate 90° Clockwise* or *Counterclockwise* (either direction is fine) as demonstrated in Figure 4.7b. Now change your *Opacity* for the top layer to 50%. You have your first plaid! Select the whole square to define it as a pattern through the *Edit* menu again. See Figure 4.7c for the new plaid.

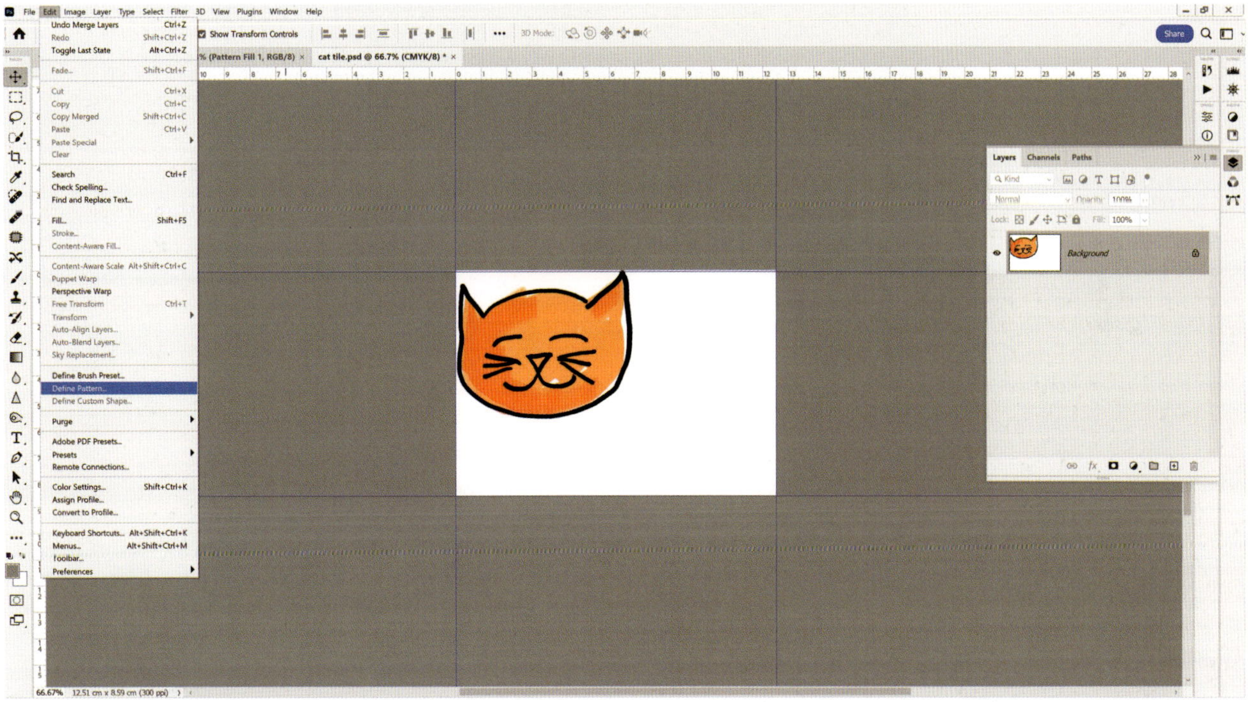

Figure 4.3 Screenshot of creating a pattern in Photoshop. The pattern image has been cropped down to precisely one repeat tile. The correct layer is selected or all layers have been flattened. We are in the *Move* tool in order to not trigger another function. Go to *Edit → Define Pattern*. The software will ask you to name your new pattern.

PRO TIP 4.1

Make a Texture into a Pattern!

This technique works well with prints as well as textured fabrics such as bouclé, corduroy, or chunky knits. Use the same techniques just described for prints but using a textured fabric instead. Apply any distorting, cropping, and color corrections needed, then offset the image to see how it repeats. You will probably see a noticeable line in the offset. Use your *Lasso* selection tool to select the visible line area and go to *Edit → Fill*. Choose *Content Aware* from the drop-down menu in the dialog box.

Try turning a few different fabrics such as the fabric shown in Figure PT4.1 into repeat patterns for your drawing application. Keep these saved in a library for use as you progress with your rendering skills. Consider whether you would rather free-hand sketch the pattern or texture or turn an existing source into a usable repeat pattern.

Figure PT4.1 You can use textured fabrics for your rendering like prints. Check how it repeats with the *Offset* filter. *Content Aware Fill* works well to correct most textures.

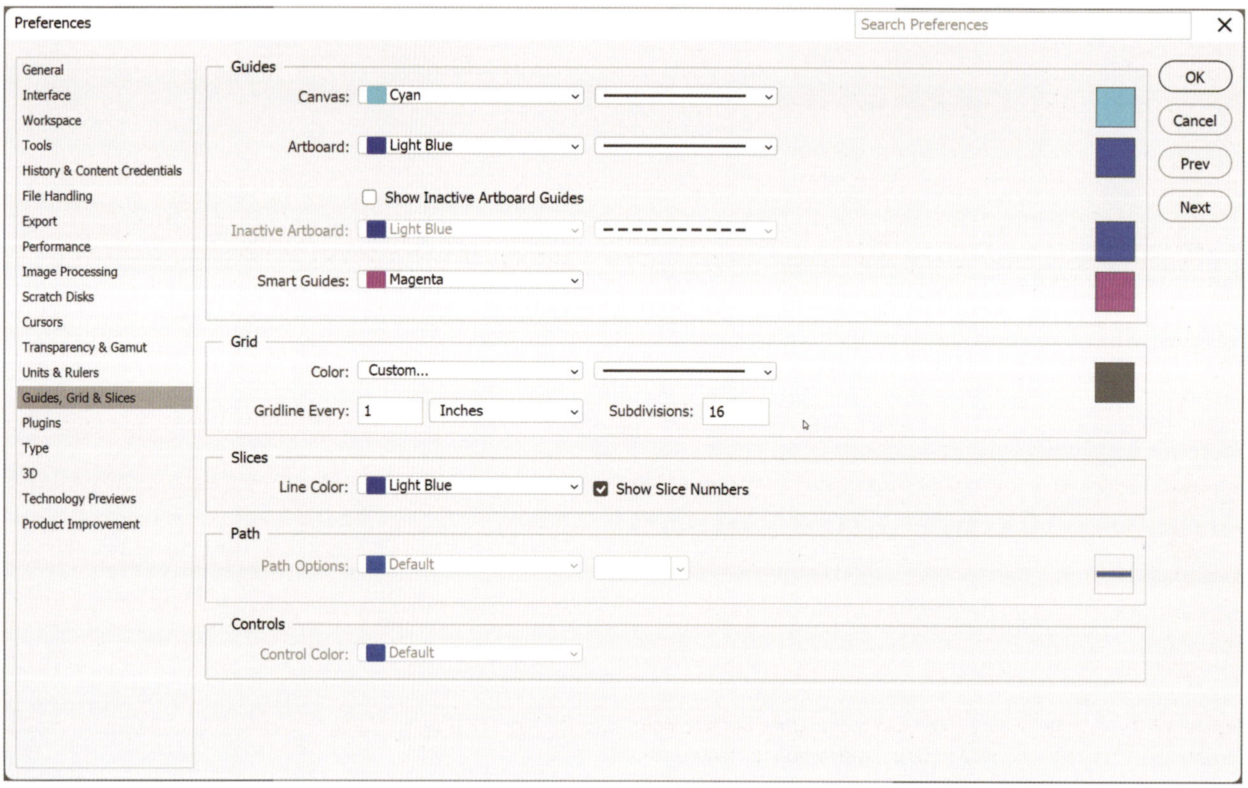

Figure 4.4 Screenshot of *Preferences* dialog box. Go to the *Guides, Grids & Slices* tab and change the grid divisions. We set ours to every 1 inch with 16 subdivisions.

Figure 4.5 Use the *View* menu to turn on the *Grid* feature.

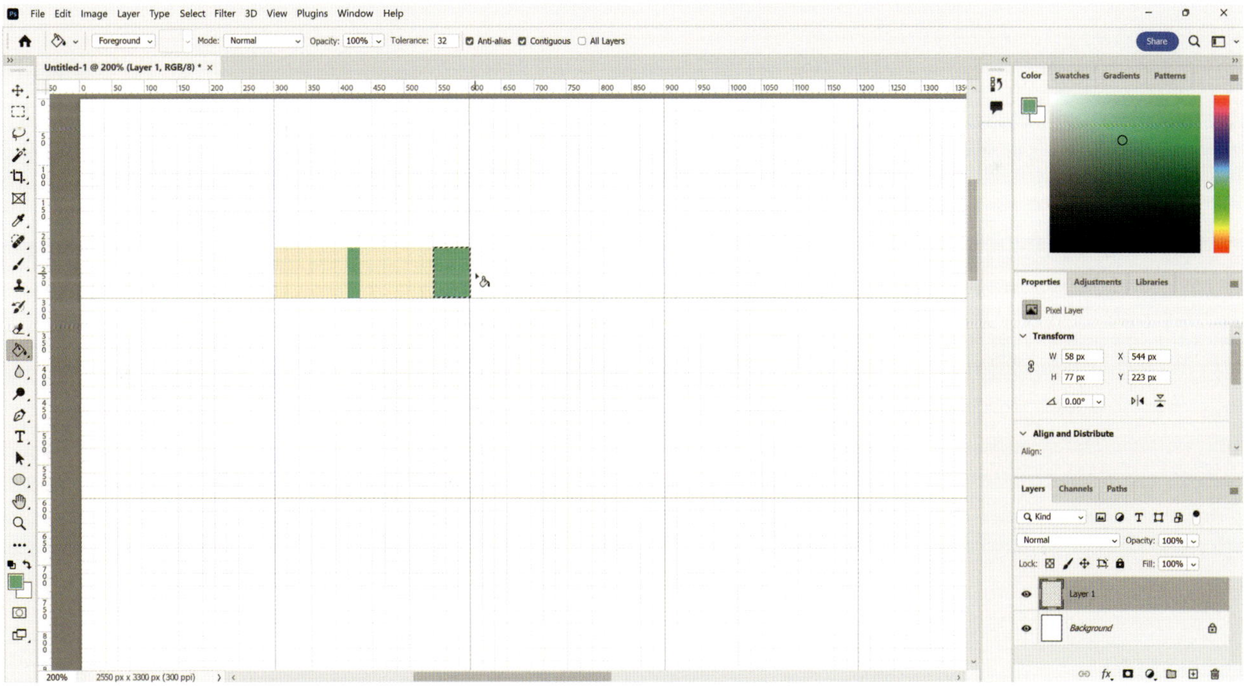

Figure 4.6 Use the *Rectangular Marquee* tool to draw out selection boxes. Fill with colors to your liking to make a stripe pattern. Remember that it does not need to be a big selection to create a stripe pattern.

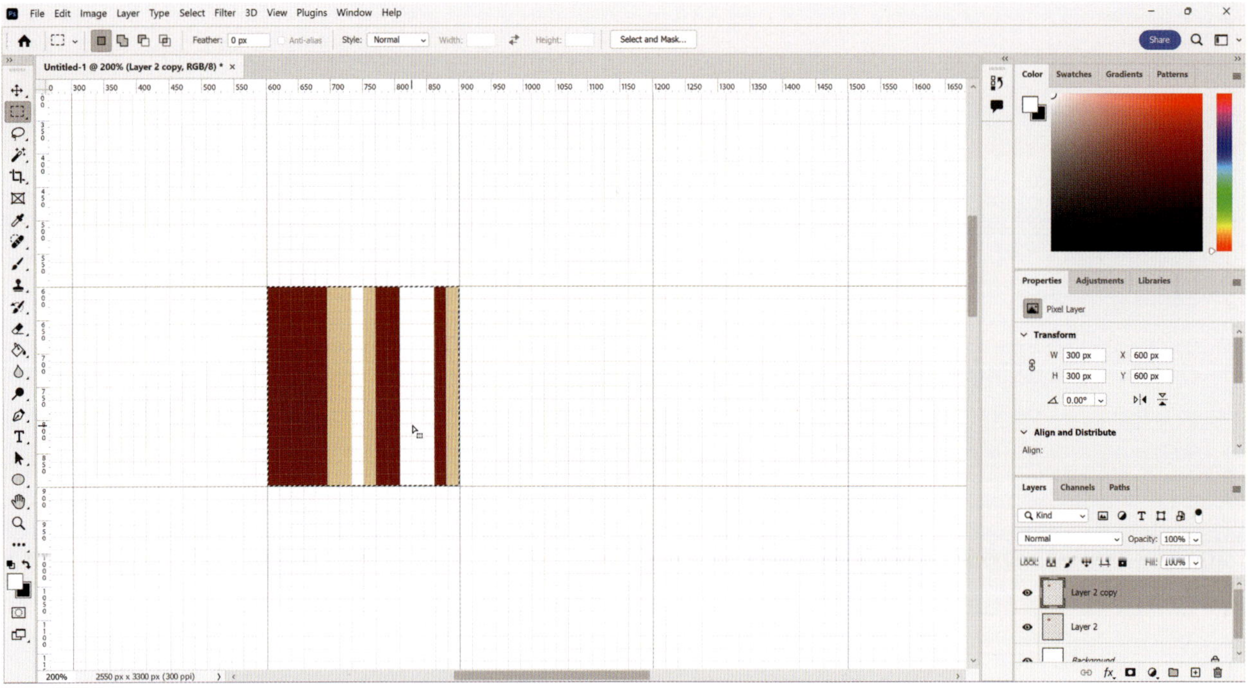

Figure 4.7a Create a square section of stripes to start your plaid.

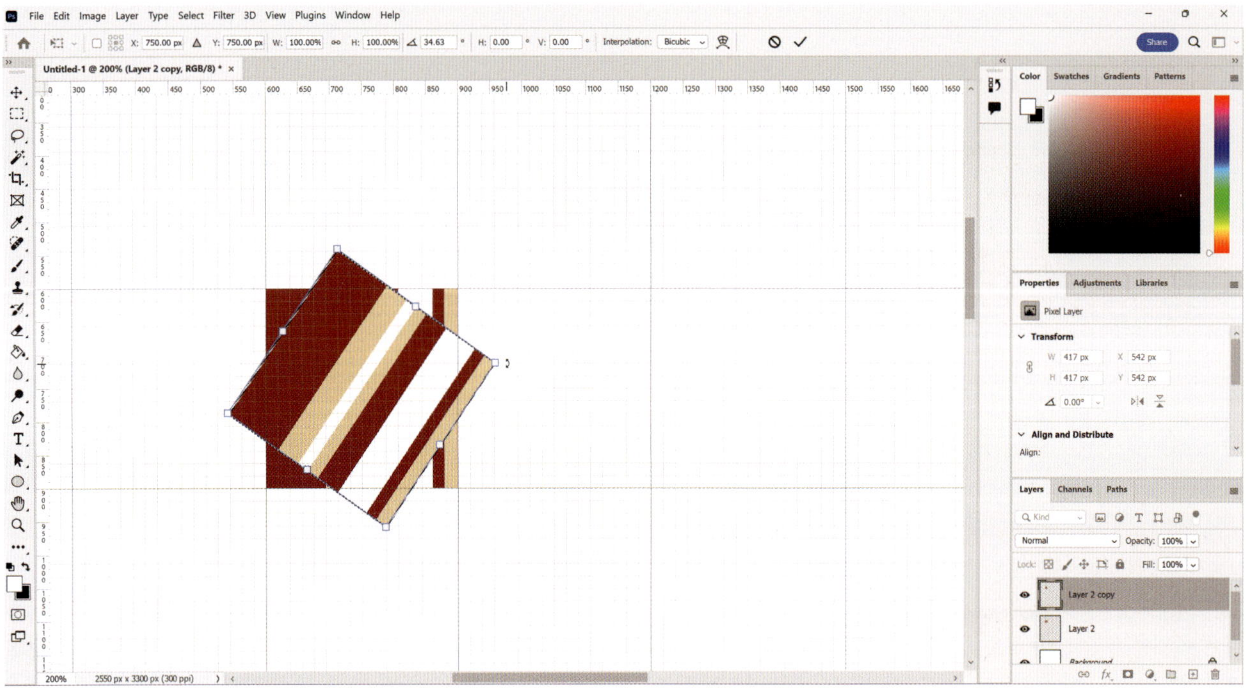

Figure 4.7b Make a duplicate of your layer, then use the *Transform* tool to rotate your top layer 90 degrees.

Print 4: If you would like to recolor your patterns, you can either recolor the original artwork and *Define* it as a new pattern, or you can add an *Adjustment Layer* to the pattern layer for a temporary fix as seen in Figure 4.8. To create a new pattern with different colors, *Open* your original artwork. *Save* a copy and recolor it using a *Paint Bucket*, *Paint Brush*, or *Adjustment Layer*. Once you are satisfied with the result, use the *Edit menu* → *Define Pattern* to turn it into another pattern. If you just want to test out a different color scheme or don't expect to use the

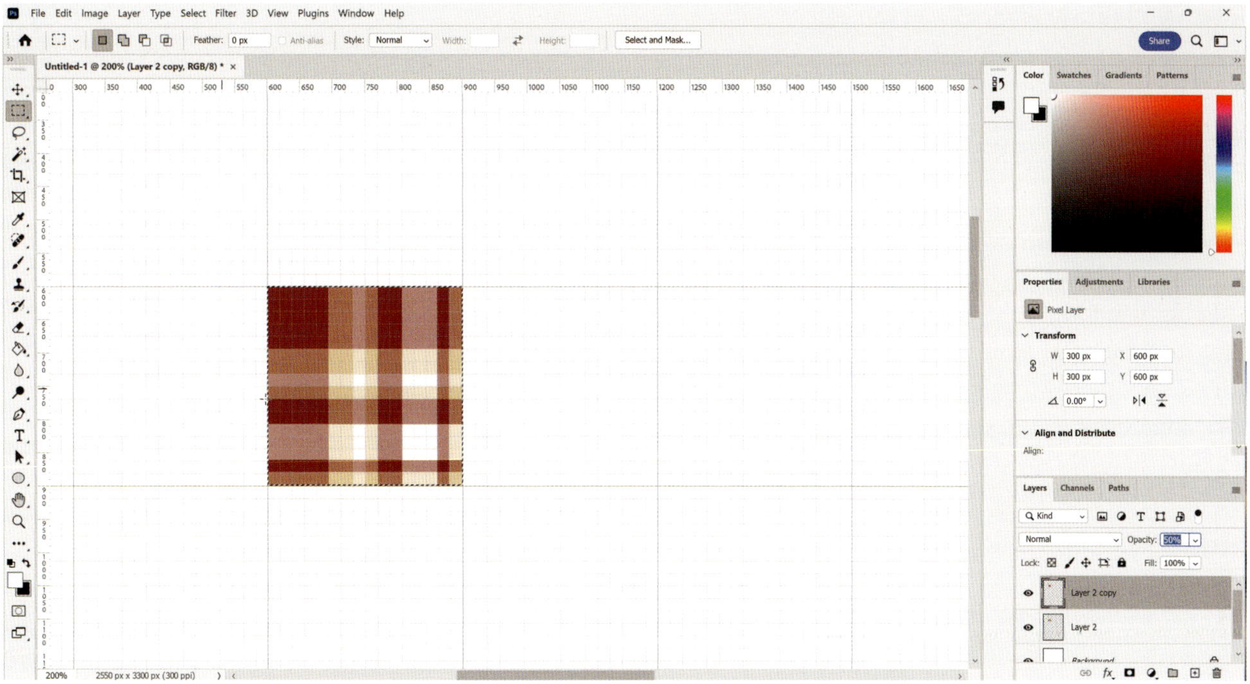

Figure 4.7c Change the top layer to 50% Opacity. *Marquee* select the square and *Define* your pattern. You now have a plaid in your library.

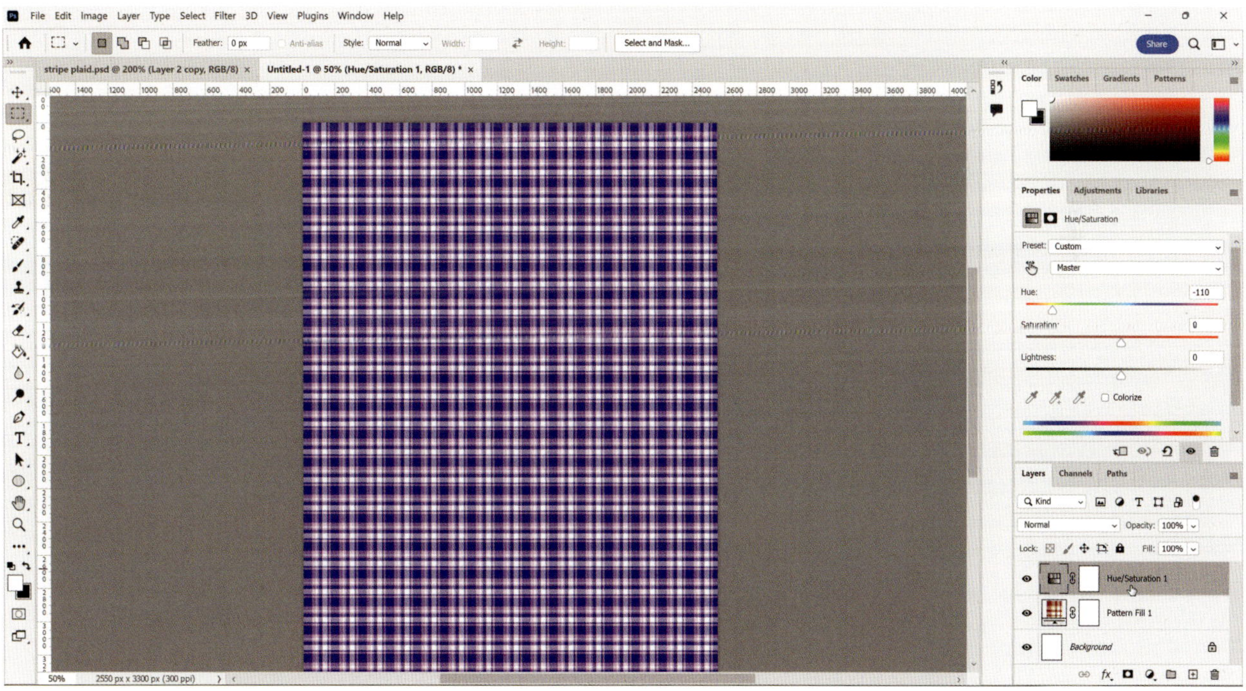

Figure 4.8 To make a quick color change, try an *Adjustment Layer* above your pattern. Be sure to clip it to the selection. If you want a reusable pattern in a different color, go back to your original artwork, change the color fills, and redefine it as a new pattern.

pattern for other renderings, you can add an *Adjustment Layer* above your current pattern layer in the rendering file. If you decide you don't like it, turn it back off!

To access the patterns on other devices, you will need to export the pattern. Look for the *Patterns* panel. You can find it under *Window → Patterns*. You will see your pattern in this panel. You can select your pattern in this panel and then *right-click* on it. This will bring up a pop-up window. In the pop-up window, select *Export Selected Patterns* as seen in Figure 4.9. This will allow you to save the pattern anywhere you wish, including on a cloud drive. Later, you can import the file to other devices.

To import a pattern or set of patterns, look again in the *Patterns* panel. In the upper right corner of the panel will be a drop-down menu below the icon of three stripes. In this menu, choose the option to *Import Patterns*. A file selection folder will appear. Navigate to the PatternLibrary.pat file provided in your STUDIO downloads for this chapter. Photoshop patterns must end with the extension (.pat) to be imported. Select the file and it will load the pattern set into your patterns panel!

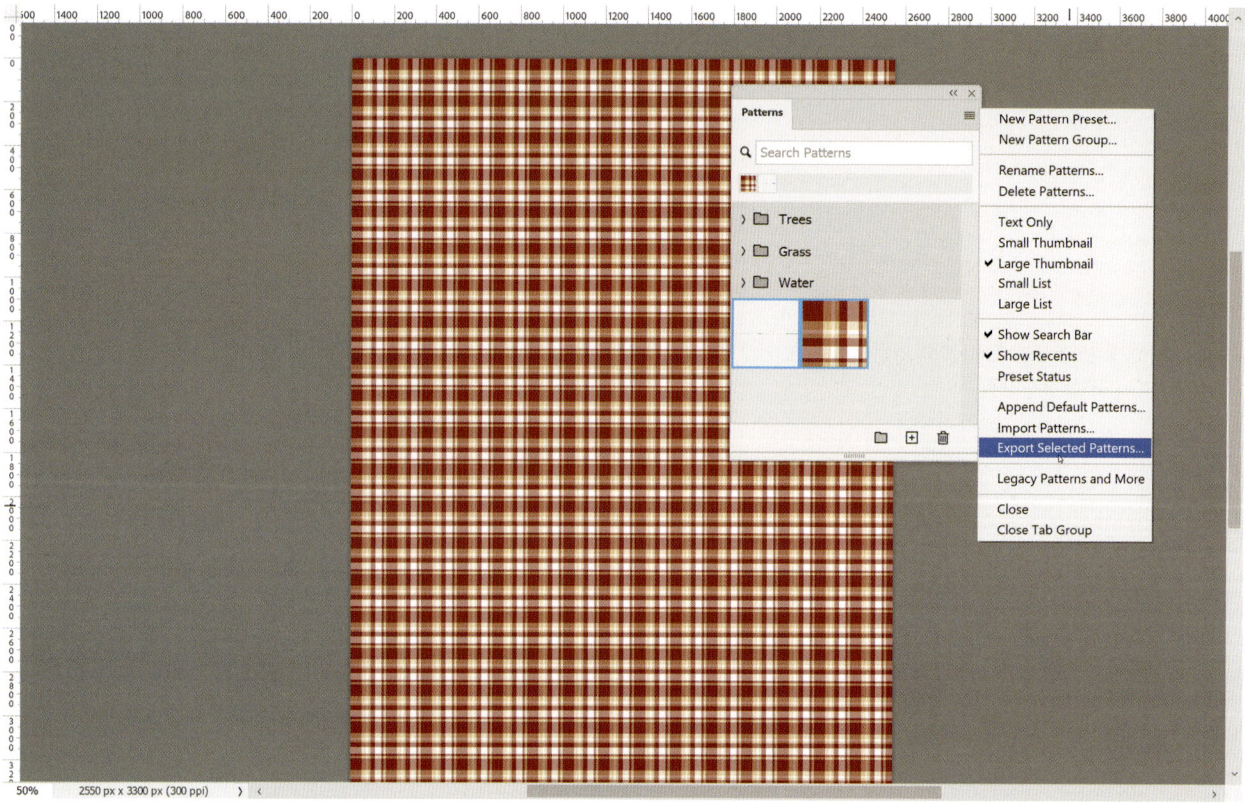

Figure 4.9 To export your patterns for use on another device, select the pattern(s) from your library. Use the drop-down menu in the upper right corner of the patterns panel. Select *Export Selected Patterns* and choose your save location.

Project 4.2: Apply, Scale, Rotate, and Warp Pattern Fills in Ps

There are multiple different ways to apply a pattern in Photoshop. Some of the most common methods include using the *Paint Bucket* tool and using a *Pattern Layer* converted to a *Smart Object*. The first method is fast whereas the second method gives you maximum control over the look of your print.

Method 1: Step 1: Let's use exercise file PatternPlay.psd and your recently created pattern from the last lesson. *Open* the exercise file. To fill an area with a pattern using the *Paint Bucket* tool, make sure the skirt surface is colored on a separate layer as discussed in Chapter 3. This will make it easy to fill with one click. It may be hard to tell in our example, but the skirt is colored with white. Turn off the visibility of the top sketch layer to see that there is a white fill.

Step 2: Next, switch to the *Paint Bucket* tool. If you don't see it, click and hold the *Gradient* tool. Before using the *Paint Bucket*, look at the settings for the tool. These can easily be found in the *Options* bar. If you do not see the *Options* bar at the top of your screen, click on the *Window* menu and scroll down to *Options* to turn the bar on. The *Options* bar shown in Figure 4.10 allows you to change the settings for the *Paint Bucket* before using the tool. You want to look for the drop-down menu on the left side of the bar that offers the options *Foreground* or *Pattern*. Choose *Pattern*. Another box will appear beside this option that will allow you to choose which pattern. Pick your pattern. Then uncheck *Contiguous* so that the *Paint Bucket* will fill all the areas you have selected.

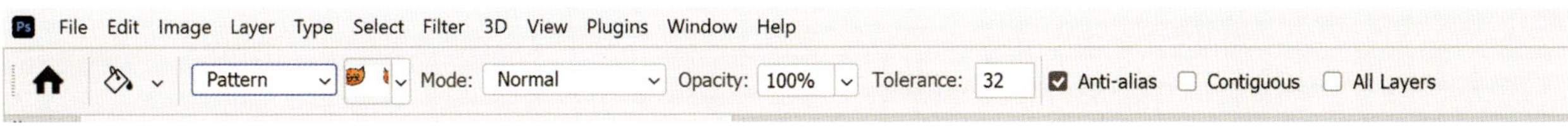

Figure 4.10 Screenshot of the *Options* toolbar when the *Paint Bucket* tool is active. Notice that we have the tool set to *Pattern* and have chosen our pattern. Additionally, we have un-checked *Contiguous* so that we can fill all the areas that are masked.

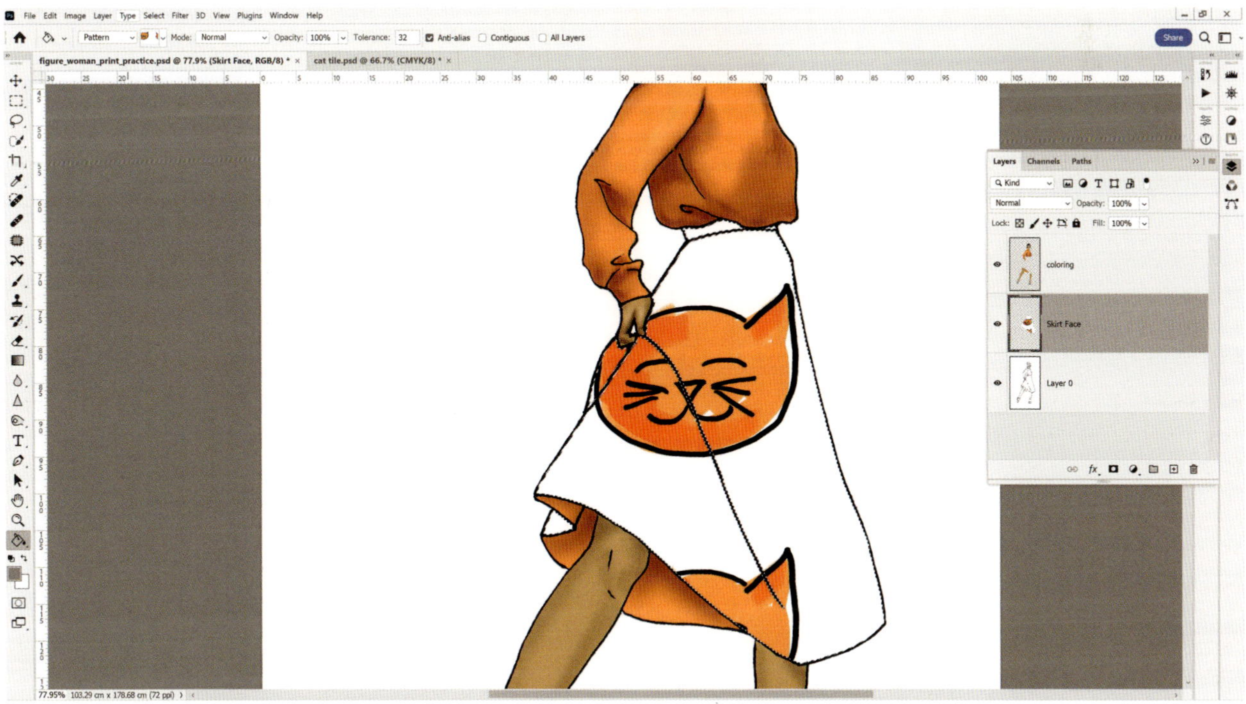

Figure 4.11 Screenshot of the skirt filled using the *Paint Bucket* tool. Notice that the pattern is large (we cannot change that without re-working the original image file) and the fill is on the original skirt layer.

Step 3: After you have made all the changes to the tool settings, make sure you are still on the skirt layer and then click inside the skirt with the *Paint Bucket* tool. This will fill the skirt with your pattern. For my example, the tool fills the skirt with a very large version of my cat pattern. The bucket uses the original size of the pattern from the original document. This can be problematic because you can't easily resize or warp the pattern. Figure 4.11 shows the incorrectly proportioned pattern fill. The only way to have the correct size pattern when using the *Paint Bucket* is to make the pattern tile the correct size to start. You will need to return to your original pattern tile file, reduce the image size through the *Image* menu, and then redefine the pattern if you want to change it. So, although the *Paint Bucket* method is a quick way to fill with a pattern, it comes with limitations. The next method is more flexible and allows you to resize the pattern as well as rotate the motif.

Method 2: Step 1: Either *Undo* your action until the skirt is white again, or *Open* the file from its original, unaltered state again. We are going to add the pattern on a new layer and use a *Clipping mask* to shape it. *Click* on the skirt layer. Make a *Rectangular Marquee* that generously covers all areas of the skirt.

Step 2. Now look at the bottom of the *Layers* panel. The center icon is a circle that is half white and half dark. Some people compare it to a black and white cookie. If you hover over it, it should give the tool tip "create new fill or adjustment layer". *Click* the icon to trigger a pop-up menu. Near the top of the menu, choose *Pattern* as seen in Figure 4.12. A pattern options pop-up menu should appear. In this box, you can choose the desired pattern. You can also change the scale and angle. Once you have the print correctly set, click *OK* to apply the pattern layer. Because you had a rectangular selection, it will automatically create a layer mask in that shape as in Figure 4.13.

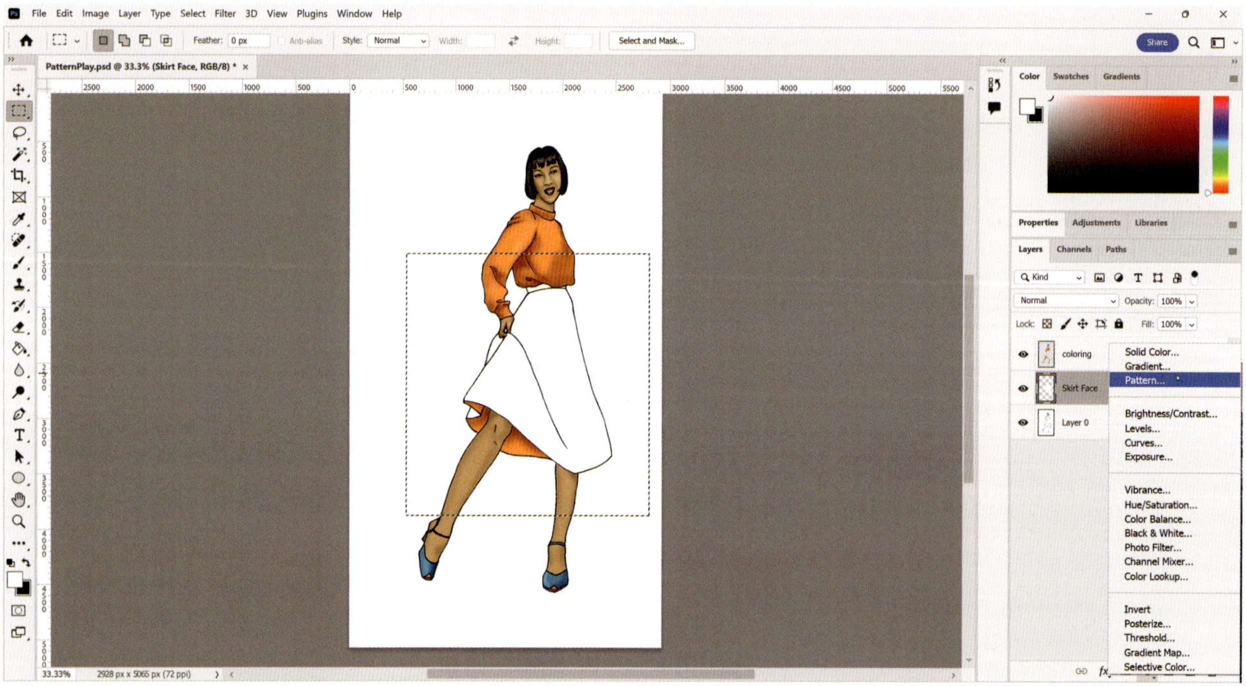

Figure 4.12 Screenshot of creating a *Pattern Fill Layer* directly from the *Layers* panel. Look for the tiny icon at the bottom of the *Layers* panel that is a half white/half black circle and click on it. It will give you an options box that includes *Pattern* as its third choice.

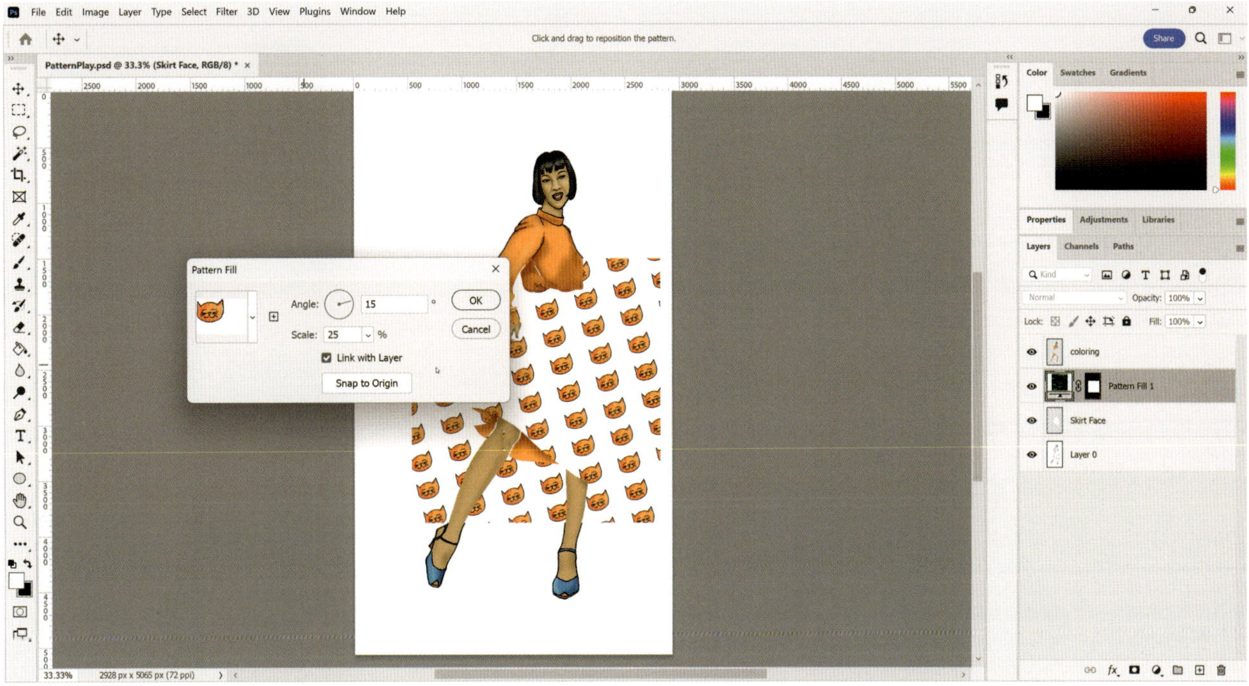

Figure 4.13 When a *Pattern Fill Layer* is applied while an area is already selected, a layer mask is applied in addition to the new fill layer. Notice the tiny black and white thumbnail to the right of pattern thumbnail on the selected layer in the panel. The black and white thumbnail is a representation of the layer mask. Also, notice the pattern options on the left of the screenshot. The pattern has not been fully confirmed. This is why the pattern thumbnail in the *Layers* panel still shows dark leaves instead of cats.

PRO TIP 4.2

Check Your Scale

You finally managed to turn your print into a repeat! That's great, but the work isn't over yet. Be sure to scale your print according to the proportions of your illustrated body. Many prints are smaller than you think. Look at a photograph of a person wearing a repeat print. Pay attention to how small the scale is compared to the body. Now think about what scale your fabric will be compared to the illustration. Figure PT4.2a shows a frog print at full scale as it was scanned. Refer back to the scan with the measuring tape. Those frogs are not that big! Figure PT4.2b shows the fabric at a more proportional scale to the rendered figure. If you are not sure of the correct scale, take a head-to-toe snapshot of a friend in the print (or something close to it if you don't have the exact print in your hands). An out-of-scale print can flag your work as amateur, so take the time to get it right!

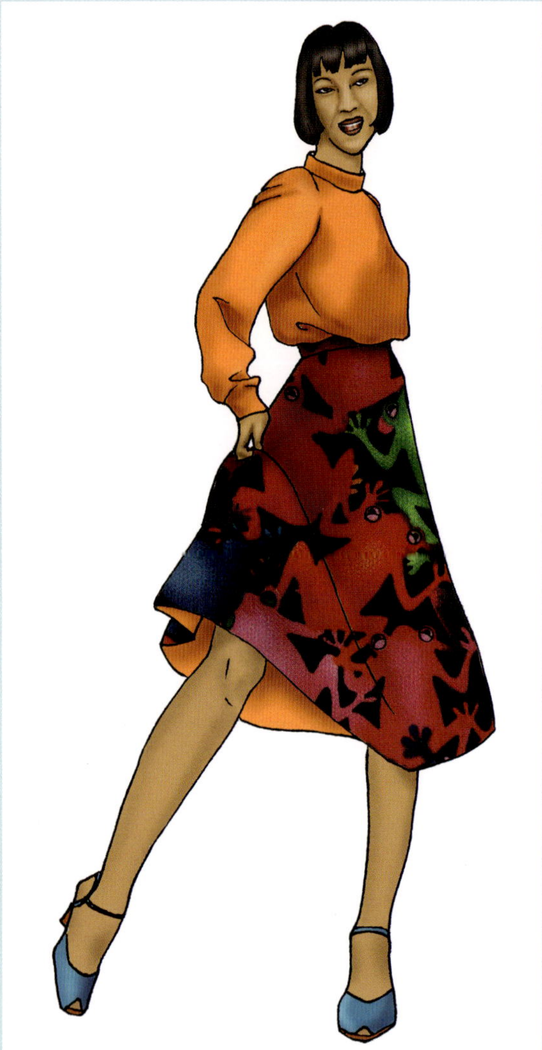

Figure PT4.2a The frog pattern was placed at the default 100%. This is way too big for our rendered figure!

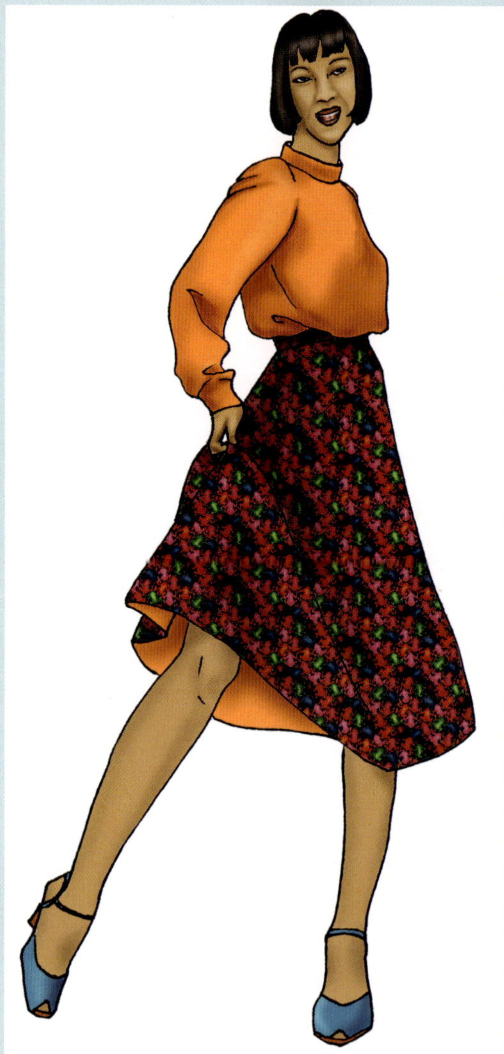

Figure PT4.2b Here, the frog pattern is to the correct scale to the figure. We brought it down to only 10% to fix the proportions.

Step 3: We will clip this layer to the skirt shape below so the rectangle is less distracting. *Right-click* on the pattern layer and select *Create Clipping mask*. Alternatively, you can hover your mouse between the pattern layer and the skirt layer while holding the *alt/option* key. Your mouse icon should change to a downward arrow with a page beside it. *Click* the mouse to clip the layer down. The *Pattern Fill Layer* will now be clipped or shaped to the layer beneath it, as can be seen in Figure 4.14.

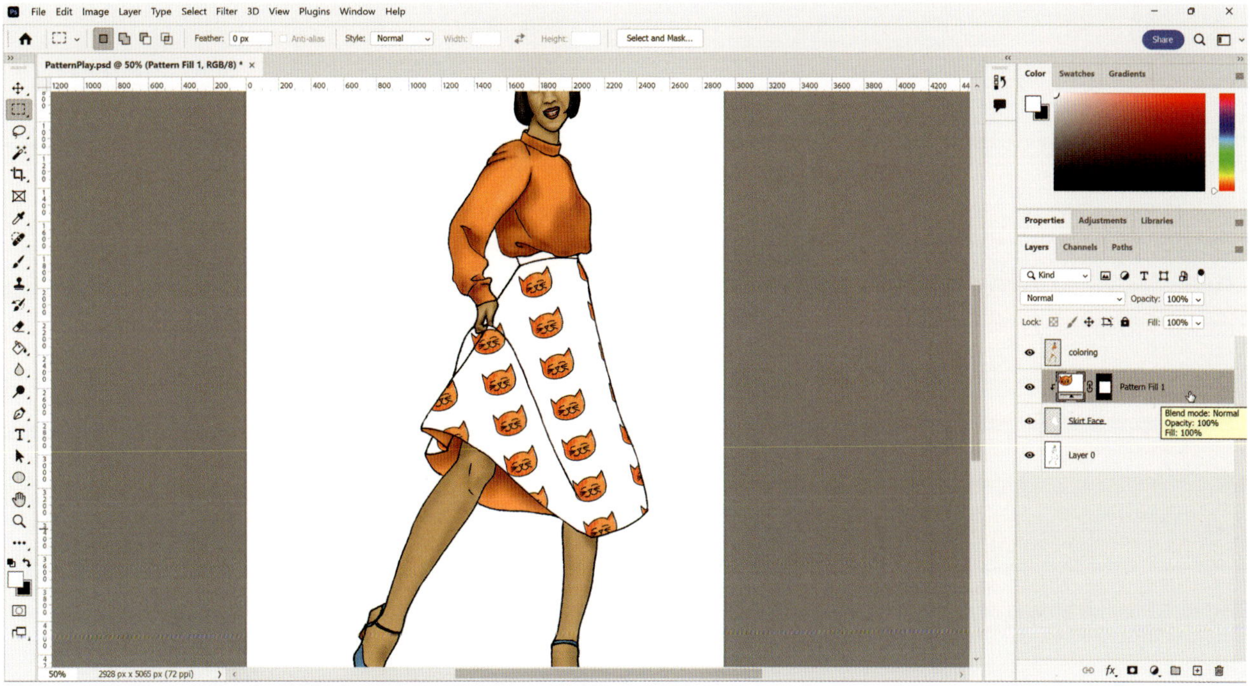

Figure 4.14 Screenshot of creating a clipping mask in Photoshop. To clip a *Pattern Fill* to a layer with an object or shape, the pattern layer must be located directly above the object layer in the *Layers* panel. Then either go to *Layer* → *Create Clipping mask* or you can *right-click* on the pattern layer in the panel and look for the same option in the pop-up menu.

Step 4: We will use the *Free Transform* tools to make the skirt look like it is moving around the body. However, if we try to transform it now, it will reshape the mask rather than the pattern inside it. Let's fix that issue. In the *Layers* panel, *right-click* on the pattern layer in the gray space next to the layer name. Choose the command to *Convert to Smart Object* as can be seen in Figure 4.15a. A **Smart Object** is a clever feature of Photoshop that allows you to make non-destructive changes by saving the settings you tweak. Essentially, it is like a mini file within your main file. When you select this, you will notice that the layer mask goes away, and a small icon appears in the corner of your layer thumbnail. Figure 4.15b shows how the icon in the *Layers* panel should look. This indicates that it is a *Smart Object*.

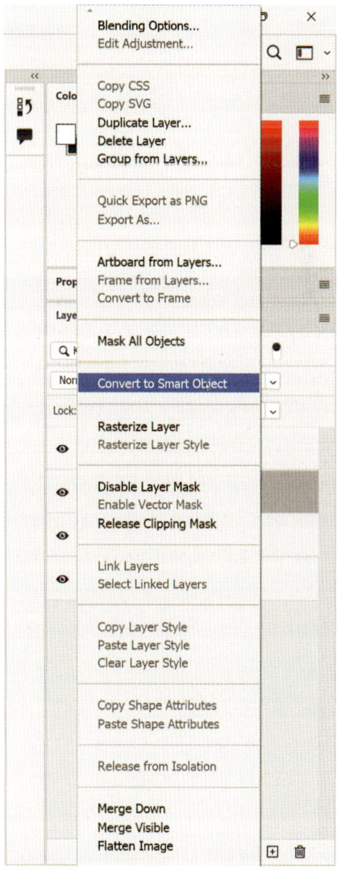

Figure 4.15a *Right-click* the layer to see the menu above. Choose *Convert to Smart Object*.

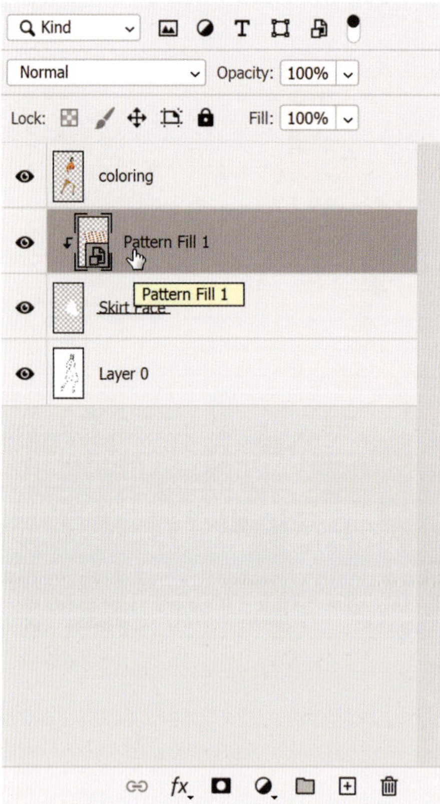

Figure 4.15b Notice the icon on your layer thumbnail. This indicates that the layer is a *Smart Object* now. You can also see the down arrow, indicating that the pattern fill is clipped into the skirt face layer.

Now you can use *control+t/command+t* to bring up the *Transform* tool. While this tool is active, *right-click* the image to bring up the options. Choose *Warp* from the menu. The **Warp** tool will bring up a grid that will allow you to manipulate the pattern in a way to make it look like it wraps around the body. You can tug and pull the image to manipulate the shape of the pattern. You may need to add more crosshairs to give you more control. If that is the case, *right-click* again while in the warp command and click on the command to *Split Warp Horizontally*, *Split Warp Vertically*, or *Split Warp Crosswise*. Click on the warp mesh to add a new section. Do this as often as needed for your preferred control level. The *Warp* tool is best for getting the overall shape of your pattern. We can refine the details and wrinkles later. Once you are happy with the results, *click* the check mark in the top options menu or just hit the *Enter/Return* key to accept the changes. Figure 4.16 demonstrates the warp tool.

Now you know how to fill an area with a pattern in Photoshop. You can even make it look more realistic with the option to warp the fill. Another advantage to the *Pattern Fill Layer* is that you can make as many versions as you like to try out different pattern looks! Let's look at one more option that allows you to affect the warping option with a different type of precision.

Project 4.3: Using Puppet Warp for Patterns

The warp feature works well for most looks, but you may occasionally find that **Puppet Warp** is better for the illustration needs. *Puppet Warp* is a feature that works particularly well for patterns that need to follow a bent knee or elbow. It creates a mesh that you can use to bend and warp the pattern while keeping other areas stationary. You can choose to clip the layer to the object below it or use a layer mask to shape the pattern. For our example, we will use a *Clipping mask*.

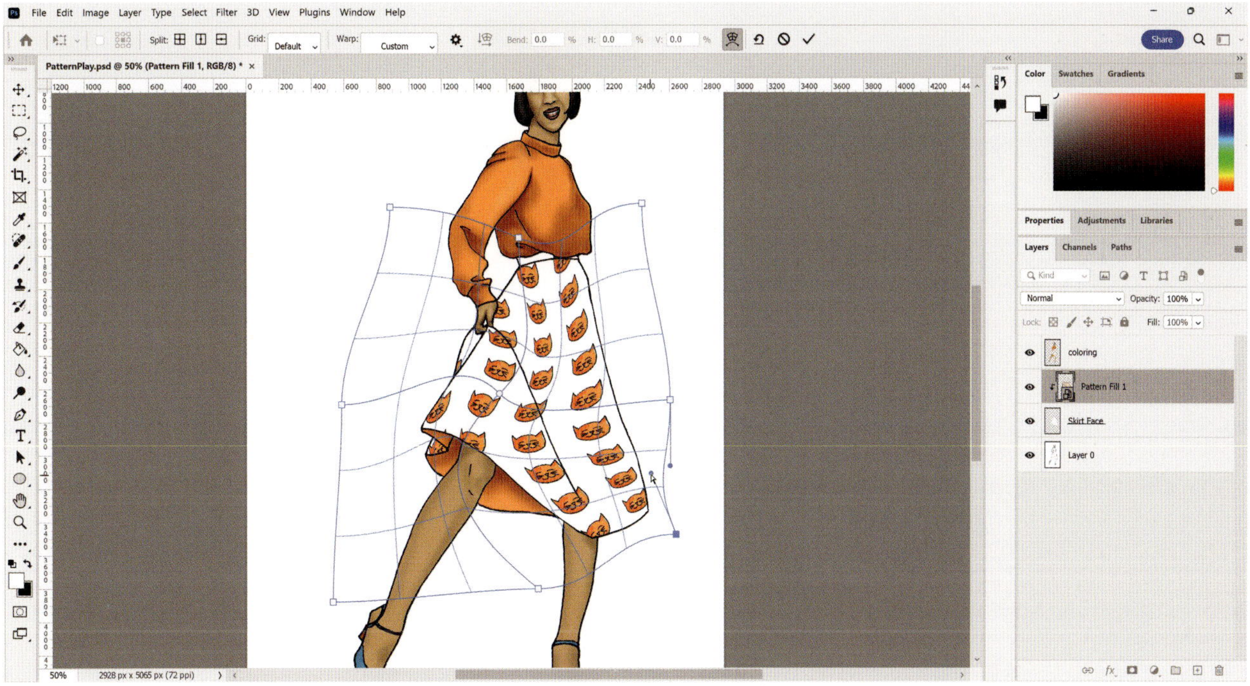

Figure 4.16 The blank layer mask has been deleted from the pattern layer and the pattern layer has been turned into a *Smart Object*. We are in the process of warping the pattern to reflect the movement of the fabric of the skirt using *Edit* ⟶ *Transform* ⟶ *Warp*. Extra crosshairs were added for more control.

Step 1: Start with a *Pattern Fill Layer* above your garment piece. You can either go through the *Layer* menu at the top or directly in the *Layers* panel. Clip the layer down to the garment layer, such as the shirt sleeve in this example. As before, you will need to convert the layer to a *Smart Object* once you are certain that you have the correct scale. Next, go to the *Edit* menu and select *Puppet Warp*. A mesh will appear over the item on that layer.

Step 2: *Click* on the mesh cross points to lay down a virtual push pin. Aim the pins for areas you want to keep stable and areas you want to move. After you play with this feature for the first time, you will get a sense of how to lay down your pins. Figure 4.17 shows the pattern rectangle manipulated in *Puppet Warp*.

Now start to move pins around with your cursor. Using this feature, you can bend a pattern around the bent elbow of the figure. Use the *Enter/Return* key or the check in the top *Options* bar to approve the adjustment. This makes it easier to control around distinctive bends in the fabric. You can see the results in Figure 4.18. How else will this feature be helpful for your illustrations?

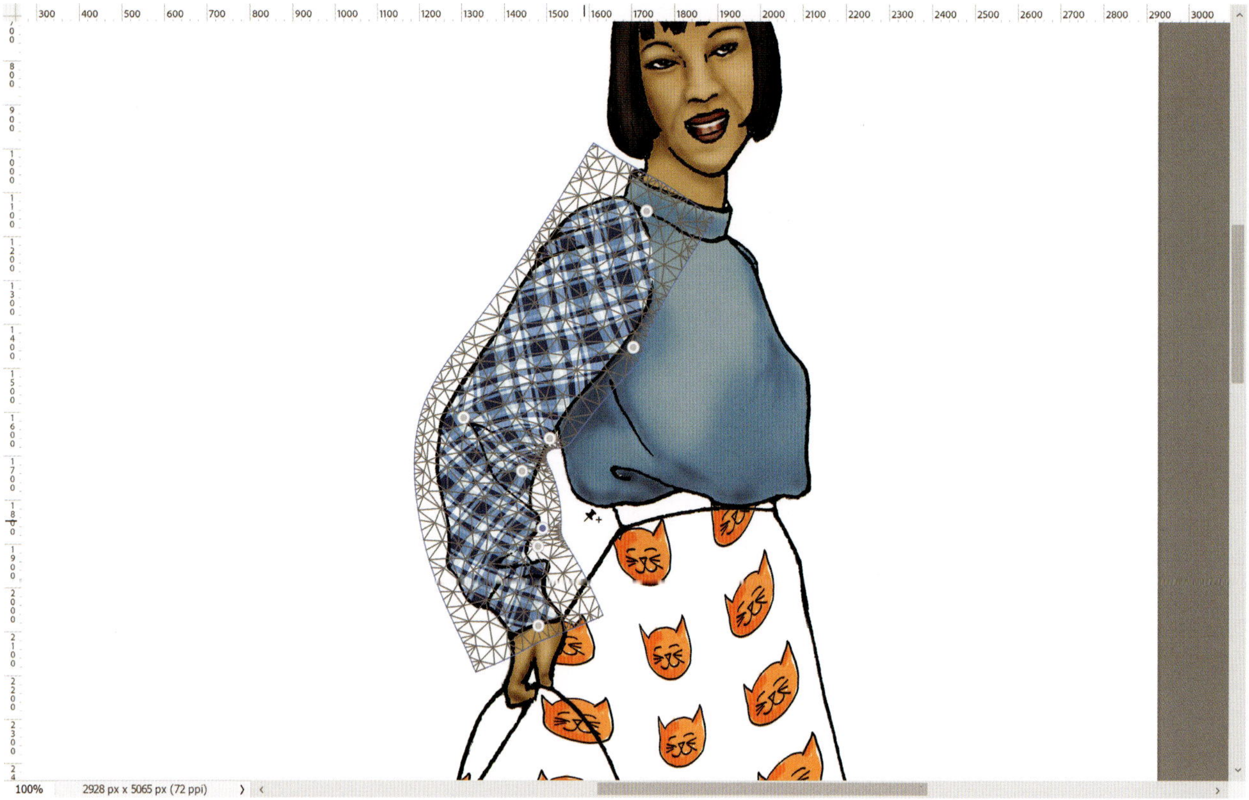

Figure 4.17 Use *Puppet Warp* on areas such as bent elbows or knees. A rectangle was filled just big enough to cover the sleeve area. Add pins with a *click* while in *Puppet Warp*. Then you can use the pins to pull the shape and pattern. Remember to convert it to a *Smart Object* before using the *Puppet Warp* feature, though.

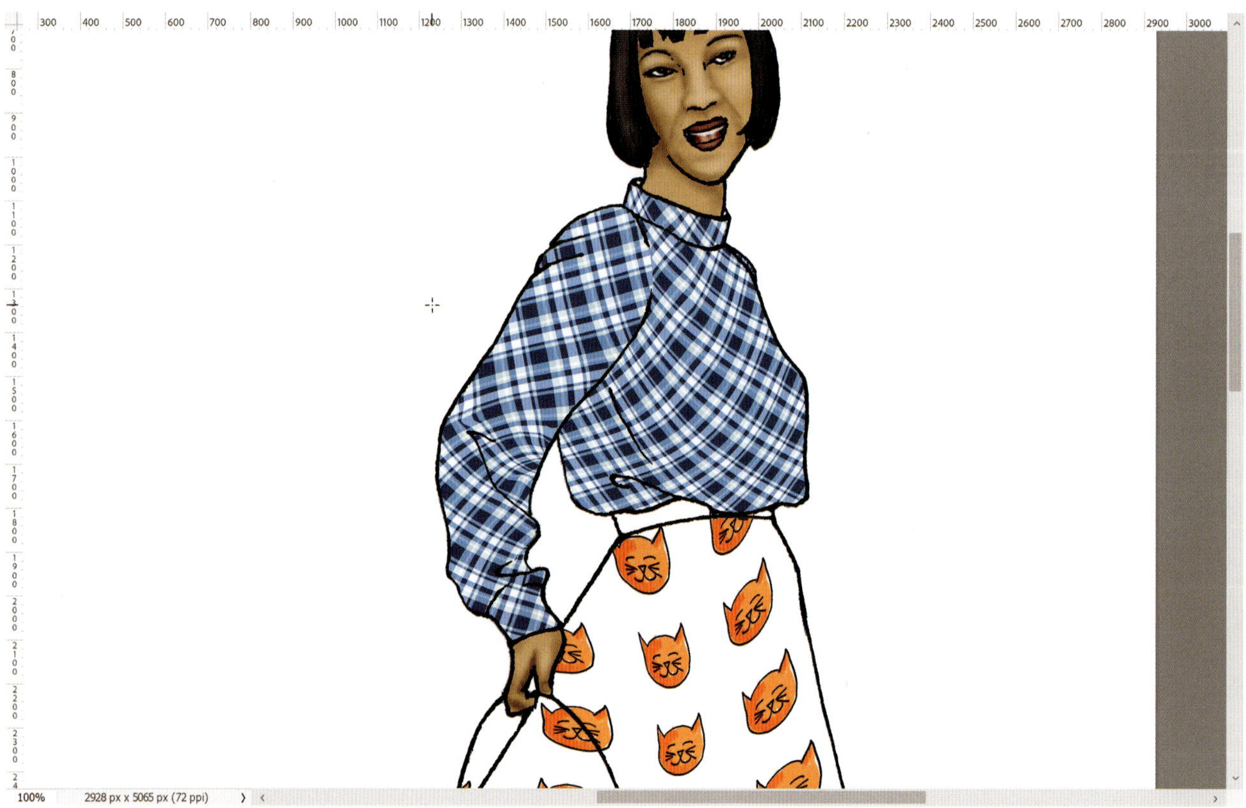

Figure 4.18 Once you commit to the distortion, the mesh will disappear, and you can fully see your results. If you need to tweak it more, just double-click the words "Puppet Warp" in your layer. You can go back in and move it more.

PRO TIP 4.3

My Drawing App Doesn't Have a Pattern Feature!

If you are using an app other than Photoshop or Illustrator, search around through the help menu or online tutorials to see if there are any tips for creating and using patterns. However, some apps simply don't support anything like a repeat pattern. If that is the case, you have a few options.

First, try free-handing a version of your pattern to scale like in the rendering in Figure PT4.3. This can be analog or digital. Sometimes the old ways are the easiest. Simplify your pattern repeat down to colors and general shapes as they would appear at the correct scale. Then try your hand at sketching them on your rendering.

If that is not for you, try laying your fabric out on the floor (iron it first and make sure your floor is clean!). Then photograph it zoomed out. *Crop* your photo to just the fabric. *Place* it in your rendering and clip it to your garment object. The trick is to zoom out enough to get several repeats and the right scale for your rendered figure.

There is always a workaround for any issue. Don't be afraid to experiment and try something new to fix your issue. If it works, make a tutorial video on it! Others in the same situation will appreciate your innovation.

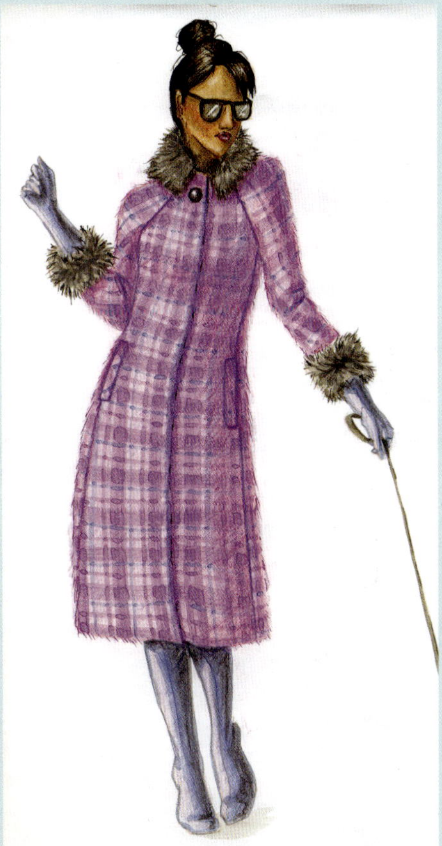

Figure PT4.3 An analog sketch with a pattern that was scanned in and altered digitally.

Project 4.4: Creating Folds with a Liquify Filter

The warp features are great for creating the general illusion of the fabric following the garment shape. However, they are difficult to control if you want to create wrinkles, gathers, pleats, or other folded effects. Before embarking down this pathway, decide if your illustration needs that level of detail. In many cases, it looks fine without. Remember, the more detail you add, the more time it takes to render. Take a moment to decide if your time or accurate illustration detail is more important for this project. There is no right answer; it entirely depends on you and your current situation.

Step 1: Let's start with the *Liquify* filter. Using the file from the last exercise, you will be able to add in the look of individual folds in your print. Make sure you are on your *Pattern Fill Layer* and that it has been converted to a *Smart Object* and already warped. Go to the *Filters menu* → *Liquify*. This will open a plugin feature window with your warped pattern fill showing. This makes it hard to see where you want to add folds, so look in the right-side menu. There is a checkbox for *Show Backdrop*. Tick this box and use the default settings. This will allow you to see where you need to manipulate the print. Figure 4.19 demonstrates the *Show Backdrop* feature.

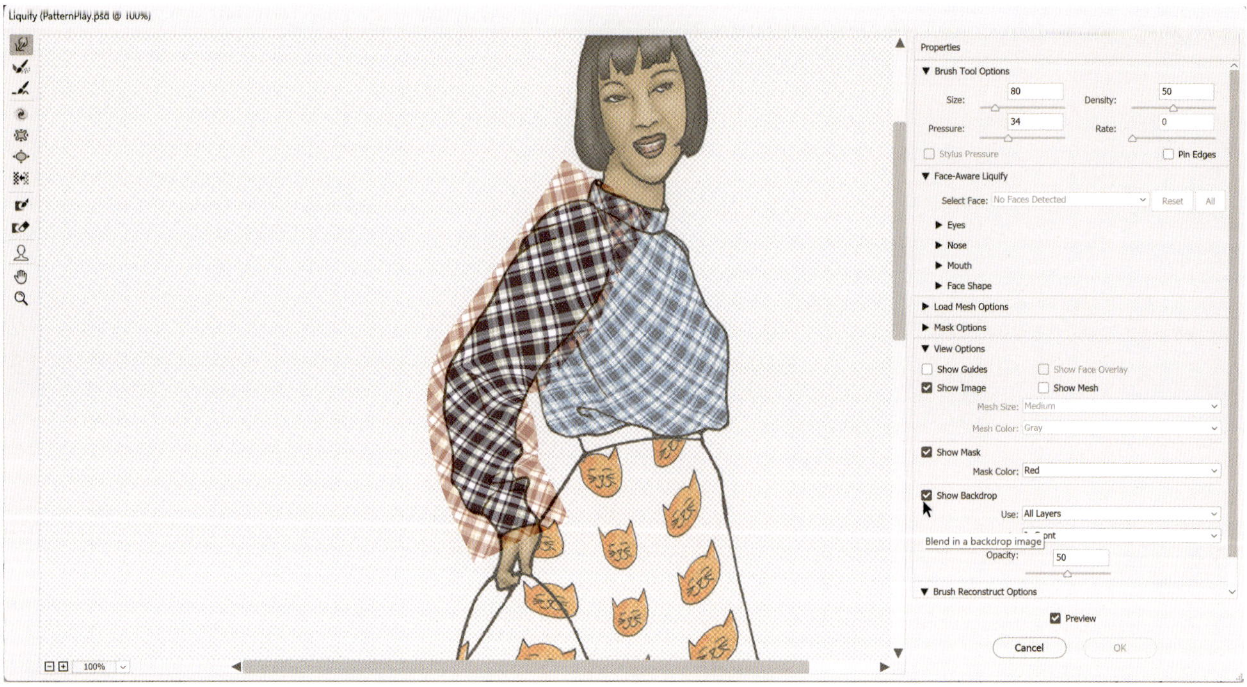

Figure 4.19 Once you enter the *Liquify* interface, be sure to turn on *Show Backdrop* in the right-hand menu. This will allow you to see your drawn folds on the sketch layer.

Step 2: Now you can use the *Forward Warp* tool (the top icon on the left-side toolbar) to push around the pattern to create fold-like effects. If you go too far, then use *control+z* or *command+z* to undo or use the second tool in the toolbar to reconstruct the area. You may need to change the pressure to something more subtle in the tool brush options. Play around until you are happy, like in Figure 4.20a. Remember you can always cancel out of it and restart the filter if you really mess it up. Figure 4.20b shows how the manipulations show in the normal interface. Even if you accept the changes, you can *double-click* on the word *Liquify* in the pattern layer to go back in and adjust or just drag it to the trash can icon to start over!

The *Liquify* tool takes some practice to get the hang of it. Be sure to practice some before jumping in on a complicated project. Once you are comfortable, you will find it to be a rewarding feature for creating folds in your prints!

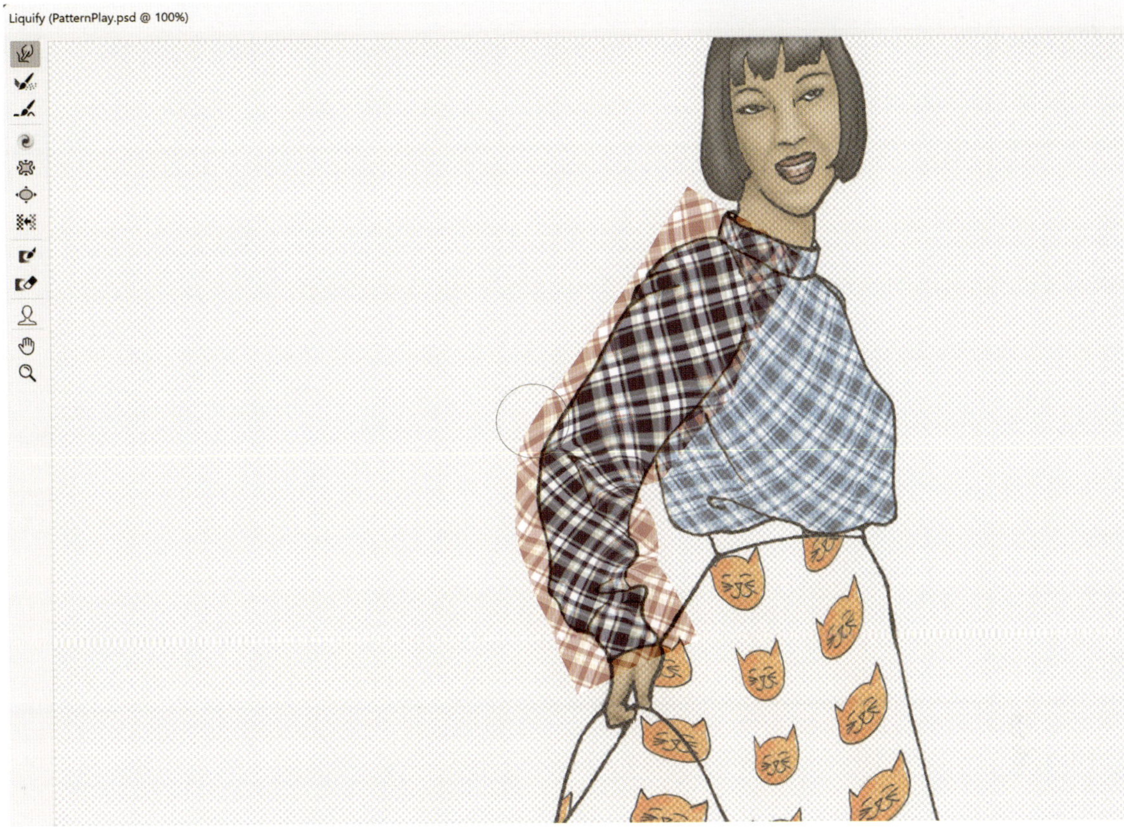

Figure 4.20a Use the *Forward Warp* tool in the *Liquify* filter to push your pattern around for the appearance of folds in the fabric. Notice how it distorts the fabric. The key is to use small strokes and not overdo it.

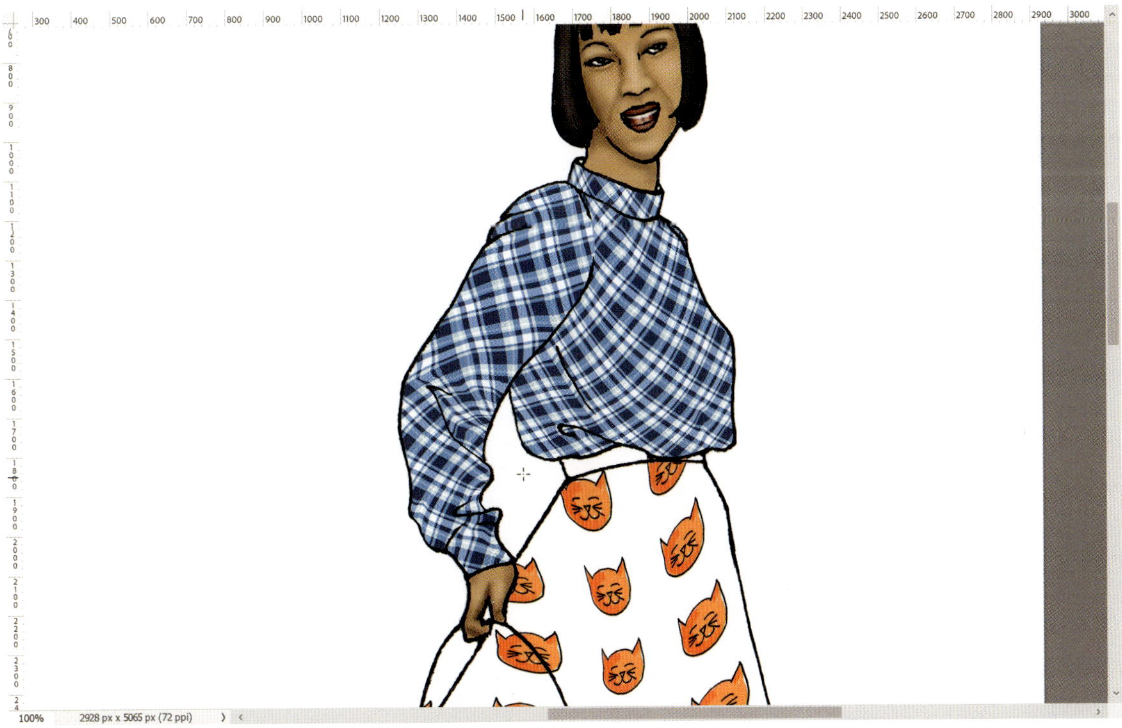

Figure 4.20b It is a little hard to see your results clearly while in the interface. You may need to accept the changes, then go back into the filter by *double-clicking* the word "Liquify" in your *Layers* panel to adjust it more.

PRO TIP 4.4

Using Displacement Maps

Displacement maps are a bit more advanced, but a great way to create the look of fabric distortion for ruffles, pleats, and dramatic folds in your pattern repeat. A displacement map uses a black and white map, such as the one shown in Figure PT4.4a, to tell the application how to displace the image. Check out Robin Schneider's tutorial on displacement maps in her Photoshop for Fashion LinkedIn Learning courses. Essentially, you set up a 50% gray layer with dark shadows and/or highlights in black and white. *Duplicate* the layer to a new document and *Save* it as a separate file. Then, on your rendering file with the *Pattern Fill Layer* selected, go to the *Filter menu → Distort → Displace.* Use the default settings and navigate to the file you just saved. See how it pushes the dark areas back and pulls the white areas forward as in Figure PT4.4b? After you take the time to become familiar with the *Liquify* filter, experiment with displacement maps. We recommend taking a short tutorial or two on them first to better understand the feature, though.

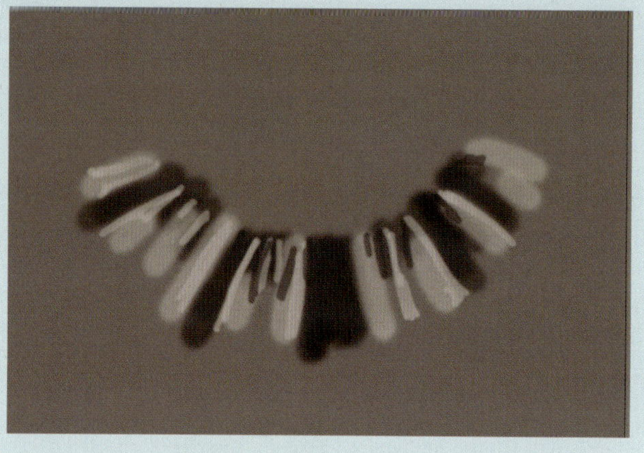

Figure PT4.4a A displacement map is created on a 50% gray layer with black and white shadows. Where the black areas show, the pattern will push back whereas it will pull forward in the white areas.

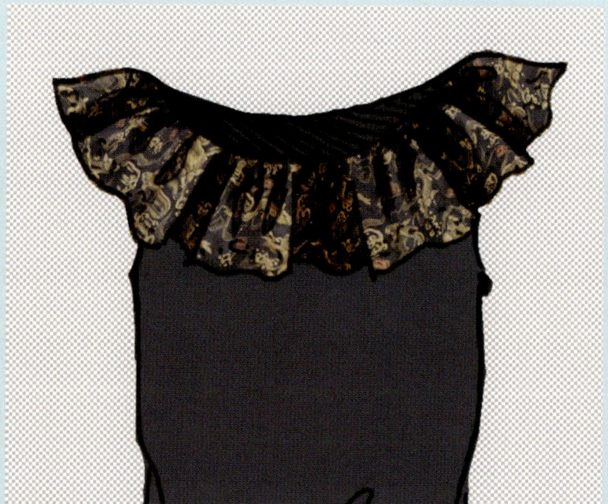

Figure PT4.4b Here the *Displacement* filter is applied using the previously completed displacement map file. It helps to create a more realistic undulation for folds in the fabric.

Troubleshooting

"Why does my *Paint Bucket* only partially fill the object?"

One of the more common issues with print layers includes when the *Paint Bucket* tool incorrectly fills the item, as seen in Figure 4.21. First, check that you are on the correct layer and that the item you want to fill has some sort of solid color covering the whole area (such as the skirt). Check that you don't have any shading at this point. Any color variation will disrupt the *Paint Bucket* coverage. Likewise, any gaps in the color will leave holes when you fill. If your tool adds the print to the entire page, it is likely that you simply didn't click on the colored area of the item and accidentally clicked the background.

"Why does the *Pattern Fill Layer* fill the whole screen?"

In this case, you need to add a mask. Make sure you either clip the pattern layer down to the layer below it or use a layer mask from the shape of the layer below.

"I tried to distort the pattern but it gets wonky. Part of the pattern disappears and it doesn't actually distort the pattern fill!"

If you tried to distort the pattern but instead it changes the layer mask as seen in Figure 4.22, you need to undo your last action. Remember to change your pattern layer into a *Smart Object*. The layer mask will disappear, and a *Smart Object* icon will show on the layer thumbnail. Now you will be able to warp your pattern fill without affecting the mask!

Should you find that your *Pattern Fill Layer* won't transform, remember to convert the layer to a *Smart Object* first. This is an easy step to miss.

"I'm in *Puppet Warp*, but every time I move the pin, the whole thing just spins around!"

When using the *Puppet Warp* feature, if you find that moving your pin rotates the whole selection then you probably need to put down more pins before moving it. That will keep one area stable while you move the other area.

Using Patterns in Ai

You can use your pattern previously corrected in Ps for use in Illustrator if you like. Bring in the small version you originally used in Ps and embed it or directly *Open* it in Ai. Then, simply click on *Object* → *Pattern* → *Make* to make it an Illustrator pattern, as seen in Figure 4.23. Accept the changes. You will see the pattern show in your *Swatches* panel. You can also create your own in Illustrator and make it a little more intricate if you like.

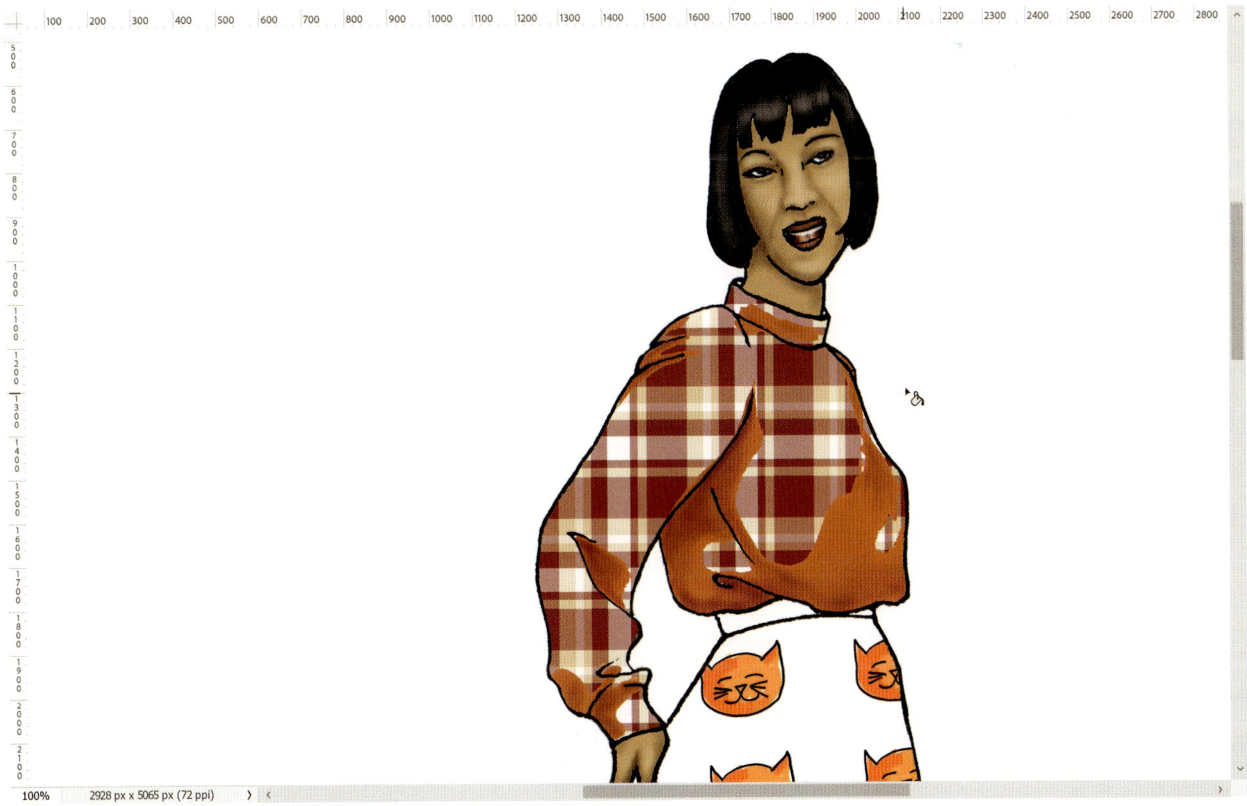

Figure 4.21 Keep your areas filled with only one flat color when adding patterns. The *Paint Bucket* tool will not make a clean fill if you have already applied shading.

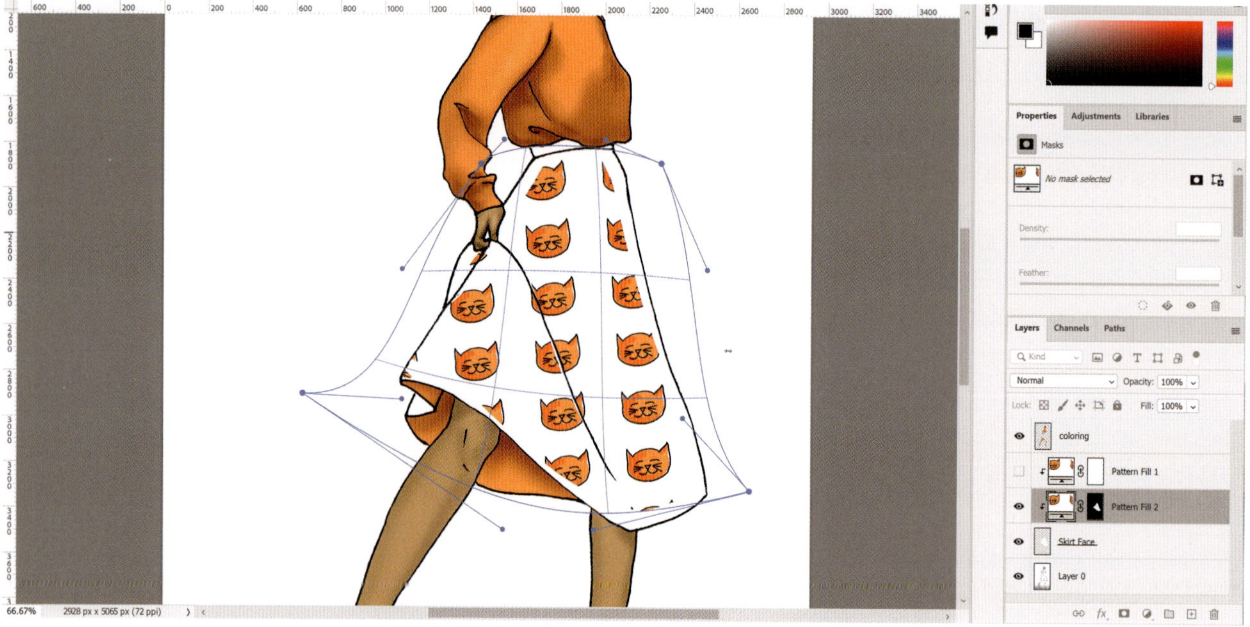

Figure 4.22 If you don't turn your pattern layer into a *Smart Object* before you use the *Transform* tool, the transformation will affect the mask but not the pattern fill. Notice here that the warp has distorted the mask shape and made it smaller than the skirt (look for the cut-off cat heads at the sides). Also notice that it has not distorted the pattern fill at all. Exit out of the transformation and convert your layer before trying again.

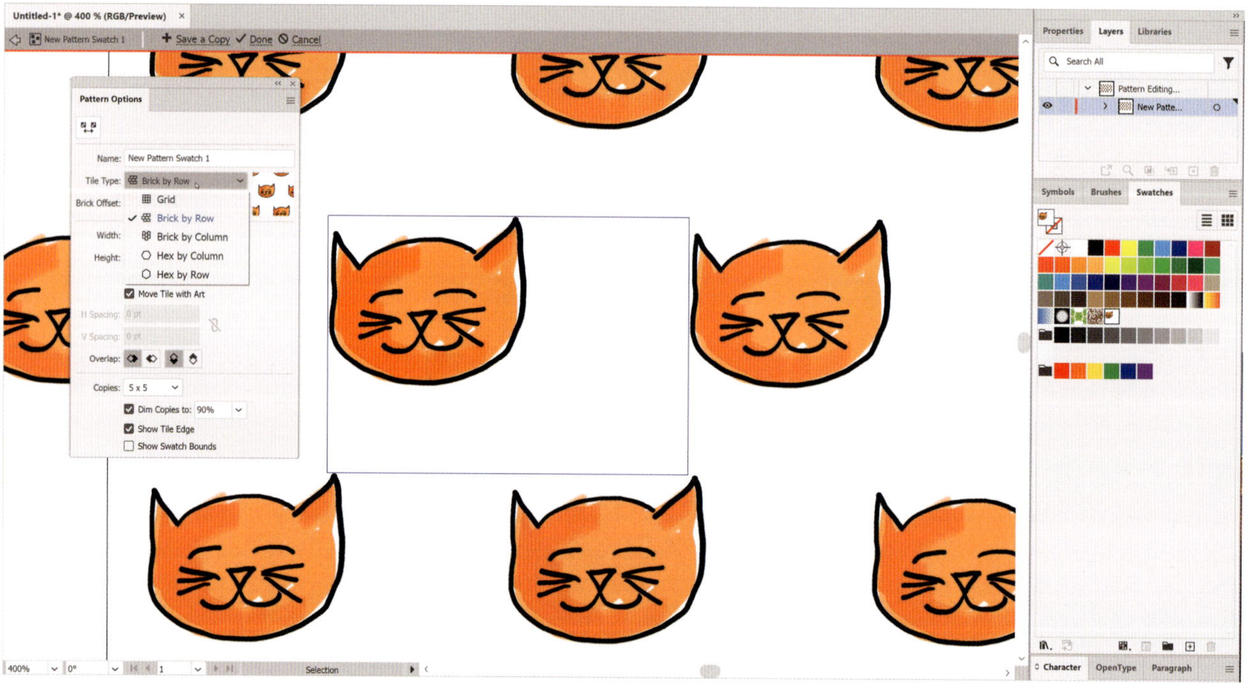

Figure 4.23 You can use any pattern artwork originally created in Photoshop or other digital art applications while in Illustrator. Place and embed your artwork on a new document. Select the art and use the *Object menu* → *Pattern* → *Make*. This will create a new pattern swatch from your artwork.

Project 4.5: Creating Patterns in Ai

In many ways, creating a print in Illustrator is easier than Photoshop. It depends on the type of pattern you want to achieve. Illustrator is more conducive to graphic prints, whereas Photoshop is better for photographic prints and fabric scans.

To create a pattern in Illustrator, *Open* a new file in a comfortable size. Make sure your *Raster Settings* are high (300 dpi) in case you apply any raster effects. If you would like a grid to help you, you can turn it on under the *View* menu. I also recommend turning on the *Snap to Grid* command under the *View* menu. Remember that to change the grid and subdivisions, go through the *Preferences* dialog box (*control+k/command+k*).

Pattern 1: Step 1: Let's start with an easy one: stripes. Use your *Rectangle* tool. Choose any fill color you like and remove the stroke. Click once on the artboard with the cursor. A dialog box will appear, asking for your width and height of the rectangle. Even though it is set to pixels, you can type in ¼" for the height and ¼" for the width (or use mm if you prefer metric). The program will convert your measurements to pixels for you. You now have a small box. Make another rectangle with a different fill, this time ¼" × 1/16". Snap the rectangles right next to each other like in Figure 4.24a.

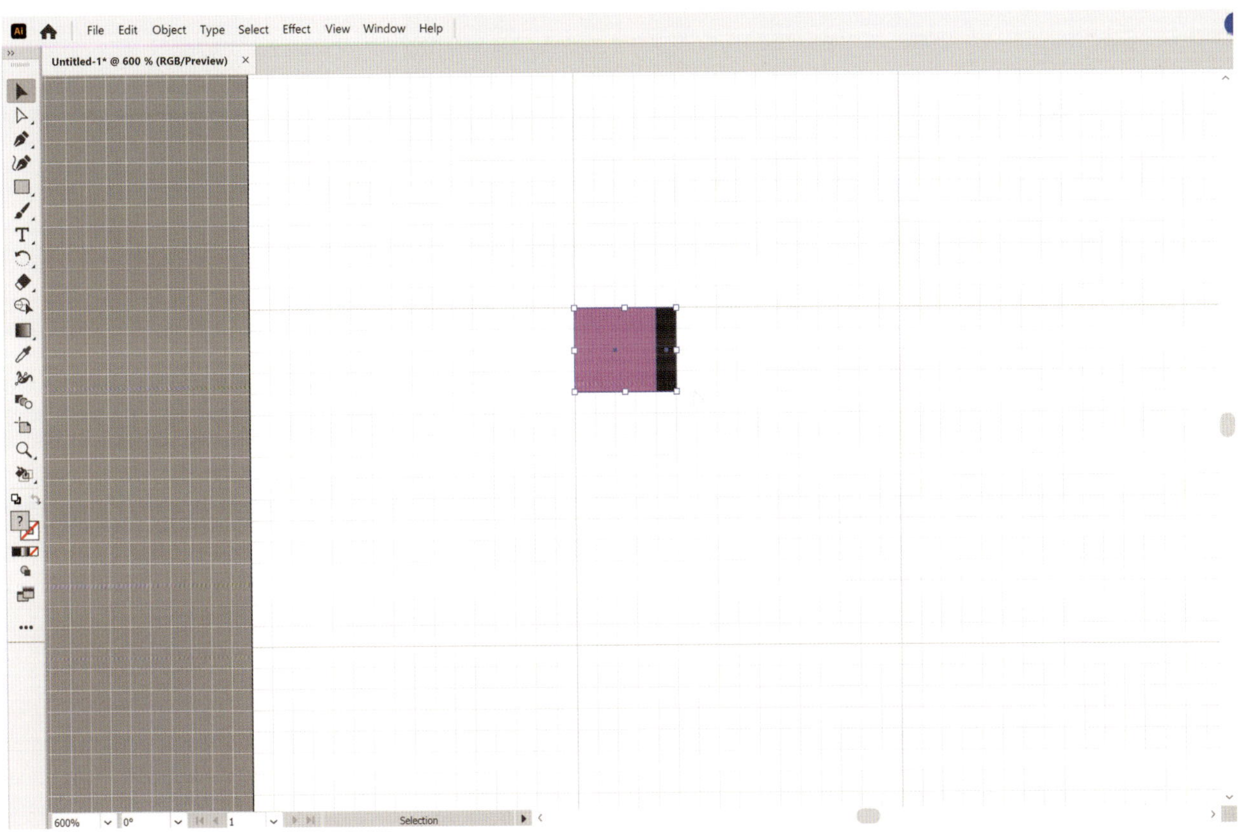

Figure 4.24a Turn on your *Grid* through the *View* menu. Use the *Rectangle* tool to create areas with a fill but no stroke. It can be as simple or complicated as you like.

Step 2: Use your black arrow (*Selection* tool) to select both rectangles together. Choose the *Object menu* → *Pattern* → *Make* to define your pattern. This brings up a mock-up of your stripe pattern. Be sure to name the pattern whatever makes sense to you. Leave all the settings to the default as seen in Figure 4.24b. Once you are happy, click *Done* in the top *Options* bar. Congratulations! You have successfully made a pinstripe print.

Step 3: As you make print patterns in Illustrator, they show up in the *Swatches* panel rather than a separate pattern panel. Draw out a new rectangle in any size you like. *Click* the last swatch in the panel before the folders for your fill. This should be your new pattern, like in Figure 4.24c.

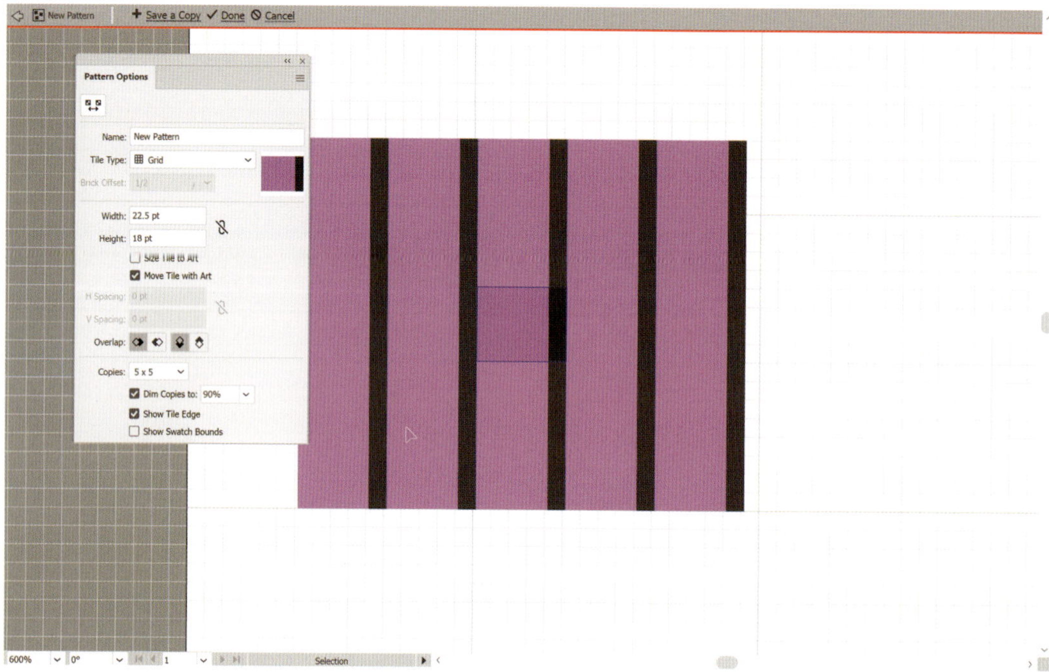

Figure 4.24b Use the *Selection* tool to select the colored rectangles. Then go to *Object* → *Pattern* → *Make* to define a new pattern. You can manipulate the pattern here, but for stripes we leave all the settings alone. Feel free to name your new pattern, though.

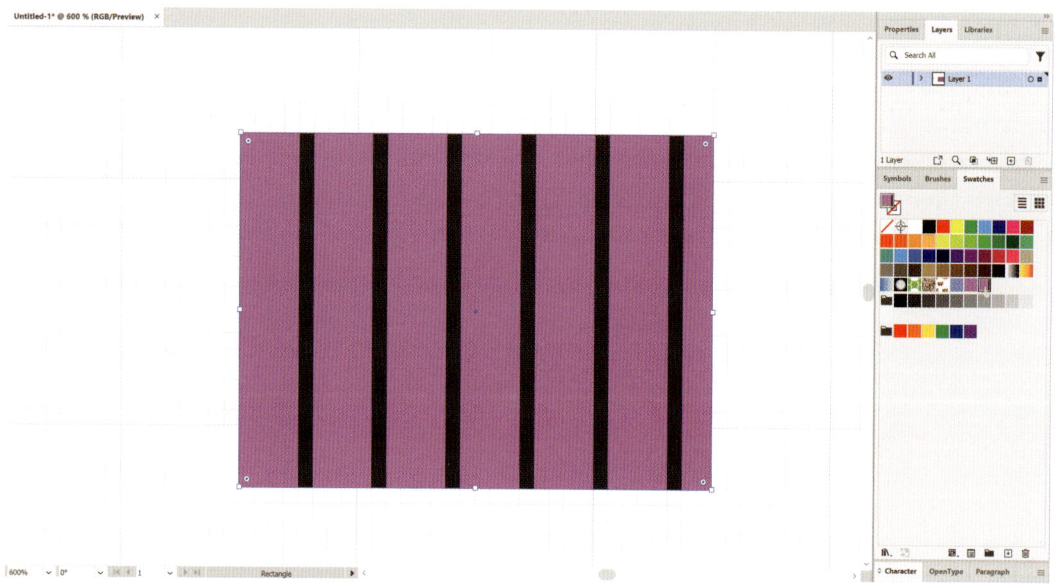

Figure 4.24c To see any of the new patterns you create as you go, draw out a new shape off to the side, then choose the fill from the *Swatches* panel. Your newly created patterns will show there.

Pattern 2: Step 1: Now let's make a plaid. Fill in a series of rectangles with the same height, but varying width and color fills. Remember to turn off the strokes. Fill in enough stripes to make the width equal to the height. In my case, I made it 1" high and filled enough stripes for it to be 1" wide. Your grid helps keep you on track with your measurements. Use the black *Selection* arrow to select all the stripes you just made. Use *control+g/ command+g* to group them together. Figure 4.25a shows our stripes grouped and in a square formation.

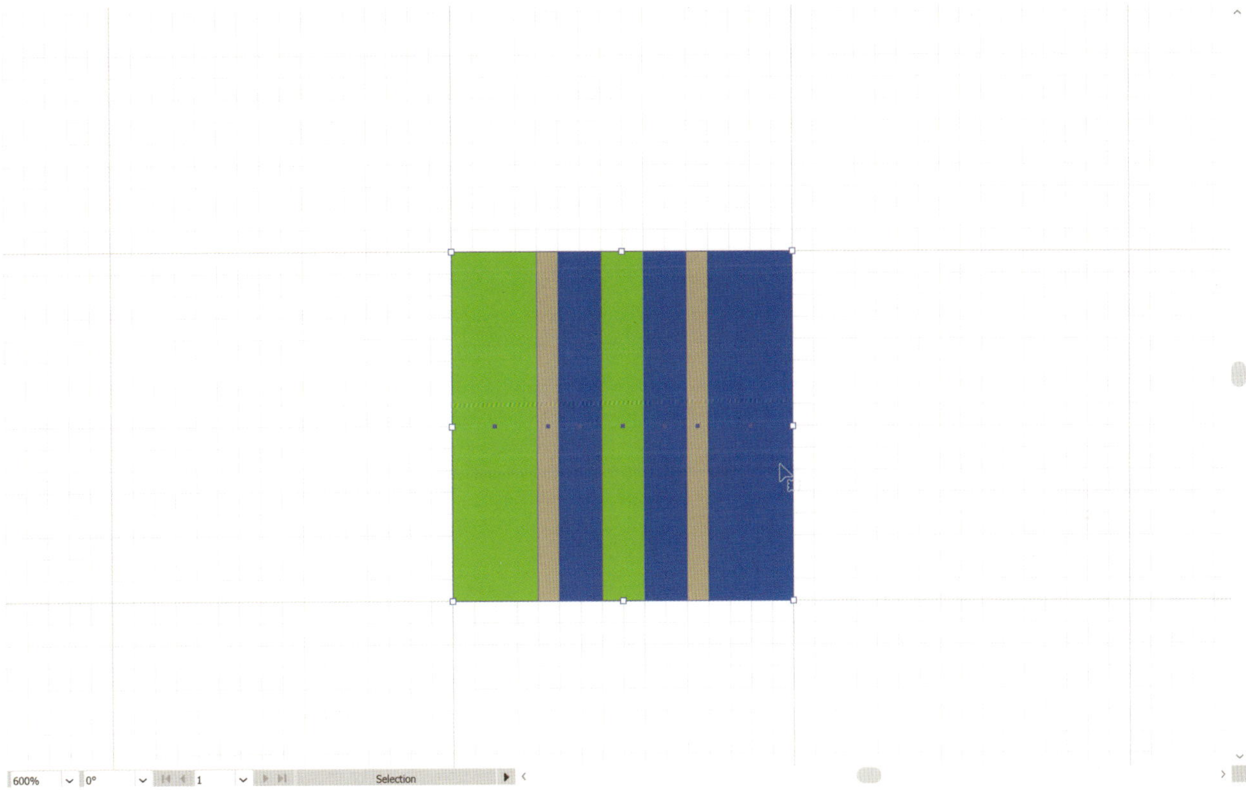

Figure 4.25a Using the same method you just learned, create a square of stripes. Group them together by selecting all the rectangles and *right-clicking* to choose *Group*.

Step 2: With the group selected, make a copy, and paste it in front using the keyboard shortcuts *control+c/ command+c*, then *control+f/command+f*. Select the *Rotate* tool (keyboard shortcut *r*) from the left Toolbar. It may be under your *Reflect* tool if you don't see it. Hit the *enter* or *return* key. This will bring up a dialog box. Type in 90 for the angle and make sure that *Transform Objects* is checked. Click *OK*. Your top stripe layer should rotate, as in Figure 4.25b. Now look in the *Properties* panel and change the *Opacity* to 50%. There is your plaid! Figure 4.25c shows our completed plaid.

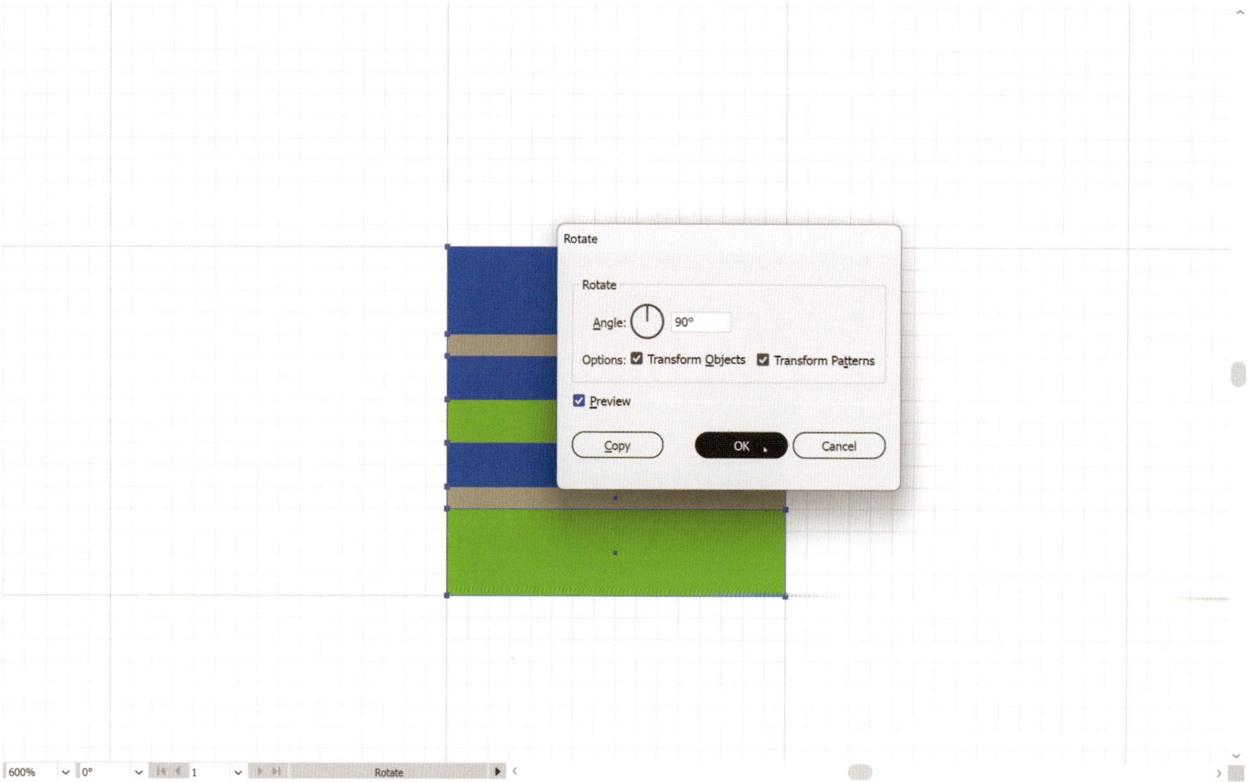

Figure 4.25b Make a duplicate of your group, then use the *Rotate* tool to turn the top layer 90 degrees.

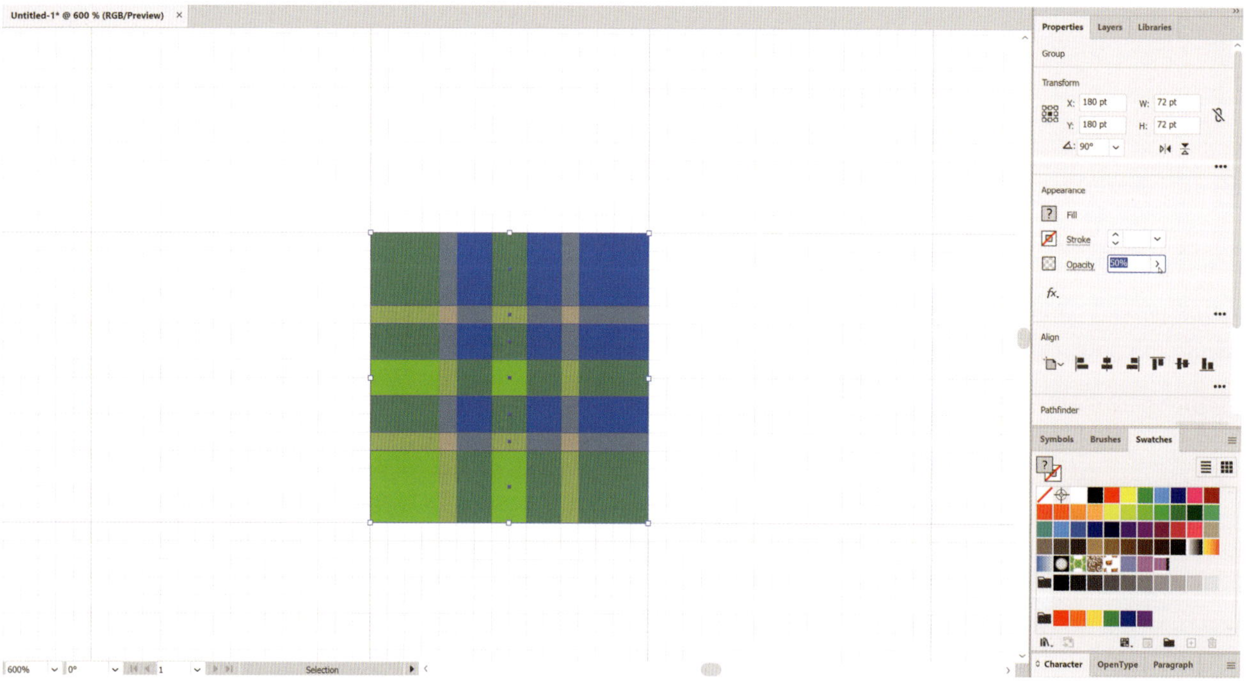

Figure 4.25c You now have a plaid. As before, turn this into a pattern swatch. This time, try *Selecting* the whole square, then drag it into the *Swatches* panel to automatically make a pattern.

Step 3. Use the black *Selection* arrow to select the whole block. This time, make sure your *Swatches* panel is open. Drag your selected plaid block into the *Swatches* panel. This will automatically create a basic pattern. *Double-click* the swatch in the *Swatches* panel to open the *Pattern* dialog box. Feel free to rename it whatever you like and click *OK*.

Pattern 3: Step 1. Let's try a more complicated pattern now. Start by pulling out *Guides* from the *Rulers* that will indicate the top, bottom, left, and right of the pattern tile. **Rulers** are onscreen measurement indicators that can be turned on for measurement reference. **Guides** are non-printing lines that can be placed to provide a visual reference. Check your *Guides* are locked (*View → Guides → Lock Guides*). If the *Grid* is distracting, turn it off through the *View* menu. Then draw your pattern tile within the guides. Use whichever tools you are comfortable with (*Pen, Pencil, Shapes*). Edit the tile to make it look how you want it to appear. You can put a rectangle with a solid fill and no stroke behind your shapes if you want your pattern to have a background as seen in Figure 4.26.

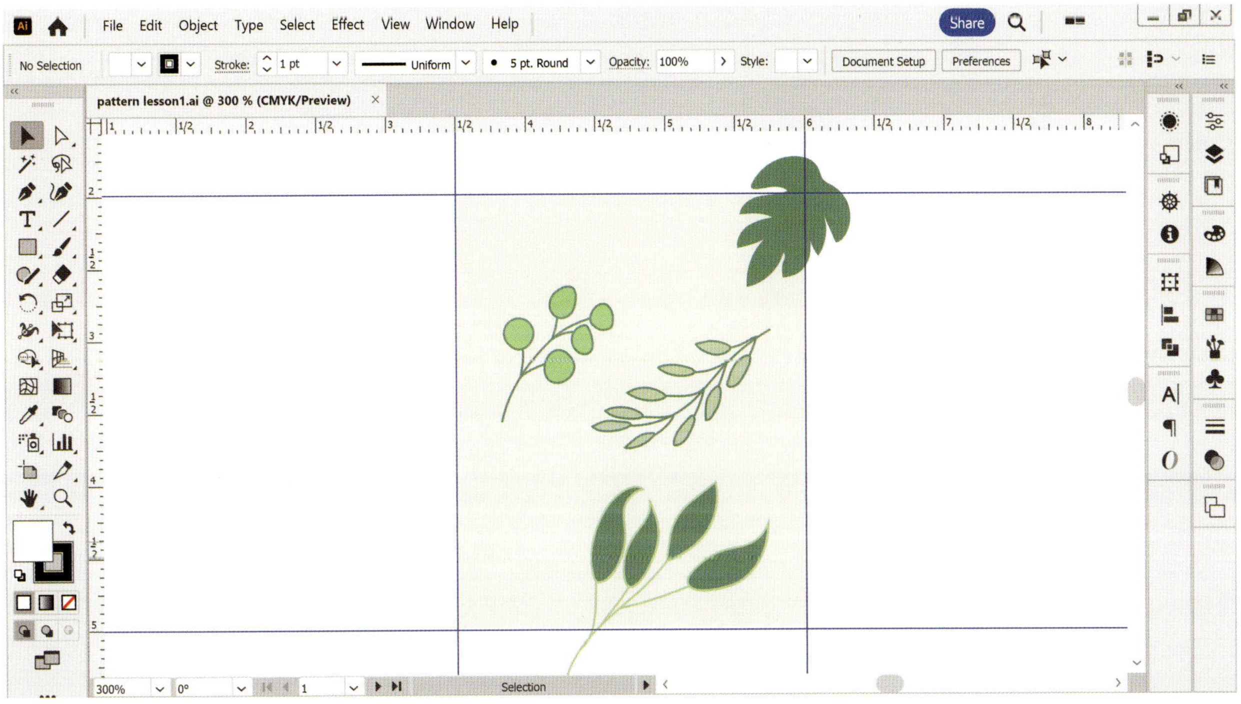

Figure 4.26 The guidelines show the limits of the tile. The motifs that extend beyond the guidelines are meant to wrap back around into the tile from the opposite direction. There is a rectangle in the back with a fill, but no stroke that will become the background color.

Step 2. Once you have drawn your pattern tile, use the *Selection* tool to select the objects that form the tile and make the swatch. To make the swatch, go to the *Object* menu, choose *Pattern* → *Make*. You have entered the *Pattern Editor* like in Figure 4.27.

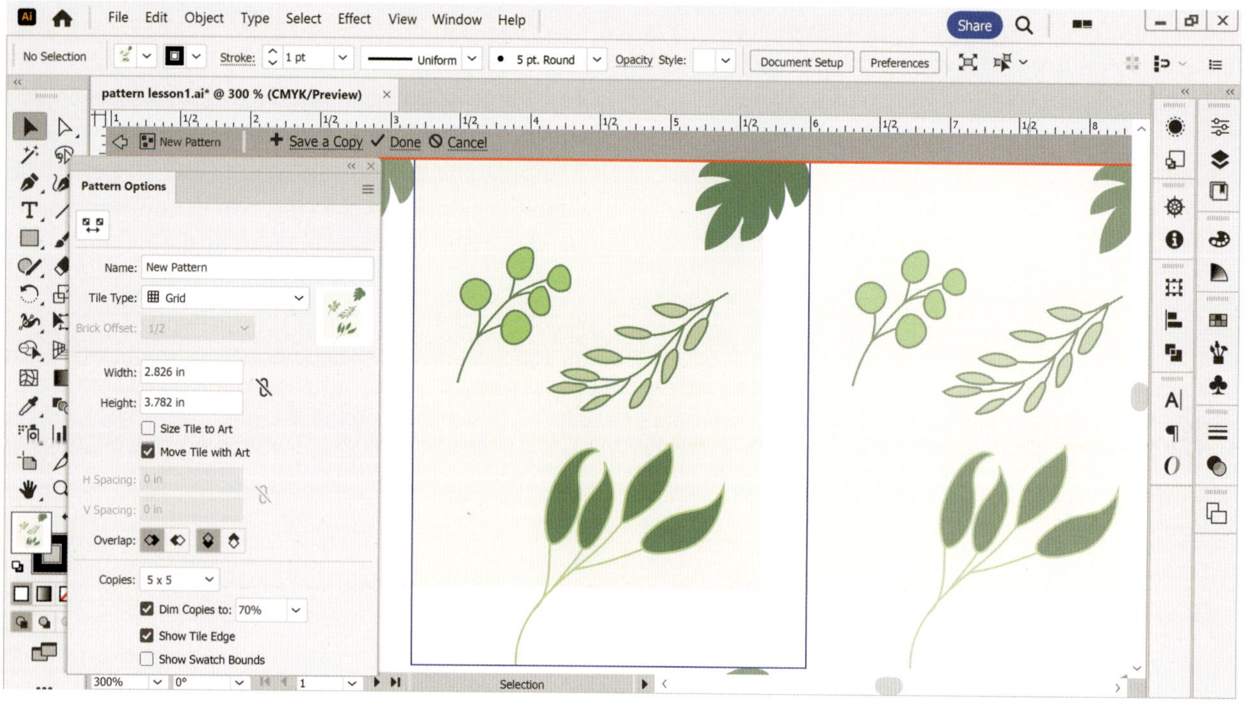

Figure 4.27 The guidelines are currently hidden (locked is also fine). All motifs and the background rectangle are selected. Go to *Object* → *Pattern* → *Create*.

PRO TIP 4.5

Analog Is Your Friend

Are you considering designing your own prints? Rather than facing the blank screen, grab some paper and a pencil! Sketch out multiple ideas. Use your resources and check out the local library for inspiration. Just because you are rendering in a digital format doesn't mean you have to do everything digitally! Do you want to design an abstract floral? Spend some time sketching in the garden. Are you inspired by Dali? Find a print book on his work. Or better yet, go to see his work in a museum!

You can adjust the width and height in the *Pattern Options* panel to omit any gaps between tiles or add more space. The easiest way to accomplish this is by clicking on the *Pattern Tile* tool in the upper left corner of the *Pattern Options* panel. A bounding box will appear when you click the tool. Grab each side of the bounding box and pull it in to match the edge of the background tile. This may result in some of the motifs being cut off. The *Overlap* direction in the panel controls which parts of overhanging element will be seen on top. Play around with these to see if there is a successful result as in Figures 4.28 and 4.29.

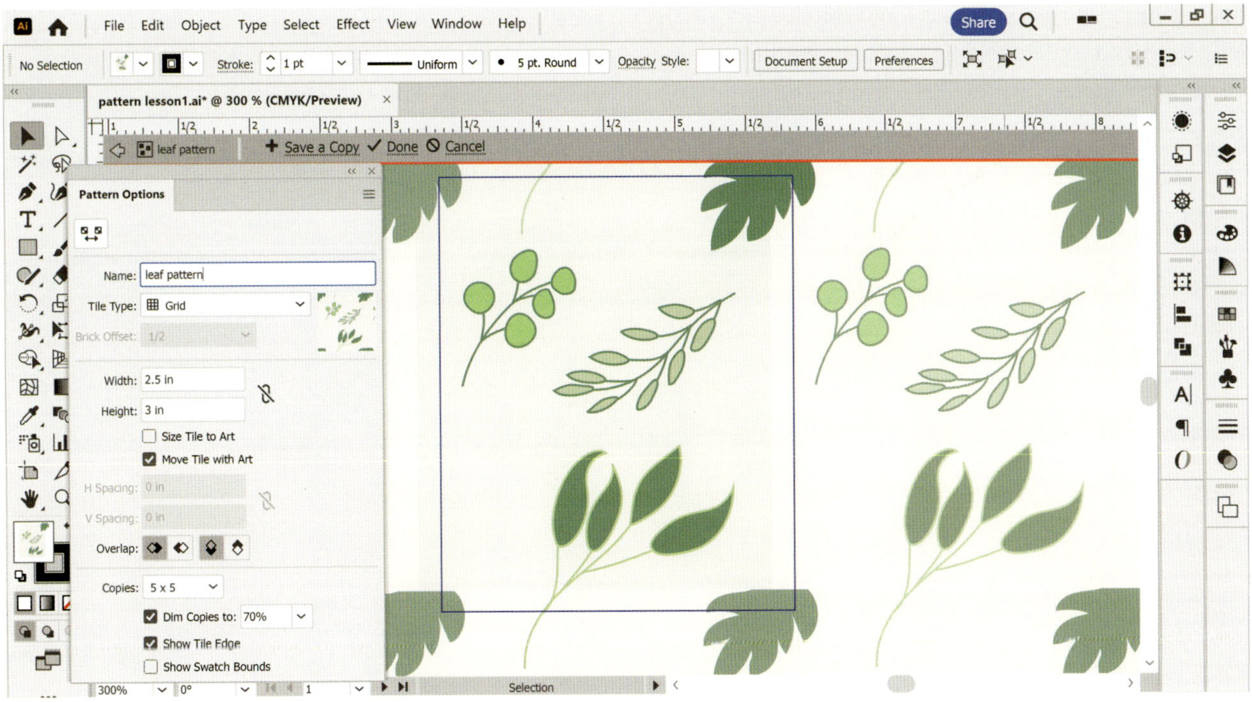

Figure 4.28 Screenshot of working with the *Pattern Editor*. Name your pattern in the *Pattern Options* panel. You can change the width and height using the *Pattern Tile* tool in the panel to add or eliminate space between tiles.

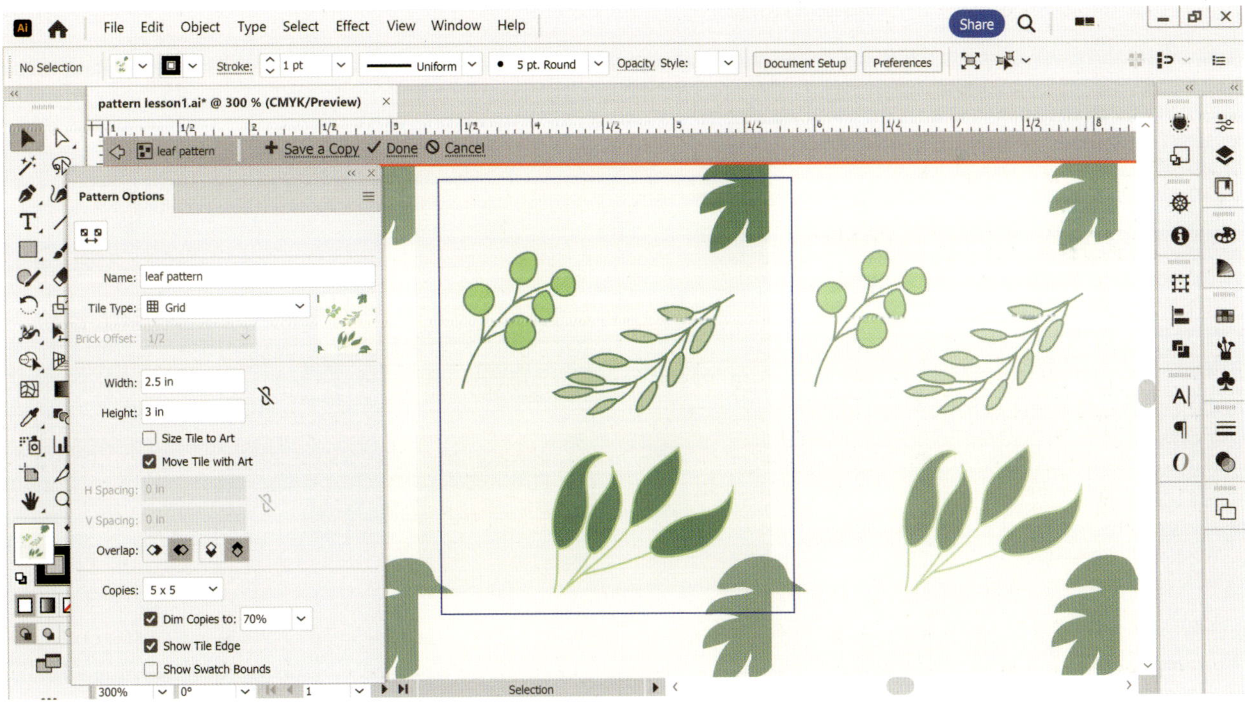

Figure 4.29 The big monstera leaf was originally lapping into the top left corner of the tile. Now it is showing in the bottom right corner of the tile. Sometimes, changing the Overlap direction will fix problems in a tile. Sometimes, you must do more work.

If a motif gets cut off regardless of the chosen overlap option, you can make a copy of the motif and paste it the correct overlap position as is shown in Figure 4.30. Use the *Selection* tool to select the motif. You can hold the *alt/option* key while moving the leaf to make a duplicate. Just remember to release your mouse before you release the key. You can also move motifs around and adjust them in this mode.

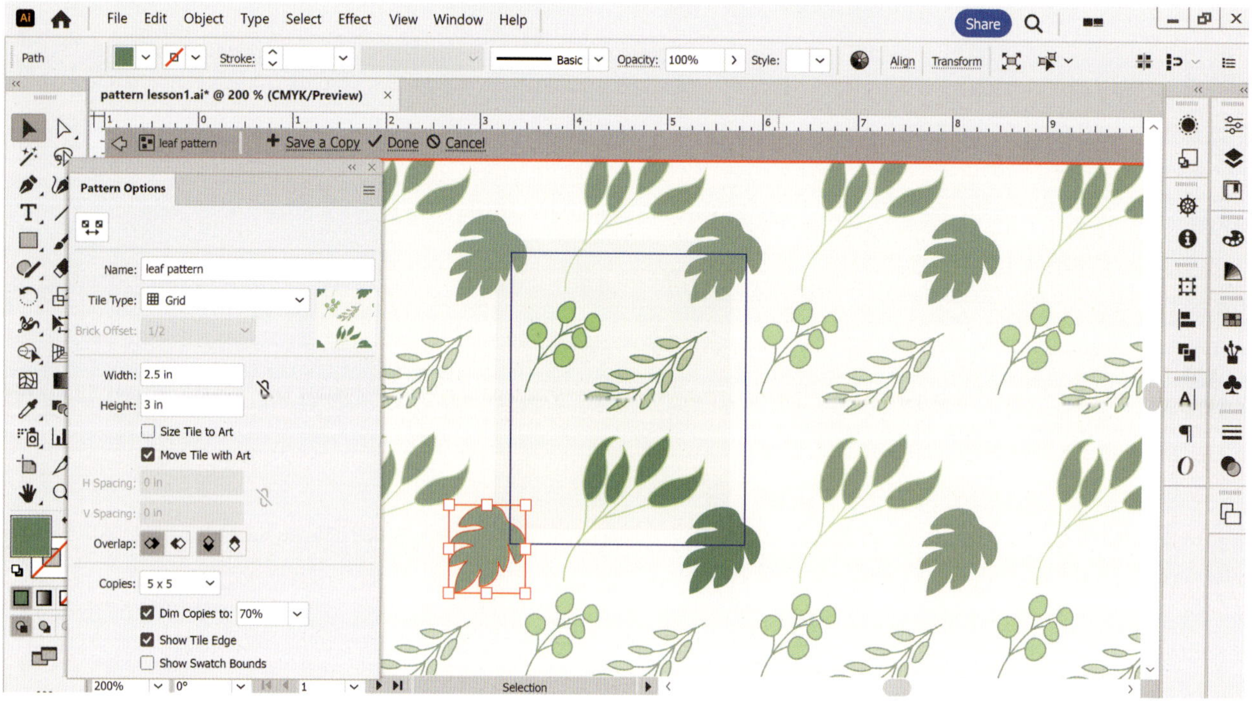

Figure 4.30 There was no perfect solution with overlap directions for this tile. Instead, the motifs that are missing parts in the overlap are selected one at a time, copied and pasted. After pasting, they are moved exactly on top of one of the partial motifs to make up the missing parts. This is done repeatedly until all motifs are complete.

Step 3. Once the pattern looks how you want it, make sure you have given the pattern a name at the top of the *Pattern Options* panel. Then either click *Done* to save the pattern or *Save a Copy* to save the changes as a new pattern. The finished pattern is saved as a swatch in the *Swatches* panel as can be seen in Figure 4.31. It can be used as a fill for any shape.

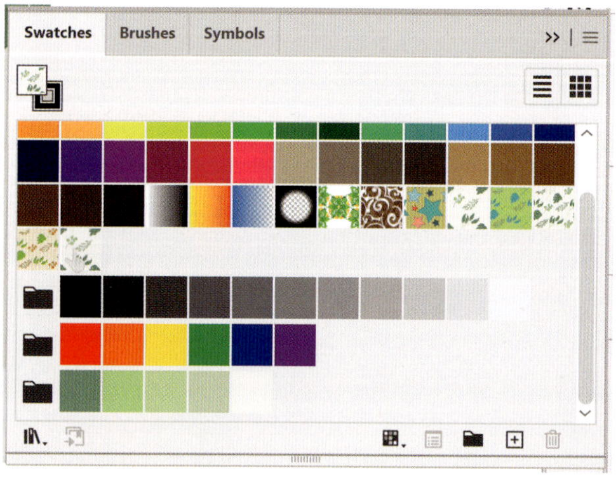

Figure 4.31 Screenshot of the *Swatches* panel. The pattern tile you made will appear in here.

Step 4. To edit a finished pattern, *double-click* the pattern in the *Swatches* panel and it will reopen in the *Pattern Editor*.

The default tile type (repeat pattern) is *Grid* in Illustrator. However, you can choose between *Grid, Brick by Row, Brick by Column* (half drop), *Hex by Column* (as seen in Figure 4.32), and *Hex by Row*. As you experiment with these, try changing the width, height, and overlaps to help your pattern. Additionally, use the *Selection* tool and move motifs around to create a more successful layout.

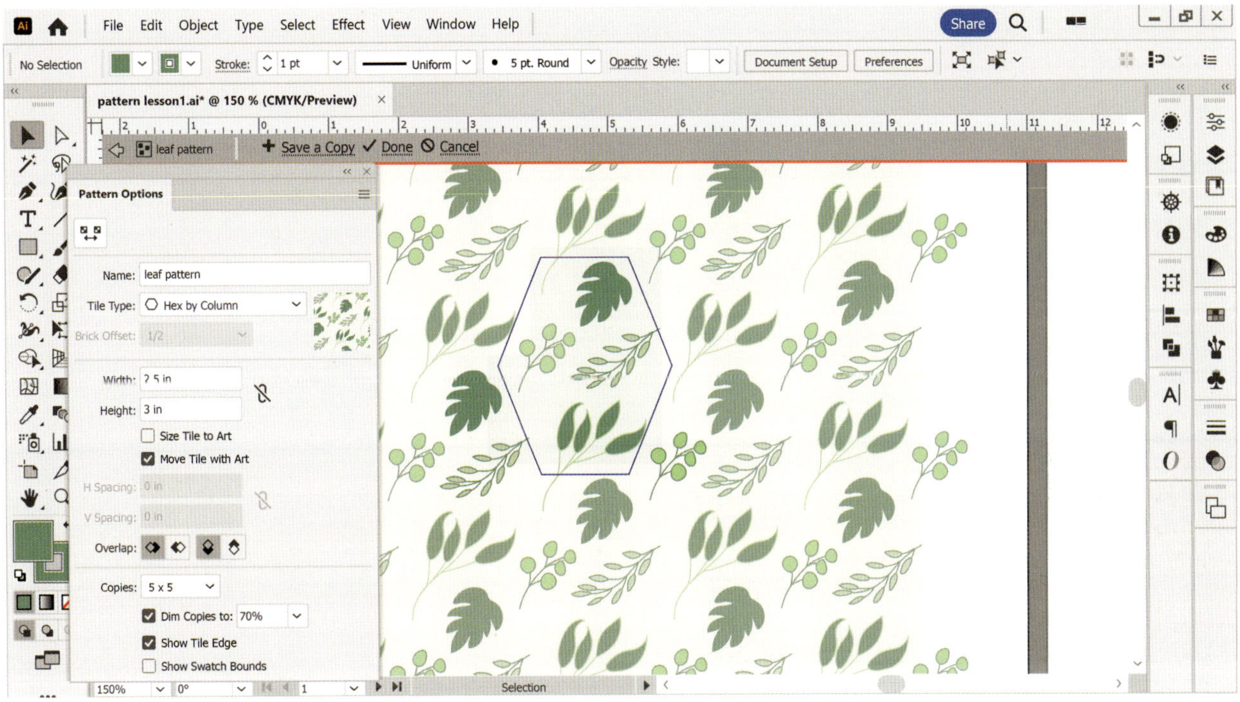

Figure 4.32 The *Tile Type* option on the *Pattern Options* panel allows you to choose between several types of pattern repeats. This is a *Hex by Column* repeat. You may have to move motifs around or copy and paste motifs to make a repeat look nice.

Pattern 4: Step 1. As your swatch (pattern tile) is a fully editable Illustrator file, you can change aspects of the pattern at any time. For instance, do you need the pattern in a different colorway? Reopen the pattern in the *Pattern Editor*, *Save a Copy* of the swatch before beginning (to keep the original colorway), then proceed to change the colors of the motifs. Then save the swatch as the new colorway. An easy way to replace the colors quickly is to select all the elements of pattern while you are in the *Pattern Editor*, then go to *Edit* → *Edit Colors* → *Recolor Artwork* as shown in Figure 4.33. The **Recolor artwork** panel will display the colors in your pattern at the bottom. You can use this panel to change individual colors. As you move the circles around in the center area of the panel, the pattern will recolor, as demonstrated in Figure 4.34.

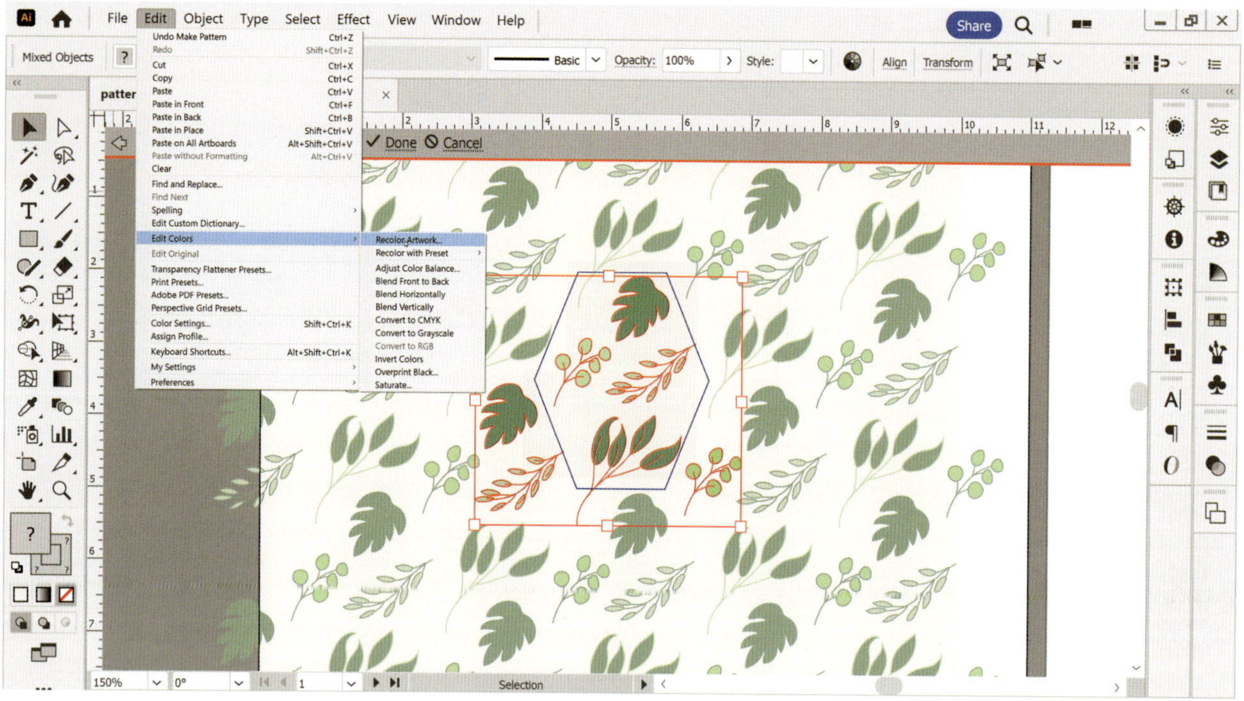

Figure 4.33 To recolor a pattern, double-click the swatch in the *Swatches* panel to open it. Either choose all the motifs, if you want to change everything at one time, or chose one element at a time to recolor one part at a time. This image show opening the *Recolor Artwork* dialog.

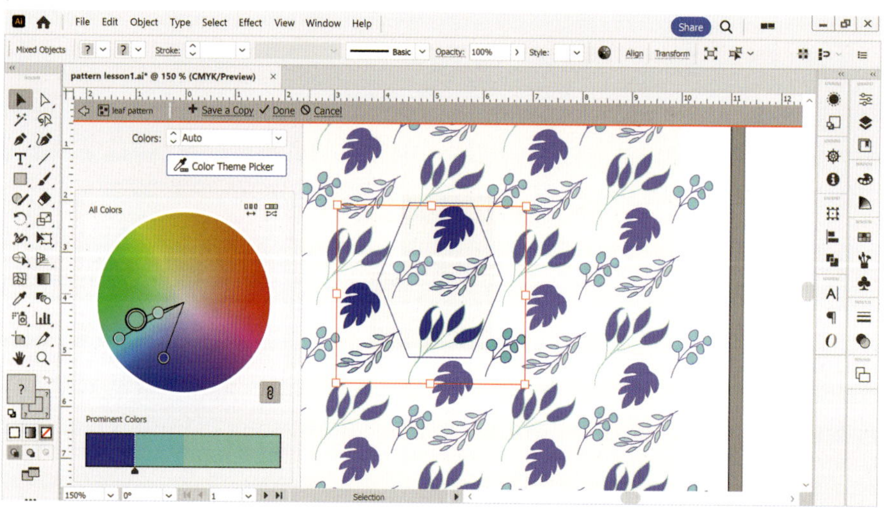

Figure 4.34 Screenshot of using *Recolor Artwork* to recolor swatches. By moving the circles in the panel, the chosen motifs in the tile will change colors. The circles in the panel can be moved around the color wheel to control hue as well as moved in and out to control intensity.

To save a print fill for future use in other documents, you can save the entire *Swatch Library*. To do this, go to the *Swatch* panel drop-down menu and choose *Save Swatch Library as AI*, like it shows in Figure 4.35. Give the library a name. This is not your Adobe Cloud Library. This is a local file that is available only on your specific device. Next time you need this swatch or set of swatches, go to the *Open Swatch Library* option and choose *User Defined*. Choose your library from the list as seen in Figure 4.36.

You can also import new patterns. When in the *Open Swatch Library* menu, choose *Other Library …* to select a file outside the Adobe presets. Navigate to the exercise file PatternLibary2.ai and select it. Select any of the patterns from the popup menu for your use. Have fun with the sample patterns!

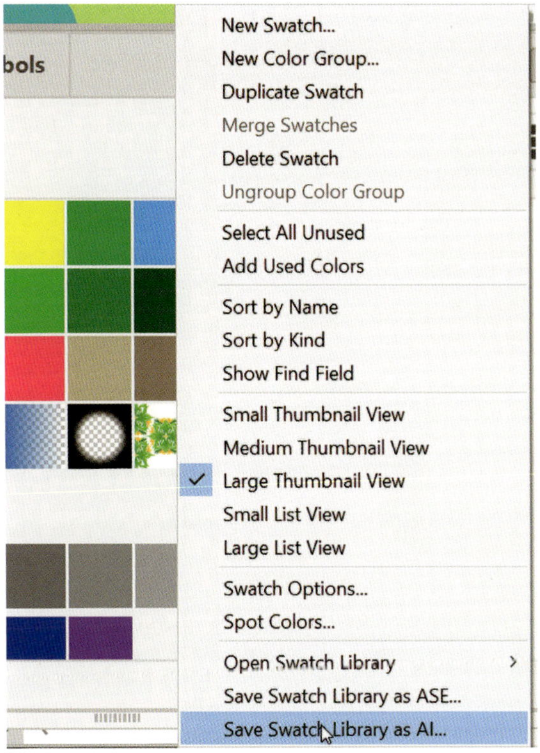

Figure 4.35 In the *Swatches* panel, go to the drop-down menu and choose *Save Swatch Library as AI*. Give your library a name.

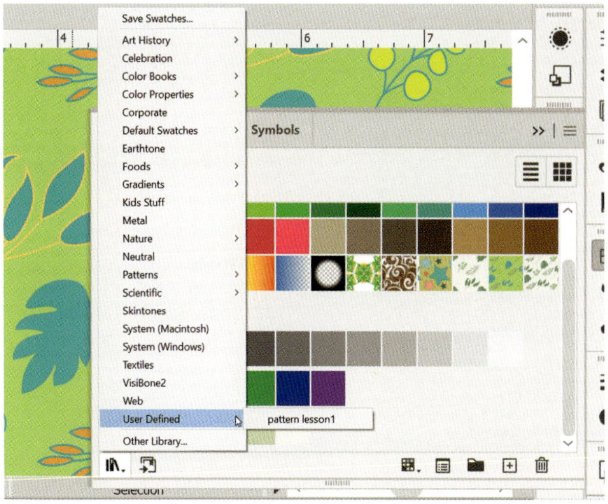

Figure 4.36 In the *Swatch* panel, go to the *Libraries* button, then scroll to *User Defined*. You should see your previously saved *Swatch Libraries* there.

PRO TIP 4.6

Ready, Set, Collect: Make a Library

Designers often aren't quite sure what the best fabric choice is until they've seen it. It is in your favor to save any previous print/texture repeats into a library for on-the-fly use. If you are the designer and illustrator, then you can easily access and try different textures or prints to see what looks best. If the designer, director, merchandiser, or some other decision-maker needs to see more than one option, you have a library ready from which to choose. Now that you know how to apply pattern repeats, it is simple enough to display different fabric choices to help yourself or others visualize.

Project 4.6: Apply, Scale, and Rotate Pattern Fills in Ai

Let's put our new patterns to use. *Open* exercise file PatternPlay2.ai. To apply a pattern to an illustration, select the shape that you want patterned (the dress body in this case). Make sure you are adjusting the fill, not the stroke. Then *click* on the pattern you made in the *Swatches* panel like in Figure 4.37.

In order to scale a pattern that you have applied to an illustration, use the *Scale* tool (keyboard shortcut *s*). Start by selecting the objects with a pattern fill with the *Selection* tool. Then switch to the *Scale* tool as shown in Figure 4.38. Hold the *alt/option* key while *clicking* on the pattern with the *Scale* tool. The addition of the *alt/option* key will trigger an options box for the *Scale* tool.

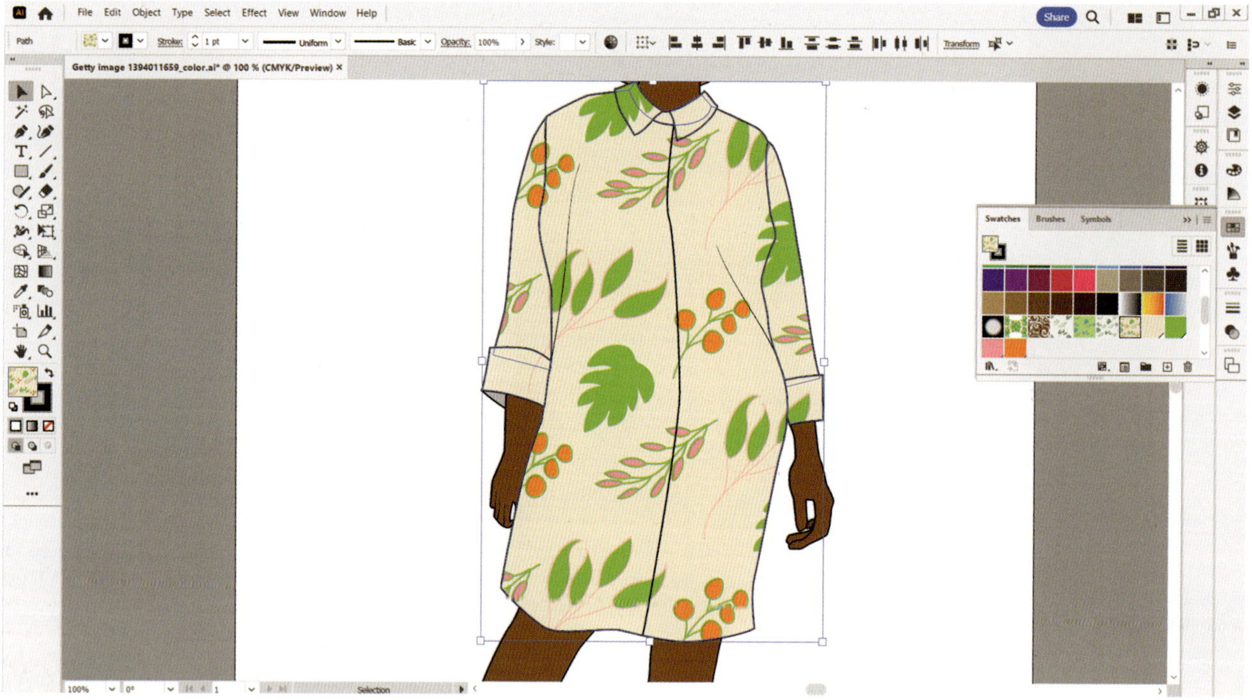

Figure 4.37 To apply a previously made pattern, make sure the pattern is open in the *Swatches* panel. Choose all the items (shapes) that you would like to apply the pattern to. Make sure you are adjusting the fill, not the stroke. Click on your pattern swatch in the panel.

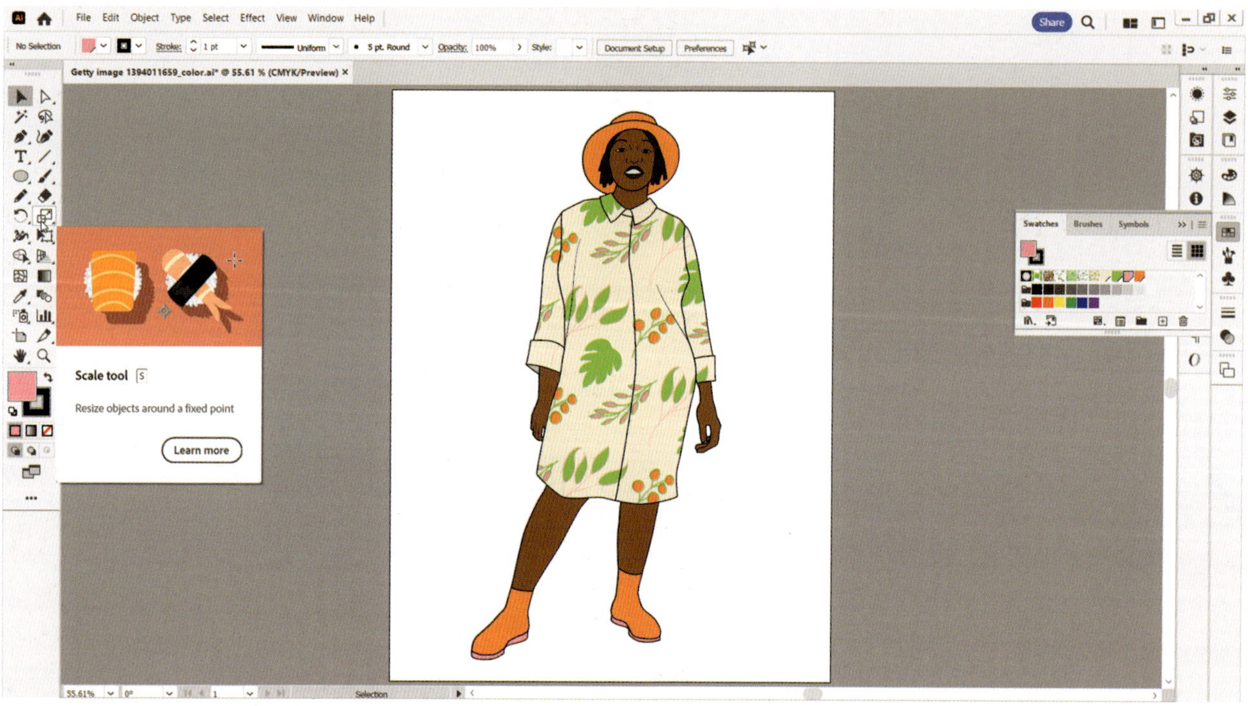

Figure 4.38 Select all items with the pattern you wish to scale. Switch to the *Scale* tool *(s)*.

In the pop-up options box, in the *Options* section, check *Transform Patterns* and uncheck everything else in that section. In the *Scale* section, you will be able to choose how much you want to scale the pattern up or down like in Figure 4.39. You can un/recheck the *Preview* box at the bottom of the menu to force a preview and review your choice before clicking *OK*.

Pattern rotation is very similar to scaling. Make sure you have selected the patterned shapes first. Change to the *Rotation* tool (keyboard shortcut *r*). Hold the *alt/*

option key when *clicking* the patterned object with the *Rotation* tool to trigger the pop-up options box. As shown in Figure 4.40, make sure *Transform Patterns* is checked and *Transform Objects* is NOT checked in the options box. Then you can choose the new angle for your pattern.

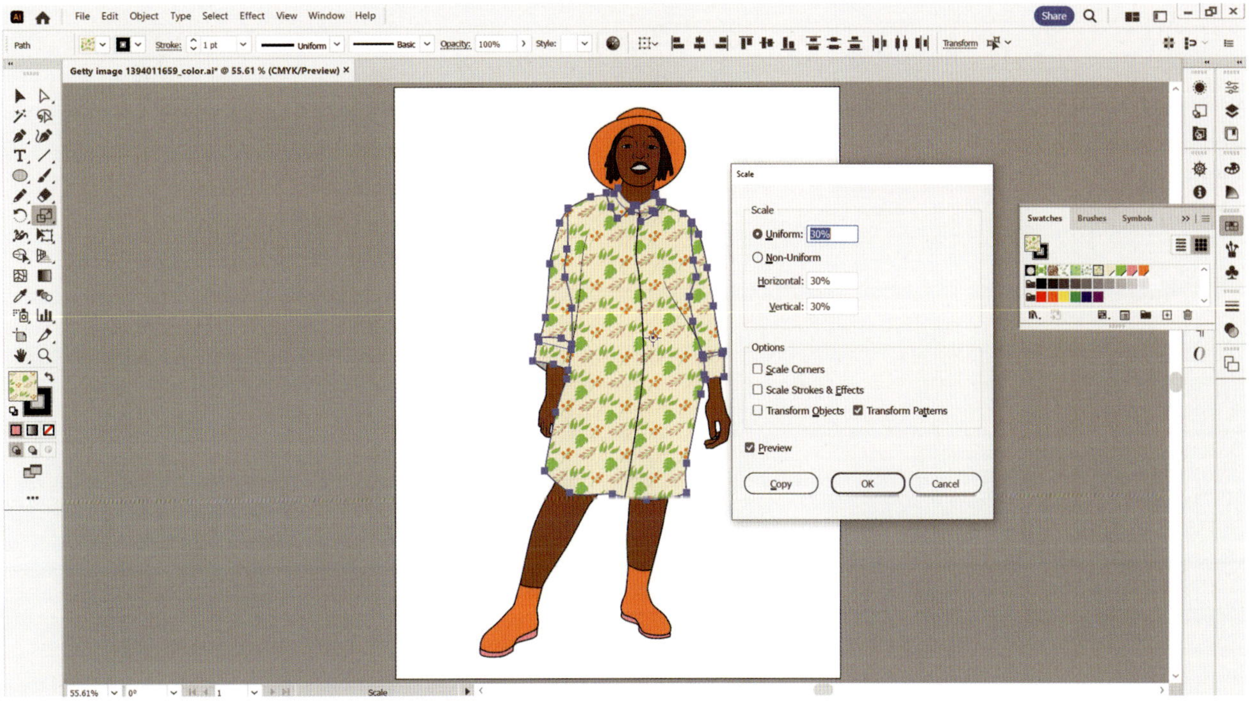

Figure 4.39 To scale a pattern, hold the *alt/option* key when clicking the objects with the *Scale* tool. This will trigger a pop-up options box. In the *Options* section of the pop-up dialog box, make sure *Transform Patterns* is checked and all other options are unchecked. In the top section of the menu, you can control how much bigger or smaller you would like to make the pattern.

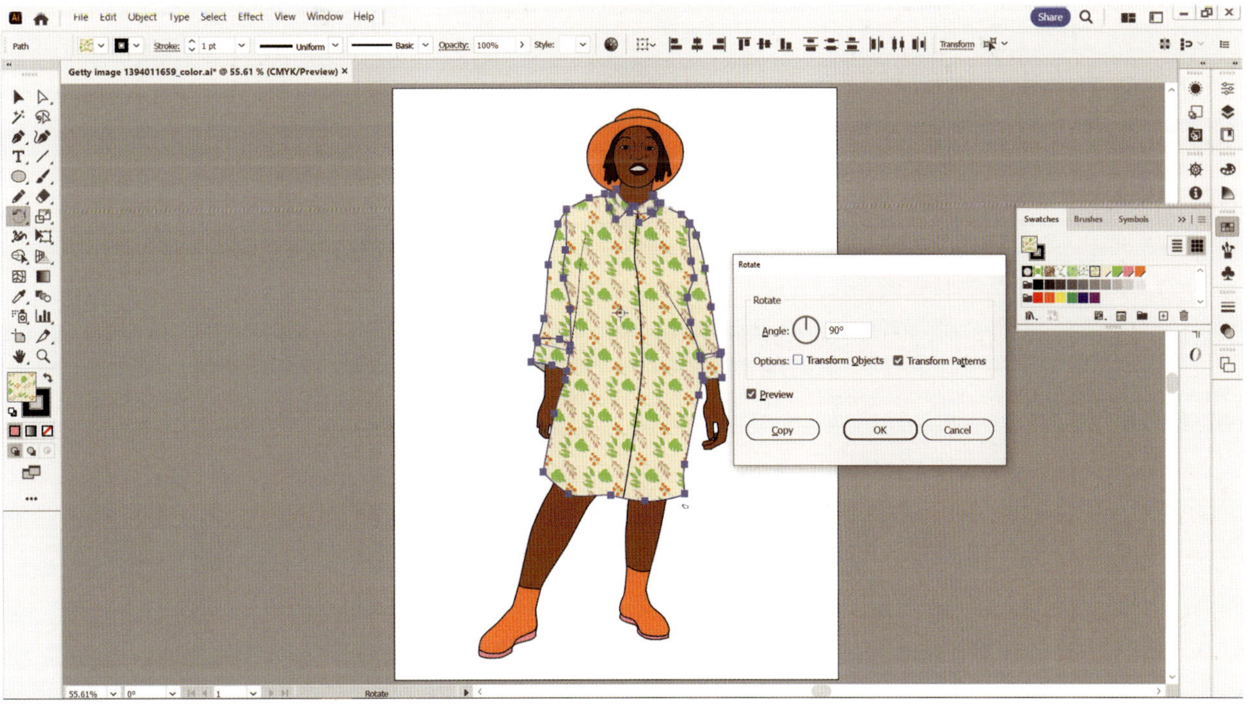

Figure 4.40 Select all objects with the pattern you would like to rotate. Switch to the *Rotation* tool. Hold the *alt/option* key when you click on the objects with the tool. In the pop-up options box, *Transform Patterns* should be checked, but *Transform Objects* should not. Use the angle to control the degree of rotation.

Project 4.7: Envelope Distort for Patterns

Warping in illustrator is less common. However, there is a way to do it through a command called **Envelope Distort**.[2] This creates an "envelope" with the pattern fill that you can manipulate to look like it is wrapping around the body. The process is similar to the way we create a pattern fill *Smart Object* in Photoshop.

Step 1: Start with your Illustrator file open. Make a new layer below your dress layer. On this layer, use the *Rectangle* tool to make a generous rectangle that covers the dress area completely. Remove the stroke and fill with your pattern of choice. As usual, you may want to choose a plaid because that will show the distortion better.

Step 2: With the rectangle selected using the black arrow (*Selection* tool), go to the *Object menu → Envelope Distort → Make with Mesh*. A dialog box will ask how many rows and columns, as seen in Figure 4.41. Add enough to give you the precision you like without so many that you spend hours fixing the warp. In our example, we kept it at four rows and four columns.

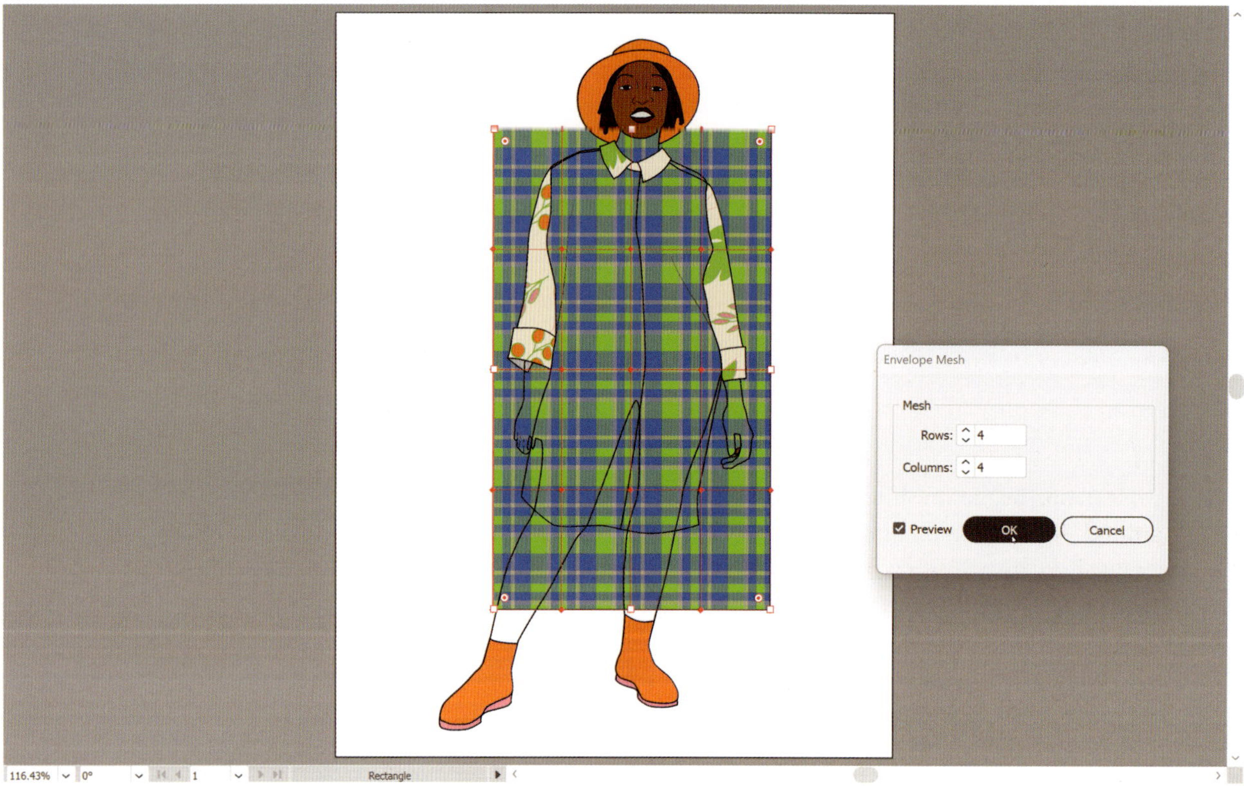

Figure 4.41 Warping a pattern fill in Illustrator is a little harder. Create a rectangle filled with your pattern below your object (in this case, the dress body). Select the rectangle and go to *Object → Envelope Distort → Make with Mesh*. Choose how many rows and columns you like. Notice that we have turned off the fill for the dress and body shapes in order to see how the pattern manipulation looks.

Step 3: Before you start to manipulate the mesh, check the settings on your distortion. Go to *Object → Envelope Distort → Envelope Options*. Unless you have raster effects in your print, don't worry about the top options. Just leave them set to the default. Make sure that *Distort Pattern Fills* is checked towards the bottom, though. Then click *OK*. Figure 4.42 shows the options box.

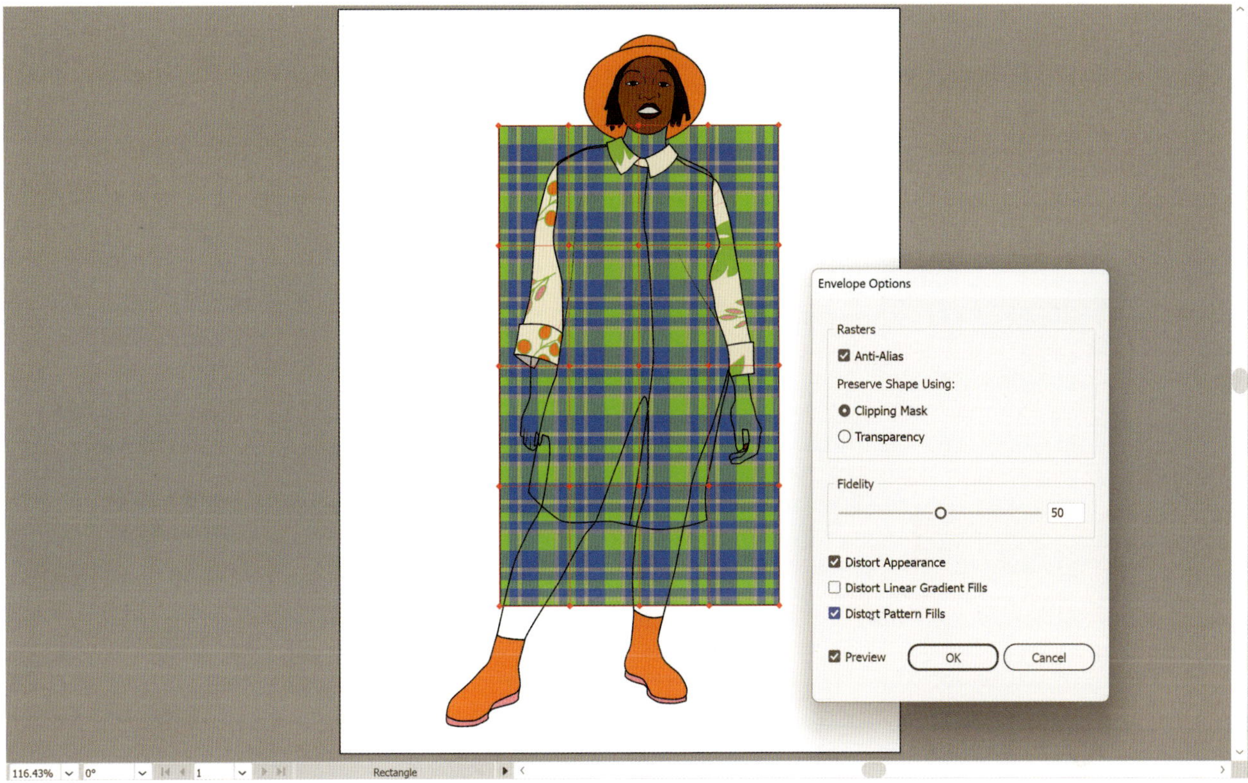

Figure 4.42 Before you warp the object, check your options panel. Go to *Object* ⟶ *Envelope Distort* ⟶ *Envelope Options*. In this box, make sure that *Distort Pattern Fills* is checked.

Step 4: Switch to the white arrow (*Direct Selection* tool). *Click* on an anchor in the mesh to push and pull your pattern around. If your whole rectangle moves, double-check that you have the white arrow tool (not the black) and that you are *clicking* on an anchor point before moving it. To see your work, you may want to switch your dress shape to no fill, and then lock the entire layer so you don't accidentally move the wrong item. Figure 4.43 shows the distortion created with no fill on the dress or body shapes. Once you have the warp adjusted to your liking, you are ready to clip it into the dress shape.

Step 5: *Unlock* your dress layer, then select both the rectangle and dress shape (hold *shift*). Make sure you are using the black arrow tool to select the entire objects. *Right-click*, then choose *Make Clipping mask*. Clipping masks in Illustrator work in the opposite layer direction from Photoshop. In Illustrator a layer clips up, whereas in Photoshop it clips down. We honestly think they did that just to mess with all of us!

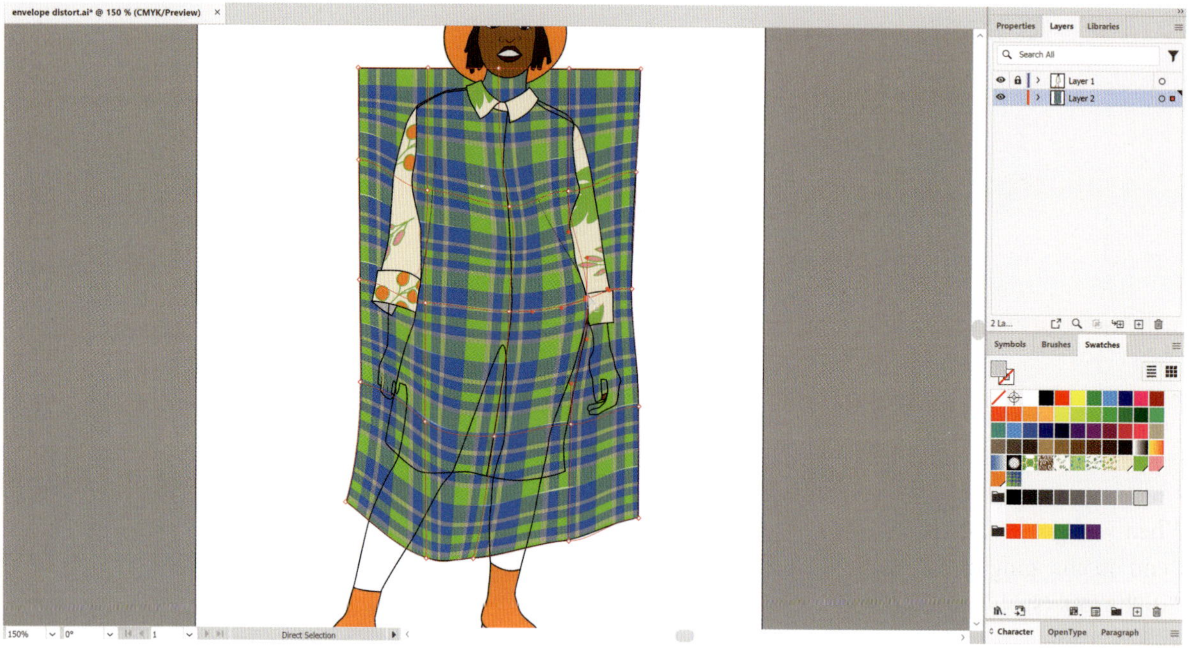

Figure 4.43 Use the *Direct Selection* tool (white arrow) to click on anchor points and handles to manipulate the warp. Notice that if you get too heavy-handed, the pattern starts to develop "cracks." There is not a good way to fix this, so be more subtle with your distortion.

Step 6: Your pattern will clip into the dress. Notice in Figure 4.44 that the stroke was changed to "none." You will need to reapply the stroke. It disappears when you use the *Clipping mask*. Repeat the process for the other parts of the dress that need a warp. If it looks fine without the warp, then just leave it as a normal fill on the object.

Sadly, there is not an easy way to create fold distortions in Illustrator directly. You can add more rows and columns to give you micro precision during the envelope distortion. However, that gets tedious. Once you finish up the rendering in Illustrator, you may want to import it into Photoshop to liquify the fold areas of your pattern fill if it is necessary to communicate them.

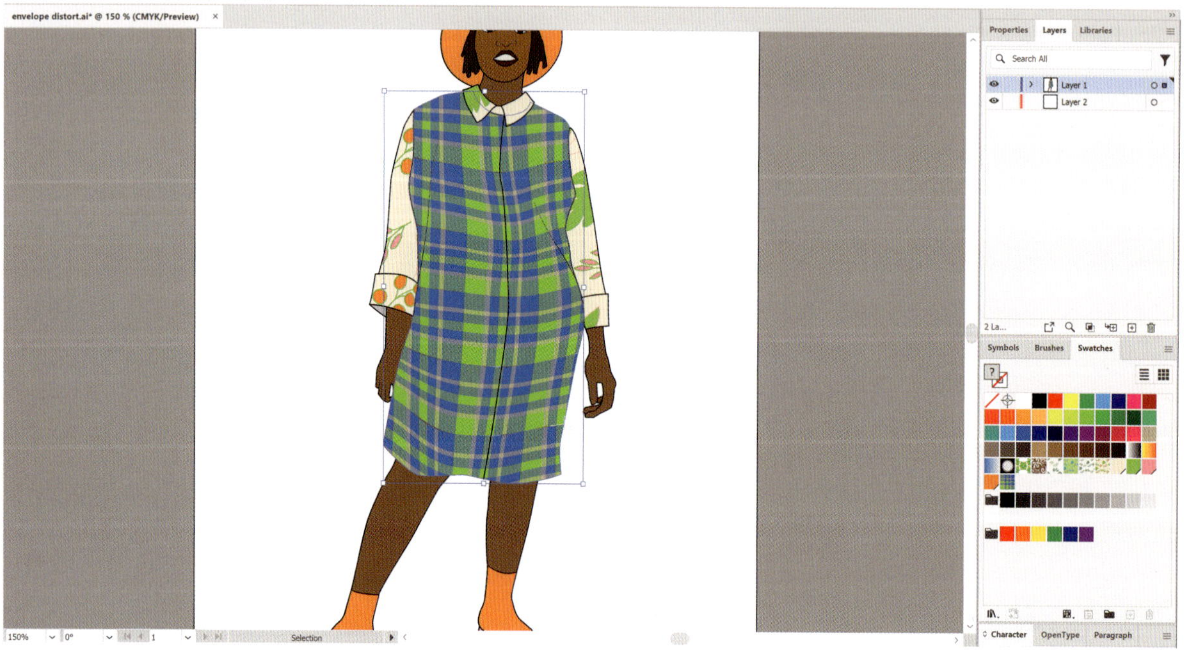

Figure 4.44 Clip your pattern fill up into your object. Use the *Selection* tool (black arrow) tool to select the rectangle and the dress shape. *Right-click* and choose *Make Clipping mask*. If you get an error message, check that you have the black arrow, not the white one. Feel free to add the stroke color back to the body shape. Now try the sleeves!

Troubleshooting

"Why does a grid appear when I turn my artwork into a pattern?"

A common mistake when creating your own prints in Illustrator is to leave the stroke on your background rectangle. If you see a weird grid that shows up in the repeat such as that seen in Figure 4.45a, go back to the original artwork. Check your background rectangle to make sure there is no stroke applied, as shown in Figure 4.45b. Then resave the pattern tile.

"When I scale/rotate my pattern, the shape changes instead of the pattern. What's wrong?"

When you go to scale or rotate your pattern fill you may end up changing the whole shape. If this is the case, go into the tool (such as *Scale*) and hit the *enter* or *return* key before you manipulate anything. It will bring up the options box. Alternatively, you can hold the *alt* or *option* keys and *click* anywhere on the screen. In the dialog box, make sure that *Transform Object* is not checked while *Transform Pattern* is checked. This should solve the issue.

"I keep getting an error when I try to clip my pattern into the object!"

When trying to clip one object into another in Illustrator, first check that the object you want clipped (such as the rectangle with the warped pattern fill) is below the object you want to clip it into. This is a little confusing if you are used to Photoshop, where the layers should be in the opposite stacking order. Make sure both objects are fully selected with the *Selection* tool (black arrow) and not the *Direct Selection* tool (white arrow). Check that you don't accidentally have one of the details of the object selected instead. Then you should be able to successfully clip the objects.

"I made a pattern with a transparent background. How can I fill the background without making a new pattern?"

Remember that when you clip your warped pattern into an object, the stroke disappears. You will need to reapply the stroke. Likewise, if you used a pattern fill with transparent areas and need to add a background color, use the *Appearance* panel to add a second fill below the group. Figure 4.46 shows a second fill applied below the pattern fill in the *Appearance* panel to create the background.

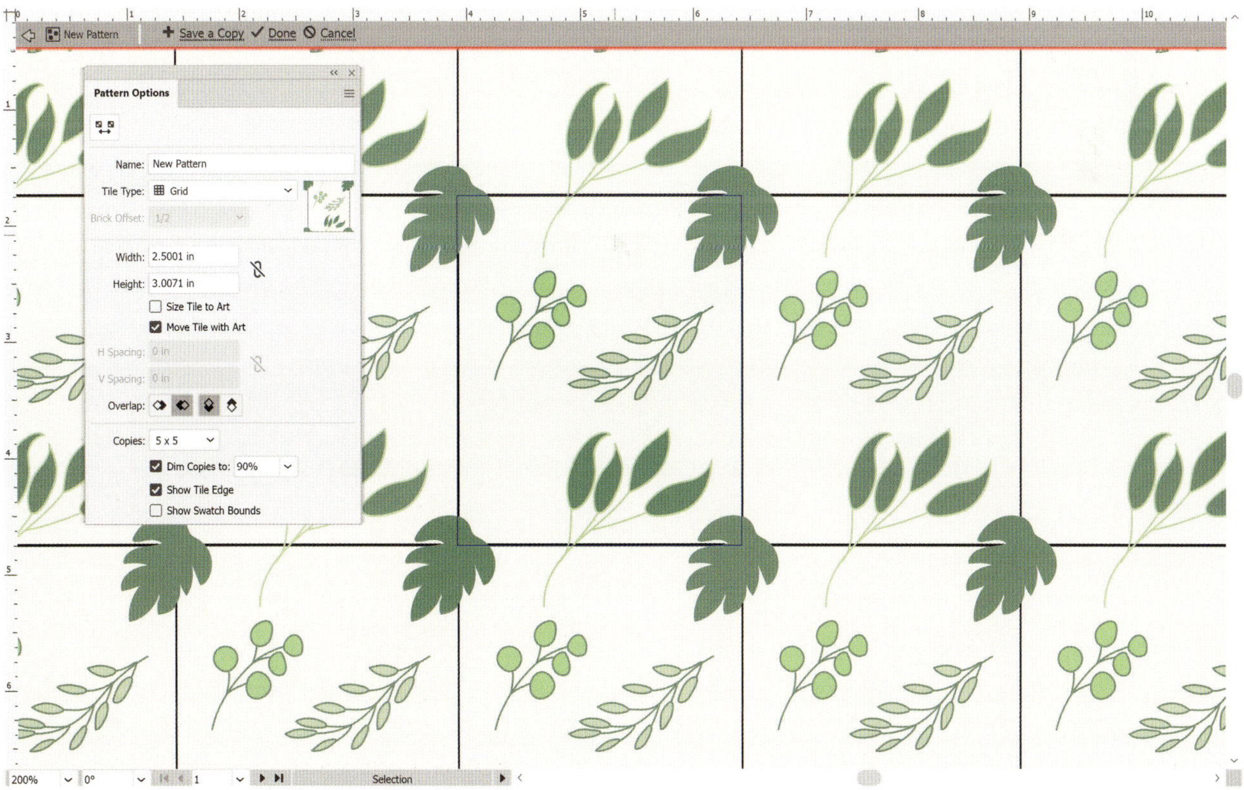

Figure 4.45a If you left a stroke on your background tile, you will see this annoying grid show up in the *Pattern Editor*.

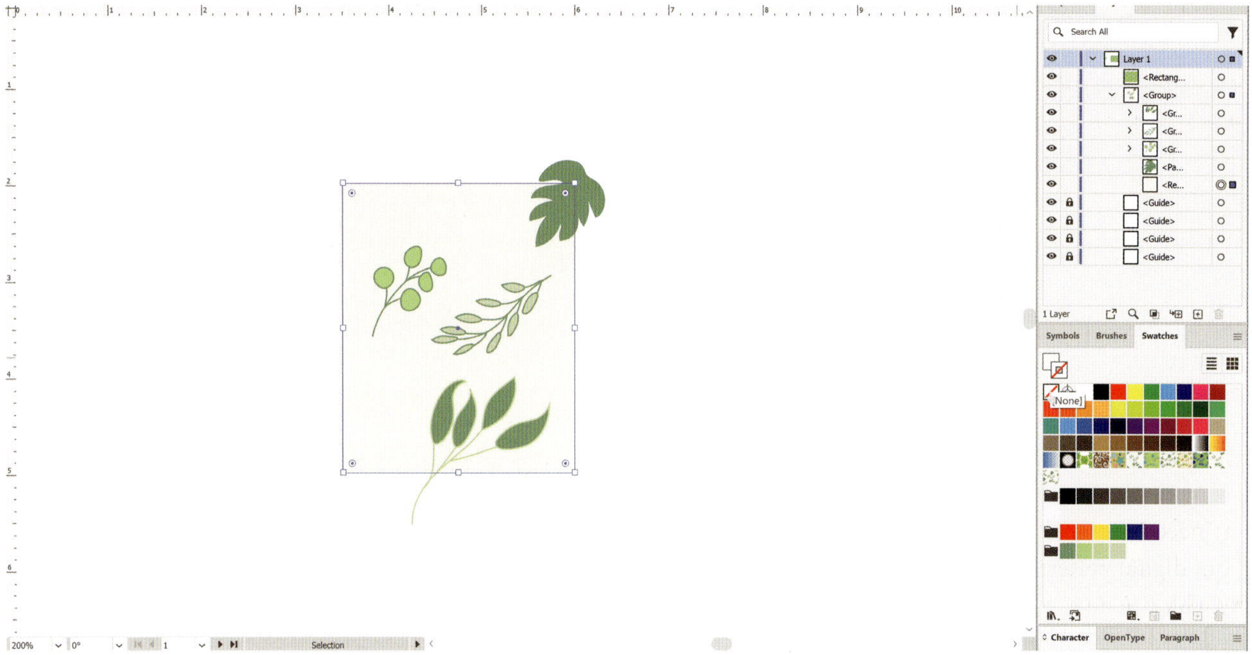

Figure 4.45b Exit out of the *Pattern Editor*, select your background tile and remove the stroke to fix the issue.

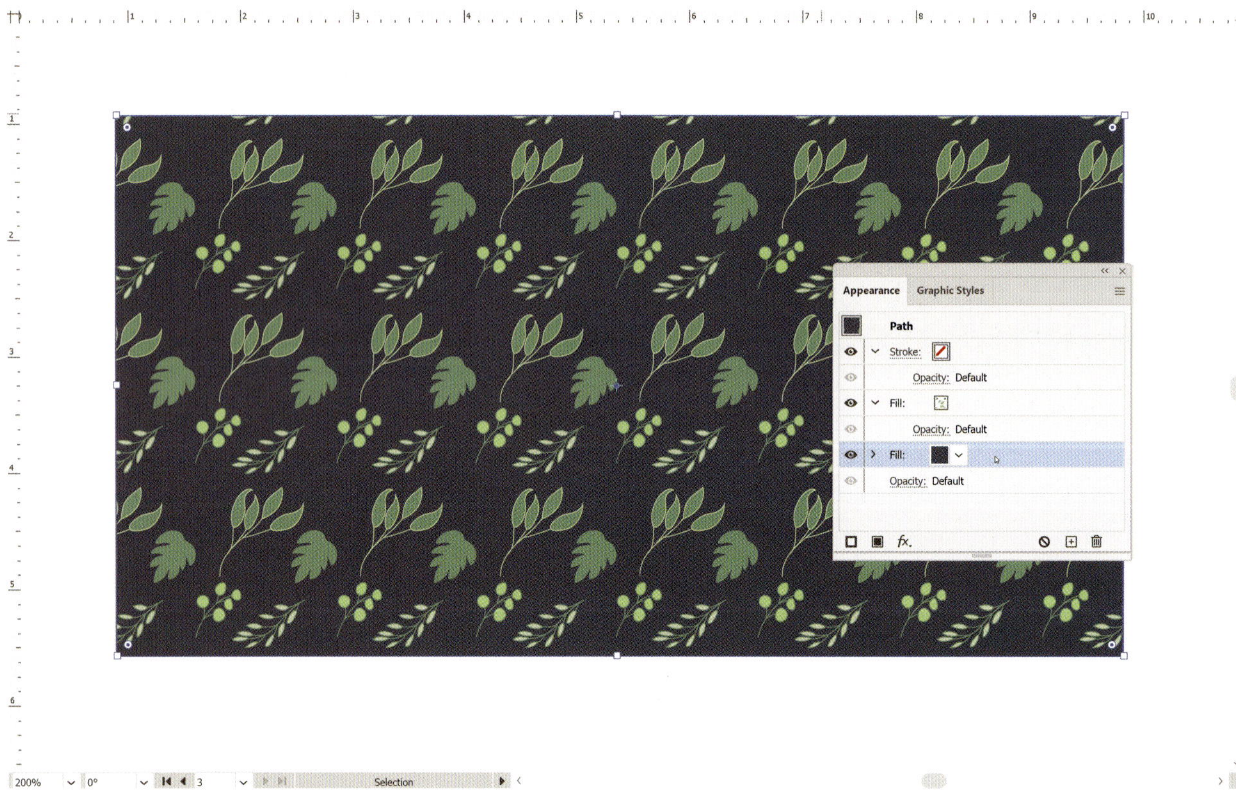

Figure 4.46 When you make a pattern without a background, it will be see-through in the spaces between your artwork. You will need to add a second fill behind the pattern fill in the *Appearance* panel. Open the panel, then add another fill using the drop-down menu in the top right of the panel. Drag the color fill below your pattern fill.

Designing Your Own Prints

Depending on your industry, you may want to consider investing more time in learning to design your own prints. Digital fabric printing is readily available these days at reasonable prices. There are plenty of online options and fabric type options. Shop around to find the best company for you if you are interested in this route. Consider designing your own print if you cannot find what you are looking for and are working in small batches or one-offs.

You may want to learn more about designing your prints. Invest the time to learn how to make prints in analog form first. This will provide the foundation you need to create intricate repeats. Then learn more about digital pattern creation from masters such as Von Glitschka.

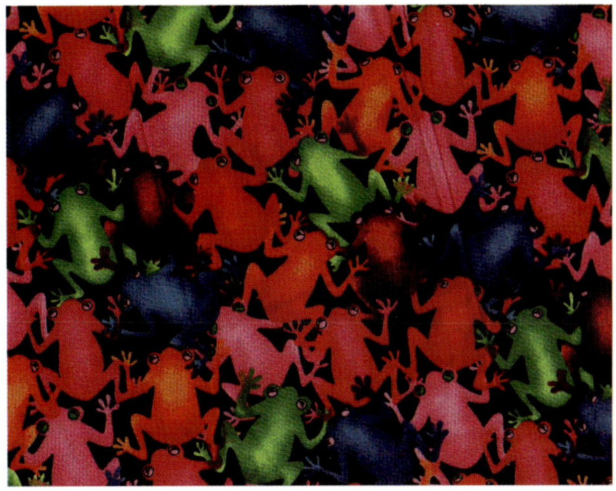

Figure 4.47a Bad flatbed scan of a patterned fabric. Notice the wrinkles in the fabric. Also, if you look closely, you will see that there is not a full repeat in the scan. Although not easily visible in this image, the fabric is also off-grain in the scan.

Project 4.8: Prep a Photo or Scan of Fabric

It's far more likely that you will need to use an existing print or textile pattern rather than designing your own. In this project, we will learn to take a scan a of fabric and turn it into a useable pattern file for use on your garment designs.

Step 1: To prepare a photo or scan of a fabric it is best to first work in Photoshop. You will need to make sure you have photographed or scanned a complete repeat of the print.

Scans (from a flatbed scanner) typically provide the best start for creating patterns from existing fabric. They are flat and more evenly colored. Photos are often shot with a slight perspective or skew that is difficult to correct. They also have variation in coloring from the environmental lighting. However, photos are often the only source of input for many students, so we learn to make them work.

When preparing a fabric for scanning or photography, it can be useful to place rulers or other straight-edged items squared-up along the four edges of the fabric or repeat, like a frame. This will provide straight lines in the image that you can align to the guides in Photoshop.

Aim to make sure that there is no skewing or other distortion in the fabric like that seen in Figure 4.47a and 4.47b. Press your fabric and try to make the grain and pattern lay as square or aligned as possible before scanning or photographing. Time spent preparing the fabric for input can save significant time and frustration with the software. When trying to troubleshoot prepping a fabric scan for repeat, the most common issue is a bad scan or photo. Often, the best solution to a frustrating photo correction is to go back and work on the original scan or photo. If at all possible, use a flatbed scanner. If you don't have one at home, work, or school, consider going into a copy shop with self-service machines. Have your fabric pressed and use double-stick tape to adhere a ruler or measuring tape to indicate the warp and weft of your fabric as well as the scale.

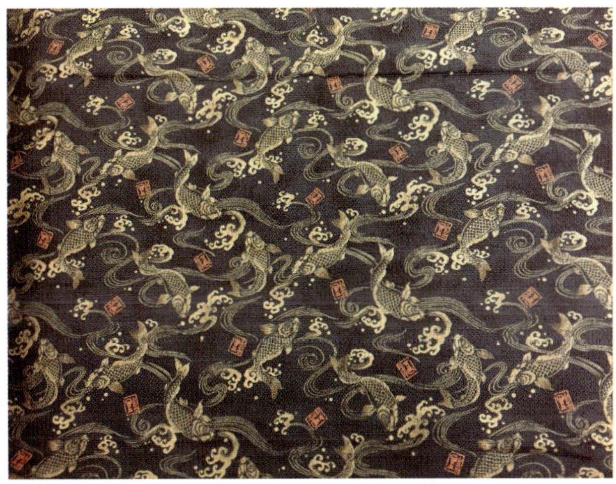

Figure 4.47b Bad photograph of patterned fabric. Notice the wrinkle near the top as well as the bad lighting. We will see in subsequent images that this photo is taken at a slight angle, creating skewing problems with the pattern tile.

STYLE SECRETS 4.1

Cultural Appropriation

Where is the line between cultural appreciation and appropriation? If you are a designer, you need to stay aware of misrepresenting a culture during your process. It is easy to choose a fabric because you think it looks pretty and accidentally insult a cultural group with the use of their heritage for your design. When using fabric, design elements, or imagery from another culture for your designs, take the time to do the research. If possible, talk to representatives of that culture to make sure you are characterizing the culture in an appropriate and acceptable way. The context is key. Be sure to be fully forthcoming when asking for guidance from cultural agents. Is it for a theatrical play or fashion? Who will be wearing the print or garment? Why are they wearing it? All these contextual variables could make a difference in the advice you receive. Remember, just because you didn't know that you appropriated from a culture doesn't mean you are excused. A lack of knowledge can be just as hurtful as intentional harm.

Inevitably, a good scan will solve 90% of the problems in this section, as seen in Figure 4.47c. You will have even lighting (due to the flatbed scanner), your weave will be flat and easy to connect in the *Offset* filter. What might take hours in Photoshop is sometimes corrected in a 10-minute fabric prep and scan!

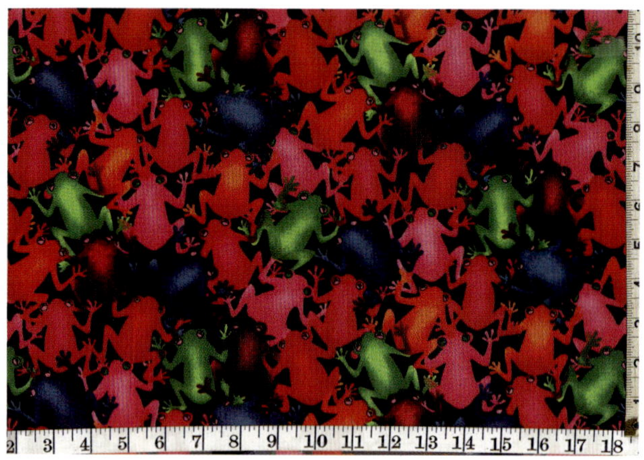

Figure 4.47c Good flatbed scan of a printed fabric. The fabric is on-grain, squared-up, and contains a full repeat of the pattern. Additionally, a set of measuring tapes were adhered to the fabric so the user would know the approximate size of the original pattern tile size and have an idea of the straight edges. If you look carefully, you will see that this tile size is about 16" × 8" or 40.5 cm × 20.5 cm.

Step 2: Once you have the image of your print opened in Photoshop, you will have to determine if the repeat tile needs to be corrected. Use exercise file FabricScan.jpg for this exercise. Turn on the *Rulers* using the shortcut *control+r/command+r* or find them in the *View* menu. Pull a guideline out from the left ruler to the left side of the repeat, then pull a second guideline out to align to the right side of the repeat. Remember that guides must be pulled from the ruler. Vertical guides come from the left side ruler whereas horizontal guides come from the top ruler. Pull guidelines from the top ruler to mark the top and bottom of your repeat as well as demonstrated in Figure 4.48. After establishing the guidelines, check to see if both top corners of your repeat tile touch the guideline. Do the same check for the bottom, left, and right guides. You may want to lock your guides by either *right-clicking* on a guide and selecting *Lock Guides* or go through the *View* menu. You will then need to crop the pattern to use it. There are multiple ways to crop the pattern; however, we recommend that you first set your guidelines precisely on the left, right, top, and bottom boundaries of the pattern repeat.

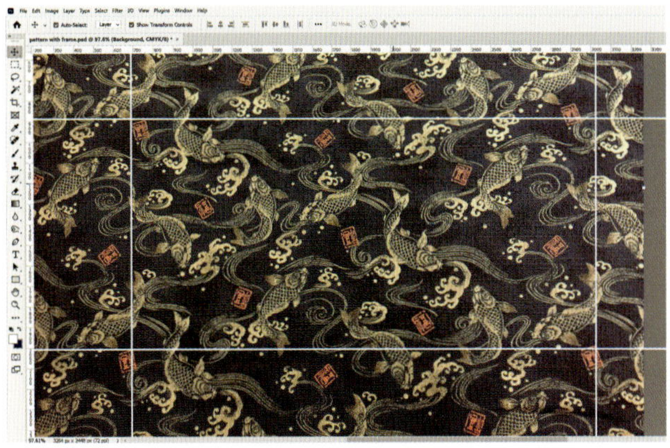

Figure 4.48 Screenshot of setting up the guidelines to mark the pattern repeat in Photoshop. Notice the four white lines that are supposed to mark the pattern. However, in this case, the repeat is not aligning correctly. This is a case in which the original image needs to be edited for the pattern to tile correctly.

Step 3: When the guides are set and if your repeat appears to align to the guides, switch to the *Crop* tool. *Click* on the top left intersection of your guides and drag your cursor to the bottom right intersection. The crop selection should automatically snap to your guides. This makes it easier to be precise. If your tool is not snapping to the guides, look in the *View* menu under *Snap To*. Make sure *Guides* have a check mark beside the word. Look in the top *Option* bar. Make sure that the box for *Delete Cropped Pixels* is selected. If you don't delete the pixels, they will show up in the repeat! Once you have selected one complete tile repeat with the crop tool as shown in Figure 4.49, press *enter* or *return* on the keyboard. The rest of the image will be cropped away.

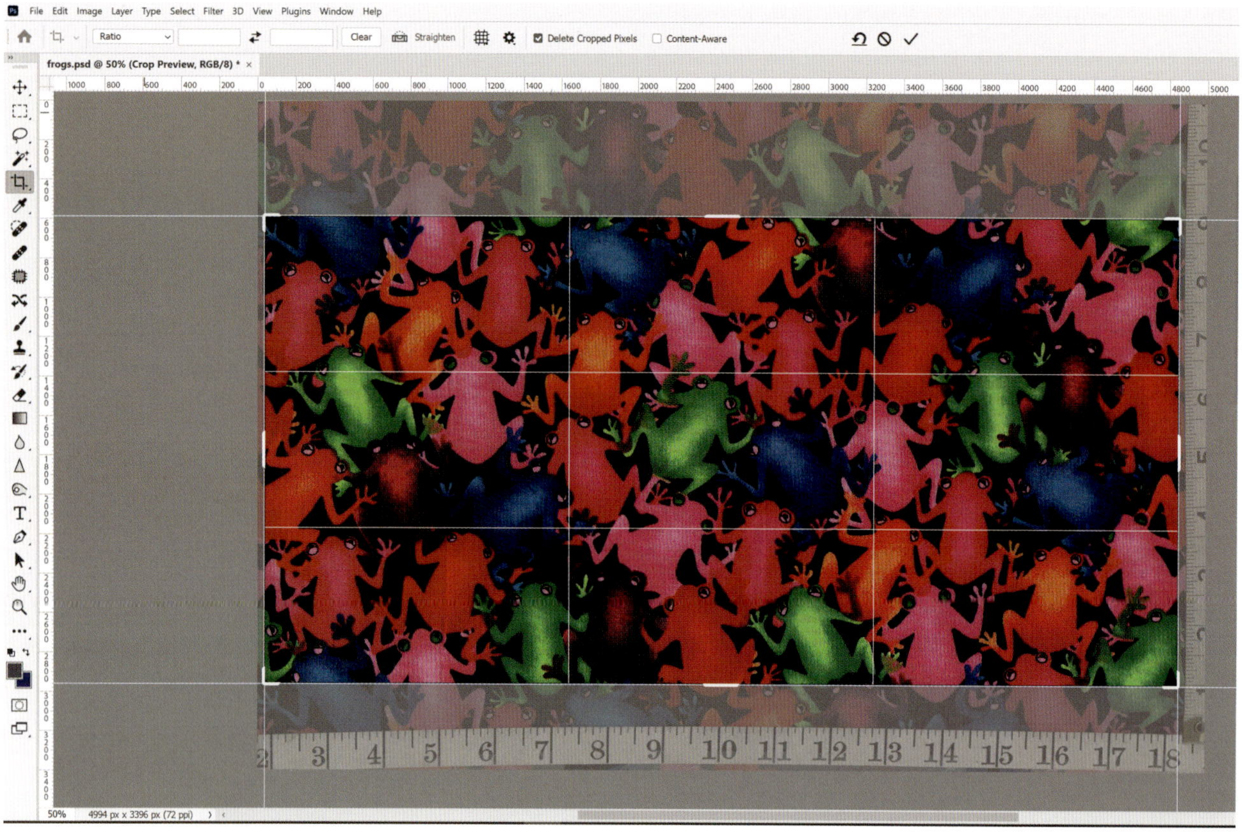

Figure 4.49 The crop box is aligned with the guidelines and *Delete Cropped Pixels* is checked on the *Options* toolbar at the top. In this image, the pattern tile aligns to the guidelines and does not need to be corrected.

Step 4: The quickest way to check how it will repeat is through the **Offset** filter. This filter allows the image to wrap back on itself so you can see how the edges connect in a repeat. Look in the *Filters menu → Other → Offset*. A dialog box will pop up. If you've never used this filter before, the horizontal and vertical fields will be set to zero (0). If you have used it, then there will be some numerical values in the fields. Go ahead and zero the fields out to reset it if you see other numbers. Make sure the *Preview* box is ticked and that the undefined areas are set to *Wrap Around*. With the *Offset* dialog box still open, *click* your mouse in one of the corners of the fabric image and drag to the middle of the image before you release it. This will scroll the image top to bottom and side to side so you can see how it will repeat. If your scan was set up correctly, you will have successful results such as those in Figure 4.50a.

Step 5: Sometimes the results are more problematic like in Figure 4.50b. Make a note of any breaks in the repeat, then undo the filter (*control+z/command+z*) and adjust as needed. You may need to undo a couple of times if you need to adjust your crop boundaries.

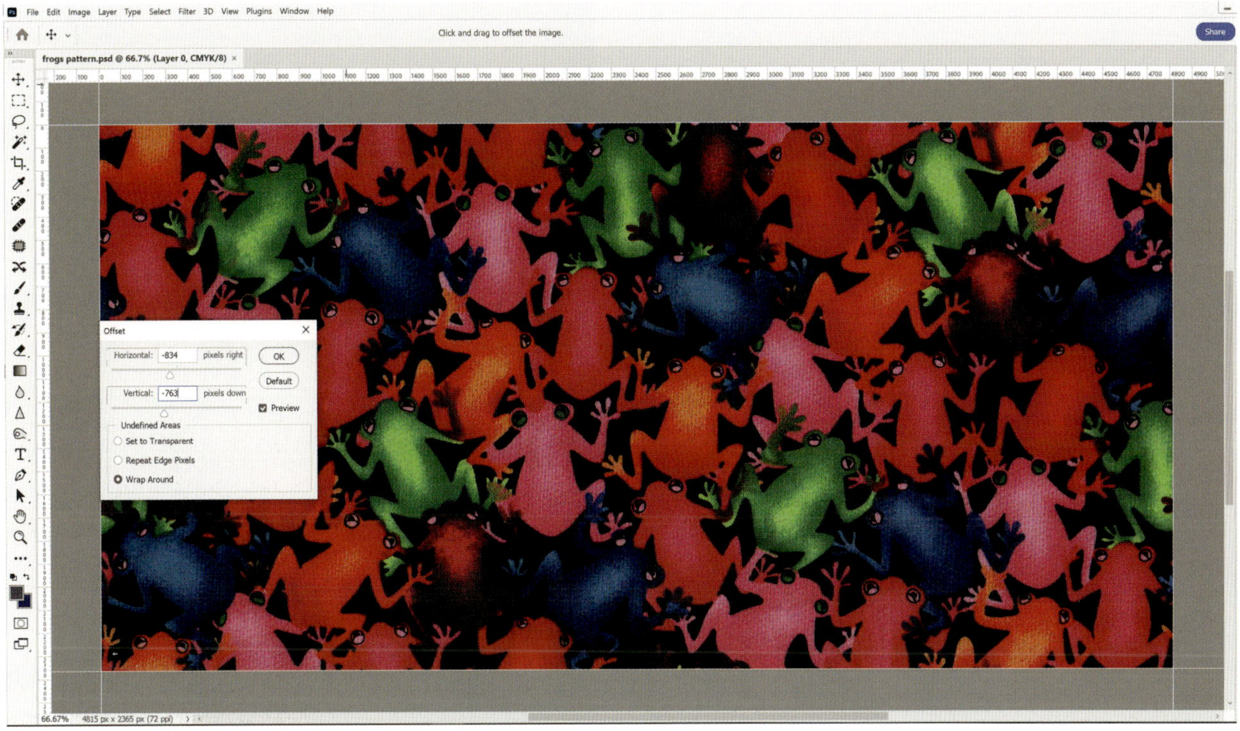

Figure 4.50a Screenshot of *Offset* filter applied to cropped patterns in Photoshop. Notice that in the first image you cannot see the join where the filter scrolled the pattern horizontally and vertically. This pattern will tile correctly.

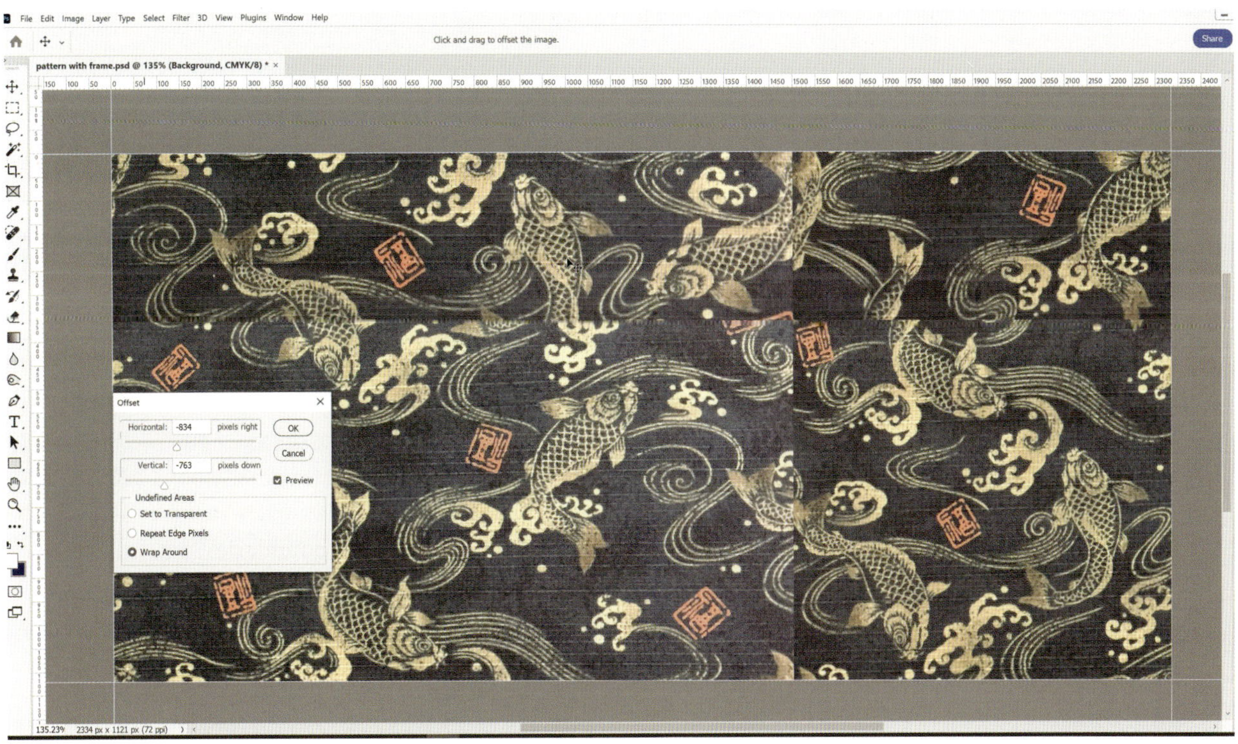

Figures 4.50b In this image, there is a distinct horizontal and vertical line where the pattern is not joining correctly in either direction after appliying the *Offset* filter. This image will need to be repaired before it can be used for a tiled pattern.

If any part of the repeat does not touch its respective guide, you will need to use the *Transform* tool to correct the image. These tools are found under *Edit → Transform*. We commonly use *Skew, Perspective, Warp*, and *Distort* to fix images that are not quite square. In Figure 4.51a, we drew a rectangular-ish shape that shows the repeat. This provides a clue as to how much distortion we will have to perform to correct the repeat tile. Figure 4.51b shows the transformation the image went through in order to correct the rectangular repeat tile.

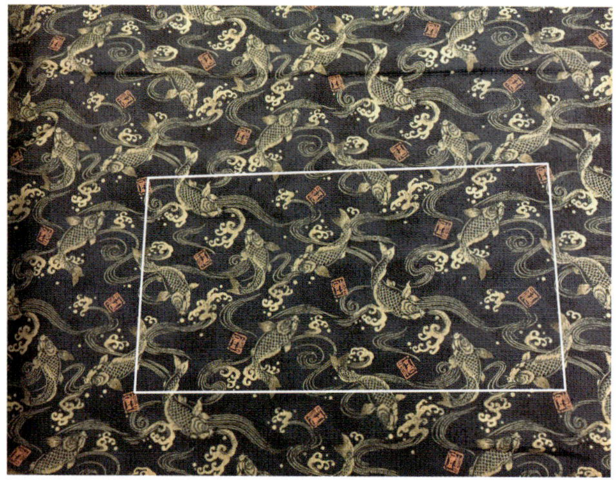

Figure 4.51a The pattern image before transformation to make the tile align. Notice the trapezoid drawn on the image. This is the repeat tile. It needs to be a perfect rectangle.

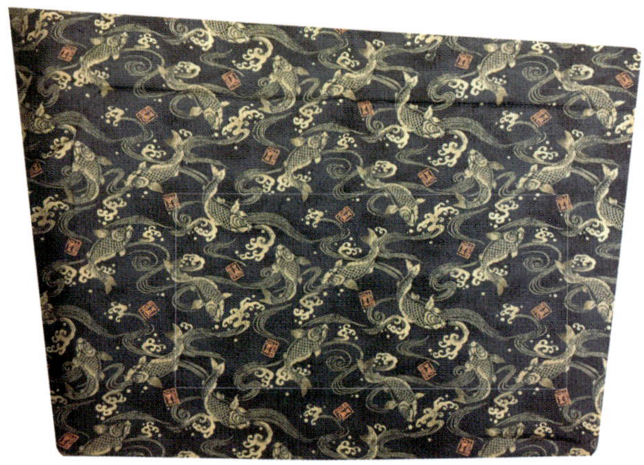

Figures 4.51b The repeat is now a perfect rectangle; however, the outside border of the image is not. This shows how much the image had to be manipulated to bring the tile into alignment.

Step 6: You may also need to do color or value corrections on your fabric image. One of the most common issues with input fabric images is a gradation in light from one side of the image to the other. This is not normally noticeable; however, when the tile is repeated, it creates an undesirable ripple or undulation in the colors as can be seen in Figure 4.52a. Figure 4.52b shows the tile corrected for all the color and lighting variations.[3]

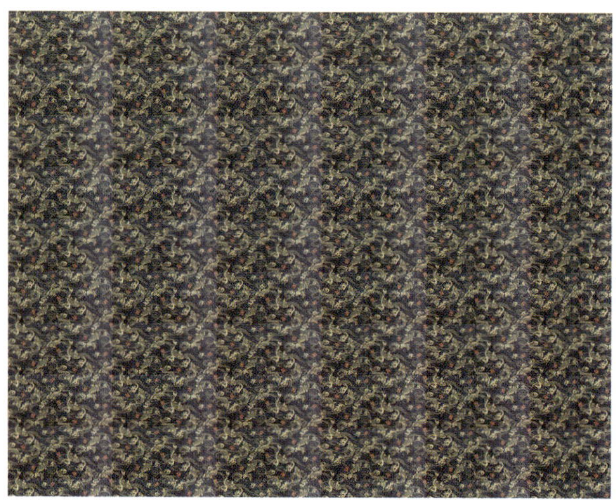

Figure 4.52a Repeat with a color gradation problem. The scan of this fabric had a lighting difference from left to right. When turned into a repeat, you can see a wave across the pattern.

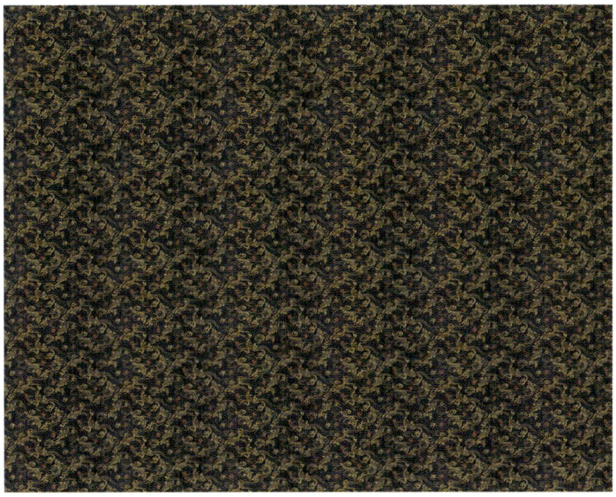

Figure 4.52b Pattern with gradation corrected. This version of the pattern has the lighting problem corrected. It looks flatter and more like the original fabric.

An easy way to correct most lighting problems is to work with **gradients**. A gradient is a transition between one color to the next. We can use this with a *Blend Mode* to change the appearance of the lighting on an image.

Create a layer on top of your motif and set the *Blend Mode* for the new layer to *Multiply*. Then get the *Gradient* tool from the toolbar. Check your foreground and background color boxes. Change them back to the default black and white colors. Otherwise, the gradient tool will pick up the colors that currently show. Now look for the gradient swatch drop-down near the left side of the *Options* bar. It will look like a gradient. *Click* on the swatch and look for a black and white gradient. It is typically filed under *Basics* as seen in Figure 4.53a. After you choose the black and white gradient, you can click *OK*.

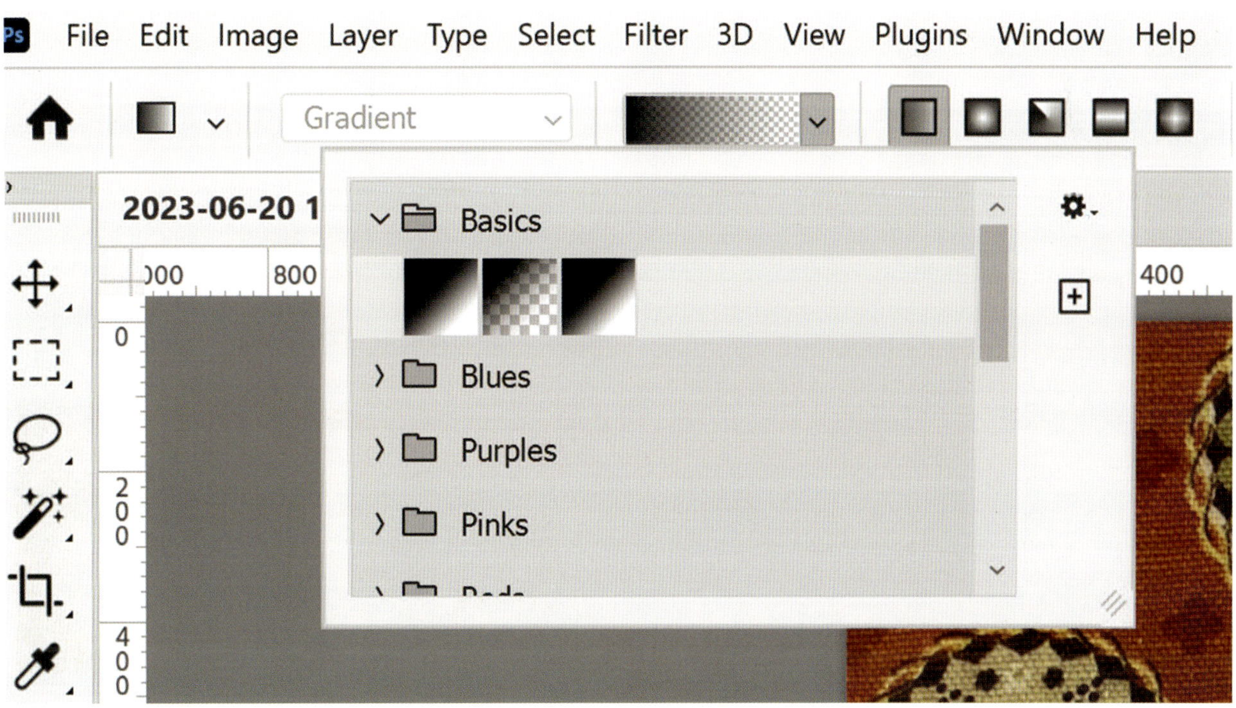

Figure 4.53a Screenshot of *Options* toolbar and *Gradient* options box.

After setting the gradient settings, you are ready to apply the gradient on your layer. Look at your image and decide which side is darker and which side is lighter. Also, is the light change from top to bottom, side to side, or diagonal? Your gradient direction will have to match the light direction change. For the default black and white gradient, the gradient is applied black leading to white like in Figure 4.53b. This means that where you first *click*, black will start. So, if you are using the default black and white gradient, first *click* in the lightest part of your motif and then *drag* your cursor to the darkest part of your motif to *release* the click.

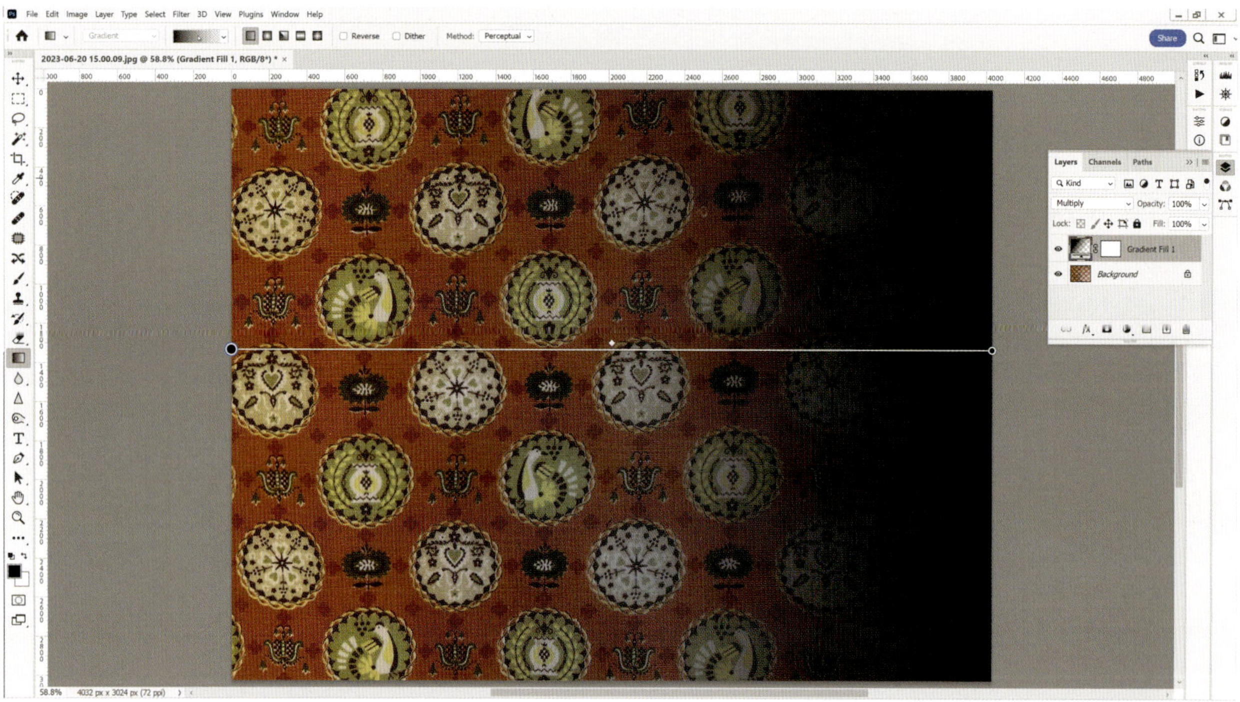

Figure 4.53b Screenshot of inserting the gradient. Notice the gradient is drawn on a new layer.

Step 7: When you first apply the gradient, the black will probably be too dark. Adjust the opacity or fill of the layer until the lighting looks more consistent from one side to the other. If the angle of your gradient does not match the angle of your lighting, you can re-drag the gradient with the gradient tool such as shown in Figure 4.53c. There is no need to start completely over. You may also need to try different blend modes as *Multiply* is not always the best option.

Step 8: You may also need to do a color correction using an *Adjustment Layer* and *Mask* like in Figure 4.53d. Refer to the color chapter for more help with adjustment layers if needed. The chances are that any color differentiation will follow the same gradation as your value differentiation. Once you make your adjustment, *control-click* or *command-click* on the gradation layer image to select the gradient. Then *click* back on the *Adjustment Layer Mask* and fill it with black to apply the same gradation. Adjust it as necessary for an even color. Remember, you can always recheck through the *Offset* filter to see how the repeat will connect to itself.

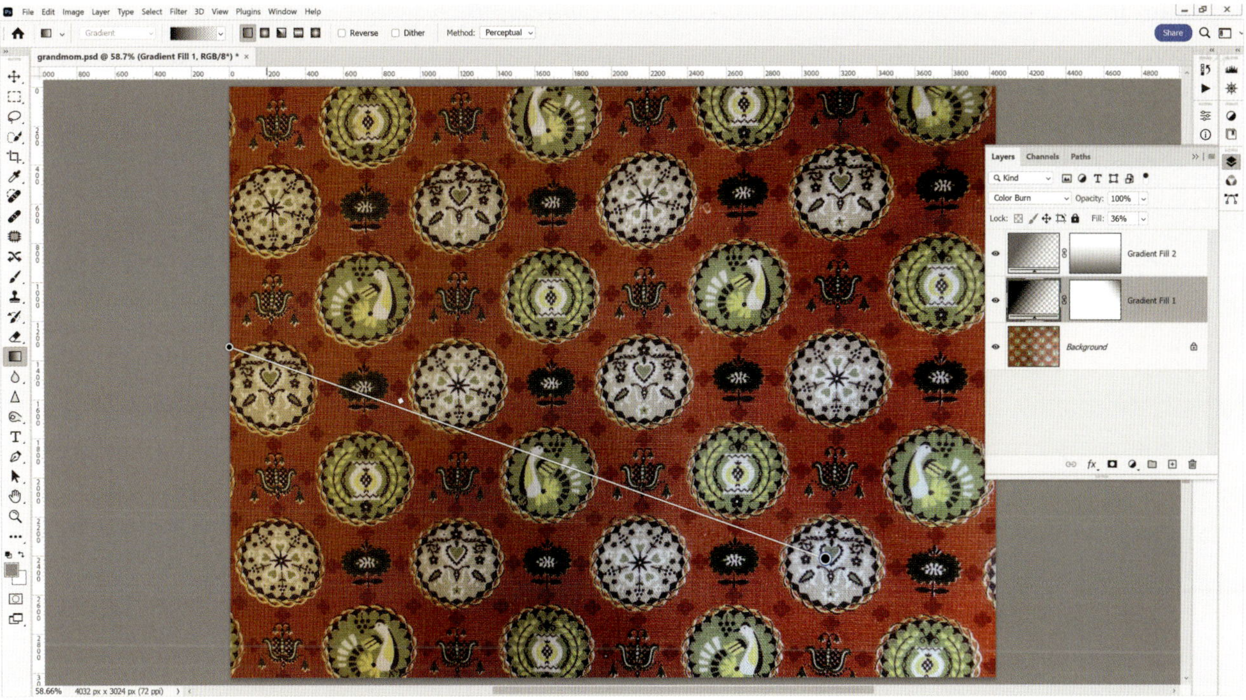

Figure 4.53c There are now two gradient layers to achieve better results with this image. The *Blending Modes* have been changed from *Multiply* to *Color Burn*, as this produced the best results with this image. The fill for each gradient layer has also been adjusted to better match the darker side of the image.

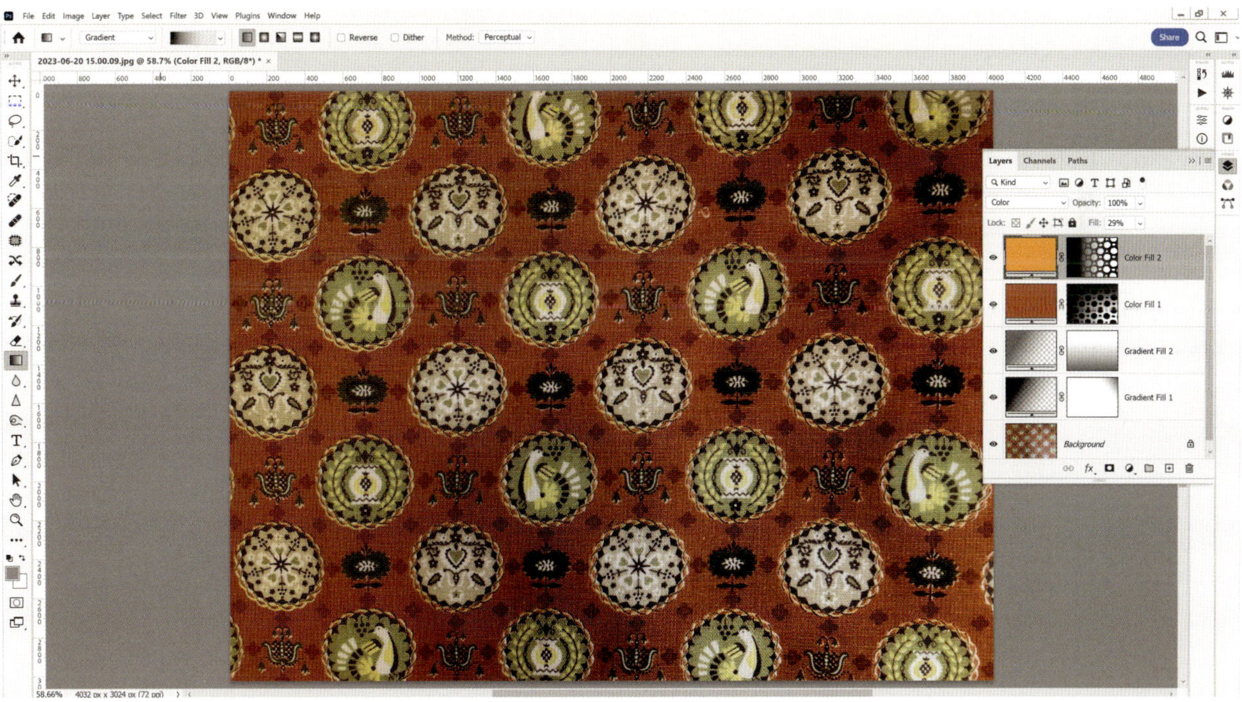

Figure 4.53d Two different color correction layers have been applied to the image in addition to the gradients. One layer affects the background and the other affects the various motifs. A gradient is applied to each layer mask so the side of the image that does not need to be corrected will not be affected.

Step 9: Once a pattern has been fully squared up and color-corrected, make sure to save it. Put it into a folder you can easily access it for use with both Photoshop and Illustrator as we progress through the chapter. Go ahead and start a print library folder.

STYLE SECRETS 4.2

Using Bold and Surprising Patterns

Bold and surprising patterns can turn a good design into a great one. Many new designers shy away from prints and patterns. However, an unexpected print usage can grab your audience's attention in a fun way. Especially with today's easy access to digital printing, try blowing up your print to something completely out of scale with the wearer. Or mix unorthodox pattern designs like those in Figure PT4.5. Have fun and try it out while in the design phase. Part of why digital rendering is so good is the flexibility to try out multiple colorways and fabric types in one rendering!

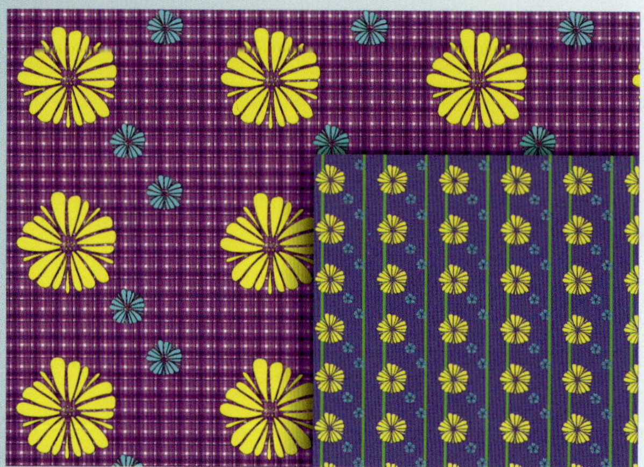

Figure PT4.5 Don't be afraid to try an unorthodox mix of scale, color, and pattern!

Summary

Patterns are as important to design communication as color. To identify a repeat tile, look for spots where the exact motif shows up again in the exact same position. To create a pattern in Photoshop once you have created a repeat tile or reduced your scanned fabric down to one repeat tile, go through the *Edit* menu. You can apply a pattern through the *Paint Bucket* tool, although it doesn't allow for much control. Creating a pattern layer yields more precision. Be sure you turn it into a *Smart Object* to be able to transform and warp the pattern. Then clip your pattern to the image.

In Illustrator, you will want to use the *Pattern Editor* panel to create your print. Patterns are stored and accessed in the *Swatches* panel in this application. Apply your pattern as a fill and use the *Scale* or *Rotate* tools to manipulate it. You can use *Envelope Distort* to apply some illusion of it wrapping around the body.

Creating your own prints can be rewarding but is not always practical. Use a flatbed scan of your fabric to create a digital pattern for use on your renderings. The *Offset* filter in Photoshop is key to test how well the tile will repeat. Adjust the image by transforming and adjusting as much as necessary to make a clean repeat tile. Then jump in and start applying your patterns to renderings to help communicate your designs!

STUDIO Companion Videos for Chapter 4

Please refer to STUDIO for accompanying chapter video(s).

Keywords

Displacement Map
Envelope Distort
Gradient
Grid
Guides
Offset
Puppet Warp
Recolor Artwork
Repeat tile
Rulers
Smart Object
Warp

Review Questions

1. Explain why Figure 4.2b is a good repeat tile and Figure 4.2a is not.
2. What is the command in Photoshop to create a pattern from an image?
3. Why is a pattern layer a better choice for applying patterns than the *Paint Bucket* tool? Provide at least three reasons.
4. Name and describe three ways to warp the pattern fill in Photoshop. What is each method best for?
5. What is the command in Illustrator to create a pattern from a graphic?
6. What must you do in the *Options* dialog box for tools such as *Scale* and *Rotate* in order to get the pattern to change rather than the whole shape?
7. Explain why it is more prudent to rescan your fabric if it is wrinkled, off-grain, or has bad lighting rather than trying to fix it in Photoshop.

Commands Introduced

- Convert to Smart Object
- Define Pattern
- Envelope Distort
- Export Patterns
- Gradient Tool
- Grids/Rulers/Guides
- Import Patterns
- Import Swatches
- Make Clipping mask
- Offset Filter
- Pattern Editor
- Pattern Fill Layer
- Preferences
- Recolor Artwork
- Rotate Patterns
- Save Swatch Library
- Scale Patterns
- Warp Transform

Keyboard Shortcuts

- AI: *control+f/command+f* (paste in front)
- AI: *control+g/command+g* (to group)
- *control+k/command+k* (preferences)
- Ai: *r* (rotate)
- AI: *s* (scale)
- PS, Ai: *control+c/ command+c* (copy)
- PS: *control+r/ command+r* (rulers)
- Ps, Ai: *control+z/ command+z* (undo)

Discussion Questions

1. If you choose to use a Kente cloth pattern on a prom dress, is this cultural appreciation or appropriation? Describe a specific situation of this scenario that would fit each description (appreciation versus appropriation).
2. Do you think it is worthwhile to spend the time making all the garment folds in a repeat pattern look realistic on an illustration?
3. Do you think it is better to use existing fabric designs or to design your own print?

Practice Exercises

1. Find the repeat tile on an existing fabric print in your collection. Use masking tape to indicate the repeat.
2. Design a simple repeat in Photoshop, Illustrator, and/or the application of your choice using your own artwork.
3. Create a sketch with a fluffy gathered skirt or a pleated skirt. Apply a pattern and spend the time correctly warping the pattern to look realistic.
4. Scan in your own fabric print and clean it up to make a good repeat pattern.

Endnotes

1. *Grids* are especially useful if you find yourself needing to make to-scale flats.
2. Illustrator's *Envelope Distort* just won't work quite as well as Photoshop's *Warp* feature. The print starts to degrade in odd ways if you push it too far. If you want more realistic print warp effects, take the piece into Ps and use the *Warp Transform*.
3. Okay, so this particular example took both authors about three hours to truly correct using many techniques (more than we described here!). A better scan of this fabric would have eliminated most of the issues presented. Seriously, just fix the scan and save yourself a lot of wasted time.

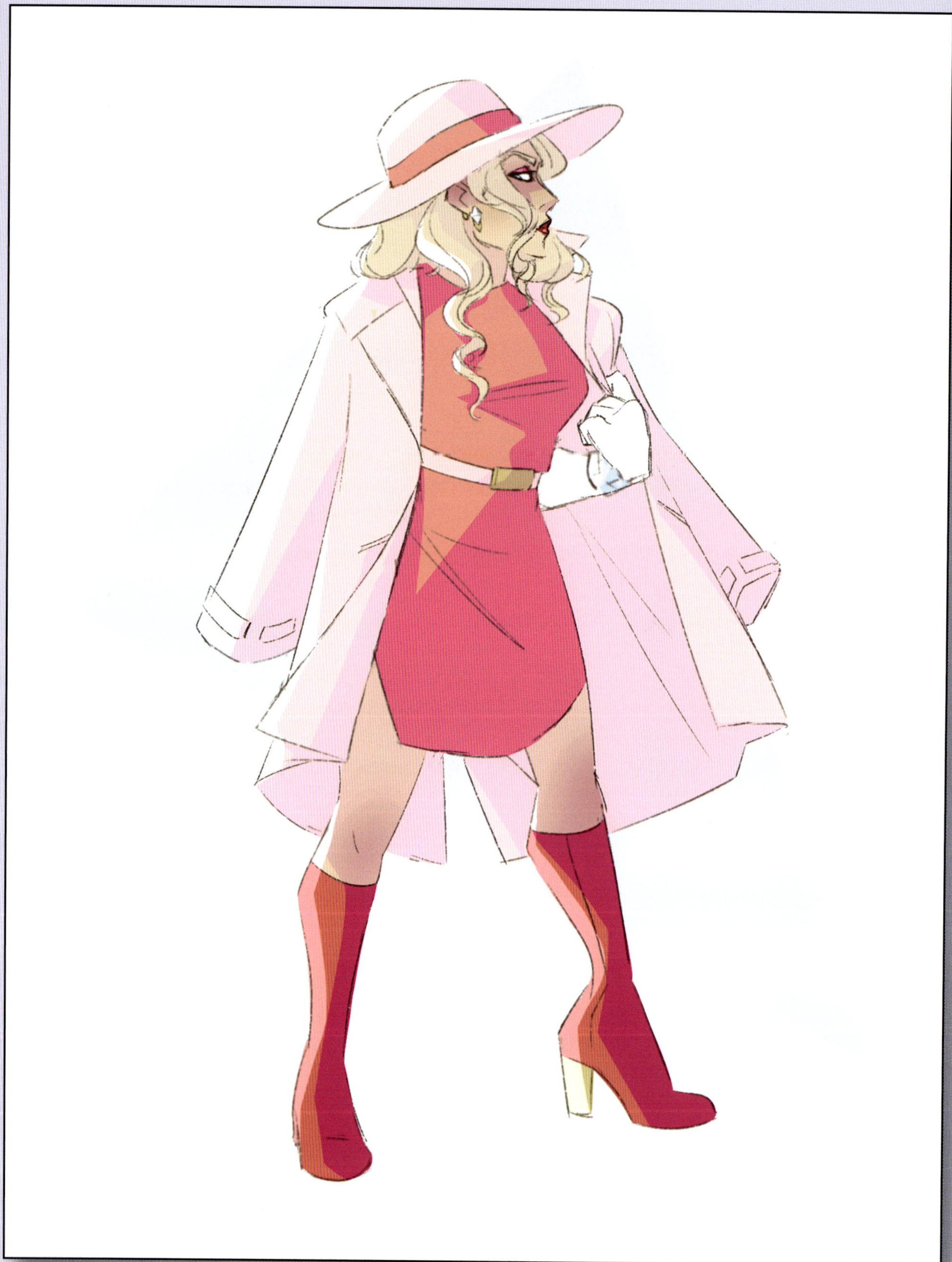

Figure 5.1 Providing light and shadow to your rendering informs the viewer about dimension and texture. Courtesy of Sam Connor.

CHAPTER 5
Shading, Highlighting, and Giving Life to the Illustration

Learning Objectives

After completing this chapter, you should be able to

- Analyze the basic components of light and shadow
- Apply lighting effects on Photoshop renderings
- Apply lighting effects on Illustrator renderings

Let's give a little life to our illustrations. Adding light and shadow can take an illustration from good to great. But remember the purpose: to communicate a design. How much time should you spend on highlights and shadows? This area presents a rabbit hole for many people. Sometimes you just need to slap some rudimentary highlights and shadows to get the work done. Take the time to learn how to apply lighting effects. Just keep the purpose in mind when rendering for communication rather than artwork.

Basics of Shading and Highlights

If you have been through any drawing or painting class, you have probably experienced a lesson or two in light and shadow. If you haven't, you may want to spend some time analyzing the shape of highlights and shading in photographs or live subjects.

Without going into too much depth, here is a sample study of a sphere. Figure 5.2 shows that even with a single light source, you still get bounce light reflections on the opposite side of the ball. You can see that the shadows and highlights can be rather complex, with areas that are lighter and darker within each.

When illustrating garments, you can simplify the lighting effects or you can make them quite realistic, depending upon your purpose. Either way, it is to your advantage to spend time studying and understanding how light affects objects. Pay attention to the shape that a highlight or shadow makes as well as casting shadows and reflected light as shown in Figures 5.3a–d.

Highlights and shadows on people and clothing are a bit more complex. Check out the Extend Your Learning appendix to learn more about portraying light and shadow if this is new territory. For practice, use an image like the one shown in Figure 5.4 to identify the light source, highlights, shadows, and any cast shadows or reflected light. You can find this image in your Studio exercise files as ShadingPractice.jpg. If using your own

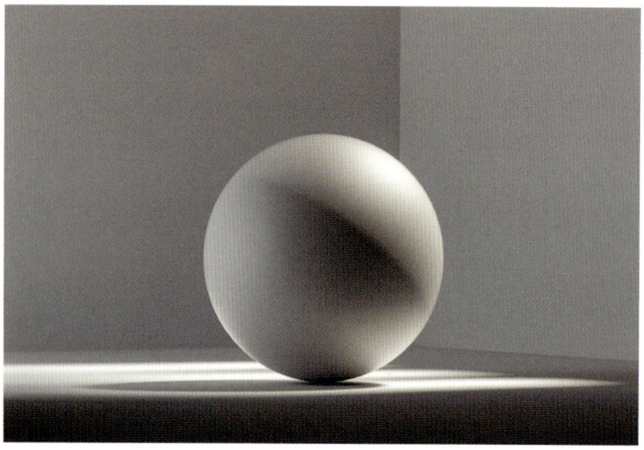

Figure 5.2 Light study. Courtesy of Milad Fakurian on Unsplash.

image, we recommend desaturating your image first if it has color. This will help you to identify the shapes easier.

Light and Shadow Colors

Not only are the shapes created by light important, but the color is as well. As discussed in the color chapter, color is made up of hue, saturation, and value. When you desaturate a photo, you are eliminating the hue and saturation, which makes it easier to see the shapes of the highlights and shadows. Let's focus on the other aspects now.

When opening a photo, use the *Eyedropper* tool to see the colors in the highlight and color areas. Boxes filled with color directly pulled from the photo in Figure 5.5 were created. What do you notice about the highlights and shadows?

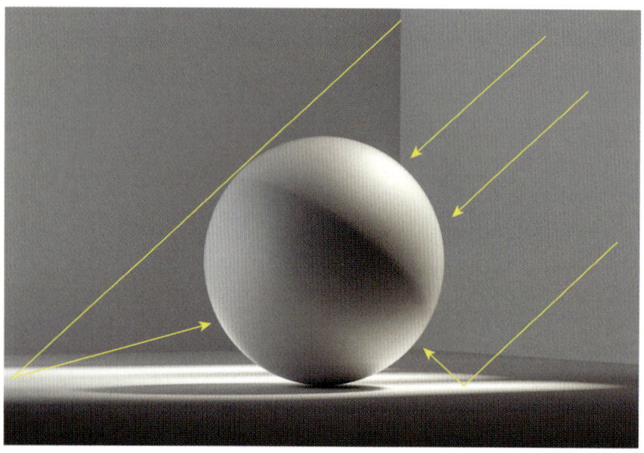

Figure 5.3a The arrows in this image show how the light comes from the upper right corner and hits the top of the sphere. Notice that it also hits the ground and reflects back up to the shadowed side.

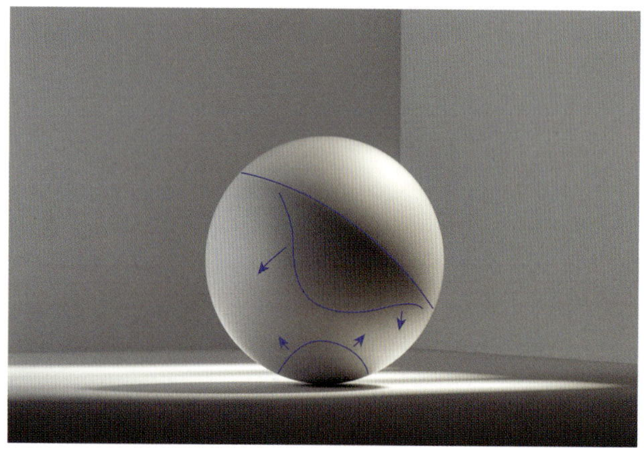

Figure 5.3c The shadows are most intense where the sphere turns away from the light source. It is also dark at the base where there is no reflected light to dissipate the shadow.

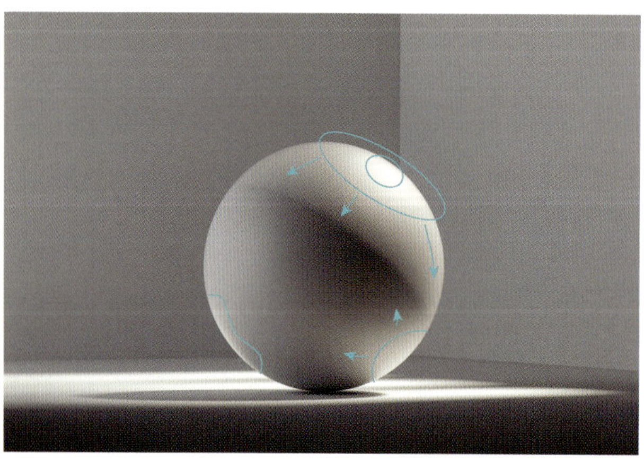

Figure 5.3b The lines here indicate how the highlight shape changes. There is an area with the brightest highlight that is closest to the light source. The highlight then fades out according to the shape of the form. There are two areas of reflected light at the base of the shape, as well.

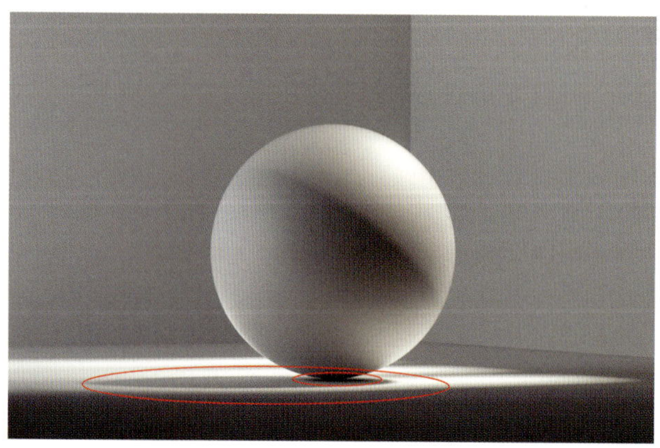

Figure 5.3d Finally, notice how the shadows are cast by the sphere where it blocks out the light source. The shadow is in the shape of the sphere but flattened on the ground to make a sharp ellipse. There is also a darker secondary shadow just below where the sphere sits.

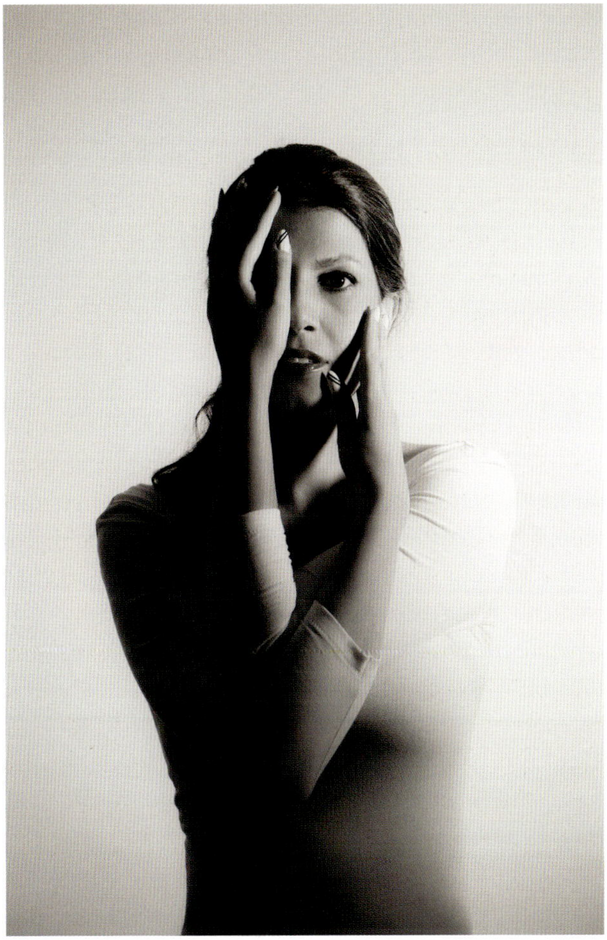

Figure 5.4 Use a desaturated image like this one to identify the highlights and shadows. Courtesy of Milad Fakurian via Unsplash.

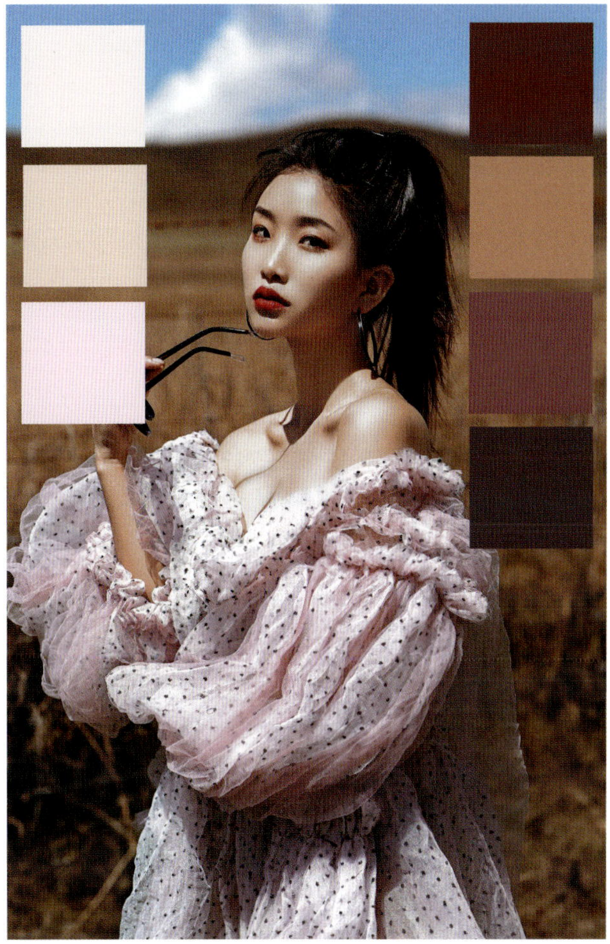

Figure 5.5 The *Eyedropper* tool was used to pick up the highlight and shadow colors in this photo. Notice that highlights are lighter and desaturated. Shadows are darker and more saturated with color. None of the colors are truly grayscale, though. Photo by 邱 严 via Unsplash.

PRO TIP 5.1

Consistent Light Sources

When making your figure renderings separate from the layout, you want to consider consistent light sources. As you place your figures into the layout, it may look odd if they have dramatically different light directions. Think of it as several models in the same room. The primary light source doesn't change for each one unless you have a separate spotlight on each. For most design communication, overly dramatic lighting isn't necessary anyway. So, you may want to keep to a general front wash for the majority of your renderings. The main exception to this is for theater design, when a garment is always meant to be viewed with specific lighting.

Can you see how the highlights are not only closer to white, but they are also less saturated than the shadow colors? Generally, highlights and shadows stay in the same general hue range as the object. However, the value and saturation change dramatically.

On the color dialog box, the highlights move up and to the left. Shadows move down and to the right towards more saturation. The hue is determined by the base color of the item. You can see the movement in Figure 5.6.

Shading/Highlighting Color Versus Shading/Highlighting Pattern Fills

Before we describe the tools to create highlight and shadow on a rendering, it is important to note that the tools won't work directly on pattern fills. You may fall in love with the *Dodge* and *Burn* tools (described momentarily), but will get the "no" symbol when you try to use them on a *Pattern Fill Layer* (see Figure 5.7) unless it has been rasterized. Remember that rasterizing a fill makes a destructive change, so you need to decide if that is the best choice for your situation.

If you want to keep a non-destructive workflow, there are other methods for shading pattern fills and *Smart Object* layers. In fact, most of the other approaches described momentarily will work fine for pattern layers. You can easily add a Clipped layer and adjust the *Blend Mode* and *Opacity* to create light and shadow. Although pattern fills require a little workaround, they are easy enough to become second nature in your rendering workflow.

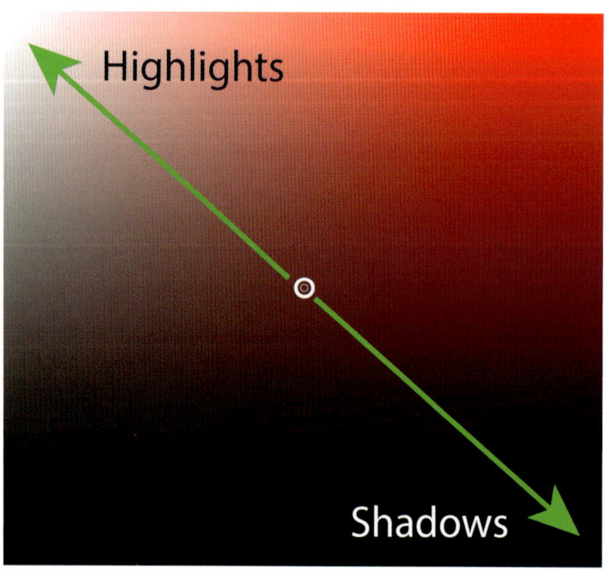

Figure 5.6 In the color dialog box, highlights move up to the top left corner and shadows move in the opposite direction.

Basics of Value Mapping

We touched on value mapping in the color chapter. Essentially, it is the practice of laying down your values before getting into hue and saturation. This workflow style works well when you are thinking about your artwork as a whole picture, background and all. Concept artists, character and game designers commonly work in this style. If you tend to render your designs that way, then value mapping may be a great choice for you. We (the authors) tend to not use it as often simply because we render our figures and garments separately, then compile them into a layout with a background towards the end of the process. Everyone works a little differently, so try out the workflow and see if it works for you.

To use value mapping, you want to sketch out the basic outline of your artwork. Think about your light sources and how it affects your subject. Start to paint in the values using a grayscale range as shown in Figure 5.8. If you don't have your own rendering to shade, you may use the exercise file ValueMapPractice.jpg.

You still want to group like objects on the same layer. For example, we are keeping the figure's body on

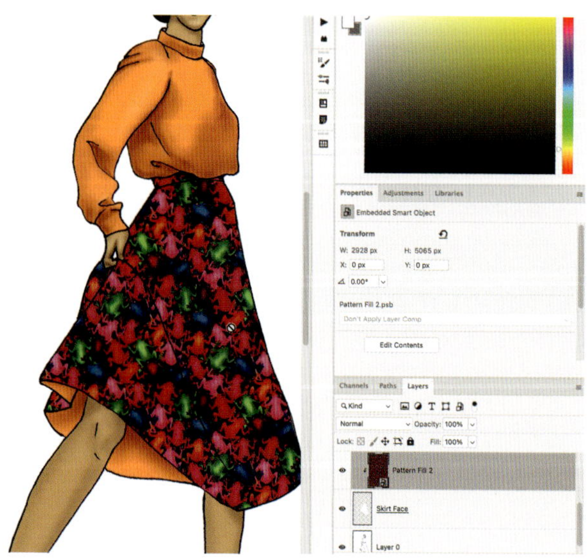

Figure 5.7 *Pattern Fill* and *Smart Object* layers will not let you use the *Dodge* and *Burn* tools directly. You will get the "no" symbol. Instead, make a new clipped layer and use one of the other methods described to create light and shadow.

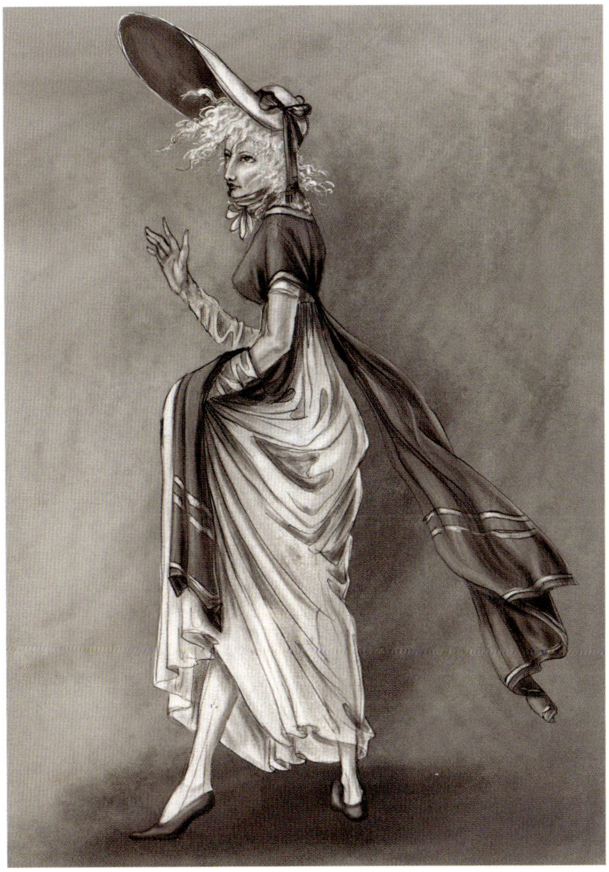

Figure 5.8 Value map grayscale rendering.

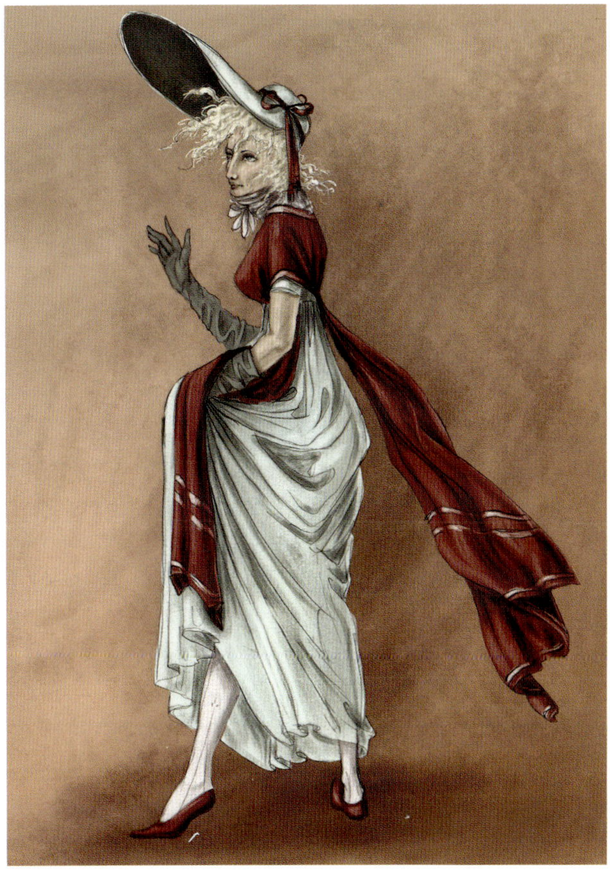

Figure 5.9 Color glazing added to the value map.

a separate layer from the garment in our image. This makes your workflow easier to keep up with when you add patterns or need to quickly change colors. Otherwise, you end up with a layer mask on every new layer, which starts to add file space.

Some folks like this method because they don't have to worry about the colors just yet while laying out the image. Others prefer it so they can look at the image in terms of the elements and principles of design without the color getting in the way. Does the image look balanced and proportional? Where is the focal point and how does the eye travel around the artwork? Is the texture balanced? We will cover texture in the next chapter, but texture is communicated primarily through light and shadow.

Once you are satisfied with the grayscale values, you can start to glaze over or simply replace the grayscale value with color. Use any method that makes you happy. You can add *Adjustment Layers*, use *Blend Modes*, or directly replace the paint color. Figure 5.9 shows the finished result with color added. Does this seem like a good fit with your workflow?

Project 5.1: Light and Shadow in Photoshop

Light and shadow can be achieved in either Photoshop or Illustrator. However, it will probably seem more intuitive in Photoshop (or other painting apps) if you are used to a painterly style. The two more straightforward approaches are painting in the highlights and shadows using the *Dodge* and *Burn* tools or the *Paintbrush* tool. You may find that creating highlight and shadow layers is the better option for you, though. For these exercises, we used exercise file ShadePractice1.psd. Feel free to use your own rendering, too.

Dodge and Burn Tools

The **Dodge** and **Burn** tools are straightforward. That's why so many people love them. Both are found in the toolbar on the left. The *Dodge* tool looks like a lollipop, although it's meant to imitate masking tape in reference to how darkroom tonal mapping was performed. The *Burn* tool is an open-handed fist, again referring to the non-digital technique.[1] These tools work by increasing or decreasing brightness of whatever color they pass over. So, you must have a layer with color already added or it won't show any results. They don't change the hue or saturation levels, so it tends to be a "flatter" look when adding dimension to your work. However, you don't have to adjust the color constantly, like you might with painting highlights and shadows with the *Paintbrush* tool.

Open one of your colored renderings in Photoshop or your digital painting app of choice. We find it easiest to block in your shadows first. Choose the layer you want to add highlights and shadows. In our example in Figure 5.10, we are on the dress layer. Make a duplicate of the layer and work on the copy. Start by selecting the *Burn* tool. In the *Options* bar at the top, you have some, well, options. You can change the size and attributes of your brush shape. Start with a big, soft brush. Then you will see a drop-down menu option for *range*. Stick with the *midtones* for the moment because you have flat color. Keep the *exposure* at 50% for the moment. As you become more familiar with the tool, you will probably want to adjust all of these settings. Think about your light source direction and start to lay down some big, soft shadows in areas that would be blocked the most from that light source.

Build up your shadows. You will quickly realize that it works better to have a low exposure and build up to the level of shadow you like. A drawback is that you cannot adjust the brush shape like the *Paintbrush* tool. You can change the basics such as size, hardness, opacity, and flow. However, you cannot change to a different tip with more texture.

Now switch to the highlights. Stay on the duplicated layer and choose the *Dodge* tool from the toolbar on the left. Change any of the settings you like but stick with the *midtones range* for the moment because we have a flat base. Build up your highlights on the lit side of your garment. See Figure 5.11 for our example.

The *Dodge* and *Burn* tools are a great way to slap down some highlights and shadows, quickly. You don't need to constantly sample and adjust colors because the tools work with the color that is already there. It is a destructive edit, though. That's why it's best to make a duplicate of your layer before you start working with the tools. However, if you decide that you darkened an area a bit too much, there's not a good way to fix it. You can undo it until the area is fixed (as long as it wasn't too many edits ago) or you can use the *Dodge* tool to try to brighten the area again. Sadly, this usually results in a muddy mess. As mentioned previously, the tools also result in flatter colors because saturation isn't part of the mix, and the tools won't work on *Pattern Fill Layers*. Let's look at some other options.

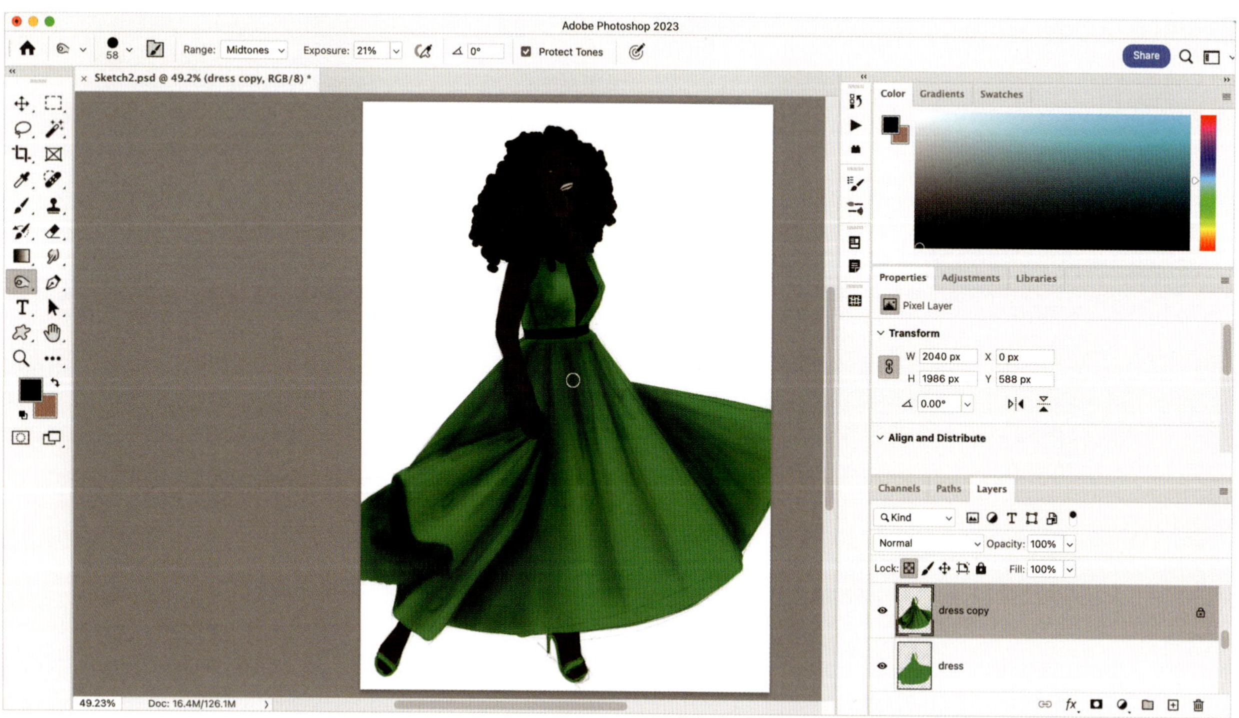

Figure 5.10 Use the *Burn* tool to lay down the shadows first. Make a duplicate of your layer before using the tool so you can always go back to the original flat color layer if needed.

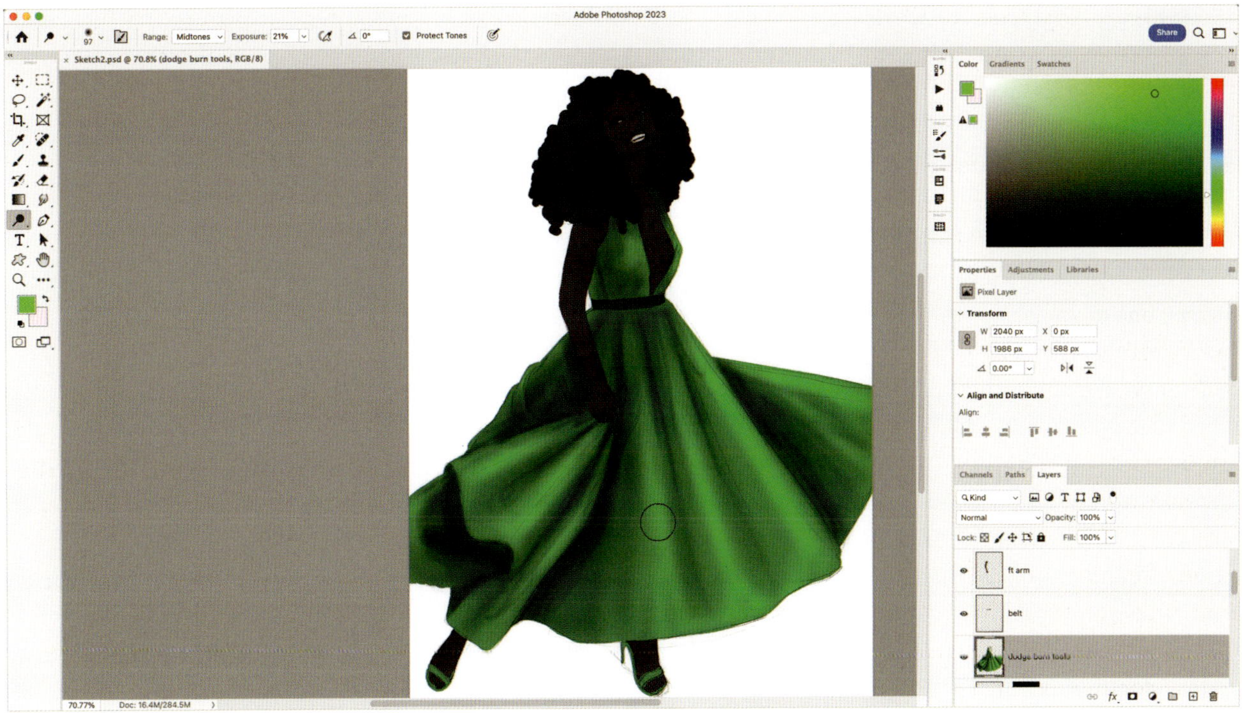

Figure 5.11 Building up the highlights with the *Dodge* tool.

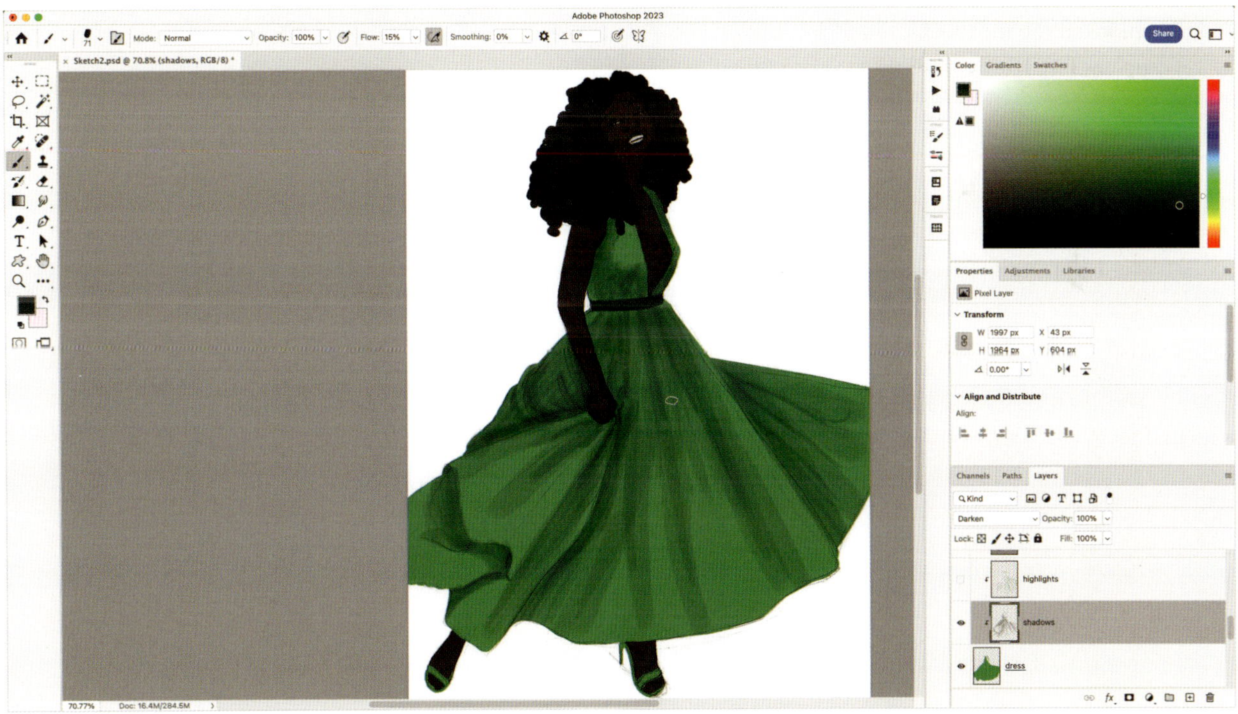

Figure 5.12 Painting in the shadows. We used a marker-style brush for this version.

Painting Layer

Step 1: Painting can result in richer, more complex highlights and shadows for your rendering. Unlike the *Dodge* and *Burn* tools, you can add an empty layer above your flat color layer to keep it non-destructive. A paint layer is adding in new paint (well, digital paint at least), whereas the *Dodge* and *Burn* tools must work with paint already on the layer. If you are working on the same file, turn off the visibility of your layer with the dodge and burn effects. Add a new layer and clip it to your color layer. This will be your shadow layer.

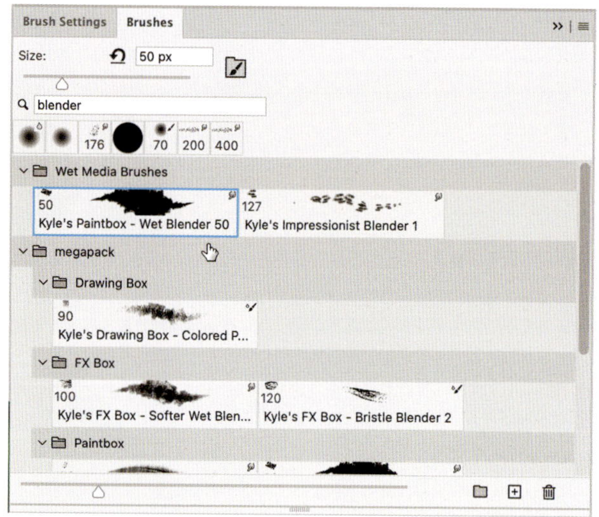

Figure 5.13 The *Smudge* tool can have brush presets, too. Search for "blender" in the brush dialog box.

Step 2: Using the *Eyedropper* tool, pick up the base layer of your artwork. We will use the dress layer again for our example. Now adjust your color to be slightly darker and more saturated. Change the blend mode of your shadow layer to *Darken* or *Multiply*. Now adjust the opacity or flow of your brush (whichever you are more comfortable adjusting) to build up your shading as seen in Figure 5.12. Remember that it helps to start with the broad shaded areas, then start adding in the detail shading. Think about where you have soft transitions versus sharper shadows. If you need more than one layer for your shading, go for it! You can always flatten your shadow layers later to save file space.

Step 3: Try playing with different brush tips to get the effect you like. Don't get too lost down this rabbit hole, though. You can easily spend hours trying different brushes. Most digital artists have a select few go-to brush tips they use for 80% of their digital painting. Also consider using the **Smudge** tool to blend your brush strokes. This tool acts the way it sounds. It digitally smudges the paint effect to soften transitional areas. You can find the *Smudge* tool in the toolbar on the left. It looks like a person's finger pointing or dragging. However, also try digging through the paintbrush presets. You'll notice that some of the brush types are called "blender" and show the *Smudge* tool in the corner of the picture as seen in Figure 5.13. These are presets for the *Smudge* tool with textured brush tips applied. Try them out and see what works for you.

Step 4: Let's add some highlights now like in Figure 5.14. Again, pick up your base color, then adjust it lighter and less saturated. Add a new clipped layer and set it to *Screen*. Start to paint in your highlights now. How is it looking? Remember to *Zoom* out and look at the picture from further away. If it is too much, you can decrease the opacity for the entire layer.

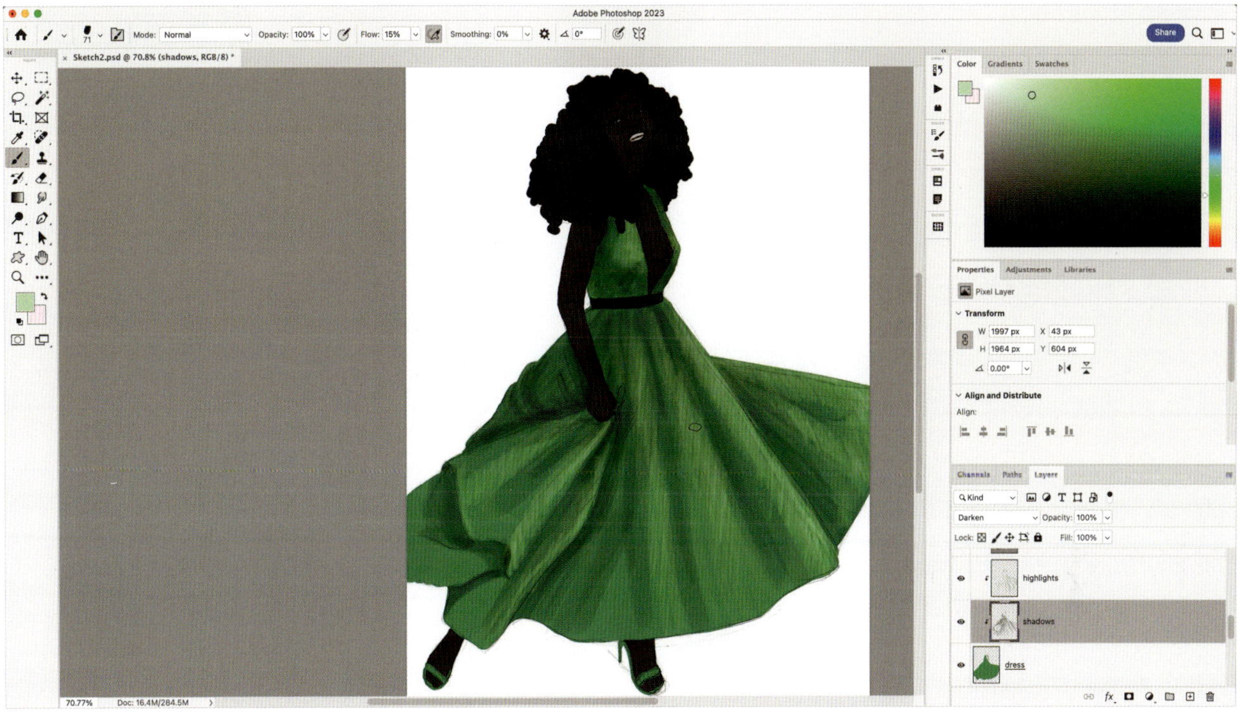

Figure 5.14 To paint in the highlights, use a paler, less-saturated color. We used a brush tip that replicated colored pencils for the highlights.

If you want to have some fun with your shading, try using complementary colors in the shadows from the base layer as we did in Figure 5.15. Or play with the hue in other ways. It adds another layer of artistry. Remember, you can change your brush attributes for more texture. Also try playing with the blend modes and opacity to see if you find a better mix for your illustration! This method has more complex and artistic results, but often takes a little more time and decision-making.

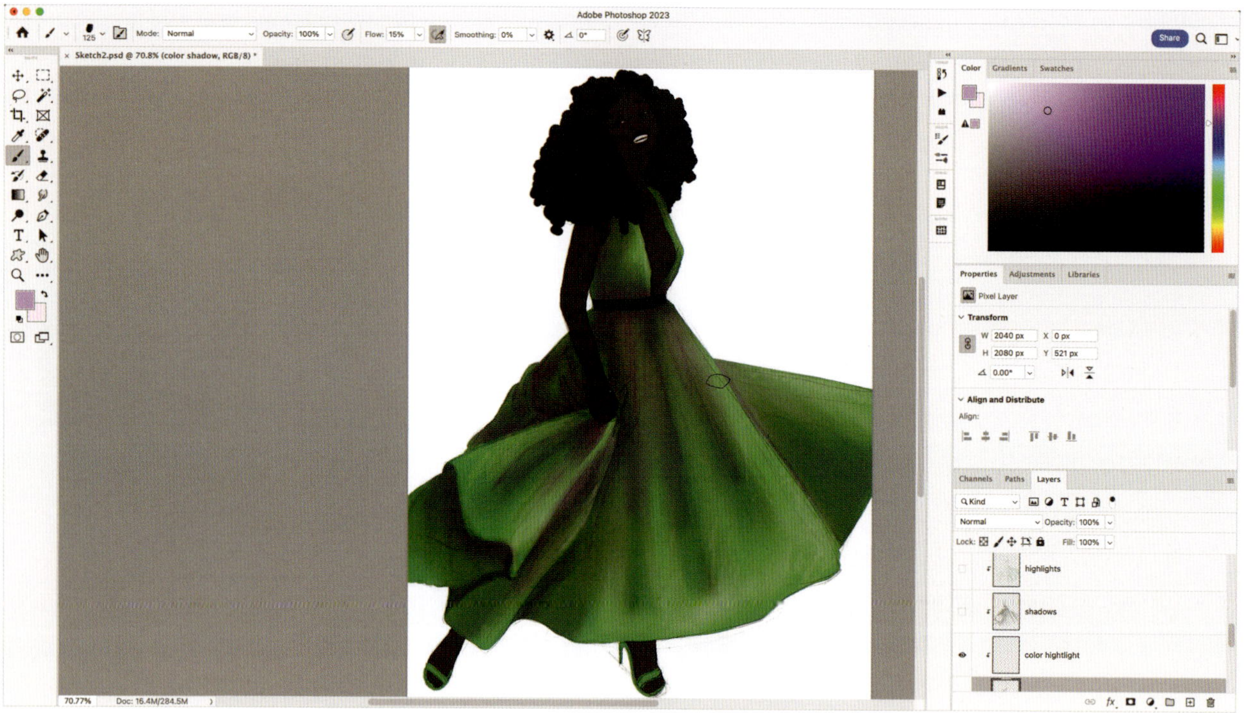

Figure 5.15 Using more artistic methods of painting highlights and shadows with violet colors and a textured brush tip.

50% Gray Layer

An alternate way to use the *Dodge* and *Burn* tools that allows for more non-destructive flexibility and use on *Pattern Fill Layers* is to use a 50% gray layer. Let's see how this works.

Step 1: Above your dress layer, add a new blank clipped layer. Go to the *Edit* menu → *Fill*. This will bring up a dialog box. In the contents, choose *50% gray*. Leave all the other settings to the default. You should have a gray layer covering the dress area now. In the *Layers* panel with the new gray layer selected, change the *Blend Mode* to *Overlay*. Your dress (or whatever garment you are coloring) should match the original color you filled when coloring.

Step 2: The *Overlay Blend Mode* darkens anything below 50% gray and lightens anything brighter than 50% gray; 50% gray exactly disappears and does not affect the layers below it. Now on this new layer, you can use the *Dodge* and *Burn* tools to paint in your highlights and shadows. As it is clipped, it won't affect anything past the dress layer as seen in Figure 5.16.

This method still results in slightly flatter colors, but this may not be an issue for your needs. It works great for pattern fills and smart objects, though. It has the bonus that you can duplicate this layer to its own file and save it to use as a *Displacement Map* as briefly described in the Patterns chapter Pro Tip.

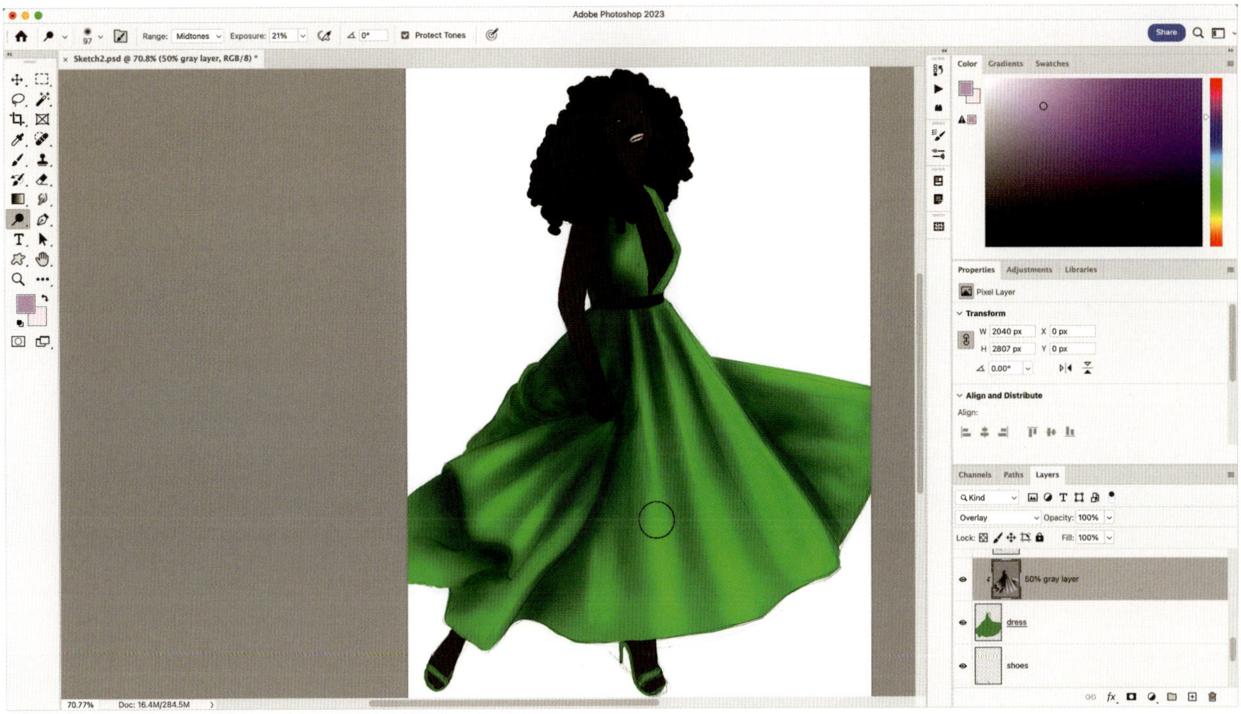

Figure 5.16 Using *Dodge* and *Burn* tools on a 50% gray layer. Be sure the layer is clipped to your object layer and the *Blend Mode* is set to *Overlay*.

STYLE SECRETS 5.1

Give Your Light and Shadow Style

The multitude of brush options in any digital art application can be overwhelming. Once you become familiar with the tools and techniques, start trying textured brushes for your highlights and shadows. You will find that these different brushes and tools can add depth to your rendering style. It is easy to get lost down the rabbit hole of trying new brushes. If you like the look of a technique, make note of what brush the artist used. This will give you a useful starting point. You can also start with one type of brush, such as the gouache category. Find one that intrigues you, and practice working with it. The more comfortable you are with your brushes, the more fun you can have with rendering your designs.

Besides brush types, don't be afraid to play with color and other tools in your light and shadow. See what the *Smudge* tool, *Blur* tool, and *Mixer Brush* can accomplish for you. Although we can't cover everything in this book, there are a lot of learning options out there to help you. Spend a little time understanding these other tools and practice. You are on your way to developing your own style through added knowledge!

Dodge and Burn Layers

The final method is commonly used for photograph retouching. The concept is the same as the *Dodge* and *Burn* tools but uses *Layers* and *Layer Masks* instead.

Step 1: Turn off the visibility of any previous highlight/shadow practice layers. Use the *Layers* panel to duplicate your color layer. You can either *right-click* on the layer and choose *Duplicate Layer* to the same document, or you can drag the layer to the plus icon (+) at the bottom of the panel. Create two duplicates and rename one Shadows and the other Highlights to keep up with your layers. Turn off the visibility of the highlights layer for the moment.

Step 2: Choose your shadows layer and go to the *Image* menu → *Adjustments*.[2] Choose whichever adjustment type you feel most comfortable with to reduce the brightness. If you are new to most of this program, use the *Brightness/Contrast* adjustment. If you are a little more advanced, you can use the *Levels* or *Curves* adjustments. We used *Curves* in Figure 5.17a. Whatever you choose, lower the brightness significantly to match what value you think your darkest darks should be.

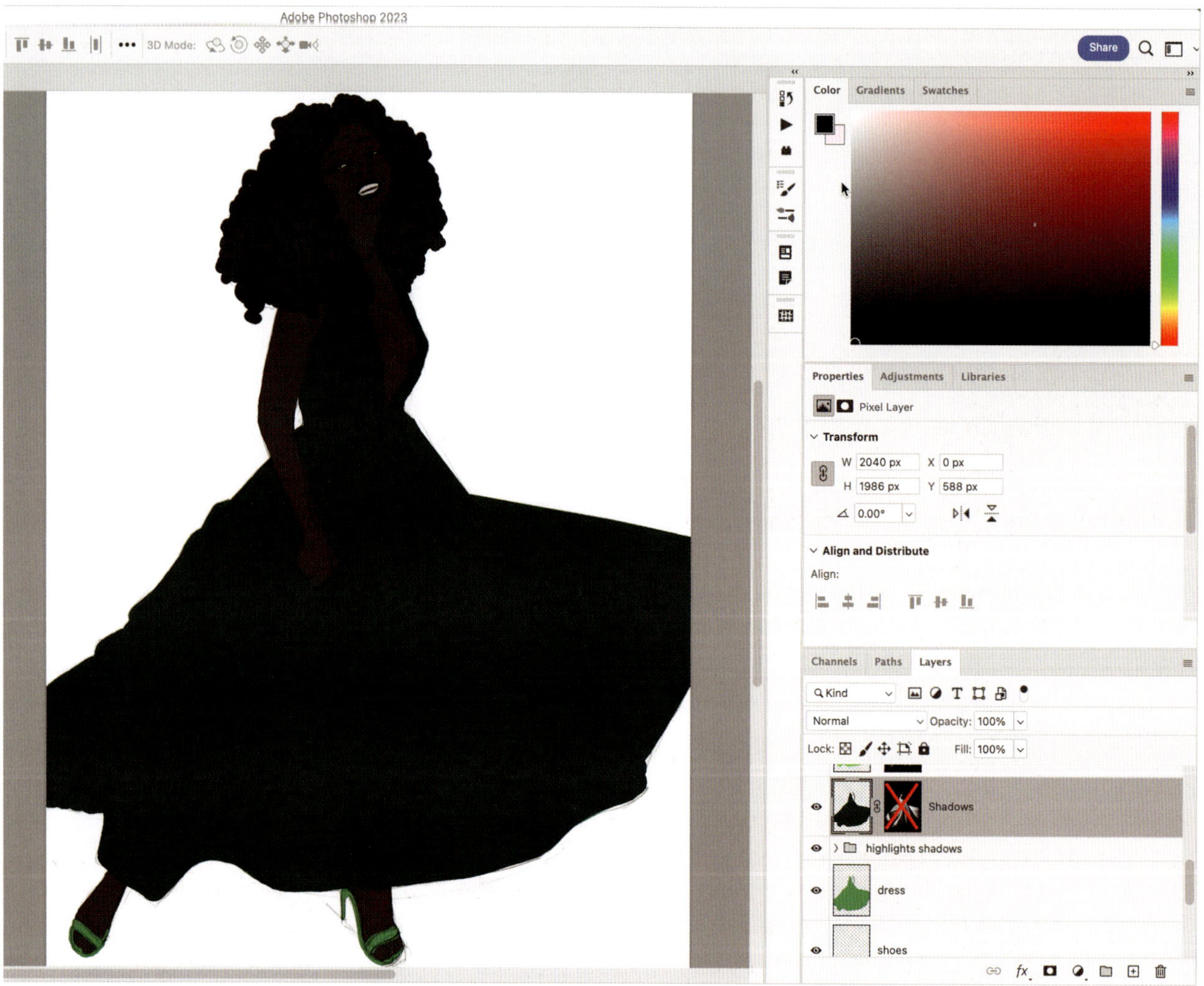

Figure 5.17a Create a burn or shadow layer by duplicating the layer and adjusting the brightness.

Step 3: With the shadow layer selected in the *Layers* panel, hold the *alt/option* key and *click* on the *Layer Mask* icon. This will apply a solid black mask to your shadow layer. Use the *Paintbrush* tool with white to control where the shadows appear by painting on the layer mask. Remember that you can adjust the brush attributes along with the *Opacity* to control how your shadows appear. Also make sure that you have the mask selected in your *Layers* panel before you start to paint. We changed the visibility to only see the mask in Figure 5.17b. You don't need to do this step, though.

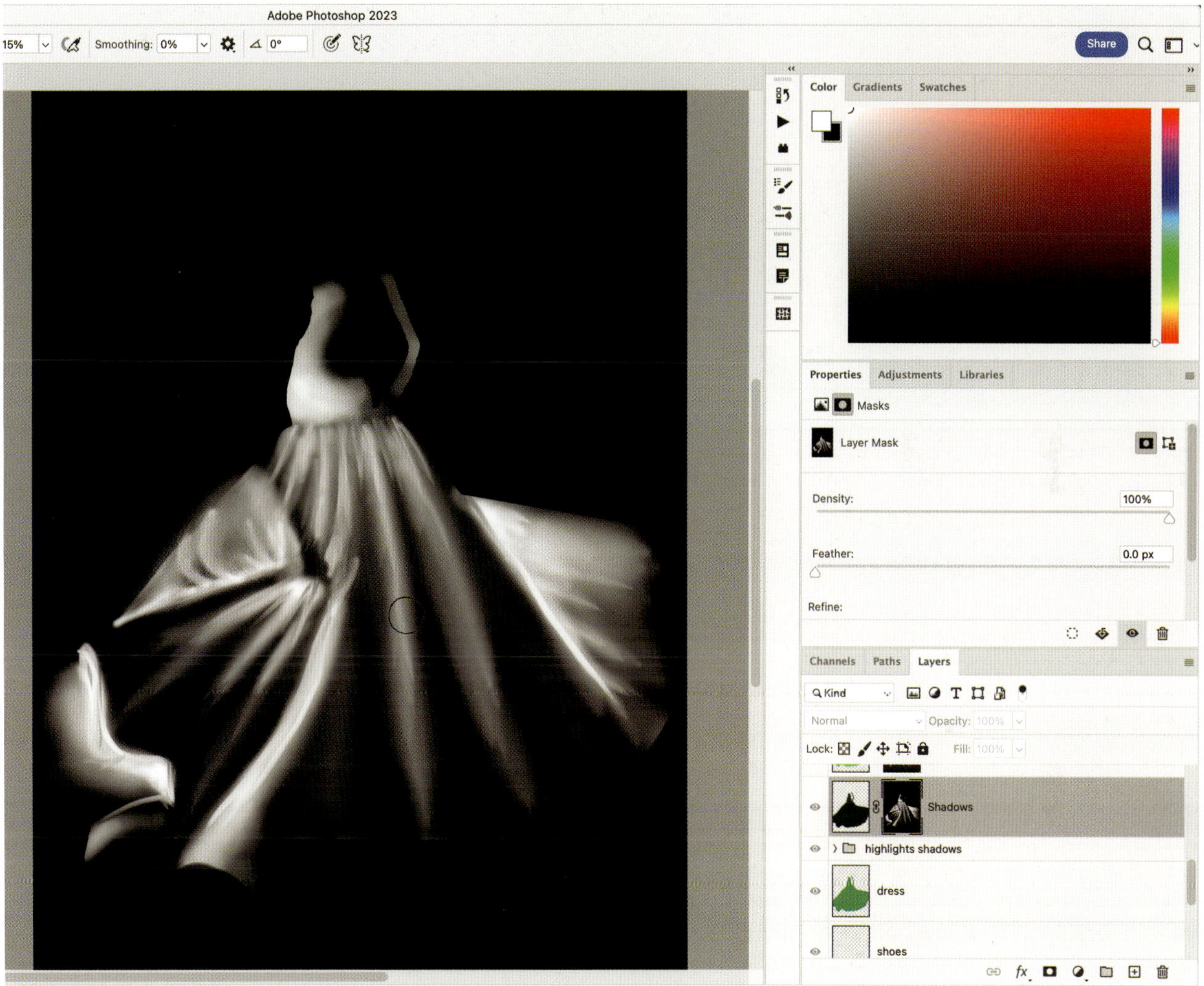

Figure 5.17b Use white to paint in your mask and allow the shadow layer to show through. For this screenshot, we made the mask visible by clicking on the mask while holding the *alt/option* key. This is usually an unnecessary action while rendering. We simply wanted to visibly show how the mask looks.

Step 4: Now work with the highlights layer. Turn the *visibility* back on for that layer. Again, make an adjustment of your choice to the brightness of the layer. Then apply a black mask by holding *alt/option* while *clicking* the *Layer Mask* icon in the *Layers* panel. Use your *Paintbrush* tool to paint white into the layer mask to reveal the highlights.

Step 5: You can also adjust the shadow and highlight *Layers Blend Modes*. See if any options such as *Darken* or *Multiply* produce better results with your shadow layer. Likewise, see if *Lighten* or *Screen* work with your highlights layer. Remember to *Zoom* out every now and then as well. If you decide that the overall effect is too much, drop the *Opacity* for the layer. If it just needs a small fix, paint some black back into your mask to correct the area. You can see our results in Figure 5.18.

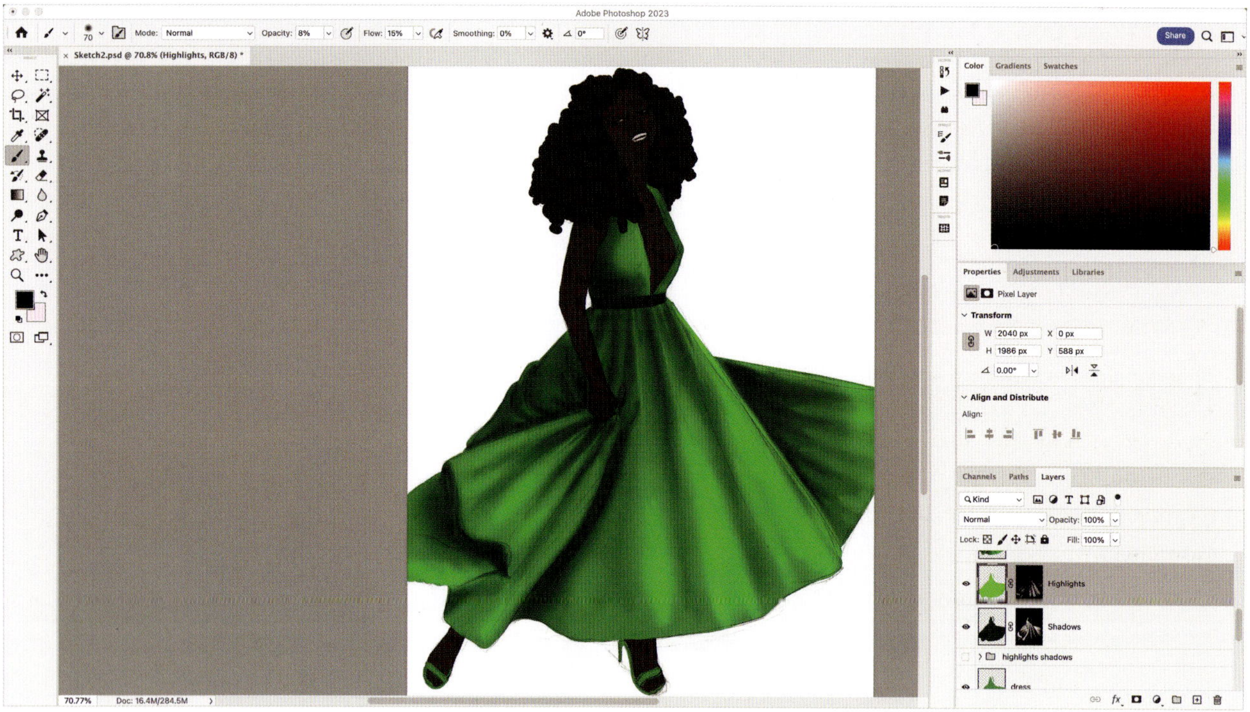

Figure 5.18 Adding brightness to your work with a *Dodge* layer.

Although this method works for a flat fill layer, it seems a little cumbersome when simply using a *Paintbrush* or the *Dodge* and *Burn* tools will suffice. It works well for pattern fills and smart objects, though. Where this technique really shines is in photographic retouching. If you need to edit any photos of your work, you may find the *Dodge* and *Burn* layers to be the best method for those finishing touches, as shown in Figure 5.19.

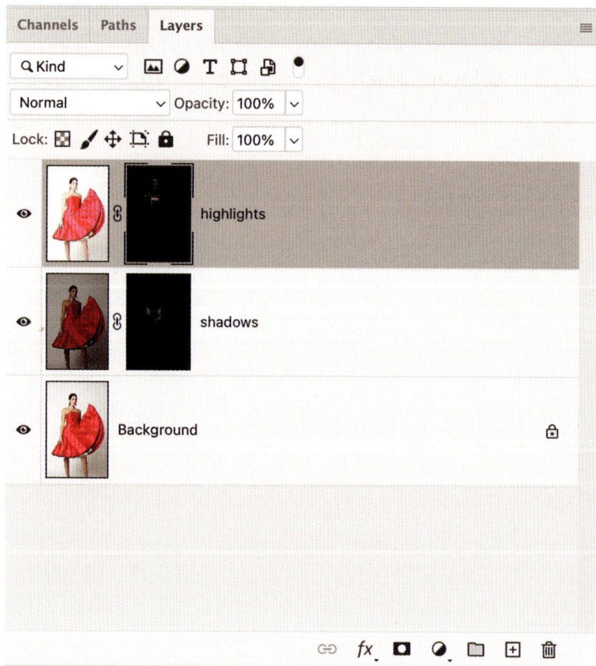

Figure 5.19 *Dodge* and *Burn* layers work best for retouching photos.

Cast Shadows in Ps

To add a cast shadow in Photoshop, you will want to first add a layer below all the other layers. How detailed or realistic do you want this shadow? For this practice, we used the exercise file CastShadow.psd.

Method 1: If you want to create a simple hint of a cast shadow, use the *Elliptical Marquee Selection* tool (often found below the *Rectangular Marquee* in the toolbar) and draw out a marquee selection below your figure. Add a shadow-colored fill or gradient of your choice. Reduce the opacity to make it transparent. Voila! You have a shadow like the one seen in Figure 5.20. You can also use the *Paintbrush* tool to shape or add to the shadow effect.

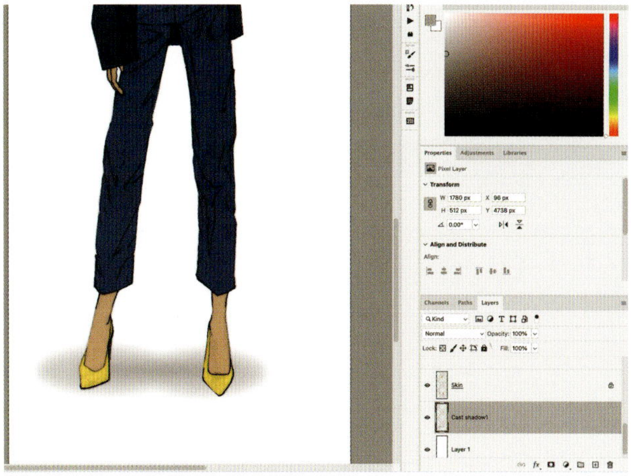

Figure 5.20 After filling an ellipse using the *Paintbucket* tool, we applied a *Gaussian Blur* filter to blend out the *Cast shadow*.

Method 2: Step 1: To add a slightly more realistic shape to your shadow, use the *Magic Wand* to select the background. *Inverse* your selection so you have a selection around your entire figure. Add a layer to the bottom of the stack if you did not do so previously and make sure you are working on that layer. Use the *Paintbucket* or *Gradient* tools to add a gray shadow color to the selection on that layer. Deselect using *control+d/command+d*.

Step 2: Now you want to transform the shadow by using *control+t/command+t*. *Right-click* and choose *Distort*. This will allow you swing the figure down to an angle that looks correct for your figure and the background. If you are not sure what sort of background you will put the figure on later, just swing the shadow off to the side so you can come back to it later in the layout phase.

Step 3: Remember to lower the *Opacity*, and to keep the feet of the shadow attached to the feet of the figure unless they are flying like Peter Pan! You can see our cast shadow in Figure 5.21.

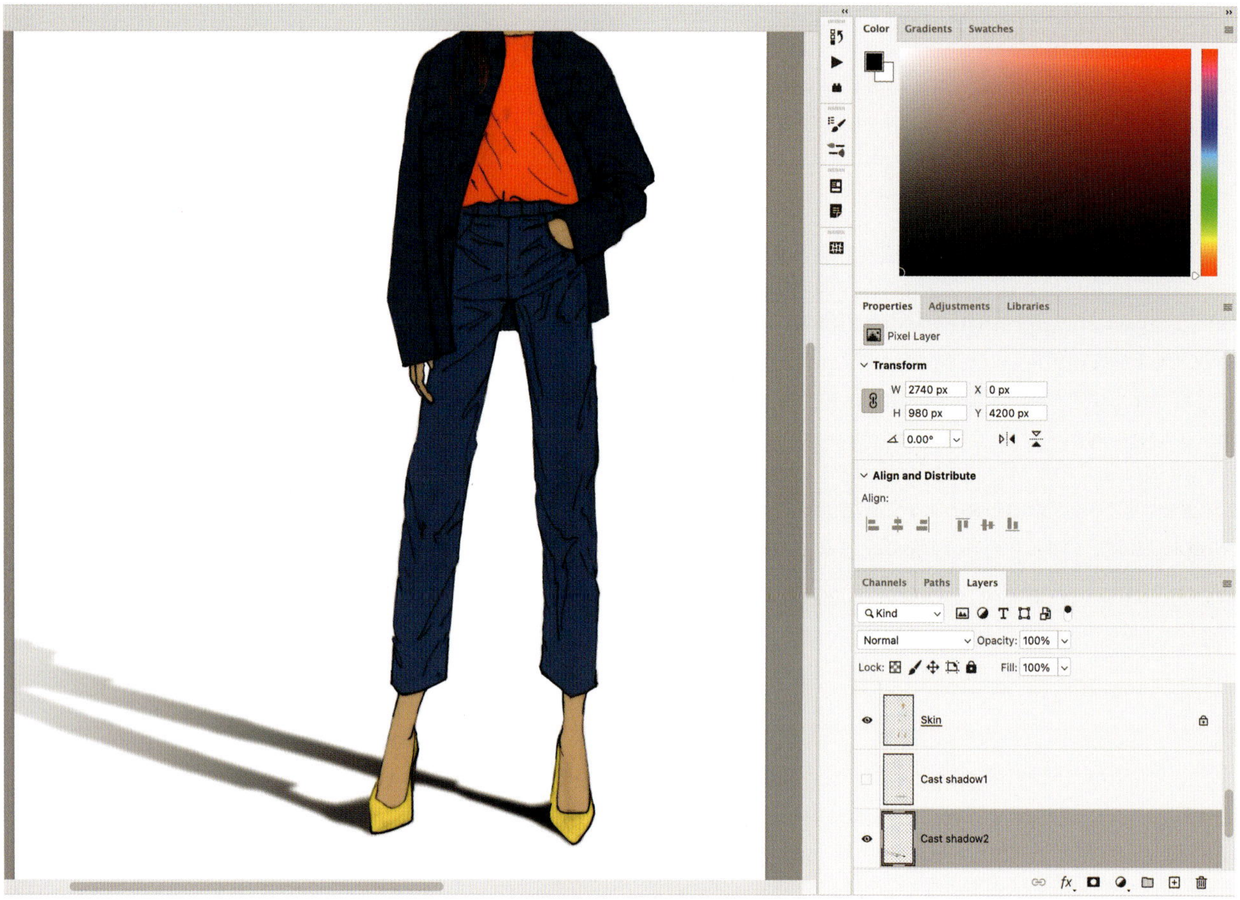

Figure 5.21 Use the *Magic Wand* tool to make a selection in the shape of your figure. Then fill it, distort it, and add a blur.

Troubleshooting

"I'm trying to use the *Dodge/Burn* tool but keep getting an error symbol?"

If you get either an error message or a little "no" symbol that won't allow you to use these tools, check your layers. There are certain types of layers that won't allow you to use tools such as these. *Pattern Fill Layers* and *Smart Object* layers fall into this category. You will either need to use another method or try rasterizing the layer. Likewise, check that the layer is not locked, or that you are not on the wrong layer altogether.

"I just realized that I was painting on the wrong layer!"

Sadly, there is no quick fix for this issue, and it is something that every digital artist has experienced at some time or another. If you just started, *Undo* your way back to the start of the error. If you are too far along or realized the mistake after saving and reopening the file, you have a few options. If the painted area happens to fall over a space of previously transparent pixels, you can probably use the *Lasso* or other *Selection* tool to select the offending paint strokes. Then cut them to the clipboard with a *right-click* command or using the keyboard shortcut *control+x/command+x*. Select the correct layer, then *Paste in Place* through the *Edit* menu or use the shortcut *shift+control+v/shift+command+v*. If it is more of a hot mess than that, you may just have to delete the layer and start over or accept the mistake and move forward without changing it.

"I just zoomed out to realize that my highlights/shadows are too heavy-handed and look weird."

Hopefully, you are using one of the methods with your highlights/shadows on a separate layer from the object. If this is the case, you can reduce the *Opacity* of your layer or try changing the *Blend Mode* to see if it fixes the issue. You can also try adding a *Layer Mask* to reduce the effect. If your effects are on the same layer as the object, you will have to try painting over the area to reduce the offending area.

STYLE SECRETS 5.2

Talk to Your Lighting Designer

If you are rendering designs for any sort of performing art costume, take a moment to talk with the lighting designer. Find out what sort of light they are considering for the moment when this garment is on stage. Because you are working with a digital medium, you have the advantage of showing the design with different types of lighting. Add a *Hue/Saturation Adjustment Layer* with the gel color.

You may even want to try a **Gradient Map**. A *Gradient Map* is an adjustment layer like *Levels* and *Curves*. It replaces the shadows with the dark value of color in the gradient, the midtones with the middle value, and the highlights with the light value. Figure SS5.1a shows the original rendering, and SS5.1b shows the image with a blue *Gradient Map* adjustment added. This helps provide the effect of a gelled lighting source. You add the map to the top of your image, then change the blend mode to *Overlay* or *Soft Light*. You may also need to adjust the opacity. These are overly simplified instructions, so take the time to look up some tutorials on *Gradient Maps* if this option interests you.

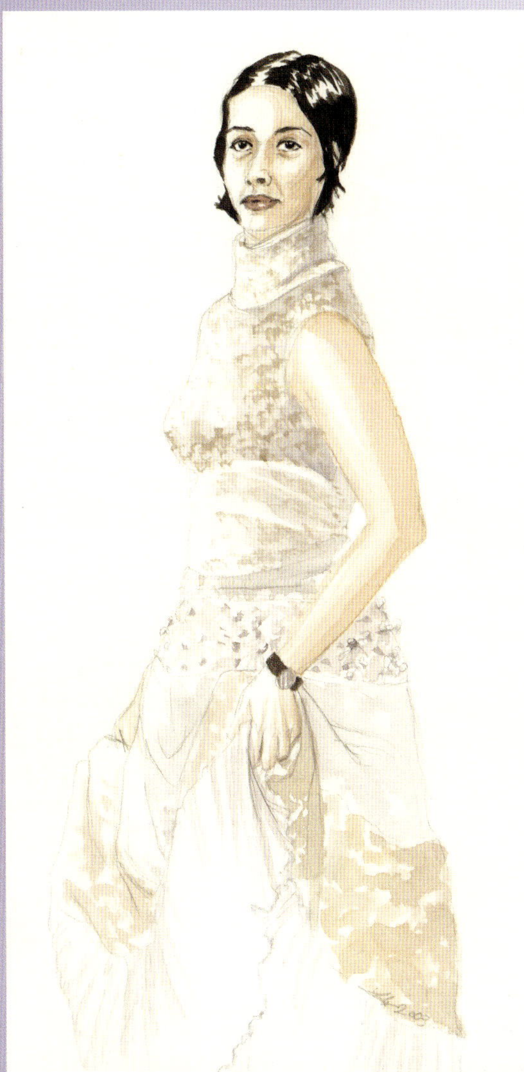

Figure SS5.1a The original rendering as it was created.

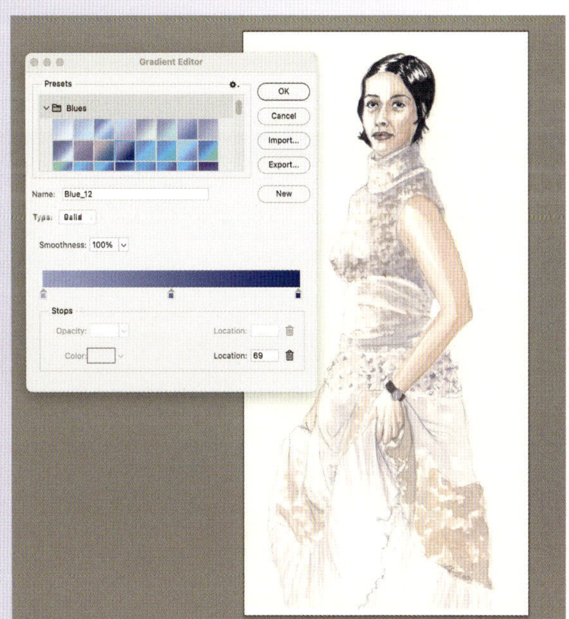

Figure SS5.1b Here the rendering has a blue *Gradient Map Adjustment Layer* added. Be sure to change your blend mode for the layer to *Overlay* or *Soft Light*. This helps to simulate a blue gel light source.

Project 5.2: Light and Shadow in Illustrator

Many beginners don't think to add light and shadow effects in vector programs like Illustrator because it isn't a digital painting application like Photoshop. Illustrator produces more graphic effects but can still result in illustrations with distinctive highlights and shadows. So, jump in and start adding dimension to your vector artwork.

The great news is that highlights and shadows are essentially new shapes and paths, so they affect solid color and pattern fills the same way. There is no need to treat patterns any differently from your solid color objects.

Paths/Shapes

Think back to earlier in this chapter about the shapes of shadows and highlights. In a vector program like Illustrator, you need to create those shapes to produce lighting effects on your rendering.

Step 1: *Open* one of your Illustrator files that has already been colored and concentrate on one object of clothing at a time. We are using an example from the patterns chapter in Figure 5.22. You will find it in the exercise files, labelled ShadePractice2.ai. In our example, we will make lighting effects for the dress. Think about your light source and how it will affect the highlights and shadows on this object. Where are your darkest shadows and brightest highlights? What shape are they? Start to draw in one of your darkest shadows with the *Pen* tool. Make a closed shape. Now choose a fill color that is darker and more saturated than your base color. Remove any stroke. You just made a shadow!

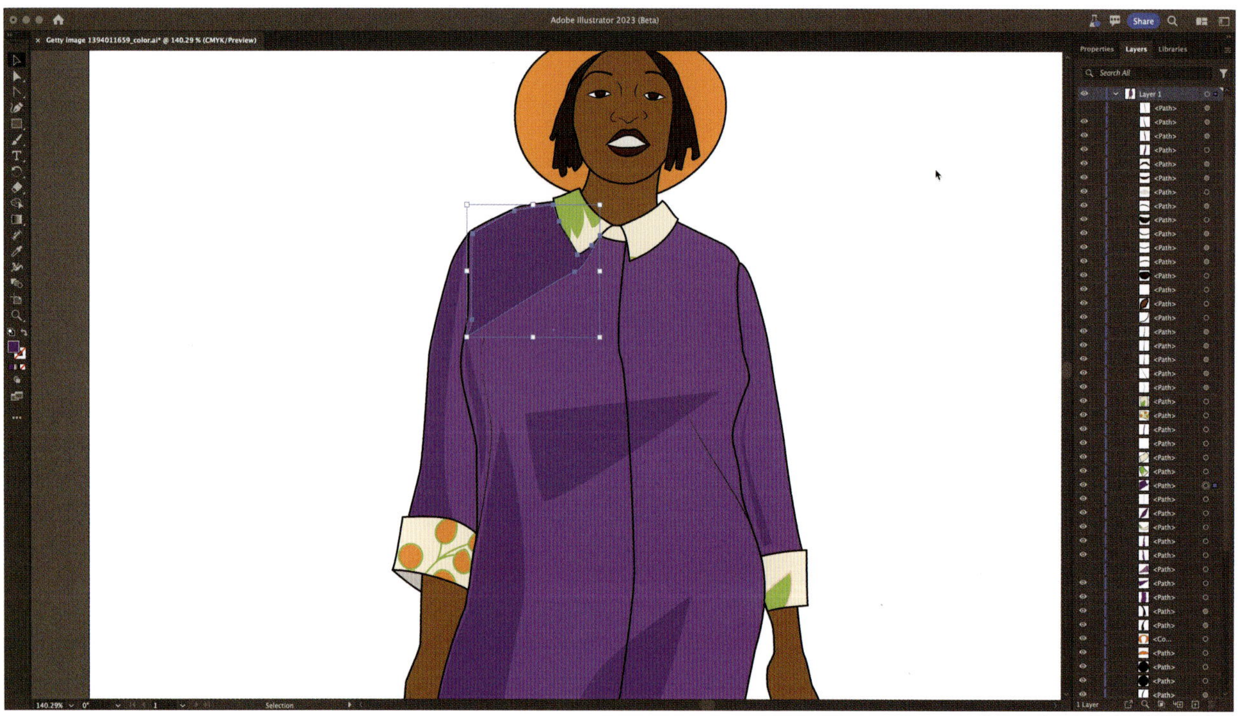

Figure 5.22 Adding a shadow shape in Illustrator.

Step 2: For thin areas of highlights and shadows, you can use an open stroke. Remove any fill and change your stroke color to match your shadow color. Make sure your corners/joins are set to *Rounded*. Look in the *Strokes* panel and try choosing one of the *Profiles* to something more suitable for your shadow as seen in Figure 5.23.

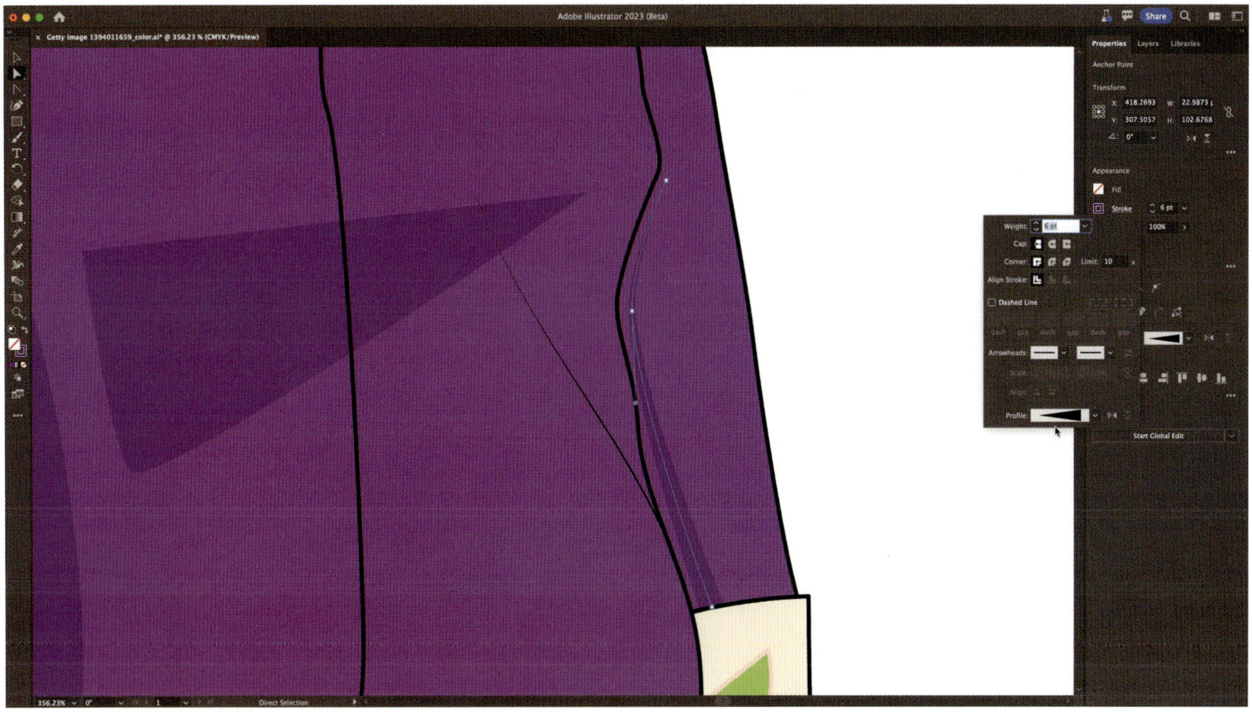

Figure 5.23 Using a path with a stroke profile for a shadow.

Step 3: That's it! Continue to go around your rendering and add in shadow/highlight shapes and strokes. You can see our final result in Figure 5.24. You will use the same concept of shape/path shadows and highlights for the next two techniques.

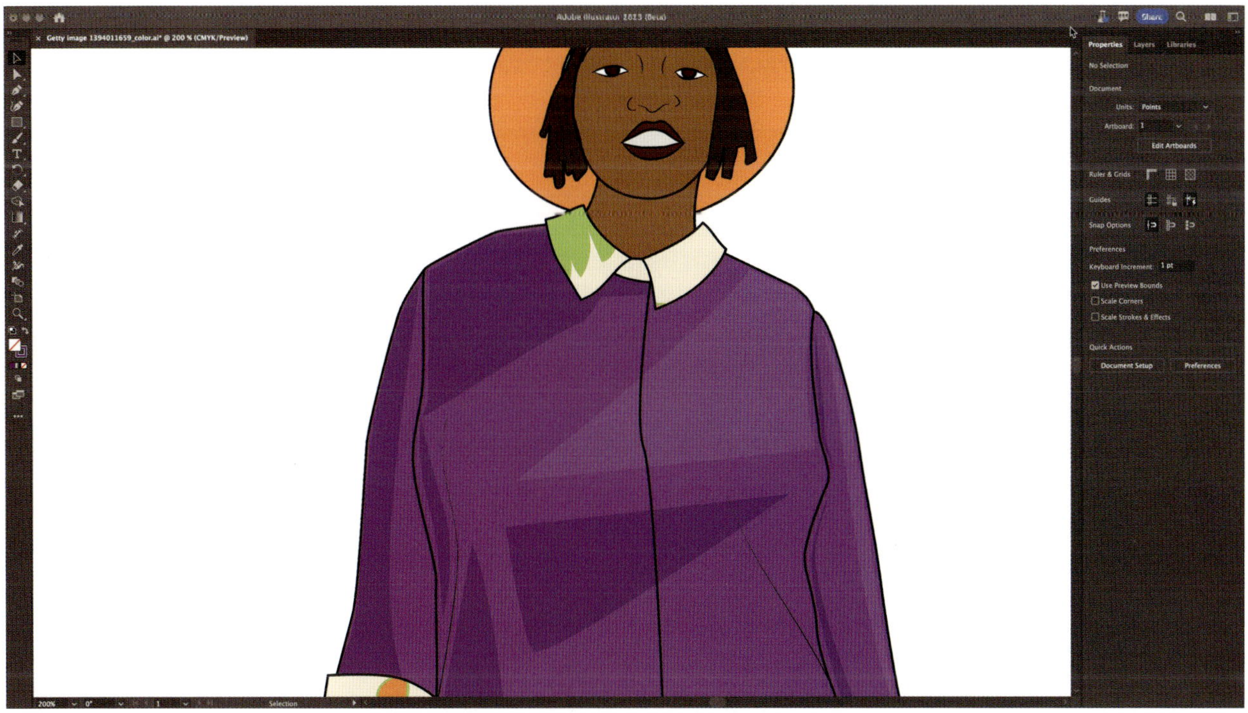

Figure 5.24 You can use this technique to create graphic highlights and shadows.

Blur

You can use a *Blur* effect in Illustrator to soften the edges of your light and shadow. This is a raster effect, so be sure to double-check that your document raster resolutions settings are set to *High (300 ppi)* in the *Effect* menu. Choose one of your shadow shapes with the *Selection* tool. In the *Effect* menu, choose *Blur* → *Gaussian Blur*. A dialog box will appear, and you can choose how blurry you want the area. Click *OK* to select the setting. If you decide to adjust that setting later, you can select the shape and reopen the effect through the *Appearance* panel as seen in Figure 5.25.

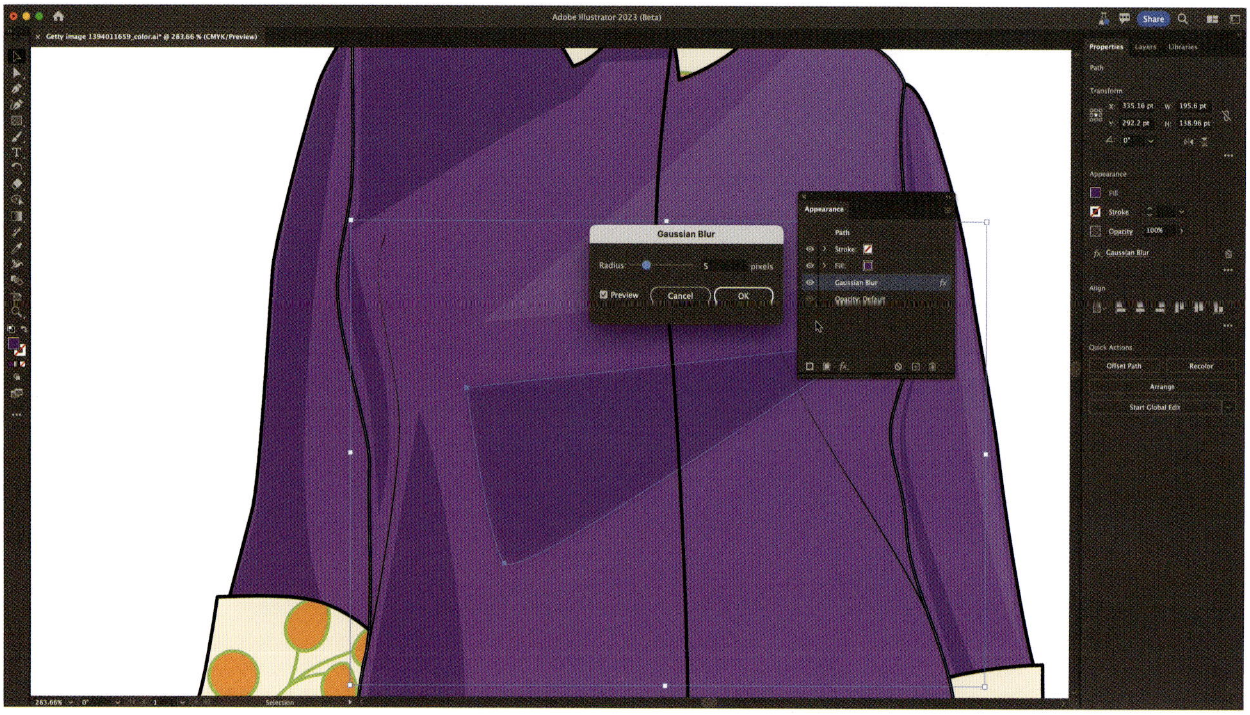

Figure 5.25 When you add a *Gaussian Blur* effect, you will be asked to choose the blur radius. You can change the blur by reselecting the effect in the *Appearance* panel.

The tricky part about this fun feature is that you may notice your blur extending beyond the boundaries of your garment. There are two methods to fix this. Start by deleting the offending shadow.

Method 1: Use the black arrow to select the outer shape of your garment area. In Figure 5.26a you can see that we selected the arm of the shirt sleeve. With the object selected, look in your toolbar on the left. Just below the fill and stroke colors, you will notice three tiny icons with a circle and square in different configurations or you may only see one icon (depending upon your version). The last one should show the square cut off by the circle and is called the *Draw Inside Mode*. If you have one icon, click on it and you will have the option to choose *Draw Inside*. When you click this mode, you will see dashed corner indicators around your selected base shape like those seen in Figure 5.26b. Now, redraw your shadow shape and add the blur. You will notice that it is bound by the base image and will not blur beyond that area as shown in Figure 5.26c. If you ever need to edit the shape, you can use the *Direct Selection* tool or go into *Isolation* mode to work with it.

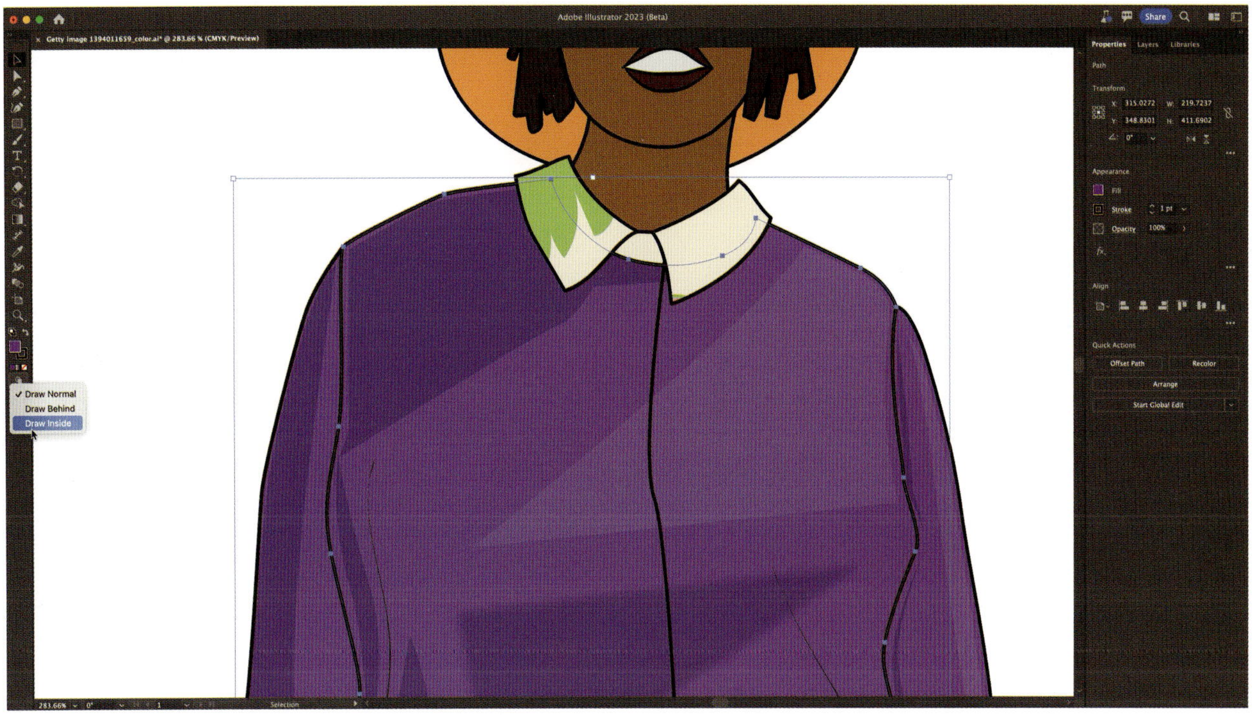

Figure 5.26a Select your main object such as the dress. Then choose the *Draw Inside* mode from the bottom of the toolbar on the left.

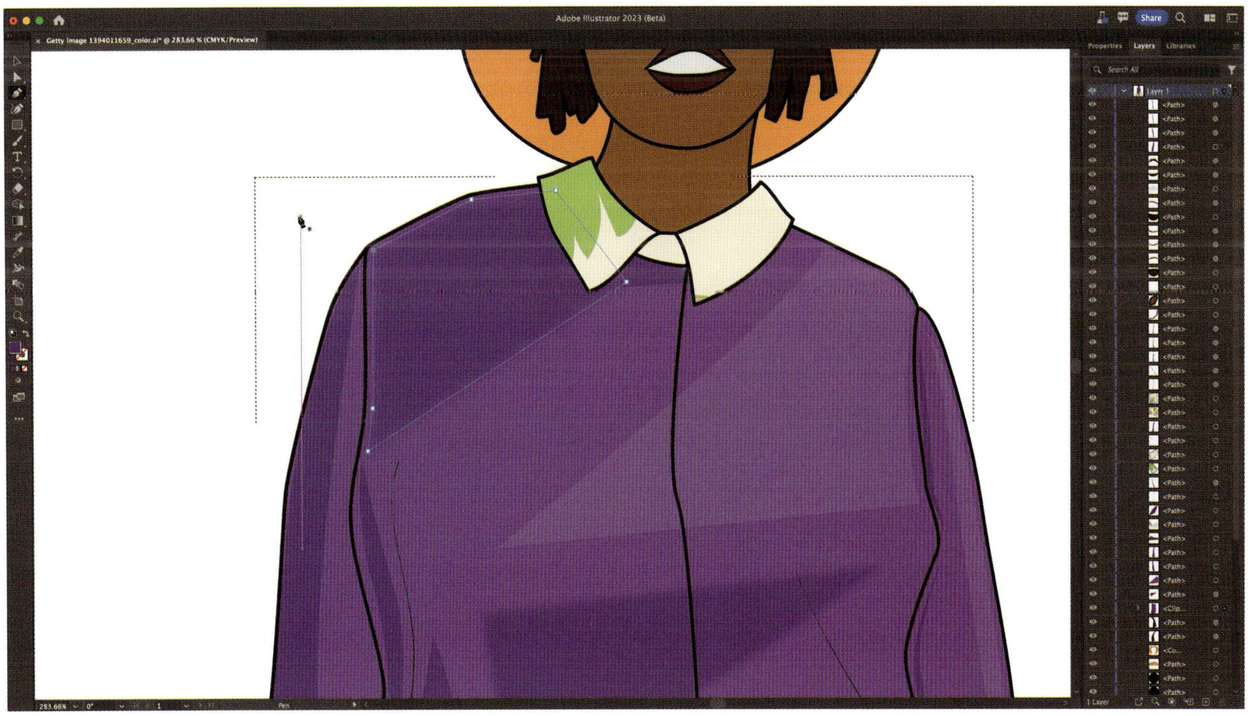

Figure 5.26b When using *Draw Inside* mode, you will see dashed crop marks around your primary object. Now you can start to draw your shadows and highlights.

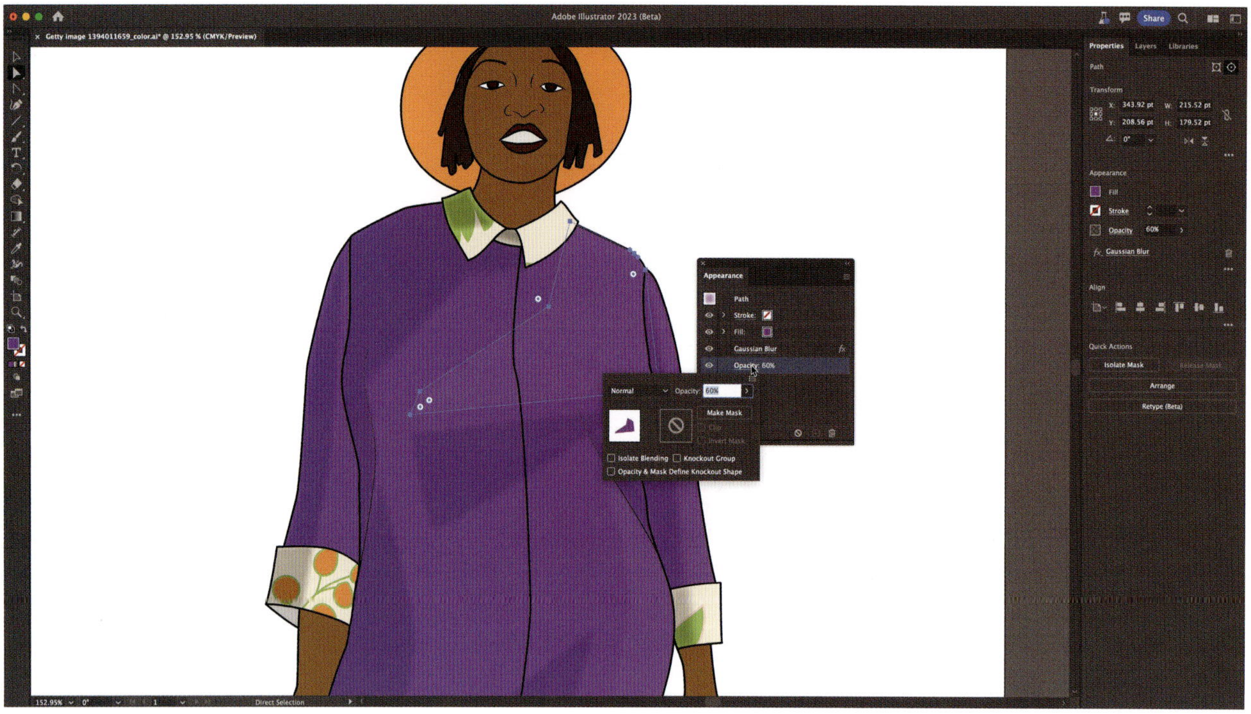

Figure 5.26c While in the *Draw Inside* mode, the *Gaussian Blur* effects will not bleed outside of your primary object.

Method 2: If for whatever reason you prefer not to use the *Draw Inside* mode, you will need to clip any blurred effects to the base image. Recall that in Illustrator, images clip up rather than down. You will also need to make a copy of your base image before you start because the clipped shape will "eat" the base image to which it is clipped. Select the base image such as the sleeve in Figure 5.27a. Use *control+c/command+c* to copy the shape. Draw your shadow shape directly below this shape and apply your blur effect. You may need to turn off the fill visibility on the shape above it to see what you are doing.

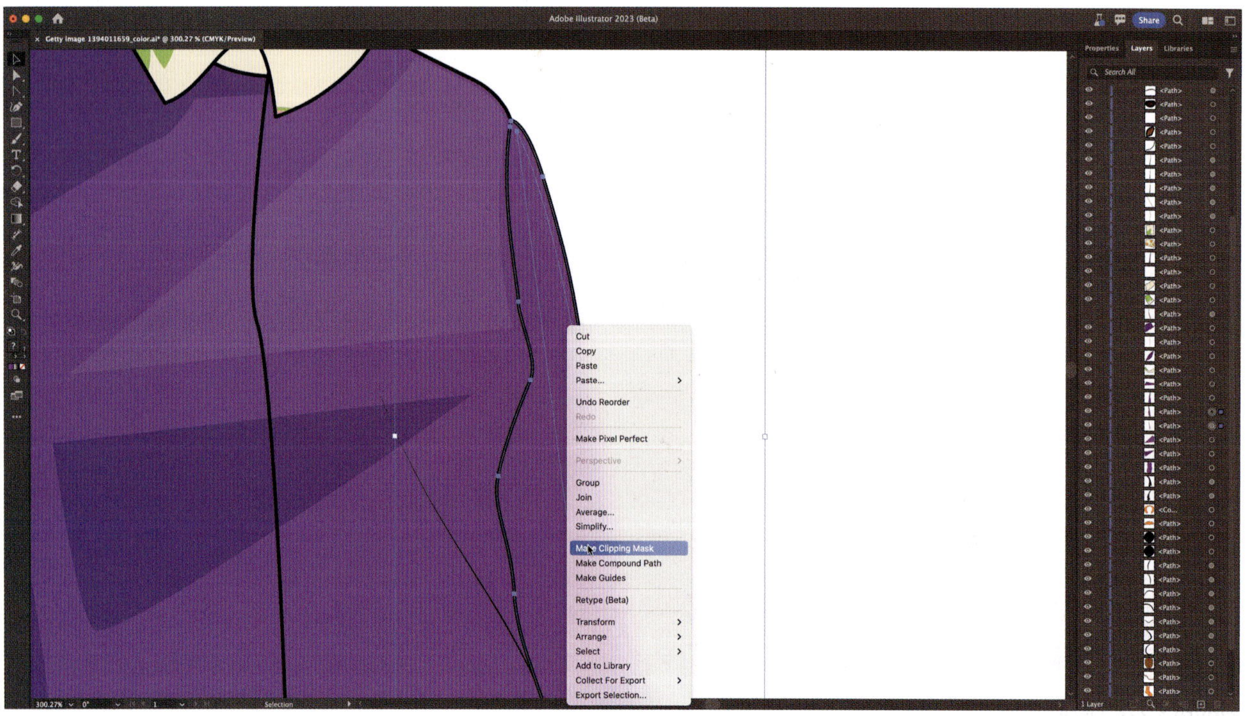

Figure 5.27a Draw your highlight or shadow, then move it below your main object in the *Layers* panel. Select both objects, then *right-click* and choose *Make Clipping mask*.

Now select both the base shape and the shadow shape. *Right-click* and select *Make Clipping mask*. Your shadow blur will be clipped into the sleeve shape. However, the sleeve just disappeared, as seen in Figure 5.27b. Use *control+b/command+b* to paste your copied sleeve behind the shadow. Figure 5.27c shows the final effect.

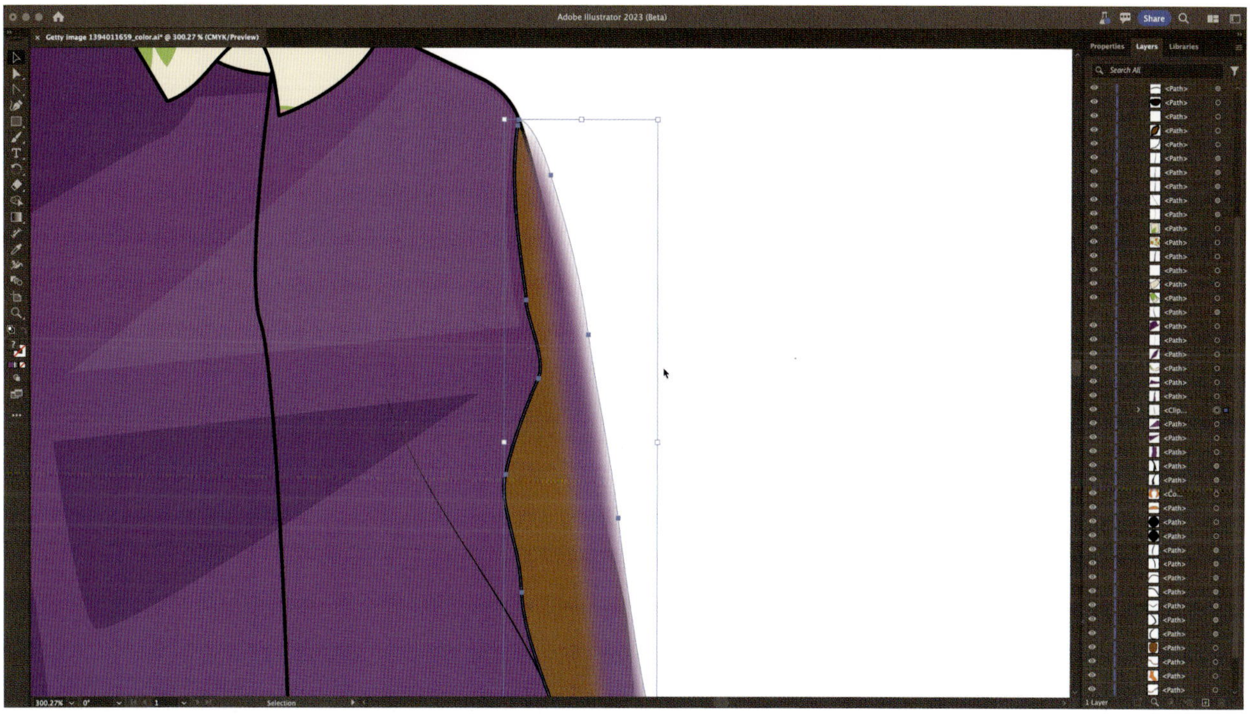

Figure 5.27b Once you create the *Clipping mask*, the top object will disappear. Paste your object in back by using *control+b/command+b*. If you forgot to copy it to the clipboard, *Undo* to reverse your steps, Copy the top object, then recreate the previous steps to get back to this point.

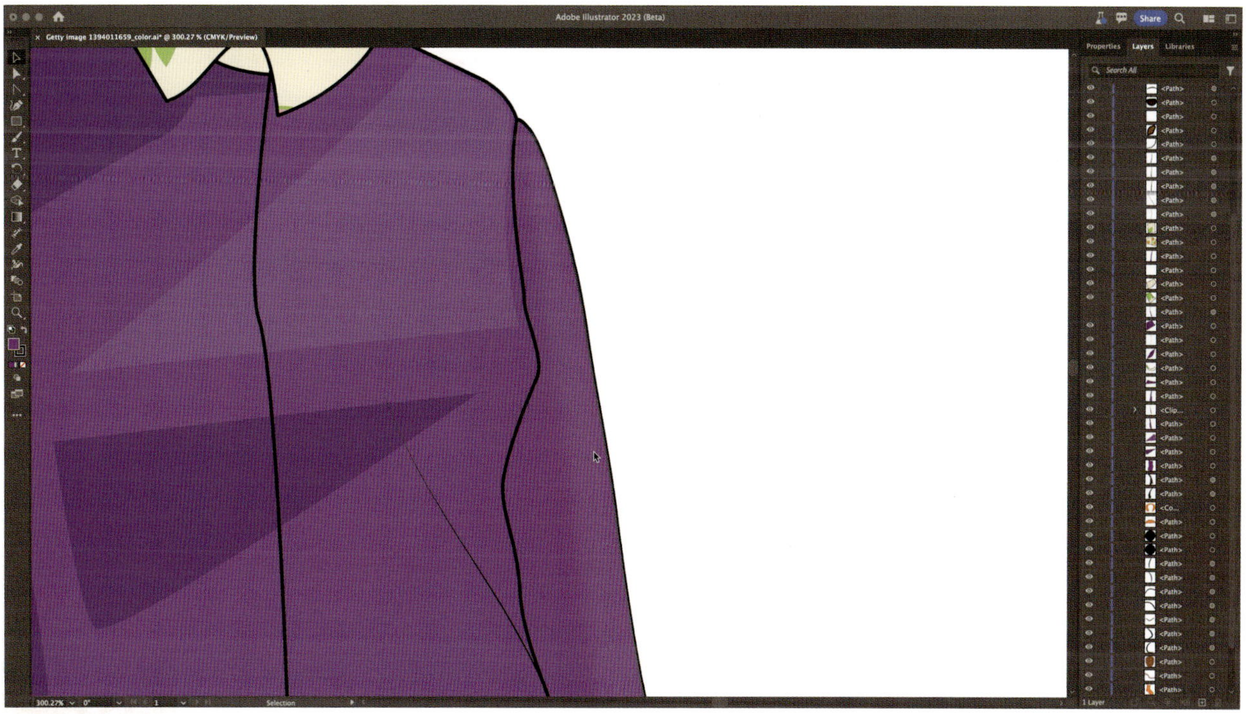

Figure 5.27c Once the primary object is pasted back in, you will have a highlight or shadow clipped into it. This works well when you don't have many highlights or shadows to clip. Otherwise, we suggest that you use the *Draw Inside* mode instead.

If you only have one or two blur effects that need to be clipped, this method works just fine. However, it can be a bit tedious to constantly go through the motions of clipping if you have a lot of blurred effects falling outside your boundaries. If that is the case, we recommend keeping to the first method of drawing your blurred lighting effects.

Opacity

Your highlights and shadows are shaping up nicely but are still too heavy-handed. This is where the *Appearance* panel and *Opacity* come into play. Whether your highlights/shadows have blur effects or not, you will probably want to reduce the opacity. Select the shadow or highlight and open your *Appearance* panel or look in the *Properties* panel. Click on the word *Opacity*. Here, you can either lower your *Opacity* to make the area more transparent or choose a *Blend Mode* such as *Multiply* or *Screen* as shown in Figure 5.28. Or you can go crazy and do both, you sly devil! Play around with the opacity through your *Appearance* panel to make your highlights and shadows more effective. You'll notice this works particularly well over pattern fills as seen in Figure 5.29.

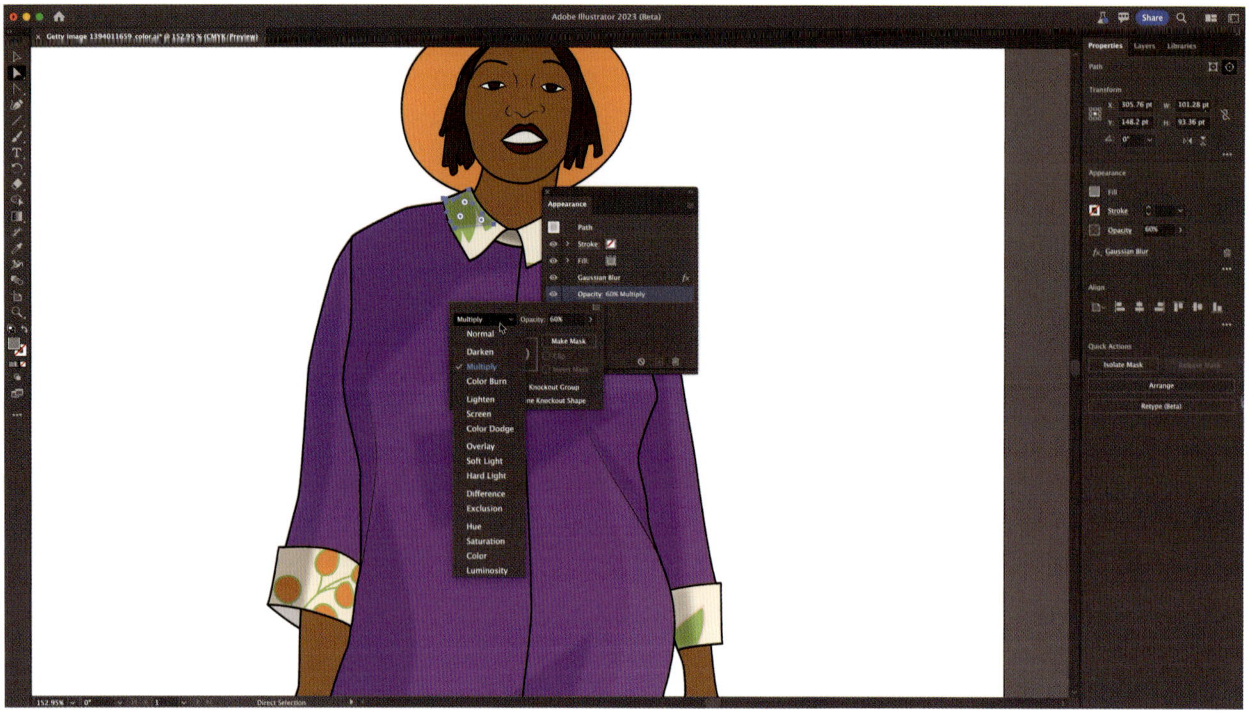

Figure 5.28 Use the *Appearance* panel to change the opacity and blend modes of your highlights and shadows. You will find that *Darken* or *Multiply* blend modes work well for shadows over pattern fills.

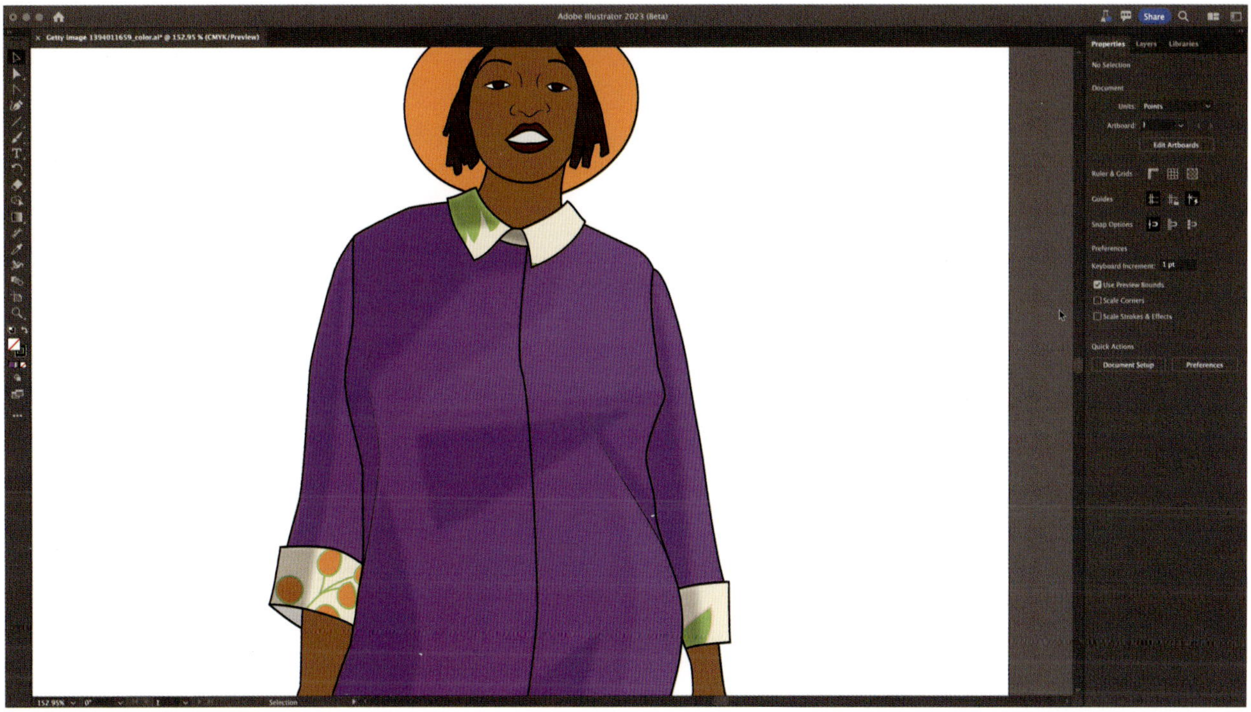

Figure 5.29 Have fun creating your shadows and highlights. Remember to think in shapes when creating them.

Cast Shadows in Ai

Method 1: Similar to Photoshop, you can create a simple elliptical shape with a shadow fill below your other shapes and paths as seen in Figure 5.30. Remove the stroke and reduce the opacity. The *Magic Wand* in Illustrator won't work for a background selection like it does in Photoshop, so to make a figure-shaped shadow, we will need to do a couple of extra steps.

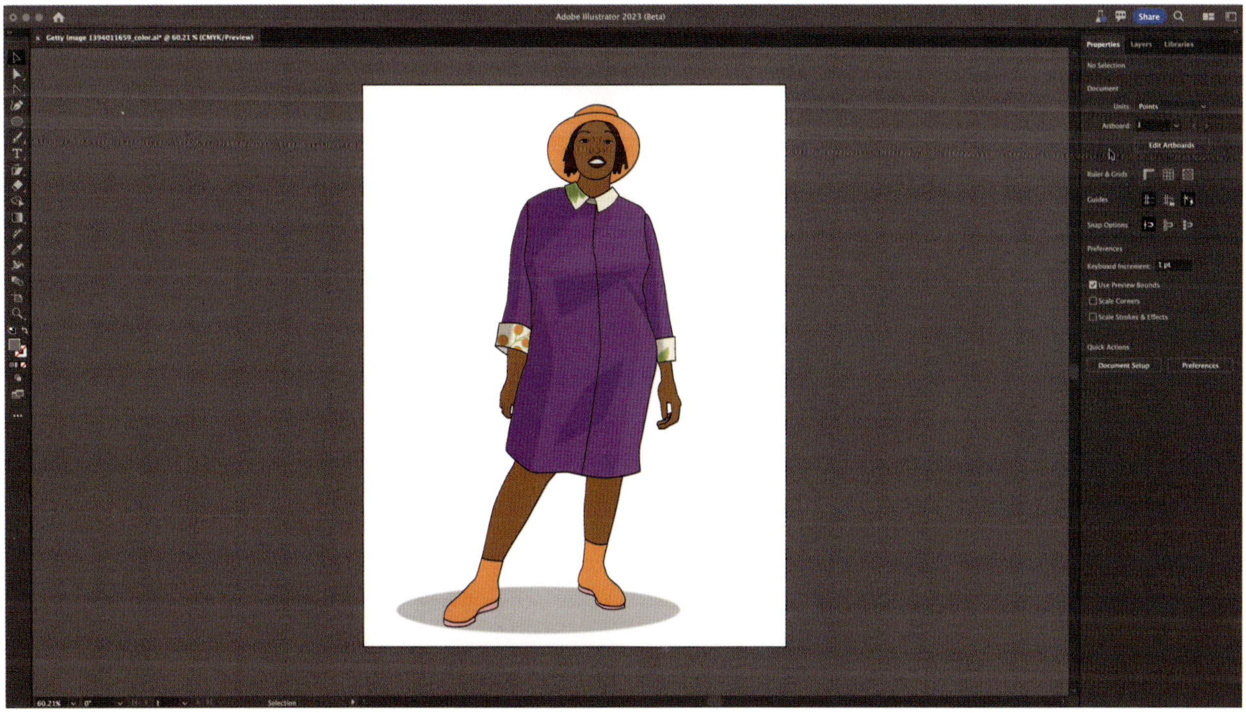

Figure 5.30 Add a simple ellipse shape to create an easy cast shadow.

Method 2: Use the *Selection* tool (black arrow) to select the entire figure. Make sure you get all of it and that none of the layers are locked. Copy it to the clipboard with *control+c/command+c*. Add a layer to the bottom of the stack and paste the copy on it using the *Paste in Back* command, *control+b/command+b* as seen in Figure 5.31a. Now go to the *Pathfinder* panel and *Combine All*. Remove your stroke and fill the shape with your shadow color. You probably can't see it below your figure, so turn off the *Visibility* on all other layers temporarily like we did in Figure 5.31b. With the object selected, use the *Shear* tool from the toolbar. It may be below your *Scale* tool. Use the *Shear* tool to swing your shadow down and move it to connect to the feet of your figure. You can see our finished shadow in Figure 5.31c. You can also use the *Direct Selection* tool to select parts of the shape and adjust it if necessary. Have fun with your new cast shadows!

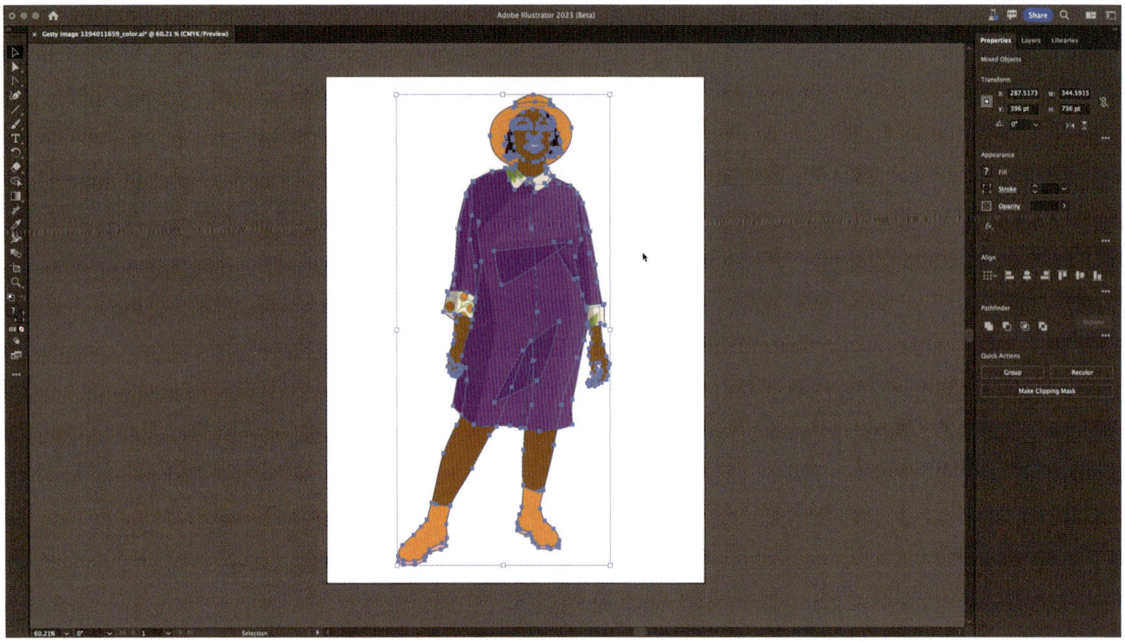

Figure 5.31a Select the entire figure with the *Selection* tool.

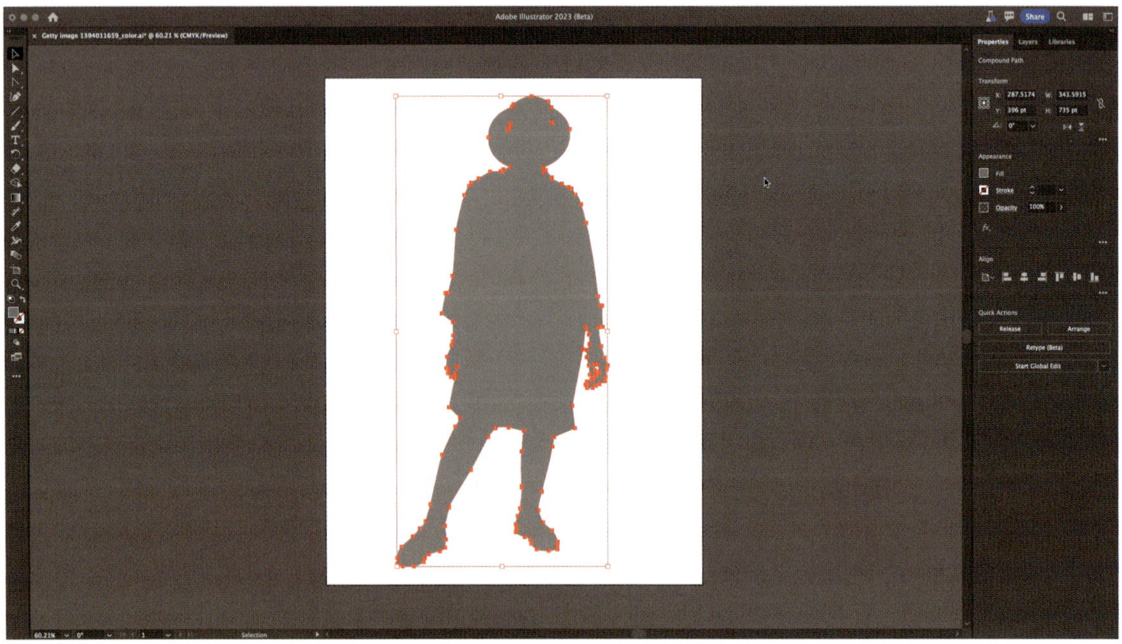

Figure 5.31b While it is still selected, use the *Pathfinder* or *Properties* panel to *Combine All*. Remove the stroke and change the fill to a shadow color of your choice. In this screenshot, we turned off the visibility of the top figure to make it easier to see the shadow.

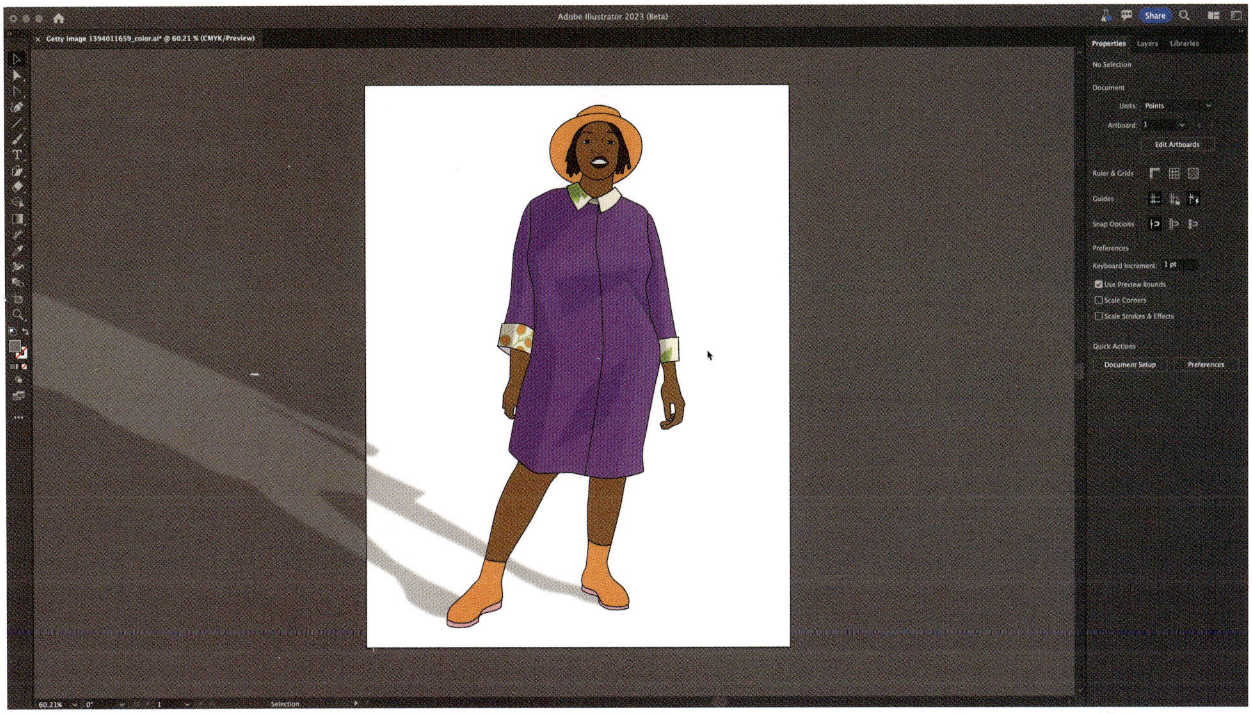

Figure 5.31c Use the *Shear* tool to distort the shadow shape. Feel free to add a *Blur* effect and change the *Opacity*.

Troubleshooting

"My blur effect looks very pixelated."

Recheck raster settings. Go to the *Effect* menu → *Document Raster Effects* and check the *Resolution*. It should be set to *High (300 ppi)*. In older versions of Illustrator, you will need to redo the blur effect after the resolution is corrected. In current versions, it will automatically correct.

"My blur goes outside the lines of my artwork!"

If you see an effect like the one shown in Figure 5.32, you'll need to either *Undo* and recreate your blurred effects using the *Draw Inside* mode, or make a *Clipping mask* as described earlier. Be sure to do this step or you will suffer a fuzzy halo of blurred shadows and highlights around the edges of your rendering. This never looks good, so take the time to contain your blurs.

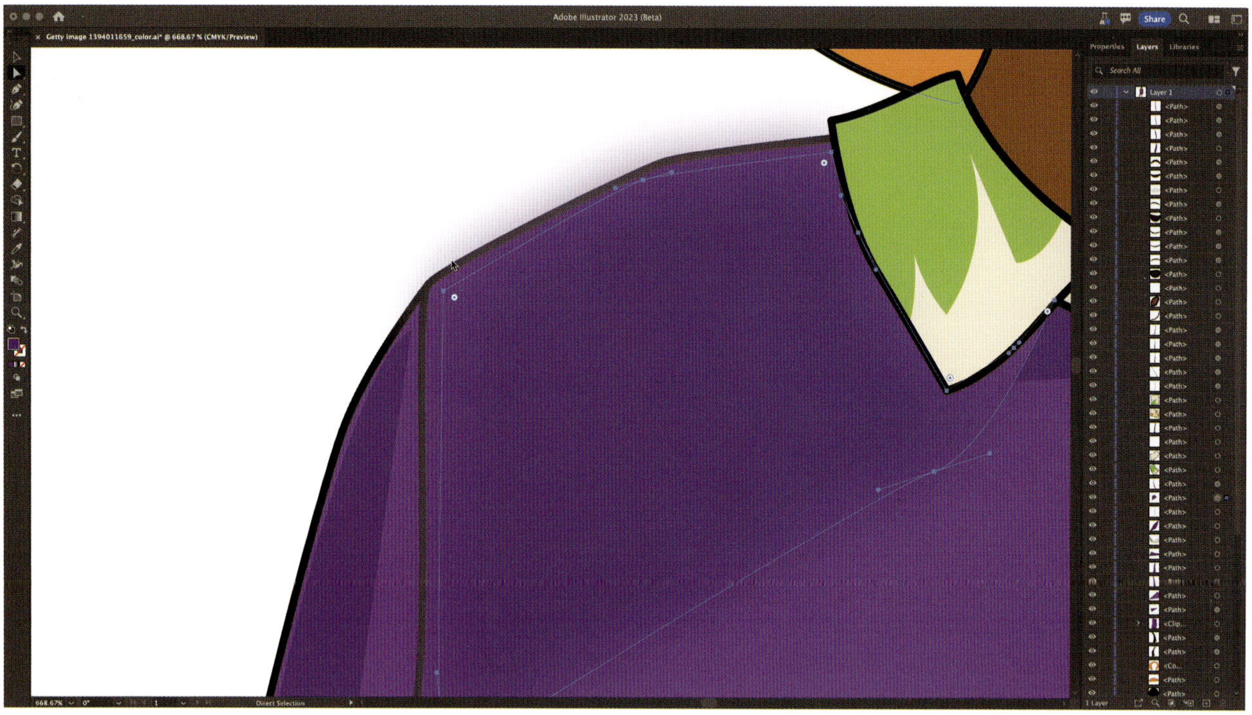

Figure 5.32 If you apply a *Blur* effect, you may see it bleed outside of your object. *Undo* your actions and either use *Draw Inside* mode or create a *Clipping mask* to contain it.

"My sleeve just disappeared after I clipped into it!"

Clipping masks in Illustrator eat the shape they are clipped into. It's just how the application works. If it is something other than a pattern fill (you can always add the stroke back in to correct it) then you will need to *Undo* the *Clipping mask*. Remember to first make a duplicate of the shape you are clipping into. Then you can create the *Clipping mask*. Now use the *Paste in Back* command to add the shape back in and make it look correct.

Summary

Adding highlights and shadows to your renderings can really step up the design communication! Be sure to spend some time understanding how light affects objects through other art classes or books. More importantly, make a point of noticing the shape and color of highlights and shadows in your everyday life.

You are welcome to try value mapping as a workflow to see if it is right for you. Regardless, you can add highlights and shadows in multiple ways. The *Dodge* and *Burn* tools and the *Paintbrush* tool are useful for painting in your effects in Photoshop or other digital painting applications. Although you can add these effects directly to your object, try adding separate layers to keep the file as non-destructive as possible.

You can also use a 50% gray layer set to the *Overlay Blend Mode* or try *Dodge and Burn* layers with masks. Although the *Dodge/Burn* tools will not directly work on a pattern fill or smart object, you can use any of the other methods on separate layers to shade your patterns. Don't forget to add a cast shadow to ground your figure.

To make highlights and shadows in a vector-based illustration, you will need to draw them in as shapes or paths. Feel free to play with the *Blur* effect and *Opacity* to change the look. You can add cast shadows in Illustrator, too. Now that you know how to add lighting effects, let's move to textures where your lighting can really shine!

STUDIO Companion Videos for Chapter 5

Please refer to STUDIO for accompanying chapter video(s).

Keywords

Dodge
Burn
Smudge
Gradient Map

Review Questions

1. What is reflected light and how might it affect your lit subject?
2. Review the pros and cons of using the *Dodge* and *Burn* tools.
3. Describe how the *Dodge/Burn* tools differ from *Dodge/Burn* layers.
4. Describe how the *Smudge* tool is useful in the highlight/shadow process.
5. Compare and contrast using the *Draw Inside* mode to using a *Clipping mask* in Illustrator.

Commands Introduced

- 50% Gray Fill
- Appearance panel
- Burn tool
- Combine All Pathfinder
- Distort
- Dodge tool
- Draw Inside Mode
- Duplicate layer
- Gaussian Blur
- Illustrator Clipping mask
- Paste in Back
- Paste in Place
- Shear
- Smudge tool

Keyboard Shortcuts

- Ai: *control+b/command+b* (Paste in Back)
- Ai, Id, Ps: *control+c/command+c* (copy)
- Ps: *control+d/command+d* (deselect)
- Ps: *control+t/command+t* (free transform)
- Ai, Id, Ps: *control+v/command+v* (paste)
- Ai, Ps: *control+x/command+x* (cut selected object)

Discussion Questions

1. Is value mapping a good workflow for you? Why or why not?
2. Is it better to shade in colors or just use *Dodge* and *Burn*?
3. How is dramatic lighting unnecessary and potentially problematic for most design communication?
4. Are cast shadows necessary for design communication layouts? Explain your thoughts.

Practice Exercises

1. Find a photograph with distinctive light and shadow. Change it to grayscale and identify the light direction(s), highlight shapes, shadow shapes, and cast shadows.
2. Using the same photo, turn the color back on. Use the *Eyedropper* tool to pick up the main highlight colors. Apply each to a selection on a new layer or a separate artboard. Do the same for the main shadow colors.
3. Create a sphere and shade it using a textured *Paintbrush* of your choice.
4. Using one of your own renderings, try two different methods for adding shadow and light in Photoshop. Which do you prefer? Why?

Endnotes

1. In film photography, you could block off a section to *Dodge* or brighten an area on the negative. Blocking the light results in less exposure, which results in a brighter area. When you "burned" an area, you exposed it longer to the light to result in darker areas.
2. This is one of those times that you probably want a destructive change to save file space. We can always adjust the layer mask and opacity to change the results.

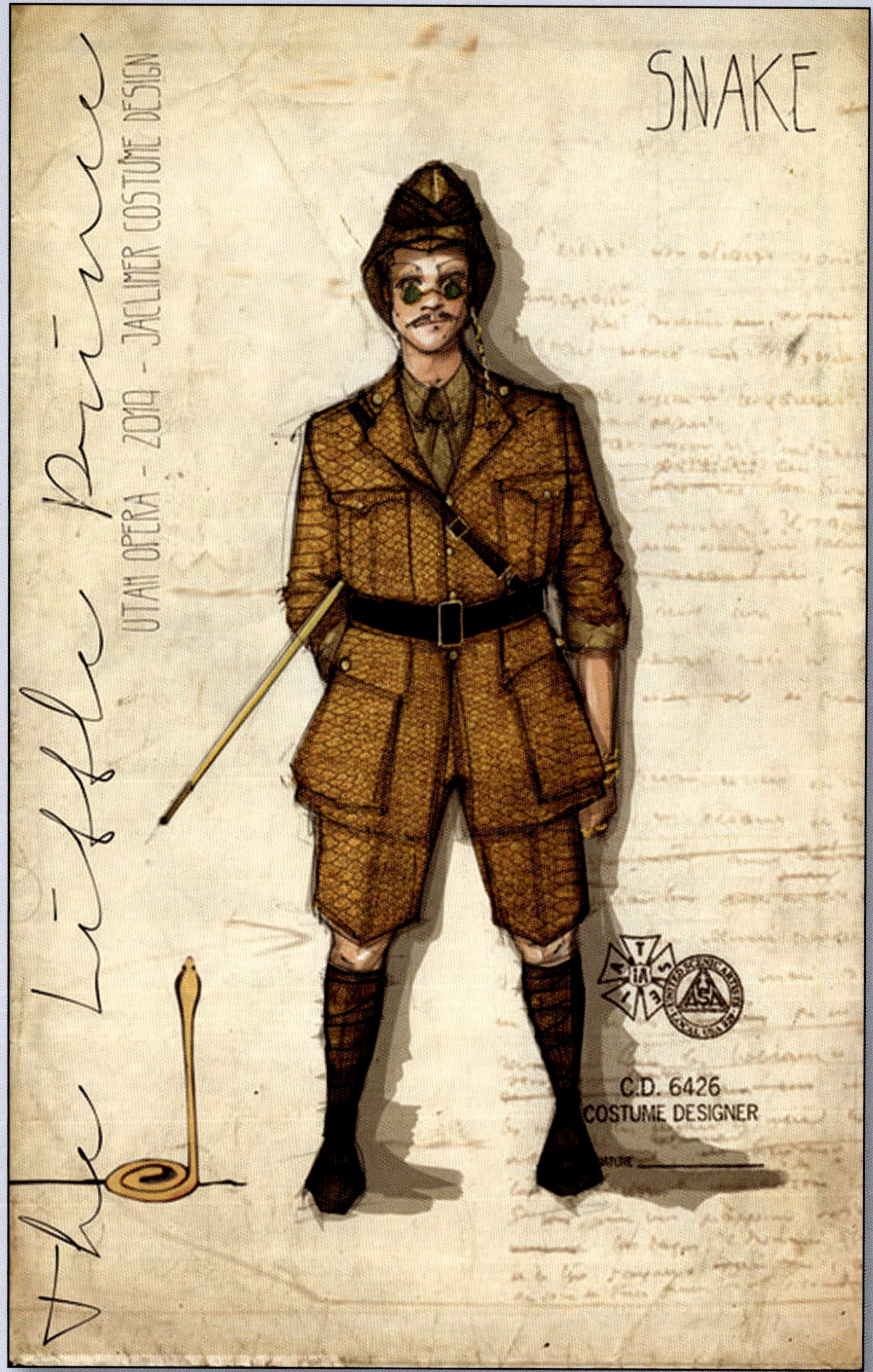

Figure 6.1 Visual texture in a rendering informs the viewer about fabric and trim expectations. Courtesy of Jacob A. Climer.

CHAPTER 6

Adding Texture for Fabrics

Learning Objectives

After completing this chapter, you should be able to

- Analyze the base elements of texture and how to portray it in a digital rendering
- Create brush, filter, pattern, and layer effect textures in Photoshop
- Create brush, pattern, and layer effect textures in Illustrator
- Investigate specialty textures and apply them

You've got color. You've got patterns. Now let's add some texture to the mix! Conveying your fabrics through texture can help to communicate your design more fully. It also provides a little thrill of excitement to see your fabric come alive through the surface interest.

Why Add Texture?

Texture, like prints, is an important part of communicating your design. Although these steps can be skipped in a pinch, you and your teammates or clients will be happier if you show your patterns and texture. The illustration will be closer to the end result of the completed garment. Not only does this make for a better illustration for your portfolio, but it also makes for better design communication.

Basic Fabric Properties

Fabric properties not only direct the visual texture, but they also play a part in how you draw the fabric in the beginning stages. Pay attention to your fabric properties. How thick or thin is the fabric? Does it drape down the body or is it stiff, standing away from the form? Is it translucent or opaque? All of these properties play a part in how you render your fabric. If you have the source in front of you, study it carefully. What would it look like once sewn into a garment? You will not succeed in communicating a silk charmeuse if you draw your garment with a stiff outline that stands away from the body.

Once you have the basic outline of the fabric sketched out, think about the visual texture. Remember that there is a difference between the hand (tactile texture) and the visual texture. Some fabrics are rough to the touch, but still look smooth, such as a wool crepe or a gabardine. How does this translate into an illustration? What about a highly textured textile like fur? Pay attention to the fabric laid flat and its profile. What does your textile look like on the edges or when it folds back on itself? Is the edge smooth, rough, or fuzzy? How lustrous is the fabric? Does it absorb light or reflect it? Is it opaque or transparent? All these factors will affect how you translate the fabric in a rendered form.

Also remember the scale of your fabric on a full person from a distance. How much detail do you really see? Do you need to show every wale of your twill, or can you simply break up the surface to give the impression of a twill? A fabric swatch right in front of your eyes will look different when you put it on a person and stand back enough to see their full length. If you aren't sure, drape the fabric (or something with a similar texture) on a form and take a full-length photo. How much detail do you see in the photo? That is how you should convey the texture in your illustration.

Project 6.1: Texture in Photoshop

Photoshop and other digital painting applications excel with textures. The features and filters are primary assets for building up layers of textures. As you become more familiar with the tools, you may find that a mixture of techniques is the best way to achieve your look. Also remember that you can turn a texture into a pattern fill as we learned in the last chapter! So, you already know one technique.

In this project, we will try several different techniques to convey a modest number of fabric types. Unfortunately, we do not have room to cover the thousands of textiles available. This chapter is extra-long as it is! However, you should be comfortable enough with the tools to think through your own renderings.

Brush Effects

See Video 6.1 on brush effects in Photoshop.

Many fabrics can be emulated simply by using the right brush. You can control the *Brush* style through the *Brush Settings* panel. In the *Windows* menu, scroll down to either *Brushes* or *Brush Settings*. Whichever you choose, the other will automatically open as well. Alternatively, if you have your *Brush* tool selected, the top *Options* ribbon will often show some of the primary controls. However you get to the controls, you will see that you can change the *Size* and *Hardness* of the *Brush*. You can select other *Brush Presets* and change the *Blend Mode* of your *Brush*. We talked about most of this already in the Color chapter, but wanted to remind you how to access the controls.

Study your fabric. If you have it physically in front of you, that's fantastic. However, a photograph often makes it easier to see the highlights and shadows. It is even better if you can take your fabric, roughly drape it on the form, and provide some lighting before photographing it. It will help you to understand how light and shadow react on your fabric and how to render it.

Let's start with a simple velvet. Physically, velvet can be a complex fabric to make, but it is fairly easy to render. Look at the photograph in Figure 6.2. Velvet has a short pile, which creates a slightly fuzzy or blurred edge. The shadows are deep and rich. The highlights are easily visible, but it is not a highly reflective material due to the pile. This leaves your highlights slightly muted and soft. Most of the transitions between light and dark are soft, except where you have a sharp fold in the fabric.

Think about how that information transitions into your rendering. Choose or create a sketch that has the right visual weight and drape of velvet. The rendering we chose was for a bias-cut dress. If we use a dress-weight velvet, it should work nicely for our purposes.

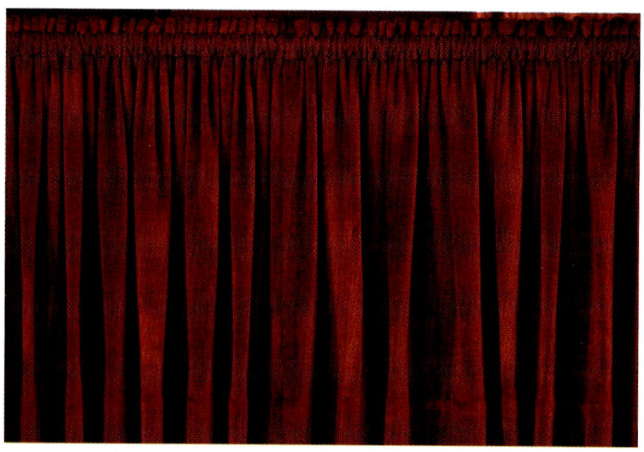

Figure 6.2 Notice that velvet has deep shadows and soft, muted highlights. The edge has a slight fuzziness to it. Courtesy of DJ Paine via Unsplash

Step 1: *Open* the exercise file BiasDress.psd. Create your garment base color. Choose a flat color in the mid-tone of your fabric and color the garment on that layer in your favorite method. You can paint it in with the *Brush* tool (shortcut *b*) and *Paint Bucket* tool (shortcut *g*), as shown in the Color chapter, or you can make a *Selection* of the shape and mask it out. Remember there are about twenty different ways to achieve the same results in these programs!

Step 2: Apply a small blur to your base color. You may want to convert your base color layer to a *Smart Object* if you are not sure how much to blur it or suspect that you might change your mind later. You can choose to do this for many of your texture layers as you build them up. Remember, *Smart Objects* give you more editability, but take up more file space. We often use them while working on a file, but then flatten the layers out once we are certain of our choices.

Whether you convert your layer to a *Smart Object* or not, you need to apply the *Blur* filter. In the top menu, go to *Filters* → *Blur* → *Gaussian Blur*. This will bring up a dialog box as seen in Figure 6.3. You don't need a higher amount. Use a lower number for your *Radius*; just enough to soften the edge so it looks fuzzy. In our example, we had a *Radius* of 5. This will change according to the size and resolution of your rendering.

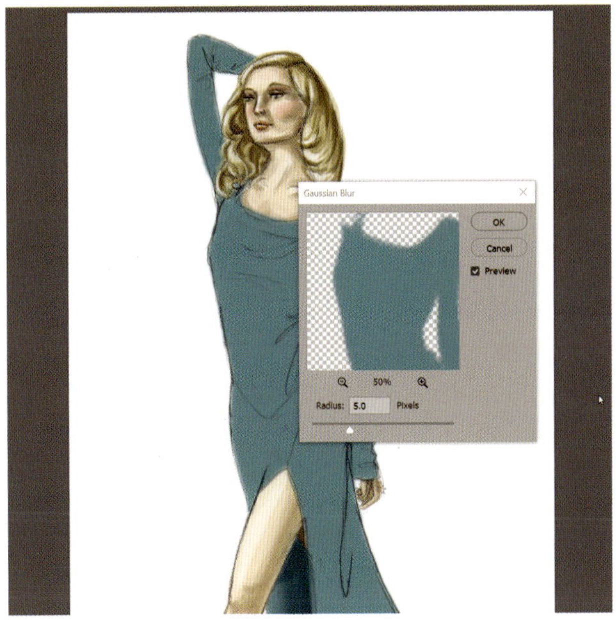

Figure 6.3 Lay down your base color. Add a *Gaussian Blur* from the *Filters* menu. For our illustration, we used a blur *Radius* of 5 pixels.

Step 3: Let's add some basic shading to the fabric. You can choose the soft, round brush found under the *General Brushes* folder of the *Brushes* panel. Adjust the *Size* to your needs as you paint. Keep the same base color you initially chose for your base. Create a new *Layer* and change the *Blend Mode* to *Multiply*. Clip your layer to the base color layer below it. Do you remember how to clip a layer? There are a couple of fast ways to do this action. Review your knowledge from the previous chapters.

Then start to paint in your shadows. You may find it too intense at first, so adjust your brush *Opacity* as needed while painting. Do this through the top *Options* ribbon or the *Brush Settings* panel rather than the *Layers* panel. Paint in the bigger shadow shapes, then adjust your brush smaller and with a higher opacity to intensify the shadow shapes. Think about how the fabric creates shadows around the body and in folds. Figure 6.4 shows the basic shadows applied.

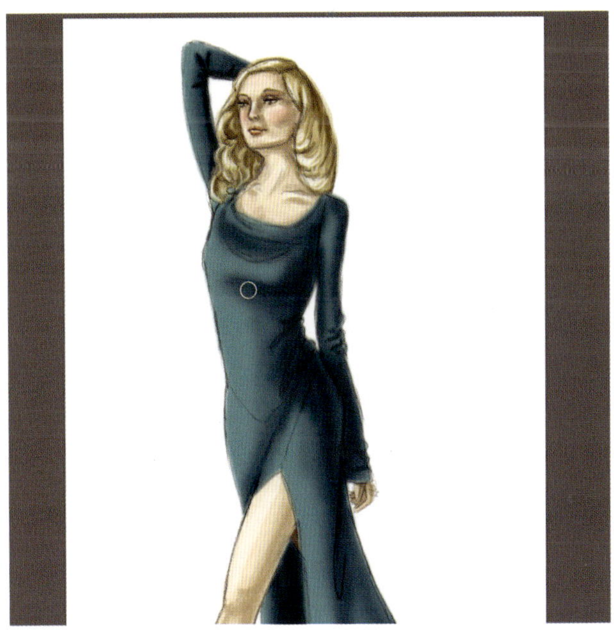

Figure 6.4 Create a new layer and set the *Blend Mode* to *Multiply*. Use a soft, round *Brush* to paint in your shadows. Velvet can get very dark in the shadow areas.

Step 4: Add in some highlights. Create a new *Layer* and set the *Blend Mode* to *Screen*. Again, use a soft, round *Brush*. You may want to lighten your color slightly. Bring down the *Opacity* of the brush to a low number such as 15–20%. Paint in your larger highlight transition areas, and slowly build up to some of the more intense lights. Don't overdo the highlights. Remember that velvet generally absorbs more light than it reflects unless it has been pressed down like a panne or crushed velvet. See the finished effect on our example in Figure 6.5. Your overall effect should be soft in appearance. If you are fighting the urge to pet the screen, you know you have done a good job! Once you are satisfied, feel free to flatten some of your layers to save file space.

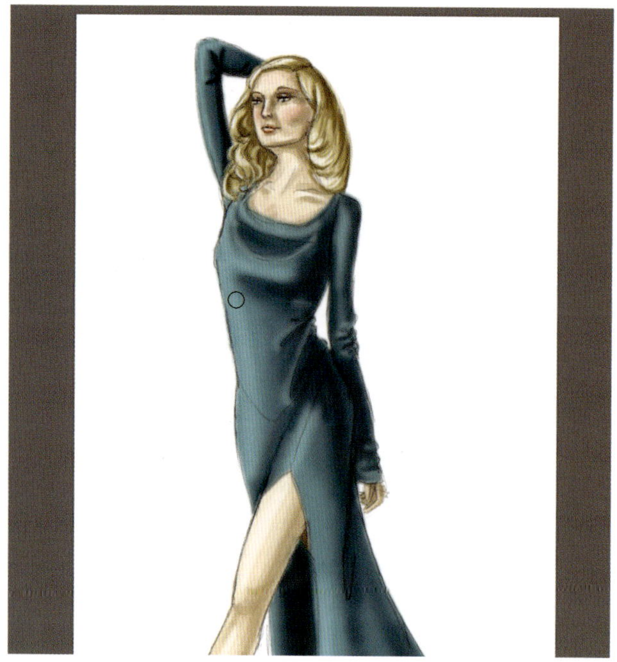

Figure 6.5 Create a new *Layer* and set the *Blend Mode* to *Screen*. Using the soft, round *Brush* again, paint in gentle highlights. You may want to lower the *Opacity* of this layer if your highlights are too strong. Velvet has soft, muted highlights.

Let's try a satin fabric next. Notice the image of satin in Figure 6.6. The surface is smooth and softly reflective. Satin shows a more intense contrast between the lights and darks, particularly around folds. When cut on the bias, it clings to the skin.

It helps to know the fiber of your satin. Synthetic fiber satins such as polyester tend to have a more intense reflection. It's almost a "brassy" effect with near-white reflections in the hot spots. Silk will have slightly softer, more muted highlights.

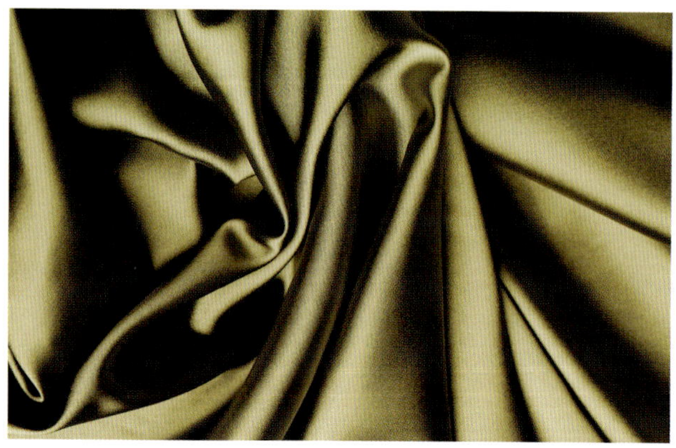

Figure 6.6 Study your satin fabric before painting. Look at how this satin reacts to the light compared with the velvet previously. Notice that there is more contrast with more intense transitions. Courtesy of Frank Winkler via Pixabay.

Step 1: As before, paint your base color on a separate layer. Create a new *Layer* and set it to *Multiply*. Clip it down to the base layer. Use a soft, round *Brush* in the same color to build up the big shadow areas as shown in Figure 6.7. Don't get too intense just yet. If it is too dark, feel free to lower the layer *Opacity* through the *Layers* Panel. You may even want to add a *Gaussian Blur* filter to the shadow layer to soften the transitions.

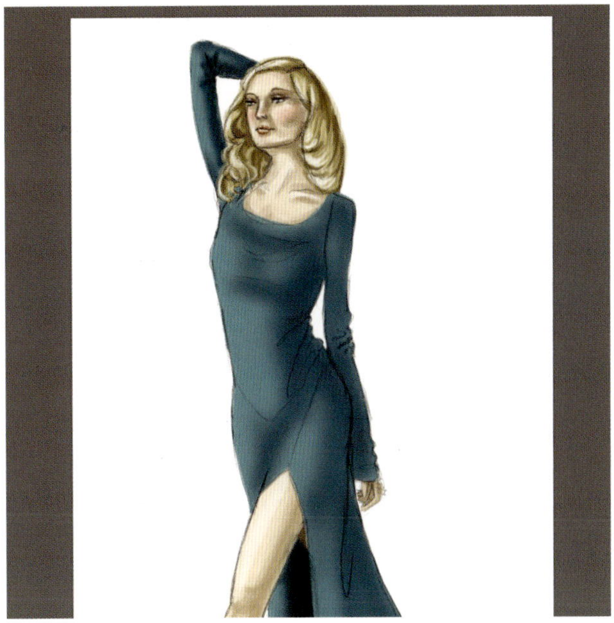

Figure 6.7 For satin, create your base color layer, then add a *Layer* set to *Multiply* to softly paint in the big shadows.

Step 2: Create another *Layer* and set it to *Multiply* again. This is to build up your more intense, sharper shadows. Keep using a soft, round *Brush*, but make it progressively smaller and with a higher *Opacity*. Focus on the darkest areas and inner folds like in Figure 6.8.

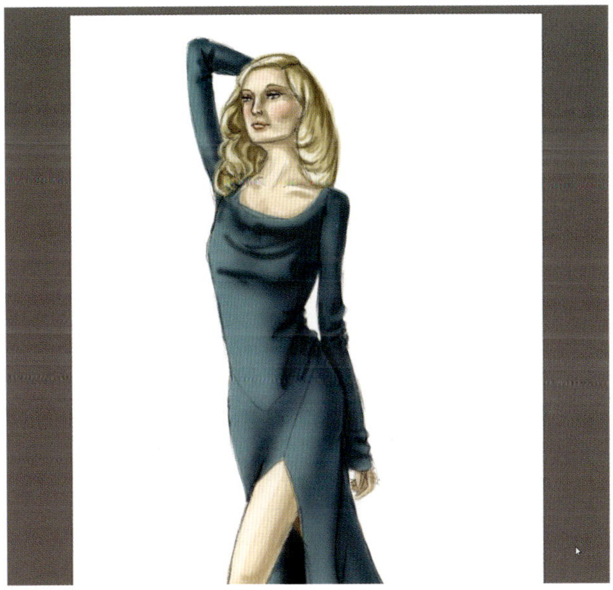

Figure 6.8 Create another *Layer* set to *Multiply* to build up the sharper, more intense shadows.

Step 3: Create a new *Layer* for your highlights. Set your *Layers Blend Mode* to *Screen*. Use a large soft, round *Brush* with lower *Opacity* and paint in the general highlights. Build them up to the hot spots of your fabric lighting as seen in Figure 6.9. This may be enough if you have a silk satin. If you are happy with the results, feel free to stop and *Flatten* some of your layers to save file space. You can do this by *right-clicking* on a layer and selecting *Merge Down*.

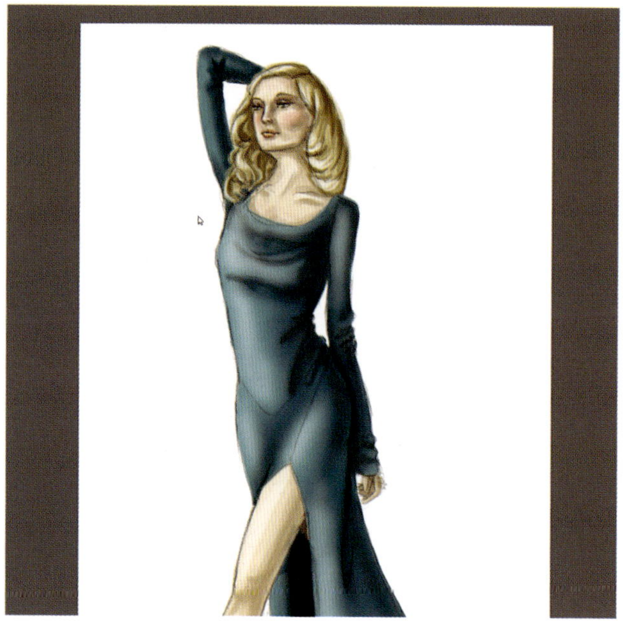

Figure 6.9 Use a layer set to *Screen* to paint in your highlights. Start with large, gentle transitions at first. This may be enough, depending on the luster of your satin.

Step 4: If you want to push your highlights a bit further, create another *Layer* and set it to *Screen* again. Reduce your *Brush Size* and increase the *Opacity*. Set your *Foreground Color* to white or near-white. Paint in the sharp highlights where the light should bounce off the fabric the most as shown in Figure 6.10. Think about how it reflects on the body and folds in the fabric. Usually, synthetic satins need this extra push to represent the fabric luster more realistically. If you overdo it, remember that you can reduce the opacity of the entire layer.

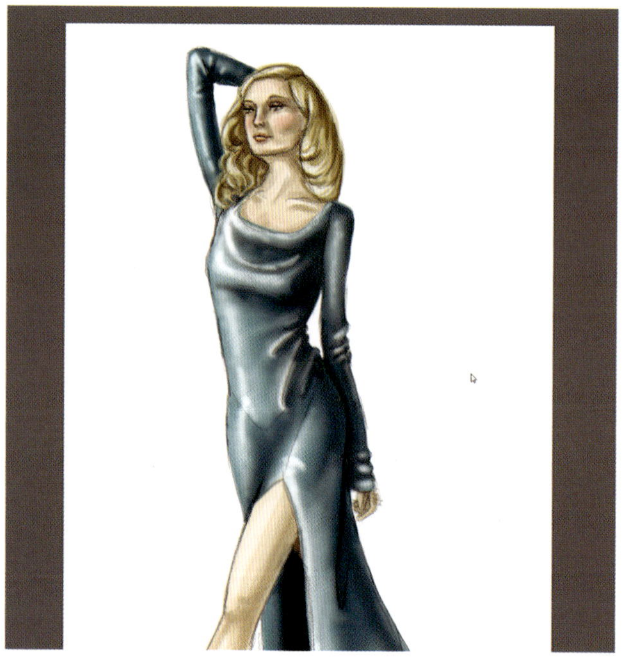

Figure 6.10 If you need to pop your highlights, repeat the process with a smaller, more opaque brush for the highly lustrous areas of the fabric.

We are just getting rolling, so let's try an iridescent taffeta while we are at it. Iridescence can be achieved in a couple of different ways, according to the color range between the two sets of yarns. If the iridescence is within an analogous range, meaning the colors are near each other on the color wheel, we can use the following technique. However, if your iridescence bounces between colors further apart on the color wheel, such as blue and yellow, you may want to use a gradient map as described later in the holographic section.

For an analogous iridescence, choose your base color. It should be highly saturated and in the brighter range such as the fuchsia color shown in Figure 6.11. Taffeta has a smooth surface and moderate luster. However, an iridescent fabric has one color of yarns running in the warp direction, with another color in the weft direction, creating a bi-color effect. Therefore, one color tends to show more in the shadows and the other color shows up more in the highlights. To achieve this look, keep the same foreground color that you just used for the base. Set the *Brush Blend Mode*, rather than the *Layers Blend Mode*, to *Multiply*. Remember the *Brush Blend Mode* can be found in the top *Options* ribbon while the *Brush* is active. This blend mode will allow you to intensify the deeper color in the shadows as you paint them. You can reduce or increase your *Brush Opacity* as needed while painting. Then create a new *Layer* for your highlights. Set the *Brush Blend Mode* to *Screen* to paint in those highlights. This will intensify the other side of that color. For our example, the fuchsia becomes redder in the shadows, and a hot pink in the highlights.

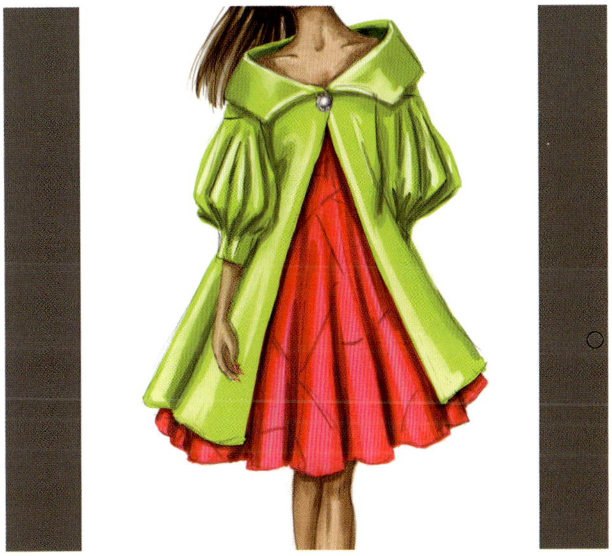

Figure 6.11 Use the same idea for an iridescent taffeta. Only set your *Brush Blend Mode* to *Multiply* or *Screen* rather than the *Layers Blend Mode*.

Filter Effects

Photoshop filters can be used to successfully give the impression of a variety of different textures. Using filters often means that you do not have to prepare special brushes or pattern texture files. This can speed up the texturizing part of the rendering process. Although we demonstrate three different textures using filters, this certainly does not mean that those are the only textures that can be rendered by filters. Take some time and experiment with filters and the filter settings. See what else you can come up with.

Denim is the first texture we will render with filters. There are many ways to create denim textures. You will even notice some of the variations in this book. However, this is an easy method that you can start with and improve upon as you get more advanced.

Step 1: *Open* JazzyGranny.psd. Before we utilize the filters, the denim object needs a base color. For this project, we will be rendering denim on a pair of jeans. *Mask* or select the entire jean area. On a new layer, *Fill* or *Paint* the area with a solid color. We used a medium denim blue as demonstrated in Figure 6.12.

Step 2: To work non-destructively, we will work with *Smart Filters* for this project. While you are on the jeans base color layer, click on *Filters* → *Convert for Smart Filters*. This converts the layer into a *Smart Object* and will clip the filters to the base layer. However, it will take more disk and processing space. So, if you don't need the filters to stay "live," you may choose to flatten the layers when you are finished with all the steps.

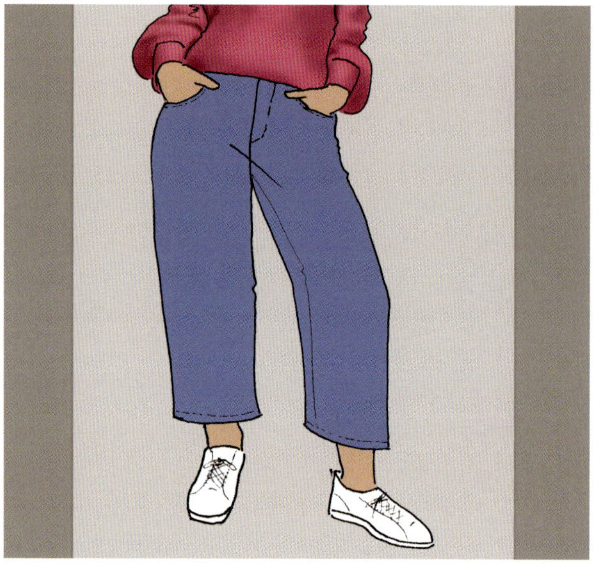

Figure 6.12 Adding the base color for the denim. *Fill* the jeans with a solid color.

Step 3: Once the layer is prepared, it is time to apply the first filter. **Noise** creates a static texture that is useful for many fabrics. Go to *Noise* → *Add Noise* as you see in Figure 6.13. In the *Noise* options box, check the *Monochromatic* option. Then you can try different settings. See whether you like *Uniform* or *Gaussian Noise* better and try different *Amount* percentages. We chose *Uniform* and 33% as shown in Figure 6.14. Click *OK* when you are done.

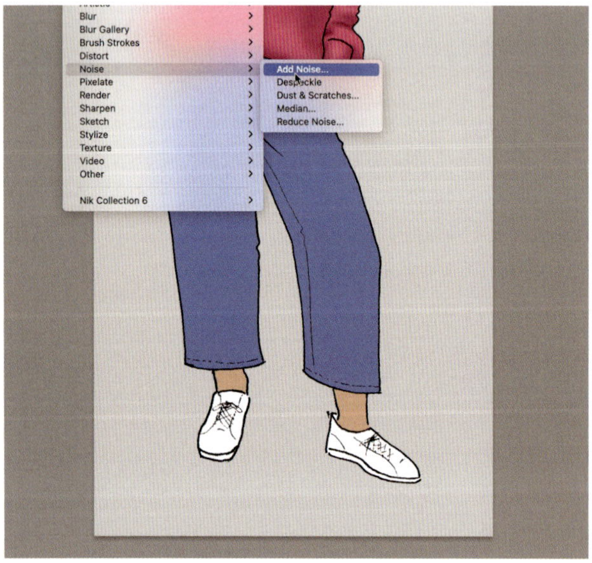

Figure 6.13 Click on *Filters* → *Convert for Smart Filters*. Then click on *Filters* again. Go to *Noise* → *Add Noise*.

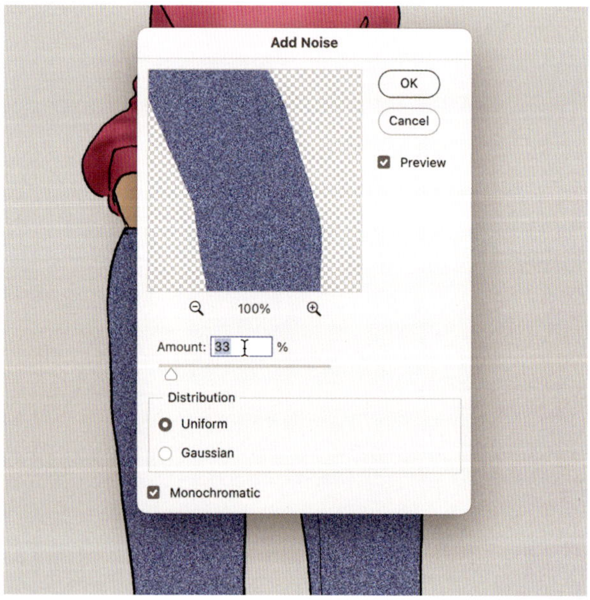

Figure 6.14 In the *Noise* options box, choose *Uniform* or *Gaussian* (whichever you like best), *Monochromatic*, and set the *Amount* to 33%. Click *OK*.

Step 4: The *Noise* filter alone could be used for denim. It also could be used for a lovely wool tweed or melton texture. To make the denim more convincing, we will add a second filter that creates a twill appearance. To start the next filter, go to the *Filter Gallery* via *Filter → Filter Gallery*.

The *Filter Gallery* will allow you to preview multiple different filters and try different settings. In the gallery, click on the *Brush Strokes* folder. Then, in the folder, click on *Angled Strokes*. You can try different settings within the *Angled Strokes* filter to see what works best for you. Figure 6.15 shows the settings *Direction Balance* 25, *Stroke Length* 15, *Sharpness* 1. Click *OK* when you are satisfied.

Upon finishing your filters, you will notice in the *Layers* panel that your filters are a sublayer labeled "Smart Filters." You can see an example in Figure 6.16. The filters can be controlled and altered individually in this format.

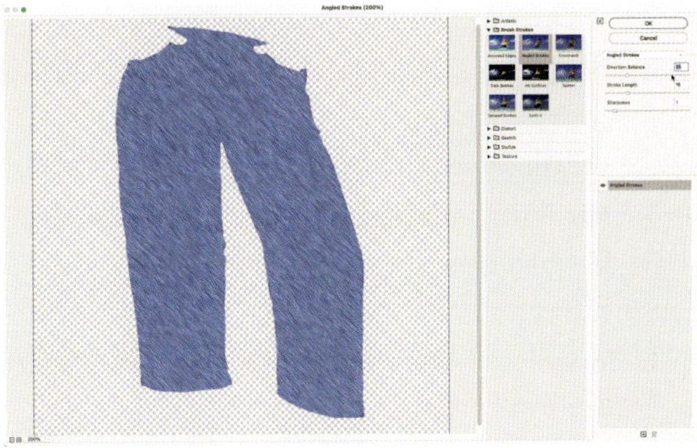

Figure 6.15 Add a second filter to make a better denim texture. Go to *Filter → Filter Gallery*. Then click on the *Brush Strokes* folder. Choose *Angled Strokes*. The settings for this filter are: *Angle Strokes*, *Direction Balance* 25, *Stroke Length* 15, *Sharpness* 1.

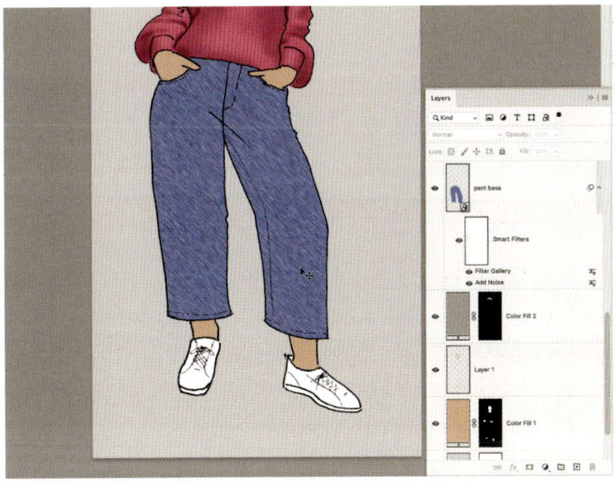

Figure 6.16 When you use the *Smart Filters*, your results will be similar to this image.

Step 5: After all the filters are completed, you will probably want to add shading for realism. As discussed in Chapter 5, you might want to put the highlights and shadows on separate layers from the rest of the jeans. This makes it easier to make corrections and alterations. The final result of our jeans is shown in Figure 6.17.

Next, we will create a rough-spun linen texture using filters. The linen texture creation process is very similar to the denim process. In fact, it starts the same way. The difference is in the second filter.

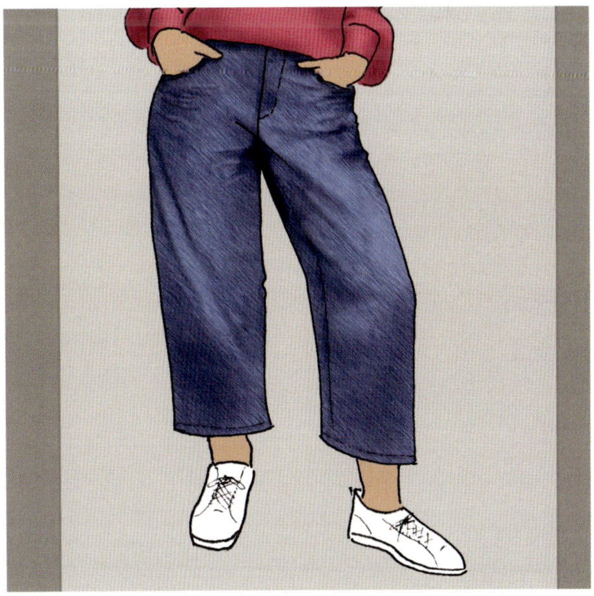

Figure 6.17 The last step is to add shadows and highlights. As discussed in Chapter 3, it is better to keep the highlights and shadows on separate layers, at least initially.

Step 1: Your linen garment needs a base color layer. We are using the same file as we used for the denim. *Mask* the pants, create a new *Layer*, and *Fill* the area with a base color. Next, we prepare the *Layer* by going to *Filter → Convert for Smart Filters.*

Step 2: Use the *Noise Filter*. Click on *Filter → Noise → Add Noise* and then adjust the settings as you did for denim. We chose *Uniform*, *Monochromatic*, and 33% in the example shown in Figure 6.18. Click *OK* when you are happy with the results.

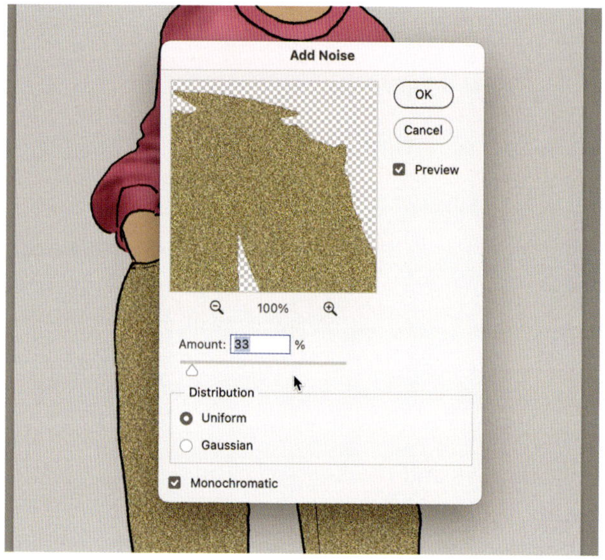

Figure 6.18 Start the linen pants the same way as the denim. Fill the space with a base color. *Convert for Smart Filters*. Go to *Filter → Noise → Add Noise*. In the *Noise options box*, choose *Uniform* or *Gaussian* (whichever you like best), *Monochromatic*, and set the *Amount* to 33%. Click *OK*.

Step 3: The next filter sets this process apart from the previous one. Open the *Filter Gallery* and go to the *Texture* folder. In the *Texture* folder, choose *Texturizer*. The *Texturizer Filter* uses pre-made Photoshop (.PSD) files to emboss the image. You can make texture files and save them to create different types of texture looks later. In this case, an existing texture works great for our needs. Choose *Burlap* in the *Texture Choice Box*. For the rest of the options, you can try different settings to see what works best. Figure 6.19 shows *Scaling* 50%, *Relief* 5%, and *Light* at *Top Right*. Click *OK* when you like the results. When you are finished with the filters, there will be a sublayer called "Smart Filters" in your *Layers* panel, as shown in Figure 6.20.

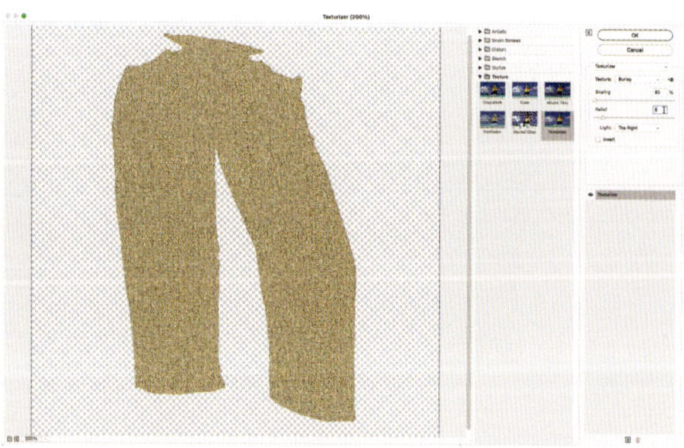

Figure 6.19 To create the linear look of linen fabric, add an additional filter. Go to *Filter → Filter Gallery*. Then click on the *Texture* folder, then choose the *Texturizer Filter*. Set the *Texture* to *Burlap*, *Scaling* to 50%, *Relief* to 5%, and *Light* to *Top Right*. Click *OK*.

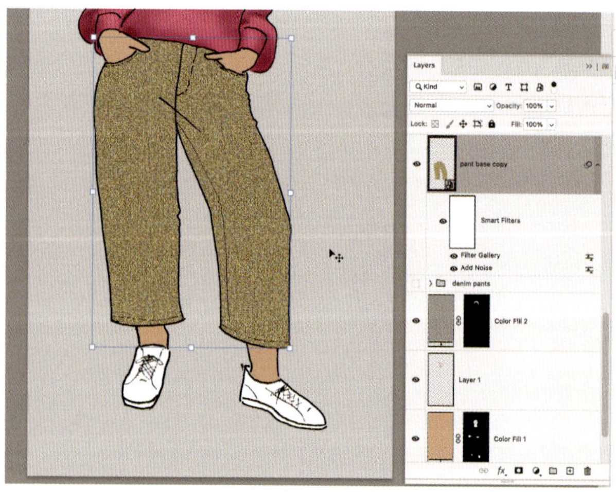

Figure 6.20 Once the filters are complete, your results should be similar to this image.

After you complete the texture work, you may want to add shading to your garment. If this is the case, try adding the shadows and highlights on separate layers, as discussed in Chapter 5. The results will be similar to Figure 6.21.

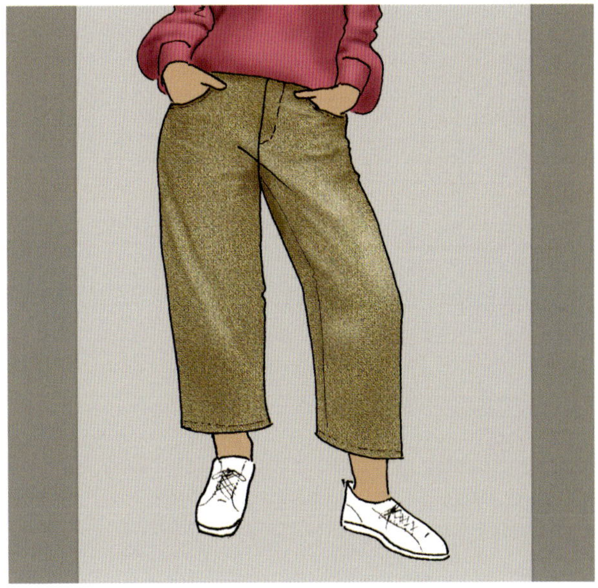

Figure 6.21 After completing the filters, create the shadows and highlights for the linen.

A good sweater texture can be achieved through a combination of filters, layers, and layer blend modes. Once you try the method below, you can experiment with other filter and blend modes to make the effect look more like your specific sweater. As with many things in Photoshop, there is not one set method.

For this project, we are starting with an illustration that already has the shadows and highlights rendered. All the sweater color layers have been *Merged* into a single layer.

Step 1: Choose a highlight color for your *Foreground Color* swatch and a shadow color for your *Background* (or paper) *Color* swatch. These two swatches will be important when rendering the effects. The entire sweater area needs to be masked. An easy way to do this is to hold the *ctrl/cmd* key and to click on the thumbnail of the sweater in the *Layers* panel as you see in Figure 6.22. This will select all the objects in that layer.

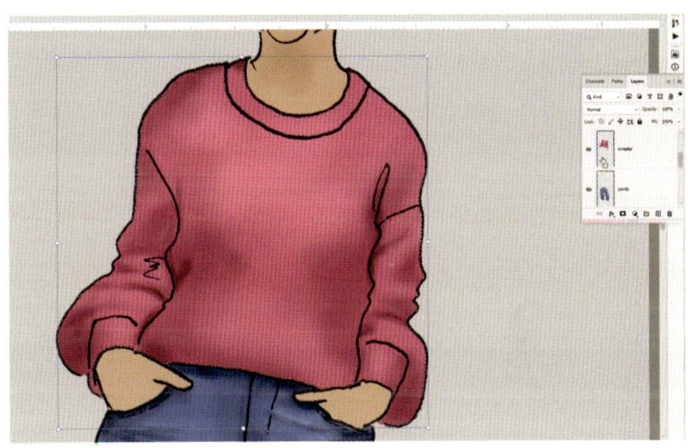

Figure 6.22 Make sure that the sweater is rendered with shadows and highlights. *Merge* all sweater color layers into one layer. Choose a highlight color from the sweater as the *Foreground Color* swatch and a shadow color from the sweater as the *Background*/paper *color* swatch. Mask the entire sweater.

All of the filters will be executed on copies of the original sweater layer. In the *Layers* panel, *right-click* on the sweater layer. On the pop-up *Options* menu, choose *Duplicate Layer*. In the *Duplicate Layer* options box that you see in Figure 6.23, name the new layer. We named the duplicate "sweater texture 1," but pick a name that makes sense to you.

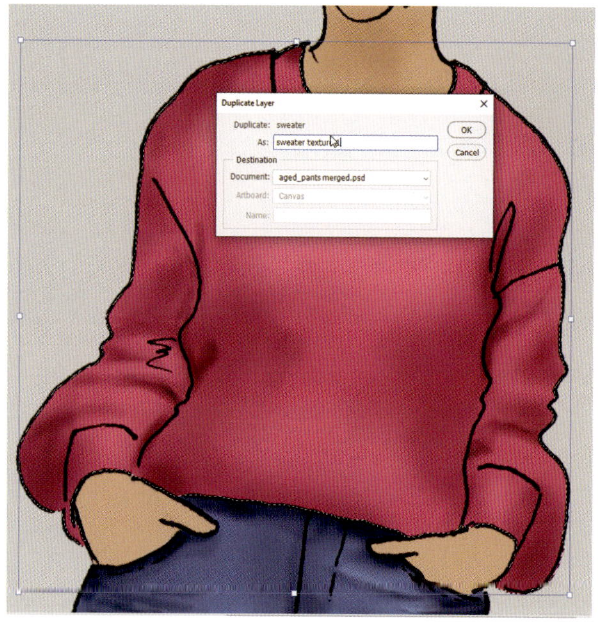

Figure 6.23 You will need a duplicate of the sweater layer for this exercise. *Right-click* on the sweater layer to bring up the *Options menu*, then choose *Duplicate Layer*. Name the new layer.

Step 2: Make sure the sweater is still masked and that you are on the new duplicate layer. For the first part of the sweater texture, we will use the **Mezzotint** filter. *Mezzotint* is a form of monochrome printmaking. The filter is meant to imitate the printmaking method by converting an image to dots or lines. The density of the dots or lines will vary according to the tone of the image.

Click on *Filter* → *Pixelate* → *Mezzotint*. In *Mezzotint*, set the *Type* to *Coarse Dots* as shown in Figure 6.24. It will use the colors from your foreground and background swatches. Click *OK*.

This filter will create a layer that initially looks like static or stippling. The layer needs to be adjusted to make it useful for the sweater texture. Try different *Blending Modes* for the layer. Then experiment with the layer *Opacity* and *Fill*. The authors settled on the *Blending Mode Soft Light*, 50% *Opacity*, and 50% *Fill*, as you can see in Figure 6.25.

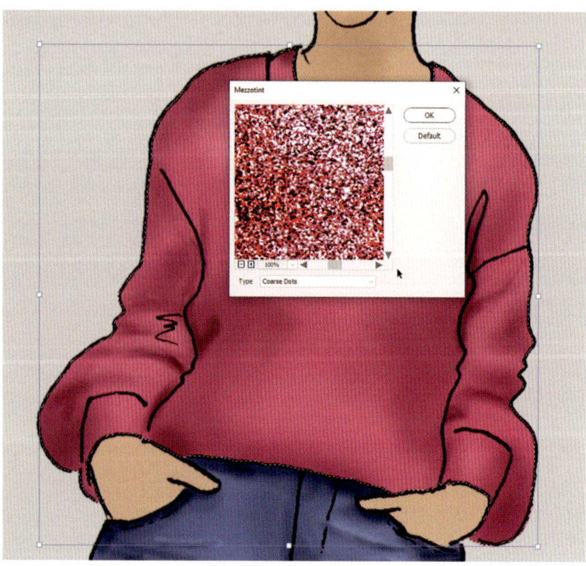

Figure 6.24 Go to the new duplicate layer. Make sure the sweater is still masked. Click on *Filter* → *Pixelate* → *Mezzotint*. In *Mezzotint*, set the *Type* to *Coarse Dots*. Click *OK*.

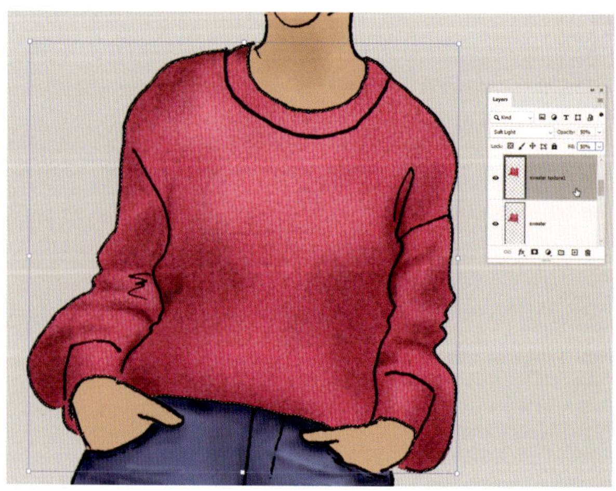

Figure 6.25 Adjusting the *Mezzotint* layer. Play with the *Layers Blending Modes*, *Layers Opacity*, and *Layers Fill* until the new texture looks good. The authors chose a *Blending Mode* of *Soft Light*, 50% *Opacity*, and 50% *Fill*.

Step 3: To help the texture look like it is a knit sweater rather than a heathered sweatshirt, we will add a second filter. *Duplicate* the original sweater layer a second time. Give the new duplicate a name. The authors used "Sweater Texture 2," but again, choose something that works for you.

Click onto the newly created duplicate layer and make sure the sweater is still masked. Go to *Filter → Filter Gallery*. The *Filter Gallery* allows you to try out many different filters before committing to them. Choose the *Artistic Folder* and click on *Rough Pastels*. Most of the settings will be default, but we will change the actual *Texture* to *Burlap*. To double check, the settings for the filter are *Stroke Length 10, Stroke Detail 9, Texture: Burlap, Scaling 100%, Relief 20, Light: Bottom*. The results should be similar to Figure 6.26. Click *OK* to confirm the filter.

Like the mezzotint layer, the rough pastel layer needs adjusting to make it work for the sweater. You can try different *Layer Blending Modes* and *Opacities*. The authors chose the *Lighten Blending Mode* and kept *Opacity* at 100%, as shown in Figure 6.27.

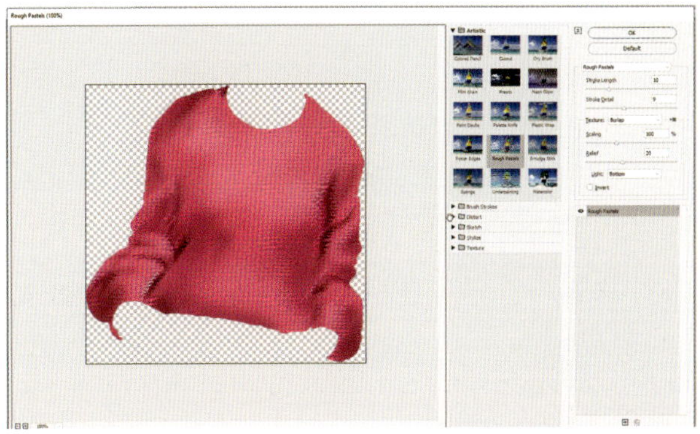

Figure 6.26 Creating the canvas filter texture. Go back to the original sweater layer and duplicate it again. Give it a name. On the new duplicated layer, make sure the sweater is still masked. Go to *Filter → Filter Gallery*. In the *Filter Gallery*, go to the *Artistic Folder* and click on *Rough Pastels*. The settings for this filter are *Stroke Length 10, Stroke Detail 9, Texture: Burlap, Scaling 100%, Relief 20, Light: Bottom*.

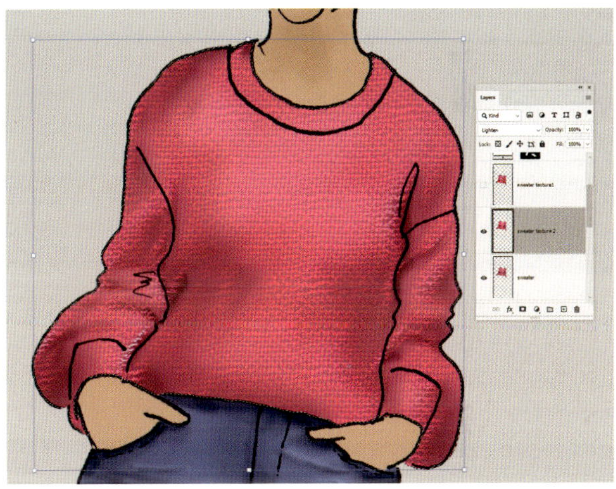

Figure 6.27 The results of the *Rough Pastels filter* need adjusting. Set the *Layer Blending Mode* to *Lighten* to adjust the effect.

Step 4: The sweater looks good at this point, but we can do better. One of the easiest ways to improve the results is to duplicate one of the texture layers and change the *Blending Modes* of the duplicate. For this example, *Duplicate* the *Rough Pastels* layer two more times for a total of three copies of this layer as you see in Figure 6.28. Each one will have different settings. As you duplicate the layers, remember to name the duplicates.

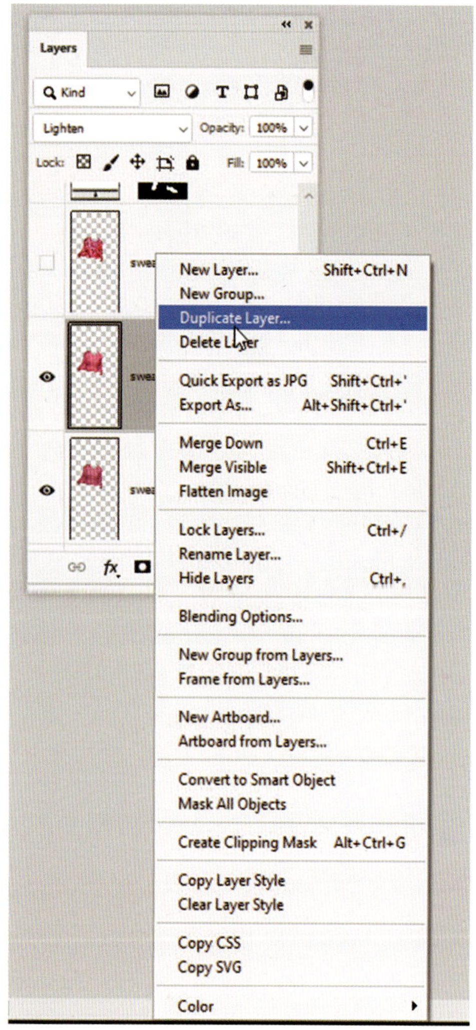

Figure 6.28 We use the *Rough Pastel* filter layer a total of three times. *Duplicate* the layer two times so you have three total copies of it. Rename the new copies.

We will improve the depth and overall texture of the sweater by adjusting the *Layer Blending Modes* of the two new copies of the Rough Pastels Layer. Switch over to one of the duplicate layers. Change its *Blending Mode* to *Darker Color* as shown in Figure 6.29. This option will emphasize the shadows in the illustration. You can also try the other darkening blending modes such as *Multiply* and *Subtraction* to see if you like the results better.

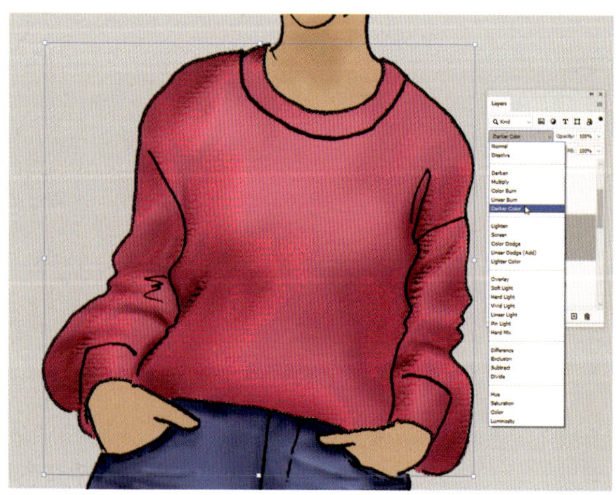

Figure 6.29 The second copy of the *Rough Pastel* layer is used to emphasize the shadows. Set the *Layers Blending Mode* to *Darker Color*.

Step 5: Now to adjust the last copy of the *Rough Pastel* layer. The purpose of this one is to soften the overall texture of the sweater. If you are illustrating a rougher sweater (e.g., slub kit), you might not want to include this layer. Go to the last duplicate layer. Set the *Blending Mode* to *Soft Light* as demonstrated in Figure 6.30. Once the filters are completed and all turned on, the results will look similar to Figure 6.31.

As mentioned previously, there are many different ways to achieve a sweater texture. This is a relatively easy method that does not require any extra preparation other than the usual base color with shadow and highlight. It is also versatile because you can try different variations with the filters and layer adjustments.

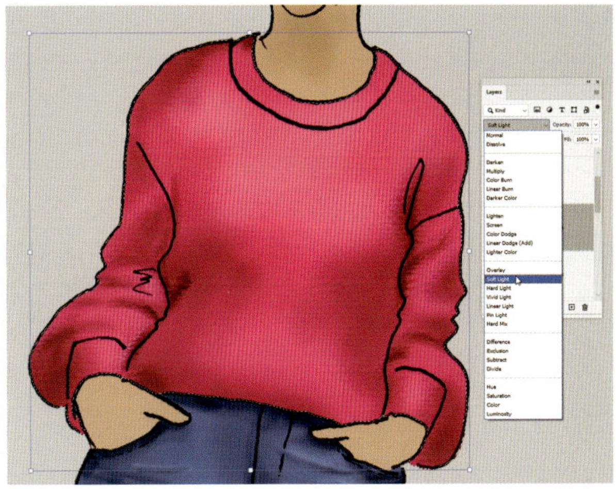

Figure 6.30 The third copy of the Rough Pastel layer is used to soften the overall texture. Set the *Layers Blending Mode* to *Soft Light*.

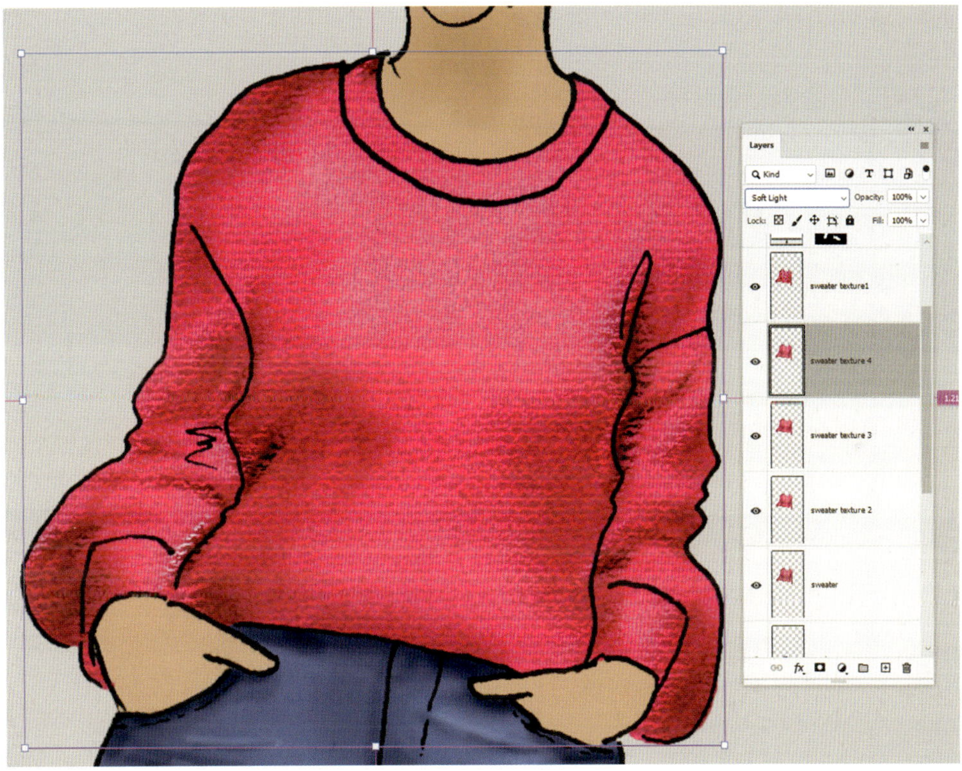

Figure 6.31 When all the sweater textures are done, there are four texture layers and one original sweater color layer.

Layer Effects

You learned how to make scanned fabric patterns into repeating seamless pattern fills in Chapter 4. Using the same methods, you can make seamless repeating textures. However, we can take this a step further and make a colorless texture file that can be used to make multiple different versions of a fabric by combining it with different layer effects.

This method can be used to make many different textures. We use corduroy to illustrate the technique. You are welcome to try it with lace, tweed, sweater knits, faille, or almost anything else with a noticeable texture. Some of the more challenging textures that do not work well are covered at the end of chapter.

Step 1: *Open* Corduroy.jpg. You need to prepare your seamless texture pattern. Find an image, take a photo, or scan a fabric. *Crop* and clean-up the image as discussed in Project 4.8. Make sure that when you tile it, it does not show the repeat or any noticeable shading. Once the repeat is prepared, remove the color by using *Desaturate* or *Black and White*. It is often best to reduce the scale of the image because you will use it on renderings that are smaller than life size. The corduroy swatch should look like Figure 6.32 when it is fully prepared. *Define* the image as a *Pattern*.

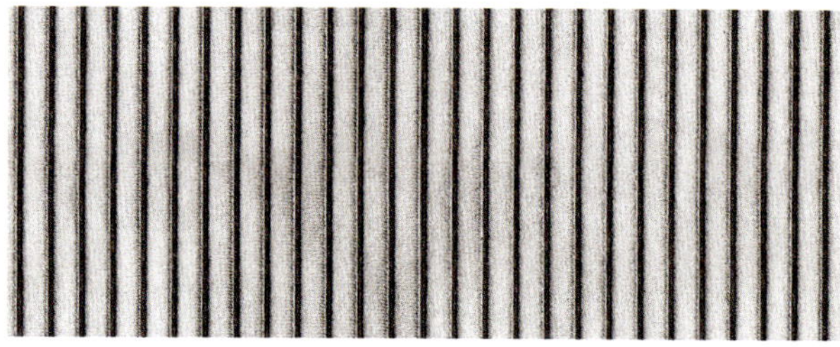

Figure 6.32 Find a photo of a swatch or scan a swatch of corduroy. Reduce the image and turn it into a pattern fill using the instructions from Project 4.8. *Desaturate* the image. *Define* the image as a *Pattern*.

Step 2: Use JazzyGranny.psd again. Create a *Pattern Fill Layer* with your new texture pattern. You can do this through the *Layers* panel or through the *Layer* menu. Choose your texture in the options box. Then adjust the *Scale* of the texture until it looks correct for your garment. In Figure 6.33, the scale was adjusted to 20%.

To make the texture show only on the desired garment, Clip the *Pattern Fill Layer* to the garment color layer. Double-check that the texture layer is directly above the color layer in the *Layers* panel. *Right-click* on the texture layer and choose *Create Clipping mask*. Alternatively, you can hold the *alt* or *option* key down and hover your mouse between the two layers. The icon will change and show an arrow pointing to the layer below. *Click* and it will clip the top layer to the bottom layer.

You will notice that the texture blocks out all the color. Adjust the *Layers Blending Mode* of the texture layer until the texture and the color blend how you want. In Figure 6.33, *Soft Light* mode was used.

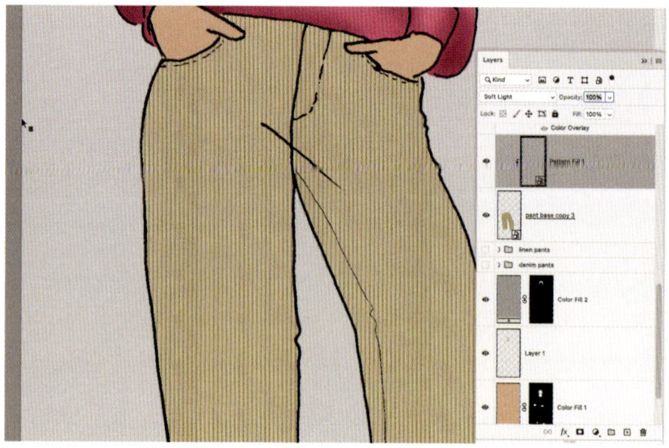

Figure 6.33 Fill the pants with a base color. Add a *Pattern Fill Layer* with the corduroy pattern fill and adjust the *Scale* of pattern as needed. Clip the pattern layer to the base color layer. Adjust the *Blending Mode* of the pattern layer to something that works well with your base color. The example shows *Soft Light*.

Step 3: You may decide this is all your work needs. However, we will take the example a few steps further. Before progressing, it is best to add shading. The shadows and highlights will show the fall of the cloth in the garment, as well as any wrinkles.

It is time to make the pattern look like it is moving with the garment. Convert the texture layer to a *Smart Object* through the *Layers* panel. Following the directions in Project 4.3, use *Puppet Warp* to alter the direction of the texture to match the movement of your fabric. Place pins, then shrink, stretch, and bend the texture. Accept the changes when you are happy with the results. In Figure 6.34, you can see that the biggest changes are over the bent knee for this exercise.

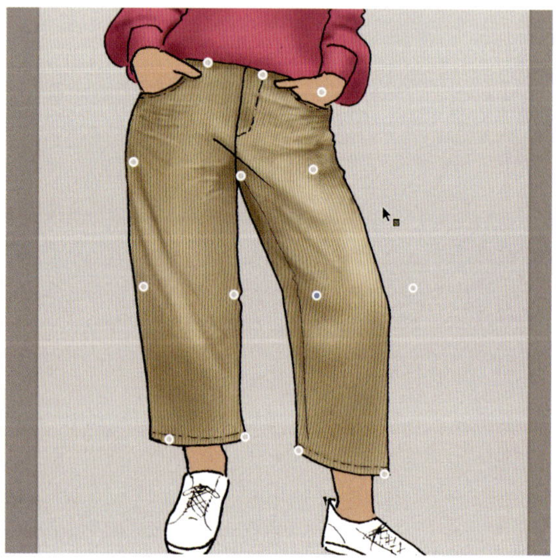

Figure 6.34 Warping the corduroy. Add the highlights and shadows to your pants so you can tell how the fabric should move or fall. Convert the *Pattern Fill Layer* into a *Smart Object*. Use *Edit* ⟶ *Puppet Warp* to bend each leg of the pattern fill.

Step 4: To really sell your texture, we will add wrinkles. Project 4.4 explains this process in more detail. Use the *Liquify Filter*. Move the mesh around in the areas that need to look like they are more bent or folded as you see in Figure 6.35. Don't go crazy. A little wrinkle work can go a long way. Click *OK* when you are done.

This completes the corduroy texture project. Your version should look similar to Figure 6.36. As noted, you may not need all these steps for every illustration. Pick and choose your needs as you feel is appropriate.

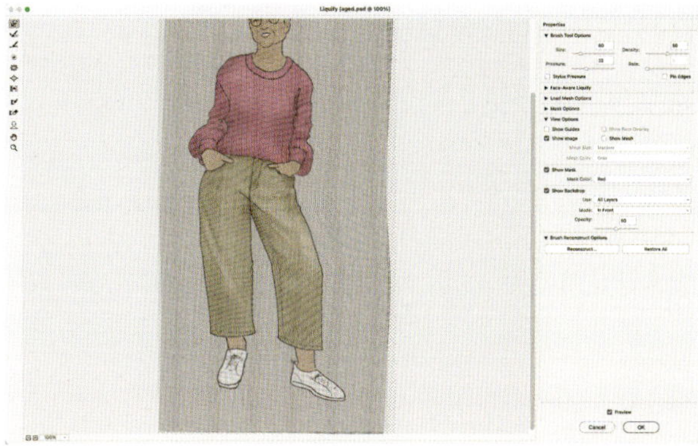

Figure 6.35 Use *Filters* → *Liquify* to add wrinkles as needed.

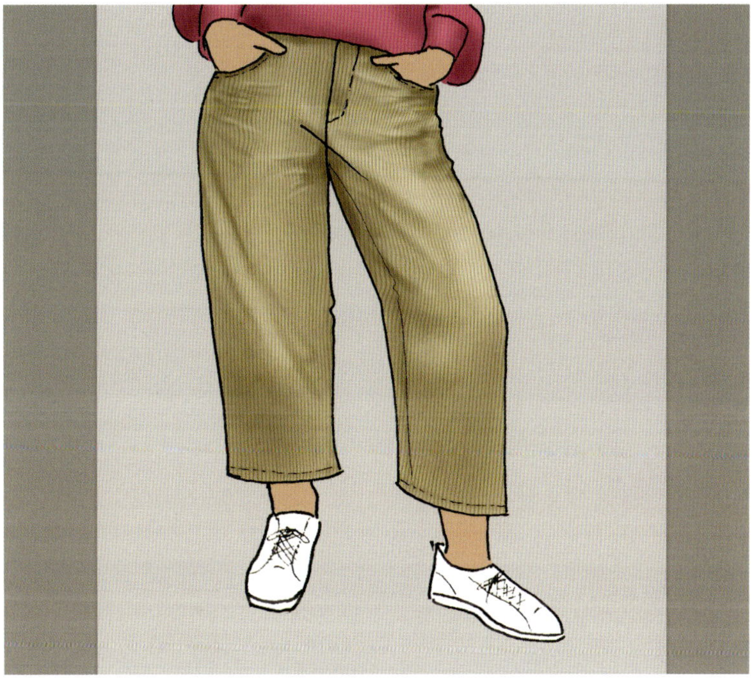

Figure 6.36 Your finished corduroy pants should look similar to this image.

STYLE SECRETS 6.1

Surprising Textures

You never know where you will come across a great texture to use for your illustrations. Don't get too caught up with using the "original source" for fabrics. A scan of burlap may work just as well for a linen texture. Or a photo of the froth on top of your fancy coffee can be the basis for a fantastic boucle! Keep your eyes and mind open when collecting textures for garments. If you see an interesting texture, snap a photo and save it. Afterall, that spiderweb you just saw may make the perfect tulle texture on your next illustration!

Troubleshooting

"What do I do when my highlights and shadows are too intense?"

If your highlights or shadows are too intense for satin or any other texture, start by adjusting the *Layer Opacity* of your highlight or shadow layers. You can also try different *Layer Blending Modes* and/or adjust the *Layer Fill.*

"Why is my *Brush* tool not acting correctly?"

1. Start by checking the brush settings. Look at the brush *Opacity, Blend Mode, Brush Tip Preset,* etc. There are many settings for a brush that affect how it works and one "wrong" setting can change how you expect it to act.
2. Next, check the *Layers* and *Layer Settings.* Are you on the correct layer? It seems like a stupid question, but we all do it. Even professionals. Then check the *Blending Mode, Opacity,* and *Fill* for the layer are set how you need them to be. Do you have a *Layer Mask* turned on that prevents you from painting? Are you working on the *Layer Mask* rather than on the *Layer* itself? Is the layer *Locked*?
3. Finally, check that you are using the correct tool. Again, it sounds like a dumb question. But Photoshop has several brush and brush-like tools. It is easy to click the wrong one. Are you trying to use the main *Brush* tool and you accidently clicked the *History Brush* or *Color Replacement* tool? These tool icons both look like brushes.

"I just can't get my *Pattern Fill Layer* to warp without getting really wonky. What can I do?"

1. First, double-check that you've made your layer into a *Smart Object.* There should be a tiny icon in the bottom right corner of the layer thumbnail that indicates if it is a *Smart Object.*
2. Are you using the best type of warp for your needs? *Puppet Warp* works best for bendy areas like arms and legs. *Transform Warp* works best for wrapping around the body. *Liquify* is good for adding folds and smaller distortions.

You may need to separate parts such as working on one leg at a time using masks or separate the top from the bottom into different layers. Then you can control each with better precision.

Project 6.2: Texture in Illustrator

Many people consider it easier to create texture in Photoshop than in Illustrator. But it is certainly not impossible to create texture in Illustrator. In fact, with a little knowledge and even more practice, it is fairly easy.

The first step is the same regardless of whether you are working in Illustrator, Photoshop, or drawing by hand: make sure your drawing reflects the texture. This could be via volume, the fall of a dress, the way a fabric folds when worn, or drawing a garment with soft lines versus angular lines.

Additionally, think about how you could adjust the outline or edge. You can use a **vector effect** such as *Roughen* to make the garment look like it is made from a rough or knobby fabric or even a gathered area. A vector effect uses vector calculations to add a distortion or other effect to a path without changing the original path and point information. The *Warp* tool can be used to create isolated areas of roughness as well as folds. These adjustments to the garment edges may be enough to portray the texture.

If you are planning on using any raster effects, raster textures, or are just not sure, you will need to set the resolution for your document. This is not a normal step for Illustrator documents; however, when you bring in raster elements, it becomes similar to working with Photoshop. You have to set the resolution to a high enough ppi before you begin to work with the raster elements, or your work will be pixelated.

To set resolution in Illustrator, go to *Effect → Document Raster Effect Settings.* An option box will pop-up that will allow you to set the *Resolution,* the *Color Mode,* and a few other options. Assuming your document is at least as large as its intended final size, then a resolution of 300 ppi is preferred for print work. Adjust for work that is either too small or will not be printed.

Brush Effects

If you are familiar with making flats in Illustrator, you are probably familiar with brushes. Brushes work well for trims and for linear textures (knit patterns, embroidery, beading, sequins). They are good for constantly used linear textures or when the texture is too complicated to make more than a small piece.

3. When creating brushes previously, you may have only created them in black and white. As we are now working on full-color renderings, we must prepare the brushes for color. One of the best ways to do this is to create your brushes with fills of 50% gray, if a fill is needed. The gray color is considered neutral and can be easily shifted to any other color if the brush is set up correctly.

We will start by creating a sequin brush. Sequins come in multiple shapes and sizes. The most common shapes are flat and cupped. Both are easy to make, although flat is considerably less work to make. We will make the flat sequin and you are welcome to try the cupped sequin on your own. This brush imitates sequins that have been embroidered in a chain or line. The same sequin images could be made into a symbol for individual placement or a brush with different settings for a scattered effect.

Step 1: The flat sequin starts with a circle and another tiny circle centered inside. The tiny circle should be subtracted from the main circle using the *Pathfinder* effects or the *Shape Builder* tool. Once you have a compound circle shape, make a second copy of the shape. One copy will have a black stroke and black fill; the second copy will have a 50% gray fill. You will place the gray circle on the top and a little to the left side of the black circle. The black circle acts as a shadow when the brush stacks the sequins on top of each other. After stacking the circles, draw a line from the center of the circle to the outside of the circle opposite the shadow side. This is the thread. Adjust the stroke of the thread to have curved ends and a weight that looks in proportion to the sequin. *Group* all the parts of the sequin. You may want to scale your sequin at this point to be the correct size for your illustration. Figure 6.37 shows the components of the sequin as well as two assembled sequins ready for making into a brush.

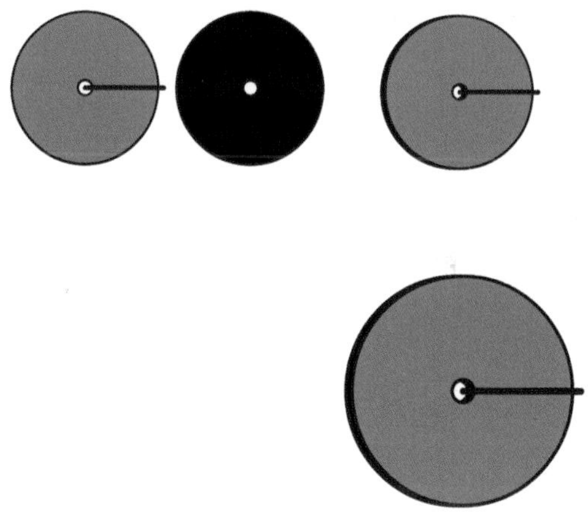

Figure 6.37 Flat sequin build and finished flat sequin. On the left side, you will see two sizes of flat sequins. On the right, you will see the components of the sequin: two compound circles and a line.

Step 2: To make the sequin brush, make sure the *Brush* panel is open. Drag the sequin image into the *Brush* panel until a plus (+) symbol appears. When you release the mouse, the first options box will appear, asking what type of brush you are making. We are making a **Scatter brush**. *Scatter brushes* are most often used to do what they imply: scatter objects. However, they can also be used like a *Pattern brush*, but with slightly different controls. In this case, we need the *Spacing Control* that allows us to overlap shapes.

For our brush controls, set the *Spacing* to 50% and set the *Rotation relative to Path*. *Colorization* needs to be set to *Tints and Shades* so the gray will color, but not the black. The rest of the settings should stay at default. You will see the options box in Figure 6.38. The results can be seen in Figure 6.39.

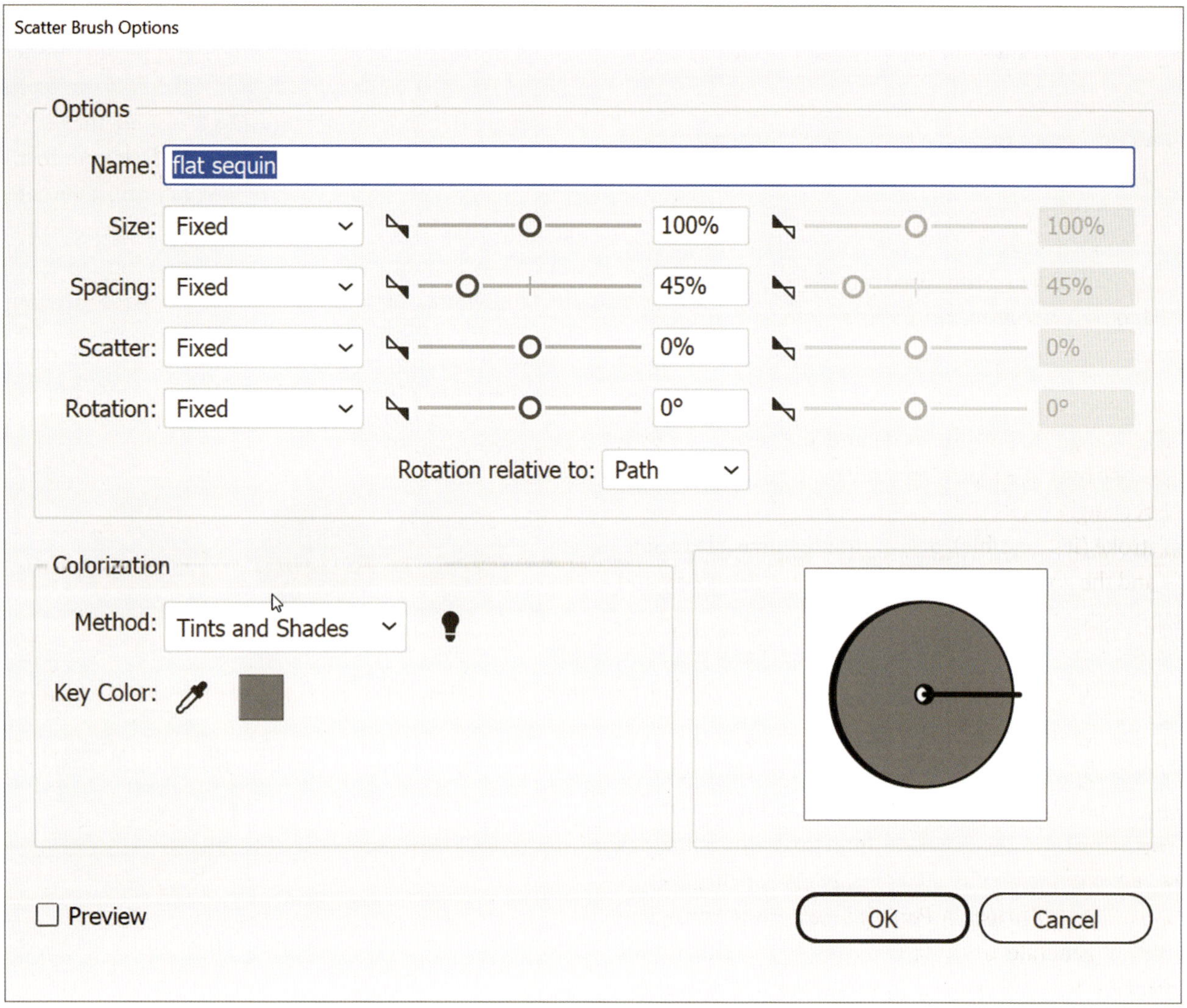

Figure 6.38 Brush options for creating sequin brush. The sequin brush is a *Scatter brush* because of the need to overlap the images. Notice Spacing is set to 45%. You will want between 40 and 50%. Additionally, *Rotation* is set *Path* so that the thread will rotate with the path. Finally, the *Colorization* is set to *Tints and Shades* so the gray will change to whatever the stroke color is set to, but the black will not change.

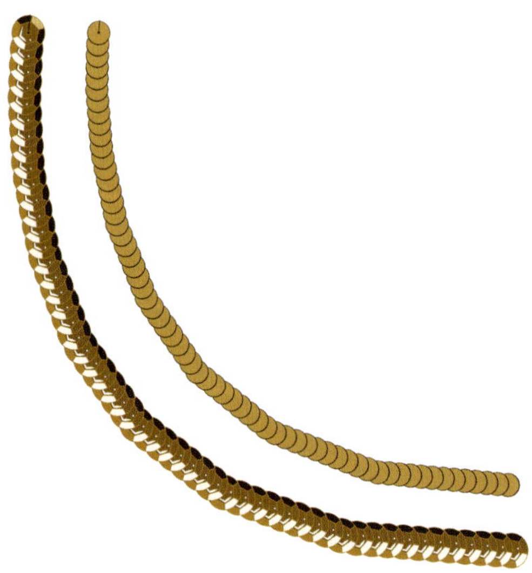

Figure 6.39 Two examples of sequin brushes. The inside curve shows the flat sequin brush. The outside curve shows an example of a cupped sequin brush. Notice the overlap and rotation on both.

Are you a knitwear designer? Quite a few knit patterns work well as brushes. We will try a basic cableknit brush.

Step 1: You may find it easier to draw a cable from a photo or to even trace the photo. The basic cable shape is a single "S" that repeats. Each shape fits into the next. Set the fill color for the shapes to 50% gray. You will need three to four links of the cable to create a small cable brush. If you want your brush to be two links, you will need four or five links. *Group* your links.

Step 2: Once you have drawn your cable, you will need to find the repeat. Look at the left image in Figure 6.40. The rectangle is positioned behind the repeat. Draw a rectangle over the repeat on your own cable. Make sure the rectangle is ON TOP. Set the rectangle to no fill and no stroke (it's invisible). Select both the invisible rectangle and the grouped cable. *Right-click* over the object and select *Make Clipping mask.* This will crop the cable to just the repeat. It will look like the right-hand image in Figure 6.40.

Step 3: Once you have the cropped repeat, double-check that the repeat is laying sideways. This is the direction needed to make a continuous brush. Open the *Brush* panel. Drag the brush repeat into the panel until you see the plus (+) symbol. When the dialog box pops up, choose **Pattern brush**. A *Pattern brush* uses a compound path to generate a continuous pattern, such as our cableknit. Name the brush and change the *Colorization method* to *Tints and Shades* so the gray will color, but not the black. You now have a cableknit brush.

Lace trim is essential to many designs, especially for children's wear, lingerie, and costumes from certain eras. It can be a little daunting at first appearance, but it is not too difficult to make if you know how. We will learn two different methods to make *Lace Brushes*.

The first way to make a *Lace Brush* is to draw the brush repeat using paths and shapes. It helps to have an actual piece of lace, either to trace or to look at as a reference. But you can also make up the lace from scratch.

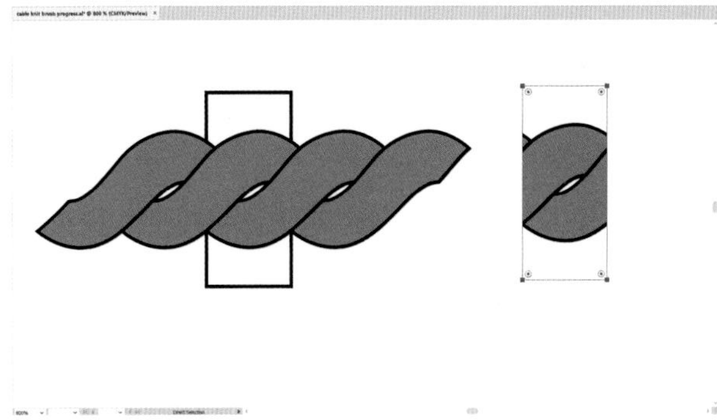

Figure 6.40 Making the cableknit brush. The image on the right shows the process of developing the cableknit links and finding the repeat. The left image shows the cropped repeat, ready to be made into a brush.

Step 1: *Open* LaceTrim.jpg. You will probably want to set up *Guides* to establish the boundaries of your repeat. In Figure 6.41, you will see that the authors are working with the repeat aligned vertically, but brush repeats must be horizontal to work. The repeat in the figure was rotated before use as a brush. With that knowledge, it is your preference whether you work horizontally or vertically.

After establishing the guides, begin to draw the lace using paths, shapes, or a combination of the two. Remember that the brush will be small, so don't try to get too detailed. Make sure that the repeat will join smoothly to the next repeat. After you finish drawing, you may want to *Scale* the drawing to a size appropriate to your rendering.

Although you can draw the lace in any color, you may want to make it black or 50% gray before turning it into a brush. Both colors are easy to tint as a brush. Once the repeat is scaled, colored, and oriented horizontally, it is time to make the brush.

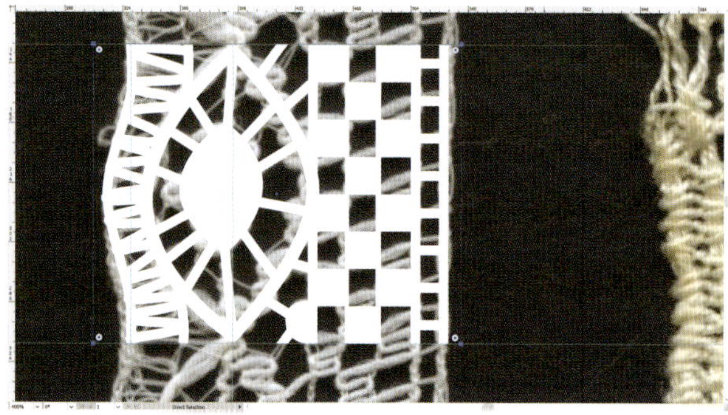

Figure 6.41 Tracing a piece of lace trim. Set *Guides* at the repeat for the lace trim. Draw the brush repeat using a combination of shapes and paths.

Step 2: Drag the repeat into the *Brush* panel. Select *Pattern brush* when the first set of options pops up. When the *Pattern Brush Options* appear, name the brush and set the *Colorization Method* to *Tints*. The rest of the settings can stay as default.

The second method we will use for creating a lace trim brush is *Image Trace*. Although this is often faster than drawing the lace, it takes more steps and typically results in a larger file size. The authors have seen traced *Lace Brushes* that continually crash less-powerful computers, so be careful when using this method.

Step 1: This method requires a scan or very clear photo of a piece of lace trim. Make sure the image is high resolution (at least 300 dpi) and contains a full repeat of the lace. It helps if it is on a black background if it is a light lace or a light background if it is a dark lace. It also starts in Photoshop to prepare the image before progressing to Illustrator.

In Photoshop, align the lace and *Crop* it to one repeat. Review Project 4.8 in Chapter 4 for instructions on how to clean up a scan or photograph to use as a repeat. Then the image needs to undergo a series of adjustments to make it strictly black and white.

Step 2: Start with *Image* → *Adjustments* → *Desaturate* to make it grayscale. Then *Image* → *Adjustments* → *Levels* and adjust the sliders until the image is mostly black and white with very little gray. Also, while adjusting the sliders, make sure the black and white are in a good balance for the lace image. Finally, click on *Image* → *Adjustments* → *Posterize* and choose two levels under the posterize options as you see in Figure 6.42. This will reduce the image to two colors.

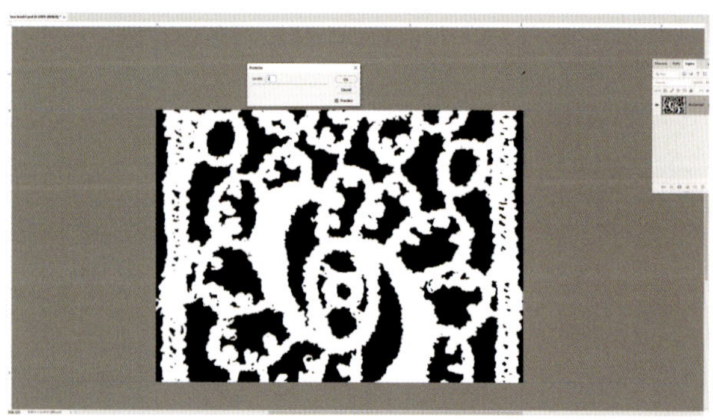

Figure 6.42 *Posterized* scan of lace in Photoshop. *Crop* the scan of the lace trim to one repeat, then *Desaturate* it. Adjust the *Levels* so it has a good balance of black and white. Finally, *Posterize* the image to two colors so there is no gray left.

If your lace is white with a black background, then you need to invert it using *Image → Adjustments → Invert.* You want black lace and a white background. Once you have the right color combination, we will remove the white background.

Step 3: If your lace layer is named "background," then rename it "layer 0" so the background can be removed. *Select* all the white background then *delete* it. The background should now show the checkerboard grid that represents transparency as you see in Figure 6.43. *Save* the image as a Photoshop document and close the document.

Step 4: Now we need to open the image in Illustrator. When you *Open* the Photoshop image in Illustrator, a dialog box will open. Choose *Flatten Layers to a Single Image.* This will keep the background deleted.

Click on the lace image with the *Select* tool then go to *Object → Image Trace* to start the tracing process. You will need to open the *Image Trace* panel. In the panel, click on *Advanced,* then select *Ignore Color* to keep the background deleted. Then adjust the sliders to get the best results.

To produce a trace with a lower file size, the authors generally recommend:

- *Mode*: Black and White
- *Threshold*: closer to less
- *Paths*: closer to less
- *Corners*: just see what produces better results. "More" has worked better for the authors
- *Noise*: higher number
- Click on *Simplify*
- *Anchors*: move towards less
- *Method*: Abutting
- *Create*: Fills (not strokes)
- *Options*: Snap Curves to Lines
- *Ignore Color* (white or whatever color is used for the background)

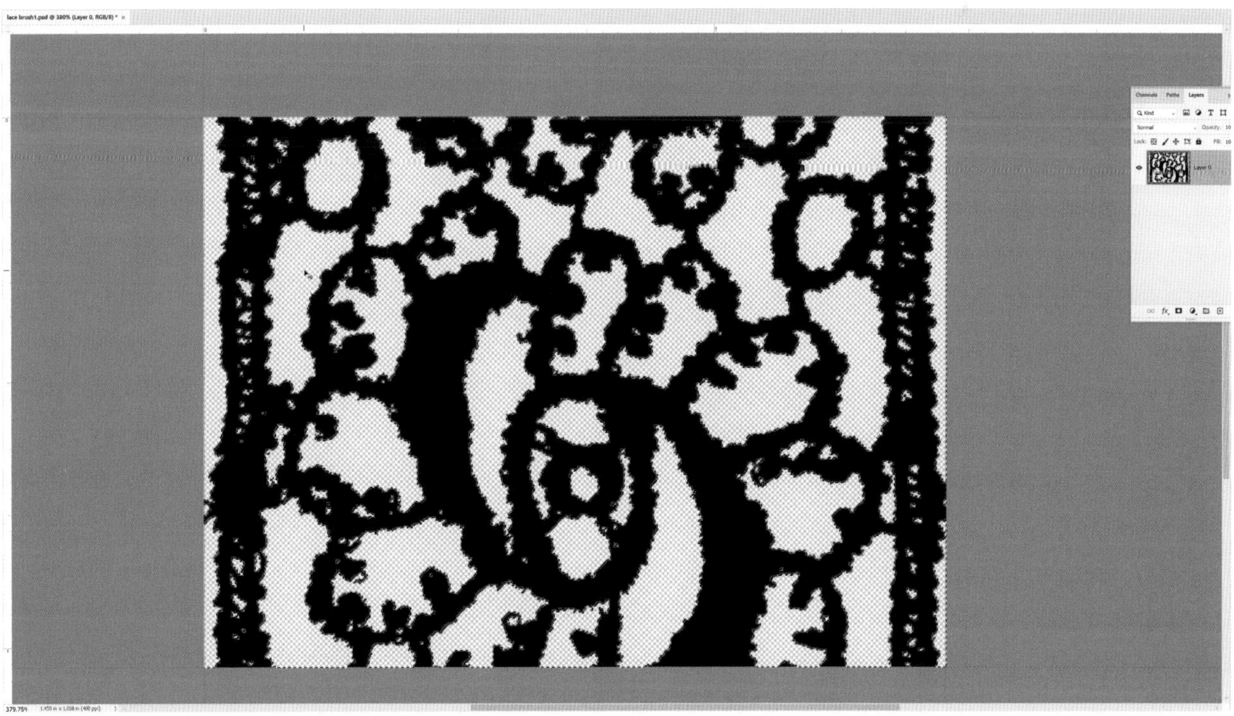

Figure 6.43 *Invert* the white lace image. Then select the white background and delete it so only the black lace remains.

Remember that the brush will be small, so you should not be concerned about every detail. You want a simplified representation of the lace. Generally, less is more in this case.

One word of caution when simplifying the tracing. Sometimes the tracing engine will round the ends of the lace where they should be squared in order to join to the next repeat tile. If you like the results of the trace other than the rounding at the tile joins, then you can *Expand* the trace. Then use the *Direct Select* tool to manually adjust the shapes. Figure 6.44 has been traced, expanded, and manually adjusted at the repeat edges.

Step 5: After creating the trace, it is time to make the brush. Make sure the image is aligned horizontally. You may need to rotate it if you have been working vertically. Open the *Brushes* panel and drag the brush repeat into the panel until a plus (+) symbol appears. When you release the image in the panel, the first option box will appear; choose *Pattern brush* as you see in Figure 6.45. Then the *Pattern Brush Options* will appear. Name the brush and set the *Colorization Method* to *Tints*, as you see in Figure 6.46. This completes the brush. To use your brushes in other renderings, save your brushes library from the brushes panel.

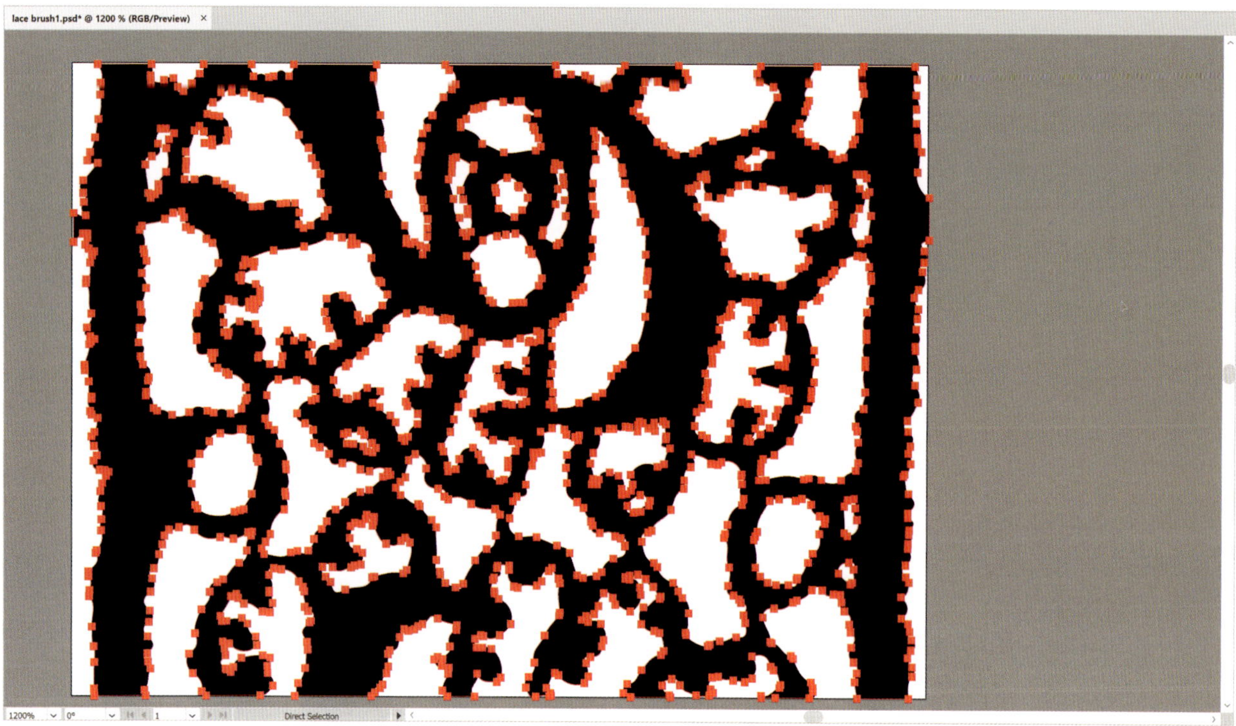

Figure 6.44 *Open* the Photoshop image in Illustrator and perform an *Image Trace*. In *Image Trace*, check *Ignore Color* to only trace the black. Adjust the settings to produce less paths and anchor points but create decent results. If you do not like any part of the traced shape, *Expand* the tracing, then manually adjust the anchor points.

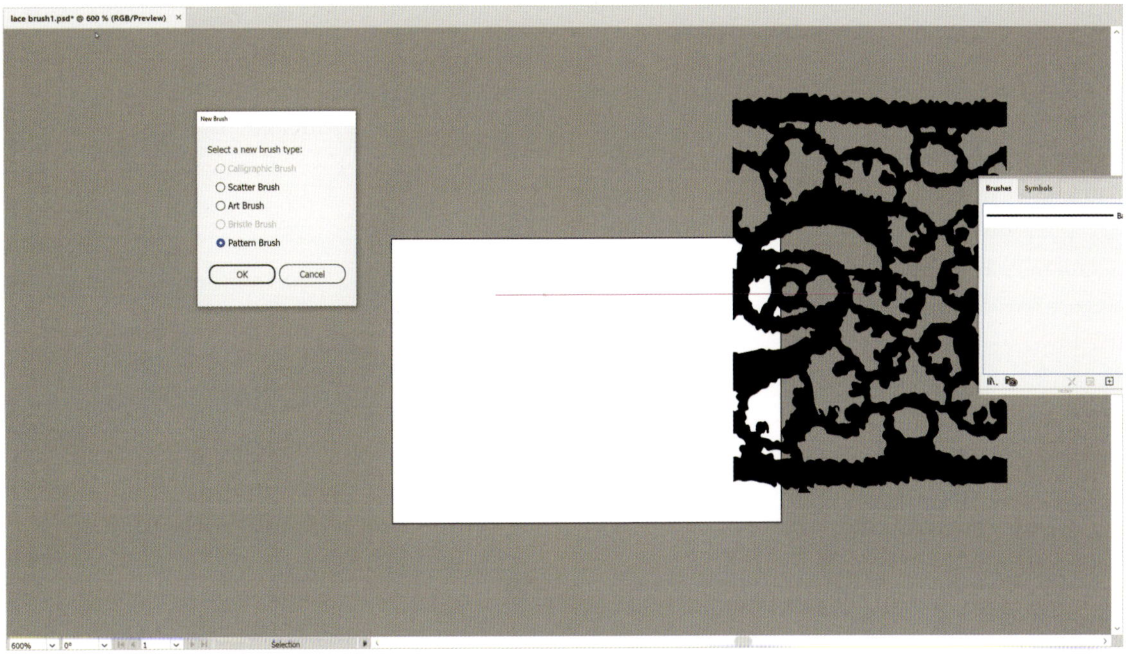

Figure 6.45 If your image is vertical, *Rotate* the traced repeat 90 degrees. Then drag it into the *Brushes* panel to create the new brush. Choose *Pattern brush*.

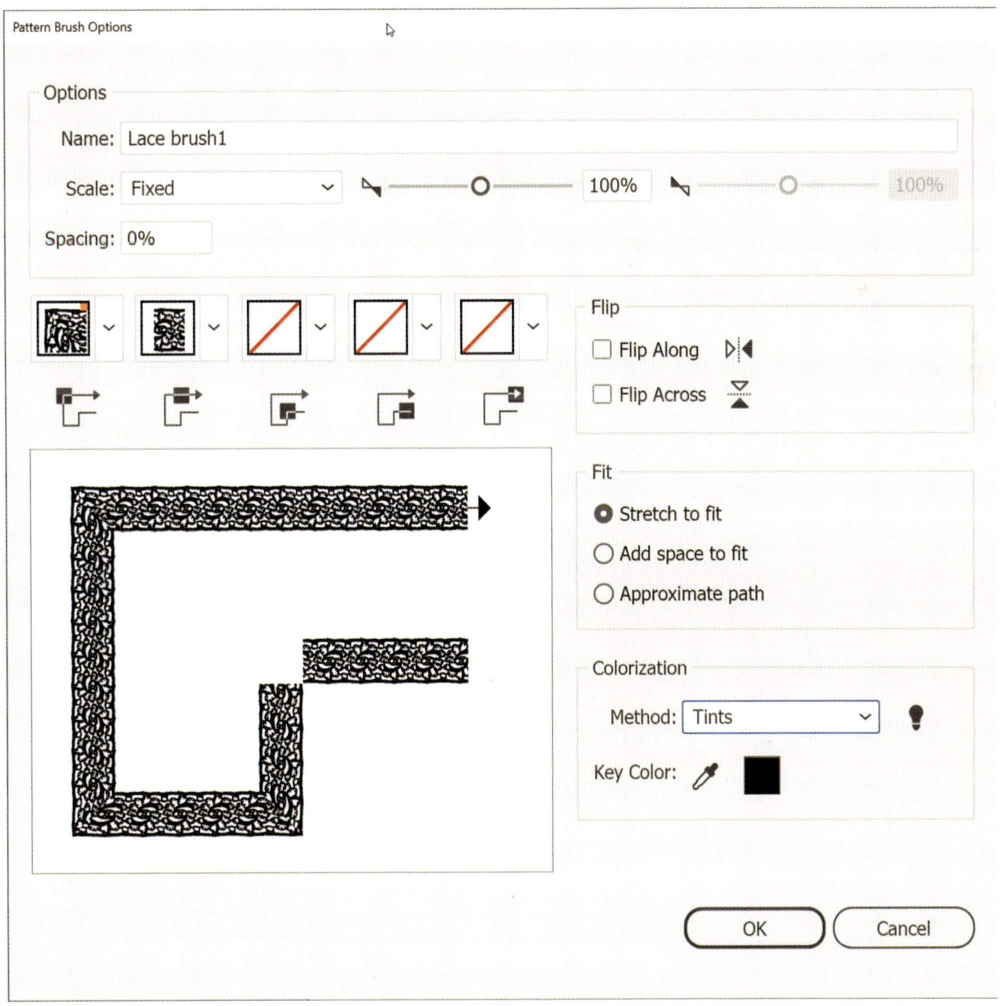

Figure 6.46 Brush settings for lace trim. Name the brush and set the *Colorization Method* to *Tints*. The rest of the settings can stay at default.

Pattern Fills

When we think about texture, we are often thinking about all-over fabric texture. In Illustrator, this usually means *Pattern Fills*. These are basically the same as the pattern fills used in Chapter 4, but now we are focusing on texture rather than on fabric design. Like before, there are many ways to make texture pattern fills. We will feature a few different methods and textures to get you started.

As the last brush we made was done with *Image Trace*, we will continue with the technique. *Image Trace* can be very useful for textures. Just be careful to reduce the number of anchors and simplify the trace so the file size is smaller. A pattern that crashes your computer because of file size is not useful.

Step 1: We will create a traced tweed. *Open* Tweed.jpg. This technique works well for boucle, houndstooth, and other highly textured fabrics. The secret is to start with an original swatch that is high contrast. That could mean that the yarns in the swatch are colors that contrast (the original tweed swatch for the example was black and white), or that the swatch was scanned or photographed with strong light that creates high contrast within the image.

When scanning or photographing the swatch, try to make sure it is squared up on grain and not skewed. This is similar to scanning and preparing a fabric repeat (Chapter 4, Project 4.8), but there is not a repeat in this case. *Open* the image in Photoshop to make any adjustments to the grain. You may also want to crop or scale the image to a more manageable size.

Step 2: After cleaning up the image in Photoshop, *Open* the image in Illustrator. Open the *Image Trace* panel (*Window* → *Image Trace*). Select the image and click *Trace*. Try different presets if you like. Otherwise, you will need to adjust the sliders to get the results you like. For the example in Figure 6.47, the authors liked the results when they reduced the number of colors to 3. Click *Expand* on the *Image Trace* panel or *Object* → *Expand* before proceeding to the next step.

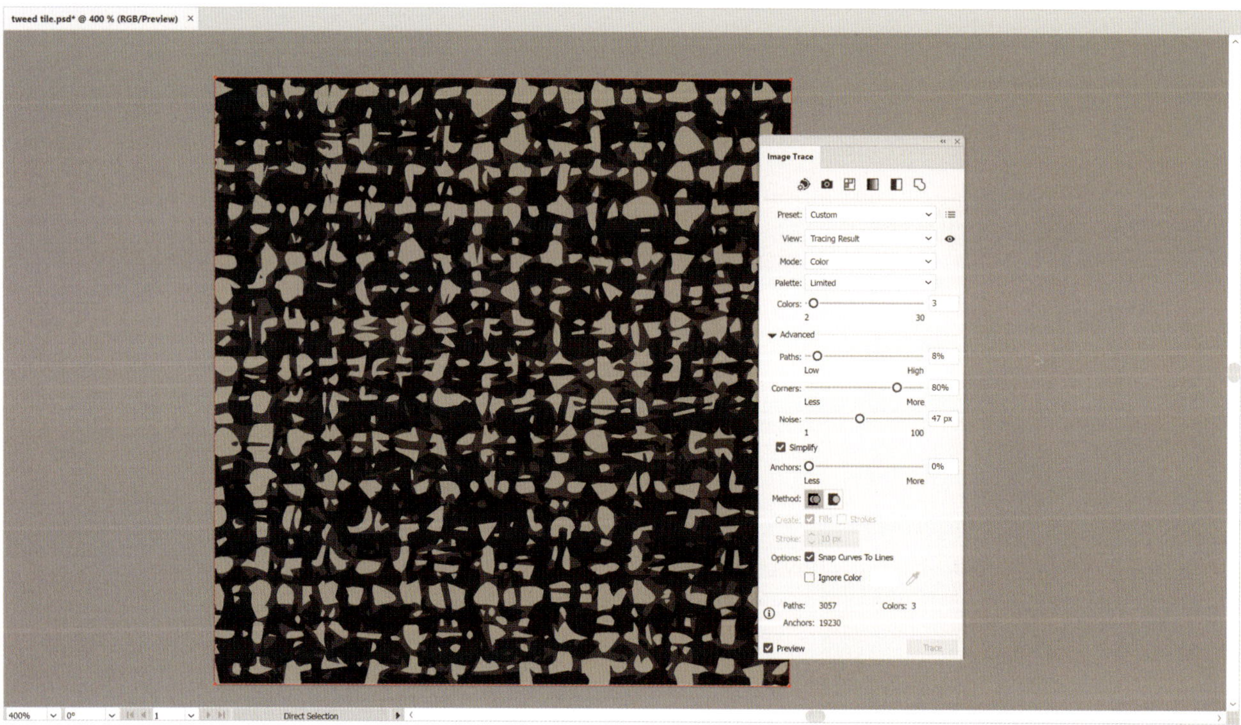

Figure 6.47 Tweed tracing results. Select the image. Perform an *Image Trace*. Adjust the sliders in the *Image Trace* panel to get good results, but with the lowest possible file size.

Because the texture is abstract and dense, the number of paths and anchors can be reduced even more without damaging the final appearance of the texture. Before we reduce the file paths, we want to make sure that the texture is the correct scale for the renderings we want to use it with. If the tile is too large, you will probably make it too detailed. *Scale* the tile to the appropriate size.

To reduce the number of paths, *Select* the tile. Then go to *Object* → *Path* → *Simplify*. Click on the ellipses (...) on the right of the option bar that pops up. This will bring up a larger options box, as you see in Figure 6.48. In the middle of the box, you will see a line that says, "Original" and "New." This will show you how well you are simplifying the file. Adjust the sliders and watch the results on the screen. The more you can simplify the image while maintaining the quality of the image, the smaller the file size.

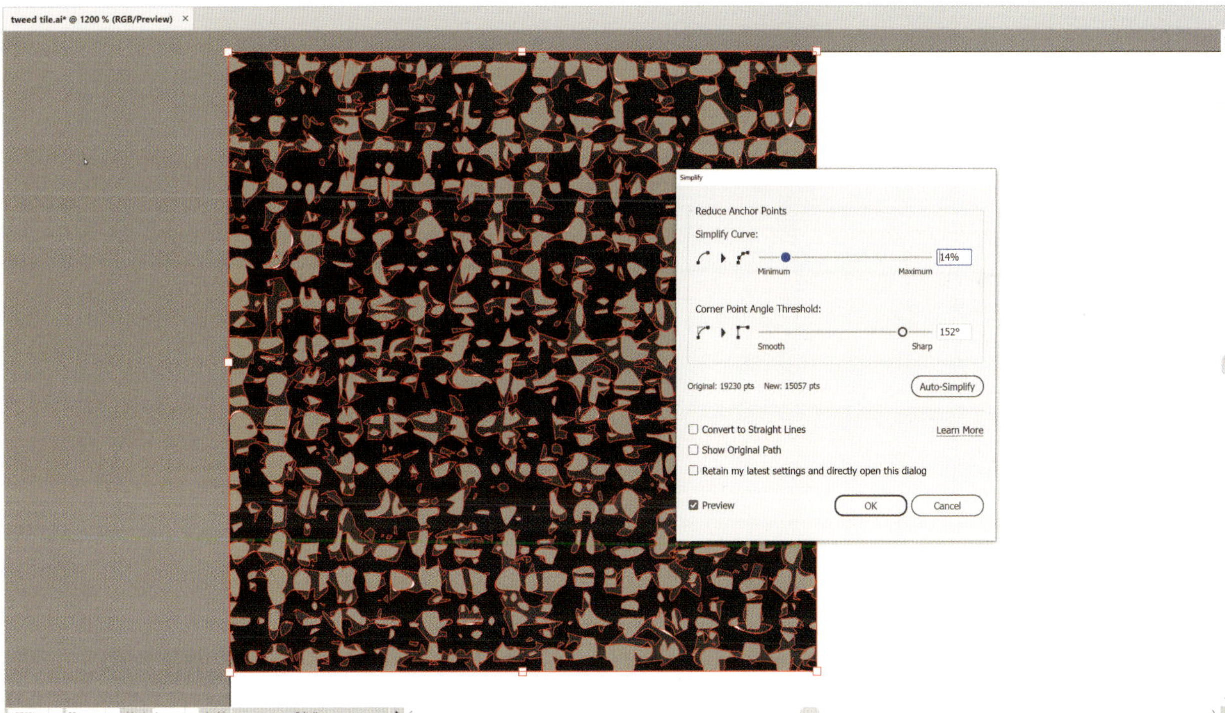

Figure 6.48 Because the texture tile is abstract, the number of paths and anchor points can be further reduced. Start by scaling the tile to an appropriate size for your renderings. Then use *Object* → *Path* → *Simplify*. This will help reduce the file size of the image.

Step 3: After the image is fully prepared, it is time to make the texture pattern fill. This part is the same as making a regular pattern fill. *Select* the tile. Go to *Object* → *Pattern* → *Make*. You can adjust for any gaps in the repeat by clicking on the *Pattern Tile Tool* button in the very top left of the *Pattern Options* panel as you see in Figure 6.49. This tool will allow you to drag the bounding box around the repeat smaller or larger. Name the texture then click *Done*. The texture is now located in the *Swatches* panel. If you want to save it for future renderings, save the *Swatch Library*.

Just as with regular pattern swatches, you can edit texture patterns by *double-clicking* on the swatch in the *Swatch* panel. Although it may be challenging to recolor the individual pieces of the texture one piece at a time, it is easy to use some of the recolor tools in Illustrator. While in the pattern swatch editor, click on the swatch. Go to *Edit* → *Edit Colors* → *Recolor Artwork* to recolor all the parts at one time as you see in Figure 6.50. You can also try *Recolor with Preset* or *Generative Recolor*, which uses artificial intelligence to come up with new color palettes.

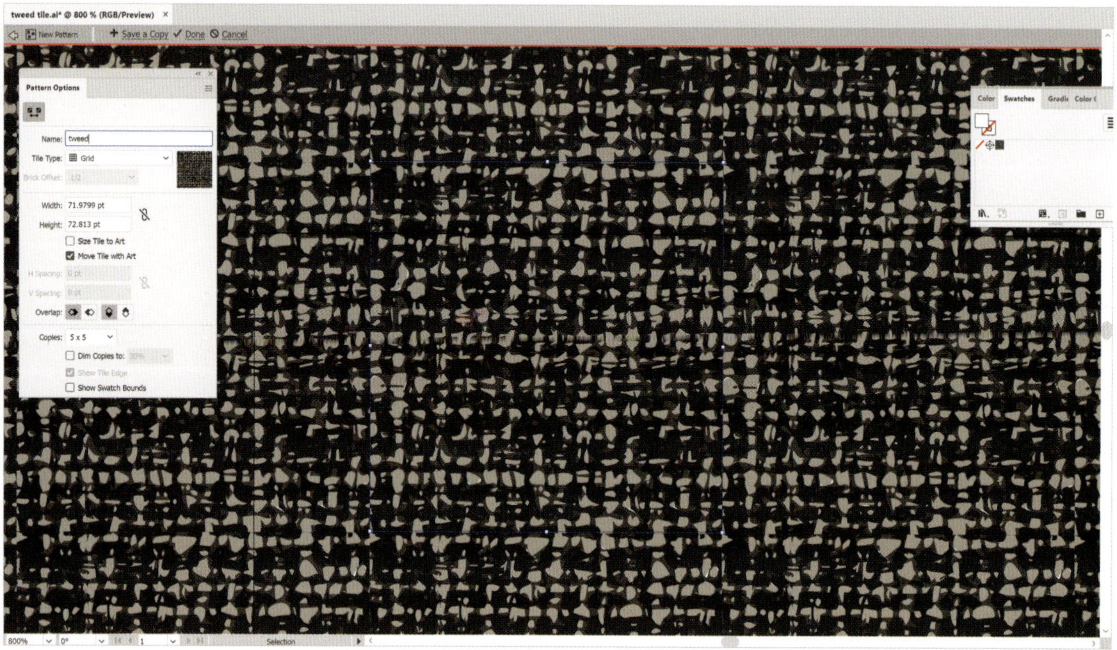

Figure 6.49 Once the texture tile is prepared, the process of making the texture pattern fill is the same as making a traditional pattern fill. Select the tile, then go to *Object* → *Pattern* → *Make*. Name the pattern and make any edits to the repeat that are needed. Click *Done* when you are finished.

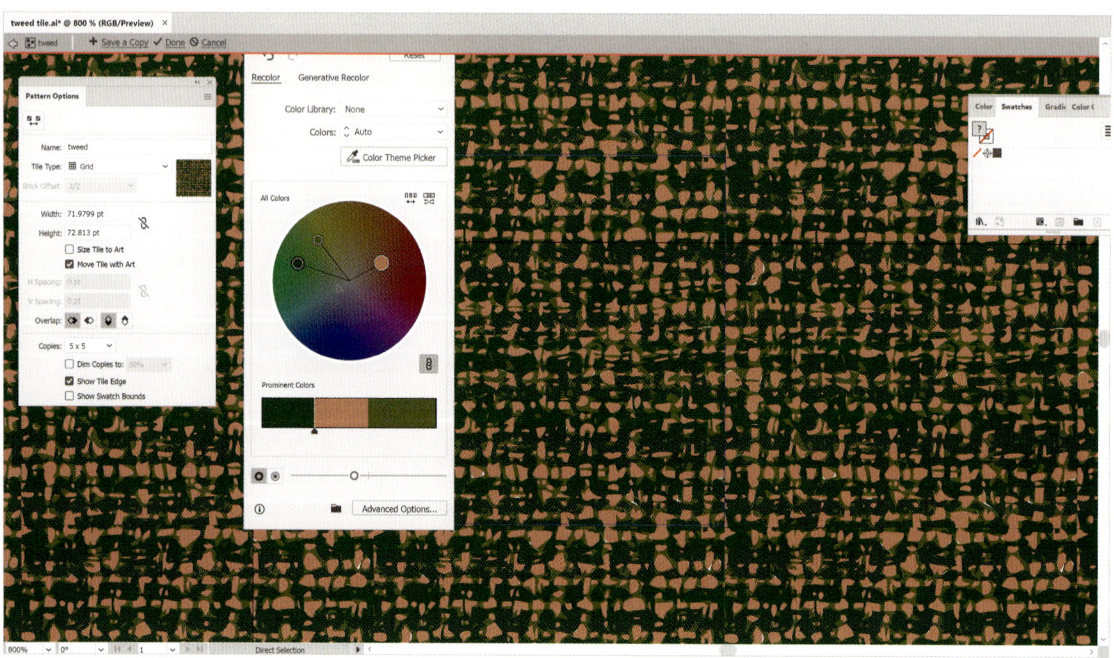

Figure 6.50 Multi-colored pattern fills can be re-colored using the *Recolor* artwork function under *Edit* → *Edit Colors* → *Recolor Artwork*, *Recolor with Preset*, or *Generative Recolor*.

Step 4: To use the texture, treat it as any fill swatch. Use one of your previous Illustrator figures from Chapters 2 or 3. Click on the area you want to fill with the texture, make sure you are changing the fill, then click on the new texture swatch. You can edit the scale, position, and angle, just as you learned in Chapter 4. You can see the tweed pattern used in Figure 6.51.

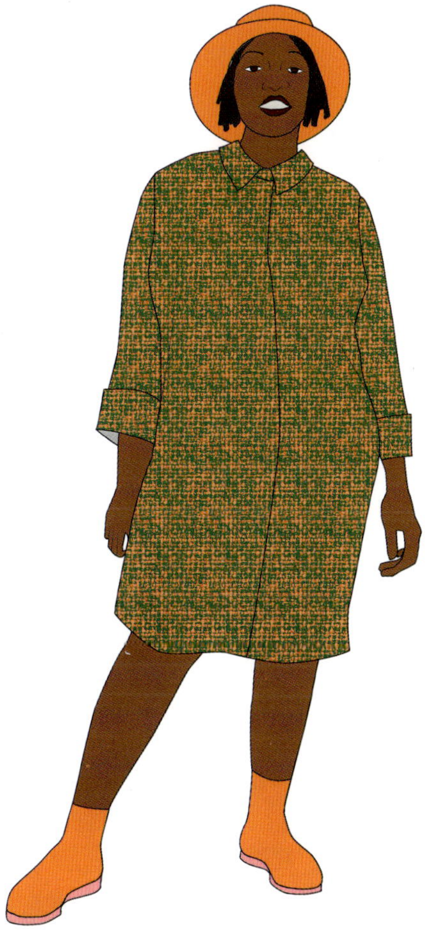

Figure 6.51 The finished tweed swatch was used for the fill texture in the figure's coat.

Next, we will make a lace texture pattern fill. The process is very similar to making the tweed pattern fill. However, lace is a cross between a repeat pattern and a texture. Therefore, the initial swatch needs more preparation than the tweed or a general texture.

Step 1: *Open* Lace.jpg. When choosing, scanning, or photographing a lace swatch, make sure that you have a full repeat in all directions. If you are not sure what that means, review Chapter 4. It is also good if it is a light lace on a dark background or vice versa. Try to ensure the swatch repeat is aligned and not skewed. *Open* the scan or photograph in Photoshop and make any transformations necessary to ensure as perfect a repeat as possible. See Project 4.8 to review instructions on how to transform a scan or photo. *Crop* your image to precisely one repeat tile as you see in Figure 6.52.

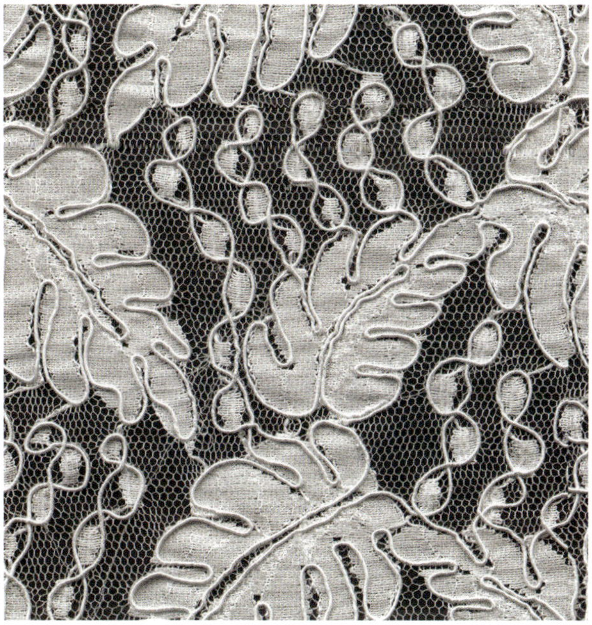

Figure 6.52 Lace is a combination of pattern and texture. You must find and crop it to the precise repeat in Photoshop, just like a pattern. However, it is also a texture because of the mesh and transparency.

Step 2: After cropping the image to one repeat tile, it will need to undergo adjustments. Start with *Desaturate* to remove color from the image. Then adjust the *Levels* to make the lace mostly black and white with little to no gray as you see in Figure 6.53. If you need, you can also *Posterize* the image to two levels. If your lace is light, you will also need to *Invert* it, as you see in Figure 6.54.

Step 3: Once the image is adjusted, it is time to remove the background. Rename the Background layer "Layer 0." Then *Select* the white background using a mask tool or one of the select options from the menu. Once all the background is selected, click *Delete* on the keyboard. The background should be deleted, as you see in Figure 6.55. Remove the selection mask before saving and closing the Photoshop document.

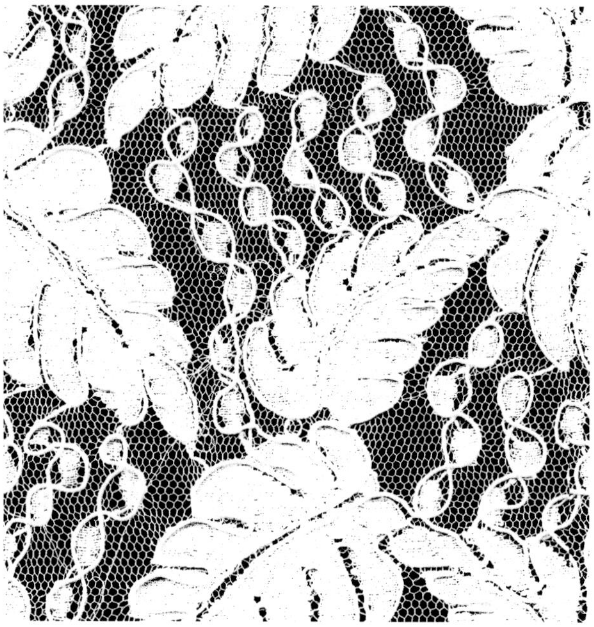

Figure 6.53 *Desaturate* the lace repeat. Then, adjust the *Levels* of your lace repeat in Photoshop so it is mostly black and white with very little gray.

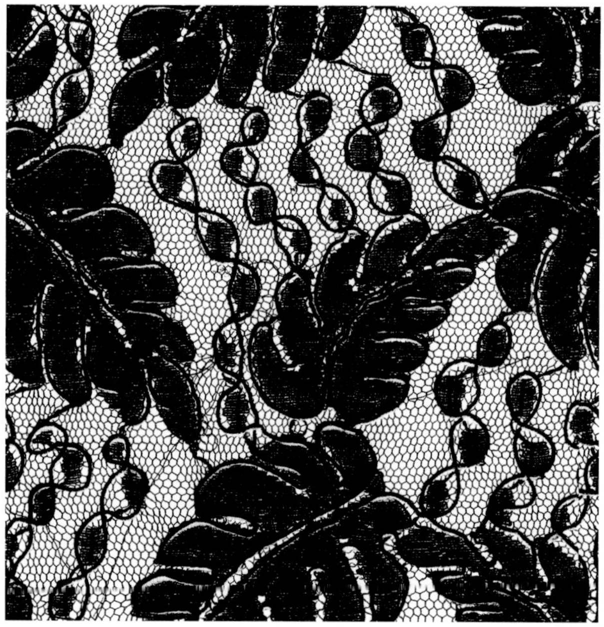

Figure 6.54 If your lace is white or light, you will need to *Invert* it, so it is black and the background is white. You can find *Invert* under *Image* → *Adjustments*.

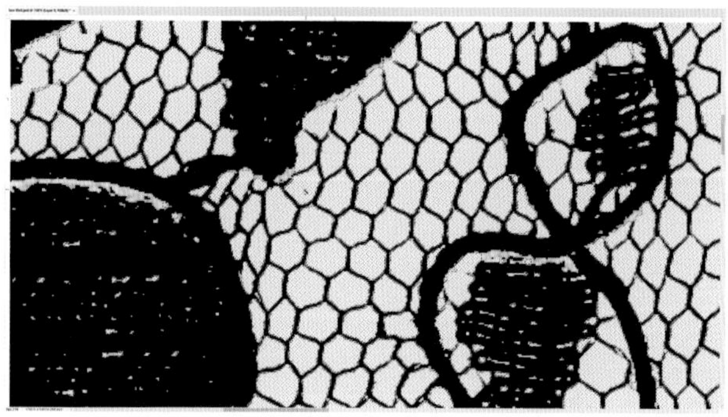

Figure 6.55 *Select* all the white background. Make sure that the layer has been renamed "Layer 0." *Delete* the selected background so only the black lace remains on a transparent background. Save and close the Photoshop document.

Step 4: *Open* the document in Illustrator and choose *Flatten Layers to a Single Image* upon opening it. Open the *Image Trace* panel. Select the lace repeat and tell the panel to *Trace*. Just like with the *Lace Brush* and with the tweed pattern, you will need to adjust the sliders in the *Image Trace* panel. Make sure the *Ignore Color* box is checked under *Advanced* to maintain the background transparency. The sliders will probably have similar settings to what we used for the *Lace Brush*, but every trace is slightly different. Remember that this lace will be reduced to a very small square, so do not try to have every detail. You will see in Figure 6.56 that the mesh is starting to disappear in places. This will not show when reduced.

You will probably want to *Scale* the image and *Simplify* it as we did with the tweed to reduce the file size. Check the edges of the tile, particularly after simplifying. If any shapes that are supposed to join to the abutting tile have been altered by the trace or simplification processes, you will need to fix them manually. *Expand* the tile and use the *Direct Select* tool to move or adjust the anchor points and paths.

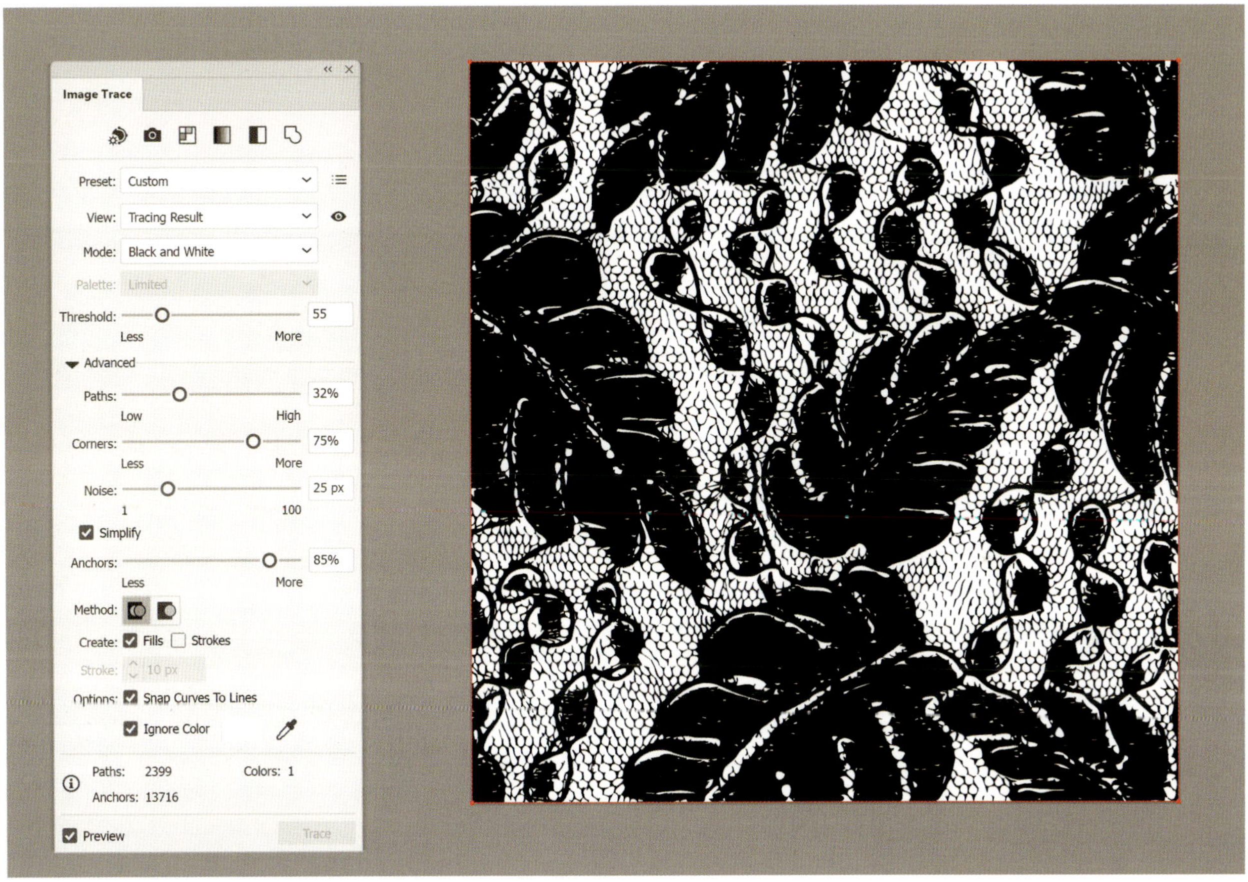

Figure 6.56 *Open* the adjusted lace tile in Illustrator. Open the *Image Trace* panel. Select the lace image and click *Trace*. In the panel, select *Advanced*. Click *Ignore Color* to keep the background deleted. Adjust the sliders to produce the best results for the smallest file size.

Step 5: After tracing, scaling, and simplifying the tile, it is time to make the pattern. Select the tile and click *Object* → *Pattern* → *Make* to create the texture pattern fill. You can adjust the bounding box of the repeat using the *Pattern Tile* tool button at the very top left of the *Pattern Options* panel. Make sure your lace looks seamless, as it does in Figure 6.57. Name the pattern and click *Done* when you are finished.

The pattern will be stored in your *Swatches* panel. To use your lace in other documents, save your *Swatches Library*. You can then reopen the library through the *Swatches* panel under *User Defined*.

Sweater knit construction can be very technical and it is important to show the texture. However, when we illustrate sweaters, remember that we are typically looking at a very reduced version of the texture. That means we can have simplified versions of the texture. We want just enough to show that we are looking at a sweater, but not so much as to clutter the illustration.

The texture pattern fill we will make is for a plain (jersey) sweater knit. You can use the same idea for reverse (purl side) knits, rib knits, and other patterns. We will create a pattern that represents the V patterns that the knit stitches create in rows and columns (wales and courses) on sweaters. The pattern can be scaled for different gauges. The original idea came from www.fashiondesign411.com.

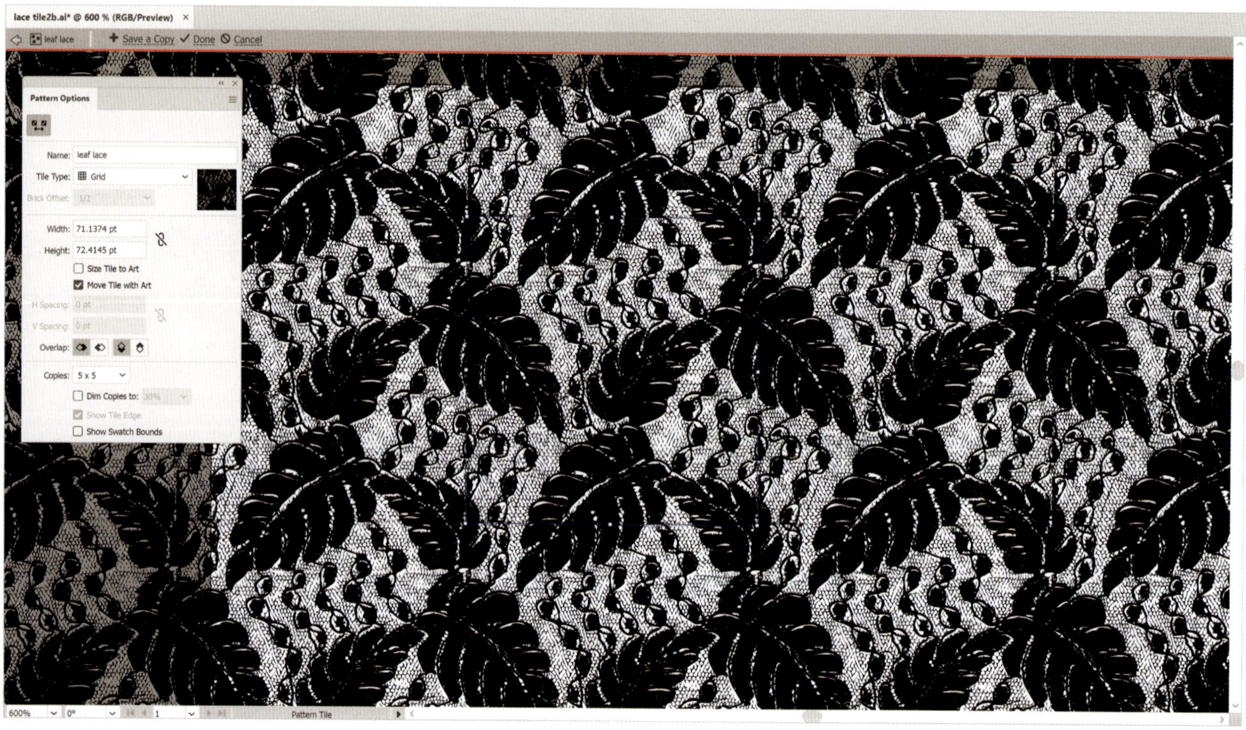

Figure 6.57 *Scale* the traced image to a size appropriate to your rendered figures. You may want to *Simplify* the image to further reduce the file size of the texture. When the tile is ready, select the tile and click *Object* → *Pattern* → *Make* to create the pattern fill. Name the texture and adjust the bounding box, if necessary. Then click *Done*.

Step 1: In Illustrator, turn on the grid by clicking *View* → *Show Grid*. Using the *Pen* tool, draw a path that represents half of one knit stitch. The authors made their stitch one grid wide by one and a half grids tall, as you see in Figure 6.58. Check that you have the stroke set to black and fill set to none. You may want the stroke set to rounded caps and rounded corners. Choose a stroke weight that works. The authors used 1 pt. *Reflect* and make a copy of the stitch from the top anchor point. *Join* the paths at the top to make a complete stitch as you see in Figure 6.59.

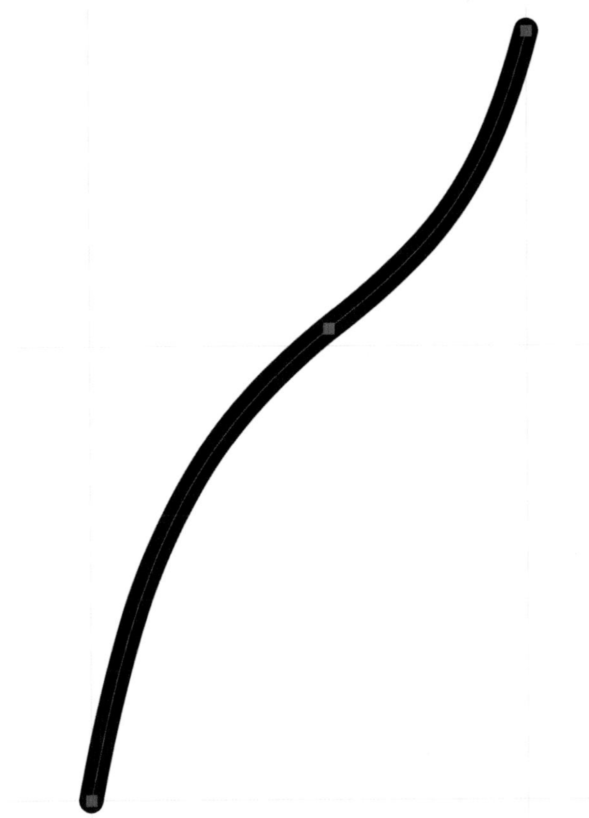

Figure 6.58 Half of the knit stitch. Using the *Pen* tool, draw a representation of the knit stitch from the base to the tip.

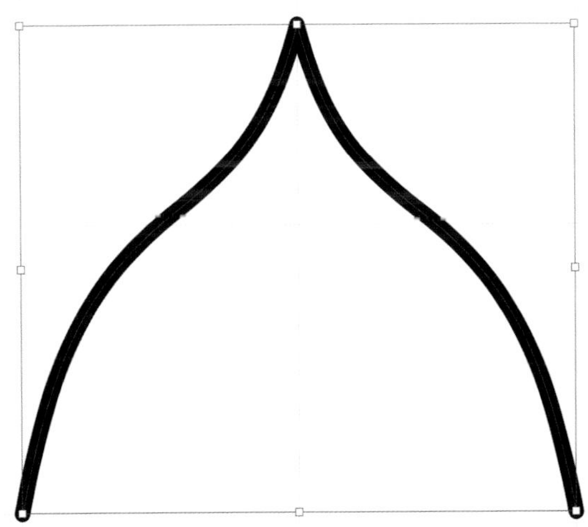

Figure 6.59 Complete knit stitch. *Reflect* and *Copy* the path from the top anchor point. *Join* the paths at the tip.

Step 2: After you have a complete knit stitch, we will prepare a grid of stitches to eventually be used for the pattern tile. Make four copies of the stitch (three new copies) and arrange the stitches in a row with the bottom anchor points overlapping, as shown in Figure 6.60. *Join* all four stitches together so they are a single path.

Make a copy of the row of stitches and place the copied row either directly above or below the original row. You should have two rows in total. *Align* the top of one row precisely with the bottom of the other row. Make sure they are aligned left to right, as shown in Figure 6.61.

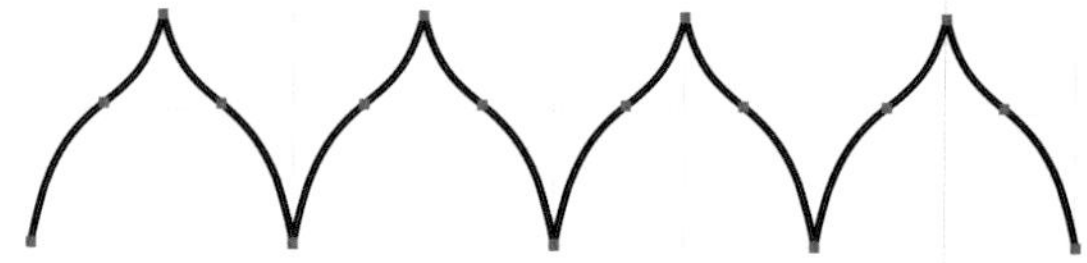

Figure 6.60 Four copies of the stitch in a row. Make four copies of the stitch. Match each copy together at the bottom anchor points. *Join* all the stitches.

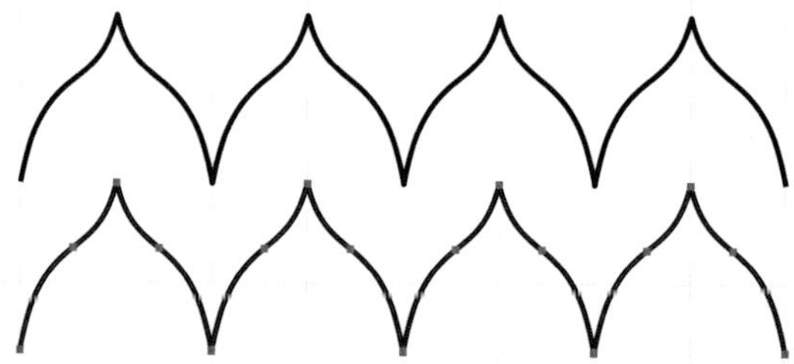

Figure 6.61 Two rows of the stitches. Make a copy of the row of stitches. The bottom of the second row should be in line with the top of the first row.

Step 3: It is now time to clip the rows into a tile. The tile will be two stitches wide by two stitches tall. The extra stitches to the left and right will be clipped off, but the clipping process will create a better join than if we had just drawn a two-by-two pattern.

Create a *Rectangle* on top of the stitch rows that is exactly two stitches wide by two stitches tall. The rectangle must touch the top and bottom of the stitches and hit exactly at the anchor points on the left and right, as you see in Figure 6.62. Make sure the rectangle is in front of the stitches.

Once you have the rectangle drawn, select the rectangle and the two rows of stitches. Click on *Object* → *Clipping mask* → *Make* to clip the stitches to the rectangle. The stitches to the left and right of the rectangle should disappear.

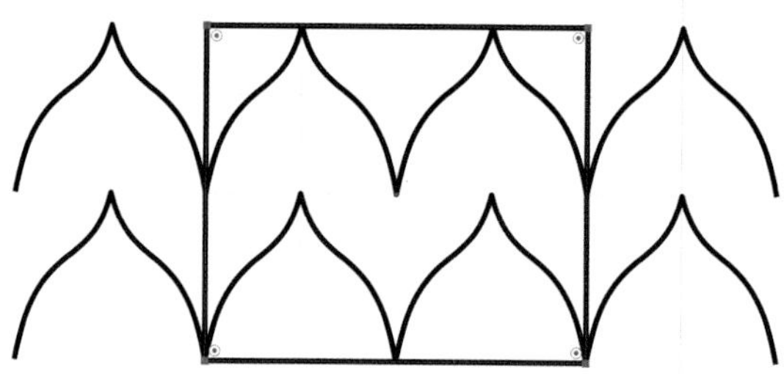

Figure 6.62 Preparing to clip the tile. Draw a *Rectangle* precisely over four of the stitches. Make sure the rectangle is directly over the stitch rows in the list of objects in the *Layers* panel. To clip the tile, select the rectangle and the two rows of stitches. Click on *Object* → *Clipping mask* → *Make*.

Step 4: To finish the tile, draw another *Rectangle* exactly the same size as the previous rectangle. Again, make sure it touches the top, bottom, and sides of the tile. This time, the rectangle needs a fill color, but no stroke. You can pick the fill. *Arrange* the rectangle and *Send to the Back*. *Group* all the parts of the tile together. The tile will look like Figure 6.63.

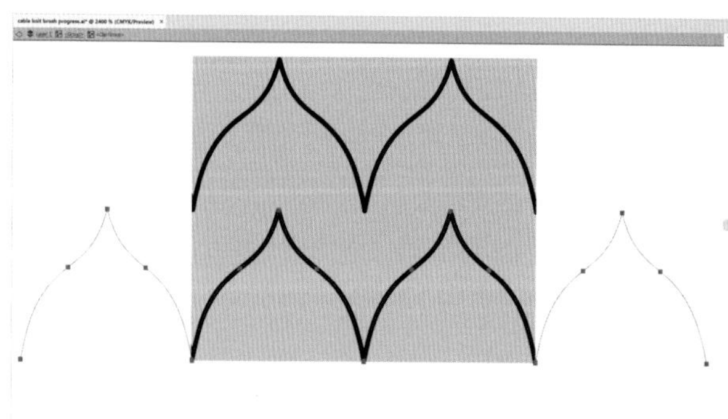

Figure 6.63 Draw a *Rectangle* the same size as the *Clipping mask*. *Arrange* it immediately beneath the clip group in the *Layers* panel (*Send to the Back*). The rectangle should have fill color, but no stroke. *Group* the clip group and the rectangle.

Step 5: When the tile is complete, make the pattern. Click on *Object* → *Pattern* → *Make* to create the pattern fill. Adjust the bounding box if you need to and name the pattern. Then click *Done* to finish the pattern. The texture pattern fill will be in the *Swatches* panel. Because the original pattern tile has a separate rectangle of color behind the stitches, it is easy to adjust the color of the fill in the pattern editor, as you see in Figure 6.64. Just select the rectangle, not the stitches, while you are in the pattern editor and adjust the fill color.

This pattern will need scaling to match the gauge of the sweater you are illustrating. However, if you make the scale too small, the pattern will look static. Figure 6.65 shows the original tile and a rectangle with a scaled version of the texture. When the pattern is scaled smaller, the reason for using a simplified version of the stitches becomes more evident. More detail would have cluttered the rendering.

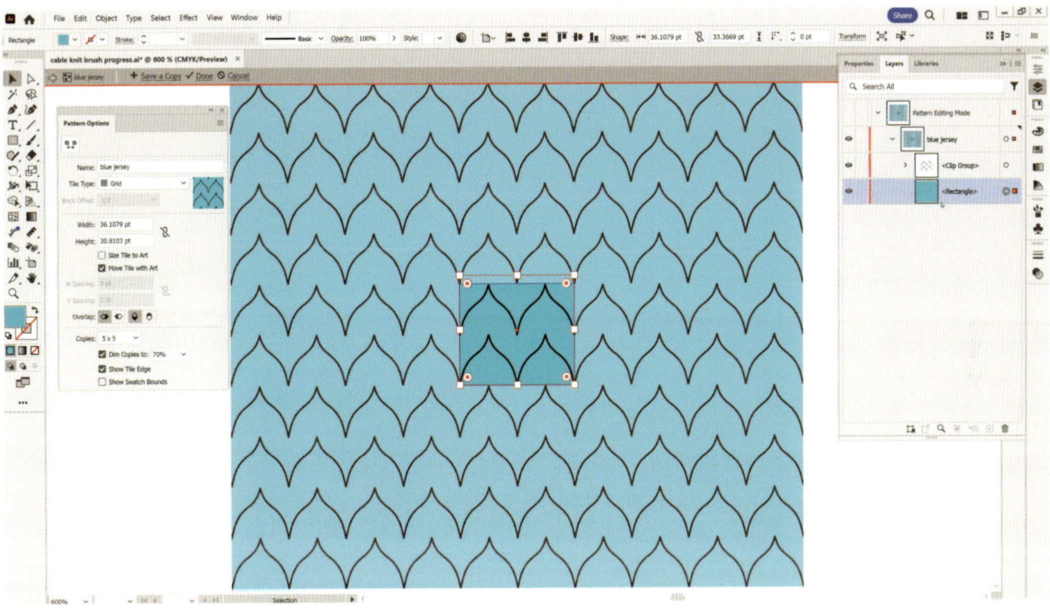

Figure 6.64 Select the grouped tile and click *Object* → *Pattern* → *Make* to create the pattern fill. Name the texture and adjust the bounding box, if necessary. Then click *Done*. Notice in the *Layers* panel that the background color is a separate rectangle. This makes it easier to change the color of your texture fill if you need to do so.

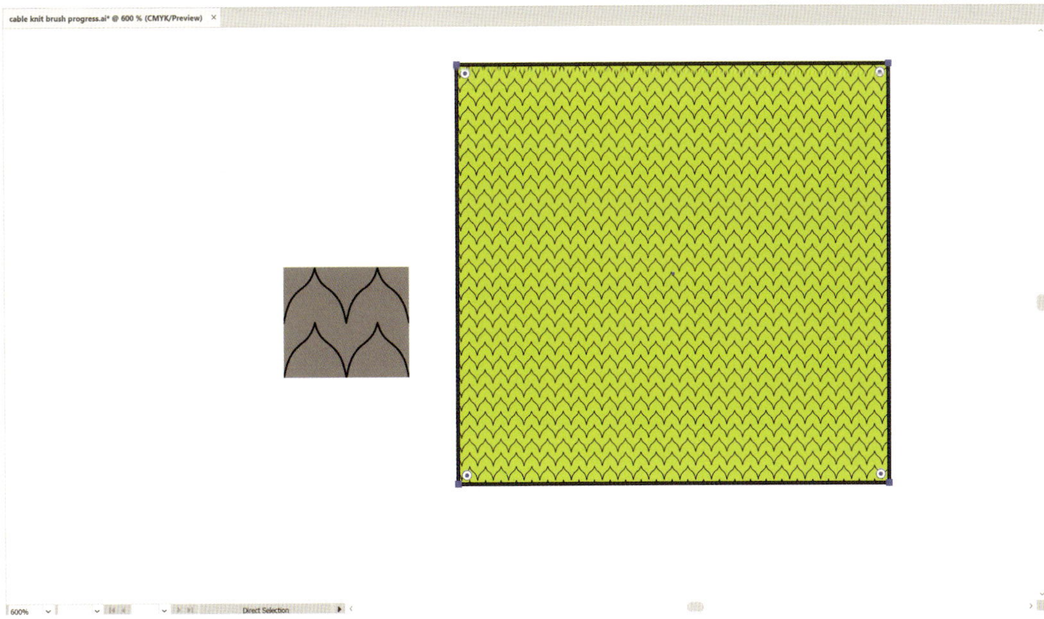

Figure 6.65 The original texture swatch and a scaled version. The image on the left is the original sweater texture repeat drawing. The image on the right shows the texture scaled and used as a fill. Once scaled, it is more apparent that the simplified version of the knit stitches works well.

To use your sweater swatch in other documents, save the *Swatch Library*. Then you can open the *Swatch Library* from the *Swatches* panel under *User Defined*. You can save multiple patterns in the same library with a little practice.

Like the tweed pattern, the knit swatch works as a fill. Figure 6.66 shows how the authors used the sweater pattern, the lace pattern, and the cableknit brush all in the same rendering. The patterns have been scaled to match the scale of the rendering. The weight of the stroke was adjusted to change the size of the brush. Because the lace pattern is transparent, there are two copies of each skirt piece. The back skirt pieces are a solid fill color and the top skirt pieces are lace fill.

A multi-purpose mesh texture pattern fill can be made in Illustrator. The mesh can be used for fishnet, sports mesh, and other types of mesh according to how you scale it and adjust the transparency. We can draw it completely from basic shapes.

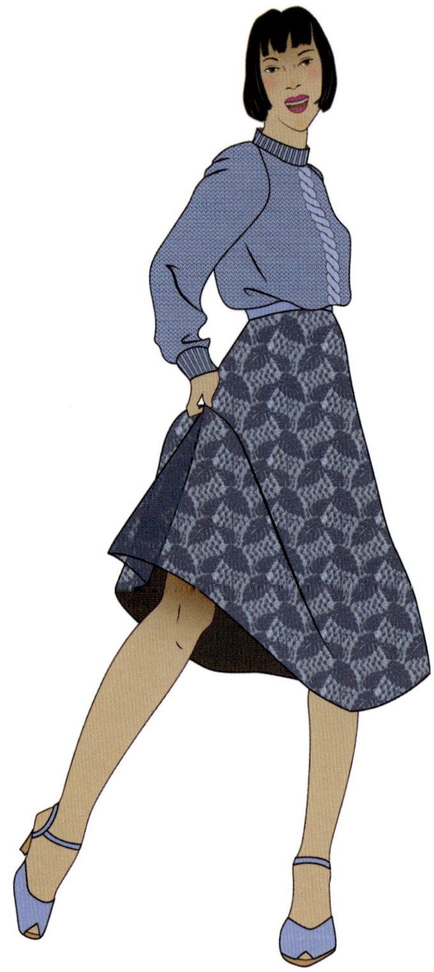

Figure 6.66 The figure uses the sweater and lace texture pattern fills. The lace was transparent, so there are two copies of each skirt piece. The bottom copy of each piece is a solid color, and the top copy is the lace. The cableknit brush was used down the front of the sweater.

Step 1: Start with a *Rectangle*. The size does not matter because you can scale it later, but the proportion of the rectangle does make a difference in the results. The authors used a rectangle that is about 50% taller than the width. (We used 18 pt wide by 24 pt high.) Give the rectangle a solid fill color, but no stroke color.

Step 2: Next, make an *Ellipse* (oval). The ellipse is about half as wide as the rectangle and about two-thirds the height of the rectangle, but this is approximate and can be adjusted to get the best results. Make a total of four copies of the ellipse. It should also have a solid fill color, but no stroke. Make sure the ellipses have a different color than the rectangle.

Place one ellipse centered across the bottom edge of the rectangle, one centered across the top edge, one centered along the right edge, and the last centered along the left edge. Either use the *Alignment* functions or the *Smart Guides* to make sure all the parts are aligned. The assembly should look like Figure 6.67. You can adjust the size of the ellipses if you need, but make sure they all match.

Step 3: To make the mesh tile, we need to remove the ellipse shapes from the rectangle shape. An easy way to do this is to use the *Pathfinder* panel. Select all the ellipses and the rectangle. Open the *Pathfinder* panel. Click on *Minus Front*, which should be the second from the top left button as you see in Figure 6.68. This will leave a modified X shape.

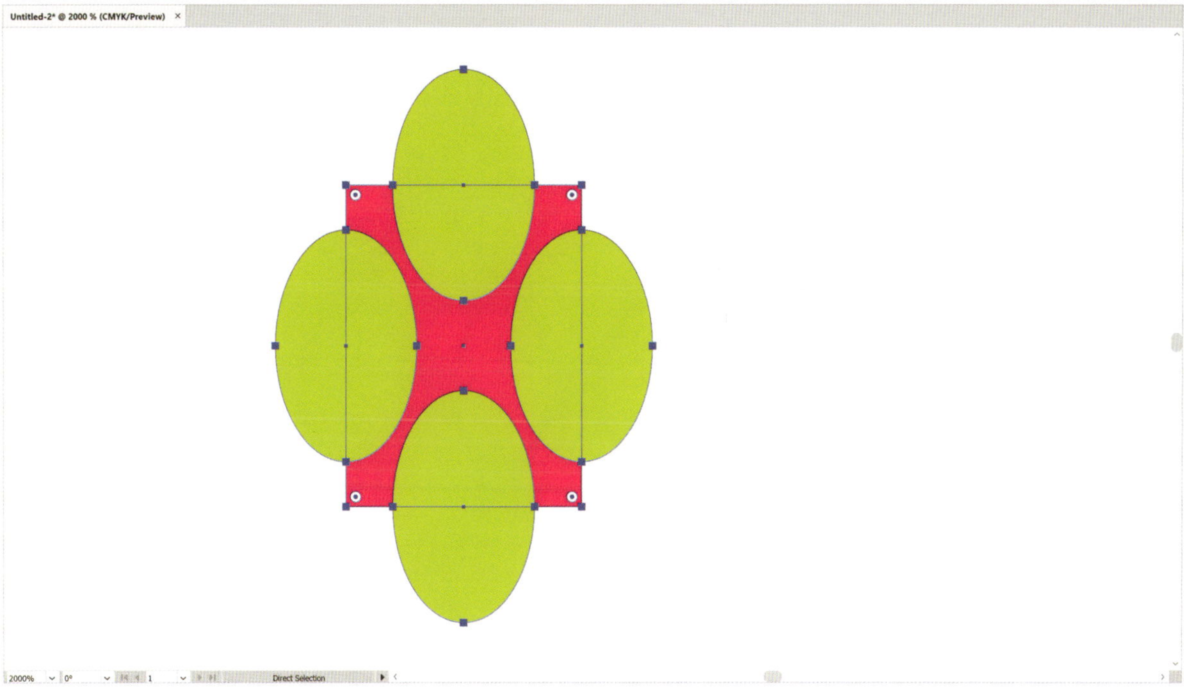

Figure 6.67 Making mesh from shapes. Make a rectangle. Then make four identical ellipses. Center an ellipse at center top, center bottom, center left, and center right.

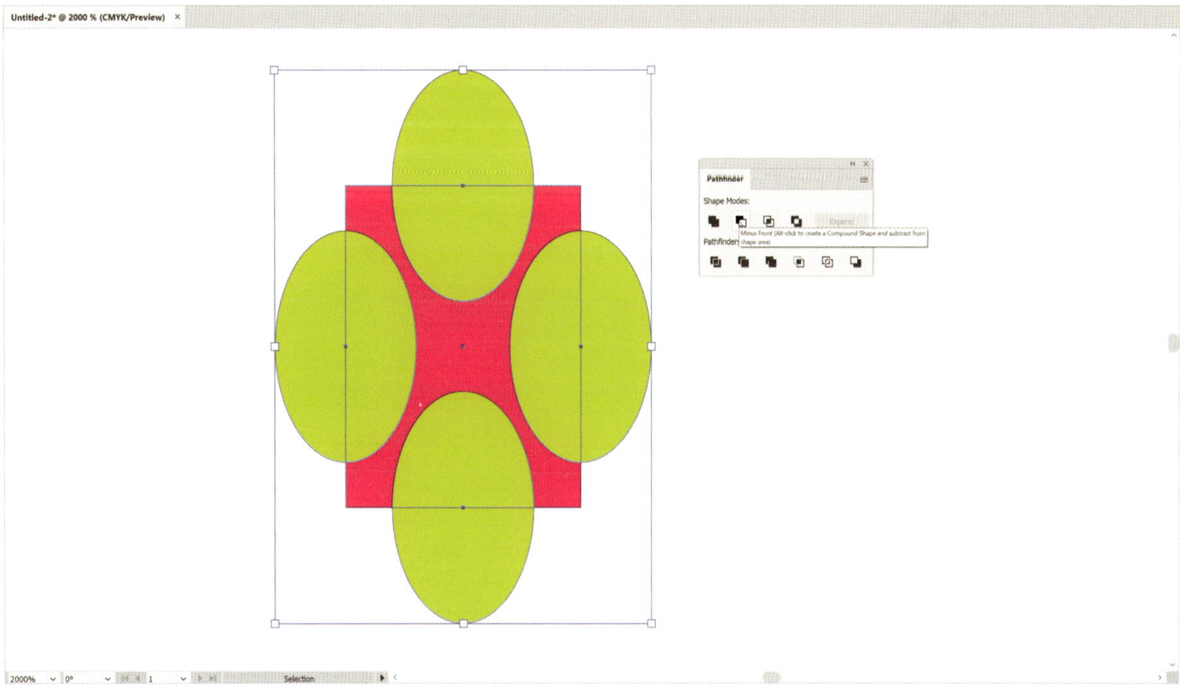

Figure 6.68 Open the *Pathfinder* panel. Select the rectangle and the four ellipses. In the *Pathfinder* panel, click on *Minus Front*, which should be the second from the top left button. You may want to change the color of the mesh and *Scale* it to an appropriate size before the next step.

Step 4: Before we make the pattern, you may want to *Scale* the tile and change the color. Once you have the tile the right color and size for what you need, make the pattern. Click on *Object* → *Pattern* → *Make* to make the pattern, as shown in Figure 6.69. Adjust the bounding box, if necessary and name the texture before clicking *Done*.

Remember that this makes a texture with transparent holes. You will typically have to use a copy of the intended shape with the mesh texture each time you use it. Figure 6.70 shows how the pattern is transparent and needs another solid shape beneath it.

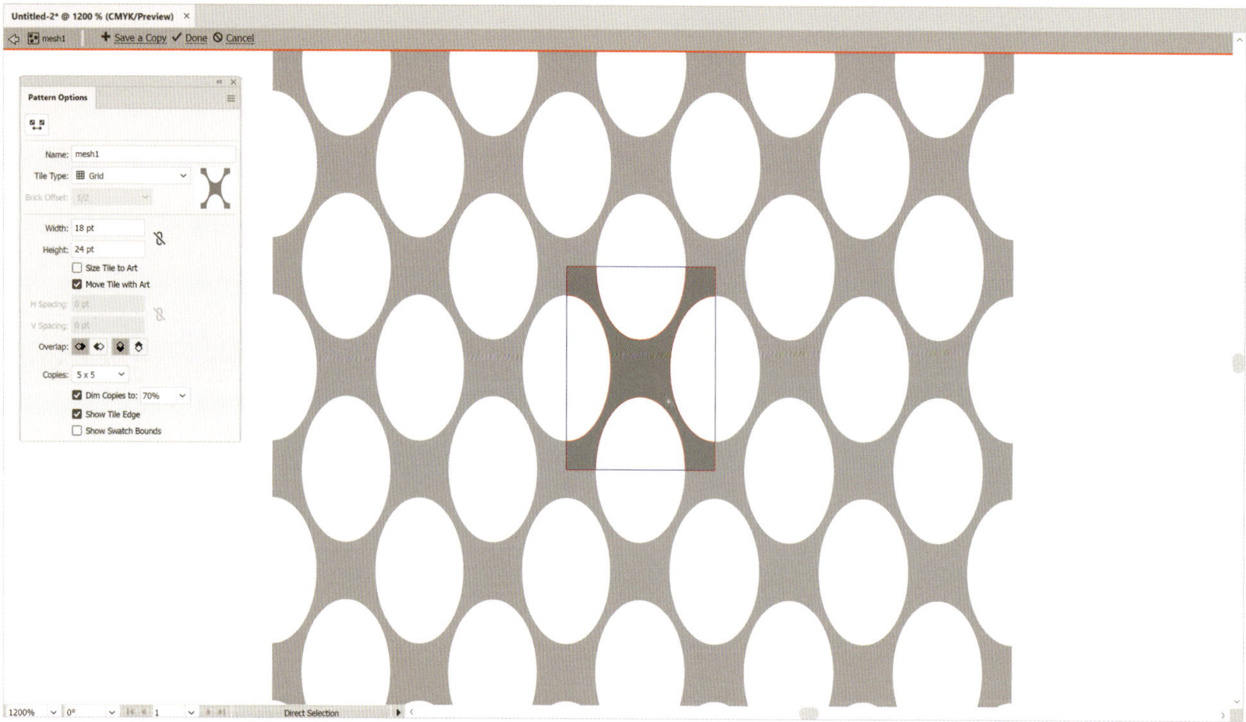

Figure 6.69 Select the shape once the ellipses have been deleted from the rectangle. Click *Object* → *Pattern* → *Make* to create the pattern fill. Name the texture and adjust the bounding box, if necessary. Then click *Done*.

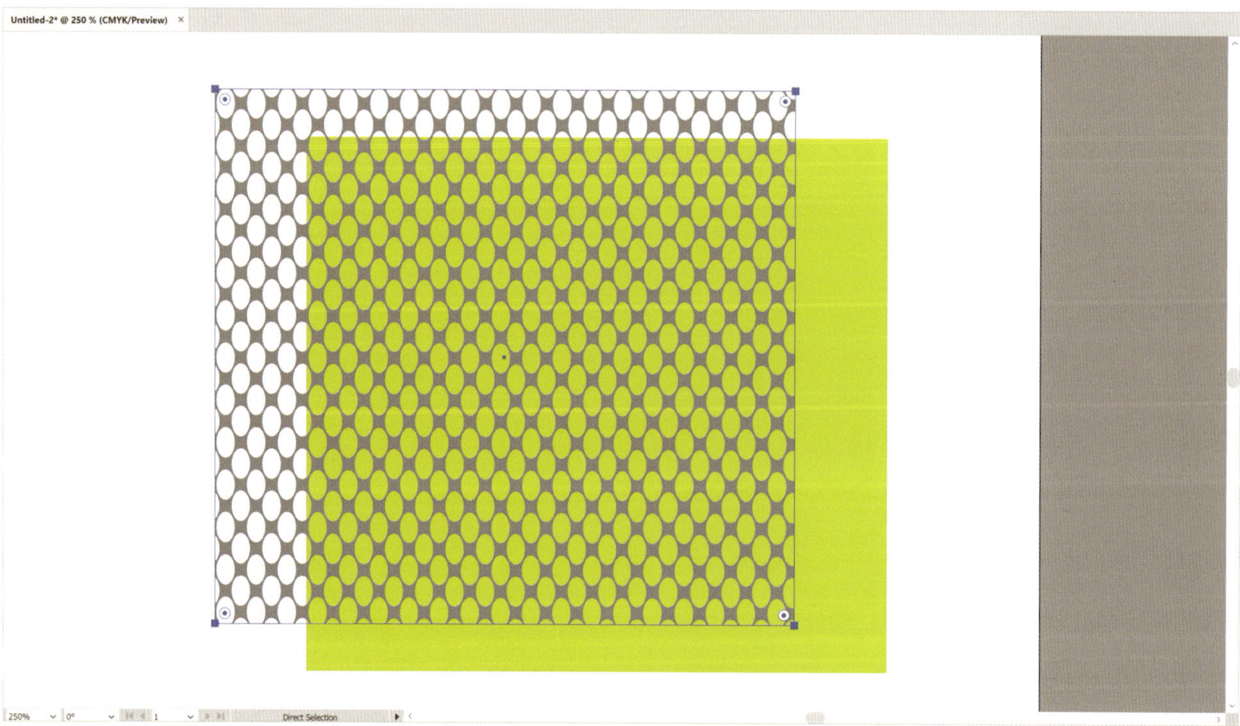

Figure 6.70 The mesh texture will be transparent. So, it will typically need to be used on top of another layer.

The next texture is made entirely in Photoshop, except for the part of making it into an Illustrator pattern swatch. However, not only is it a very useful pattern swatch, but it is also the base for the layered Illustrator sequin texture that follows. This technique makes a glitter swatch that can also represent sparkle knit.

Figure 6.71 The glitter texture is created in Photoshop. Draw a vector square to use as the base. The authors used 30% gray as the fill and no stroke. The square was drawn at 288 pts square, but it can be smaller.

Step 1: In Photoshop, make a vector rectangle. Make sure the rectangle has a gray fill and no stroke color. The authors used 30% gray as the fill color. Make the *Rectangle* somewhere between 144 pts square and 288 pts square. This makes a solid rectangle, like Figure 6.71. We are going to add texture to the rectangle, but to do this, we need to rasterize it. In the *Layers* panel, *right-click* on the rectangle layer and click on *Rasterize Layer*.

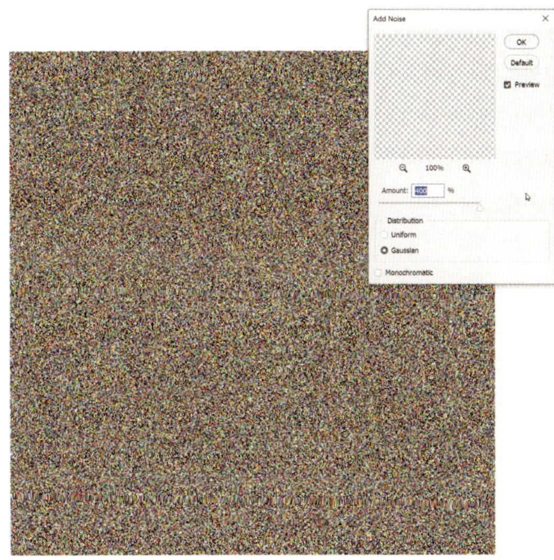

Figure 6.72 In the *Layers* panel, *right-click* on the rectangle layer and choose *Rasterize Layer*. Then, click *Filter* → *Noise* → *Add Noise*. Choose *Gaussian* and move the slider up to the maximum amount. Click *OK*.

Step 2: Once the square is rasterized, apply a noise filter. Go to *Filter* → *Noise* → *Add Noise*. Once the options box comes up, choose *Gaussian*, then move the slider up to the maximum amount of noise. Click *OK*. The results will look like rainbow static, as shown in Figure 6.72.

Step 3: The rainbow colors are not very effective as a glitter texture except in a few special cases. However, the monochromatic option of noise is *too* black and white. We need some grayscale in the results. So, we will convert the colored image to black and white. Go to *Image → Adjustments → Black and White*. You will need to try different presets or adjust the sliders to find the best settings. The goal is to make the swatch look like glitter. The result should look similar to Figure 6.73.

Step 4: *Save* the Photoshop document. Then *Open* it in Illustrator. You may want to *Scale* the image to make the glitter speckles a little larger. After you are satisfied with the look of the swatch, make the pattern. Save the *Swatch Library* so we can use it when making the next pattern.

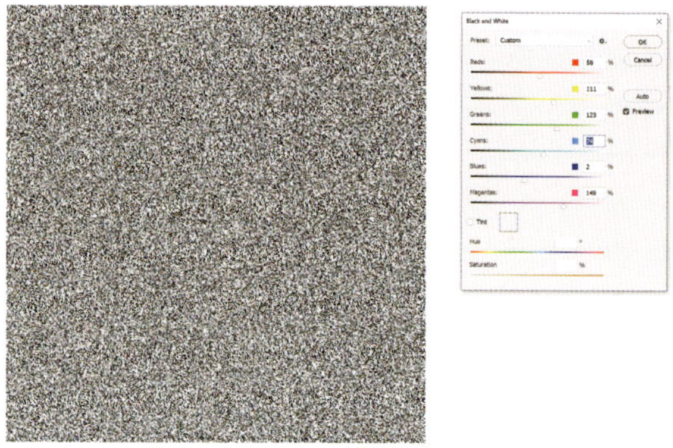

Figure 6.73 Click on *Image → Adjustments → Black and White*. Try different presets then adjust the sliders until you get a good balance of black and white. The result should resemble silver glitter. *Save* the Photoshop document. *Open* the document in Illustrator. Adjust the scale as needed, then make the pattern.

This next technique makes a fabric that resembles glitter knit fabric with foiled sequins. It is also our first layered texture. This is another pattern build that works best with the grid turned on. Click *View → Show Grid*. You will also want to turn on *View → Snap to Grid* so the objects align to the grid.

Step 1: Start by making a perfect circle using the *Ellipse* tool and holding the *Shift* key. Open the *Swatches* panel and go to *Open Swatches Library → Gradients → Metals*. Pick a metal gradient you like and fill the circle with the gradient. The authors used Silver. Adjust the gradient fill so only part of it shows. The circle should look mostly dark or mostly light. You may also want to adjust the angle. Use the *Gradient* tool to make these adjustments.

Step 2: Make a *Copy* of the circle and move the copy two grids over. Use the *Gradient* tool again and adjust the gradient on the new circle. Make sure the angle stays the same but adjust the light versus dark positioning of the gradient. Make a third copy of the circle and move it to the next position in the grid. Adjust the gradient again. You will want three to four versions of the circle in total. At least one should be very light and at least one should be dark.

Step 3: Using these three to four master circles, *Copy* and *Paste* circles randomly in a grid pattern. The second row of circles should be offset from the first row, as you see in Figure 6.74, and should have the same number of circles. Work the circles into a tile that is big enough that a repeat in the circles will not be easily noticeable. Have an even number of rows so the repeat will work correctly.

Step 4: When you have all the circles in place, *Group* the circles. Then draw a *Rectangle* around the group. Make sure the rectangle aligns with the *grid*, not the circles. *Arrange* the rectangle and *Send to the Back* (behind the circle group). *Select* the rectangle and the circle group. *Group* again. Your group should look similar to Figure 6.74.

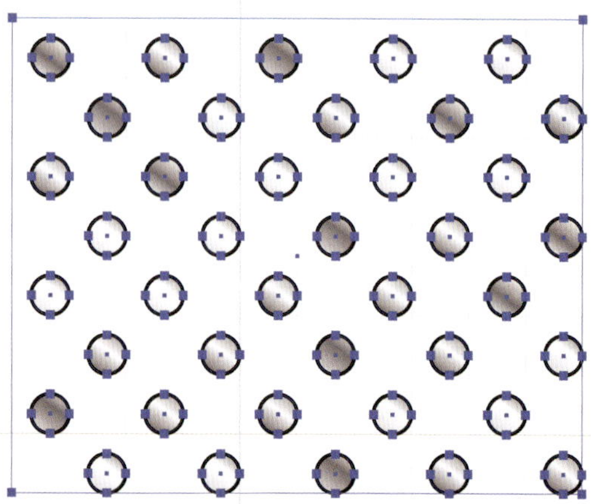

Figure 6.74 Turn on *View → Show Grid* and *View → Snap to Grid* before starting this build. Draw one circle that is on the grid. Set the fill to a gradient. The authors used a premade metal gradient from the Illustrator *Swatches Library*. Use the *Gradient* tool to manipulate the gradient to look how you want. *Copy* the circle and *Paste* it so there is one grid between the first and second circle. Manipulate the gradient fill so it is different from the first. *Copy* and *Paste* the circle again. Make at least three different versions of the circle. Start filling the grid with copied versions of the circle, changing which version of the circle goes in each spot. Fill a large enough swatch that the repeat is not easily noticeable.

Step 5: The completed tile has no background, as you will notice in Figure 6.75. So, before we make the pattern, we will give it a background using the glitter pattern we previously made. In *Isolation Mode*, select the rectangle that is located at the bottom of the group. *Fill* the rectangle with the glitter pattern fill we previously made and set the stroke to none. Exit *Isolation Mode*. *Select* the finished tile and make the pattern.

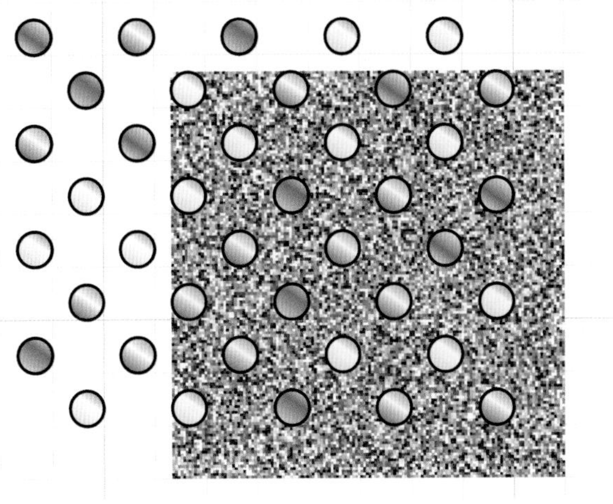

Figure 6.75 The sequin swatch on top of the glitter swatch. The sequins are most effective on top of the glitter texture. To make the final sequin texture fill, place a rectangle of glitter fill behind the sequin swatch. Make sure the rectangle is exactly the size of the repeat. Choose both swatches and *Group* them before making the pattern.

Recoloring the pattern can be more complicated because of the full range of grays from full black to full white. Plus, we have two sets of images. There are a few easy tricks to try and one method that is almost always successful. These techniques can be executed in the *Pattern Editor* or on the original tile.

First, you can try placing an additional rectangle on top of the tile. Make the rectangle a solid color (of the color you want) with no stroke. Experiment with the *Blend Modes* of the rectangle in the *Transparency* panel to see if any of the modes will create a successful coloring effect. Modes that may work include *Color*, *Darken*, *Multiply*, *Overlay*, among others. The success of each mode depends on the color you are working with.

The next method you can try for recoloring the pattern is using *Edit → Edit Colors*. *Recolor*, *Recolor with Preset*, and *Generative Recolor* can all be used. However, these may be more successful on the circles than the glitter background. You may also need to start with the *Generative Recolor* to get color to register instead of gray. Try prompts like "gold sequins" to get good results. Once the sequins are colored, it is easier to adjust the colors by hand.

As mentioned, *Edit Colors* may not adjust the background color and you may not like the results of a colored rectangle placed on top of the entire tile. However, with just a little more work there is a method to recolor the swatch more successfully by blending the two techniques. You will use *Edit Colors* to recolor the sequins again. Once the sequins are satisfactory, we will work on the background.

To color the glitter background, use the colored rectangle method. Make a rectangle the same size as the tile. Set the fill of the rectangle to the color you need and set the stroke to none. This time, *Arrange* the rectangle so it is behind the sequins, but in front of the glitter background. Adjust the *Blend Mode* of colored rectangle in the *Transparency* panel until it gives the color effect you want. This double technique method should give you a successful colored swatch in most cases.

To help sparkly textures look more convincing, you may want to add a few little starbursts to your rendering when you use the textures. You can also add tiny, blurred circles of white instead of starbursts, if you want a more realistic effect. The rendering in Figure 6.76 uses the sequin texture on her coat and the glitter texture on her boots. Starbursts were added to both. The rendering also uses the mesh pattern on her legs to represent fishnet stockings. Because the mesh pattern is transparent, there are two copies of each leg. The back copy of each leg is filled with skin color and the top copy of each is filled with the mesh pattern.

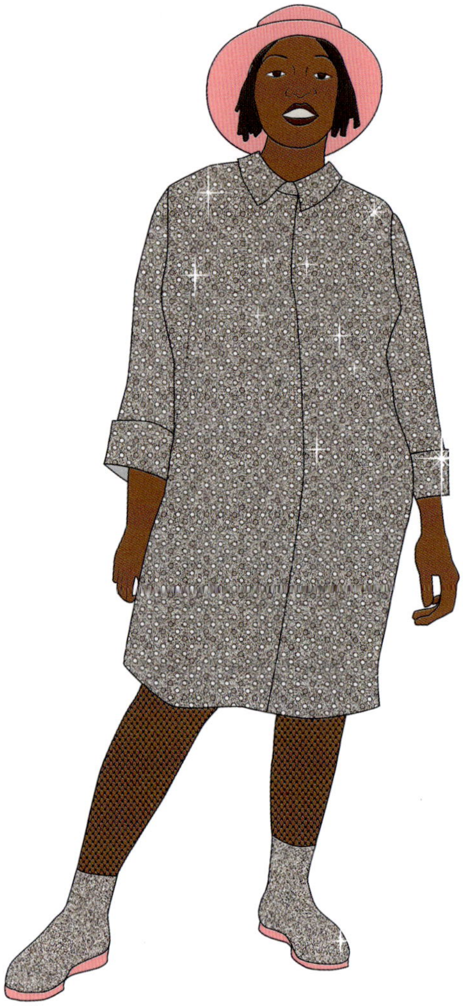

Figure 6.76 Rendered figure using various texture pattern fills. The figure's coat is filled with the sequin texture pattern fill. Her shoes are filled with glitter fill. Her legs have a second copy of each leg. The bottom copy is the original skin color, and the top copy contains the mesh fill to mimic fishnet hose. Finally, a few starbursts were added on the coat and one shoe to help make the sparkle effect more convincing.

Layer Effects

Just as with Photoshop, we can use layer effects to create different texture looks in Illustrator. One of the most useful applications for layer effects is for using and customizing generic or grayscale texture patterns. Pattern tiles can be made in Illustrator or Photoshop and imported into Illustrator. If the tiles are made in black and white, they can be easily reused every time you need that texture. It takes less time and effort to make a black-and-white texture match your custom color than it does to recolor a previously colored texture tile. We will create a herringbone texture to explore layer effects in Illustrator.

Herringbone is an easy texture to make in Illustrator because it is a repeating V shape. The herringbone we make will be a continuous V pattern; however, a broken herringbone is just as easy to make. Just adjust the initial V shape.

Step 1: It is easy for herringbone to disappear in a rendering when it is drawn too small. To prevent this problem, we will use precise measurements. Feel free to adjust the measurements to meet your needs.

Using the *Rectangle* tool, click on the page so you can enter a measurement. The square should be 60 pt by 60 pt. The square should have no stroke and a solid fill. White may give the best results for a herringbone background. However, our examples show a gray background because white does not show well in print.

With the *Pen* tool, draw the V. It should start at the upper left corner of the square, go to the mid-point on the bottom of the square, and end at the upper right corner of the square, as shown in Figure 6.77. Set the stroke weight to 1 pt with rounded caps and rounded joins. The fill is set to none, but the stroke is a solid color and probably black.

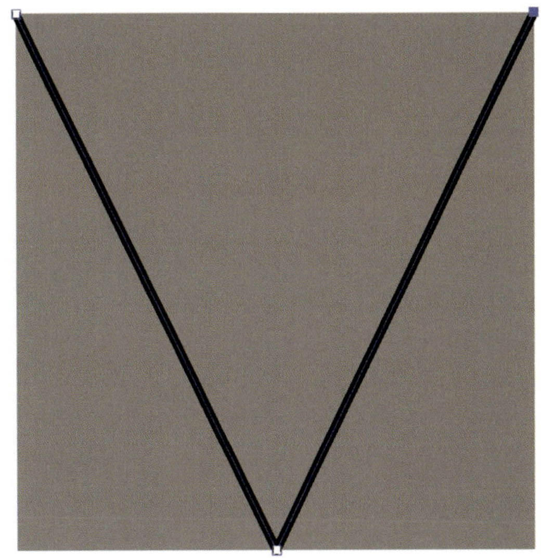

Figure 6.77 Starting the herringbone texture pattern. Create a square (*Rectangle*) that is 60 pt by 60 pt. It should have no stroke and a solid fill. The example shows a gray fill (because it shows up in print), but a white fill often works better. Draw the first V of the pattern using the *Pen* tool. The line goes from the upper left corner of the square to the bottom center and back up to the upper right corner. The *Stroke* is 1 pt in weight with no fill. Use rounded caps and rounded joins. Black stroke works well.

Step 2: We will *Copy* the V in measured vertical steps both upward and downward until the Vs cover the entire square. The step increment (measurement) must be a number that divides into the size of the square. Otherwise, the repeat will not work. For the exercise, we use steps of 6 pt because that divides evenly into the square height of 60 pt. (Math! Egad!)

Select the V. *Move* and *Copy* (in a single action) new Vs 6 pts apart in the vertical direction. A good way to do this is to use *Object → Transform → Move*. The *Horizontal Position* box entry should be zero because we are only moving vertically. Enter 6 pt in the *Vertical Position* box (as you see in Figure 6.78a) then click *Copy*. This will make a copy of the V in the downward direction. To make additional copies, you can use the shortcut *control+d / command+d* for *Transform Again*. This repeats the most recent transformation action. Copy the Vs downward until the Vs completely clear the bottom of the square.

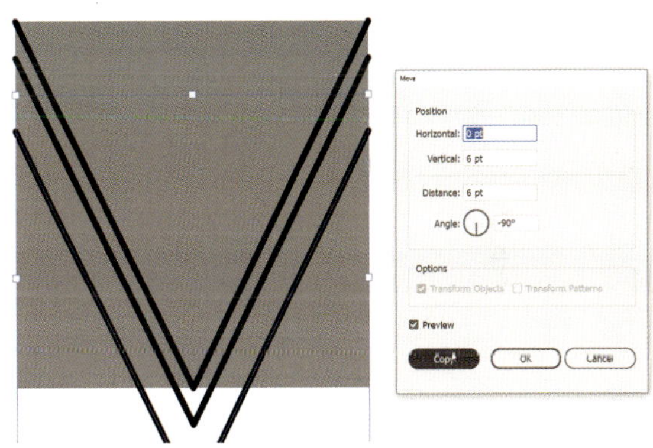

Figure 6.78a Building out the texture. *Copy* the V vertically upward and downward until the Vs cover the full square. Use the *Move* function under *Object → Transform*. Enter 6 pt in the *Vertical Position* box and 0 in the *Horizontal* position box and click *Copy* to copy the V downward. Repeat the action by using the shortcut *control+d / command+d* until the top legs of the V clear the bottom of the square. To start copying upward, *Re-Select* the original V. Go to the *Move* function again. This time, enter -6 pt (negative) in the *Vertical Position* box. Then *Copy*.

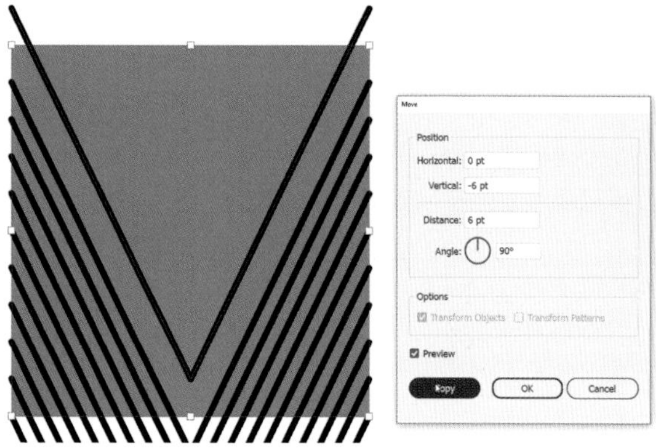

Figure 6.78b *Control+d / command+d* to repeat until the bottom point of the V clears the top of the square.

To copy the Vs in the other direction, reselect the original V. Then repeat the *Object → Transform → Move* action. This time, use negative (–) 6 pt as the *Vertical Position* amount as displayed in Figure 6.78b. After the first upward copy is made, use the *Transform Again* shortcut (*control+d / command+d*) to copy Vs upward until the Vs complete clear the top of the square as shown in Figure 6.78c. Select *all* the Vs and *Group* them.

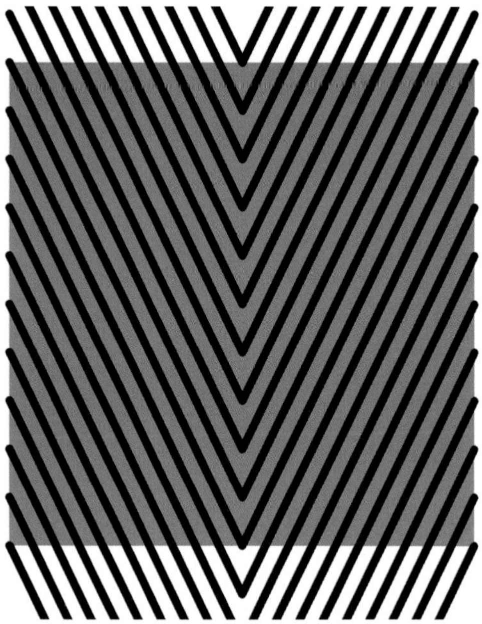

Figure 6.78c Select all the Vs and *Group* them.

Step 3: To remove the parts of the Vs that extend past the base square, we must make a *Clipping mask*. If you remember, Illustrator requires that the clipping shape (the cookie cutter) goes on top of what needs to be trimmed. It also removes the color from the clipping shape.

Make a copy of the original base square and paste it on top of the group of Vs. An easy way to do this is to select the square in the *Layers* panel, hold the *alt/opt* key and drag the square the thumbnail of the square to the top of object stack in the panel as you see in Figure 6.79a. The *alt/opt* key will create a copy of the object as you are dragging it.

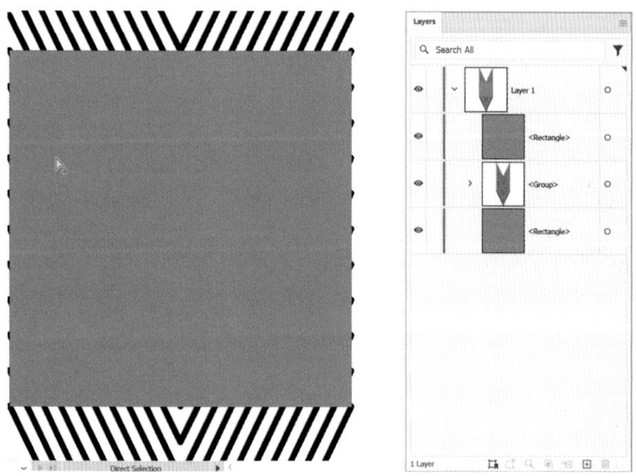

Figure 6.79a Clipping the texture to make a tile. Make a *Copy* of the base square and *Place* it in front of the group of Vs.

Select the new top square and the group of Vs. Make a *Clipping mask* using these two objects. You can do this through the *Layers* panel *Options* menu or, as shown in Figure 6.79b, through the *Object* menu. This will trim away the extending parts of the Vs and the clipping square will no longer be visible. *Select* all the parts of the new herringbone tile, including the base square, and *Group* them.

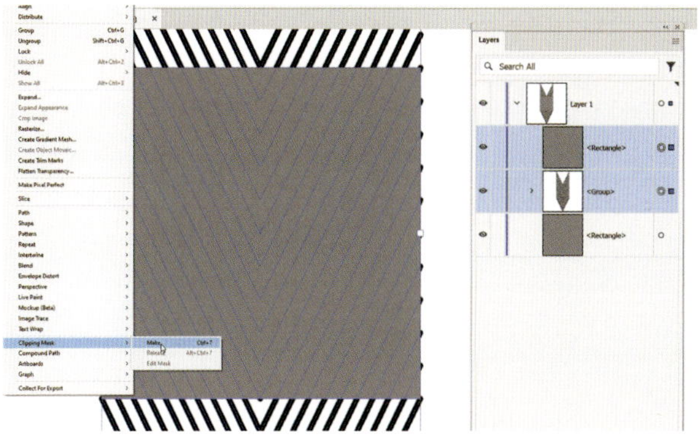

Figure 6.79b *Select* the new top square and the group of Vs. Make a *Clipping mask* to clip away the portions of the Vs that extend beyond the square.

Step 4: Time to make the tile into a pattern, using the methods previously learned. *Select* the tile and make it into a pattern. While you are in the *Pattern Editor*, adjust the tile *Bounding Box* so the repeat size matches the tile. You can use the *Pattern Tile* tool to fix the *Bounding Box*. The tile size should be 60 pt by 60 pt, which is the size of the original base square. Figure 6.80 shows how the pattern should look when it is adjusted correctly. The pattern is now located in the *Swatches* panel. If you need to use the pattern in other documents, save the *Swatches Library*.

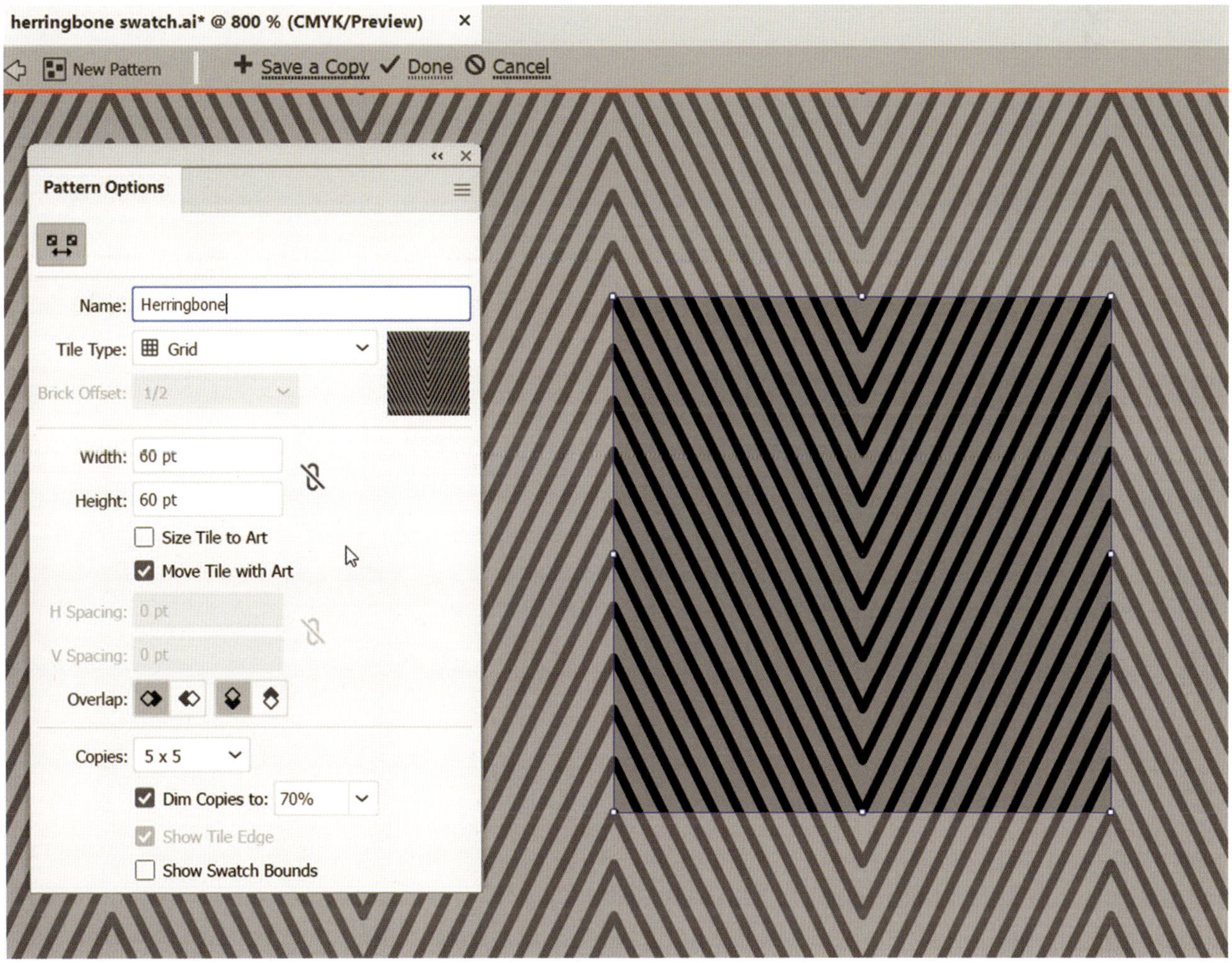

Figure 6.80 Making the texture pattern tile. *Select* and *Group* all the parts of the tile together. Make the pattern tile as discussed in Chapter 4. Use the *Pattern Tile* tool to make sure there is no white space between the tiles and that the repeat is 60 pt by 60 pt (the size of the square).

Step 5: Now we finally use our texture pattern fill and utilize layer effects. The essence of layer effects is that the layers, or in this case objects, will interact with each other using *Blending Modes*, *Opacity*, and similar adjustments. This requires more than one layer or object for the interaction to work. For this project, we will use double copies of each object that we are working on.

We will use the skirt for this project. Fill each shape that makes the skirt front with a solid color. Make a duplicate copy of each of these objects. The duplicate should be directly above the original in the *Layers* panel, as you can see in Figure 6.81. Fill the duplicates with the herringbone texture. The original color will not be visible at this point. If you need to change the *Scale* or *Rotation* of the texture pattern, use the methods you learned in Chapter 4. You can also *Warp* the pattern if you like.

Now, *Select* the objects that contain the texture pattern fill. Using the *Transparency* panel, adjust the *Blending Mode* and the *Opacity* until the texture blends with the background color successfully. Different base color and texture pattern combinations will require different *Blending Modes* and *Opacities*. The example in Figure 6.82 has a light blue base and the texture is black and white. The *Blending Mode* is set to *Color Burn* and the *Opacity* is 50%.

To ramp up this technique, you can try adding an additional copy of an object and apply a filter to the duplicate layer. Then adjust the *Blending Mode* and the *Opacity* again. For instance, maybe you want a tweedy herringbone. You could add a layer of noise (such as a *Mezzotint* filter). Then blend the objects together. Many of the techniques in this chapter can be combined. It is just a matter of experimentation.

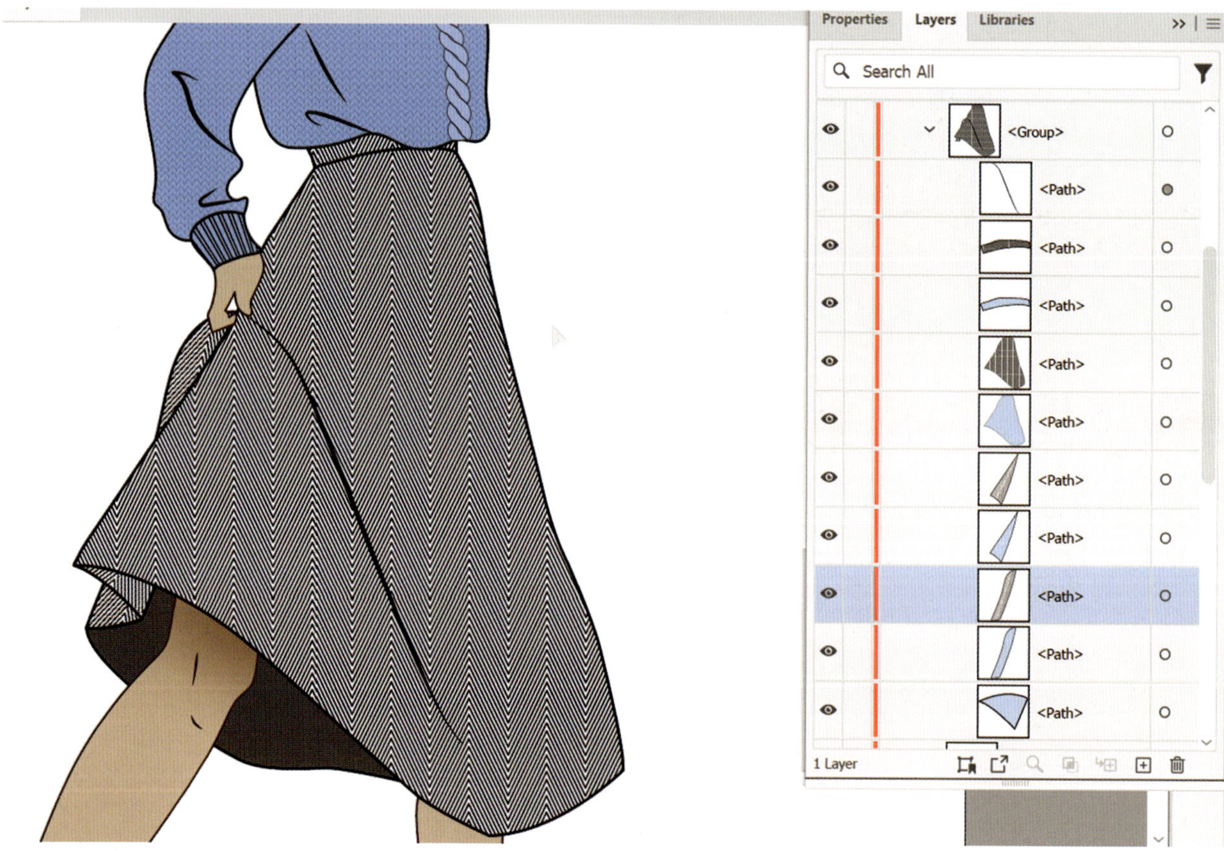

Figure 6.81 Preparing the texture for use in a rendering. To use a colorless texture pattern in Illustrator, make two copies of every object that needs the texture pattern. Make the bottom copy of each object with a solid color fill. Fill the top copy with the texture pattern fill.

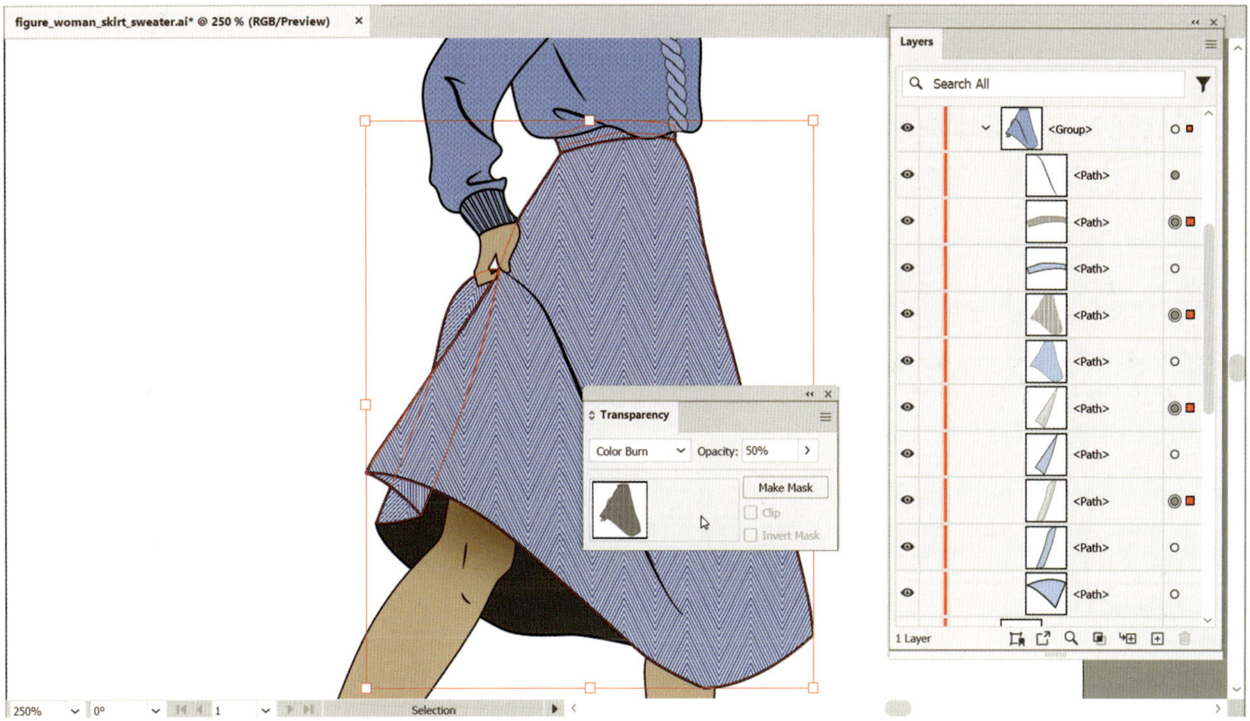

Figure 6.82 Select the texture pattern filled objects. Using the *Transparency* panel, try different *Blend Modes* and *Opacities* to achieve the desired look. This example shows a *Color Burn Blend Mode* and *50% Opacity*.

Troubleshooting

"Why won't my sequins overlap?"

Make sure it's a *Scatter brush*. A *Pattern brush* will not allow overlaps. Then check *Brush Settings*. The *Spacing* should be set at approximately 50%. Check the *Size* in the settings. If the *Size* is not set at 100%, the *Spacing* will need adjusting.

Finally, make sure that you did not include any random objects when grouping the parts of the sequin. A stray anchor point will affect the size of the bounding box and, therefore, the spacing.

"Every time I use my new texture or brush, Illustrator freezes up. What did I do wrong?"

Traced brushes and patterns can be troublesome if the number of anchor points generated during the tracing process hasn't been reduced enough. *Open* the pattern swatch or original brush tile to try different ways of reducing the size of the pattern of brush. Before you attempt to reduce the anchor points, *Scale* the swatch or tile smaller, if design allows.

Try *Simplify*. *Select* the objects you want to simplify. Then go to *Object* → *Path* → *Simplify*. Click on the ellipses to get the advanced controls. Then work with the sliders to try different results.

If *Simplify* does not work well for you, you can remove anchor points manually. Use the *Pen* tool or the *Delete Anchor Point* tool to remove the extra points. Then use the *Direct Select* tool to adjust and reshape the paths as needed.

Sometimes you can delete whole shapes. Because the pattern or brush is going to be small, details are often unnecessary or lost. Get rid of any unneeded shapes.

After you reduce the details of your brush tile or pattern tile, you will have to remake the brush or pattern. You probably want to delete the old version from your library so you don't try to use it and subsequently crash the computer again.

If all these efforts still do not result in a usable brush or pattern, realize that (1) some brushes or patterns will not work well, and it is better to find a simpler version as a substitute, and (2) some computers are just not robust enough to handle complicated files.

"What do I do if my texture does not work well with any combination of *Layer Blending Modes* and Opacity for layer effects?"

1. There are a few basic changes you can make that may give you better results. Try different colors on your pattern swatch. Different combinations of black/white/gray may give better results. If you started with black and white, try gray and black or white and gray.
2. Adjust the base colors of base shapes. Try a lighter, darker, brighter, or duller version of your base color. The variation may work better with the *Blend Mode* of the texture.

Special Textures

There are a lot, and we mean a LOT, of textures out there. For the most part, you need to start to combine your knowledge of the program with a good dose of imagination for each unique texture. Look to photographic sources and consider the properties of the materials. Does it reflect or absorb light? Is it smooth or rough? Does color play into the texture? What does the edge look like? Is it transparent? All of these questions help lead you to rendering possibilities.

We have a few suggestions for some fun textures here. We used Photoshop for the examples simply to provide a variety of solutions; however, we often explain how to make the texture in Illustrator. Remember, there are many ways to achieve similar results in these programs. Feel free to try alternative methods demonstrated by other instructors. As you build your knowledge and familiarity with the tools, try experimenting to create your own texture effects!

Project 6.3: Leather

There are many different types of leather and pleather options available. Spend time studying your leather. Many times, you do not need to create a "special" texture as the effect does not show from the distance of looking at a full-length figure. However, you may want to incorporate texture into close-up views of specific garments or accessories. Or perhaps it shows "just enough" to make a difference. You will have to make that call.

Leather tends to show some color variation, so we often start with the *Render Clouds* filter effect in Photoshop. We can use this as the basis for suede, a smooth leather, slightly textured leather, or heavily textured leather. These weight variations affect where and how you use the leather in adornment. Some leathers are primarily used for accessories rather than clothing. So, keep the weight of the leather in mind as well as the texture when designing with it.

We will start with the simplest texture and lightest weight of leather: suede. There are weights within suede, as well, but the texture tends to have the same "scuffed" appearance. For this project, we will create textures that can then be defined as a pattern in Photoshop. Alternatively, you can apply the filters directly to your rendering or even simply paint in a similar texture with your *Brush* tool. Keep in mind that every texture we address in this book can be achieved in many different ways.

Step 1: create a new 1000 by 1000 pixel document in Photoshop. You can keep the document settings at 300 ppi and RGB color mode.[1] Select a *Foreground* and *Background* color that are near to each other on the color spectrum that coincide with your leather color.

Step 2: In the top menu bar, go to *Filter* → *Render*→ *Clouds*. This is a lovely little filter that has been with Photoshop for many, many years. There are no settings to adjust. It simply uses your foreground and background colors to create a fuzzy, mottled effect. Figure 6.83 shows our result from the *Render Clouds* filter using two brown colors.

Figure 6.83 Set your Foreground and Background colors, then use the *Render Clouds* filter found in the *Filters* menu to create this effect.

Step 3: Add some noise to break up the smoothness of the effect. Go to the *Filters* menu and choose *Noise → Add Noise*. When the dialog box appears, adjust your settings until the image looks more like the scuffed appearance of suede as shown in Figure 6.84. We chose to set the *Amount* at 7%, *Uniform Distribution*, and tick the box for *Monochromatic*.

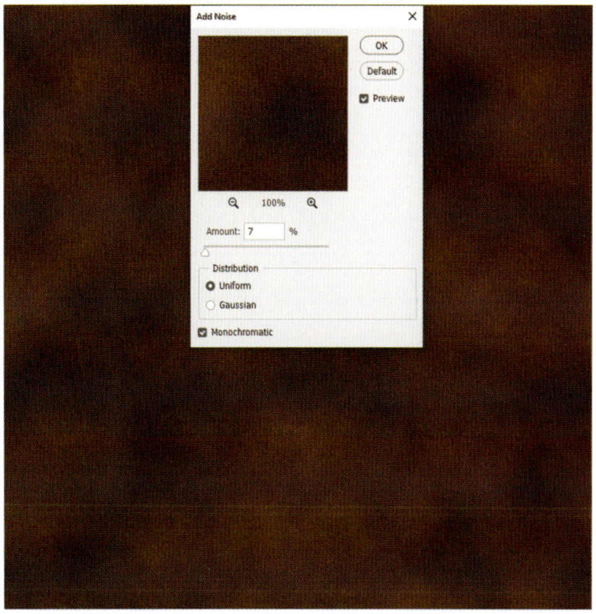

Figure 6.84 Adjust your settings to create the rougher texture of suede.

Step 4: Turn your image into a pattern. In the top menu bar under *Edit*, choose *Define Pattern* and name your pattern. Now it is ready to apply as a *Pattern Fill Layer* to your garment rendering. You can use SwankPants.psd or your own figure. Figure 6.85 shows our suede texture applied with some shading. Suede mostly absorbs light, so don't be too heavy-handed with the highlights on this texture.

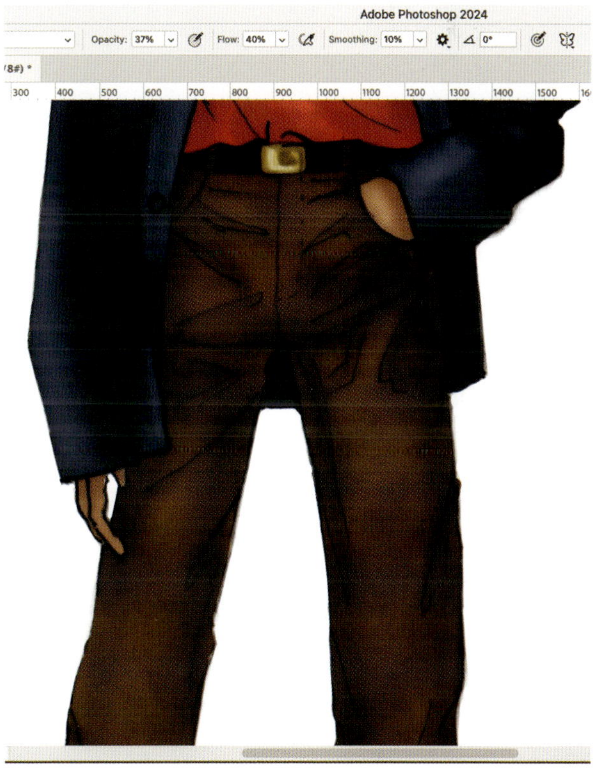

Figure 6.85 Apply your suede texture to the garment. Add shading and highlights. Suede absorbs light, so keep your highlights minimal to communicate the correct texture.

Smooth leather for jackets or pants is often heavier than suede. It has a slight grain and can have a soft shine. Let's take a look at leather now.

Step 1: Start the smooth leather the same way as the suede, by creating a mottled base. Create a 1000 by 1000 pixel document with a 300 ppi resolution. Choose a *Foreground* and *Background* color that are close to each other. Render a *Clouds* filter on the document.

Step 2: It is time to create a leather texture. Open the *Filter Gallery* through the *Filters* menu. As you can see in Figure 6.86, we will use the *Texturizer* filter in the *Texture* folder. Choose the *Sandstone* texture for this leather. You can try different settings until you get the effect you like. Although the texture does not show well in the screenshot, you should have a slightly grainy or porous texture. We used 100% *Scaling*, *Relief* 2, and *Top Right Light*. Click *OK* when you are satisfied with the texture.

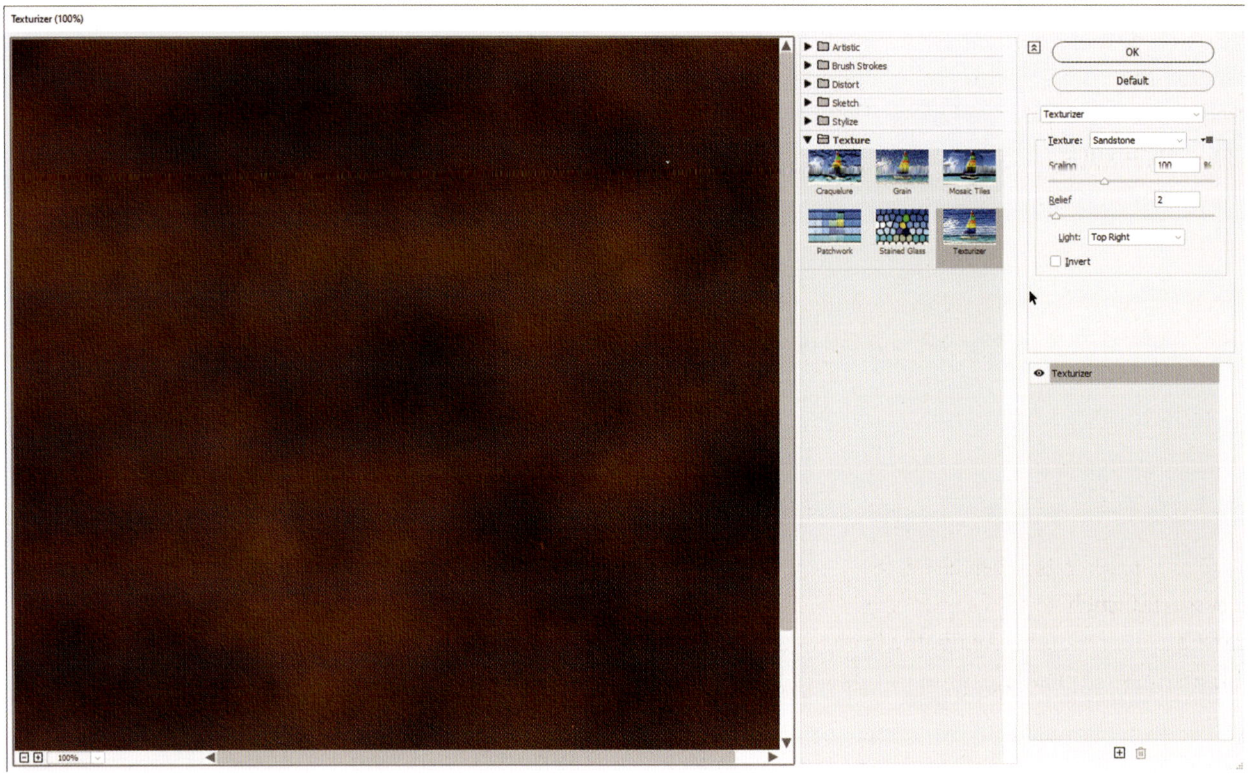

Figure 6.86 Use the same *Render Clouds* filter as your base for regular leather. You can then add the *Texturizer* filter on the *Sandstone* setting to convey the right texture.

Step 3: *Define* your new leather swatch into a *Pattern* through the *Edit* menu. To use the pattern, create a *Pattern Fill Layer* with the pattern fill. Then clip it to the defined shape. Make shadow and highlight layers as needed. Figure 6.87 shows the smooth leather swatch used on the same pants as before. This version has very subtle highlights.

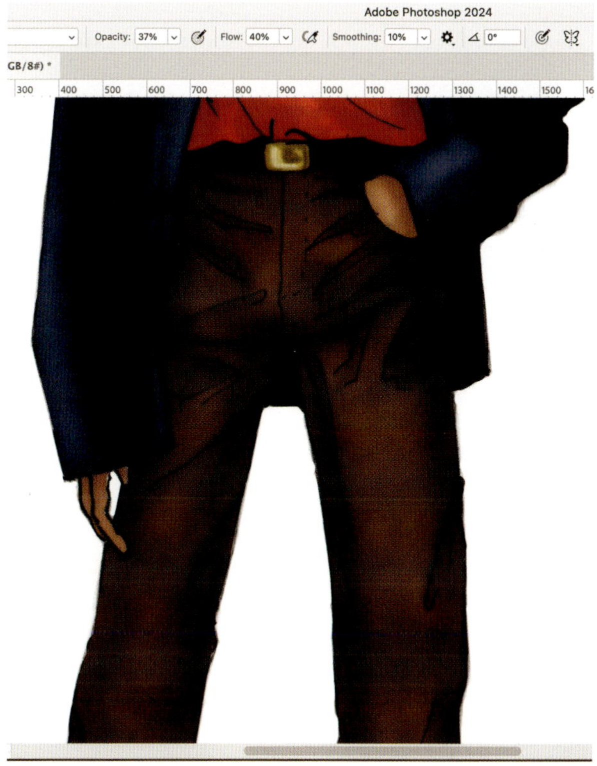

Figure 6.87 Apply your leather texture. Depending on the finish of the leather, it will probably have more highlights than suede. As you can see there is minimal texture difference between suede and leather on a full-sized rendering.

Heavy leather is often used for jackets, coats, and accessories, such as shoes and bags. This version has a more distinctive grain. Again, the leather can have a soft shine or more muted highlights.

Step 1: We need to create the texture for embossing the leather before making the rest of the swatch. Create a 1000 pixel square document with 300 ppi resolution and a white background. Set the *Foreground* and *Background* colors to Default (keystroke *d*).

Step 2: Open the *Filter Gallery* through the *Filter* menu and click on the *Texture* folder. Choose the *Stained Glass* filter. This creates a texture of pebbles or polygons that resemble heavy leather texture. Try different settings until you find a combination that you like. The example in Figure 6.88 uses *Cell Size* 2 and *Border Thickness* 1. The *Light Intensity* does not matter when working in black and white. Click *OK*.

Save the document as a PSD file. If you see lines in the pattern when you use it, return to this original texture file and use *Filter* → *Other* → *Offset*. Use the *Lasso* tool to select around the lines created by the repeat. Then use *Edit* → *Content Aware Fill* to fix the issue.

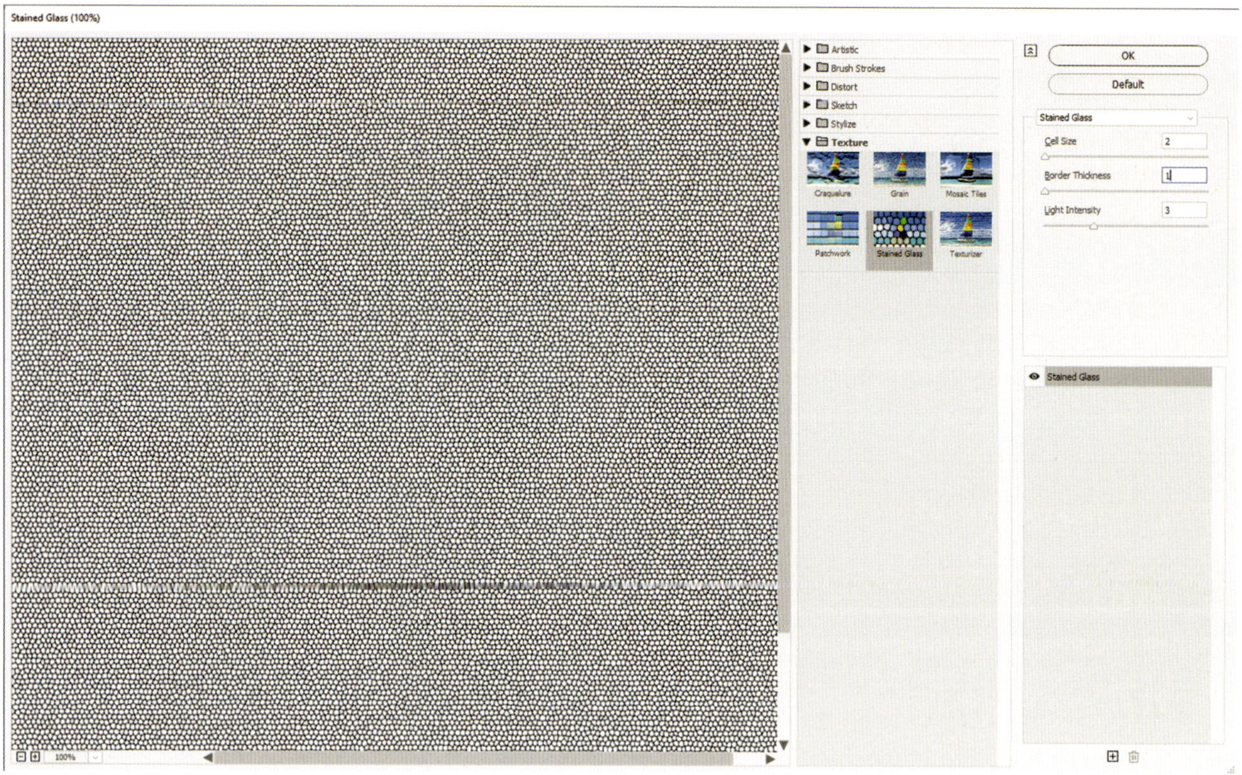

Figure 6.88 Start your accessory weight texture by creating a separate texture file. Texture files are in black and white. Use the *Stained Glass* filter to create the texture and then save your file.

Step 3: Create a 1000 by 1000 pixel square with *Render Clouds*. Use the same methods as outlined in suede or smooth leather.

Step 4: Now it is time to apply the texture we made. Open the *Filter Gallery* and navigate to the *Texturizer Filter* in the *Texture Folder*. Click the tiny *Options* menu button to the right of the *Texture* box. Click *Load Pattern* and then navigate to your saved PSD leather texture file. Adjust the settings for the filter as needed. Figure 6.89 shows the texture with *Scaling* set at 100%, *Relief* at 2, and *Light* as *Top Right*. Click *OK* when you are done.

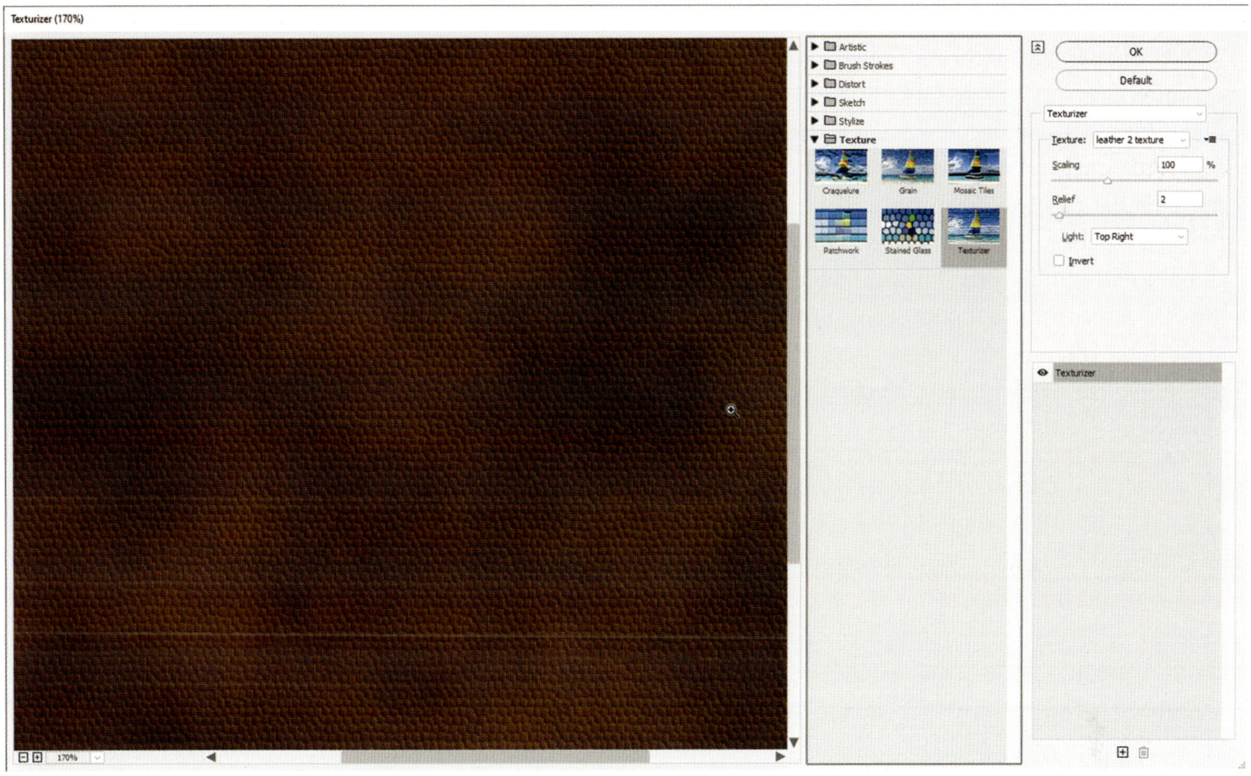

Figure 6.89 After you create a new file and apply the *Render Clouds* filter, load your recently created texture file into the *Texturizer* filter. Adjust the settings to your needs.

Step 5: To use the texture, *Define* the tile as a *Pattern*. Then, create a *Pattern Fill* layer on your rendering with the new pattern. Clip the pattern layer to the defined object. Create shadow and highlight layers as needed. Figure 6.90 demonstrates the heavy leather texture on a jacket.

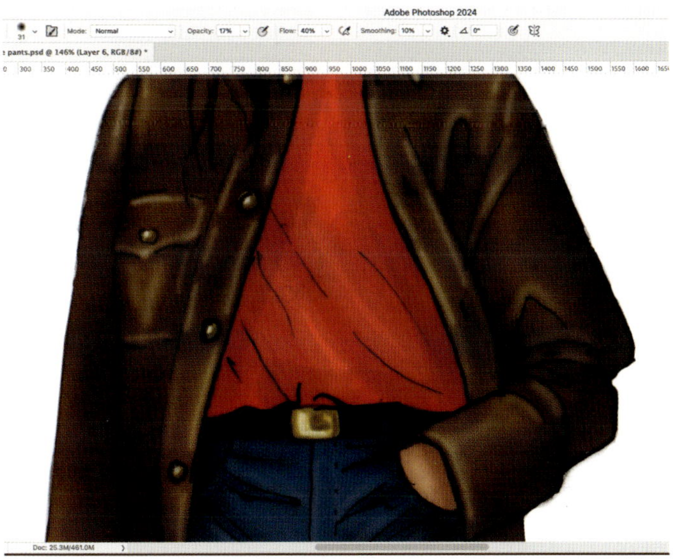

Figure 6.90 Apply your heavy leather texture. This weight is more likely to be used for shoes, bags, and jackets rather than pants or shirts. It is also more likely to show shine and wear around the seams.

Snake, alligator, ostrich, and other specialty leathers require a few extra steps, but still are not difficult to make. One of the most challenging steps is finding a good source image of the leather you want to emulate. You need a flat image of the leather that has even lighting, even coloration, and will be reasonably easy to make a seamless pattern tile with. It helps if the leather texture is similar on the top and bottom edges of the image and similar on the left and right edges, such as the image in Figure 6.91. This will make it much easier to remove obvious breaks in the tiles.

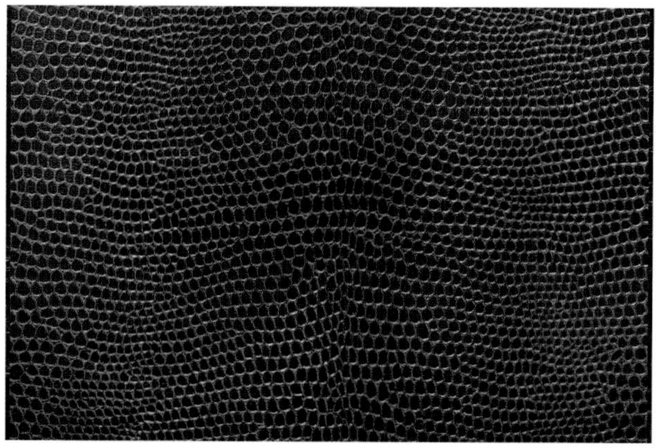

Figure 6.91 Use a flat image of the leather texture you want to emulate. Courtesy of Jacques Barrette via Pixabay.

Step 1: Once you have a good source image for your texture, you need to alter it for use as an embossing texture tile. Start by *Desaturating* it or converting it to *Black and White*. If your image is colored leather, you will probably need to *Invert* the image, so the face is light and the creases are dark, like in Figure 6.92. Adjust the *Levels* so the image is mostly black and white. Some grayscale is fine, but the closer to pure black and white you set the image, the more effective it will be.

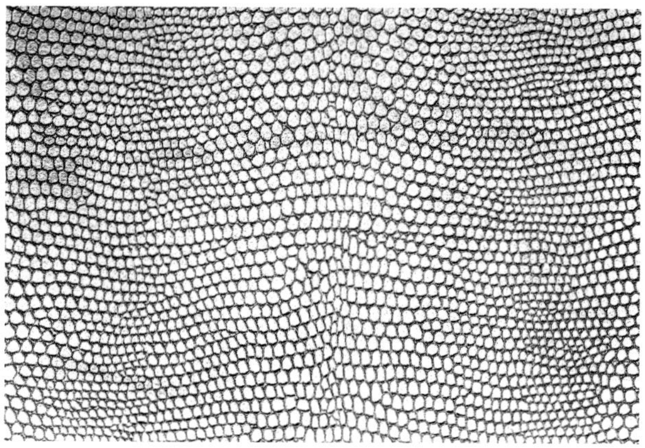

Figure 6.92 Convert your image to black and white by *Desaturating* it, or another method of your choice. *Invert* the image if necessary. Adjust the levels to strengthen the contrast and save your texture.

Step 2: To turn the image into a seamless tile, start by *Cropping* away any part of the image you do not want in the repeat. For the example, we cropped off the narrow solid bars that are visible on the left and right sides of the original image (see Figure 6.91). Go to *Filter → Other → Offset* and adjust the sliders until you can easily see and access the tile repeat vertically and horizontally. If needed, repair the repeat. You can select the problem area with the *Lasso* tool (or similar) and use a *Content Aware Fill* to repair the area. You can also use the *Clone* stamp tool, or you can use a combination of tools. Once you have a seamless texture tile, *Save* the image as a PSD file.

Step 3: Let's now make the specialty leather swatch. This part will be familiar. Start with a 1000 pixel square document set to 300 ppi. Choose two similar colors for your *Foreground* and *Background Swatches*. These will be used to render the base texture. Remember that exotic leathers come in a wide variety of colors. Don't be afraid to play with the swatch choices. *Render Clouds* using the filter again.

Step 4: Open the *Filter Gallery* and go to the *Texture* folder and to the *Texturizer* filter. Load your new exotic leather texture file in the *Texture Box*. Adjust the settings to what works best for your leather. Figure 6.93 shows *Scaling* at 100%, *Relief* at 4, and *Light* at *Top Right*, but different variations can be just as effective. Click *OK* when you like the results. You may want to try the *Offset Filter* again to see if your new tile has any visible seams before using it. If it does, correct the seams as you did before. *Define* the image as a *Pattern*.

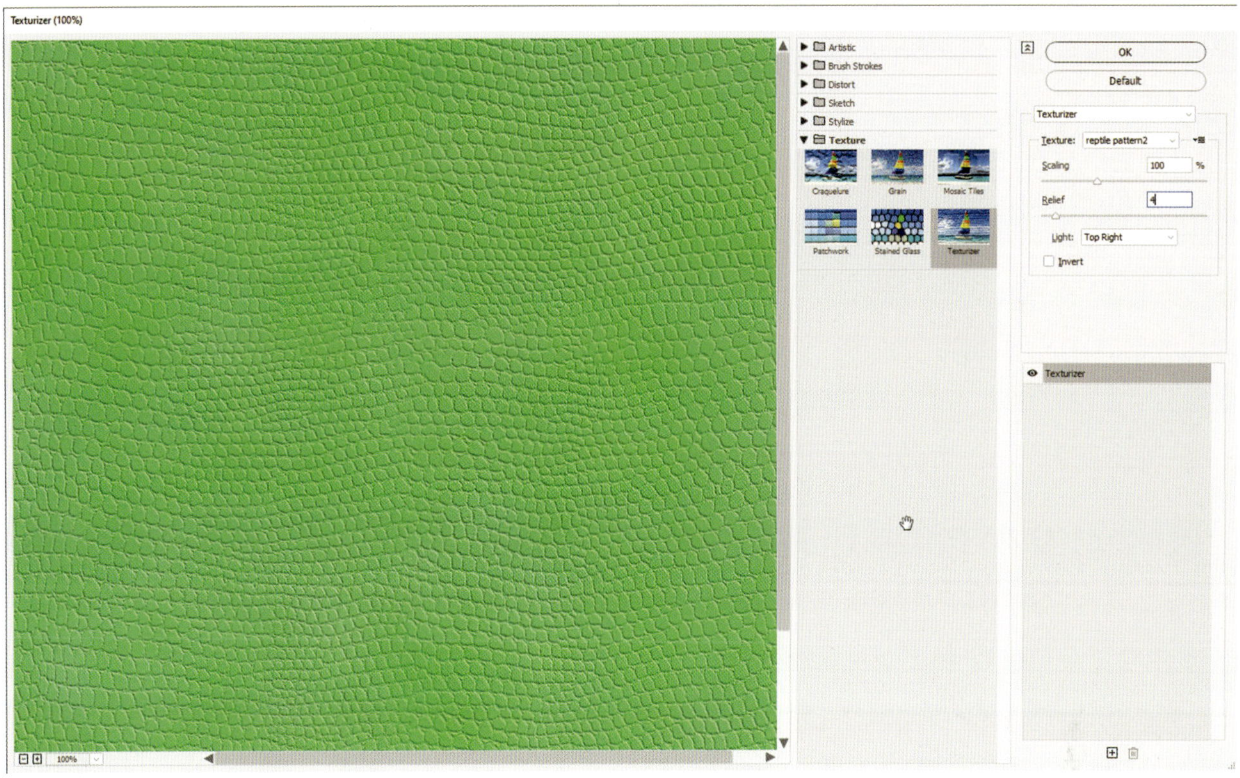

Figure 6.93 Chose your background color or use the *Render Clouds* filter. Apply the *Texturizer* filter and load your recently created texture from the previous step. Adjust the settings to your needs.

Step 5: To use the new exotic leather swatch, create a *Pattern Fill Layer*. Set the pattern to your new texture and adjust the scale of the pattern and blend mode of the layer as needed. Clip the layer to your defined object. You will probably want to create shadow and highlight layers to finish your rendering. Remember to pay attention to the specific reflective qualities of your leather. Figure 6.94 shows the reptile leather used on pants.

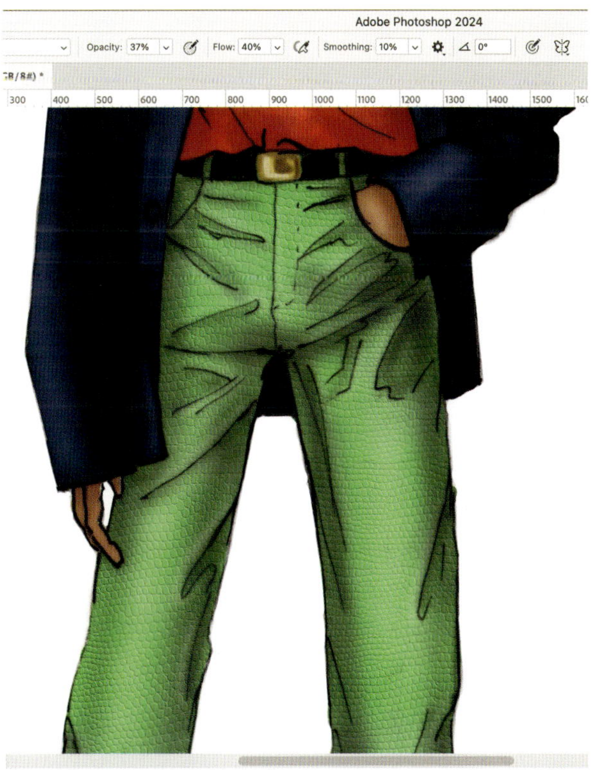

Figure 6.94 Adjust the light and shadows as needed for the reflective properties of your textured leather!

While we made all these leather textures in color, remember that it is easy to adjust the colors with *Adjustments* or *Adjustment Layers*, such as *Hue/Saturation* or *Curves*. You can also create as many textures as you like and add them to your texture library. Just make sure you keep your files organized.

Even though it is easy to create leather pattern fills in Photoshop, in most cases, it is not recommended for Illustrator. It takes up too much file space for too little visual impact. For the more generic leathers, concentrate on creating highlights and shadows that match the reflective quality of your leather.

Exotic and heavily textured leather are the exceptions in Illustrator. When texture is a key part of the identity of the material, then it is worth creating a special texture. You can use the textures created in Photoshop, just as we did for other Illustrator projects above. For example, for exotic leather, you can use either the completed leather texture tile or you can use the black-and-white texture tile (pre-embossing). The tiles can be traced or used in their raster format. Just remember that you will be increasing the size of the document in either case.

Project 6.4: Patent Leather and Latex

Patent leather and latex have similar textures; both are very shiny with smooth, highly reflective surfaces. The main difference (texturally) is that patent leather has a very slight grain. When illustrating either texture, the focus is on creating the strong highlights and shadows.

Step 1: For latex or patent leather in Photoshop, start by creating a well-defined base layer. Show the seams and any wrinkles or folds because all these will show strong highlights. Using a hard, round *Brush*, paint in the shadows on their own layer, like you see in Figure 6.95.

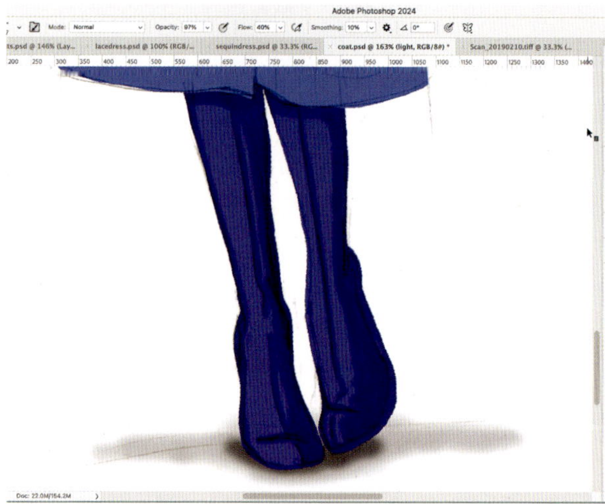

Figure 6.95 Patent leather and latex tend to have high shine and hard shadows. Create your base layer, then start to paint in your shadows with a hard, round *Brush*.

Step 2: After the shadows, create a highlight layer. Use the hard, round *Brush* again, but use white or light colors to build in the highlights. Adjust the *Size* and *Opacity* of the brush as needed to achieve the correct look for the highlights. Notice in Figure 6.96 that the highlights have hard edges. If your highlights are too strong when you finish, you can adjust the *Opacity* of the highlights layer, as shown in Figure 6.97. The highlights will appear at seams, folds, and wrinkles. They should have a very strong contrast with the surrounding area, as seen in Figure 6.98.

For the Illustrator version of patent leather or latex, use layered shapes to create high shine. The *Blob Brush* could be another method for building up the layered shapes. Remember to pay attention to your light source and the shape of your object when drawing the highlight shapes.

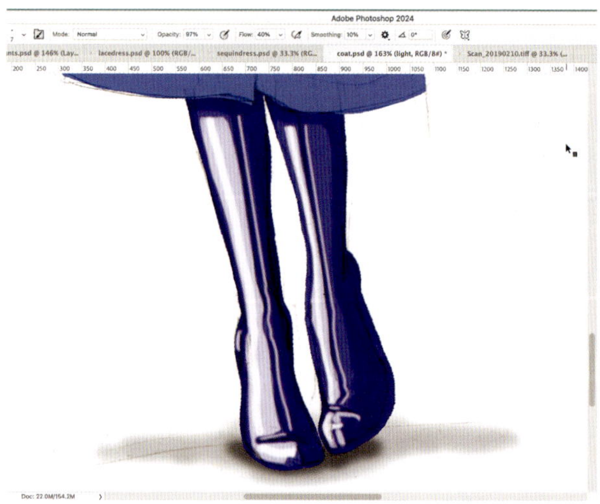

Figure 6.96 Add in your highlights. Use a hard, round *Brush* and vary your *Opacity* as needed.

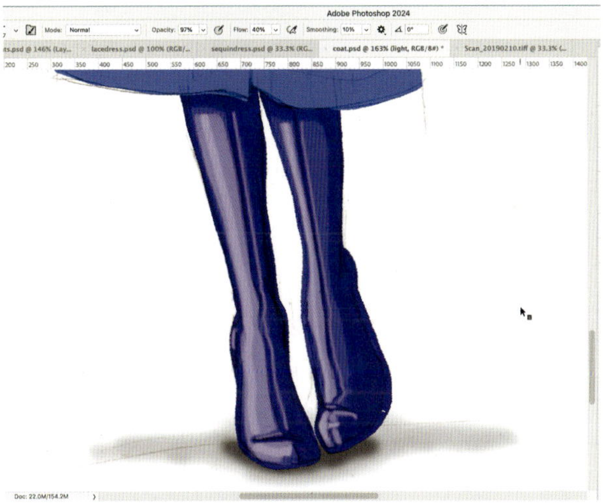

Figure 6.97 Lower the *Opacity* of your highlights layer if the effect is too stark for your intended texture.

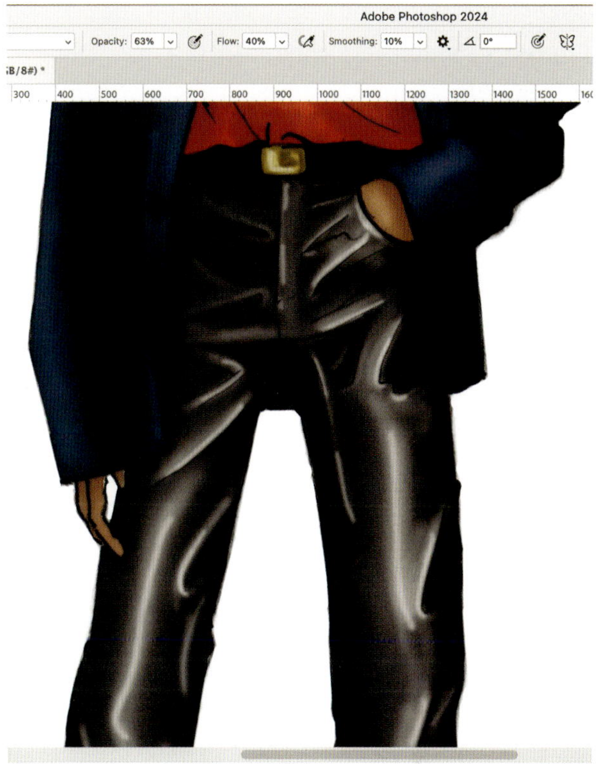

Figure 6.98 Remember that creases and folds will have a sharp contrast in the light and shadow of latex and patent leather.

STYLE SECRETS 6.2

Different Types of Texture Applications

Remember that texture is everywhere. As you render your garments, consider the texture of accessories, props, and even skin and hair! Do the boots have a hard, leathery surface? Should that cowboy hat look like felt? Do you have metal jewelry? Is your character carrying a sword? Are they a mature model/character that needs some wrinkled skin texture? All of these little details can enhance your illustration.

You will work on developing your style later in this text, but also think about the texture of your brush style and how you want to portray your rendering. For example, if you want to render in a watercolor style, you may not want to use a photorealistic texture for your fabric. You need to think about how to illustrate that fabric in a way that aligns with the watercolor look of the rest of your painting.

Project 6.5: Feathers, Fur, and Fleece

Soft, fuzzy textures, such as feathers, fur, and fleece, start with the garment drawing. In many cases, drawing the feather trim, fur collar, or soft fleece jacket well is 90% of the illustration battle. This is particularly true in Illustrator where it is more difficult to make a texture for fur, feathers, or fleece.

Feathers can be made with brushes or with pattern fills. Before making any decisions about how to make the texture, determine what type of feather you are trying to render and what the feather looks like. Is it fuzzy? Smooth? Do you see the individual feathers? Or just a nebulous mass?

Soft, fluffy feathers work well as a brush. This type of feather includes marabou and similar types of downy, airy feathers. These feathers are typically used in a strand or a semi-solid covering for an area.

Step 1: Find a source photo. To make a feather brush, you will need a good-quality photo of a soft, fuzzy feather. It is best if the feather is in high contrast against the background, such as the black feather on the white background in Figure 6.99. Regardless of the original color of the feather and background, you will need to make some adjustments to the image. *Desaturate* the image and adjust the *Levels*. If needed, *Invert* the image. When finished, you should have a black feather on a completely white background. You may also have to clean up the background. If there is any gray in the background, it will appear in the brush.

After the feather image is adjusted and cleaned up, *Define Brush Tip* through the *Edit* menu. This will create the new feather brush.

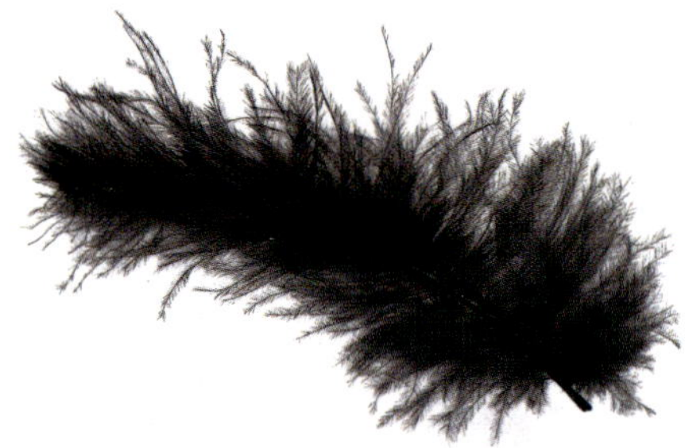

Figure 6.99 Use a photo of a soft, fluffy feather of your choice to create a new *Brush*. Be sure that the background is totally white when *Defining* the *Brush*, or you will end up with the background as part of the brush tip shape. Courtesy of Petra via Pixabay

Step 2: Before using the brush, make sure the base of the feathered garment is prepared. The outline of the area should be rough or uneven to reflect the uneven texture of the fuzzy feathers. *Fill* or *Paint* in a base color for the area. The base color should be a slightly darker color than you plan to use with the feather brush to create depth.

Step 3: Pick the main feather color and start using your feather *Brush*. You can stamp or paint with the brush. Adjust the *Size*, *Rotation*, *Opacity*, *Spacing*, *Scatter*, and other *Brush Settings* in the *Brush Settings* Panel as needed to achieve the desired look. *Size*, *Rotation*, and *Opacity* may need to be adjusted often. The goal is to make the area look like the feathery texture you have in mind. Figure 6.100 shows how the brush can be used to create a feathered collar and cuffs.

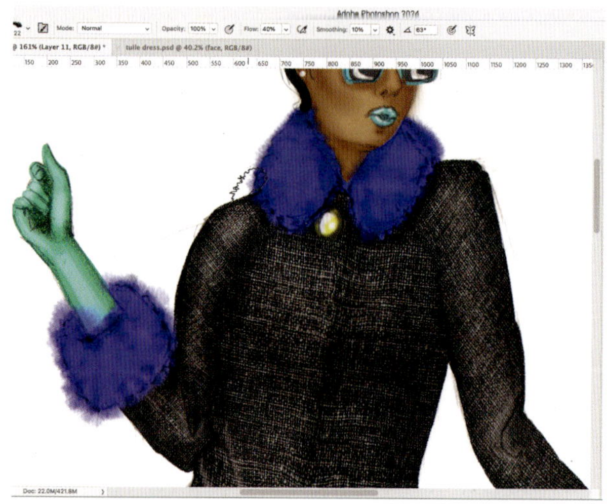

Figure 6.100 You can stamp the *Brush* to create your feathered area or paint with it. This will depend upon your brush settings and the effect that you want. You can adjust the *Size* and *Rotation* and other aspects through the *Brush Settings* panel.

As the texture develops, you can change colors. Use a darker color to create shadows and a lighter color to create highlights. You will want to keep these colors on separate layers for ease of adjustment. Then set the shadow layer to *Multiply* and the highlight layer to *Screen* as shown in Figure 6.101.

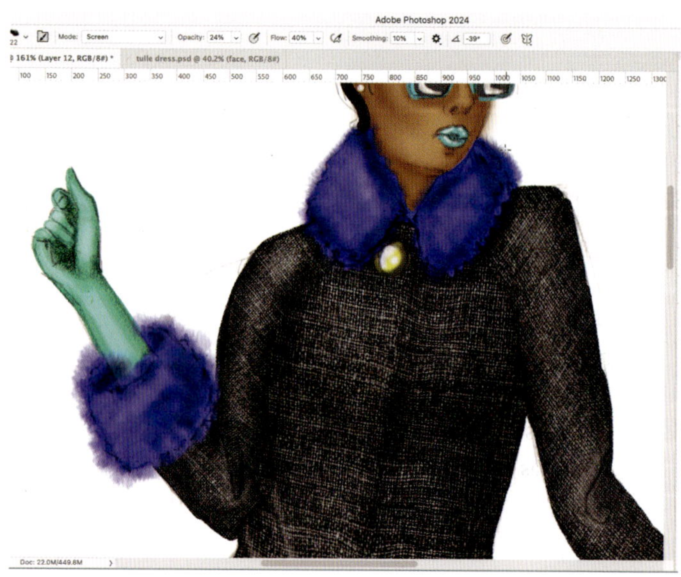

Figure 6.101 Add a layer set to *Multiply* to paint in some shading feathers and one set to *Screen* to paint in highlight feathers as needed.

Surfaces made of smooth feathers often work better with a texture fill than with a brush. Start by finding a good image of feathers similar to the surface you are trying to illustrate. Look for an image that you can make a seamless texture with, such as Figure 6.102. Be careful of too much color change from top to bottom or left to right as this will make it harder to make the image seamless.

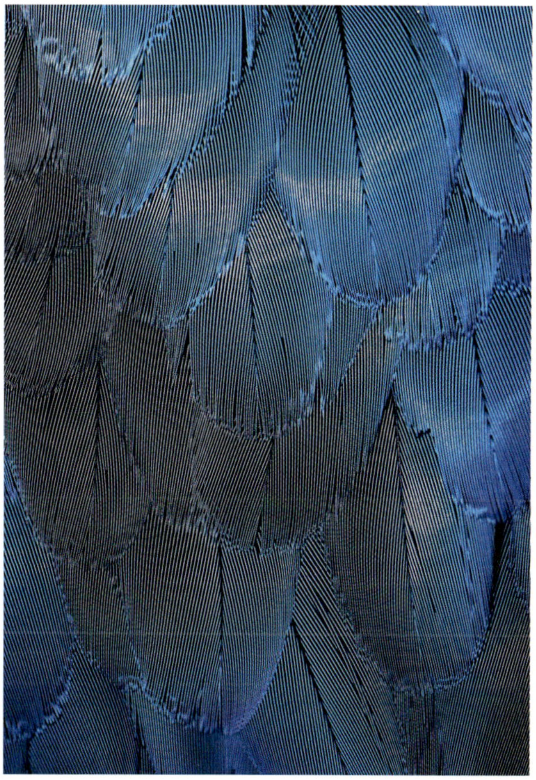

Figure 6.102 Find a picture that suits your needs. Courtesy of David Clode via Unsplash.

Step 1: Once you have a feather image, you need to prepare it. Desaturate the image or convert it to *Black and White*. You may need to adjust the *Levels* so the image is more white than black. Use the *Offset Filter* to move the repeat seams to the middle of the document. You can use the **Clone stamp** and/or *Content Aware Fill* to repair the seams. The *Clone* stamp tool uses a source spot on the image to duplicate, or clone, that spot onto other areas.

If the coloring is uneven throughout the tile, try using *Dodge* and *Burn* tools or *Dodge* and *Burn* layers to correct the issue, like you see in Figure 6.103. You can mask areas to help your precision when repairing the coloring. Every feather image is different and has different needs. Be prepared to take some time to get the repair work right. But remember that the texture tile will be small when you use it, so don't get too stressed about precision. When you finish adjusting the image, *Scale* it to a reasonable size for your renderings. Then *Define* the image as a *Pattern*.

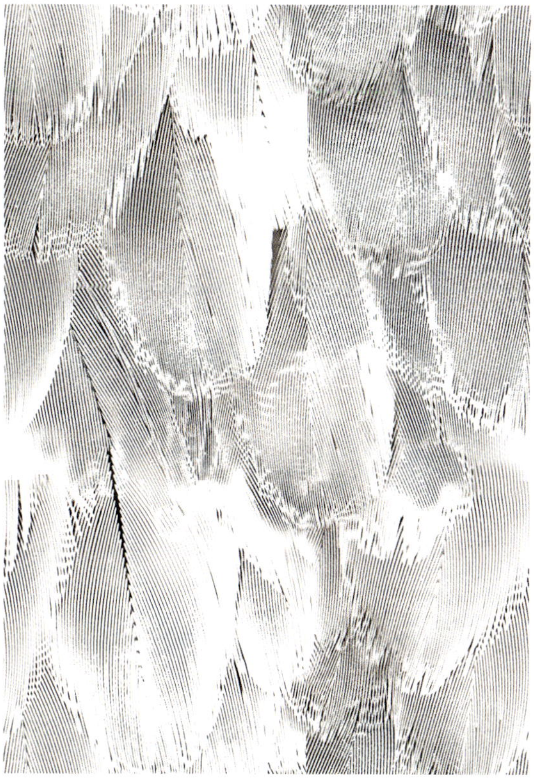

Figure 6.103 *Desaturate* your image and make sure it repeats successfully by using the *Offset* filter. Use the *Clone* stamp or another tool to fix seams that appear when the image wraps around itself. Once you complete this, *Define* your image as a new *Pattern* through the *Edit* menu.

Step 2: It's time to use the texture. Prepare a good base for the feathered area on your rendering. The edges of the area should be uneven, as if the feather ends are sticking out, such as on the cuff in Figure 6.104. *Fill* the area with a solid or mottled color. Create a *Pattern Fill Layer* with your feather texture pattern and clip the layer to your intended feather area. Adjust the *Scale* and *Angle* of the pattern so they match the garment part you are inserting the feathers into. Figure 6.105 shows the *Scaled* and *Rotated* feather pattern on the sleeve cuff.

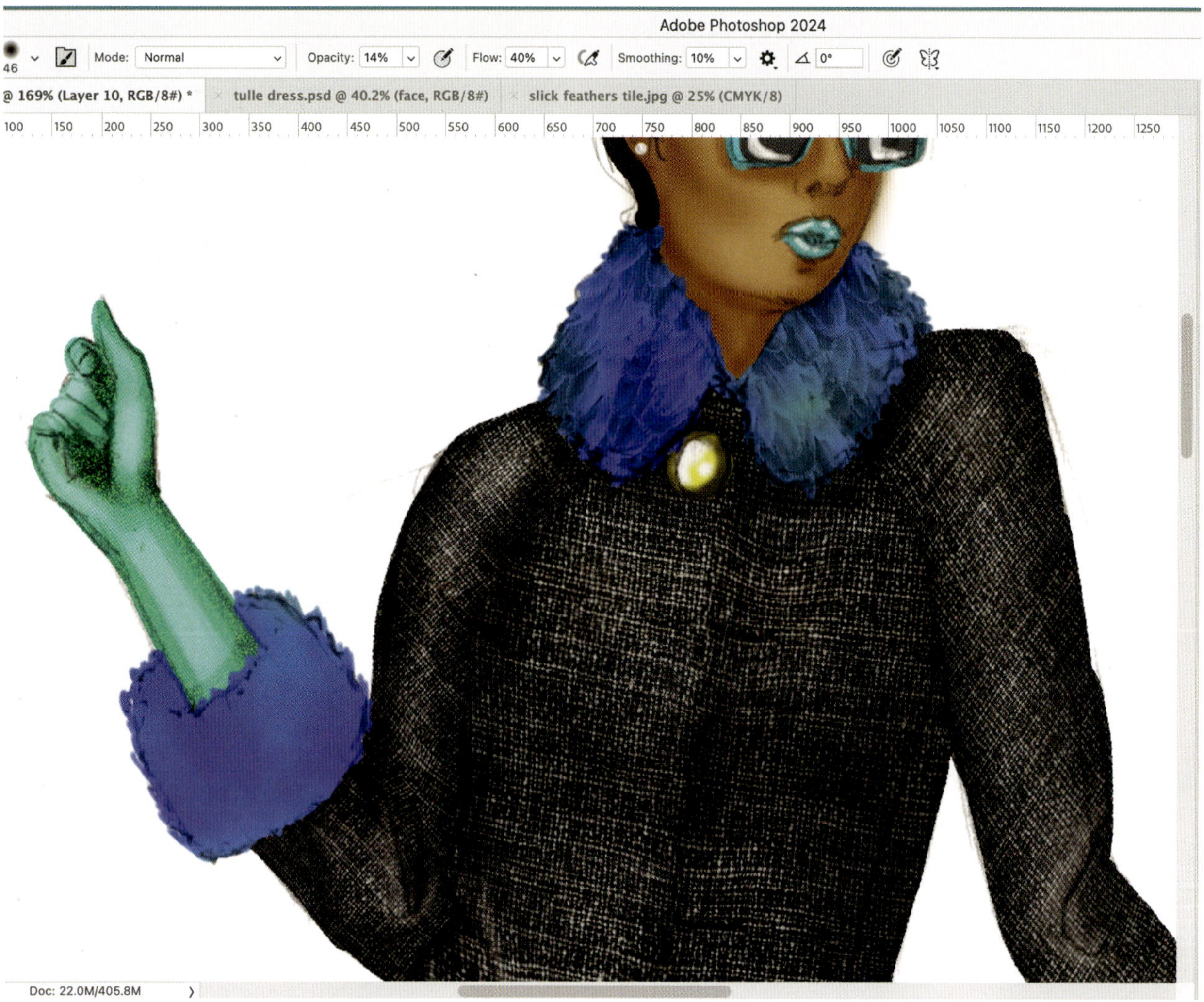

Figure 6.104 After turning your image into a pattern, paint in your base layer with the correct edges to emulate the feather texture.

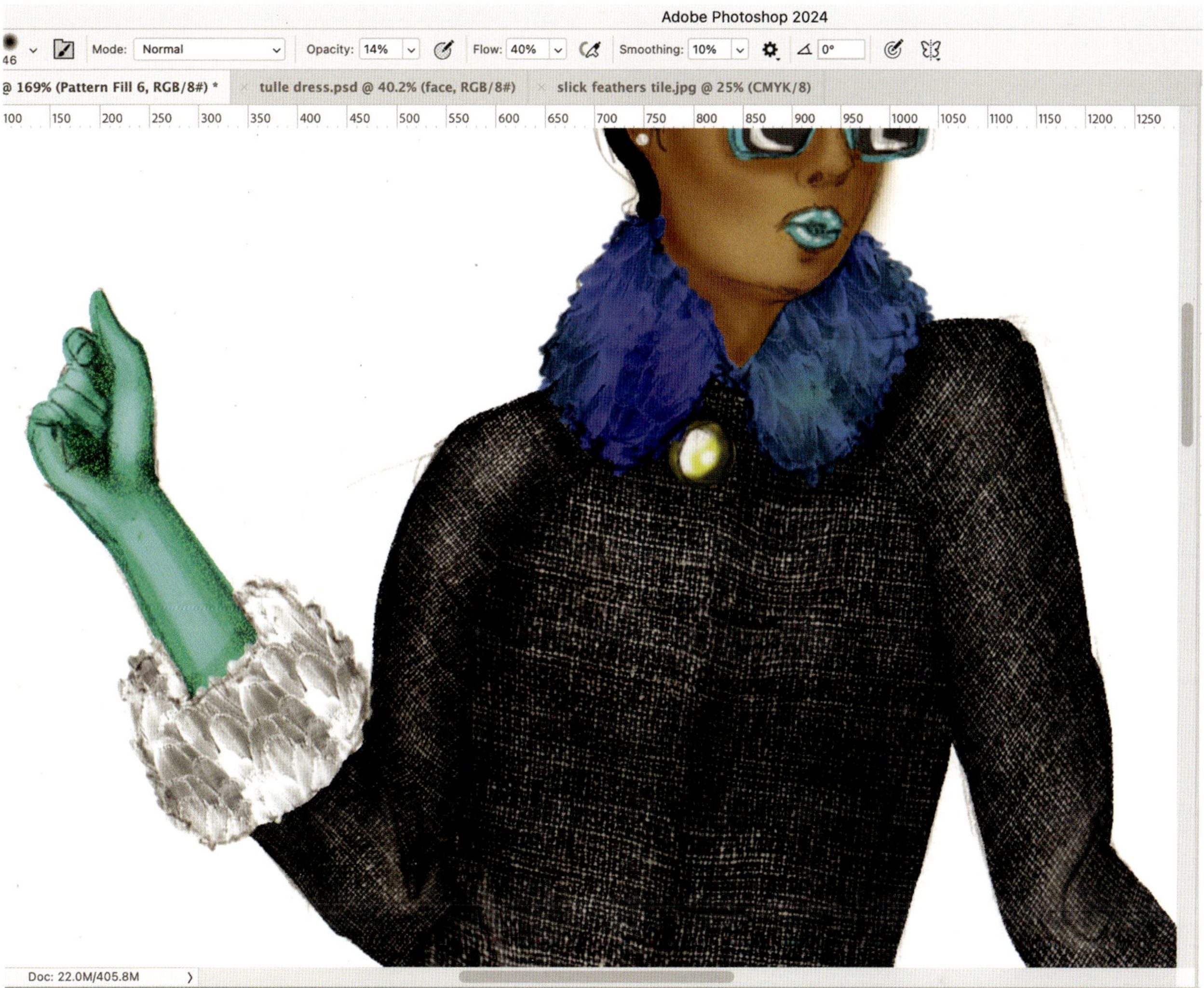

Figure 6.105 Clip your new pattern to the correct area. Be sure to adjust the scale and rotation when you initially add your fill layer.

Adjust the *Layers Blend Mode* and *Opacity* to what ever works well for your texture and color combination. You may need to do some more corrections to the edges to make it look more realistic. Figure 6.106 shows the pattern fill with the *Blend Mode* set to *Multiply* and edges reshaped.

Step 3: After inserting the feather texture and adjusting the edges of the feather area, you may decide to add some highlights or shadows. As with most situations, it is best to create a separate layer for the shadows and for the highlights. If either layer looks too strong, you can adjust the intensity with *Opacity* or *Blend Modes*. Figure 6.107 shows both the cuff and collar fully shaded.

When illustrating fur, start by analyzing the type of fur you are trying to render. What is the texture? How does the coloration work? Is the underfur color different from the color of the guard hairs? How does the fur lay? Make sure the original garment drawing matches the shape and fall of the fur you are trying to represent. The coat in Figure 6.108 is made of fake fur, but it still gives a good idea of the texture and coloration properties you need to look at. It is good to work from a reference photo.

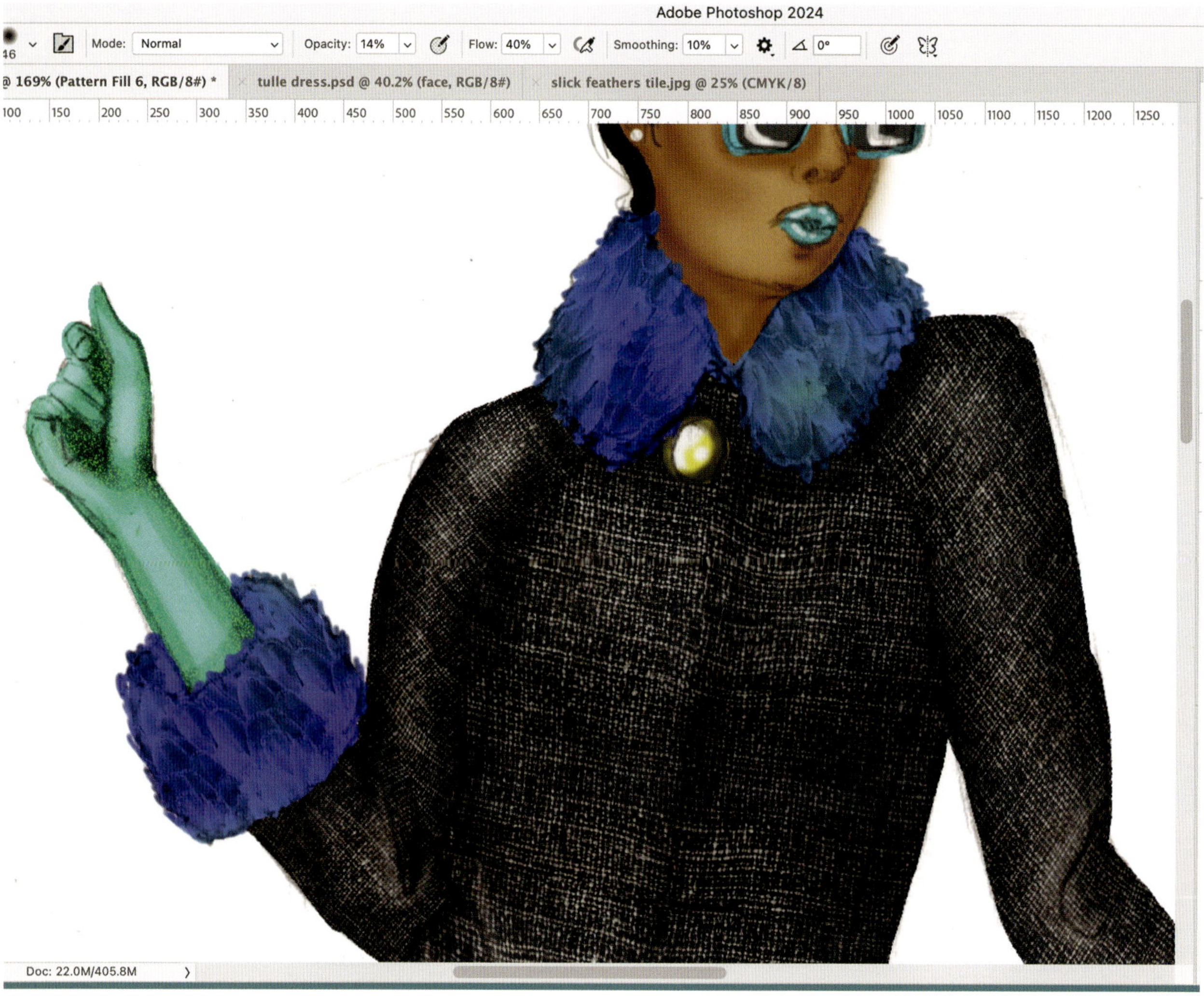

Figure 6.106 Change the *Blend Mode* of your layer to something that works with your image. We used *Multiply*.

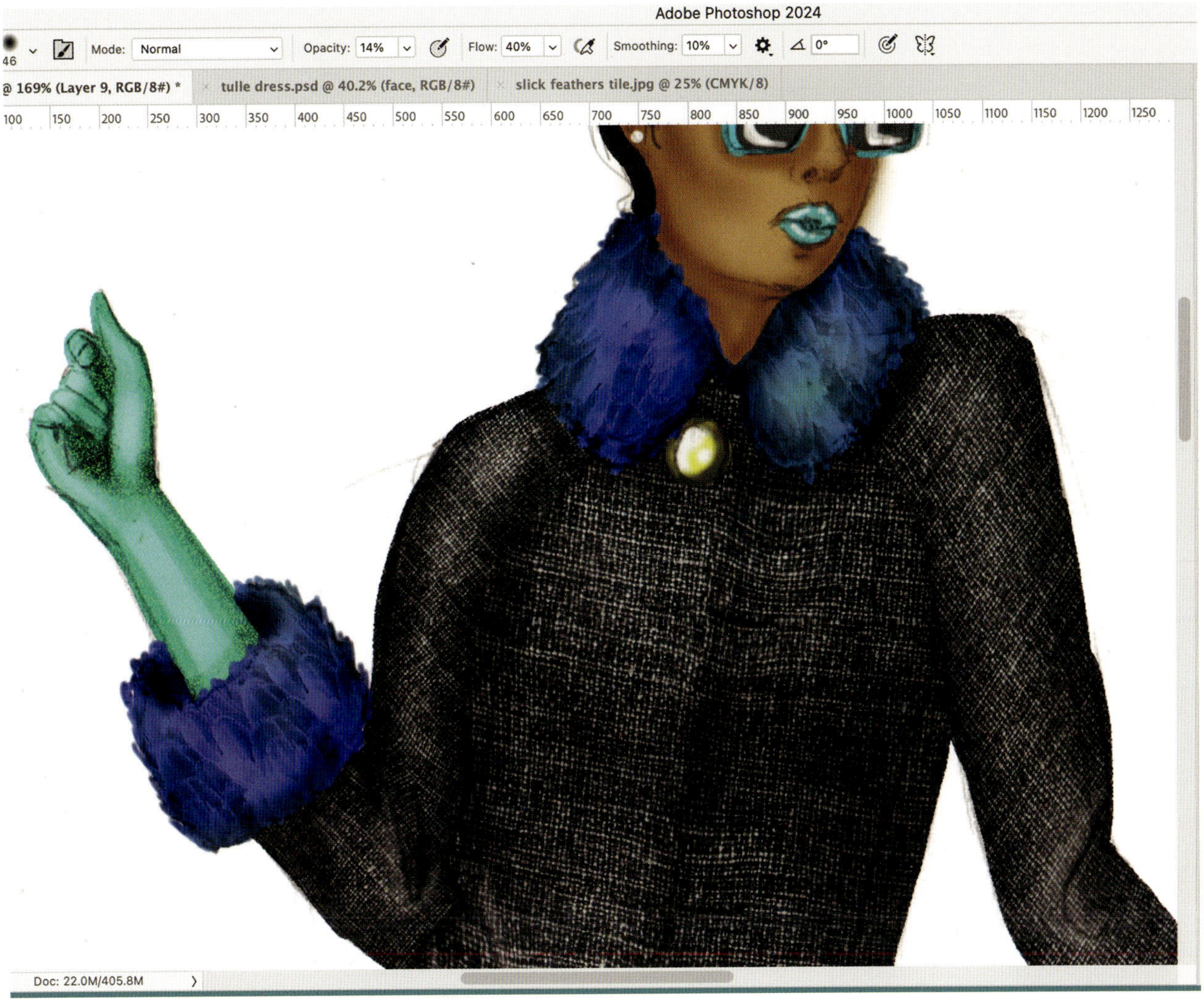

Figure 6.107 Add shading and highlights as needed.

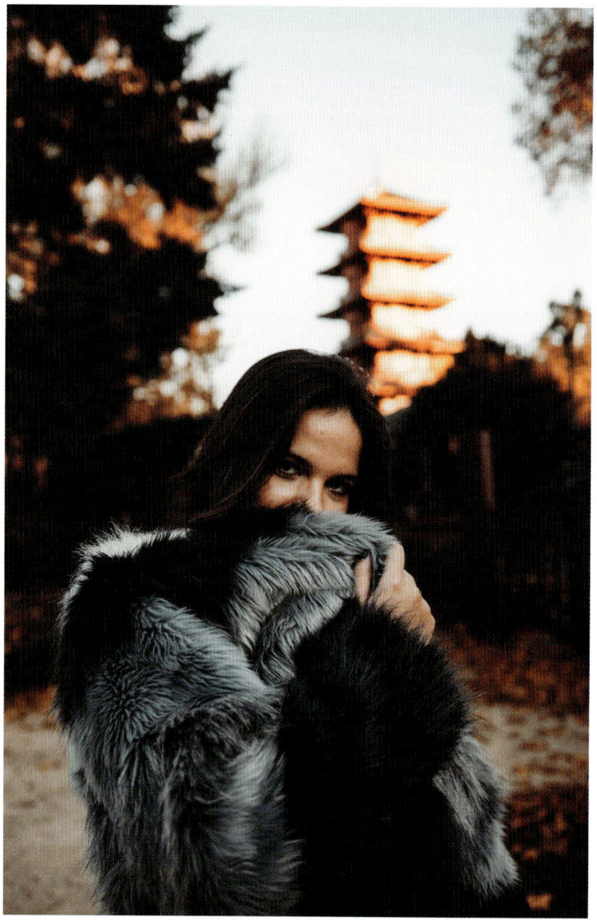

Figure 6.108 Reference photo of a fur coat. Courtesy of Roman Laschov via Unsplash.

We will demonstrate two types of fur: wolf fur and fleece or shearling. Wolf fur has a darker underfur and lighter tips. The fur lays in multiple directions due to its length and it has long fine ends.

Step 1: Paint a base color in for the fur. Use a medium or light color so it will show through the dark underfur layer. You may want to add some basic shading on this layer to guide the placement of fur on the next few layers.

Step 2: We need to find a brush that imitates the texture of the fur. There is a good brush in the **Legacy** *Brushes Library*. These are some older settings, brushes, and patterns that Photoshop has essentially "retired." These Legacy settings are usually still available by telling your program to load them. We have found many fun texture uses for these older brushes. They do not compare to the current realism of available brushes, but they are great at creating unintended effects! To load this *Brush Library*, open the *Brushes* panel and click on the panel *Options* menu. Scroll down to *Legacy Brushes* and click on it. When it asks, choose *Append Brushes*. In the *Legacy Brushes* folder, open the *Default Brushes* subfolder and find the *Grass Brush Preset*. It does not make the best grass, but, with some tweaking, it creates a fun shaggy fur. Through trial and error, adjust the *Brush Settings* until it works as a good *Fur Brush*. You may want to save this as a new *Preset*.

Make a new layer for the underfur. Switch to a darker color. Using your new *Fur Brush*, paint in the underfur. Adjust the *Rotation* as needed to follow the fall of the fur. Make the fur denser in shadows and less dense in the highlights. Figure 6.109 shows what an underfur layer looks like.

Step 3: Make another new *Layer*. This one is for the lighter part of the fur. Change to a lighter color, then paint the light fur. Pay attention to the highlights. Work with the *Brush Rotation* to best imitate the fur direction. Figure 6.110 shows the finished wolf fur rendering.

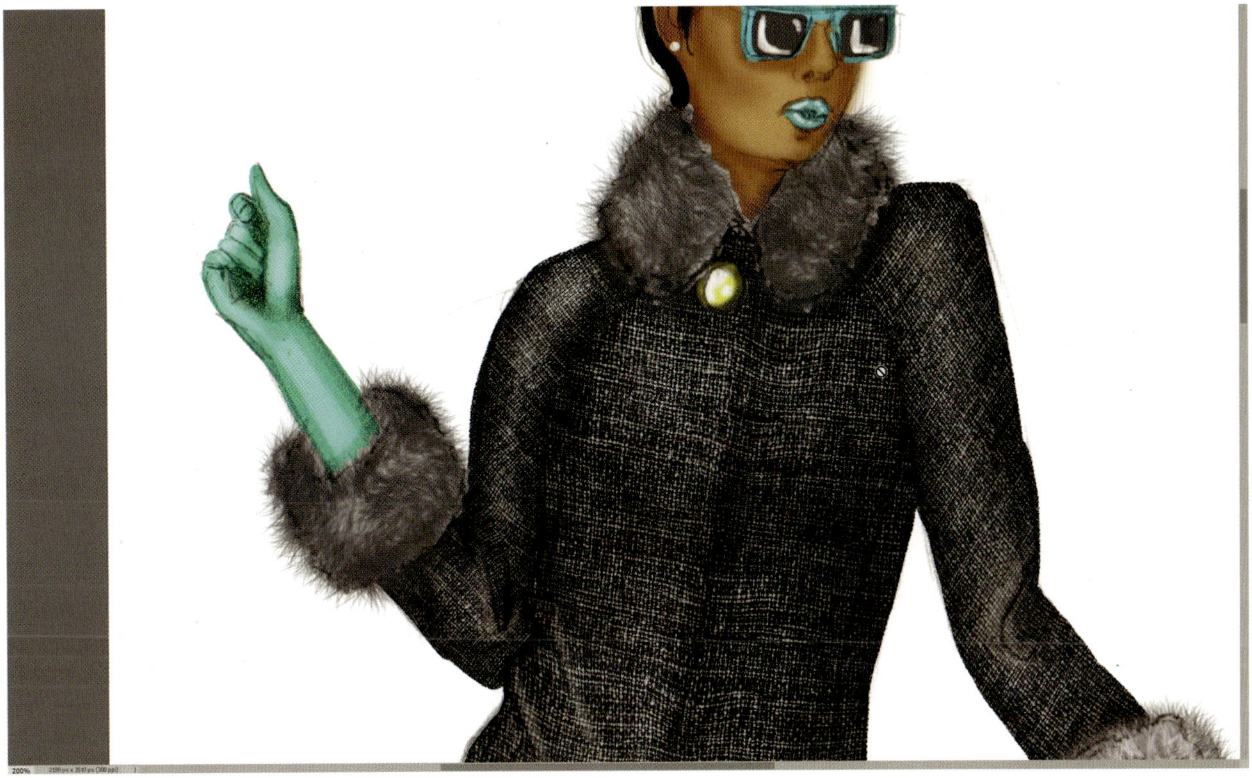

Figure 6.109 Underfur layer of wolf fur collar and cuffs. *Paint* a lighter base layer for the fur areas. Switch to a darker color. Create a new *Layer*. Use a *Fur Brush* to paint the underfur layer following the fall of the fur.

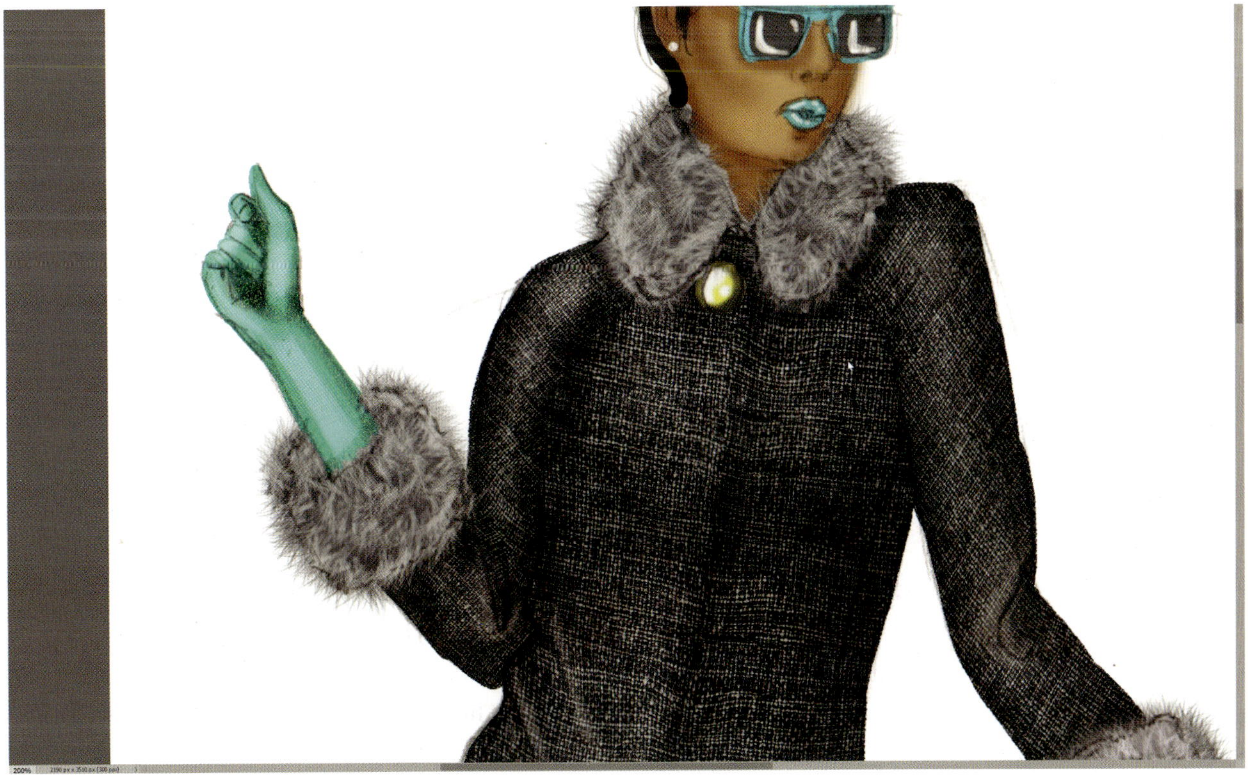

Figure 6.110 Finished wolf fur rendering. Make a new layer for the light-colored fur. Switch to a light color. Paint using the *Fur Brush*.

Fleece or shearling is typically a uniform color, but very textured. It should look soft and curly when done correctly. When preparing a drawing for fleece, draw the of the fleece areas with rough or bumpy lines to mimic the texture of the fur.

Step 1: Fill the fleece garment sections with a solid color. You can add some simple shading or highlighting at this point to help guide the creation of the fur texture. Do not overdo the shadow work because the fleece absorbs more light than many other textures.

Step 2: Find a brush that imitates the fleece texture. We recommend *Legacy Brushes* → *M Brushes* → *Frosted Glass*. Adjust the *Spacing* of the brush so it looks more like curls when used.

Make a new *Layer* for the texture. Choose a lighter color for painting the texture. Start painting and dabbing on this layer to create the texture. You may want to adjust the *Brush Size* and *Density* as you work to make the texture look more realistic. Some of the paint dabs should go past the perimeter of the garment area to make the edges look more authentic. Figure 6.111 shows the finished fleece texture on the collar and cuffs.

To create fur in Illustrator, play with the edge texture of your garment. You can use *Effects* such *Roughen* to adjust the edge. Changes to the line drawing may be enough to convey the idea of fur. You can also make a fur brush or a fur texture fill. However, these options will greatly increase the file size of your document due to the increase in points and paths.

Project 6.6: Sequins and Beading

Sequined and beaded fabrics are composed of thousands of reflective objects. Each sequin or bead moves at least slightly independently of all the others on the fabric. This means that even in the darkest shadows, there will be at least one sequin or bead that is reflecting full light. In the brightest highlights there will be a few sequins or beads that are turned so they show dark shadow instead of light. The effect is broken or dotted highlights and shadows, as you can see in the photo in Figure 6.112.

Sequined and beaded fabrics are also textured. Depending on the type of material application (fully

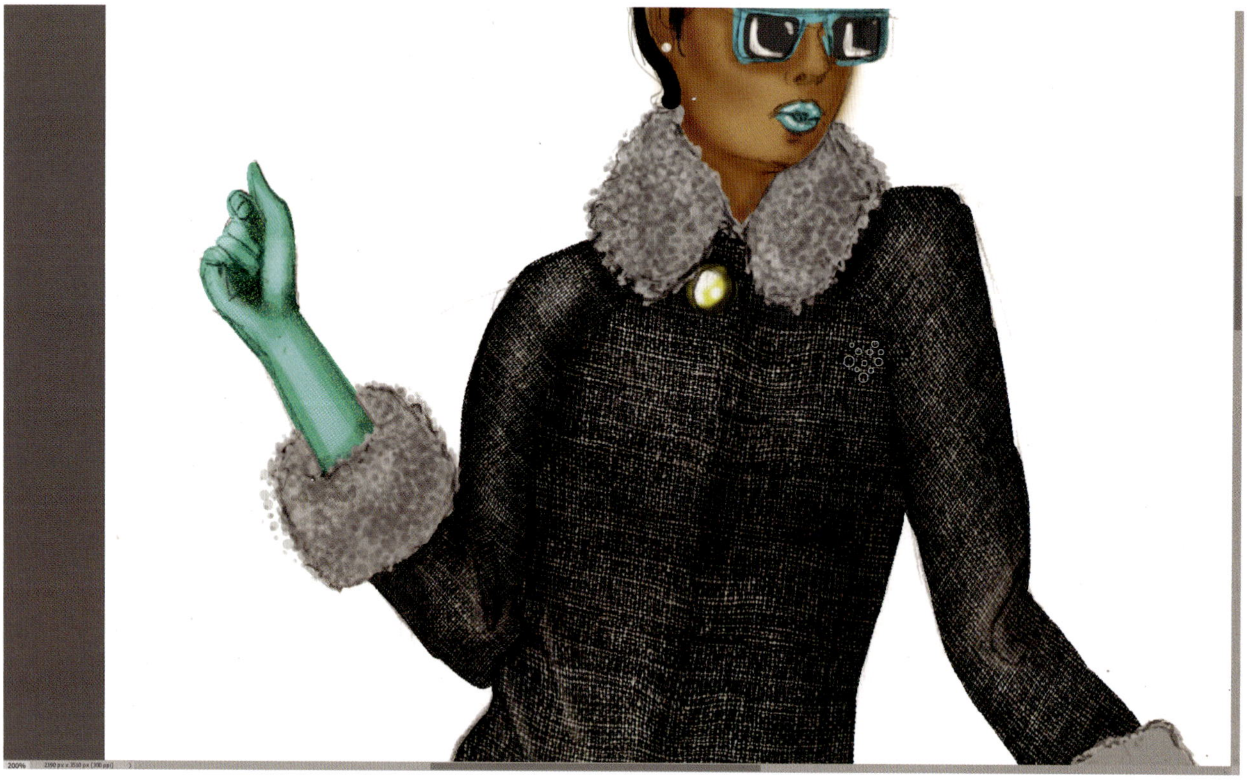

Figure 6.111 Example of shearling texture on cuff and collar.

sequined, scattered, patterned) the fall of the garment will be affected by the sequins or beads. The original drawing needs to show this. Fully sequined fabrics often look "crunchy" and show more wrinkles when worn. Fully beaded fabrics are heavy and will create drag on the body. We will be demonstrating sequined fabric, but beaded fabrics are rendered in a similar manner, with just a few adjustments.

Step 1: Before rendering your sequin garment, take time to develop a sequin brush. You may eventually want several sequin brushes to meet your needs. But we will start with one basic brush. A sequin brush should look like a scattering of dots with some color variation. This mimics the texture and broken reflection of sequins.

There are multiple brush settings that need adjusting to make a sequin brush. However, like everything, we will give you a general set of adjustments and you will have to experiment to find what works best for you and your specific illustration.

To create a sequin brush, start with a basic hard round brush. Then, open the *Brush Settings* panel. There are four sets of settings that we adjust to make a successful sequin brush. The first group of settings is the *Brush Tip Shape* settings. This is typically the first thing you see when you open the *Brush Settings* panel. Figure 6.113a shows this view of the panel. Set the *Size* to 6 pixels for a start. Check that this looks like a good size for a sequin on your rendering. Then adjust the *Spacing* to 10%.

Next, *Shape Dynamics* needs to be adjusted. This is the second group of settings on the left side of the panel. Figure 6.113b shows the setting group highlighted, if you are unsure where to find it. Adjust the *Size Jitter* until you see enough variation in the size of the brush dots to be interesting. We used 68%. If you have a tablet, set *Control* to *Pen Pressure*. Otherwise, leave it on *Off*. Again, use trial and error to find a *Minimum Diameter* that works well for you. Our brush is set at 13%. The other settings in this group can be left alone.

The third group of settings for the brush is *Scattering*. These settings will allow the brush to have multiple dots, as shown in the preview area of Figure 6.113c. Start by setting the *Scatter* at the maximum amount of 1000%. Again, if you have a tablet, set *Control* to *Pen Pressure*. If not, set it to *Off*. Adjust *Count* until the preview of the brush begins to show enough fill or coverage. The higher the *Count*, the more dots the brush will create and therefore, the more solid it will be. The lower the *Count*, the more scattered it will look. The number will need to be adjusted if you change the tip size or *Scatter* amount. We set the *Count* at 7. To create a little variety, adjust the *Count Jitter*. We chose 12% and left the *Control* on *Off*.

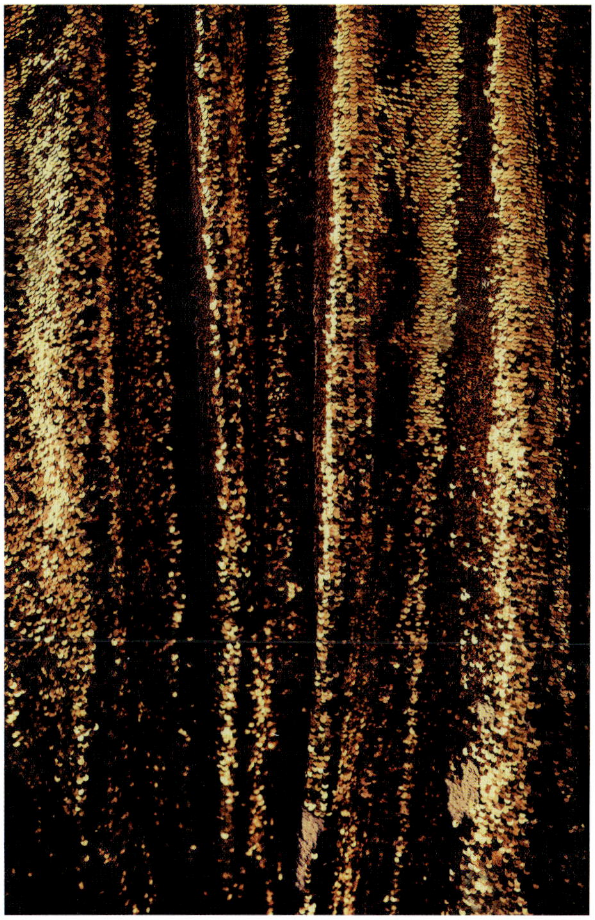

Figure 6.112 Sequined fabric. The photo of sequined fabric shows that while there are distinct highlights and shadows on the fabric, there are still individual dark sequins in the light areas and vice versa in the dark areas. Courtesy of Tim Mossholder via Unsplash.

For the fourth group of settings we will skip down to the *Color Dynamics* settings. These settings are adjusted to create color variations within the brush that mimic the sparkle variations of sequins. These settings will likely need to be adjusted every time you use the brush on a different set of colors. The settings we give were developed for medium gray to imitate silver sequins.

You will notice in Figure 6.113d that almost all the settings are adjusted in this group. Start by checking *Apply Per Tip* so each dot will have independent color variations. The rest of the settings are based on trial and error as well as personal taste. However, these are the settings the authors chose. *Foreground/Background Jitter*

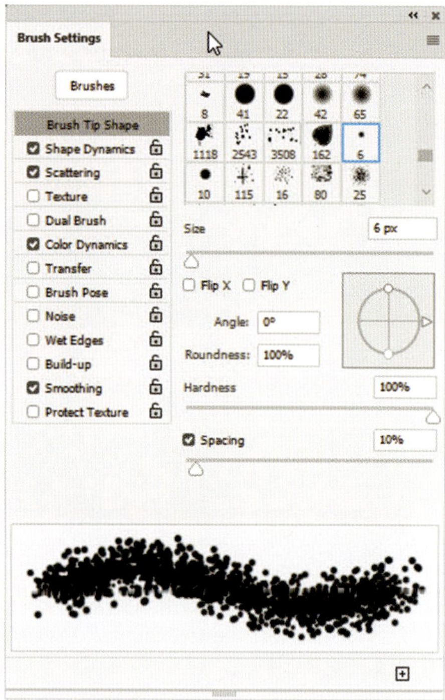

(a)

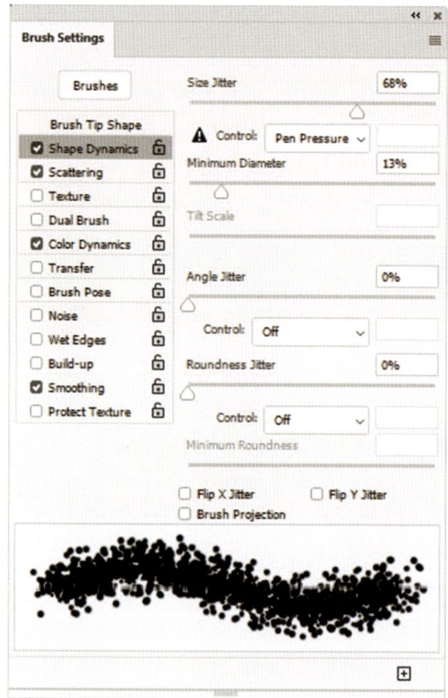

(b)

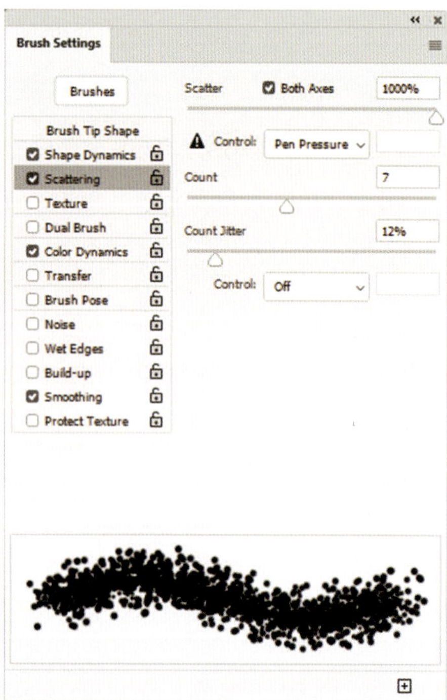

(c)

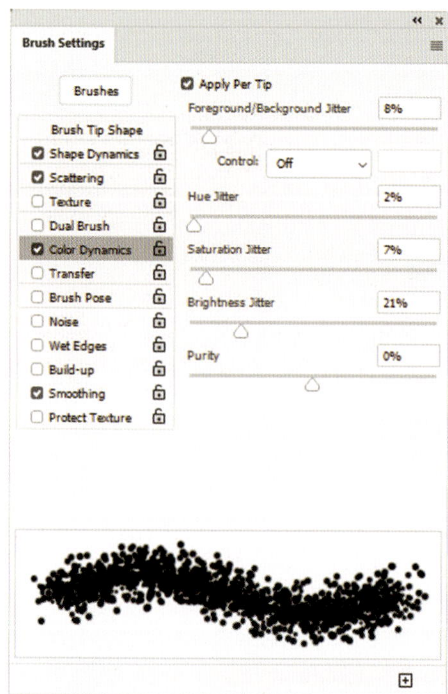

(d)

Figures 6.113a–d *Brush Settings* panel for a sequin brush. You may want to create several different sequin brushes for specific uses. These settings create a generic sequin brush. Part (a) shows the *Brush Tip Shape Settings*. The tip *Size* is set to 6 pixels and *Space* to 10%. Image (b) contains the settings for *Shape Dynamics*. *Size Jitter* is 68% and *Control* is set to *Pen Pressure*. If you do not have a tablet, leave *Control* on *Off*. *Minimum Diameter* is 13%. Image (c), *Scattering*, is key to making a sequin brush. *Scatter* is set to the maximum amount of 1000%. Again, you can set *Control* to either *Pen Pressure* or *Off*. Set *Count* to 7. *Count Jitter* is set at 12% and the *Count Control* is *Off*. Part (d) shows the *Color Dynamics* settings. *Apply Per Tip* is checked. *Foreground/Background Jitter* is 8% and the *Control* is *Off*. *Hue Jitter* is 2%, *Saturation Jitter* is 7%, and *Brightness Jitter* is 21%. *Purity* remains at 0.

is set to 8% because the *Foreground* and *Background* swatches are set to two similar colors. This is a useful and easy to control setting. The *Control* is left on *Off. Hue Jitter* is set to 2%. This setting would introduce variations in the color in terms of hue (more pink, blue, etc.), so we chose to limit this jitter. It could even be left at 0, if preferred. *Saturation Jitter* is how vibrant or dull a color is. We chose 7%. *Brightness Jitter* controls how light or dark a color is. This is key to getting random light or dark dots in the brush and works well with gray. Other colors may require more experimentation. We chose 21%. We left *Purity* at 0.

When you have all the settings how you like, save the new brush. Go to the panel *Options* menu and click on *New Brush Preset*. As you make changes to your brush for different needs, you may want to save the adjusted brushes as additional sequin brush presets.

Step 2: Now you can start rendering the sequin garment. Make sure the original drawing reflects the fall of the garment, including wrinkles or folds on the edges. Then fill the garment or garment area with a solid fill of the main sequin color.

To make the base look like sequins, apply a noise filter. Select the base fill layer, then go to *Filter* → *Convert for Smart Filters*. Then go back to *Filter* and choose *Noise* → *Add Noise*. The goal is to break up the base color with just enough color variation that it looks like a very flat version of sequins or glitter. Figure 6.114 shows what this should look like. We used the filter settings of *Amount* 10%, *Gaussian*, and *Monochromatic*. However, you may need to adjust these settings for your base color and the size of your rendering.

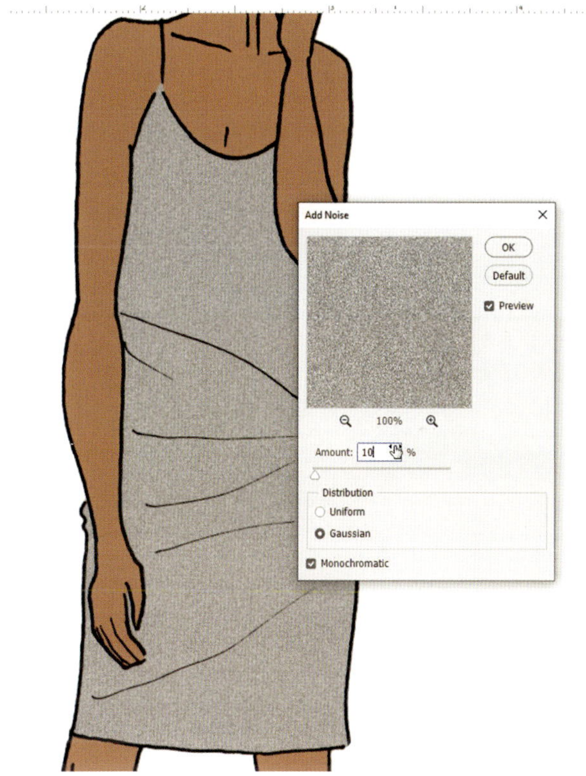

Figure 6.114 When creating a fully sequined garment, start with a textured base layer. After filling your dress with a base color, create a *Smart Filter Layer*. Use the *Add Noise Filter* to make a basic texture. Set the *Noise Filter* to *Monochromatic*. You can choose *Uniform* or *Gaussian*. Adjust the *Amount* to meet your needs. The example shows 10% and *Gaussian*.

Step 3: Once you have established the base layer, you can start using the sequin brush to make the rendering more realistic. Set your *Foreground* and *Background Colors* to two similar shadow colors for your sequins. The *Foreground Color* should be the slightly lighter of the two colors. For instance, our shadow colors are approximately 60% gray in the *Foreground* and 70% gray in the *Background*.

Create a new *Layer* for shadow or dark tones. *Mask* the garment area. An easy way to do this is to hold the *ctrl/cmd* key and click on the thumbnail of the garment on the base layer in the *Layers* panel. You want to keep the area masked the entire time you are working on the texture.

Using the *Brush* tool set to your new *Sequin Brush* preset, start painting in the dark and shadow areas of your garment. If you cover too much, don't worry, the lighter layers will cover the dark layer. You could fill the entire layer with dark paint, but you might want part of the original base layer to show through in places, as shown in Figure 6.115.

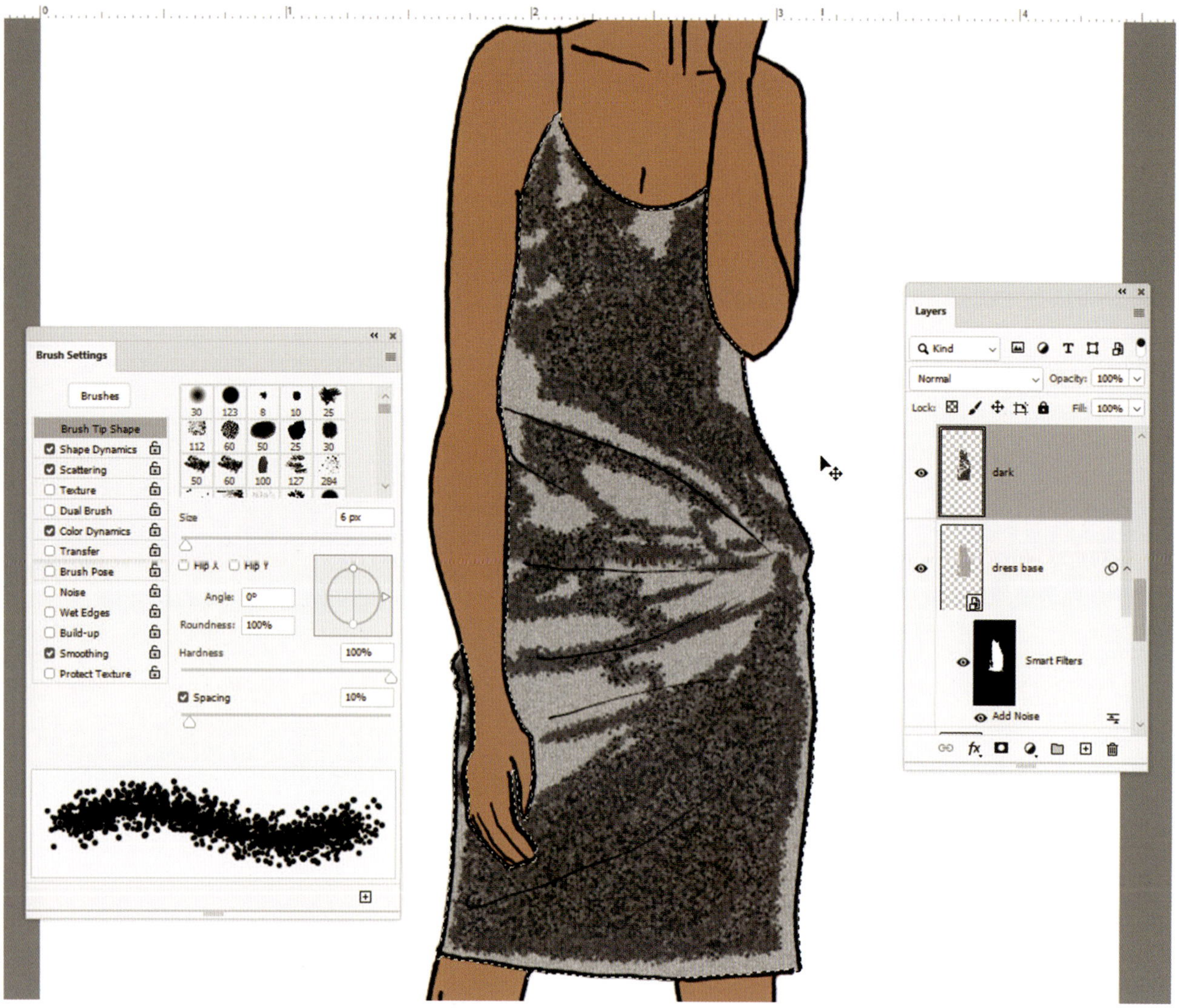

Figure 6.115 Create a new *Layer*. Set your *Foreground* and *Background* colors to two similar shadow colors for your sequins. Using your *Sequin Brush*, paint in the shadows. You can cover extra area, if you need to, because the lighter layers will sit on top.

Step 4: Rinse and repeat. To make the mid-tone layer, follow the same steps as for the dark tone layer. Set your *Foreground* and *Background Colors* to two versions of your main sequin color. Create a new *Layer*. Make sure the *Selection Mask* is still on, otherwise re-mask your garment. Use your *Sequin Brush* to paint the mid-tone areas of the garment. At this point, start to really pay attention to folds and wrinkles. There will be areas that you must NOT cover so the shadows show through. Figure 6.116 demonstrates how the folds begin to develop at this stage.

After the mid-tones, make a layer for the highlights. Set your colors to two highlight colors. These may be white and near-white or two pastel versions of your sequin color. Paint the highlights on this layer. Currently, you are concerned with the solid areas of highlights, such as along folds or on body curves. Figure 6.117 shows how this layer should look. The scattered highlights will come next.

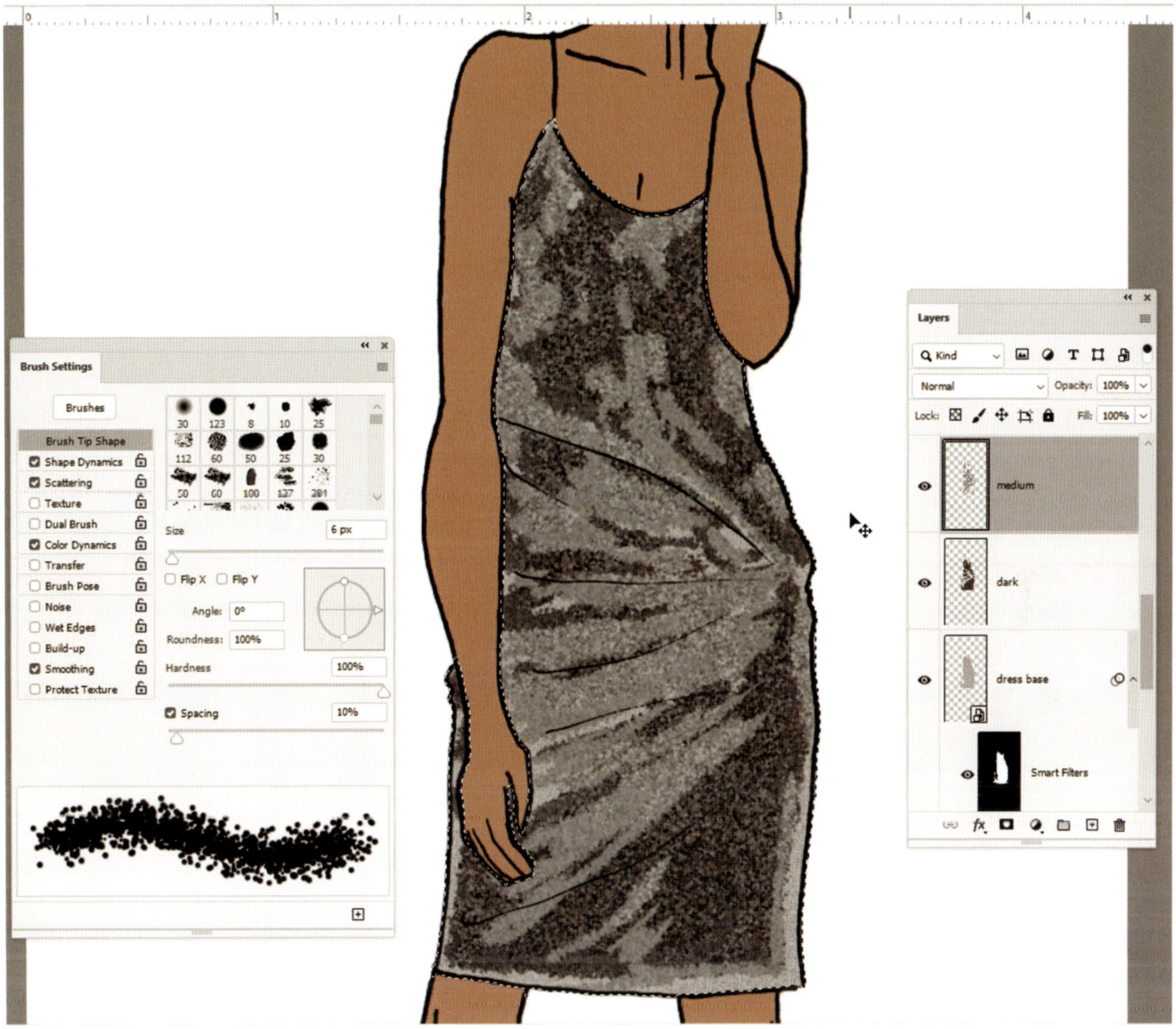

Figure 6.116 Make a separate *Layer* for the mid-tones. Set the *Foreground* and *Background* colors to two similar versions of your main sequin color. Use the *Sequin Brush* to paint the middle tone areas of your garment. Do not worry about the highlights. These will be added on a separate layer and can cover this layer.

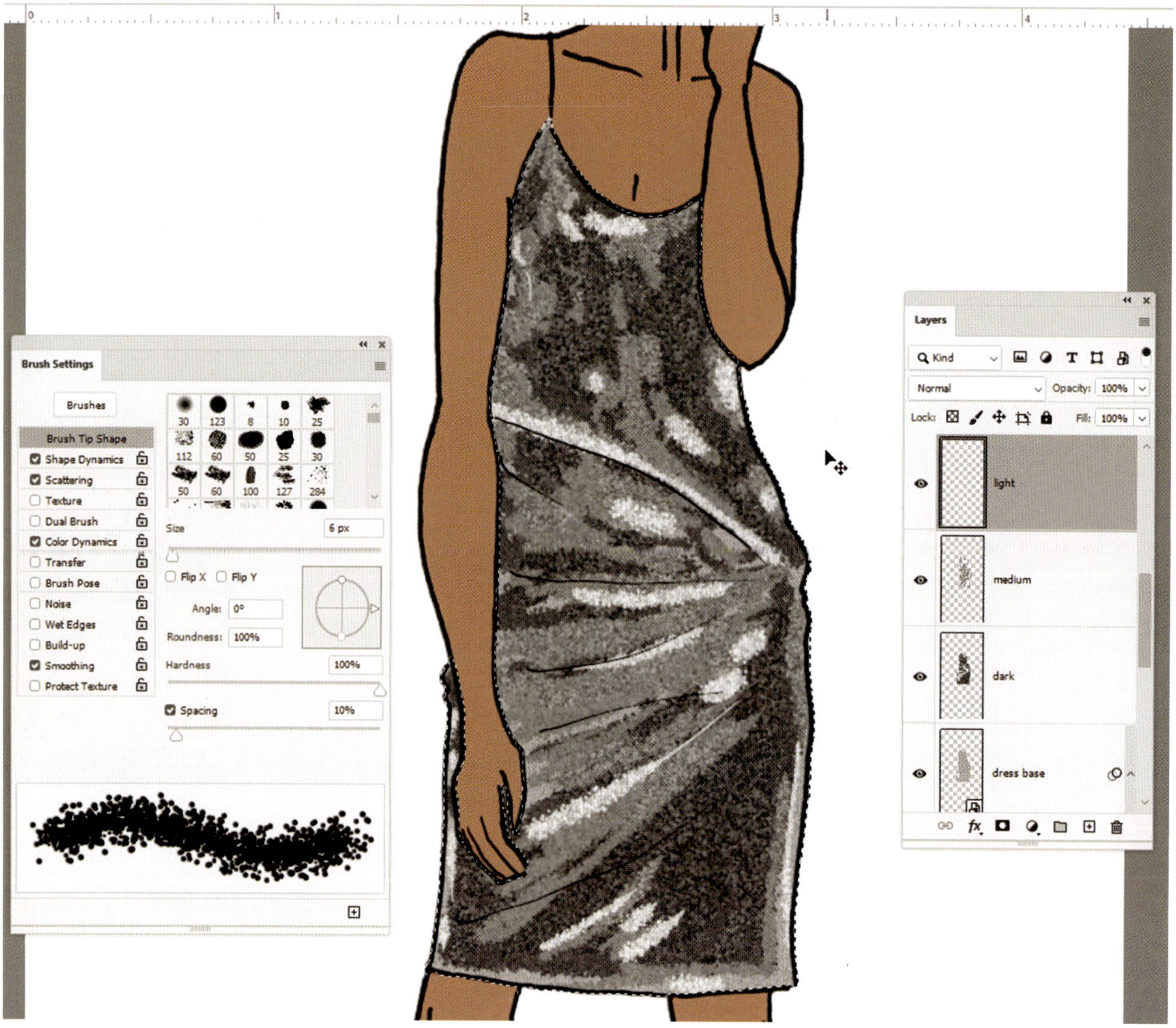

Figure 6.117 Add an additional *Layer* for the highlights. Choose two highlight colors to work with. This may be white and a near white or two pastel versions of your sequin color. Use your *Sequin Brush* to paint the highlights. Pay attention to folds, wrinkles, and body curves.

Step 5: Because sequins are known for broken or scattered highlights and shadows, we cannot stop yet. Our current effect is more similar to glitter metallic. Adjust your sequin brush so it has less fill power. You can do this by reducing the *Count* under *Scattering*. You may also want to increase the tip *Size* some. You can see a preview of the authors' *Scattered Sequin Brush* in Figure 6.118. You may want to save your new *Brush Preset*.

You can use the *Scattered Sequin Brush* on the highlights layer or on a new layer, depending on how you prefer to work. The colors should still be the highlight colors, or very similar. Use the new brush to break up the edges of the highlight areas. Then dab some random sparkles wherever you think the garment needs them so it looks more like sequins. Figure 6.118 shows the full sequin effect with the scattered sparkles.

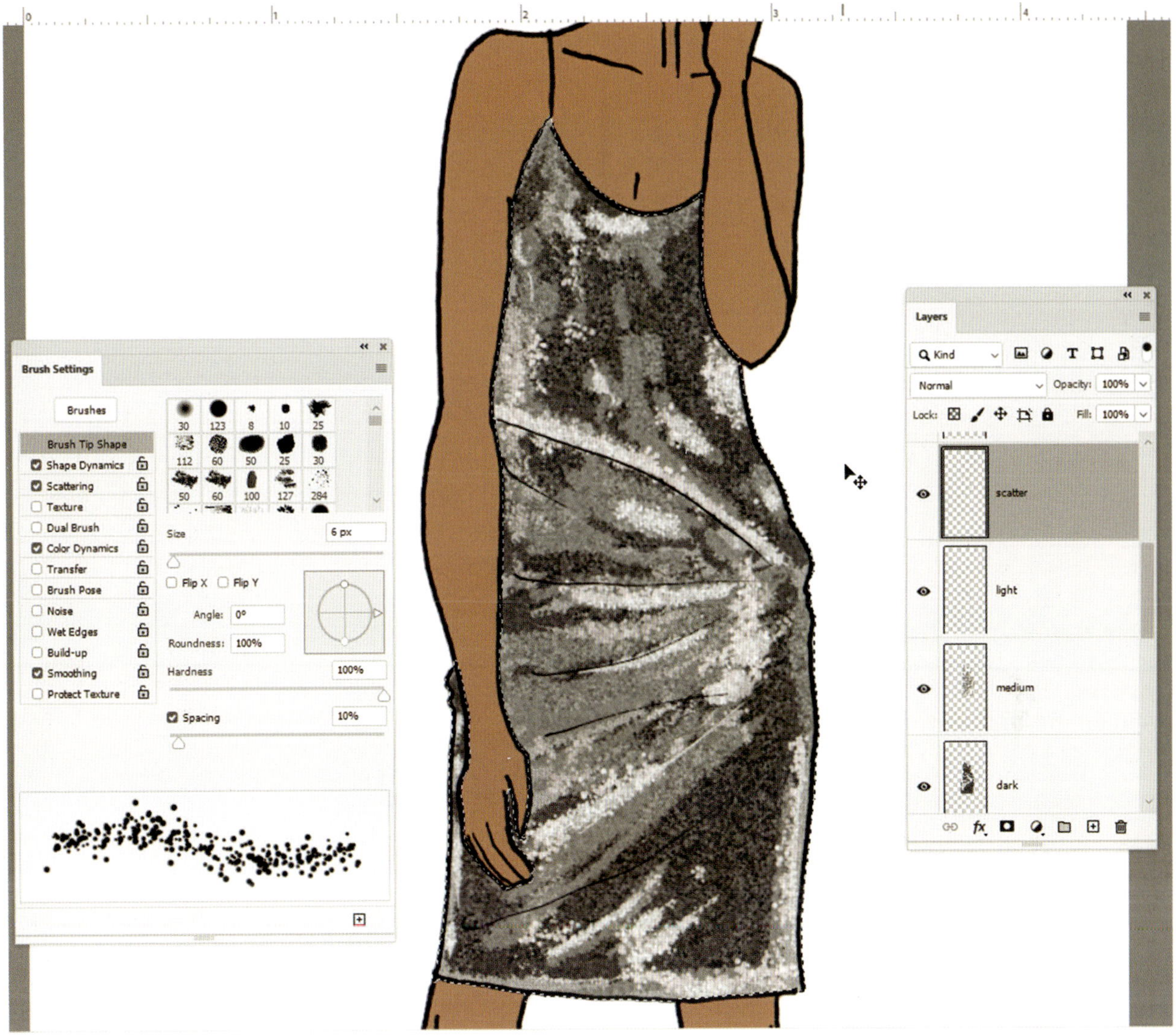

Figure 6.118 Because sequins have a scattered or broken look, the highlights need more work to make the effect convincing. Adjust the *Sequin Brush* so it is less dense (lower the *Count*). You may also want to make the *Tip Size* larger and introduce more variation in *Size Jitter*. Try a few different versions to find what works best. Use the new version of the brush to break up the highlights. Then stamp the *Brush* in a few places to add random sparkles, especially on the dark areas.

Step 6: You may consider your sequin garment done at this point. That's fine. Or you can take it a step further and add a few starbursts to emphasize the sparkle effect of the texture. You can draw the starbursts by hand, use a *Legacy Brush* (*Assorted Brushes* folder), or make a custom sparkle brush.

To make a sparkle brush, use a small round brush and black paint. Draw at least one starburst. You can have one starburst, a group of starbursts (as in Figure 6.119), or you can have a series of different starbursts. Once you have drawn the starburst(s), select the image and go to *Edit* → *Define Brush Preset* to make the new brush. You can adjust the *Brush Settings* after you have made the new brush tip.

To put starbursts/sparkles on your garment, make a new layer. Set your paint color to white. If you have *Sparkle Brush*, dab the brush in places where you want a sparkle. You can adjust the *Size* and *Rotation* of the *Brush* to obtain more variety. If you don't have a custom brush, use a small round *Brush* and draw the starbursts or use the Legacy starburst brush where you want on the layer. In either case, you may want to adjust the *Layers Blend Mode* when you are done. The example in Figure 6.120 uses the *Screen Blend Mode*.

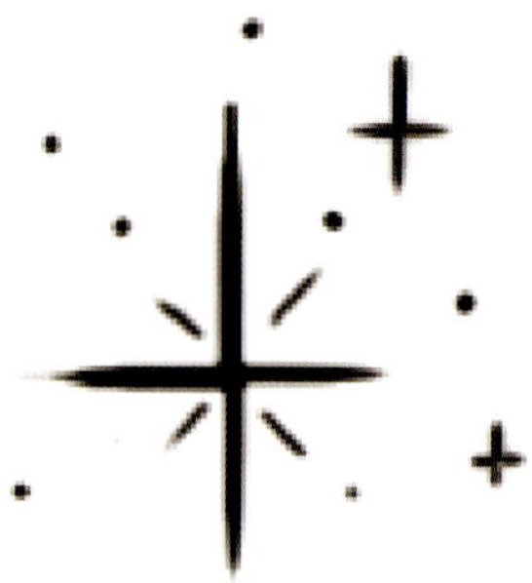

Figure 6.119 If you want to take your shine effect to the next level, you can develop a *Sparkle Brush*. Draw a few starbursts in black. You can make a few different brushes with individual stars, or one brush with all the stars in one cluster. Define the star(s) as a new *Brush Tip* to use them.

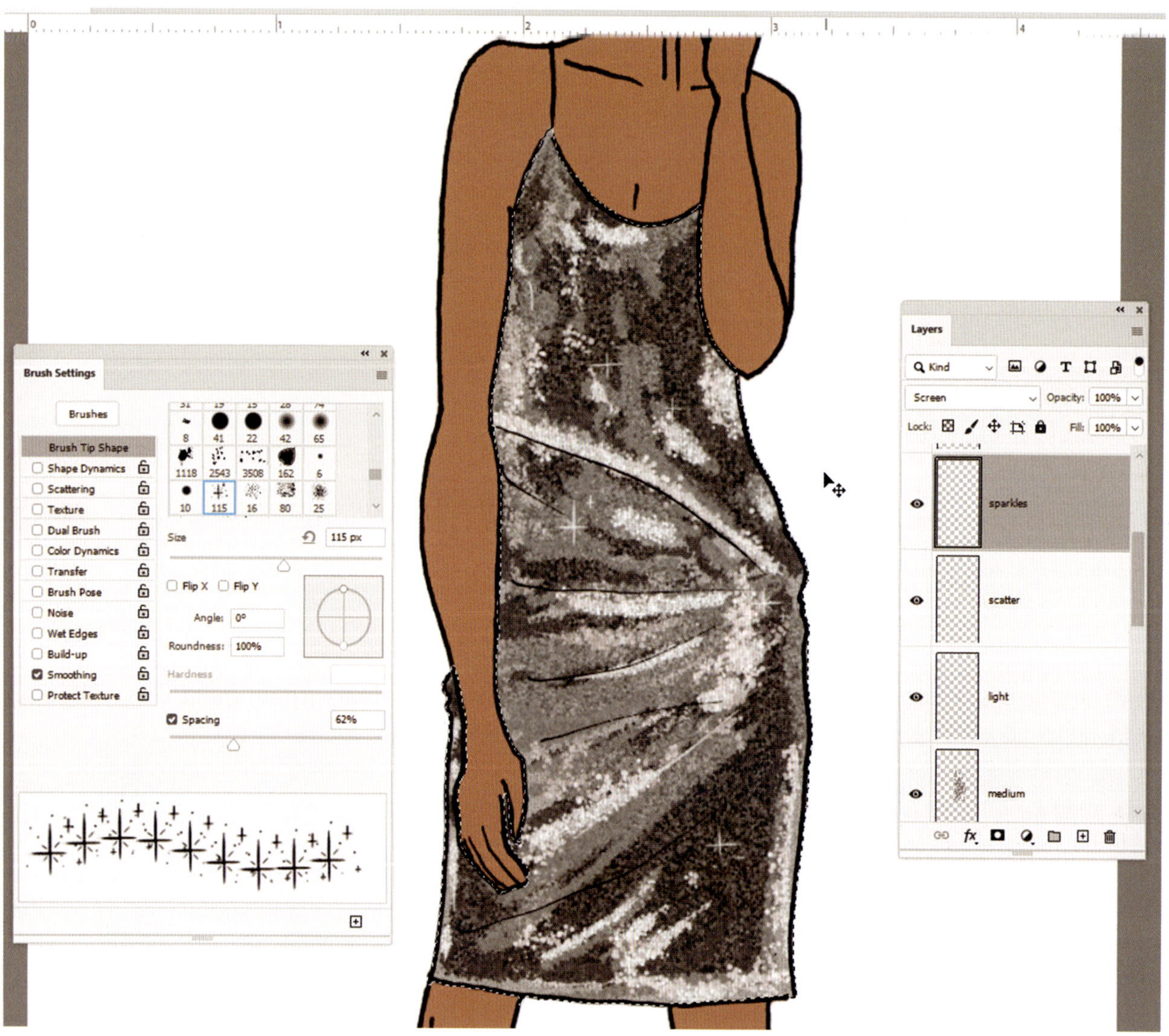

Figure 6.120 Create a *Layer* for the sparkles. Use the new *Sparkle Brush* and stamp it in a few places that need extra shine. You can adjust the *Brush Tip Size* and *Rotation* as needed to make it more interesting. You can also adjust the *Layer Blend Mode*. The example shows the *Blend Mode* set to *Screen*.

Project 6.7: Lace

We have already done several versions of lace in Illustrator. We can take those lessons and use them in Photoshop. In fact, the *Lace Pattern Fill* we made for Illustrator started in Photoshop. That pattern tile is perfect for use in Photoshop as pattern fill for PS renderings.

If you want to make a *Lace Pattern Fill*, clean up the lace image. *Desaturate* it and work with the *Levels* so it is strictly black and white (for a generic pattern). *Crop* the image to a seamless repeat. Then use *Edit menu → Define Pattern* to make the pattern. You can use it as a *Fill* or a *Pattern Fill Layer* as we have done for several of the other lessons. Now, as we have already done the pattern fill version of lace, let's try making a *Lace Brush*.

Step 1: Find or take a photo of the lace you want to work with. The lace in the image needs to be flat and preferably on a high-contrast background, such as black for white lace. Clean up and adjust the image. You may need to *Invert* the image if the lace is white or light colored. It is best if the finished image is black lace on a white background, such as in Figure 6.121.

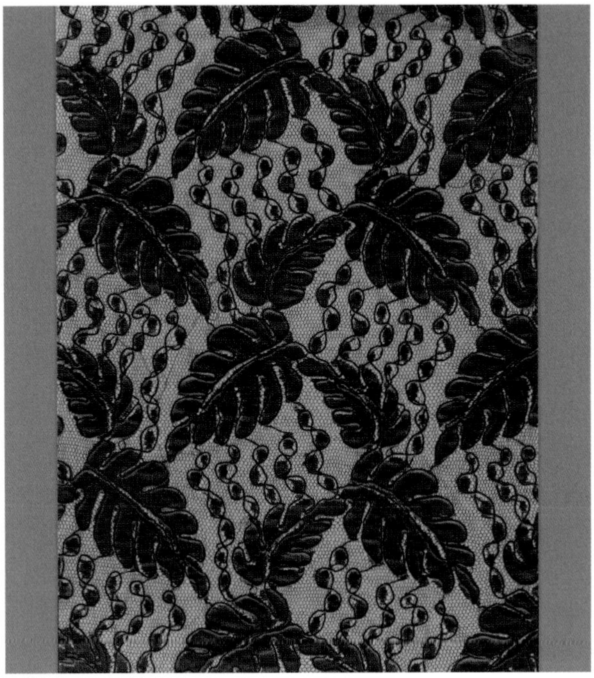

Figure 6.121 Cleaned lace image. *Desaturate* the image and *Adjust Levels* to make the image is black and white. *Invert* the image, if needed.

Step 2: Isolate the part of the image needed for the brush. The brush should be organic in shape rather than a square or rectangle. You can work with a full repeat, as shown in Figure 6.122, or just one motif. *Delete* or *Paint* white over the parts of the image that you do not need in the brush. If needed, adjust the *Levels* some more until the brush image is true black and white.

Go to *Edit menu → Define Brush Preset* to make your new *Lace Brush*. In the *Brush Settings* panel, adjust the *Spacing* and *Angle Jitter* amount until you have the results you like. Save the *Brush Preset* so it keeps the settings.

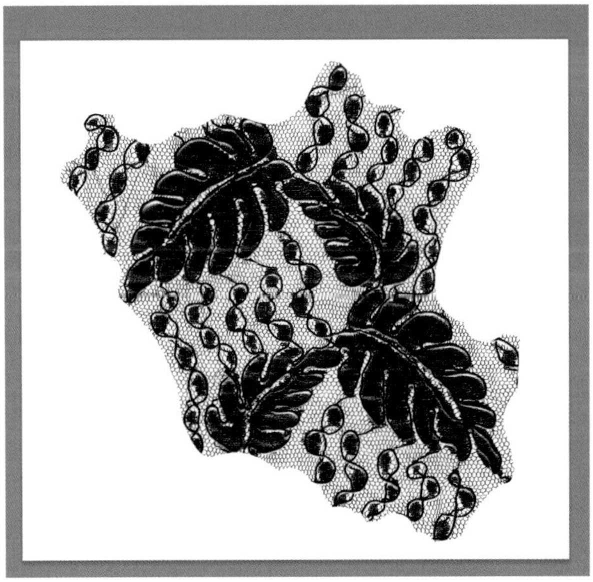

Figure 6.122 Image prepared for making a *Lace Brush*. Isolate an irregular, organically shaped area of the lace to use as the brush. *Paint* out with white or *Delete* the areas that you do not need for the brush. Click on *Edit menu → Define Brush Preset* to make the brush.

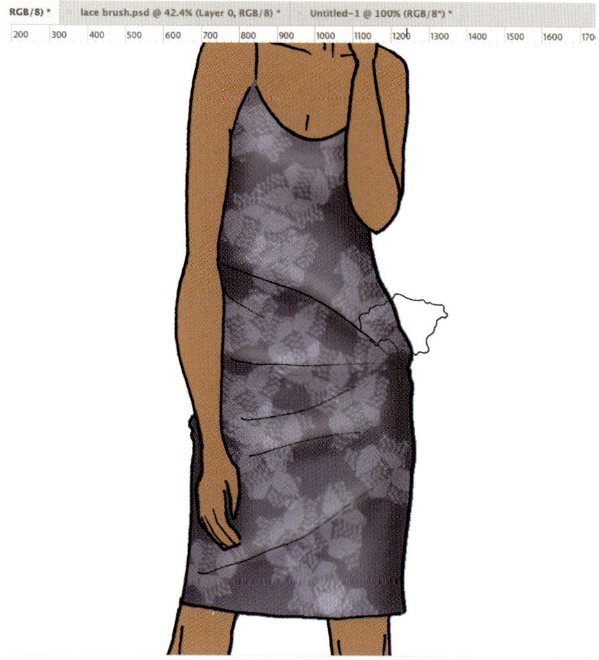

Figure 6.123 Using the *Lace Brush* on a rendering. Make a new *Layer*. Use the *Lace Brush* on the layer to create the lace texture. Adjust the *Layer Opacity* and *Blend Mode* as needed.

Step 3: Working on a prepared image, create a *Layer* for the lace. Remember to clip your layer to the garment layer! Use the *Lace Brush* to paint or stamp the lace texture where you would like it. The lace can cover the entire garment or just be used strategically as a hint of lace. Adjust the *Layer Opacity* and *Blend Mode* as needed. Figure 6.123 shows the *Lace Brush* application.

Project 6.8: Webbing, Mesh, and Fishnet

In Photoshop, webbing, mesh, and fishnet can be rendered using a variety of methods, including *Pattern Fills*, *Custom Brushes*, or even just drawing the texture using a *Basic Brush*. The main objective is to show the webbed texture of the fabric and its transparency. For this example we will develop a *Textured Pattern Fill*.

Step 1: Find or take a close-up flat photo of the type of mesh you are trying to illustrate. It works best if the mesh is black on a white background. For this project, we are working with fishnet. Using previous lessons, turn the image into a seamless repeat. If there is some wrinkling in your repeat (such as in Figure 6.124), that is usually fine. The pattern will be small when you use it, and the wrinkles are typically hard to see. *Select* and remove the background from the mesh image, leaving only the material. Then *Define* the image as a *Pattern* so it can be used as a *Pattern Fill*.

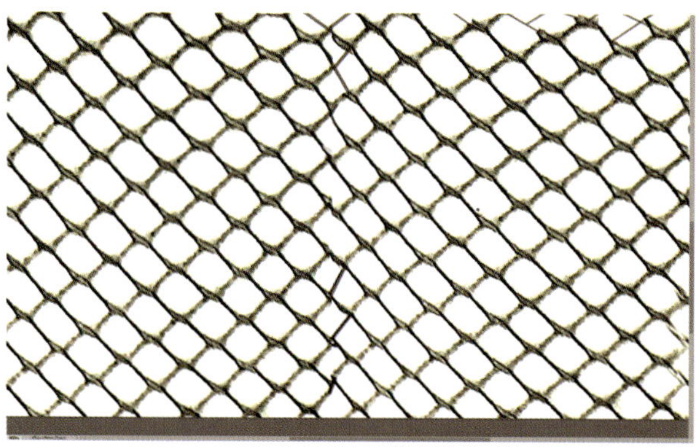

Figure 6.124 Fix the repeat of the mesh image using the *Clone stamp* tool or by manually painting in the repairs. It does not have to be perfect.

Step 2: Make a *Rectangular Selection* that is large enough to cover one of the legs. While the selection is active, create a *Pattern Fill Layer* using the new mesh pattern. Adjust the *Scale* of the pattern so it is the correct size for the garment and figure. *Right-click* on the *Layer* and convert the layer to a *Smart Object*. Using the *Move Tool*, *Move* and *Rotate* the rectangle of mesh into position over the leg. Figure 6.125 shows the mesh rectangle in position over the first leg.

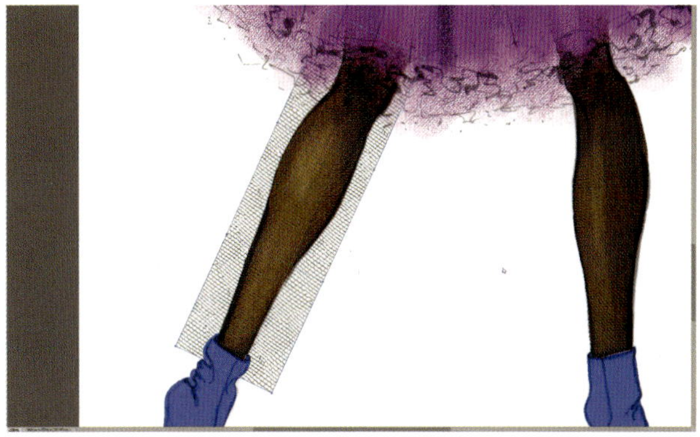

Figure 6.125 Mesh applied as a pattern fill over the leg. Make a *Rectangular Selection* and make a *Texture Pattern Fill Layer*. Adjust the *Scale* of the fill as needed. *Convert* the *Layer* to a *Smart Object*. *Move* and *Rotate* the fill shape over the leg.

Step 3: To make the mesh look like it is part of a garment, use *Warp* to bend the texture around the leg. Bring up your *Free Transform* tools with the shortcut *control+t* or *commandI+t* for a Mac. *Right-click* for the *Transform Options* menu while in the tool and select *Warp*. Manipulate the cross points and handles to make the rectangle look like it is wrapping around the leg. Allow the sides to collapse the pattern as that is how fishnet looks when viewed from an angle. Figure 6.126 shows how the shape will begin to collapse. You can also use the *Liquify* filter to manipulate the shape if needed.

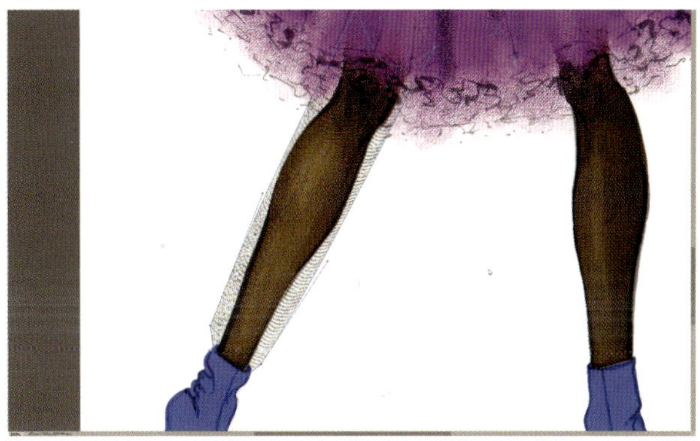

Figure 6.126 Warping the pattern fill over the leg. Use the *Free Transform* command and choose *Warp* from the menu when you *right-click*. Manipulate the cross points to make the mesh look like it wraps around the leg.

Step 4: Once you are satisfied with the shape of the texture, you can add a layer effect to increase the realism of the texture. As this particular texture is transparent in areas, the *Drop Shadow* effect will nicely pop out the hexagons and make them look three-dimensional. In the *Layers* panel, *double-click* the space beside the name of the layer to bring up the *Layers Style* dialog box. On the left side of the dialog box, click on the word for *Drop Shadow*. If you only tick the box beside the word, it will turn it on but not show the options to adjust the settings. The area in the middle should change to the *Drop Shadow* settings. Decrease your *Distance*, *Spread*, and *Size* options to very low amounts, as seen in Figure 6.127. This is a small texture, so the cast shadow will be quite small.

Step 5: Clip your pattern layer down into the painted shape layer below it. You can use the shortcut key of *alt* or *option* while hovering your cursor between the two layers. Likewise, you can *right-click* on the texture layer and choose *Make Clipping Mask* from the options. If you have a close-up of your texture, you should adjust the edge profile to match the raised texture created by the mesh. Figure 6.128 shows our finished fishnets.

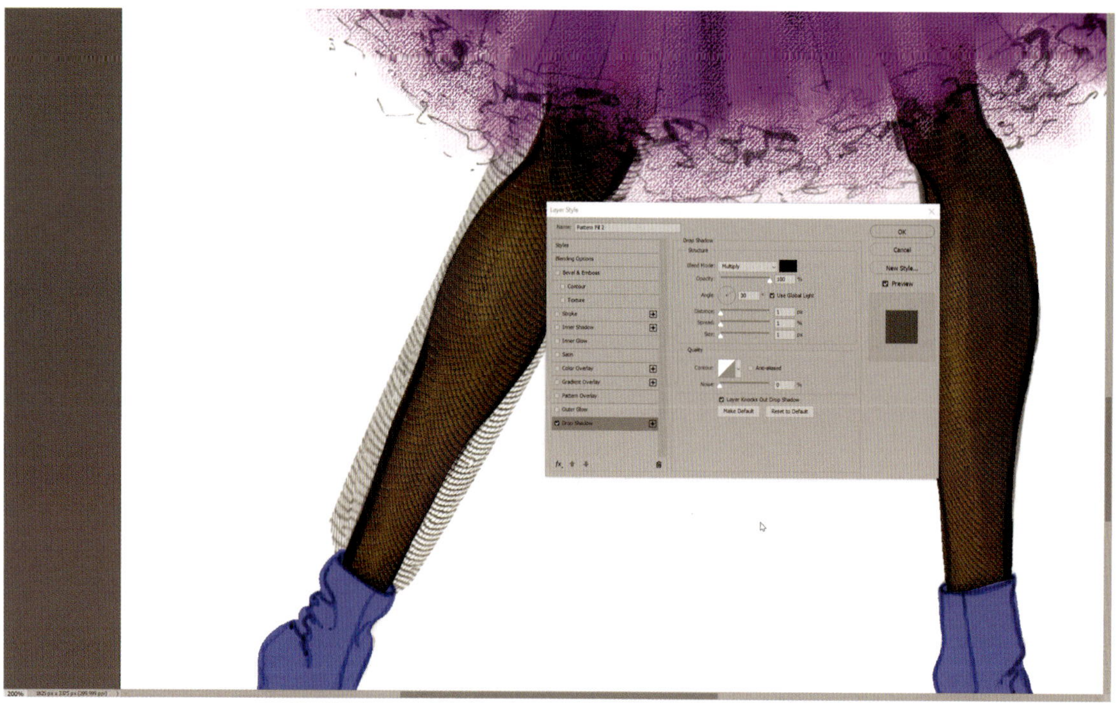

Figure 6.127 Mesh with a *Drop Shadow* effect applied through the *Layer Style*. Keep the settings very low for your *Distance*, *Spread*, and *Size* as the texture is quite fine.

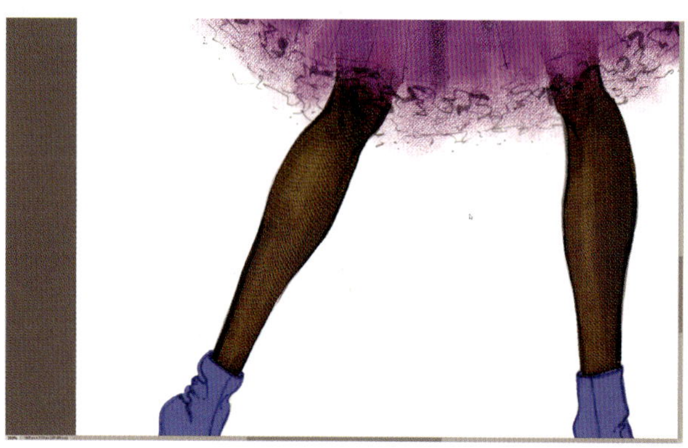

Figure 6.128 Finished mesh texture application. Clip the *Pattern Layer* to the leg layer below to contain the shape of the texture.

Project 6.9: Chiffon and Tulle

Chiffon, organza, tulle, organdy, gazar, and a variety of other fabrics are defined by their translucence. Tulle has the addition of texture; however, that is the main difference between it and other fabrics. Any of these fabrics are sheer or semi-sheer in a single layer. As you build up layers or folds, the fabric becomes more opaque. A skirt with five layers of organza or tulle may be completely opaque except around the edges where you may only see one or two layers. In contrast, a negligee made of a single layer of chiffon may be completely transparent.

To show a difference between each type of sheer fabric, make sure you draw it correctly from the beginning. Each fabric has very different properties other than translucence. Chiffon is soft and flowing; organza, organdy, and gazar have more body. Tulle has a unique way of folding, especially along the outer edges of gathered areas. Make a study of garments made of these fabrics to gain a better understanding of how to draw them.

We will illustrate organdy first. Chiffon, organza, and gazar are rendered the same way. As noted, the difference is the original line drawing of the garment and the opacity adjustment. The sample image we are working on has body, but sharp wrinkles, which gives it the properties of cotton organdy.

Step 1: When illustrating sheer fabrics, you must underpaint anything under the sheer garment that will show through the garment. Commonly, this means painting in the body or parts of the body. Sometimes, you also have undergarments that also need to be underpainted. For the example in Figure 6.129, we have painted in the figure's body with some basic shading.

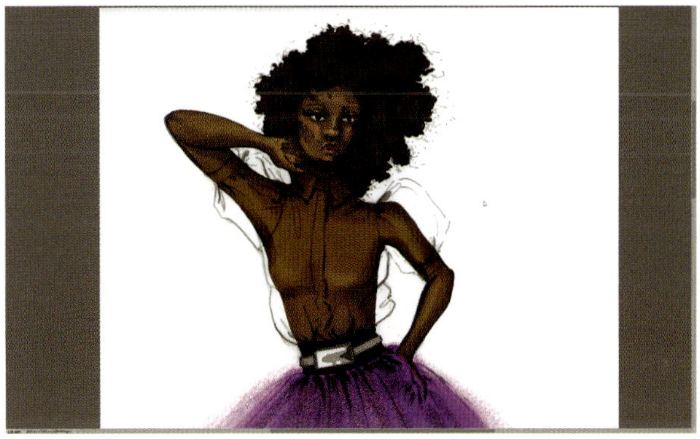

Figure 6.129 Draw the garment so it reflects the qualities of the fabric. Underpaint the body where it will be visible beneath the sheer fabric.

Step 2: Make a layer for the base color of the fabric. *Fill* or *Paint* in the garment area. If you are painting, use a hard, round *Brush*. Lower the *Opacity* of the *Layer* to match the translucency of the fabric. Some fabrics are more sheer than others and will need to have the *Opacity* of the *Layer* adjusted more. The organdy we are working on is less sheer than chiffon. Figure 6.130 shows the base layer of the organdy top painted in and the *Layer Opacity* lowered.

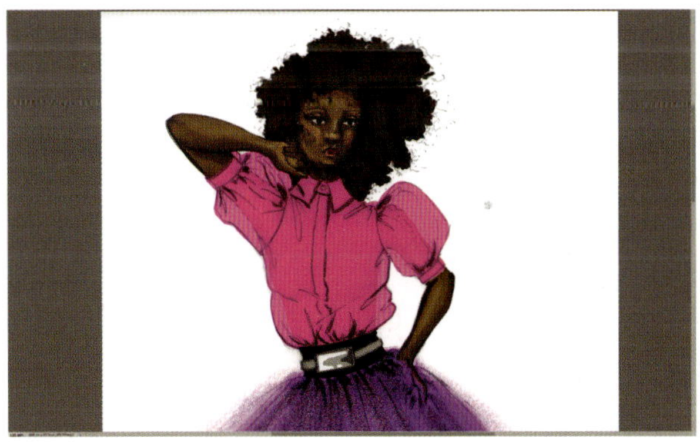

Figure 6.130 Make a new *Layer*. *Fill* or *Paint* in the base color of the fabric. Lower the *Layer Opacity* of the base color layer to match the sheerness level of the fabric.

Step 3: After creating the base fabric layer, make highlight and shadow layers as needed. If you have overlapping or folded areas, you may also need a separate layer for these. Overlaps, folds, and wrinkles have more intense color and are more opaque. If you paint these sections on a separate layer, you can control the *Layer Opacity* for these sections separately from the rest of the garment. Figure 6.131 demonstrates the completed organdy sample with shading.

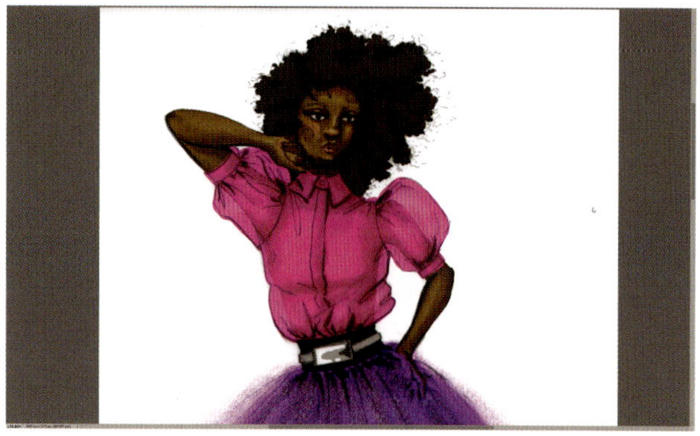

Figure 6.131 Create *Layers* for highlights and shadows. If there are any areas with layers, overlaps, or folds, create a layer for these. *Paint* in color representing the layering, overlaps, or folds, then adjust the *Layer Opacity* for this layer.

Tulle, illusion, netting, and other textured sheers require a few extra steps beyond what smooth sheers require. However, the initial drawing is still one of the most important parts of the entire rendering process. If a tulle garment is not drawn correctly, no one will understand that it is meant to be tulle. For our example, we will create a tulle skirt because that is one of the most common uses for the fabric.

Step 1: Tulle and textured sheers begin the same way as other sheers. After drawing the garment, underpaint anything that will show through from beneath the tulle garment. In Figure 6.132, you see that part of the figure's legs and her hand are painted in. The hand is considered underpainting because the skirt will cover part of it. The legs are only painted part of the way because the tulle reaches full opacity before the top. However, if you are not sure if or where this happens, you can paint all the body parts completely.

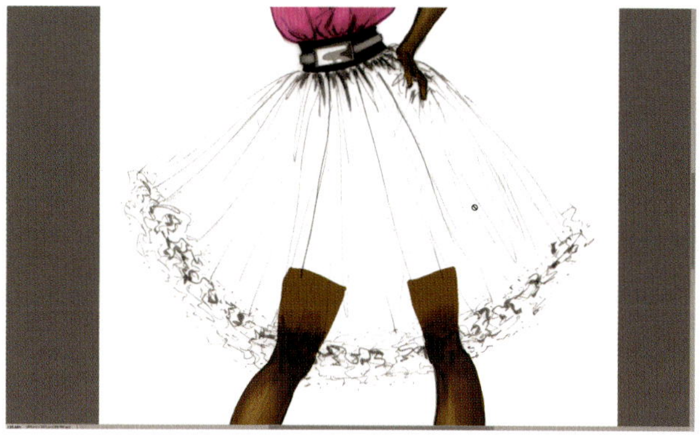

Figure 6.132 Paint any garment or body parts that will show through from beneath the tulle.

Step 2: The tulle garment needs a base layer of color. Because of the multiple layers of fabric in this garment, we will approach the base differently than we did for the organdy. Start with a new *Layer* for the color. Using the *Brush* tool, paint the base color of the skirt. Use an *Opaque Hard Round Brush* for the inner parts of the skirt, where it is completely opaque. Switch to a *Soft Round Brush* as you move out from the core of the skirt to soften the edges of the opaque area. Begin to drop the *Opacity* of the *Brush* as you move outward. The bottom edge of the skirt should be uneven because you are imitating the folds of a gathered skirt. Do not paint all the way to the translucent edges of the skirt on this layer. Keep the painting where the skirt is opaque and mostly opaque. Figure 6.133 shows what a tulle base layer looks like.

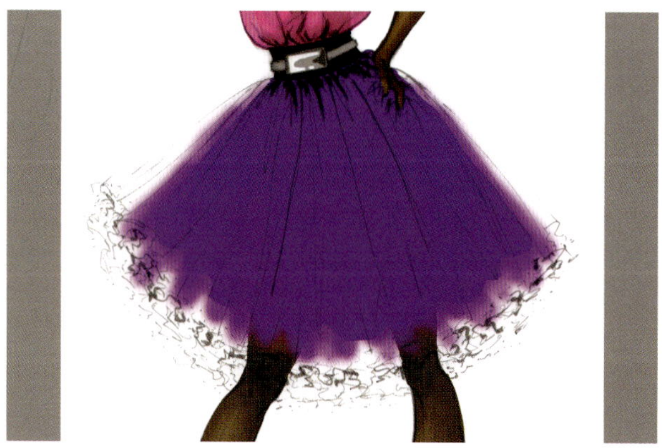

Figure 6.133 Create a *Layer* for the base color of the tulle. Using a combination of a *Hard Round Brush* and a *Soft Round Brush*, paint the opaquest part of the skirt. Avoid the sheer areas of the skirt.

Step 3: The base layer needs to be softened and blended. Switch to a slightly lighter color so shadows and texture will begin to develop. Create a new *Layer* for the softening work so it can easily be manipulated or corrected. Use a textured brush, such as *Legacy Brushes → Dry Media → Pastel Medium Tip*. This *Brush Library* comes with Photoshop but will need to be loaded from the panel *Options* menu.

Paint in strokes that follow the fall of the skirt. The painting on this layer will be denser on the inner part of the skirt and should extend a little further out than the original base layer. However, as you can see in Figure 6.134, it still does not fully fill the translucent areas.

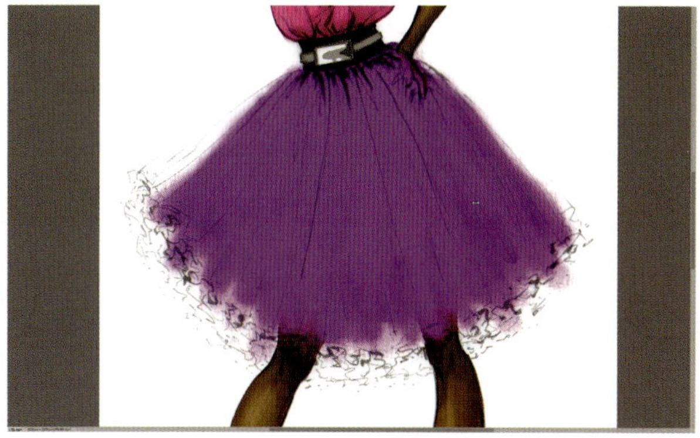

Figure 6.134 Softening the base layer of tulle. Create a new *Layer* and choose a slightly lighter color. Use a textured *Brush* and paint over the entire base color area. Extend the painting a little past the original base color edges, but do not paint into the sheerest areas of the skirt.

Step 4: Create a new *Layer* for shadows. Using the same *Brush Preset*, build up shading using a series of progressively darker colors. Work with the fall of the skirt. Use strong colors because a lighter texture layer will cover and mute this layer. Figure 6.135 shows strongly colored radiating shadows on the example.

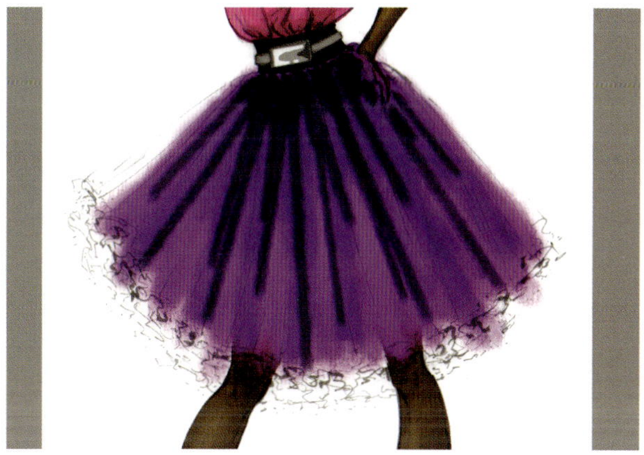

Figure 6.135 Create a new *Layer* for the shadows. Use the same textured *Brush* as before and paint the shading for the skirt. Use progressively darker colors and follow the fall of the skirt. The colors should be very strong because they will get muted by a lighter texture layer.

Step 5: Time to texture the tulle. Create a separate *Layer* for the texture. Switch to a lighter color. Use a *Brush* that looks like tulle texture. We recommend *Legacy Brushes → Dry Media → Charcoal Scraping Paper*. Paint in strokes following the fall of the skirt. This time you will cover the entire skirt area, all the way to the edges. This will create the illusion of more translucence along the outer areas, as shown in Figure 6.136.

Step 6: Finally, add highlights. Create a *Layer* for the highlights so you have better control over adjustments and corrections. Use the same textured *Brush* as you did for creating the previous texture layer. Switch to a light or white color. Paint a few streaks for highlights. Be careful not to overdo this layer. Also, pay attention to which side of the body the light source is on. Try setting the *Layer Blend Mode* to *Screen* for better results. Figure 6.136 shows the finished tulle skirt.

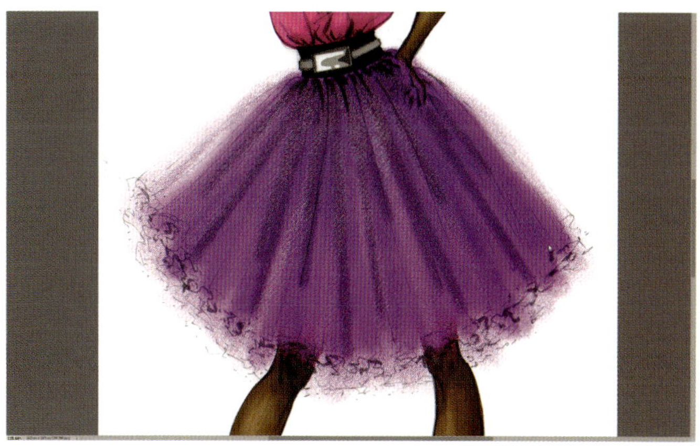

Figure 6.136 Create a new *Layer* for texture. Find a *Brush Preset* that looks like tulle texture and switch to a lighter color. Following the fall of the skirt, paint the entire skirt, all the way to the edges. Create a *Layer* for highlights. Using the same *Brush*, but a lighter color, paint the highlights. Set the *Layer Blend Mode* to *Screen*.

Project 6.10: Metallic, Holographic, and Reflective Effects

Reflective effects such as metal, metallic, holographic, and other similar surfaces can be created a number of ways depending on the luster of the material. Metallic fabric is not as reflective and can be created in a similar method as the sequin effect. A bit of *Noise* in the right color can go a long way to hint at lurex or lamé.

For something more reflective such as a foiled jersey or actual metal, you have some options. For those with an artistic background and more experience, you may want to directly paint in the look. Use a reference image to help you get the detail and color effects correct. Usually, an acrylic style *Brush* tip will serve you well for this texture. If you are short on time or less comfortable with painting, you may want to try using a *Gradient Map* effect. We learned this effect from an artist called Sinex through YouTube. Many other artists referenced this same lesson to incorporate holographic effects, so we want to acknowledge the source!

Step 1: Paint your object in the general color of your choice with highlights and shadows. You want to stick to the lighter colors to make the effect work correctly. We will make a liquid silver effect, so we painted ours in the white/gray range using a soft, round brush as shown in Figure 6.137.

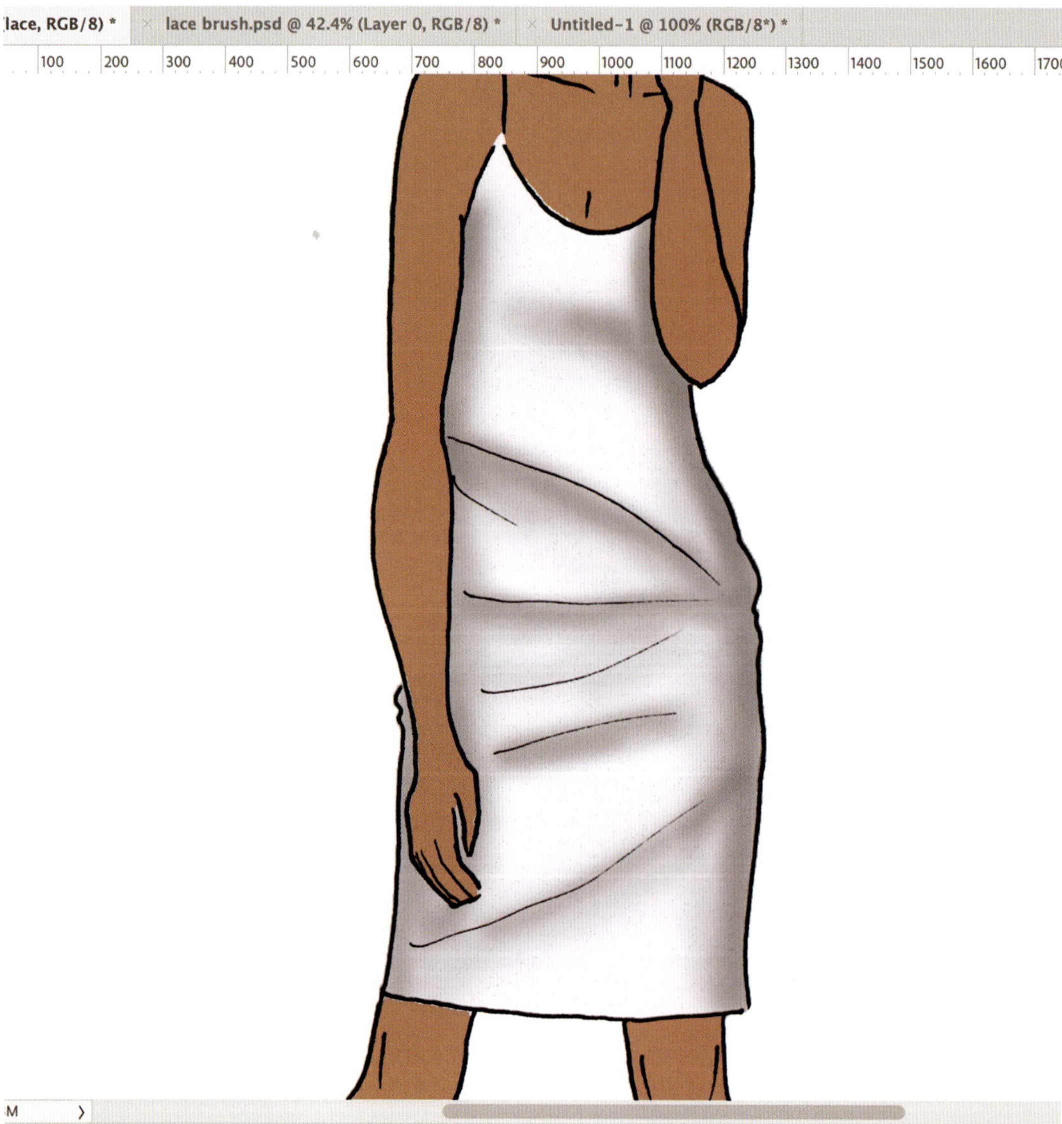

Figure 6.137 To create a reflective textile like foiled jersey, sometimes called liquid lamé, start by painting a light-colored surface with the highlights and shadows.

Step 2: Open your *Gradients* panel through the *Windows* menu. You need to append the list of gradient presets with the *Legacy Gradients*. In the *Gradients* panel, open the *Options* menu found in the upper right corner of the panel. Choose *Legacy Gradients* from the list.

Step 3: Add a *Gradient Map Adjustment Layer* through the *Layers* panel just above your garment item layer. This will apply a default gradient to your layers. Look in the *Properties* panel to adjust the gradient settings. Click the down arrow next to the gradient and navigate to the *Spectrum* folder inside the *Legacy Gradients* folder. Choose one of the rainbow effects. Be sure to clip your *Gradient Map* layer to the garment layer below it.

Step 4: Adjust the colors and positions in the gradient by clicking once on the gradient bar found in the *Properties* panel. You want to adjust it to look like an over-the-top holographic effect. Unfortunately, there is not a simple recipe for the settings. The effect depends on your base color and shading. Simply keep moving around your colors and positions on the gradient bar until it looks right. You can see the effect we created with our dress in Figure 6.138.

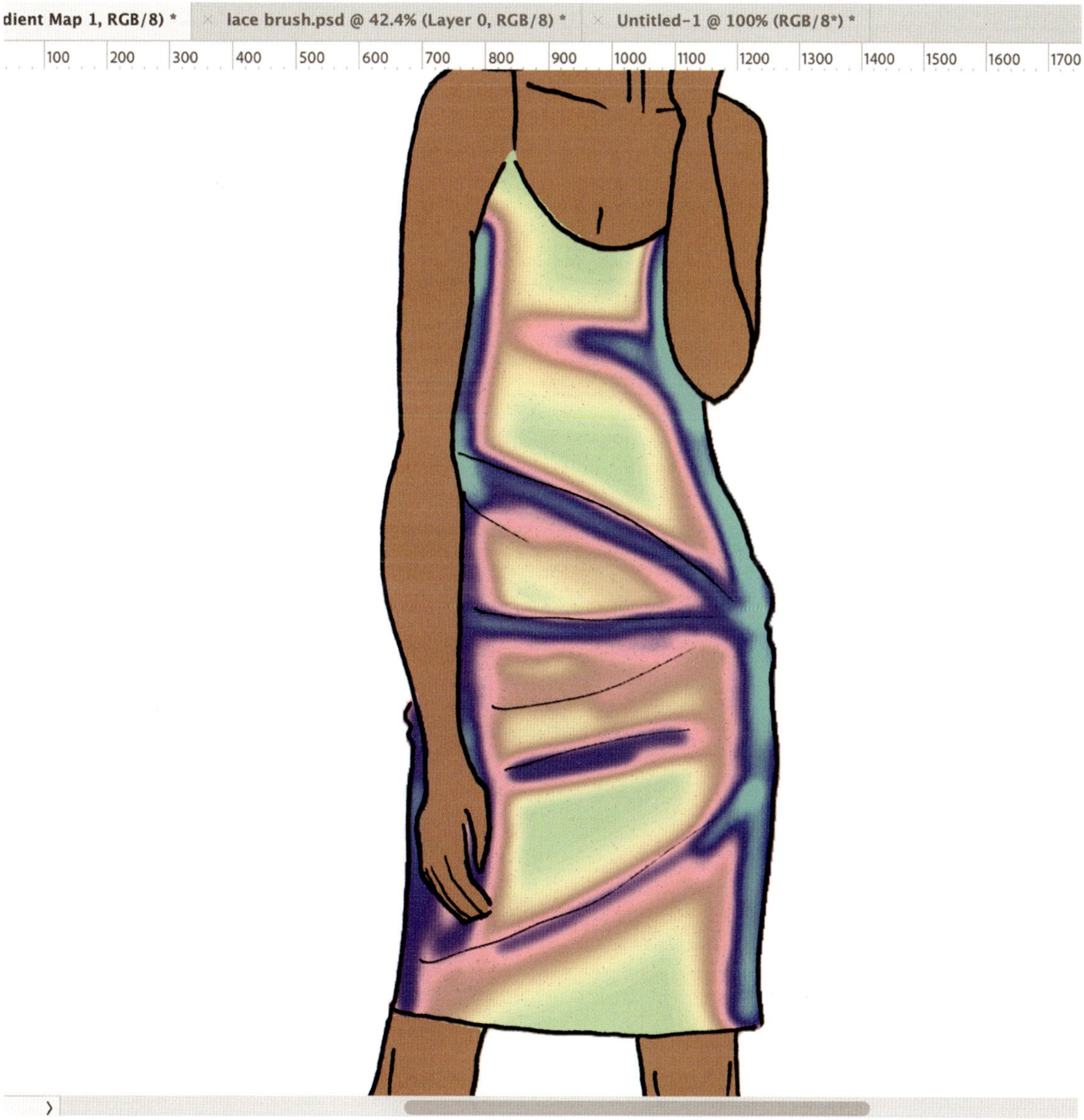

Figure 6.138 Use one of the rainbow gradients found in the *Spectrum* folder of the *Legacy Gradients*. Clip it to your garment below and adjust the colors and positions until it looks like a crazy holographic effect.

Step 5: Here is the magic part. On the *Gradient Map* layer, change your *Blend Mode* to *Luminosity*. Now your garment should look like metal, like the one in Figure 6.139. You may need to adjust your gradient a bit until you get the desired effect. Sometimes it helps to adjust the original shading on the garment layer, too. Unfortunately, this is a trial-and-error process so be prepared to face a little frustration if it doesn't work out on the first try.

Let's take this effect further to create a more realistic holographic effect. Start with the metal effect you just completed. It should look like the liquid lamé fabric in Figure 6.140. If you study holographic fabric, the rainbow effect collects in the transition areas between highlight and shadows. Therefore, we will work with each separately.

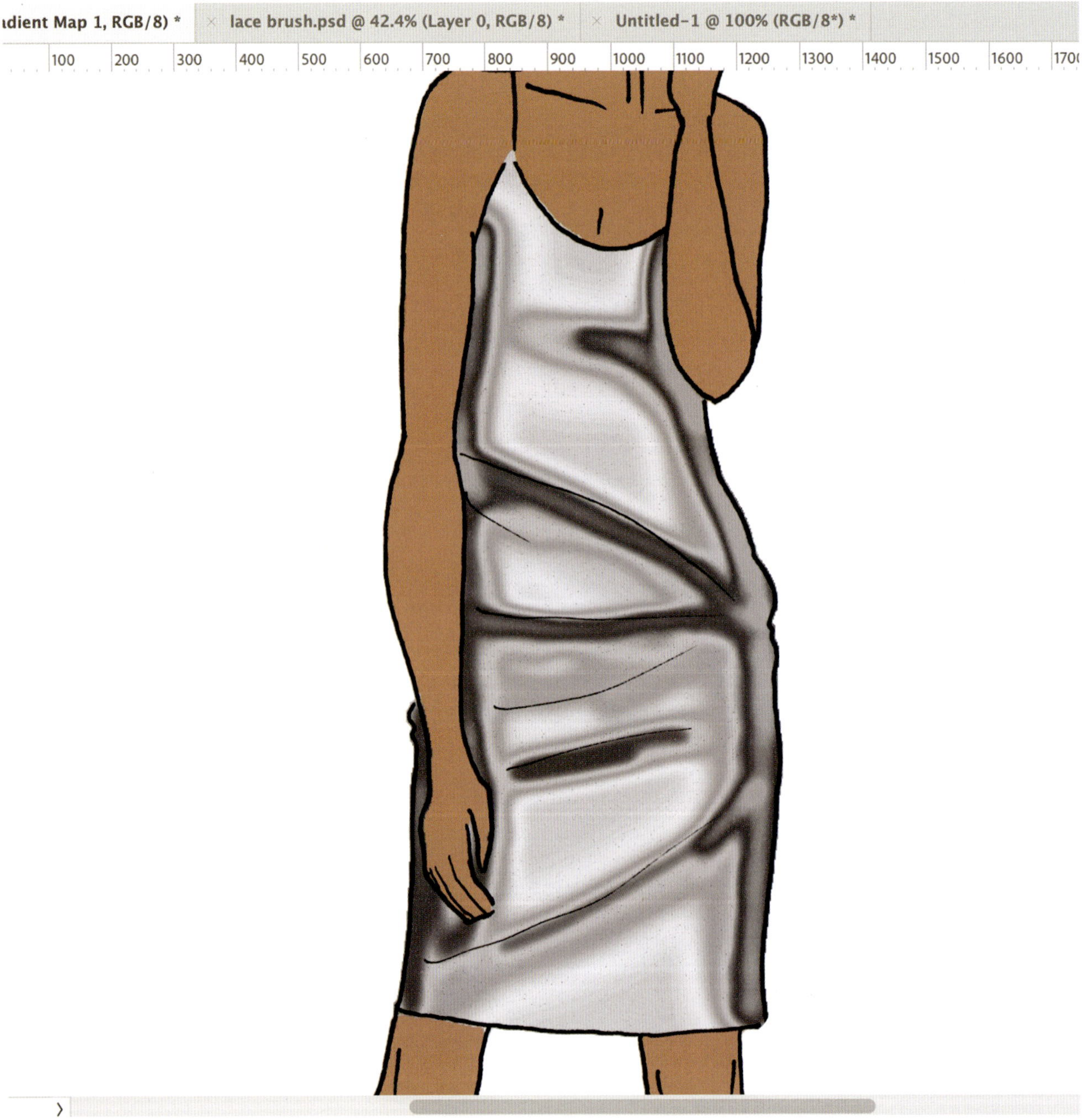

Figure 6.139 Change the *Gradient Map* layer to the *Blend Mode* of *Luminosity*. It should now look like metal! If you need to, go back and tweak the *Gradient* to make the effect look right.

Step 1: *Duplicate* the basic garment paint layer two times. This action generally releases the *Clipping mask* you made with the *Gradient Map*, so you will need to rearrange your layers and reapply the mask. Drag the two new garment layer copies above your *Gradient Map* layer in the *Layers* panel. Now clip the *Gradient Map Layer* back down to the original garment paint layer.

Step 2: Adjust the *Levels* of your first garment paint copy layer. We want to first focus on the highlights. While we are here, change the name to "holo highlights" to help you keep up with each layer. Now use the keyboard shortcut *control+l* or *command+l* for a Mac to bring up your *Layers* adjustment. It's okay to make a destructive change on this to keep the file size down. Pull up the shadow slider to darken them and pull your mid-tone slider down to increase the highlight information. You can see the effect on our example in Figure 6.140. Again, there are no magic number settings. It will take some experimentation to get the right look for your rendering.

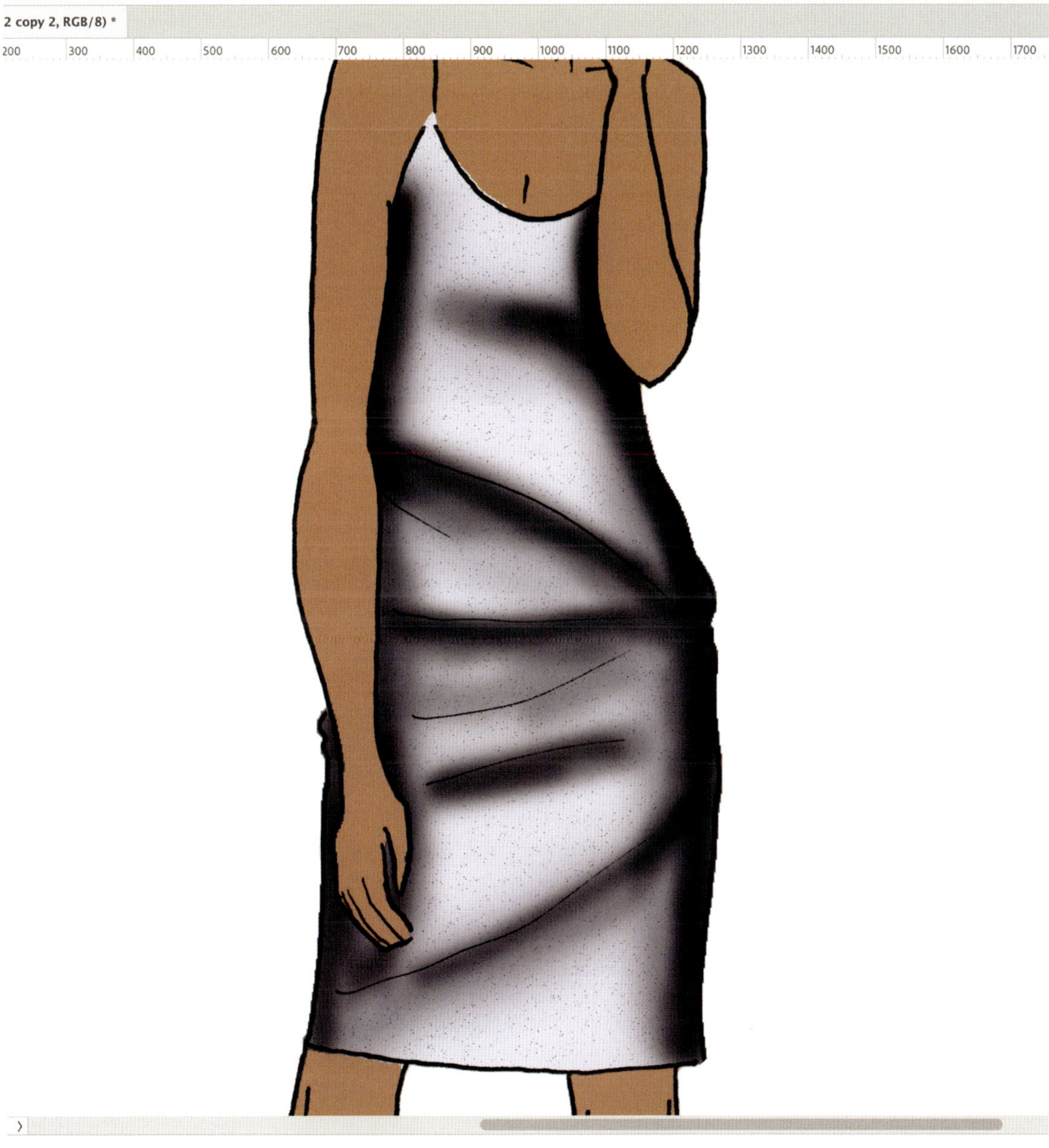

Figure 6.140 Make a duplicate copy of your painted garment layer and name it "holo highlights." Adjust the *Levels* so that there is more variation in the highlights. Your shadows should be darkened.

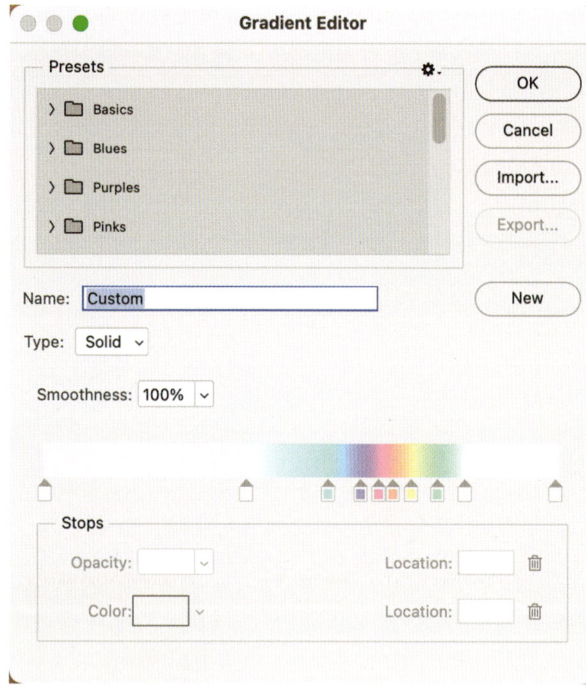

Figure 6.141 Adjust your gradient through the *Gradient Editor* panel. Add white to either end of the gradient and push the spectrum closer together in the mid-tone area. Save your gradient preset by changing the name and clicking *New*.

Step 3: Apply the same *Gradient Map* you just made for the metal effect. Adjust the *Gradient* to squeeze the spectrum into the lighter mid-tones and bookend it with white as shown in Figure 6.141. Be sure to save your preset if you want to use the effect again in the future. While your *Gradient Editor* panel is active with the adjusted gradient, fill in the name field, then click the *New* button. You can see how the *Gradient Map* changes our garment in Figure 6.142.

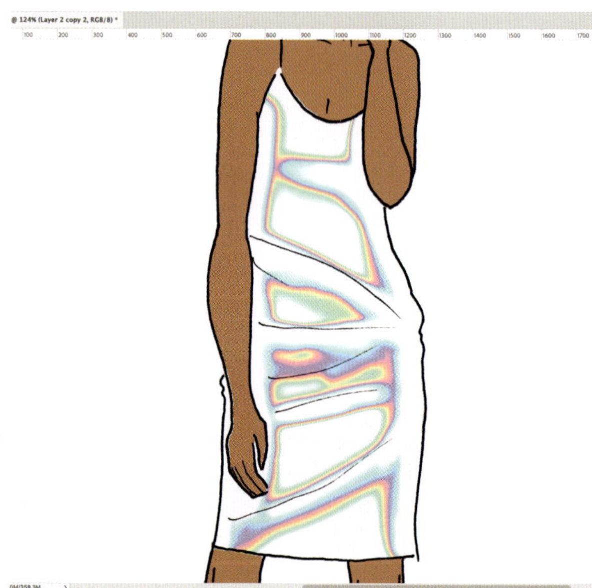

Figure 6.142 This is how our *Gradient Map* affects the highlight areas. The colored spectrum should not overpower the lightest lights. It should mostly change the transitional areas between highlight and shadow.

Step 4: Change the holo highlights *Layer Blend Mode*. In the previous effect for metal, we changed the *Gradient Map* layer. However, this time you want to leave the *Gradient Map* blend mode at normal and change the *Gradient Map* mode. We used *Soft Light* for our example shown in Figure 6.143. However, cycle through the modes to see what works best for your rendering.

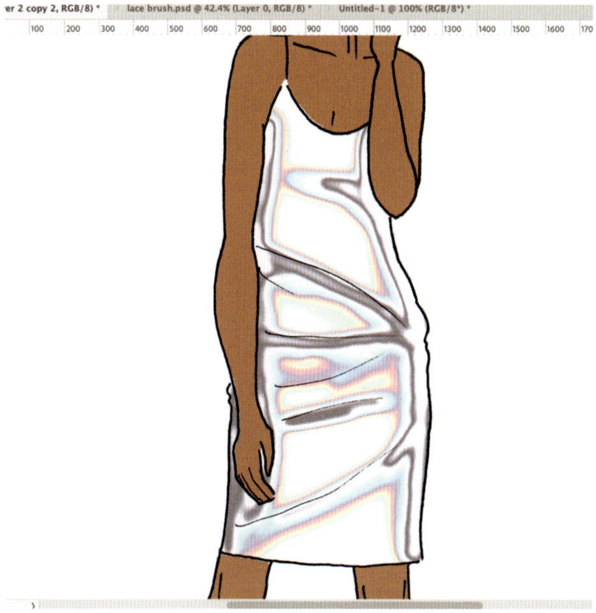

Figure 6.143 Change the *Blend Mode* of your garment holo highlights layer to *Soft Light* or another mode that works for your needs.

Step 5: Repeat this process for the shadows. Rename your second duplicate garment paint layer to "holo shadows." Adjust the *Levels* to focus on the shadow information. To do this, **clip** your highlights by bringing down the highlight slider and moving the mid-tone slider up toward the highlight end. When you bring in your shadow or highlight slider beyond the edge of the histogram information, it's called clipping the highlights or clipping the shadows. This means that you are eliminating the value information in those areas and replacing them with solid black or white. The terminology can be confusing since we also use "clipping masks." These are two different references, though.

Add a *Gradient Map Adjustment Layer* on top of your holo shadows layer. Use the previous gradient for the highlights but replace the white areas with pure black as shown in Figure 6.144. Tweak and adjust as needed, then save the preset for later use with the *New* button.

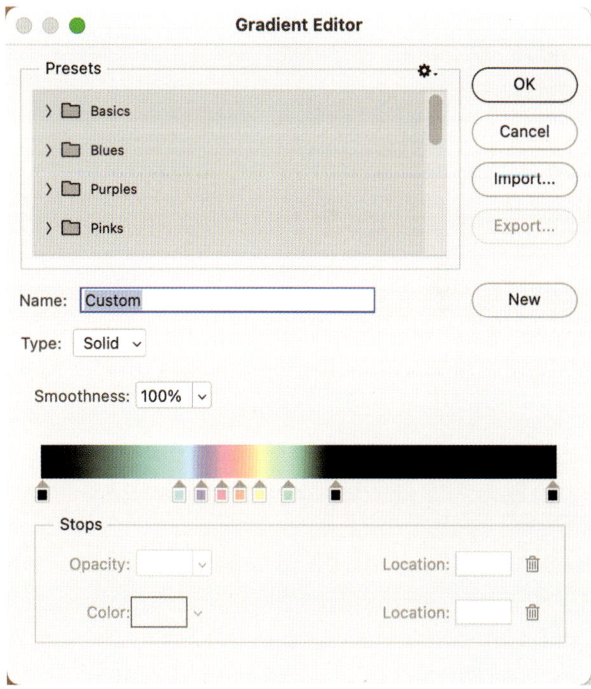

Figure 6.144 Adjust your shadow gradient by replacing the white areas with pure black. Adjust your gradient until it looks right on the garment. Save your preset with the *New* button.

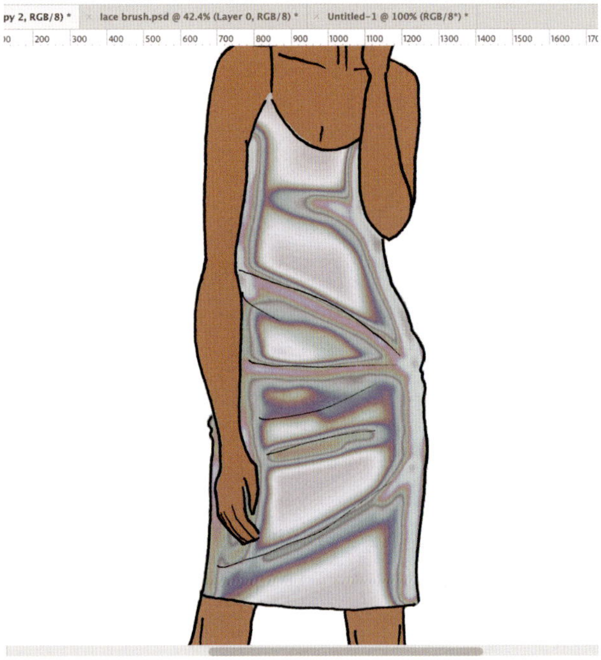

Figure 6.145 Repeat the process for your shadows to create the final holographic effect.

Step 6: Once again, change the blend mode of your holo shadows layer. We used soft light for the final effect shown in Figure 6.145. Leave the *Gradient Map Blend Mode* on *Normal*. Go back and adjust the *Gradient Maps*, shading, or levels as needed until you get the desired effect!

Project 6.11: Glowing and Lighted Effects

If you work for an athletic wear company, this section is written for you! Runners need a way to signal their presence in the dark. Reflective tape or small LED lights help make them stand out and avoid major traffic snafus. You won't always want a lighted effect, but when you do, you use a *Layer Style*.[2] Anything that is either highly reflective or emits its own light will have a soft glow around it. Let's find out how to achieve this look.

Step 1: Reflective tape is primarily a medium gray color with glass beads or microprisms that reflect light with exponential power. Start by painting in the shape of your reflective surface with 50% gray on a separate layer. Figure 6.146 shows our running pants with a reflective stripe down the sides and across the midsection.

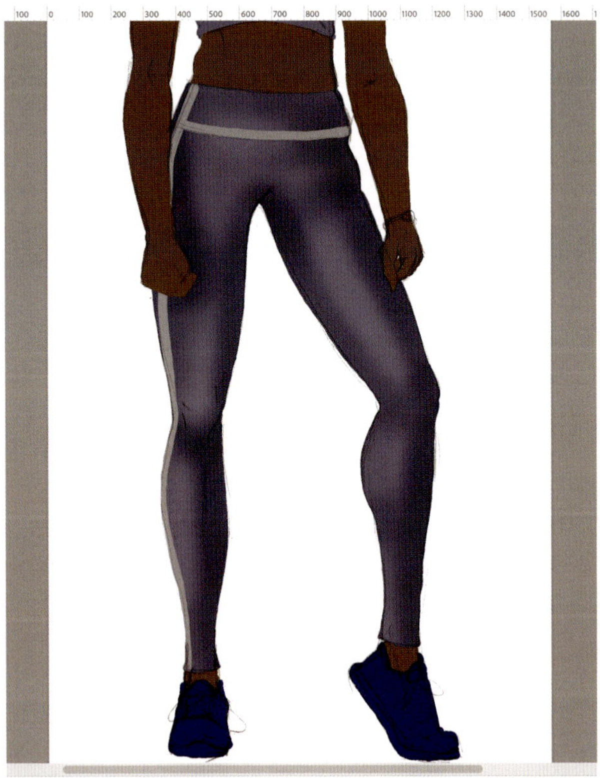

Figure 6.146 Paint in your reflective tape or material on its own layer.

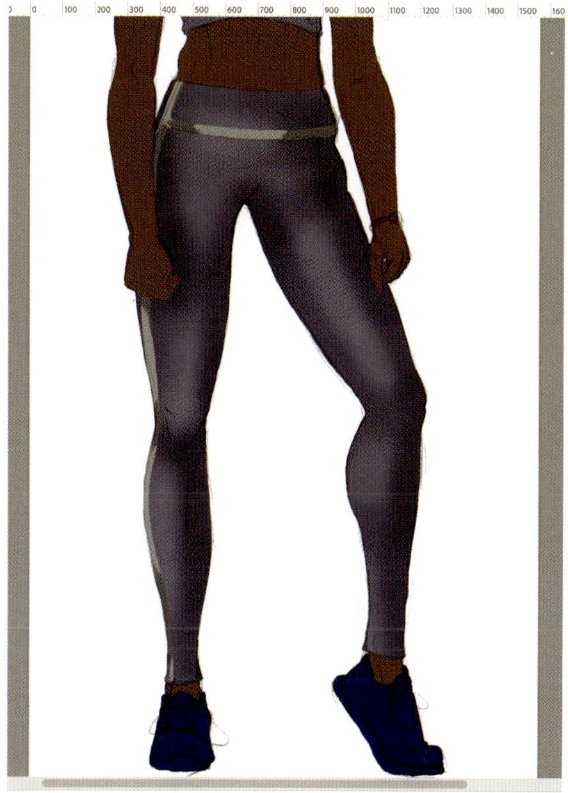

Step 2: Paint in the shadows. Unless your tape is on a totally flat surface directed toward a light source, it will pick up shadows in the areas turned away or blocked from the light. Because of the reflective material, the shadows tend to be dark with very little transition to the adjacent color. You can see the shadows we painted on our tape in Figure 6.147. The shadows can be on the original tape layer or their own layer.

Figure 6.147 Paint in your shadows. These tend to be dark with very little transitional softness.

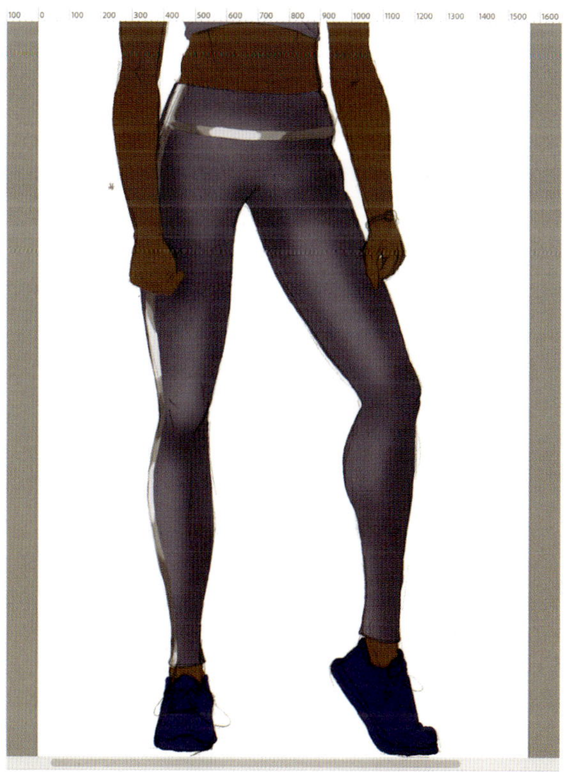

Step 3: Paint in your highlights as shown in Figure 6.148. Use a pure white color. Again, the transition is quite sharp. This should be on its own layer so we can add a *Layer Style* momentarily.

Figure 6.148 Paint in the highlights using white.

Step 4: Here comes the fun part! *Double-click* in the space beside your highlights layer to bring up the *Layer Style* options box. Add an *Outer Glow* by clicking on the words “Outer Glow” on the left side of the dialog box. You can copy our settings in Figure 6.149 or adjust them to your rendering. We have a modest amount of *Opacity* and a small amount of *Noise* in the *Structure* section. We changed the *Technique* to *Precise* with a low *Spread* and *Size* in the *Elements* Section. The rest of the settings we left at the default amounts. See the effect in Figure 6.150.

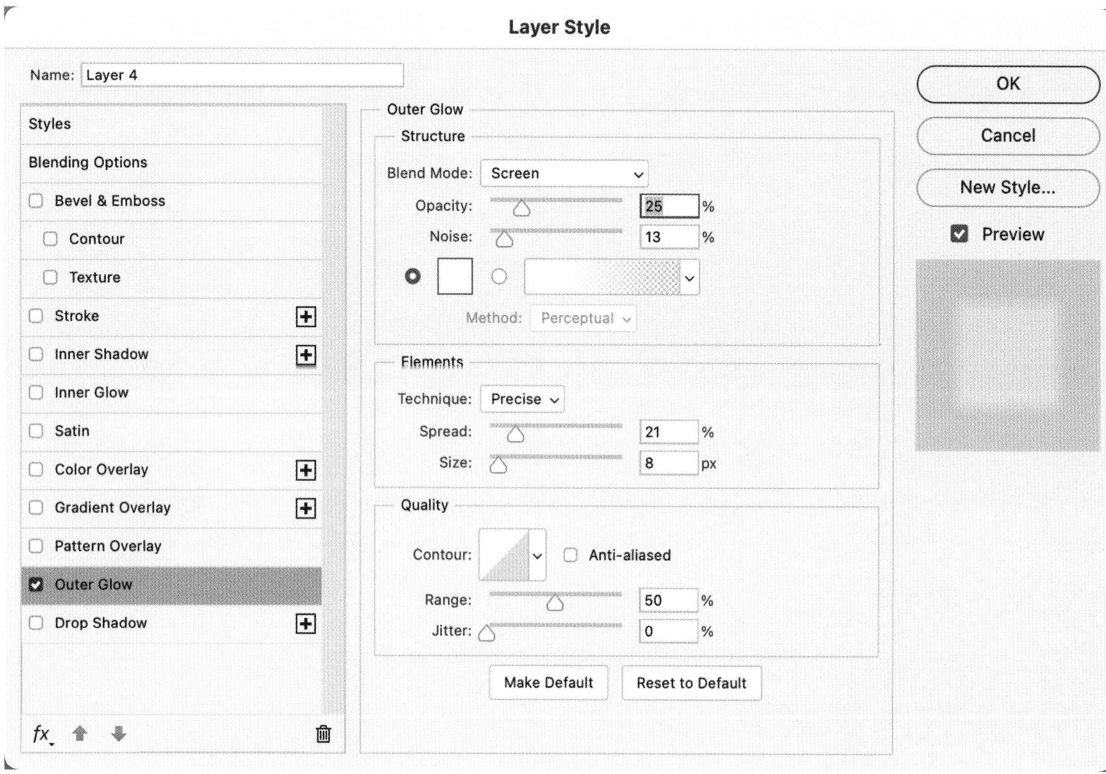

Figure 6.149 In the *Layer Style* options box, add an *Outer Glow* and adjust your settings as needed.

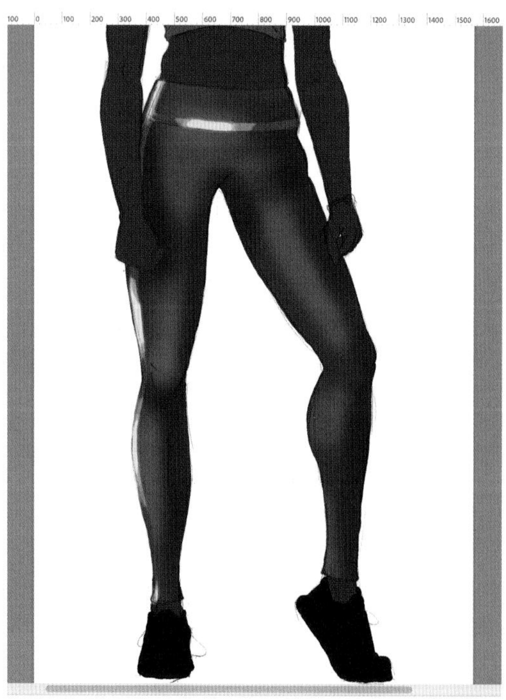

Figure 6.150 The results of adding an *Outer Glow Layer Style* to our highlights.

That creates your reflective tape effect! Of course, any lighted effect shows better in the dark, so you may want to view it against a dark background like in Figure 6.151. Consider how you want to display your designs when you get to the layout section. You will most likely want a dark background to get the full effect of the lighting.

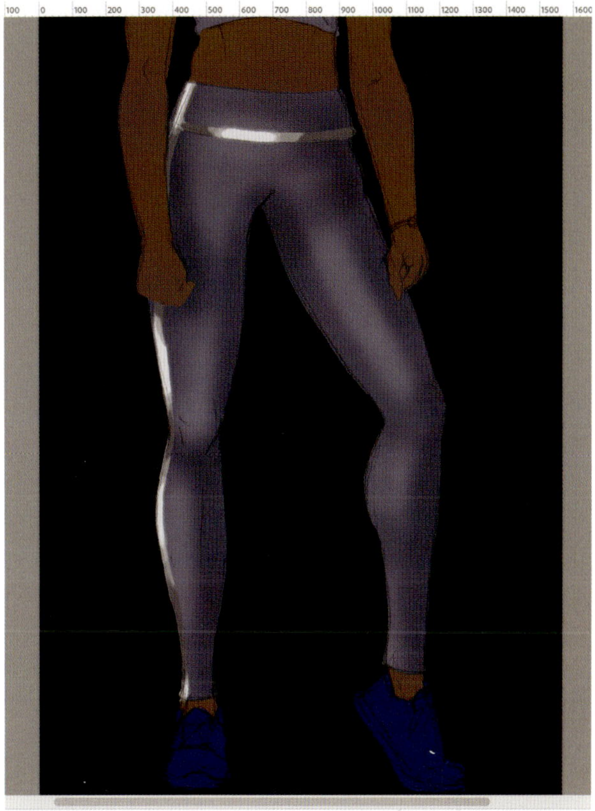

Figure 6.151 The final technique seen on a dark background for full effect.

Okay, let's take this a step further and create a trim with emitted light. LED technology makes this sort of trim much more accessible and is available in a wide variety of colors. The technique is very similar to what we just used for the reflective tape.

Step 1: Paint in your trim in a saturated version of your light source hue. You can see in Figure 6.152 we are using a bright red color. The trim is the source of light, so there are no shadows and highlights necessary for the trim.

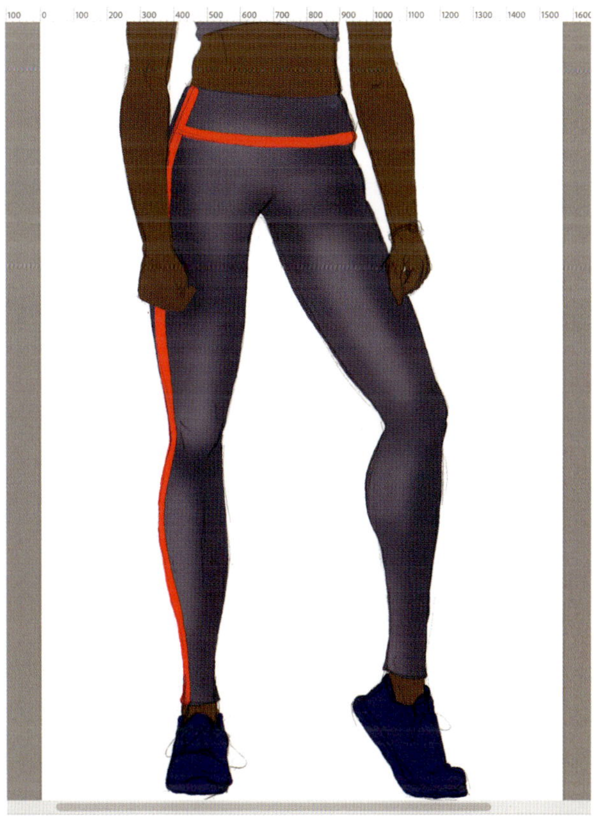

Figure 6.152 Paint in your trim in the general color of the light source. Choose a brightly saturated color for the best effect.

Step 2: Make a duplicate of this layer by dragging the layer to the plus icon at the bottom of the *Layers* panel. Set the *Layer Blend Mode* to *Screen*. On the duplicate layer, open your *Layer Style* options box by *double-clicking* in the gray space beside your layer name. As before, you want to add an *Outer Glow* effect.

Change the color of the glow to a light version of your main hue. Keep the *Opacity* and *Noise* low but increase the spread and size of your glow. You can see the effect of our glow in Figure 6.153 and our settings for this effect in Figure 6.154.

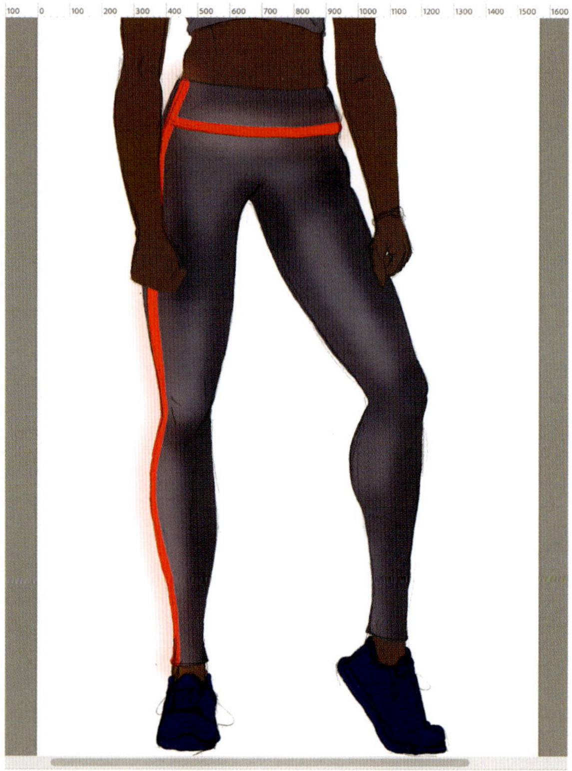

Figure 6.153 Make a duplicate of your trim layer and apply an *Outer Glow Layer Style*.

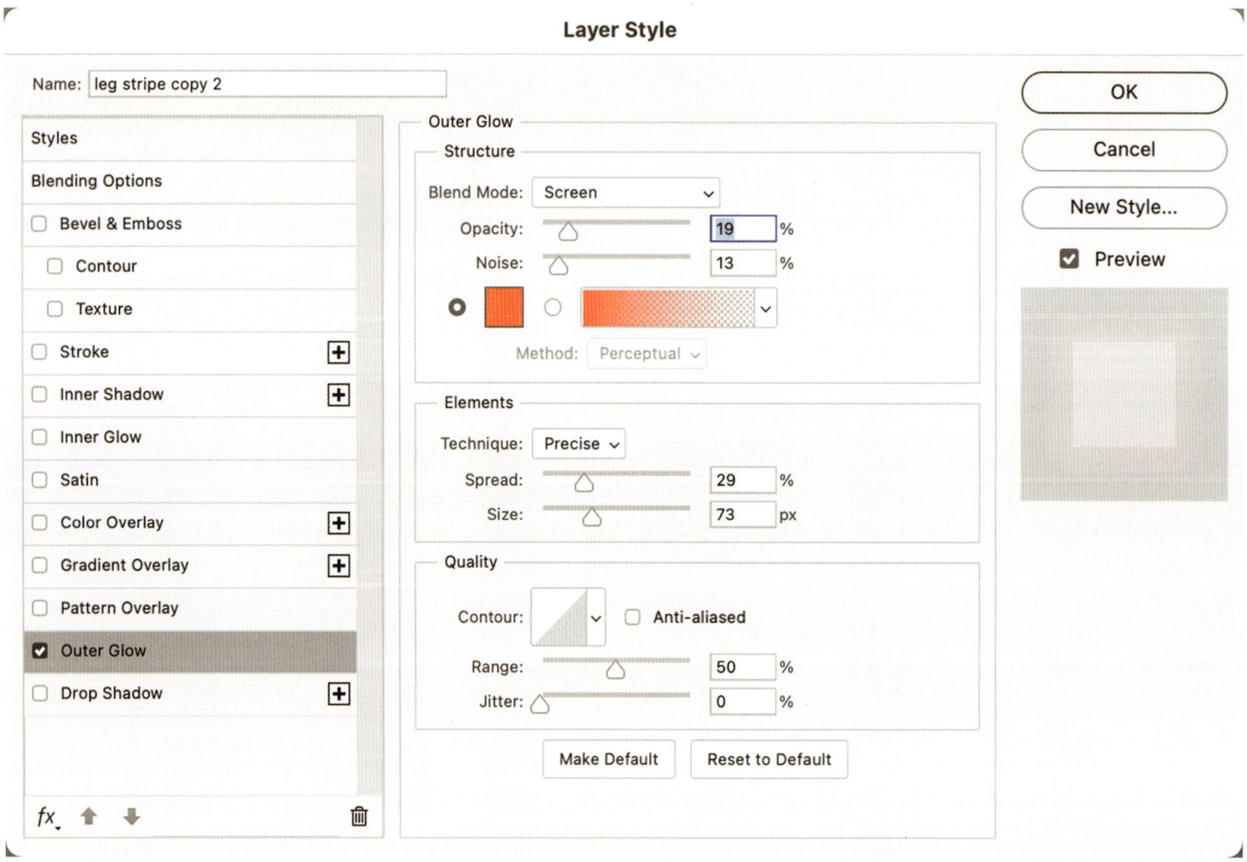

Figure 6.154 Adjust your settings of the *Outer Glow*. Keep the *Opacity* low while increasing the *Spread* and *Size*. Change the color of your glow to a light version of your trim hue.

Step 3: To increase the effect, make a duplicate of your glowing trim layer. Make sure this layer is also set to *Screen* for the blend mode. *Double-click* the layer to open the *Layer Style* box. Increase your *Opacity* and decrease the *Spread* and *Size*. Two glow layers may be enough, or you may need to repeat step 3 a few times to build up the right amount of glow for your illustration. You can see our effect in Figure 6.155.

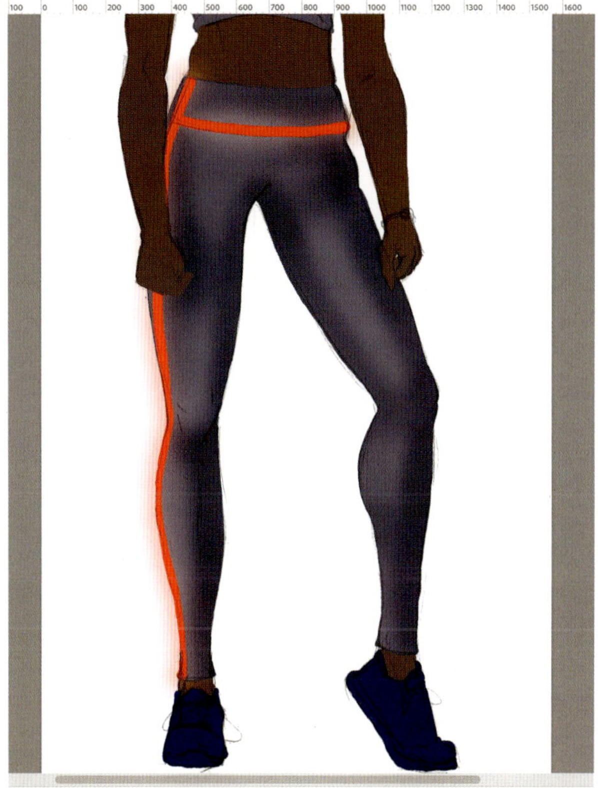

Figure 6.155 Build up duplicate glow layers. Keep the *Layer Blend Mode* set to *Screen*, and adjust your *Layer Style* settings to a smaller, more intense effect each time.

Step 4: Now click back on your original trim layer. *Double-click* the layer to open the *Layer Style* box one more time. This time, select *Inner Glow* and adjust your settings. You can see the effect on Figure 6.156a. In the settings, we increase the *Opacity* significantly. Change the *Source* from *Edge* to *Center*. Then adjust the size as needed to create the best effect of a glowing light source. you can see the settings we used in Figure 6.156b.

As before, change your background to something dark to appreciate the full effect of your lighting! If you are happy with your results, you may want to collapse all the glow layers to save some file space. If you prefer flexibility, then select all the layers and click the *New Folder* button at the bottom of the *Layers* panel. This will keep your layers neater.

Figure 6.157 shows the effect of our lighted trim on the leggings. To truly sell the effect, you will need to go in and paint some light reflection on areas of the skin or other garments affected by the light source. And before you get too excited about this technique, remember to evaluate the practicality of such a gimmick on your fashion or costume design. Will a lighted effect actually enhance your design or just make you look silly?

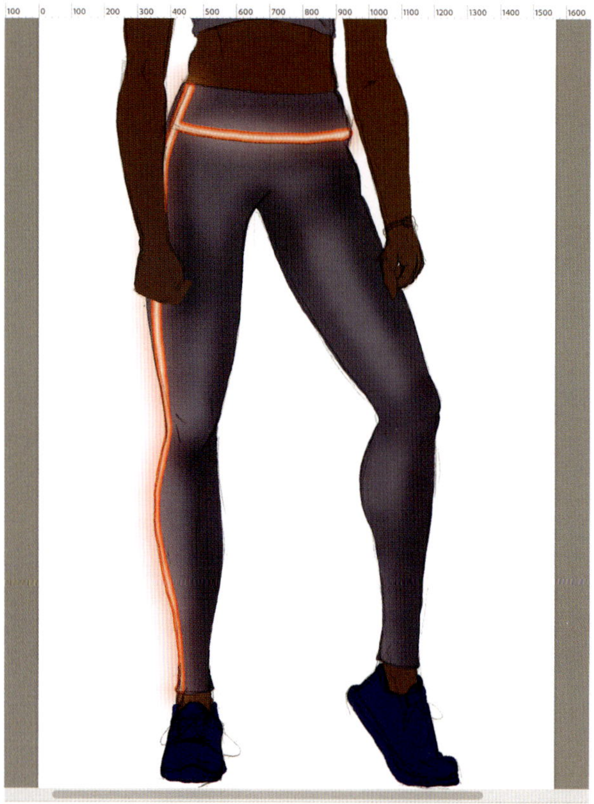

(a)

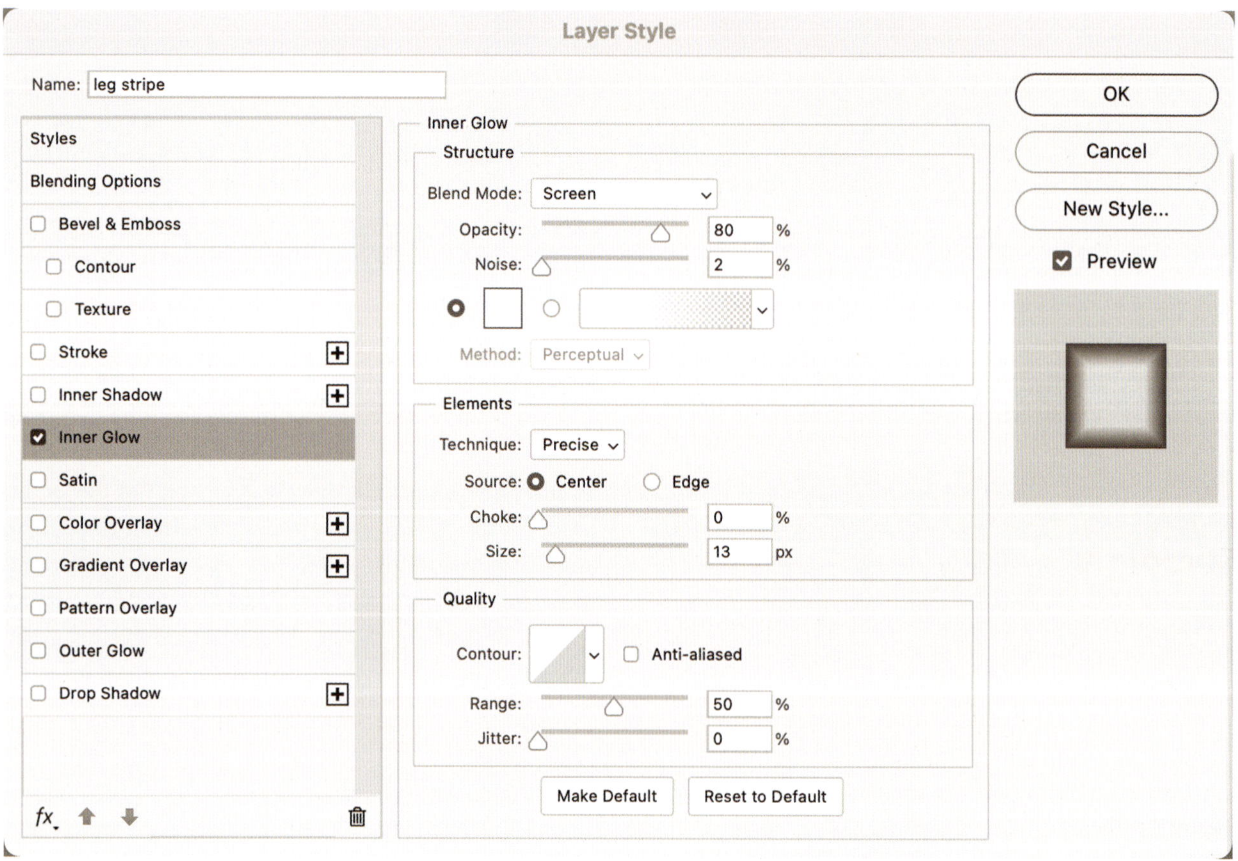

(b)

Figure 6.156a–b *Inner Glow Layer Style*. Part (a) shows the inner glow effect. Part (b) shows the settings for the *Inner Glow Layer Style* effect. This effect makes the LED strip appear to glow. Set the *Source* to *Center* and increase the *Opacity*.

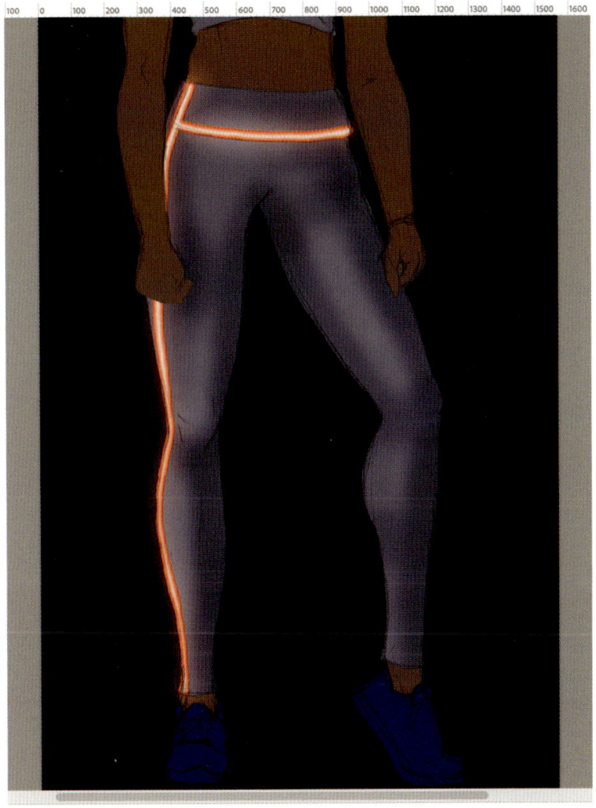

Figure 6.157 Put your rendering on a dark background to appreciate the full effect of your lighted trim.

PRO TIP 6.1

Pattern or Texture: How about Both?

As you develop your knowledge and skills, you will start to develop your own methods and tricks for rendering. To take your style to the next level, consider combining your textile patterns with some texture techniques. For example, you may have a plaid brushed mohair coat. Apply the plaid pattern, then consider how to create the brushed mohair texture. Perhaps you have a printed satin shirt. Add your print, then start to create your highlight and shadow layers to incorporate the satin texture. Feel free to go crazy with it!

Summary

Textures are not always a necessary part of an illustration. However, when you choose to include texture, Photoshop and Illustrator provide a wealth of tools and effects that can aid you in rendering the texture. Regardless of what software you are planning on using, the most important stage of illustrating texture is typically the original drawing phase. You must ensure that the garments you draw look like they are made of the fabrics you are trying to represent. Should you draw them clingy, flowy, puffy, crisp, or bulky? Imitate the fabric's visual drape in your drawing before you begin to add color and texture.

Photoshop is a powerful tool when it comes to rendering texture. You can use brushes, pattern fills, filters, layer effects, and combinations of any of these to create beautiful and even realistic textures. Plus, Photoshop's generative artificial technology (AI) is quickly developed. It is already helpful in repairing and creating textures. Soon it will be much more advanced.

Creating textures in Illustrator is often considered more challenging. However, a little practice with fills and brushes can make the task much easier. The more you work with Illustrator, the more you see that all textures are possible.

Developing textures is a never-ending task. As you make good pattern fills, brushes, or filter settings, save them. If you develop a series of steps that result in a fabric representation that you like, type up the instructions and save them somewhere. Keep all your notes and files where you can easily access them when you need them. Practice, practice, practice! You will soon be a professional at textures.

STUDIO Companion Videos for Chapter 6

Please refer to STUDIO for accompanying chapter video(s).

Keywords

Clip highlights/shadows
Clone stamp
Legacy brushes/patterns/etc.
Mezzotint
Noise
Pattern brush
Scatter brush
Vector effects

Review Questions

1. How do brushes, filters, patterns, and layer effects differ when creating textures? Why and when might it be beneficial to combine these tools and effects?
2. Why are traced texture pattern fills sometimes problematic in Illustrator?
3. Where is a good place to find old brushes that make useful textures?
4. If making a pattern for a texture, how do you make sure it will seamlessly repeat?
5. What is the difference between a *pattern brush* and a *Scatter brush*?

Commands Introduced

- Add Noise
- Brush Blend Modes
- Clone Stamp
- Document raster resolution
- Filter Gallery
- Legacy Brushes
- Legacy Gradients
- Mezzotint Filter
- Pathfinder
- Pattern brush
- Posterize
- Render Clouds
- Scatter brush
- Simplify Path
- Snap to Grid
- Vector effects

Keyboard Shortcuts

- Ps: *b* (Brush tool)
- Ai: *control+d/command+d* (Transform Again)
- Ps: *d* (Default colors)
- Ai: *g* (Paint Bucket tool)

Discussion Questions

1. In your opinion, is texture important to your renderings? Why or why not?
2. Is it better to enlarge a texture for display or omit it completely when it won't display well at its correct scaled size?
3. What is your favorite method for adding texture: brushes, pattern fills, or layers? Why?
4. Do you prefer Illustrator or Photoshop for adding texture?

Practice Exercises

1. Build a reference library—up close and on a figure.
2. Pick three new textures not described in the text—try to recreate them on an illustration.
3. Make a new texture brush. Reduce a texture such as snakeskin and turn it into a new brush.
4. Pick one of the textures described in the book and create a different way to make the same texture. For example, try making a Photoshop sequin pattern fill rather than using the brush tool.
5. Pick one of the methods described in the textbook for either Photoshop or Illustrator. Use the opposite program to try to recreate the texture.

Endnotes

1. Okay, so many readers will shout out that the resolution doesn't matter when we use pixels for our document proportions. Technically, that is true. Assigning a resolution simply assigns a measurement to the pixels rather than the other way around when you start with measurements, then assign the density of pixels within that space. Meh. Six of one, a half dozen of the other.
2. You probably need to be at least thirty years old to get this joke. Look up "The Most Interesting Man in the World" if you are curious, bored, or both.

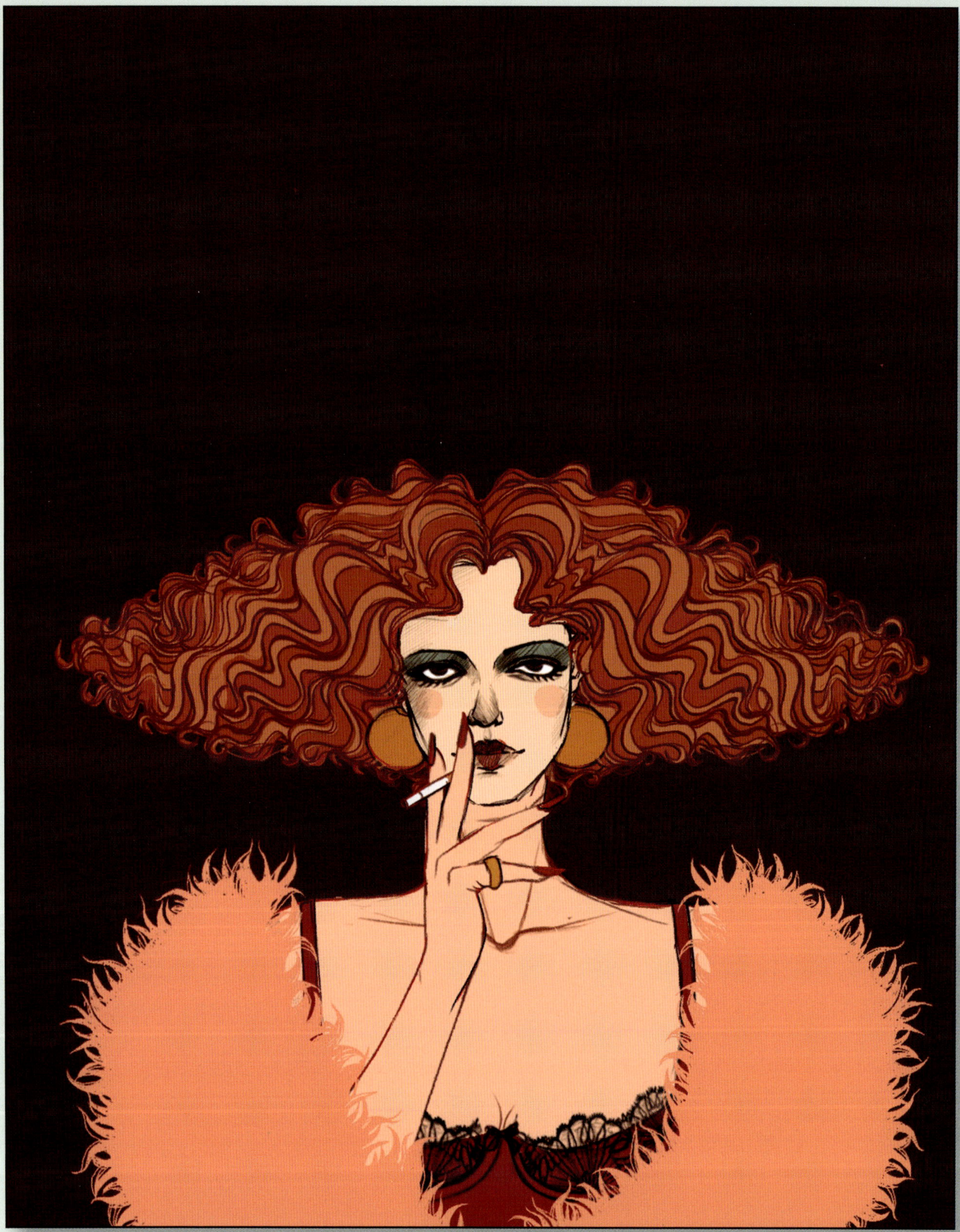

Figure 7.1 Faces and hair may or may not be important to your design communication needs. However, improving your rendering skills in this area can go a long way to making your portfolio more impressive. Courtesy of Hannah Delmore. Instagram: @hannahdelmoreillustration. Hannahdelmore.com.

CHAPTER 7

Faces and Hair

Learning Objectives

After completing this chapter, you should be able to

- Create faces and hair in Photoshop using various techniques
- Create faces and hair in Illustrator using various techniques
- Apply faces to the figure

Are faces important to what you need to accomplish? Some designers will immediately answer, "yes." However, the debate is split among many others. Faces (and hair) can do so much more than just show off illustration skills. Facial expressions, makeup, and hair impart mood, styling, and other messages that the figures alone cannot. They also give a final touch of professionalism.

How much time should you spend on faces and hair? Do you avoid faces just because they are hard? Like everything in illustration, practice makes better. But there are ways to speed up your work and to make faces and hair less of a challenge. We will cover several techniques for faces and hair from those that work well for the artistically gifted to those who need shortcuts.

Consider the Style

Faces can vary from realistic to amplified, overembellished, cartoonish depending on what type of illustration you are aiming to create. Expressions can be hinted at with a brush stroke for eyes or big cartoon lips. Features can be exaggerated, collaged or composited, or taken from photos. But the important thing is to match the style of your face rendering to the style of your figure rendering and to the mood of your clothes or costume. Make sure your message is consistent.

Hair can also be exaggerated or non-realistic. Whatever style you decide to use for your hair illustration, it is generally best to draw hair as shapes. Don't try to draw the entire hairdo as individual strands as it can look scraggly. Like with the faces, make sure that your hair illustration style matches the illustration style and look for the rest of the rendering.

In costume design, makeup and hair styling are often equally important to the costume. You can certainly make separate makeup charts and wig designs showing all the necessary detail. It often helps to show a hint of what that styling should look like when paired with the figure and garment, though. It helps to convey the whole look to your actors, directors, other designers, and costume team.

STYLE SECRETS 7.1

Do You Need a Face?

This entire chapter is about faces. What is meant by "do you need a face?" We mean, do what works best for you as a designer. Remember that for garment design this type of digital rendering is a form of design communication, rather than art. If faces are just too difficult and take too much time, feel free to skip them. Draw a head, maybe give it a hint of some hair, and move on to the important stuff: the clothing. Disproportionate faces can often be a distraction from your designs, so don't get caught up in the mechanics of the illustration itself. Sometimes, it really isn't worth it, and that's okay.

Creating Faces and Hair in Photoshop

There are many ways to create faces and hair in Photoshop. It is easy to find a method that fits your drawing style or ability. Like with figures, some artists prefer to work analog and scan in their work. Others prefer to work digitally from the beginning. Then there are the illustrators that work in a combination of analog and digital, moving between the methods freely.

In addition to differences with how much an illustrator relies on software when drawing, there are also varying levels of how much they rely on their own drawing skill for creating faces and hair. Some artists prefer to draw the entire face and all the hair themselves. Some prefer to trace from a source. Still others prefer to obtain their faces or hair from a photo or an existing drawing. These are all acceptable methods of working and Photoshop can make it easier.

Why create faces or hair in Photoshop? Consider the fact that you can put different parts of a face or hair on different layers. This makes it easier to make corrections or changes without having to rebuild the entire rendering. If we have the base skin color or hair color on an independent layer, we can easily change the color of these without affecting the shading layers or the detail layers. Or maybe we discover that one eye isn't shaped right. If the eyes are on a separate layer, we can fix this without damaging the rest of the face.

Project 7.1: Sketch/Paint a Face

One of the most straightforward methods of creating a face in photoshop is to paint it. You can work from a scanned sketch or from a digital sketch. They will both work the same way.

Step 1: Painting a face from a sketch in Photoshop is very similar to painting a figure. You first want to clean up the sketch, whether it is scanned or of digital origin. In Figure 7.2, you can see the original sketch the authors worked with, exercise file SketchedFace.jpg. It is a pencil sketch and needs a lot of cleaning. Once a sketch has been cleaned, create a new layer for the skin base layer. As you learned in the previous chapters, there are multiple ways to ensure that the color will only be applied to the area you wish it. You may also want to set the *Layer Blending Mode* of the sketch to *Multiply* if you want the original lines to be visible, as they are in the example.

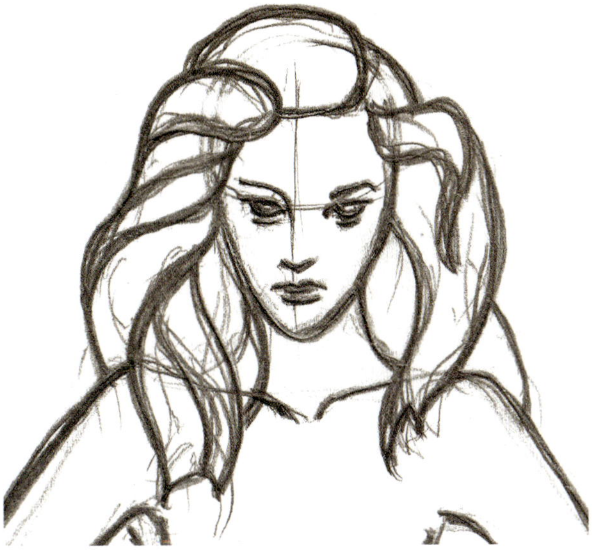

Figure 7.2 Scanned sketch for basis of painting face in Photoshop. Artwork by the authors.

Step 2: After creating the base layer for the skin (and any other base color layers you want to work with), create a layer for the skin shading. Using large, soft brushes with the *Opacity* set very low, work shadows and dimension into the face. Reduce the *Size* of the brush as you need to work into smaller areas. You can also add a layer for highlights if you need it.

The style of rendering you wish to achieve should determine the types of brushes you choose and the smoothness of your strokes. You will notice in the example, Figure 7.3, that not all the strokes are perfectly smooth. Instead, there is a painterly quality to the work. This was the choice of the illustrator, to complement the strong pencil lines of the sketch.

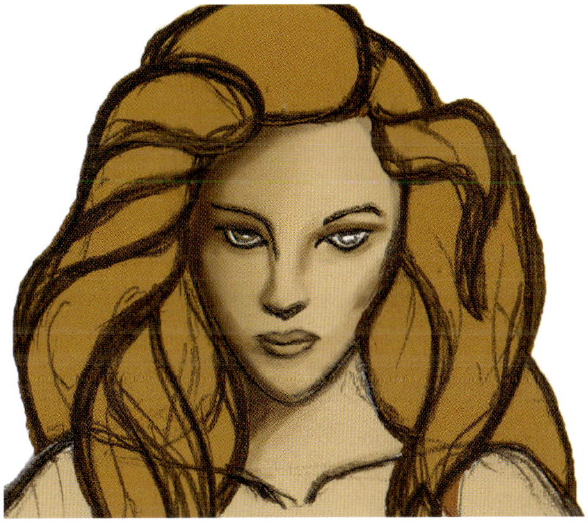

Figure 7.3 The sketch was cleaned up and kept on a separate layer. A layer was added for a solid skin color. Add a separate layer for shading. Build up shadows slowly using large, soft brushes.

Step 3: After shading and highlights have been added, it is time to add color. You will probably want a new layer for the face color, like makeup. It is up to you whether you want all face coloring on a single layer, or if you want to create separate layers for eye color, lip color, and so on. The authors used one layer for all color in Figure 7.4.

Adding color is like shading. Use large, soft brushes and build the color up. Reduce the *Size* of the brush and increase the *Opacity* as needed. Remember to be true to your illustration style as you paint. You may also have to adjust the *Blend Mode* on all the painting layers if you want to see through them.

The key to painting a face in Photoshop is not to make something that is photo-perfect, but to make something that looks good and works as a whole illustration. You can identify many errors in the original sketch for Figure 7.2, but as a finished face in Figure 7.4 it is convincing.

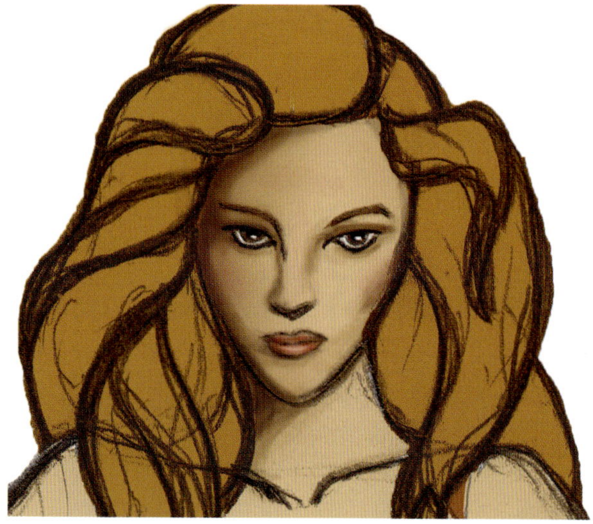

Figure 7.4 An extra layer was added for color. The eyes and lips were colored slowly by building in color with low opacity brushes. Color was added to the cheeks, forehead, and nose with a large, soft brush.

Project 7.2: Composite Face

There's no denying it, faces can be very intimidating. But software can make the situation much better. One solution is to take a face or head from another source and collage it into your illustration. It doesn't have to look human. You will notice that our example in Figure 7.5 uses the head of a hare.

The key to compositing or collaging is to make the style of all the parts mesh together. This often means that you will need to alter the face or head that you are compositing in order for it to look more like your illustration style. In Figure 7.5, the hare's head has been *Posterized* through a filter, altered in color, and had several other filters applied to make it look more like the oil pastel technique of the original illustration.

Other ideas for compositing include collaging the facial features on a head, compositing individual facial features, or just the hair. This is a technique that holds limitless possibilities. Our students have used skulls, cartoon heads, and space helmets, just to name a few examples. Search for a fun head to attach to the exercise file SketchedFace.jpg or add it to your own sketch!

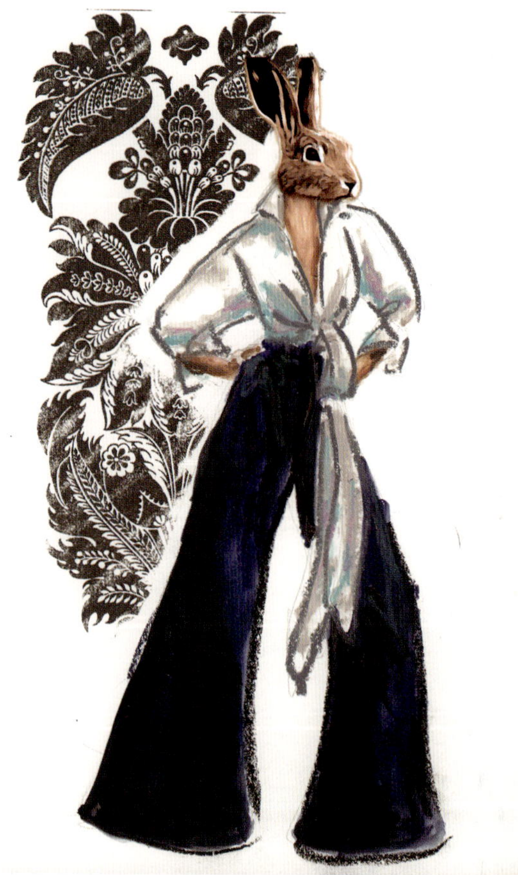

Figure 7.5 Faces can be sourced from existing photos or drawings. In this case, a photo of a hare was used for a non-traditional face. The photo was placed on the figure in Photoshop. The head of the hare was *Selected*, and a *Layer Mask* was applied to isolate it from the rest of the photo. Various adjustments and filters were applied to make the photo blend better with the original oil pastel rendering. Artwork by the authors.

Project 7.3: Reduce the Face from a Photo

The authors learned this next technique from Robin Schneider of AdobeforFashion.com.[1] It involves a few more steps, but illustrators who struggle with faces often like the technique. It also works well for costume designers who want to include accurate facial features of the actors in the costume.[2] As the project title indicates, you need a photo of a face to execute this technique. Make sure the face in the photo fits the intended figure in terms of shape and angle.

Step 1: Remove the color in the photo. *Open* the exercise file ReduceFace.jpg. The easiest way to remove the color is to use the *Desaturate* action under *Image* → *Adjustments*. If *Desaturate* does not produce good results, you can use the *Black and White* command instead. The goal is to have good contrast between the facial features and the skin. In Figure 7.6 you will notice that skin is very light, and the features are dark. This makes the next steps easier.

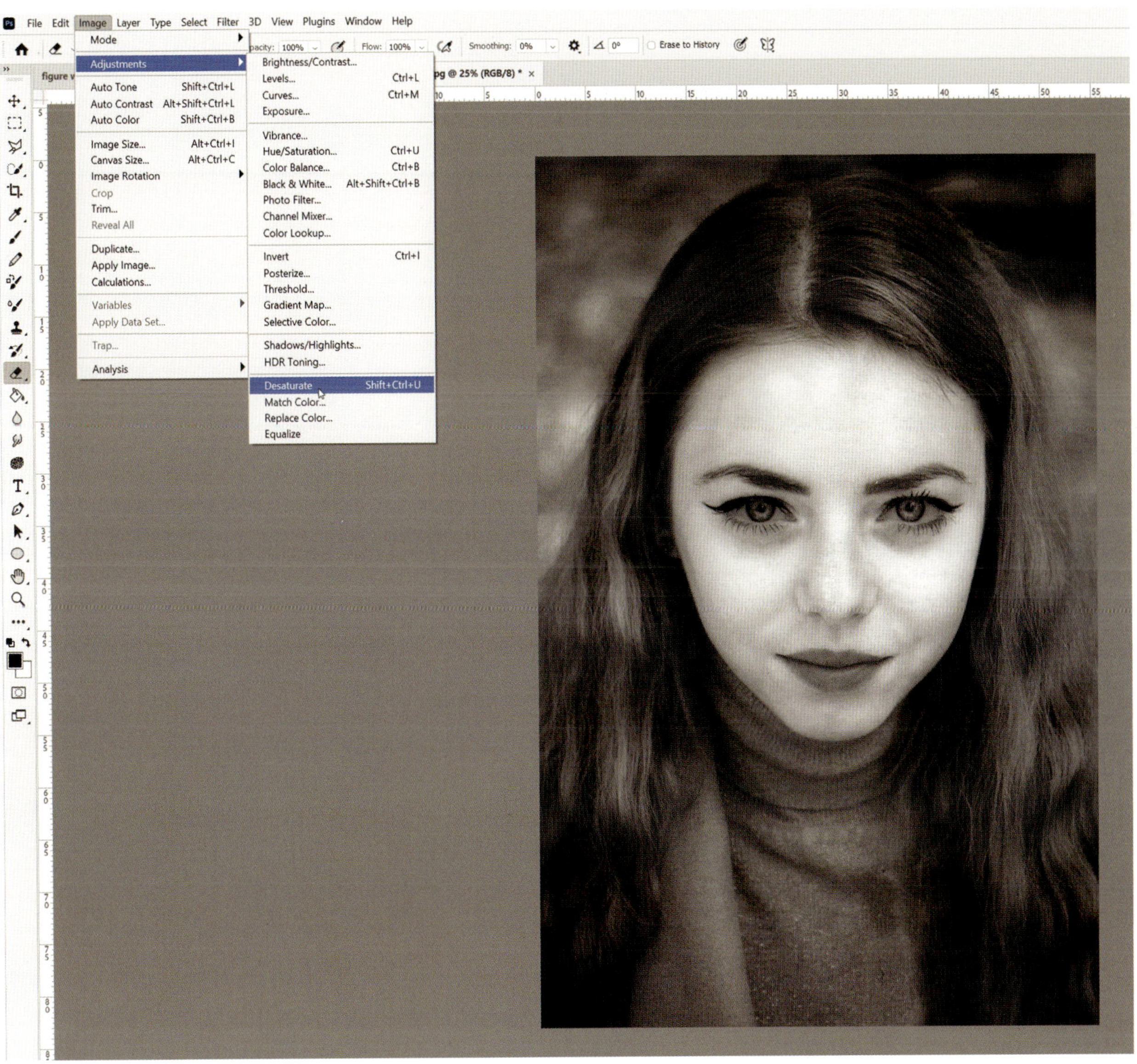

Figure 7.6 Desaturating a photo for use as a face. Color is reduced to black and white by using the *Desaturate* function. Courtesy of Vlad Rudkov via Unsplash.

Step 2: After desaturating your image, you will use the **High Pass filter** to reduce the photo to something resembling lines. This filter blocks the low-frequency signals.[3] In layman's terms, it detects the edges of an image such as between the skin and the eyelashes of our portrait. This makes it easier to reduce the face to just the features as outlines. The filter can be found under *Filter → Other → High Pass*. As you see in Figure 7.7, you will adjust the radius in the filter until most of the texture is gone and the image appears flat except for the facial features. Typically, this means keeping the radius size low. The trick is to avoid any **color halos** that may show when you move the radius too high. A *color halo* is a bright rainbow or holographic-like ring that softly surrounds areas of high contrast. If you start to see a halo distortion around your features, back off the radius and pull the numerical value down further. If you do not get good results in high pass no matter how much you tweak the radius, you may need to go back and readjust the contrast between the skin and the facial features when converting the image to black and white.

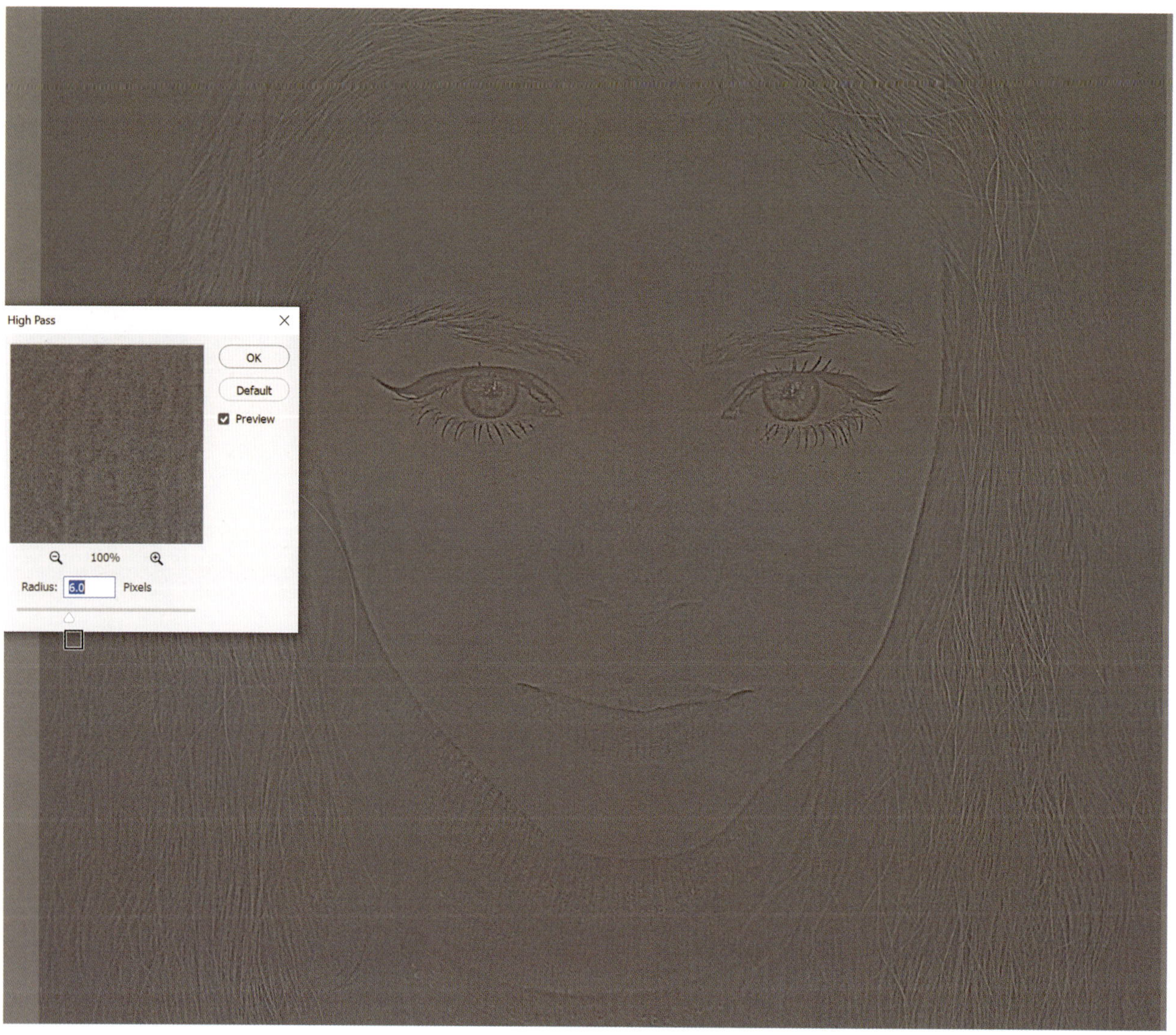

Figure 7.7 The goal with the *High Pass* filter is to reduce the photo to an image resembling line art. Lower the radius in the filter until just enough details in the image show for the facial features to still be useful. The less texture, the better.

Step 3: The *High Pass* filter will leave some artifacts or grains that can make using the face challenging. A good way to reduce the texture of the image is to apply a *Gaussian Blur* filter. The goal is to find a balance between blurring out the texture but not overblurring the facial features. To do this, keep the radius of the blur low, as seen in Figure 7.8.

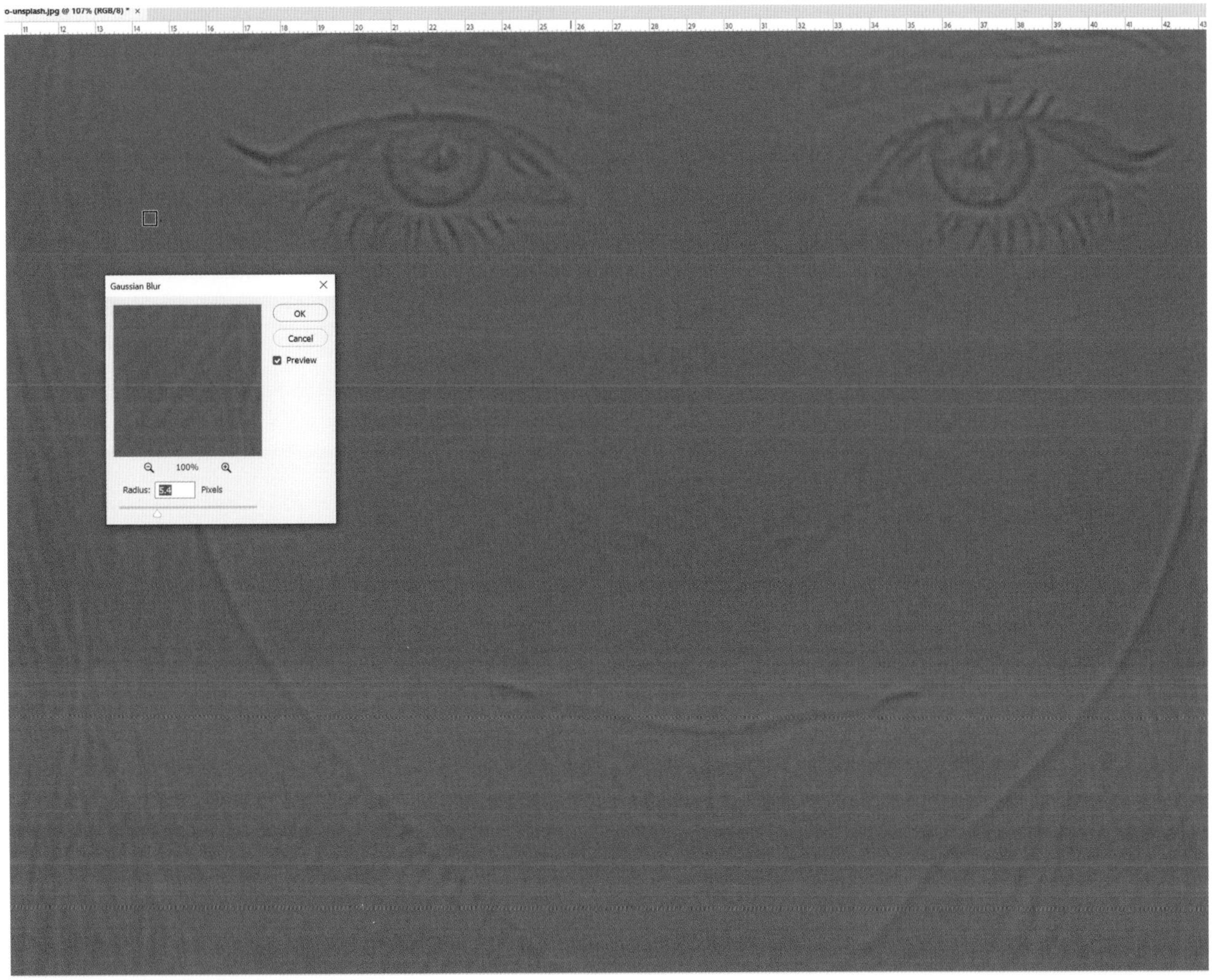

Figure 7.8 Use the *Gaussian Blur* filter to reduce any remaining grain and texture in the image. Adjust the radius of the filter until there is a good balance between the reduction of texture and the facial features still being useable.

Step 4: The point of the process is about to become apparent. We will use *Levels* to remove the gray from the image, reducing it to black and white lines. Open *Levels* under *Image → Adjustments*. Move the white slider to the left until it is under the peak of the histogram. Then move the black slider to the right until it is also under the peak of the histogram. Adjust the two sliders until the image is similar to Figure 7.9. The goal is to have a mostly white image with strong black lines and little to no gray. Make sure you keep the detail in the facial features. Admittedly, all these adjustments take some practice. Sometimes you have to start over to get the initial contrast strong enough to have good results at this stage.

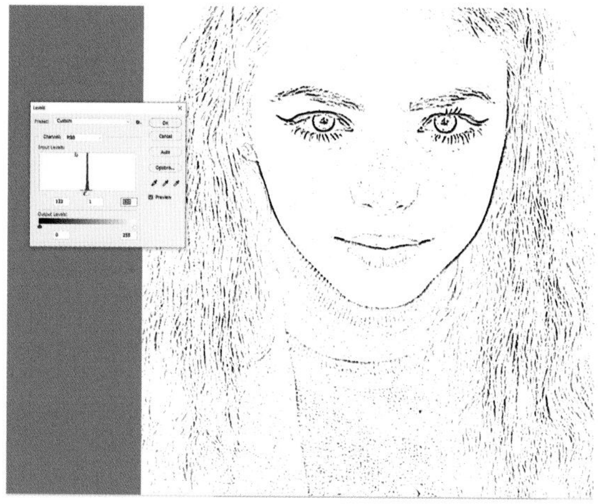

Figure 7.9 Open *Levels* under *Image → Adjustments*. Bring the white slider underneath the peak of the histogram. Do the same with the black slider. Adjust these sliders until the image is mostly white with black lines and looks like a line drawing

Step 5: Once you get good results from the levels adjustment, you need to clean up the image and prepare it for use. Use the *Crop* tool to reduce the image down to just the part you want to use, typically just the features. Then use the *Brush* tool with the paper color to paint out any digital artifacts or items you don't want to show. You may need to strengthen the lines of the features with a dark colored Brush tool. Sometimes finding that sweet spot in the *High Pass* filter means that key lines are eliminated. You can always draw them back in. Figure 7.10 shows a cleaned and cropped face, ready to use. The authors saved this image for easy use on future renderings.

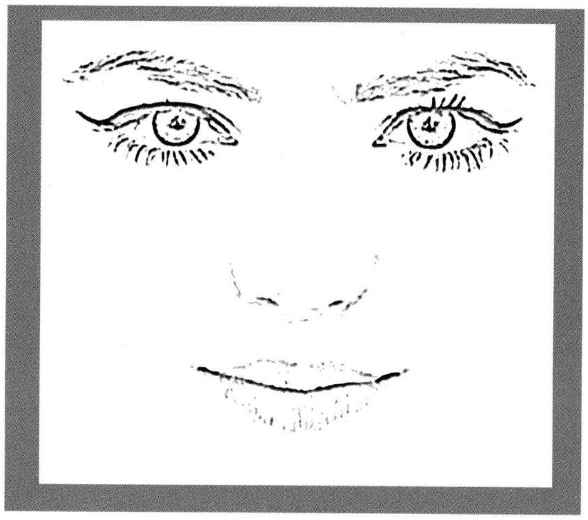

Figure 7.10 *Crop* the image to just the facial features. Then use either a brush with white paint or the *Eraser* tool to clean up the image.

Step 6: To use the new face, *Open* the figure you wish to receive the face. You can use the exercise file SketchedFace.jpg or your own figure. We set up *Guides* on the head of the figure to make it easier to place and scale the face on the figure. Once the figure is ready, you can either copy and paste the face from the original file or you can place the file, as the authors did in Figure 7.11. The face will probably need to be *Scaled* and *Moved* into position. You may also want to set the *Blending Mode* for the face layer to *Multiply* so any white space on the face does not interfere with the rest of the figure.

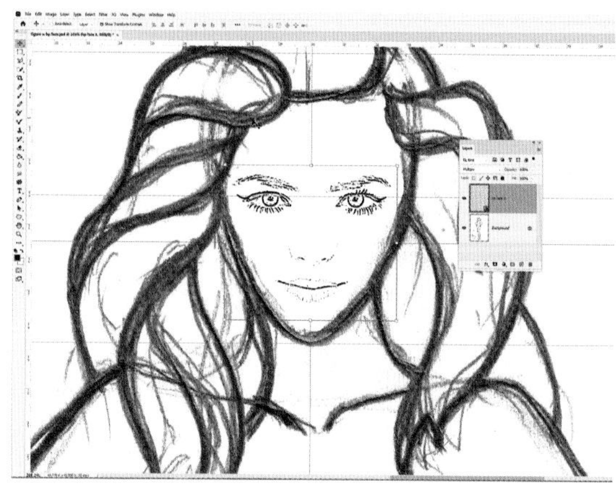

Figure 7.11 We applied the face to a scanned sketch, but this type of face could be applied to any type of Photoshop image from unfinished to fully rendered. To aid placement, we used *Guides*. Then we *Scaled* the face and set the *Blend Mode* to *Multiply* so the white space would not interfere with the original figure.

Although the authors applied the face to a pencil sketch, this technique can be applied to any form of rendering from unfinished sketch to fully finished rendering. The face could be considered done at this stage, but most artists would rather the face match their illustration style. This can be done easily and without much more work.

Step 7: To make the face look more like the original rendering, make a new layer above the placed face. Choose a brush that replicates the strokes used in the original drawing (or the same brush). In Figure 7.12, the authors used a pencil-style brush to look like the original pencil drawing. Paint or draw over the facial features until they blend with the original rendering. It usually doesn't take much to disguise the placed image as your own drawing or painting.

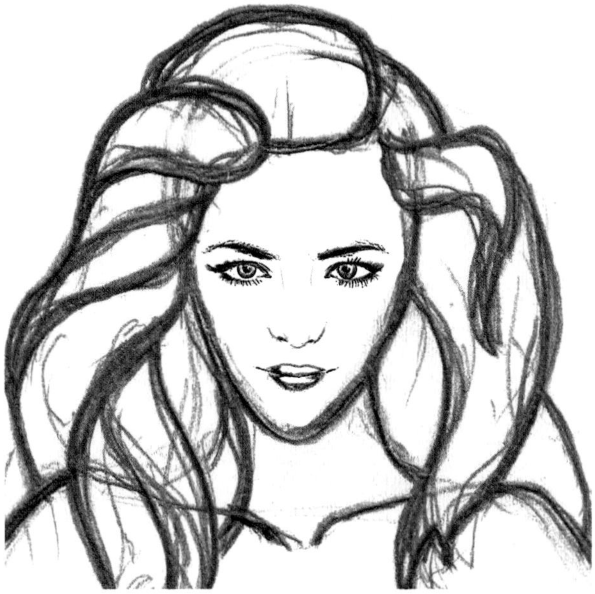

Figure 7.12 Making the face match the figure style. Often the placed face does not match the style of the original figure. This is easily remedied by painting over the placed face on a separate layer using a brush that complements the style of the original drawing. In this case, we used a pencil-style brush to make the face look more like the original pencil drawing.

PRO TIP 7.1

Use Your Actor's Face

Actors have egos. Well, actually, everyone has some sort of ego, but it is rather prevalent with actors. Here's a little secret for all the costume designers in the audience: if your actor has a positive relationship with their costume, they are much easier to work with. When you make the costume rendering look like the actor, they have an easier time connecting to the costume of the character. It is also flattering for them.

When the actors are cast, try to get a headshot or snap a quick photo of their face when they come in for measurements. Use this photo for reference, or use the other techniques listed in this chapter to help you draw a similar visage. Give it a try and see if your actors start to become more congenial, overall. Some may not notice, but we bet the majority will react positively.

Project 7.4: Draw a Face Separately

This is for those of you who want a hand-drawn face but are a bit intimidated by drawing directly on the figure. Draw the figure without the face as in Figure 7.14. Once again, you can use the exercise file SketchedFace.jpg or your own drawing. Then draw the face separately on a much larger scale as in Figure 7.13. Use exercise file NewFace.jpg or create your own. Scan both images and clean them up. Then *Place* the features into the figure file. *Scale* and adjust the face image as needed to make it fit the figure, as you see in Figure 7.15.

This method allows you to draw the face in much higher detail. It also helps by reducing the fear factor that comes with drawing a face on a figure. The face is now separate and can be fixed or restarted as many times as needed.

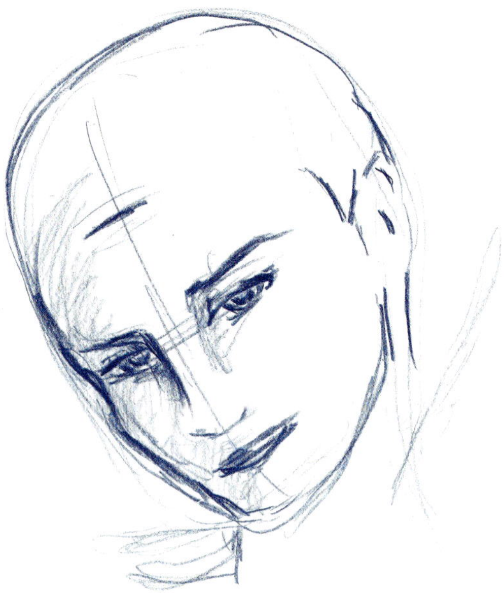

Figure 7.13 Scan of separately drawn face. Artwork by the authors.

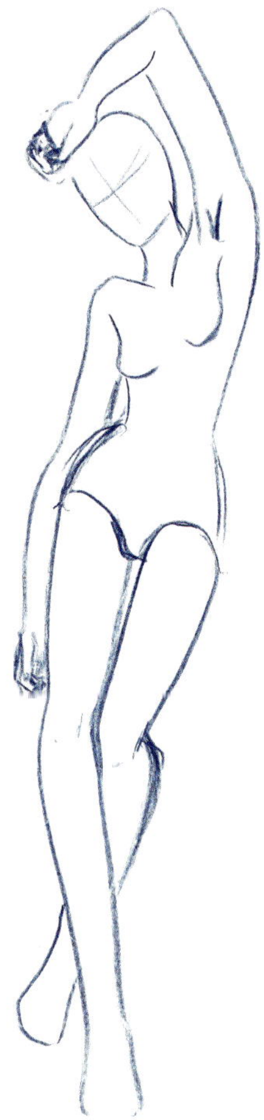

Figure 7.14 Scan of figure drawn without face. Artwork by the authors.

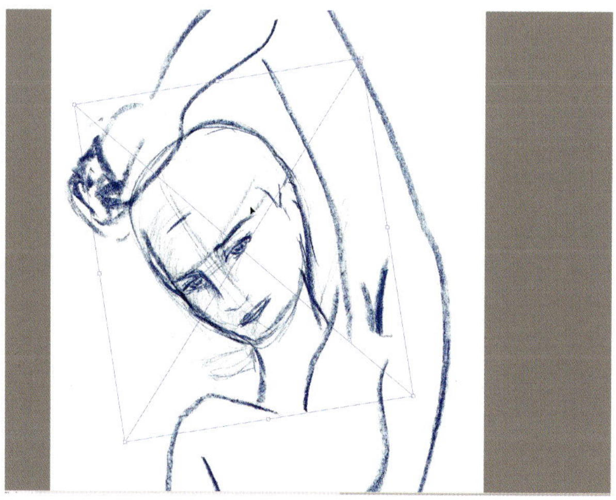

Figure 7.15 The *Blending Mode* of the face layer is set to *Multiply* so we can see through the white space to the body layer behind it. The face needed to undergo a few transformations, such as *Scale* and *Rotate* to fit on the figure convincingly. The completed figure is now ready to paint in Photoshop, trace in Illustrator, or print and hand render.

Project 7.5: Hair Techniques

As with faces, painting is one of the most common and straightforward ways to achieve hair in Photoshop. That's not to say it is the only way. Most of the methods outlined for faces also work for hair.

Keep in mind that hair, seen from a distance of any kind, is just a collection of highlight and shadow shapes. Individual strands can't be seen, except on the peripheral of the hair shape. If you try to draw hair strand by strand, you will get a "straw" hair effect. Analyze a photo of a full-length figure. What shapes do you see to indicate the hair? Where can you make out individual strands? How can reduce this information to indicate hair on your renderings?

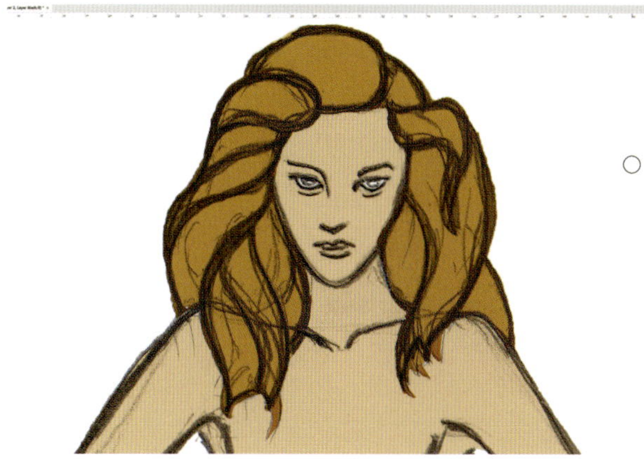

Figure 7.16 The sketch was cleaned up. A separate layer was made for the base color layer. Notice that the sketch separates the hair into large shapes rather than individual hair strands. Artwork by the authors.

Step 1: Start by cleaning up the original sketch if it needs it. Use exercise file SketchedFace.jpg again. To paint the hair, you will want to start with a base color layer. This can be placed behind or on top of the figure, depending on how you work. You can use a *Selection Mask* or a *Layer Mask* to keep the color confined to an area. You may want to adjust the *Layer Blend Mode* if you need the sketch layer to show through, as seen in Figure 7.16.

Step 2: After the base color is applied, it is best to create separate layers for shading and highlighting. You may want to set the *Blend Mode* for the shading layer to darken or multiply and the highlight layer to lighten, or something similar. Experiment and find what works best for you. Paint in the shadows using a large, soft brush with low opacity. Build in color slowly. Adjust the brush *Size* and *Opacity* as needed. Then do the same for the highlights. You may want to have a *Layer* or *Selection Mask* turned on to keep all the brush strokes contained within the area of the hair. This can create a sharp edge on the hair shape, as you will notice on Figure 7.17, but you can soften the edge later if you need.

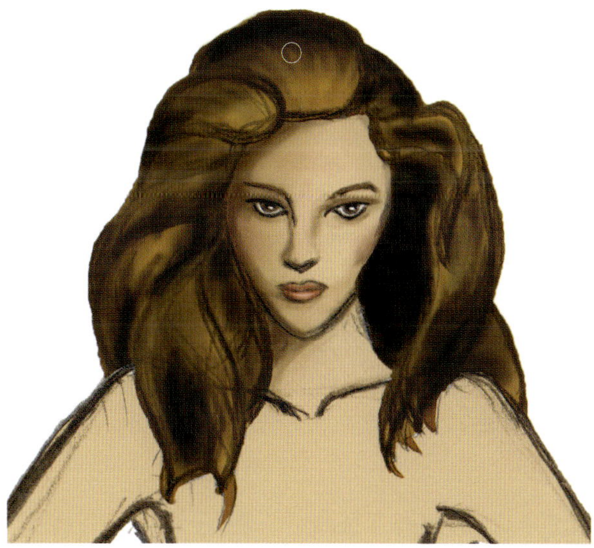

Figure 7.17 Two new layers were made: one for shading and one for highlights. The shading and highlights were painted in on their respective layers using large, soft brushes and low opacity. The size of the brush was decreased as we worked into the detail areas. Color was built up slowly.

Step 3: Once the highlights and shadows are completed, create a new layer for details. At this point, you want the mask turned off. Use a smaller, more opaque brush to draw in individual strands of hair and other details. Some of the tendrils should extend outside of the original hair outline.

This is also a good time to re-evaluate the edges of the hair. If necessary, go back to the highlight or shadow layer and use a soft brush to diffuse the edges of the hair. You will notice in Figure 7.18 that the edge around the face has been softened with a dark color, making the hair look more natural.

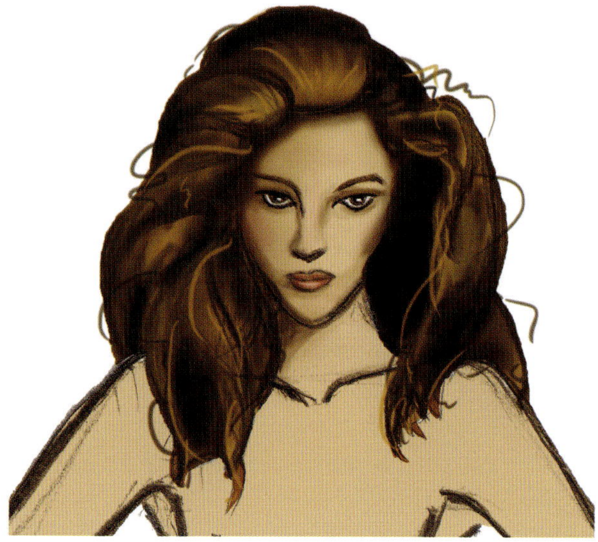

Figure 7.18 An extra layer was created for hair details. Using a smaller brush with higher opacity, individual strands were painted in to give the hair life and more realism.

Troubleshooting

"Why can't I get my photo face to look like a line drawing after *High Pass* and levels?"

1. Some photos do not have enough contrast to work well and need extra work before the *High Pass* filter. Use the *Black and White* adjustment instead of *Desaturate*. Try some of the presets to see which gives you the highest contrast between the face and the features. You may want to adjust the sliders even more to get better contrast.
2. If you can't get high enough contrast with *Black and White*, you can utilize *Curves*. First try *Curves* after *Black and White* and see if you can achieve enough contrast. If this doesn't work, backtrack to the original image and use *Curves* on the colored version. You can even use *Curves* on the individual color channels. If you can get a strong contrast between the skin and the features while it is in color, then it should work when you proceed to *Black and White*.
3. Finally, some photos just do not work well for this technique. Sometimes it is better to cut your losses and find another photo with better contrast. You may want to find a photo in which the model has strong makeup. This might make it easier to get good results.

Creating Faces and Hair in Illustrator

As with Photoshop, there are many ways to create faces and hair in Illustrator. However, the process can sometimes feel less intuitive than painting a face or hair in Photoshop. The trick, like everything in Illustrator, is to work in shapes.

For faces, look at how various parts of the eyes and lips create layered shapes. The nose is often a series of lines worked with profiles or with the width tool. Do not try to include every detail and every color nuance. Individual eyelashes will look clunky once you shrink the face to fit the figure. Simplify the features to just a few key shapes that indicate the correct features.

Hair is sometimes one big shape, sometimes several smaller shapes, and sometimes a series of layered shapes. It all depends on the texture of the hair, the lighting, and how the hair is styled. But again, do not try to include everything. Part of the beauty of Illustrator drawings is their cleanliness.

Project 7.6: Trace a Photo or Sketch of a Face

One of the easiest-to-understand methods is to draw the face and hair directly on the figure in Illustrator, just as you would paint the face or hair in Photoshop. This results in a less repeatable but more personalized look for each figure, as you will see in Figure 7.19.

However, it is sometimes nice to have a set of go-to faces that can be used repeatedly or other easier ways of putting faces and hair on an Illustrator figure than to draw the whole thing from scratch each time. It is less noticeable if a face is repeated than a figure or pose. Illustrator excels in making actions repeatable. The key is to choose a good set of source faces and hair to begin with.

A face that is meant to be repeatable can be made into a *Symbol* and saved as a *Symbol Library* that can be opened into any Illustrator document. *Symbols* are commonly used when creating flats or technical drawings because we can save zipper sliders or buttons as symbols for easy reuse. But symbols can also be useful for figure rendering. A **symbol** is a small drawing in Illustrator that is saved in a *Symbol Library* and is prepared for rapid reuse. A **Symbol Library** is a collection of symbols that can be saved and reopened in any Illustrator drawing. Symbols are scalable and editable.

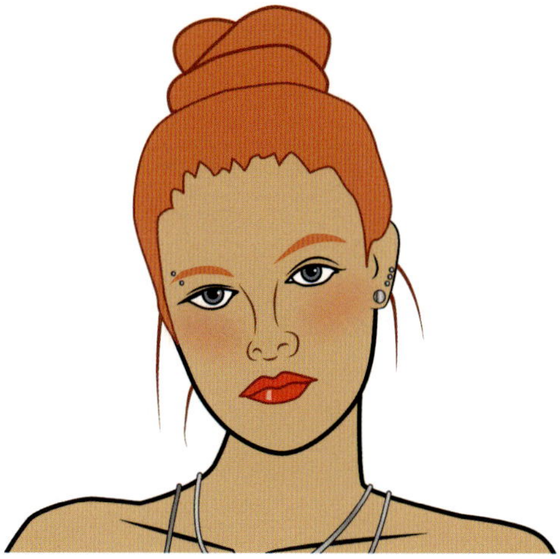

Figure 7.19 This face and the hair were drawn directly on the Illustrator figure using the *Pen* tool and a variety of different stroke weights, profiles, and fills. The hair was kept as a few simple shapes and was illustrated in only one color. Artwork by the authors.

Step 1: To prepare a face for use as a *symbol*, start with a clear photo or use your own sketch of a face that will work for many of the figures that you draw. You can use the exercise file ReduceFace.jpg as a template or import your own photo. You will notice that the photo used in Figure 7.20 is a forward face with little to no tilt or turn. This makes it a good choice for all figures with straight-facing heads. Trace or draw the major facial features. If you are planning on making hair into symbols, see Project 7.8 for hair specifics.

As you begin to complete the tracing, check the drawing without the photo or sketch, as shown in Figure 7.21. Notice how the shapes of each feature are simplified. Use what you learned in the figure, color, and shading chapters to make your features look nice. Make sure that all the curves are smooth, strokes are the correct weight, and fills are complete. You can use a *Blur* effect to indicate shadow as we did on the teeth. As this is a face you are using repeatedly, the proportions need to be as perfect as you can get them. Remember to test the face for size. Chances are that the face will be small when you place it on a figure. So, scale the face to an appropriate size and make sure all the details still look in proportion and uncluttered.

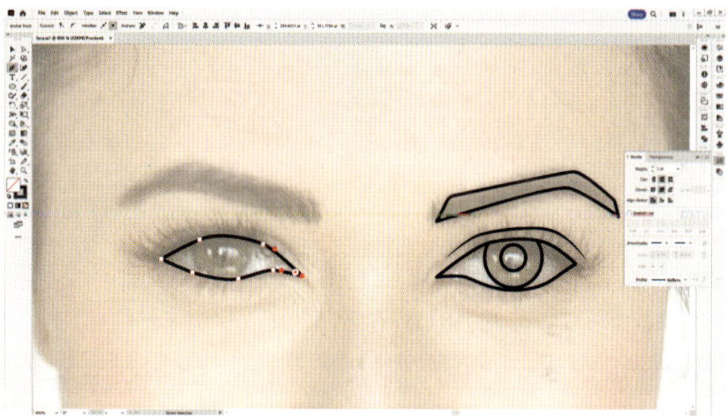

Figure 7.20 A photo was opened in Illustrator and the opacity of the photo was reduced to make it easier to see the tracing. A new layer was made for tracing and the features were traced using the *Pen* tool. Courtesy of Jake Nackos via Unsplash.

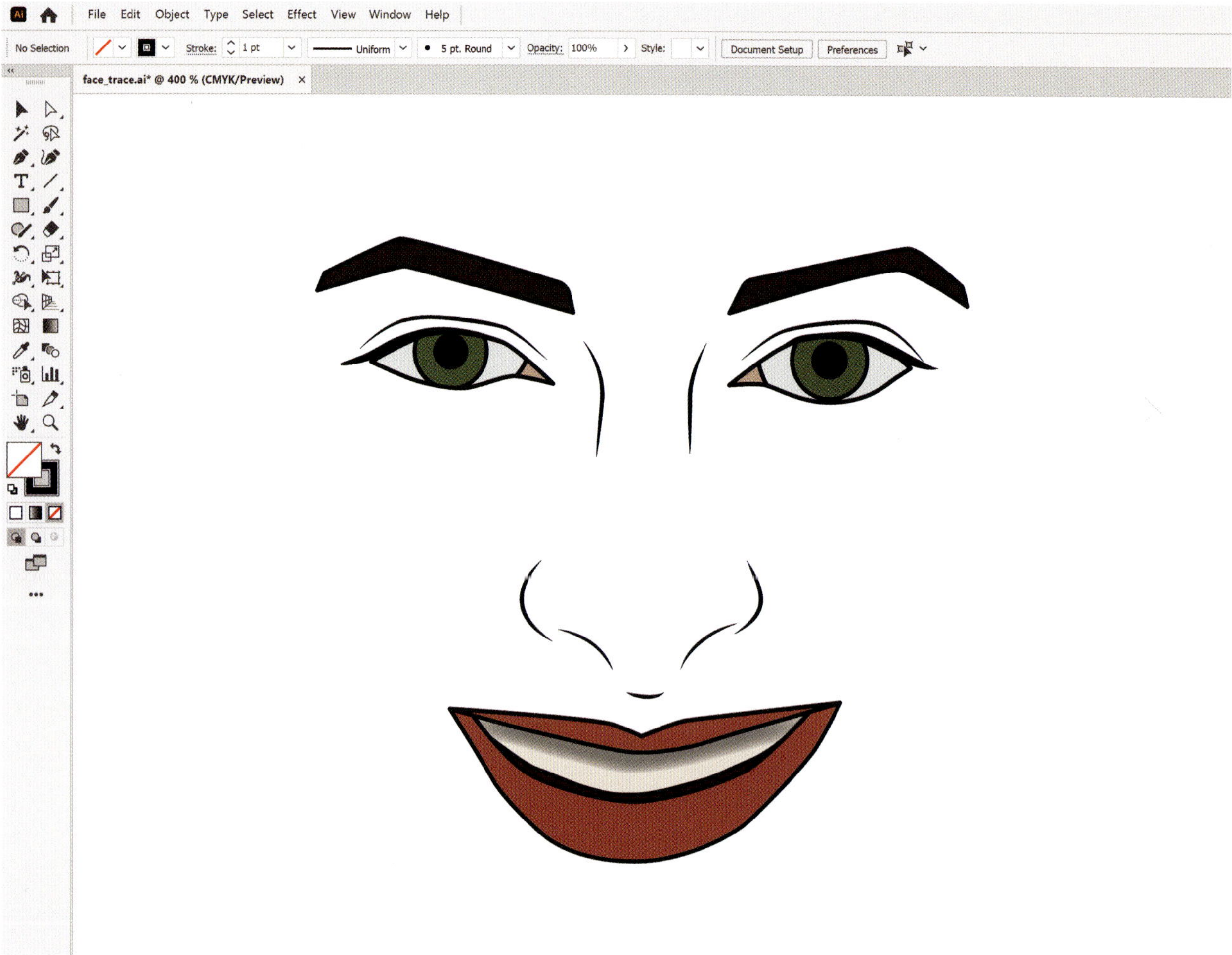

Figure 7.21 Fills were added and stroke weight and style were adjusted to make a convincing face. The position of a few features were adjusted to make the face more usable as a generic face.

Step 2: To save your new face (or hair) as a symbol, select all the parts of the face and *group* them. Then open the *Symbols* panel. You can find it under the *Window* menu. With the *Select* tool, drag the face drawing into the *Symbols* panel until you see a plus (+) symbol. When you release the drawing in the panel, an options box will appear. Most of the options will not affect the symbol as we intend to use it. You only need to name the symbol in this box before clicking *OK*. At this point, you will see your new symbol in the symbols panel. You can see an example of this in Figure 7.22.

Step 3: Next you will need to save the symbols library so it can be retrieved from any Illustrator drawing (on the same computer). To save the library, click on the panel *Options* menu button in the top right corner of the panel. From the drop-down menu, choose *Save Symbol Library*. Let Illustrator pick where the file will be saved. It will always look in that location first, so it is generally best to use the default file location. Name your new symbol library and click *Save*.

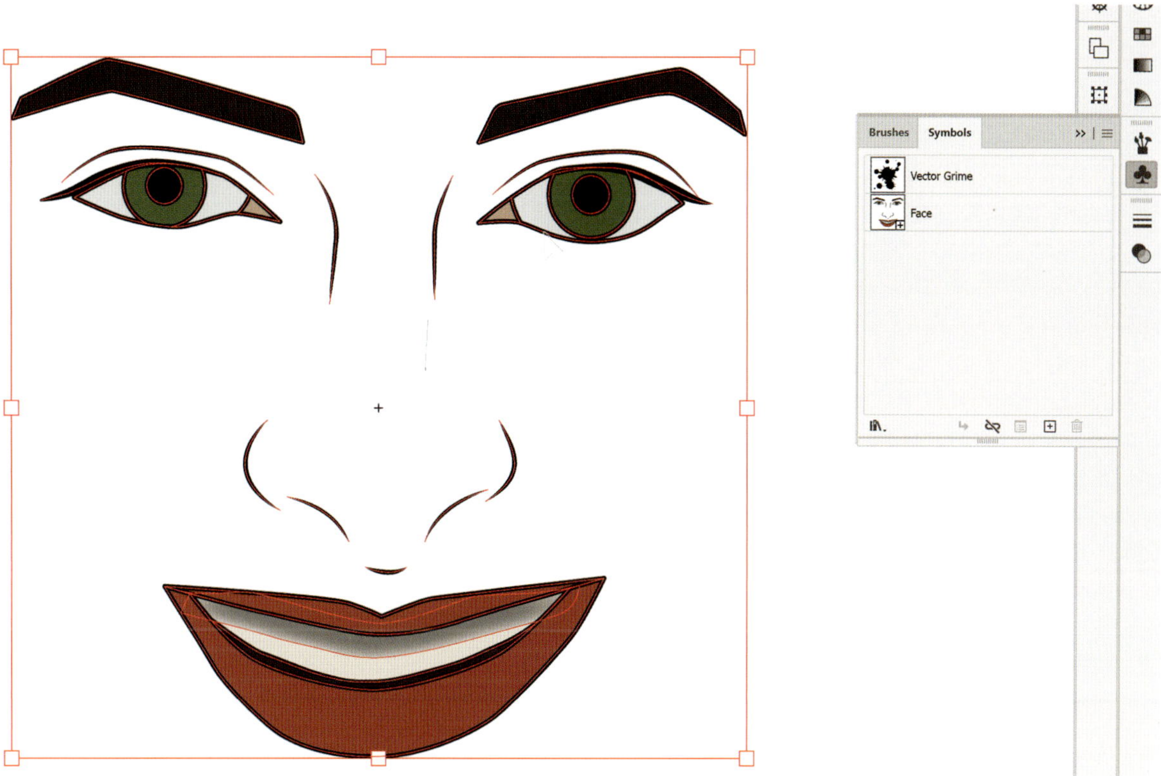

Figure 7.22 All the parts of the face were grouped together. Then the face was dragged into the *Symbols* panel to create a new symbol. The *Symbol Library* was saved so the face symbol can be accessed again in other files.

Step 4: To use your new face (or hair) symbol, *Open* the destination figure illustration first. Use one of your traced figures from Chapter 2. This can be a sketch, a finished rendering, or anything in between. The authors recommend preparing the destination figure's head with guidelines to aid the placement of face. We used a vertical center guide, and three horizontal guides representing the top and bottom of the head and the eyeline (middle), but use what makes sense to you.

Step 5: Open the *Symbol* panel. Go to the *Open Symbol Library* button at the bottom left of the panel (or you can access the command through the panel options menu). Scroll down to *User Defined* on the list. You should see the name of your symbol library under *User Defined*. *Click* on your symbol library.

Step 6: Drag your face symbol onto the figure. Remember to hold the *Shift key* to constrain the proportions as you adjust the scale of the symbol to fit your figure. It is best to work with the width and height of symbol constrained while doing the initial resizing, even if the proportions are not quite correct for your new figure. This will keep you from overstretching the drawing in one direction or another. You will see in Figure 7.23 that

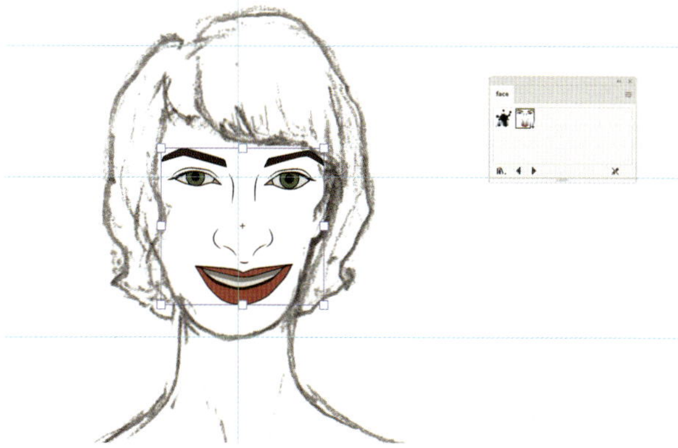

Figure 7.23 A sketched figure was opened in Illustrator with the *Symbol Library* panel. To make placement and sizing easier, guides were set up on the face of the figure, marking the center of the face, and the top, bottom, and middle of the head. Drag the face symbol onto the figure's head and *Scale* it to the correct size. Notice that the face *Symbol* is still too wide for the figure's head.

the symbol has been placed and scaled using the guides, but the width of the face does not match the new figure. Our model looks like she is trying out for the role of the Joker!

After putting the face on the figure and scaling it, take the time to really look at the proportions and make adjustments. Does the face need to be slightly narrower? Wider? Higher? Lower? Remember to zoom out and look at the figure as a whole. Figure 7.24 shows where the authors have made the *Symbol* face narrower to match the destination figure. This looks more natural.

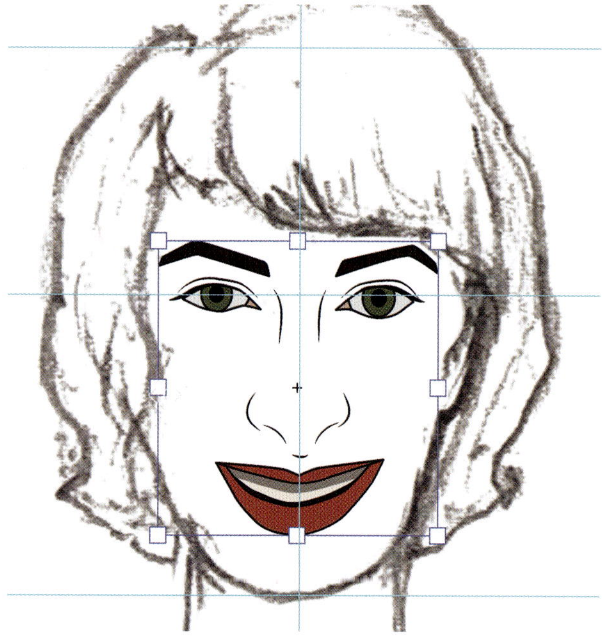

Figure 7.24 The face symbol was made narrower using the controls on the bounding box. The symbol now looks like it fits the face. The figure can be traced in Illustrator or painted in Photoshop to create a fully rendered illustration.

Project 7.7: Place a Photoshop Face in Adobe Illustrator

Time for a little software mash-up. If you prefer drawing figures in Illustrator but find making faces or hair easier in Photoshop, this method is for you. As with drawing a face in Illustrator for reuse, you can create a face in Photoshop for reuse (or single-use placement).

Step 1: You will need to paint a face in Photoshop, or like the authors did, take a face from an existing Photoshop rendering. It is best if the face is on a transparent background and only includes the facial features or fades out around the edges. *Crop* the painting to just the part you need as seen in Figure 7.25 and *Save* or *Export* it. It is easiest if you save it as a flattened PNG file that supports transparency, but Illustrator also supports PSD files.

Step 2: In Illustrator, the painted face can be placed as-is or can be made into a *Symbol*. If you want to make a *Symbol*, *Open* the face in Illustrator. In the opening dialog box, click on *Flatten Layers to a Single Image* if you did not already flatten it in Photoshop. Now you should be able to follow the previous instructions on making a symbol and saving the *Symbol Library*.

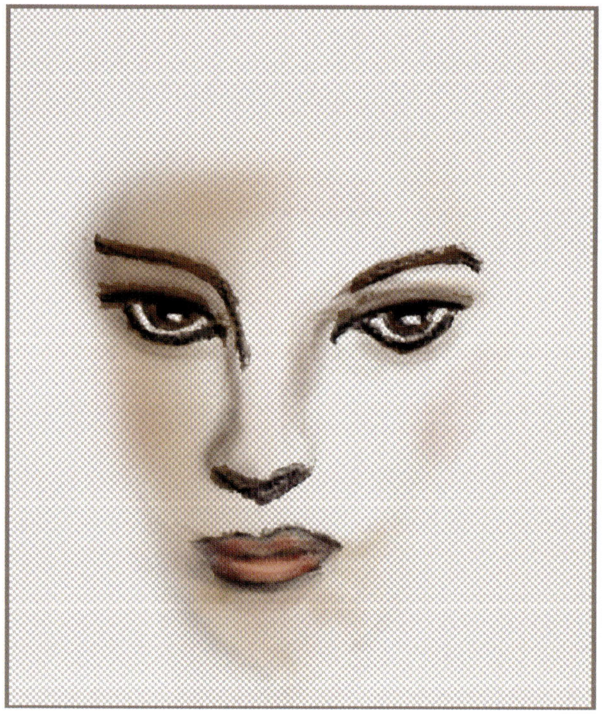

Figure 7.25 Photoshop face prepped for use in Illustrator. This face was taken from the digitally painted version of the face in Photoshop. We removed the base color layer. Then all details around the face were either erased or softened with a big, soft eraser brush. Crop the face to just the facial features.

Step 3: To use the new Photoshop face, *Open* the destination figure. You may want guides to help you place the face. If the face is a symbol, open your *Symbol Library* panel and *drag* the symbol onto the figure. If the face is still a Photoshop document, select *File* → *Place* and select your file to place.

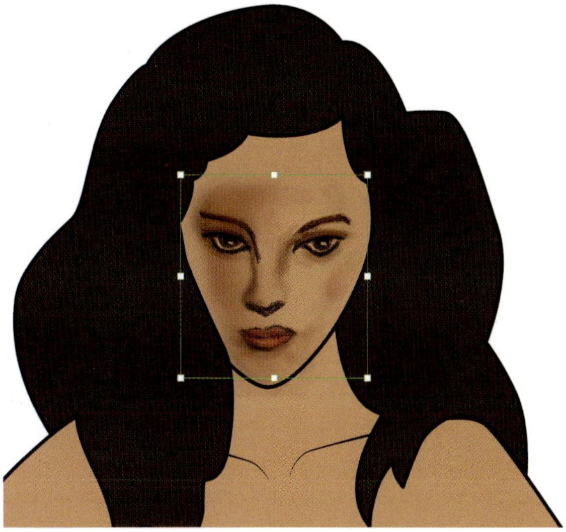

Figure 7.26 Photoshop face *Placed* on Illustrator figure. In this example, the face was *Placed* on the figure, *Scaled* to the correct size, and set to a *Blend Mode* of *Multiply*. For faces you would like to use repeatedly, first make them into a *Symbol*.

Step 4: Once the face is on the drawing, *Scale* it and adjust the shape and position as needed. You may need to adjust the blending mode of the face object to make it blend into the Illustrator drawing successfully. The example in Figure 7.26 has the *Blend Mode* for the face set to *Multiply*.

Step 5: After placing the face, you may decide to make a few more adjustments to make the face more successful. For instance, in Figure 7.27, white shapes were drawn behind the eyes. All white color was lost when we set the *Blend Mode* to *Multiply*.

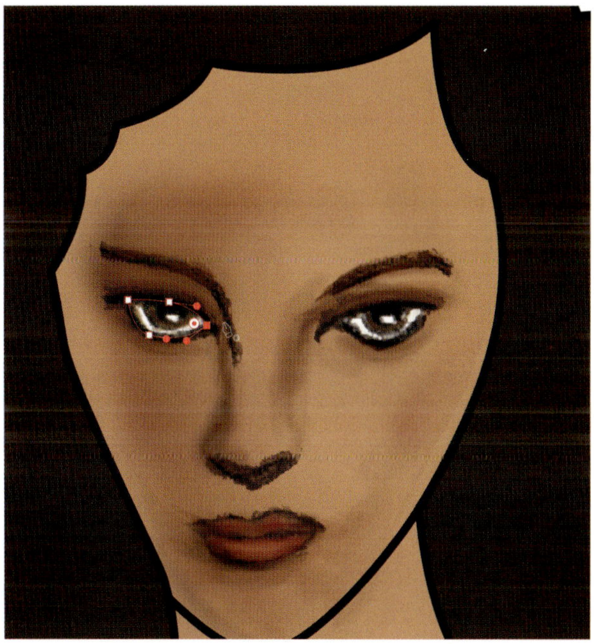

Figure 7.27 Finishing details. With the face set to multiply, the white portions of the eyes disappeared. To make the eyes look better, we drew white shapes using the *Pen* tool behind the eyes that show through.

Project 7.8: Hair Techniques

Any of the Illustrator techniques for faces can be used to create or place hair. The hard part about drawing hair in Illustrator is understanding how to reduce it down to simplified shapes. Let us start by looking at a photo of hair and how it can be simplified.

At first glance, the hair in Figure 7.28 can be a little intimidating. There are stray hairs everywhere and the main mass of the hair is tied in a messy bun. Plus, the model has fine hair laying over her forehead. Start by mentally filtering out all the stray hairs. Look for the major shapes.

Step 1: If you look at Figure 7.29, you will notice that the hair has been reduced to three shapes—the hair on the skull and the two parts of the bun knot. These three shapes are drawn to form the base of the hair. Arrange the shapes with the top shape in the back and the skull portion in the front. This is generally how we start drawing hair; find the main shapes, draw them, and decide what order they should be in.

Step 2: Once you have the main shapes drawn, you must decide how much of the detail to draw in and how to approach them. In general, simpler is better with Illustrator. If you try to draw everything the rendering will look messy and cluttered.

As for the how, do shapes or lines work better? Is the *Pen* tool still your best choice if you are trying to imitate very organic lines? Do you need to try a filter such as *Blur*? This is when trial and error plus practice comes in handy.

In Figure 7.30, you will notice that the fringe across the forehead has been drawn as a single, continuous shape rather than as multiple lines. Although this is less delicate than the original fringe, the result is less messy than trying to draw the individual hairs. Most illustrators have difficulty with such delicate work until they are more advanced with the software. This is a simple solution to a challenging shape.

As for individual tendrils or strands of hair, reduce these to just what is most important for the look of the hair. Sometimes these need to be drawn as a shape, such as a curl. Other times, a line works better, like with stray hairs. In Figure 7.30, the stray hairs have been reduced to three tendrils. They were drawn with paths that are thicker at the base and tapered to a point at the end. This keeps the look of the hair neat.

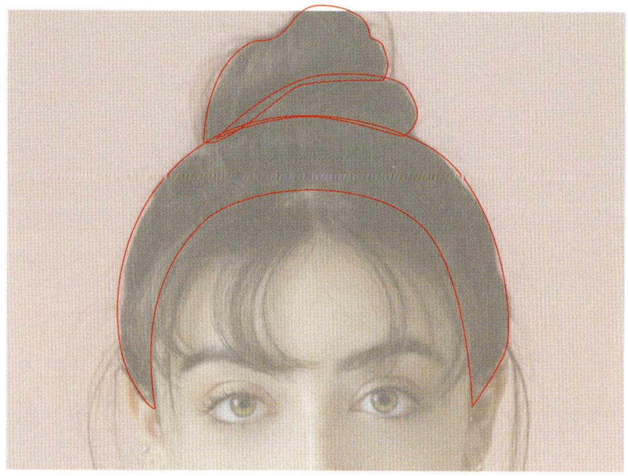

Figure 7.29 Hair reduced to three main shapes. If we ignore all the individual tendrils and loose hair, there are three main shapes. These can be drawn to create the base of the hair. Courtesy of Jimmy Fermin via Unsplash.

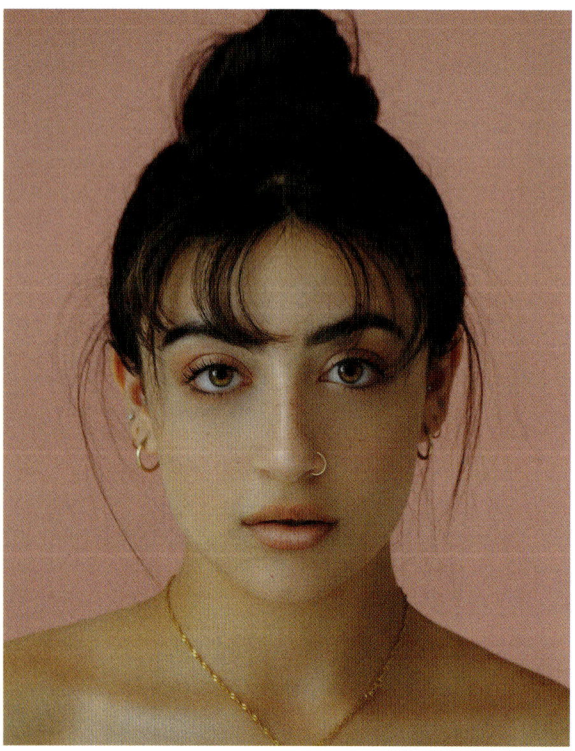

Figure 7.28 Headshot of model with updo. The model's hair in this photo is pulled into a casual bun. She has fringe across the forehead as well as tendrils of loose hair hanging down in all directions. Courtesy of Jimmy Fermin via Unsplash.

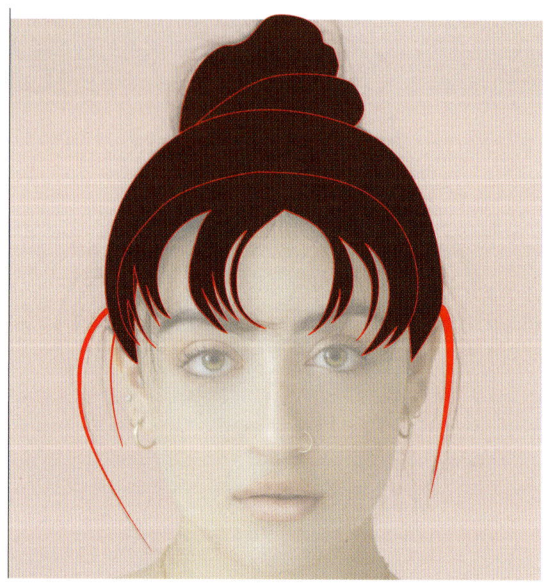

Figure 7.30 Final shapes for hair. We reduced the fringe to one single shape rather than individual hairs. This is less delicate, but still successful and much easier to draw. Only three stray tendrils were drawn in to reduce the messiness. The tendrils use paths with no fill. The *Width* tool was used to make them wider at the base and tapered to a point at the end. Courtesy of Jimmy Fermin via Unsplash.

PRO TIP 7.2

Age, Race, and Gender of the Face

Representation matters on so many levels. When analyzing skin colors, sample from photographs if possible. Skin varies widely in undertones, value, and saturation. Take a color sample from a photo of your subject to look for an accurate undertone. Some skin has warm undertones whereas others are cool. Look for prominent discolorations like freckles or vitiligo that you may want to show on your illustration. Age and gender can also affect the base colors and values.

Aside from representative skin tones, pay attention to how underlying bone structure changes between races, ethnicities, ages, and genders. Closely look at the facial structure of your subject when using a photographic reference. How do the proportions of the cheekbones, nose shape, and jawline relate? Are the eyes tilted up or down? Are the lips fuller or thinner? The face is a difficult subject for many budding artists to learn. Make it a personal goal to be able to represent a range of different facial types as you grow in this area. Not only will you be a better artist, but your clients will also know that you care about representation.

Once you get the basics of hair shapes, you can try your hand at more challenging hair shapes. One of the tricks is to not just look at the overall shape of the hair, but to look at the shapes of the highlights and shadows in the hair. For the next example, you may want to skip down to Figure 7.34 and look at the finished product first. This will help you to understand the process better. The original image featured a model with her hair backlit by the sun. This created areas of strong highlight and shadow.

When drawing hair shapes, do not worry about which order you should do the drawing. For instance, in Figures 7.31–7.33 the images show the hair shapes as they are arranged front to back, but this is not the order in which we drew them. Draw the shapes in whichever way makes sense to you and you can re-arrange the order as you need. This is the beauty of Illustrator. For the example below, the authors drew the shapes in Figure 7.32 first because the black and dark brown shapes make the main hair silhouette. This made it easier to understand where the other shapes needed to be. The gold shape in Figure 7.31 was the last one added.

Figures 7.31–7.34 are also good examples of when to try other tools in Illustrator. The *Pencil* tool was used rather than the *Pen* tool for drawing each base hair shape. The *Pencil* tool allows the user to draw free-form

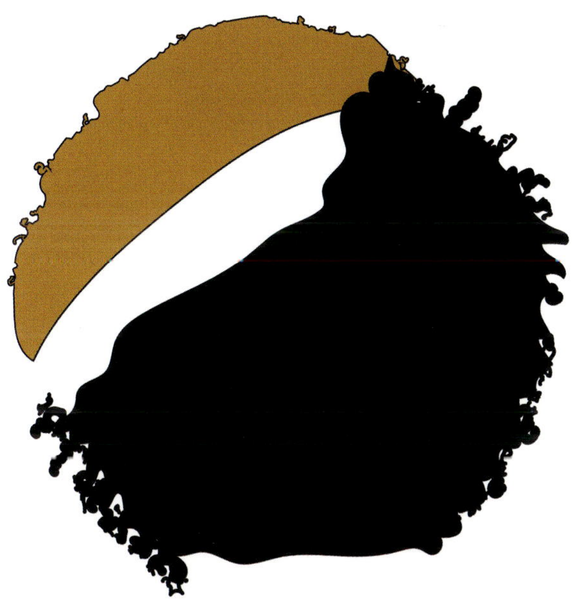

Figure 7.31 First layer of hair for Illustrator figure. In Illustrator, hair is drawn in shapes and the shapes are arranged back to front. This image shows the back two shapes for hair that requires four shapes. These two shapes go behind the head. The original shapes were drawn using the *Pencil* tool to allow for a more organic shape. We added the curls using the *Blob Brush*. The individual blob shapes were joined to their respective shape using the *Unite* command in the *Pathfinder* panel. This reduced the number of shapes in the drawing and eliminated distracting outlines around the individual curl shapes.

and results in a more organic shape. This was useful for the curly texture. To achieve the individual curls, we utilized the *Blob Brush*. The **Blob Brush** draws shapes that are the diameter of the brush, rather than paths. This resembles painting with a traditional Photoshop brush. Change the diameter of the brush to have variety in curl size. However, the blobs were individual shapes with their own strokes and we merged them with the base hair shapes using the *Unite Command* in the *Pathfinder* panel. The **Unite Command** welds selected shapes together where they touch or overlap.

These are just a few of the tools that can help you achieve more successful hair in Illustrator. Continue to try more tools. You can also add effects and filters such as *Blur*.

Remember that once you have perfected your hair, you can *Group* all the elements and turn it into a *Symbol* for repeated use. You can also *Open* the hair file in Photoshop and add finishing touches, such as blending and painted tendrils. The key is to know when to stop and to call your work done.

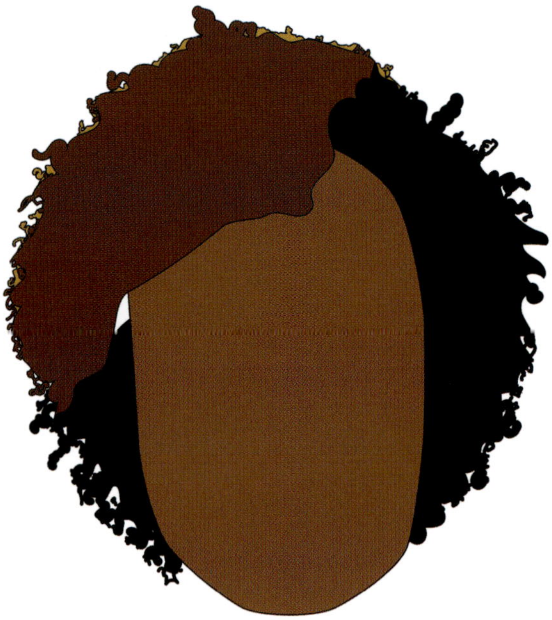

Figure 7.32 Middle layer of hair. This is the first layer of hair that is arranged on top of the face. We can now see the face as well.

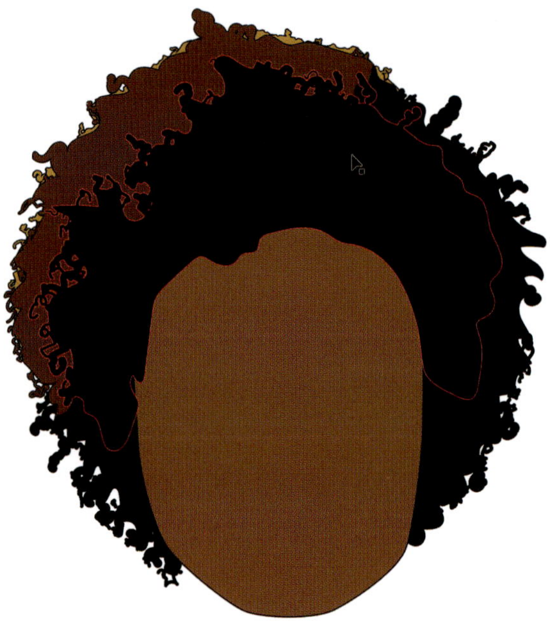

Figure 7.33 Top layer of hair. The top layer of hair is shown in this image. We can see how it sits on top of the forehead and creates a better face shape. It also sits in front of the ears, which are not shown in this image.

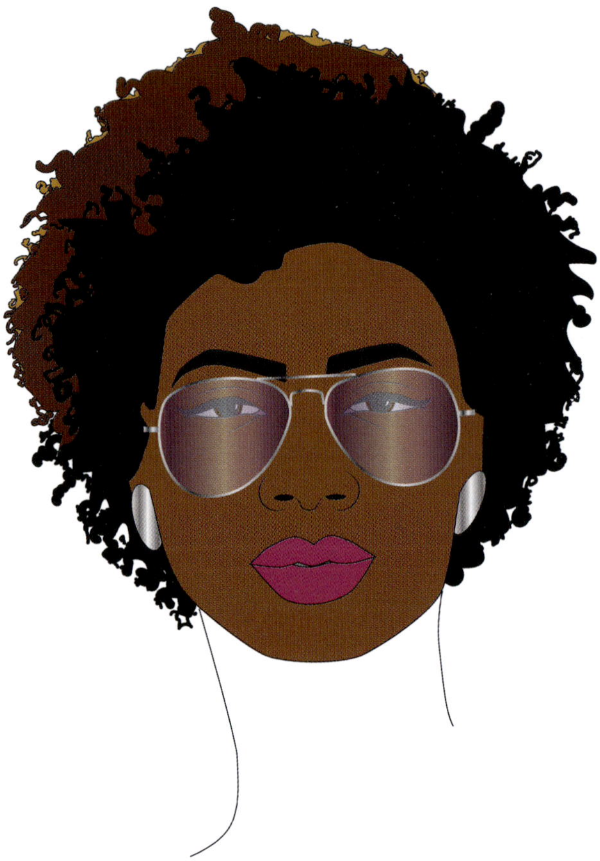

Figure 7.34 Final face. This image shows all the facial features turned on. Artwork by the authors.

PRO TIP 7.3

Facial Hair

Do you need to show facial hair such as a mustache or beard? Like other hair, don't get caught overthinking it. How can you simplify the shape of the highlights and shadows found in the facial hair to communicate it without getting bogged down with details? Remember, on a full-length figure, that level of detail won't show. Facial hair can often be simplified to a single shape. In Figure PT7.1, we reduce the mustache and beard to two shapes of a single color in Illustrator. Draw out the basic shape with the *Pen* tool, then apply an effect called *Roughen*. This command can be found through *Effect → Distort and Transform → Roughen*. Once the pop-up dialog box appears, take the *Size* down to 0.05–1%, and the *Relative Detail* up to 30–40. Collect some resource photos and draw the primary shape(s) you see.

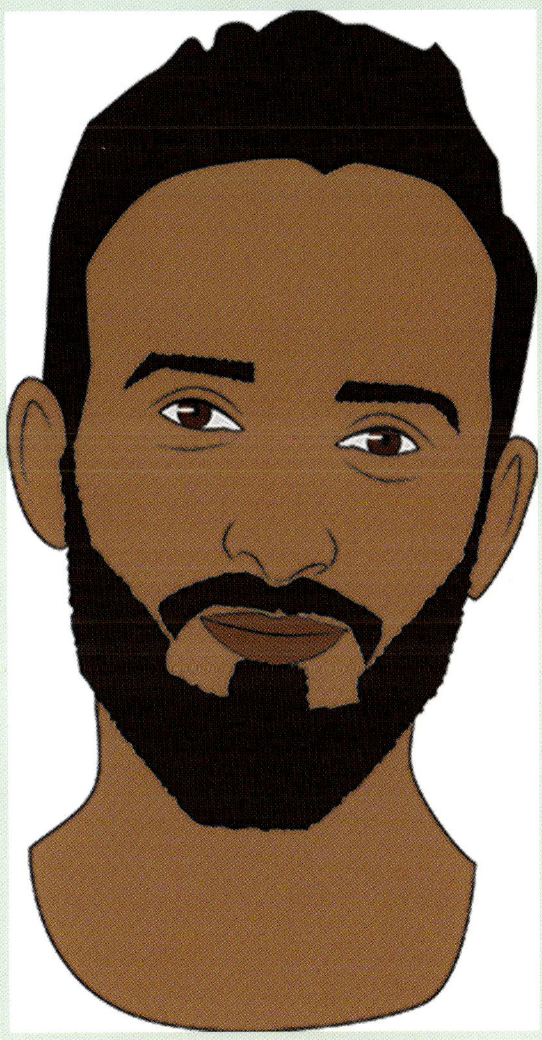

Figure PT7.1 In this Illustrator face, we made the beard one shape and the mustache another but in the same color. Break up the edge of the path with the *Roughen* effect. Once the face is reduced to a smaller figure, it will be enough to communicate the facial hair.

Troubleshooting

"Why can't I find my face symbol?"

1. Did you save the *Symbol Library*? You may need to go back to the original face drawing file. The symbol should be in that file. You can save your *Symbol Library* from there.
2. Did you try to open your *Symbol Library* under *User Defined*? The *Symbol* file will not automatically open. Remember to go to the *Open Symbol Library* button and scroll down to *User Defined* to find your saved *Symbol Library*.
3. Did you accidentally save your *Symbol Library* somewhere other than the default location? If this is the case, you can search for the library, but it may be easier to resave it from the original face drawing file and let the symbol panel save operation put the library in the default file location.
4. Did you change computers since you made the *Symbol*? If that is the case, the easiest thing to do is to *Open* the face drawing file on the new computer and save the *Symbol Library* again on the new computer.

1. "Why can't I turn my Photoshop face into a *Symbol*?"

When you opened the Photoshop face in Illustrator, did you click on *Flatten Layers to a Single Image?* If not, don't worry. The layers can be flattened in Illustrator. Go to the *Layers* panel and click on the *Panel Options* button. Choose *Flatten Artwork*. You should be able to select all the parts of your artwork and drag it into the *Symbols* panel now.

Summary

Faces and hair are intimidating for many illustrators, but Photoshop and Illustrator can make the task easier and often faster. Faces and hair can be painted or drawn from scratch or a sketch in either program by the more confident artist. Photoshop can be used to superimpose hair or a face from a drawing, a photo, or another source onto an existing rendering. The software can even be used to reduce a photo to line art for the base layer of a face or hair. In Illustrator, faces and hair can be created and saved for repeated use.

Like everything, creating good faces and hair takes practice. You must also make sure the face and hair as well as the rendering style are cohesive with the rest of the illustration. With some experience, your illustrations can look much more professional with faces and hair than they did without.

STUDIO Companion Videos for Chapter 7

Please refer to STUDIO for accompanying chapter video(s).

Keywords

Blob Brush
Color halo
High Pass filter
Symbol
Symbol Library
Unite

Review Questions

1. What filter do you use to reduce a photo of a face?
2. How can you speed up your workflow regarding faces in Photoshop? In Adobe Illustrator?
3. Explain why the *Blob Brush* works so well for hair in Illustrator.

Commands Introduced

- Create Symbol
- Roughen effect
- Save Symbol Library
- Unite

Keyboard Shortcuts

- Ai: *N* (Pencil tool)
- Ai: *Shift+B* (Blob Brush)

Discussion Questions

1. Do you think it is important to include faces for design communication? Why or why not?
2. Explain which software application you prefer for making faces and hair and why.
3. Is it "cheating" to use a photo to reduce or trace a face? Why or why not?
4. Which facial features do you think are hard to draw and why? Which features are easier for you? Analyze what makes certain features hard and others easier.

Practice Exercises

1. Compile a folder of faces for drawing and color reference. Aim to collect a variety of genders, races, ethnicities, and ages.
2. Using a photograph of a figure's hair and tracing paper, trace over with a pencil or pen how you can simplify and break down the hair into color shapes.
3. Prepare the same face (using one of your sketches or a photo reference) in Photoshop and Illustrator. Which looks better? Was one faster or easier than the other?
4. Make three different face symbols in Illustrator that can be used on your figures. Make sure the face angle matches your most commonly drawn head angle. Save this as a *Symbol Library* that you can add to later.
5. Make three different hair symbols in Illustrator that can be used on your figures. Save as part of your symbol library.

Endnotes

1. Robin Schneider has a Photoshop rendering tutorial available if you have access to LinkedIn Learning. Check out her course for more ideas.
2. We can say from personal experience that it often helps to appeal to the ego of your actor by making the costume rendering actually look like them! The actors have an easier time visualizing themselves in the costume and representing the character.
3. The *High Pass* filter is commonly used in photography for sharpening images, reducing noise, and for a technique called frequency separation. This is a nifty solution that allows you to color-correct on the low-frequency layer and fix the texture on the high-frequency layer. This is just another example of how learning about peripheral subjects such as photography retouching can help spark ideas to use in your illustrations!

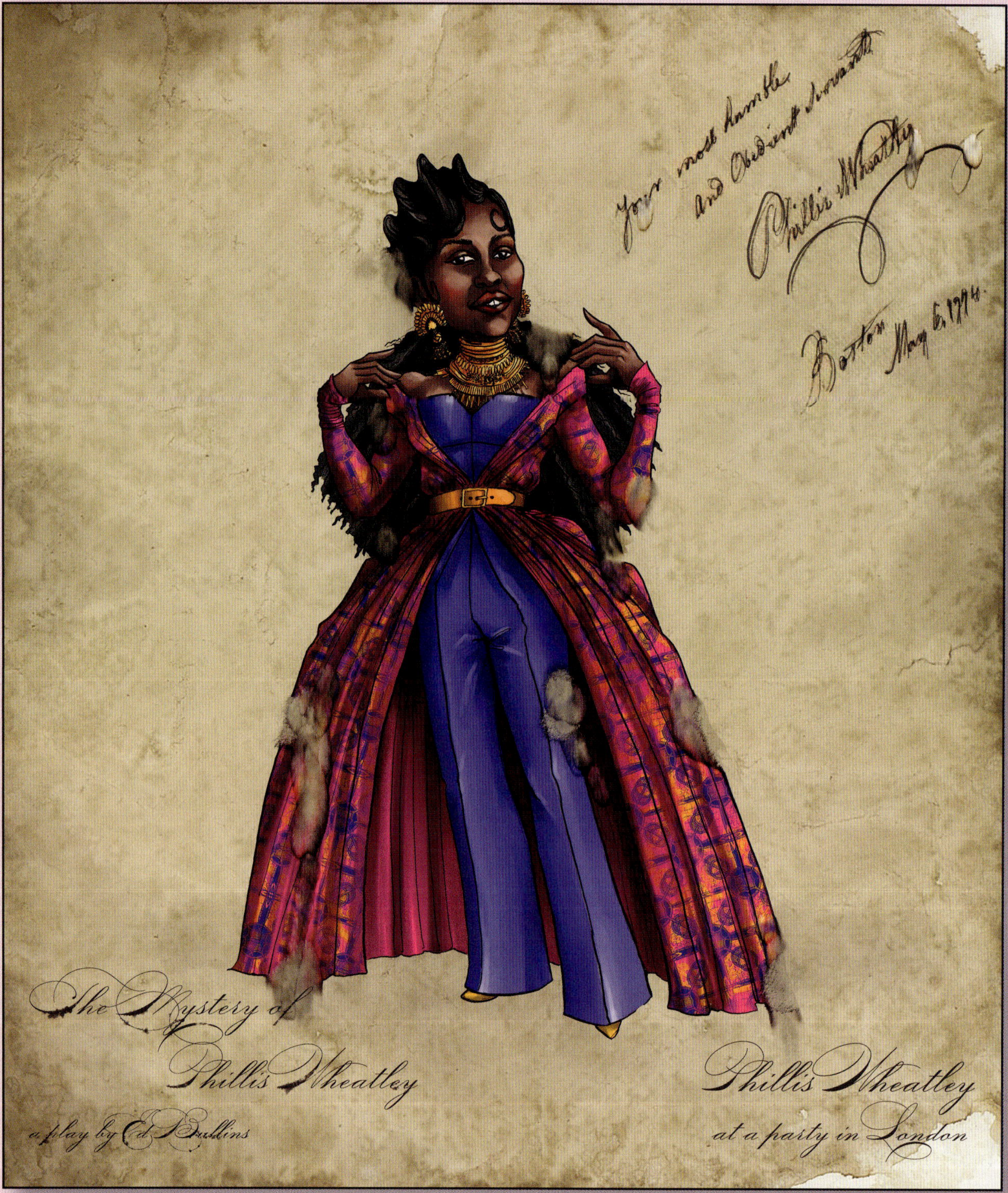

Figure 8.1 Your style will distinguish your work from that of your colleagues. Remember to keep the design communication clear, though. Courtesy of David Arevalo.

CHAPTER 8
Style

Learning Objectives

After completing this chapter, you should be able to

- Create a rendering in marker style
- Create a rendering in gouache style
- Create a rendering in watercolor style
- Create a rendering in a realistic style
- Create a rendering in graphic style
- Create a rendering in a composite style

Style is something you can develop over time. If you are skilled at analog renderings, you probably already have a style type. Feel free to let this transfer to your digital work. If you are just starting to discover illustration, then you may want to try your hand at several standard style types to see if any of them feel right to you.

Styles

Style is the sweet middle spot between straight design communication and artistic illustrations. We are all drawn to particular styles or adaptations of rendering. What's your favorite? Is there an illustrator or artist you particularly admire for their work? What is it about that artwork that stands out for you? The quality of line work? Which medium is used to apply color? The proportions or characterization of the figures? Perhaps it is in the layout. All of these factors contribute to style. Start to pay attention to the specific qualities that appeal most to you.

As mentioned earlier, if you have already developed an analog rendering style, it can easily transfer to digital medium. If you are used to working in watercolor or gouache, feel free to continue with digital brushes meant to emulate those mediums. You can even apply paper textures to your work to make it look more realistic and less digital. If you don't see the right style of brush in your application, check to see if the parent company offers free brushes and textures for you to download. You can also purchase brushes and paper textures through third-party vendors. See the resources section for online options. Likewise, you can create your own brushes after you become more familiar with your application!

Perhaps you have a drawing style but never ventured into colored rendering. Carefully consider your drawing style and choose a digital rendering style that aligns. For example, if you use a graphic caricature style, then you may want to use Illustrator because it lends itself to flat graphic fills. Likewise, you might also try the marker look in Photoshop or try a halftone comic-style approach using specialized actions and filters. Reference analog artwork to help inform your choices.

And if you just have no idea what style to use, try several to see what works best for you. This can be a very fun exercise! Just don't lose sight of the main objective: design communication. Developing a style is enjoyable, but remember to clearly display your garment design so that others can understand it easily. Keep in mind how much time can be lost in artistic style. Sometimes it is better to keep it simple and move on when time is of the essence.

Project 8.1: Marker Style in Photoshop

When planning to digitally emulate an analog rendering technique, it helps to take a moment to analyze the medium in its natural form. Look at the marker rendering in Figure 8.2. What qualities signal that it uses marker to create the color? In this case, the open white space is used for highlights, while the area with marker provides both color and the sense of shadows. Other marker renderings do not use white space but instead create depth through building up the color with overlapping strokes. Although the rendering is detailed, it does not attempt to create a photo-realistic look. Markers lend themselves to a graphic style of rendering, such as comics or manga. Also note that there is a little bit of noise or paper tooth to the rendering.

Figure 8.3 shows a digital fashion rendering by Ana Stoyanova. She used digital prints on the garments but feathered out the edges with a soft brush to give it the look of a marker rendering.

Marker style works best in Photoshop or another digital painting application. Use the *Brush* tool to mimic the look of layered marker strokes. This can be a fast way to lay down color, which is why analog markers are so readily used in the fashion industry. It also produces a more minimal and commercial look.

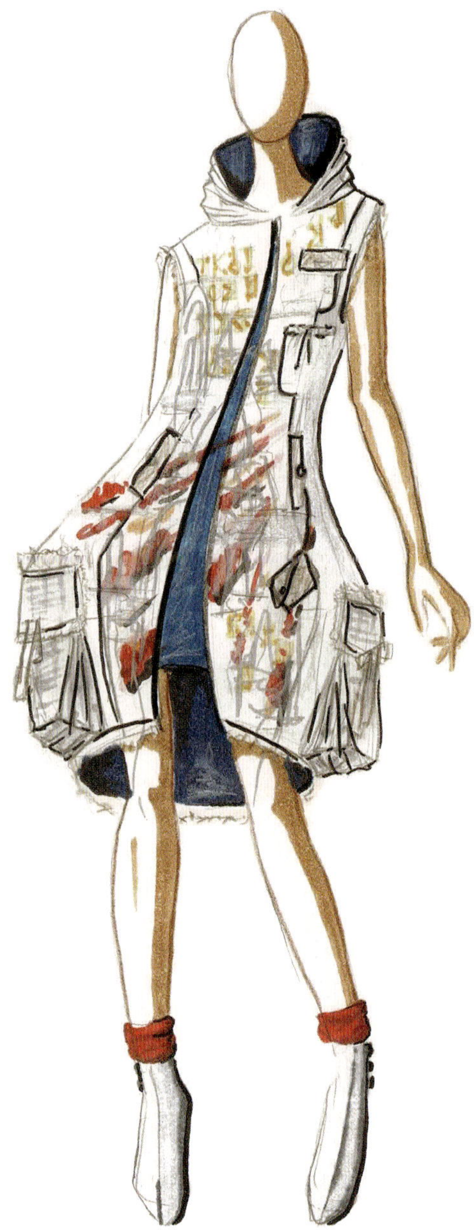

Figure 8.2 Use an analog marker rendering to analyze the qualities of the medium. What makes it look like marker? Artwork by the authors.

When trying out any new style of rendering, or using any new brush for that matter, be sure to test your brush options. Open a blank document and just play around with the brush to get the feel for how it handles. Try rendering something simple, such as the brush exercise page provided with your downloads and shown in Figure 8.4. Use the image as a template to trace or change the *Layer Blend Mode* to *Multiply* and color on the layers below it. Use whichever method that makes the most sense to you.

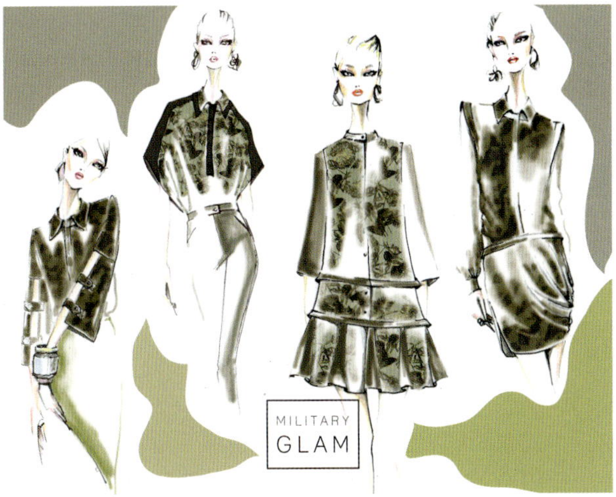

Figure 8.3 Digital brushes can keep the same artistic qualities of analog work. Digital marker-style rendering courtesy of Ana Stoyanova.

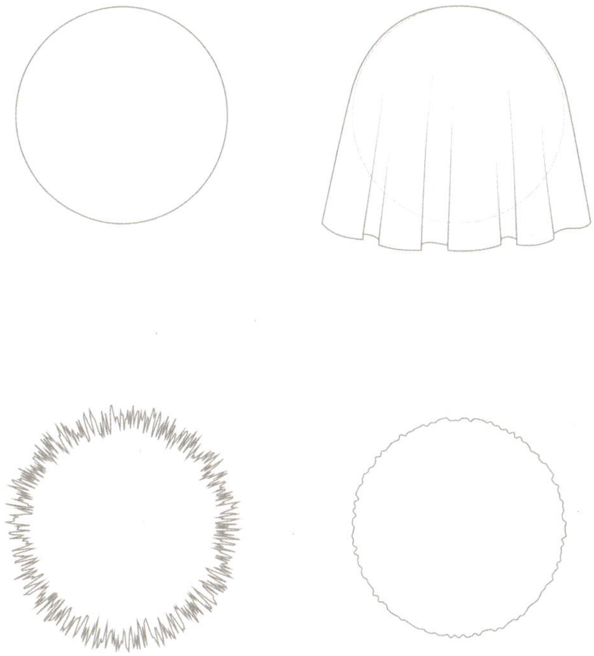

Figure 8.4 Use this brush practice sheet from your exercise files when using a new brush for the first time.

In the example seen in Figure 8.5, we used *Kyle's AM DigiMagic Square* brush in Ps. The Art Marker brush pack can be downloaded for free if you have an Adobe subscription.[1] See how the layers build up with multiple passes of the digital brush?

If you prefer to keep it simple or don't have access to an excess of brush options, then try the default plain round brush that is available with almost any digital painting app. You will need to make some adjustments, though. Lower your *Opacity* to about 50% and take the brush *Hardness* down to 75%. You can get a very similar effect to that of the specialty marker brushes. Don't be afraid to tweak the settings to your liking. You may also find that changing the blend mode of the brush options to *Multiply* will help. Play around and find something that works for your needs, then try it out on the brush practice exercises.

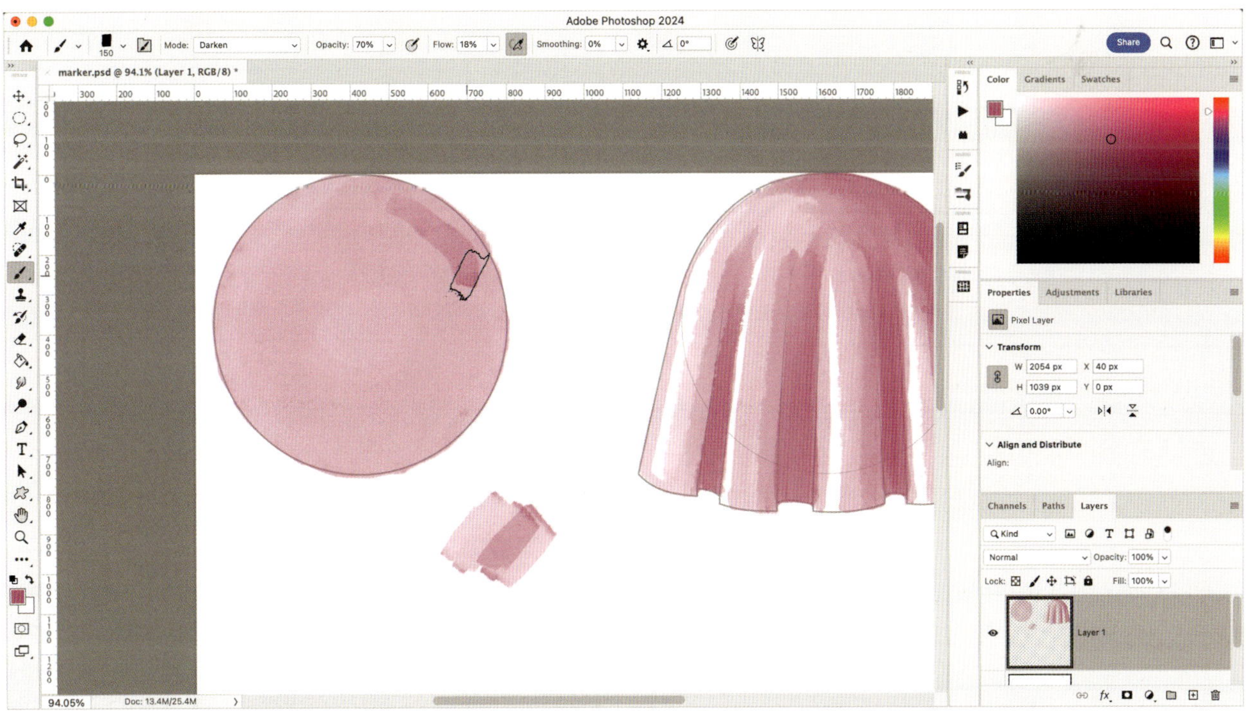

Figure 8.5 Use the brush tester exercise file to try out a new brush. We tried the art marker brush to render the sphere and fabric.

To use the brush for a flat fill, you will need to keep your mouse or stylus engaged. That means you shouldn't lift your stylus from the tablet or release the mouse button while coloring the area that should be flat. Once you lift/release and re-engage the brush, it will start to create a darker color in that area. Note the difference in an engaged fill versus when we lift the stylus and engage the brush again over an area in Figure 8.6. If you are using a stylus, it works best to turn off the pressure sensitivity settings for an even fill.[2] You can also lay down your first layer with the *Opacity* up to 100% and then adjust it to 50% for shading effect. Everyone works the program a little differently. Try a few versions and go with the one that feels the most natural to you.

When the opacity is set lower, you can easily build shading effects by lifting and engaging the stylus/mouse multiple times to layer up a color as you would with an analog marker. If you changed the brush settings to turn off pressure sensitivity of your stylus for filling with a flat color, you may want to turn it back on to have more control over how subtly your color builds up.

Analog marker paper such as Bristol board tends to be rather smooth, but you might see a slight tooth or texture. Try adding a low *Noise* filter to create the same effect. Refer back to Chapter 6 on textures if you need a reminder of how to apply noise. See Figures 8.7a and 8.7b for a design rendered in marker style with a little noise added to create the paper texture. Use StyleFigure1.jpg if you do not have your own figure on which to practice.

To complete the look, try one of the inking brushes for outlines and accents. You can also use colored pencil-style brushes for adding details just as you would on analog rendering. In Figure 8.7c, we left the pencil lines because they were so strong and had a nice texture. However, we use the *Kyle's Drawing Box Wet Crayon* brush to add a colored pencil effect for additional shading and blending.

PRO TIP 8.1

Brush Gluttony

There are a lot of fun brushes out there! Too many, really. You may be on the lookout for the one perfect brush for a project, and end up with twenty, or even 200. Too many brush choices can be overwhelming. Instead of piling up your brushes in the virtual drawer, spend time getting used to just four or five options. Find a handful of go-to brushes that work for you. Then practice working with them until they are second nature to you. If you are new to digital art and not sure which brushes to choose, aim for one pencil-style brush, one inking brush, and two to three in your favorite style of painting (marker, gouache, watercolor, etc.). It's just too easy to lose time hunting for the "perfect" brush. The brush you are already using is perfect, so learn how to use it effectively. If you really want to explore other brush options, try making your own for fun!

PRO TIP 8.2

Accessories

Don't neglect your accessories when styling the garment. Shoes, jewelry, headwear, and other accessories can make an illustration look more polished. A common student mistake is to completely ignore the accessories. They draw the figure, add some clothes, and call it done! Is your model really going to walk around barefoot? The accessories should not detract from your garment design, but rather accentuate your design. It doesn't take much to hint at these items, so remember to include them in your illustrations.

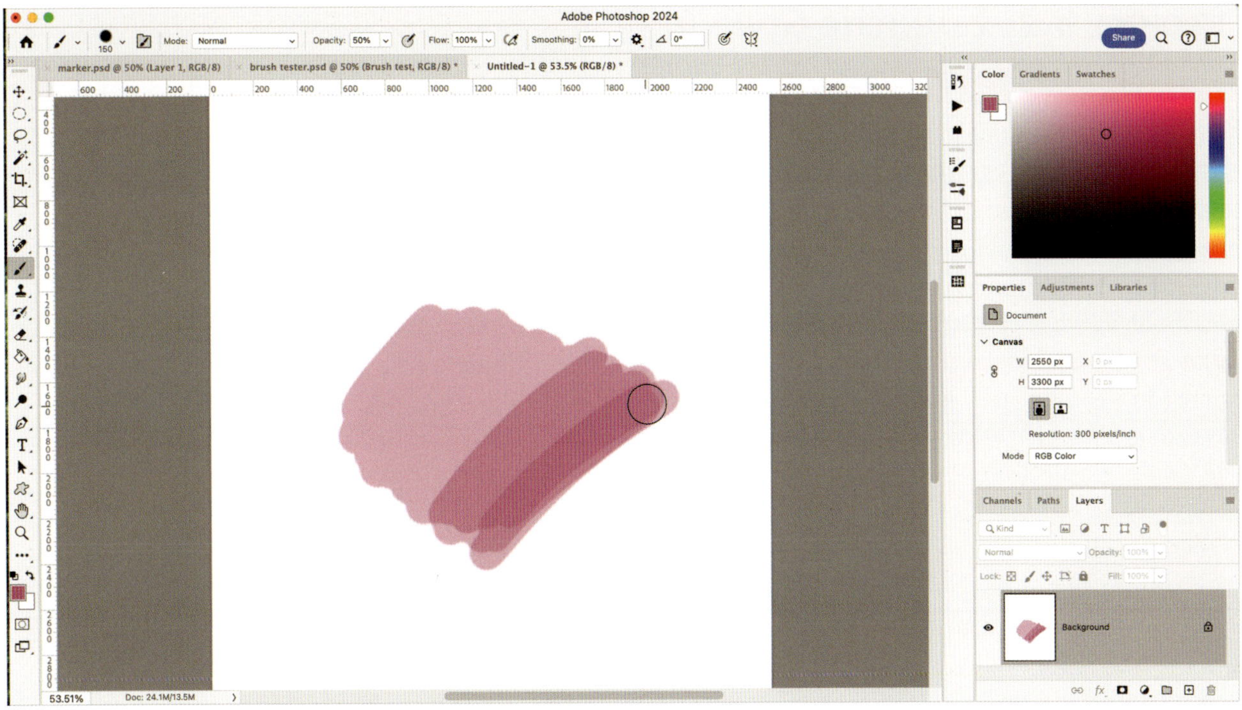

Figure 8.6 The area to the left was filled by scrubbing the stylus back and forth multiple times without lifting it from the tablet. The area on the right shows the effect when the stylus is lifted and re-engaged. If you want to create a flat fill, be sure to keep the stylus or mouse engaged for the whole area.

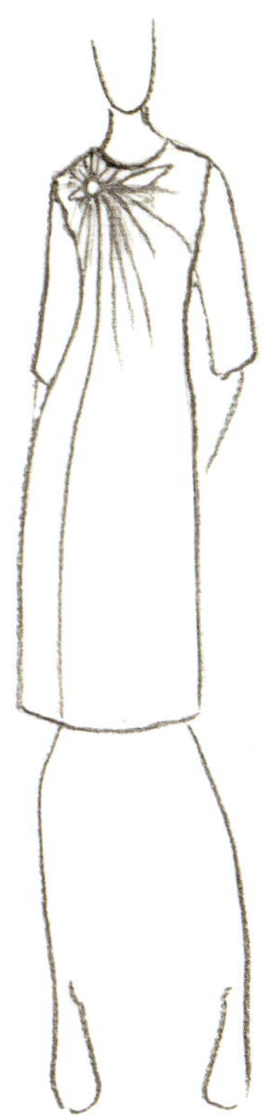

Figure 8.7a We started with a stylized sketch that works well for a fashion marker style. The body is simplified to a few suggestive lines, but the garment is still clear. Artwork by the authors.

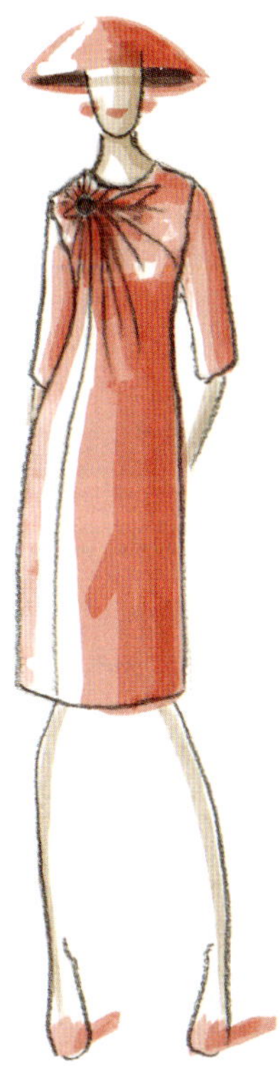

Figure 8.7b We used *Kyle's AM DigiMagic Square* brush to render the figure. Bold, loose strokes help convey a marker style, along with blank areas where the "paper" shows through. Then we added a small amount of noise to give the impression of a paper tooth.

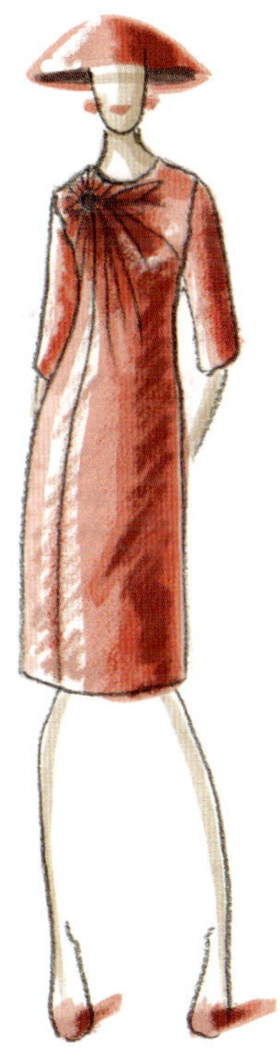

Figure 8.7c Completed rendering with *Kyle's Drawing Box Wet Crayon* brush to mimic colored pencils.

Project 8.2: Gouache Style in Photoshop

Gouache is the traditional analog medium for many designers. The paint acts a little like watercolor and a little like acrylic. However, it has more opacity and a chalky appearance, making it a great choice for colored papers. The analog rendering seen in Figure 8.8 used gouache and a white gel pen on black paper. Because the darkness of the paper creates the shadows, we mostly painted in the highlights and mid-tones. Like marker, this can be a fast way to lay down color and communicate the design effectively.

Figure 8.9 is a digital costume rendering by Jacob Climer. Note how he built up color and left the sketchy quality of the line work. He also incorporated a paper texture to complete the gouache effect. Bright whites help to indicate sequin effects like a gel pen, while a soft white brush creates feather effects.

As expected, there are specific brushes created to emulate the feel and appearance of gouache. Pick one or

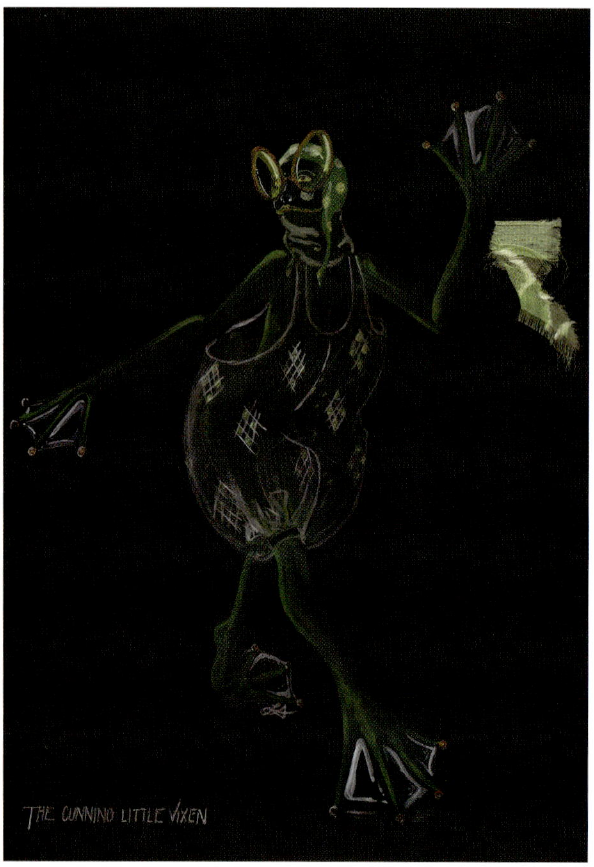

Figure 8.8 This analog gouache rendering shows the chalky and graphic quality of gouache. Artwork by the authors.

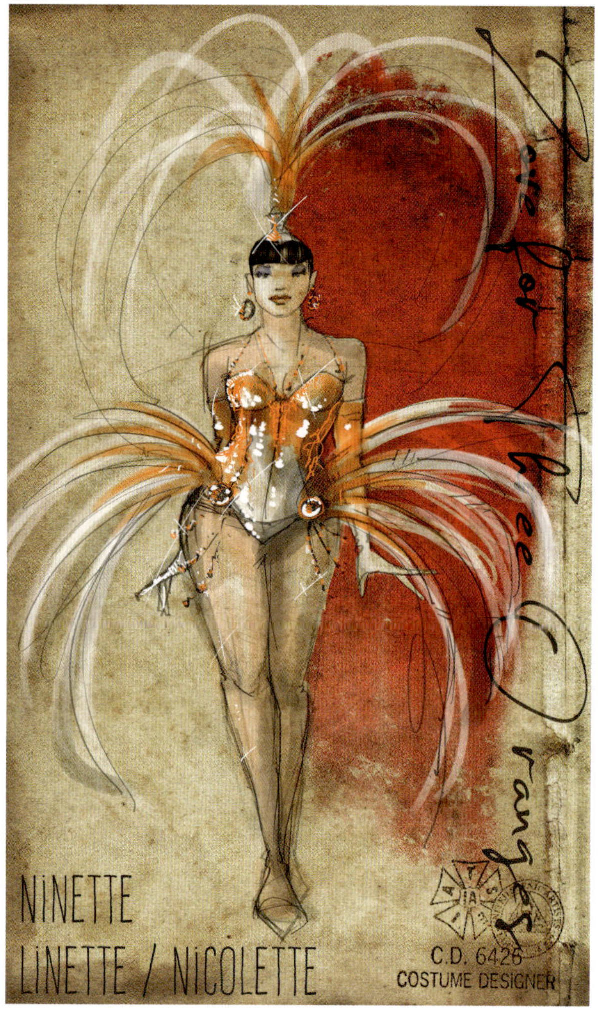

Figure 8.9 Use brushes to convey the desired medium. Don't be afraid to experiment. Gouache-style digital rendering courtesy of Jacob Climer.

two gouache-style brushes and practice as you did with the marker brushes. We used *Kyle's Paintbox Gouache A Go Go* brush in Photoshop with the brush exercise file in Figure 8.4. You can build up the digital paint just as you would on an analog gouache rendering.

Note that there are "wet" brushes and "dry" brushes in the gouache style. If you have ever worked physically with gouache, you are familiar with the concept of wet and dry brushing. As it sounds, wet painting has more water and flows easily. Dry brushing uses thicker, drier paint that lays down with a certain amount of roughness. Additionally, there are stipple and crosshatch brush effects available for many digital gouache brush types as these techniques are often used by commercial artists. Try a few out to see if you like the effect. You can see in Figure 8.10 that we used *Kyle's Paintbox Gouache A Go Go* with the brush tester file.

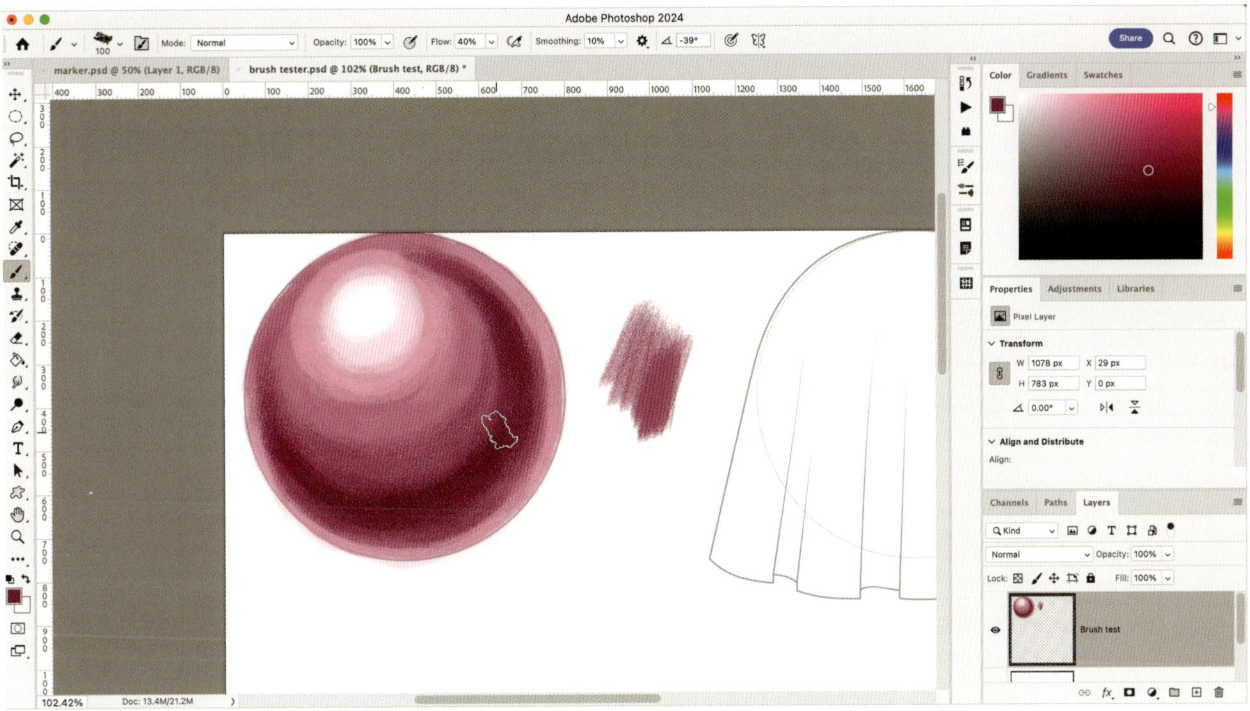

Figure 8.10 We used *Kyle's Paintbox Gouache A Go Go* brush for the brush tester exercise file.

As before, feel free to use inking brushes and colored pencil brushes to add some finishing effects. Figure 8.11a shows a digitally rendered design in progress using the gouache style. You can use StyleFigure2.jpg or your own figure to practice your gouache-style rendering. Figure 8.11b shows a closeup of the figure to display the texture a little better.

Part of the fun of gouache is using a colored paper or background. If doing single design plates for costumes, try adding in a slightly textured and colored background (Figure 8.11c). If you plan to group figures together such as for a fashion portfolio layout, you may want to wait until you get to the backgrounds and layout chapters to take this step.

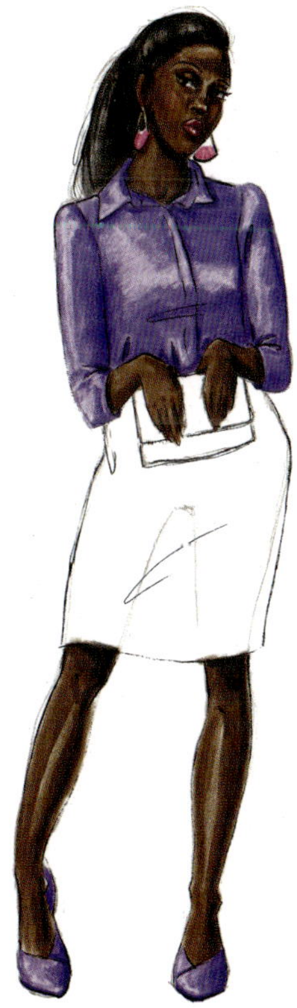

Figure 8.11a This fashion rendering was started using *Kyle's Paintbox Gouache A Go Go* brush. Artwork by the authors.

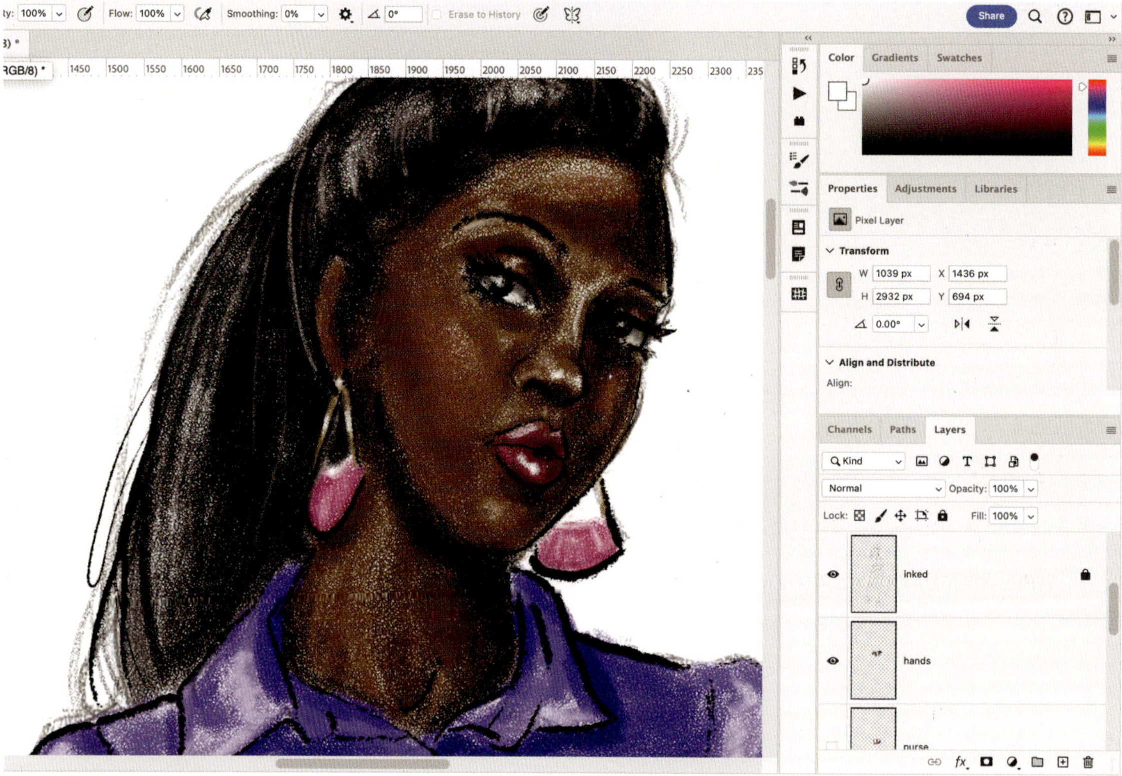

Figure 8.11b In this closeup, you can see how the texture of the digital brush emulates a slightly dry brush and creates a full but gritty stroke effect.

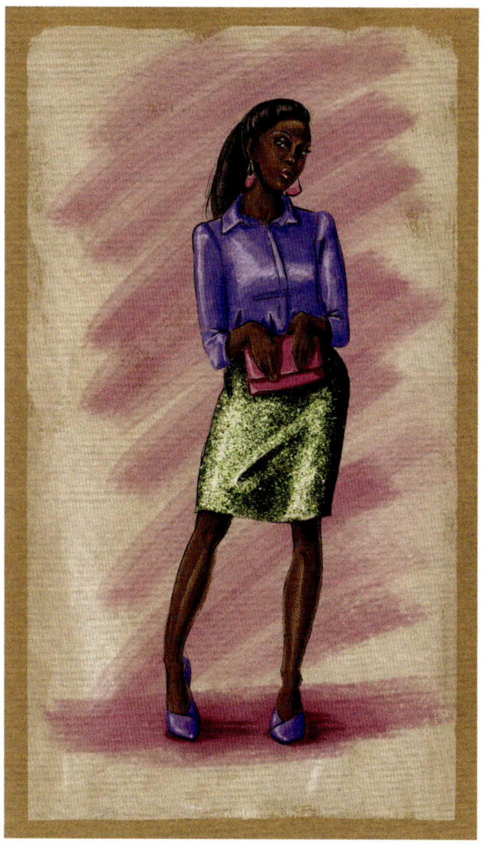

Figure 8.11c The design finished with a colored paper background to add texture and depth.

STYLE SECRETS 8.1

Paper Fun!

Illustration style can be enhanced tenfold by adding a paper texture. If you are making singular garment layouts, you can add it directly to your illustration. If you plan to include multiple illustrations/figures in a layout, then add the texture to the layout file instead. There are several ways to add a paper texture. You can scan an image of a paper texture and place it behind your figure so long as the illustration background is transparent. You can also apply it over the illustration and change the *Blend Mode* to *Multiply* so the shadows of the texture show on the rendering. You can also purchase paper texture options if that is in your budget.

Project 8.3: Watercolor Style in Photoshop

Painting with analog watercolors can be simultaneously freeing and frustrating. The paint has a slightly uncontrolled quality that leads to this dichotomy. It creates beautiful blooms of paint and a light, airy quality. However, like gouache, you can also achieve sharp, detailed work through a slightly drier brush.

Figure 8.12 shows an analog watercolor rendering with both the loose uncontrolled edges and sharp detail work. The paper used for watercolors usually has a bit of a texture or rough tooth that shows with the applied paint. You can also create special textural effects with water, alcohol, or even salt. Many specialized digital brushes can mimic these qualities.

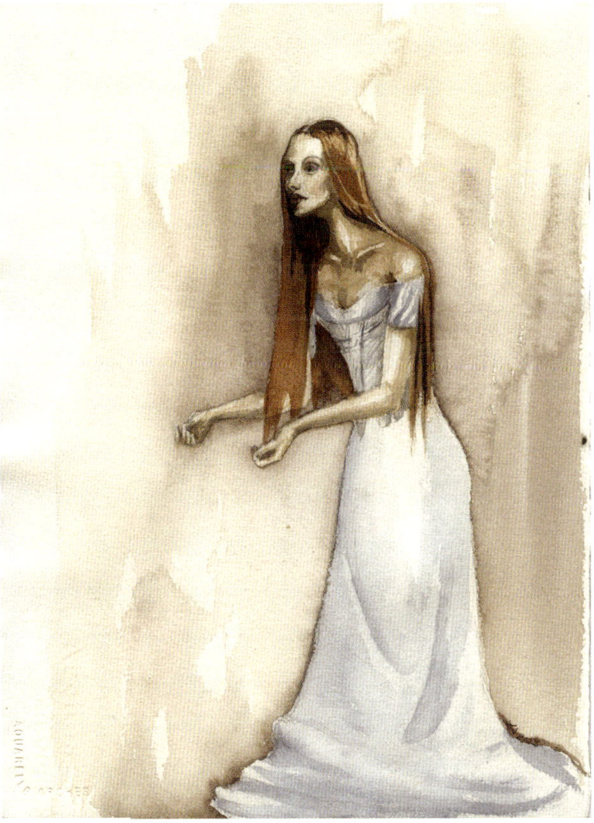

Figure 8.12 Watercolor can be both tightly controlled and wildly chaotic. Notice how much the paper affects the color quality of this analog rendering. Consider how to replicate that in a digital form. Artwork by the authors.

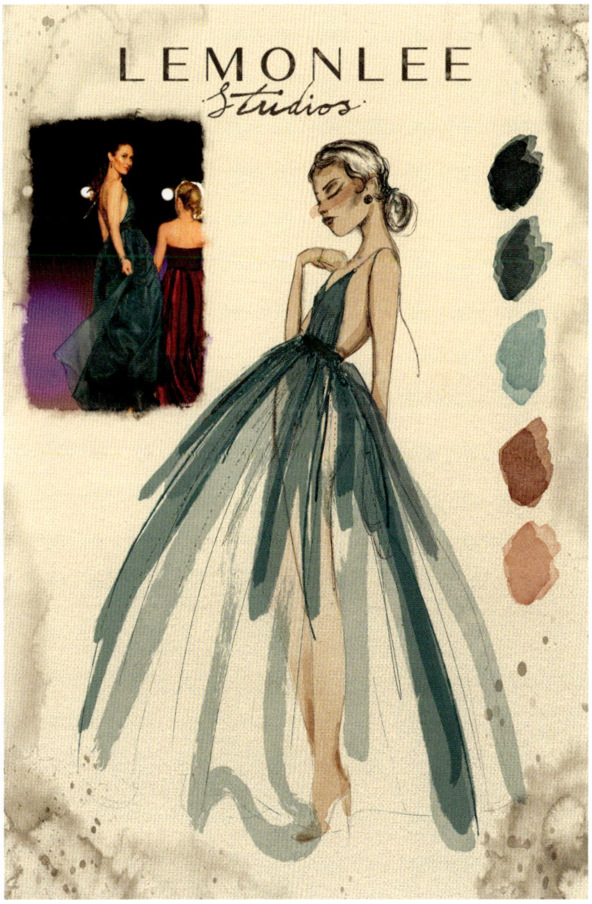

Figure 8.13 Most digital painting applications have a large selection of brushes and filters to create realistic analog effects. Watercolor-style digital rendering courtesy of Liana Hinojosa of LemonLee Patternmaking Studios.

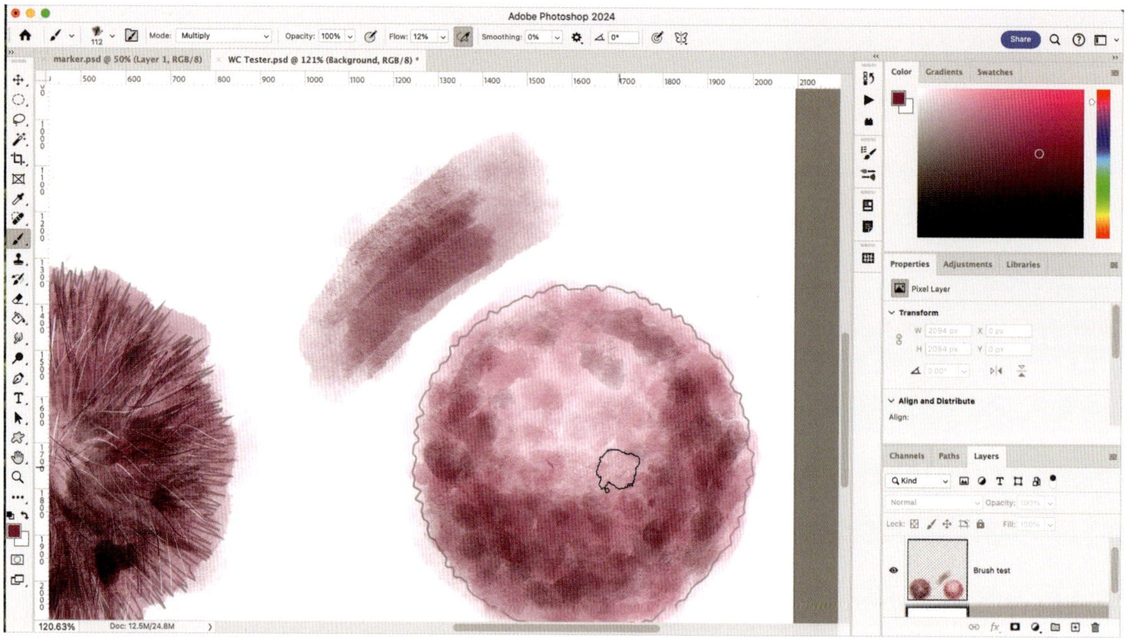

Figure 8.14 Testing brushes on the exercise file. Here we are using *Kyle's Paintbox Watercolor Fill* to practice on the fur and soft textured exercises.

In the digital watercolor-style rendering by Liana Hinojosa shown in Figure 8.13, less is more. The artist used Procreate for this with a loose drawing style and loose painting. Just a few strokes indicate the sheerness of the skirt fabric. The added texture on the background adds to the free painting effect.

There are a lot of watercolor-style digital brushes out there to explore. Some create the soft texture, some can mimic the bleeding effect, and others act like a drier brush for detail work. There are also blenders and erasers that have a watercolor style. If you are already comfortable with analog watercolor, there is a brush (or several brushes) just for you! If you've never worked with analog watercolors, then digital watercolor-style brushes may be more frustrating for you. It never hurts to try, though! Try some experimentation with the brushes to see if they work for you as we did in Figure 8.14.

Robin Schneider uses a technique of laying down a color, then revealing it through a mask with a watercolor-style brush.[3] This may work better for you than using the brush to lay down the color in a watercolor style initially. Don't be afraid to experiment with different ways to achieve similar results.

To create the sharper detailed work, use a drier-style brush in a smaller size. Likewise, you can let the inker show the detail and just use the watercolor style brushes to lay down a wash of color. In Figure 8.15a, we used *Kyle's Inkbox Amazing Cartoon Nib* brush for the detail and outline work. The layer is set to multiply, so we painted on a layer below using *Kyle's Paintbox Watercolor Fill* in varying sizes for the color.

Again, the paper texture plays an important part of watercolor medium. Therefore, you can scan your own paper or purchase a paper texture to place in the background. Watercolor washes also make a great background, even if you don't use that style for rendering your figures. Try out some of the salt or alcohol brushes that move the paint around. They are great for a fun texture! Figure 8.15b has a watercolor paper background for texture, and a big wash with *Kyle's Real Watercolor Salt Course* brush for added texture.

Project 8.4: Realistic Style in Photoshop

With the current abundance of digital and artificial intelligence-generated art, hyper-realism is a popular look these days. It looks very cool, but it takes a lot of time to create. So, is it worth it? As the artist, you need to weigh that question for yourself.

Realism has a few different levels or nuances. **Photo-realism** is art created in a way that looks nearly identical to a photograph. It takes a high level of technical skill to reproduce but leaves many artists asking, "What's the point?" when photographs already exist.

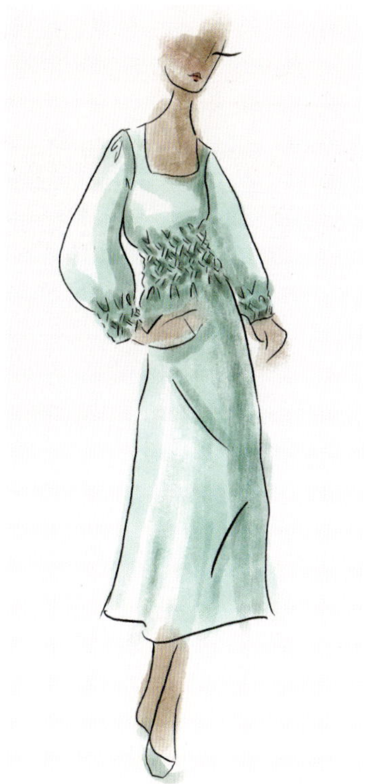

Figure 8.15a After inking the figure using *Kyle's Inkbox Amazing Cartoon Nib* brush, we painted it with a slightly loose watercolor brush. This is a fast way to lay down color.

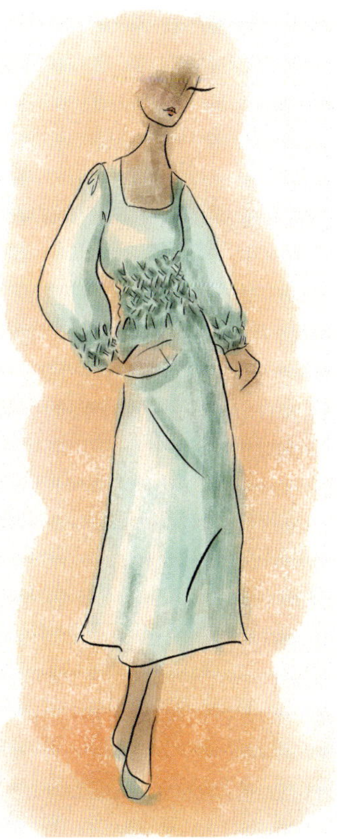

Figure 8.15b The finished rendering in watercolor style with paper texture and a big wash added.

Hyper-realism refers to an art style that is depicted to mimic high-definition photography, but with an artistic twist added such as imaginary details. Hyper-realism is very prevalent in artificial intelligence-generated art, often showcasing photo-realistic images of non-realistic scenes. **Semi-realism** utilizes analog-like tools with the detail and accuracy of a photograph.

The oil painting by Jean Auguste Dominique Ingres in Figure 8.16 shows an analog oil-painted portrait. Although the face has a soft quality, the fabrics are rendered in such detail as to look like a photograph. Photography was in its early stages when this was painted, and realistic portraits were still highly sought by the upper class in Western society.

Grace Kang created the rendering seen in Figure 8.17. This is in a semi-realistic artwork that incorporates gouache- and colored pencil-style tools but mixed with a detailed, photorealistic drawing style. The accuracy of the drawing to the actor's proportions and face along with the attention to detail in the fabrics looks quite realistic. When paired with the colored pencil style of rendering, it creates an excellent example of mixing analog artistic medium styles with realistic drawing.

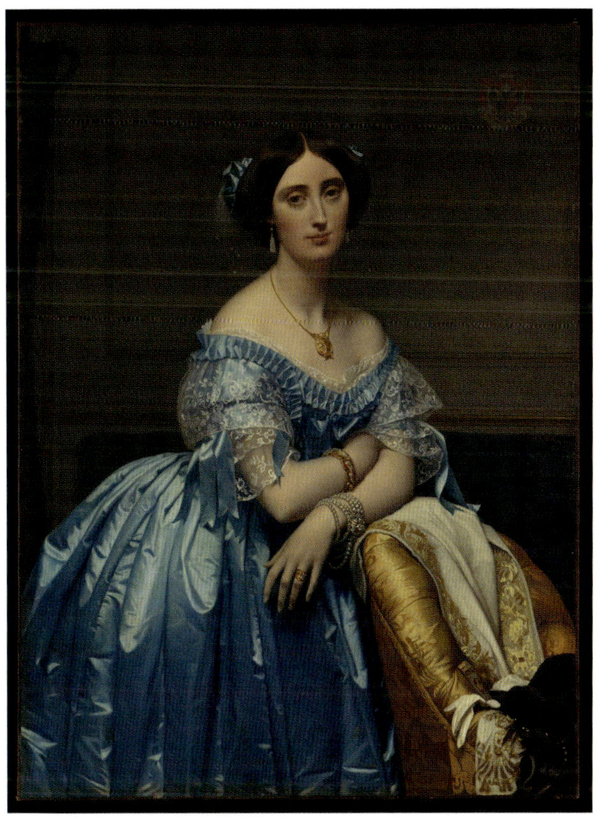

Figure 8.16 This Ingres portrait in oil was painted between 1851 and 1853. Notice the attention to detail in the fabrics. Robert Lehman Collection, 1975/The Metropolitan Museum of Art.

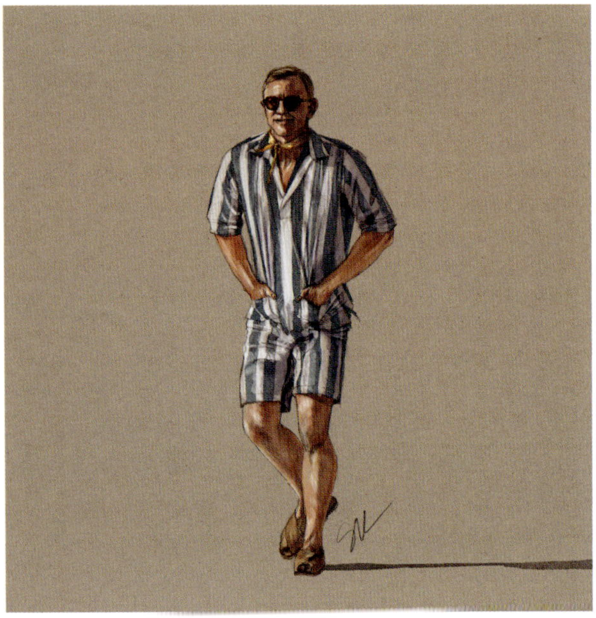

Figure 8.17 Digital rendering by Grace Kang. Costume design by Jenny Eagan. She uses a colored pencil-style rendering to create a semi-realistic style. There is still a painterly quality about the artwork that takes the image beyond photo-realism.

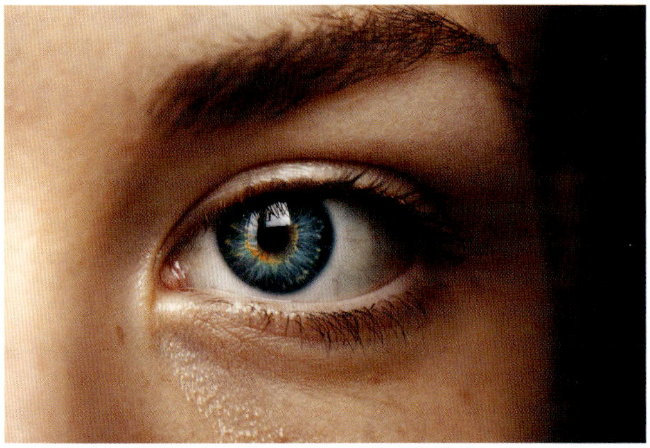

Figure 8.18 Notice the contrast in textures, color variations, and focus in this photo of an eye. Courtesy of Amanda Dalbjörn via Unsplash.

As noted previously, any sort of realistic style takes time. It also takes extraordinary attention to detail. Regardless of whether you use the style on a regular basis for your design communication or not, there is no doubt that you can vastly improve your technical skills by practicing photo-realism. The benefits of exercising this style include improved observation skills along with artistic coordination. So, even if you don't want to use realism in your garment rendering regularly, it is certainly advantageous to practice the style in your downtime.

If you have never attempted anything like this, find a simple photo as reference. Try something like a closeup of an eye or a shoe. Attempting a full figure can be overwhelming when first focusing on realism. Spend time analyzing the photograph. Where is it in focus and where do you see some blur? Where is there a contrast in texture? Look at the photograph of an eye in Figure 8.18. You can find this photo in your exercise files called RealisticPractice.jpg. Notice that the edges become unfocused around the outer corner of the eyelashes. Do you see the shadow of the eyelashes reflected in the eyeball? What about the fine wrinkles and texture under the eye? These are all observations that will aid your endeavor to create a photo-realistic style and help you to become a better artist, overall.

As you master photo-realism, you will learn where to shortcut the information artistically as well as how to create such details by imagination rather than copying a photograph. You will need to be able to draw accurate proportions by hand, digitally, or both. This is a skill that takes time to develop, so don't be discouraged if you aren't there yet. Make it a long-term goal.

For digital rendering, you need to understand your brushes and filters well. Keep the photo reference handy on your screen. Once you sketch the outline shapes, start looking at the values. It helps to squint or temporarily blur the photo reference for this. Where is it darkest and lightest? Build up your colors in layers. Remember that some areas stay blurry while others are sharp. Figure 8.19a demonstrates a photo-realistic painting of the eye photograph. See how we build up the color first? Figure 8.19b shows how the realism starts to kick in when we add in the sharp details through painting and filters.

This is not the most practical of rendering styles for design communication, but it depends on your goals. This style helps to build your technical and observation skills, certainly. However, it generally takes too long to render to be useful on a regular basis in fashion and costume design. If you are strictly a fashion illustrator it may be a worthwhile endeavor, though. Or you simply need this level of detail to communicate your ideas to the client. Only you know your situation and can make that call! Regardless, now you have some artistic reference to help you on your way.

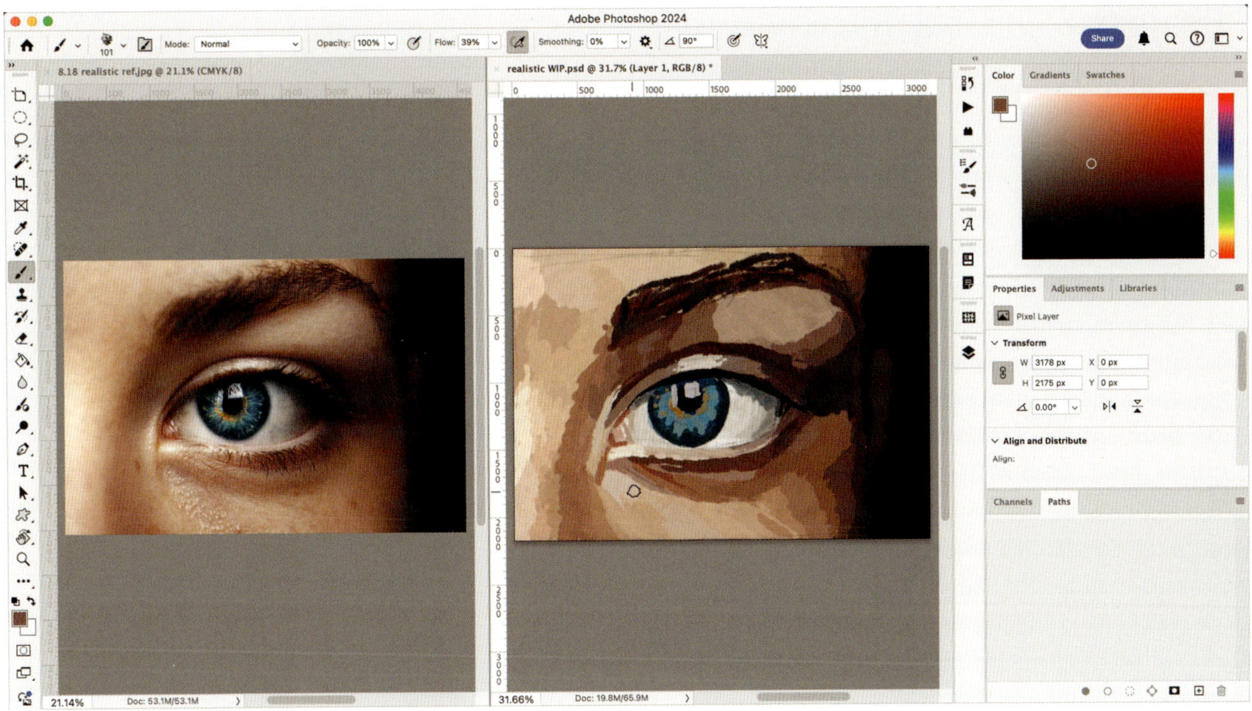

Figure 8.19a Laying down the color of the rendering. Squint your eyes to see the base colors in the photograph and apply a similar pattern to your rendering.

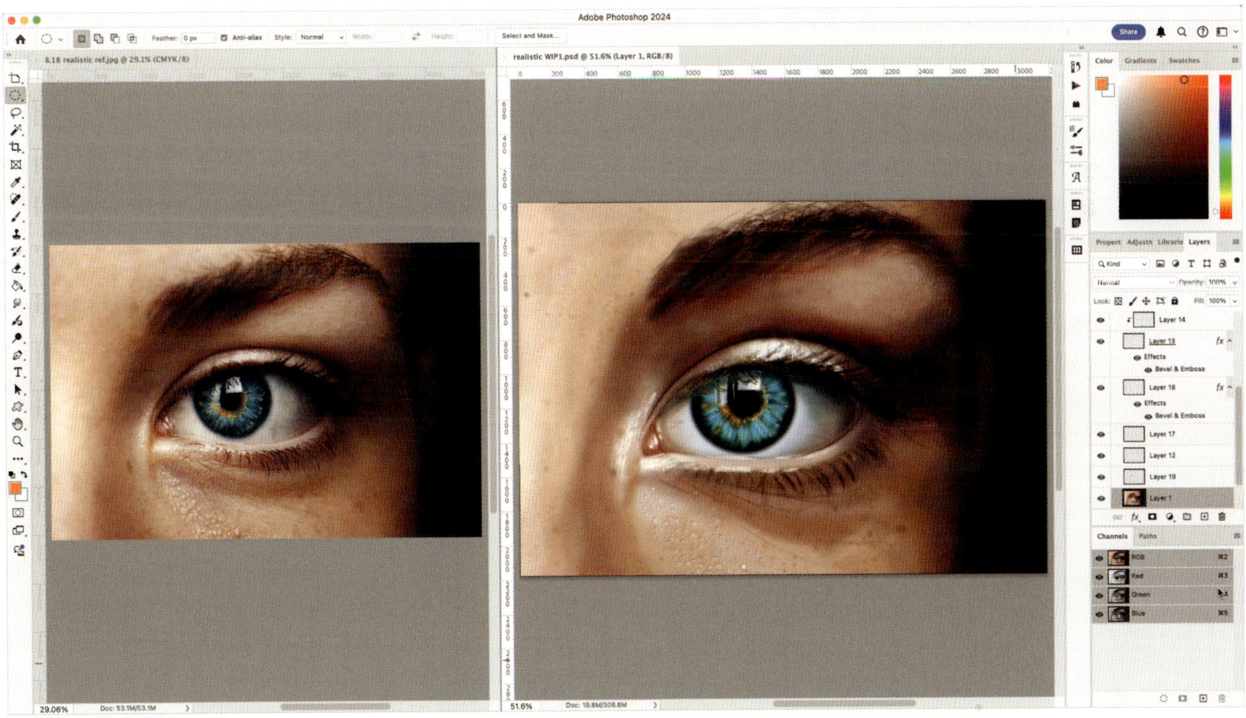

Figure 8.19b Photo-realistic rendering of the eye photograph with full detail.

Project 8.5: Graphic Style in Adobe Illustrator

See Video 8.5 on rendering graphic style in Illustrator.

If you are a wiz with Illustrator, you will probably prefer a graphic style of design communication. Understand that a graphic style does not mean lack of features, though. You can simplify lines, colors, and textures but still convey an astonishing amount of detail; and while these attributes may be simplified, they are not altogether absent.

Consider the analog graphic-style rendering in Figure 8.20. This was created with markers, which naturally lend themselves to this style. The color is blocked in with minimal shadows and clean, simplified lines. The hand inking has a varied line weight, but it smoothly transitions from thick to thin.

The rendering in Figure 8.21 by Arti Sandhu demonstrates a different graphic style. She uses a stylized figure but still shows impressive detail in the fabric designs. Graphic styles lend themselves well to fun proportions of the body and face.

Both Photoshop and Illustrator can be used to create a graphic-style rendering. However, this is one area where Illustrator shines, so we will focus on that application. As you are trying to convey a certain design, you may wish to have some fun with the figure wearing the clothing. In Figure 8.22a, we rendered the model with bright green skin to compliment the pink garment. The heavy outline also lends to the comic-book feel of the illustration. Consider the many features of Illustrator and how to use them for your rendering. Use one of your figures from Chapters 2 or 3 for practice.

To create the heavy outline, we use a technique commonly used for fashion flats. Select all the artwork with your *Selection* tool. Make sure none of your layers are locked. Group them using the menu command *Object* → *Group* (*control+g/command+g*). Open the *Appearance* panel. With the entire group selected, add a new stroke by *clicking* the empty frame in the lower right corner of the panel. Then *click* and *drag* the stroke below the contents in the group as shown in Figure 8.22b. Adjust the stroke however you like. We changed the *Weight* to 4 points, black, with *Rounded* corners for the effect seen.

If you would rather use Photoshop or another digital painting application, think about the brushes you use. Use the *Paint Bucket* tool to fill areas with flat color while trying out some of the half-tone *Pattern brushes* for a "Zap! Pow!" comic style as seen in Figure 8.23.

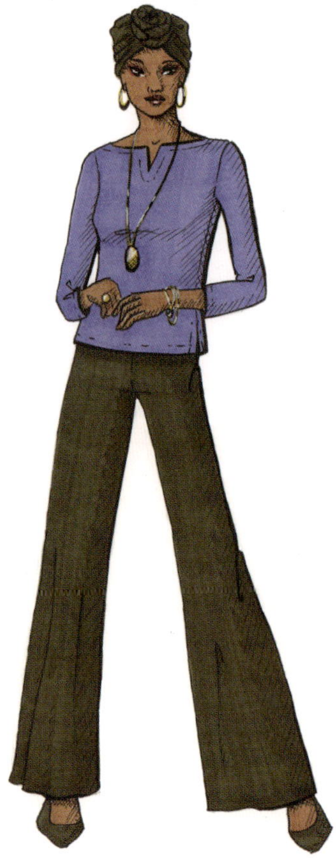

Figure 8.20 This figure was hand-rendered in a graphic style using alcohol markers with inked cross-hatching for shading. Notice that the simplified line quality and coloring does not mean a lack of details.

STYLE SECRETS 8.2

Align Your Styles

We've been approaching your illustration one step at a time but keep the big picture in mind with your style. It's easy to draw the figure and garment in one style, paint it in another, then put it into a background and layout that is something else altogether. As you progress through the lessons and start to find your personal style, be sure to keep it cohesive within a single illustration or layout.

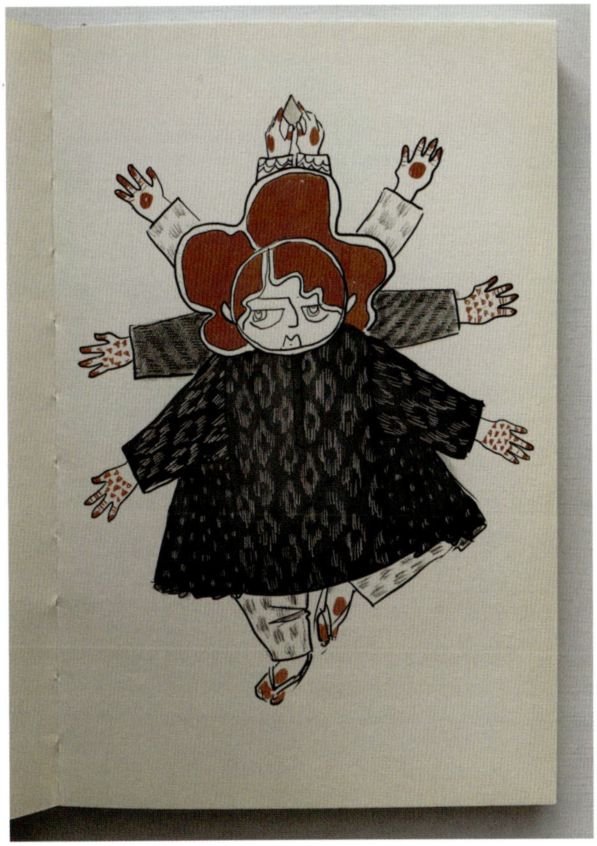

Figure 8.21 Graphic styles can be created in multiple applications. Courtesy of Arti Sandhu.

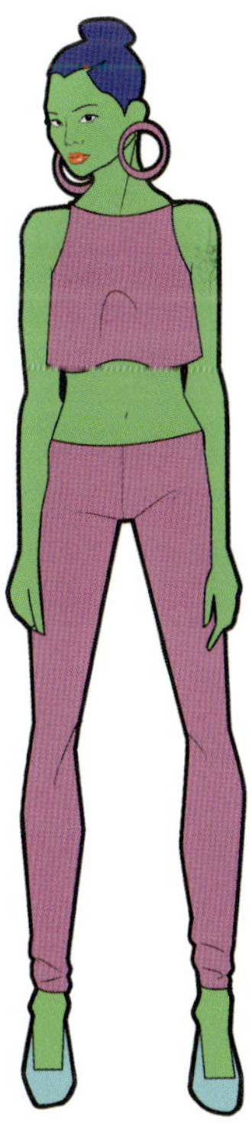

Figure 8.22a A graphic fashion rendering created in Illustrator. A fun quality of comic-style rendering is that out-of-place features like green skin seem perfectly natural. Artwork by the authors.

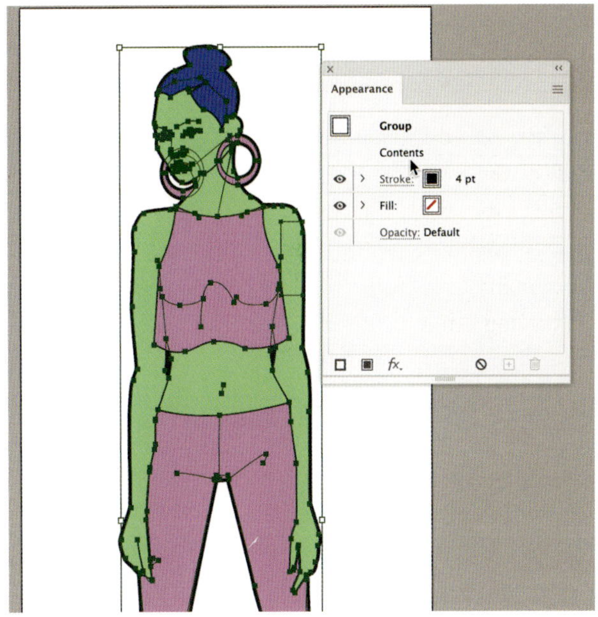

Figure 8.22b Create a heavy outline through the *Appearance* panel in Illustrator. *Group* the entire figure first. Then add a stroke to the group. Be sure to pull the stroke below the contents in the panel.

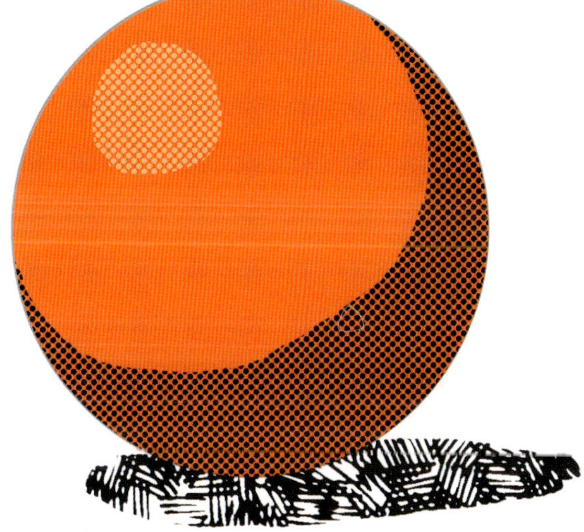

Figure 8.23 Try using some of the halftone brushes for a fun graphic style in Photoshop.

Project 8.6: Composite Styles

Collage has been a fun and creative way to build design communication for many decades. When creating an analog collage, you may mix photographs, different papers, found objects, or other sources of color and texture. The analog collage in Figure 8.24 uses a pencil sketch for the base. Then we glued ripped bits of magazines to create the fabric color and texture. The rips help indicate seams, folds, and fabric direction.

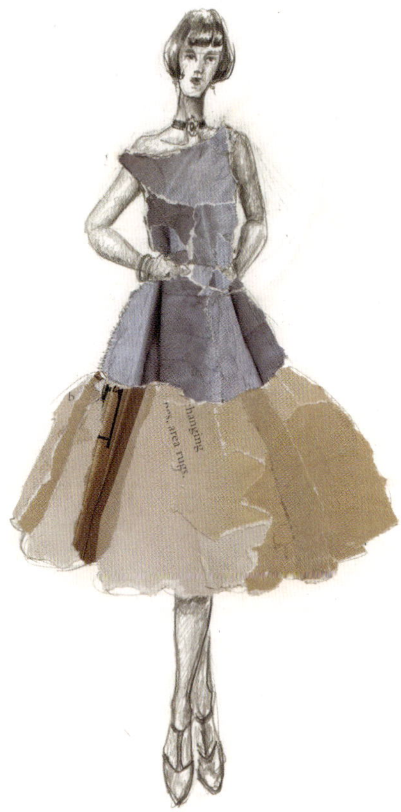

Figure 8.24 This analog collage uses a pencil-sketched figure with ripped bits of glossy magazine to create the effect of the dress.

Digital collage is not much different from analog collage. Instead of physical cut and paste, you create a digital version through masks and layers. Pull from a variety of source material for figures, faces, textures, fabrics, shapes, etc. It helps to build digital folders of possible imagery as you go. Watch out for copyrighted imagery, though. Be sure to source responsibly. Scan in fabrics and organic matter, take your own photos, use royalty-free images, and get permission when using someone else's material. Once you build up a resource library, it will make your rendering process faster. If you think, "I need a gingham for that apron," then you can quickly find a suitable image from your resource folders to *Clip* into the apron shape.

Collage is a great way to play with ideas and make quick mock-ups. Use the fast photobashing style by masking around shapes and layering them digitally. The trick to photobashing is not to get too hung up on perfect selections or realistic overpainting. Just start pulling sources together. If you aren't sure about a look, then turn off the layer and make another on top. Flip between the options to consider which looks best. You can see Hannah Delmore's process in Figure 8.25. She uses the same figure multiple times to try out different looks.

When using this style for finished renderings, you may want to incorporate more painting and filters to communicate the design. In Danny Guerra's rendering seen in Figure 8.26, he mostly sketched the garment design over the collage elements. The great thing about collage is that there is no wrong answer!

Start by roughly sketching your idea. *Open* some source material, either in separate windows or directly *Place* them off to the side of your current artwork. Just make sure they are in easy reach. Try different methods of *Selecting* and *Masking* your source material. Don't forget to use *Transform*, *Blend Modes*, and *Opacity* on your layer to help blend items into the artwork. In Figure 8.27a, we imported a snakeskin texture, changed the color through a *Hue/Saturation Adjustment Layer*, *Warped* the image through *Free Transform* (*control+t/command+t*), and used a layer mask to fit it to the figure's midriff. The layer mask is turned off in this image.

As a final note about collage style, this is one area where AI-generated art may come into play. Consider uploading one of your own design sketches and tease your keywords to see if the results spark any ideas. Or use AI to create interesting textures for you to mask and *Clip* into your artwork. You can use a process called **inpainting**, which is called *Generative Fill* in Adobe Ps. Inpainting utilizes generative AI and deep learning to analyze a digital photograph or drawing and then replace a selection using text-to-image prompts. For example, you can select the hat of your figure and try replacing it with other hat styles using the feature. At the time of writing this text, *Generative Fill* is only available in the Beta version of Ps, but we expect it will soon be implemented in the full version.[4]

You may also want to try Photoshop's **Neural Filters**. These filters are another new feature that uses artificial intelligence. This is less generative and is closer to the algorithms of *Content-Aware Fill* that simply analyze the image and try to "fix" it using the surrounding pixel information. *Neural Filters* are currently part of the full version of Ps, and can be found in the top ribbon menu under *Filters* → *Neural Filters*. Once selected, the program will open a new panel with several options such as *Skin Smoothing*, *Makeup Transfer*, and *Colorize*. You will need to activate each by downloading the filter and *toggling* the button to the right of the filter type. We

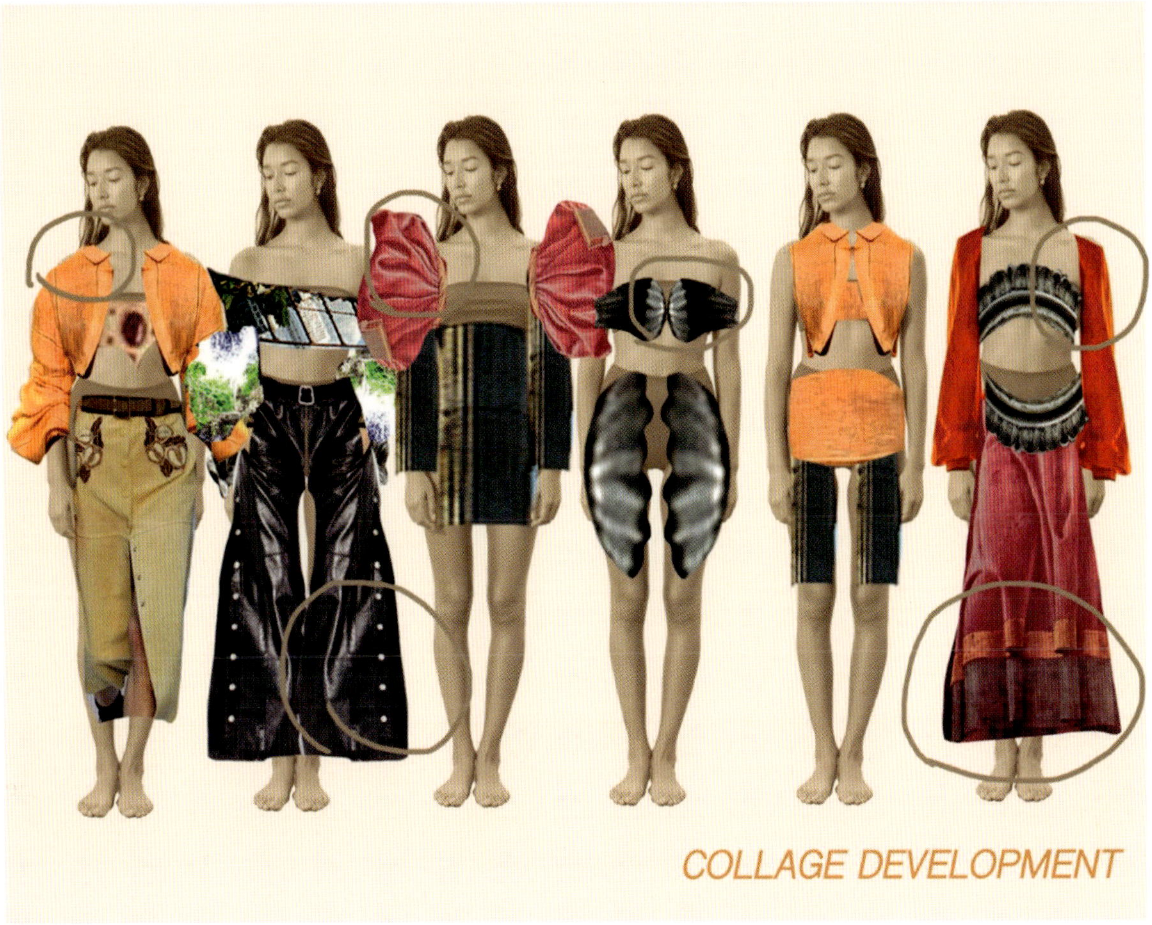

Figure 8.25 Collage can be used to test design ideas before further elaboration. Photo collage development courtesy of Hannah Delmore. Instagram: @hannadelmoreillustration. Hannahdelmore.com.

haven't experimented with this much yet, but it certainly looks enticing for the photobashing style of rendering!

Try the various programs to boost your creativity and look at your artwork in a different way. In our collage, we used artificial intelligence to create the tulle skirt, the snakeskin texture, and the background using Adobe Firefly (Figure 8.27b). The rest of the collage was digitally painted with *Kyle's Paintbox Gouache A Go Go* brush and *Kyle's Inkbox Amazing Cartoon Nib* brush.

Other Style Options to Explore

The list of styles presented here are far from finite. Think about other styles that you admire. Try to mimic historic artistic style like pointillism or mosaics. Study the style of another artist that sparks your interest. Play around with other digital medium brushes such as acrylic or oil pastel. Keep in mind the point of your renderings, though. A particular style may be fascinating, but does it accurately communicate the garment design (Figure 8.28). Is it relevant to what you need to accomplish?

Would an animated rendering help communicate your design? Or a 3D rendering that shows all sides of the garment? These are other possibilities that only you can answer for yourself. If you want to explore such options, you will most likely need to access other programs. These styles could be useful for designing animated characters or gaming costumes. If it works for your needs, go for it!

Observation and exposure to other artworks are the best way to develop your own style. If you are just getting into rendering, allow yourself the freedom of time to find your style. Play around with your options to find what works best for you and your situation.

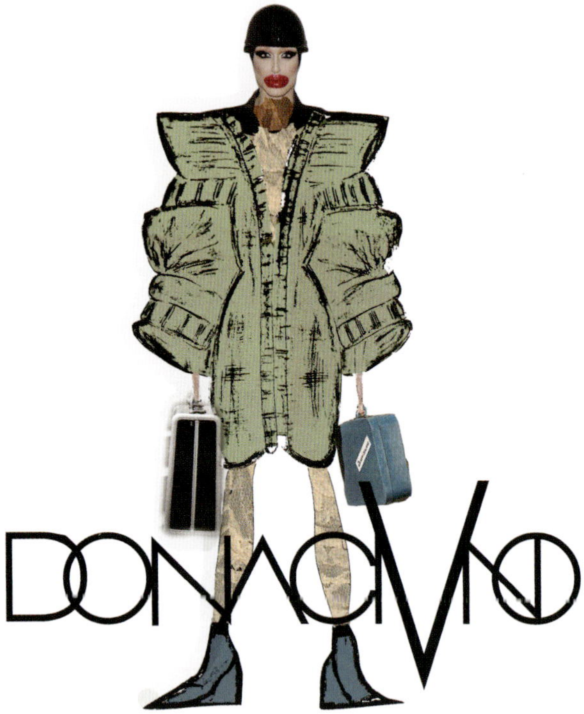

Figure 8.26 Collage can also be used for polished, final renderings. Digital collage and design by Donny Guerra V. Instagram: @donnyguerrav. Texas Tech University. College of Human Sciences. Apparel Design & Manufacturing. Model: Milk. Instagram: @bigandmilky.

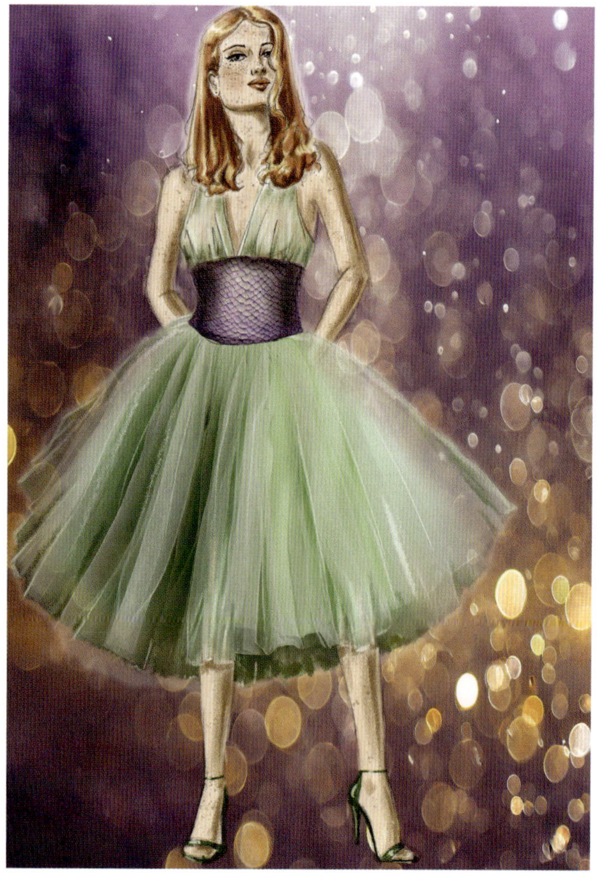

Figure 8.27b Try using AI for parts of your collage. You can create garment textures, specific parts like collars or pockets, backgrounds, or accessories!

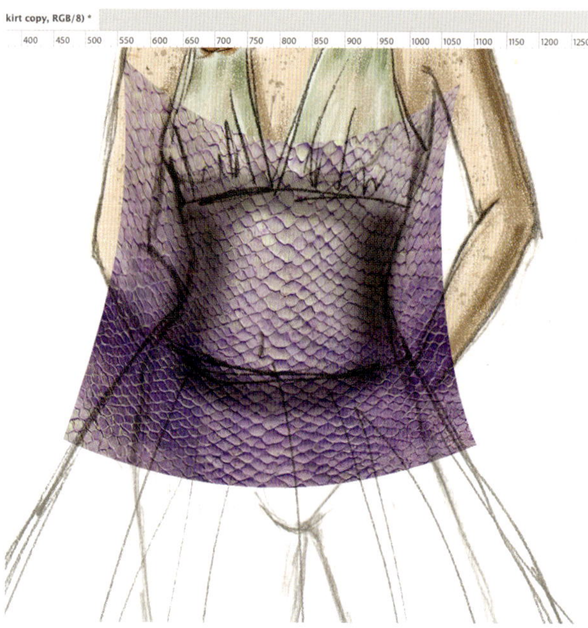

Figure 8.27a For our collage, we *Placed* an image of snakeskin and adjusted the shape to wrap around the body using the *Warp* feature in *Free Transform*. The snakeskin texture was created using AI in Adobe Firefly. Artwork by the authors.

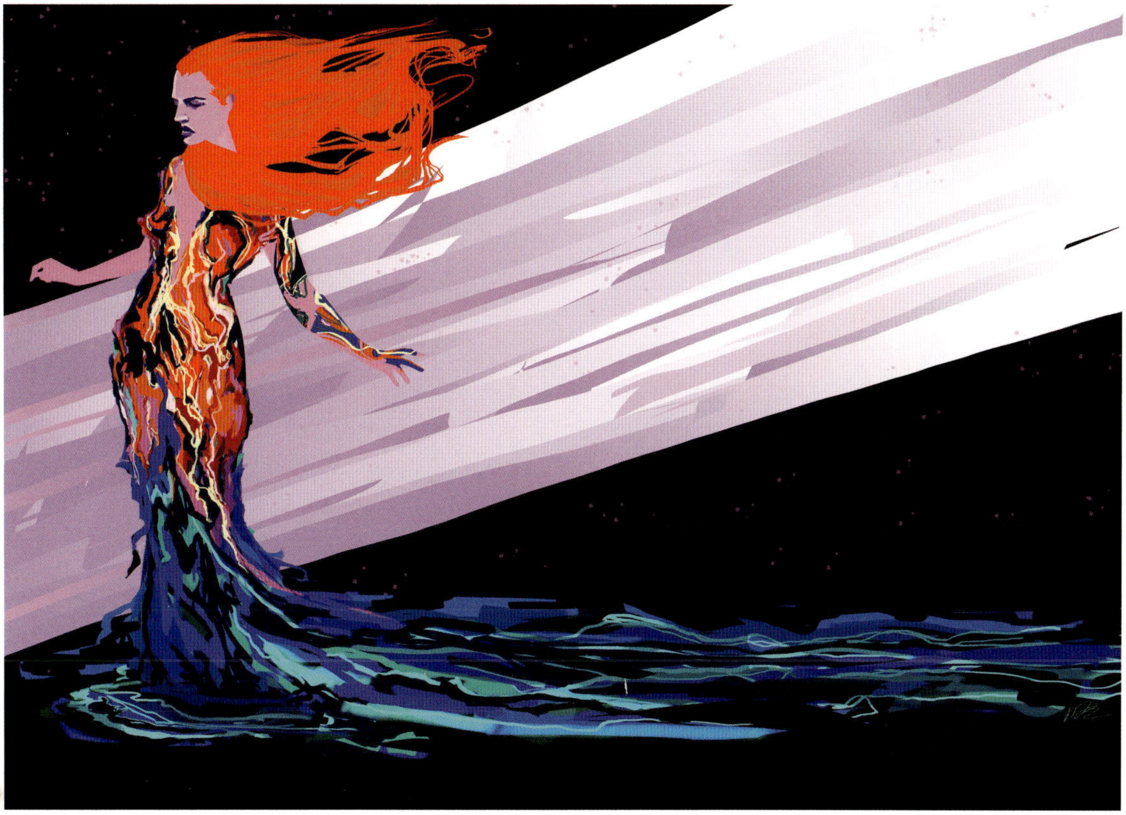

Figure 8.28 This rendering is a great example of design exploration. However, depending on the context, it may not be the best way to communicate the design. Artwork by Julianne D'Errico @julianne.derrico. Juliannederrico.com.

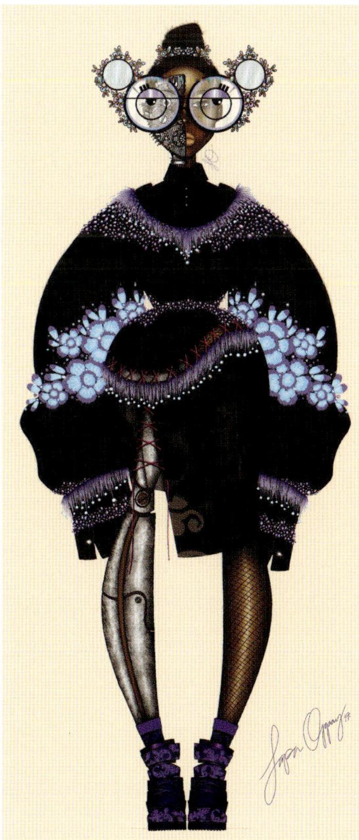

Figure 8.29 This artist uses a mix of styles to convey his design. "Clockwork: Look 10" by Papa Oppong. 2017. Made with Procreate for iPad.

STYLE SECRETS 8.3

How Often Should I Change Styles in a Portfolio?

Are you having fun playing around with different styles? That's great for personal exploration and learning! However, as you start to develop your portfolio, you may want to rein it in a bit. Too many style types tend to communicate inconsistency with your designs. As a general rule, we recommend keeping your style shifts to a maximum of three.

Now with that said, there are trends within portfolios. In the 1990s, it was expected that you could show a range of illustration styles, so more styles were considered better. Currently, the focus is on your design ability rather than the illustration style. Therefore, you probably want to be more selective and consistent. Pay attention to industry trends and adjust your portfolio accordingly. Context may also dictate the need for more style types. The moral of this story is to do your homework and determine the best solution for you and your situation.

Troubleshooting

"There are too many brush options to choose from. I just want a simple [insert type of brush here]."

Tell us about it. There are a LOT of brush options. Look online for the specific brush used by an artist whose work you admire. It's just practice and experimentation mixed with a healthy dose of time to find the "right" brush for you. See the Pro Tip about Brush Gluttony.

"I want to try this textured brush, but it keeps acting weird."

1. Check that your brush is not a blender or eraser. The brush tip is only one part of the settings. See if it is set to a brush action rather than a blending or erasing action first.
2. Look through the other settings. There are a lot of them! See what settings are turned on or off. Play around with them until you start to get the action you expect. If you tweaked a brush and want to use it how you just set it up to run, be sure to save the brush or you will have to repeat the setting changes!
3. Sometimes there is just a weird glitch. *Save* your work. *Close* and reopen the program.

"When I add a heavy outline to my artwork in Illustrator, it never works right."

1. First, make sure the full artwork is selected and grouped together. Make sure you don't have any layers or objects locked when grouping.
2. Make sure you drag the word *Contents* below your new stroke in the *Appearance* panel list.

Summary

There are many fabulous styles out there for design communication. The best way to find your style is through observation and experimentation. Try using a marker- or watercolor-style brush to lay down color quickly in a looser style of rendering. Try gouache for a little more body to your painting. Illustrator lends itself well to a graphic style of rendering. Collage is a great way to try out ideas through photobashing mock-ups. You can also use it as a full rendering style by adding your own sketches and painting. There are many other styles out there to try. Play around and find the one that suits you best.

STUDIO Companion Videos for Chapter 8

Please refer to STUDIO for accompanying chapter video(s).

Keywords

Hyper-realism
Inpainting
Neural Filters
Photo-realism
Semi-realism
Style

Review Questions

1. Describe one way to make your own marker-style digital brush if you do not have access to pre-made art marker brushes.
2. Describe how to fill an area with flat color when your brush has the *Opacity* turned lower than 100%.
3. Where can you find more Photoshop brushes as part of your Adobe subscription?
4. Describe two different ways to obtain a watercolor paper texture for your digital needs.
5. To add a heavy outline to your rendering in Illustrator, what steps must you take?
6. What are the benefits to learning a realistic style of rendering?
7. List four different ways to responsibly resource material for your collage.

Commands Introduced

- Appearance panel

Keyboard Shortcuts

- Ai: *control* + *g*/*command* + *g* (Group objects)
- Ps: *control* + *t*/*command* + *t* (Free transform)

Discussion Questions

1. Is it better to have a detailed rendering style or a fast rendering style? Explain your thoughts.
2. Is there any benefit to developing multiple styles of design communication? Why or why not?
3. Is it still your design if you *Clip* other garments into your collage? Explain your decision.
4. Have you tried using artificial intelligence in your artwork? Do you feel it was successful or not successful and why? How could it be improved?
5. Research three other historic artistic styles. Try your rendering in each of those styles.

Practice Exercises

1. Use one of your figures and garment designs. Try rendering it in at least three different styles. Which was fastest? Which one looks best? Which do you like best and why?
2. Create an analog rendering however you like. Now try to digitally recreate it. Compare the experience and results of the two renderings.
3. Compile a folder of rendering styles that you admire. Note the specific elements you like about each.

Endnotes

1. In the *Options* menu of the *Brush* panel, choose *Get More Brushes*. This will take you to a section of the Adobe website. Log in with your Adobe ID and you can download hundreds of brushes developed by Kyle Webster, a Ps brush guru.
2. For flat fill, go into the brush settings for opacity. In the *Transfer* settings, be sure that *Opacity Jitter* control is set to *off*.
3. Robin Schneider has a Photoshop rendering tutorial available if you have access to LinkedIn Learning. Check out her course for more ideas!
4. As quickly as the software updates, these features will probably be implemented into the full version of Photoshop by the time this text is printed. Look for tutorials through your favorite Adobe learning channel on the most recent features of Adobe Illustrator.

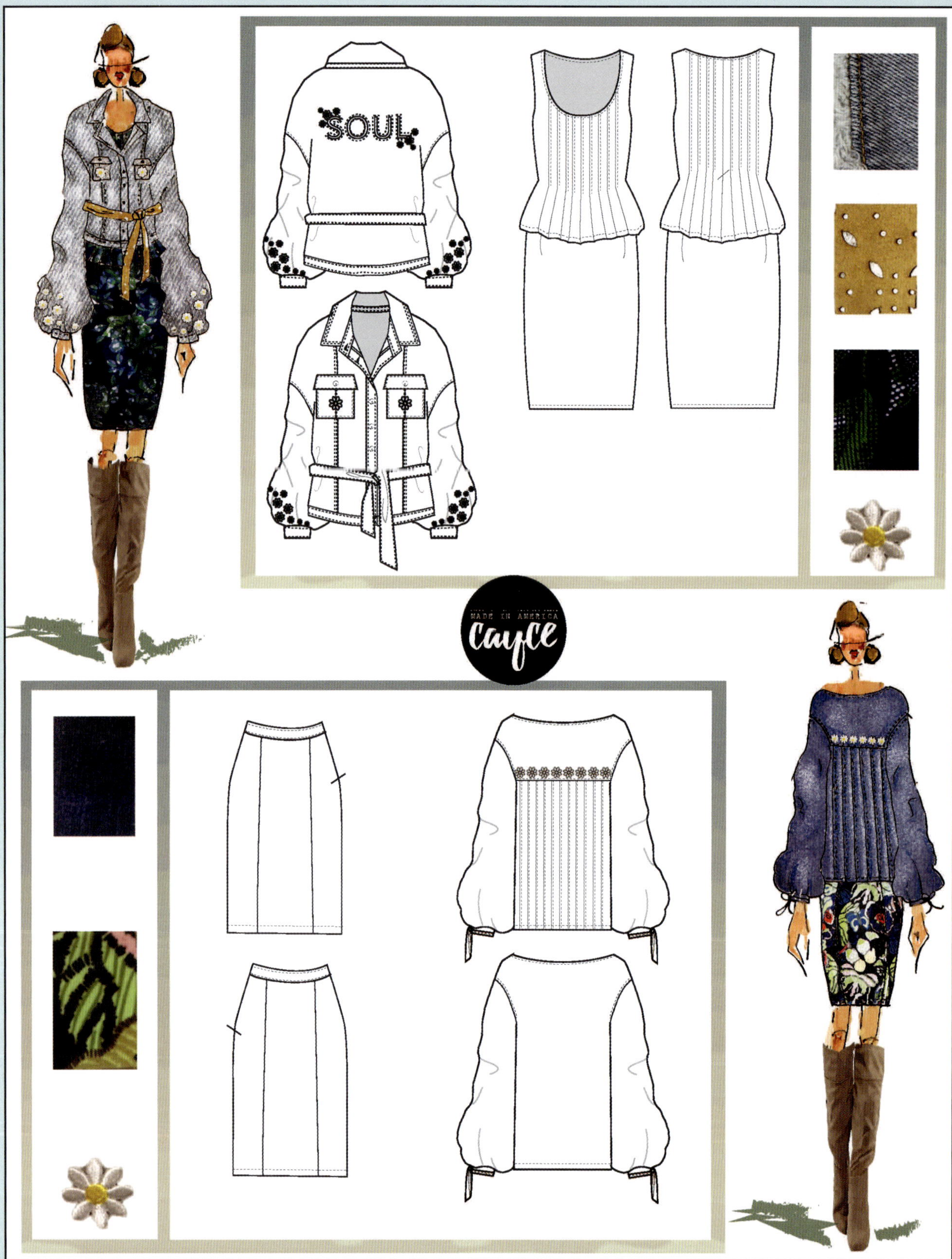

Figure 9.1 Illustration layout needs vary somewhat between the fashion and costume industries. However, similar elements are present in both layout types. Courtesy of Cayce Atwood, Texas Tech University. College of Human Sciences. Apparel Design & Manufacturing.

CHAPTER 9

Basics of Layouts for Fashion and Costume

Learning Objectives

After completing this chapter, you should be able to

- Construct a mood or inspiration page that communicates your design process
- Compile a fabric page for your layout
- Create a photoshoot of your completed garments to include with your layout
- Investigate possible layouts for your design work

Let's think about how your figures will work in a portfolio layout. Even if you don't need a portfolio, layouts help professionalize the look of your illustration work and pull your ideas into a clear form of communication for others. Think about how you want to present your ideas to everyone else. What are the most important ideas you need to communicate? Let's investigate here.

Components of a Fashion Portfolio Project

We are starting to enter the main territory where fashion and costume industries treat design communication a little differently. For the most part, fashion portfolios communicate fashion lines while costume portfolios focus on shows or performances. We will start with the fashion layout needs.

Besides the illustration of the garment, the focus of this text so far, fashion portfolio layouts have common elements. They often include the inspiration, or at least hint at it through the background, title, and other elements of the layout. There are several ways to communicate your inspiration. The most obvious is a page devoted to a composite of your inspirational images, colors, and so on. This is the target of our first project in this chapter, Project 9.1.

For most fashion brands, they create a large board of inspiration for all the designers to reference when generating ideas and developing the line. In this case, the inspiration board is not necessarily part of a portfolio layout. Of course, if you are already working for a brand, you often cannot include your work for that company in your personal portfolio according to how they handle intellectual property in your contract. Read carefully if you are in this situation so you don't breech your contract!

For student or theoretical projects, you can also incorporate your inspiration into the choice of background, your title, or include small elements throughout the layout rather than devoting a single page to inspiration. It looks quite professional to mix your inspiration in with your title page or your fabrics/color page if there is room. Don't overcrowd it if not, though!

Which leads us to the next part of a fashion layout: the fabrics and color page. The garments you design need to exist in the context of the fabrics that work best for them. Know your fabrics well. What is the fiber content? What is the fabric construction? These are two different aspects of textiles that should always be communicated. Show images of each fabric in the colors you plan to use for your line. It helps to indicate where the fabrics are used if it is not clear through the illustration or flats, too.

As mentioned in Chapter 1, technical flats are the bread and butter of the fashion industry. Most of your fashion layouts should include clear, clean flats of the garments (Figure 9.2). It's okay to have layouts without rendered figures so long as you have all the flats present. However, it's not very useful to have rendered figures without flats unless you are applying for an illustration position. Good flats will generally get you the job faster than great renderings, if all other considerations are equal.[1] Be sure to work on your technical flats in class or through the Extend Your Learning appendix.

The final tangential element of a fashion portfolio is a photo of your garment(s) if you made it/them. This is not strictly necessary, and certainly not if you did not make a sample garment. However, if you completed a sample as a class project (and it looks professional), consider shooting it on a model and incorporating a photo into your layout. It can add a touch of professionalism that sets you apart from other job applicants.[2]

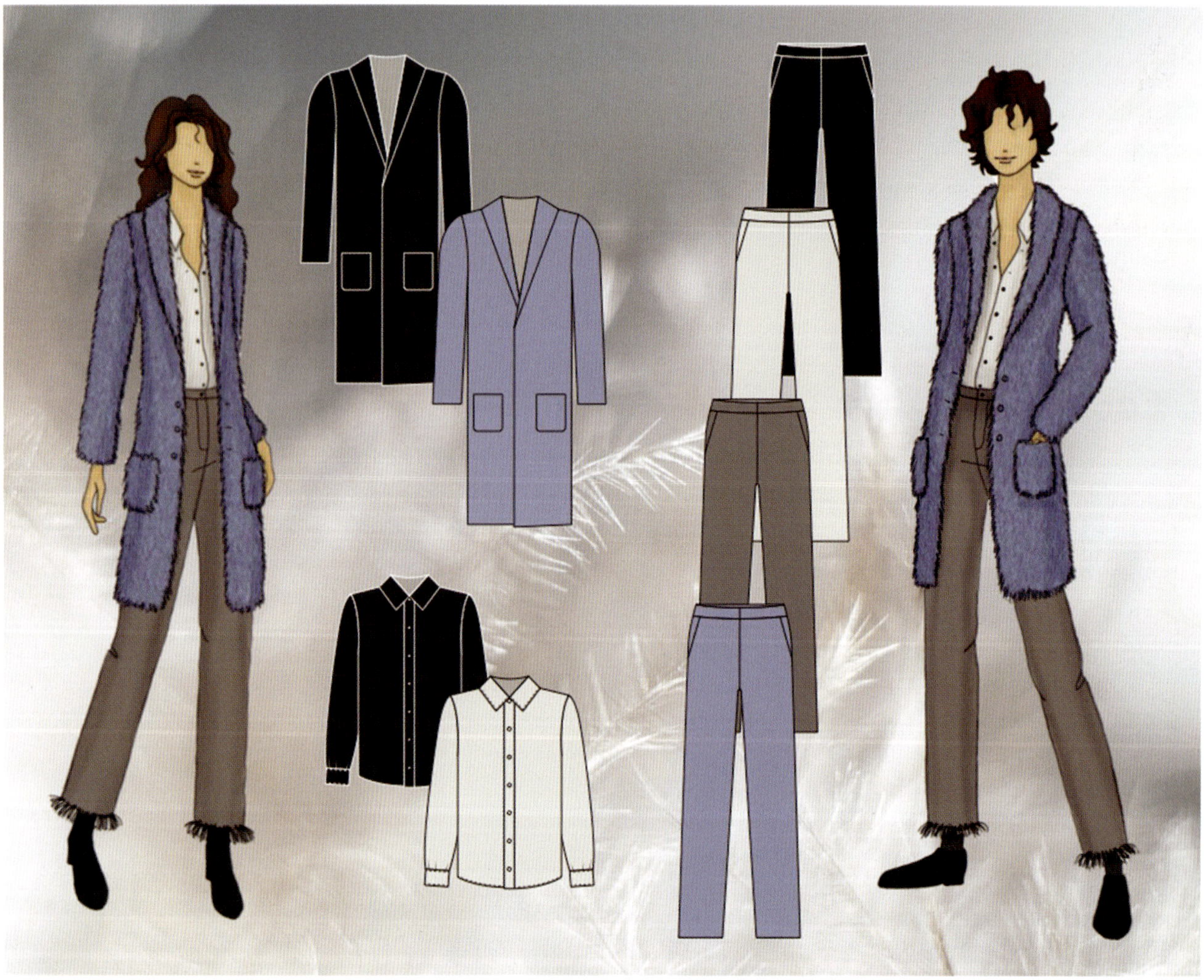

Figure 9.2 You will frequently show the technical flats next to your illustrations in a fashion layout. Courtesy of Adrianna Martinez.

Components of a Costume Portfolio Project

Costume portfolios are a bit less standardized than fashion portfolios but still have necessary core elements. Like fashion portfolios, it helps to show some of your inspiration and research for the production. You can create an image composite as described in Project 9.1, or you may bring your research journal. We cover design journals more in Chapter 12.

Also like fashion layouts, you want to include your fabric swatches with the necessary fiber and fabric information. In costume design, these tend to be included as a swatch ring or directly attached to the illustration. However, for a smaller show, you may want to include a swatch page like the one in Project 9.2.

If the show was produced, you can include **still shots** or **production shots**. Still shots are photographed during a run of the show and display the costumes in action on stage. Production shots are studio photographs of an actor in full costume and makeup.

You may also want to include other research such as complicated makeup designs, masks, wig designs, specialized embroidery, or accessories that help bring the character to life. These elements can help to demonstrate your design skills in other ways.[3] They also provide more context for the research and costume designs.

We will discuss the portfolio needs more in Chapter 12. For now, let's focus on how to construct your layouts for each project.

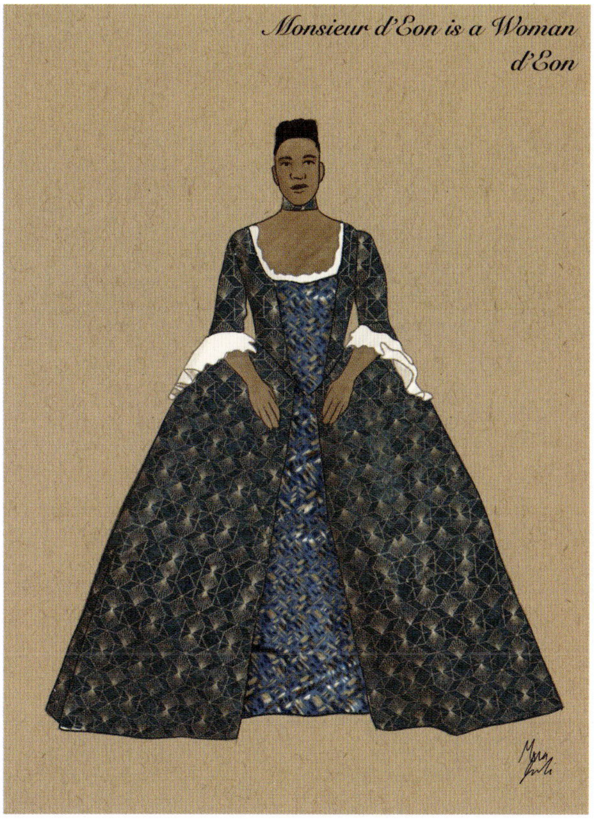

Figure 9.3 Costume plates or illustrations need to communicate the character. Often, costume renderings are not only used by the costume shop to produce the garments, but also by the director, actors, and set or lighting designers to better understand the vision of a production. Courtesy of Mona Jahani, Michigan State University.

STYLE SECRETS 9.1

A Note about "Borrowing" Inspiration for Your Portfolio

Where is the line between borrowing inspiration and appropriation? Unfortunately, there is no clear-cut answer to this. With the widespread use of images on the internet, many people have come to rely on image searches for the majority of their visual research. Often this leaves you with a plethora of images and no idea where they came from. Although this is fabulous to spark creative inspiration, it leaves the illustrator in the tenuous position of stealing someone else's artistic work. If these images are part of your personal workflow and are never displayed to the public, it is generally okay. Just make sure that you do not "borrow" from another artist to the point that it could be confused with your work.

If you are using this work to create mood/inspiration layouts, then you need to seek permission if possible, and give named credit at the very least. Part of this is dependent upon how much you change the image from the original look. If you use a photobashing or collage illustration method, check with others to see if they would recognize the original artwork within your rendition. If you fully sketch your work, make sure that the illustration style is different enough from your style inspiration sources to not be mistaken for the work of the influencing artist.

When in doubt, either do not use another's work, or at the very least, give credit. You do not want others stealing your work without permission, so please do not do it to others.

Project 9.1: Mood/Inspiration Composites

Although mood or inspiration pages are not strictly necessary for a design layout, they do help to communicate your thought process. Inspiration pages also can be tricky to manage correctly. Inspiration can come from many different sources, including copyrighted images. And how can you show your inspirational images without it looking cluttered?

Copyrighted imagery is a delicate issue. On one hand, a specific picture was so helpful and provided significant direction for your work. On the other hand, you don't want it to look like you are stealing another artist's work. Creativity rarely occurs in a vacuum, so you cannot and should not avoid inspiration that was produced by others. But you should treat it with the respect that you hope others will extend to your work. Keep up with the original sources as you gather research. Yes, many of us like to peruse the vast vault of images available without tracking all the details. But make the effort to track your sources as you go.[4] Soon it will be second nature.

Consider how you will use your inspiration. This will make a difference in the copyright issue. If you utilize it strictly for personal use and the inspiration will not be shown to others, then do whatever you like! However, if you intend to use the inspiration in your portfolio, especially a digital portfolio, you need to give proper credit. Because most digital portfolios are websites, you need to be particularly careful. A website is considered a form of publication, and your sources may come under more scrutiny than with a physical portfolio. You probably will not be able to show any manipulation of the work, such as incorporating it into a composition. It may be safer to simply reference the work as a form of inspiration through writing rather than showing it. If, however, you plan to keep the inspiration strictly in your physical portfolio that will only be seen during in-person interviews, you have more leeway as it is not published. Be sure to still give credit, though. You can't expect others to respect artists if artists don't respect each other.

Consider other sources of inspiration that are less problematic, too. Take your own photos of interesting textures or scenes (Figure 9.4). Paint your own picture for inspiration, such as an abstract or dream image. Look through royalty-free image banks or consider paying for specific stock images to help convey your thoughts. Take those stock images and make an artistic composite that conveys your inspiration.

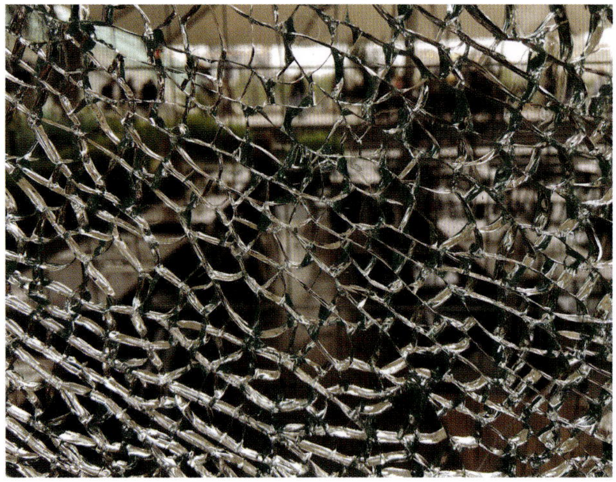

Figure 9.4 Take pictures of interesting textures you see, such as this shattered window we saw while in London. You can utilize it for your inspiration page. Photo courtesy of the authors.

So how do you keep it looking professional and organized? As you designed your garments, consider which images influenced you the most. You probably had a slew of images from your research, but narrow it down to just a few of the most influential (Figure 9.5). Or perhaps use the images that summarize your inspiration best. This may be one key picture, or a small bank of four to eight.

Think about your inspiration and any keywords that come up. Is it structured, severe, and crisp? Try using straight edges in your composition. Is it organic and airy? Use more blend modes and delicate masking to put it together. Look at your collected inspiration and give yourself three to five keywords that describe it. Think in terms of descriptive words like dark, playful, or grounded. Use these words to help design the inspiration layout.

Creating a Composition

An inspiration composition works best with photography software like Photoshop. You will need to use your masking and blending skills to keep it looking professional. Use the exercise files found in the Chapter 9 folder for an inspiration theme of "The American Dream." You can try to match yours to our examples shown below, but feel free to try to come up with your own compositions.

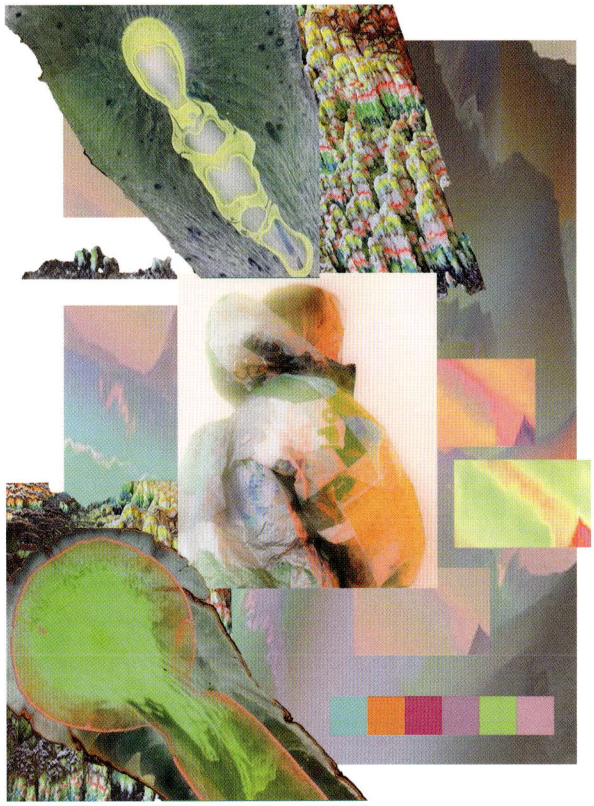

Figure 9.5 Some compositions work well with straight lines mixed with organic shapes. Other inspiration pages need a more chaotic look for the theme. The inspiration should still be clear, even through the chaos, though. Courtesy of Latisha Francis. Texas Tech University. College of Human Sciences. Apparel Design & Manufacturing.

Step 1: We assume that you have already collected your research by this point as you needed it to design your garments. If you have not already, determine your keywords as described previously. This will provide direction to your layout. If you are using the exercise files, use the keywords: classic, shattered, and illusionary. The premise is the hidden fractures behind the "American Dream."

Comb through the visual research. Was there a key image that drove your designs more than the others? This picture should probably be the keystone for your inspiration composition. Make sure your image is high-enough resolution to not be pixelated in your final arrangement.

Now choose three to five supporting images such as textures, silhouettes, or other mood images. Make note of your color palette, too. It is just as important for this as it is for the designs. You may have more supporting images, but don't go overboard. It's not necessary to show every piece of inspiration. If you have too much going on, the direction is lost.

Step 2: Now that you have your main elements, sketch some thumbnail layouts (Figure 9.6). These won't be shown to anyone, so don't get self-conscious about how they look. Just sketch out some ideas of how you want to arrange the inspiration onto a single page. Keep it rough and avoid too much attention to detail at first. More sketches equate to a better selection. We recommend a minimum of ten ideas, but sketch as many ideas as you can.

Think more about the focus and values at this stage. Where are your darks and lights? Where should your eye land first and how will it move around the page? Keep your elements and principles in mind with layouts as much as with your garment designs. How is the balance? Use artistic proportions such as the **rule of thirds** in mind. The rule of thirds is a way of framing the subject or focus of a composition in an interesting way. Keep your keywords in mind, too. The layout should match the inspiration.

Choose one or two of your thumbnails to explore in more depth. Start to think about the details more at this point. Start to roughly lay out the images in Photoshop or another photo-editing software. Get a sense of your proportions and balance before you start to refine the composition.

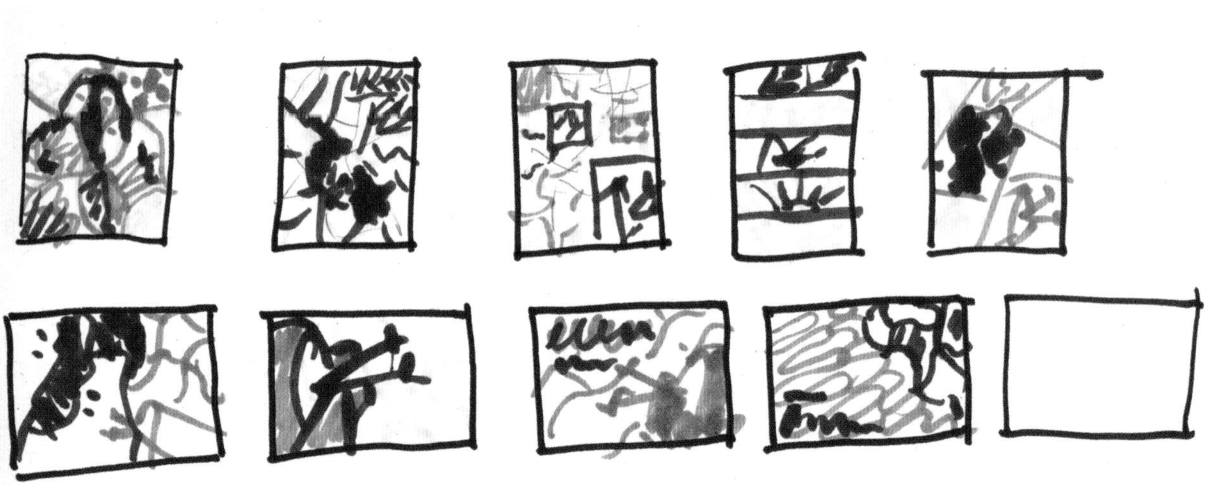

Figure 9.6 Sketch out layout thumbnails once you have gathered your inspiration elements. These are just layout ideas. Don't get too caught up in details at the moment. Your thumbnails may not make sense to anyone else viewing them, but you should have an idea of what each represents.

Step 3: Start working on the details. Isolate the images and textures through layer masks or by eliminating the unnecessary information in the picture (Figure 9.7). Make a color palette off to the side as a reminder of your color scheme. You may need to adjust colors to help unify the visual elements if they do not already convey the correct colors for your composition.

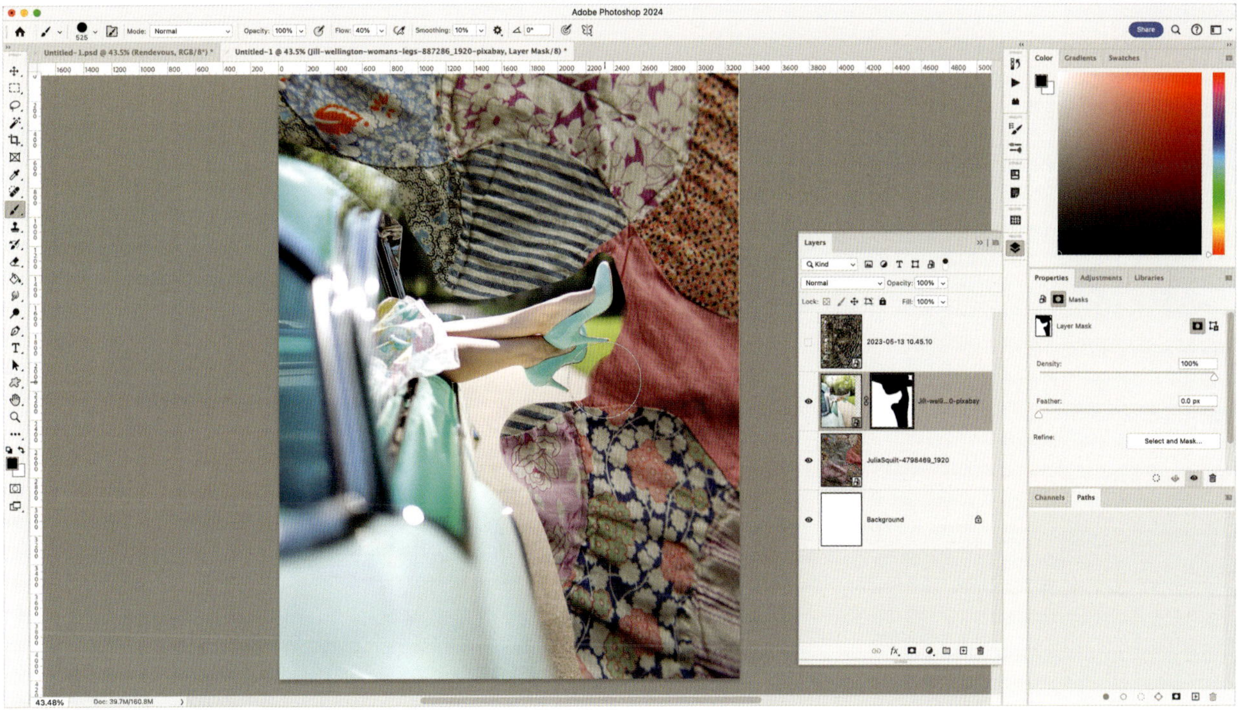

Figure 9.7 Use rough masks to start to lay out your composition. In our example, we are not using all the photos from our library. We chose to focus on a few key images.

Step 4: Work with layers, selections, masks, adjustments, overlays, blend modes, gradient maps, and so on to pull it together. Inspiration pages are a great way to build your Photoshop skills if you are not already intimate with the many ways to layer an image. Flip through the *Blend Modes* to see if one works for your needs. Try the *Blend If* sliders in the *Layer Blending Options* dialog box. Duplicate layers to compound effects. In essence, play around with the many, many options until you reach the desired effect for your composition.

Step 5: Step back and assess. *Zoom* out to fit your work on the screen (Figure 9.8) and then *Zoom* out more to make it close to the same size as your thumbnail from step 2. Do the values and basic composition align? Try flipping the direction of the image to see it from a different angle. If you have a little time, sleep on it and come back another day. These exercises will help provide perspective. You may see something that needs a tweak.

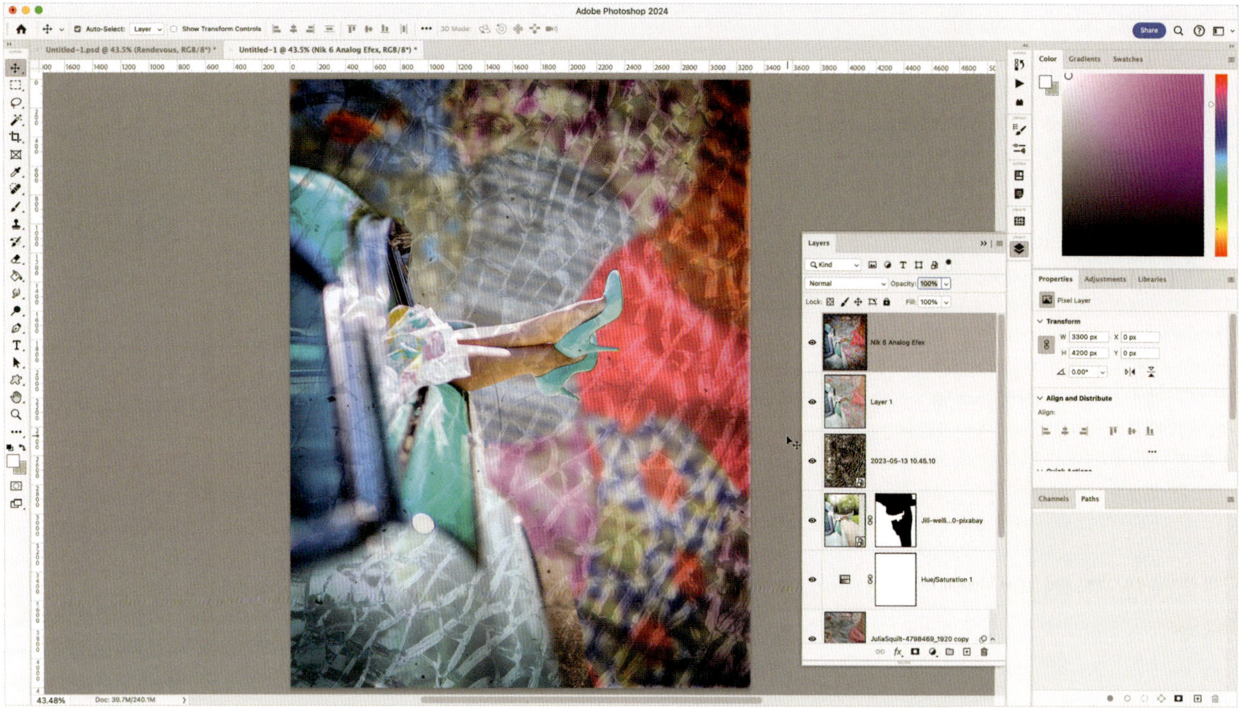

Figure 9.8 Take a step back to look at the outcome. What is working and what is not?

Try asking for feedback. Can your friend determine the theme without verbal direction? Is it unified and harmonious? Is the color palette clear? Are the textures clear? Is it cluttered or imbalanced? Is it interesting and eye catching? Does it make sense? Is the story clear? Does it introduce the designs? Ask specific questions like these so your friend can give specific feedback to help you.

Inspiration compositions are one of those items that it is easier to see when something is wrong than when it is right. There are a few common mistakes to avoid as you arrange your compositions. Too many images are the primary mistake. Students commonly try to put in every single image, and it quickly becomes cluttered with no clear direction. Even by limiting your imagery, there can still be a lack of direction. It may be an arrangement of interesting pictures, but it fails to tell a story about the design inspiration. Or you may have a lovely and unified composition, but it doesn't seem to relate to the designs at all. Does your inspiration need footnotes to explain? Remember this is a visual journey of your process. You can include one to two descriptive statements about your inspiration, but don't make it too complicated or convoluted. The other side of that issue is if you make it too literal. These are all considerations in your design process, as well. Hopefully, most of this was worked out in the initial inspiration and design stages rather than at the end when you are pulling the inspiration into your portfolio layout!

Incorporating Text

Your inspiration composition may work well on its own page. However, you may want to incorporate some text with it (Figure 9.9). Is the text decorative such as keywords or a quote infused into the layout? If this is the case, use fonts that work with the overall arrangement and elements. If you plan to include the title of the project here, use an appropriate font. It should match the overall aesthetic but still be readable. Make sure there is enough contrast between the text and the background, too.

You may want to include the element credits as well. If this is the case, choose a clear, readable font. The point is to make the information available, but not steal focus from your composition. Add the info in an unobtrusive area.

Project 9.2: Fabric and Color Information

Your designs depend on proper fabric choices. Be sure to incorporate those choices into your layout. Your fabric knowledge is often part of the job interview. Use the

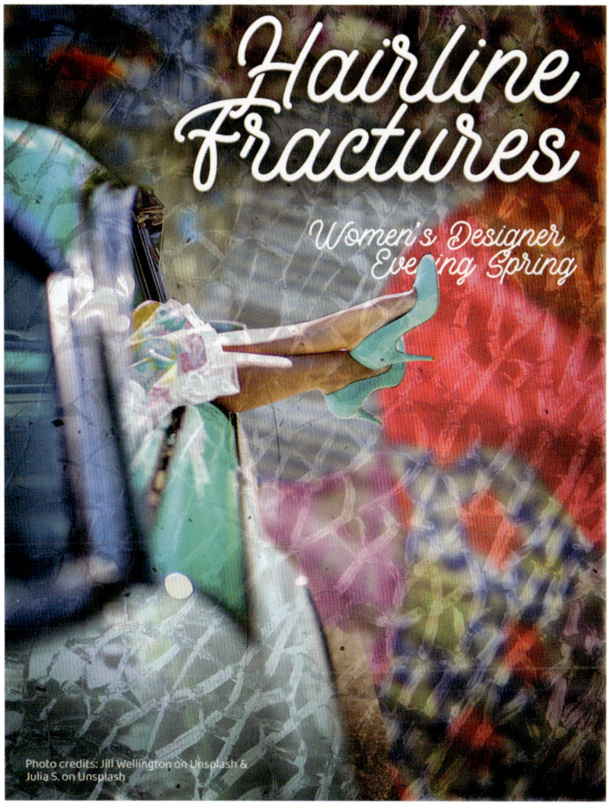

Figure 9.9 Incorporating title information is treated differently from credit information. Think about your font styles, size, and contrast. Both should look like they belong in the composition. However, title information can be part of the artwork with more flourish. Photos courtesy of Jill Wellington/Unsplash and Julia S./Unsplash; composition by the authors.

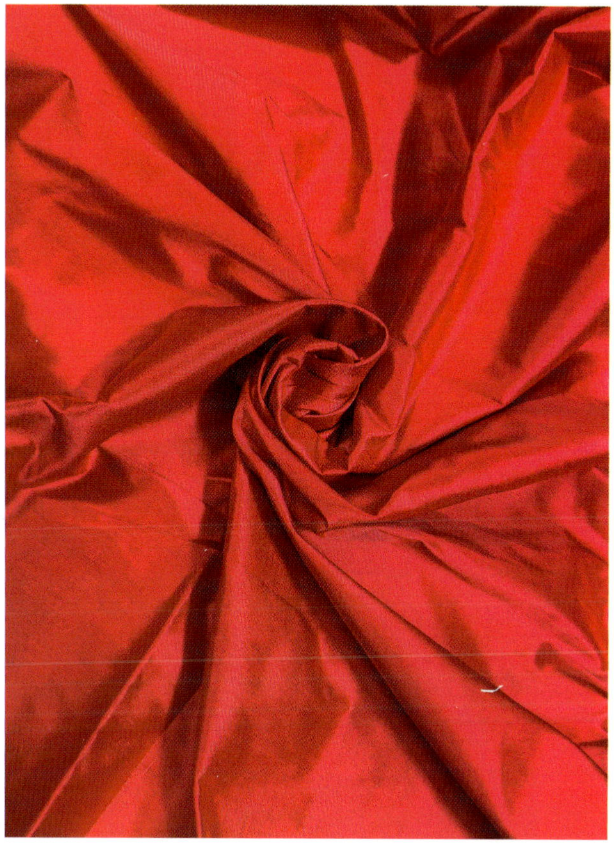

Figure 9.10 Use the provided fabrics like the one above and color scheme included in your exercise files to make a fabric page that goes with your inspiration page. Photo courtesy of the authors.

fabrics page in your layout to show how well you understand fiber and fabric properties, weights, drape, and so on.

Fashion and costume layouts incorporate fabrics in distinctly different ways, though. The fashion layout tends to utilize a more formalized display. Whether you use physical swatches or digital images of them, keep it neat and informative. Label each swatch with the fiber content and fabric construction. Indicate true color information, meaning don't show your fabrics in a color that is not part of your line. If you have garments in multiple colorways, show the fabric in each color offered.

In the costume industry, fabric swatches are not expected to be neatly trimmed and boxed into a single page. Generally, fabrics are attached to the individual costume plates or kept on a single ring that shows the whole show at a glance. Pulled costumes, meaning costumes pulled from a stock and not constructed specifically for the production, will not usually have swatches. When you do have swatches, though, it is best to keep up with the fiber content and fabric construction for the rendering.

Regardless of your industry, make sure the swatches match the information and look like the correct fabric construction (Figure 9.10). It is a clear sign that you don't understand textiles if you show a corduroy fabric and call it a taffeta.[5] This is a bit of a "rookie" mistake that students sometimes make, and it is a fast way to end your interview quickly!

Color

You may want to include a color palette with color chips, but it is more important to show your fabrics in the correct colors offered (Figure 9.11). When you use digital fabrics, it is easy enough to use an *Adjustment Layer* to correct the color of the fabric image. If you use physical swatches, you will need to obtain the correct color from your vendor or apply any dye/distressing techniques you intend for the fabrics.

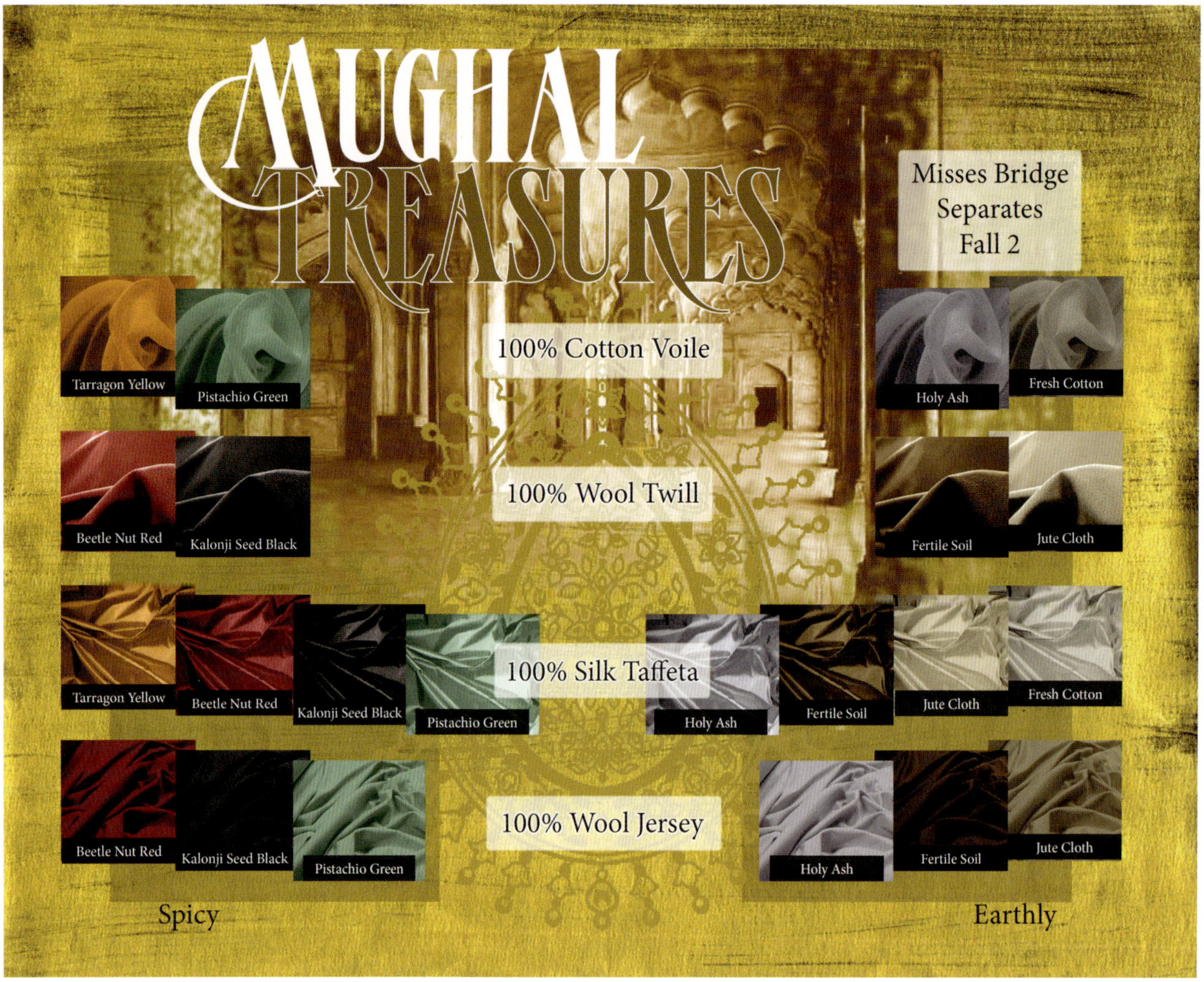

Figure 9.11 Notice that the fabrics are shown in the correct color and named. There are two color palettes for this line, and the colors are clearly grouped. Each textile has the fiber and fabric information. This fabric page also incorporates the inspiration images and title page in one. Although the title looks a bit like a romance novel, all the information is clear. Artwork courtesy of the authors.

Layouts

Try your hand at creating a fabric swatch page using the colors and fabrics in the exercise folder for Chapter 9. Try to match it to the inspiration page you made in Project 9.1. In fashion, keep your fabrics to one page of the portfolio layout. If it works with the theme, you may integrate the fabric and color information with your individual designs in the line.

If you have multiple color stories for your fashion line, cluster the colors physically on the page. Also make sure that the colors you use for your renderings match what you have on the fabrics page. It doesn't make sense to the viewer if you show a yellow–orange color on your fabrics page, but it looks red on your rendering.

For costumes, use the fabrics to provide as much information as possible per costume (Figure 9.12). You may need to add some notes about how it is used. There is less of a "norm" for how fabrics are used in costume design. Just be sure to show them in an informative way.

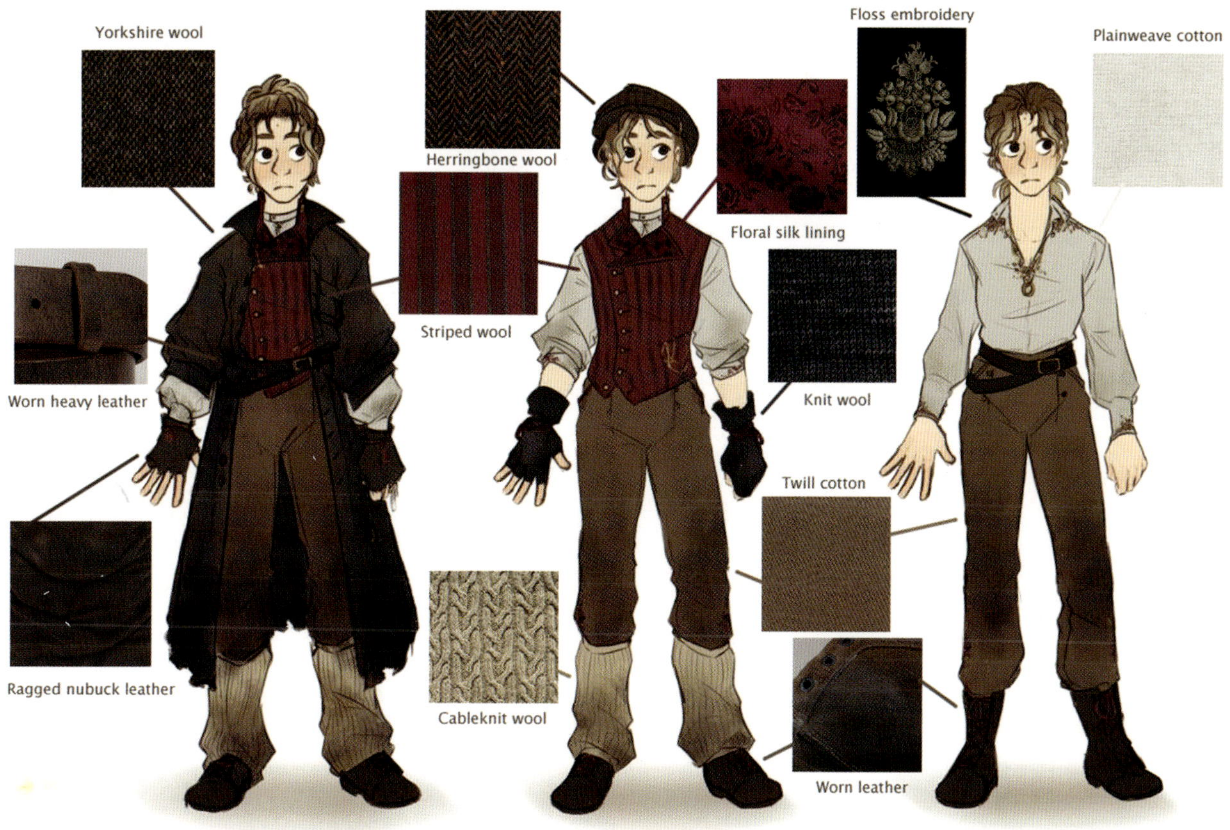

Figure 9.12 Consider providing more information about how the fabrics are used and where. This will help your costume shop as they create the costumes. Courtesy of Sam Connor.

PRO TIP 9.1

Know Your Textiles

Whether you are in fashion or costume design, you need to build your knowledge of fabrics. We think this is one of the most highly underestimated classes that students take. We make a habit of asking alumni which classes they wish they could take again after graduation, and 100% of them list textiles! Industry professionals expect that you know this subject during design conversations, so it is worth putting in extra time to study your fabrics.

If you are new to the subject, there are a couple of key lessons to focus your attention. Primarily, make sure you understand the difference between the **fiber** and the **fabric** construction of a textile. Fibers are the physical material(s) from which a fabric is made. The fabric construction is how the textile is made. Example fibers are silk, polyester, and cotton. Example fabrics are satin, denim, and taffeta. The fiber content of a fabric is generally listed with a percentage. The fabric is sometimes harder to determine without a lot of experience.

Once you have that first distinction down, learn to quickly tell the difference between major categories of fibers and fabrics. Spend some time learning the properties of natural fibers and manufactured fibers. Also learn how to tell the difference between a knit and a woven fabric. This bank of knowledge will take some time to build up, and really only makes sense by working with fabrics first-hand. Start now if you have not already. Afterall, you don't want to be "that" person who can't decide if they want to use "a silk or a satin." Cue the eyeroll.

Step 1: Gather your fabrics. Use the exercise files found in your STUDIO resources or use your own collection. Will you use physical or digital swatches? Physical swatches are more engaging during an in-person interview, but harder to come by these days. You will also need to scan them in and make them digital files for any online portfolios. Digital swatches are easy to manipulate and add to a layout but may not be as interesting as physical swatches. You decide, though.

Step 2: Adjust the swatches if necessary. Acquire the correct color or dye your swatches to match the intended color and effect. For digital swatches, adjust the colors to accuracy (Figure 9.13). Trim your swatches neatly, if necessary, regardless of physical or digital swatches. Remember that neat trimming is less expected in the costume industry, but make sure they are big enough to see the character of the fabric. Tiny swatches do not provide enough information.

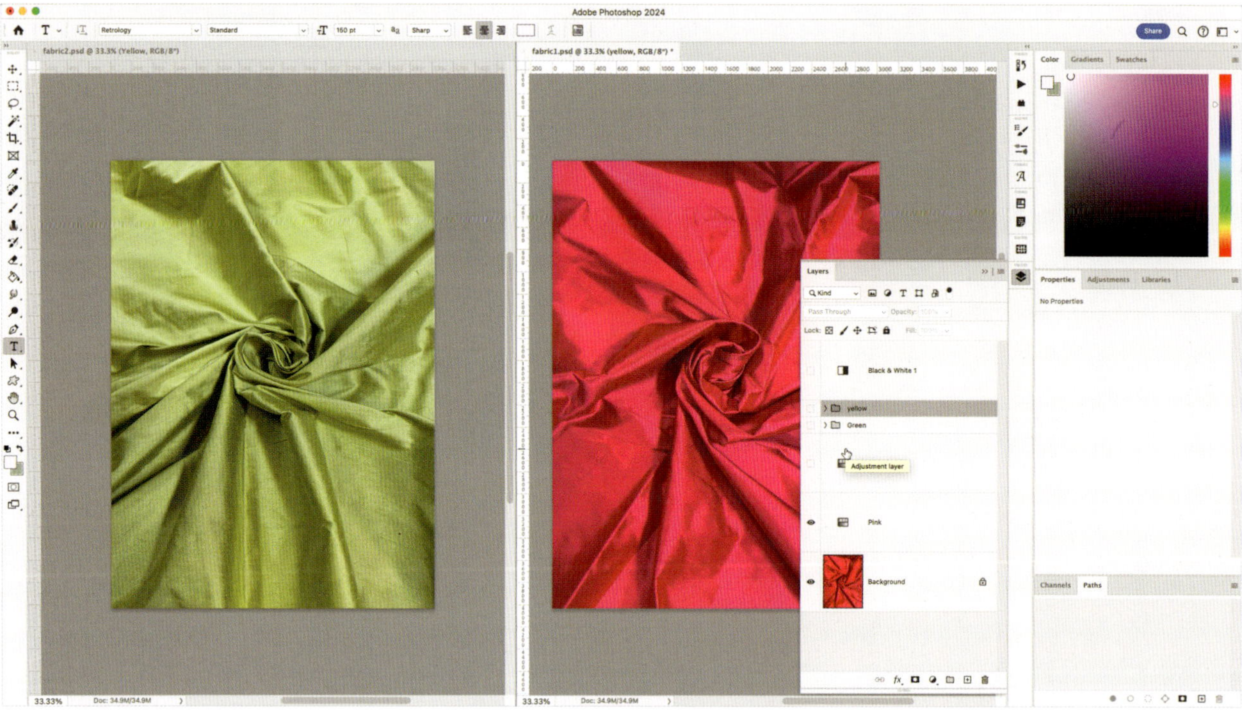

Figure 9.13 Digitally adjust the colors of your swatches to match the palette.

Step 3: Guess what? You need to create thumbnail layouts again! Think about how to incorporate your fabric and color information. Keep the layout in line with the inspiration and design layouts. This should look like one seamless project rather than individual pages that "sorta" go together. You may not need as many layout options because fabric information is a bit more limited than an inspiration composition. Keep all your thumbnails for later, though. You may want to reuse some of those other layout ideas in another project!

Step 4: Choose the layout that works best for your needs. Composite the layout (Figure 9.14). Digitally add the fabrics in the correct colors with the written information. If you want to use physical swatches, create a layout that leaves space for the swatches to be adhered to the printout.

Step 5: Again, step back and check your work. Does it look like the same project as your inspiration page and your designs? Is the information clear and readable. Apply the same lessons about text that we covered in the inspiration page section. Check your font style, size, and contrast. Is it clear which information goes with which swatch? Does the background integrate with the project but not detract from the swatches and information? If so, you are ready to move on to the next part.

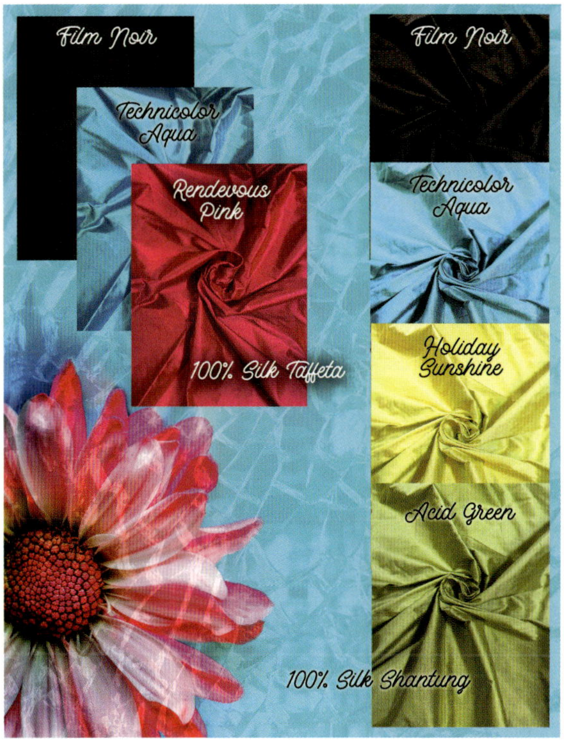

Figure 9.14 Add in your fabric swatches and information. Check that the layout works with your project, overall. Composition courtesy of the authors.

STYLE SECRETS 9.2

Let's Get Physical (Swatches)

You may be shocked to learn that there was a time when students could obtain physical fabric swatches from stores with minimal effort! Unfortunately for students today, two issues hindered this access. There simply are not as many brick and mortar (meaning physical) fabric stores around. A large percentage of them closed their doors over the last few decades. The other issue is that previous students took advantage of fabric swatching with the existing stores. They would cut large chunks out of very expensive textiles without any concern for the damage they caused. The stores often lost a lot of money on unsanctioned student swatching. So if you get a dirty look from a fabric store employee when you admit to being a student, now you know why!

This doesn't mean that it is impossible to obtain swatches, though. It's just harder than it used to be. There are a number of online fabric vendors that send a certain number of swatches if you are looking for a particular fabric. They expect you to purchase something, though. Whether you ask for swatches from an online vendor or a physical one, you should expect to buy some fabric along the way. Try to build a relationship with your fabric vendors. Talk with them regularly about your upcoming projects and what fabrics you are looking for.

Alternatively, keep a box of fabrics from previous projects. Over time, you will build a library of some great swatches. You can use these for theory or unrealized projects. They don't work so great for projects you want to produce and need fabric yardage, so contact your vendors for such a project.

Sometimes, a physical sample is just not an option, though. This is one more reason to beef up your textile knowledge. You will need to use digital swatches, which means you need to know how that fiber and fabric will act in a realized sample. Will it perform the way you expect and show in your rendering? If not, the professionals you interview with will probably notice it.

Project 9.3: Photoshoots of Garments

A physical sample of your garment can help you to stand out from the competition in an interview. Beware, because a poorly executed sample can make you stand out in bad way, though. This is one of those things that if you have it, great. If you don't, do not fret. It's not strictly necessary.

A common student mistake is to plop their garment onto a school dress form and take a picture in the classroom. Photoshoots can be expensive and time-consuming. But this sort of photo never shows your garment well and looks unprofessional in your layout next to your highly professional designs! Take the time to show it in the best possible way. If you don't have a professional photographer or model, consider creating a nice backdrop with fabric. Make sure the dress form is clean and neat. Add some extra lighting to make it look good. Clamp lights from your local hardware store can create wonderful lighting.

If at all possible, photograph your work on a person, though. It adds a level of professionalism that is difficult to achieve with a dress form. Consider your background and lighting, too. Does it show the details of your garment well? Does it mix in with the style of your layout? All of these are considerations for your photoshoot.

Style

What style works best for your needs? If you are in fashion, consider if you want a **lookbook-style** photograph or an **editorial style**. Lookbook-style photos are generally shot in a studio with a minimal background (Figure 9.15). This is the primary style you see for brand lookbooks, or images used by buyers to determine which styles they want to purchase for their stores. The models are relatively static in order to show the garment accurately.

Editorial-style photography, however, uses a more artistic approach (Figure 9.16). Think of the spreads in fashion magazines like *Vogue* and *Harper's Bazaar*. The garment may not be as clear, but the photograph conveys a rich mood or attitude. You will need to plan ahead to think about the environment and lighting. If you are working with a photographer, talk to them about what you would like to express with the photos.

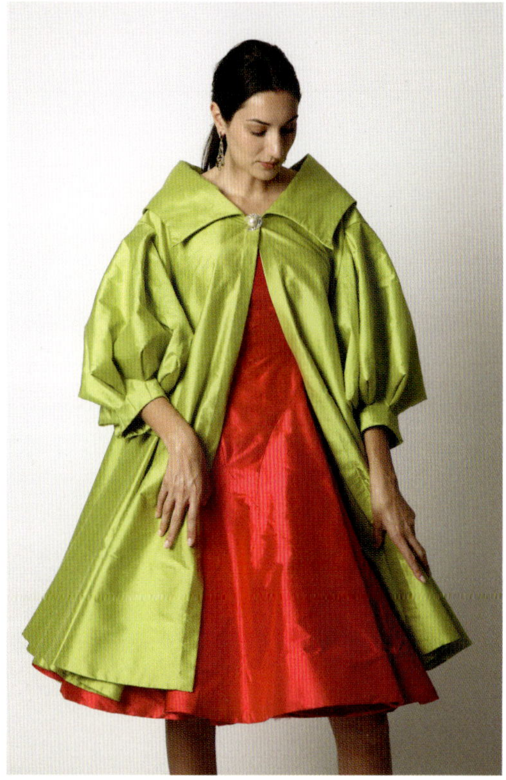

Figure 9.15 Use studio photography for a lookbook-style photoshoot. This type shows your garment details best. Design courtesy of the authors. Photography courtesy of Ricardo Gutierrez. Model: Paige of R Models.

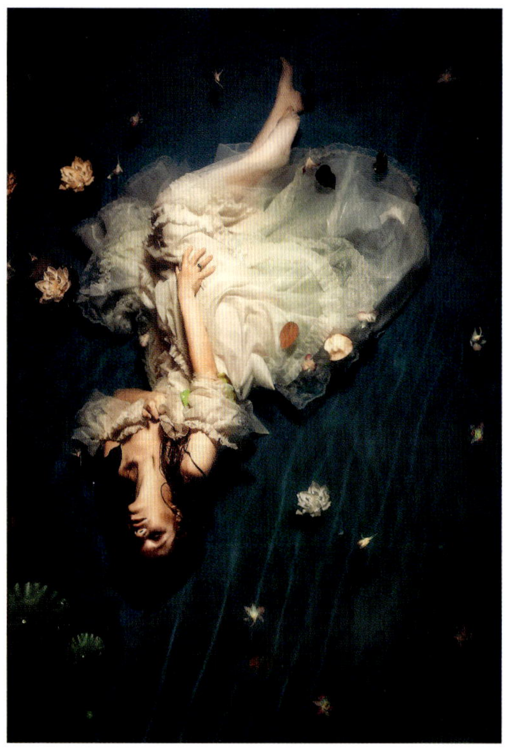

Figure 9.16 Editorial-style photography is often shot on location with stylized flair. It does not always show the garment well but helps convey the mood of the piece. Courtesy of Alice Alinari via Unsplash.

PRO TIP 9.2

Hire a Photographer

You're on a budget. We get it. Who has the money to hire a fancy-schmancy photographer when you have a handy camera phone and a dress form? Unfortunately, amateur photography always looks, well, amateur. This is one area where you should strive to hire a professional.

Remember at the beginning of the book how we discussed that many people mix up good illustration for good design? The same transference happens with photography. A good photograph can make a mediocre sample look fantastic, while a bad photograph can make an excellent sample look terrible. A professional photo rubs off on your design portfolio, making you look more professional in turn. They can show your garment in the best light. Literally. They have professional lighting equipment! Aside from that, you are supporting another artist. As you move from the role of student to working professional, you want to start incorporating professional behaviors like paying others for their art.

But of course, you are still a student living on Ramen noodles! Think of some creative ways to incorporate professional photography on your student budget. Contact a fellow student majoring in photography. You should still pay them for the work, but for a fraction of the price of an established professional. Or try negotiating with a professional. You can be their assistant in exchange for a photoshoot. Perhaps offer to help with a job and tag your work onto the end so they don't have to spend the time setting up the studio for you. Use a friend or family member as your model. This is still a little tricky as there is a pretty big difference in the professionalism of a paid model versus a friend, though. Try using backdrops that are readily available such as a brick wall. This will depend on the look of your garment and theme, though. If you are using a fabric drape, make sure it is well ironed before photographing. Those wrinkles are a big distraction, especially to those who work with fabric regularly! Find a friend to do the makeup and hair styling but beware of overdoing it. Simpler is better. Remember the focus should be on your garment and not the model. There are plenty of ways to achieve a professional photoshoot on a small budget. Brainstorm with your friends for more ideas.

In terms of costumes, production shots equate to a fashion lookbook style and stills are somewhat like editorial-style photos. The tradeoff is the same. Production shots show the costume and character more in-depth with a studio shot. You will need to coordinate with your actors and makeup/hair team to schedule the photography. Alternatively, it still portrays the costume in action and in the context of the set and lighting design. You can often take stills during one of the last technical rehearsals before opening night. Check with the production team about the best timing for your photos.

Clean Up and Retouching

Photography retouching is an entire career in itself. There are many, many online and in-person courses as well as books and other resources about retouching. So, we won't go too in-depth here. The first and most important rule is to get it right while shooting, though. Press your garments, make sure they are finished, and don't have threads hanging (unless they are supposed to!). Try to get the makeup and hair as perfect as possible. Make sure there are no oddities in the background of your photography angle. The more you can fix pre-production, the better. These things can be fixed in Photoshop post-production, but it often takes twice the time. Just get it right before you take the shot!

Sometimes, though, there are things that just can't be "fixed," such as removing a street sign from the background. This is when you bring out your arsenal of photo-editing tools such as the *Spot Healing* tool, *Content-Aware Fill*, and *Liquify* filter. The trick to good photo editing is that it should not look like it's been edited at all. This takes time, practice, and an eye for detail. Your goal should be to show the best version of the model and garment without changing the character or features.

You may need to tweak the colors, so they stay true to the original. Unfortunately, if you are keeping your images digital, you will always be at the mercy of the color skewing that occurs from one monitor to the next. You can make the colors true on your device, but they may not show accurately on someone else's monitor. However, if you plan to print your image, you will need to check the color adjustments with a few prints along the process. It may look right on screen but print too dark.

Aside from color corrections, you may want to add some artistic touches. Use subtle tools such as vignetting, *Dodge* and *Burn* layers, or add a *Noise* filter for some grain. Make sure your effects aren't over the top and help bring the focus to your garment (Figure 9.17).

Layout

How will you incorporate the photos into your layout? There's no perfect formula for this, but there are a few tips that will help you. First, don't overdo it. Yes, you have twenty fantastic shots of your garment, but in most cases you only need to show one. Pick your shot that shows the garment the best and include it near the rendering of the garment. If you have an alternative view such as with the coat off or displaying a detail of the sleeve, you can add one more in there. But we don't need another angle of the same garment on every page of your layout. You certainly don't want to show the photo next to a rendering of a different garment—it creates confusion. We expect the two to be the same (Figure 9.18).

Consider how you frame it into the layout, as well. Will you leave it as a hard-edged rectangle, fade the edges into the background, or create a faux Polaroid? If your layout has a Western theme, should you show the photo as a wanted poster or a faded daguerreotype? If you have a futuristic theme, can you make your model look like a hologram? These all sound super cool, but make sure the garment is still clear and the photograph is not a distraction from your designs. Remember, this is meant to enhance your design communication. Take a step back and review it critically. Ask for feedback if you are not sure.

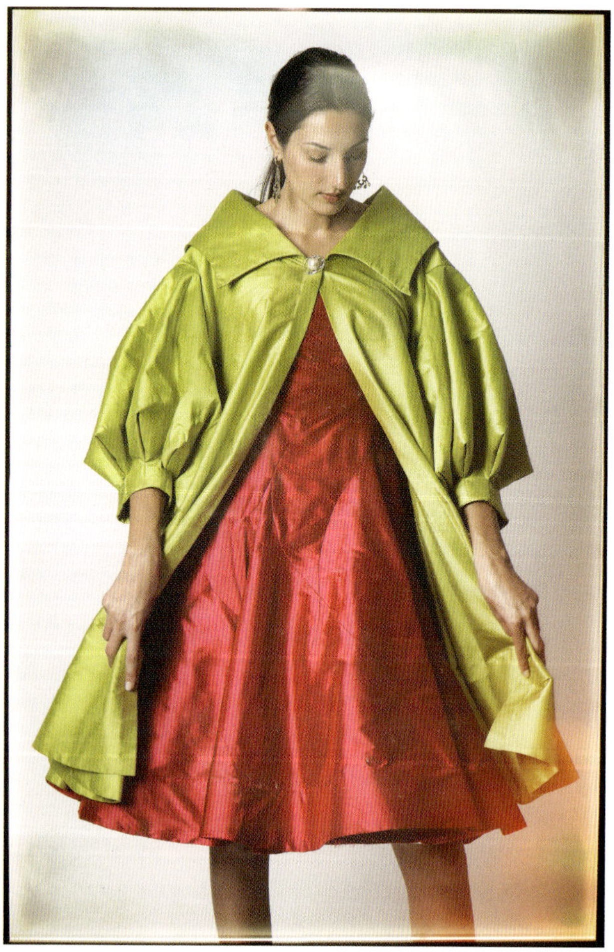

Figure 9.17 In this edit of our photo, you can see that we added some effects to make the photo seem antique to fit with the degraded retro theme.

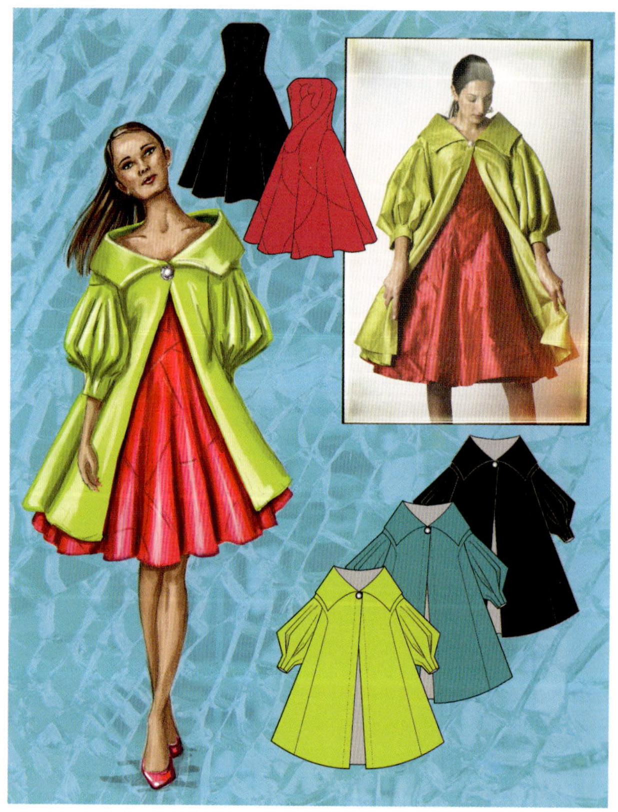

Figure 9.18 We added the photo to our design sketch and flats for the same garment. Artwork and design courtesy of the authors.

Use the exercise files or your own photos and designs to create a layout that integrates the design with the photo. Figure 9.18 shows how we combined them into our layout. How does yours look?

Project 9.4: Sketching Your Layouts (Concept Thumbnails)

You finally made it to the design layouts. You may want to start here, then return to the inspiration page, fabric page, and so on. This is a chicken or egg problem. Sometimes it works best to think about the layout as a whole and sometimes it works best to start with your inspiration and let that influence the rest of the layout. Feel free to switch around your starting point.

Step 1: As you start to figure out your design layout, have your elements in front of you for the project: the rendering(s), flats, fabrics, any text, inspiration, etc. Let the elements help to inform the layout. If you have already completed your inspiration and fabric pages, have those front and center. Remember this should look like one cohesive project rather than a collection of individual pages.

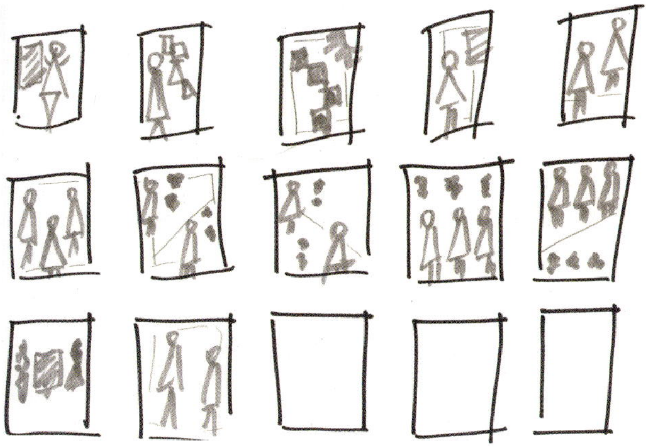

Figure 9.19 Thumbnail sketches of potential layouts.

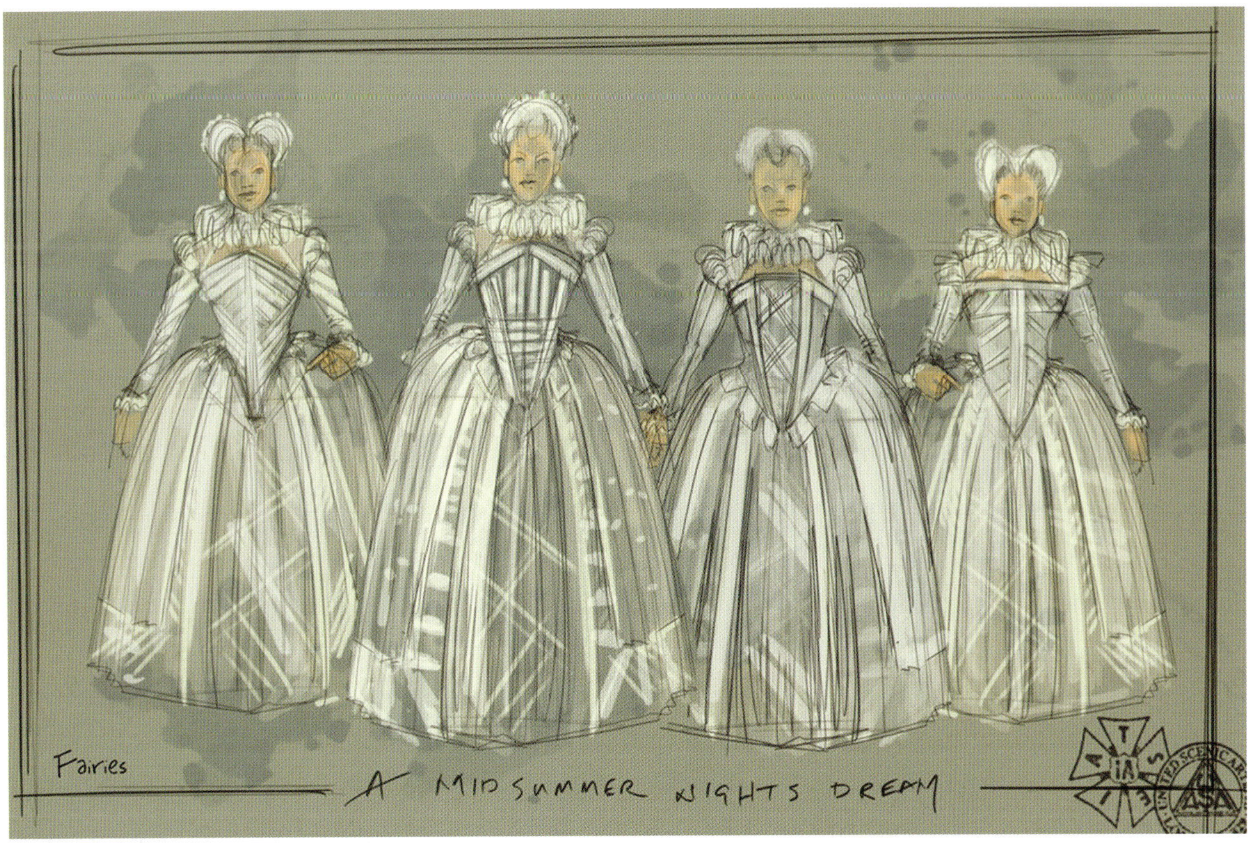

Figure 9.20 For costumes, use consistent or similar backgrounds and title treatments to create a sense of cohesion for the entire production. Courtesy of Jacob A. Climer.

Step 2: Then start sketching some thumbnail layouts (Figure 9.19). Just like before, don't get hung up on details too much. Think about the overall composition and how to incorporate your elements in a harmonious way. Consider how many pages you will need for the project. For fashion, the number of pages matters somewhat. You don't want too many pages that seem like a book or entire portfolio in one project. Generally, you don't want to go above eight pages. If you plan to use it for a physical portfolio, you want to keep to an even number of pages. We discuss this more in Chapter 12, but you don't want to end one project and start another in facing pages. Essentially, it is better for a new project to start with the turn of a page. This is less problematic in a digital portfolio as there is no page-turning action.

As you start to think about the layout, consider if your theme works with repetitive pages or if you need to change the organization page to page. Some themes lend themselves well to a static layout with a recurring look (Figure 9.20). It may be that you only need to refine one of your thumbnails and repeat the look of your different renderings on each page. Other themes require more organic, or even chaotic, looks. It just depends on your theme. Go back to your keywords for guidance.

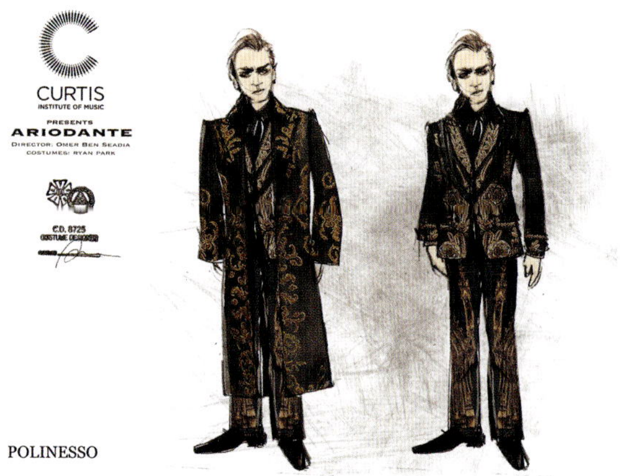

Figure 9.21 You may need to show a few different views of your character if the look changes during the scene. You may also want to incorporate information about the production such as the theater, show, scene, and character information. Courtesy of Ryan Park.

Step 3: Start to pull your elements into the layout. Refer to Chapter 11 for more technical help with adding your elements using Photoshop, Illustrator, or, preferably, InDesign. You may want to pause here and review that chapter before proceeding with your layout. Use the book how it best suits you.

Consider your background, color scheme, font usage, and other elements. Remember to keep referring to your keywords and any previous layouts such as your inspiration page. Also keep in mind that the point is to communicate your designs. Don't get lost in too much fluff that obfuscates the information.

Do your renderings work better in groups or as individuals? Consider if you can create clusters of figures to better convey the line or show (Figures 9.22 and 9.23).

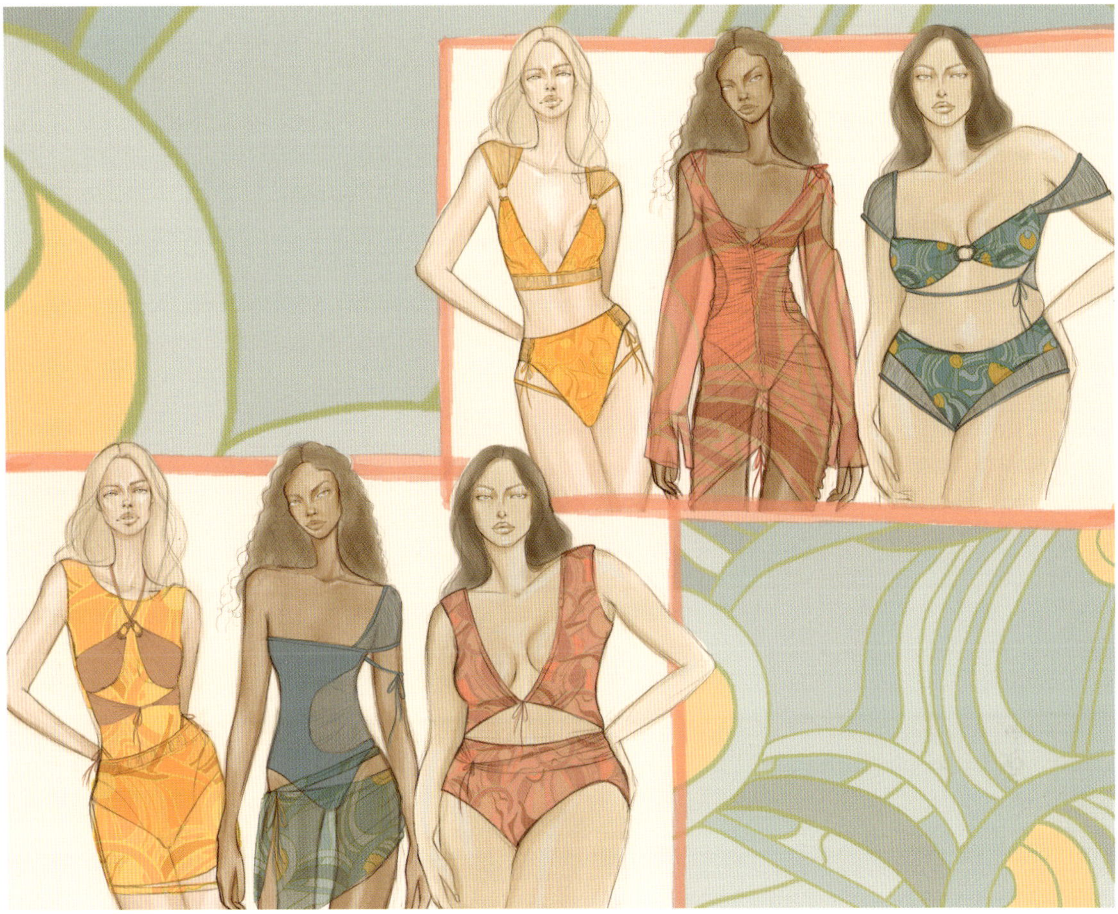

Figure 9.22 You can use repetitive figures and layout if it works with the theme of your designs. Courtesy of Hannah Delmore @hannahdelmoreillustration. Hannahdelmore.com.

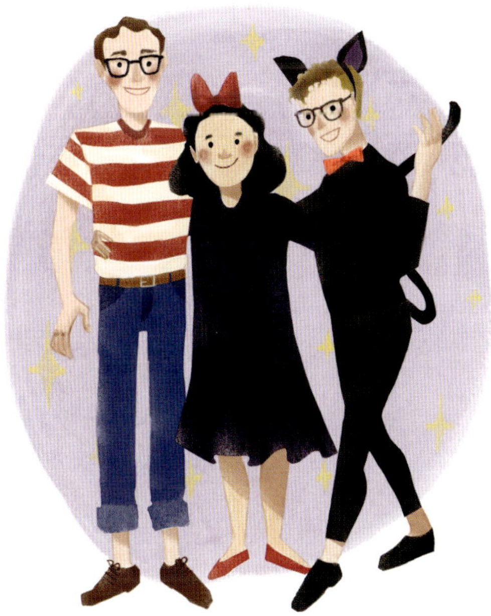

Figure 9.23 If it works for your production, consider showing some characters on the same page if they are frequently seen onstage together. Artwork and design courtesy of Grace Kang.

Step 4: Refine your layouts. Clean up any masking, adjust colors, add layout texture if needed, and direct the focus. If you need help with backgrounds or layout textures, jump to Chapter 10. Check the flow from page to page. If you have costume renderings, you will probably have similar layouts between the plates. Check that you are directing the focus to the design communication, though.

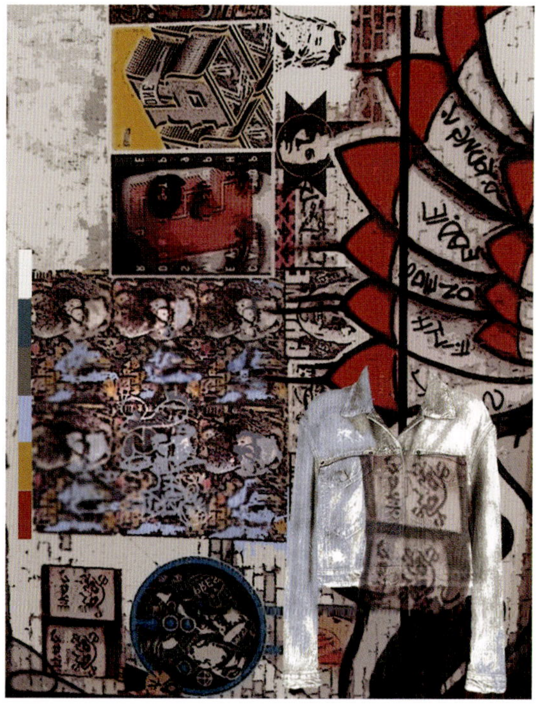

Figure 9.24a This inspiration artwork incorporates street art. Artwork courtesy of Rachel Anderson. Instagram: @rachelandersonfashion. Texas Tech University. College of Human Sciences. Apparel Design & Manufacturing.

Step 5: Look at the whole picture. Does the project flow from one page to the next (Figures 9.24a–f)? Does it make sense without explanation? Is it cohesive and harmonious? Are the designs clear? Can you tell how the fabrics are used, or do you need to add some directional notes? Again, ask for feedback if you're not sure about the look.

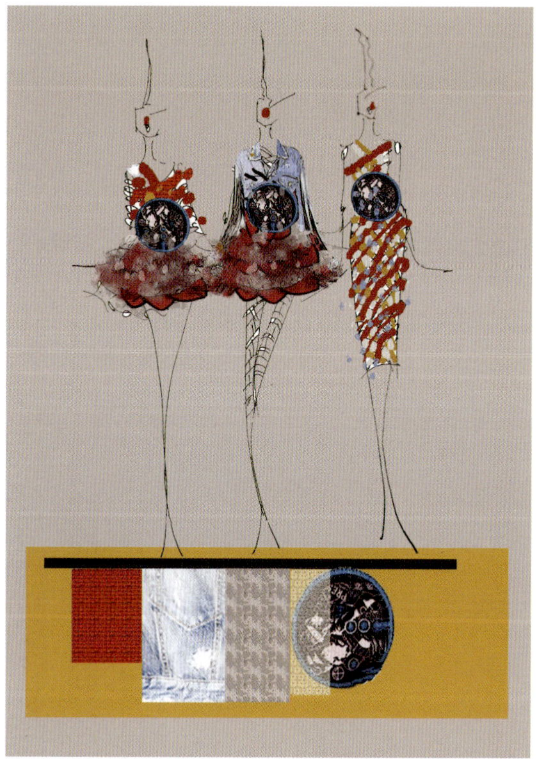

Figure 9.24b See how the designs, illustration style, and theme all work cohesively? This layout is only two pages, but it works together as a whole. Artwork and designs courtesy of Rachel Anderson. Instagram: @rachelandersonfashion. Texas Tech University. College of Human Sciences. Apparel Design & Manufacturing.

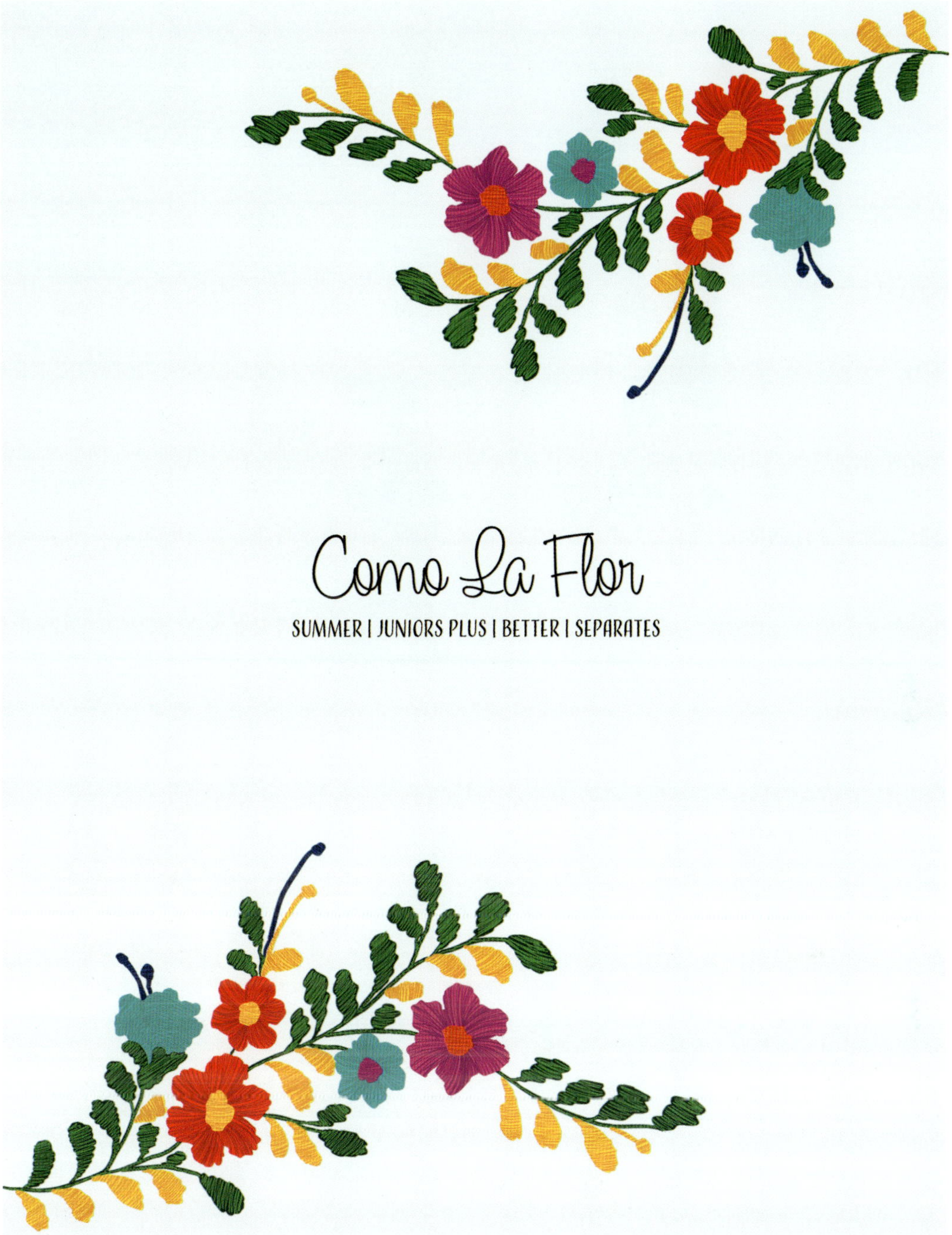

Figure 9.25a Portfolio project courtesy of Arlette Benavides. This is her title page. The background is relatively plain but the decorative elements of the flower embroidery help liven it up. Notice that the font is readable while still adding to the decorative nature of the project. Her line information uses a font with less flourish for readability. Courtesy of Arlette Benavides.

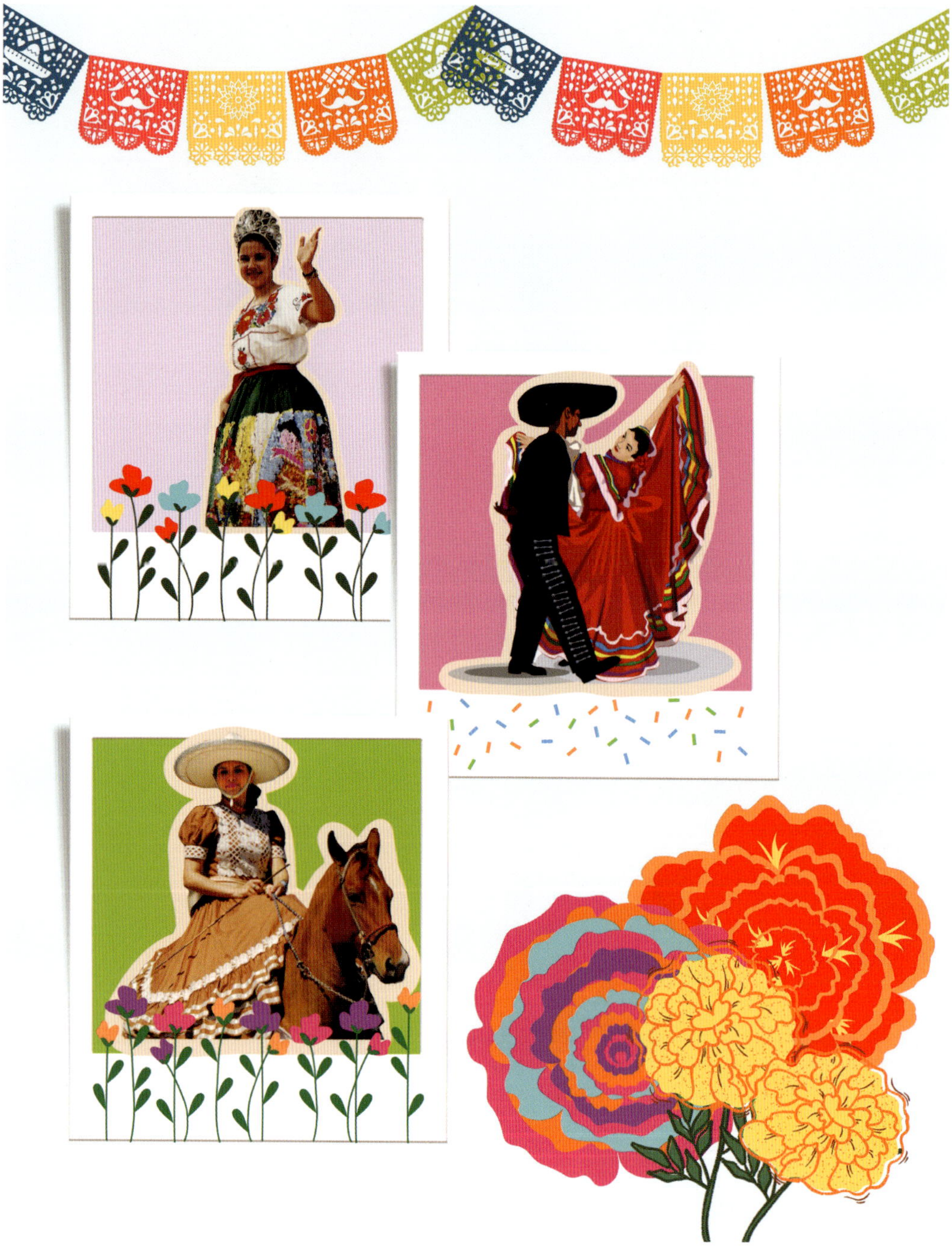

Figure 9.25b Arlette's inspiration is clean and clearly conveys the cultural inspiration. She pulled from her heritage for this collection. Courtesy of Arlette Benavides.

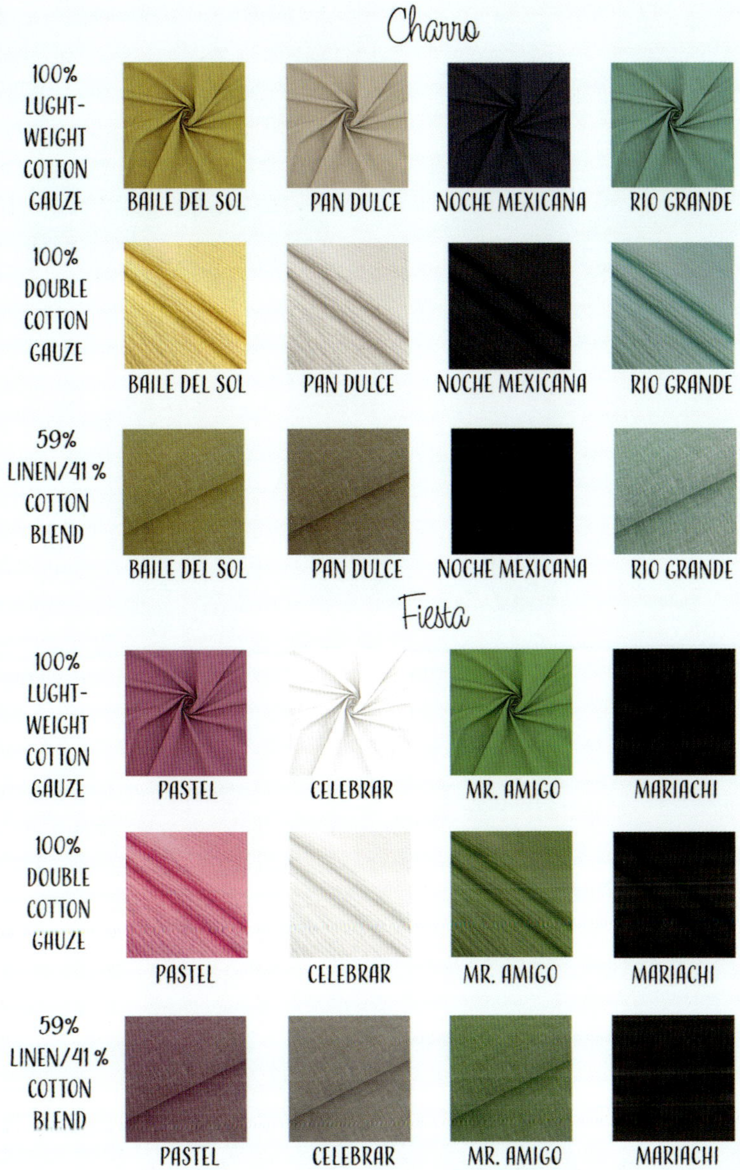

Figure 9.25c For her fabrics page, Arlette offers the designs in two color stories. The information is clear and easy to relate to the designs. Notice that her color names match the theme. Courtesy of Arlette Benavides.

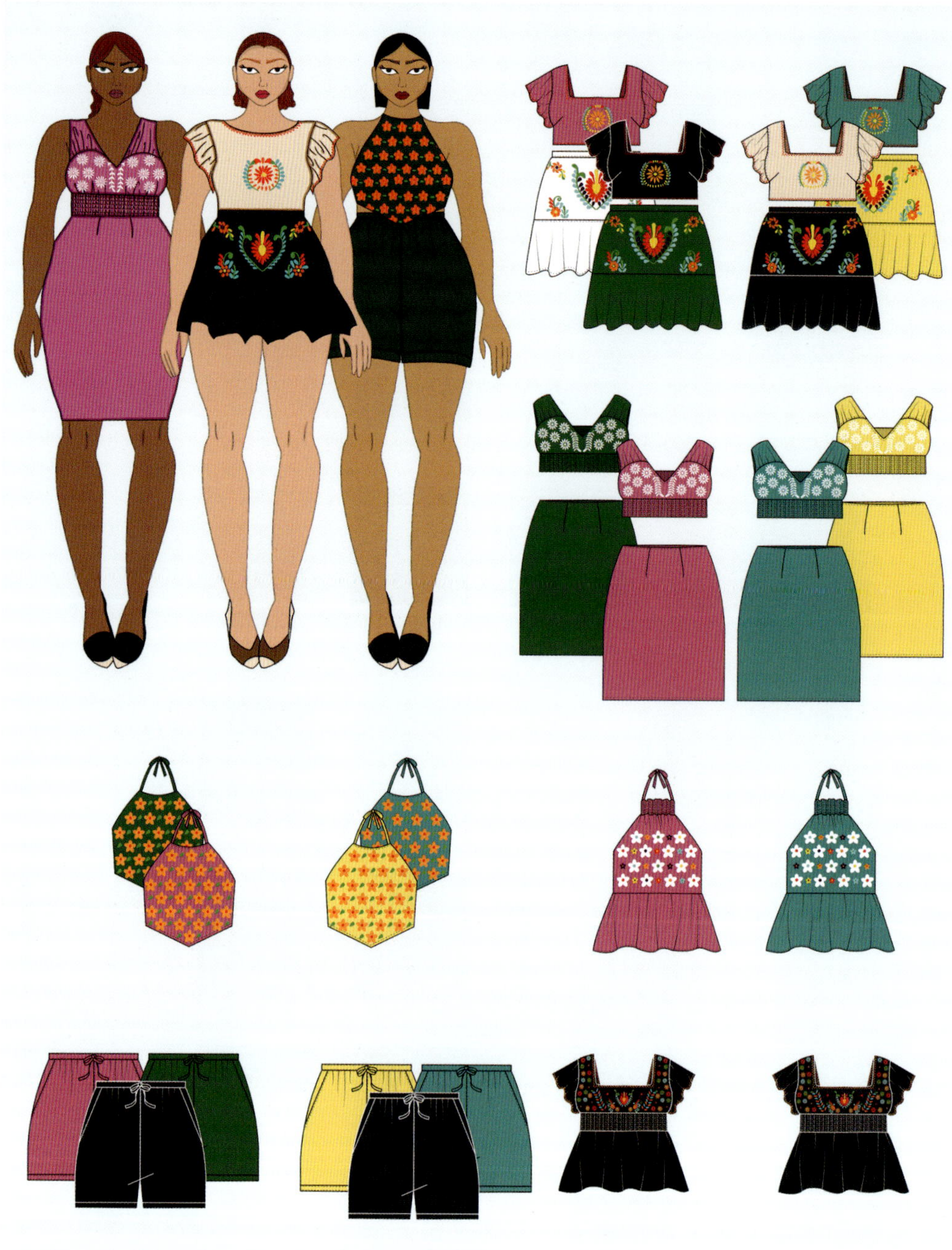

Figure 9.25d To show the designs, she focused on clear flats. She shows some of the possible styling combinations on her figures. An important consideration with flats is to keep them all to the same proportions. Meaning, the flats should look like they came off the same figure so we have a sense of scale. Courtesy of Arlette Benavides.

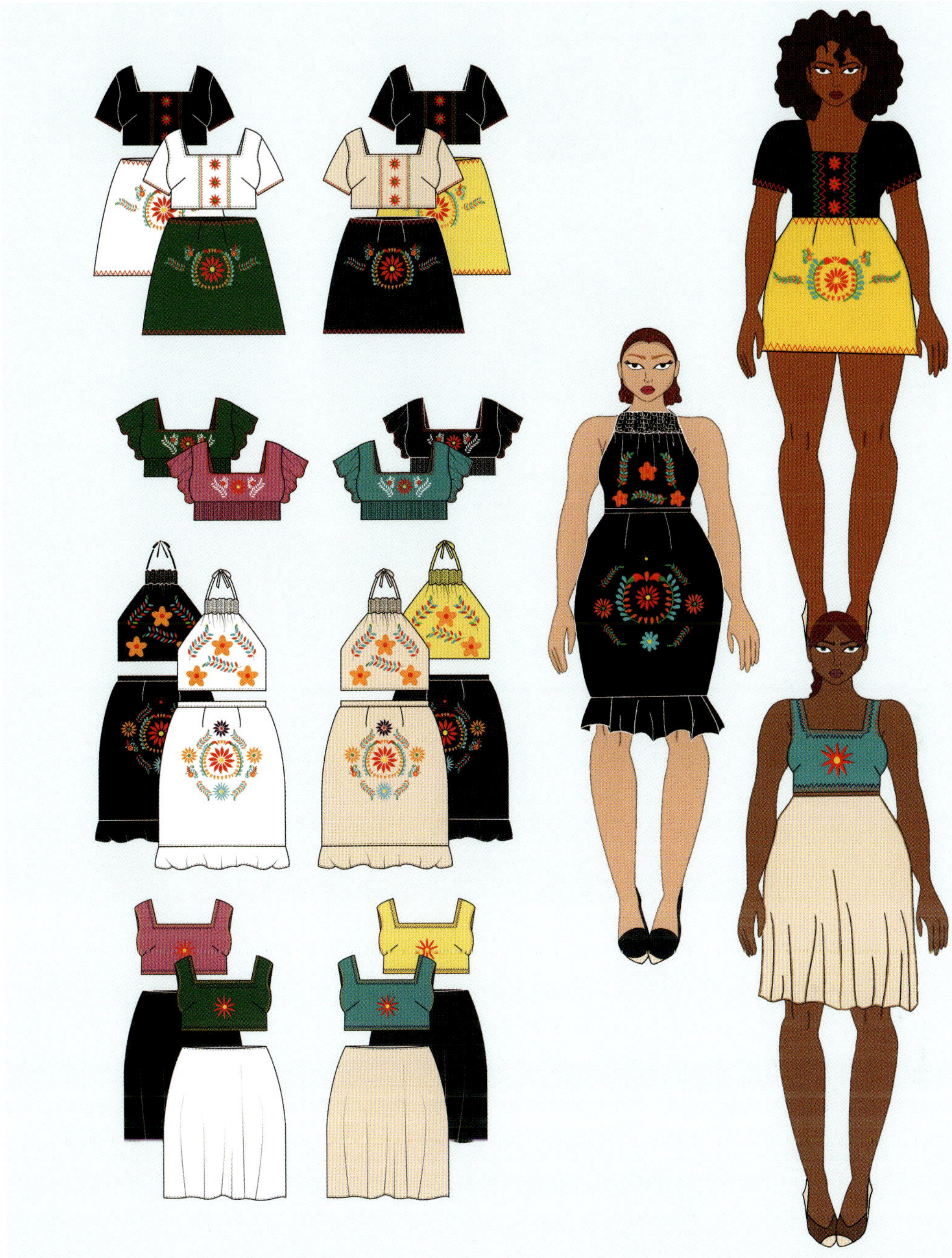

Figure 9.25e Arlette varies the layout somewhat between each page of designs, but the background and drawing style is consistent. This helps to make the project cohesive. Courtesy of Arlette Benavides.

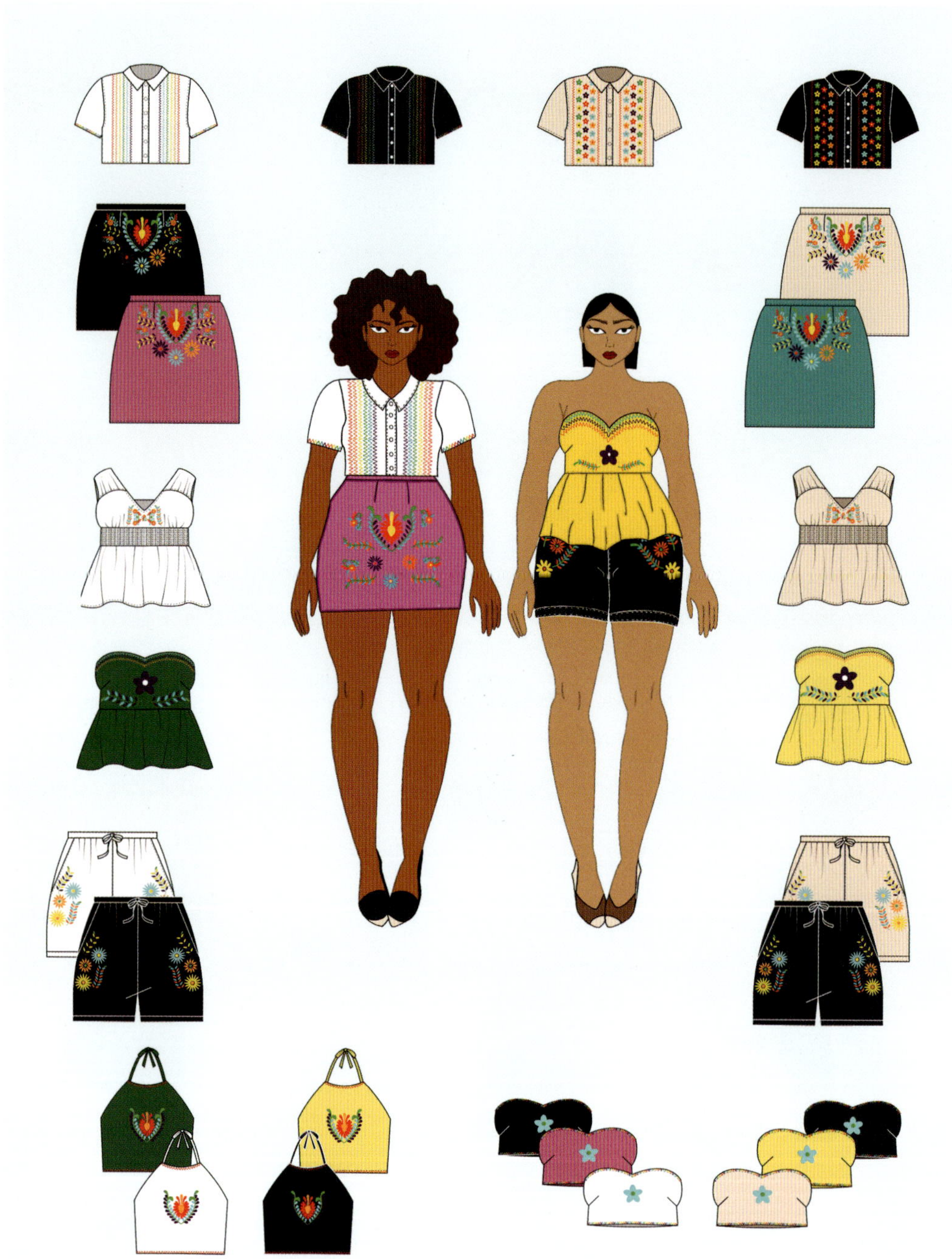

Figure 9.25f This is a large line with two colorways. However, she still keeps the entire project to six pages. Each page is clear without being too cluttered. There is a sense of organization while it remains fun, as a Juniors market line should be. Courtesy of Arlette Benavides.

Summary

Now that you've completed some renderings, you should think about how to lay out a project. Mood pages are not necessary but help to introduce your design process and inspiration. Fabric and color pages provide important information about the fabric choices for your designs. If you have completed garments, consider photographing the work. Aim for a professional look and then think about how to best integrate it into your design layout. Create thumbnail layouts to ideate the best way to display your work. The layout can be just as important as your designs if it does not show the work advantageously. Remember to frequently step back to look at the project as a whole.

STUDIO Companion Videos for Chapter 9

Please refer to STUDIO for accompanying chapter video(s).

Keywords

Editorial style
Fabric
Fiber
Lookbook style
Production shots
Rule of thirds
Still shots

Review Questions

1. What are the pros and cons of a fashion lookbook-style photo versus an editorial-style photo?
2. What are the pros and cons of costume still shots versus production shots?
3. Explain why it is important to be aware of fiber and fabric information in your industry.
4. What is the best way to fix issues for your photographs?
5. What is the point of creating thumbnail sketches for layouts? Why bother?
6. Why should you seek feedback about your layout?

Discussion Questions

1. Do you feel that inspiration pages are helpful or a waste of space? Explain your thoughts.
2. Discuss other ways to incorporate your fabric and color information besides a fabric page.
3. Is it fair that most fabric shops no longer allow students to take swatches? Explain your viewpoint.
4. Why do you think there are so few physical fabric stores around the USA now? Are online fabric stores comparable to physical stores?
5. Which do you personally like more: lookbook style or editorial? Why? (Substitute production shots or stills if you are in costume.)
6. Brainstorm ideas to achieve professional-quality photographs of garments if you are on a severely limited budget.

Practice Exercises

1. Use your own source material to compile an inspiration page for one of your shows or lines.
2. Start a digital folder of your own photographs. Make subfolders for textures, color inspiration, and different types of imagery that makes sense to you.
3. Start a digital folder of fabric photographs for reference. Create subfolders for each category of fabric types however it makes sense to you.
4. Start a digital folder of photography inspiration: lookbook and editorial styles or stills and production shots.

Use these for reference as you start to style your own garment photographs.

5. Take your project from this chapter and create an entirely new layout for it. Which do you like better and why?

Endnotes

1. A good tech pack will get you a job the fastest, though. See Chapter 12.
2. Poorly executed garments can cost you a job, too. It's okay to not be an expert in all aspects of your industry. If construction or pattern work is just not part of your skillset, don't include those items in your portfolio.
3. This depends on your training and expertise, too. Are you trying only for design-related jobs such as assistant designer? Or are you open to costume tech jobs such as first hand or draper? If you are open to production jobs, then show some of your construction and pattern work.
4. It is also useful to have this information when you need to look up that artist later. We can't tell you how many times we recalled the perfect image but had no idea how to find it again!
5. This is not a hypothetical. It actually happened. Feel free to laugh.

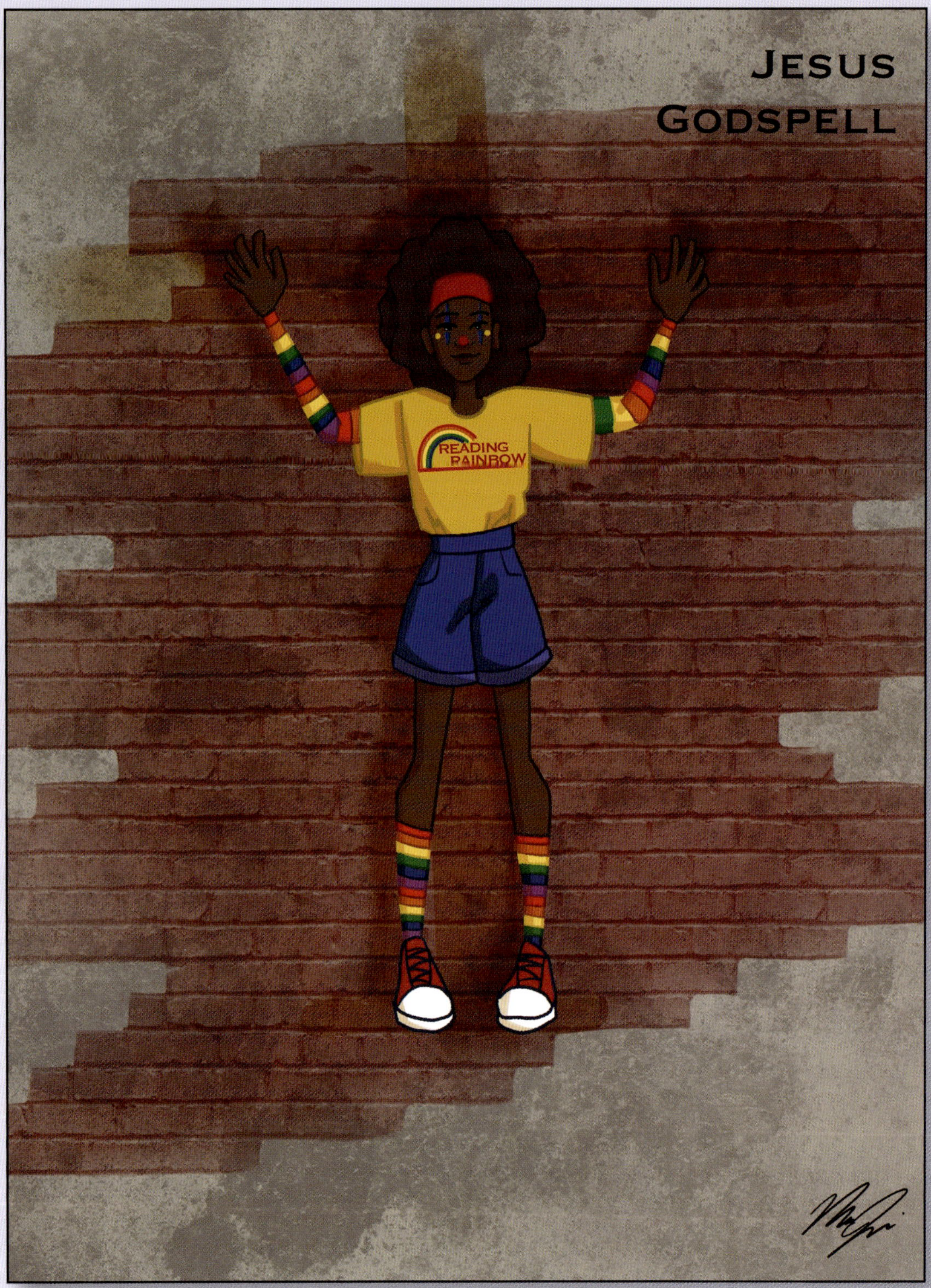

Figure 10.1 The background should help communicate your design without distracting from it. Courtesy of Mona Jahani for Michigan State University.

CHAPTER 10
Backgrounds and Textures for Layouts

Learning Objectives

After completing this chapter, you should be able to

- Create backgrounds that support the overall layout of an illustration
- Utilize textures to alter the look of a layout

You saw how paper textures can make a digital style look more realistic, but what about other background types? Why does a background matter? Why pay any attention to backgrounds or overlaying textures? What's the point? These are all good questions. They may, in fact, not matter for your needs. For many fashion and costume designers, though, backgrounds help sell the garments. They are especially helpful for making your portfolio more professional. If you want to learn more about taking your illustrations to the next level, keep reading!

Project 10.1: Scene Background

Scene backgrounds are often the first type of background that novice illustrators are drawn to. There are some amazing scenic images that just seem to beg to be used. Because who doesn't want to situate their figures in a fairy grotto or on the edge of an active volcano?

However, scene backgrounds can easily overwhelm the figure if the composition is not executed well. Remember that the point of the illustration is to communicate the clothing. The background should support the figures, not be the focus.

When choosing a scene background, you can create your own or select a background from an existing source. If you are using a pre-made background, remember to check the resolution and size of the image. Make sure it will not be **pixelated** when you use it. Pixelated images are easily recognized by the square pixels that appear when viewed with higher than 100% zoom ratio. Check the pixel size of your rendering. If the background image you want to use is smaller than your rendering, it will not work well for this purpose.

Check the proportions of your figures against the background. Do the figures look like they fit in the background? Ground your figures into the background unless it is abstract. Make sure the figures are not randomly floating above the ground unless that is your intention, such as a jumping figure or if the runway is in zero gravity.

Look at the lighting and coloring of the background versus the lighting and coloring you used for your figure. Does the light come from the same direction? If not, you may want to either adjust the shading of your figure or just pick a different background. You can try horizontally flipping either the figure or the background to see if they align that way. Lighting color can be adjusted by using color overlays and blend modes either on the background or the figures. Lighting differences are subtly distracting to viewers, so you don't want to ignore them.

Other actions you may want to consider when preparing a scene background include reducing opacity or saturation to make the background less distracting. You can also apply filters to make the background's visual style better match the style of your figure illustrations, as you see in Figure 10.2. The archway serves to provide a sense of the scenery as well as framing the subject. In the end, remember who the star is.

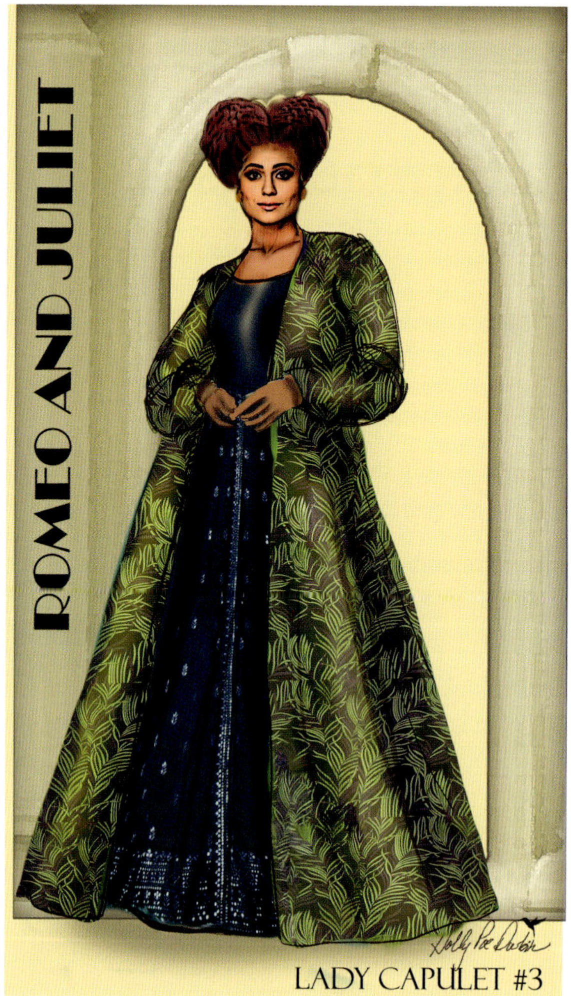

Figure 10.2 Illustration with a simple scenic background. Artwork and design courtesy of Holly Poe Durbin @hollypoedurbin.com.

For the background and texture projects in this chapter, we will use the same figure for each exercise. This way, you can compare the different effects the backgrounds and textures have on the figure without being distracted by figure differences. We will start by creating a layout with a scenic background.

As mentioned, you often need to adjust scenic images to make them work better for backgrounds. The scenic image provided has already been adjusted by the authors. It began as a photograph. The authors ran several Photoshop filters on it, including *Poster Edges* and *Surface Blur* to make it look like the figure's illustration style.

If the image you want to use is not wide or tall enough, generative artificial intelligence in Photoshop is getting considerably better. You can now do a technique called **Outpainting**, which is painting or continuing the image beyond its original borders. This still works better with relatively simple additions beyond the borders, but this limitation is quickly changing.

PRO TIP 10.1

Depth of Field

As you start to work with backgrounds and layouts, consider the depth of field. What is in sharp focus and what starts to get fuzzy? Of course, you want your designs to be clear. The easiest way to play with this is to make your background slightly blurred and the figure(s) in focus. As you get more experienced, you may want to play with making parts of the image slightly blurred like a photographic effect. Even when a figure is fully in focus, some textures blur slightly. Pay attention to photography and the depth of field. Collect examples for inspiration. You may get some interesting ideas!

The image in Figure 10.3 was chosen because it is plain, not distracting, and is a good proportion for the figure. It also frames the figure well and the overall look of the image works with the look of the figure. Several different images were tried before the authors decided this was the best choice. Some images were rejected for being too distracting and some for being the wrong proportion or camera angle for the figure.

To prepare the background for this project, create a page the size of your preferred portfolio layout. Fill the page with a white color fill or a white rectangle. The white will enable you to lighten the images you place on top.

Place the scenic background image file. You can choose whether to embed it or leave it linked. Adjust the size and position of the image until it covers the page, and the casement (door opening) is mostly centered on the page. This layer should be directly above the white page. Adjust the *Opacity* of the background image layer to 50% as you see in Figure 10.3. This will make the background appear lighter.

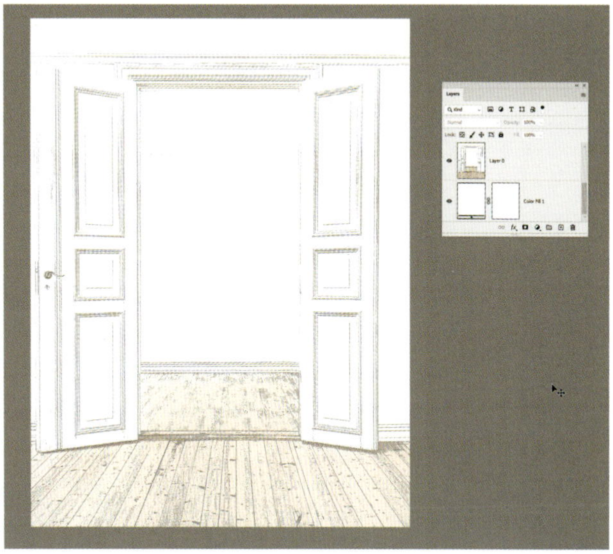

Figure 10.3 The original background image was a photograph. The image was altered using several filters to make it look more like the illustration style of the figure, with heavy outlines and flatter color. To prepare the background, *Place* it over a solid white page. Set the *Opacity* of the scene layer to 50%. Original photograph courtesy of Phil on Unsplash.

After preparing the background, *Place* the figure. Again, you can choose whether you want to embed or link the figure file. The figure layer should be above the background image layer. Adjust the size and position of the figure. The figure needs to look like it is a natural part of the scene. Check the size of the figure against the size of the background elements. Then make sure the figure looks like it is standing on the ground, not floating or tilting. You will notice in Figure 10.4 that the figure needs to be set close to the bottom of the scene image to make the size work. If you want to move the figure back, you will need to make it smaller.

After placing your figure in the scenic background, you may notice that it still does not look like it is part of the scene. You will need to adjust the lighting, coloring, or in this case, add a shadow to ground the figure. You can create shadows using any of the techniques discussed in Chapter 5. For Figure 10.5, the authors painted in the shadows.

Create a new layer between the background and the figure. Switch to the *Brush Tool* and choose a large, soft brush with low opacity. Set the paint color to black or a dark gray. Paint in the shadow. The shadow should be darkest where it touches the feet and fades out as it moves away from the feet, as you see in Figure 10.5. Pay attention to the direction of the light, which is from the right of this figure. The *Blending Mode* for the layer can be set to *Multiply* for better results.

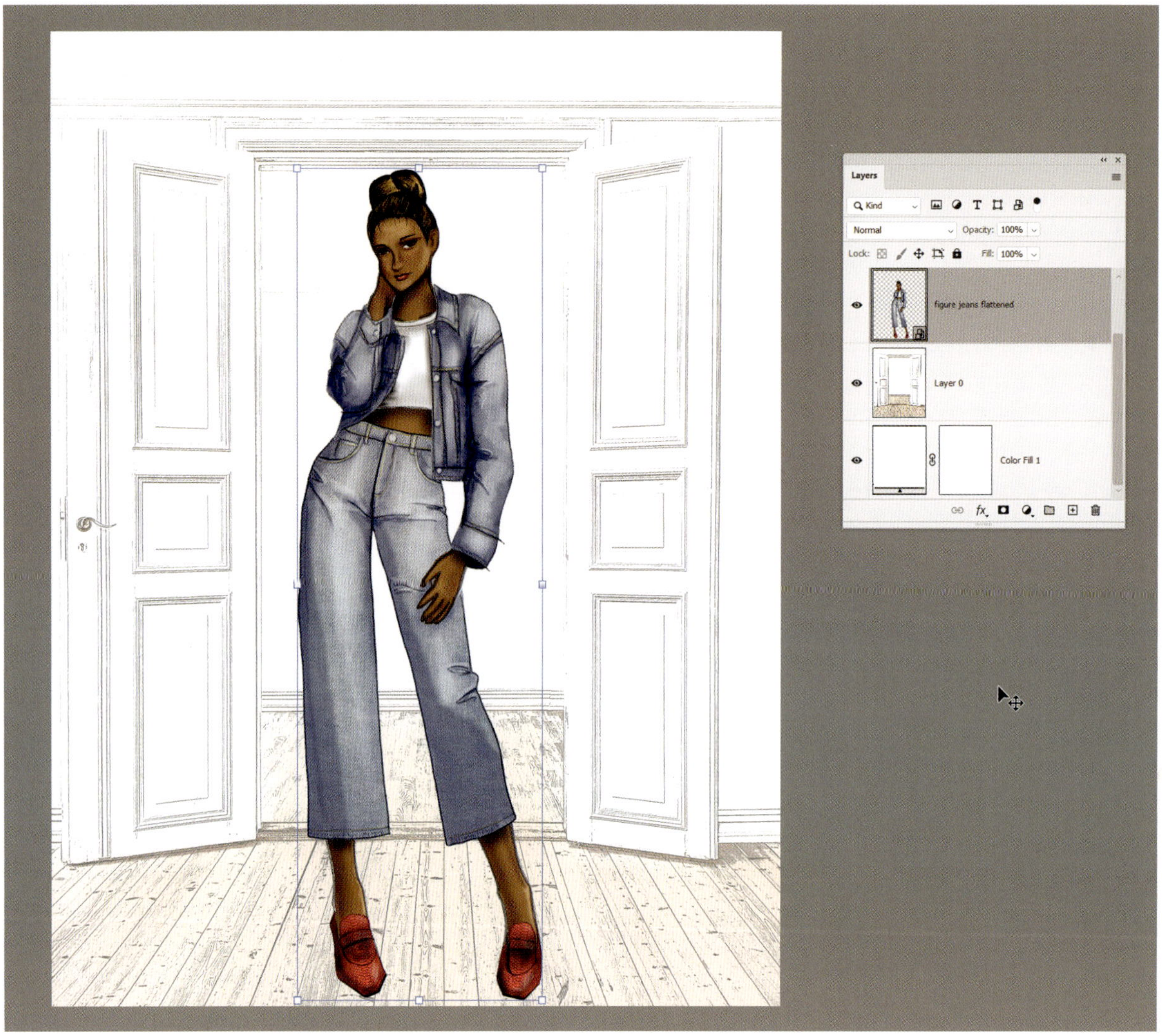

Figure 10.4 *Place* the figure in the document. Move it around until the figure looks like it is standing in the scene, not floating. You may need to resize the figure to keep it in proportion to the background elements. Figure artwork by the authors.

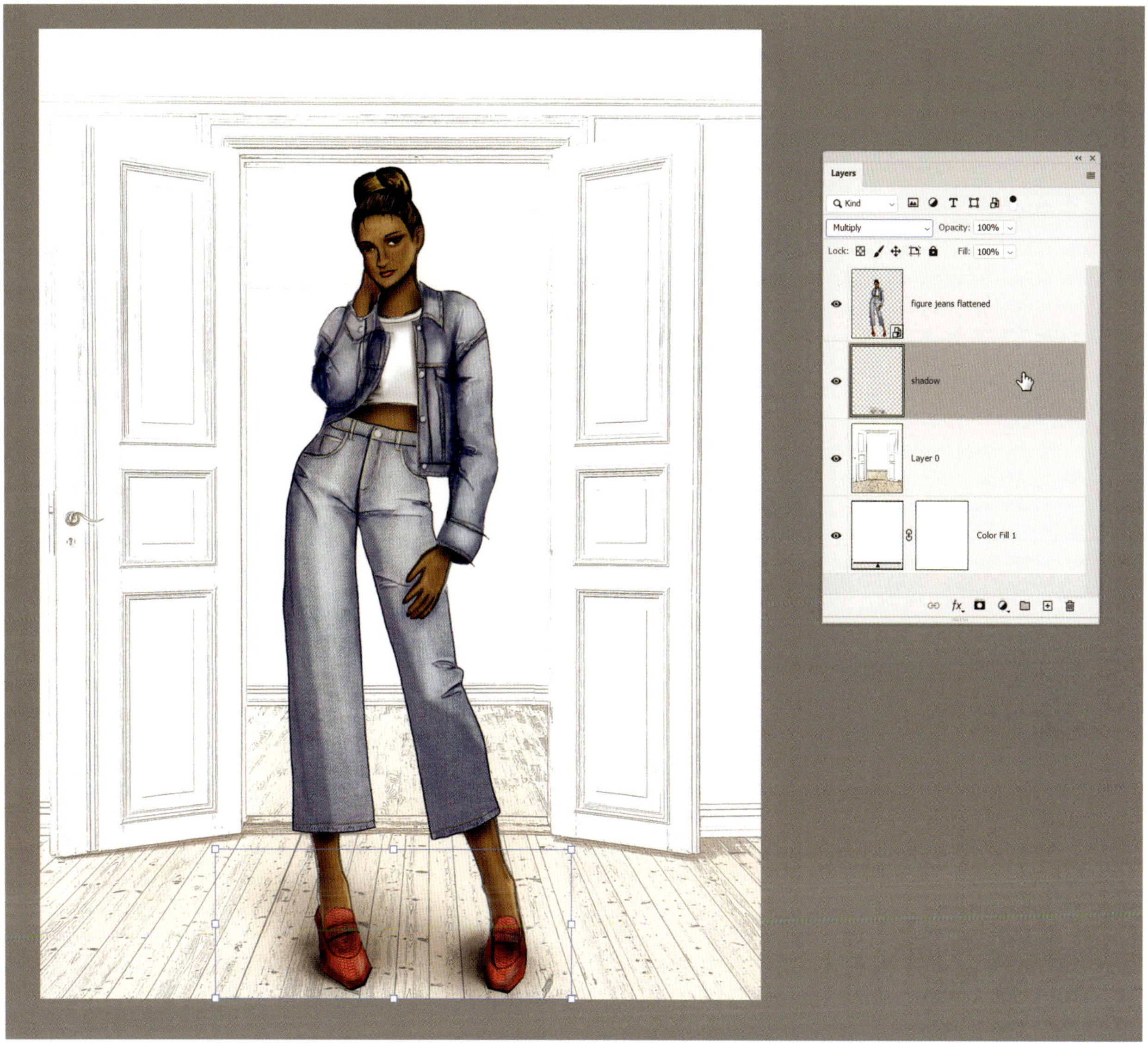

Figure 10.5 Often figures need shadow or lighting adjustments to make them look like they are part of the scene. For this example, we need to add shadows around the figure's feet. Create a new *Layer* between the figure and the background. Using a large soft *Brush* with low *Opacity*, paint in a shadow around the feet. The authors used black paint and set the layer to *Multiply* in this example.

PRO TIP 10.2

Keep to Scale

Think about the scale of your figure to your background. Also consider the scale of separate figures if you have more than one in a layout. Think about how they relate, spatially. Any figures "standing" further back will be smaller than those closer to the viewer or fourth wall. Just make sure they are still big enough to clearly see the designs. You can even have some figures falling outside of the frame if that part of the garment does not matter. For example, if you have a line of swimwear, you may have one or two figures that are much bigger, and their legs are cut off by the frame because the legs do not have any clothing covering them. If you are not sure that you have the hang of getting the proportions correct, then just keep them in a line. Poor proportions can really distract the viewer from your great designs!

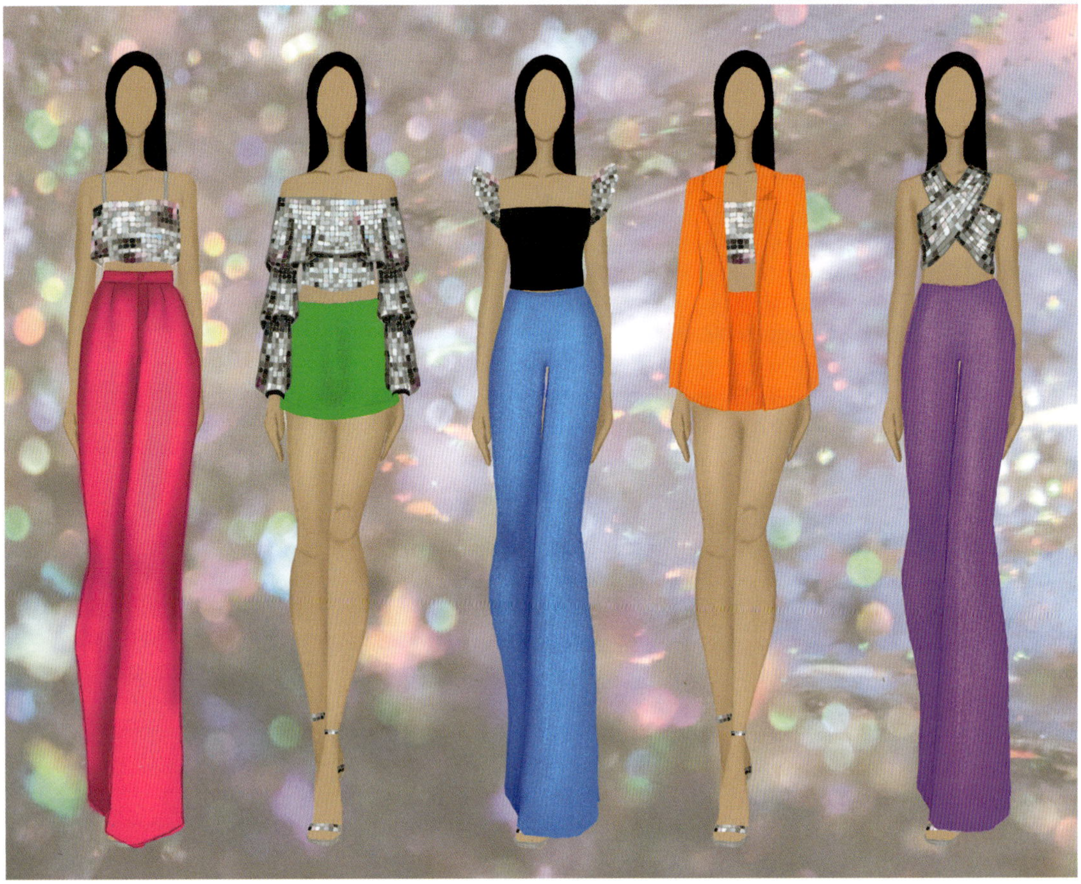

Figure 10.6 Illustration with an abstract glitter texture background. Courtesy of Rebecca Salinas @byrebeccasalinas.

Project 10.2: Texture Background

A texture image is easy to use and often less distracting than other background choices. Textures can set the mood of the illustration without being the focus. You could choose a gritty wall texture or close-up of graffiti for an edgy streetwear line or something as simple as a paper texture for a more classic look. A bokeh background can give a very soothing feel whereas a confetti texture can be fun or youthful.

As with the scene backgrounds, you may need to adjust the image before use. Check the size of the background to make sure it will fit your illustration without pixelation. You can reduce saturation or opacity, or increase blur. You will notice that the opacity has been reduced in the background for Figure 10.6. Color can also be adjusted using color overlays and blending modes. Make sure that the background does not overwhelm the figures. It should tie everything together and set the mood.

For our texture background project, the texture image was altered by the authors. The color was changed to complement the figure. This is a common and easy change when working with texture backgrounds.

For this project, *Open* the texture background image. Place the figure on the background. You can decide whether to embed or to link the placed figure. Resize and reposition the figure as needed, as shown in Figure 10.7.

The project could be considered done at this stage. However, when you look at Figure 10.7, it needs something else to make it look more cohesive. For this example, we will add a graphic element, which will create visual interest through line and color.

Use the *Pen* tool to draw the shape. In Figure 10.8, you will see that the authors drew a shape across the bottom of the page that angles up to the right more than the left. The shape is set to a black fill with no stroke. Try different *Blending Modes* for the shape layer until you find a result you like. In Figure 10.9, the authors used the *Saturation* mode.

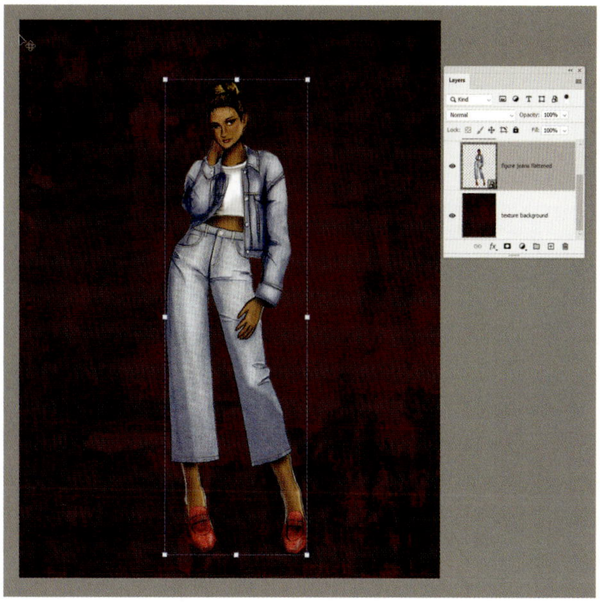

Figure 10.7 While this example is executed in Photoshop, the same steps work in Illustrator, and with a little adjustment, InDesign. To start, *Open* the textured background and *Place* your figure. Arrange the figure where you want it.

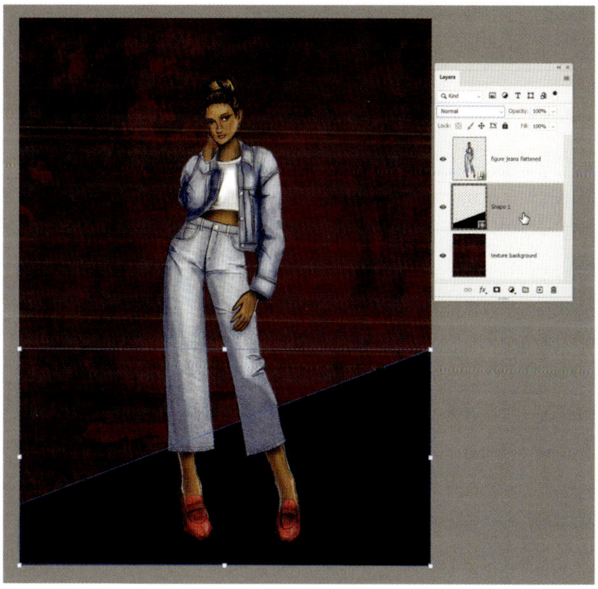

Figure 10.8 The image can be used with just the figure and the textured background. However, sometimes it needs a little something extra to make it look more professional. In this case, we will add an angled shape that mimics the floor or ground. Use the *Pen* tool and draw the angled shape from margin to margin. Set the *Fill* to black and the *Stroke* to none. The shape should be between the figure and the background.

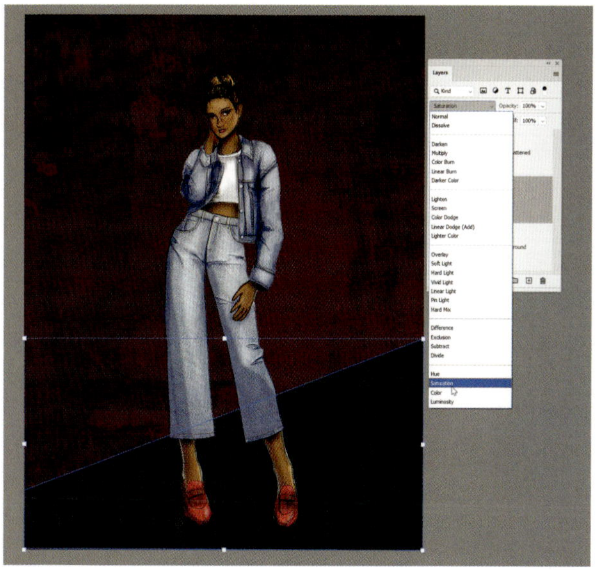

Figure 10.9 To make the shape mesh with the background better, we will change its *Blending Mode*. You can try different *Blending Modes* and opacities to see what you like best. The authors used *Saturation* and left the *Opacity* at 100%.

Project 10.3: Clean/Graphic Background

Sometimes all your illustration needs is a solid color background, a gradient, or a color block. Less can be more in many cases. All attention will be on the figures, and this indicates a classy professionalism.

Graphic elements come in a variety of styles. You will notice in Figure 10.10 that part of the color blocking was done in a pencil texture. You can also add a few abstract brush strokes or other random shapes to help pull your layout together and draw the eye around the page.

Our graphic background project starts very simply. Create a page with solid color fill or a solid rectangle that fills the page. The authors used a dark navy color fill in Figure 10.11. Place the figure on the page. Resize and reposition it as needed.

To add a graphic element to the background, draw a shape on a layer between the figure and the background fill. This could be any shape. You could also create a frame around the page instead of a filled shape.

For Figure 10.12, the authors chose to draw a rectangle that is a little wider and shorter than the figure. The shape has a solid fill of bright red and no stroke. The rectangle is centered to the page. However, these are the choices of the authors, and you can adjust as you desire. The point is to make something that looks good with the figure.

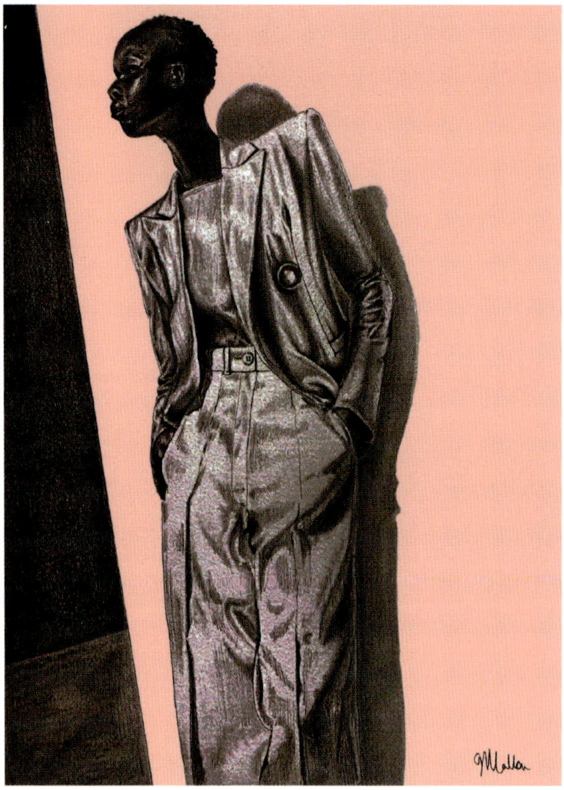

Figure 10.10 This figure has a color-blocked background to make the rendering more interesting. Courtesy of Jackie Mallon @ jackie_mallon1. Jackiemallon.com.

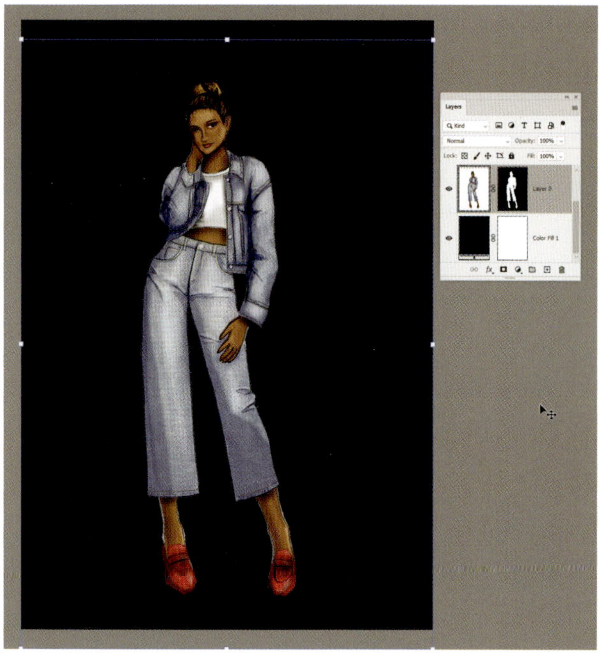

Figure 10.11 Making a color-blocked background for a rendering. This project works the same in Photoshop, Illustrator, and InDesign. Start with a page with a *Color Fill* layer or a solid-fill *Rectangle* for the page color. *Place* the figure on the page.

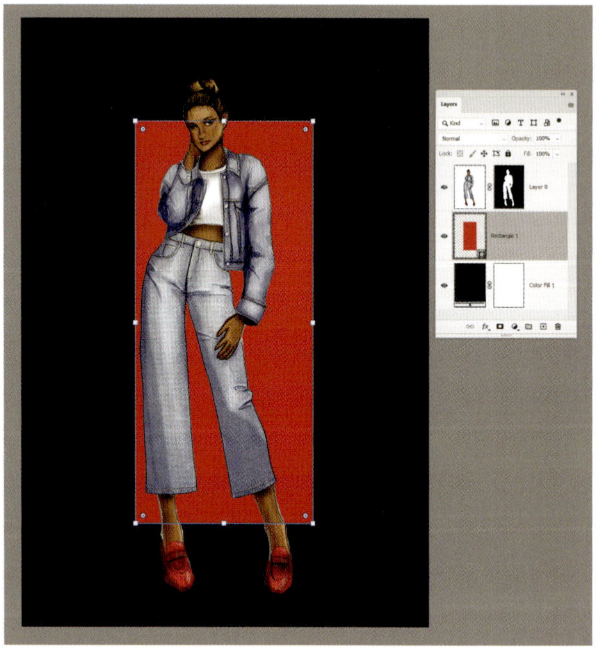

Figure 10.12 Color-blocking the background. We will make a simple rectangle block, but you can make any shape or group of shapes. For this project, use the *Rectangle* tool and draw a rectangle behind the figure. Set the rectangle to a solid-fill color with no stroke. The authors used a dark navy page with a bright red block. We also centered the block on the page but place it where you think it looks best. Adjust the placement of both the block and the figure until you are satisfied.

STYLE SECRETS 10.1

Don't Make Your Background the Star!

As students learn to incorporate backgrounds and layouts, inevitably someone will pick an elaborate background because it looks "cool." Remember that you are trying to show off your designs, not what is behind them. Make sure that your background enhances rather than distracts from your figures and garments. Sometimes it is simply too busy and detailed to be used well, even with a blur filter and opacity mask. Chuck it and pick a plainer solution to show off your work. You should never be more married to your background than your designs. Remember who is the star of this show.

Project 10.4: Overlay Texture

Texture overlays can be used to make an illustration look like it was created on handmade paper or for distressing a layout. Overlays are a good way to blend hand illustrations into a background or to give a page a feeling of age. Texture brushes can enhance the overall effectiveness of the overlay or can be used separately to add distressing or other subtle elements to a layout.

When choosing a texture, look for subtle textures without noticeable repeating elements. Also check for hidden watermarks that will appear when you utilize the texture if you are using a free source. There are many professionally made textures that can be purchased for a reasonable price from sources such as Adobe Stock. See the resources section in the appendix for more sources.

To utilize a texture overlay, place the image on a different layer and experiment with different blend modes and opacity. This works in Photoshop, Illustrator, and InDesign, as well as in many other rendering programs that utilize layers. If your program does not have blend modes, you can try working with just opacity. Sometimes that is enough to be effective.

If you are only working with a texture overlay and a plain background, you may want to add a vignette to further highlight your figure. A **vignette** is an effect that darkens or lightens the area outside your main subject, typically around the borders of the layout. Sometimes vignettes also include a blur effect. This effect is meant to help draw the eye to the main subject. Figure 10.13 uses a vignette to add interest to the otherwise plain background.

Photoshop has an automatic *Vignette* action that can be accessed through the *Discovery* panel. However, you can also create a vignette using a highly feathered selection mask and a color overlay or color fill. You can also paint a vignette on a layer using a very large, soft brush.

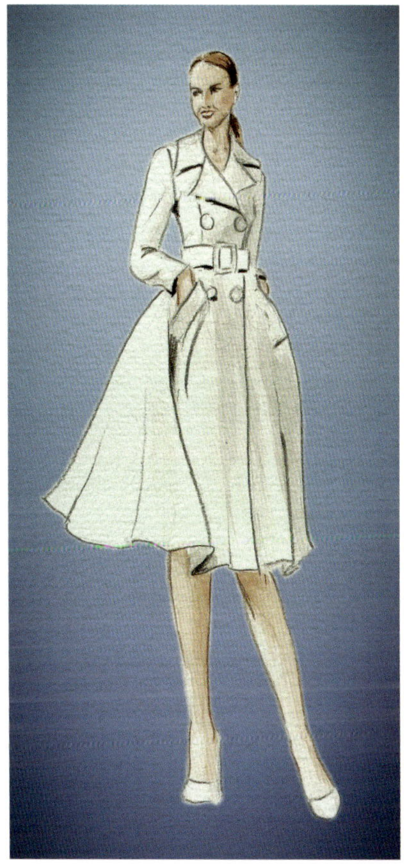

Figure 10.13 Figure with watercolor paper texture overlay. The original figure was rendered in watercolor and superimposed on a simple gradient background. Place a watercolor paper texture on top and set the *Blending Mode* for the paper layer to *Multiply*. Then add a vignette to draw the eye to the figure. The added texture allows the watercolor rendering to blend with the background. Artwork by the authors.

When choosing texture images for an overlay it is important that the visual style of the texture complements the style of the figure. For our texture overlay project, we will use an image of a distressed wall.

The gentle ruggedness of the texture image works well with the stone-washed denim on the figure.

To use a texture overlay, start by placing your figure on a background. For this project, we will place our figure on a solid color background. In Figure 10.14, the authors used a burgundy color fill for the background.

After arranging your figure, place the texture overlay image on top of the figure. This can be embedded or linked. Resize and reposition the texture image as you need, as shown in Figure 10.15.

To make the overlay work, try different *Blending Modes* and *Opacities* for the texture image layer. You may find several combinations that you like and will have to choose which one works best. If none of them work, try inverting the texture image, then experiment with the *Blending Modes* and opacity again. In Figure 10.16, the authors used the *Divide Mode* and *75% Opacity*.

Textures are very easy to create yourself. In fact, many professional illustrators habitually take pictures of interesting textures they come across in "the wild" for possible use later. Textures can come from photographs, scans, or can be produced digitally. Are you looking for a texture of a certain type of paper? Scan it in! Do you need a tree bark texture? Go outside and take photos, as seen in the texture photo in Figure 10.17.

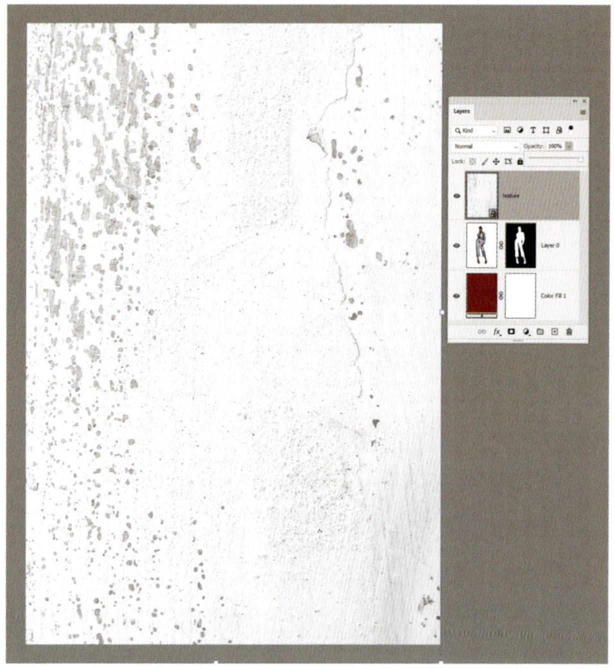

Figure 10.15 *Place* the texture overlay image on top of the figure. Arrange it so it covers the entire page and is rotated to the angle you prefer. The texture image we are using is a photo courtesy of NordWood Themes on Unsplash.

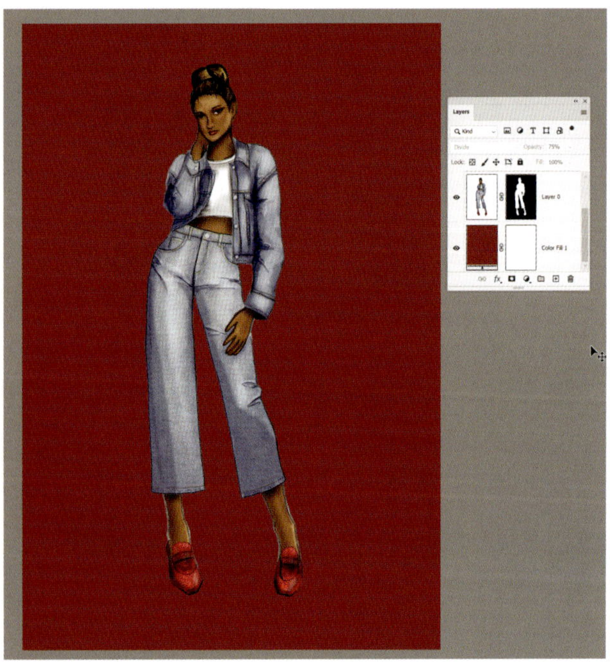

Figure 10.14 This project works the same way in Photoshop, Illustrator, and InDesign. You can have any kind of background. However, for this project, start a page with a color fill or a solid-fill rectangle for the page color. *Place* the figure on the page.

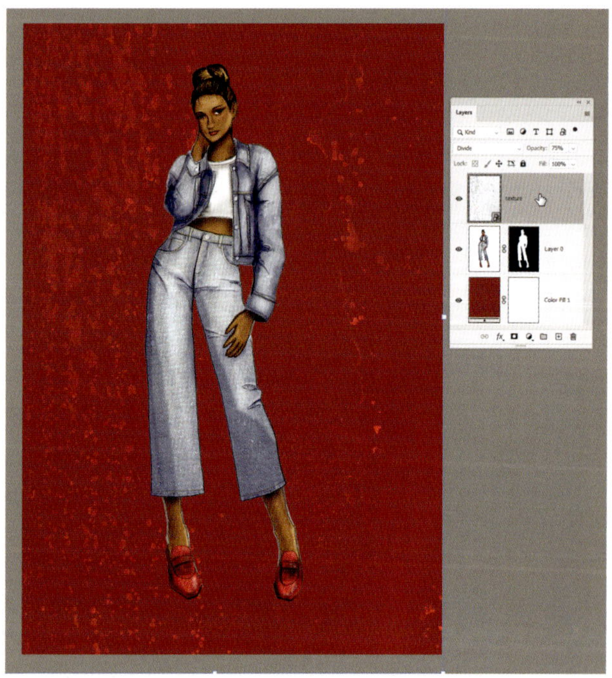

Figure 10.16 To make a texture overlay work, you must adjust the *Blending Modes* and/or *Opacity* of the overlay layer. Try different *Blending Modes* and *Opacity* settings until you find something you like. The authors chose the *Divide Blending Mode* and a 75% *Opacity*.

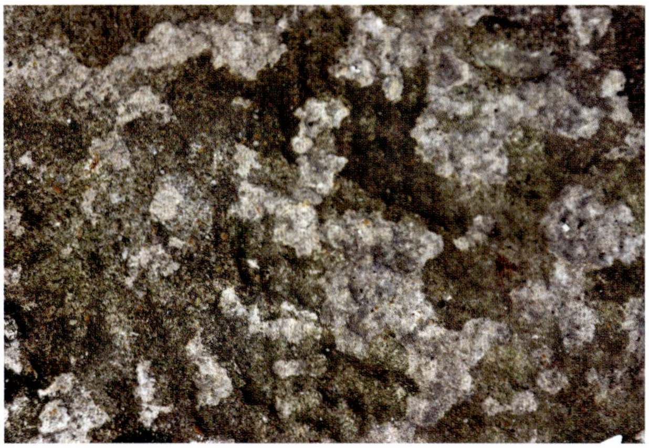

Figure 10.17 The authors regularly photograph interesting textures, such as this lichen-covered concrete, to use later in renderings.

When you want to use your homemade textures, you may need to clean up the images and make adjustments. It is common to remove unwanted parts of the image when working with photos. Scanned images also require some manipulation if there are parts that do not meet your needs. You may want to desaturate the image or convert it to black and white. Sometimes the colors can be distracting when a texture is used as an overlay.

A good trick for working with dark textures is to *Invert* them. Figure 10.18 is an example of a homemade texture of photocopy crackle. You will see the inverted image in Figure 10.19. By inverting the image to mostly white, it is less likely to overpower the image. Depending on your needs, you make want to take it a step further and adjust the levels. Images can be reduced to strictly black and white with no gray, if this works better for you.

You can also find or create a texture brush to selectively add texture to your layout. This technique works best in Photoshop. It is less successful in Illustrator and generally does not work in InDesign. In both cases, it would be better to either apply the brushes in Photoshop or create an image with the brush strokes that can be used in Illustrator or InDesign.

There are many free and commercially available texture brushes for Photoshop. It is almost as easy to create your own texture brush. Sometimes creating your own is the only way to get what you really want.

To make a texture brush in Photoshop, you will either need to find or create a source image that has the texture you want to use. If the texture image is dense, without clearly accessible edges, you may want to erase or paint out some of the area around the part of the texture you want to use as a brush. You can see an example of an image that needs to be cleaned and the result of the cleaning in Figures 10.20a and 10.20b.

Figure 10.18 Scan of a crumpled piece of solid black photocopier paper. This is an example of a homemade texture. This texture was developed by copying a solid black sheet of paper on an old electrostatic (non-laser) photocopier. The authors then crumpled the page until some of the toner began to flake off. Textures can be scans, photographs, or hand-generated. Texture created by the authors.

Once the brush tip shape is cleaned and selected, go to *Edit → Define Brush Preset* to create the new brush. The brush tip is now part of the *Brush Library* on your computer and can be applied with the *Brush* tool. You will probably need to adjust the size, opacity, and rotation of the brush tip to get it to look how you envisioned. In Figure 10.21 you will see two brushes that the authors made from the photocopy texture. You will notice the brush instance on the right is darker than the one on the left. In Figure 10.22, the authors adjusted the brush so the color strength more closely matched. The tips were also rotated to best fit with the layout.

For our texture brush project, we will start with a photo of rust. Texture brushes can be made from any image. However, it is easier if the source image has areas that can be easily isolated. Also, does the image

Figure 10.19 Many times, when a texture is dark, it will work better if you *Invert* the image and/or adjust the *Levels*. Light images are typically easier to apply over a rendering using *Blending Modes*.

have sections that look like they would make interesting brushes? The image in Figure 10.23 has nice rust spots that will make good brushes. The area around the rust spots does not have a lot of texture, which will make it easier to clean up and isolate the spots.

To make a texture brush, we must convert colored images to black and white. For the project, use *Image → Adjustments → Black and White* so you can control the contrast. The goal is to have dark rust spots, but not so dark that they lose their detail. The surrounding area should be as light as possible. You will see in Figure 10.24 that the authors used the *High Contrast Blue Filter*.

The conversion to black and white may not create enough contrast, as is the case with our example. If this happens, either adjust the *Levels* or use *Curves* to further adjust the contrast. For our project, we will use *Curves* so we do not lose the details in the rust spots. You can see the curve adjustments and the results in Figure 10.25.

Once the image is adjusted, decide if you need to clean around the areas you want to make into brushes. You can use the eraser tool (set to white) or a white brush. When you are satisfied with the image, choose one of the *Selection* tools and *Mask* the first area you want to make into a brush nib, as you see in Figure 10.26. The authors used the *Lasso* tool to mask their image, but use whichever tool you are most comfortable with.

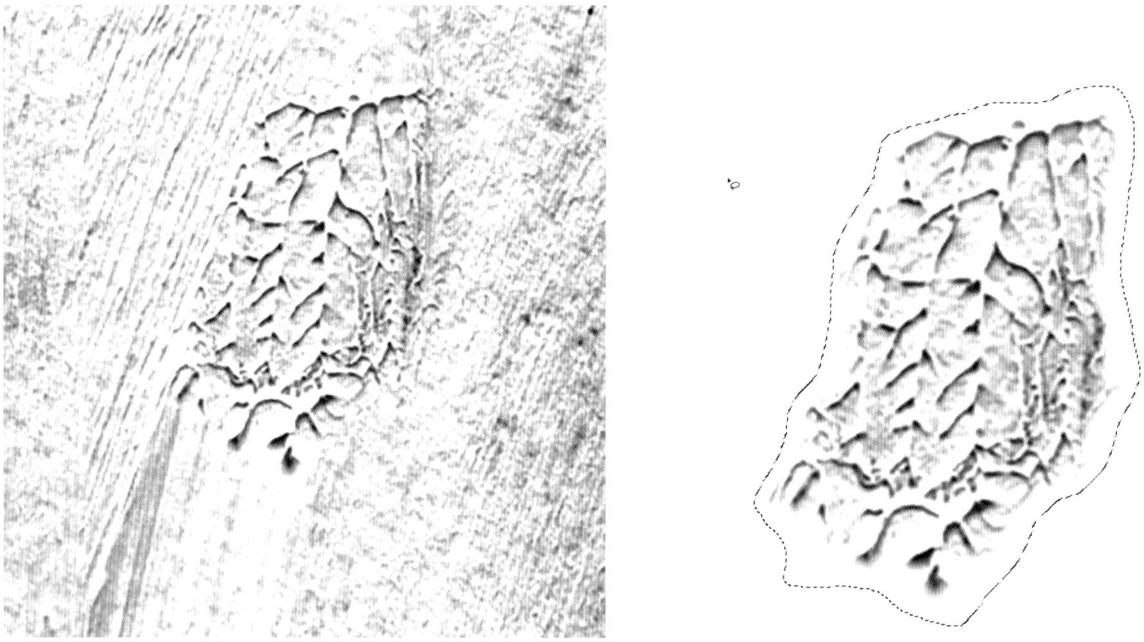

Figures 10.20a, b A texture image and the same texture image cleaned up and masked for brush creation. The first image shows a scan of a paint texture that has been *Inverted*, *Desaturated*, and had *Levels* adjusted. The second image is the same texture with the area around the brush print erased. Once the image was cleaned up, the desired brush tip shape was selected using the *Lasso* tool in preparation for making the brush.

Figure 10.21 Two brushes made from the photocopy scan. Texture images can be good sources for unique texture brushes. Select interesting areas of the photocopy scan using the *Lasso* tool and *Define a New Brush* for each of these brush tips. They can be used to distress renderings.

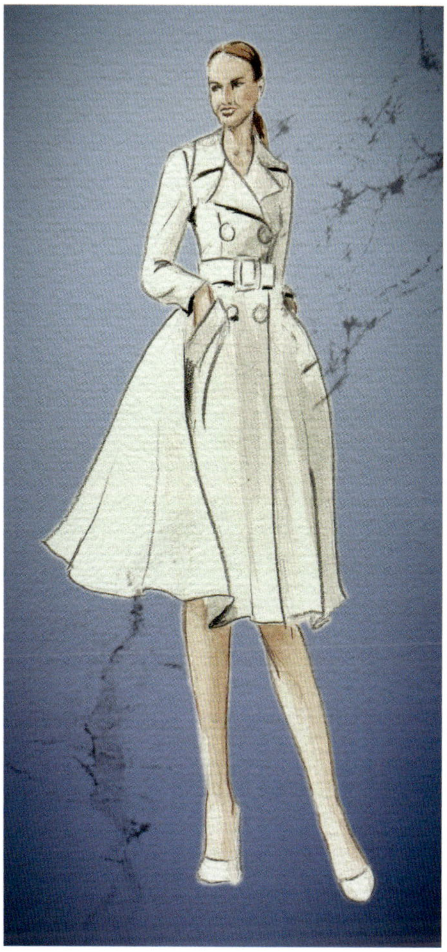

Figure 10.22 The two brushes made from the photocopy scan were used to distress the rendering.

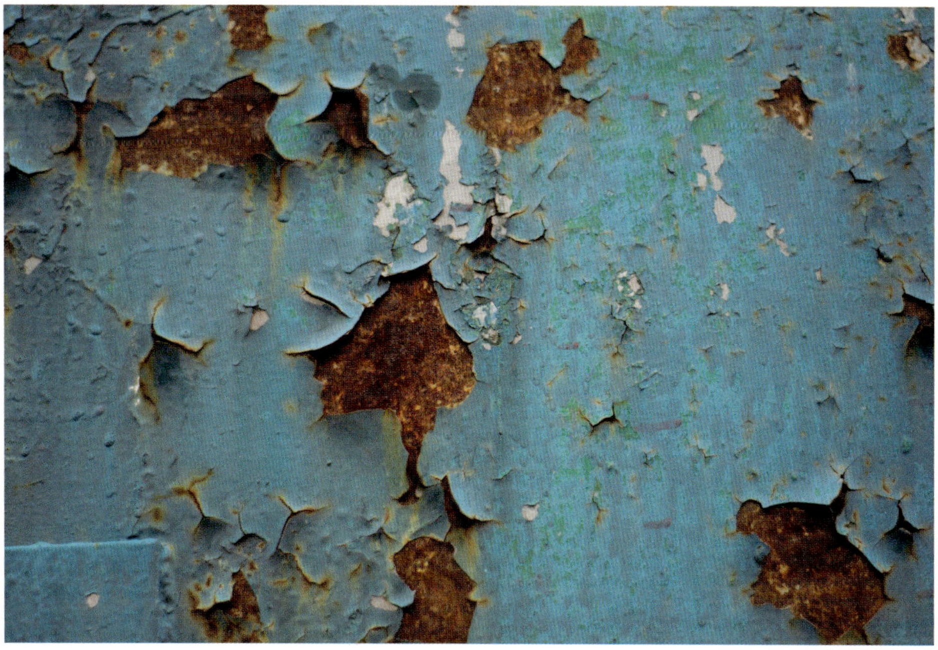

Figure 10.23 Choosing an image to make a texture brush. When looking for a source image, look at the various elements in the image. Are there parts in the image that can be isolated to make interesting brushes? We will use this image of rust and peeling paint courtesy of Marie P of Unsplash.

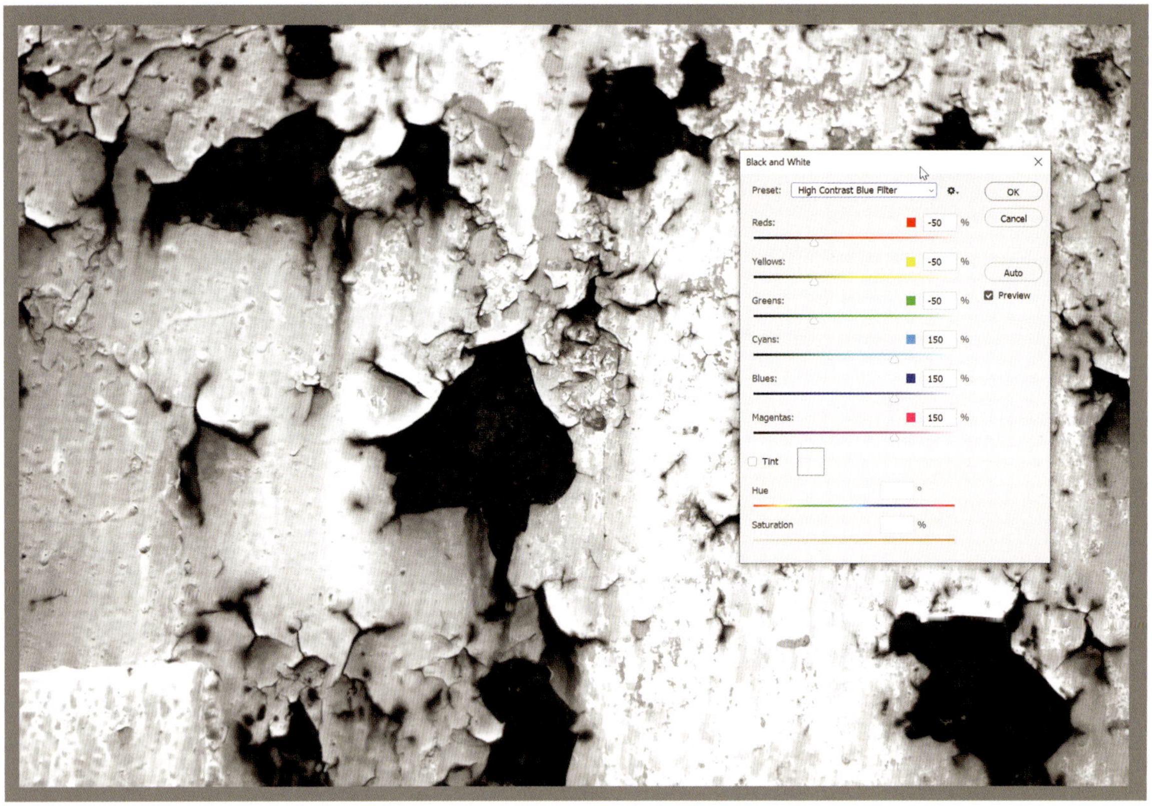

Figure 10.24 To create a brush nib, *Open* the source image in Photoshop. The image will need to be converted to black and white. You can use *Desaturate* or *Black and White*. For this image, *Black and White*, set to *High Contrast Blue Filter*, works best. This setting produces nearly black rust spots, and the rest of the image is closer to white. Typically, the higher the contrast, the better.

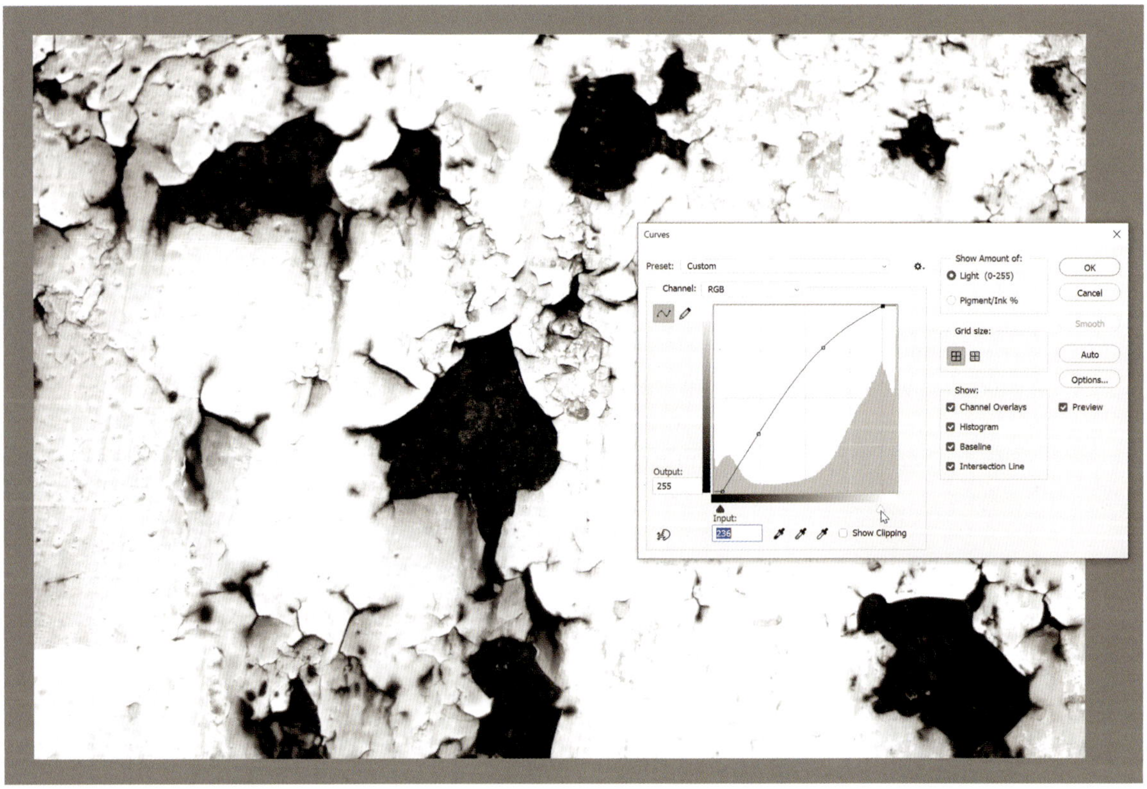

Figure 10.25 To successfully create a brush nib, it is best if the area surrounding the desired brush nib is white or close to white. Use *Curves* on this image to increase the white without losing the detail of the dark areas.

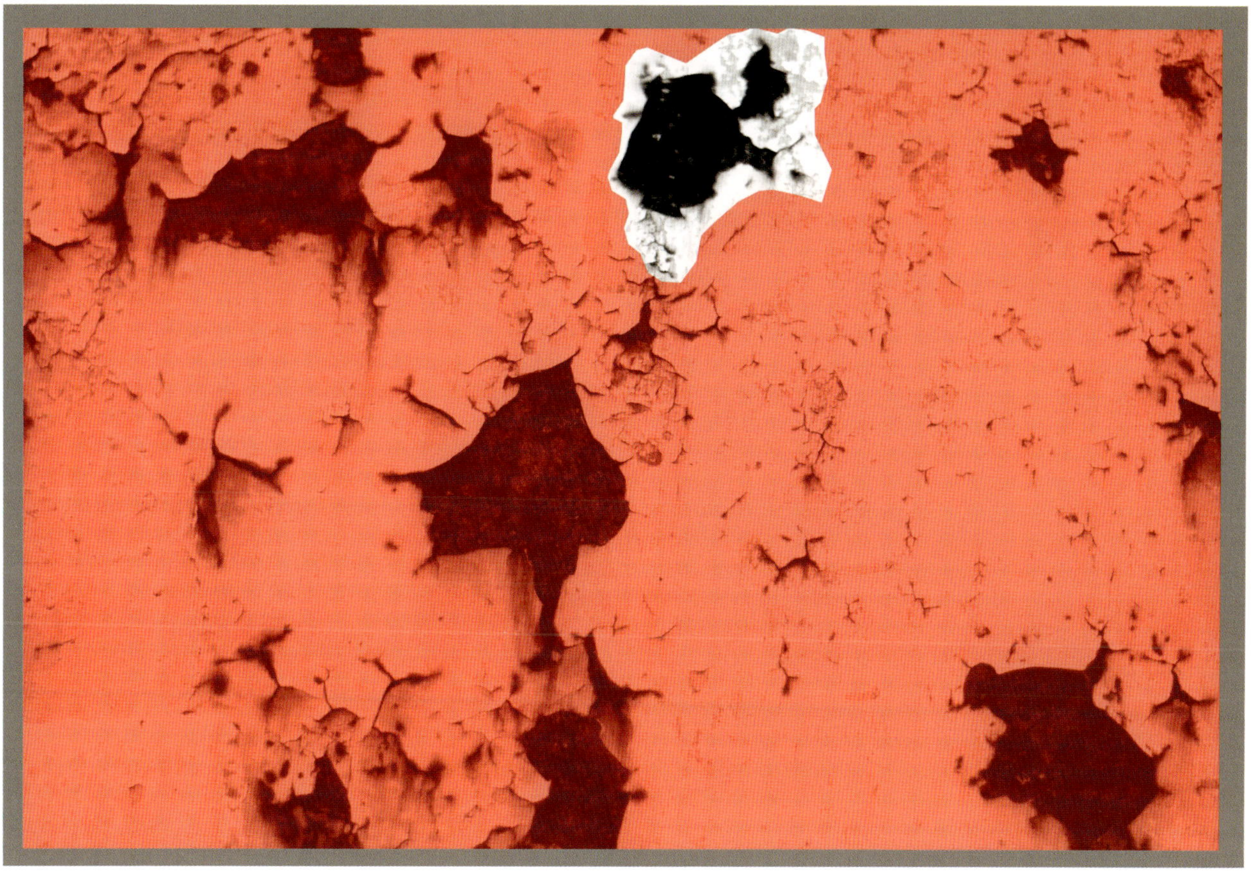

Figure 10.26 Once you have made all the necessary adjustments, use one of the *Selection* tools to mask the area you want to make a brush from. The authors used the *Lasso* tool.

While the area is selected, go to *Edit → Define Brush Preset*. Name your brush in the dialog box. You now have a new brush nib, as seen in Figure 10.27. You can deselect your rust spot and select a new spot to make other brushes. The nibs are located in the *Brushes* panel and can be adjusted in the *Brush Settings* panel.

To use your brush nib, select the *Brush* tool. Set the tool to your new brush nib in the *Brushes* panel. You may want to adjust the size, opacity, and rotation of the brush to meet the needs of your illustration. Figure 10.28 shows the rust spot brush used on the figure with the texture overlay. You can see how this adds a little more distressing to the layout.

Figure 10.27 Keep the image selected. Go to *Edit → Define Brush Preset* to make your brush. Name the brush. You now have a texture brush. You are welcome to make several different texture brushes for variety.

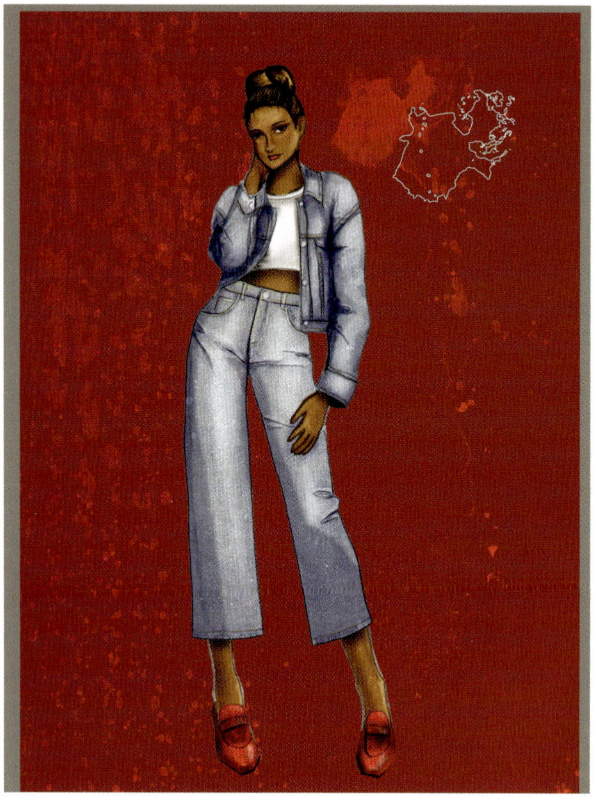

Figure 10.28 After you have made your new texture brush, *Open* your rendering. Using the *Brush* tool set to your new texture brush nib, you can add interesting textures to enhance your layout. The authors added a rust splotch to the top of this layout.

Troubleshooting

"Why is my background pixelated or fuzzy?"

1. This probably means that your background image is either low resolution or not large enough for your page, which in turn makes it low resolution. Although there are plugins and software programs for enlarging and sharpening images, they can only do limited work with the missing pixels. The best solution is to pick a new image that is an appropriate size and resolution for your needs.

"Why won't my texture overlay work?"

2. If your overlay blocks out the rest of the page check the blending modes and opacity for the layer. These probably need to be adjusted.
3. If your overlay is not affecting the figure, first check that the overlay layer is on top of the figure layer. Next, check the blending modes and the opacity for the texture layer. The settings may work well for the background but not the figure, and need further adjusting.

Summary

Backgrounds are not always necessary, but in many cases, they can help pull the rendering together and sell the garment or costume. A background can be any type of image; however, there are three basic categories that meet most needs: scenic, texture, and clean or graphic. Remember to choose a background that complements your rendering without overwhelming it. Use filters, adjustments, blending modes, and opacity to help make your backgrounds work better.

Textural overlays and brushes can have similar effects as backgrounds but are applied on top of the figures. These can be paper textures, distressing textures, or just about anything else you can think of. The texture should enhance the rendering, not distract. Textural overlays require the use of blending modes and/or opacity reduction to work. Settings for texture brushes change on a case-by-case basis.

STUDIO Companion Videos for Chapter 10

Please refer to STUDIO for accompanying chapter video(s).

Keywords

Outpainting
Pixelated
Vignette

Review Questions

1. How do you ground a figure in a scenic background?
2. Name at least three different ways you can adjust a background to make it less distracting or blend better with your figure.
3. How is a texture overlay different from a background?

Commands Introduced

- Define Brush Preset

Discussion Questions

1. When is a background a distraction instead of an asset?
2. Is it better to make your own textures or buy professionally made textures?

Practice Exercises

1. Place a figure on three different backgrounds. Explain the pros and cons of each background. Which background is superior for your needs and why?

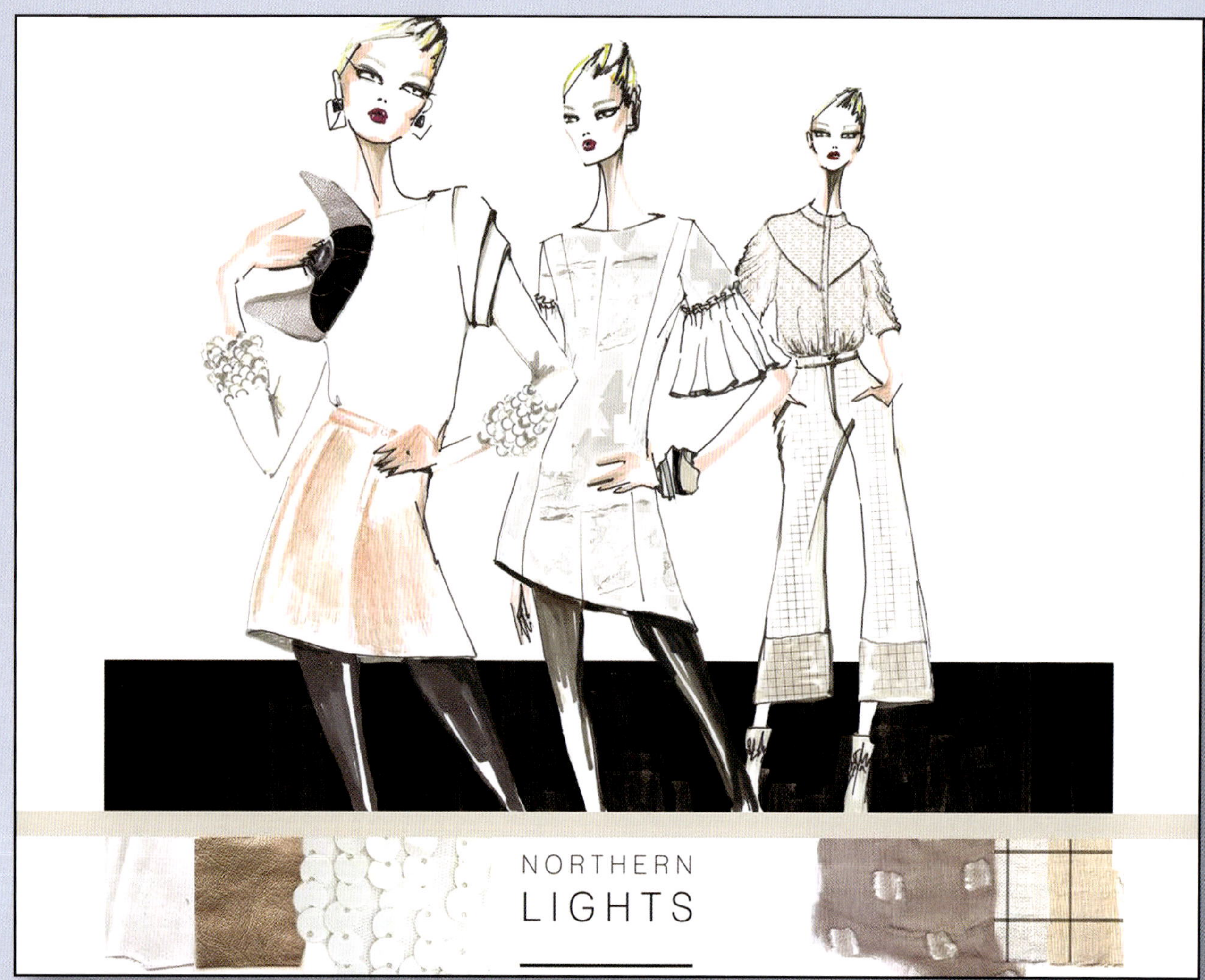

Figure 11.1 Compile your designs, fabrics, and other essential design information into a professional portfolio project. Courtesy of Ana Stoyanova. Anasotyanova.com.

CHAPTER 11
Putting it All Together

Learning Objectives

After completing this chapter, you should be able to

- Apply Photoshop tools for creating compiled layout projects
- Apply Illustrator tools for creating compiled layout projects
- Apply InDesign tools for creating compiled layout projects
- Evaluate the best saving method for your choice of publishing

Once you gather your digital files of figures, backgrounds, fabrics, and inspiration, you can pull them together into a project. In this chapter we will compile everything into one file. We will show how to use Photoshop and Illustrator for compiling your layout, but InDesign excels here. If you have not used InDesign before, get ready for a fun experience!

Project 11.1: Photoshop Layout

Although Adobe Photoshop can be used for multi-page layouts, it is best for single pages or for creating and/or editing components of a layout. Because of the size of Photoshop files, it is often better to place linked Photoshop files into an InDesign document or, if the Photoshop files are small, into an Illustrator document. This helps the software (and your computer) manage the file size and the computer resources needed to process the layout file.

If you decide to proceed with a multi-page Photoshop layout, make sure to save your document often. Due to the file size and memory requirements, the file is more likely to crash your computer. It can be very frustrating when you lose your work, so just make sure you do not lose much by saving frequently.

Artboards

Artboards, or separate pages within one file, are now available in Photoshop. However, they are more challenging to manipulate in Photoshop than in Illustrator or InDesign. Artboards in Photoshop are currently designed to create multiple phone/mobile device app screens. They are not meant to handle multiple large print pages due to the generally large file size of Ps documents.

To use artboards in Photoshop, it is best to instigate artboards from the document creation. Artboards can be added after initial document creation, but it seems to eliminate any artwork on your initial document upon switching to artboard mode. To start a document with artboards, look for the *Artboards* checkbox in the *New Document* dialog box. Make sure to check this box as seen in Figure 11.2.

A document that has artboards enabled will have "Artboard 1" labeled over the first page. To add more artboards, use the *Artboard* tool. It will be under the *Move* tool at the top of your toolbox. With the *Artboard* tool, *click* to one side of the existing artboard and drag out a new artboard. Once you have a new artboard, you can specify its size through the *Properties* panel while you are still in the *Artboard* tool. You can also click the original artboard and adjust its size.

Another way to add artboards is to first *click* the artboard with the *Move* tool, then switch to the *Artboard* tool. Upon switching tools, you will notice that plus symbols inside circles appear outside the artboard as seen in Figure 11.3. If you *click* on the symbols, a new artboard blank will be generated. If you hold the *alt/option* keys and *click* on the symbols, a duplicate of the artboard with any artwork will be made.

To delete an artboard, click on the board with the *Move* tool to select it. Then click *Backspace* or *Delete* on the keyboard.

Placing Files

While in Photoshop, you can place many different file types including other Ps documents, Ai documents, JPEGs, PNGs, and so on. When placing files in Photoshop, you must choose whether you want to place your files as linked or embedded files. Remember from Chapter 2 that linked files have the advantage that they will result in smaller file sizes in Ps and enable the software to process actions more quickly. Additionally, they are live, meaning that any changes you make to the original file will be reflected in the Ps file you have placed them in. The disadvantage is that the host file (the file you placed it into) must always "know" where the original file is located. If you move

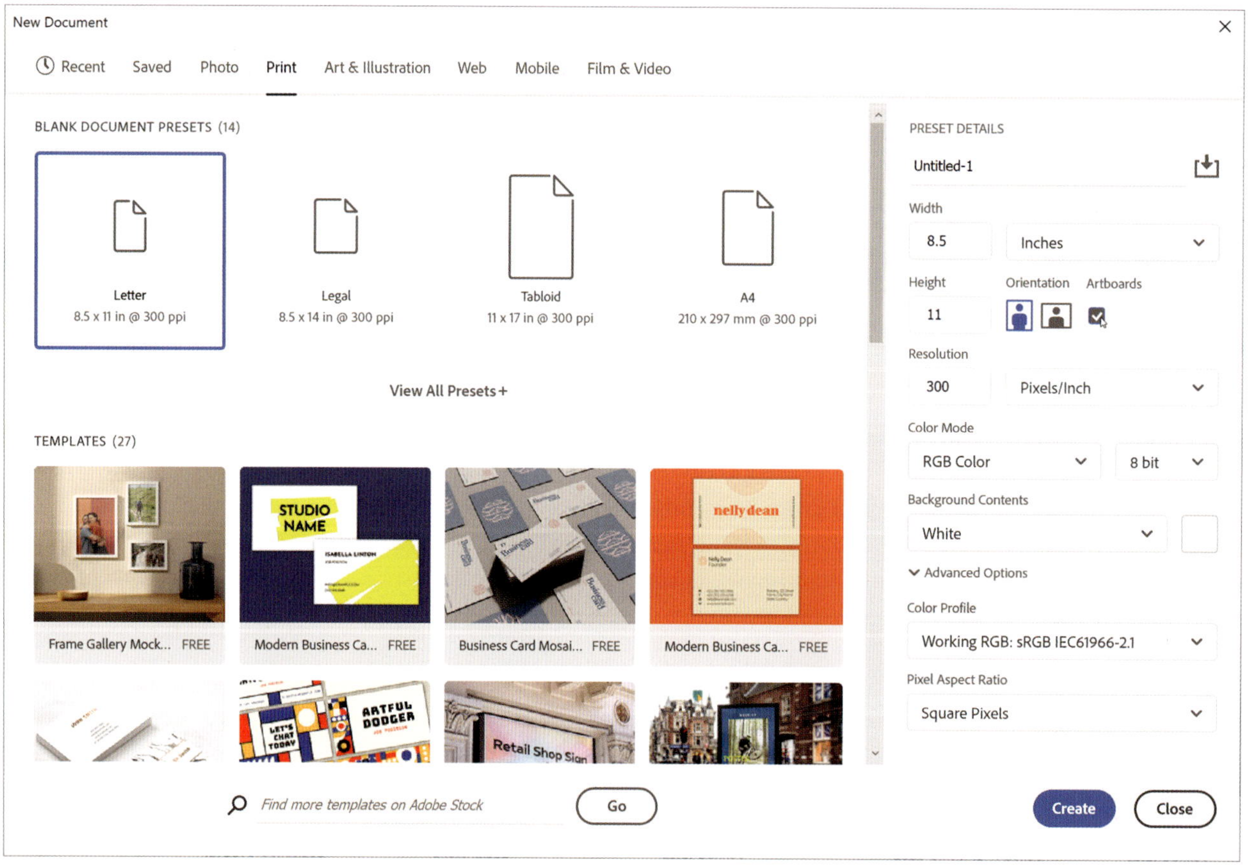

Figure 11.2 Screenshot of *New Document* window in Photoshop. Notice the tiny checkbox for *Artboards* on the right side, next to the *Orientation* choices.

Figure 11.3 An active artboard in Photoshop will be labeled "Artboard" above the page. To add more artboards, you can select the board with the *Move* tool, then switch to the *Artboard* tool. This will trigger a series of plus symbols in circles to appear around the board. These can be used to create new artboards.

the original file or if you send the host file to someone without the linked file, there will be an error.

Embedded files have essentially the opposite advantages and disadvantages. They are permanently located inside the host file, so you do not have to worry about anything getting lost. However, this results in a larger file size and slower processing time. It also means that the placed version of the file is independent of the original version of the file. Subsequent changes made to the original version will not be reflected in the placed version. You choose what works best for you.

Step 1: We will create a one-page layout to try placing files. Create a new document in Photoshop. Go to the *Print* tab on the new document dialog box and choose either *Letter* or *A4*. Set *Orientation* to *Portrait*. You can leave the rest of the settings alone for this practice. Go to *File → Place Embedded* to place the background image: Background1.jpg. *Click* once on the page to place it. When a placed image comes in, it will have a blue "X" across it as well as its normal bounding box. Resize and move your image into place. In this case, we will slightly stretch our background to fit the entire page.[1] When you are finished manipulating the image, click *Enter/Return* on the keyboard.

Step 2: Next, we will place a linked file. Go to *File → Place Linked* and choose SportyFigure1.psd. Again, the image will come in ready to be resized and moved around on the page. We will make our figure a little smaller and recenter her on the page, but you can decide what you want to do. Press *Enter/Return* once your figure is placed where you want her.

Once we have the two images placed, look in the *Layers* panel. Notice that there are tiny icons on the thumbnails and that the icons are different. The background, which was embedded, has a page icon. The figure, which was linked, has a chain icon, as can be seen in Figure 11.4.

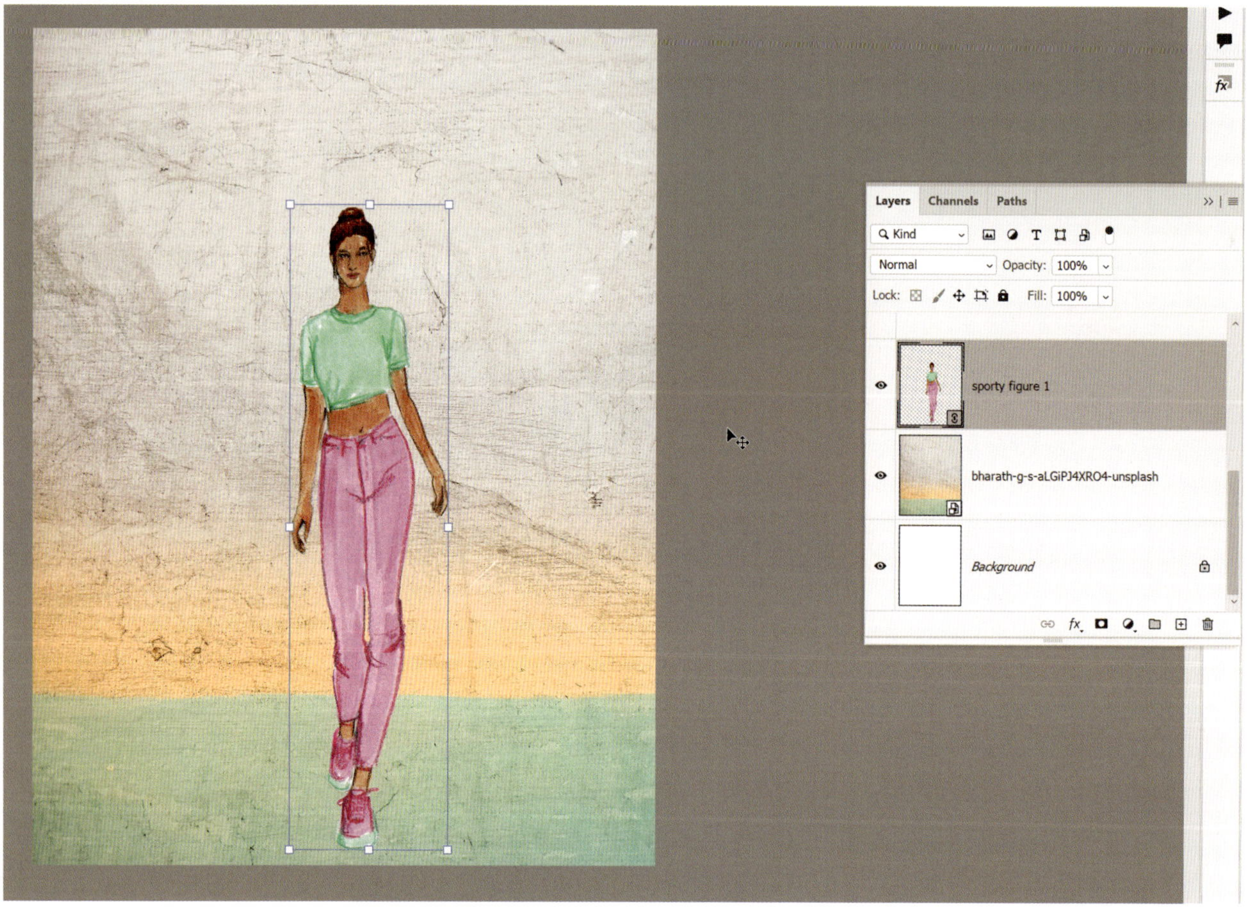

Figure 11.4 The *Layers* panel shows one image that has been placed as an embedded file (the background) and one image that has been placed as a linked file (the figure). Notice in the *Layers* panel, the thumbnail of the figure has a tiny icon of a chain in the bottom right corner while the thumbnail of the background has a tiny icon of a page in the bottom right corner. These indicate whether a file is embedded or linked.

Step 3: So, you can see the benefit of a linked file, let's change the color of the original. In the *Layers* panel, *double-click* the thumbnail of the linked figure layer. It will open a new window with the linked file. Change the color of one area like the t-shirt. In our example shown in Figure 11.5a, we used a *Hue/Saturation Adjustment Layer* to make the t-shirt blue. *Save* the file.

When you click back over to your layout file, the figure should automatically update to the new color. If for some reason it does not, *right-click* on the layer and select *Update Modified Content*. Figure 11.5b shows the updated layout.

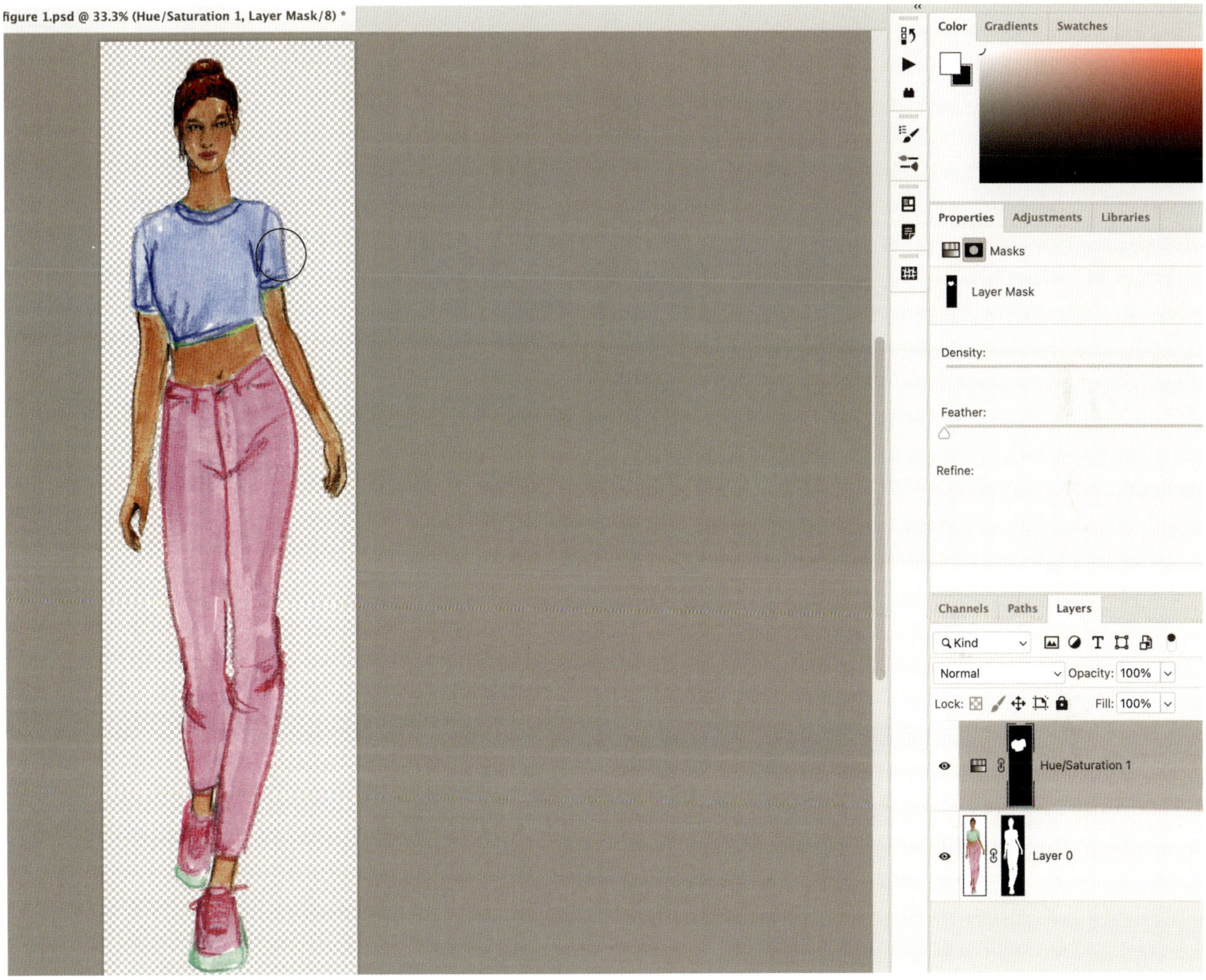

Figure 11.5a After *double-clicking* the layer thumbnail of the linked figure in your layout file, Ps will open the linked file in a new window. You can make any adjustments and save the file.

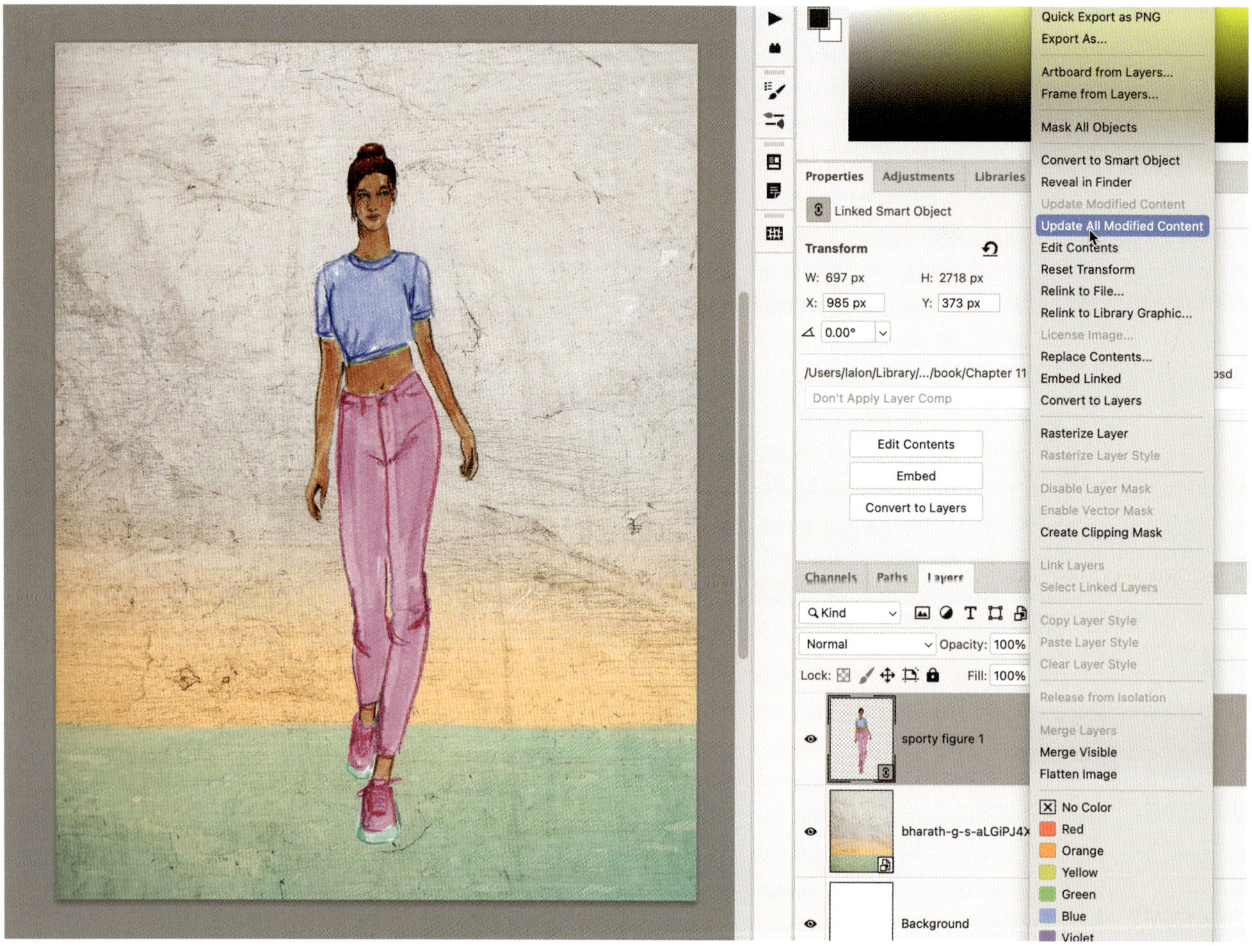

Figure 11.5b The layout file should automatically update. If it does not, *right-click* on the layer and choose *Update All Modified Content*.

Text

In layouts, we often need to add text, whether it is a title, description, or other information. To add text to a Photoshop page, get the *Type* tool from the toolbox and *click* on the page. Then start typing. The type will be in your foreground color and will either be in a default font and size, or your last used, depending on your recent actions.

To change the text properties, make sure you are on the same layer as the text. Then use the *Text* tool to highlight/select your text. Once the text is selected, you can change it through the *Options* toolbar, the *Properties* panel as shown in Figure 11.6, or the *Character* and *Paragraph* panels.

One of the benefits of Ps is the layer styles. You can *double-click* on your text layer and choose from a bevy of interesting layer styles such as *Drop Shadow*, *Emboss*, or *Outer Glow* as seen in the options box in Figure 11.7.

Also consider that you may add a texture layer to your text in the way described in Chapter 10. Only use these options if they enhance and match your layout style. Adding effects for the sake of the effect tends to distract from your design communication. However, it is good to note that the options are there if the occasion calls for it!

Project 11.2: Illustrator Layout

Adobe Illustrator is good for layouts, particularly if the files you want to display are all (or mostly) vector files, although that is not to say that it cannot handle PSDs, JPEGs, or other pixel-based file types. Illustrator permits you to have multiple pages and to specify your page sizes. Let's create a practice layout project to learn some of the key processes.

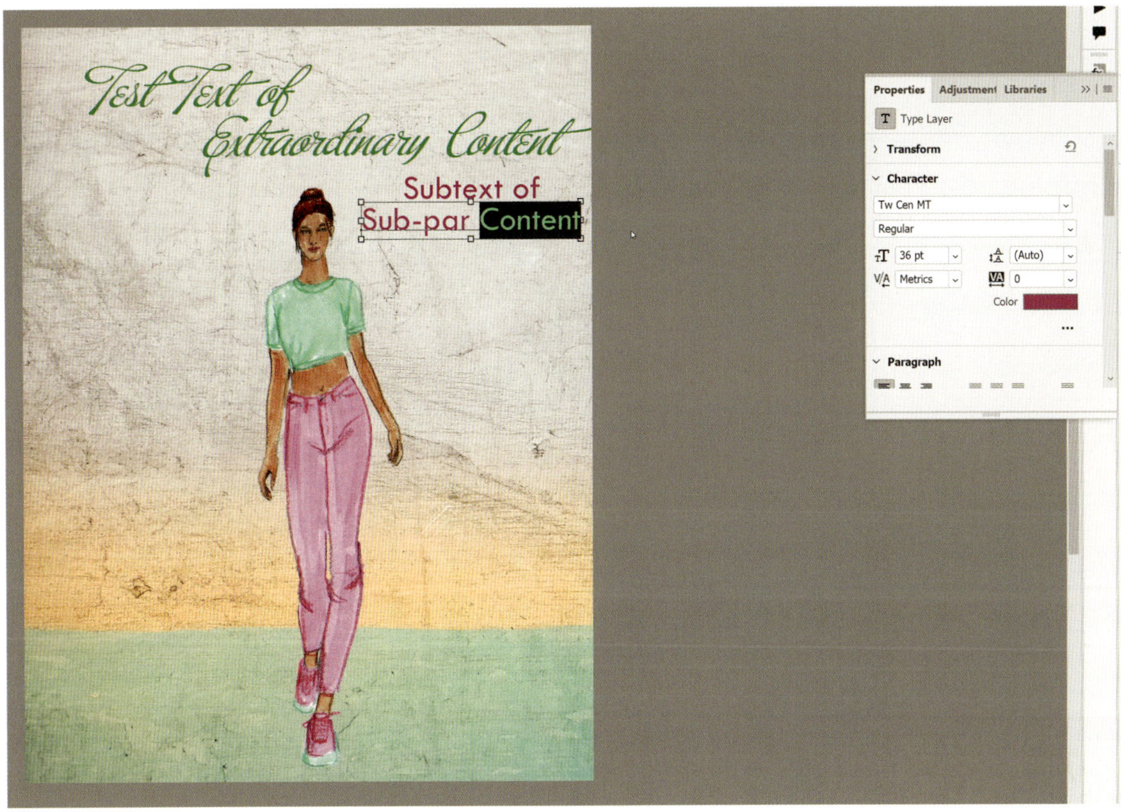

Figure 11.6 Setting the character preferences through the *Properties* panel.

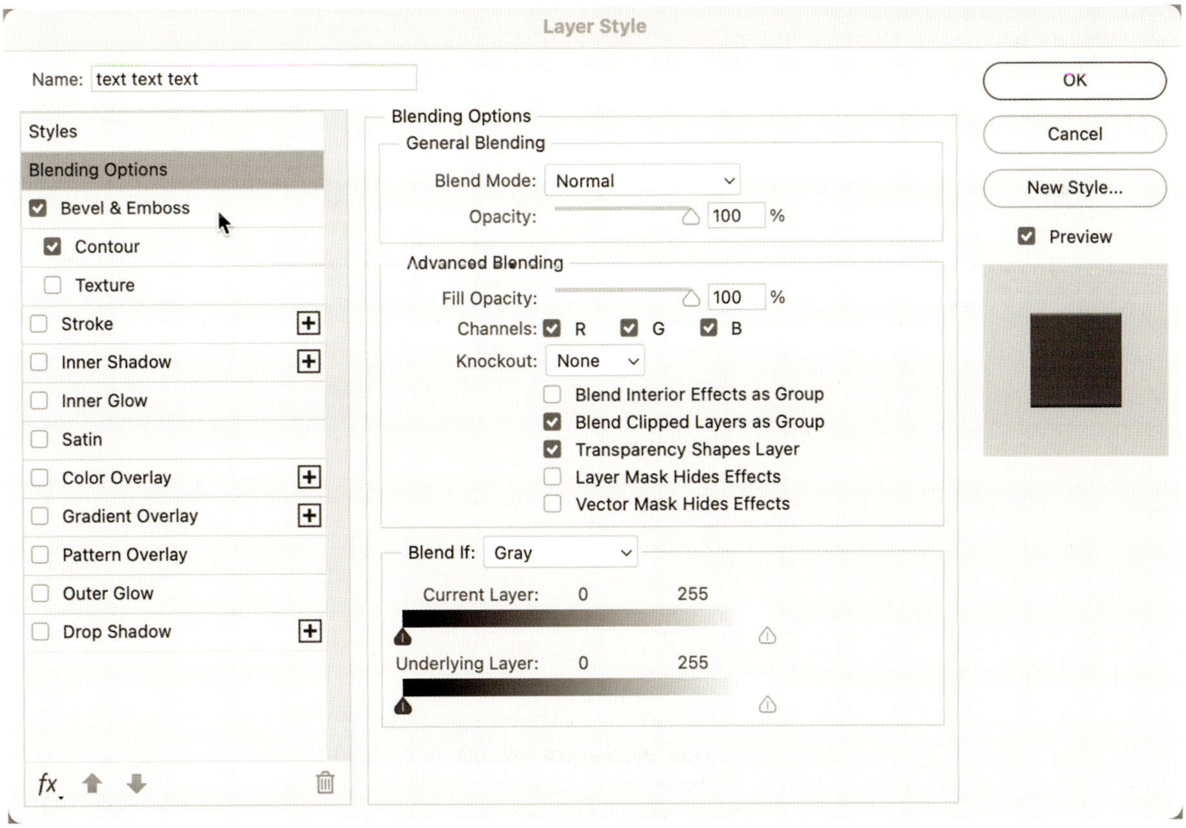

Figure 11.7 The *Layer Style* options box. Consider if a *Drop Shadow* or *Emboss* will enhance your text on your layout.

STYLE SECRETS 11.1

The Tao of Graphic Designers

If you want to create a more impactful portfolio, take a graphic design course. Learn about layout design and typography. How you present your designs is often as important as the designs themselves. We mentioned at the start of this book that good/bad design is often confused with good/bad illustration. A good layout can present your designs in a favorable light that may or may not affect others' perception of your garment design. However, a bad layout almost always becomes a distraction and certainly detracts from your garment design.

Artboards

We will create a new document and look at artboards on the new document dialog box first. Then we will look at how to add and change artboards to an existing document. Create a *New Document* in Illustrator. In this dialog box, you will see several options. Across the top, there is a menu of preset sizes, including *Print* and *Web*. If you look under *Print*, you will see both US and International size standards. Let's start with the *A4* size.

On the right, there are several settings we need to look at. First, you can name the file in the top blank. We will call this file Illust_layout_pract (or whatever you prefer). Then you will see the size of the page. The dimensions probably defaulted to points. You are welcome to switch to a different unit such as centimeters or inches, if you prefer, to check the size of your page.

Next, there are two icons that indicate the orientation of the page. Do you want the page to be *Portrait* (upright) or *Landscape* (horizontal)? We'll set ours to portrait for the practice. Last on this row is a box labeled *Artboards*. This is asking how many pages you want. Let's set this to two (2).

We'll skip over bleed.[2] However, we recommend that you look at the color mode. Because we clicked on the *Print* presets, your color mode is set to *CMYK*, which is what you would need for printing. If you are intending to publish digitally, we recommend that you switch this to *RGB*. Refer to Chapter 3 for more information on color modes.

Raster Effects are concerned with any images that are not vector-based, such as imported Photoshop or JPEG images. If you are intending to print your work, set this to *High*. If you are only publishing on the web, you can set the *Raster Effects* at *Medium* or *Low* to save file space. Leave the *Preview Mode* to *Default*. Once you have everything set, click *Create*. Figure 11.8 shows the new document window.

If you have already created your document and need to change your artboards, add an artboard, or delete an artboard, we can do that. One of the best places to control the artboards is from the *Artboards* panel. Go to *Window → Artboards* to find it. This will look a little like the *Layers* panel.

Go to the upper right corner of the panel and click the drop-down *Options* menu to look for *New Artboard* as shown in Figure 11.9. There's also a plus (+) icon at the bottom of the panel that will allow you to create a new board with one click. Create a new artboard so you have a total of three boards.

We can change the size of our artboard from here as well. Make sure artboard 3 is highlighted in the panel (click on its name once). You will see in the panel a little icon beside each artboard name that looks like a little page. Click on the icon beside artboard 3 and this should trigger the *Artboard Option* box to come up as seen in Figure 11.10. In the box, you can type in a new size, a new name for the board, and give a new orientation. This is a fast way to make changes. Change the preset for this board from *A4* to *Letter* so it no longer matches the others.

Deleting an artboard is similar to adding one. You can find the *Delete* option under the panel drop-down menu or you can click the trash can icon at the bottom of the panel. Just make sure that you have highlighted the correct artboard first, as shown in Figure 11.11. Otherwise, you can also *drag* your artboard to the trash can. Go ahead and delete artboard 3. Now we are back to two pages.

Placing Files

To put multiple images in your new layout, you will need to *Place* files into the document. Like Photoshop, there are two types of placed files in Ai: *Linked* and *Embedded*.

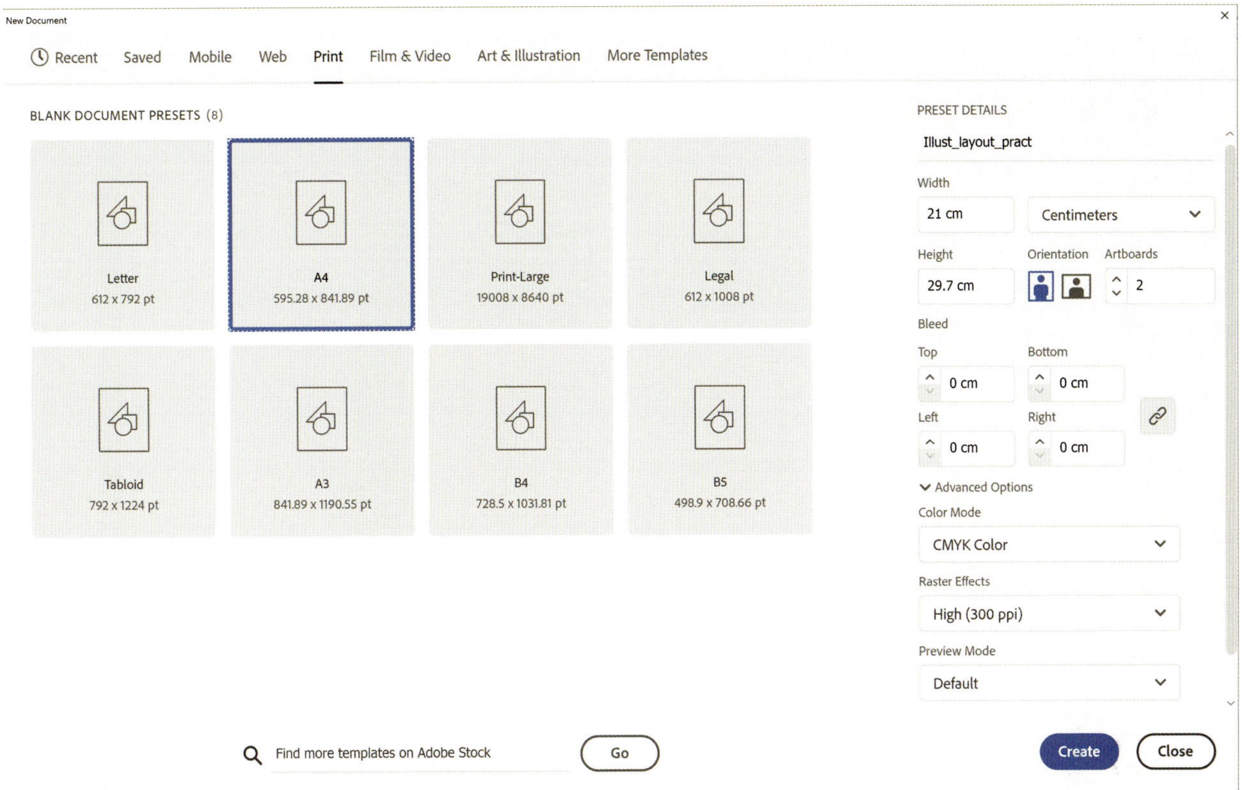

Figure 11.8 Screenshot of *New Document* window in Illustrator. For the exercise, we have selected the *A4* preset under the *Print* tab. The pages are in *Portrait* orientation, and we have entered 2 *Artboards*. The color mode defaulted to *CMYK* and raster effects defaulted to *High* when we chose a *Print* preset.

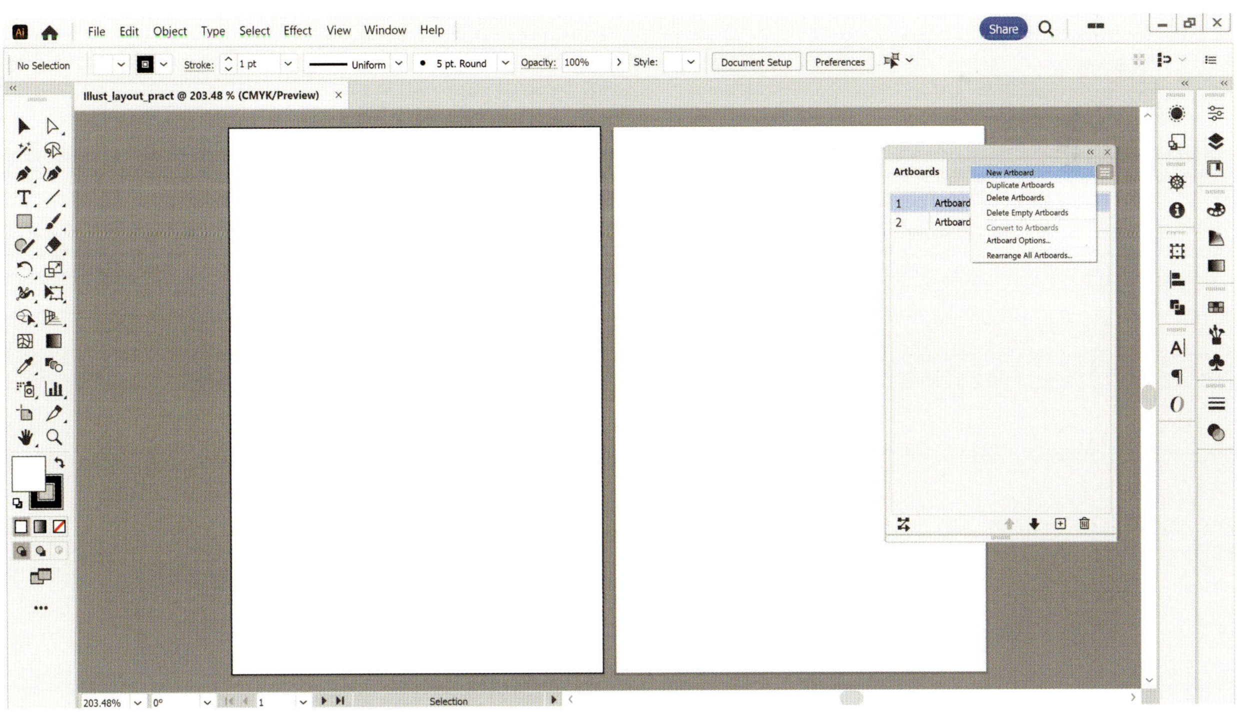

Figure 11.9 Screenshot showing the *Artboards* panel and the panel *Options* menu. *New Artboard* is currently highlighted as we are in the process of creating a third artboard. The tiny *Plus* (+) symbol at the bottom of the panel beside the trashcan icon is another way to create a new artboard.

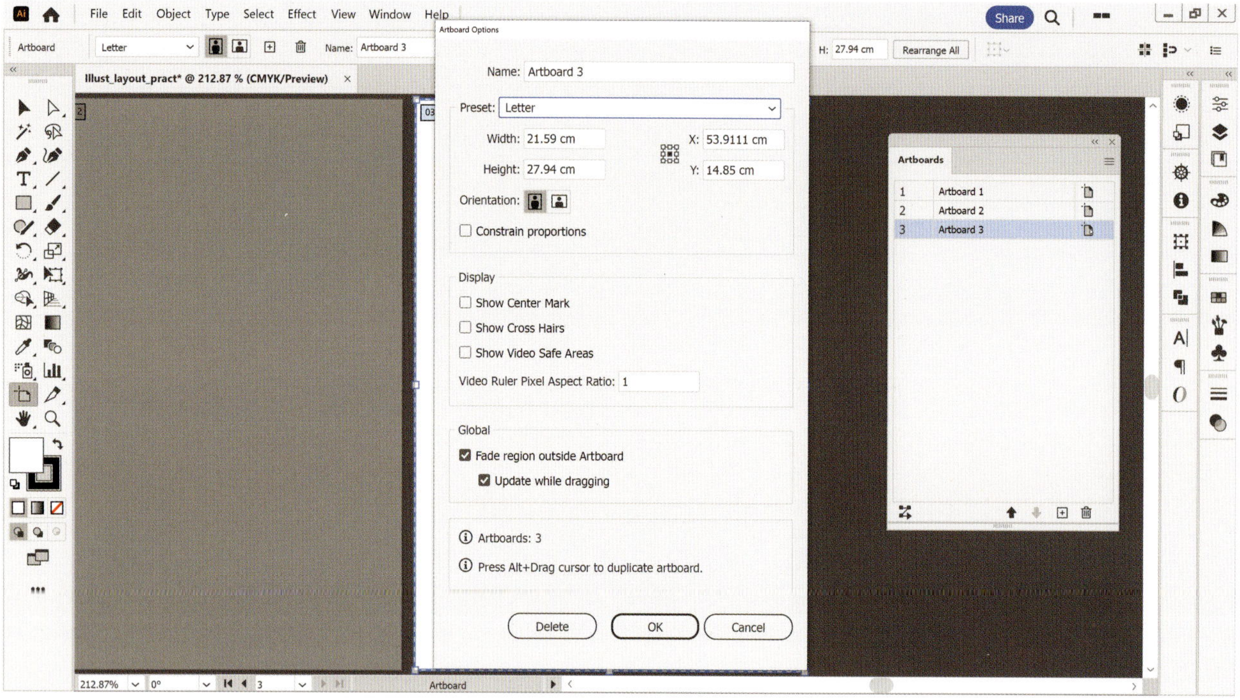

Figure 11.10 Screenshot of the *Artboard Editor*. The editor can be accessed courtesy of clicking on the tiny page icon beside the artboard's name in the *Artboard* panel or through the drop-down *Artboard Options* menu for the panel. In this view, we have changed the preset size of the third artboard to *Letter*. We can also name each artboard, prescribe custom sizes, and change the page orientation through the editor.

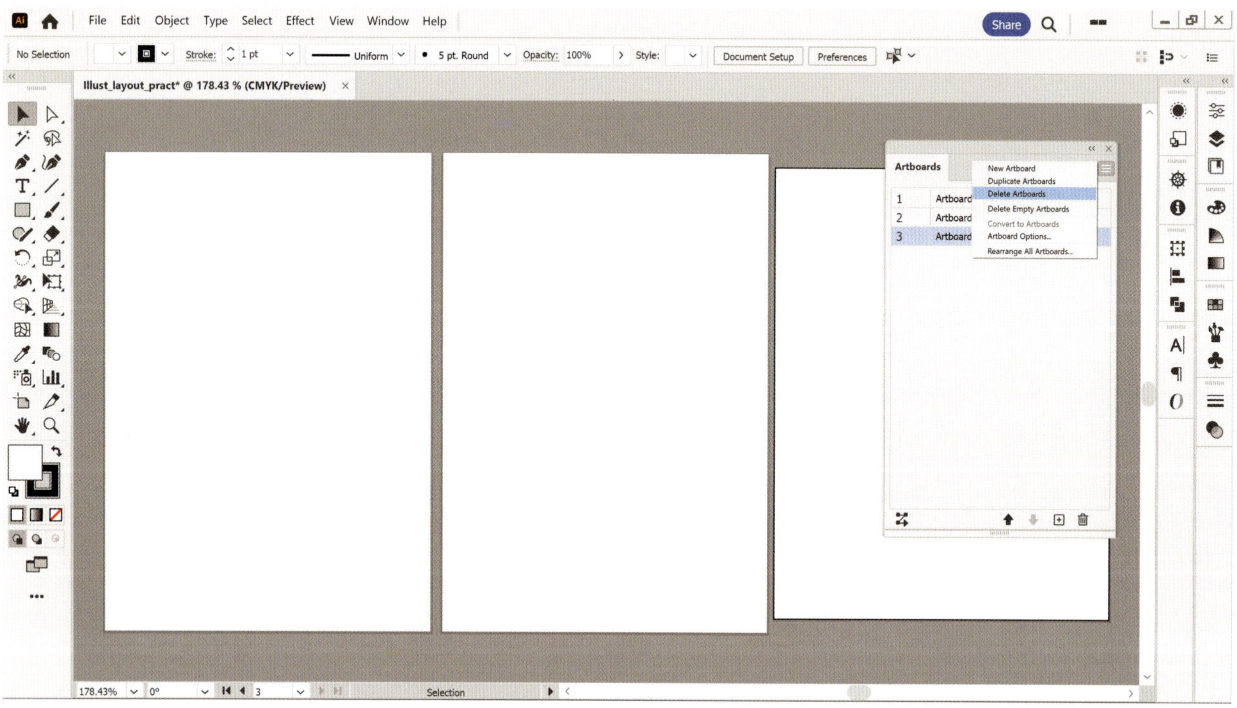

Figure 11.11 Screenshot showing the process of deleting an artboard. We have the third artboard highlighted in the *Artboards* panel, so we know that we are deleting the correct artboard. Then we can delete the artboard through the *Options* menu of the *Artboards* panel, or we can *click* the trash can icon at the bottom of the *Artboards* panel.

The pros and cons of embedding versus linking are the same regardless of the software. Whether you decide your placed files should be embedded or linked, the process of placing starts the same way.

Step 1: Go to *File* → *Place* and look for the file you wish to place. For our practice document, we will place AiFigure1.ai. Once you click *Place* on the dialog box, a cursor with a preview of your image will appear. Place the cursor where you would like the upper right corner of your image to be and *click*. Don't worry if you are not sure; you can move your image afterwards.

Step 2: Let's place our image somewhere on the first page. You will see your image surrounded by the bounding box and with a large "X" over it like in Figure 11.12. Using the *Selection* tool (*v*), you can move and resize your image. Remember to hold the *Shift* key when resizing to constrain the height to width ratio and keep from distorting the proportions.

Step 3: Once you have your image resized and moved into position, it is time to decide whether you want a linked image or an embedded image. It is currently linked. If you want to keep it that way, no further action is needed. To convert it to an embedded image, make sure you have the *Selection* tool and that the image is selected (highlighted). On the *Control* bar, you will see a button towards the left side that says *Embed*, as shown in Figure 11.13. Simply *click* the button.

Step 4: Let's try this a second time. Place the file AiFigure2.ai in the practice document. Feel free to add other elements such as a background, fabric swatches, or flats to enhance your layout.

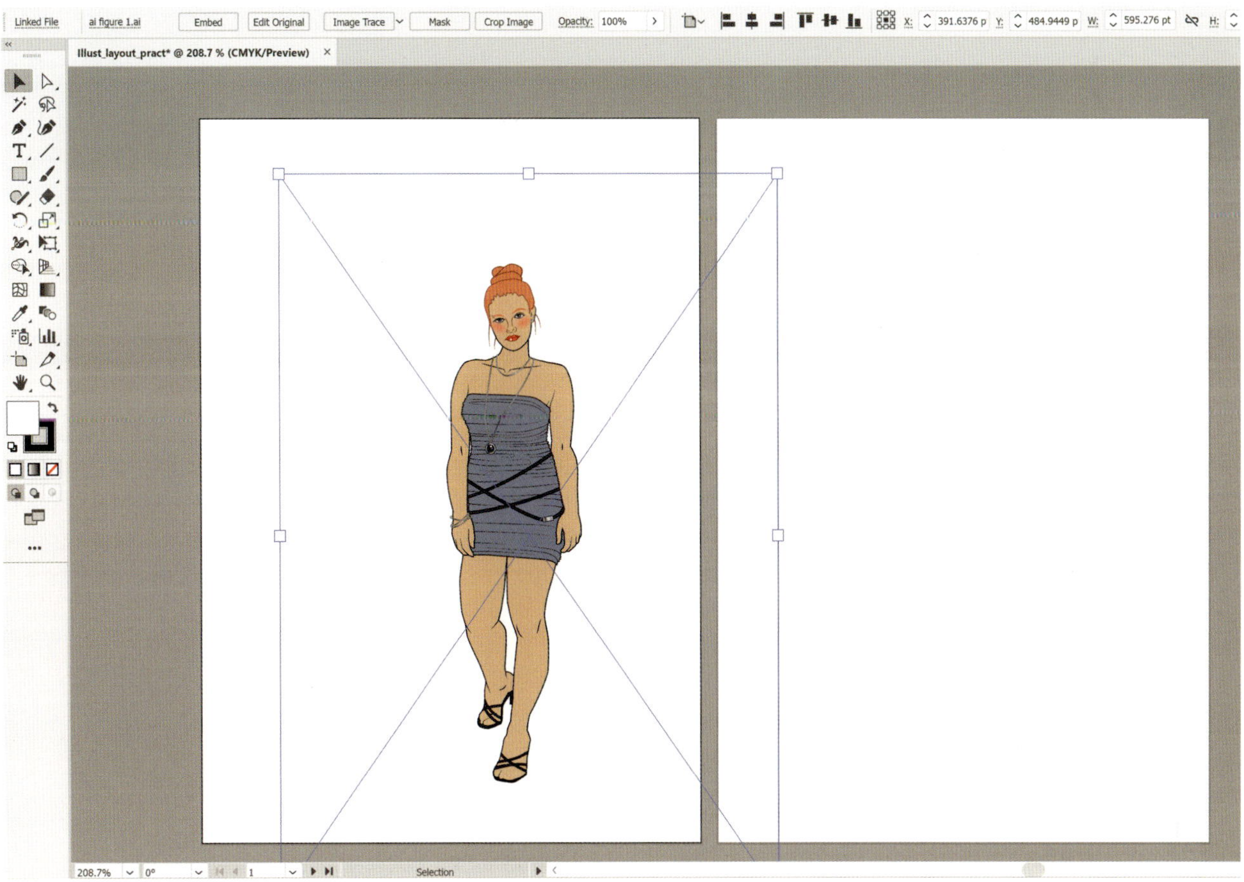

Figure 11.12 Notice the "X" across the figure. This means that placed file is linked. If you *Embed* the file, the "X" will go away.

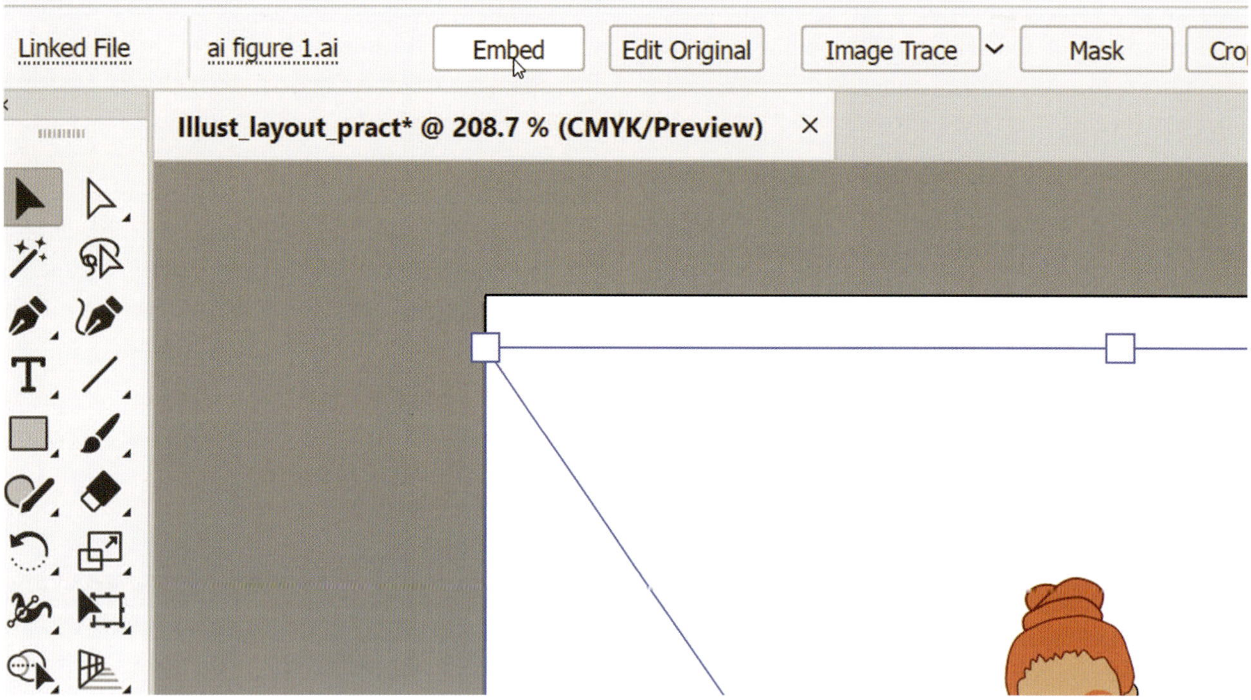

Figure 11.13 The *Embed* option can be found on the *Control* toolbar. The option can also be found in the *Links* or *Properties* panel while the image is selected.

Text

Step 1: There are a variety of text tools available in Illustrator, the most commonly used one being the *Type* tool (*t*). To add basic text, select the *Type* tool from the toolbox, then *click* on the artboard. You will see "Lorem ipsum" appear on the page. As long as the text is highlighted and you are in the *Type* tool, you can start typing your text as seen in Figure 11.14.

Step 2: To change the size, color, and format of your text, you will also need to be in the *Type* tool and have the text selected. Then go to the *Properties* panel. The first thing you will want to do is to change the size so you can see the text better. You can find text size under the *Character* section of the *Properties* panel or in the *Character* panel (found under *Type* in the *Windows* menu). The default size is 12 points. For a title on an A4 page, you will probably want around 72 points. You can choose a size from the drop-down menu, or you can type a custom size in the box.

Step 3: Font style is also found in the *Character* section of the *Properties* panel as shown in Figure 11.15. You can choose a font from the list available from Adobe, download a font from the Adobe Cloud, or install a font from a different source. Often, fonts come with different style variations, such as regular, italic, or bold. These variations can be found in the box directly below the font choice box in the *Character* section.

Step 4: Above the *Character* section in the *Properties* panel, you will find the *Appearance* section. Here, you can control the fill color as well as the stroke color and weight of the text. *Click* on the swatch beside *Fill* to change the fill color. If you want your font to have an outline, then set a stroke color and weight. You can also control the opacity of text in this section.

Step 5: You may need to change the alignment of the text. It will default to left alignment. However, if you are typing multiple lines, you may want more control. *Alignment* is in the *Paragraph* section of the *Properties* panel. You can choose from left, center, and right alignment, as well as a selection of justified alignments. Figure 11.16 shows a clean version of the project.

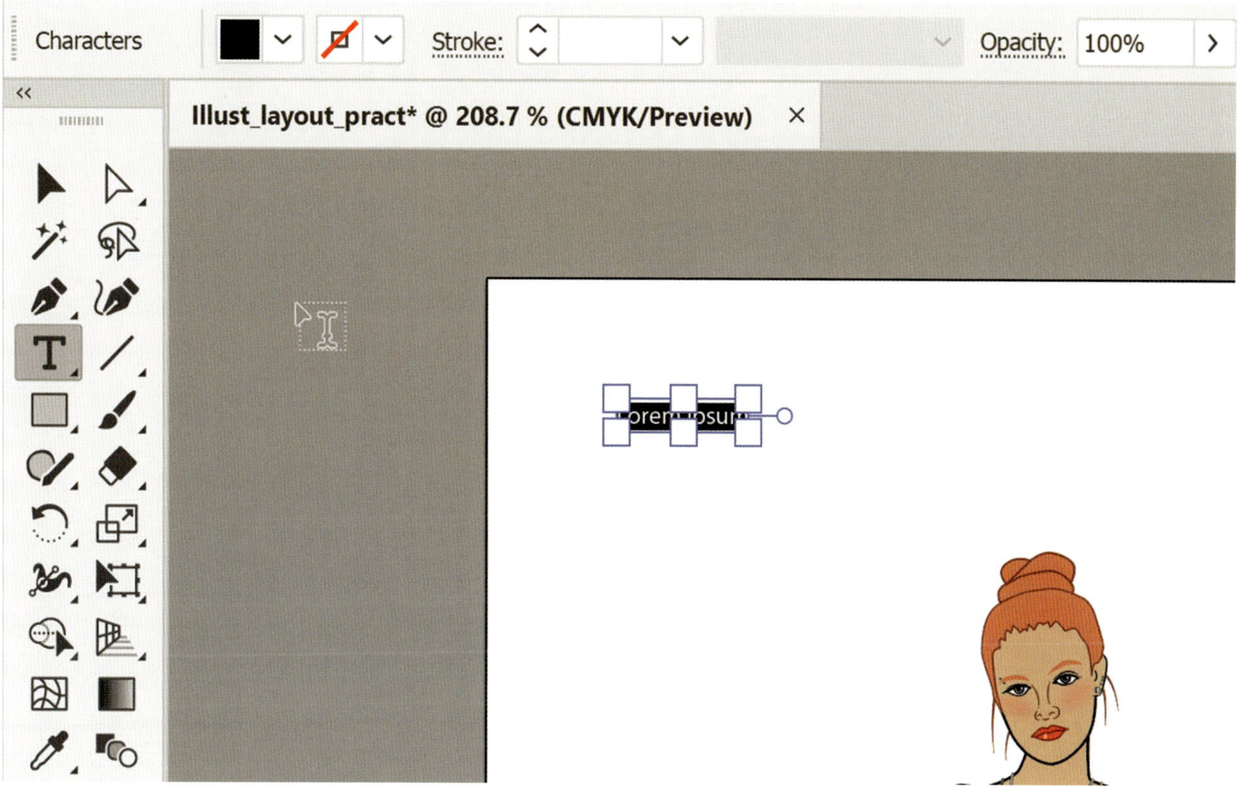

Figure 11.14 When using the *Type* tool in Illustrator, place-holder text (Lorem Ipsum) will be inserted on your page until you start typing unless you have changed this in the preferences. Once you click to start the text, you can immediately start typing.

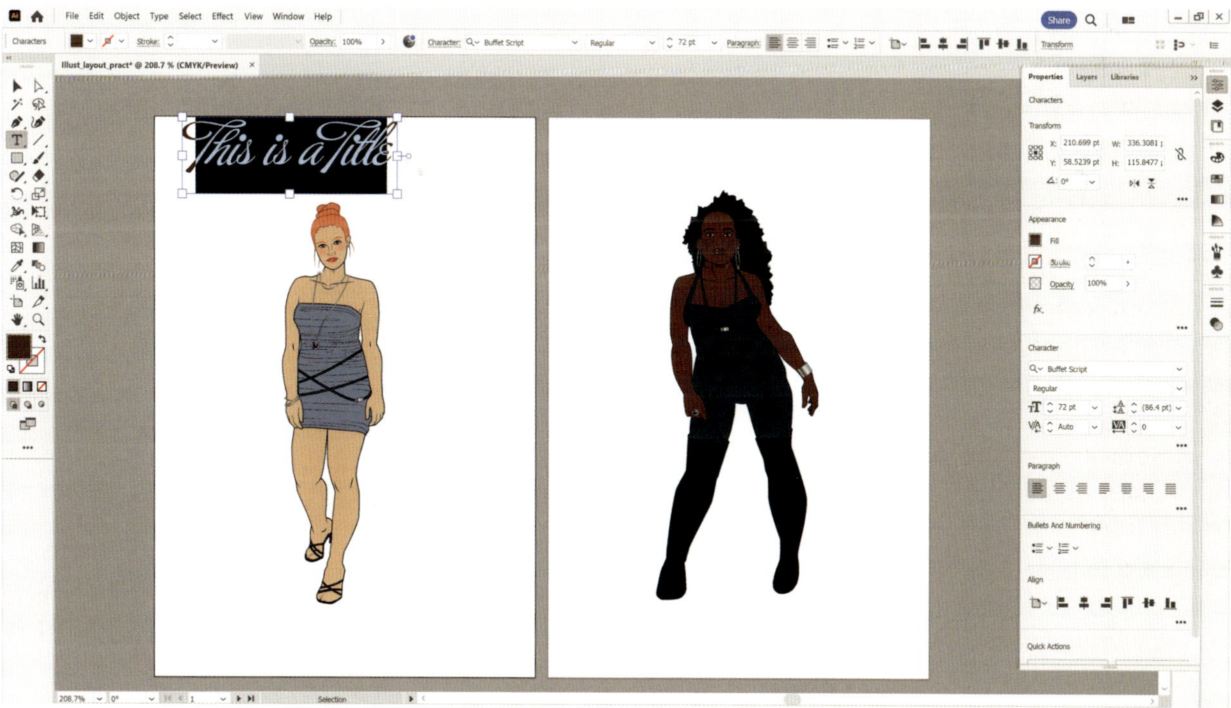

Figure 11.15 You will probably want to format your text once you type it. To do this, make sure the text is highlighted with the *Text* tool or use the keystrokes *control+a/command+a* to select all of your active text. Character, paragraph, and alignment characteristics can be found in the *Properties* panel, the *Control* toolbar, or the *Type* panels.

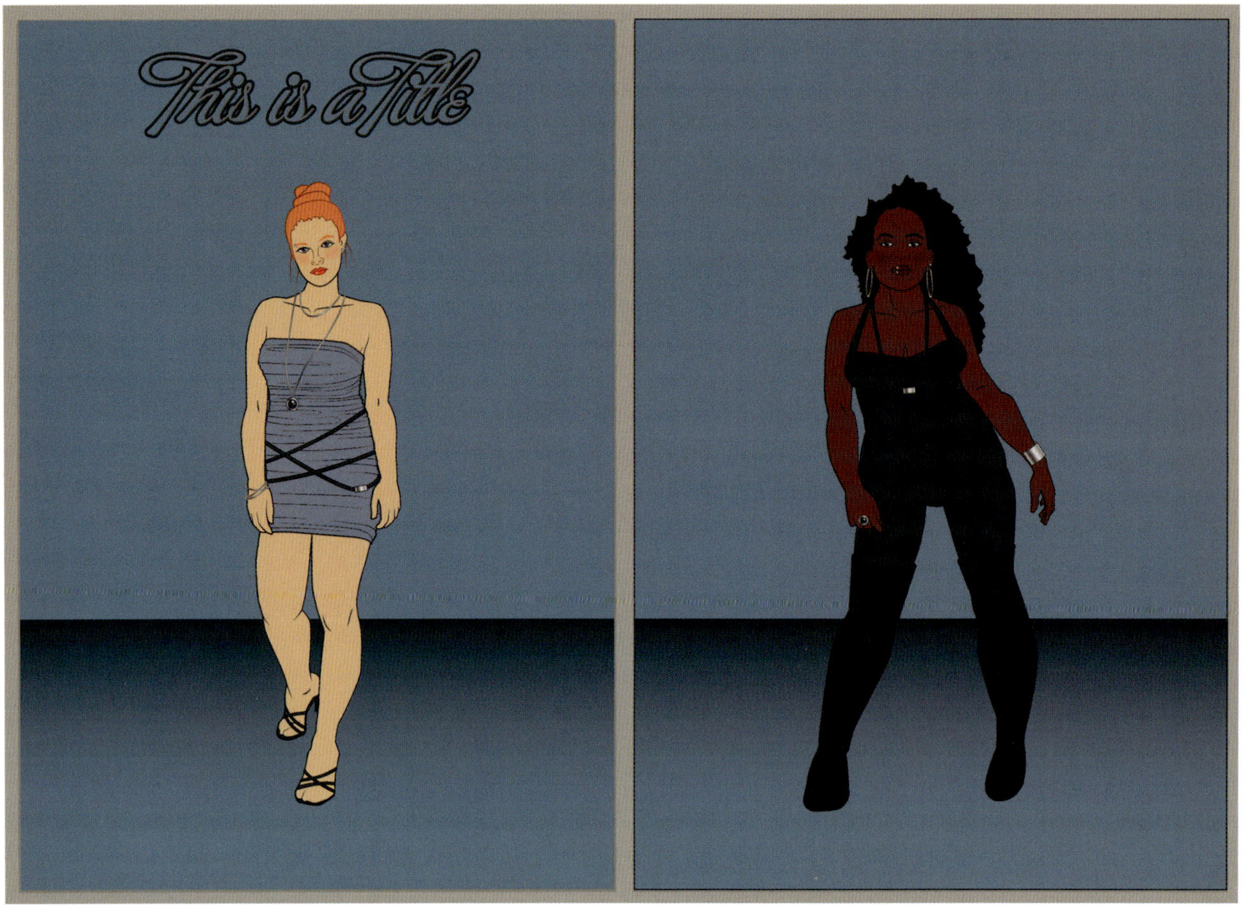

Figure 11.16 Example of the practice Illustrator layout with a few simple Illustrator elements (such as gradient-filled rectangles) added to make the layout more interesting.

STYLE SECRETS 11.2

Look at the Whole Picture

Just like analog artwork, you want to step back and look at your work from a bird's-eye perspective. Remember as you are working to occasionally zoom out to see how it looks as a whole. You may even want to zoom out so the layout is thumbnail size to see how the balance and contrast are working for you. When working on a layout, look at all the pages together. Do they look like a cohesive group? Does one page stand out from the others? It's easy to get caught in the detail work when on a digital screen. Take 5 to admire your work from afar!

In some ways, Illustrator allows for more flexibility with text than Photoshop, depending on the result you are looking for. For example, you have the ability to align your text to a path or shape area in Illustrator. Look for these tools below the standard text tool in your toolbar on the left. You can also add effects such as a *Drop Shadow* or *Artistic Effect*. Select the text layer with your *Selection* tool, then choose an effect from the *Effects* menu, or add it through the *Appearance* panel.

Project 11.3: InDesign Layout

InDesign is a page-layout application for print and digital publication. It is used by publishers to create magazine, book, and web layouts. It is also ideal for creating portfolio layouts due to its control over text and highly flexible nature when working with both Photoshop and Illustrator files.

Introduction to InDesign (Id)

Step 1: Let's learn about InDesign by creating a simple portfolio layout. After opening the application, click on *New File*. There are several items you need to be aware of in the *New File* dialog box. First, you can name your file in the blank field at the top right of the dialog box. By naming your file now, it helps prevent accidentally naming it "Untitled-1" or something similar. We will name our practice file Indd_layout_pract.

Step 2: File size dimensions are directly under the file name. You can choose which units to view the dimensions in. We recommend millimeters, centimeters, or inches if you are not familiar with picas or points. You want to set your dimensions to the true final size, rather than trying to upsize the document later. For instance, if I want to print the pages as 11 inches by 14 inches, I will set the pages as that size from the very beginning. InDesign also has a series of preset page sizes, if you look across the top of the dialog box, where the menu items say *Print*, *Web*, and *Mobile*. After you enter or choose a size, you can choose whether you want to have the pages displayed as landscape (horizontal) or portrait (vertical) orientation by clicking on the corresponding icons. For this introduction project, let's choose letter or A4 size (under the *Print* tab) and set the orientation to landscape.

Step 3: How many **pages** do you want? Pages are like artboards in the other applications. However, they are referred to as pages in InDesign. If you aren't sure, you can add or subtract pages later. However, it is good if you enter a starting guess. This will give you pages to work with upon starting the project. If you have more than one page, you will have to decide if you want your pages to face each other, like book pages, or if you want single pages, like stapled handouts. If you want facing pages, *Check* the corresponding box, otherwise, make sure the box is *unchecked*.

Step 4: Next in the section, there's a box labeled *Start #* as seen in Figure 11.17. This is a little less straightforward. In InDesign, page 1 is always a lone page, like the front cover of a book. Therefore, if you want your layout to start in a left-hand layout, as if the book were opened and you are looking at both pages, your start page is actually page 2. This does NOT affect the page count. We will ignore the checkbox for *Primary Text Frame* for the moment. For our intro project, let's set the *Pages* to 2, check *Facing*, and set *Start #* to 2. We will leave the rest of the options on default, so, click *Create*.

PRO TIP 11.1

The Importance of InDesign

InDesign is often overlooked in the fashion and costume industries but can be a valuable addition to your skillset. Don't discount it because of fear or simply because it's not often listed on job call skill lists. The software is relatively easy to learn compared with other Adobe applications. Once you get the hang of frames and where to find your tools, it makes layouts super quick and easy. It is also the best software for creating your resumé and cover letters. Take a little time now to become proficient in this excellent layout software. Your company will be grateful when you can create beautiful reports and help with marketing materials. You can even create a tech pack template in InDesign if your company does not have dedicated software for their tech packs. It's one more skillset on your resumé to make you an invaluable asset!

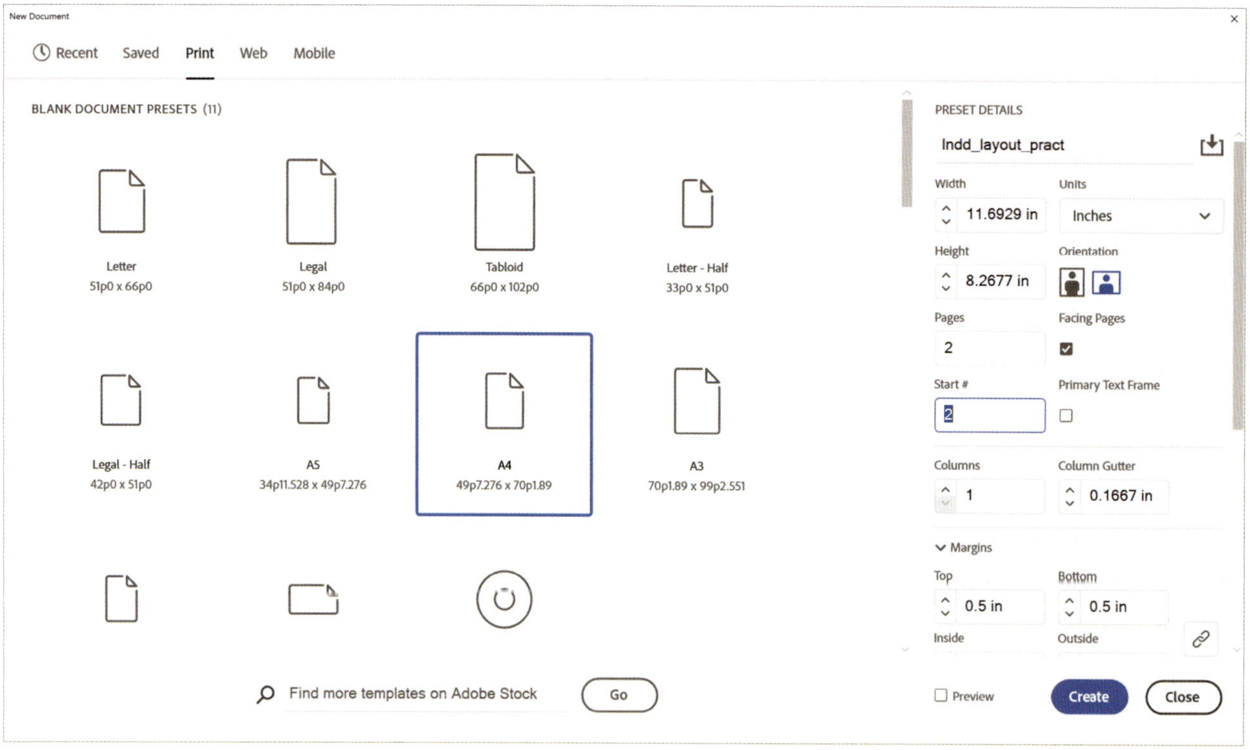

Figure 11.17 *New Document* options box for InDesign. For the practice project, we are choosing the preset for *A4* under the *Print* tab. The project name will be Indd_layout_pract and the *Orientation* is set to landscape. Set the *Pages* to 2, the *Start #* to 2, and check the box for *Facing Pages*.

Pages

When your new introduction project opens, you should see two horizontal pages butted against one another on the screen. These are your two **working pages**. Working pages are what they sound like. These are individual pages to which you add artwork. The pink and purple rectangles around the inside of the pages are the margins. The margins can be changed when setting up the initial document in the *New Document* dialog, or after creation through *File → Document Setup*.

Let's look at the pages in more detail in Figure 11.18. Open the *Pages* panel. You can find the panel by clicking on the *Window* menu and scrolling to *Pages*. The top section of the panel shows **parent pages** and the lower section shows working pages. Parent pages are master pages that allow you to add consistent elements on all the pages such as headers, footers, and backgrounds. Parent pages are not necessary for portfolio layouts with different elements on all pages. So, we will ignore the parent pages (top) section for now. The pages panel shows all the pages in your document. Your current document will show that you have a page 2 and a page 3, and that they are facing each other. There will be a tiny down-pointing arrow over the page that you are currently editing in the panel.

You can move from page to page in the panel. For instance, if the arrow is over my page 2 and I double-click on the thumbnail of page 3, I will jump to page 3 on the main screen, too. To change the order of the pages, grab the thumbnail of a page in the panel and drag it in front of or behind the thumbnail of a different page. For instance, if I grab the thumbnail of page 3, I can drag it in front of the thumbnail of page 2 and they switch positions. You may not see much of an effect unless you have added artwork to one or the other page.

To delete a page, *drag* the thumbnail of a page down to the trash can at the bottom of the pages panel. Another option is to *click* on the thumbnail of a page, then click on *Layout → Pages → Delete Pages*. Try deleting page 3.

There are a few different ways to add a page. Look at the bottom of the *Pages* panel. There is a + symbol in a square. This is the *Add Page* icon, a good way to add single pages. Another way to add pages is to look at the top right corner of the *Pages* panel. There is an icon with four horizontal lines that represents the drop-down

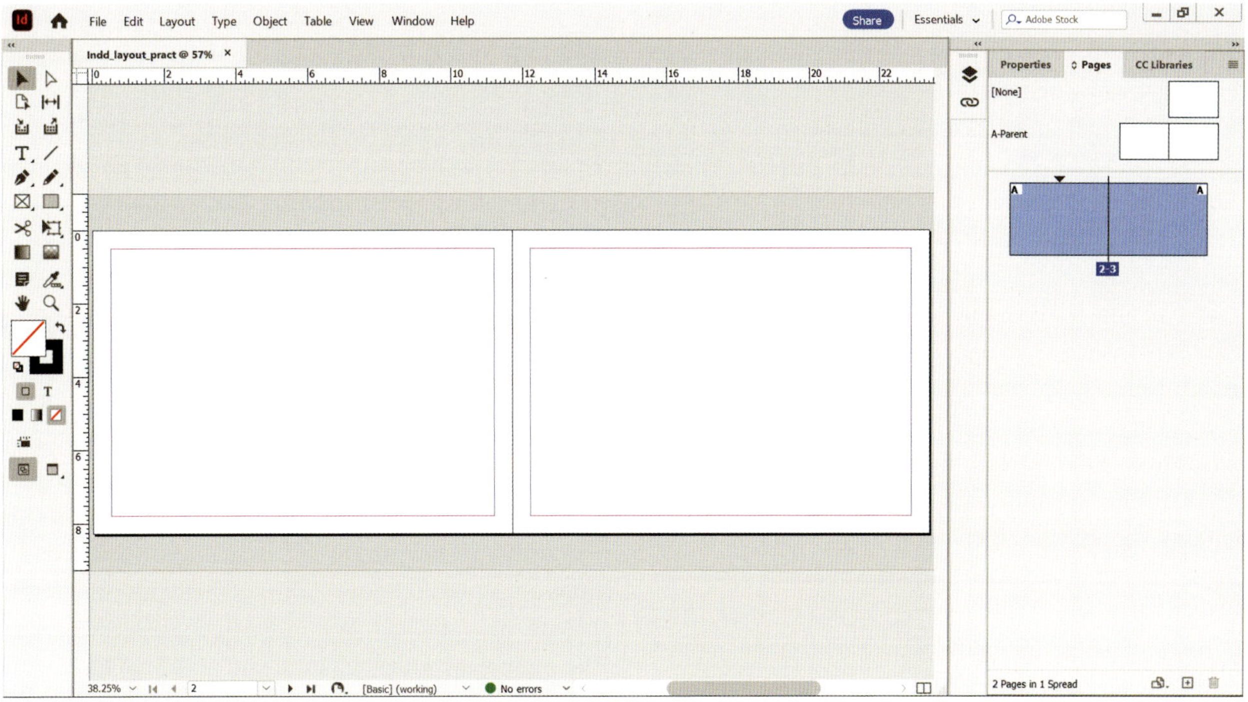

Figure 11.18 The lower section of the *Pages* panel (currently highlighted) shows the main pages for the document in thumbnail format. The tiny downward pointing arrow over a page indicates which page you are working on.

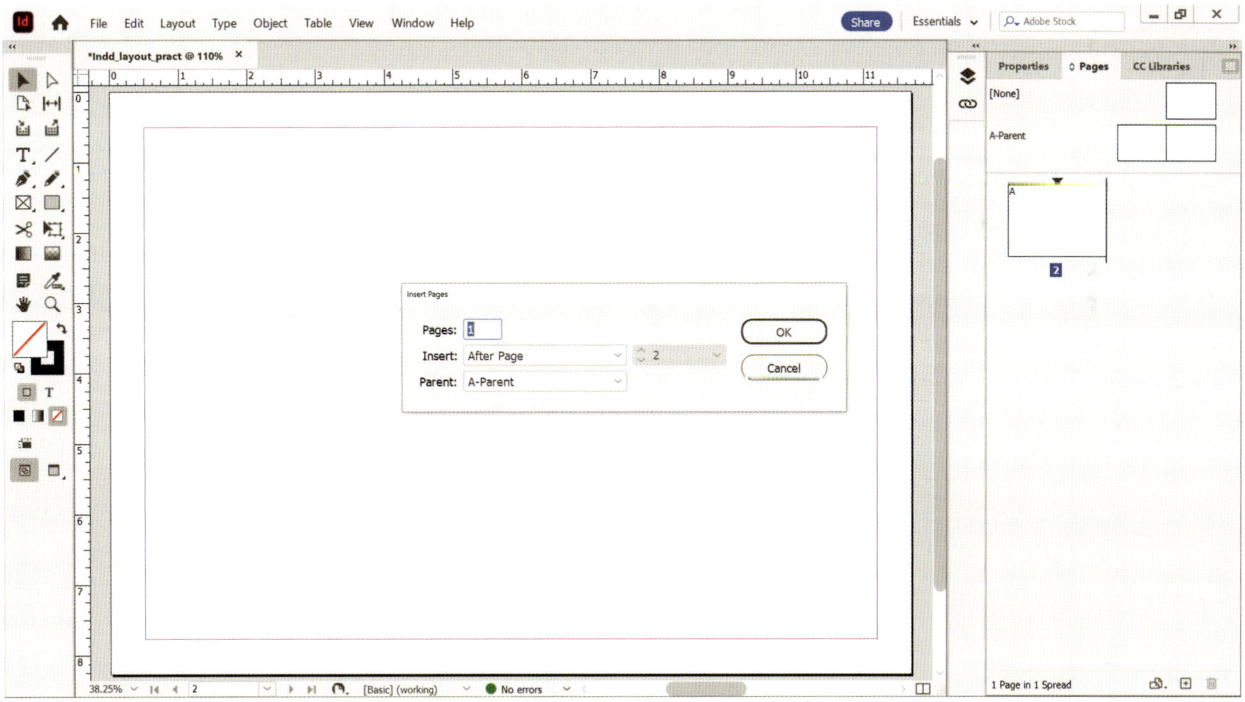

Figure 11.19 Page 3 has been deleted and as indicated in the options box in the middle of the screen, we are in the process of adding a page to the layout. We can control how many pages to add as well as where in the layout to add the pages.

Options menu. If you click this button, a dialog box pops up that allows you to choose how many pages to add and to specify where to add them. If you deleted page 3, try adding it back as shown in Figure 11.19.

Placing and Frames

InDesign does NOT like cut and paste to add elements. We are all tempted to work like that due to developed habits in other software. Get out of the habit while in InDesign. You will not like the results and will end up very frustrated when glitches constantly occur. Instead, we must create **frames**, then place objects in the frames. Frames are digital containers that can show and block parts of placed images or other objects.

There are three types of frames that you will commonly use in InDesign: the **basic frame**, the **text frame**, and the **basic shape**. A basic frame is a container. It holds files such as images. The text frame does what it sounds like; it holds text. The basic shape can hold files or text, but mostly it is used for color fills or for making a visual frame or border using strokes.

We like to explain frames as being like windows in a building. Windows can come in all different sizes and shapes, and they let you see into the building. However, a single window typically does not let you see everything in the entire building. Frames can also be made in practically any size or shape. They let you see through to the image or object they contain. Yet, like the window frame, the edges of the frame may restrict how much of the image or object is visible.

This can be confusing at first when you are trying to figure out why you don't see all the image or part of your text is missing, no matter how many times you have typed it. However, the more you work with frames, the more you are likely to enjoy the control. In time, you can learn to use frames to hide objects in images without having to edit the original image, make text flow on pages in shapes that complement your design, and, in general, create much better layouts with less work.

Frame 1: Let's start with most basic frame using a shape: the *Rectangle* tool (*m*). Draw a rectangle that fills the first page from margin to margin. To change the fill and stroke of the rectangle, it works like Illustrator. Change to the *Selection* tool (*v*) and make sure the rectangle is still selected. Go to the *Properties* panel and look for the *Fill* section. *Click* on the fill swatch and the fill dialog pops up. You can choose a fill via a swatch, a color on the palette, or a gradient. You can change stroke properties the same way, with the additional ability to change the stroke weight and type. Basic shapes are good ways to create a background behind objects or for a whole page. For our project, make sure your rectangle has a fill like the one seen in Figure 11.20.

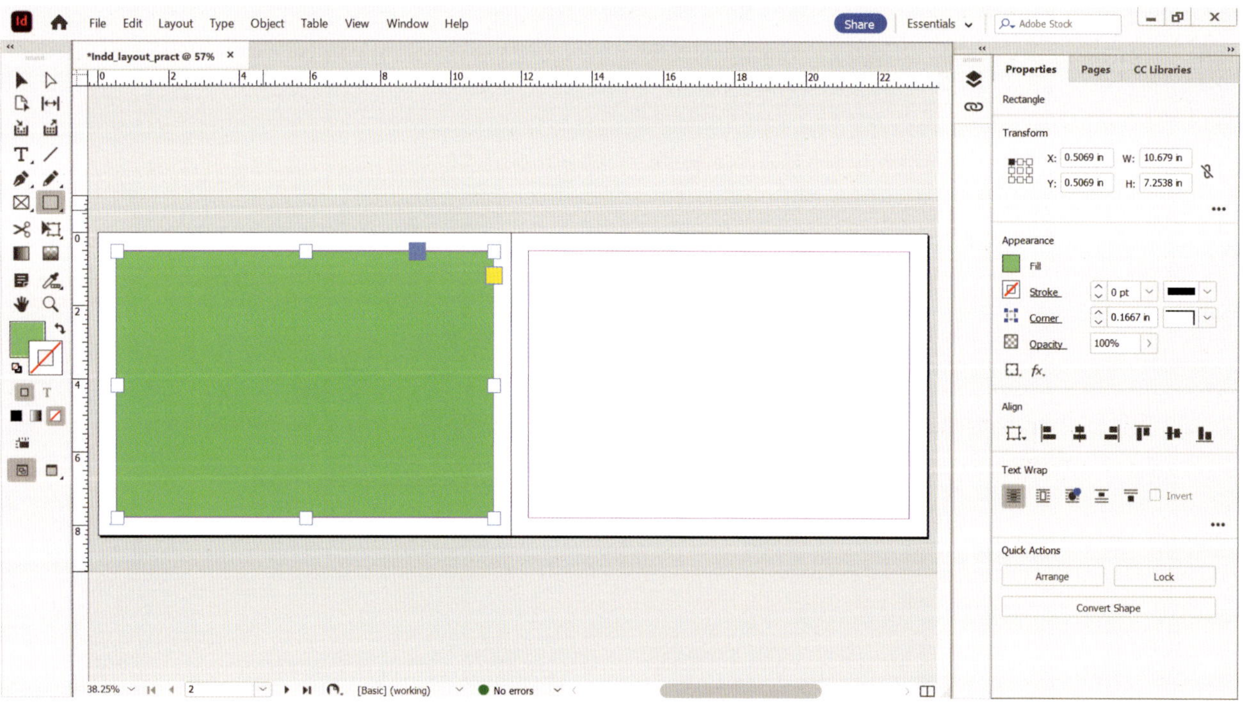

Figure 11.20 The rectangle has a fill, but no stroke. Shapes, such as rectangles can be used as frames, backgrounds, or color accents.

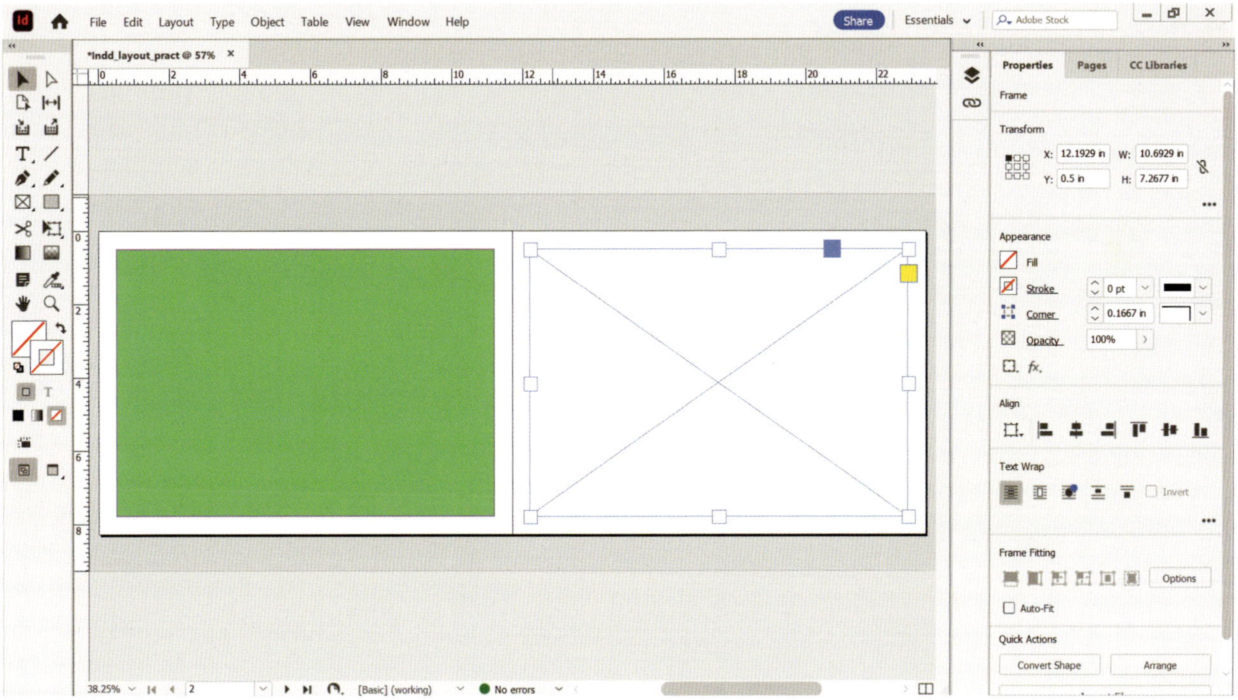

Figure 11.21 Screenshot showing an empty frame on the second page. This was drawn with the *Rectangle Frame* tool (*f*) and is intended to hold images.

Frame 2, Step 1: Now let's explore the basic frame. We will use the *Rectangular Frame* tool (*f*). Using the tool, draw a rectangle from margin corner to opposite margin corner on the second page. It will look like the basic rectangle shape, except there will be a big "X" across the frame as seen in Figure 11.21. This means that the frame is currently empty. Switch to the *Selection* tool (*v*) and make sure the frame is still selected. To fill a frame with an image, you must *Place* files into the frame. Do NOT be tempted by the paste function. Go to *File* → *Place*. Then search for the file you want to insert.

When a file is properly placed, you will see a chain icon on the top left corner of the frame as seen in Figure 11.22a. This means that what you see on the screen is linked to the original file in its original location on your computer or the cloud. This can be confusing at first. What is happening is that a representation of the file is showing in InDesign. However, the image is not a fixed part of the InDesign document. If we place an Illustrator file into an InDesign document, the Illustrator image is linked to the original Illustrator file. So, if we change something (like a color) in the original Illustrator file, then the change will also show up in the InDesign document as shown in Figure 11.22b. On the downside, if we accidentally move a file, then the link is broken, and the InDesign document will not display or print correctly.

For our project, place the file Background1.jpg. You will probably notice that the image looks pixelated and is too large for the frame. We will discuss why momentarily.

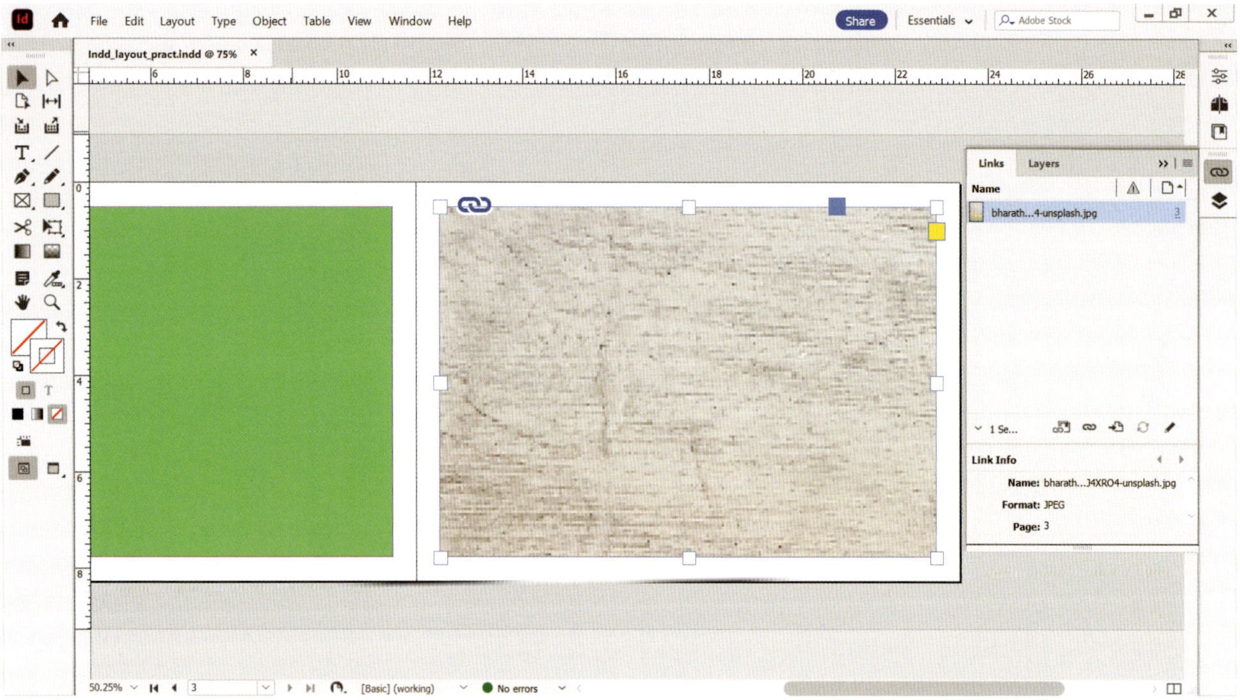

Figure 11.22a Screenshot of a placed imaged. The first screenshot shows a properly linked placed image. Notice the chain icon at the top left of the image's frame.

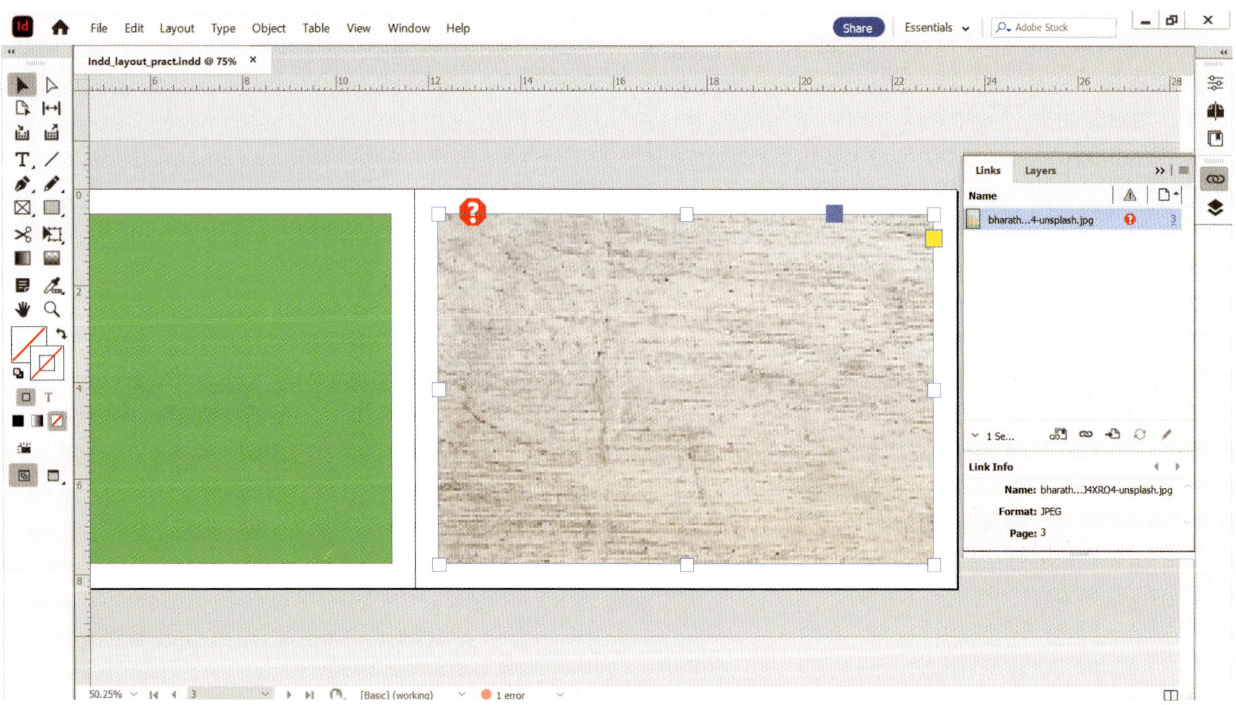

Figure 11.22b The second screenshot shows the same image, but with a broken link. There is now a question mark at the top left of the image's frame. Additionally, there is a question mark in the *Links* panel next to the name of the image. This means that the original image file has been moved, deleted, or lost since it was originally placed. The link will have to be re-established for the file to be viewed or printed correctly.

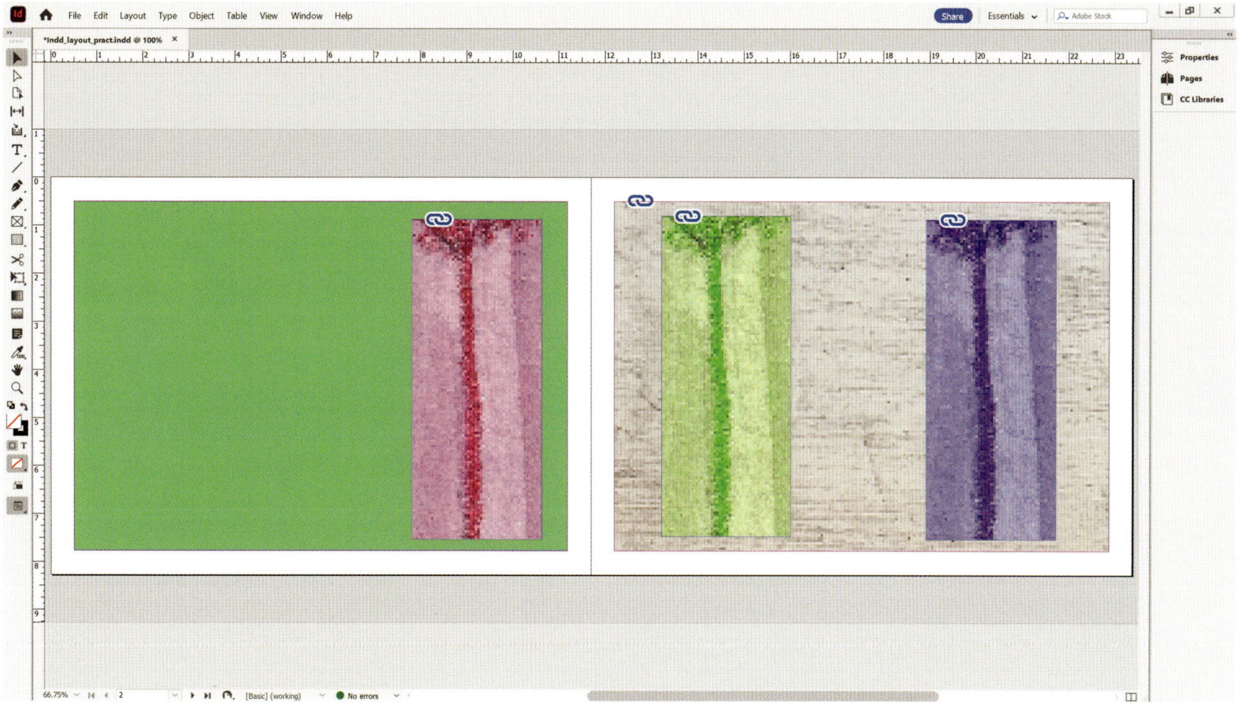

Figure 11.23 Layout with the three figure files placed in three separate frames. Notice that the figures are currently much too large for their frames. We will have to fix this.

Step 2: The basic frames are used for placing almost all files in InDesign. So, if we want to place figures from Illustrator or Photoshop, we will make a frame for each file or image on the InDesign document. Before placing files, you want to do all or most of the illustration work in whichever application(s) you are using. Make 1 frame on the first page and 2 frames on the second page of our intro project for containing figures. Switch to the *Selection* tool (*v*) and select the first frame. Place the file SportyFigure1.psd into the frame by going to *File → Place*. Repeat the steps to place the following files in the rest of the frames. Remember to select the frame first each time. Use the files SportyFigure2.psd and SportyFigure3.psd. Notice when you insert the images that, like the background image you inserted, these images are too large for the frames like in Figure 11.23.

Step 3: Often the file you place into a frame is either too large or too small for the frame. There are a few easy ways to resize the image as well as the frame using **Fitting options**. InDesign has multiple preset *Fitting* options that change the relationship of content to its frame. Let's start with resizing the image. Use the *Selection* tool to click on one of the images first. Then go to the *Object* menu and scroll down to *Fitting*. You will see several choices as shown in Figure 11.24. *Fill Frame Proportionally* will completely fill the frame with your image without distorting its height to width ratio as shown in Figure 11.25a. However, because it is completely filling the frame, part of the image may be cut off by the frame. *Fit Content Proportionally* is similar. It maintains the height to width ratio of the image, but instead of filling the entire frame, it grows or shrinks the image until one of the dimensions matches the frame. This means that the other dimension is typically smaller than the frame and some white space is left in the frame, as shown in Figure 11.25b.

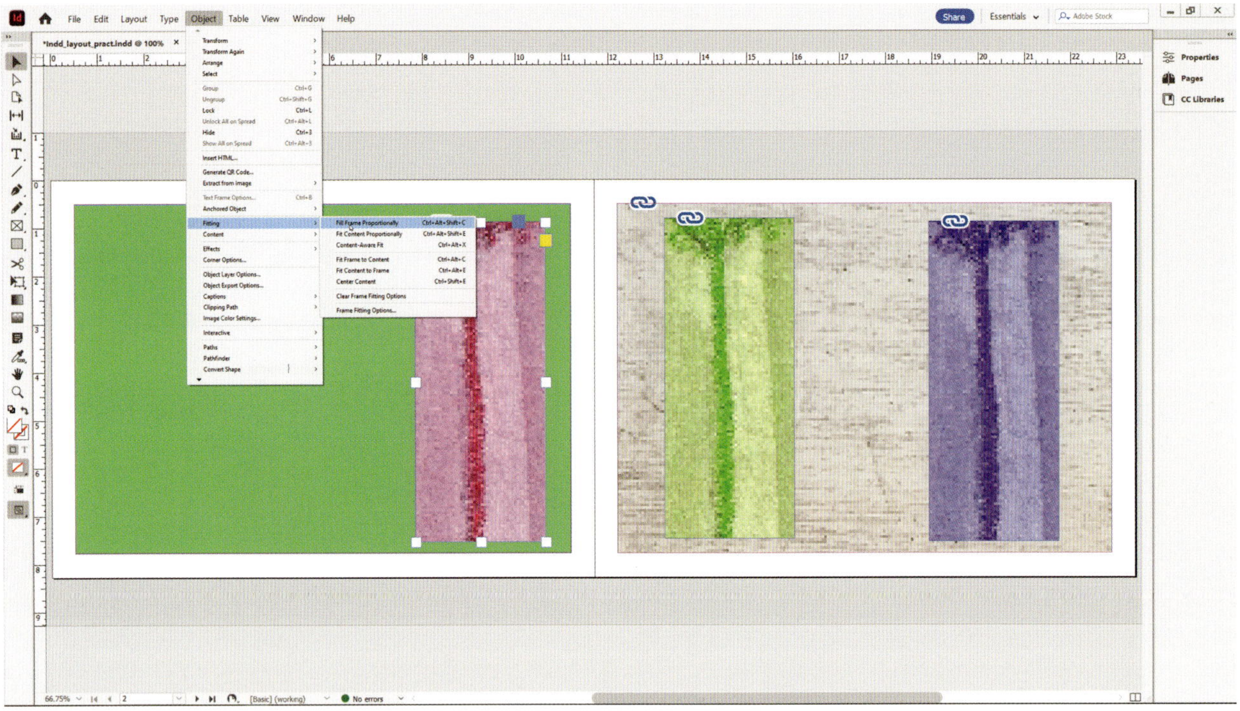

Figure 11.24 Screenshot of *Object* menu showing *Fitting* options. Select the object(s) that you want to apply the *Fitting* options to before selecting the options.

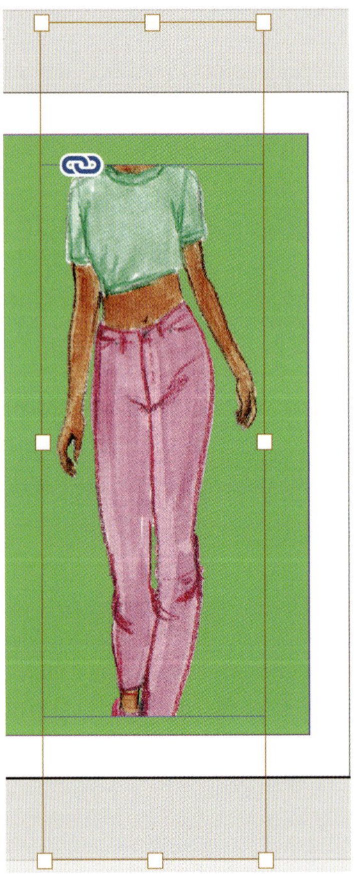

Figure 11.25a Screenshot showing *Fill Frame Proportionally*. In this case, the figure overflows the frame and the top and bottom of the model is cut off.

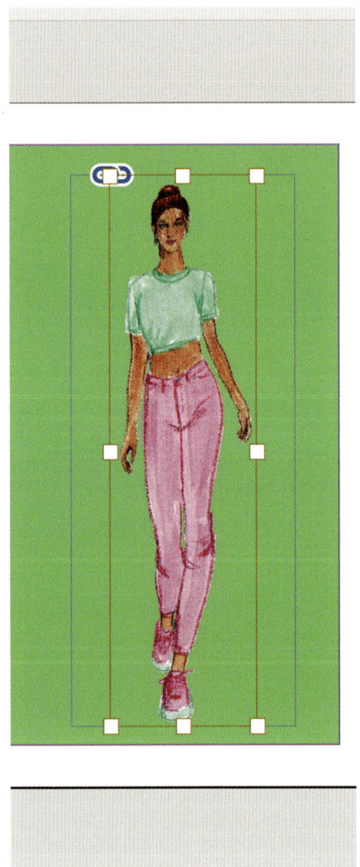

Figure 11.25b The second image shows *Fit Content Proportionally*. The figure is enlarged or shrunk until the entire figure fits within the frame, without distorting the image proportions.

If you don't care about the height to width ratio of your image (if it is abstract or textural) you can choose *Fit Content to Frame*. This option will fill the frame edge to edge with your image like in Figure 11.26a. However, it does not work well for proportional images like our figure.

Finally, if you like the size of your image and you just need to change the size of the frame, you can choose *Fit Frame to Content*. This option will snap your frame to the edges of your image without changing the image size, as shown in Figure 11.26b. Just remember that it sees the whole image size, including any white background around a figure.

Step 4: Sometimes the autofitting options do not provide the resizing options you want. Another easy way to resize an image is to use the *Selection* tool and the *Control* bar. With the *Selection* tool (*v*), make sure the frame of the object is selected. We suggest using the *Fit Frame to Content* option before resizing the image. This way you will see the entire image and the frame will be resized along with the image as you work.

Once the frame is fit to the object, look along the *Control* bar at the top. There is a series of boxes along the bar from left to right that contain numbers. The first set is the *X/Y* position of the object on the page. The second set is the actual *Width* and *Height* of the frame. This can be very useful if you know the precise size you want an image to be. You can adjust your frame as seen in Figure 11.27.

The third set is *Scale*, displayed as a percentage. This may be the easier set of controls to use initially. When you first click on your frame with the *Selection* tool, both boxes probably display *100%*. You can move

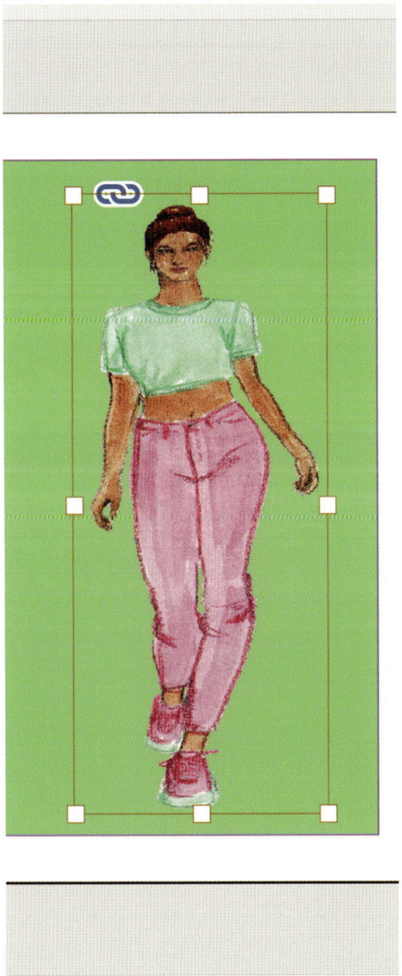

Figure 11.26a This image shows *Fit Content to Frame*. With this option, the image is enlarged or shrunk without any regard to proportion until it fills the frame in all directions. This often results in a distorted image.

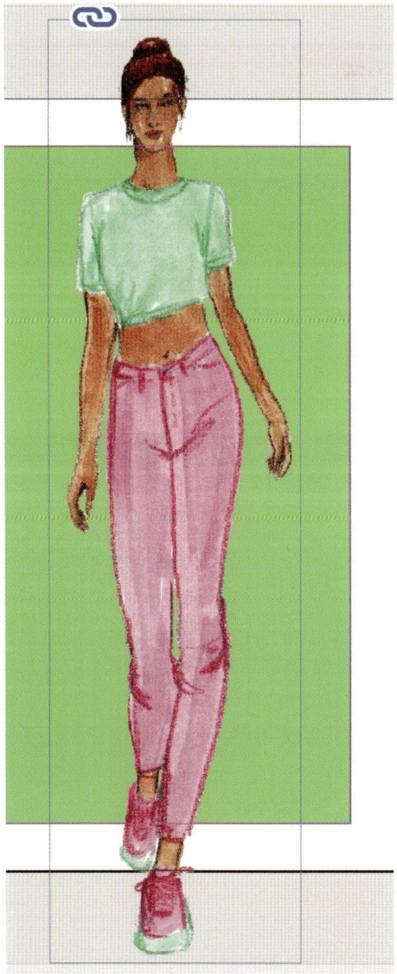

Figure 11.26b This image shows *Fit Frame to Content*. With this option, the content size is not altered. Instead, the frame size is changed to match the image. Notice that the image is larger than the page.

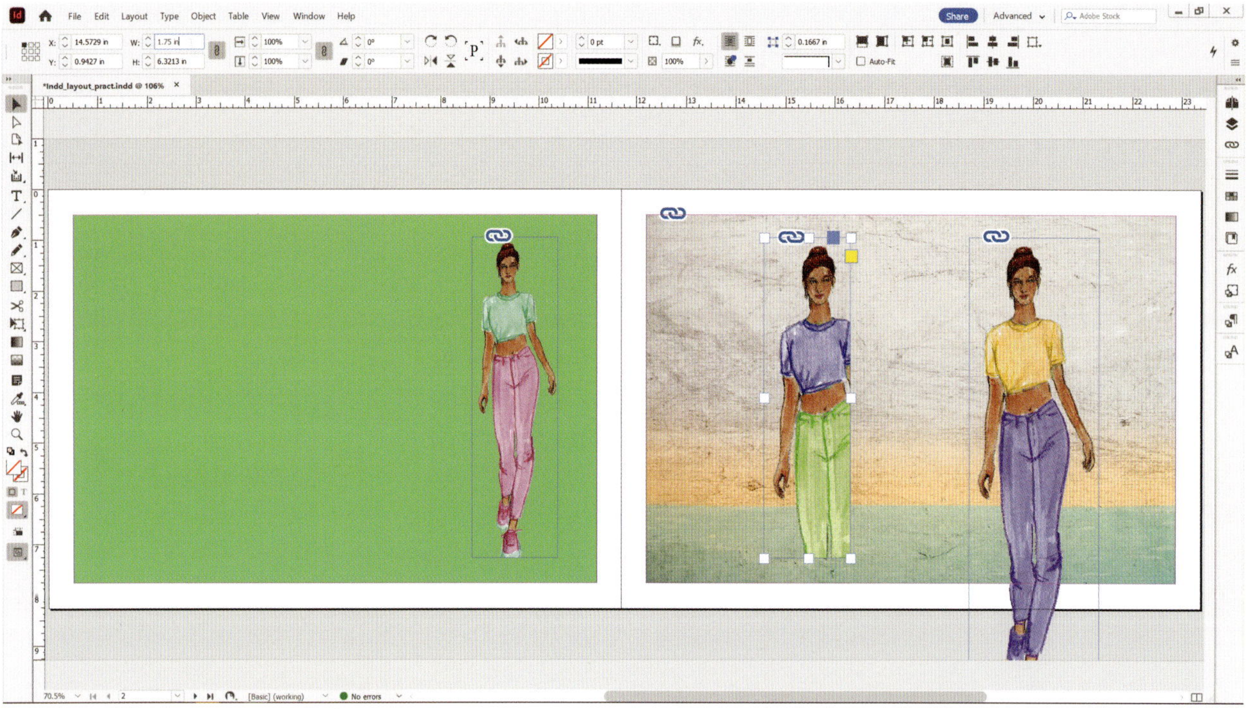

Figure 11.27 The *Width* and *Height* boxes are on the *Control* toolbar or on the *Properties* panel. This allows the user to dictate the size of the frame very precisely. However, the contents do not change size with the frame with this action. You will have to use a fitting option such as *Fit Content Proportionally* to keep all the image visible. Notice that the left-hand figure frame and the middle figure frame are now the same size. They have the same width and height. However, the figures within the frames are not the same size. This will have to be fixed.

the percentage to a higher number to make your image and frame larger or you can reduce the percentage to reduce the frame and image as shown in Figure 11.28. You can also enter a custom scale if the preset jumps are too much or too little for your needs.

Step 5: If you need to resize multiple items, select all the items you need to change using the *Selection* tool while holding the *Shift* key. Make sure to NOT click on the center circle that appears when you hover over the frame. Then you can use the same method to resize all items at once as you would to resize a single item.

Up to now, we have only used the *Selection* tool or black arrow. To check the proportions of images, we need to learn a little about the *Direct Selection* tool (*a*) or white arrow. As with Illustrator, the *Direct Selection* tool controls details. With InDesign, this means that the tool controls the contents of the frame instead of the frame itself. If a frame is selected with the *Selection* tool (*v*) you will notice that the frame is highlighted in blue. This is the window that we referenced in the earlier analogy.

Switch to the *Direct Selection* tool (*a*) and click on the image in the frame. You will notice that the image is now highlighted with a brown frame. Additionally, the brown frame may extend past the original blue frame. When using the *Direct Select* tool, you are controlling the actual image (or the items inside the window). Also note that if you click on the circle target inside the frame with the regular *Selection* tool (*v*), it will act like the *Direct Selection* tool and select the object rather than the frame, as shown in Figure 11.29.

To check if multiple images are the same proportion to one another, click on one with the *Direct Selection* tool and look at the *Scale* on the *Control* bar. Then click on the next image and check its scale. If they have the same scale while you are selecting them with the *Direct Selection* tool, then they are in proportion to one another. This is useful for checking the proportions of figures or flats, assuming that the original files were drawn in the same proportions.[3]

To move an object and its frame, use the *Selection* tool (*v*) and click on the object so the frame highlights in blue as seen in Figure 11.30. Then click and *drag* your object to wherever you want it. To move an object within its frame, use the *Direct Selection* tool (*a*) and click on the image in the frame so the object highlights in brown. Then *drag* the object around within the frame to reveal/hide the desired part of the object as shown in Figure 11.31.

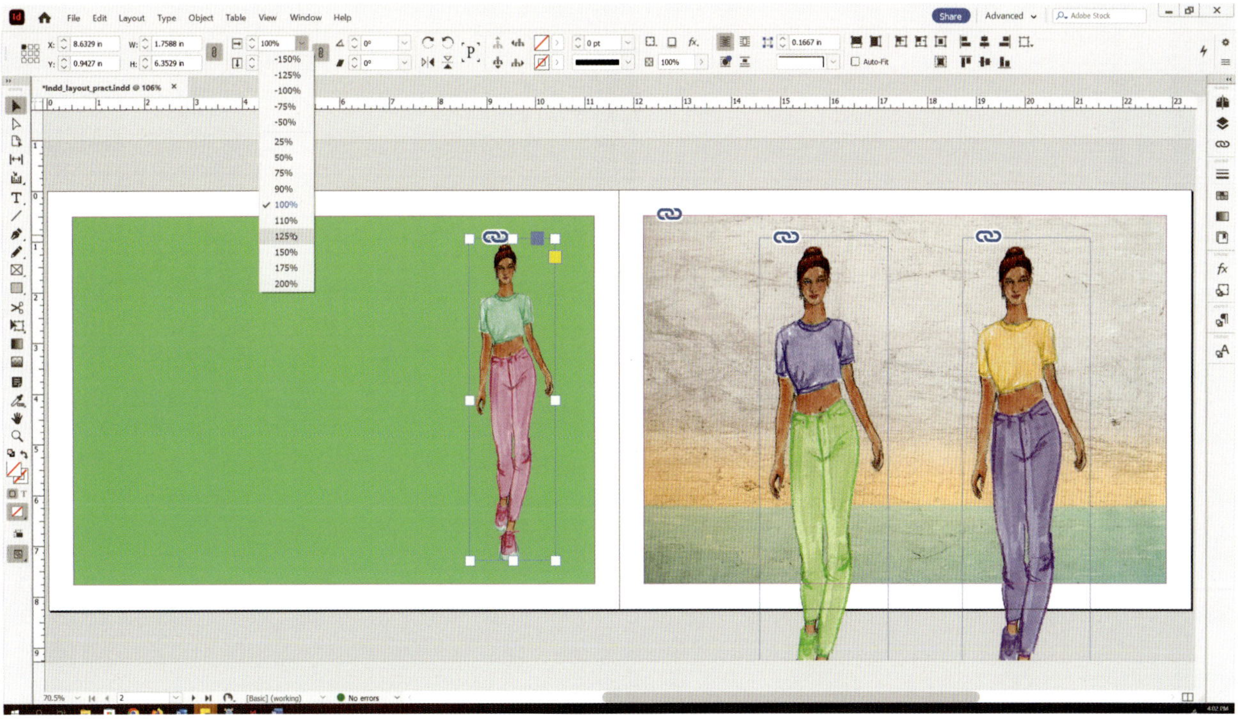

Figure 11.28 Using the *Scale X Percentage* and *Scale Y Percentage* options on the *Control* toolbar, the size of the frame and the contents (image) can be changed in preset jumps or by custom amounts. If the chain icon beside the percentage boxes is selected, the proportions of the image will be constrained.

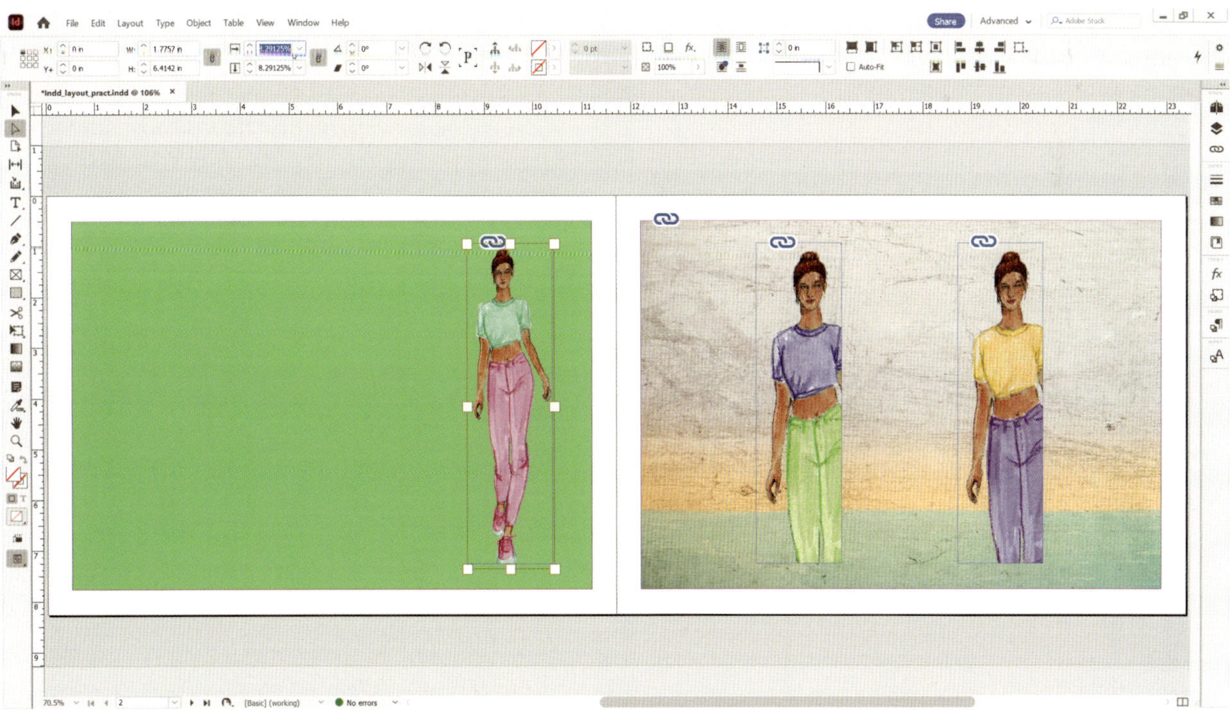

Figure 11.29 We have selected the first figure with the *Direct Selection* tool (*a*) and there is now a brown frame around it instead of a blue frame. Now the numbers in the *Control* toolbar or the *Properties* panel reflect the size of the image instead of the frame. If we want to manually match the proportions or sizes of multiple images, we can use these numbers.

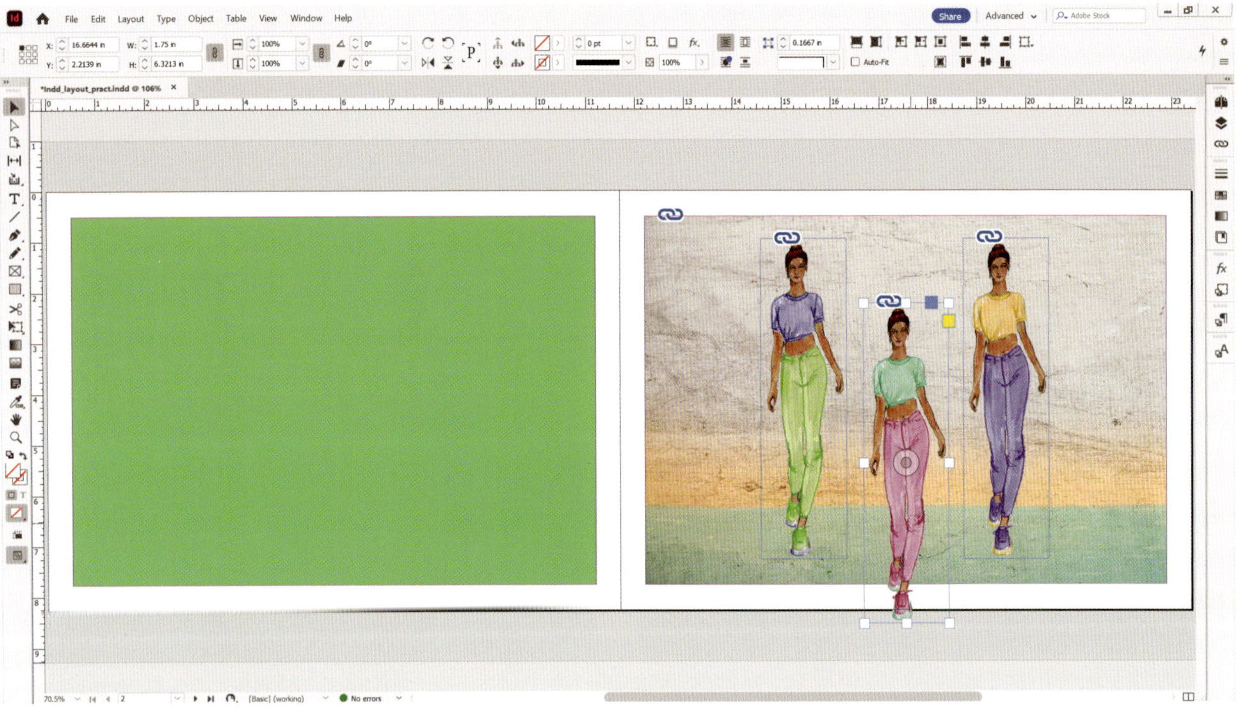

Figure 11.30 Moving a frame and image together. Using the *Selection* tool (*v*), click on the object you want to move. Make sure not to click on the center, where the target appears, as this will trigger a different option. Click and *drag* your object to its new location.

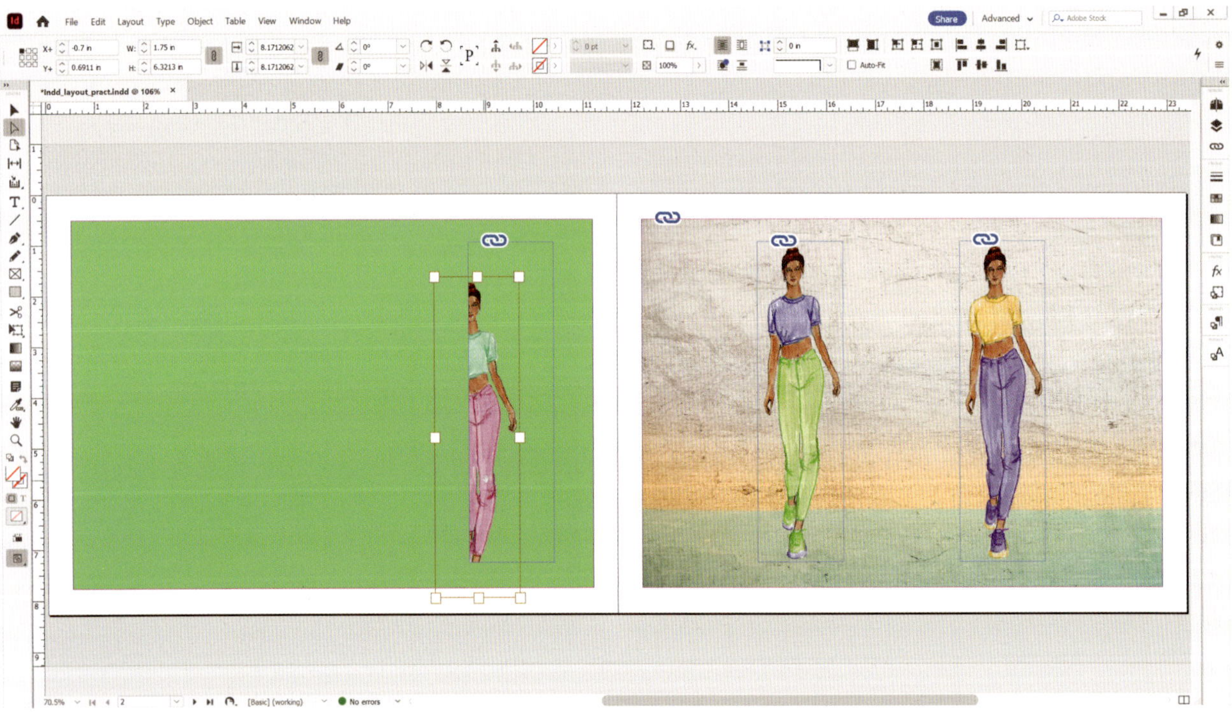

Figure 11.31 Moving an image within a frame. Using the *Direct Selection* tool (*a*), click on the image you want to move. Click and *drag* your image to where you want it within the frame. Remember that the frame will not move during this action.

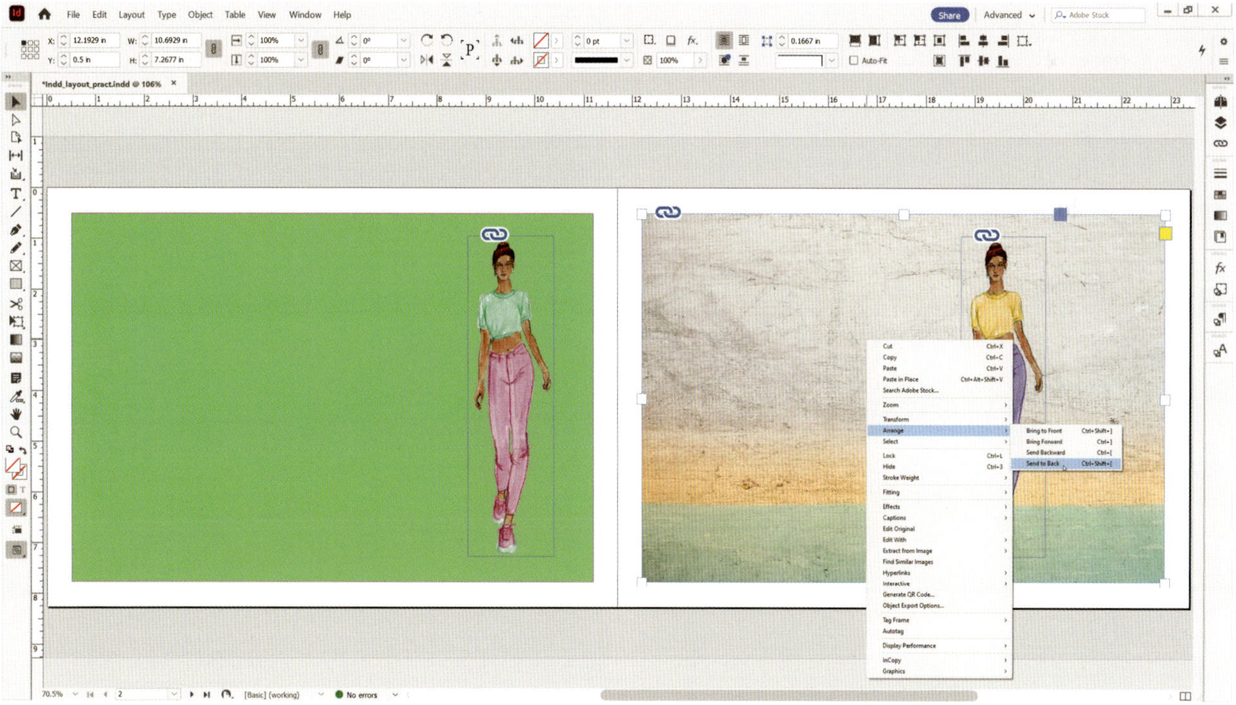

Figure 11.32 Arranging the object order. Notice that the second figure is missing. It is actually hiding behind the background. To make the figure visible again, we need to either bring the figure to the front or send the background to the back. *Click* on the background to select it. Then *right-click* on it to bring up the options box. Look for *Arrange → Send to Back*. This will enable you to see the figure again.

Step 6: What if one object is on top of another and you want it reversed? Maybe you accidentally put the background on top of the figures. If this is the case, the order can be rearranged easily. Use the *Selection* tool to click on the object so it is highlighted, then *right-click* on it. One of the options in the pop-up menu is *Arrange*. Under *Arrange*, you will find the options: *Send to Back*, *Send Backwards*, *Send to Front*, and *Send Forwards* as shown in Figure 11.32. Not all options are always available, depending on where an object is in the arrangement (e.g., already at the top of the stack). *Send Backwards* and *Send Forwards* moves the object one step down or up in the order. *Send to Back* and *Send to Front* moves the object all the way to the top or bottom of the stack. This function can also be found under the *Object* menu.

Let's try something slightly more advanced than moving objects around: working with opacity and blend modes. These concepts should be familiar to anyone who works with Photoshop and with many Illustrator users. However, opacity and blend modes are one of those functions that do not stay in the same place between applications. In InDesign, these two functions hide in the *Effects* panel.

Step 1: Select the object you want to affect. Then go to *Window → Effects* to bring up the *Effects* panel as shown in Figure 11.33. At the top left of the panel, you will see an options box that probably says *Normal*. This is the *Blend Modes* options box. Next to this, on the top right, is the *Opacity* options box.

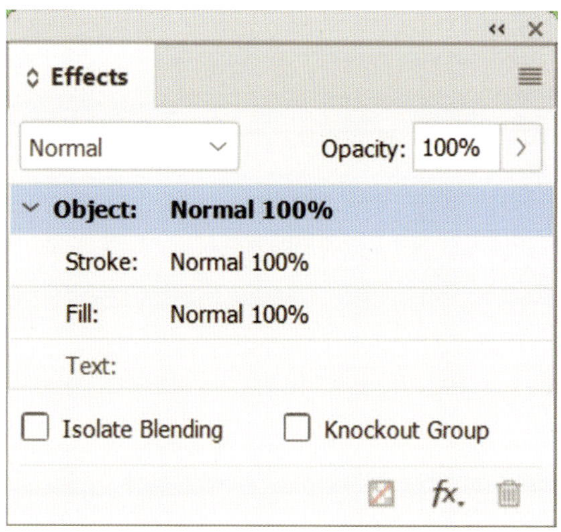

Figure 11.33 *Effects* panel. Notice that *Blend Modes* and *Opacity* are at the top.

Step 2: For a quick experiment, create a rectangle on the second page of your practice project and send it to the back of the object stack using *Arrange* as shown in Figure 11.34a. Then select the frame holding the textured background image using the *Selection* tool. You can either do this by first clicking off your page then clicking back onto your image or you can select the image by clicking the tiny square next to the image name in the *Layers* panel. Once you have selected the textured background image, try adjusting the look of the page by choosing a different blend mode and opacity for the image as shown in Figure 11.34b. The final outcome does not matter because this is just practice.

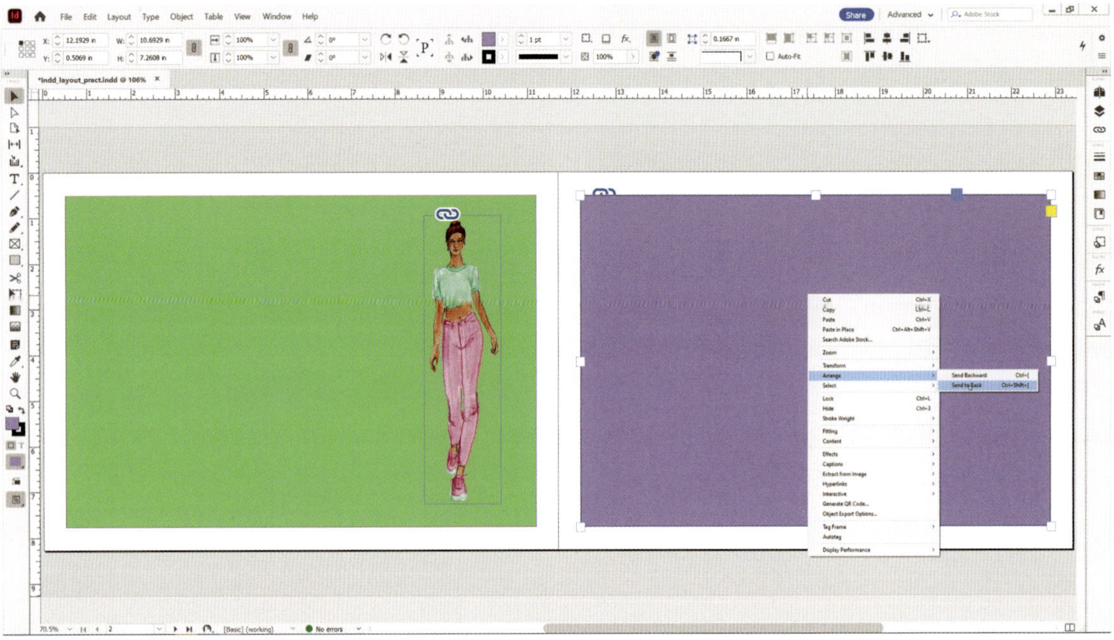

Figure 11.34a Preparing to experiment with blend modes and opacity. Make a rectangle with a solid fill and no stroke on the second page. Then send it to the back.

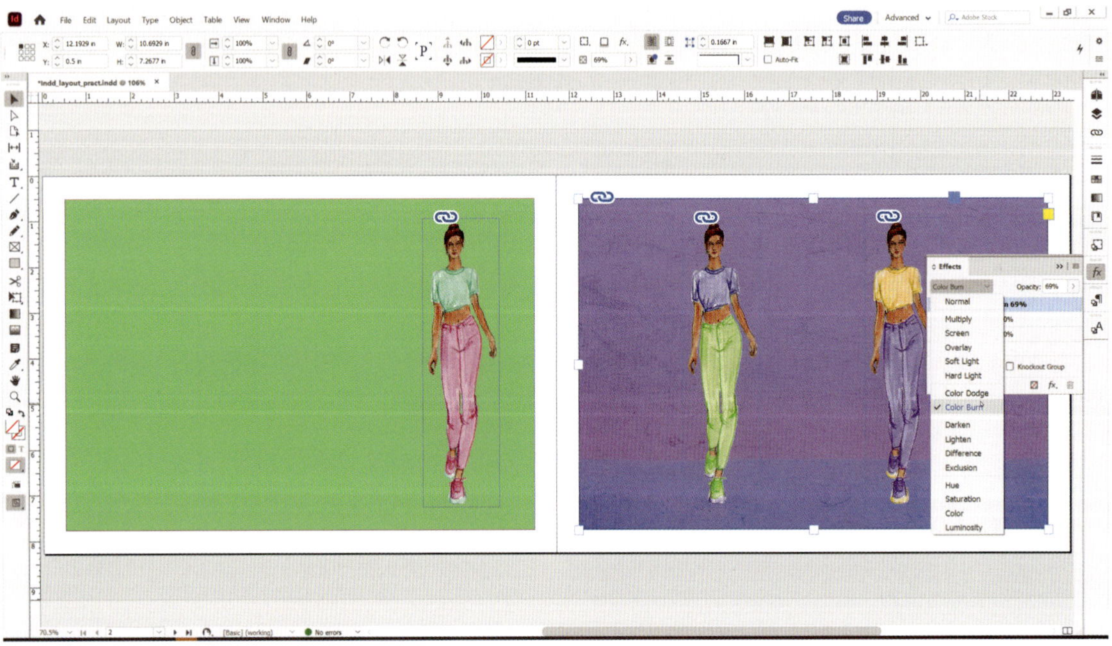

Figure 11.34b Deselect everything on your page, then click on the textured background image. Using the options in the *Effects* panel, try different *Blend Modes* and *Opacities* to achieve different effects.

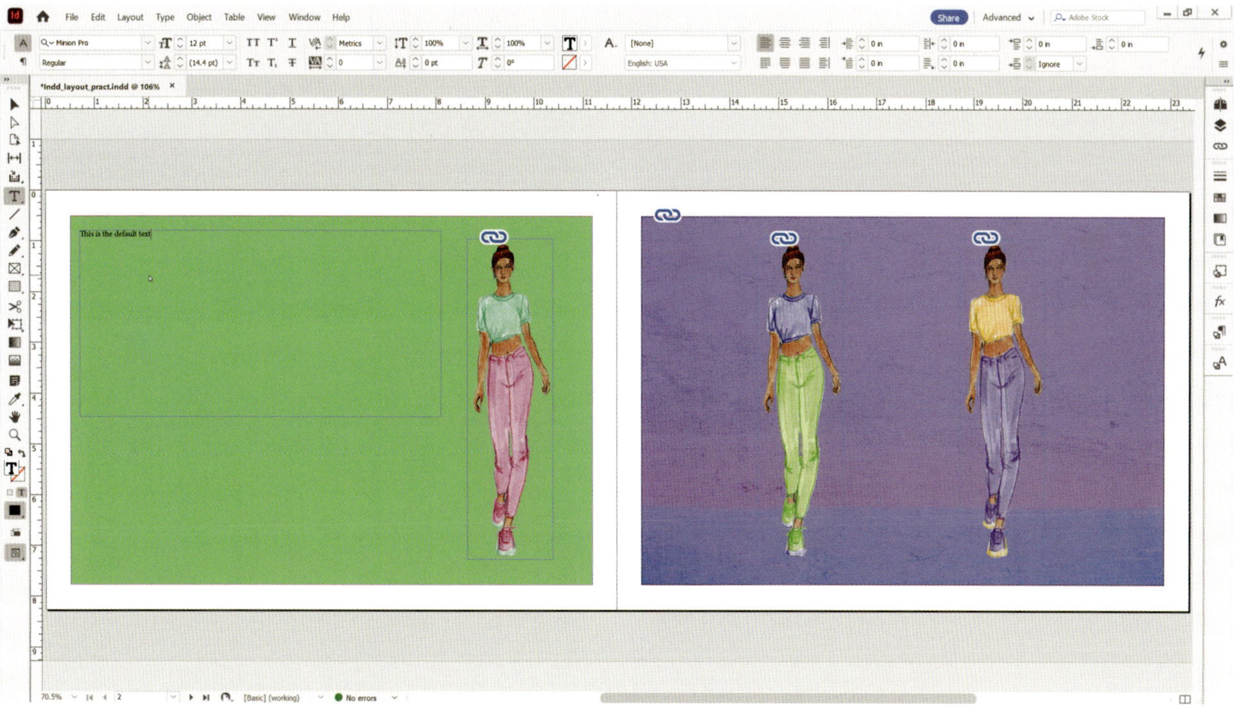

Figure 11.35 The *Type* tool enables you to draw a text frame, create the text, and edit the text. You will need a frame before creating the text, so it is best to use the *Type* tool to draw the frame. Once you have drawn the frame, your cursor will be blinking inside the frame and you can start typing. Default text is typically black and 12 pt, so sometimes it can be hard to see.

Text

Step 1: To add text to an InDesign document, you will need to add a text frame or box first. This can be done with the *Type* tool (*t*). Once you switch to the *Type* tool, click and drag a box on your page where you would like your text such as in Figure 11.35. Then click inside the text frame with the same tool to establish your cursor and start typing. The text will be in the default font, color, and size initially. This means that it is sometimes difficult to see, especially if you are working on a dark background.

Step 2: To make changes to your text style, make sure you are in the *Type* tool and highlight your text. In the *Properties* panel, you will see a section for *Appearance*, a section for *Character*, and a section for *Paragraph* while the text is highlighted. Alternatively, you can open the panel for each under the *Windows* menu. Figure 11.36a shows the *Character* panel open. In the *Appearance* section or panel, you can control the fill and stroke color of the text as well as the stroke weight. To change the font or font size, look in the *Character* section or panel. Lastly, to control alignment, look in the *Paragraph* section or panel as shown in Figure 11.36b.

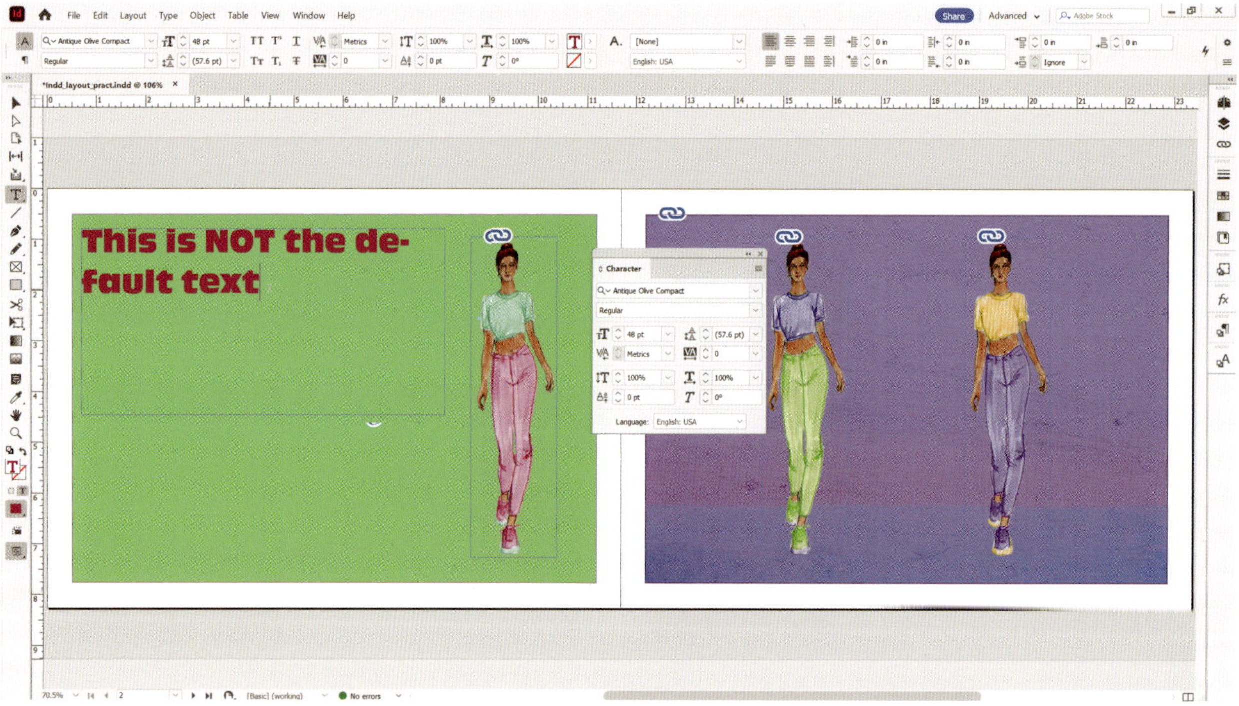

Figure 11.36a In the first image, the character has been altered in the *Character* panel. A new font was chosen, a new character color, and a new text size was selected.

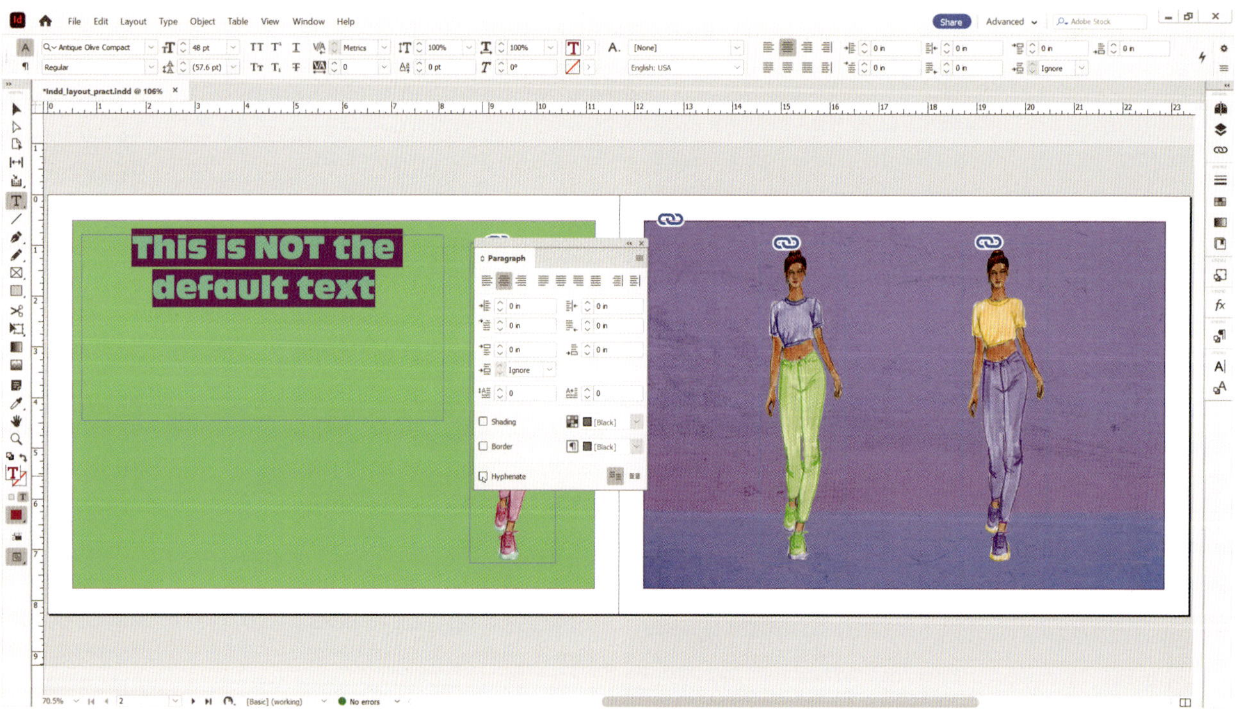

Figure 11.36b Altering the character and paragraph properties of type. In the second image, the paragraph characteristics were changed. The text is now centered, and hyphenation is turned off. *Character* and *Paragraph* properties can be controlled through the *Control* toolbar, the *Properties* panel, or individually through the *Character* panel and *Paragraph* panel.

Step 3: If you don't see all your text, it may not fit inside the frame. Look for a yellow square with a plus (+) symbol in the bottom right corner of the frame like in Figure 11.37. This symbol means that there is more text in the frame than is currently showing. Switch to the *Selection* tool and try dragging the frame larger. Warning: do not use keyboard shortcuts while you are in the text typing mode. You will accidentally add the shortcuts as text to the end of whatever you were typing!

If making the frame larger doesn't work, try making the text smaller. This can be tricky when you cannot see all the text. So before changing the size, press *control+a/command+a* to select all the text. Then reduce the font size.

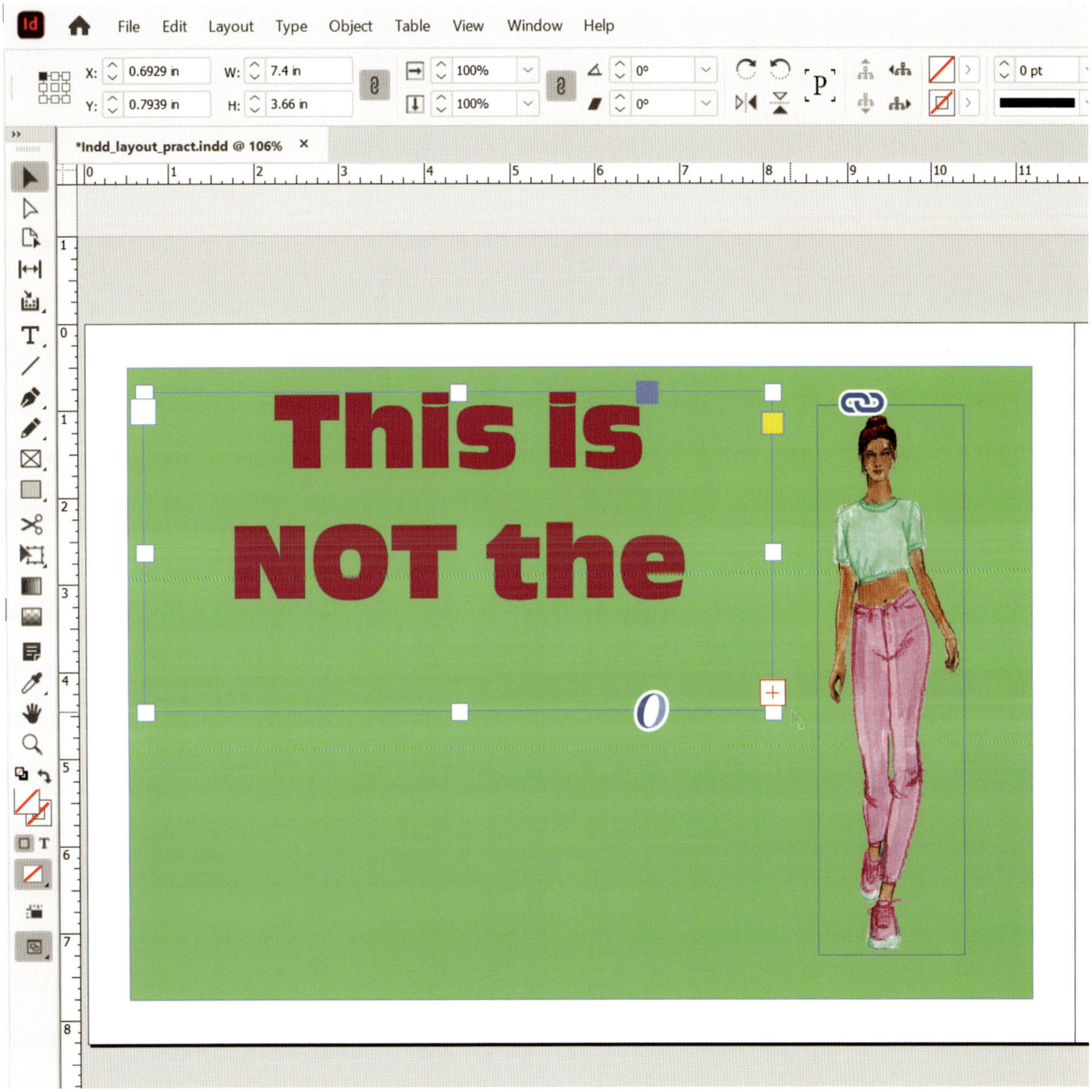

Figure 11.37 Example of overrun text. The selected text is not a complete phrase; part of the text is missing. Notice the plus (+) symbol in the bottom right corner of the text frame. This indicates overrun text or that the text does not fit in the frame. The frame needs to be enlarged or the text reduced.

PRO TIP 11.2

Character and Paragraph Styles

As you become more familiar with InDesign, you will hear about **character** and **paragraph styles**. InDesign has the capability to "memorize" repetitive settings for your text. This means that you can set a style for a particular font, font size, spacing, color, alignment, and so on. When you find yourself constantly changing the settings between a heading style and the body copy style, you should probably set a character and paragraph style. There are plenty of online tutorials to help you achieve this if you like. It will really help speed up your workflow!

Screen Modes/Display Performance

One of the most common complaints from new InDesign users is "My images are pixelated!" InDesign defaults to displaying work at a lower resolution to speed up the refresh rate and be less taxing on memory and video cards. This does not mean that your work is lower quality. Instead, you must get into the habit of checking your work occasionally in *High Quality Display* or in *Presentation Mode* as in Figure 11.38. The latter choice is often the fastest to get to.

To view your work in *Presentation Mode*, go to *View → Screen Mode → Presentation* or use the keyboard shortcut *shift+w*. You can navigate from page to page using the arrow keys on your keyboard. To exit this view, press *Escape* on the keyboard.

If your work is still pixelated when you look at it in *Presentation Mode*, then your work will print or export pixelated. You will need to recheck if your linked files were saved at a high resolution or not stretched beyond their original scale.

Now, there is a caveat to the *Presentation Mode* and its use for judging print quality. If you are working on a document with a very large page size, like a poster, *Presentation Mode* will not show the document at 100% zoom size. You will be looking at a reduced version of the document. By the time you print the document at 100%, it may still be pixelated. To determine the quality of a large document, we have to look at it a little differently.

For this type of document, go to *View → Display Performance → High Quality Display*. Then select *View → Actual Size* so you are looking at the document at 100%. You will have to scroll up and down on the document to see all the parts, but at least you can tell if it is pixelated. Remember to return the *Display Performance* back to *Typical* when you are done.

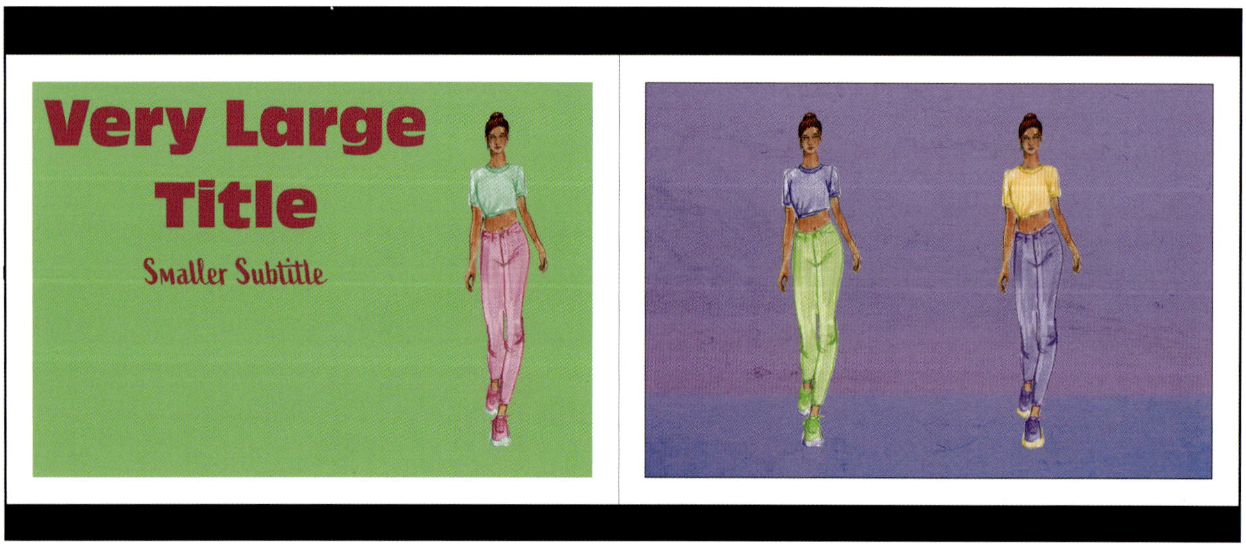

Figure 11.38 Check your work in *Presentation Mode* to view it at a better resolution.

Troubleshooting

"I don't see some/all of my text/image."

1. In terms of an image, you need to fit your content to the frame. In terms of text, it is probably overrun, meaning it doesn't fit in the text frame. Try making the frame bigger or the text smaller. If you cannot access your text to make it smaller, press *control+a/command+a* on the keyboard first to select all.
2. Another problem that causes overrun text is that sometimes there are spaces or line breaks before the beginning of the text. This is more common with copy and pasted text. You can find out if there are extra spaces by clicking *Type → Show Hidden Characters*. Delete your extra spaces.
3. Your text or image could have inadvertently ended up in a different frame than the one you intended. Look around the document and see if it is somewhere else. You can also look in the *Layers* panel. If you see your text or image in the panel, select it in the panel by clicking on the tiny square beside the title of your layer. This will highlight the text in the document.

"I have a broken link."

If you have a broken link, Open the *Links* panel and click on the item that needs to be relinked. It will have a question mark beside it to indicate that the link has a problem. Then you can either *right-click* on it and choose *Relink* or you can click the relink button at the bottom of the panel. An options box will come up and you will need to direct InDesign to the file's location.

"Everything on the screen is pixelated."

1. Check the *Display Performance* under the *View* menu. Set it to *High Quality*. Then check your zoom and make sure you are not zooming higher than 100%. If this fixes the problem, remember to set your *Display Performance* back to *Typical* before continuing to work as the higher resolution will slow your computer.
2. If you are still having trouble, check if your images are linked in the *Links* panel. If there are any unlinked images, relink them.
3. Finally, if everything else is good, your images may just be too low of resolution. You may need to either find better images or attempt to fix them in Photoshop.

"Every time I click on the object with the *Selection* tool it switches from editing the frame to editing the object."

1. Make sure you are using the *Selection* tool (black arrow). You can type *v* on the keyboard to double-check this.
2. If you *click* the very center of an image, there is a target. This target will cause the *Selection* tool to act like the *Direct Selection* tool and the object will highlight instead of the frame. Just avoid the center of the image and this will not trigger. If the target proves to be a constant source of aggravation for you, you can turn off the option through the *Preferences* menu.

"When I place my figures, they have a white rectangle behind them that I don't want."

1. Generally, there is one solution for this. You need to go back to the original file and make sure any backgrounds are eliminated and/or have the visibility turned off.
2. There is a *clipping path* option in InDesign, but it can be tricky to use. However, if you are working with very clean artwork on a very flat background, you can try it. You will find it under the *Object* menu.

Saving and Packaging Files

Now that you have compiled your artwork into a portfolio layout, consider how to share your work. Do you need to have a friend or teacher look at it one last time? Do you need to print it out? Are you going to add it to your social media page or website? Each of these uses may result in saving the file a little differently.

Method 1: There are a few good ways to share your files with others for review. In recent editions of the Adobe software, they have added a *Share* button in the upper right corner of your application. This creates a link to a file in your cloud file management system with Adobe through your Adobe ID. When you share the link, others may make comments as needed, which are then visible to you. They cannot, however, make edits to the file.

Method 2: To share a file for editing, check first if your company has a cloud file management system within their network. Most do. This is probably the easiest and safest way to share your work for edits. Be sure that all linked files are also in a shared folder. You may want to make a duplicate in an unshared folder in case your colleague makes an irreversible edit or deletes the file accidentally, though.

Method 3: However, if you need to share with someone outside of your network, you may want to **package** the file. The packaged file creates a folder with the native file, any linked object files, and the fonts used.[4] If you are turning in your work to a teacher for grading or feedback, they will probably ask for it to be packaged. That allows them to see all your work and give the best feedback to help you improve.

You must understand that compiled documents are basically pages with frames and links. The contents of the frames still reside with other files. So, if you move one of the linked files or move the master document without its linked files, it no longer works correctly. Before saving or printing anything, make sure that all your files are still linked (no broken chain icons on frames).

Additionally, packaging works a little differently for each of the software applications. InDesign makes packaging very easy and provides the most options when you do so. Go to *File* → *Package*. An options box comes up. Our best advice for packaging is to keep clicking on whatever the affirmative answer is for each new screen. This generally will get you through the packaging process, if all your links are unbroken. When the process is done, there will be a new folder that was created, wherever you told the app to put it. Typically, this folder ends up in the same folder you were saving the original document.

Inside the folder, you should see another folder for links, another for fonts, the master document file, and a PDF copy of the file as shown in Figure 11.39. The extra PDF is particularly good in case you did not properly link your files. Your teacher can see how you intended the layout to look even if it does not properly show in the indd file. You will want to send this entire folder if you want to share it. Let's repeat that one more time: you need to send the ENTIRE FOLDER, not just the indd file!

Illustrator works much the same way. Once you have saved your file in its native format, go to *File* → *Package*. Tick all the options that show in the pop-up box. The main difference is that Illustrator does not automatically create a PDF copy in your folder like InDesign does. You can always manually save a PDF copy within your packaged file by going through the *Save As* command in the *File* menu. As before, be sure to share the entire folder rather than just the single file.

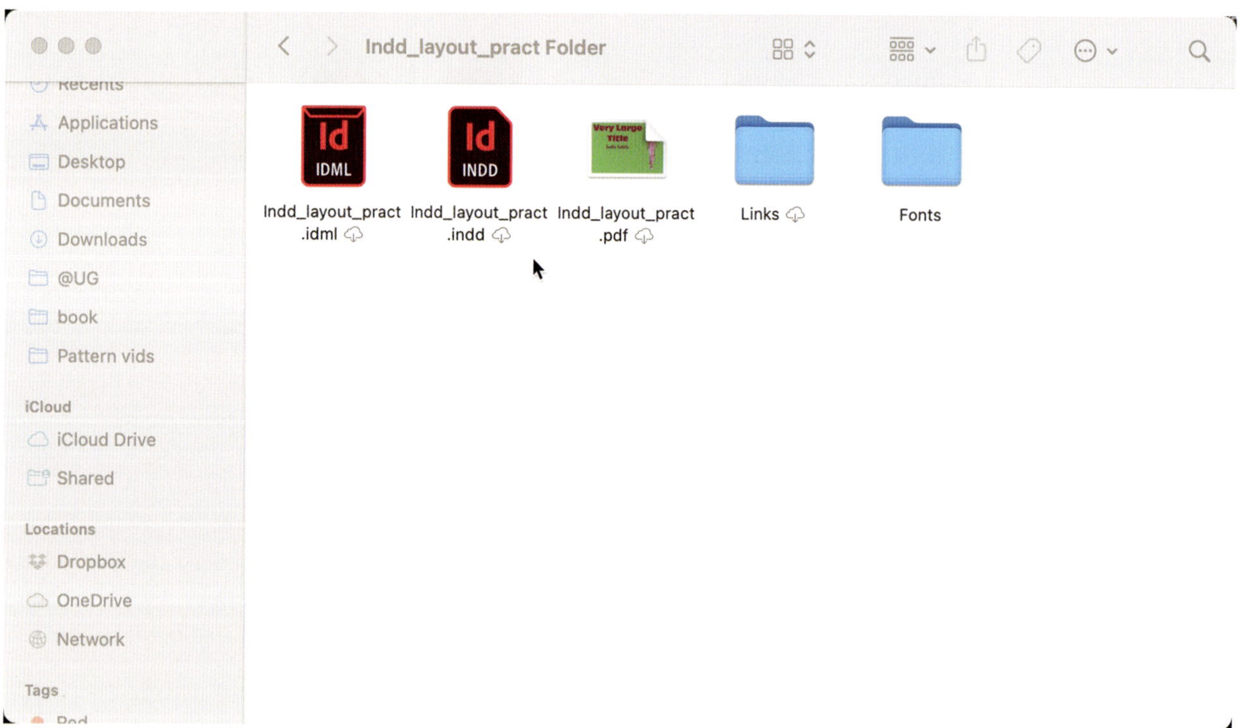

Figure 11.39 Using *Finder* or *Explorer* to see the files created when packaging your layout. Within the folder you should see an indd file, an idml file, a PDF copy, a links folder, and a fonts folder. You must send the parent folder containing all of these items for the receiver to properly use the file for edits.

Photoshop, for some reason that baffles many users, does not currently package fonts with the rest of the file. Perhaps they will add that feature in the future, but in the meantime, you will need a workaround. Some prefer to migrate their Photoshop document to Illustrator or InDesign to get a full package. You can also manually include a copy of your fonts with your packaged folder. The next person opening the file will have to install and apply the font, though. This makes it a less-than-ideal way to share files. You will also need to manually make a PDF copy if you want to include it with the working files.

Project 11.4: Save for Print

Let's try saving our practice file for printing. First you want to save your work using *File → Save*. Make sure you know where you are saving the file and that you give the file a name. It will save in the native file format (.ai, .psd, or .indd). This is the editable version of your file that you can reopen in the original application anytime you need to make a change.

In many cases, exporting your file as an Acrobat file (.PDF) will result in a good print that can be read by most print companies. In Illustrator and Photoshop, you can use the command *Save As* under the *File* menu and choose the *PDF* format to save your file as a PDF. Make sure it saves at a high resolution for printing.

In InDesign, you need to export your file as a PDF. Go to *File → Export*. Choose where you want to save the file and what to name the file; then make sure the file type option is set to Adobe PDF (print). Another options box will come up where you can make further changes to your PDF settings. Typically, *High Quality Print* is a good setting for prints. After you click Export at the bottom of the box, a PDF will be generated. This file can then be sent to the printer.

We often recommend that students have a backup file format when printing in case something happens with the PDF. Occasionally, PDFs will have some odd error that only shows once it is printed. Printers generally only need a flat copy of the final image, so you can convert your files to high-resolution JPEGs as a backup.

Project 11.5: Save for the Web

Generally, images saved for consumption over the internet do not require a high resolution. In fact, smaller, lower-quality files are ideal so they do not take as long to load.

First, consider why you are sharing your images. Is this for an online portfolio of your work? If so, you may want to add a **watermark** to help prevent others from stealing your work and claiming credit for it. Watermarks use small or low-opacity images or text that sit on the primary image and indicate that it is your work, as shown in Figure 11.40. Smaller, low-resolution images also make it extremely difficult for others to download and print your work without it looking like a mess.

Are you sharing through a particular social media platform? Then you probably want to crop it to the correct aspect ratio of that venue. Look up the correct ratio for your desired social media application and crop your flattened image to fit that ratio in the most flattering way. Use *Save As* or *Export* to change it to a JPEG or other image format that works for that application.

JPEGs work well for web distribution because they are small and carry limited information. Make a copy of your finalized work, then reduce it to web resolution of

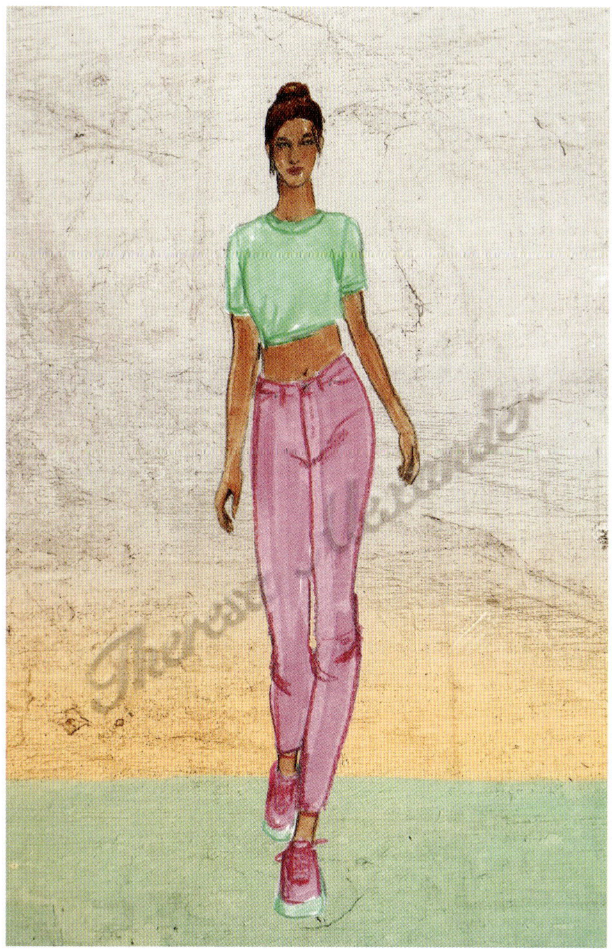

Figure 11.40 You can add a watermark to your artwork to help deter those who might try to use your artwork without your permission when posting on the web.

72 ppi and add a watermark if you like. Flatten the layers and save each page as a separate JPEG file. JPEGs do not support multiple pages, so you need to save each page individually. For all three Adobe software applications, you can find *Export* or *Export As* under the *File* menu.

Troubleshooting

"My images are not printing/exporting correctly."

1. You probably have broken links. Double-check in the *Links* panel that none of the links indicate a problem. If they have a broken link, relink them.
2. Sometimes PDFs coming out of InDesign have printing errors. We don't know why. For this reason, if you are sending your printing to a printing service, we always recommend having an alternate version of the file. If you are sending your file to a professional printer, have the packaged folder for the best results. If you are sending your file to a printing service at an office supplies store, or similar, then have a high-resolution JPEG version of the file.

"I tried to *Open* an InDesign file on another computer and now nothing looks right."

1. Make sure you packaged your file on the original computer. Before you packaged the file, all the images needed to still be linked.
2. Bring the whole packaged folder over to the new computer, not just the original file. *Open* the .indd file that is in the folder.
3. You may have to relink the images when you *Open* the file. Typically, once you relink one file, Id will find all the others if they are in the same folder.
4. You may also have to activate any Adobe fonts that did not come over with the folder.

Summary

Compiling content for your layouts can occur in Photoshop or Illustrator, but InDesign is generally the best application for this task. Both Photoshop and Illustrator use the term "artboard" for multiple pages within the same file. Photoshop sometimes has trouble handling artboards due to the tendency for large files within the application, though. You can place linked or embedded files to each artboard as needed to compile the individual elements of your project into one file. Adding text is easy through the text tool. Remember to adjust character and paragraph attributes for more professional text results. You also have the option to add effects or layer styles to your text.

InDesign uses the term "pages" for multiple pages within a file. When placing objects or text in InDesign, you need to use frames. These are containers that act like windows in a building. The content in a frame can be revealed or hidden according to the position and size of the frame related to the content inside the frame.

How you save your file depends on how you intend to use it. You can use the *Share* option available within the Adobe applications, share the file through an in-network file share application, or package your file. To send your file to a printer, you can save-as or export it to a PDF. For web publishing, reduce the resolution and file size, then export it to a JPEG. You are ready to pull your portfolio together, now!

STUDIO Companion Videos for Chapter 11

Please refer to STUDIO for accompanying chapter video(s).

Keywords

Artboards
Basic frame
Basic shape
Character/paragraph styles
Fitting options
Frames
Package
Pages
Parent pages
Text frame
Watermark
Working pages

Review Questions

1. Why are artboards not used as often for Photoshop as they are in the other software?
2. What tool(s) would you use if you want to move the frame and content together in InDesign? What tool(s) would you use if you only want to move the content inside the frame?
3. Explain the difference between a basic frame, a text frame, and a basic shape in InDesign.
4. What does InDesign do when packaging that Illustrator does not?
5. Why would you reduce your resolution for web distribution?

Commands Introduced

- Arrange
- Artboard tool
- Effects
- Effects panel
- Export
- Fitting Options
- Frames
- High Quality Display
- Layer Styles
- Package
- Presentation Mode
- Share
- Show Hidden Characters
- Type tool
- Update modified content

Keyboard Shortcuts

- Ai, Id, Ps: *control+a/command+a* (Select All)
- Ps, Ai, Id: *t* (Type tool)
- Id: *f* (Rectangular Frame tool)
- Id: *m* (Rectangle tool)
- Id: escape (exit Presentation Mode)
- Id: *shift+w* (Presentation Mode)

Discussion Questions

1. Why would Photoshop, Illustrator, or InDesign be better for layout in different situations? Explain when and why you would want to use one and not the other for three different situations.
2. Is the act of sharing a font with a colleague who did not pay for the font unethical? Defend your opinion.
3. Is using others' artwork for your mood/inspiration/research ethical or unethical? Defend your opinion. Now consider if someone else uses your artwork for their projects without asking. How do you feel about that?

Practice Exercises

1. Recreate your mood board from Chapter 9 using InDesign.
2. Create the same multi-page layout in Photoshop, Illustrator, and InDesign. Be sure to package each for practice. Compare and contrast the experiences. What did you like about each? What did you dislike?
3. Prepare and save at least one portfolio project for web publishing. Try adding a watermark to each page.

Endnotes

1. Generally, you do not want to stretch or enlarge a photo only using the *Transform* tools. If the object is not the correct size for your layout, you will need to choose a new image or it will be pixelated, distorted, and generally look bad. For this instance, the image only needs to be stretched slightly to fit, and it is an abstract background that does not show the distortion easily. Please note that we rarely do this, though.

2. Bleeds are printing conventions that allow your artwork to extend slightly beyond the page size. Generally, the artwork is printed on a piece of paper that is bigger than the intended size, then cut down to the correct size. This allows the printing to extend to the edges of the cut paper without any blank space or margins.
3. Be consistent with your figure sizes in relation to your layout page size. This provides consistency between figures when you place them into a layout. It also prevents you from making figures that are significantly smaller than your layout, which in turn results in pixelated images when you stretch them to fit the page.
4. Please share fonts responsibly. Many artists make a living by selling their font artwork. If you purchased a font, you should not share it with someone who did not purchase it. Check with whomever you are sharing your packaged files with to see if they need the fonts or not for their part of the edits.

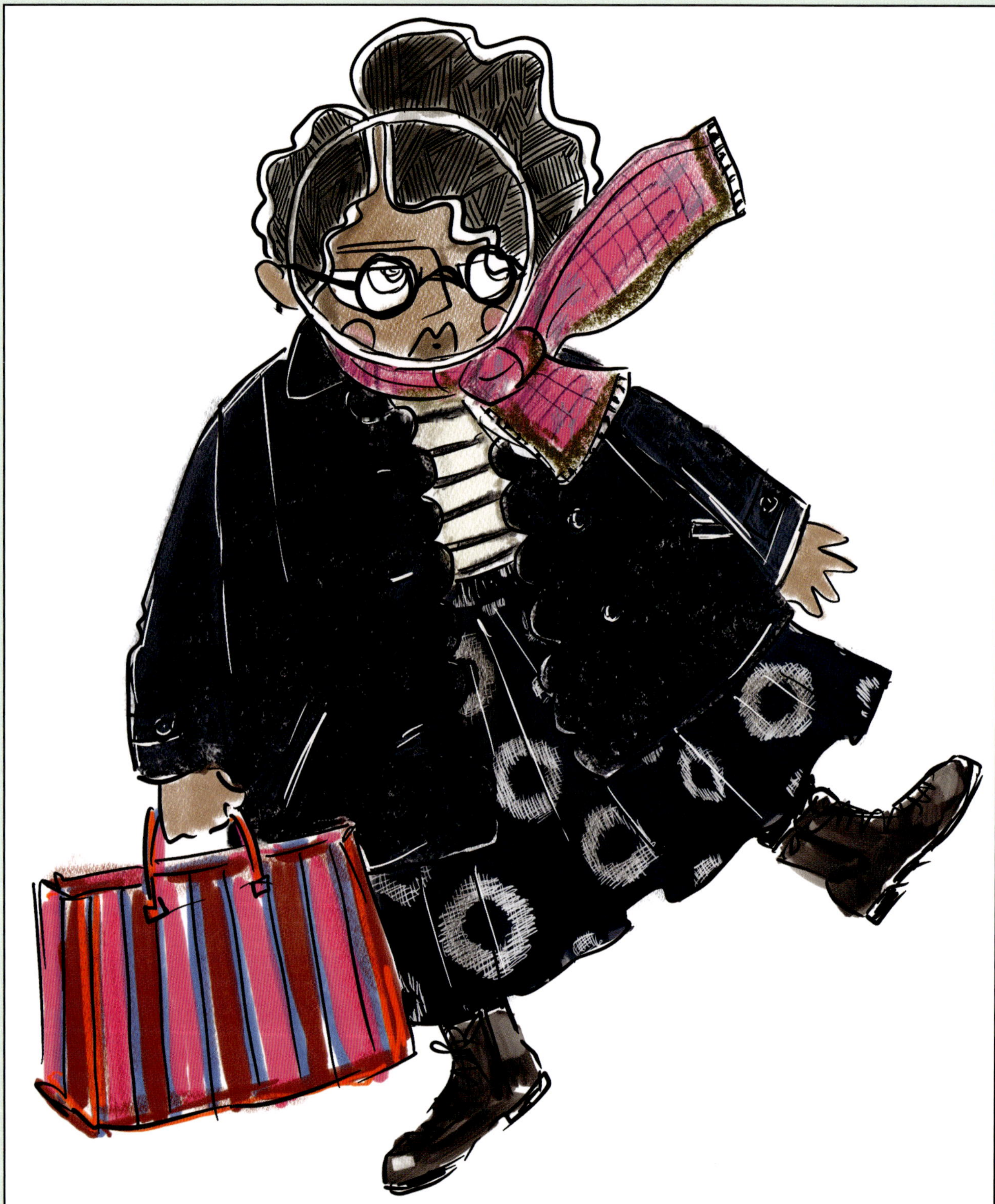

Figure 12.1 Your portfolio is part of your personal brand in the professional world. Courtesy of Arti Sandhu.

CHAPTER 12
Portfolios

Learning Objectives

After completing this chapter, you should be able to

- Determine if a physical portfolio, digital portfolio, or combination works best for you
- Construct a mini mock-up portfolio
- Generate a wireframe or mini mock-up digital portfolio
- Curate your online presence
- Align your resumé and other marketing collateral to your personal brand
- Prepare to use your portfolio in job interviews

To have a portfolio or not to have a portfolio seems to be the debate among many students, faculty, and professionals these days. In times past, every fashion and costume design graduate was expected to have a portfolio. Now it depends more on what type of job for which you intend to apply and your personal situation. If you want to be a designer, then yes, you need a portfolio. Are you just starting out in the industry or returning after an extended hiatus? Yep. A portfolio will help. Portfolios help to visually describe your ability as a designer. It can be just as vital as a resumé in the job hunt. If you plan to go into development, some aspect of tech, or another variation of the fashion/costume industries, then you will need to talk to other professionals in that area about the need for a portfolio. It can help you stand out from the competition, but may be seen as overkill for some jobs. However, we generally recommend you have a portfolio when applying for entry-level jobs, so when an interviewer asks to see it, you are prepared.

The Image You Present to the World

Now that you have completed some projects, you need to start pulling it all together. Start to think of yourself as a brand: How do you want the professional world to see you? Do you have a specific design style? Are there particular positions or companies you would like to work for? What is their design style? Whether you are just entering the industry or simply upskilling, you need to think about the image you present. Consider the whole package: your designs, portfolio, resumé, online presence, and even your personal look to a degree.

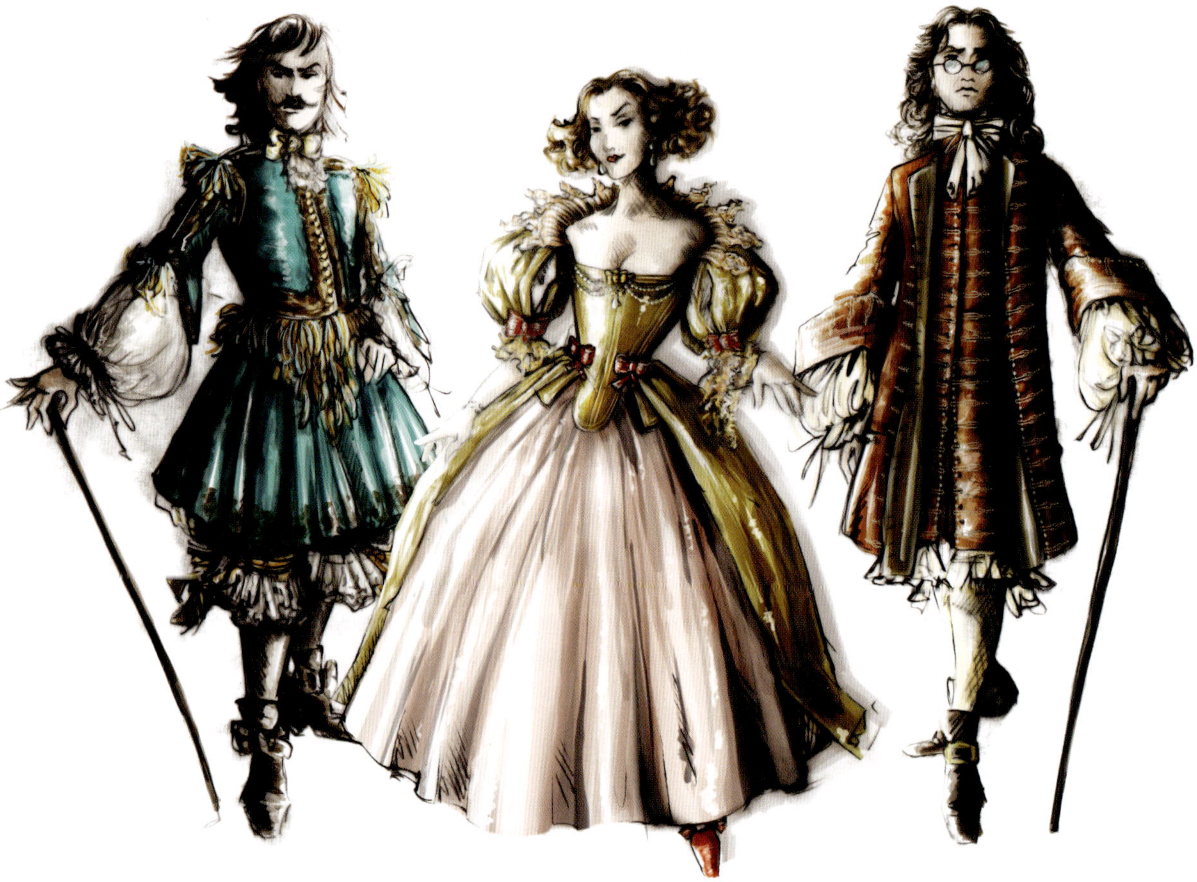

Figure 12.2 Consider your rendering and design style as part of your personal brand. Courtesy of Fabio Toblini.

Start with some reflection. Think about words that you want others to associate with your work. Choose three or four keywords. Consider descriptive words such as luxury, sustainable, quirky, quality, and so on. Your visual branding should reflect your chosen keywords. For example, perhaps you enjoy designing active and casual wear for the moderate plus-size industry. You may choose words such as affordable, comfortable, and reliable. Or if you love to design costumes for children's shows you may choose playful, imaginative, and nurturing as your words. Keep your specific words at the center of your work as you compile your portfolio and other branding materials in this chapter.

Let's briefly discuss some other little things that contribute to your image. Consider your web address and email. Having a professional email is best to support your career. Keep your fun email address personal. For example, Hottiesparklegurl23@email.com does not convey the professional image you are trying to nurture at this time in your life. Create a more suitable email for your career correspondence. A professional email address works best if it includes your first and last name. The same principle applies if you want a web portfolio. Consider the website address. Avoid anything "cutesy" or downright unprofessional when choosing your domain name.

Think about your voicemail and email signature lines as well. It all plays into your personal branding. Make sure your voicemail clearly states your name and your request for the message such as, "Please leave your name, number, and a brief message, and I will get back to you soon." It's simple, clear, and professional. Your email signature line should include a closing salutation, your name, and contact information. Images may not show with all email programs, so just use text. Avoid quotes and inspirational sayings. They create clutter and many professionals consider them as pet peeves. It's generally best practice to not annoy any potential employers before you meet them!

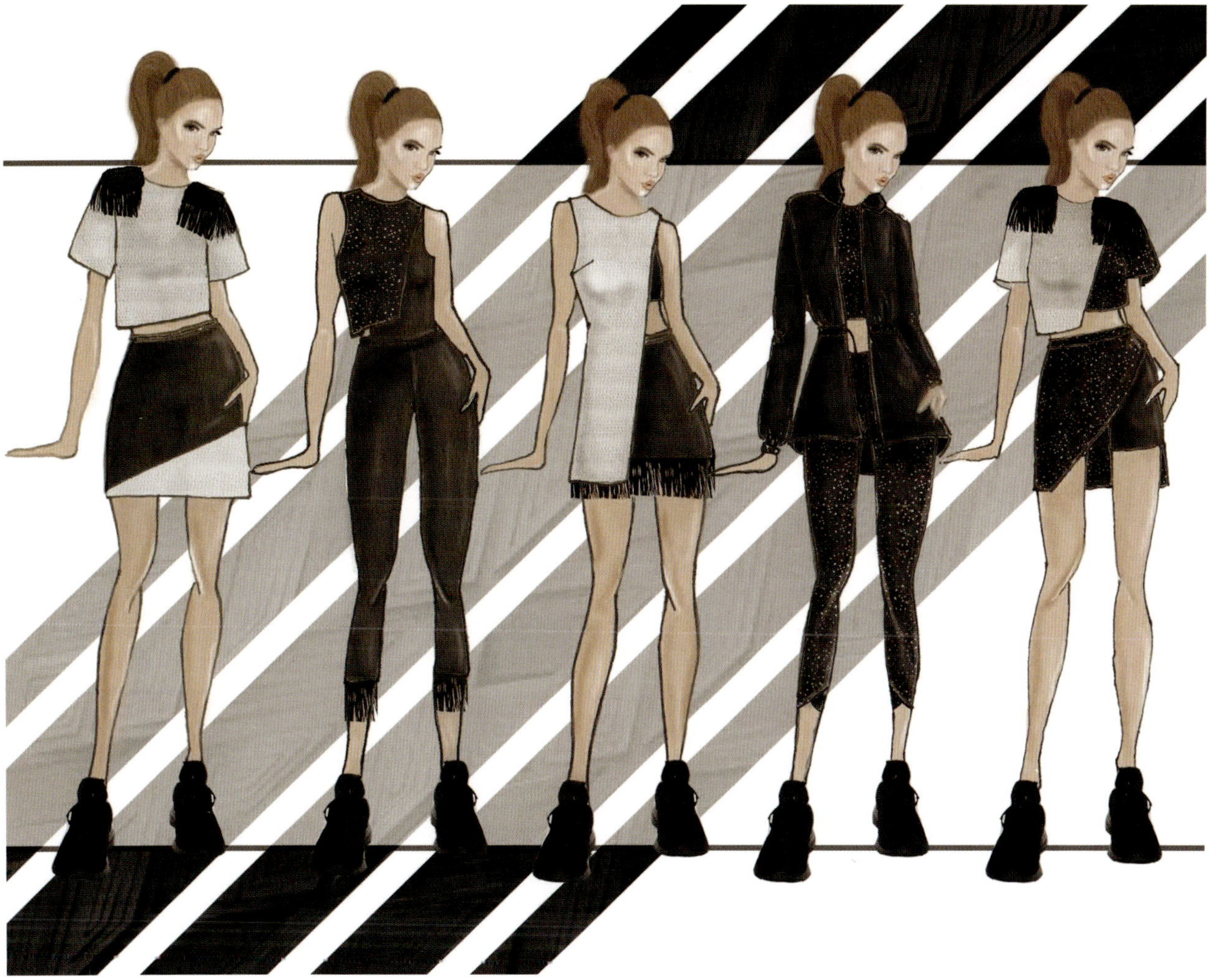

Figure 12.3 Should you focus your portfolio or show flexibility with your projects? Discuss your career goals with your instructor. Courtesy of Raegan McGuire Tocco @reagan.mcguire Texas Tech University, College of Human Sciences, Apparel Design & Manufacturing.

You should also consider your personal image and how you dress in the professional world. This may seem odd, but it can play into the branding. Others will judge you based on how you look, whether it is right or wrong. So, it is beneficial to control your message. Think about your keywords again. Do you project to adjectives? You don't need to be over the top with it. Primarily, you want to make sure you don't convey mixed messages. For example, your portfolio and resumé may indicate luxury and prestige. If you look more "street goth," though, others will be confused about your personal brand. We have noticed over the years that previous students who looked like their niche market excelled. Are you interested in the western-wear market? Dress professionally with a western flair. Do you want to go into luxury? Upscale your look. Demonstrate you understand the customer better than the average bear. This is a bit above and beyond, but it is something to consider.

Portfolios

So, you've decided you need a portfolio. What type do you need? Digital or physical? Adaptable or targeted? It is time to make some decisions.

If you are still in school, talk with your professor to get suggestions. Talk over your career goals and your target employers. Discuss your skills: what you do well and what you need to improve.

If you are already in the industry, check with industry professionals: what is most useful? Ask your co-workers and industry friends if you can look at their portfolios. Get feedback from them about what has worked for them and what has not. Ultimately, you must make your own decisions.

When deciding on the type of portfolio, keep in mind the upkeep. How often will you need to update them and how difficult will it be to do the updating? Portfolios should look fresh, not dated. Old work can send the wrong message to potential employers that you either are not up to date with the current styles and trends or that you do not value their time enough to put effort into your portfolio.

Digital, Physical, or Both?

Let us look at the differences between a digital and a physical portfolio. As this is a book about digital rendering, you might immediately think "digital portfolio!" However, it is best to make an educated decision. Both formats have benefits and downsides. You want to choose what is best for your needs.

You will see the pros and cons of digital portfolios outlined in Table 12.1. Most of these points are self-explanatory, however, some need a little more clarification. Under pros, we stated that a digital portfolio allows you to post other types of work. If you have degrees, skills, or professional hobbies other than fashion or costuming, you can have sections in a digital portfolio dedicated to these. Are you an artist, a jewelry maker, or an expert at surface design? You can include these. Potential employers can choose whether they want to view these sections. However, a physical portfolio must be more focused and generally cannot include extra sections. Instead, you would have to have separate portfolios if you wanted someone to see evidence of these skills.

We also included the benefit that people can send your digital portfolio to their own contacts. Perhaps you sent your digital portfolio to someone in hopes of an interview, but you were not right for the job. If the interviewer likes your work and knows someone else who might be looking for your skillset, they can forward your portfolio to that contact.

Under cons, we listed that your work can be stolen and typically you have no control over who sees your work. However, you can make your website or files password protected or have a hidden website. A hidden website means that your page is not listed with Google or other search engines and is not easy to come across without the specific URL. Just remember that you may be missing the opportunity to have potential employers come across your work on their own. Also, once you have shared a password or a hidden website address, they can still be shared by others. There is nothing foolproof. To mitigate this, remember that you can add a watermark to your work and use lower-resolution files that look fine on screen, but will not print well. It will not stop potential thieves from stealing your design ideas, but it can prevent them from claiming your artwork as their own.

What about a physical portfolio? Isn't that "old school" and outdated? Remember that you are likely to be interviewed by people older than you that thrive on "old school." So, be careful with such assumptions. As with digital portfolios, whether you choose to have a physical portfolio depends on your needs.

Table 12.2 lists the pros and cons of a physical portfolio. Generally, these points are easy to understand, but a couple of points could use more explanation. We state that you can include 3D, tactile, or interactive work in a physical portfolio. This is an important point. Many potential employers want to see that you have handled actual fabric when making design and sourcing choices. In a digital world, it is easy to pull the image of a fabric

Table 12.1 Pros and Cons of Having a Digital Portfolio

PROS	CONS
• Easy to email a link to potential employers remotely	• Work is published on the Internet and can be stolen
• Easy to change/update work	• Typically, have no control over who sees your work
• Can include other work, such as photography, art, or technical work	• Can only show 2D images of any 3D items such as fabrics or garments
• Can include animations	• Analog work must be scanned
• Can set up a contact page	• Must update digital portfolios regularly
• Can easily connect work to resumé	• Cannot include any copyrighted material from other artists
• Can connect to your social media accounts	
• Other people can send your website or file to people they think should know about your work	

swatch and place it alongside our renderings. However, without the real fabric swatch, we have not proven our understanding of fabric weight and hand.

Additionally, there is the interest factor that comes with tactile, 3D, and interactive objects in a portfolio. Many designers and costumers have a need to touch things. If there are elements in your portfolio that they can touch, flip in a different direction, pull out, or somehow interact with, it stops the monotony of turning pages and brings the interest back to the portfolio and back to you.

Sketch books and research journals can be very interesting but are often too lengthy to scan and place in a digital portfolio in their entirety. If you carry one of your best examples to an interview along with your portfolio, these can be great ways to demonstrate how you work. Many interviewers can glean more information from your unfinished work than from your polished portfolio.

If you want the portability of the digital portfolio but the ultimate security of the physical portfolio (or another combination of benefits), consider having both. There is nothing stopping you other than your own efforts.

Many fashion and theatre professionals keep both digital and physical portfolios. The digital portfolio contains a few key renderings or projects as well as information about themselves. It acts like an elaborate business card to introduce themselves and draw in interest. Today, a digital portfolio is expected. So, you may miss out on some opportunities by not having a digital presence. The bulk of your work should be saved for the physical portfolio, though. The benefit of this approach is that you can use your digital portfolio to entice potential employers to call you in for an interview to see more of your work in the physical portfolio. The two should not be exact duplicates of each other, though. Otherwise, what is the point?

Adaptable or Targeted?

What are adaptable or targeted portfolios? A **targeted portfolio** is one that contains work curated for a specific job or company. In fashion, you may be interested in an assistant designer position with a big-name sportswear brand. You would make sure all the items in your portfolio are in line with the brand's aesthetic and market in a targeted portfolio.

In theatre, targeted portfolios are less common. It means that you specialize in a type of production such as large-scale musicals or historical plays. If applying to be an assistant designer, this type of portfolio may help you to entice a particular designer by showing them that you excel in the same type of shows that they typically design.[1]

An **adaptable portfolio** is not built with a specific job in mind and is more versatile. It will show more variety in work. However, you may know what areas of the industry you are most interested in. In this case, you can limit your work to these areas. For example, maybe you are more interested in denim and casual sportswear. All your work could focus on these two categories without being oriented around a specific job or company.

Adaptable portfolios are very common for costume design. You generally want a variety of production types to show your flexibility. Costume designers can be typecast just as easily as actors. Sometimes you inadvertently create a reputation for designing only certain types of shows. An adaptable portfolio helps to demonstrate your versatility if you do not want to be pigeon-holed into a limited genre of productions.

The popularity of adaptable versus targeted changes with the times. However, like everything else, the choice is ultimately yours. Base that choice on what best fits your needs.

Let us look at the pros and cons of each, starting with the adaptable portfolio. Many students start with an

Table 12.2 Pros and Cons of a Physical Portfolio

PROS	CONS
• Can control who sees your work	• Can be heavy
• Easier to keep your work from being copied/stolen	• Can be damaged or lost
• Can include 3D, tactile, or interactive work	• Can be expensive (both the case and the pages)
• You can easily show your research journals or sketch books	• Digital work must be printed
• You will stand out in a digital world	

adaptable portfolio because they have a limited amount of work. As they grow, they may begin to create more work that allows them to develop a targeted portfolio.

Table 12.3 outlines the major benefits and drawbacks to an adaptable portfolio. Let us look at two points that are directly opposed. The benefit in which an adaptable portfolio can show interviewers potential for alternative job opportunities is in direct conflict to the drawback that the portfolio does not show how well you work with a specific company in a specific job. These are two points you will have to weigh and decide which is more important to you.

The advantages and disadvantages of a targeted portfolio are listed in Table 12.4. These are essentially the opposite of those for the adaptable portfolio. One of the most important points to keep in mind is that you will have to change out the work in your portfolio for each job interview to keep it on target. Although a targeted portfolio can be very effective, it is also a lot of work.

To make yourself more flexible, you will need to have multiple adaptable projects. Keep them ready to go in portfolio sleeves (if you use them) so you can take one project out and substitute it with a better fit for the upcoming interview. Of course, if you have multiple interviews in a day for jobs with different needs, this can be cumbersome and time-consuming. You are probably better off just sticking with an adaptable portfolio. Be sure to verbally connect a project or two to the company, though. We will cover this more when we briefly discuss interviews in this chapter.

Physical Portfolios

What do you need for a physical portfolio? For many, a physical portfolio starts with the case. This could be the traditional black leather or plastic case, a special order or handmade case,[2] or even just a box. One of the most important things to consider when choosing your portfolio case is size. The size of your case impacts the size of the work you will present. The case should be easily portable. Can you easily transport it to appointments? Can you carry it on flights (and will the case pass through security)? Will the work it contains be large enough to show detail? This can be a difficult balance.

We recommend 11" × 14" or A3 for the size. This size allows you to show detail without the layouts being too cluttered. You can easily spread it on a table for an interview where all can see. It is also easy to carry without constantly whacking strangers in the kneecaps as you walk!

But what if your physical portfolio is lost, damaged, or stolen? It is typically best to use copies in the portfolio rather than your original work. This is a safety net in case anything happens to it. For some reason, copies

Table 12.3 Pros and Cons of an Adaptable-Style Portfolio

PROS	CONS
• Do not have to change out the work as often • Shows versatility • Can show potential for other jobs in case the interviewer has other openings • Sometimes it is easier for students and graduates that do not have enough targeted work for a targeted portfolio	• Does not show how well you can work with a specific company • Can indicate a lack of willingness to put extra effort into the interview

Table 12.4 Pros and Cons of a Targeted-Style Portfolio

PROS	CONS
• Shows you are prepared for the interview and dedicated to the potential job • Shows capability within the requirements of the job • Makes it easier for the interviewers to see you assimilating into the company and job	• Limits the types of jobs you can be considered for • Must change out the pages if you need to interview for a different type of job • Sometimes you may not have enough high-quality work that matches the target • Makes you look unprepared or uninterested in the position if your portfolio is not aligned with the current company/job for which you are applying

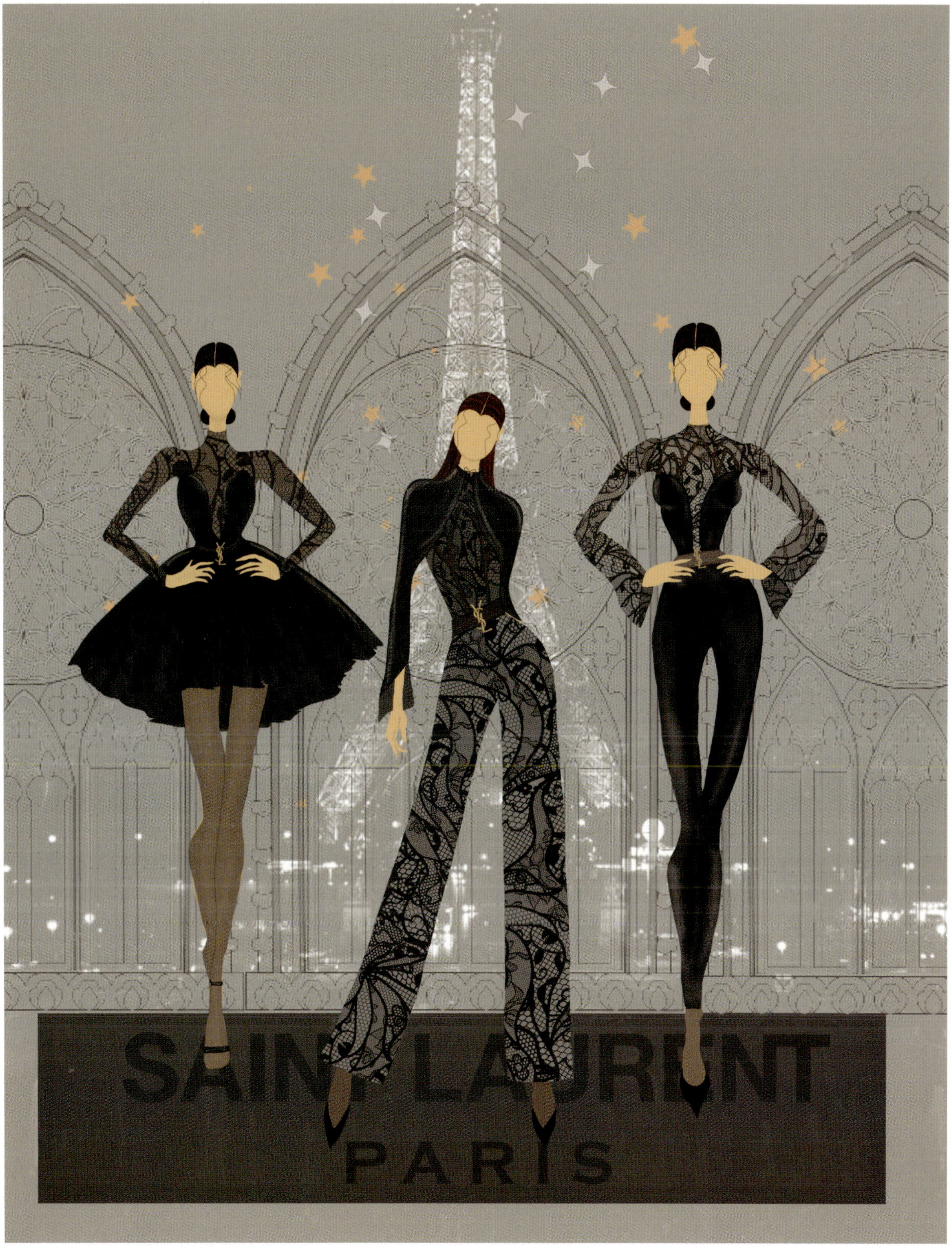

Figure 12.4 Projects can be interchanged according to the interview needs. Update your portfolio for the job description. Courtesy of Shelby Gomez.

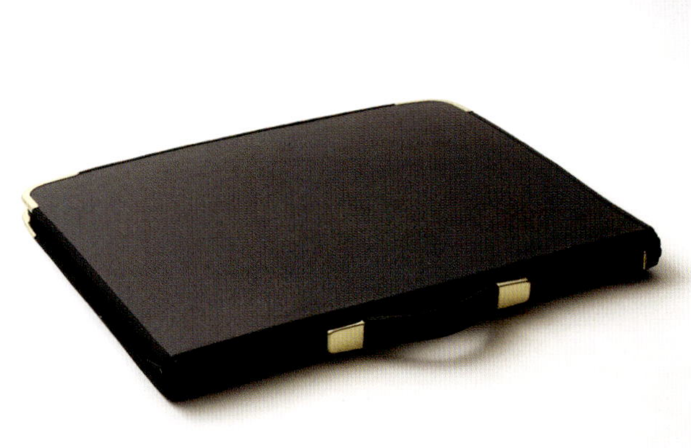

Figure 12.5 When looking for physical portfolio cases, you want to consider the size and how easy it is to handle during an interview. kyoshino/iStock.com

also tend to look better than the physical artwork of any hand-rendered layouts. So keep any original artwork safe at home and use printouts of the work in your portfolio. If anything happens to it, you will still have the original work and can rebuild the portfolio.

As a side note, never, ever leave your physical portfolio with a company after an interview. It is a sadly common practice for less-scrutable businesses to steal student designs without credit or payment. If they insist that you should leave your work with them, direct them to your online portfolio or offer to return for another interview. You and your portfolio are a package deal. We discuss this more in the section on interviews.

Does your portfolio need page protectors or sleeves? If so, make sure they are all the same type and that they are not scuffed or scratched. Although it can be expensive, replace the sleeves as needed so they look fresh. You don't want to lose out on a potential job because of old page protectors.

Components of a Physical Portfolio

The contents of your portfolio will vary depending on the type of job for which you are applying. Some jobs will require more variety than others.

Fashion students and professionals, do you need a portfolio that is creative, technical, or business-oriented? A portfolio for an assistant designer, a stylist, and a technical designer are very different. Ask yourself what the employer needs to see and what work best showcases your applicable skills. This could include design group layouts, tech or specification packs, fabrics, inspiration journals, and lookbooks. The interview may also specify what type of work you need to show.

Costume students and professionals, show your costume renderings, stills and photoshoots, research inspiration, and any technical skills you want to advertise. Think about the jobs you would like to pursue. If you truly want to stick solely with design, avoid showing too much technical work. Highly skilled drapers, craftspersons, and stitchers are always in demand. If a designer or shop sees that you have talent in that area, you will likely be directed that way. If you are open to different types of job opportunities, then show off your work!

Project 12.1: Mock-Up Portfolio

It can be very helpful to make a mock-up of your portfolio before you put the time and effort into the full-sized version. This seems like a waste of time to students who want to jump directly to the end, but it helps catch time-consuming and costly mistakes before they are made. This will allow you to see how the portfolio

STYLE SECRETS 12.1

Tech Packs Can Be an Advantage

In the fashion industry most entry-level jobs are in technical design. A strong technical package is your golden ticket to the job. A solid tech pack will get you in the door faster than a well-illustrated, well-designed collection. This may not be your dream job, but you are in the design department regardless. With time and reliable work, you can climb your way up to more creative positions!

will "read" when organized a certain way and what its impact will be. It will also allow you to see what should be included, discarded, and what is missing.

Making mock-up portfolios is similar to making flowcharts or a storyboard. It is a combination of organization and determining the narrative about you as a designer or maker. What do you want the portfolio viewer to know or see about you? How do you organize your materials to tell this tale?

It is most effective if you make a physical mock-up of your portfolio so that you have to turn the pages. This gives you a better understanding of how the portfolio will look and how viewers will see and interact with the pages. You can use small pieces of paper, index cards, printouts, or whatever works.

The pages should show rough sketches or actual prints of what you want on each portfolio page. Consider whether you need to include other items besides the renderings and layouts and remember to include those items. You can staple, tape, or clip the pages together.

Organization matters. Start and end strong, no matter what. Viewers will be most strongly impacted by what they see first and last. The first item encourages them to keep perusing and the last item sticks in the memory. Put your best work at the beginning and end.

If you have enough high-quality work, you may want to put some of your best work in the middle. This works to re-ignite the viewer's interest as they move through your projects. As with any good work, it only helps to make a better impression.

How many projects or pages should you include? You want enough high-quality work to show your talents and skills, but not so many that you become repetitive or tiresome to the viewer. The general number is probably somewhere between ten and thirty pages or three to six projects, but there is no hard-and-fast rule.

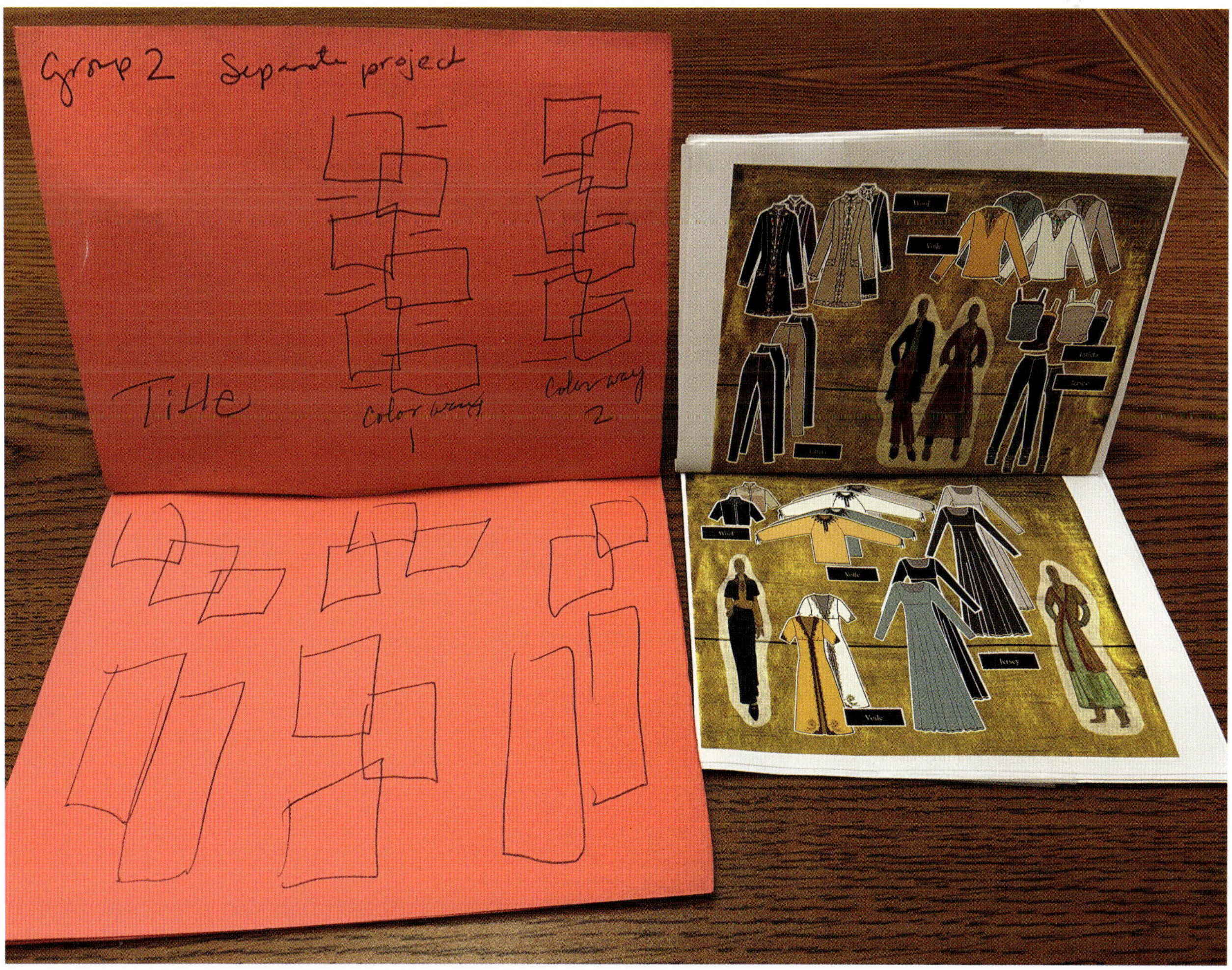

Figure 12.6 A mini mock-up portfolio can be as simple as some sketches cut out and stapled together to give an idea of the flow of your work. You can also print out reduced-size versions of your projects for a more accurate visual representation.

STYLE SECRETS 12.2

Make it Touchable

Design people love things they can touch. This is an easy way to make yourself memorable during an in-person interview. Add physical fabric swatches. Include surface design samples. Bring a garment you designed and constructed. Add tactile elements to your design journals.

They also like to play and love to be surprised. Have parts of the portfolio that pull or fold out. Use extra portfolio sleeves and black masking tape to create a barn-door interaction. Are you feeling really creative? Try a pop-up effect! Just make sure the effects do not outshine your design work. All effects should enhance your content rather than distract from it.

The mock portfolio should help you determine if you have too many or too few pages.

Make sure to have several people give you feedback on the mock portfolio. Rely more on professional colleagues or mentors rather than friends and family.[3] Check with people who know what should be in a fashion or costume portfolio. Ask them:

- If the organization makes sense
- If it feels like anything is missing or repetitive
- If there are too many or too few pages
- If the renderings/projects/items chosen seem appropriate for the intended job

After the feedback, make some corrections. Remember that feedback is just advice rather than final directives. Sort through what you learned from others and focus on the comments that came up multiple times. Sometimes you will hear conflicting advice, too. That's okay, as portfolios are very subjective. If you are not sure, trust your gut feeling. It is your work, after all. No one knows it better than you. Start organizing your full-scale portfolio based on your mock-up edits.

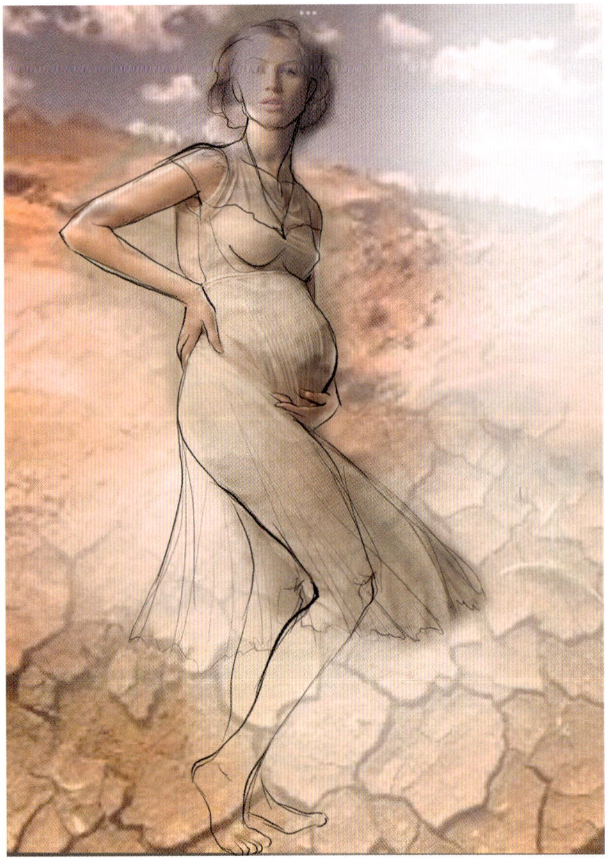

Figure 12.7 Digital portfolios are essential in today's world. Carefully curate your projects shown online to entice potential employers without giving away everything for free! Artwork by Olivera Gajic.

Digital Portfolios

When we think about digital portfolios, most people immediately think about a website or a similar online presence. However, a digital portfolio could be as simple as a PDF file that can be emailed to potential employers. They can also be videos or fully interactive websites.

If you choose to have a website, should you have a public or hidden website? You can also choose to have a password-protected website. These decisions are based on your need to protect your work compared to your desire for exposure.

Components of a Digital Portfolio

Because digital files can be copied, you must consider how much work you give away "free." Often, a digital portfolio is used as an appetizer; a way to entice potential employers and make them want to call you for an interview. This means that you may want to put one or two excellent examples and a few good examples of your work, but not *all* your best work in the digital portfolio. Especially if you have a physical portfolio, save some of your best work for the physical portfolio and for the interview.

If your digital portfolio is a file, research file formats and how you want to present your work. Do you want to have a simple series of images, such as a slide-show presentation that has been converted to a PDF? Do you want something more sophisticated, such as a short movie or animation of your work? There are many options available, and many more being developed every day, so do your homework.[4] However, make sure what you choose will show your work well rather than distract the viewer. Also use a format that the viewer can easily open. Your chances of an interview will plummet if they have to download a specialized app just to see your work.

If you want to use a web-based portfolio, do research on what hosting services are available and what each service offers. There are free services, but they may not offer what you need. They also severely limit your control over the layout. Consider security, your URL name, ease of making and editing the pages, how well you can make the look of the site match your personal branding, navigation capabilities, and ability to create a contact page.

What do you need to have in a digital portfolio? Obviously, you will need examples of your work. Typically, this will be three to five collections, shows, or projects. None of these need to be complete collections or shows. Again, you want just enough to make people interested in you. You may want to show other components of these projects, such as photographs of finished pieces, partial tech packs, inspiration, or other items that are essential to the job you want.

You will probably want an "About Me" page. Make sure this is written with a professional tone. It should outline your skills and accomplishments related to your potential job. Remember to include your education, experience, and any specialized training. This page should not give personal details about your life, such as where you are from, who your family is, whether you are married or have children, your ethnicity, age, or any other details that can either be used against you in an interview or used by identity thieves. It should also not include anything about your social life. Remember that this is for professional use.

Make sure you have a contact page or make your contact information very easy to find. The last thing you want is for someone to love your work, but not be able to find your contact information! If your digital portfolio is a PDF or file, this could be a page with a link to your email. If you have a website, you may not want to post your email or other contact information directly as this information can be picked up and used for spam. Never list a physical location, though. It creates a safety issue and can limit your job offers by location. If your website host gives you an option, a contact form is a better choice. Just make sure to have several people test the form to double-check that everything is set correctly and that you are not going to miss important connections.

Then you should decide whether to post your resumé. It can be very beneficial to have the resumé posted with your portfolio. If your resumé is a PDF, security is less of a concern. However, if your portfolio is a website, the information on your resumé can sometimes be used for identity theft.

There are some options. First, you can post an **abbreviated resumé**. This could have the details of what you did at your jobs without listing your employers. For instance, you could list an employer as Major Retailer, Small Women's Sportswear Manufacturer. Or you can list the shows you have designed without naming the specific theatre. If you are concerned, you could also list generic versions of your educational institutions also. At the top or bottom, make sure to include the disclaimer that specifics have been removed for identity protection and the full resumé is available upon request.

Another option is to put your resumé on a password-protected page. The downside is that no one can see an indication of your resumé unless they have the password. The upside is that it may be less confusing than the version without specifics.

Project 12.2: Mock-Up Website Portfolio

This is the same concept as the physical mock-up. You want to **wireframe** your website or mock-up your file (digital book). A website wireframe is the skeletal layout and organization of your potential website. In your mock-up the organization, navigation, and contents should all be considered.

If you are wireframing a website, it really is a combination of flowchart and storyboard. The flowchart aspect shows how you plan to build and navigate the website, from the home page to each subsequent page. Make sure the navigation is logical. Have other people check your navigation and provide suggestions. Also consider problems such as how to get back to the home page and how to jump from one section to another. Look at other websites that you consider easy to navigate to get ideas.

Once you have decided how you want to set up the basic website navigation, start drawing in pages. You can have sketches, digital mock-ups, or actual renderings, but you want to see what your website will look like. Make sure it visually flows. This is when you can tell if you need to add or subtract pages as well as if color schemes, layouts, and fonts work.

For portfolios that are files instead of websites, the process is similar. However, you are probably less concerned about navigation, unless you have developed an interactive file. Typically, you will organize the pages within the file the same way you would a physical portfolio. Make sure you use very strong renderings for the start and end of your digital portfolio file so you will be well remembered. Then map out what contents you want in the middle.

As with the website and the physical portfolio, use sketches or actual renderings as placeholders for each page so you can see how your portfolio will look. Check the flow, the length, and if the contents are enticing. Also consider how you want the portfolio to begin and end (think about covers of a book) and how you want the pages to transition.

Once you have completed your mock-ups, have several people give you constructive feedback. Again, stick with professional colleagues or mentors rather than friends and family. Make changes that you think will most benefit you and the job you want. Then it is time to make the actual digital portfolio.

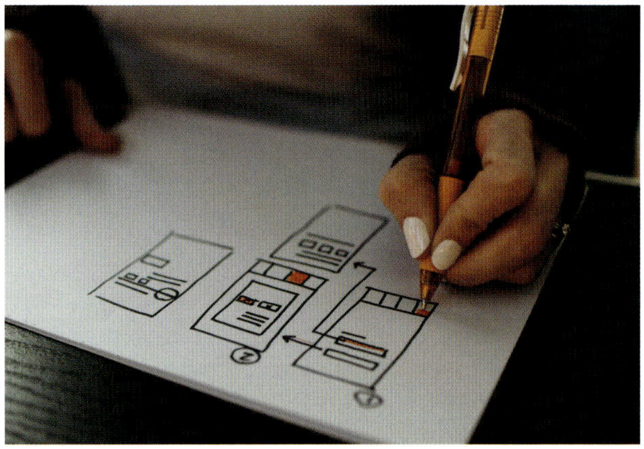

Figure 12.8 Use a wireframe to plan out the navigation of your portfolio website. Look at other sites and study their navigation for ideas. Courtesy of Kelly Sikkema via Unsplash.

Resumés and Letterheads

As you pull together your portfolio, you need to consider the look of your resumé and any **marketing collateral**. Marketing collateral is the assortment of your promotional materials such as the letterhead you use for cover letters, your resumé, business cards, and other items you use to promote yourself in the industry. There are plenty of sources available to help you with the content of your resumé and any cover letters. We have a few notes that are specific to the fashion and costume industries to help you out.

PRO TIP 12.1

Device-Responsive Design

You never know how someone will access your digital materials. Consider how your digital portfolio will look on a smart phone or tablet. Look into websites with **device-responsive design** options. This means that the website will visually change proportions in response to the specific device on which it is accessed to make it easier to read. Your website may look fantastic on a laptop screen but may be impossible to navigate on a phone. Some build-your-own websites offer solutions for this issue.

If you can afford one, you may alternatively consider a web designer. As trained graphic designers, they can help you look your best. Web and user experience (UX) designers know how to make your website aesthetically pleasing, easy to navigate, and device-responsive. Not everyone has the budget for a website designer, but it is money well spent if you can. Either way, check into your options for device-responsive design.

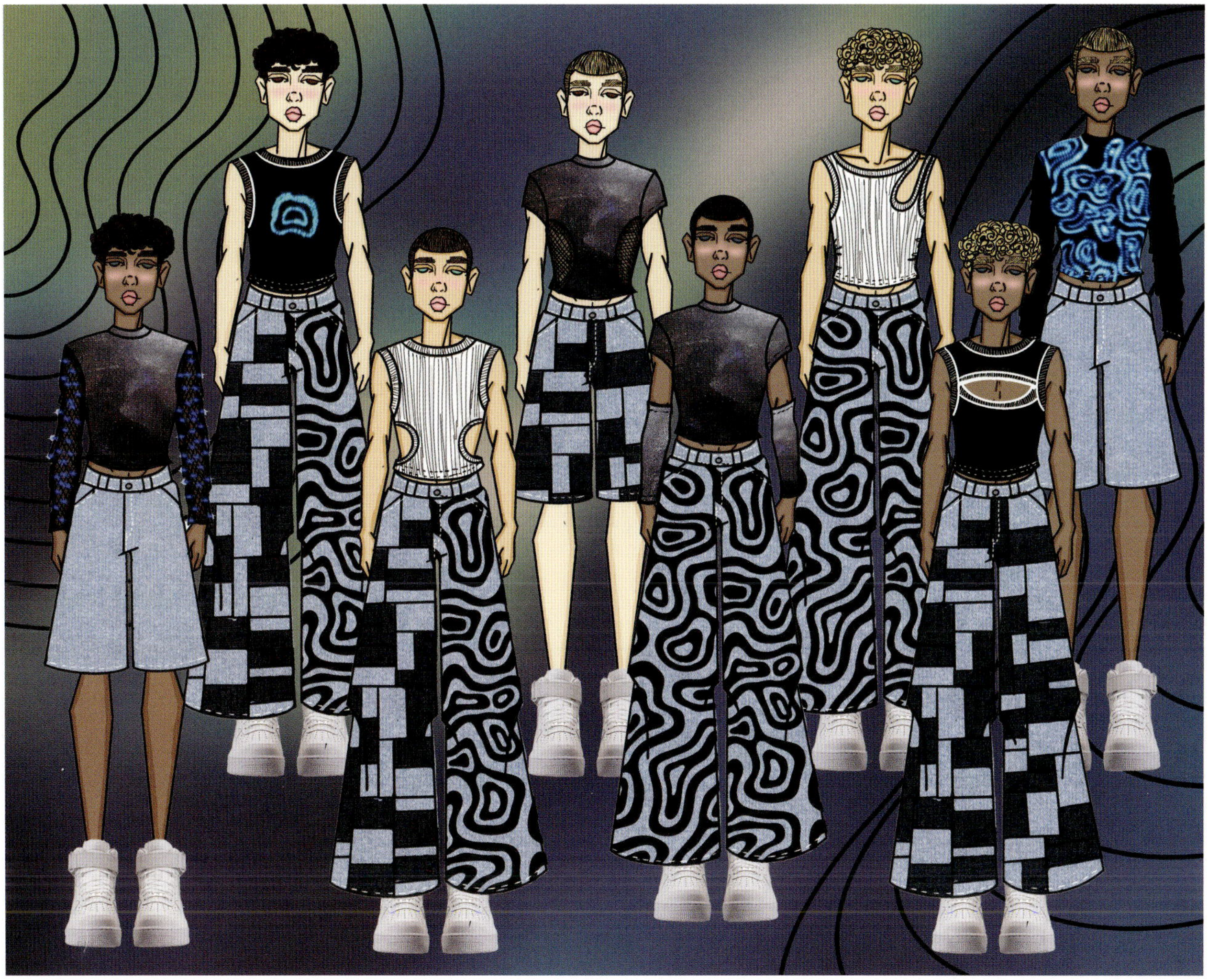

Figure 12.9 Your illustration and design styles should be reflected in your choice of marketing collateral design. Carefully consider what your work says about you and how that translates graphically to your letterhead and business cards. Courtesy of Frankie Rivera.

First and foremost, make sure you have a professional resumé, business card, and cover letter. Keep it in line with your personal brand discussed in the beginning of this chapter. A graphic **style sheet** will make your life much easier as you design these materials. Style sheets are a quick reference guides containing a specific color palette, fonts, and logo information. Consider the colors, typefaces, and mood you want to portray. Refer to your personal keywords frequently.

Yes, you should design your own resumé and other marketing collateral. Don't rely on graphic design shortcuts such as Canva. The designs look great but are easily recognizable. As a costume or fashion designer, it sends a message that you either cannot successfully design your own brand or simply won't spend the time to do so. Neither of these messages instill confidence in your abilities as a designer for your potential employers.

Instead, use existing personal marketing as inspiration when designing your own. If you are not comfortable with the task of designing it yourself, consider hiring a professional graphic designer to help you. Look at their other work to see if their style lines up with your own. Talk with them about your keywords and let them see your garment designs. This will help them to present viable options for you. Also check that they are in your budget before fully committing.

What makes a good resumé in fashion or costume? We have included an example resumé in Figure 12.11a and an annotated version in Figure 12.11b. If you are just starting out, focus the attention on your education as that is probably your most valuable asset fresh out of school. If you have good experience, focus on that instead. Don't be humble, but don't be disingenuous either. If you are

Style Sheet
Lalon Alexander Marketing Collateral

Fonts:

Alabama 30 pt

Alabama 48 pt

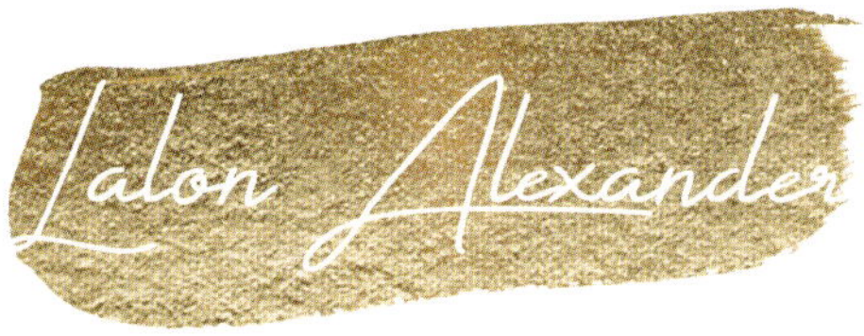

Graphic: Gold Swish
Text: Alabama 48 pt; 110% Vertical scale; 125% Horizontal scale

Cheltenham Pro 12 pt
Cheltenham Pro Bold 12 pt
Cheltenham Pro Light Italic 12 pt

Cheltenham Pro 14 pt
Cheltenham Pro Bold 14 pt

Graphic: Criss Cross Pattern; Full scale

White
#ffffff
C **0**
M **0**
Y **0**
K **0**

Black
#231f20
C **0**
M **0**
Y **0**
K **100**

Graphic: Criss Cross Pattern; Full scale; 25% Opacity

25% Gray
#c7c8ca
C **0**
M **0**
Y **0**
K **25**

Gold
#e5cca4
C **10**
M **18**
Y **38**
K **0**

Margins: 3p
Column gutter: 2p

Figure 12.10 Create a style sheet to make sure you use consistent colors, fonts, and other graphic elements in all of your marketing collateral.

Lalon Alexander

Seeks to contribute to a lively, sustainable fashion brand. Team player with experience in creative problem solving and generating innovative solutions to complex problems. Excels in both technical and creative design.

Contact

+1 (123) 456-7890
lalonsemail@abc.com

Portfolio

www.lalonalexander.com

Software Proficiency

- MS Excel
- Adobe Illustrator
- Adobe Photoshop
- Adobe InDesign
- Gerber Accumark
- Optitex Pattern Design
- Browzwear

Specialty Aptitudes

- Menswear
- Knitwear
- Tech packs
- Creative problem-solving
- Collaboration
- Written & verbal communication

Education

- Happy Snappy University, **Bachelor of Science:** Fashion Design 2028
  - Minor: Underwater Basketweaving
  - GPA: 3.65

Experience

- Assistant Technical Designer, Children's Knitwear Division, **Namby-Pamby Design, Inc.** 2024–present
  - *Create minimum of 10 tech packs for production each month*
  - *Responsible for all technical flats in children's knitwear division*
  - *Assisted with design decisions for Fall 2025 line*
- Sales Associate, **Sappy Bridal** 2022–2024
  - *Exceeded monthly sales quota consistently*
  - *Awarded Employee of the Month (July 2020 & Jan. 2021)*
  - *Assited in alterations department regularly*

Award & Honors

- Dean's List 2023–2025
- 2nd place in Happy Snappy University Red Dress Fashion Competition 2023
- Recipient of Big Cheese Academic Scholarship 2023–2025

Volunteer Experience

- Habitat for Humanity volunteer 2022–2025
- Backstage dresser for various fashion shows 2022–2024

Figure 12.11a An example resumé. Notice that all the information fits on one page.

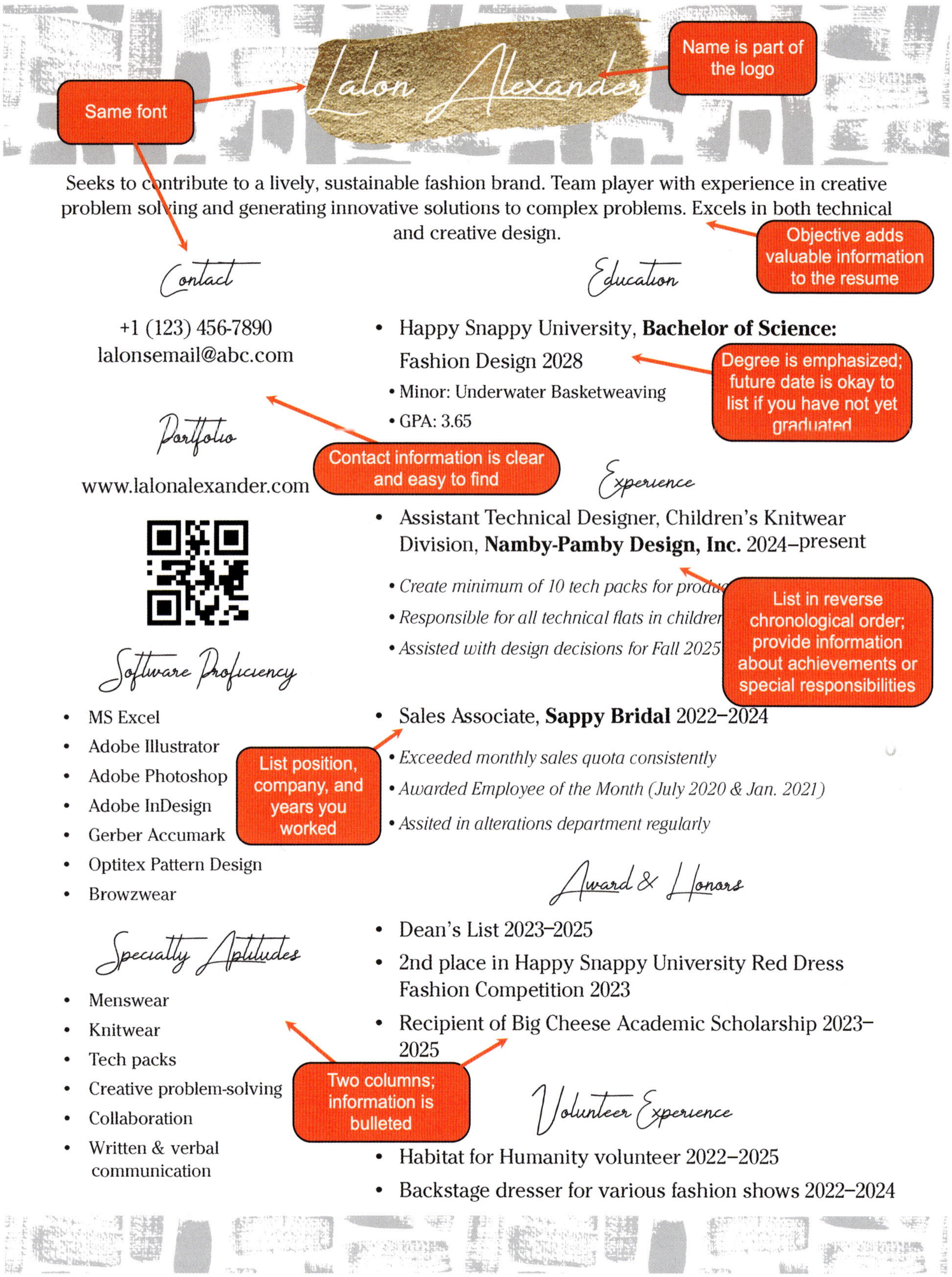

Lalon Alexander

Seeks to contribute to a lively, sustainable fashion brand. Team player with experience in creative problem solving and generating innovative solutions to complex problems. Excels in both technical and creative design.

Contact

+1 (123) 456-7890
lalonsemail@abc.com

Portfolio

www.lalonalexander.com

Software Proficiency

- MS Excel
- Adobe Illustrator
- Adobe Photoshop
- Adobe InDesign
- Gerber Accumark
- Optitex Pattern Design
- Browzwear

Specialty Aptitudes

- Menswear
- Knitwear
- Tech packs
- Creative problem-solving
- Collaboration
- Written & verbal communication

Education

- Happy Snappy University, **Bachelor of Science: Fashion Design 2028**
  - Minor: Underwater Basketweaving
  - GPA: 3.65

Experience

- Assistant Technical Designer, Children's Knitwear Division, **Namby-Pamby Design, Inc.** 2024–present
  - *Create minimum of 10 tech packs for produ*
  - *Responsible for all technical flats in childre*
  - *Assisted with design decisions for Fall 2025*
- Sales Associate, **Sappy Bridal** 2022–2024
  - *Exceeded monthly sales quota consistently*
  - *Awarded Employee of the Month (July 2020 & Jan. 2021)*
  - *Assited in alterations department regularly*

Award & Honors

- Dean's List 2023–2025
- 2nd place in Happy Snappy University Red Dress Fashion Competition 2023
- Recipient of Big Cheese Academic Scholarship 2023–2025

Volunteer Experience

- Habitat for Humanity volunteer 2022–2025
- Backstage dresser for various fashion shows 2022–2024

Figure 12.11b Here, we annotated the resumé with some tips to help you design yours.

still learning to use Photoshop, list yourself as beginner or intermediate rather than advanced.

Currently, there seems to be a trend to use your photo on the resumé or cover letter. Please don't. Like an excess of selfies on social media, it comes across as narcissistic and immature. You should be hired for your skills, not the way you look.

Add your contact information to all marketing collateral. Stick to a cell phone and email address. Add your website and any social media accounts you want the interviewers to see, too. There is no need to add a physical address though. So little professional correspondence occurs through regular mail these days there is no need. It can also limit you to a particular location. Some companies will not consider you if you do not already reside nearby, so don't offer the information unless it is specifically requested.

Keep your resumé and cover letter to one page each, particularly in the fashion industry. If you go beyond one page, most recruiters will simply toss your application into the trash without a second look. Avoid any mention of high school or allude to personal information such as your marital status, religion, or political views. Focus on your skills, particularly those that help differentiate you from the competition. If your working experience is limited, add in some volunteer work. Objectives are not necessary and can signal that you are trying to fill space on your resumé. If you have an objective, make sure it adds value to your resumé. "Seeking an entry-level position in the fashion industry" is a waste of valuable real estate on your resumé. It's obvious. You wouldn't apply for the job if you were not looking for it. Instead, focus on your soft skills and ambitions. Make sure you add something that isn't already apparent in your resumé.

Likewise, consider what makes a good cover letter in the industry. It should not be a repeat of your resumé. Be sure to tell a story about who you are. Give examples and mini stories that demonstrate your skills. This is your sales pitch to the company to entice them to call you in for an interview. Focus on the skills listed in the job qualifications. Make their job easy for them by showing how well you fit their need.

In today's world of artificial intelligence, don't be tempted to have AI create a cover letter for you. You have to speak and write like you do in the letter. It is a

PRO TIP 12.2

Asking for References

You don't need to include "references available upon request" on any of your materials anymore. It is an outdated practice. We know you will provide references if asked. In most cases, you won't need those references until you are in the last round of interviews and filling in forms with the human resources department. When you are at that point, know how to appropriately ask for a reference.

Contact your past employers or teachers. Make sure they remember you and ask if they are willing to provide a reference for you. In theory, this should be someone who knows you well and with whom you maintain a positive relationship. Have a conversation and bring up your current career aspirations. If they are willing to help you out, provide at least two weeks' time for them to write the letter. Give them the deadline, to whom and where to address the letter, background information about the job qualifications, and your current resumé. This will give them the appropriate information to write a good letter. If the employer prefers phone calls to letters, make sure to get the most appropriate contact information from your reference. They may be willing to share their office phone but not their cell phone.

Never assume when getting references. Don't provide their name and contact information if you have not checked with your reference. Also ask every time or be clear that you are asking for an extended period of time. Just because they said yes a month ago does not mean they have the time to help you out this month.

Finally, remember to write a thank-you note to your reference each time they assist you. It is good manners and helps maintain a positive, professional relationship. You never know when you will need them again!

Lalon Alexander

+1 (123) 456-7890 lalonsemail@abc.com

Billie Burke, Internship Coordinator
Big Bubba's BeOtchin Babes Brand
1234 8th Ave
New York City, NY 10018

March 1, 2026

Dear Ms. Burke,

The moment I saw the design internship position open, I immediately had to write to you to apply! I cannot tell you how much the prospect of working for Big Bubba's BeOtchin Babes Brand means to me. I would honestly be over the moon to be considered for this prestigious position. The BBBBB label has been a staple in my closet since high school. Please allow me to introduce and present myself:

As a senior in the Snappy Happy University's fashion design bachelor's degree program, I have acquired many of the skills you seek for this position. Along with the standard design, patternmaking, and construction classes, I have sought many of the specialized courses to diversify my skillset. For example, the fashion department offered a menswear class this semester. I have never thought much about menswear before taking this class. However, I found that it really helped me to push my flexibility and problem-solving skills in design. I have also become more aware of global fashion trends as a result.

Additionally, as part of my class learning and my part-time experience, I am quite proficient with Microsoft Excel. Your position announcement stated that you use Excel for your technical packages. Along with creating tech packs for our regular production class assignments, I am trusted with the privilege of creating them in my current position with Namby-Pamby Design, Inc. I would love the opportunity to see, learn, and quickly adapt to BBBBB's team tech pack process.

Collaboration comes naturally to me, and I am thrilled to imagine myself as part of your crew. I grew up in a large family of 6 brothers and sisters, so I had to become a team player practically at birth. Even when collaborations break down, I enjoy using creative problem-solving to overcome strife. Just last semester, one of our key team members on a class project had to back out unexpectedly right before the project was due. That was really stressful, but I helped to organize and distribute the unfinished work amongst our remaining members to complete the task. Our teacher even commented that we had one of the best projects!

Thank you so very much for your time and consideration of my application for the design internship. I have included my resumé for your review and hopefully to entice you into an interview. I will call next week to confirm receipt of these materials, to see if you have any questions for me, and to possibly schedule an interview date. I hope you have a fantastic week in the meantime!

Warmly,

Lalon Alexander

Figure 12.12a An example cover letter.

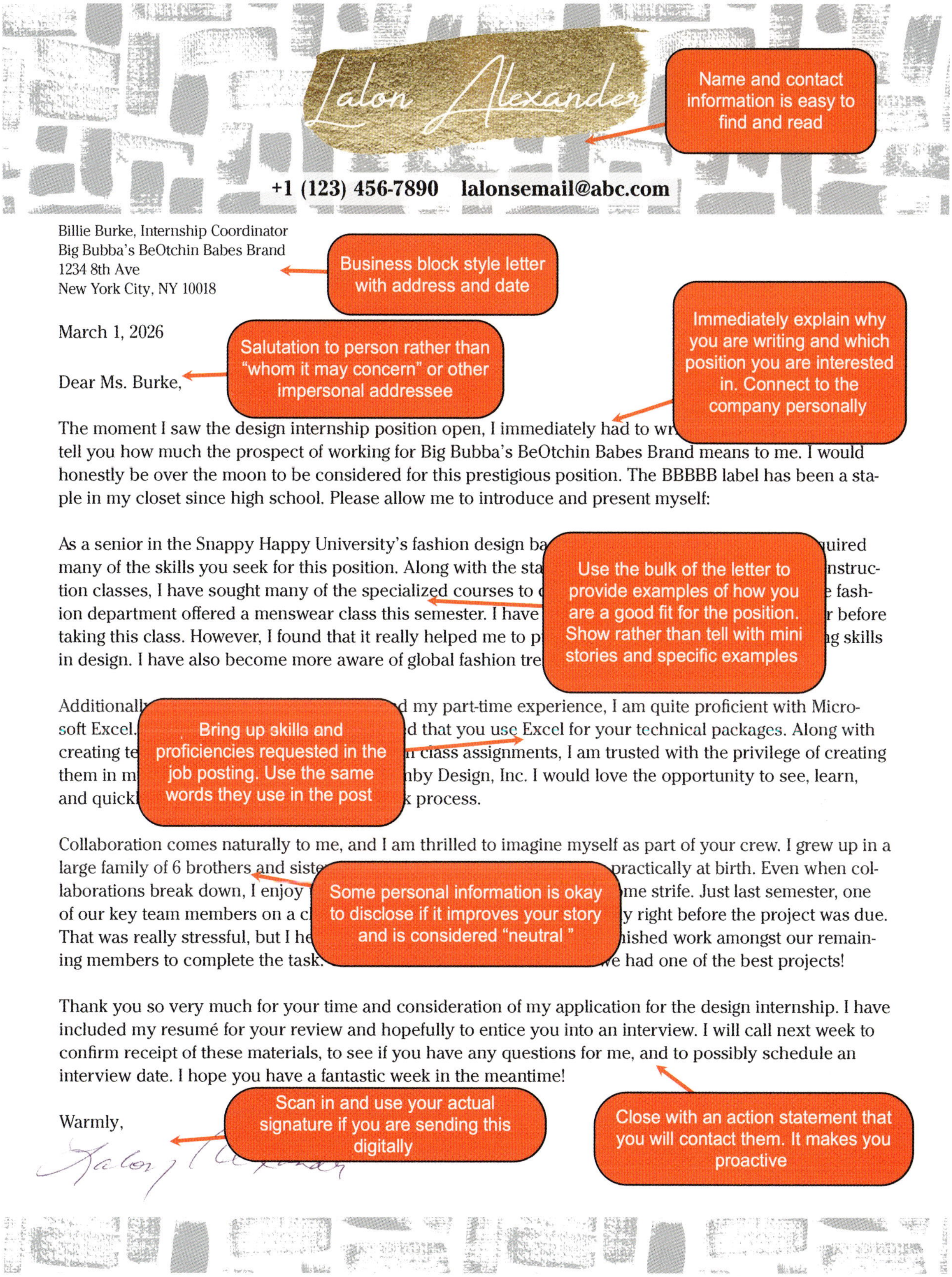
Lalon Alexander

+1 (123) 456-7890 lalonsemail@abc.com

Billie Burke, Internship Coordinator
Big Bubba's BeOtchin Babes Brand
1234 8th Ave
New York City, NY 10018

March 1, 2026

Dear Ms. Burke,

The moment I saw the design internship position open, I immediately had to wr… tell you how much the prospect of working for Big Bubba's BeOtchin Babes Brand means to me. I would honestly be over the moon to be considered for this prestigious position. The BBBBB label has been a staple in my closet since high school. Please allow me to introduce and present myself:

As a senior in the Snappy Happy University's fashion design ba… …uired many of the skills you seek for this position. Along with the sta… …nstruction classes, I have sought many of the specialized courses to … …e fashion department offered a menswear class this semester. I have … …r before taking this class. However, I found that it really helped me to p… …g skills in design. I have also become more aware of global fashion tre…

Additionall… …d my part-time experience, I am quite proficient with Microsoft Excel. … …d that you use Excel for your technical packages. Along with creating te… …n class assignments, I am trusted with the privilege of creating them in m… …nby Design, Inc. I would love the opportunity to see, learn, and quickl… …k process.

Collaboration comes naturally to me, and I am thrilled to imagine myself as part of your crew. I grew up in a large family of 6 brothers and siste… …practically at birth. Even when collaborations break down, I enjoy … …me strife. Just last semester, one of our key team members on a c… …y right before the project was due. That was really stressful, but I he… …ished work amongst our remaining members to complete the task. … …e had one of the best projects!

Thank you so very much for your time and consideration of my application for the design internship. I have included my resumé for your review and hopefully to entice you into an interview. I will call next week to confirm receipt of these materials, to see if you have any questions for me, and to possibly schedule an interview date. I hope you have a fantastic week in the meantime!

Warmly,

Figure 12.12b The annotated version provides tips to help you write your letter. Remember to customize it to each job position.

clear sign that something is up when your cover letter sounds more sophisticated than you do when speaking during your interview. In fact, this is how many teachers identify that you used AI for your homework! It is not uncommon for some companies to ask for a writing sample if it relates to the position for which you are applying. You can also be quickly black-balled in the industry for not submitting your own work during a job application. Even if you do not consider it "cheating," your potential employers may.

Likewise, don't copy heavily from example cover letters available on the internet. Write your own story. There is a well-shared sample that starts with, "In my pursuit of creative endeavors, I came across this job announcement … ." Please avoid borrowing too much from such examples. Recruiters easily recognize the "creative endeavors" letter. It shows a lack of imagination and initiative when your letter is clearly a knockoff.

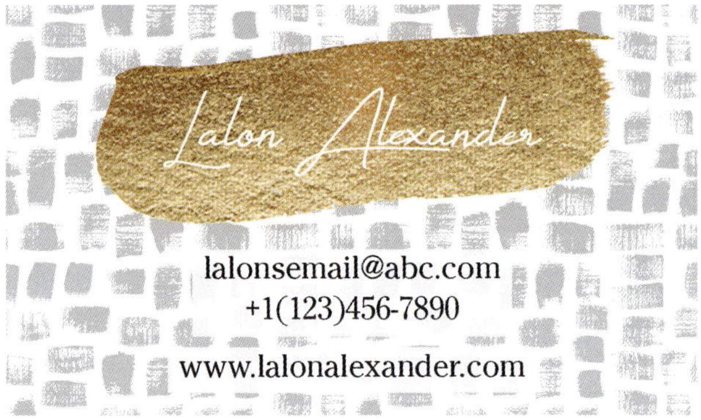

Figure 12.13 An example business card that goes with the other materials shown in this chapter. This one was designed to standard American business card size. Notice that the contact information is clear and legible.

Project 12.3: Create a Resumé, Letterhead, and Business Card Layouts

Like your portfolio layouts, you should roughly sketch out several ideas. If you have not yet created a personal brand logo, start with that. Keep your branding keywords handy. Perhaps even create a trend board to direct yourself. Feel free to create the logo in Illustrator, Photoshop, or another favorite drawing application. Seek feedback and tweak it as needed.

If you have something already created, create a style sheet for yourself. Include colors, typefaces, and other visual elements to keep your look consistent. This will be invaluable as you create your other marketing collateral. You are welcome to use Photoshop, Illustrator, or another illustration application for your resumé and letterhead, but InDesign truly excels in this type of document. You can easily manage the content in a word processor like Microsoft Word. Then import and place that content into the InDesign document. As you update the Word document, the linked file will update the next time you *Open* your InDesign document.

Step 1: Setup your document for a standard size such as 8.5" × 11" or A4. Keep to standard sizes for your marketing collateral. Potential employers will be annoyed if they must resize your document or locate special paper just to print your documents. Annoying your potential employers is never a good idea: especially before you meet them!

Set up your *Margins* while you are in the *New Document* dialog box. Find the sweet spot that works best for you. You don't want to print your content to the edge as it will most likely get cut off during printing and looks overcrowded. You also don't want extra-large margins that are clearly meant to take up space and "fluff" your content. Generally, ¼–½ inch or 5–10 millimeters makes a good margin. If you want multiple columns, set them up in your *New Document* dialog box. Add a *Gutter* space so the columns do not butt up against one another. The bleed does not matter unless you plan to print multiple copies professionally. Otherwise, the digital copy of your documents won't include a bleed, so there is no point.

Step 2: Set up the visual elements of your resumé or letterhead. Consider if you want the logo and contact information at the top, bottom, or sides. Again, you want it large enough to be seen and is easily legible. However, it should not be so big as to be obviously trying to take up space. Students often make this mistake thinking that it will be less noticeable that they do not have a lot of experience. However, it tends to have the opposite effect. Rather than using visuals to fill in for a lack of content, try adding different content such as volunteer work, special skills, or a good objective that makes you stand out.

Step 3: For your resumé, add any headings you need for the various sections such as education and experience. It is okay for your headings to have more flourish. Just make sure that they are still readable. Check it with a friend or two.

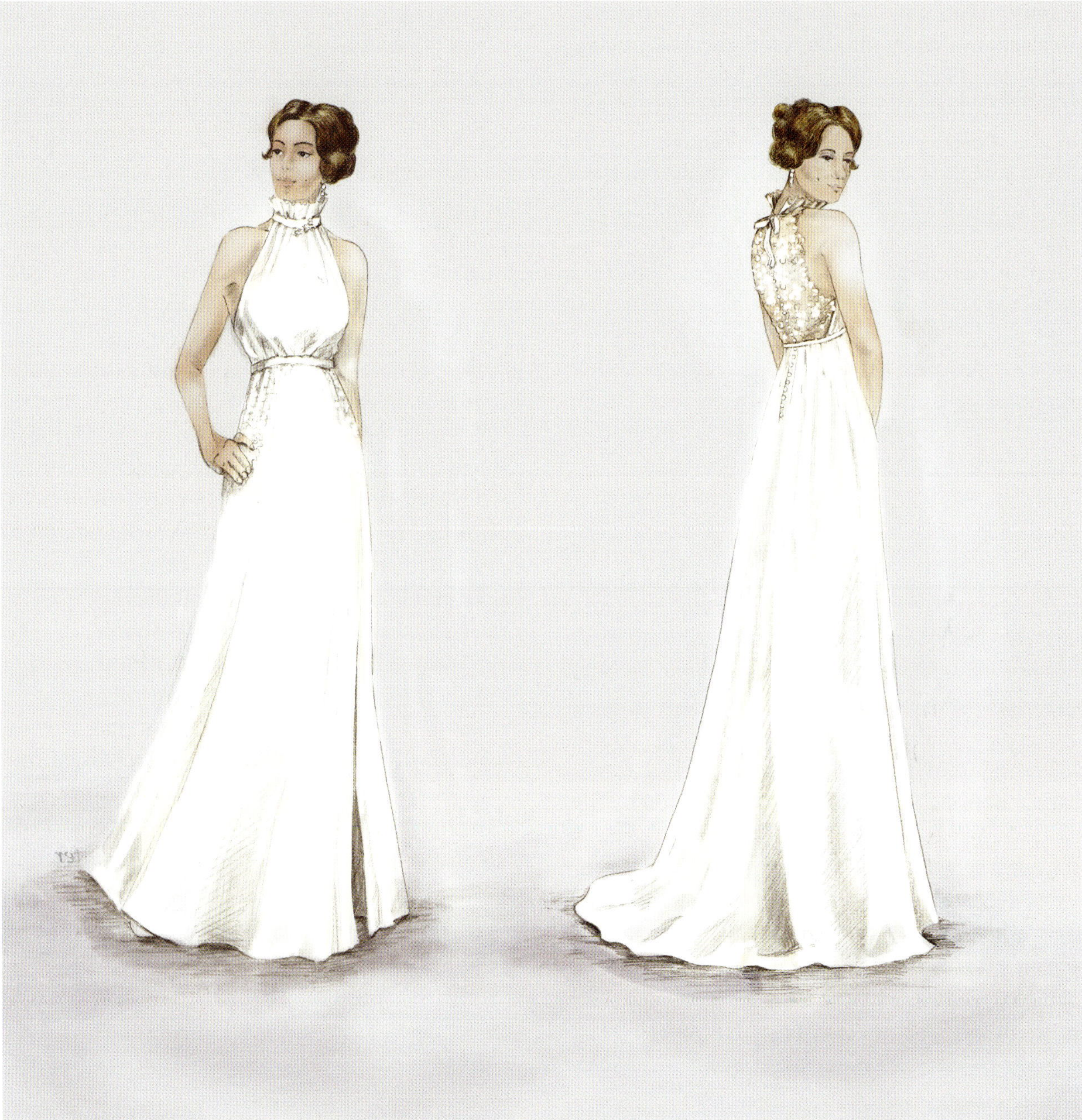

Figure 12.14 When entering the workforce for the first time it can be very daunting, but let your portfolio help to sell your skills. Courtesy of Carla Bellisio.

Step 4: Import and place your content. Keep it linked so it is easy to update your information as it changes. The primary content should be in a very easy to read font.

Step 5: Export each page. Stick with a PDF format. You want a file format that is easy to read, not too large, and will print well. A PDF works best for this. It also has the advantage that the viewer can make their own notes on the file during the interview process.

For your business card, repeat the basic steps outlined for resumés and your letters. Consider if you want to keep your business card to a standard size. Non-standard sizes and shapes have the advantage of quickly capturing attention. However, they are harder to put into a wallet. Many people still practice this often-overlooked business practice. Look around at design industry business card trends. Aim for something that fits your personal brand.

You can probably just manually type your contact information directly into the file rather than linking it. It is less likely to change, and the information is minimal. A business card should only include your name and contact information. We don't recommend adding a job title as it can limit your prospects. If you list something like "assistant designer," others may think you are not experienced enough for certain jobs. If you say something like "fashion designer," they may see you as pretentious. Make your life easier and just leave it off.

Troubleshooting

"I don't have enough experience for my resumé."

Although not a software issue, this problem frequently comes up with students preparing for the professional world. As mentioned before, you can add volunteer experience or list some of your specialized skills gained through class. Are you bilingual? List your fluent spoken and written languages. Enumerate some duties below any jobs you have had. If you haven't had any jobs, try for an internship. Internships and apprenticeships always look good on a resumé and are a great way to gain more experience. Don't worry too much if you have jobs outside of your chosen career. For example, working as a waitperson at a restaurant is a great way to learn customer service and thinking on your feet. It also shows longevity as a valuable employee if you have had that position for more than a year. There are multiple ways to add to your resumé when you lack job experience. Talk to your teachers and mentors for more ideas.

"Can I add columns to my document after I created it?"

Yes, certainly. Look under the *Layout* menu in InDesign. Select the *Margins and Columns* command. A dialog box will appear and you can add or adjust your columns and margins here.

Social Media

Are you a social media guru? Or perhaps you avoid it altogether. We promise you; your potential employers will check you out online one way or another. So be prepared for it. Curate your online presence.

There are a couple of ways to handle your social media activity. The first is to keep all your accounts completely private or simply avoid any social media activity. Some of us just do not have the know-how or energy to keep up with the plethora of social media, and that's okay. Although this approach sounds easy enough, it can be harder than you may think. Keeping your settings private seems to be a constant battle for the average user. Social media applications constantly refresh their privacy settings and policies, which means you need to stay vigilant and check your settings frequently. Avoiding any contact with social media can also prove troublesome as it can hinder you in other ways such as keeping up with trends, visual research, company news, and colleagues.

The other option is to engage in social media publicly. If you are new to social media, or are not great at keeping up with it, then restrict yourself to one or two applications. As you become more proficient and prolific, then branch out into others. An empty profile can be just as off-putting for potential employers as an inappropriate or directionless profile. Keep yourself limited so you are not overwhelmed or losing excessive time keeping up with your accounts. Try starting with LinkedIn first, as it is an application for professionals.[5] When you feel ready, branch into Instagram or another platform that is prevalent in your industry.

If you are a social media maverick, then carefully curate your posts and edit your profile to a professional audience. Create a schedule of posting that you can keep up with regularly. Stick to posts about industry news and trends. Think about the image you are presenting to your potential employers.

You need to start making hard decisions. You may have political views and a lifestyle that you feel are important parts of your image and what makes you, you. That is fantastic that you know yourself! However, potential employers may or may not agree with that image. You need to decide if it is more important to you to have as many job opportunities as possible, or to be true to your image. There is no right or wrong answer to this decision. Just be aware that others will judge you no matter the situation.

When applying for professional positions, your potential employers will look for a professional image. You need to eliminate photos of your "party" days if you have them. They don't care what you ate for lunch, which celebrities you think are hotties, or if that nail color "slays." And they certainly don't want to see you passed out drunk in your bestie's back seat. An abundance of selfies can come across as narcissistic and immature. Essentially, start to think like a responsible, professional adult and make sure your online profile(s) align with that image.

Now if you believe that an employer should stay out of your personal business and not care what you do on your own time, that's okay too. Make the decision and stand by it. However, do not be shocked if you receive fewer callbacks or if they ask you about certain activities during your interview. Again, there is no right or wrong answer. You simply need to decide if it is more important to you at this point in your life before someone else makes the decision for you.

You may choose to find the middle ground, as well. Perhaps reduce or eliminate the less-professional activities but stick to your convictions with activities that are truly important to you. For example, showing support by marching in an LBGTQ+ parade may be a huge part of your personal identity. Yes, some more conservative employers may feel that should not be part of your professional profile. However, you may not want to work with anyone that takes that stance. So, the tradeoff is perfectly acceptable to you in this case. The point is to be conscious of, and make definitive choices about, what your online profile says about you.

Presenting Your Work

You have a portfolio! You have a resumé and a cover letter! You just landed an interview! Wait ... now what?! The work doesn't end with creating all this stuff. You have to present yourself, too.

In terms of nailing the interview, there is a lot of help out there for techniques. Practice is the main tip. Remember to look the part, too. How you dress for an interview with Ralph Lauren is different from how you might dress if you have an interview for Urban Outfitters. You need to look professional for both, but with slightly different style to show that you understand their aesthetic.

The one area specific to designers that is rarely covered in interview technique help sources is how to handle your portfolio. It is a very common student/early professional mistake to not correctly use your portfolio during an interview.

How to Handle Your Portfolio During Interviews

Is your interview in person or conducted online or through the phone? This will obviously change how you engage with your portfolio for the interviewers. Either way, you must involve your portfolio.

It may seem obvious how to use your portfolio in a face-to-face interview. However, we find that young professionals are often too nervous to utilize it well. When you walk into an interview, put your portfolio on the table so it is hard to ignore or forget. Introduce and engage with your interviewers as usual. If asked about your portfolio, walk through it as described momentarily.

Sometimes, they don't ask, though. Use their questions to bring up your work. For example, if they ask about your ability to work in teams, bring up a team-designed project in your portfolio. As you are talking, open it and turn to the project. Then ask if they would like to see the rest of your work while you have the portfolio open. Essentially, find an opportunity to slip one of your projects into the conversation. If the opportunity simply does not show up and it seems like the interview is about to wrap up, simply ask, "Would you like to see some of my design work?" There's nothing wrong with jumping to the point. What you should absolutely not do under any circumstance is to walk out of the interview without showing them your portfolio. An unopened portfolio is a sure sign that you will not get that design job.

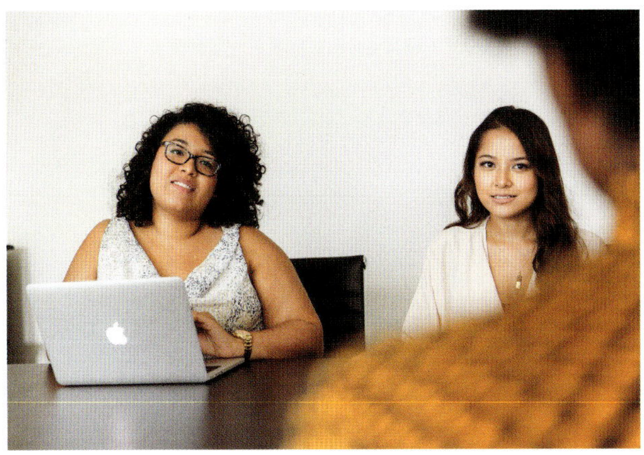

Figure 12.15 Take the opportunity to introduce your portfolio during the interview questions. Remember to face your work to the interviewers. Courtesy of Christina @ wocintechchat.com via Unsplash.

Once you have the portfolio open, remember to face it towards the interviewers. You'd be surprised how many young professionals start to talk about the work with the portfolio facing themselves! Lay it down so everyone can easily see the pages. Be sure to keep your hands out of the way of the artwork. The interviewers may let you direct the presentation, or they may start to flip through the pages at their own pace. Either way, provide information about each project. Talk about your inspiration, what you learned from the project, and how such designs could benefit the company or brand. Discuss your fabric choices and if you worked with a team. Remember that the best interviews are conversations, so engage with your interviewers while showing your work.

There are some don'ts to handling your portfolio during an interview, too. Don't let the conversation fizzle out while the interviewers are looking at your work. You don't have to ramble or be a chatterbox. Brief pauses are perfectly fine. However, total silence indicates that you are not that interested in the position or that you lack initiative.

Likewise, don't quiz your interviewers about your work. It may seem like you are motivated by asking, "Do you have any recommendations for improving my work?" However, it tends to be disturbing to most interviewers by putting them on the spot for instant feedback. When walking your interviewers through a project, you shouldn't simply describe what they are looking at. Tell a story that involves the project rather than simply describing that, "this dress has short sleeves and uses the cotton print." They can see that for themselves. And as mentioned previously, never, EVER leave your portfolio with your interviewers.

A digital portfolio is a major advantage should your interview be online or via the phone. Have a fast way for your interviewers to get to your work. A website works best for this, but you can also email a PDF of your digital portfolio to them just before your interview. Consider having a printed QR code on your business card or a clickable link on your resumé that leads to your online portfolio. If you are meeting online, ask to share your screen so everyone is looking at the same thing as you walk them through the portfolio. Like a face-to-face interview, you want to describe your design process or lessons from each project. Involve the interviewers by connecting your work to the company/brand/people with whom you are interviewing. Make their position easy by demonstrating how well you fit with them and how ready you are to do the job!

PRO TIP 12.3

Don't Underestimate the Power of a Thank-You

Job opportunities are won and lost by thank-you notes. Seriously. This has to be the most underestimated and overlooked professional game-changer. Send a thank-you note for interviews, references, mentors, or anyone who assisted you along the way. Even if the interview went badly, always send a thank-you note. It will show a different side of you. No matter which industry you are in, it is a small world. Professionals know each other and share stories. You want them to share the positive stories rather than the embarrassing ones.

Consider the level of their time. You should always provide a quick verbal thanks for in-person situations but reflect if you want to follow up with a more lasting form of thank-you. You may want to send a quick email thanks for those that provided a little verbal help or suggestions. For more involved help, think about sending a handwritten thank-you note. Handwritten notes sent through the mail have a powerful impact on people. It is so infrequently practiced these days that you will immediately stand out as someone who is considerate and willing to go the extra mile. We know of employers who changed their minds about the best candidate for the job based on the one who sent a handwritten card.

In your note, remind them of who you are. Bring up points discussed at your meeting or interview. For interviews, offer to meet with them again. Above all else, make yourself human and memorable to them.

Consider writing notes to admins who helped you or colleagues who recommended the job to you. You never know who has the boss's ear or who you will run into again in the future. Along those lines, be nice to everyone during the interview visit!

Networking with Your Portfolio

Interviews are not the only place to use your portfolio. When networking with other professionals, be sure to direct them to your work. Website portfolios work best for this. Have your website easily accessible on your business card. If you don't have a digital portfolio, consider making some postcards of one of your renderings. It's a great teaser for your work and gives them a physical reminder they can take to the office.

Try approaching industry professionals for advice as it often leads to job possibilities. Don't just corner them and ask them to provide advice on the spot; start a conversation by asking more about how they got to where they are now. See if they are open to a longer conversation to learn more and provide career advice to you. Offer to buy coffee or even lunch. Many people are flattered by this approach and more likely to take you up on it. Ask if they would mind viewing your portfolio and providing some feedback. If they know it is coming, they feel more prepared to give you pointers. All of this can lead to a positive professional relationship. They may be willing to continue to mentor you for some time. The greatest advantage is that these professionals are now familiar with your work and can direct potential jobs your way as they hear about them!

No matter how you hear about a job, be sure to follow up on it within the week. Seriously. Don't let the opportunity fly by. The fastest way to lose out on a job is to not apply. And if a mentor hears that you never acted on their advice, they will stop recommending you.

Summary

Now that you have improved your digital illustration skills significantly, you should consider how you want to present your work. Consider the whole package of your designs, portfolio, resumé, cover letter, business card, and personal image. Consider if a physical or digital portfolio fits your needs. You may choose to have both so they complement each other. Also think about whether a targeted or adaptable portfolio is best in your situation. Consider the layout of your work through a mini mock portfolio or a wireframe of your potential website. Make sure your resumé and other marketing collateral match your brand. Create a style sheet to help you. Think about your online image, particularly through social media. Employers will check during interviews. Curate your image consciously. Remember to implement your portfolio into your interviews as well. Walk your interviewers through your projects and show rather than tell them how well you will do the job.

STUDIO Companion Videos for Chapter 12

Please refer to STUDIO for accompanying chapter video(s)

Keywords

Abbreviated resumé
Adaptable portfolio
Device-responsive design
Marketing collateral
Style sheet
Targeted portfolio
Wireframe

Review Questions

1. List three pros and three cons of a physical portfolio. Do the same for a digital portfolio.
2. List three pros and three cons of a targeted portfolio. Do the same for an adaptable portfolio.
3. Why should you not include a physical address on your resumé or website these days? Provide at least two reasons.
4. What are three things you should do with your portfolio during an interview?
5. If you are new to social media, which platform should you start with first and why?
6. Why should you not ask for feedback during your interview?

7. Why should you never leave your physical portfolio with a prospective employer?
8. Which file format is best for your resumé and cover letter, and why?

Discussion Questions

1. Do you prefer a digital or physical portfolio? Why?
2. Do you think an adaptable or a targeted portfolio is better for you? Why?
3. Are objectives outdated? Defend your answer.
4. Do you believe it is okay to use artificial intelligence for your cover letters? Defend your answer and provide scenarios that support your opinion.
5. How important is a social media presence for your chosen career? Defend your opinion.
6. What is your opinion in the social media debate? Is it okay for potential employers to judge future employees by their social media presence or should they mind their own business? Defend your answer.
7. How do you think you should dress for an interview in your chosen career? Make a list of what you believe is okay and what is not okay.

Practice Exercises

1. Look up three websites of designers you admire. Track the navigation and make notes about the visuals that you like. Compare and contrast each. List the features and visuals you would like to include on your own website.
2. Use your keywords and personal brand to build a style sheet. Create a limited color palette and choose no more than two fonts. One can be decorative while the other is clear and legible. Think about what elements should be consistent in all of your marketing collateral such as frames, borders, or logo placement.
3. Evaluate your current portfolio. Create two more projects to fill in any holes or provide alternate options when switching projects between interviews.
4. Contact a professional whose career you admire. Reach out to ask about their personal story. See if they are willing to meet you personally and if they are willing to look over your work for advice.
5. Scout for at least five different jobs you are interested in and qualified for. List the specific qualifications and keywords such as collaboration, creativity, or communication. Make sure your cover letter touches on these areas.
6. Trade resumés and cover letters with a classmate or professional colleague. Provide critical feedback to each other. Pay attention to the visuals as well as the content.
7. Work in teams or small groups. Take turns interviewing each other. Talk about what was good and what needs some tweaking. Workshop possible answers together.

Endnotes

1. Costume designers are always interested in your design work, but are probably more interested in your ability to stay organized if you are interviewing as an assistant designer. Be sure to show that you have a good knowledge of fabrics and excellent communication skills. Direct the interview in those directions rather than focusing on your designs.
2. Handmade cases can be very impressive but also very expensive. At the end of the day, the content of the portfolio is what really matters. Make sure what's inside the portfolio leaves a better lasting impression than the outside. Don't feel that you need a fancy case to get the job. It's just icing, and the employers know it.
3. Friends and family do not provide good feedback unless you have a relative in your specific industry with a good perspective of what to look for. Inevitably, family and friends feel it is their job to either support you or criticize you. So, the feedback either leans towards a rainbow report of how fantastic you are, or leaves you sobbing in the corner contemplating a career change to the fast-food industry. Either way, it's just not useful or productive.
4. Don't get too caught up with gimmicky presentations. It can be off-putting for many professionals. Remember it's about your design work and ability to do the job for which you are interviewing.
5. Actually, it is a good practice for any professional to have a solid LinkedIn profile. It is not the most exciting social media platform, but employers expect to be able to find you. We have experienced some search committees that become highly suspicious of non-existent or bare profiles on LinkedIn. It does not take much to create a professional profile, and you are not expected to post frequently. LinkedIn is used more for the contacts than the feed.

Appendix 1 Resources

Many of these resources cost extra money. Consider carefully what you truly need for your workflow and what fits your budget. Remember to shop around holidays as well. For example, most of these resources have big sales around "Cyber Monday" in the United States. You will be able to get deals on both software and hardware at that time. But keep in mind that just because you see a big discount doesn't always mean that you are getting a good deal! Do some research before you buy. Read the reviews and watch some tutorial videos to see if that resource is something you will use regularly.

Also remember for each of these resources to check the computing requirements. Some require very little, but others may take significant memory, disk space, processing power, and a powerful graphics card. Check the recommended system requirements against your computer. Will your device be able to support this program or peripheral hardware?

Note that websites provided for all resources are for US-based customers. For our friends outside of the United States, please search for the company name using your normal browser to see if it is available in your region. If not, try general searches for resources using specific keyword phrases such as "Photoshop brushes." You may even find resources that we don't have here in the States!

Some of the companies will have educational discounts for students. You may have to hunt around their website. The information is not always easy to find. Search for "educational discount" or "student discount." If you are a teacher, sometimes they extend the discount to teachers, and sometimes it is only for students. It is always worth checking, though.

Most software offer some sort of free trial, as well. You can try it out without payment for seven to ninety days, depending on the company. Be careful, though. You often have to supply payment information so they can charge you as soon as the trial is up. If you decide you don't want to buy-in, cancel it before the trial ends!

Software

- Adobe: https://www.adobe.com/
  - Look for the educational discount: https://www.adobe.com/creativecloud/buy/students.html
- Affinity Designer/Photo/Publisher: https://affinity.serif.com/en-us/
- ClipStudio Paint: https://www.clipstudio.net/en/
- Corel: https://www.corel.com/en/ Corel produces Painter along with CorelDRAW and PaintShop Pro
  - Painter Educational license: https://www.painterartist.com/en/product/education/
- Krita: https://krita.org/en/
- Procreate: https://procreate.com/ Purchase it directly through the App Store on your iPad or iPhone.

Hardware

- Tablets: We are referring to tablets that you plug (physically or through a wireless connection) into your computer, rather than a standalone tablet such as the iPad. These additions make digital illustration much more user-friendly compared to working with a mouse. Some models are simple slates with a stylus, and you see your results on the screen. Other, more expensive models include a screen slate and touch-screen capabilities. Prices range dramatically according to the features involved. The technology in this area is rapidly updating with screen resolution, stylus responsiveness, and touch-screen ability. Be sure to do your research in terms of reviews, quality, and price before you invest.
  - HUION: https://www.huion.com/
    - HUION Educational Program: https://store.huion.com/pages/education-program

- Wacom: https://www.wacom.com/en-us
    - Wacom educational discount: https://www.wacom.com/en-us/promos/education-discount
  - XP Pen: https://www.xp-pen.com/
    - XP Pen Education Program: https://www.xp-pen.com/store/education-program.html
- Editing consoles: Consoles are great additions to your tablet or even just a keyboard and mouse. They allow you to program shortcuts and commands onto buttons and wheels that you can control with your non-dominant hand to speed up your workflow when working on illustrations for long periods of time. They can be expensive, so if you only dabble in digital illustration, it's probably not worth the investment. If you start to illustrate for hours on end, you may want to look into them.
  - Loupedeck: https://loupedeck.com/us/
  - Shuttle Pro (Contour Design): https://contourdesign.com/
  - TourBox: https://www.tourboxtech.com/en/
- Scanners
  - Epson: https://epson.com/usa
- Printers
  - Canon: https://www.usa.canon.com/
  - Epson: https://epson.com/usa

Plugins

Plugins are software applications that work within other software. They will do specific tasks. Some can perform multiple actions whereas others will only do one thing. Plugins run the gamut from free (yay!) to a few hundred dollars in the United States. These are all above and beyond what is necessary to create the illustrations discussed in this text. However, some can be quite useful for speeding up your workflow or expanding your creative reach. Shop around to see if any spark your interest enough to invest!

- Astute Graphics: https://astutegraphics.com/
- Brushbox: https://derrickbarth.gumroad.com/l/brushbox
- Exposure Software: https://exposure.software/
- GuideGuide: https://guideguide.me/
- Nik Collection (DxO): https://www.dxo.com/
- ParticleShop (Corel): https://www.painterartist.com/en/product/particleshop/
- Portrait AI (ON1): https://www.on1.com/
- Portraiture: https://www.imagenomic.com/Products/Portraiture
- PixelSquid: https://www.pixelsquid.com/
- Retouch Ninja: https://exchange.adobe.com/apps/cc/4b69c6fc/retouch-ninja
- Topaz Labs: https://www.topazlabs.com

Assets: Brushes, Patterns, Textures, Etc.

- Brushwarriors: https://brushwarriors.com/
- Creative Market: https://creativemarket.com/
- Cubebrush: https://cubebrush.co/
- DesignCuts: https://www.designcuts.com/
- Envato Elements: https://elements.envato.com/
- Fashion Designer 411: https://www.fashiondesign411.com/
- Freepik: https://www.freepik.com/
- Kyle's brushes through Adobe: https://www.adobe.com/products/photoshop/brushes.html
- Real-Ink Digital Brushes: https://realink.digital
- Retro Supply Co.: https://www.retrosupply.co
- True Grit Texture Supply: https://www.truegrittexturesupply.com
- Vector Stock: https://www.vectorstock.com/

Fonts

- Adobe Type: https://fonts.adobe.com/
- DaFont: https://www.dafont.com/
- Font Squirrel: https://www.fontsquirrel.com/

Stock Photos

- Adobe Stock: https://stock.adobe.com
- Dreamstime: https://www.dreamstime.com
- Getty Images: https://www.gettyimages.com/
- iStock: https://www.istockphoto.com/
- Pexels: https://www.pexels.com/
- Pixabay: https://pixabay.com/
- Unsplash: https://unsplash.com/

Appendix 2 Extend Your Learning

Although this is a more advanced text for digital illustration, there are resources available for those who need to brush up their skills in one area or another. Or if you mastered the lessons in this book and wish to learn more, try some of the resources we have listed for you. To extend your learning, you may want to enroll in a traditional schooling format such as university or other formal classrooms. There are non-traditional choices as well, such as community classes, online classes, books, or finding a mentor. If you don't have access to such resources, try to follow an expert or artist you admire through social media. You can learn a lot from simple observation. Remember that learning can come from unexpected sources. In the meantime, try to join a local or online community for support and feedback.

Online Software Training

- Class 101+: https://class101.net
- CreativeLive: https://www.creativelive.com
- Domestika: https://www.domestika.org
- KelbyOne: https://kelbyone.com
- LinkedIn Learning: https://www.linkedin.com/learning
- Paintable: https://paintable.cc/
- Schoolism: https://schoolism.com
- Skillshare: https://www.skillshare.com/en/
- Udemy: https://www.udemy.com
- Wingfox: https://www.wingfox.com
- YouTube: https://www.youtube.com/

Software Training Books

Anton, Kelly Kordes, & DeJarld, Tina (2024). *Adobe InDesign Classroom in a Book 2024 release.* Adobe Press.

Beginner's guide to digital painting in Photoshop: characters. (2015). 3DTotal Publishing.

Chavez, Conrad (2024). *Adobe Photoshop Classroom in a book* (2024 release). Adobe Press.

Hoppe, Jason, & Safari, an O'Reilly Media Company (2020). *Adobe Illustrator* (1st edition). Rocky Nook Inc.

Hume, Robert (2020). *Fashion and textile design with Photoshop and Illustrator: professional creative practice* (2nd edition). Bloomsbury Visual Arts.

Inko & Staley, Liz (2024). *Learn Clip Studio Paint: a beginner's guide to creating compelling art in manga, comics, and animation* (4th edition). Packt Publishing Ltd.

Jelezky, Dimitri (2021). *Fashion design: digital drawing with Adobe Illustrator: techniques & tips* (1st edition; English 1st edition). Jelezky Publishing.

Laskevitch, Stephen (2019). *Adobe InDesign CC* (1st edition). Rocky Nook Inc.

Laskevitch, Stephen (2023). *Adobe Photoshop: a complete course and compendium of features* (2nd edition). Rocky Nook Inc.

Schneider, Robin (2012). *Adobe for fashion: Illustrator CS6: the ultimate guide to drawing flats.* New York Cookie Graphics LLC.

Ulichney, Max, Grünewald, Simone, Stokart, Aveline, & Nassour, Sam (2020). *Beginner's guide to digital painting in Procreate: how to create art on an iPad.* 3DTotal Publishing.

Wood, Brian (2023). *Adobe Illustrator classroom in a book 2024 release.* Adobe Press.

Figure Drawing and Rendering Books

Baeza, Juan (2014). *Fashion drawing course: from human figure to fashion illustration* (Thomas Corkett, Trans.). Promopress.

Faigin, Gary (2008). *The artist's complete guide to facial expression*. Watson-Guptill; GMC Distribution [distributor].

Gurney, James (2010). *Color and light: a guide for the realist painter*. Andrews McMeel Publishing.

Hamm, Jack (2020). *Drawing the head and figure*. Jack Hamm. Reprint of 1963 Grosset & Dunlap book.

Hogarth, Burne (2002). *Dynamic wrinkles and drapery*. Watson-Guptill.

Loomis, Andrew (2011). *Figure drawing for all it's worth*. Titan Books. Reprint of 1943 Viking Press book.

Robertson, Scott, & Bertling, Thomas (2014). *How to render: the fundamentals of light, shadow and reflectivity* (1st edition). Design Studio Press.

Seok, Junghyun (2020). *Stonehouse anatomy note: anatomy for all artists* (Hans Olo, Trans.). Superani.

Simblet, Sarah, & Davis, John (2020). *Anatomy for the artist* (American edition). DK Publishing.

Fashion Illustration Books

Abling, Bina (2019). *Marker rendering for fashion, accessories, and home fashion*. Fairchild Books, an imprint of Bloomsbury Publishing Inc.

Abling, Bina (2023). *Fashion sketchbook* (8th edition). Fairchild Books, an imprint of Bloomsbury Publishing Inc.

Bryant, Michel Wesen (2016). *Fashion drawing: illustration techniques for fashion designers* (2nd edition). Laurence King Publishing.

Hagen, Kathryn (2011). *Fashion illustration for designers* (2nd edition). Prentice Hall.

Kiper, Anna (2011). *Fashion illustration: inspiration and technique*. David & Charles.

O'Neal, Lamont (2023). *Illustrated men: drawing and rendering the male fashion figure*. Bloomsbury Visual Arts.

Paci, Tiziana (2018). *Colour in fashion illustration: drawing and painting techniques* (Katherine Kirby, Trans.). Promopress.

Riegelman, Nancy (2016). *9 Heads: a guide to drawing fashion* (4th edition, revised). 9 Heads Media.

Tallon, Kevin (2008). *Digital fashion illustration with Photoshop and Illustrator*. Batsford.

Tallon, Kevin (2013). *Creative fashion design with Illustrator* (New edition). Batsford.

Theater Illustration

Jaen, Rafael (2017). *Digital costume design and collaboration: applications in academia, theatre and film*. Routledge.

Tan, Huaixiang (2010). *Character costume figure drawing: step-by-step drawing methods for theatre costume designers* (2nd edition). Elsevier/Focal Press.

Portfolio and Professional Development Books

Barrett, Joanne Ciresi (2013). *Designing your fashion portfolio: from concept to presentation*. Fairchild Books, an imprint of Bloomsbury Publishing Inc.

Hagen, Kathryn, & Hollinger, Julie (2013). *Portfolio for fashion designers* (1st edition). Pearson.

McKelvey, Kathryn, & Munslow, Janine (2007). *Illustrating fashion* (2nd edition). Blackwell Publishing.

Tain, Linda (2018). *Portfolio presentation for fashion designers* (4th edition). Fairchild Books, an imprint of Bloomsbury Publishing Inc.

Design Books

Albers, Joseph, & Weber, Nicolas Fox (2013). *Interaction of color* (50th anniversary edition. 4th edition). Yale University Press.

Cooperman, Marcie (2013). *Color: how to use it* (1st edition). Pearson.

Edwards, Betty (2004). *Color: a course in mastering the art of mixing colors*. Jeremy P. Tarcher/Penguin.

Ellinwood, Janice Greenberg (2022). *Fashion by design* (2nd edition). Fairchild Books, an imprint of Bloomsbury Publishing Inc.

Holtzschue, Linda (2017). *Understanding color: an introduction for designers* (5th edition). Wiley.

Appendix 3 Shortcuts

ADOBE® PHOTOSHOP® KEYBOARD SHORTCUTS

Command		**Shortcut**	
Tools			
	Move Tool	V	
	Artboard Tool	V	
	Rectangular Marquee Tool	M	
	Elliptical Marquee Tool	M	
	Lasso Tool	L	
	Polygonal Lasso Tool	L	
	Object Selection Tool	W	
	Quick Selection Tool	W	
	Magic Wand Tool	W	
	Crop Tool	C	
	Eyedropper Tool	I	
	Color Sampler Tool	I	
	Brush Tool	B	
	Pencil Tool	B	
	Color Replacement Tool	B	
	Mixer Brush Tool	B	
	Clone Stamp Tool	S	
	Pattern Stamp Tool	S	
	History Brush Tool	Y	
	Art History Brush Tool	Y	
	Eraser Tool	E	
	Background Eraser Tool	E	
	Magic Eraser Tool	E	

ADOBE PHOTOSHOP SHORTCUTS			
Command		**Shortcut**	
	Gradient Tool	G	
	Paint Bucket Tool	G	
	Sponge Tool	O	
	Horizontal Type Tool	T	
	Vertical Type Tool	T	
	Pen Tool	P	
	Freeform Pen Tool	P	
	Content-Aware Tracing Tool	P	
	Curvature Pen Tool	P	
	Path Selection Tool	A	
	Direct Selection Tool	A	
	Rectangle Tool	U	
	Ellipse Tool	U	
	Triangle Tool	U	
	Polygon Tool	U	
	Line Tool	U	
	Custom Shape Tool	U	
	Hand Tool	H	
	Rotate View Tool	R	
	Zoom Tool	Z	
	Adjustment Brush Tool		
	Selection Brush Tool	L	
	Magnetic Lasso Tool	L	
	Perspective Crop Tool	C	
	Slice Tool	C	
	Slice Select Tool	C	
	Ruler Tool	I	
	Note Tool	I	
	Count Tool	I	
	Spot Healing Brush Tool	J	
	Remove Tool	J	
	Healing Brush Tool	J	
	Patch Tool	J	

ADOBE PHOTOSHOP SHORTCUTS

Command		Shortcut	
	Content-Aware Move Tool	J	
	Red Eye Tool	J	
	Dodge Tool	O	
	Burn Tool	O	
	Vertical Type Mask Tool	T	
	Horizontal Type Mask Tool	T	
	Frame Tool	K	
	Default Foreground/Background Colors	D	
	Switch Foreground/Background Colors	X	
	Toggle Standard/Quick Mask Modes	Q	
	Toggle Screen Modes	F	
	Toggle Preserve Transparency	/	
	Decrease Brush Size	[	
	Increase Brush Size	]	
	Decrease Brush Hardness	{	
	Increase Brush Hardness	}	
	Previous Brush	,	
	Next Brush	.	
	First Brush	<	
	Last Brush	>	
	Toggle Preview Mode	N	
	Show Previous Layer Boundary	]	
	Show Next Layer Boundary	[	
Application menus			
File			
	New	Ctrl/Cmd+N	
	Open	Ctrl/Cmd+O	
	Browse in Bridge	Alt/Opt+Ctrl/Cmd+O	Shift+Ctrl/Cmd+O
	Open As	Alt/Opt+Shift+Ctrl/Cmd+O	
	Close	Ctrl/Cmd+W	
	Close All	Alt/Opt+Ctrl/Cmd+W	
	Close Others	Alt/Opt+Ctrl/Cmd+P	
	Close and Go to Bridge	Shift+Ctrl/Cmd+W	

ADOBE PHOTOSHOP SHORTCUTS			
Command		**Shortcut**	
	Save	Ctrl/Cmd+S	
	Save As	Shift+Ctrl/Cmd+S	
	Save a Copy	Alt/Opt+Ctrl/Cmd+S	
	Revert	F12	
	Export>		
		Export As	Alt/Opt+Shift+Ctrl/Cmd+W
		Save for Web (Legacy)	Alt/Opt+Shift+Ctrl/Cmd+S
	File Info	Alt/Opt+Shift+Ctrl/Cmd+I	
	Print	Ctrl/Cmd+P	
	Print One Copy	Alt/Opt+Shift+Ctrl/Cmd+P	
	Exit	Ctrl/Cmd+Q	
Edit			
	Undo	Ctrl/Cmd+Z	
	Redo	Shift+Ctrl/Cmd+Z	
	Toggle Last State	Alt/Opt+Ctrl/Cmd+Z	
	Fade	Shift+Ctrl/Cmd+F	
	Cut	Ctrl/Cmd+X	F2
	Copy	Ctrl/Cmd+C	F3
	Copy Merged	Shift+Ctrl/Cmd+C	
	Paste	Ctrl/Cmd+V	F4
	Paste Special>		
		Paste in Place	Shift+Ctrl/Cmd+V
		Paste Into	Alt/Opt+Shift+Ctrl/Cmd+V
	Search	Ctrl/Cmd+F	
	Fill	Shift+F5	
	Content-Aware Scale	Alt/Opt+Shift+Ctrl/Cmd+C	
	Free Transform	Ctrl/Cmd+T	
	Transform>		
		Again	Shift+Ctrl/Cmd+T
	Color Settings	Shift+Ctrl/Cmd+K	
	Keyboard Shortcuts	Alt/Opt+Shift+Ctrl/Cmd+K	
	Menus	Alt/Opt+Shift+Ctrl/Cmd+M	

ADOBE PHOTOSHOP SHORTCUTS			
Command		**Shortcut**	
	Preferences>		
		General	Ctrl/Cmd+K
Image			
	Adjustments>		
		Levels	Ctrl/Cmd+L
		Curves	Ctrl/Cmd+M
		Hue/Saturation	Ctrl/Cmd+U
		Color Balance	Ctrl/Cmd+B
		Black and White	Alt/Opt+Shift+Ctrl/Cmd+B
		Invert	Ctrl/Cmd+I
		Desaturate	Shift+Ctrl/Cmd+U
	Auto Tone	Shift+Ctrl/Cmd+L	
	Auto Contrast	Alt/Opt+Shift+Ctrl/Cmd+L	
	Auto Color	Shift+Ctrl/Cmd+B	
	Image Size	Alt/Opt+Ctrl/Cmd+I	
	Canvas Size	Alt/Opt+Ctrl/Cmd+C	
Layer			
	New>		
		Layer	Shift+Ctrl/Cmd+N
		Layer Via Copy	Ctrl/Cmd+J
		Layer Via Cut	Shift+Ctrl/Cmd+J
	Quick Export as JPG	Shift+Ctrl/Cmd+'	
	Export As	Alt/Opt+Shift+Ctrl/Cmd+'	
	Create/Release Clipping Mask	Alt/Opt+Ctrl/Cmd+G	
	Group Layers	Ctrl/Cmd+G	
	Ungroup Layers	Shift+Ctrl/Cmd+G	
	Hide Layers	Ctrl/Cmd+,	
	Arrange>		
		Bring to Front	Shift+Ctrl/Cmd+]
		Bring Forward	Ctrl/Cmd+]
		Send Backward	Ctrl/Cmd+[
		Send to Back	Shift+Ctrl/Cmd+[
	Lock Layers	Ctrl/Cmd+/	

ADOBE PHOTOSHOP SHORTCUTS			
Command		**Shortcut**	
	Merge Layers	Ctrl/Cmd+E	
	Merge Visible	Shift+Ctrl/Cmd+E	
Select			
	All	Ctrl/Cmd+A	
	Deselect	Ctrl/Cmd+D	
	Reselect	Shift+Ctrl/Cmd+D	
	Inverse	Shift+Ctrl/Cmd+I	Shift+F7
	All Layers	Alt/Opt+Ctrl/Cmd+A	
	Find Layers	Alt/Opt+Shift+Ctrl/Cmd+F	
	Select and Mask	Alt/Opt+Ctrl/Cmd+R	
	Modify>		
		Feather	Shift+F6
Filter			
	Last Filter	Alt/Opt+Ctrl/Cmd+F	
	Adaptive Wide Angle	Alt/Opt+Shift+Ctrl/Cmd+A	
	Camera Raw Filter	Shift+Ctrl/Cmd+A	
	Lens Correction	Shift+Ctrl/Cmd+R	
	Liquify	Shift+Ctrl/Cmd+X	
	Vanishing Point	Alt/Opt+Ctrl/Cmd+V	
View			
	Proof Colors	Ctrl/Cmd+Y	
	Gamut Warning	Shift+Ctrl/Cmd+Y	
	Zoom In	Ctrl/Cmd++	Ctrl/Cmd+=
	Zoom Out	Ctrl/Cmd+-	
	Fit on Screen	Ctrl/Cmd+0	
	100%	Ctrl/Cmd+1	Alt/Opt+Ctrl/Cmd+0
	Extras	Ctrl/Cmd+H	
	Show>		
		Target Path	Shift+Ctrl/Cmd+H
		Grid	Ctrl/Cmd+'
		Guides	Ctrl/Cmd+;
	Rulers	Ctrl/Cmd+R	

ADOBE PHOTOSHOP SHORTCUTS			
Command		**Shortcut**	
	Snap	Shift+Ctrl/Cmd+;	
	Guides>		
		Lock Guides	Alt/Opt+Ctrl/Cmd+;
Window			
	Actions	Alt/Opt+F9	F9
	Brush Settings	F5	
	Color	F6	
	Info	F8	
	Layers	F7	
Panel menus			
Layers			
	New Layer	Shift+Ctrl/Cmd+N	
	Quick Export as JPG	Shift+Ctrl/Cmd+'	
	Export As	Alt/Opt+Shift+Ctrl/Cmd+'	
	Lock Layers	Ctrl/Cmd+/	
	Create/Release Clipping Mask	Alt/Opt+Ctrl/Cmd+G	
	Merge Layers	Ctrl/Cmd+E	
	Merge Visible	Shift+Ctrl/Cmd+E	
Taskspace			
Select and Mask			
	Tools>		
		Quick Selection Tool	W
		Refine Edge Brush Tool	R
		Brush Tool	B
		Object Selection Tool	W
		Lasso Tool	L
		Polygonal Lasso Tool	L
		Hand Tool	H
		Zoom Tool	Z
	Properties and Tool Options>		
		Cycle Tool Mode	E
		Show Edge	J
		Show Original	P

ADOBE PHOTOSHOP SHORTCUTS			
Command		**Shortcut**	
		Cycle View Mode	F
		Disable Views	X
		Marching Ants	M
		Overlay	V
		On Black	A
		On White	T
		Black and White	K
		On Layers	Y
		Onion Skin	O
Content-Aware Fill			
	Tools>		
		Sampling Brush Tool	B
		Lasso Tool	L
		Polygonal Lasso Tool	L
		Alignment Tool	A
		Hand Tool	H
		Zoom Tool	Z
	Properties and Tool Options>		
		Cycle Tool Mode	E
Neural Filters			
	Tools>		
		Hand Tool	H
		Zoom Tool	Z
		Sampling Brush Tool	S
		Selection Brush Tool	B
		Selection Removal Brush Tool	E

ADOBE ILLUSTRATOR SHORTCUTS

Command		Shortcut	
Tools			
	Selection	V	
	Direct Selection	A	
	Magic Wand	Y	
	Artboard	Shift+O	
	Lasso	Q	
	Pen	P	
	Add Anchor Point	=	
	Delete Anchor Point	-	
	Anchor Point	Shift+C	
	Curvature Tool	Shift+~	
	Line Segment	\	
	Rectangle	M	
	Ellipse	L	
	Paintbrush	B	
	Blob Brush	Shift+B	
	Pencil	N	
	Shaper Tool	Shift+N	
	Symbol Sprayer	Shift+S	
	Column Graph	J	
	Slice	Shift+K	
	Perspective Grid	Shift+P	
	Perspective Selection	Shift+V	
	Type	T	
	Touch Type	Shift+T	
	Gradient	G	
	Mesh	U	
	Shape Builder	Shift+M	
	Live Paint Bucket	K	
	Live Paint Selection	Shift+L	
	Rotate	R	
	Reflect	O	
	Scale	S	

ADOBE ILLUSTRATOR SHORTCUTS			
Command		**Shortcut**	
	Width	Shift+W	
	Warp	Shift+R	
	Free Transform	E	
	Eyedropper	I	
	Blend	W	
	Eraser	Shift+E	
	Scissors	C	
	Hand	H	
	Rotate View Tool	Shift+H	
	Zoom	Z	
	Toggle Fill/Stroke	X	
	Default	D	
	Swap Fill/Stroke	Shift+X	
	Color	,	
	Gradient	.	
	None	/	
	Toggle Screen Mode	F	
	Show/Hide All Palettes	Tab	
	Show/Hide All But Toolbox	Shift+Tab	
	Increase Diameter	]	
	Decrease Diameter	[	
	Symbolism Tools - Increase Intensity	Shift+}	
	Symbolism Tools - Decrease Intensity	Shift+{	
	Toggle Drawing Mode	Shift+D	
	Presentation Mode	Shift+F	
Application menus			
File			
	New	Ctrl/Cmd+N	
	New from Template	Shift+Ctrl/Cmd+N	
	Open	Ctrl/Cmd+O	
	Browse in Bridge	Alt/Opt+Ctrl/Cmd+O	
	Close	Ctrl/Cmd+W	
	Close All	Alt/Opt+Ctrl/Cmd+W	

ADOBE ILLUSTRATOR SHORTCUTS			
Command		**Shortcut**	
	Save	Ctrl/Cmd+S	
	Save As	Shift+Ctrl/Cmd+S	
	Save a Copy	Alt/Opt+Ctrl/Cmd+S	
	Revert	F12	
	Place	Shift+Ctrl/Cmd+P	
	Export>		
		ExportforScreens	Alt/Opt+Ctrl/Cmd+E
		SaveforWeb(Legacy)	Alt/Opt+Shift+Ctrl/Cmd+S
	Package	Alt/Opt+Shift+Ctrl/Cmd+P	
	Scripts>		
		OtherScript	Ctrl/Cmd+F12
	Document Setup	Alt/Opt+Ctrl/Cmd+P	
	File Info	Alt/Opt+Shift+Ctrl/Cmd+I	
	Print	Ctrl/Cmd+P	
	Exit	Ctrl/Cmd+Q	
Edit			
	Undo	Ctrl/Cmd+Z	
	Redo	Shift+Ctrl/Cmd+Z	
	Cut	Ctrl/Cmd+X	
	Copy	Ctrl/Cmd+C	
	Paste	Ctrl/Cmd+V	
	Paste in Front	Ctrl/Cmd+F	
	Paste in Back	Ctrl/Cmd+B	
	Paste in Place	Shift+Ctrl/Cmd+V	
	Paste on All Artboards	Alt/Opt+Shift+Ctrl/Cmd+V	
	Paste without Formatting	Alt/Opt+Ctrl/Cmd+V	
	Spelling>		
		CheckSpelling	Ctrl/Cmd+I
	Color Settings	Shift+Ctrl/Cmd+K	
	Keyboard Shortcuts	Alt/Opt+Shift+Ctrl/Cmd+K	
	Preferences>		
		General	Ctrl/Cmd+K
Object			

ADOBE ILLUSTRATOR SHORTCUTS			
Command		**Shortcut**	
	Transform>		
		TransformAgain	Ctrl/Cmd+D
		Move	Shift+Ctrl/Cmd+M
	Arrange>		
		BringtoFront	Shift+Ctrl/Cmd+]
		BringForward	Ctrl/Cmd+]
		SendBackward	Ctrl/Cmd+[
		SendtoBack	Shift+Ctrl/Cmd+[
	Group Ungroup	Ctrl/Cmd+G Shift+Ctrl/Cmd+G	
	Lock>		
		Selection	Ctrl/Cmd+2
	Unlock All	Alt/Opt+Ctrl/Cmd+2	
	Hide>		
		Selection	Ctrl/Cmd+3
	Show All	Alt/Opt+Ctrl/Cmd+3	
	Join	Ctrl/Cmd+J	
	Average	Alt/Opt+Ctrl/Cmd+J	
	Edit Pattern	Shift+Ctrl/Cmd+F8	
	Blend>		
		Make	Alt/Opt+Ctrl/Cmd+B
		Release	Alt/Opt+Shift+Ctrl/Cmd+B
	Envelope Distort>		
		MakewithWarp	Alt/Opt+Shift+Ctrl/Cmd+W
		MakewithMesh	Alt/Opt+Ctrl/Cmd+M
		MakewithTopObject	Alt/Opt+Ctrl/Cmd+C
	Live Paint>		
		Make	Alt/Opt+Ctrl/Cmd+X
	Clipping Mask>		
		Make	Ctrl/Cmd+7
		Release	Alt/Opt+Ctrl/Cmd+7
	Compound Path>		
		Make	Ctrl/Cmd+8

ADOBE ILLUSTRATOR SHORTCUTS			
Command		**Shortcut**	
		Release	Alt/Opt+Shift+Ctrl/Cmd+8
Type			
	Create Outlines	Shift+Ctrl/Cmd+O	
	Bullet	Alt/Opt+8	
Select			
	All	Ctrl/Cmd+A	
	All on Active Artboard	Alt/Opt+Ctrl/Cmd+A	
	Deselect	Shift+Ctrl/Cmd+A	
	Reselect	Ctrl/Cmd+6	
	Next Object Above	Alt/Opt+Ctrl/Cmd+]	
	Next Object Below	Alt/Opt+Ctrl/Cmd+[	
Effect			
	Apply Last Effect	Shift+Ctrl/Cmd+E	
	Last Effect	Alt/Opt+Shift+Ctrl/Cmd+E	
View			
	Preview	Ctrl/Cmd+Y	
	GPU Preview	Ctrl/Cmd+E	
	Overprint Preview	Alt/Opt+Shift+Ctrl/Cmd+Y	
	Pixel Preview	Alt/Opt+Ctrl/Cmd+Y	
	Zoom In	Ctrl/Cmd+=	
	Zoom Out	Ctrl/Cmd+-	
	Fit Artboard in Window	Ctrl/Cmd+0	
	Fit All in Window	Alt/Opt+Ctrl/Cmd+0	
	Reset Rotate View	Shift+Ctrl/Cmd+1	
	Hide Bounding Box	Shift+Ctrl/Cmd+B	
	Show Transparency Grid	Shift+Ctrl/Cmd+D	
	Actual Size	Ctrl/Cmd+1	
	Hide Gradient Annotator	Alt/Opt+Ctrl/Cmd+G	
	Hide Edges	Ctrl/Cmd+H	
	Smart Guides	Ctrl/Cmd+U	
	Perspective Grid: Show Grid	Shift+Ctrl/Cmd+I	
	Hide Artboards	Shift+Ctrl/Cmd+H	
	Show Template	Shift+Ctrl/Cmd+W	

ADOBE ILLUSTRATOR SHORTCUTS			
Command		**Shortcut**	
	Rulers>		
		ShowRulers	Ctrl/Cmd+R
		ChangetoArtboardRulers	Alt/Opt+Ctrl/Cmd+R
	Show Text Threads	Shift+Ctrl/Cmd+Y	
	Guides>		
		HideGuides	Ctrl/Cmd+;
		LockGuides	Alt/Opt+Ctrl/Cmd+;
		MakeGuides	Ctrl/Cmd+5
		ReleaseGuides	Alt/Opt+Ctrl/Cmd+5
	Show Grid	Ctrl/Cmd+'	
	Snap to Grid	Shift+Ctrl/Cmd+'	
	Snap to Point	Alt/Opt+Ctrl/Cmd+'	
Window			
	Align	Shift+F7	
	Appearance	Shift+F6	
	Attributes	Ctrl/Cmd+F11	
	Brushes	F5	
	Color	F6	
	Color Guide	Shift+F3	
	Gradient	Ctrl/Cmd+F9	
	Graphic Styles	Shift+F5	
	Info	Ctrl/Cmd+F8	
	Layers	F7	
	Pathfinder	Shift+Ctrl/Cmd+F9	
	Stroke	Ctrl/Cmd+F10	
	Symbols	Shift+Ctrl/Cmd+F11	
	Transform	Shift+F8	
	Transparency	Shift+Ctrl/Cmd+F10	
	Type>		
		Character	Ctrl/Cmd+T
		OpenType	Alt/Opt+Shift+Ctrl/Cmd+T
		Paragraph	Alt/Opt+Ctrl/Cmd+T
		Tabs	Shift+Ctrl/Cmd+T

ADOBE ILLUSTRATOR SHORTCUTS

Command		Shortcut	
Help			
	Illustrator Help	F1	
	Switch Selection Tools	Ctrl/Cmd+ '	
Other panel			
	New Symbol	F8	
	Add New Fill	Ctrl/Cmd+/	
	Add New Stroke	Alt/Opt+Ctrl/Cmd+/	
	New Layer	Ctrl/Cmd+L	
Other text			
	Point Size Up	Shift+Ctrl/Cmd+.	
	Point Size Down	Shift+Ctrl/Cmd+	
	Font Size Step Up	Alt/Opt+Shift+Ctrl/Cmd+.	
	Font Size Step Down	Alt/Opt+Shift+Ctrl/Cmd+	
	Spacing	Alt/Opt+Shift+Ctrl/Cmd+O	
	Uniform Type	Shift+Ctrl/Cmd+X	
	Left Align Text	Shift+Ctrl/Cmd+L	
	Center Text	Shift+Ctrl/Cmd+C	
	Right Align Text	Shift+Ctrl/Cmd+R	
	Justify Text Left	Shift+Ctrl/Cmd+J	
	Justify All Lines	Shift+Ctrl/Cmd+F	
	Toggle Auto Hyphenation	Alt/Opt+Shift+Ctrl/Cmd+H	
	Subscript	Alt/Opt+Shift+Ctrl/Cmd+=	
	Superscript	Shift+Ctrl/Cmd+=	
	Bold	Shift+Ctrl/Cmd+b	
	Italic	Shift+Ctrl/Cmd+i	
	Underline	Shift+Ctrl/Cmd+u	
Other object			
	Lock Others	Alt/Opt+Shift+Ctrl/Cmd+2	
	Hide Others	Alt/Opt+Shift+Ctrl/Cmd+3	
	Repeat Pathfinder	Ctrl/Cmd+4	
	Average & Join	Alt/Opt+Shift+Ctrl/Cmd+J	
	Isolate Selected Object	Double-click	

ADOBE ILLUSTRATOR SHORTCUTS			
Command		**Shortcut**	
	Exit Isolation Mode	Esc	
Other misc			
	Switch Units	Alt/Opt+Shift+Ctrl/Cmd+U	
	New File (No Dialog)	Alt/Opt+Ctrl/Cmd+N	
	Cut (Secondary)	F2	
	Copy (Secondary)	F3	
	Paste (Secondary)	F4	
	Zoom In (Secondary)	Ctrl/Cmd++	
	Navigate to Next Document Navigate to Previous Document	Ctrl/Cmd+F6 Shift+Ctrl/Cmd+F6	
	Navigate to Next Document Group	Alt/Opt+Ctrl/Cmd+F6	
	Navigate to Previous Document Group	Alt/Opt+Shift+Ctrl/Cmd+F6	
	Subscript (Secondary)	Alt/Opt+Shift+Ctrl/Cmd++	
	Superscript (Secondary)	Shift+Ctrl/Cmd++	

ADOBE INDESIGN SHORTCUTS			
Command		**Shortcut**	
Tools			
	Add Anchor Point Tool	=	
	Apply Gradient	.	
	Apply None	Num /	
	Apply default fill and stroke colors	D	
	Color Theme Tool	Shift+I	
	Convert Direction Point Tool	Shift+C	
	Delete Anchor Point Tool	-	
	Direct Selection Tool	A	
	Ellipse Tool	L	
	Eyedropper Tool	I	
	Free Transform Tool	E	
	Gap Tool	U	
	Gradient Feather Tool	Shift+G	
	Gradient Swatch Tool	G	
	Hand Tool	H	
	Line Tool	\	
	Measure Tool	K	
	Page Tool	Shift+P	

ADOBE INDESIGN SHORTCUTS

Command		Shortcut	
	Pen Tool	P	
	Pencil Tool	N	
	Rectangle Frame Tool	F	
	Rectangle Tool	M	
	Rotate Tool	R	
	Scale Tool	S	
	Scissors Tool	C	
	Selection Tool	V	Text: Escape
	Shear Tool	O	
	Swap fill and stroke activation	X	
	Swap fill and stroke colors	Shift+X	
	Toggle Content Collector and Content Placer	B	
	Toggle Text and Object Control	J	
	Toggle view setting between default and preview	W	
	Type Tool	T	
	Type on a Path Tool	Shift+T	
	Zoom Tool	Z	
Application menus			
File			
	New>		
		Document	Ctrl/Cmd+N
	Open	Ctrl/Cmd+O	
	Browse in Bridge	Ctrl/Cmd+Alt/Opt+O	
	Close	Ctrl/Cmd+W	
	Save	Ctrl/Cmd+S	
	Save As	Shift+Ctrl/Cmd+S	
	Save a Copy	Ctrl/Cmd+Alt/Opt+S	
	Place	Ctrl/Cmd+D	
	Export	Ctrl/Cmd+E	
	Document Setup	Ctrl/Cmd+Alt/Opt+P	
	Adjust Layout	Shift+Alt/Opt+P	
	File Info	Shift+Ctrl/Cmd+Alt/Opt+I	
	Package	Shift+Ctrl/Cmd+Alt/Opt+P	
	Print	Ctrl/Cmd+P	
	Exit	Ctrl/Cmd+Q	
Edit			
	Undo	Ctrl/Cmd+Z	
	Redo	Shift+Ctrl/Cmd+Z	
	Cut	Ctrl/Cmd+X	
	Copy	Ctrl/Cmd+C	

ADOBE INDESIGN SHORTCUTS

Command		Shortcut	
	Paste	Ctrl/Cmd+V	
	Paste without Formatting	Shift+Ctrl/Cmd+V	
	Paste Into	Ctrl/Cmd+Alt/Opt+V	
	Paste in Place	Shift+Ctrl/Cmd+Alt/Opt+V	
	Clear	Backspace	
	Duplicate	Shift+Ctrl/Cmd+Alt/Opt+D	
	Step and Repeat	Ctrl/Cmd+Alt/Opt+U	
	Deselect All	Shift+Ctrl/Cmd+A	
	Select All	Ctrl/Cmd+A	
	Edit in Story Editor	Ctrl/Cmd+Y	
	Edit in Copy Editor (Beta)	Shift+Alt/Opt+Y	
	Quick Apply	Ctrl/Cmd+Enter	
	Find/Change	Ctrl/Cmd+F	
	Find Next	Ctrl/Cmd+Alt/Opt+F	
	Spelling>		
		CheckSpelling	Ctrl/Cmd+I
	Preferences>		
		General	Ctrl/Cmd+K
	Check In	Shift+Ctrl/Cmd+F9	
	Check In All	Shift+Ctrl/Cmd+Alt/Opt+F9	
	Check Out	Ctrl/Cmd+F9	
	Toggle search direction	Ctrl/Cmd+Alt/Opt+Enter	
	Update Content	Ctrl/Cmd+F5	
Layout			
	Pages>		
		Add Page	Shift+Ctrl/Cmd+P
	First Page	Shift+Ctrl/Cmd+Page Up	
	Previous Page	Shift+Page Up	
	Next Page	Shift+Page Down	
	Last Page	Shift+Ctrl/Cmd+Page Down	
	Next Spread	Alt/Opt+Page Down	
	Previous Spread	Alt/Opt+Page Up	
	Go to Page	Ctrl/Cmd+J	
	Go Forward	Ctrl/Cmd+Page Down	
	Go Back	Ctrl/Cmd+Page Up	
	Left Spread Presentation Mode:	LeftArrow	
	Right Spread Presentation Mode:	RightArrow	
Type			
	Character	Ctrl/Cmd+T	
	Paragraph	Ctrl/Cmd+Alt/Opt+T	
	Tabs	Shift+Ctrl/Cmd+T	

ADOBE INDESIGN SHORTCUTS

Command		Shortcut	
	Create Outlines	Shift+Ctrl/Cmd+O	
	Create outlines without deleting text	Shift+Ctrl/Cmd+Alt/Opt+O	
	Show Hidden Characters	Ctrl/Cmd+Alt/Opt+I	
Object			
	Transform>		
		Move	Shift+Ctrl/Cmd+M
	Transform Again>		
		TransformSequenceAgain	Ctrl/Cmd+Alt/Opt+4
	Arrange>		
		Bring Forward	Ctrl/Cmd+]
		Bring to Front	Shift+Ctrl/Cmd+]
		Send Backward	Ctrl/Cmd+[
		Send to Back	Shift+Ctrl/Cmd+[
	Select>		
		Container	Escape
		Content	Shift+Escape
		First ObjectAbove	Shift+Ctrl/Cmd+Alt/Opt+]
		Last Object Below	Shift+Ctrl/Cmd+Alt/Opt+[
		Next ObjectAbove	Ctrl/Cmd+Alt/Opt+]
		Next Object Below	Ctrl/Cmd+Alt/Opt+[
	Group	Ctrl/Cmd+G	
	Ungroup	Shift+Ctrl/Cmd+G	
	Lock	Ctrl/Cmd+L	
	Unlock All on Spread	Ctrl/Cmd+Alt/Opt+L	
	Hide	Ctrl/Cmd+3	
	Show All on Spread	Ctrl/Cmd+Alt/Opt+3	
	Text Frame Options	Ctrl/Cmd+B	
	Fitting>		
		CenterContent	Shift+Ctrl/Cmd+E
		Content-Aware Fit	Ctrl/Cmd+Alt/Opt+X
		Fill Frame Proportionally	Shift+Ctrl/Cmd+Alt/Opt+C
		FitContent Proportionally	Shift+Ctrl/Cmd+Alt/Opt+E
		FitContent to Frame	Ctrl/Cmd+Alt/Opt+E
		Fit Frame toContent	Ctrl/Cmd+Alt/Opt+C
	Effects>		
		DropShadow	Ctrl/Cmd+Alt/Opt+M
	Clipping Path>		
		Options	Shift+Ctrl/Cmd+Alt/Opt+K
	Paths>		
		MakeCompound Path	Ctrl/Cmd+8
		ReleaseCompound Path	Shift+Ctrl/Cmd+Alt/Opt+8

ADOBE INDESIGN SHORTCUTS

Command		**Shortcut**	
Table			
	Table Options>		
		Table Setup	Shift+Ctrl/Cmd+Alt/Opt+B
	Insert Table	Shift+Ctrl/Cmd+Alt/Opt+T	
View			
	Overprint Preview	Shift+Ctrl/Cmd+Alt/Opt+Y	
	Zoom In	Ctrl/Cmd+=	Ctrl/Cmd+Num +
	Zoom Out	Ctrl/Cmd+-	Ctrl/Cmd+Num -
	Fit Page in Window	Ctrl/Cmd+0	
	Fit Spread in Window	Ctrl/Cmd+Alt/Opt+0	
	Actual Size	Ctrl/Cmd+1	
	Entire Pasteboard	Shift+Ctrl/Cmd+Alt/Opt+0	
	Screen Mode>		
		Presentation Presentation Mode: Escape	Shift+W
		Set Presentation Background to Black Presentation Mode:	B
		Set Presentation Background to Gray Presentation Mode:	G
		Set Presentation Background to White Presentation Mode:	W
	Display Performance:		
		Fast Display	Shift+Ctrl/Cmd+Alt/Opt+Z
		Typical Display	Ctrl/Cmd+Alt/Opt+Z
		High Quality Display	Ctrl/Cmd+Alt/Opt+H
		Clear Object-Level Display Settings	Shift+Ctrl/Cmd+F2
	Hide Rulers	Ctrl/Cmd+R	
	Grids & Guides>		
		Show Guides	Ctrl/Cmd+;
		Lock Guides	Ctrl/Cmd+Alt/Opt+;
		Snap to Guides	Shift+Ctrl/Cmd+;
		Smart Guides	Ctrl/Cmd+U
		Show Baseline Grid	Ctrl/Cmd+Alt/Opt+'
		Show Document Grid	Ctrl/Cmd+'
		Snap to Document Grid	Shift+Ctrl/Cmd+'
	Structure>		
		Show Structure	Ctrl/Cmd+Alt/Opt+1
Windows			
	Color: Color	F6	
	Color: Swatches	F5	
	Control	Ctrl/Cmd+Alt/Opt+6	
	Effects	Shift+Ctrl/Cmd+F10	

ADOBE INDESIGN SHORTCUTS

Command		Shortcut	
	Info	F8	
	Interactive: EPUB Interactivity Preview	Shift+Alt/Opt+Enter	Shift+Alt/Opt+Num Enter
	Layers	F7	
	Links	Shift+Ctrl/Cmd+D	
	Object & Layout: Align	Shift+F7	
	Output: Preflight	Shift+Ctrl/Cmd+Alt/Opt+F	
	Output: Separations Preview	Shift+F6	
	Pages	F12	Ctrl/Cmd+F12
	Stroke	F10	Ctrl/Cmd+F10
	Styles: Character Styles	Shift+F11	Shift+Ctrl/Cmd+F11
	Styles: Object Styles	Ctrl/Cmd+F7	
	Styles: Paragraph Styles	F11	Ctrl/Cmd+F11
	Text Wrap	Ctrl/Cmd+Alt/Opt+W	
	Type & Tables: Character	Ctrl/Cmd+T	
	Type & Tables: Glyphs	Shift+Alt/Opt+F11	
	Type & Tables: Index	Shift+F8	
	Type & Tables: Paragraph	Ctrl/Cmd+Alt/Opt+T	
	Type & Tables: Table	Shift+F9	
	Utilities: Scripts	Ctrl/Cmd+Alt/Opt+F11	
Help			
	InDesign Help	F1	
Panel menus			
	Character Styles>		
		Redefine Style Text:	Shift+Ctrl/Cmd+Alt/Opt+C
	Character>		
		All Caps	Shift+Ctrl/Cmd+K
		Small Caps	Shift+Ctrl/Cmd+H
		Strikethrough	Shift+Ctrl/Cmd+/
		Subscript	Shift+Ctrl/Cmd+Alt/Opt+=
		Superscript	Shift+Ctrl/Cmd+=
		Underline	Shift+Ctrl/Cmd+U
	Paragraph Styles>		
		Redefine Style Text:	Shift+Ctrl/Cmd+Alt/Opt+R
	Paragraph>		
		Drop Caps and Nested Styles	Ctrl/Cmd+Alt/Opt+R
		Justification	Shift+Ctrl/Cmd+Alt/Opt+J
		Paragraph Rules	Ctrl/Cmd+Alt/Opt+J
Object editing			
	Decrease scale by 1%	Ctrl/Cmd+	
	Decrease scale by 5%	Ctrl/Cmd+Alt/Opt+	
	End Path Drawing	Enter	

ADOBE INDESIGN SHORTCUTS

Command		Shortcut	
	Increase scale by 1%	Ctrl/Cmd+.	
	Increase scale by 5%	Ctrl/Cmd+Alt/Opt+.	
	Nudge down	DownArrow	
	Nudge down 1/10	Shift+Ctrl/Cmd+DownArrow	
	Nudge down 1/10 duplicate	Shift+Ctrl/Cmd+Alt/Opt+DownArrow	
	Nudge down duplicate	Alt/Opt+DownArrow	
	Nudge down x10	Shift+DownArrow	
	Nudge down x10 duplicate	Shift+Alt/Opt+DownArrow	
	Nudge left	LeftArrow	
	Nudge left 1/10	Shift+Ctrl/Cmd+LeftArrow	
	Nudge left 1/10 duplicate	Shift+Ctrl/Cmd+Alt/Opt+LeftArrow	
	Nudge left duplicate	Alt/Opt+LeftArrow	
	Nudge left x10	Shift+LeftArrow	
	Nudge left x10 duplicate	Shift+Alt/Opt+LeftArrow	
	Nudge right	RightArrow	
	Nudge right 1/10	Shift+Ctrl/Cmd+RightArrow	
	Nudge right 1/10 duplicate	Shift+Ctrl/Cmd+Alt/Opt+RightArrow	
	Nudge right duplicate	Alt/Opt+RightArrow	
	Nudge right x10	Shift+RightArrow	
	Nudge right x10 duplicate	Shift+Alt/Opt+RightArrow	
	Nudge up	UpArrow	
	Nudge up 1/10	Shift+Ctrl/Cmd+UpArrow	
	Nudge up 1/10 duplicate	Shift+Ctrl/Cmd+Alt/Opt+UpArrow	
	Nudge up duplicate	Alt/Opt+UpArrow	
	Nudge up x10	Shift+UpArrow	
	Nudge up x10 duplicate	Shift+Alt/Opt+UpArrow	
	Pin Bottom Edge	Ctrl/Cmd+Alt/Opt+DownArrow	
	Pin Left Edge	Ctrl/Cmd+Alt/Opt+LeftArrow	
	Pin Right Edge	Ctrl/Cmd+Alt/Opt+RightArrow	
	Pin Top Edge	Ctrl/Cmd+Alt/Opt+UpArrow	
	Resize Horizontally	Shift+Alt/Opt+H	
	Resize Vertically	Shift+Alt/Opt+V	
	Select all Guides	Ctrl/Cmd+Alt/Opt+G	
	Toggle Live Edit Mode	4	
Text and tables			
	Align center	Shift+Ctrl/Cmd+C	
	Align force justify	Shift+Ctrl/Cmd+F	

ADOBE INDESIGN SHORTCUTS

Command		Shortcut	
	Align justify	Shift+Ctrl/Cmd+J	
	Align left	Shift+Ctrl/Cmd+L	
	Align right	Shift+Ctrl/Cmd+R	
	Align to baseline grid	Shift+Ctrl/Cmd+Alt/Opt+G	
	Apply bold	Shift+Ctrl/Cmd+B	
	Apply italic	Shift+Ctrl/Cmd+I	
	Apply normal	Shift+Ctrl/Cmd+Y	
	Auto leading	Shift+Ctrl/Cmd+Alt/Opt+A	
	Auto-hyphenate on/off	Shift+Ctrl/Cmd+Alt/Opt+H	
Views	Navigation		
	200% size	Ctrl/Cmd+2	
	400% size	Ctrl/Cmd+4	
	50% size	Ctrl/Cmd+5	
	Activate last-used field in panel	Ctrl/Cmd+Alt/Opt+'	
	Close all	Shift+Ctrl/Cmd+Alt/Opt+W	
	Close document	Shift+Ctrl/Cmd+W	
	First Spread	Shift+Alt/Opt+Page Up	
	Fit Selection in Window	Ctrl/Cmd+Alt/Opt+=	
	Force redraw	Shift+F5	
	Go to first frame in thread	Shift+Ctrl/Cmd+Alt/ Opt+Page Up	
	Go to last frame in thread	Shift+Ctrl/Cmd+Alt/ Opt+Page Down	
	Go to next frame in thread	Ctrl/Cmd+Alt/Opt+Page Down	
	Go to previous frame in thread	Ctrl/Cmd+Alt/Opt+Page Up	
	Last Spread	Shift+Alt/Opt+Page Down	
	New default document	Ctrl/Cmd+Alt/Opt+N	
	Next window	Ctrl/Cmd+Tab	
	Open context menu	Shift+F10	
	Open/Close all panels in side tabs	Shift+Ctrl/Cmd+Alt/Opt+Tab	
	Previous window	Shift+Ctrl/Cmd+Tab	
	Save all	Shift+Ctrl/Cmd+Alt/Opt+S	
	Scroll down one screen	Page Down	
	Scroll up one screen	Page Up	
	Show 1st spot plate	Shift+Ctrl/Cmd+Alt/Opt+5	
	Show 2nd spot plate	Shift+Ctrl/Cmd+Alt/Opt+6	
	Show 3rd spot plate	Shift+Ctrl/Cmd+Alt/Opt+7	
	Show Black plate	Shift+Ctrl/Cmd+Alt/Opt+4	
	Show Cyan plate	Shift+Ctrl/Cmd+Alt/Opt+1	
	Show Magenta plate	Shift+Ctrl/Cmd+Alt/Opt+2	
	Show Yellow plate	Shift+Ctrl/Cmd+Alt/Opt+3	

ADOBE INDESIGN SHORTCUTS

Command		Shortcut	
	Show all plates	Shift+Ctrl/Cmd+Alt/Opt+'	
	Show/Hide all panels	Tab	
	Show/Hide all panels except toolbox	Shift+Tab	
	Toggle Character and Paragraph Modes in Control Panel	Ctrl/Cmd+Alt/Opt+7	
	Toggle Keyboard Focus in Control Panel	Ctrl/Cmd+6	
	Toggle Measurement System	Shift+Ctrl/Cmd+Alt/Opt+U	
	Toggle between current and previous views	Ctrl/Cmd+Alt/Opt+2	

Glossary

Abbreviated resumé Refers to an abridged version of your resumé that eliminates specifics such as company names from your work experience that can be used for identity theft.

Adaptable portfolio Contains a versatile range of design work that is flexible for multiple job types and companies.

Adjustment layer Layers apply changes specific to the layer such as hue shifts, value adjustments, and saturation adjustments.

Adobe libraries A collection of assets that is connected to your Adobe ID.

Analog Meaning non-digital.

Anchor point Mathematical coordinates on a vector artboard.

Artboards The term Photoshop and Illustrator use to indicate separate pages within one file.

Autotrace A tool available in Adobe Illustrator. The Autotrace function will scan your artwork while applying points, paths, and fills.

Background color What your eraser will fill in where you erase. This is sometimes called paper color.

Basic frame A visual digital container for image files within InDesign.

Basic shape Refers to a frame in InDesign that only holds a fill and/or stroke rather than text or image files.

Blend mode A tool that affects how the colors of one layer interacts with the colors of the layer below it.

Blob brush Will draw filled shapes in Illustrator. The size of the shape can be controlled by double-clicking on the tool button.

Brushes Images applied to a pathway (vector or raster). These generally mimic analog brush strokes.

Burn A way of decreasing the brightness by way of the *Burn* tool or a burn layer.

Character/paragraph styles A function within InDesign that allows you to set a style for a particular font, font size, spacing, color, alignment, and so on when you use the same styles multiple times in a document.

Clip highlights/shadows Means that you are eliminating the value information in those areas and replacing them with solid black or white.

Clipping mask A mask that is applied to the boundaries of the layer to which it is clipped. When a layer is clipped, the layer below it acts as the mask.

Clone stamp Uses a source spot on the image to duplicate, or clone, that spot onto other areas.

Closed path A vector path that connects to make an enclosed shape.

CMYK Color using pigment utilizes subtractive color and is called CMYK for cyan, magenta, yellow, and key color or black.

Color calibration The process of aligning the color consistency across your devices.

Color gamut The range of colors available within that mode.

Color halo Refers to a ring of bright distortion that can show around high contrast areas.

Contiguous When the contiguous box is ticked, it will only select areas that are touching the color you selected with your wand.

Design communication Illustrations of clothing used to communicate the garment design.

Destructive workflow A way of working in any application that saves file space, but does not allow an artist to go back and change certain steps after a file is saved and closed.

Device-responsive design Refers to web design or app development that will visually adjust to the device on which it is accessed.

Digital Meaning incorporating computer software and hardware.

Displacement map A feature in Photoshop that uses a grayscale map to distort or displace an image.

Dodge A way of increasing the brightness by way of the *Dodge* tool or a *Dodge* layer.

Editorial style Refers to fashion photographs styled with an artistic flair. These are meant to convey a mood and do not always show the garment clearly.

Embedded image A placed image within another file that is stored in the document file. This will increase the file size but does not require the artist to transfer multiple files when sharing a document.

Envelope distort An Illustrator feature that allows you to distort or warp individual objects.

Expand Transforms an image trace, paint strokes, text and patterns into editable shapes with anchors, paths, and fills.

Fabric Usually refers to the fabric construction of a textile such as denim, satin, or jersey knit.

Feather A way to soften the transition between the selected and unselected area.

Fiber Refers to the content of a textile such as silk, cotton, or polyester.

Fitting options Preset styles that change the relationship of content to its frame within InDesign.

Flow Refers to how much "paint" is loaded onto your digital brush.

Foreground color The active color you use when painting.

Frames Digital containers that can show and block parts of placed images, text, or other objects within InDesign.

Generative AI A form of artificial intelligence that creates new content such as images.

Glazing Applying hue to a painting after the values are established.

Global color When part of your artwork is colored with a global color swatch, you can open the swatch to change it and it will automatically adjust all items colored with that global color swatch.

Gradient A transition between one color and another.

Gradient maps Adjustment layers with a gradient applied. When set to the correct blend mode, it replaces the shadows with the dark value of color in the gradient, the midtones with the middle value, and the highlights with the light value.

Grid A non-printing tool to assist with alignment.

Guides Non-printing lines that can be placed to provide a visual reference. Guides must be pulled from the *Rulers*.

High Pass Filter A filter option in Photoshop under *Filter → Other*. The high pass filter reduces subtle areas of color change to a semi-solid gray color while emphasizing the areas of strong color change. It is useful for converting black and white images into an image that resembles line art.

Histogram A graph indicating an approximate representation of the distribution of numerical data related to an image. Histograms are commonly used to indicate color and value information in Adobe Photoshop.

Hue/saturation adjustment layer An adjustment layer based on the properties of hue, saturation, and brightness.

Hyper-realism An art style that is depicted to mimic high-definition photography, but with an artistic twist added such as imaginary details.

Inpainting A generative AI term referring to a program that analyzes an image and replaces a selection of it using text to image prompts.

LAB Stands for lightness-axis, a-axis, and b-axis.

Layer mask A mask that allows you to direct how much of that layer shows; a mask that is applied to an entire layer.

Layer-color mapping The process of keeping items of similar color (usually items of illustrated clothing or parts of the body) on separate layers.

Layers A common feature in most artistic software applications that keeps information segregated to a section of the file and allows for more flexibility with the program.

Legacy brushes/patterns/etc. are older settings, brushes, and patterns that Photoshop has essentially "retired."

Levels Adjustment Layer The *Levels Adjustment* panel can effectively alter an image's value scale. The levels adjustment layer is an applied layer with the stored adjustment information. Having that information on a separate layer allows the artist to make changes to the levels in a non-destructive workflow.

Libraries A collection of assets. Libraries can be connected to your Adobe ID or can be localized on a specific computer.

Linked image A placed image within another file that is not stored in the file. Instead, the image stores the path to that image and must import the information each time the file is opened. This saves file space, but requires that the artist include all linked images with the working file when sharing it.

Liquify A filter available through Photoshop and other similar applications. The liquify filter allows the artist to manipulate pixels by moving them in what is perceived as a "liquid" motion. This is a good tool for making small changes in a sketch or rendering such as moving the placement of a feature slightly.

Live Paint Allows you to add color in an image without creating closed paths with a pen tool.

Lock transparency A feature that prevents the artist from making changes outside the boundary of the artwork on that layer.

Lookbook style Refers to fashion photographs used for a brand's lookbooks. These are generally shot in a studio with a minimal background to show the garment details clearly.

Marketing collateral The assortment of your promotional materials such as letterhead and business card design used to promote yourself in the industry.

Mezzotint A form of monochrome printmaking. The *Mezzotint* filter is meant to imitate the printmaking method by converting an image to dots or lines. The density of the dots or lines will vary according to the tone of the image.

Neural Filters Filters in Photoshop that utilize deep-learning algorithms for image enhancement.

Noise Creates a static texture that is useful for many fabrics in Photoshop.

Non-destructive workflow A way of working that allows the artist to return to previous changes within parts of the file. This allows the artist flexibility but increases the file size.

Offset A filter in Photoshop that allows your image to wrap back on itself. This is especially helpful when determining if your pattern repeat will look correct.

Opacity The transparency of a fill, stroke, layer, or effect.

Open path A vector path that does not connect to a make an enclosed shape.

Outpainting Painting or continuing the image beyond its original borders. This is now a technique that generative AI can accomplish.

Package Refers to a file save system that puts a file, any linked files, and fonts into a folder to share with others.

Pages The term InDesign uses to indicate separate pages within one file.

Parent pages Master pages within InDesign that allow you to add consistent elements on all the working pages such as headers, footers, and backgrounds.

Path A vector feature that indicates a connection between two anchor points.

Pattern brush A brush that uses a compound path to generate a continuous pattern along a path in Illustrator.

Pencil tool In Illustrator, the *Pencil Tool* is similar to the *Pen Tool*, but lets you draw free-form shapes and paths.

Photomerge This feature is available in Photoshop, and allows an artist to merge multiple image files that overlap into on single image. This feature is useful when scanning in oversized renderings that do not fully fit on a scanner bed.

Photo-realism Art created in a way such that it looks nearly identical to a photograph.

Pixelated Means the grid of individual color pixels or squares is visible. This happens when an image is low resolution or has been enlarged too much.

Production shots Studio photographs of an actor in full costume and makeup.

Puppet Warp A feature in Photoshop that allows you warp the object with more precision and distortion.

Raster Refers to a pixel-based image. The pixel grid carries color and value information. Photos and painterly images are pixel-based.

Recolor artwork A panel in Illustrator that allows you to change individual colors within your artwork.

Repeat tile Means that you have the same motif, in the same color and orientation, in all four corners of a rectangle.

RGB An acronym for red, green, and blue. This is an additive system used for describing how colors interact through light.

Rule of thirds A way of framing the subject or focus of a composition in an interesting way for photography and art.

Rulers Onscreen measurement indicators that can be turned on for measurement reference.

Scatter brush A brush that uses a compound path to scatter the image along a path in Illustrator. The controls allow the user to increase or decrease the spacing between each iteration of the compound path.

Selection mask A mask applied to a particular selection made with a selection tool.

Selection tools Tools used to select certain aspects of an image. These tools vary for raster and vector images.

Semi-realism An art style that utilizes analog-like tools with the detail and accuracy of a photograph.

Smart object A feature of Photoshop that allows you to make non-destructive changes by saving the settings of filters, transformations, adjustments, and blending options.

Smudge A tool that "pushes" the previously applied digital paint around the canvas. Smudge tools can have brush tip attributes and presets, often called "blenders" in the *Brush* panel.

Still shots Photographs taken of costumes during a run of show and display the costumes in action on stage.

Style Refers to a way of illustration that mixes artistic expression and design communication.

Style sheet Refers to a visual reference of the graphic elements used in your marketing collateral.

Symbol A premade image in Illustrator that is made for reuse and part of a symbol set or library. Symbols are generally small images that you plan on using repeatedly.

Symbol Library A saved set of symbols in Illustrator. The symbol library is typically saved on the user's computer for easy retrieval. Good illustrators will save symbols into libraries with a common theme, such as a face symbol library and a hair symbol library.

Targeted portfolio Contains design work curated for a specific job or company.

Technical flats A form of clear technical drawings that show all details and visible stitching. These are frequently used in the fashion industry for design communication.

Template A starting file to aid the rendering process. It can either be a file set up with appropriate parameters such as canvas size, background color, and/or labels, or it can indicate the use of a reference image that is placed on the bottom layer of a file as you build it.

Text Frame A visual digital container for text within InDesign.

Text to image is one tool of generative artificial intelligence that creates new images by analyzing human-generated keywords against the data set of images available on the internet.

Transform tools Tools that allow you to transform part or all of an image, depending upon the selection. Transformation tools include scaling, rotating, distorting, flipping, and other alterations.

Unite In Illustrator, this command is sometimes called *Add*. It will merge all the selected touching objects and draw the outline around the outside. Unite can be found in the *Pathfinder* panel or in the *Effects* menu.

Value-mapping The process of laying down your grayscale values before applying the hue, or glazing.

Vector Artwork created in a vector system uses mathematical coordinates to create the image. These images have a more graphic quality than raster images.

Vector effects Use vector calculations to add a distortion or other effect to a path without changing the original path and point information.

Vector mask A mask that follows a vector path.

Vignette An effect that darkens or lightens the area outside your main subject, typically around the borders of the layout. Sometimes vignettes also include a blur effect. This effect is meant to help draw the eye to the main subject.

Warp A subtool within the *Transform* tool that allows you to distort the object using a mesh.

Watermarks Small or low-opacity images or text that sits on the primary artwork image to indicate that it is your work.

Wireframe A skeletal layout and organization of a potential website or application.

Workflow How you approach your illustration and coloring process.

Working pages Individual pages within InDesign to which you add artwork.

Index